PLATO
The Man and His Work

A. E. Taylor

DOVER PUBLICATIONS, INC.
Mineola, New York

Bibliographical Note

This Dover edition, first published in 2001, is an unabridged, unaltered republication of the 4th edition (1937) of the work originally published in 1926 by Methuen & Co. Ltd., London.

Library of Congress Cataloging-in-Publication Data

Taylor, A. E. (Alfred Edward), 1869–1945.
  Plato : the man and his work / A.E. Taylor.
    p. cm.
  Originally published: London : Methuen & Co., 1926.
  Includes bibliographical references and index.
  ISBN 0-486-41605-4 (pbk.)
    1. Plato. I. Title.

B395 .T25 2001
184–dc21
[B]
                                                        00-065955

Manufactured in the United States of America
Dover Publications, Inc., 31 East 2nd Street, Mineola, N.Y. 11501

TO

ALL TRUE LOVERS OF PLATO, QUICK AND DEAD,

AND IN PARTICULAR TO

PROFESSOR CONSTANTIN RITTER

Vagliami il lungo studio e 'l grande amore

PREFACE

I HOPE two classes of readers may find their account in this book—"Honours students" in our Universities, and readers with philosophical interests, but no great store of Greek scholarship. What both classes most need in a work about Plato is to be told just what Plato has to say about the problems of thought and life, and how he says it. What neither needs is to be told what some contemporary thinks Plato should have said. The sense of the greatest thinker of the ancient world ought not to be trimmed to suit the tastes of a modern neo-Kantian, neo-Hegelian, or neo-realist. Again, to understand Plato's thought we must see it in the right historical perspective. The standing background of the picture must be the social, political, and economic life of the age of Socrates, or, for the *Laws*, of the age of Plato. These considerations have determined the form of the present volume. It offers an analysis of the dialogues, not a systematization of their contents under a set of subject-headings. Plato himself hated nothing more than system-making. If he had a system, he has refused to tell us what it was, and if we attempt to force a system on a mind which was always growing, we are sure to end by misrepresentation. This is why I have tried to tell the reader just what Plato says, and made no attempt to force a "system" on the Platonic text. My own comments are intended to supply exegesis, based as closely as may be on Plato's own words, not to applaud nor to denounce. The result, I hope, is a picture which may claim the merit of historical fidelity. For the same reason I have been unusually careful to determine the date and historical setting assumed for each dialogue. We cannot really understand the *Republic* or the *Gorgias* if we forget that the Athens of these conversations is meant to be the Athens of Nicias or Cleon, not the very different Athens of Plato's own manhood, or if we find polemic against Isocrates, in talk supposed to have passed at a time when Isocrates was a mere boy. If it were not that the remark might sound immodest, I would say that the model I have had before me is Grote's great work on the *Companions of Socrates*. Enjoying neither Grote's superb scholarship nor his freedom from limitations of space, I have perhaps the compensation of freedom from the prejudices of a party. Whatever bias I may have in metaphysics or in politics, I have tried to keep it out of my treatment of Plato.

I must apologize for some unavoidable omissions. I have been unable to include a chapter on the Academy in the generation after Plato and Aristotle's criticisms of it; I have had to exclude from consideration the minor *dubia* and the *spuria* of the Platonic *corpus*; I have passed very lightly over much of the biology of the *Timaeus*. These omissions have been forced on me by the necessity of saying what I have to say in one volume of moderate compass. For the same reason I have had to make my concluding chapter little more than a series of hints. This omission will, I trust, be remedied by the publication of a study, "Forms and Numbers," which will, in part, appear in *Mind* simultaneously with the issue of this volume. The details of the *Timaeus* are fully dealt with in a Commentary now in course of printing at the Clarendon Press. A brief account—better than none—of the transmission of the Platonic tradition will be found in my little book, *Platonism and its Influence* (1924; Marshall Jones Co., Boston, U.S.A.; British Agents, Harrap & Son).

Want of space has sometimes forced me to state a conclusion without a review of the evidence, but I hope I have usually indicated the quarters where the evidence may be sought. May I say, once for all, that this book is no " compilation " ? I have tried to form a judgment on all questions, great and small, for myself, and mention of any work, ancient or modern, means, with the rarest of exceptions, that I have studied it from one end to the other.

There remains the grateful duty of acknowledging obligations. I am a debtor to many besides those whom I actually quote, and I hope I have not learned least from many whose views I feel bound to reject. In some cases I have echoed a well-known phrase or accepted a well-established result without express and formal acknowledgment. It must be understood that such things are mere consequences of the impossibility of excessive multiplication of footnotes, and that I here, once for all, request any one from whom I may have made such a loan to accept my thanks. The recommendations at the ends of chapters are not meant to be exhaustive nor necessarily to imply agreement with all that is said in the work or chapter recommended. The last thing I should wish is that my readers should see Plato through my spectacles. I wish here to make general mention of obligation to a host of scholars of our own time, such as Professors Apelt, Parmentier, Robin, Dr.

Adolfo Levi, the late Dr. James Adam, and others, besides those whose names recur more frequently in my pages. The immense debt of my own generation to scholars of an earlier date, such as Grote, Zeller, Diels, Baeumker, Bonitz, is too obvious to need more than this simple reference.

To two living scholars I must make very special acknowledgment. How much I owe to the published writings of my friend and colleague in Scotland, Professor Burnet, will be apparent on almost every page of my book ; I owe even more to suggestions of every kind received during a personal intercourse of many years. I owe no less to Professor C. Ritter of Tübingen, who has given us, as part of the work of a life devoted to Platonic researches, the best existing commentary on the *Laws* and the finest existing full-length study of Plato and his philosophy as a whole. One cannot despair of one's kind when one remembers that such a work was brought to completion in the darkest years Europe has known since 1648. It is a great honour to me that Dr. Ritter has allowed me to associate his name with this poor volume. Finally, I thank the publishers for their kindness in allowing the book to run to such a length.

A. E. TAYLOR

EDINBURGH, *July* 1926

NOTE TO SECOND EDITION

THIS Second Edition only differs from the first by the correction of misprints, the addition of one or two references and the modification of a few words in two or three of the footnotes.

A. E. TAYLOR

EDINBURGH, *March* 1927

NOTE TO THIRD EDITION

APART from minor corrections and some additions to the references appended to various chapters, this edition only differs from its precursors by the presence of a Chronological Table of Dates and an *Appendix*, dealing briefly with the *dubia* and *spuria* of the Platonic tradition. (I have, for convenience' sake, included in this a short account of a number of Platonic epistles which I myself believe to be neither dubious nor spurious, but have not had occasion to cite in the body of the book.) I should explain that this essay was substantially written in 1926, though it has been revised since.

I take this opportunity of mentioning the following recent works, to which I should have been glad to give more specific references in the text, had they come into my hands a little sooner. All will be found valuable by the serious student of Plato.

STENZEL, J.—*Platon der Erzieher.* (Leipzig, 1928.)

SOLMSEN, F.—*Der Entwicklung der Aristotelischen Logik und Rhetorik.* (Berlin, 1929.)

WALZER, R.—*Magna Moralia und Aristotelische Ethik.* (Berlin, 1929.)

TOEPLITZ, O.—*Das Verhältnis von Mathematik und Ideenlehre bei Plato,* in *Quellen und Studien zur Geschichte der Mathematik I. 1.* (Berlin, 1929.)

ROBIN, L.—*Greek Thought and the Origins of the Scientific Spirit.* (E. Tr. from the revised edition of the author's *La Pensée Grecque,* London, 1928.)

A. E. TAYLOR.

EDINBURGH, *July*, 1929

NOTE TO FOURTH EDITION

I HAVE made few changes in this new edition of the text, though I have been led to rewrite one or two paragraphs in the chapter on the *Timaeus* by study of Professor Cornford's valuable commentary on his translation of the dialogue. I have tried to remove misprints and detected errors throughout. Among works important for the student of Plato published since the earlier editions of this book I could mention in particular the following :

FRUTIGER, P.—*Les Mythes de Platon.* (Paris, 1930.)

SHOREY, P.—*What Plato Said.* (Chicago, 1933.)

NOVOTNÝ, F.—*Platonis Epistulae.* (Brno, 1930.)

HARWARD, J.—*The Platonic Epistles.* (E. Tr. Cambridge, 1932.)

FIELD, G. C.—*Plato and His Contemporaries.* (London, 1930.)

CORNFORD, F. M.—*Plato's Cosmology, the Timaeus of Plato translated with a running commentary.* (London, 1937.)

SCHULL, P. M.—*Essai sur la Formation de la Pensée Grecque.* (Paris, 1934.)

A. E. TAYLOR.

CONTENTS

THE following abbreviations have occasionally been used:

E.G.Ph.[3] = BURNET, *Early Greek Philosophy* (3rd edition), 1920.

E.R.E. = HASTINGS, *Encyclopaedia of Religion and Ethics*, 1908–1921.

R.P. = RITTER AND PRELLER, *Historia Philosophiae Graecae* (9th edition), 1913.

PLATO
THE MAN AND HIS WORK

CHAPTER I

THE LIFE OF PLATO[1]

PLATO, son of Ariston and Perictione, was born in the month Thargelion (May–June) of the first year of the eighty-eighth Olympiad by the reckoning of the scholars of Alexandria, 428–7 B.C. of our own era, and died at the age of eighty or eighty-one in Ol. 108.1 (348–7 B.C.). These dates rest apparently on the authority of the great Alexandrian chronologist Eratosthenes and may be accepted as certain. Plato's birth thus falls in the fourth year of the Archidamian war, in the year following the death of Pericles, and his death only ten years before the battle of Chaeronea, which finally secured to Philip of Macedon the hegemony of the Hellenic world. His family was, on both sides, one of the most distinguished in the Athens of the Periclean age. On the father's side the pedigree was traditionally believed to go back to the old kings of Athens, and through them to the god Posidon. On the mother's side the descent is equally illustrious and more his-

---

[1] The chief extant lives are : (a) Apuleius, de Platone, i. 1–4 ; (b) Diogenes Laertius, iii. 1 (critical edition, Basle, 1907) ; (c) Olympiodorus (Platonis Opera, ed. Hermann, vi. 190–195). The least bad of these is (b), which appears to have been originally composed for a lady amateur of Platonic philosophy (φιλοπλάτωνι δέ σοι δικαίως ὑπαρχούσῃ, § 47), not before the latter part of the first century of our era. The one or two references to the scholar Favorinus of Arles may possibly be later marginal annotations by an owner or copier of the text. If they are original, they would bring down the date of the Life to the latter part of the second century A.D. In the main Diogenes Laertius appears to give the version of Plato's life accepted by the literati of Alexandria. But we can see from what we know of the work of Alexandrians like Sotion, Satyrus, and Hermippus, that biographies were already being ruined by the craze for romantic or piquant anecdote before the end of the third century B.C. In Plato's case there is a peculiar reason for suspicion of Alexandrian narratives. The writers were largely dependent on the assertions of Aristoxenus of Tarentum, a scholar of Aristotle who had known the latest generation of the fourth century Pythagoreans. Aristoxenus has long been recognized as a singularly mendacious person, and he had motives for misrepresenting both Socrates and Plato. See Burnet, Greek Philosophy, Part I., p. 153.

torically certain, and is incidentally recorded for us by Plato himself in the *Timaeus*. Perictione was sister of Charmides and cousin of Critias, both prominent figures in the brief " oligarchic " anarchy which followed on the collapse of Athens at the end of the Peloponnesian war (404–3 B.C.). The grandfather of this Critias, Plato's maternal great-grandfather, was another Critias, introduced in the *Timaeus*, whose own great-grandfather Dropides was a " friend and kinsman " of Solon, the great Attic legislator. The father of this Dropides, also called Dropides, the first member of the house who figures in authentic history, was the archon of the year 644 B.C. Besides Plato himself, Ariston and Perictione had at least three other children. These were two older sons, Adimantus and Glaucon, who appear as young men in Plato's *Republic*, and a daughter Potone. Ariston appears to have died in Plato's childhood ; his widow then married her uncle Pyrilampes, whom we know from the allusions of the comic poets to have been a personal intimate of Pericles as well as a prominent supporter of his policy. Pyrilampes was already by a former marriage the father of the handsome Demus, the great " beauty " of the time of the Archidamian war ; by Perictione he had a younger son Antiphon who appears in Plato's *Parmenides*, where we learn that he had given up philosophy for horses.[1]

These facts are of considerable importance for the student of Plato's subsequent career. Nothing is more characteristic of him than his lifelong conviction that it is the imperative duty of the philosopher, whose highest personal happiness would be found in the life of serene contemplation of truth, to make the supreme sacrifice of devoting the best of his manhood to the service of his fellows as a statesman and legislator, if the opportunity offers. Plato was not content to preach this doctrine in the *Republic* ; he practised it, as we shall see, in his own life. The emphasis he lays on it is largely explained when we remember that from the first he grew up in a family with traditions of Solon and accustomed through several generations to play a prominent part in the public life of the State. Something of Plato's remarkable insight into the realities of political life must, no doubt, be set down to early upbringing in a household of " public men." So, too, it is important to remember, though it is too often forgotten, that the most receptive years of Plato's early life must have been spent in the household of his stepfather, a prominent figure of the Periclean *régime*. Plato has often been accused of a bias against " democracy." If he had such a bias, it is not to be accounted for by the influence of early surroundings. He must have been originally indoctrinated with " Periclean " politics ; his dislike of them in later life, so far as it

[1] See the family tree in Burnet, *Greek Philosophy, Part I.*, Appendix I., p. 357. For Pyrilampes, cf. *Charmides*, 158a, and for Demus, *Gorgias*, 481d 5, Aristophanes, *Wasps*, 98. According to *Ep.* xiii. 361e, Perictione was still alive at the date of writing (*i.e.* about 366), but her death was expected, as Plato speaks of the expense of the funeral as one which he will shortly have to meet. Nothing is known of Pyrilampes after the battle of Delium (424 B.C.).

is real at all, is best intelligible as a consequence of having been
" behind the scenes." If he really disliked democracy, it was not
with the dislike of ignorance but with that of the man who has
known too much.

The actual history of Plato's life up to his sixtieth year is almost
a blank. In his own dialogues he makes a practice of silence about
himself, only broken once in the *Apology*, where he names himself as
one of the friends who urged Socrates to increase the amount of the
fine he proposed on himself from one mina to thirty and offered
to give security for the payment, and again in the *Phaedo*, where
he mentions an illness as the explanation of his absence from the
death-scene.[1] Aristotle adds the one further detail that Plato had
been " in his youth familiar with " the Heraclitean Cratylus, though
we cannot be absolutely sure that this is more than a conjecture of
Aristotle's own. The later writers of the extant *Lives* of Plato add
some details, but these are mainly of a purely anecdotal kind and
not to be implicitly trusted. In any case their scraps of anecdote
throw no light on Plato's life or character and we may safely
neglect them here. All we can be sure of, down to Plato's twenty-
sixth year, is that the influence of friendship with Socrates must
have been the most potent force in the moulding of his mind. (We
may add that if Aristotle's statement about Cratylus[2] really is
more than an inference, the Heraclitean doctrine, learned from
Cratylus, that the world disclosed to us by our senses is a scene of
incessant and incalculable mutability and variation, was one which
Plato never forgot. He drew, says Aristotle, the conclusion that
since there is genuine science, that of which science treats must be
something other than this unresting " flux " of sense-appearances.)

The gossiping Alexandrian biographers represented Plato as
" hearing " Socrates at the age of eighteen or twenty. This cannot
mean that his first introduction to Socrates took place at that age.
We know from Plato himself that Socrates had made the close
acquaintance of Plato's uncle Charmides in the year 431, and was
even then familiar with Critias.[3] Presumably Plato's acquaintance
with Socrates, then, went back as far as he could remember. The
Alexandrian tales will only mean that Plato became a " disciple "
of Socrates as soon as he was an ἔφηβος or " adolescent," a period
of life currently reckoned as beginning at eighteen and ending at
twenty. Even with this explanation the story is probably not
accurate. Both Plato and Isocrates, his older contemporary,
emphatically deny that Socrates ever had any actual " disciples "
whom he " instructed," and Plato himself, in a letter written nearly
at the end of his life, puts the matter in a truer light. He tells us
there that at the time of the " oligarchical " usurpation of 404–3,
being still a very young man, he was looking forward to a political
career and was urged by relatives who were among the revolu-
tionaries (no doubt, Critias and Charmides) to enter public life

[1] *Apology*, 38b 6. *Phaedo*, 59b 10. [2] Aristotle, *Met*. 987a 32.
[3] See the opening pages of the *Charmides*.

under their auspices, but waited to see first what their policy would be. He was horrified to find that they soon showed signs of lawless violence, and finally disgusted when they attempted to make his " elderly friend Socrates," the best man of his time, an accomplice in the illegal arrest and execution of a fellow-citizen whose property they intended to confiscate. The leaders of restored democracy did worse, for they actually put Socrates to death on an absurd charge of impiety. This, Plato says, put an end to his own political aspirations. For in politics nothing can be achieved without a party, and the treatment of Socrates by both the Athenian factions proved that there was no party at Athens with whom an honourable man could work. The suggestion clearly made here is that Plato did not regard Socrates as, properly speaking, a master. He loved him personally as a young man loves a revered elder friend, and he thought of him as a martyr. But it was not until the actual execution of Socrates opened his eyes once for all that he gave up his original intention of taking up active political life as his career. His original aspirations had been those of the social and legislative reformer, not those of the thinker or man of science.[1]

Hermodorus,[2] an original member of Plato's Academy, stated that for the moment the friends of Socrates felt themselves in danger just after his death, and that Plato in particular, with others, withdrew for a while to the neighbouring city of Megara under the protection of Euclides of that city, a philosopher who was among the foreign friends present at the death of Socrates and combined certain Socratic tenets with the Eleaticism of Parmenides. This temporary concentration at Megara presumably would only last until the feelings aroused in connexion with the *cause célèbre* had had time to blow over. The biographers narrate that it was followed by some years of travel to Cyrene, Italy, and Egypt, and that the Academy was then founded on Plato's return to Athens. How much of this story—none of it rests, like the mention of the sojourn in Megara, on the evidence of Hermodorus—may be true, is very doubtful. Plato himself, in the letter already alluded to, merely says that he visited Italy and Sicily at the age of forty and was repelled by the sensual luxury of the life led there by the well-to-do. His language on the whole implies that most of the time between this journey and the death of Socrates had been spent at Athens, watching the public conduct of the city and drawing the conclusion that good government can only be expected when " either true and genuine philosophers find their way to political authority or powerful politicians by the favour of Providence take to true philosophy." He says nothing of travels in Africa or Egypt, though some of the observations made in the *Laws* about the art and music, the arithmetic and the games of the Egyptian children have the appearance of being first-hand. The one fateful result of Plato's " travels," in any case, is that he won the whole-hearted devotion of a young man of ability and

[1] See the full explanation of all this at *Ep.* vii. 324b 8–326b 4.   [2] D.L., iii. 6.

promise, Dion, son-in-law of the reigning "tyrant" of Syracuse, Dionysius I.[1]

The founding of the Academy is the turning-point in Plato's life, and in some ways the most memorable event in the history of Western European science. For Plato it meant that, after long waiting, he had found his true work in life. He was henceforth to be the first president of a permanent institution for the prosecution of science by original research. In one way the career was not a wholly unprecedented one. Plato's rather older contemporary Isocrates presided in the same way over an establishment for higher education, and it is likely that his school was rather the older of the two. The novel thing about the Platonic Academy was that it was an institution for the prosecution of *scientific* study. Isocrates, like Plato, believed in training young men for public life. But unlike Plato he held the opinion of the "man in the street" about the uselessness of science. It was his boast that the education he had to offer was not founded on hard and abstract science with no visible humanistic interest about it ; he professed to teach "opinions," as we should say, to provide the ambitious aspirant to public life with "points of view," and to train him to express his "point of view" with the maximum of polish and persuasiveness. This is just the aim of "journalism" in its best forms, and Isocrates is the spiritual father of all the "essayists," from his own day to ours, who practise the agreeable and sometimes beneficial art of saying nothing, or saying the commonplace, in a perfect style. He would be the "Greek Addison" but for the fact that personally he was a man of real discernment in political matters and, unlike Addison, really had something to say. But it is needless to remark that an education in humanistic commonplace has never really proved the right kind of training to turn out great men of action. Plato's rival scheme meant the practical application to education of the conviction which had become permanent with him that the hope of the world depends on the union of political power and genuine science. This is why the pure mathematics—the one department of sheer hard thinking which had attained any serious development in the fourth century B.C.—formed the backbone of the curriculum, and why in the latter part of the century the two types of men who were successfully turned out in the Academy were original mathematicians and skilled legislators and admini-

---

[1] I have said nothing of the story related, *e.g.*, in D.L., iii., 18–21, that Dionysius I had Plato kidnapped and handed over to a Spartan admiral who exposed him for sale at Aegina, where he was ransomed by an acquaintance from Cyrene. The story, though quite possible, seems not too probable, and looks to be no more than an anecdote intended to blacken the character of Dionysius, who in fact, though masterful enough, was neither brute nor fool. In spite of the counter-assertion of Diels, it is pretty certainly *not* referred to in Aristotle, *Physics*, B 199*b* 13. Simplicius seems clearly right in supposing that Aristotle's allusion is to some situation in a comedy. The statement that Dionysius *attempted* to kidnap Plato is made earlier by Cornelius Nepos, *Dion*, c. 2, and perhaps comes from the Sicilian historian Timaeus.

strators, a point on which we shall have a word or two to say in the sequel. It is this, too, which makes the Academy the direct progenitor of the mediaeval and modern university : a university which aims at supplying the State with legislators and administrators whose intellects have been developed in the first instance by the disinterested pursuit of truth for its own sake is still undertaking, under changed conditions, the very task Plato describes as the education of the " philosopher king." The immediate and perceptible outward sign of the new order of things in the Greek world is that whereas in the age of Plato's birth aspiring young Athenians had to depend for their " higher education " on the lectures of a peripatetic foreign " sophist," in the Athens of fifty years later aspiring young men from all quarters flocked to Athens to learn from Isocrates or Plato or both. The travelling lecturer was replaced by the university or college with a fixed domicile and a constitution.

Unfortunately the exact date of the foundation of the Academy is unknown. From the obvious connexion between its programme and the conviction Plato speaks of having definitely reached at the time when he visited Italy and Sicily at the age of forty, we should naturally suppose that the foundation took place about this time (388–7 B.C.) ; and it is easier to suppose that the visit to Sicily preceded it, as the later biographical statements assume, than that it followed directly on its inception. If there is any truth in the statement that the real object of Plato's journey was to visit the Pythagoreans, who were beginning to be formed into a school again under Archytas of Tarentum, we may suppose that it was precisely the purpose of founding the Academy which led Plato just at this juncture to the very quarter where he might expect to pick up useful hints and suggestions for his guidance ; but this can be no more than a conjecture.

We have to think of Plato for the next twenty years as mainly occupied with the onerous work of organizing and maintaining his school. " Lecturing " would be part of this work, and we know from Aristotle that Plato did actually " lecture " without a manuscript at a much later date. But the delivery of these lectures would be only a small part of the work to be done. It was one of Plato's firmest convictions that nothing really worth knowing can be learned by merely listening to "instruction " ; the only true method of " learning " science is that of being actually engaged, in company with a more advanced mind, in the discovery of scientific truth.[1] Very little in the way of actual " new theorems " is ascribed to Plato by the later writers on the history of mathematical science, but the men trained in his school or closely associated with it made all the great advances achieved in the interval between the downfall of the original Pythagorean order about the middle of the fifth century and the rise of the specialist schools of Alexandria in the

---

[1] *Ep.* vii. 341*d–e*. See the comments on this passage in Burnet, *Greek Philosophy, Part I.*, 220–222.

third. In estimating Plato's work for science it is necessary to take account first and foremost of the part he must have played as the organizer and director of the studies of this whole brilliant group. It was, no doubt, this which induced the first mathematician of the time, Eudoxus of Cnidus, to transport himself and his scholars bodily from Cyzicus to Athens to make common cause with the Academy. Probably we are not to think of Plato as writing much during these twenty years. He would be too busy otherwise, and, as we shall see, there is the strongest reason for thinking that most of his dialogues, including all those which are most generally known to-day, were all composed by his fortieth year, or soon after, while the important half-dozen or so which must be assigned to a later date most probably belong definitely to his old age.

In the year 367 something happened which provided Plato, now a man of sixty, with the great adventure of his life. Dionysius I of Syracuse, who had long governed his native city nominally as annually elected *generalissimo*, really as autocrat or " tyrant," died. He was succeeded by his son Dionysius II, a man of thirty whose education had been neglected and had left him totally unfitted to take up his father's great task of checking the expansion of the Carthaginians, which was threatening the very existence of Greek civilization in Western Sicily. The strong man of Syracuse at the moment was Dion, brother-in-law of the new " tyrant," the same who had been so powerfully attached to Plato twenty years before. Dion, a thorough believer in Plato's views about the union of political power with science, conceived the idea of fetching Plato personally to Syracuse to attempt the education of his brother-in-law. Plato felt that the prospect of success was not promising, but the Carthaginian danger was very real, if the new ruler of Syracuse should prove unequal to his work, and it would be an everlasting dishonour to the Academy if no attempt were made to put its theory into practice when the opportunity offered at such a critical juncture. Accordingly Plato, though with a great deal of misgiving, made up his mind to accept Dion's invitation.

If the *Epistles* ascribed in our Plato MSS. to Plato are genuine (as I have no doubt that the great bulk of them are), they throw a sudden flood of light on Plato's life for the next few years. To understand the situation we must bear two things in mind. Plato's object was not, as has been fancied, the ridiculous one of setting up in the most luxurious of Greek cities a pinchbeck imitation of the imaginary city of the *Republic*. It was the practical and statesman-like object of trying to fit the young Dionysius for the immediate practical duty of checking the Carthaginians [1] and, if possible, ex-pelling them from Sicily, by making Syracuse the centre of a strong constitutional monarchy to embrace the whole body of Greek com-munities in the west of the island. Also, Plato's belief in the value of a hard scientific education for a ruler of men, wise or not, was absolutely genuine. Accordingly he at once set about the task

---

[1] *Ep.* vii. 333*a* 1, viii. 353*a*.

from the beginning and made Dionysius enter on a serious course of geometry. For a little while things looked promising. Dionysius became attached to Plato and geometry the "fashion" at his court. But the scheme wrecked on a double obstacle. Dionysius was too feeble of character and his education had been left neglected too long, and his personal jealousies of his stronger and older relative were easily awakened. In a few months the situation became strained. Dion had to go into what was virtually banishment and Plato returned to Athens. Relations, however, were not broken off. Dionysius kept up a personal correspondence with Plato about his studies and projects, and Plato endeavoured to reconcile Dionysius and Dion. This proved not feasible when Dionysius not only confiscated Dion's revenues but forced his wife, for dynastic reasons, to marry another man. Yet Plato made another voyage to Syracuse and spent nearly a year there (361–360) in the hope of remedying the situation. On this occasion something was really done on the task of drafting the preliminaries to a constitution for the proposed federation of the Greek cities, but the influence of the partisans of the old *régime* proved too strong. Plato seems at one time to have been in real personal danger from the hostility of Dionysius' barbarian body-guards, and it was with difficulty and only by the mediation of Archytas of Tarentum that he finally obtained leave to return to Athens (360 B.C.).

At this point Plato's personal intervention in Sicilian politics ceases. The quarrel between Dion and Dionysius naturally went on, and Dion, whose one great fault, as Plato tells him, was want of "adaptability" and *savoir-faire*, made up his mind to recover his rights with the strong hand. Enlistment went on in the Peloponnese and elsewhere, with the active concurrence of many of the younger members of the Academy, and in the summer of 357 Dion made a sudden and successful dash across the water, captured Syracuse, and proclaimed its "freedom." Plato wrote him a letter of congratulation on the success, but warned him of his propensity to carry things with too high a hand and reminded him that the world would expect the "You-know-who's" (the Academy) [1] to set a model of good behaviour. Unfortunately Dion was too good and too bad at once for the situation. Like Plato himself, he believed in strong though law-abiding personal rule and disgusted the Syracusan mob by not restoring "democratic" licence ; he had not the tact to manage disappointed associates, quarrelled with his admiral Heraclides and at last made away with him, or connived at his being made away with. Dion was in turn murdered with great treachery by another of his subordinates, Callippus, who is said by later writers to have been a member of the Academy, though this seems hard to reconcile with Plato's own statement that the link of association between the two was not "philosophy" but the mere accident of having been initiated together into certain "mysteries." Plato still believed strongly in the fundamental honesty and sanity of

[1] *Ep.* iv. 320 *c–e*, and for Dion's want of " tact," *ibid.* 321*b*, vii. 328*b*.

Dion's political aims and wrote two letters to the remnants of his party, justifying the common policy of Dion and himself and calling on them to be faithful to it, and making suggestions for conciliation of parties which were, of course, not accepted. As he said in one of these letters, the fatal disunion of parties seemed likely to leave Sicily a prey either to the Carthaginians or to the Oscans of South Italy.[1]

It is not necessary to follow the miserable story of events in Syracuse beyond the point where Plato's concern with them ends. But it is worth while to remark that Plato's forecast of events was fully justified. The " unification of Sicily," when it came at last, came as a fruit of the success of the Romans in the first two Punic wars; and, as Professor Burnet has said, this was the beginning of the long series of events which has made the cleavage between Eastern Europe, deriving what civilization it has direct from Constantinople, and Western Europe with its latinized Hellenism. If Plato had succeeded at Syracuse, there might have been no " schism of the churches " and no " Eastern problem " to-day.

Nothing is known, beyond an anecdote or two not worth recording, of Plato's latest years. All that we can say is that he must still have gone on from time to time lecturing to his associates in the Academy, since Aristotle, who only entered the Academy in 367, was one of his hearers, and that the years between 360 and his death must have been busily occupied with the composition of his longest and ripest contribution to the literature of moral and political philosophy, the *Laws*. Probably also, all the rest of the dialogues which manifestly belong to the later part of Plato's life must be supposed to have been written after his final return from Sicily. A complete suspension of composition for several years will best explain the remarkable difference in style between all of them and even the maturest of those which preceded. It may be useful to remember that of the years mentioned as marking important events in Plato's life, the year 388 is that of the capture of Rome by the Gauls, 367 the traditional date of the " Licinian rogations " and the defeat of the Gauls at Alba by Camillus, 361 that of the penetration of the Gauls into Campania.

See further:

BURNET, J.—*Greek Philosophy, Part I.*, Chapters xii., xv.
BURNET, J.—*Platonism* (1928).
FRIEDLANDER, P.—*Platon: Eidos, Paideia, Dialogos* (1928).
GROTE, G.—*Plato and the other Companions of Socrates*, Chapter v.
RITTER, C.—*Platon*, i., Chapters i.–v. (Munich, 1914.)
WILAMOWITZ-MOELLENDORFF, U. v.—*Platon*. (Ed. 2. Berlin, 1920.)
STENZEL, J.—*Platon der Erzieher*. (Leipzig, 1928.)
   The general historical background of Plato's life may be studied in any good history of Greece. Specially excellent is
MEYER, E.—*Geschichte des Altertums*, vol. v. (Stuttgart and Berlin, 1902.)
ROBIN, L.—*Platon*, pp. 1–8.

CHAPTER II

THE PLATONIC WRITINGS

I

PLATO is the one voluminous author of classical antiquity whose works seem to have come down to us whole and entire. Nowhere in later antiquity do we come on any reference to a Platonic work which we do not still possess. It is true that we know nothing of the contents of Plato's lectures except from a few scanty notices in Aristotle or quotations preserved from contemporaries of Aristotle by the Aristotelian commentators. But the explanation of this seems to be that Plato habitually lectured without any kind of manuscript. This explains why Aristotle speaks of certain doctrines as taught in the " unwritten teaching " (ἄγραφα δόγματα) of his master, and why at least five of the auditors of a particularly famous lecture (that on " The Good "), including both Aristotle and Xenocrates, published their own recollections of it. We must suppose that Plato's written dialogues were meant to appeal to the " educated " at large and interest them in philosophy ; the teaching given to Plato's personal associates depended for its due appreciation on the actual contact of mind with mind within the school and was therefore not committed to writing at all. As we shall see later on, this has had the (for us) unfortunate result that we are left to learn Plato's inmost ultimate convictions on the most important questions, the very thing we most want to know, from references in Aristotle, polemical in object, always brief, and often puzzling in the highest degree.

When we turn to the contents of our manuscripts, the first problem which awaits us is that of weeding out from the whole collection what is dubious or certainly spurious. We may start with the fact that certain insignificant items of the collection were already recognized as spurious when the arrangement of the dialogues which we find in our oldest Plato MSS. was made. By counting each dialogue great or small as a unit, and reckoning the collection of *Epistles* also as one dialogue, a list of thirty-six works was drawn up, arranged in " tetralogies " or groups of four. It is not absolutely certain by whom or when this arrangement was made, though it certainly goes back almost to the beginning of the Christian era and perhaps earlier. It is commonly ascribed by later writers to a certain Thrasylus or to Thrasylus and Dercylides The date of neither of these scholars is known with certainty. Thrasylus has been usually identified with a rhetorician of that name living under Augustus and Tiberius. But it is notable that Cicero's contemporary, the antiquary M. Terentius Varro, refers [1] to a passage of the *Phaedo* as occurring in the " fourth roll " of Plato, and the *Phaedo* actually happens to be the fourth dialogue of the first " tetralogy." Hence it has been suggested that the arrangement is older than Varro. If this is correct, it will follow that either Thrasylus has been wrongly identified or the arrangement was merely adopted, not originated, by him. On the other hand, this grouping cannot be *earlier* than the first or second century B.C. For Diogenes Laertius [2] informs us that an earlier arrangement of the dialogues in " trilogies " had been attempted, though not carried completely through, by the famous third-century scholar Aristophanes of Byzantium. There is no hint anywhere that the " tetralogies " of Thrasylus admitted any work not regarded as Platonic by Aristophanes or excluded any which he had admitted. We may fairly conclude that the thirty-six " dialogues " were currently regarded as genuine by the librarians and scholars of the third century B.C. As far as the extant dialogues omitted from the " tetralogies " go, there is no question that they are one and all spurious, and no one proposes to reverse the judgment of antiquity on any of them. The same thing is true of the collection of " definitions " also preserved in Plato MSS. There is no doubt that in the main the definitions of the collection are genuinely ancient and Academic. Some of them are actually extracted from the Platonic dialogues ; others are shown to be Academic by their coincidence with Academic definitions used or commented on by Aristotle in his *Topics*. But since some of them can be pretty clearly identified with definitions we can prove to be characteristic of Plato's immediate successors, Speusippus and Xenocrates, we cannot regard the collection as the work of Plato. Our only real problem is whether the list of the thirty-six dialogues must not be further reduced by the elimination of spurious items. Even in antiquity there were doubts about one or two dialogues. The *Alcibiades II* [3] was thought to be unauthentic by some, and the Neoplatonist Proclus wished to reject the *Epinomis*. In modern times doubt has been carried much farther. In the middle of the nineteenth century, especially in Germany, the " athetizing " of Platonic dialogues became a fashionable amusement for scholars ; the *Laws* was pronounced spurious by Ast and, at one time, by Zeller, the *Parmenides, Sophistes*, and *Politicus* by Ueberweg and others; extremists wished to limit the number of genuine dialogues to nine. Fortunately the tide has turned, since the elaborate proof of the genuineness of the *Sophistes* and *Politicus* by Lewis Campbell. There is now a general agreement that every dialogue of any length and interest in the list of the thirty-

---

[1] Varro, *de lingua Latina*, vii. 88. [2] D. L., iii. 61–62.

[3] Athenaeus (506e) records an opinion which ascribed the dialogue to Xenophon.

six is Platonic, and an equally general agreement about the spuriousness of a number of the smaller and less interesting, though there
still remain one or two works about which opinion is divided.   Thus
there is little doubt of the un-Platonic character of the following
works : *Alcibiades II, Hipparchus, Amatores* (or *Rivales*), *Theages,
Clitophon, Minos.*   Opinion may be said to be divided about *Alcibiades I, Ion, Menexenus, Hippias Major, Epinomis, Epistles.*
The scope of the present work allows me only to make one or two
very brief remarks on the subject.

As to the now generally rejected dialogues it may be observed
that they are all brief and of no great moment.   Our conception
of Plato as a thinker and a writer is not seriously affected by the
rejection of any of them.   If it were possible to put in a word on
behalf of any of these items, I should like personally to plead for
the short sketch called the *Clitophon,* which seems to be in any case
a mere unfinished fragment, the main purport of which can only be
conjectured.   The style and verve are not unworthy of Plato, and
I believe I could make out a case for the view that the point to which
the writer is working up is also Platonic, as well as important.   Yet
there is the difficulty that the little work appears on the face of it
to be in form a criticism of the parts played by Socrates and Thrasymachus in *Republic I,* and it is hard to think of Plato as thus playing
the critic to one of his own writings.

About all these dialogues we may say at least two things.
There is only one of them (the *Alcibiades II*) which does not seem
to be proved by considerations of style and language to be real
fourth-century work.   And again, there is no reason to regard any
of them as " spurious " in the sense of being intended to pass falsely
for the work of Plato.   They are anonymous and inferior work of
the same kind as the lighter Platonic dialogues, and probably, in
most cases, contemporary with them or nearly so, not deliberate
" forgeries."   Hence this material may rightly be used with caution
as contributing to our knowledge of the conception of Socrates
current in the fourth century.   *Alcibiades II* is probably an exception.   It is the one dialogue in the list which exhibits anything
very suspicious on linguistic grounds, and it appears also to allude
to a characteristic Stoic paradox.[1]   But, even in this case, there is
no ground to suppose that the unknown writer intended his work
to pass current as Plato's.   A little more must be said of the
dialogues which are still rejected by some scholars, but defended
by others.   The *Alcibiades I* has nothing in its language which
requires a date later than the death of Plato, and nothing in its

---

[1] There seems to be a definite polemic running through the dialogue
against the Stoic thesis that every one but the Stoic " sage " is insane.   Cf.
in particular *Alc. II*, 139c–140d.   (Personally I regard the attack on this
paradox as the main object of the work.)   Hence it cannot date from any
period of the Academy before the presidency of Arcesilaus (276–241 B.C.), with
whom anti-Stoic polemic became the main public interest of the school
For a discussion of the question see *Appendix*, pp. 528–9.

contents which is not thoroughly Platonic. In fact, it forms, as the Neoplatonic commentators saw, an excellent introduction to the whole Platonic ethical and political philosophy. It is just this character which is really the most suspicious thing about the dialogue. It is far too methodical not to suggest that it is meant as a kind of " textbook," the sort of thing Plato declared he would never write. And the character-drawing is far too vague and shadowy for Plato even in his latest and least dramatic phase. In the interlocutors, though they bear the names Socrates and Alcibiades, there is no trace of any genuine individuality—far less than there is even in the anonymous speakers in the *Laws*. It is a further difficulty that on grounds of style and manner the dialogue, if genuine, would have to be assigned to a late period in Plato's life when he is hardly likely to have been composing such work. On the whole, it seems probable that *Alcibiades I* is the work of an immediate disciple, probably written within a generation or so of Plato's death and possibly even before that event.

The *Ion*, so far as can be seen, has in its few pages nothing either to establish its authenticity or to arouse suspicion. It may reasonably be allowed to pass as genuine until some good reason for rejecting it is produced.

The *Menexenus* offers a difficult problem. It is referred to expressly by Aristotle in a way in which he never seems to quote any dialogues but those of Plato, and it seems clear that he regarded it as Platonic.[1] On the other hand, the contents of the work are singular. It is mainly given up to the recital by Socrates of a " funeral discourse " on the Athenians who fell in the Corinthian war. Socrates pretends to have heard the discourse from Aspasia and to admire it greatly. Apparently the intention is to produce a gravely ironical satire on the curious jumble of real and spurious patriotism characteristic of the λόγοι ἐπιτάφιοι, which are being quietly burlesqued. The standing mystery for commentators is, of course, the audacious anachronism by which Socrates (and, what is even worse, Aspasia) is made to give a narrative of events belonging to the years after Socrates' own death. To me it seems clear that this violation of chronological possibility, since it must have been committed at a time when the facts could not be unknown, must be intentional, however hard it is to divine its precise point, and that Plato is more likely than any disciple in the Academy to have ventured on it. (As the second part of the *Parmenides* proves, Plato had a certain " freakish " humour in him which could find strange outlets.) And I find it very hard to suppose that Aristotle was deceived on a question of Platonic authorship. Hence it seems best to accept the traditional ascription of the *Menexenus*, however hard we may think it to account for its character.

The *Hippias Major*, though not cited by name anywhere in Aristotle, is tacitly quoted or alluded to several times in the *Topics* in a way which convinces me that Aristotle regarded it as a Platonic

[1] Aristot. *Rhetoric*, 1415b 30.

work.[1] As the "athetizers" have really nothing to urge on the other side except that the dialogue is not Plato at his best, and that there are an unusual word or two to be found in it (as there are in many Platonic dialogues), I think Aristotle's allusions should decide the question of genuineness favourably.

The *Epinomis* and *Epistles* are much more important. If the *Epinomis* is spurious, we must deny the authenticity of the most important pronouncement on the philosophy of arithmetic to be found in the whole Platonic *corpus*. If the *Epistles* are spurious, we lose our one direct source of information for any part of Plato's biography, and also the source of most of our knowledge of Sicilian affairs from 367 to 354. (As E. Meyer says, the historians who reject the *Epistles* disguise the state of the case by alleging Plutarch's *Life of Dion* as their authority, while the statements in this *Life* are openly drawn for the most part from the *Epistles*.) Documents like these ought not to be surrendered to the "athetizer" except for very weighty reasons.

As to the *Epinomis* the case stands thus. It was certainly known in antiquity generally and regarded as genuine. Cicero, for example, quotes it as "Plato." On the other hand, the Neoplatonic philosopher Proclus (410–485 A.D.) wished to reject it as spurious because of an astronomical discrepancy with the *Timaeus*. Diogenes Laertius also tells us that Plato's *Laws* were "copied out from the wax" by the Academic astronomer Philippus of Opus, adding "and his too, as they say, is the *Epinomis*." It has become common in recent times to assert, on the strength of this remark, that the *Epinomis* is an appendix to the *Laws* composed by Philippus. It ought, however, to be noted that Proclus was apparently unaware that any doubt had been felt about the *Epinomis* before his own time, since he based his rejection wholly on argument, not on testimony. His argument is, moreover, a bad one, since the "discrepancy with the *Timaeus*" of which he complained is found as much in the *Laws* as in the *Epinomis*. The internal evidence of style seems to reveal no difference whatever between the two works. And it may be urged that since the state of the text of the *Laws* shows that the work must have been left at Plato's death without the author's final revision and then circulated without even the small verbal corrections which the editor of a posthumous work commonly has to make in the interests of grammar, it is most unlikely that disciples who treated the *ipsissima verba* of a dead master with such scrupulous veneration would have ventured on adding a "part the last" to the work on their own account. Hence it seems to me that Hans Raeder is right in insisting on the genuineness of the *Epinomis*, and that the remark of Diogenes about Philippus of Opus only means

[1] Twice for the unsatisfactory definition of τὸ καλόν as τὸ πρέπον (*Topics*, A5. 102a 6, E5. 135a 13) ; once for the still worse definition of καλόν as τὸ δι' ὄψεως ἢ ἀκοῆς ἡδύ (*Topics*, Z6. 146a 22). That both these bad attempts at definition occur in the dialogue seems to make it clear that Aristotle is alluding to it and not to any other source.

that he did for this work was also transcribed by, or perhaps dictated to, him. (The now customary disparagement of the *Epinomis* seems to me due to mere inability to follow the mathematics of the dialogue.[1])

Professor Werner Jaeger [2] has incidentally done a service to the student of the *Epinomis* in his recent work on the development of Aristotle's thought by showing that there is an intimate connexion between the *Laws* and *Epinomis* and Aristotle's work περὶ φιλοσοφίας, of which only fragments are now extant. In particular, as he shows, there is an immediate connexion between the " fifth " or " etherial " bodily region of the *Epinomis* and Aristotle's famous " celestial matter " of which the " heavens " are assumed to be made (the *essentia quinta* or *materia coelestis*). Professor Jaeger interprets the connexion thus. We have first the *Laws* circulated promptly after Plato's death, then Aristotle's proposals for modifications of Platonic doctrine in the περὶ φιλοσοφίας, finally (all in the course of a year or two), the *Epinomis*, rejoining to Aristotle, and composed by Philippus. While I regard Professor Jaeger's proof of the intimate relation between *Epinomis* and περὶ φιλοσοφίας as important, I think it more natural to interpret the facts rather differently by supposing the *Laws* and *Epinomis* together to have been transcribed and circulated shortly after the death of Plato, and then followed by Aristotle's criticism of Platonic doctrine in the περὶ φιλοσοφίας. This at least leaves Aristotle more leisure than Professor Jaeger's hypothesis for the composition of a work which, as we know it ran to three " books," must have been of considerable compass. Whatever the truth about the *Epinomis* may be, I am at least sure that it is premature to assume that it is known not to be Plato's.

As for the *Epistles*, it is not necessary now to argue the case for their genuineness as elaborately as one would have had to do some years ago. Since Wilamowitz in his *Platon* declared for the genuineness of the very important trio VI, VII, VIII, those who depend on " authority " for their opinions have been in a hurry to protest that these three at least must be accepted. But the acceptance of the three logically carries with it recognition of the correspondence between Plato and Dionysius (II, III, XIII) and the letter of congratulation and good advice to Dion (IV) ; and when these are accepted as Platonic, there remains no good ground for rejecting any of the thirteen letters of our MSS. except the first, which is written in a style wholly unlike the others, and by some one whose circumstances, as stated by himself, show that he can be neither Plato nor Dion, nor have any intention of passing for either. Presumably this letter got into the correspondence by some mistake at a very early date. The twelfth letter (a mere note of half a dozen lines) was apparently suspected in later antiquity, since our

---

[1] For a good recent defence of the dialogue see the discussion in H. Raeder, *Platons philosophische Entwickelung*, 413 ff. and cf. *infra*, pp. 497-8.

[2] Jaeger, *Aristoteles*, c. 2.

best MSS. have a note to that effect.   No grounds have ever been produced for questioning the authenticity of any of the rest which will bear examination.   Most of the difficulties raised in modern times, especially those alleged in connexion with II and XIII, rest on mere misunderstandings.   It is safe to say that the present tendency to accept only VI, VII, VIII is a consequence of mere servile deference to the name of Wilamowitz.   None of these documents should have needed the imprimatur of a professor as a recommendation ;   their acceptance is bound to lead logically to that of the rest with the exception of I and *possibly* XII.   As far as external testimony goes, it is enough to say that Aristophanes of Byzantium included in his " trilogies " *Epistles* (pretty obviously our thirteen, or we should have heard more about the matter), and that Cicero quotes IV, IX, and especially VII (*nobilissima illa epistula*, as he calls it) as familiar Platonic material.   This, taken together with the thoroughly Platonic style of the letters, disposes of the notion that they can be " forgeries."   The art of writing such prose was already dead in half a century after Plato's death, and the revival of " Atticism," which might make such a production barely conceivable, belongs to a time some generations later than Cicero.[1]

II

To understand a great thinker is, of course, impossible unless we know something of the relative order of his works, and of the actual period of his life to which they belong.   What, for example, could we make of Kant if we did not know whether the *Critique of Pure Reason* was the work of ambitious youth or of ripe middle age, whether it was written before or after the discourse on the *Only Possible Demonstration of the Being of a God* or the *Dreams of a Ghost-seer* ? We cannot, then, even make a beginning with the study of Plato until we have found some trustworthy indication of the order in which his works, or at least the most significant of them, were written.   Even when we have fixed this order, if it can be fixed, we need, for a completer understanding, to be able also to say at what precise period of life the most important dialogues were written,

---

[1] The reader will find an elaborate collection of linguistic and other arguments against the *Epistles* in the section devoted to them in H. Richards' *Platonica*, 254–298, and, as regards most of the series, in C. Ritter, *Neue Untersuchungen ueber Platon*, 327–424.   Most of the alleged objections appear frivolous, or at best based on misreading of the Syracusan situation.   Why the German critics in general think that it is in some way " unworthy " of Plato to have had a " business settlement " with Dionysius such as that to which *Ep.* xiii. relates is to me as unintelligible as Wilamowitz's assertion that the statements of the same letter about the great age of Plato's mother and the existence of four nieces for whom he may have to provide must be fiction. Old ladies do sometimes live to over ninety, and any man of sixty may quite well have four nieces.   The names of Bentley, Cobet, Grote, Blass, E. Meyer, are enough to show that there is plenty of good " authority " for belief in the *Epistles*.   See *Appendix*, pp. 541–544, for further discussion.

whether in early manhood, in mid life, or in old age, and again whether they are an unbroken series of compositions or whether there is evidence of a considerable gap or gaps in Plato's literary activity. These are the questions which we have now to face.

The external evidence supplied by trustworthy testimony only assures us on one point. Aristotle tells us (*Pol.* 1264*b* 26), what could in any case never have been doubted, that the *Laws* is later than the *Republic*. There was also an ancient tradition, mentioned by Proclus and implied in the statement of Diogenes Laertius about Philippus of Opus, that the *Laws* was left by Plato " in the wax," and the " fair copy " for circulation made after his death. The statement is borne out by the frequency in the dialogue of small grammatical difficulties which cannot reasonably be ascribed to later " corruption," but are natural in a faithfully copied first text which has never received the author's finishing touches. Trustworthy testimony takes us no farther than this. Comparison of certain Platonic dialogues with one another yields one or two other results. Thus the *Republic* must be earlier than the *Timaeus*, where it is referred to and the argument of its first five books briefly recapitulated. The *Politicus* must be not earlier than the *Sophistes*, to which it is the professed sequel ; and the *Sophistes*, for the same reason, later than the *Theaetetus*. These are all the certain indications furnished by the matter of the dialogues themselves. There *may* be an allusion in the *Phaedo* to a point more fully explained in the *Meno*, and the *Republic* has been supposed to allude to both. Both the *Theaetetus* and the *Sophistes* refer to a meeting between Socrates, then extremely young, and the great Parmenides ; and there must be some connexion between these references and the fact that the *Parmenides* professes ostensibly to describe this encounter. But we cannot say that the allusions enable us to determine with certainty whether the *Parmenides* is earlier than both the others, later than both, or intermediate between the two. Raeder has tried to show at length that the *Phaedrus* contains allusions which would only be intelligible to readers who already knew the *Republic*; but there are gaps in his argument, and it has not completely convinced some prominent Platonic scholars. Clearly, if we are to arrive at results of any value, we need a clue to the order of composition of the dialogues which will take us much farther than the few certain indications we have so far found.

In the earlier part of the nineteenth century more than one unsatisfactory attempt was made to provide such a clue. Thus it was at one time held that we can detect signs of comparative youth in the gorgeous rhetoric of certain dialogues, and the *Phaedrus* in particular was often assumed to be the earliest of the dialogues on this ground. But it is obvious that reasoning of this kind is inherently untrustworthy, especially in dealing with the work of a great dramatic artist. Inferences from the manner of the *Phaedrus* are, for example, to be discounted partly on the ground that its rhetoric is largely parody of the rhetoricians, partly because so much of its content is imaginative myth which lends itself naturally to a high-flown diction. The assumption that works in which there is a large element of semi-poetical myth must be "juvenile" obviously rests on another assumption, for which we have no evidence at all, that we know independently what the personal temperament of the youthful Plato was. We have only to think of the known chronological order of the works of Goethe to see how unsound a method must be which would require us to regard the second part of *Faust* or *Wilhelm Meisters Wanderjahre* as juvenile productions. A still more arbitrary assumption underlies the attempt of E. Munk to arrange the dialogues in order on the assumption that the age ascribed to Socrates in a dialogue is an indication of its date. On the theory that dialogues which represent Socrates as a young man must be early, those which represent him as old, late, we should have to put the *Parmenides*, where Socrates is " very young," at the opening of the series, the *Theaetetus*, which narrates a conversation held just before his trial, at the other end, though the allusion in the one dialogue to the meeting which provides the setting for the other shows that they are probably not to be separated by too long an interval.

The serious scientific investigation of the internal evidence for the order of composition of the dialogues really begins in 1867 with Lewis Campbell's philological proof of the genuineness of the *Sophistes* and *Politicus*. It has been further developed, sometimes with too much confidence in its results, by a whole host of writers, notably Dittenberger and C. Ritter in Germany, and W. Lutoslawski in this country. The underlying and sound principle of the method may be simply stated thus. If we start with two works which are known to be separated by a considerable interval and exhibit a marked difference in style, it may be possible to trace the transition from the writer's earlier to his later manner in detail, to see the later manner steadily more and more replacing the earlier, and this should enable us to arrive at some definite conclusions about the order of the works which occupy the interval. The conclusion will be strengthened if we take for study a number of distinct and independent peculiarities and find a general coincidence in the order in which the various peculiarities seem to become more and more settled mannerisms. The opportunity for applying this method to the work of Plato is afforded by the well-authenticated fact that the *Laws* is a composition of old age, while the *Republic* is one of an earlier period, and forms with certain other great dialogues, such as the *Protagoras, Phaedo, Symposium,* a group distinguished by a marked common style and a common vigour of dramatic representation which experience shows we cannot expect from a writer who is not in the prime of his powers. Growing resemblance to the manner of the *Laws*, if made out on several independent but consilient lines of inquiry, may thus enable us to discover which of the Platonic dialogues must be intermediate between the *Laws* and the *Republic*. There are several different peculiarities we may obviously select for study. Thus one obvious contrast between *Republic* and *Laws* is to be found in the marked decline of dramatic power. A second is that the *Laws* conforms carefully to a whole number of the graces of style introduced into Attic prose by Isocrates, the *Republic* and the other great dramatic dialogues neglect these elegancies. A third line of study which has been very minutely pursued, especially by Lutoslawski, is the examination of special uses of connecting particles throughout the dialogues. Without going into detail, it is enough to say here that the result of these converging lines of study has been to convince students of Platonic language and idiom, almost without an exception, that we can definitely specify a certain group of very important dialogues as belonging to the post-*Republic* period of Plato's life. The group comprises *Theaetetus, Parmenides, Sophistes, Politicus, Timaeus, Philebus, Laws*. The identification of this group of " later " dialogues may be taken as a pretty assured and definite result, not likely ever to be seriously modified.

It is another question whether the employment of the same method would enable us to distinguish more precisely between the earlier and later dialogues belonging to either of the two great groups, so as to say, *e.g.*, whether the *Philebus* is earlier or later in composition than the *Timaeus*, the *Symposium* than the *Phaedo*. When two works belong to much the same period of an author's activity, a slight difference of style between them may easily be due to accidental causes. (Thus in dealing with the *Symposium* we should have to remember that a very large part of it is professed imitation or parody of the styles of others.) Lutoslawski in particular seems to me to have pushed a sound principle to the pitch of absurdity in the attempt, by the help of the integral calculus, to extract from considerations of " stylometry " a detailed and definite order of composition for the whole of the dialogues. It may fairly be doubted whether " stylometric " evidence can carry us much beyond the broad discrimination between an earlier series of dialogues of which the *Republic* is the capital work and a later series composed in the interval between the completion of the *Republic* and Plato's death.

It is possible, however, that some supplementary considerations may take us a little further. Plato himself explains, in the introductory conversation prefixed to the *Theaetetus*, that he has avoided the method of indirect narration of a dialogue for that of direct dialogue in order to avoid the wearisomeness of keeping up the formula of a reported narrative. Now the greatest dialogues of the earlier period, the *Protagoras, Symposium, Phaedo, Republic*, are all reported dialogues, and one of them, the *Symposium*, is actually reported at second-hand. So again is the *Parmenides*, where the standing formula, as Professor Burnet calls it, is the cumbrous " Antiphon told us that Pythodorus said that Parmenides said." The original adoption of this method of narration of a conversation is manifestly due to the desire for dramatic life and colour.

It permits of the sort of record of the by-play between the personages of the story which contributes so much to the charm of the *Phaedo*. But the labour required to keep up the " formula " is so great that it is not surprising that Plato finally dropped it, and that the *Theaetetus* and all the works we find reason to place later are in the form of direct dialogue. To me it seems highly probable, though not certain, that it was the special complication of the formula required for the *Parmenides* which led to the final abandonment of the method, and that we may plausibly infer that the *Parmenides* was written either simultaneously with the *Theaetetus* or immediately before it. Another inference which I should draw with some confidence is that, since no young writer is likely to have made his first prentice experiments in dialogue with so difficult a form, the popular view that the *Protagoras* is one of the earliest of the Platonic dialogues must be erroneous. The certainty and vigour of the dramatic handling of the characters there should prove that the *Protagoras* belongs as a fourth with the *Phaedo*, *Symposium*, and *Republic* to the period of Plato's supreme excellence as a dramatist and stylist. In particular, it must be a considerably later work than the comparatively undramatic and rather unduly diffuse *Gorgias*, a point which has some bearing on the interpretation of the purpose and ethical teaching of the *Protagoras*.

We may turn next to the question whether it is possible to fix any definite date in Plato's life as a *terminus ad quem* for the earlier series of dialogues, or a *terminus a quo* for the later. Something, I believe, may be done to settle both these questions. I have already referred in the last chapter to the statement made by Plato in *Ep.* vii., written after the murder of Dion in the year 354, that he came to Sicily in his forty-first year already convinced that the salvation of mankind depends on the union of the philosopher and the " ruler " in one person. The actual words of the letter are that Plato had been driven to *say* this " in a eulogy on true philosophy," and this seems an unmistakable allusion to the occurrence of the same statement in *Rep.* 499 ff. It should follow that this most philosophically advanced section of the *Republic* was already written in the year 388–7, with the consequence that the *Republic*, and by consequence the earlier dialogues in general, were completed at least soon after Plato was forty and perhaps before foundation of the Academy. If we turn next to the dialogue which seems to prelude to the later group, the *Theaetetus*, we get another indication of date. The dialogue mentions the severe and dangerous wound received by the mathematician Theaetetus in a battle fought under the walls of Corinth which cannot well be any but that of the year 369. It is assumed tacitly all through that Theaetetus will not recover from his injuries and is clear that the discourse was composed after his death and mainly as a graceful tribute to his memory. Thus, allowing for the time necessary for the completion of so considerable a work, we may suppose the dialogue to have been written just before Plato's first departure on his important practical enterprise at Syracuse. This, as Professor Burnet has said, seems to be the explanation of the magnificent eulogy of the retired and contemplative life, a passage confessed by Plato himself to be an irrelevance so far as the argument of the dialogue is concerned. Plato is giving expression to the reluctance with which he leaves the Academy, at the bidding of duty and honour, for the turmoil and sordidness of the political arena.

Once more, the *Sophistes* seems to give us an approximate date. It is the first of the series of dialogues in which the deliberate adoption of the Isocratean avoidance of hiatus occurs. This would naturally suggest a probable break of some length in Plato's activity as a writer just before the composition of the *Sophistes*. Now it is antecedently probable that there must have been such an interruption between 367 and 360, the year of Plato's last return from Syracuse. His entanglements with Dionysius and Sicilian affairs, combined with his duties as head of the Academy, are likely to have left him little leisure for literary occupation in these years.

Thus we may say with every appearance of probability that there are two distinct periods of literary activity to be distinguished in Plato's life. The first cannot have begun before the death of Socrates ; apart from the absurdity of the conception of Plato as " dramatizing " the sayings and doings of the living man whom he revered above all others, it is fairly plain that the original motive for the composition of " discourses of Socrates " by the *viri Socratici* was to preserve the memory of a living presence which they had lost. It apparently continued down to Plato's fortieth or forty-first year and the opening of the Academy, and it includes all the work in which Plato's dramatic art is most fresh and vigorous. The main object of this incessant activity seems to be to immortalize the personality of Socrates. For twenty years after the foundation of the Academy Plato seems to have written nothing, unless the *Phaedrus*, a difficult dialogue to account for on any theory, falls early in this period. This is as it should be : the President of the Academy would for long enough after its foundation be far too busy to write. Then, probably on the eve of the Sicilian adventure, after twenty years of work the Academy is sufficiently organized to leave its head, now a man of some sixty years, leisure to write the *Theaetetus* and *Parmenides*; but an opportunity for continuous writing does not present itself until Plato's final withdrawal from active personal participation in " world politics." The composition of five such works as *Sophistes, Politicus, Timaeus, Philebus, Laws,* is a notable achievement for any man between the ages of sixty-seven and eighty-one. But we must think of this work as being executed simultaneously with regular oral exposition of the doctrine described by Aristotle as the " philosophy of Plato." It is an entire misconception to relegate this last stage in the development of Plato's thought, as the textbooks often seem to do, to a " senile " year or two subsequent to the close of Plato's activity as a writer. It must have been contemporary with the writing of the whole

" later " group of dialogues, and the man who was still at his death labouring on the *Laws* can never have sunk into " senility."

See further:

BURNET, J.—*Platonism*, Ch. 1, 4.

CAMPBELL, L.—" *Sophistes* " and " *Politicus* " of Plato (1867), General Introduction.

HACKFORTH, R.—*The Authorship of the Platonic Epistles*. (Manchester, 1913.)

RAEDER, H.—*Platons philosophische Entwickelung*. (Leipzig, 1905.)

LUTOSLAWSKI, W.—*Origin and Growth of Plato's Logic*. (1897.)

PARMENTIER, L.—*La Chronologie des dialogues de Platon*. (Brussels, 1913.)

RITTER, C.—*Untersuchungen ueber Platon*. (Stuttgart, 1882.) ; *Neue Untersuchungen ueber Platon*. (Munich, 1910.)

LEVI, A.—*Sulle interpretazioni immanentistiche della filosofia di Platone*. (Turin, N.D.)

SHOREY, P.—*The Unity of Plato's Thought*. (Chicago, 1903.)

SHOREY, P.—*What Plato Said*, pp. 58–73.

ROBIN, L.—*Platon*, pp. 19–48.

NOVOTNÝ, F.—*Platonis Epistulae*.

HARWARD, J.—*The Platonic Epistles* (Introduction).

NOTE.—I do not deny that Plato's " first period " may have extended into the opening years of his career in the Academy. On my own reasoning this must be so if the *Phaedo* should, after all, be later than the *Republic*. It has been argued (*e.g.* by M. Parmentier) that the *Symposium* must be later than 385, the year of the death of Aristophanes. I doubt, however, whether too much has not been made of the supposed Platonic rule not to introduce living persons as speakers. Callias was alive and active years after any date to which we can reasonably assign the *Protagoras*. Euclides, who was alive and apparently well when Theaetetus received his wound, is more likely than not to have survived the writing of the *Theaetetus*. Socrates " the younger " can hardly be taken to have been dead when the *Politicus* was written. Gorgias *may* have lived long enough to read the *Gorgias*. Simmias, if we may believe Plutarch *de genio Socratis,* was alive and active in 379. That the majority of Plato's personages are characters already dead when his dialogues were written, seems to me a mere consequence of the fact that the dialogues deal with Socrates and his contemporaries.

[It might be urged against the reasoning of the first paragraph of p. 20 *supra* that several, if not all, of the dialogues of Aeschines (certainly the *Aspasia, Alcibiades, Callias, Axiochus*) were of the " narrated " type. But they were narrations of the simplest kind of which the *Charmides* and *Laches* are examples, and such evidence as we have suggests that they are all later in date of composition than the earliest work of Plato.]

CHAPTER III

MINOR SOCRATIC DIALOGUES : *HIPPIAS MAJOR,*
HIPPIAS MINOR, ION, MENEXENUS

LOVERS of great literature have every reason to be whole-heartedly thankful that once in the world's history a supreme philosophical thinker should also have been a superb dramatic artist. But what is to them pure gain is, in some ways, gain at the expense of the average student of " metaphysics." For several reasons it is quite impossible to construct a neatly arranged systematic handbook to the " Platonic philosophy." In the first place, it is doubtful whether there ever was a " Platonic philosophy " at all, in the sense of a definite set of formulated doctrines about the *omne scibile.* Plato has done his best to make it quite clear that he took no great interest in " system-making." To him philosophy meant no compact body of " results " to be learned, but a life spent in the active personal pursuit of truth and goodness by the light of one or two great passionate convictions. It is not likely that, even at the end of his life of eighty years, he fancied himself to have worked out anything like a coherent, clearly articulated " theory of everything." Systematization of this kind commonly has to be paid for by intellectual stagnation ; the vitality and progressiveness of Platonism is probably largely owing to the fact that, even in the mind of its originator, it always remained largely tentative and provisional. If there ever was a Platonic " system," at least Plato himself resolutely refused to write an exposition of it,[1] and we of later times, who do not possess any record of the oral teaching which was clearly intended to be the vehicle of Plato's most personal and intimate thinking, are not in a position to make the lack good. The dialogues will tell us something of Plato's fundamental life-

---

[1] *Ep.* vii. 341c : " There does not exist, and there never shall, any treatise by myself on these matters. The subject does not admit, as the sciences in general do, of exposition. It is only after long association in the great business itself and a shared life that a light breaks out in the soul, kindled, so to say, by a leaping flame, and thereafter feeds itself." *Ep.* ii. 314c : " I have never myself written a word on these topics, and there neither is nor ever shall be any treatise by Plato ; what now bears the name belongs to Socrates beautified and rejuvenated." That is, all that a teacher can do in philosophy is to awaken in a younger mind the spirit of independent personal thinking ; the dialogues are meant not to expound a " Platonic system," but to preserve the memory of Socrates. One of Plato's grounds for dissatisfaction with Dionysius II was that he had circulated a work professing to expound " Platonism " (*Ep.* vii. 341b).

long convictions ; of his " system," if he had one, they hardly tell us anything at all. With Aristotle we are in a very different position. We have lost the " works " in which he recommended his " views " to the world at large, and possess the manuscripts of courses of lectures in which we see him, for the most part, feeling his way to his results through the criticism of others.

Further special difficulties are created for us by certain peculiarities of Plato's literary temperament. Unlike Aristotle, he does not introduce himself and his opinions into his dialogues. He is, in fact, at great pains, with the instinct of the great dramatist, to keep his own personality completely in the background. Socrates is present as one of the speakers in all the dialogues except the *Laws*, and in all except those which we have seen reason to regard as written in late life, Socrates is not only the chief speaker but dominates the whole dialogue by his vivid and strongly marked personality. It can hardly be doubted that in the long list of works written before Plato had found his real vocation as head of the Academy, the main conscious object of the writer is to preserve a faithful and living portrait of the older philosopher.

Even if we accept the view originated about the beginning of the nineteenth century, that Plato has transfigured the personality and teaching of Socrates out of recognition, we are bound, I think, to hold that the transfiguration has been unconscious. We cannot seriously ascribe to Plato deliberate and pointless mystification. This means, of itself, that Plato carefully devotes himself to reproducing the life and thought of a generation to which he did not himself belong, and that whatever indications he may have given us of his personal doctrines have to be given under restrictions imposed by this selection of a vanished age as the background of the dialogues. (Thus we cannot read the *Republic* intelligently unless we bear carefully in mind both that the whole work presupposes as its setting the Athens of the Archidamian war and that this setting had vanished into the past by 413, when Plato was still no more than a boy. So to understand the *Protagoras* we have to remember that we are dealing with a still earlier time, Athens under Pericles shortly before the outbreak of the great war, and that Plato was not even born at the date of the gathering of the "wits " in the house of Callias.) There are only two characters among the host of personages in Plato's dialogues of whom one can be certain that they are not actual historical figures of the fifth century, the unnamed Eleatic of the *Sophistes* and *Politicus* and the unnamed Athenian of the *Laws*. They have been left anonymous apparently on purpose that their creator may be at liberty to express thoughts of his own through them with a freedom impossible in the case of figures who are " kennt men," with characters and views of their own which have to be taken into account.

This is generally admitted on all hands except for the one most important figure of all, that of Socrates. Him, it is still maintained in many quarters, though not so confidently as it used to be maintained thirty or forty years ago, Plato treated without scruple, to the point of putting into his mouth all sorts of theories invented by Plato himself after the death of their ostensible exponent. I cannot myself believe in this extraordinary exception to the general rule, but even if one does believe in it, the general situation is not very seriously affected. Even those who most freely credit Plato with fathering his own views on Socrates commonly admit that some of the views ascribed to Socrates in the dialogues (if only those expressed in the *Apology*) are those of the actual Socrates, and to admit this means admitting at least that we have somehow to distinguish between those utterances of " Socrates " which are really deliverances of " Plato " and those which are not, and it becomes a difficult problem to know on what principle the distinction is to be made. Finally, there is a further difficulty arising from the very life-likeness of the dialogues of the earlier groups. In nearly all of them except the shortest, the conversation wanders, as actual talk does, over a wide field of topics. Metaphysics, ethics, the principles of government, of economics, of art-criticism, of education, may all come under consideration in one and the same conversation. If we try to isolate the topics, putting together under one head all Plato has to say anywhere about economics, under another all his utterances about religion, under a third his views on beauty and the arts, we run the very serious risk of confusing what may be views learned early in life, and very largely taken over receptively from a predecessor, with the very ripest fruits of a life of intense personal thought. (Thus it would be rash to confound in one amalgam utterances about early education taken from the *Republic*, written probably before Plato was forty and at any rate *possibly* more Socratic than Platonic, with others taken from the *Laws*, the *magnum opus* of Plato's old age, where there is no Socrates in question to cause any difficulty.) A work on Platonic philosophy composed on these principles may be an admirably digested " cram-book " ; it is certain to obliterate every trace of the development of Plato's thought. For all these reasons, it seems the better choice between evils, to deal with the different dialogues *seriatim*, even at the cost of some repetition.

Accordingly I propose first to consider what we may call the " Socratic " group among the dialogues, the series of works culminating, so far as ripeness of thought and compass of subjects are concerned, in the *Republic*, grouping the slighter dialogues together but dwelling more fully on the detail of the greater and richer. Next I propose to treat separately each of the great dialogues of Plato's later age in the same way. In both cases I must remind my reader that I do not believe that many results of anything like certainty can be reached in the determination of the precise order of composition of particular dialogues. In the case of the earlier group, which I call Socratic in the sense that they are dominated by the personality of Plato's Socrates, I make no assumption about this order beyond the general one that the four great dialogues which have the widest range of subject-matter and are also reported at second-hand are maturer work than the slighter dialogues which have the form of direct conversation, and presumably also than shorter "indirect" conversations like the *Charmides* and *Euthydemus*. Beyond this, the order in which I shall examine the dialogues has no merit except that of convenience. Similarly the arrangement I shall adopt for the dialogues of later life is not meant to carry any silent chronological implications.

With one or two trifling exceptions most of the dialogues we shall have first to review have an ethical purport. (Perhaps the only complete exception of any importance is afforded by the *Cratylus*.) The interest of many of them is by no means exclusively ethical, sometimes (as in the case of the *Euthydemus*) not ostensibly primarily ethical, but we commonly find that the discussion either begins with, or is found as it proceeds to involve, the great practical issue of the right direction of conduct. It is therefore advisable to begin at the outset by formulating very briefly and in a way which brings out their interconnexion, a few simple principles which we shall find running through the whole of Plato's treatment of the moral being of man. Since we find these principles taken for granted in what has every mark of being Plato's earliest work as well as in his ripest and latest, we may fairly regard them as a legacy from Socrates ; and the most characteristic of them are, in fact, specifically attributed to Socrates by Aristotle, though we have no reason to suppose that Aristotle had any reason for the attribution beyond the fact that the principles in question are put into the mouth of Socrates in the Platonic dialogues, notably in the *Protagoras*. The most bald and straightforward statement of these principles as a whole in the Platonic *corpus* is perhaps that of the *Alcibiades I*, which has every appearance of being intended as a compendium of ethics composed by an immediate disciple and possibly during Plato's lifetime. We may reproduce the main line of argument adopted there and elsewhere much as follows.

The one great standing aim of men in all they do is to attain happiness (*eudaimonia*), in other words to make a success, in the best sense of the word, of life. Every one wants to make a success of his private life ; if a man is conscious of abilities and opportunities which open the way to prominence as a public man, he is anxious to make a success of the affairs of his " city," to be a successful states- man. This is what we mean by being a *good* man ; the *good* man is the man who "conducts his own affairs, those of his household, those of the city, *well.*" And the words *good* and *well* are not used here in a narrowly moralistic sense. To conduct your business well means to make a thorough success of it ; the good man is the thoroughly effective man. But to make a thorough success of life means to achieve and possess *good.* We may say then that all men alike desire *good* and nothing but good. A man may conceivably prefer the appearance or reputation of some things to their reality ; *e.g.* a man may prefer a reputation for a virtue he does not possess to the possession of the virtue, or he might prefer being thought handsome or witty to being really so. But no one ever prefers being thought to enjoy good to the actual enjoyment of good. Where good is concerned, every one wishes really to have it, and not to put up with a counterfeit. If a man chooses, as many men do, what is not really good, the reason must be that he wrongly supposes it to be good. No one would ever knowingly choose evil when he might choose good, or leave a good he might have had unchosen. This is the meaning of the famous " Socratic " paradox that " all wrongdoing is involuntary." It is involuntary in the sense that the man who chooses what is bad only chooses it because he wrongly thinks it good. And so with the other " paradox " that no one ever knows the good without acting on his knowledge. It cannot be true that men "know the good but do the bad "; that would imply choice of an evil known to be evil, and such a choice is impossible.

Now when we come to consider the different things which men commonly call " good " and wish to have, we see at once that they are of various kinds. Some of them are material possessions. Many men think that good means just plenty of things of this sort. But we can easily see that material things are not good except for a man who knows how to use them. It would be no good to a man, for example, to have flutes, or musical instruments of any kind, unless he knew how to use them. Flutes are good—for the man who knows how to play on them. Similarly it would be no real good to you to possess all the gold in the world, unless you know how to *use* it. Again, men think that bodily beauty, strength and agility, robust health, are very good things. But health and strength again may be misused ; they are good only for the man who knows how to make the proper use of them. If a man has not this knowledge, but " abuses " his physical advantages, it might be much better for him if he had been less robust and active. The same thing is true of intellectual " parts." A man is not really the better for parts and accomplishments which he does not know how to use rightly. In fact we may say that if health, wealth, and the recognized " good " things are to be really good, it is first of all necessary that the user of these things should be good. Now that which uses all other things, even a man's body, is his *soul*. The soul *is* the man, and everything else that is his is merely something he has or owns. A man, in fact, is a " soul *using* a body " (this is the standing Academic definition of " man ").[1] Hence the first condition of enjoying real good and making a real success of life is that a man's soul should be in a good or healthy state. And the good or healthy state of the soul is just the wisdom or knowledge (*sophia, phronesis*) which ensures that a man shall make the right use of his body and of everything else which is his. Hence the first duty of every man who means to enjoy good or happiness is to " tend his soul," " to

---

[1] For this reasoning see *Alc. I* 119a–133d, *Euthydemus,* 278e–282d, 288d–292e. For the soul as the real " man " which " uses " the body see *Alc. I* 130c.

see to it that his soul is as good as it possibly can be," that is, to get the knowledge or insight which ensures his using everything rightly. And before a man can develop this quality of soul, he must be brought to " know himself," that is, to recognize the imperative need of moral wisdom and the dreadfulness of his present state of ignorance.[1] This is why Socrates taught that " all the virtues are one thing," wisdom or moral insight, and why he insisted that the necessary preparation for the private man or the statesman who means to make life a success is the " tendance of his own soul," and the first step towards this " tendance " is true self-knowledge. The same considerations explain the peculiar character of the mission Socrates believes himself to have received from heaven. He does not claim, like the professional teacher of an " art " such as medicine or music, to have ready-made knowledge to impart to anyone, and hence he denies that he has ever had " disciples." For he does not profess to have attained the wisdom or insight of which he speaks, but only to have attained to the perception that it is the one thing needful for the conduct of life. He claims only that he makes it the business of his life to " tend his own soul " and exhorts all his fellow-citizens, high and low, old and young, to do the same, and that he has a certain power of bringing home to others by his questions the grossness and danger of their ignorance of themselves. His function is simply to impress on all and sundry the misery of the state of ignorance in which they find themselves " by nature " and the importance of " coming out of it." How a man is to come out of this state of nature is not explained anywhere,[2] but in proportion as he does come out of it and advance to true insight, true knowledge of moral good and evil, all the different " virtues " or excellences of character and conduct will automatically ensue from this knowledge.

These fundamental elementary notions will suffice to explain the general character of most of the earliest " Socratic " dialogues. The procedure adopted is commonly this. Some term of moral import for the conduct of life, one of those words which everybody is using as familiar expressions daily without much consideration of their precise meaning, such as " courage," " self-mastery," or even " virtue " itself, is taken and we ask the question whether we can say exactly what it means. A number of answers are suggested and examined, but all are found wanting. None of them will stand careful scrutiny. Usually the result arrived at is a negative one. We discover to our shame that we do not really know the meaning of the most familiar epithets which we use every day of our lives to convey moral approval or censure. This revelation of our own ignorance is painful, but it has the advantage that we have taken a

---

[1] This is the message with which Socrates regarded himself as charged by God to his fellow-citizens and mankind in general (*Apol.* 29*d–e*, 36*c*, 41*c*).

[2] Naturally not. An answer to this question would raise the issues covered in Christian theology by the doctrine of " grace." We must not look for an anticipation of Augustine in Hellenic moral philosophy.

step forward. At any rate, our knowledge of our own ignorance will henceforth prevent our fancying that we really knew when we were repeating some of the formulae which our inquiry has condemned. Now that we know that we do not know what it is so necessary for the conduct of life to know, we are at least left with a heightened sense of the importance of " tendance of the soul " ; we shall not, like the rest of mankind, suppose ourselves to be in spiritual health when we are really inwardly diseased ; our very knowledge of the gravity of our spiritual malady will make us all the more unremitting in our determination to make the attempt to escape from our ignorance the great business of life. This, rather than anything more specific in the way of " positive results," is the conclusion Plato means us to draw from these " dialogues of search." It has been objected to Plato by unsympathetic critics, as he makes some of his characters object it to Socrates, that such a conclusion is not satisfactory. Socrates, Grote thinks, should have exchanged the easier part of critic for that of defender of theses of his own. He would have found that they could be subjected to a dialectic like his own with effects as damaging as those produced on his rivals' theories by himself. The objection misses the mark. Plato's object is not to propound theorems in moral science for our instruction, but to rouse us to give our own personal care to the conduct of our moral life by convincing us of the ignorance we usually disguise from ourselves by acquiescence in uncriticized half-truths and the practical gravity of that ignorance. He wishes to make us think to the purpose about the great concern of life, not to do our thinking for us. From his point of view, complacent satisfaction with false conceptions of good is the deadliest of all maladies of the soul ; if he can make us honestly dissatisfied with our customary loose thinking, he has produced exactly the effect he designed.

We may now, bearing these few simple ideas in mind, consider the arguments of some of the early dialogues.

The Greater Hippias.—The form of the dialogue is the simplest possible ; it is a direct colloquy between Socrates and a single speaker, the well-known polymath Hippias of Elis, who figures also in the *Lesser Hippias*, the *Protagoras*, and a conversation, perhaps suggested by the opening remarks of our dialogue, in the fourth book of Xenophon's *Memorabilia*.[1] The presence of Hippias at Athens implies that the time is one of peace, and, as the first visit of Gorgias to the city is referred to as a past event (282*b*), the supposed date must be after 427 B.C., and therefore during the years of the peace of Nicias. Hippias is depicted as childishly conceited on the strength of the great variety of topics he is able to expound, and the brilliant financial success which attends him wherever he goes. Even at Sparta—a city where he is often called on matters of state— though no interest is taken in his astronomy and mathematics, he has made a resounding success with a more immediately practical

[1] Xenophon, *Memor.* iv. 4.

subject, a set homily put into the mouth of Nestor on " the kind of fine achievements by which a young man may win high reputation " (286*b*). This remark leads on to the main subject of the dialogue, the question what is really meant by the word καλόν, beautiful, which was commonly employed, like its Latin equivalent *honestum*, and our colloquial " fine," to express both physical and moral beauty. Socrates professes to have much trouble in satisfying the question of a certain combative and ill-mannered acquaintance who has reproached him for constantly using the epithets καλόν and αἰσχρόν, " fine " and " ugly," in judgments of value without being able to explain their exact meaning. Can Hippias help him out of his perplexity ? (It does not call for much perspicacity to see that the imaginary " rude fellow " who insists on asking awkward questions is no other than Socrates himself.[1]) The precise problem is this. We call an act of remarkable courage a " fine " act, and we say the same thing about an act of outstanding and remarkable justice. The use of the same word " fine " in both cases implies that there is a something (a certain εἶδος, form, or character—the word is little more than a synonym for a " something ") common to both cases, or why do we give them the same name, " fine " ? What is " the fine itself," " the just fine " (αὐτὸ τὸ καλόν), *i.e.* what is it which is exactly and precisely named when we use the word " fine " ?[2] Hippias, like many interlocutors in Plato, underrates the difficulty of the problem because he confuses the *meaning* of a term with an *example* of it. He answers that a " fine girl " is, of course, something " fine " (287*e*). But this clearly tells us nothing about the *meaning* of " fine." There are also " fine " horses, " fine " musical instruments, even " fine " pots and pans, like those made by the masters of Attic pottery (288*d*), and, after all, the beauty of the " fine girl " is relative. She would not be " fine " by comparison with a goddess (289*b*). What then is " the just fine," the character which all " fine " things exhibit ? (289*d*). Here again Hippias makes an elementary blunder. Anything, he says, is made " fine," if it is gilded, and so " that which by its presence makes a thing fine " may be said to be just *gold* (289*e*).

But then the objection occurs that Phidias notoriously did not gild the features of his famous chryselephantine Athena, and surely Phidias may be presumed to have known his own business as an artist (290*b*). This leads, at last, to a real attempt to *define* " the fine." The " fine " is " the becoming " or " fitting " or " appropriate " (τὸ πρέπον, 290*c*). It would follow from this at once that a soup-spoon of wood, because more " fitting," is more beautiful or " fine " than a golden spoon (291*c*). Note that Socrates does not

---

[1] See 288*d*, where Socrates humorously describes his pertinacious questioner as " no wit, one of the *canaille* who cares nothing for anything but the truth," and 298*b* 11, where he as good as identifies him with " the son of Sophroniscus."

[2] The characteristic phrases αὐτὸ τὸ καλόν and εἶδος are introduced at 289*d* without explanation, as something quite familiar. They bear the same

positively assert this conclusion, as he is represented as doing by interpreters who are determined to see nothing in him but a commonplace utilitarian. He obviously intends to raise a difficulty. It seemed a satisfactory explanation of the procedure of Phidias to say that a statue with a gilded face would not be " beautiful " because the gilding would not be " befitting." Yet, though a common wooden spoon would be more " in place " where one is eating soup than a golden one, it is a *paradox* to say that because the wooden spoon is " in place," it is a thing of beauty. Whatever may be the true answer to the question what " beauty " is, the identification of the aesthetically " fine " with the " befitting " is far too crude a solution.

Hippias evidently feels the difficulty, and is made to fall back again on an illustration, this time from the moral sphere. It is eminently " fine " to live in health, wealth, and honours, to bury your parents splendidly, and to receive in the fullness of days a splendid funeral from your descendants (291*d*). But this, again, is manifestly no true definition. A definition must be rigidly universal. But every one will admit that Heracles and Achilles and others who preferred a short and glorious to a long and inglorious life, and so died young and left their parents to survive them, made a " fine " choice (292*e*–293*c*). The illustration has thus led nowhere, and we have still to discuss the definition of the " fine " as the " fitting " or " becoming " on its own merits. When a thing has the character of being " becoming," does this make it " fine," or does it only make the thing *seem* " fine " ? Hippias prefers the second alternative, since even a scarecrow of a man can· be made to look " finer " if he is " becomingly" dressed. But, obviously, if " propriety " makes things seem finer than they really are, " the appropriate " and the " fine " cannot be the same thing (294*b*). And we cannot get out of the difficulty, as Hippias would like to do, by saying the " appropriateness " *both* makes things " fine " and makes them seem " fine." If that were so, what really *is* " fine " would always *seem* fine too. Yet it is notorious that communities and individuals differ about nothing more than about the question what sort of conduct is " fine " (294*c*–*d*). Thus if " appropriateness " actually makes things " fine," the proposed definition may possibly be the right one ; but if it only makes them " seem " fine— (we have seen that the alternatives are exclusive of one another)— the definition must clearly be rejected. And Hippias is satisfied that this second alternative is the true one (294*e*). (Hume's well-known ethical theory affords a good illustration of the point of this reasoning. Hume sets himself to show that every society thinks the kind of conduct it " disinterestedly " likes virtuous and the

meaning which they have in dialogues where the so-called " ideal theory " is expounded. They mean that which is denoted without excess or defect by a significant name, a determinate character. This is a good illustration of the way in which the " ideal theory " is directly suggested by the everyday use of language. It is assumed that if several things can each be significantly called *x*, then *x* has a determinate significance which is the same in all the cases.

conduct it " disinterestedly " dislikes vicious. He then assumes that he has proved that these two kinds of conduct really *are* virtuous and vicious respectively, and that because a society knows certainly what it likes and what it dislikes, it is infallible in its judgments about virtue and vice. There is manifestly no connexion between the premises of this reasoning and its conclusion.) Socrates now (295c) throws out a suggestion of his own for examination. Perhaps it may be that the " fine " is the same as the " useful." At any rate, by " fine eyes " we seem to mean eyes which do their work of seeing well, by a " fine " or " handsome " body one which discharges its various functions well, and the same considerations seem to hold good of " fine " horses, ships, implements of all kinds, and " fine " social institutions. In all these cases we seem to call " fine " that which serves the use to which it is to be put well, and " ugly " that which serves that use badly. The examples, drawn from a wide range of facts, thus suggest an obvious generalization, and the use of them to suggest it is an illustration of what Aristotle had in mind when he specified " inductive arguments " as one of the contributions of Socrates to philosophical method.[1]

If the definition once given were magisterially proposed for our acceptance, Socrates would thus stand revealed as a pure utilitarian in moral and aesthetic theory. But it is, in fact, put forward tentatively as a suggestion for examination. The examination is conducted in strict accord with the requirements of the dialectical method as described in the *Phaedo*.[2] The first step is to see what consequences follow from the suggested " postulate " ($\dot{\upsilon}\pi\dot{o}\theta\epsilon\sigma\iota\varsigma$). If the consequences are found to be in accord with known facts, and thus so far " verified," the postulate will be regarded as *so far* justified ; if some of them prove to be at variance with fact, it must be modified or dismissed, it cannot hold the field as it stands.

What consequences follow, then, from the identification of the " fine " with the " useful " ? There is one at least which must give us pause. A thing is useful for what it *can* do, not for what it cannot ; thus our formula apparently leads to the identification of τὸ καλόν with *power* to produce some result. But results may be good or they may be bad, and it seems monstrous to hold that power to produce evil is " fine." We must, at the least, modify our statement by saying that the " fine " is that which can produce *good, i.e.*, whether the " useful " is " fine " or not will depend on the goodness or badness of the end to which it is instrumental. Now we call that which is instrumental to good " profitable " (ὠφελιμόν) ; thus our proposed definition must be made more specific by a further determination. We must say " the fine "

[1] Aristot. *Met.* M1078b 27. Note that neither Socrates nor Aristotle regards the " induction " as a proof. The generalization τὸ καλόν = τὸ χρησιμόν has yet to be tested and may have to be rejected. The testing is the work of intellectual analysis, or, as Socrates and Plato call it " dialectic."
[2] *Phaedo*, 100a–b, 101d.

is that which is profitable (instrumental to the production of good) (296e).

Even so, we have a worse difficulty to face. We are saying in effect that the " fine " = that which causes good as its result. But a cause and its effect are always different (or, in modern language, causality is always transitive). Hence, if the " fine " is the *cause* of good, it must follow that what is " fine " is never itself good, and what is good is never itself " fine," and this is a monstrous paradox (297a). It seems then that the attempt to give a utilitarian definition of τὸ καλόν must be abandoned.

Possibly we may succeed better with a hedonist theory of beauty. The pictures, statues, and the like which we call " fine " all give us pleasure, and so do music and literature. In the one case the pleasure is got from sight, in the other from hearing. This suggests the new theory that the " fine " is " that which it is pleasant to see or hear " (298a). And we may even get in " moral beauty " under the formula, for " fine conduct " and " fine laws " are things which it gives us pleasure to see or to hear. But there is a logical difficulty to face. We are trying to define the " fine " as " that which it is pleasant to see *and* hear." But, of course, you do not hear the things which it is pleasant to see, nor see the things which it is pleasant to hear. Thus our proposed definition will not be true of either of the classes of things which are " fine," and, being true of neither, it cannot be true of both. We assumed that τὸ καλόν, whatever it may be, must be a character common to all ' fine ' things, but " to be seen and heard " is not a character either of the " pleasures of sight " or of the " pleasures of hearing " (300a, b).

Aristotle comments on the fallacy, formally committed in this argument, of confusing " and " with " or," but the real trouble lies deeper. When the reasoning has been made formally sound by substituting " or " everywhere for " and," it still remains the fact that it is hard to say that the " pleasures of sight " and those of hearing have anything in common but their common character of being pleasant, and it has been the standing assumption of the dialogue that all " fine " things *have* some one common character. But the conclusion, which might seem indicated, that the " fineness " which all " fine " things have in common is just " pleasantness " is excluded by the firm conviction of both Plato and Aristotle that there are " disgraceful," morally " ugly " pleasures, *e.g.* those of the sexual " pervert." At the same time, the proposed formula is at any rate suggestive. There must be some reason why the two unmistakably " aesthetic " senses should be just sight and hearing, though the utilization of the fact demands a much more developed aesthetic psychology than that of our dialogue. The equivocation between " and " and " or " is, on Socrates' part, a conscious trap laid for his antagonist, as he shows when he goes on to remark that, after all, it is possible for " both " to have a character which belongs to neither singly, since, *e.g.*, Socrates and Hippias are a couple, though Socrates is not a couple, nor is Hippias. Thus it would be logically possible that " the pleasures of sight and hearing " might collectively have some character which belongs to neither class separately ; but the possibility is nothing to *our* purpose. For we agreed that the " fine " is a character which makes all " fine " things " fine," and obviously a character which " fine sights " do not possess, (though the collection " fine sights *and* sounds " may possess it,) cannot be what makes " fine " sights fine (303*d*). If we look for some common character which distinguishes both pleasures of sight and pleasures of hearing from other pleasures, and so justifies our calling them in particular the " fine " pleasures, the only obvious character is that both are " harmless " and therefore better than other pleasures, (indulgence in which may easily harm our health or character or repute). But this brings us back to our old formula that the " fine " is the " profitable " with the added specification that it is " profitable pleasure " (303*e*). And thus we are faced once more with the difficulty that the " fine " is made productive of good, or a cause of good, with the consequence that the " fine " is not itself good nor the good itself " fine " (304*a*). Thus the result of the whole discussion is negative. We have only learned that though we are always talking about " fine conduct," as though we knew our own meaning, we are really in a state of mental fog of which we ought to be ashamed. We have discovered our own ignorance of what it is most imperative we should know and what we fancy ourselves to know exceptionally well.

It is in this salutary lesson and not in any of the proposed definitions of the " fine " that we must look for the real significance of the dialogue. But it is also suggestive in other ways. The lesson it gives in the right method of framing and testing a definition is more important than any of the tentative definitions examined. Yet it is a valuable hint towards a more developed aesthetic theory that sensible " beauty " is found to be confined to the perceptions of the two senses of sight and hearing, and the illustration of the golden and wooden spoons might well serve as a warning against the dangers of an unduly " rationalistic " aesthetic theory. A wooden porridge-spoon is not necessarily a thing of beauty because it may be admirably " adapted " for the purposes of the porridge-eater. It is a still more important contribution to sound ethics to have insisted on the impossibility of reducing moral excellence (the " fine " in action) to mere " efficiency," irrespective of the moral quality of the results of the " efficient " agent.[1] And the emphatic insistence on the " transitive " character of all causality—a view which pervades all the best Greek metaphysics from first to last— may be regarded as the opening of a discussion which has continued to our own time and has issues of the most momentous kind for the whole interpretation of existence.[2]

---

[1] Mr. Chesterton remarks somewhere that Fagin was probably an exceptionally " efficient " educator of boys ; the trouble was that he was efficient in teaching them the wrong things.

[2] *E.g.* the cause of Theism is bound up with the position that all genuine causality is " transitive," and that purely " immanent " causality is not caus-

The Lesser Hippias.—This short dialogue, though less ambitious m its scope, is much more brilliantly executed than the *Hippias Major*. Its authenticity is sufficiently established by the fact that Aristotle, though not mentioning the author, quotes the dialogue by name as " the Hippias " ; such explicit references never occur in his work to writings of any " Socratic men " other than Plato.[1] The conversation discusses a single ethical paradox, and its real purport only emerges in the closing words of Socrates.

Socrates opens the talk by quoting an opinion that the *Iliad* is a finer poem than the *Odyssey*, as the hero of the former, Achilles, is a morally nobler character than Odysseus, the hero of the latter. The moralistic tone of this criticism is characteristically Athenian, as we can see for ourselves from a reading of the *Frogs* of Aristophanes, but does not concern us further. The remark is a mere peg on which to hang a discussion of the purely ethical problem in which Socrates is really interested. The transition is effected by the declaration of Hippias that Achilles was certainly a nobler character than Odysseus, since Achilles is single-minded, sincere, and truthful, but Odysseus notoriously *rusé* and a past master of deceit. We see this from the famous lines in the ninth book of the *Iliad*, where Achilles pointedly tells the " artful " Odysseus that he hates the man who says one thing and means another " worse than the gates of Hades " (365a). Socrates replies that, after all, Achilles was no more " truthful " than Odysseus, as the context of this very passage proves. He *said* he would at once desert the expedition, but, in fact, he did nothing of the kind, and, what is more, he actually told his friend Aias a different story. To him he said not that he would sail home, but that he would keep out of the fighting until the Trojans should drive the Achaeans back to their ships (371b). (This is meant to negative the suggestion of Hippias that Achilles honestly meant what he said when he threatened to desert, but changed his mind afterwards because of the unexpected straits to which his comrades-in-arms were reduced.) It looks then as though Homer, unlike Hippias, thought that the " truthful man " and the " liar " are not two, but one and the same.

This is the paradox which Socrates proceeds to defend, and Hippias, in the name of common sense, to deny. Or rather it is the application of a still more general paradox that the man who " misses the mark " (ἁμαρτάνει) on purpose (ἑκών) is " better " than the man who does so " unintentionally " (ἄκων). Popular morality rejects

ality at all. This becomes specially obvious from a study of the famous Aristotelian argument for the " unmoved Mover."

[1] It is barely credible that Aristotle should not have read the admired " Socratic discourses " of Aeschines of Sphettus or the *Alcibiades* of Antisthenes, and it is therefore significant that he never mentions any of these works. We may take it that a named dialogue introducing Socrates *always* means to him a dialogue of Plato, or one regarded by the contemporary Academy as Plato's. And I cannot believe that the Academy itself can have been liable to error about the Platonic authorship of dialogues within a quarter of a century of Plato's death.

a view of this kind as monstrous.   It holds that we ought, as
Hippias says, to show συγγνώμη (to "make allowances") for
involuntary wrong-doing, but that for deliberate wrong-doing there is
no excuse.   The main interest of the dialogue lies in the line of argument by which Socrates impugns this generally accepted thesis.
He proceeds, as usual, by an "inductive" argument, *i.e.* an appeal
to analogy.   In general, the man who knows most about a subject
is of all men the one who can mislead you in his own subject if he
chooses to do so.   An able mathematician, like Hippias, would be
much better able to impose a false demonstration on others than a
non-mathematician, who would only commit fallacies unintentionally
and incidentally, and thus be led into visible self-contradictions.
And the same thing holds good for astronomy (366*d*–368*a*).   The
same thing is true about arts involving manual dexterity (368*b*–
369*b*).   The man who only fails when he means to fail is a much
better craftsman than the man who fails unintentionally from in-
competence.   It is true also of all forms of bodily dexterity.   The
runner who falls behind only when he means to do so, the wrestler
who is thrown when he means to let himself be thrown, is a better
runner or wrestler than the man who falls behind his competitor
or is thrown against his will, because he "can't help it" (373*c*–
374*b*).   So with physical "talents."   The man who only makes a
false note when he means to do so is a better singer than the man
who can't help singing out of tune.   And in the world of industry,
a tool with which you can make a bad stroke when you mean to do
so, is a better tool than one with which you can't help making false
strokes.   And to come to living "implements," a horse or a dog
which does its work badly only when the owner means that it shall,
has a "better soul" than one which does the wrong thing when the
owner means it to do the right one (374*c*–375*c*).   The same thing
would be true of a servant.   (Bob Sawyer's boy, who took the medicines to the wrong houses because he was ordered to do so, was much
more efficient than the sort of boy who blunders about errands
because he is too stupid to do what he is told.)   We may argue by
analogy that our own souls are better if they "go wrong" on purpose than if they do so unintentionally (375*d*).   In fact, we may
condense the principle of the argument thus.   Righteousness or
morality (δικαιοσύνη) is either "power" (δύναμις), or "knowledge"
(ἐπιστήμη), or both.   But the man who *can* do right is better in
respect of "power," a more "able" man than the man who
cannot ; and the man who knows how to do it has more knowledge
than the man who does not.   And we have seen that it takes more
ability and more knowledge to "go wrong" when you mean to do so,
than to blunder unintentionally.   And the better man is the man
who has the better soul.   Hence it seems to follow that "the man
who does wrong on purpose, if there is such a person, is a better man
than the man who does wrong unintentionally" (375*d*–376*b*).   Yet
this is such a paradox that Socrates hesitates to assert it, though
he does not see how to escape it.

What is the real point of this curious argument ? It is clear, of course, that the main assumption on which it is based is the famous Socratic thesis that " virtue is knowledge," and again, that the method by which the conclusion is reached is the appeal to the analogy of the arts and crafts so constantly employed by Socrates. It is clear also that Plato does not mean us to accept the alleged inference ; he does not seriously think that the deliberate " villain " is morally better than the man who does wrong, in an hour of temptation, against his settled purpose in life ; it is the impossibility of such a doctrine which leads Socrates to say that he cannot commit himself consistently to the conclusion. Yet we cannot take the dialogue as intended to expose and refute either the doctrine that virtue is knowledge, or the use of the analogy from the " arts " as valuable in ethical reasoning. That a man who knows " the good " will, of course, aim at it is a standing doctrine of all Greek ethics ; to suppose that Plato means either to deny this or to reject reasoning from the " arts," would be to treat nearly the whole of the *Republic*, to name no other Platonic dialogues, as a prolonged bad joke. We must therefore find some other method of interpretation.

On reflection we see that the key to Plato's meaning is really supplied by one clause in the proposition which emerges as the conclusion of the matter : " the man who does wrong on purpose, *if there is such a person*, is the good man." The insinuation plainly is that there really is no such person as " the man who does wrong on purpose," and that the paradox does not arise simply because there is no such person. In other words, we have to understand the Socratic doctrine that virtue is knowledge, and the Socratic use of the analogy of the " arts," in the light of the other well-known Socratic dictum, repeated by Plato on his own account in the *Laws*, that " all wrong-doing is involuntary." It is this, and not the formulated inference that the man who does wrong on purpose is the good man, which is the real conclusion to which Plato is conducting us. And we need have no difficulty about admitting this conclusion, if we bear in mind the true and sensible remark of Proclus about the Platonic sense of the word " voluntary " (ἑκούσιον). In Plato, the voluntary, as Proclus says,[1] means regularly what we really wish to have. Now no man wishes to have what he knows or believes to be bad for him. Many men wish for what, in fact, would be bad for them, but they can only do so because they falsely think the thing in question good. To wish to have a thing *because* you know it would be bad for you would be impossible. As Aristotle puts it, " every one wishes for what *he* thinks good." Many men choose evil in spite of the fact that it is evil, no one chooses it *because* it is evil and he knows it to be so. (Of course he may know or believe that he will be sent to prison or to hell for choosing as he does, but at heart he thinks that it will be " worth his while " to take these consequences, he will be " better off " even after paying this price

[1] Proclus, *in Remp.* ii. 355 (Kroll).

for what he desires.[1])   Thus the proposition " all wrong-doing is
involuntary," has nothing to do with the question of human
freedom ; it is merely the negative way of stating that a man who
really knows what his highest good is, will always act on this knowledge.   The man who really knows the good but chooses something
else is as much of a nonentity as a round square, and it is just because
" there is no such person " that the wildest paradoxes can be asserted
about him.

It follows that knowledge of the good is, in one respect, different
from every other kind of knowledge, and this difference affects the
employment of the analogy from professional and technical knowledge, the sort of thing the " sophists " meant by " knowledge."
It is the only knowledge which *cannot* be put to a wrong use ; every
other kind of knowledge can be abused, and is abused when it is
put to a bad use, as, *e.g.*, when the medical man employs his special
professional knowledge to produce disease or death, instead of
curing the one or preventing the other.   There is a real analogy
between " goodness " and the " arts " ; false beliefs about what is
good or bad will ruin the conduct of life, as surely as false beliefs
about what is wholesome will ruin a man's practical success as a
medical man ; but if you press the analogy to the point of arguing
that a man can use his knowledge of good for the deliberate doing of
evil, as he might use his knowledge of medicine to commit a clever
murder, you will be led astray, a truth with which Socrates is made
to show himself familiar in Book I. of the *Republic*, when he urges
this very point against Polemarchus ; that the analogy has its limits
does not prevent it from being a sound analogy within those limits ;
that it becomes unsound when you forget them is no reason for
denying that virtue really is knowledge, though it is not, like the
" goodness " taught by the sophists, mere technical knowledge
how to produce certain results, if you happen to wish for them.

Ion.—Little need be said about this slight dialogue on the nature
of " poetic inspiration."   The main ideas suggested are expounded
much more fully in those important Platonic works with which we
shall have to deal later.   We may, however, make a few remarks
about the current conceptions of poetry against which Socrates is made
to protest.   It is important to remember that the whole conception
of " inspiration," so familiar to ourselves, is foreign to the way of
thinking of poetry characteristic of the age of Pericles and Socrates.
Poets were habitually reckoned, along with physicians, engineers,
engravers, and others, as σοφοί, " wits " or " clever men."   This
means that what was thought distinctive of the poet was not what
we call " native genius," but " craftsmanship," " workmanship,"
" technique."   He was conceived as consciously producing a
beautiful result by the deft fitting together of words and musical
sounds, exactly as the architect does the same thing by the deft
putting together of stones.   Of all the great Greek poets Pindar is

---

[1] Cf.   " To reign is worth ambition though in Hell :
         Better to reign in Hell, then serve in Heav'n."

the only one who pointedly insists on the superiority of φυά, " native genius," to the craftsmanship (τέχνη) which can be taught and learned; but to our taste conscious workmanship, rather than untaught "inspiration," is the characteristic quality of Pindar himself. *We* should never dream of talking of *his* "native wood-notes wild," or of comparing him with a skylark pouring out its soul in "*unpremeditated* art." Also it was held commonly that the service the poet does us is definitely to "teach" us something—how to fight a battle, how to choose a wife, to retain a friend, or something of that kind. This explains why, in the *Apology*, when Socrates is speaking of his attempts to discover a "wiser man" than himself, he mentions poets along with statesmen as the two classes of recognized σοφοί to whom he first turned his attention (*Apol.* 22c). Since he found that the most admired poets were quite helpless at explaining the meaning of their own finest passages, he came to the conclusion, which he repeatedly maintains in Plato, that poets are not deliberate "craftsmen" at all, (do not compose in virtue of σοφία, *ibid.* 22b,) but that poetry is a matter of "natural endowment" (φύσις) and non-rational "inspiration," and thus became the originator of the conception of the "poet" conventional among ourselves.

Ion, who is represented as an eminent professional rhapsode, shares the current views of the "wisdom" of the poets; it is a matter of "skill" or "art" (τέχνη), and he assents at once to the inference that the professional reciter of poetry absorbs from his study of the poet's works a special measure of their author's "skill." The interpreter of the poet to the audience is, like the poet himself, the possessor of a "craft" or "profession." Yet he has to admit that his own skill as an interpreter is confined to the poetry of Homer; he cannot succeed in declaiming any other poet or explaining the "beauties" of his work; in fact, his interest flags as soon as any poet but Homer is made the topic of conversation. This, as Socrates says, serves to show that the rhapsode's accomplishment is not the result of specialist skill. All the poets, as Ion admits, treat of much the same topics—the conduct of men and women in the various occupations of life, the "things in the heavens and the underworld," and the births and doings of "gods," though Homer treats all these topics better than any one else. Hence if the exposition of a poet were a matter of professional expert knowledge, the same knowledge which makes a man able to appreciate and expound Homer, would equally make him a good critic and expositor of poetry in general. Consequently, Socrates suggests that the conception of the interpreter of the poet as a conscious "craftsman" is mistaken. The poets themselves are not self-conscious "artists"; they compose their works in a mood of "inspiration" in which they are "taken out of themselves," and are temporarily, like "seers" or Bacchanals, vehicles "possessed" by a higher power of which they are the unconscious mouthpieces. In the same way, the "rhapsode" with a special gift for reciting Homer is "inspired" by the poet at second-hand. He becomes

temporarily himself the "mouthpiece" of the poet, as the poet is
the mouthpiece of the god.   And he in turn "inspires" his hearers
by communicating to them, in a non-logical way, something of the
"inspiration" he has received from the poet.   Thus poet, reciter,
audience, are like so many links of iron, the first of which is "attracted" by a magnet, and in its turn attracts another.   It is evidence
for the non-rational character of this influence that the rhapsode
for the time actually enters into the feelings of the characters whose
speeches he is declaiming, shudders with their fears and weeps
over their distresses, and makes his audience do the like, though
neither they nor he may really be faced with any danger or distress.
So far Ion is not unwilling to go with Socrates, but he is less ready
to follow him when Socrates turns to the other chief feature in the
popular conception of the poet, and denies that the poet as such is
a "teacher" with knowledge to impart to us.   If Homer were
really a great teacher of wisdom human and divine, it should follow
that a rhapsode, whose profession compels him to be intimately
acquainted with Homer's poetry, is also a high authority in all
fields of knowledge.   But it is undeniable that a physician would
be a sounder judge of Homer's statements about medicine than a
rhapsode, and again that a racing man would be better able to
appreciate and criticize the advice Nestor gives in the *Iliad* about
horse-racing than a professional rhapsode, unless the rhapsode
happens incidentally to be a specialist in horse-racing.   If then
there really is any department of specialist knowledge which can be
acquired by a study of Homer, what is it ?

Ion falls back on the traditional view that at any ʳate Homer is
a specialist in the art of warfare, and that a close student of Homer,
such as he himself has been, learns from Homer the "art of the
general."   The *Iliad*, in fact, is a first-rate manual of military science,
and Ion professes, on the strength of his familiarity with it, to be a
great general *in posse*.   But how comes it, then, that he has never
attempted to distinguish himself in so eminently honourable a
profession ?   If there is no opening in his native city of Ephesus,
which is now a subject-ally of Athens, why has he never, like some
other aliens, entered the military service of Athens herself ?

Nominally the little dialogue is concerned with the question
whether rhapsodes and actors owe their success to professional
or expert knowledge, or to some kind of "genius" or non-rational
"inspiration."   But it is clear that the real points intended to be
made are that the poet himself is not an "expert" in any kind of
knowledge and, as poet, has not necessarily anything to teach us.
These points are enforced more impressively in other Platonic
works, notably in the *Phaedrus*, but the *Ion* has its value, both as a
contribution to the psychology of the "rhapsode" (or, as we should
say to-day, the actor), and as a particularly clear and simple refutation of the never-dying popular delusion that the function of the
poet himself, and consequently of his exponent, is primarily didactic.
The type of critic who conceives it to be his business to find

" morals " and " lessons " in the plays of Shakespeare, and regards it as the object of *Hamlet* or *Macbeth* to warn us against procrastination or ambition, has something to learn even from the *Ion*.

Menexenus.—The *Menexenus* offers, in a way, a worse puzzle to the reader than any other work of the Platonic *corpus*, and it is not surprising that its authenticity should be doubted by students of Plato who are in general on the conservative side in questions of genuineness. Externally the evidence for it is good. It is twice cited by Aristotle,[1] and once with a formal title, " the Funeral Discourse," and this seems to show that Aristotle at least believed it to be Platonic. Now the systematic production of works falsely ascribed to eminent authors seems not to occur in the history of Greek literature until long after the time of Aristotle. And again it is not likely that Aristotle, of all men, should have been misinformed about the real authorship of an Academic dialogue. Thus it is hard to believe either that the dialogue is a deliberate forgery or that it is a production of some lesser member of the Academy which has been ascribed by a simple mistake to Plato, as seems to be the case with a few of the minor items of the " canon of Thrasylus." Nor have modern stylometrical investigations given any reason to suspect the little work. Aristotle's allusion thus seems to compel us to accept it as genuine. On the other hand, there are two notorious difficulties which we have to face when we admit Plato's authorship. One is that it is at least hard to see what Plato's object in such a composition can be. The other is that the dialogue commits an anachronism to which there is no parallel anywhere in Plato, and which cannot be unconscious. The body of it is made up of a recital by Socrates of a " funeral oration " on the Athenians who fell in the Corinthian war, and Socrates professes to have heard the speech from the lips of the famous Aspasia, the wife of Pericles. It is certain that Socrates was put to death in the summer of the year 399 B.C., long before the opening of the Corinthian war (395 B.C.). Yet he is made to carry his review of Athenian history down to the pacification dictated by the Persian king, which ended the war in the year 387. Aspasia, the nominal speaker, must have died *before* Socrates. This is implied in the structure of the *Aspasia* of Aeschines, on which see H. Dittmar, *Aeschines von Sphettus*, 45–56. Plato must have violated chronology quite deliberately and with a view to producing a definite effect. But what can we suppose the intention to have been ?

It is idle to suggest that the whole affair is a mere Aristophanic jest, and that Plato only wants to show that he can rival the comedians on their own ground by putting ludicrous " topical allusions " into the mouth of his hero. We cannot reconcile such a use of Socrates, for purposes of pure burlesque, with the tone of reverence and devotion in which Plato continues to speak of Socrates in the letters written at the very end of his own life ; even

---

[1] *Rhetoric*, 1367*b* 8, 1415*b* 30.

if one could, we have to remember that Socrates is not being made, as he might be made in a burlesque, to offer a remarkably intelligent " anticipation of the course of events " ; he is represented as commenting on the events of the twelve or thirteen years after his own death *ex post facto*. And we still have to explain why Socrates should pretend that Aspasia too is still a well-known figure at Athens, and that he has learned his discourse from her. Again, we cannot account for this use of Aspasia by appealing to the passage (*Menexenus*, 236*b*) where Socrates is made to credit her with the authorship of the famous " funeral speech," delivered by Pericles in the first year of the Archidamian war, and reported by Thucydides. Plato's object is not to ridicule oratory of this kind by the insinuation that its tone is what might be expected from a woman and an *hetaera*. The remains of the *Aspasia* of Aeschines of Sphettus, make it clear that the view, which underlies the proposals of *Republic* v., that " the goodness of a woman and that of a man are the same," was a genuine doctrine of Socrates, and that he quite seriously believed in the " political capacity " of Aspasia. His profession of owing his own " Funeral Discourse " to her is, no doubt, only half-serious, but it is quite in keeping with what we know to have been his real conviction. We have therefore to discover the object of the whole singular mystification, if we can, from an analysis of the oration itself.

It will not be necessary to insert here a full analysis, but there are certain points, well brought out in such a commentary as Stallbaum's, which we have to bear in mind. The discourse is framed on the lines we can see from comparison with the extant examples to have been conventional on such occasions. It treats first of the glorious inheritance and traditions of the community into which the future warriors were born and in which they were brought up, then of their own achievements, by which they have approved themselves worthy of such an origin, and finally of the considerations which should moderate the grief of their surviving friends and relatives. In this respect it exhibits a close parallel with the discourse of Pericles in Thucydides, the " funeral speech " included in the works ascribed to Lysias, the *Panegyricus* of Isocrates, the discourse of Hyperides on Leosthenes and his companions in the Lamian war. There are direct verbal echoes of the speech of Lysias, perhaps of that of Pericles, and, I suspect, also of the Isocratean *Panegyricus*, a work of the year 380. The diction again has clearly been modelled on that actually adopted in real encomia of the fallen, and it is this which makes it impossible to use evidence from style to date the dialogue. " Funeral orations " belong to the type of oratory called by the Greeks " epideictic," and demand an artificial elevation of diction and use of verbal ornament avoided in " forensic " pleading and political speaking. Hence all the extant specimens exhibit, to a greater or a less degree, the high-flown and semi-poetical character distinctive of the Sicilian " show declamation " introduced to Athens by Gorgias, and Plato has been careful to preserve this peculiarity. When we examine the contents of the discourse, we see that he has been equally careful to conform to the accepted model. His oration, like those of Lysias and Isocrates, but unlike the really statesmanlike discourse of Pericles, dwells on the topics afforded by mythology for the glorification of Athens, the origination of the cultivation of corn and of the olive in Attica, the contest of Athena with Hephacstus for the patronage of the city, the public spirit and chivalry displayed in such legendary exploits as the protection of the family of Heracles and the rescuing for burial of the corpses of the champions who fell before the gates of Thebes. Lysias and Isocrates both expatiate on these prehistorical events at great length—a length apparently satirized by Socrates in the remark (239*b*) that they have already received their due meed of celebration from the poets. The speech then proceeds, like those which are apparently its immediate models, to a sketch of the history of Athens down to date, the object of which is to glorify the city on two grounds—its rooted and inveterate antipathy to "barbarians," (242*c–e*, 245*d*,) and its unselfish Panhellenism, shown by its readiness always to make sacrifices to preserve the "balance of power" between the different Greek cities by supporting the weaker side in these internal quarrels (244*e*). The demonstration of the second point in particular leads to a bold falsification of history, by which the fifth century attempts of Athens to dominate Boeotia and the Archidamian war itself are made to appear as heroic struggles against the "imperialism" of other communities. We know enough from Plato of the real sentiments both of himself and of Socrates to understand that this version of history cannot represent the serious convictions of either ; it has all the appearance of satire on the "patriotic" version of history given by Isocrates in an inconsistent combination with Panhellenism. Similarly, after reading the *Gorgias* and *Republic* and the sketch of Athenian history given in *Laws* iii., we shall find it impossible to take the *Menexenus* seriously when it glorifies the existing constitution of Athens as a true aristocracy in which the men who are reputed to be "best" govern with the free consent of the multitude (238*d–e*). When we are told that at Athens, as nowhere else, "he who has the repute of wisdom and goodness is sovereign," the emphasis must be meant to fall on the words "who has the repute," and the encomium is disguised satire. Probably, then, the real purpose of the discourse is to imitate and at the same time, by adroit touches of concealed malice, to satirize popular "patriotic oratory." It is no objection to such an interpretation to say, what is true enough, that the speech contains noble passages on the duty of devotion to one's State and the obligation of perpetuating its finest traditions. Even the "flag-flapper" who distorts all history into a romantic legend of national self-glorification, usually has some good arguments, as well as many bad ones, for his "patriotism," and we may credit Plato with sufficient penetration to have seen that satire misses its designed effect unless it is accompanied by intelligent recognition of the good which is mingled with the evil in its objects. (This is why so much of the writing of Juvenal, Swift, Victor Hugo, merely wearies a reader by the monotony of the invective.[1])

If Isocrates is the person against whom the satire of the *Menexenus* is largely directed, we can see an excellent reason why that satire should be so liberally mixed with sympathy. Isocrates was honourably distinguished by his real superiority to mere particularism and his real concern for the interests of Greek civilization as a whole, and in this he and Plato were wholly at one. But, unlike Plato, who regarded the hard and fast distinction between Greek and " barbarian " as unscientific superstition, Isocrates takes the antithesis seriously and tends to regard hate of the barbarian as equivalent to love for civilization. The combination of the two points of view in the *Menexenus* is a fair representation of his lifelong attitude towards affairs. So again the distortion of history by which the most aggressive exploits of Attic imperialism, such as the attempt of Pericles and his friends to dominate Boeotia, and the Archidamian War as a whole, are represented as " wars of liberation," is no very violent parody of the methods of Isocrates when he is anxious, as in the *Panegyricus*, to gratify Athenian partiality for Athens or Athenian dislike of Sparta. One may suspect the same purpose of parody in the false emphasis which is laid in the *Menexenus* on the naval exploits of Athens in the Sicilian expedition as efforts for the " liberation " of the oppressed. Isocrates notoriously held the view that the naval ascendancy of Athens had been a national misfortune, since it had led to the lust for empire, and there are passages in the *Laws* which show that Plato sympathized with this conviction. But it would be a telling criticism of the Isocratean way of manipulating history to show that it could easily be employed for glorifying precisely the side of Athenian history which gave Isocrates himself least satisfaction. You have only to sit as loosely to facts as Isocrates habitually allows himself to do when he wishes to praise or to abuse some one, and you can make Alcibiades into a hero of chivalry who was only doing his duty by the oppressed when he lured Athens on to its ruin by the prospect of the conquest of Sicily ![2] If we read the *Menexenus* in this light, we can perhaps understand the point of the curious anachronism in its setting. The satire of the actual " Funeral Discourse " is so subtly mixed with sympathetic appreciation that it would be easy to mistake the whole speech for a serious encomium—a mistake which has actually been made by a good many interpreters of Plato. The ordinary reader needs some very visible warning sign if he is to approach the discourse with the required anticipation that

[1] Cf. the excellent remarks of Sir A. Quiller-Couch, *Studies in Literature*, p. 290 ff.

[2] Lysias takes care to " skip " the Peloponnesian War entirely ; Isocrates does worse. He actually justifies the two great crimes of the enslavement and massacre of the Melians and the destruction of Scione !

its purpose is satirical. The warning is given, for any intelligent reader, by the amazing introduction of Socrates at a date years after his death. It is as though Plato were telling us in so many words that we are dealing with the utterances of a mere puppet who has nothing to do with the great man to whose memory the dialogues in general are a splendid tribute. Even so, the fiction is singular, and hardly to be accounted for unless we realize the presence in Plato himself of a peculiar vein of freakish humour which comes out notably in the singular " antinomies " of the *Parmenides* as well as in the whimsicalities of the *Sophistes* and *Politicus*. It was an " impish " trick to put the discourse of the *Menexenus* into the mouth of a puppet Socrates, and we may be glad that the trick was never repeated, as we are glad that Shakespeare never perpetrated a second *Troilus and Cressida*. The very audacity of the trick is some additional evidence of the genuineness of the dialogue. We can understand that Plato might take such a liberty—once, and in an unhappy moment ; it is surely incredible that a younger member of Plato's *entourage* should have ventured on it at all.

See further :

RITTER, C.—*Platon*, i. 297–308 (*Hippias II*), 359–361 (*Hippias I*), 485–496 (*Menexenus*).

RAEDER, H.—*Platons philosophische Entwickelung*, 92–94 (*Ion*), 94–95 (*Hippias II*), 101–106 (*Hippias I*), 125–127 (*Menexenus*).

APELT, O.—*Beiträge zur Geschichte der griechischen Philosophie* (1891), 369–390 (*der Sophist Hippias von Elis*) ; *Platonische Aufsätze* (1912), 203–237 (on *Hippias I and II*).

KRAUS, O.—*Platons Hippias Minor*. (Prague, 1913.)

DITTMAR, H.—*Aeschines von Sphettus* 1–59 (on the connection of the *Menexenus* with the *Aspasia* of Aeschines. The connection is clearly made out, but I think it an exaggeration to find the purpose of Plato's dialogue mainly in a " polemic " against Aeschines).

CHAPTER IV

MINOR SOCRATIC DIALOGUES : *CHARMIDES*, *LACHES, LYSIS*

WE may group the three dialogues which form the subject of this chapter together for several reasons. From the dramatic point of view all show an advance upon what is likely to have been the earliest form of the Platonic dialogue, the direct presentation of Socrates in conversation with a single interlocutor. The *Lysis* and *Charmides* both profess to be reports of recently held conversations given by Socrates to an unnamed friend or friends, and thus conform to the type of such masterpieces of literary art as the *Protagoras* and *Republic*. The fiction that the dialogue is reported enables Socrates to draw a highly dramatic picture of the persons engaged in the conversation and the circumstances in which it is held. This device is not adopted in the *Laches*, where the method of direct reproduction of the conversation is maintained, but the same advantage is obtained by adding to the number of the interlocutors, so that we have a vivid characterization of three persons, two of them notabilities, besides Socrates himself. All three dialogues, again, are connected by the fact that they deal with Socrates in the special character of older friend and adviser of the very young, and two of them, the *Charmides* and *Lysis* give us an attractive picture of his personal manner as mentor to his young friends. In the cases of *Charmides* and *Laches* Plato has been careful to indicate approximately the period of life to which Socrates has attained, and we see that both are meant as pictures of the master as he was between the ages of forty and fifty, and thus take us back to a time when Plato himself was either an infant or not yet born. It is closely connected with this that both dialogues, and especially the *Laches*, are pervaded by the atmosphere of the Archidamian war and remind us of the fact that Socrates was, among other things, a fighting man. A further point of connexion between these two dialogues is, that they are both concerned at bottom with a difficulty arising directly out of the Socratic conception of virtue as identical with knowledge. Each deals with one of the great recognized virtues demanded from a Greek " good man "—the *Charmides* with "temperance," the *Laches* with " valour " or " fortitude "—and in both cases the discussion follows the same general lines. We are gradually led up to the point of identifying the virtue under consideration with knowledge of the good, and then left to face the difficulty that the identification seems to involve the further identification of this particular virtue with all virtue. If valour, for example, is knowledge of the good, how can we continue to distinguish the soldier's virtue of valour from any other virtue, and what becomes of the popular belief that a man may have one virtue in an eminent degree, and yet be deficient in another— may be, for example, a very brave soldier but very " licentious " ? This problem of the " unity of the virtues " forms the starting-point for the discussion of the *Protagoras*, and cannot be said to receive its full solution until we come to the *Republic*. Thus, by raising it, the *Laches* and *Charmides* prelude directly to what must have been the great achievements of Plato's literary prime of manhood ; this is an additional reason for holding that they must not be placed among his earliest compositions. It is, for example, quite possible, if not even probable, that both may be later works than the *Gorgias*, which still retains the method of simple direct reproduction of a conversation and, for all its impressive eloquence, shows less insight into the more difficult philosophical problems raised by the Socratic conception of morality.

The *Charmides*.—Formally, like several of the dialogues, the *Charmides* has as its object the finding of a *definition*. To us it seems at first pedantic to attach importance, in morals at any rate, to mere definitions of the different virtues. A definition, we are inclined to think, is at best a matter of names, whereas ethical thinking should concern itself directly with " concrete realities." If a man recognizes and practises a noble rule of life, it matters very little by what name he calls the right act, whether he looks at it as an exhibition of courage, or of justice, or of " temperance." The " fine " deed can, in fact, easily be made to wear the semblance of any one of these " virtues." This is true enough, but it would be out of place as a criticism on the Socratic demand for " definitions " in matters of conduct. From the Greek point of view, the problem of definition itself is not one of names, but of things. If our moral judgment is to be sound, and our moral practice good, we must approve and disapprove rightly. We must admire and imitate what is really noble, and must not be led into false theory and bad practice by confused thinking about good and evil. The problem of finding a definition of a " virtue " is at bottom the problem of formulating a moral ideal, and it is from this point of view that we ought to consider it. The important thing is that we should know quite definitely what we admire in conduct and that our admiration should be rightly given to the things which are really admirable. Failure in finding the definition means that we really do not know what we admire, and so long as we do not know this, our moral life is at the mercy of sentimental half-thinking.

The particular virtue selected for discussion is one which bulks very large in all Greek thought about the conduct of life—the beautiful characteristic called by the Greeks *sophrosyne*, and by the Romans *temperantia*. It is easier to indicate from the usage of the language what this moral excellence is, than to find any one name for it in our modern English.   In literature we find *sophrosyne* spoken of chiefly in the following connexions.   As its derivation implies, the word means literally the possession of a " sane " or " wholesome " mind ; *sophrosyne* is thus contrasted with the " folly " of the man who " forgets himself " in the hour of success and prosperity, and " presumes on " his advantages of wealth or power, pushes them to the full extreme in his dealings with the less fortunate.   Or it may equally be contrasted with the " unbalanced " conduct of the fanatic who has only one idea in his head, can only see one side of a situation and is blind to all the others.   In this sense, as the virtue opposed to the pride of the man who forgets that the gods can cast him down as low as they have raised him high, the recklessness of the successful man who forgets that he may himself come to be as much at the mercy of another as others are now at his, the pitilessness of the fanatic who can only see one side to every question, *sophrosyne* covers very much of what we call humility, humanity, mercy. Again, the word is a name for the kind of conduct thought becoming specially in the young towards elders, soldiers towards their superior officer, citizens towards their magistrates.   In this sense it means proper modesty and even covers such minor matters as a becoming outward deportment in speech and gesture.   In still a third sense, it is the characteristic of the man who knows how to hold his imperious bodily appetites, " the desire for meat and drink and the passion of sex," in easy and graceful control, as contrasted with the man who offends us by unseemly and untimely greed of these appetitive enjoyments.   In this aspect, *sophrosyne* is what in good English is still called " temperance," if we take care to remember that it is part of the virtue itself that it is not the imperfect self-restraint of the man who holds himself in check ungracefully and with difficulty, but the easy and natural self-restraint of the man who enjoys being " temperate." [1]   If it does not seem an affectation to use such a phrase, we may say that *sophrosyne* is the spirit of the " disciplined " life.   It is not, as Hume insinuates,[2] a " monkish " virtue, except in the sense that you certainly cannot be a good monk without it.   Neither, as Hume forgot, can you be a good soldier, and that is why in the *Laws* [3] Plato throws *sophrosyne* and valour together, and insists that the former is the major and the harder part of the lesson every good " fighting man " has to master.   The very wide range of the use of the word in literature goes a long way to explain the importance Socrates attaches to a clear and coherent statement of its meaning, and the difficulty the company have in producing such a statement.   The introductory narrative provides an opportunity for a clear indication of the date

[1] Hence Aristotle's sharp distinction throughout the *Ethics* between the σώφρων and the ἐγκρατής or morally " strong " man in whom judgment and " will "—in the Elizabethan sense—are at variance though he habitually compels himself to follow judgment.
[2] *Inquiry into the Principles of Morals*, Section IX. Part I.
[3] *Laws*, 634a–b.

at which the conversation is supposed to take place. Socrates has been serving before the walls of Potidaea, in the campaign of the year 431 with which hostilities between Athens and the members of the Peloponnesian confederacy opened, and has just returned safe and sound, after having displayed his courage and coolness in danger, as we learn from the *Symposium*,[1] by saving the life of Alcibiades. He is then a man of some forty years (Plato, we must remember, is not yet born). He goes direct, on his arrival, to his " wonted haunts," the *palaestrae*, and begins at once to ask questions about the way in which " philosophy and the young people " have been faring in his absence on service (*Charm.* 153*d*). (This, we observe, implies that the interest of young men of promise in Socrates as a wise counsellor was already a reality, eight years before Aristophanes burlesqued these relations in the *Clouds*.) Critias, cousin of Plato's mother, afterwards to be unhappily known as a leader of the violently reactionary party in the " provisional government " set up after the capitulation of Athens to Lysander, but at present simply a young man of parts but with a touch of forwardness and self-confidence, thereupon promises to introduce Socrates to his own cousin Charmides (Plato's uncle, subsequently associated with Critias and his party as the head of the commission set up to dominate the Piraeeus), as a lad of exceptional promise.[2] Socrates had already seen him as a mere child, but he has now grown to be a youth of wonderful beauty and equally wonderful *sophrosyne*. It is agreed that Socrates shall have some conversation with the lad and judge of him for himself.

Socrates leads up playfully to his real purpose, the examination of the boy's spiritual state. Charmides has been complaining of headaches. Socrates professes to have brought back from his northern campaign a wonderful remedy which he has learned from a Thracian.[3] The Thracian, however, had explained that not only can you not treat a local disorder properly without treating the patient's whole body, you cannot treat the body successfully without treating the soul, which is the real seat of health and disease. Hence Socrates is under a promise not to practise the recipe against headache on anyone who is not spiritually sound in constitution. It would be useless if employed on a subject with a deep-seated spiritual disorder. *Sophrosyne* is presupposed in spiritual health ; before Charmides can be treated for his headaches, then, we must find out whether he has *sophrosyne* (*Charm.* 155*e*–158*e*). Now if a man has this or any other character of soul, it must, of course, make

---

[1] *Symposium*, 219–220.

[2] According to Xenophon (*Mem.* iii. 7, 1), it was Socrates himself who first persuaded Charmides to enter public life. But this looks like a mere inference from what is said in our dialogue of the modest and retiring disposition of Charmides in boyhood. If the fact were so, it is singular that no one ever seems to have accused Socrates of " corrupting " Charmides, though he was made responsible for Critias and Alcibiades.

[3] For the reputation of Thrace as a home of this kind of lore—it was the land of Orpheus, we must remember—cf. Eurip. *Alc.* 986 ff.

its presence *felt*, and its possessor will therefore have an opinion of some kind about its nature. (It is not meant, of course, that the possessor of the character need have a " clear and distinct idea " of it, but only that he must have some acquaintance with it ; language about it will have some meaning for him, exactly as language about sight or hearing will mean something to anyone who can see or hear, though it would be meaningless to beings born blind or deaf.)   Thus we are led to the question what kind of thing Charmides takes *sophrosyne* to be.   As is natural in a mere lad, Charmides fixes first of all on an exterior characteristic, and equally naturally it is a characteristic of *sophrosyne* in the form which would be most familiar to a boy—the form of decent and modest bearing towards one's elders and " good behaviour " generally.   One shows *sophrosyne* by walking, talking, doing things generally, in an " orderly and quiet " fashion ; so perhaps we may say that it is " a sort of quietness " (ἡσυχιότης), a " slowness " which may be contrasted with undignified and ungraceful " hurry " (159b).   This, of course, is true, so far as it goes, only it does not go very far.   There is a " hurry " which means that one's limbs or one's tongue are not really under control as they should be.   But we want to get behind such mere outward indications to the interior condition of soul from which they spring ; and besides, clearly " slowness," " deliberateness," does not always arise from being " master of one's soul."   As Socrates says, in the various physical and mental accomplishments it is what is readily and quickly done, not what is done slowly and with difficulty, that is " well " or " fairly " (καλῶς) done.   He who reads or writes, or wrestles or boxes well, does these things quickly ; he who can only make the proper movements slowly does not do them well.   So with accomplishments of the mind.   A fine memory or judgment or invention is a quick, not a slow, memory or judgment or invention. Now it is admitted that *sophrosyne*, whatever it is, is something " fine " (καλόν).   Clearly then it cannot be right to fix on " slowness " as what is specially distinctive of *sophrosyne* (159c-160d). The point is that, in small things as well as in great, the man who is master of his soul is free from " hurry."   There is, in a sense, a spacious leisureliness about his behaviour.   But this freedom from " haste " and " hurry " is not the same thing as slowness : slowness *may* be, and often is, a mere consequence of awkwardness, of *not* being master of yourself.

Charmides next makes a suggestion which shows a real attempt to get behind the externals of behaviour to the spirit and temper they reveal. *Sophrosyne* makes a man quick to feel shame, and perhaps it is the same thing as modesty (αἰδώς, 160e).   The boy is still clearly thinking of the form in which *sophrosyne* would be most familiar to a well-bred boy—the sense of being " on one's best behaviour " in the presence of one's parents, one's elders, and in general of those to whom respect is due.   (We may compare Kant's well-known comparison of the reverence for the moral law which is, according to him, the specific *ethical* feeling, with the sense of restraint we feel in the presence of an exalted or impressive personage—the sort of feeling an ordinary man would have if he were suddenly summoned to an interview with the King or the Pope. There is a real analogy between the two things ; as Kant says, our feeling in both cases is primarily one of inhibition or restraint. You don't " loll ' in the King's presence, and a good man is not " free and easy " in the presence of a moral obligation.) But again, the analogy is only an analogy, not an identity. *Sophrosyne* cannot be simply identified with *shamefacedness* (αἰσχύνη) or *modesty* (αἰδώς).[1] For, by general consent, it is something which is always not merely " fine " (καλόν) but good (ἀγαθόν), and there is a false modesty which is not good. As Homer says, " Modesty is not good in a beggar." (Cf. the Scots saying, " Dinna let yer modesty wrang ye.") The shame or modesty which makes a man too bashful to tell his full need on the proper occasion is not good, but *sophrosyne* is always good (160e-161a).

This leads to a third suggestion which is more important than any we have yet met. Charmides has heard some one—it is hinted that this some one is Critias—say that *sophrosyne* means "attending to one's own matters " (τὸ τὰ ἑαυτοῦ πράττειν, 161b),[2] and this, perhaps, may be the true account. It does obviously present one advantage. The formula is a strictly universal one, applicable to the whole conduct of life in all its different " ages," not merely to the kind of conduct appropriate to the young in particular. In a boy the shyness, or backwardness, of which we have just been speaking is a laudable thing, and "forwardness " a fault, but " shyness " is far from being a laudable characteristic in a grown man. But at any age of life it is laudable to " mind your own affairs " and censurable to be a " meddler " or busybody. Unfortunately, as Socrates goes on to point out, the phrase " to attend to one's own matters " is so ambiguous that the new suggestion is something of a " conundrum " ; we have to guess, if we can, what its author may have meant (161d). Clearly he cannot have meant that a man should only read and write his own name and no one else's, or that the builder or the physician should build his own house or cure his own body and no other, on pain of being noted for a " meddler." Life would be intolerable to a community where the rule was that every one should " attend to his own matters " in the sense that he must " do everything for himself " (161e). The alleged saying, then, is what we called it, a pure conundrum. In the *Republic*, as

---

[1] Strictly, αἰδώς is the name for laudable modesty, αἰσχύνη for the backwardness which is not laudable, *mauvaise honte*. But the words are freely treated as interchangeable.

[2] τὸ τὰ ἑαυτοῦ πράττειν is the conduct which is the opposite of τὸ πολυπραγμονεῖν, " having a finger in everyone's pie." In Attic life πολυπραγμοσύνη would show itself, *e.g.*, in that tendency to quarrel with one's neighbours and drag them into law-suits about trifles which Aristophanes regularly ascribes to his *petits bourgeois*. Hence ἀπράγμων is in Attic sometimes an epithet of censure— " inert," " lazy "—but often one of approval—" a quiet decent man," a man who " keeps himself to himself."

we all know, this very phrase "to mind one's own matters" is adopted as an adequate definition not merely of one type of "virtue," but of δικαιοσύνη, "right-doing," the fundamental principle of the whole moral life. There is no inconsistency between the two dialogues. The point made in the *Charmides* is simply that the phrase as it stands, without further explanation leaves us in the dark. In the *Republic* the necessary explanation has been supplied by the educational theory and moral psychology which precede its introduction, so that when we come to it, it has a very definite significance, and is seen at once to embody the whole content of the Socratic ideal that a man's business in life is the "tendance of his soul." If it had been sprung upon us, without this preparation, in the course of *Republic* i. as an answer to the ethical nihilism of Thrasymachus, it would then have been exactly what Socrates calls it in the *Charmides*—a conundrum.

The defence of the proposed definition is now taken up by Critias. He replies to the objection of Socrates by making a distinction between " doing " (τὸ πράττειν, τὸ ἐργάζεσθαι) and " making " (τὸ ποιεῖν). The shoemaker " makes " shoes for his customers, but in " making " their shoes he is " doing " his own work. The shoes he makes are not his own shoes, but the making of them *is* his " own " trade or work. Here again we are dealing with a real and important distinction ; in the *Republic* we shall learn the true significance of the conception of a " work " or " vocation " which is a man's " own," not because the products of it are to be his " own " property for his own exclusive use, but because it is the contribution he and no one else can make to the " good life." Critias has not, however, thought out the implications of his own distinction, and goes wrong from the start by an elementary confusion of ideas. He appeals in support of the distinction to the saying of Hesiod that " no work is disgraceful," [1] on which he puts a glaringly false interpretation. Hesiod, he says, cannot have meant that no occupation is a base one, for there are base trades like those of the shoemaker and fishmonger, not to mention worse ones. By " work " Hesiod must have meant " making what is honourable and useful," and similarly, when we say that *sophrosyne* is " minding your own matters " or " doing your own work " we mean that it is doing what is " honourable and useful " (163b–c).

We might expect that Socrates would fasten at once on the obvious weakness of this definition ; it presupposes that we already know what we mean by " good and useful." We should then be led direct to the conclusion which it is part of Plato's purpose to drive home, that we cannot really know the character of *sophrosyne*

---

[1] ἔργον δ' οὐδὲν ὄνειδος (Hesiod, *O.D.* 311). Xenophon (*Mem.* i. 2, 56–57) states that Socrates was fond of the saying, apparently taking it in the sense that " honest work is no disgrace." His " accuser " twisted it to mean that no one need feel ashamed of anything he does. Comparison with the similar charges of getting an immoral sense out of the poets considered in the *Apologia Socratis* of Libanius, seems to show that what Xenophon has in view is the pamphlet of Polycrates against Socrates.

or any other virtue until we know what good and evil are, and when we know that we have answered the question what virtue is. In point of fact, Socrates prefers to make an unexpected deviation from the direct line of the argument, which raises a still more general issue, and apparently takes us out of the sphere of ethics into that of epistemology. The length of this section shows that it is meant to be the most important division of the dialogue, and we shall need therefore to consider it with some care.

According to the explanation of Critias, a physician who cures his patient is doing something good and useful for both himself and the patient and is therefore acting with *sophrosyne*. But he need not know that he is doing what is " good and useful." (The physician cannot be sure that he will really be the better, or that his patient will be the better, for his services. It *might* be better for the patient that he should die, or for the physician that he should not make the income he does make.) Thus it would seem that a man may have *sophrosyne* without being aware that he has it (164*a–c*). This would not only seem inconsistent with the assumption Socrates had made at the beginning of his conversation with Charmides, but also flatly contradicts the generally accepted view, with which Critias agrees, that *sophrosyne* actually is the same thing as " self-knowledge." (The thought, of course, is that " sanity of mind " is precisely a true understanding of yourself, your strength and your weaknesses, your real situation in relation to gods and men, the kind of self-knowledge which was inculcated by the *Nosce teipsum* [1] inscription in the Delphic temple.) We thus find ourselves embarked on a double question : (1) Is self-knowledge possible at all ? (2) If it is, is it profitable ; has it any bearing on the practical conduct of life ? Or again : (1) What is the object apprehended by self-knowledge ? (2) What is the result it produces ?

The second question is met by Critias with the reply that self-knowledge, like such " sciences " or " arts " as arithmetic and geometry, and unlike such "sciences " or " arts " as building or weaving, has no " product." This is, in untechnical language, the distinction which is more clearly drawn in the *Politicus* and finally takes technical form in Aristotle as the distinction between " speculative " knowledge, which has no further end than the perfecting of itself, and " practical " knowledge, which has always an ulterior end, the making of some thing or the doing of some act. Critias is unconsciously assuming first that self-knowledge is ἐπιστήμη or τέχνη, knowledge of universal rules or principles of some kind, and next that it is " speculative," not " practical " science. The result is that he is virtually confusing the direct acquaintance with one's own individual strength and weaknesses really meant in the Delphian inscription with the " science " of the psychologist. He is taking it for granted, as too many among ourselves still do, that to know psychology and to have a profound acquaintance with your own " heart " are the same thing (*Charm.* 165*d–e*.) Socrates lets this

[1] γνῶθι σαυτόν.

confusion of "direct acquaintance" with "knowledge about" go uncriticized, because his immediate purpose is to raise a more general issue, one which concerns not the *effect* of knowledge, but the *object* apprehended. In all other cases, he urges, that which is apprehended by a "knowledge" or "science" is something different from the knowing or apprehending itself. Arithmetic for example is knowledge of "the even and odd," as we should say, of the characters of the integers. But "the even and odd" are not the same thing as the knowing which has them for its object. (In fact, of course, arithmetic is a mental activity, the integers and their properties are not.) We shall find the same distinction between the "knowing" and the object known in the case of any other "knowledge" we like to take (166a–b). Critias admits the truth of this in general, but asserts that there is one solitary exception. The self-knowledge of which he had spoken is this exception; it is quite literally a knowing which "knows itself and all other knowledges," and the virtue *sophrosyne* is no other than this "knowing which knows itself" (166c). In effect this amounts to identifying *sophrosyne* with what is called in modern times "theory of knowledge."

We proceed to test this thesis in the true Socratic way by asking what consequences would follow from it. It would follow that the man who has *sophrosyne* would know what he knows and what he does not know but merely "fancies" (οἴεται), and also what other men know and what they only "fancy." Let us once more put our double question, Is such knowledge as this possible, and if it is, is it of any benefit to us?

There is a grave difficulty even about its possibility. For, in all other cases, we find that a mental activity is always directed on some object other than itself. Sight and hearing do not see or hear sight or hearing; they see colours and hear sounds. Desire is never "desire of desire" but always desire of a pleasant object; we do not wish for "wishing" but for *good*. What we love is not "loving" but a beloved person, what we fear, not fear but some formidable thing, and so forth. That is, it is characteristic of mental activities of all kinds that they are directed upon an object *other than themselves* (167c–168a). It would be at least "singular" (ἄτοπον) if there should be a solitary exception to this principle, a "knowing" which is not the knowing of a science (μάθημα) of some kind, but the "knowing of itself and the other knowings" (168a). Knowing, in fact, is always a knowing of something, and so *relative* to an object known; its "faculty" is to be *of* something (168b), and so where there is knowing there must be a known object, just as where there is a "greater than" there must always be a "less" *than* which the greater is greater. Hence, if there is anything which is greater than itself, it must also be less than itself; if anything which is double of itself, it must also be half itself, and so on. If "seeing" can see itself, "seeing" itself must be coloured. Some of these consequences are patently absurd, *e.g.* that there should be a number which is greater than, and by consequence also less than itself ; if it is not so obvious that seeing cannot see itself, and that sight, by consequence, is not a colour, the position is at any rate difficult to accept. It would require a great philosopher to decide the question whether any activity can be its own object, and if so, whether this is the case with the activity of knowing, and we have not the genius needed to determine the point (168*b*–169*b*). But in any case, we may say that such a supposed " knowing of knowing " cannot be what men mean by *sophrosyne* unless it can be shown that it would be " beneficial " to us, as *sophrosyne* admittedly is (169*b*–*c*).

(So far then, the point of the argument has been the perfectly sound one that no mental activity is its own object. Manifestly this is true of the knowing of the epistemologist, as much as of any other activity. If there is such a science as the " theory of knowledge," its object will be " the conditions under which knowledge is possible." But these conditions are not the same thing as anyone's knowing about them. The doctrines of the *Critique of Pure Reason*, for example, are one thing and Kant's knowing or believing these doctrines is another.)

We can now take a further step. Let us concede, for the purposes of argument, that there is such a thing as a " knowing of knowing." Even if there is, it is not the same thing as " knowing *what* you know and *what* you do not know," and therefore is not the self-knowledge with which Critias has been trying to identify *sophrosyne*. Critias does not readily take in the distinction, which has therefore to be made gradually clearer by illustrations. Suppose a man to " know about knowing," what will this knowledge really tell him ? It will tell him that " this is knowledge " and " that is not knowledge," *i.e.* that this proposition is true, that proposition is not certainly true. But to know so much and no more would certainly not be enough for the purposes of the practitioner in medicine and statesmanship. The physician needs not merely to know that " I know such and such a proposition," he needs to know that the true proposition in question is relevant to the treatment of his patients. In other words, it is not enough for him to know what *knowledge* is, he needs to know what *health* is, and the states-man similarly must know not merely what knowledge is, but what *right* is. *Ex hypothesi* they will not learn this from a science which has knowledge as its object, but from medicine, of which the object is health in the body, or from politics, which knows about " right." Thus we must not say that the man who has only " knowledge of knowledge " will know *what* he knows and *what* he does not ; we may only say that that he will know the bare fact *that* he knows or does not know. (The meaning is, for example, that a man who was a mere epistemologist and nothing more might be aware that when he says, " So many grains of arsenic are fatal, " he is saying something which satisfies all the conditions required for genuine scientific knowledge ; but, if he only knew epistemology and nothing else, he would not even know that he must not administer fatal doses of arsenic to his fellow-men.) Thus if *sophrosyne* is the same thing as

a " knowledge of knowledge," the man who has it will not be helped
by it to distinguish a genuine practitioner from a pretender in
medicine or in anything else.   To distinguish the true physician
from the quack, you need to know not epistemology, the " knowledge of knowledge," but medicine, the " knowledge of things
wholesome and unwholesome."   The true judge of medical theory
and practice is not the epistemologist but the medical specialist, and
no one else (169d–171c).   And this conclusion seems to dispose of
the worth of *sophrosyne*, if we were right in identifying it with a
" knowledge of knowledge."   A self-knowledge which taught us to
know, in the first instance, our own strength and weakness, and, in
the second place, the strength and weakness of others, and so
enabled us to be on our guard against self-delusion and imposture,
would be of the highest value for the conduct of life.   But we have
just seen that all that the epistemologist as such could possibly
tell about himself or anyone else would be merely whether he really
knew epistemology (171c–e).

The point to which all this leads us up is manifestly that though
sophrosyne is a knowledge of something, it cannot be a " knowledge
about knowledge," nor can this be what was really meant by those
who have insisted on self-knowledge as the one thing needful for a
happy life.   It is clearly indicated that the sort of knowledge of
ourselves really needed as a guide to practice is knowledge of good and
evil and of the state of our souls in respect of them, a view which
would immediately lead to the further result that all the genuine
virtues are at bottom one and the same thing, knowledge of the good,
and the distinctions commonly made between the different types
of virtue at best conventional.   (It is incidentally a further valuable
result of the argument that it has vindicated the autonomy of the
various sciences by exposing the pretensions of the " theory of
knowledge " to judge of scientific truths on *a priori* grounds, and
making it clear that in every case there is no appeal from the verdict
of the expert in a specific science, so long as he claims to be the final
authority *in his own speciality*.)

The main purpose of the discussion becomes apparent when we
reach its final section.   Even if we waive all the difficulties we have
raised, and admit that *sophrosyne* really is a " knowledge of knowledge," and that such a knowledge is, (as we just said that it is
not,) " knowing *what* we do know and what we do not," would this
supposed knowledge be of any value for the direction of life ?
It is clear, of course, that if we had such a knowledge, and directed
our actions by it, everything would be done " scientifically " (κατὰ
τὰς ἐπιστήμας, ἐπιστημόνως).   Our medical men, our soldiers, our
sailors, all our craftsmen in fact, would be real experts ; lives would
not be lost by the blunders of the incompetent physician or strategist
or navigator, clothes would not be spoiled by the bungling of their
makers ; we may even imagine that " prophecy " might be made
" scientific," and that we could thus have confident anticipations of
the future, and, if you like, we may suppose ourselves equally

correctly informed about the past (a suggestion which curiously recalls Du Bois-Reymond's fanciful picture of his omniscient " demon "[1]). But we should be none the happier for all this knowledge unless we had something more which we have not yet mentioned—knowledge of good. Without this we might know all about healing the sick, sailing the sea, winning battles, but we should not know when it is *good* that a sick man should recover, or that a vessel should come safe to port, or a battle be won. If our life is to be truly happy, it is this knowledge of our good which must take the direction of it; apart from that knowledge, we may be able to secure the successful accomplishment of various results, but we cannot make sure that anything will be " well and beneficially " done. But *sophrosyne* by our assumed definition is not this knowledge of good ; even when we waived all other difficulties about it, we still retained the thesis that it is a " knowledge about knowledges," a " science of sciences." Thus *sophrosyne* seems to fall between two stools ; it is not the knowledge of good which would really ensure happiness. It is not even a knowledge which will ensure that the practitioners of the various " arts " shall be experts and practise their callings with success ; for we have just seen that it is the specialist in each department and not the man who knows the " theory of knowledge " who is the final judge in his own department. *Sophrosyne*, if we accept the proposed definition of it, even with the most favourable interpretation, thus seems to be of no practical value whatever (171*d*–175*a*). Yet this conclusion is so extravagantly paradoxical that it clearly cannot be sound. We can only suppose that the fault is with ourselves ; our notions on the subject must be hopelessly confused. This is unfortunate, as it makes it impossible to employ the Thracian's recipe for the cure of Charmides, but there is no help for it. (Of course, the real, as distinct from the dramatic, conclusion has already been reached in the suggestion that what is really needed for the direction of life is the knowledge of good, and that this knowledge is something quite different from any of the recognized special " sciences " or " arts." The purpose of the dialogue is to show that serious examination of the implications of the current conceptions of *sophrosyne* conducts us straight to the two famous Socratic " paradoxes " of the unity of virtue and its identity with *knowledge* of good.)

The Laches.—The *Laches*, which we may now treat more briefly, aims at reaching these same results by starting with the current conceptions of the great fighting-man's virtue—courage or valour or fortitude. As in the *Charmides*, the discussion is accompanied by an interesting introduction which enables us to refer it to a definite period in the life of Socrates. Lysimachus and Melesias, the undistinguished sons of two of the greatest Athenians of the early fifth century, Aristides " the just " and Thucydides, the rival of Pericles, are both anxious that their own sons should rise to distinction, and therefore that they should receive the careful education which

[1] Du Bois-Reymond, *Ueber die Grenzen des Naturerkennens,* 17 ff. ; Ward, *Naturalism and Agnosticism,* i. 40 ff. (ed. 1).

their own parents were prevented by their preoccupation with public affairs from bestowing on themselves. They have just witnessed a public exhibition given by one Stesilaus, who professes to be able to teach the art and mystery of fighting in full armour, and have brought with them two of the most famous military men of the day, Laches and Nicias, in order to get their opinion on the advisability of putting the lads under such an instructor.

Socrates also has been present at the display, and at the recommendation of Laches, who witnessed and highly admired his presence of mind and courage in the disastrous retreat of the Athenian forces from Delium (424 B.C.), he is taken into consultation (*Laches*, 180a–b). It now comes out that Sophroniscus, the father of Socrates, had been a lifelong friend of Lysimachus, and that Socrates himself is a person of whom Lysimachus has heard the boys speak as an object of great interest to themselves and their young companions (180d–e). Laches, as it comes out later, knows nothing of him except his admirable behaviour on the field of Delium (188e), but Nicias is perfectly familiar with him and his habit of turning every conversation into a searching examination of the state of his interlocutor's soul (187e–188b). These allusions enable us to date the supposed conversation pretty accurately. It falls after Delium in 424, but not long after, since it is assumed that Laches, who fell at Mantinea in 418, is still burdened by the cares of public office (187a–b). The references to the comparative poverty of Socrates—it is not said to be more than comparative (186c)—may remind us that Aristophanes and Amipsias both made this a prominent feature in their burlesques of him (the *Clouds* of Aristophanes and the *Connus* of Amipsias), produced in 423. It points to the same general date that the two old men should be thinking of the speciality of Stesilaus as the thing most desirable to be acquired by their sons. After the peace of Nicias, which was expected to put an end to the struggle between Athens and the Peloponnesian Confederation, it would not be likely that fathers anxious to educate their sons well should think at once of ὁπλομαχία as the most promising branch of education. We thus have to think of the conversation as occurring just about the time when Aristophanes produced his delightful caricature of Socrates as a guide of youth ; Socrates is a man of rather under fifty ; Nicias and Laches, as Plato is careful to remind us (181d), are older men, and Lysimachus and Melesias quite old and " out of the world." [1]

The two military experts, as it happens, are of different minds

---

[1] The same approximate date is suggested by the allusion to the famous Damonides, or Damon, of Oea. Nicias expresses gratitude to Socrates for having procured an introduction to Damon for his son Niceratus. Laches professes to think Damon a mere spinner of words and phrases, but Nicias retorts that it is not for him to judge, since he has never even met the man (200b). The assumption is that Damon is living in retirement from society generally. Since he was one of the two " sophists " who " educated " Pericles (Isocr. xv. 235), he must have been born, like his colleague Anaxagoras, about 500 B.C., so that his advanced age will account for his seclusion

about the practical value of the proposed instruction in the conduct of spear and shield. Nicias, who is represented all through as the more intellectual of the two, is inclined to recommend it on the grounds that a soldier needs to know how to handle his weapons, that he is likely to find skill of fence serviceable in actual fighting, that it may awaken in him an interest in other branches of the military art, such as strategy, finally that the training produces grace and agility and banishes awkwardness (181e–182d). Laches, a brave fighting-man with no intellectual capacity, takes a different view. He holds that the " proof of the pudding is the eating of it." There cannot be much in this technical skill, for we see that the Spartans, who ought to be the best judges of things military, set no store by its professors, and the professors themselves avoid Sparta like the plague. They reap their harvest from communities who, by their own admission, are backward in warfare. (This is an excellent little bit of dramatic characterization ; Laches is mentally too dull to see the obvious explanation that the professionals take their wares to the market where the need for them is likely to be most felt.) Besides, in actual warfare, the professional masters of fence never distinguish themselves.[1] Laches remembers having seen this very professor make himself a laughing-stock by his clumsy handling of a complicated weapon of his own forging (182d–184c).

In this disagreement of the experts, Socrates is now called upon to give the decisive opinion. But, as he says, a question of this kind is not to be settled by a majority of votes. The deciding voice should be left to the expert, the man who really knows, even if he were found to be in a minority of one. But who is the expert to whom we ought to appeal in the present case ? Not the mere expert or connoisseur in ὁπλομαχία. The problem is really concerned with the " tendance " of the young people's souls, and the expert to whom we must appeal is therefore the expert in " tending " his own soul, the man who can achieve " goodness " in himself and, by his influence, produce it in others (185a–e). Now, if a man really is an expert, he may take either of two ways of convincing us of his claims. If he has learned his skill from others, he can tell us who his teachers were, and convince us that they were competent.[2] If he has picked it up for himself, as expert knowledge is often picked up, he can point to its results, can give us examples of persons who have been made better by his influence on them (186a–b). Socrates confesses himself to be no expert, but maliciously suggests that the case may be different with the two generals. They are richer than he, and may have been able to pay " sophists " for instruction in the art of " tending the soul " ; they are older and more experienced, and so may have discovered the secret for themselves

---

[1] In the *Republic* Socrates himself is made to propose a training for his young men from which all specialism of this kind is expressly excluded (*Rep.* iii. 404a ff.).

[2] We shall see the full significance of this when we come to examine the *Protagoras*.

(186c). At any rate, they must be experts, or they could not pronounce on a question in which only the expert is competent with such confidence and readiness. (The insinuation, of course, is that, as we might expect from their disagreement, neither is a real " expert "; both are talking about what they do not understand.)

We may, however, contrive to avoid the demand for direct evidence that there is an expert among us. For if a man really knows what, e.g., good sight is, and how to produce it in a patient, he can tell us what sight is ; if he cannot, he is manifestly not a specialist in the treatment of the eye. So, in the present case, the man whose judgment we need is the expert in " goodness," which makes our souls better souls. If a man cannot even say what goodness is, it would be waste of time to take his advice on the kind of education which will produce it. Thus the original question whose judgment is authoritative in the problem of education may be replaced by the question who knows what goodness is. And this question may be, for convenience, further narrowed down. For our present purpose, judging of the worth of the art of the professional teacher of skill with shield and spear, it will be sufficient to consider only one " part " of goodness—courage or valour. A competent judge on the question whether the accomplishment makes its possessor a better soldier must at least be able to say what courage is (189d–190e). We have now got our ethical question fairly posed : What is it that we really mean to be talking about when we speak of ἀνδρεία—manliness, valour, courage—as one of the indispensable points of manhood ? Laches, the less thoughtful of the two professional soldiers, thinks that any man can answer so simple a question off-hand. " A man who keeps his place in the ranks in the presence of the enemy, does his best to repel them, and never turns his back—there is a brave man for you " (190e). Thus, just as in the Charmides, we start with a proposed definition of an interior state of soul which confuses the state itself with one of its common and customary outward expressions. The further course of the discussion will reveal the double defectiveness of this formula. It is not even adequate as a description of the conduct of the fighting-man himself, and fighting is far from being the only business in life which demands the same qualities as those we expect from the good soldier. As usual, Plato is anxious to insist upon the real identity of the spiritual state under the great apparent variety of its outward manifestations. To discover that other occupations than those of warfare also call for the " soldierly " virtues is a long step towards discovering the essential unity of the " virtues " themselves.

Even Laches is ready to admit at once that a feigned withdrawal is a proper manoeuvre in warfare, as is shown by the practice of the Scythians, the pretended retreat by which the Lacedaemonians drew the Persians from their defences at Plataea, and other examples (191a–c). He is even ready to allow that fighting is not the only situation in which courage may be shown. A man may show himself a brave man or a coward by the way he faces danger at sea, poverty, disease, the risks of political life ; again, bravery and cowardice may be shown as much in resistance to the seductions of pleasure and the importunities of desire as in facing or shirking pain or danger, a consideration which, incidentally, shows the artificial nature of the popular distinction between valour, the virtue of war, and *sophrosyne*, the virtue of peace and non-combatants (191*d–e*). (It is this passage of the *Laches* which Aristotle has in view in the *Ethics* where he distinguishes valour in the " primary " sense of the word from the very kind of conduct here called by the name.[1] The disagreement, however, is a purely verbal one. Aristotle does not mean to deny that the qualities in question are indispensable to the good life, nor that there is a close analogy between them and the quality of the soldier, which justifies a " transference " of the name *valour* to them. He is concerned simply, in the interests of precise terminology, to insist that when we speak of " putting up a good fight " against disease, financial distress, temptation, and the like, we are using language which originally was appropriated to the actual " fighting " of actual soldiers, and Aristotle's purpose in giving the series of character-sketches which make up this section of the *Ethics* requires that he shall describe the various " virtues " in the guise in which they are most immediately recognizable by popular thought.)

Now that he sees the point, Laches replies very readily that there is a certain spirit or temper which is to be found universally in all the examples of courageous behaviour Socrates has produced. They are all cases in which a man " persists " in the face of opposition or risk of some kind. Hence he proposes as the definition of courage that it is in all cases a certain καρτερία, " persistence," " endurance," " sticking to one's purpose " (192*c*). This definition clearly has some of the qualities of a good definition. When you speak of courage as a " persistence of soul," just as when we commonly use the word " resolution " as a synonym for it, you are really trying to indicate the spirit which underlies all the manifold expressions of the quality. And it is, of course, true that persistence or resolution is a characteristic of courage ; the brave man is one who " sticks it out." But, as a definition, the formula is still too wide. All courage may be persistence, but all persistence is not courage. In the technical logical language which makes its appearance in Plato's later dialogues, we need to know the " difference "[2] which discriminates persistence which is courage from persistence which is not. Since unwise persistence, mere obstinacy, is a bad and harmful thing, whereas we certainly mean by courage something we regard as eminently good, it looks as though we might remedy the defect of our formula by saying that " wise persistence " (φρόνιμος καρτερία) is courage (192*d*). But the question now arises *what* wisdom we mean. A man may wisely calculate that by persisting in expenditure he will make a commercial profit, but we should hardly regard this as an example of courage. When a

---

[1] *E.N.* iii. 6, 1115*a* 7 ff.　　[2] διαφορά, διαφορότης (*Theaetet.* 208*d* ff.).

physician persists in refusing the entreaties of his patient for food which he knows would be bad for the patient, we do not think the physician has shown any particular courage. In warfare, we do not commend the courage of a force which " holds out " because it knows that it is superior in numbers and still has the stronger position and is certain of reinforcement. It is just the " persistence " of an inferior force, with a worse position and no hope of relief, that impresses us as singularly courageous. So we think more of the courage of the man who acquits himself well in the cavalry though is he an unskilled rider, or the man who makes a plucky dive into deep water though he is a poor swimmer, than we do of the persistence of the man who acquits himself well because he has mastered these accomplishments. (E.g., we think Monmouth's raw countrymen showed great courage at Sedgemoor in putting up a fight against the Household troops; we do not commend the courage of the Household troops because they " held out " against a crowd of peasants.) This looks as if, after all, it is " unwise " persistence (ἄφρων καρτέρησις) rather than " wise " which is the true courage. We have plainly not found the right formula yet, and shall have to call on ourselves for the very quality of which we have been speaking, " persistence " in the inquiry, if we are to approve ourselves " courageous " thinkers (192c–194a). We must not miss the point of this difficulty. Socrates does not seriously mean to suggest that " unwise " resolution or persistence is courage. His real object is to distinguish the " wisdom " meant by the true statement that courage is " wise resolution " from specialist knowledge which makes the taking of a risk less hazardous. The effect of specialist knowledge of this kind is, in fact, to make the supposed risk unreal. The man whom we admire because we suppose him to be rightly taking a great risk is, in reality, as he himself knows, taking little or no risk. Our belief in his courage is based on an illusion which he does not share. But it is true that we do not regard the " unwise " persistency of the man who takes " foolish " risks as true courage. What we really mean is that the brave man faces a great risk, being alive to its magnitude, but faces it because he rightly judges that it is good to do so. The " wisdom " he shows is right judgment of good and evil, and this is what Socrates means to suggest.

At this point Nicias comes into the discussion. He has " often " heard Socrates say that a man is " good " at the things he " knows " (ἄπερ σοφός, 194d) and "bad" at the things he does not know (ἃ ἀμαθής). If this is true, as Nicias believes it to be, courage, since it is always a good quality or activity, will be a σοφία or ἐπιστήμη, a knowledge of some kind. It is clearly not the same thing as any form of specialist technical knowledge, for the reasons we have already considered. But it may well be that it is " the knowledge of what is formidable and what is not " (ἡ τῶν δεινῶν καὶ θαρραλέων ἐπιστήμη, 194e); i.e. the truly brave man may be the man who knows, in all the situations of life, what is and what is not a proper object of fear. This suggestion is plainly a step in the right direction, as it incorporates the important distinction between specialist knowledge and the kind of knowledge which might conceivably be the same thing as virtue, the distinction which would be made, in the fashionable terminology of our own day, between knowledge of facts and knowledge of values.   Laches, however, who is in a bad temper from his own recent rebuff, treats the theory as a mere piece of mystification, and can hardly be brought to express his objections to it in decently civil language.   A physician or a farmer knows the dangers to which his patients or his cattle are exposed, but such knowledge does not constitute courage (195b).   The objection shows that Laches has missed the whole point of the definition, as Nicias goes on to observe.   The physician may know that a patient will die or will recover ; he does not know whether death or recovery is the really " formidable " thing for the patient.   It may be that it is recovery which would in some cases be the " dreadful " thing, but medical science cannot tell us which these cases are; (e.g. a man might use his restored health in a way which would bring him to public disgrace worse than death, and, of course, his medical man cannot learn from the study of medicine whether this will happen or not [1]).   Even the " seer " can only predict that a man will or will not die, or lose his money, that a battle will be won or lost ; his art cannot tell him which event will be better for the man or the State (195e–196a).   This is, of course, exactly the reply which might be made to Laches' criticism from the Socratic standpoint.   But it still leaves something to be said which Socrates is anxious to say.   In the first place, if courage is knowledge of some kind, we must deny that any mere animal can be brave.   In fact, the truly brave will be a small minority even among men.   Must we say, then, that there is no difference in courage between a lion and a deer, a bull and a monkey ?   Laches thinks the suggestion a sufficient refutation of what he regards as the sophisticated nonsense of Nicias, but, as Nicias observes, its edge is turned if we distinguish between natural high temper and fearlessness (τὸ ἄφοβον) and genuine courage (τὸ ἀνδρεῖον, 196d–197c).   So far Nicias is simply insisting on what we shall see from the *Phaedo* and *Republic* to be the Socratic view.[2] Native fearlessness is a valuable endowment, but it is only in a human being that it can serve as a basis for the development of the loyalty to principle we call courage, and it is only in " philosophers " that this transformation of mere " pluck " into true valiancy is complete.   But there is a further difficulty which Nicias has left out of account.   By a " formidable thing " or " thing to be feared " we mean a *future* or impending *evil*.   Now there is no science of *future* good and evil distinct from the science of good and evil

---

[1] So in Dickens's *Great Expectations* it is " better for " the returned convict that he dies in the prison hospital, since, if he had recovered, he would have been sent to the gallows for returning from transportation.   The hero is *glad* to hear on each inquiry that the patient is " worse."

[2] The distinction is more obvious to a Greek than to ourselves, since the *vox propria* for " brave " is ἀνδρεῖος, " manly," and to call a brute " manly " is felt to be at least a straining of language.

simpliciter, just as there is no special science of "*future* health and disease" or of "*future* victory and defeat." There is simply the science of medicine or of strategy, and these sciences apply indifferently to past, present, and future. So our definition, if we are to retain it, must be amended ; we must say that courage is "knowledge of good and evil," without any further qualification (198*d*–199*e*). But as now amended our formula covers not merely a part but the whole of goodness. If it is a definition at all, it is the definition of "goodness," not of one of several different varieties or departments of "goodness" (199*e*). Yet it is commonly held that courage is not the whole of "goodness"; a good man needs to display other virtues, such as "justice" and *sophrosyne*. It appears then that, after all, we have not answered the question what *courage* is. So far from being competent to choose masters for the education of the boys, we all need to go to school ourselves, if only we could find a teacher (201*a*).

Thus the dialogue has led us to the same result as the *Charmides*. If we try to explain what any one great typical moral virtue is, we find ourselves driven on to define it as "the knowledge of what is good." Every virtue thus seems on examination to cover the whole field of the conduct of life, and none can be in principle distinguished from any other. Yet it is commonly thought, and we shall see in dealing with the *Republic* that there are facts of experience which strongly support the view, that the different virtues are so really distinct that a man may be eminent for one and yet no less eminent for the lack of another, (as the typical soldier is commonly thought to be at once braver and more licentious than the ordinary peaceable civilian). We are forced by our intellect to accept the Socratic "paradox" of the unity of virtue, but we have to explain how the "paradox" is to be reconciled with the facts upon which popular moral psychology is based. How the reconciliation is effected we shall be able to say when we have studied the *Protagoras*, *Phaedo*, and *Republic*. The all-important point, on which too many interpreters went wrong in the nineteenth century, is to understand that, to the end of his life, Plato never wavered in his adherence to the "paradox" itself.

Lysis.—The dialogue is linked with the *Charmides* by its setting, which presents another charming picture of the manner of Socrates with promising boys ; some of the problems of moral psychology it suggests point forward to one of the supreme achievements of Plato's literary prime, the *Symposium*. It is specially interesting as the unnamed source from which Aristotle derives most of the questions discussed in a more systematic way in the lectures which make up the eighth and ninth books of the *Nicomachean Ethics*. (The extensive use of the *Lysis* in these books of itself disposes of the misguided attack made on its authenticity by some nineteenth-century scholars.)

The subject of the discussion is Friendship, a topic which plays a much more prominent part in ancient than in modern ethical literature, for easily assignable reasons. It is quite untrue to say that the Greeks " had no family life," but it is true that owing to the neglect of the education of their women, the family tended to be more a close " business partnership " than a centre of intellectual interests and spiritual emotions. Again, though conjugal affection could be a real thing in the Hellenic world, for the same reasons, romantic love between the sexes had little scope for the moralizing and spiritualizing effects we are accustomed to ascribe to it. " Passion " was relatively more prominent, " affection " much more secondary, in the sexual life of Periclean Athens than in that of any community which has been stamped by Christian traditions. In the Greek literature of the great period, Eros is a god to be dreaded for the havoc he makes of human life, not to be courted for the blessings he bestows ; a tiger, not a kitten to sport with.[1] Love, as known to the classical writers, is a passion for taking, not for giving. Hence in life, as seen from the Hellenic point of view, there are just two outlets for the spirit of eager unselfish devotion. It can show itself in a high impersonal form, as absolute devotion to the ·. city " which is the common mother of all the citizens. For the man who, like most of us, needs a personal object of flesh and blood for passionate affection and self-sacrifice, there is the lifelong friend of his own sex, whose good is to him as his *own*. This is why, in Aristotle's *Ethics*, an elaborate study of friendship immediately precedes the culminating picture of the " speculative life," in which man puts off the last vestiges of his human individuality to lose himself in the contemplation of God. We may suspect that those who condemn the tone of Greek ethics as " self-centred "have usually " skipped " these books in their reading of the *Ethics*, and forgotten that they are only the remains of what was once a vast literature.[2]

Plato's interest in the *Lysis* is partly a psychological one. He is fascinated by the mystery of the attraction which can draw two human beings so close, that each is to the other as dear or dearer than himself, as modern philosophers have been by the mystery of the attraction of a particular woman for a particular man. What does *A* see in *B* rather than in *C*, to account for this attraction ? But he has also a more specifically ethical purpose, as will appear from an analysis of his argument. As usual, we shall find the fundamental conceptions of the Socratic morality, the doctrine

[1] Cf. Bevan, *Hellenism and Christianity*, 93–94.

[2] There are linguistic difficulties about any precise reproduction of the argument of the *Lysis* in English. φιλεῖν can only be rendered " to love," *i.e.* with the love of affection (not that of sexual desire). But for φίλος, used as a substantive, we have to say " friend," while the adjective has to be rendered in various ways. If we said regularly either " friendly " or " dear," we should obscure the reasoning, since " friendly " means definitely " a person feeling affection," and " dear " a " person towards whom affection is felt." Either rendering would make nonsense of the question, whether our φίλοι are those whom we " love " or those who " love us." Further, when the adjective is used about things, like wine and the like, we cannot render it by either. We have to say that a man " likes " wine or horses. This must be my apology for the shifts to which I have been driven.

of the " tendance " of the soul and the dependence of happiness
upon *knowledge* of good, emerging from the paradoxes in which the
discussion appears to entangle itself.

The introduction of the dialogue closely resembles that of the
Charmides.   Socrates is taking a walk outside the city wall from
the suburb of the Academy on the N.W. to the Lyceum on the
E., when he is accosted by some of his young friends and drawn
into a *palaestra* to make the acquaintance of Lysis, a beautiful and
modest boy passionately admired by Hippothales, one of the elder
lads.   Hippothales, in fact, as the others complain, makes a nuisance
of himself by inflicting on them endless bad poems, in which he
belauds the antiquity, wealth, and splendid renown of the family of
Lysis.   Socrates good-naturedly banters Hippothales on the mal-
adroitness of attempting to make a " conquest " by flatteries which
would be more likely to spoil the recipient, by making him arrogant,
conceited, and domineering, and is then invited to enter the *palaestra*
and give a practical example of the kind of conversation really
appropriate to a " lover " (*Lysis*, 203a–207c).

(The tone which Socrates adopts in his conversation with Lysis
discloses quietly but unmistakably the difference between his own
conception of a romantic attachment and that of his fashionable
young companions.   The tacit presupposition is that the " true
lover's " desire is for the real felicity of the beloved ; his passion is
thus an entirely pure and disinterested thing, a form of φιλία, " affection," not of selfish lust ; and this, no doubt, is why Socrates can open
the argument by examples drawn from wise parental affection.[1])

Lysis has parents who love him dearly.   Since they love him so
well they are, of course, anxious for his " happiness."   Now a man
cannot be happy if he is not his own master and cannot " do what
he desires," " have his own way."   Yet the very parents who are
so devoted to the boy's happiness will hardly let him have his own
way about anything.   He is not allowed to drive his father's
horses or mules, though a hired coachman or a groom who is a slave
is allowed to do as he thinks good with them.   He is even made to
go to school under the conduct of a *paedagogus* and, though the
man is a slave, has to do what he tells him.   When he comes back
from school, he may not do as he pleases with his mother's wools and
implements for spinning and weaving ; he would even be whipped
if he meddled with them.   This does not look like being happy or
being one's own master (207e–209a).

Lysis gives the boyish explanation that he is not yet old enough
to meddle with such matters.   But the real reason cannot be one of
age.   There are things in which he is allowed to have his own way.
When his parents want him to read aloud, to write or to sing, he is
allowed to have his own way about the order in which he reads or

[1] The brutal selfishness of the fashionable ἐραστής is the theme of Socrates
homily in the *Phaedrus*, on the text " that one's favours should not be granted
to a ' lover.' "   Cf. the proverb quoted at the end of the homily, that this sort
of " love " is the " love of the wolf for the lamb " (*Phaedrus*, 238c–241d).

writes words and about tuning the strings of his instrument, because
these are things which he *knows* how to do. Any man, or any body
of men, will be ready to let us manage any kind of business at our
own discretion, if only it is believed that we know *how* to do it
better than anyone else. When you *know* how to handle an
affair, every one will trust you to handle it ; no one will interfere
with your action if he can help it ; the affair will really be *your*
affair and you will be *free* in dealing with it. But our best friends
will be the first persons to check us from having our own way in
matters we do not understand ; they will not be *our* affair, and we
shall be " under the control of others," " not our own masters " in
handling them (209*a*–210*b*). The reason is that we are " unprofitable," " useless " (ἀνωφελεῖς), in matters we do not understand.
But we cannot expect anyone to " love " us for our " uselessness."
If we are " wise," everybody will be our friend, because we shall
be " good and useful " ; if we are not, even our parents and relatives
will not be our friends. Thus the sample conversation is made to
lead up to the point that to be happy and to be free is the same
thing as to have true knowledge. Socrates adds, with a sportive
play on words, that it is absurd, μέγα φρονεῖν, " to have a high mind,"
to be conceited, about matters we do not know, and where, therefore, we haven't a " mind " of our own at all (ἐν οἷς τις μήπω φρονεῖ).
This is, of course, directed against the vanity of the pride of family
which we were told Hippothales encouraged in Lysis (210*b*–*d*).

Some by-play follows here, and when the argument is resumed
it is with a different interlocutor. This is a device for calling our
attention to the fact that the main issues of the dialogue have not
yet been raised ; they are to be looked for, not in the example of the
right way of conversing with an ἐρώμενος, but in the apparently more
desultory talk which is to follow. Socrates remarks that though he
has always thought a good friend the most precious possession a
man can have, he himself does not so much as understand how a
friend is acquired. Young people who have had the good fortune
to form a passionate friendship in their earliest days could, no doubt,
enlighten him out of their experience. In this way we make the
transition to the main problem of the dialogue, the question :
What is the foundation of the personal attraction of one man for
another ?

" If one man loves another, which is the friend of the other—the
lover of the loved, or the loved of the lover, or does this make no
difference ? " *I.e.*, where there is a one-sided affection of *A* for *B*,
does this entitle us to say that *A* and *B* are " friends " ? If not,
does it entitle us to call *one* of them a " friend," and, if so, which is
the friend ? Are my friends the persons who love me or the persons
whom I love ? The difficulty lies in the existence of unrequited
affection. *A* may be strongly attracted to *B*, while *B* is indifferent to
A, or even repelled by him. Can we talk of friendship in cases of
this kind ? Or should we say that there is not friendship unless
the attraction is reciprocal ? It seems most reasonable to hold that

the relation of friendship only exists when there is this reciprocal affection. In that case nothing is φίλον to you unless it "loves you back." To a Greek this creates a linguistic difficulty. When he wishes to say that a man is "fond of" anything—wine, for example, or wisdom—he has to form a compound adjective with φιλο for its first component, φίλοινος, φιλόσοφος, or the like, much as when a German wishes to say that he is fond of animals he has to call himself a *Tierfreund*. Language thus seems to be against the view just suggested, but there are undeniable facts on its side ; very young children may feel no love for their parents, and may feel actual "hate" when they get a whipping, but the parent, even when he punishes the child, is its "best friend." This suggests that it is being loved that makes a friend. If you love me, I am your friend, whether I love you or not (212*b*–213*a*).

But a difficulty arises when we remember that, by parity of reasoning, it should follow that it is *being* hated which makes a man an enemy : (if you hate me, I am your enemy, though my heart may be full of nothing but goodwill to you, or though I may not know of your existence). This leads to the paradox that when A feels love to B, but B hates A, A is being hated by a friend and B loved by an enemy, and thus the same couple may be said to be at once friends and enemies, a contradiction in terms (213*b*).

If we revise our view and say that it is not being loved but loving that makes a friend, so that he who loves me is my friend, whatever my attitude to him may be, the same paradox equally follows, since I may love a person who cannot abide me. Since we began by setting aside the view that reciprocal affection is necessary for friendship, we seem thus to have exhausted all the possibilities, and to have shown that there is no such relation as friendship (213*c*).

The absurdity of this shows that we must have made a false start. We must go over the ground again, and we may take a hint from the poets, who talk of friendships as "made in heaven.' God, they say, "draws like to its like." The scientific men who write cosmologies also make use of this principle of "like to like ' to account for the distribution of bodies in the universe. Perhaps this may be the secret of friendship ; the drawing of A to B may be one case of a great universal principle which underlies the structure of the universe. Yet, on closer examination, we see that unfortunately, so far as the relations of men are concerned, the principle of "like to like" cannot be, at best, more than half the truth. Bad men are not made friends by being "drawn together." The more closely they are drawn together, the more each tries to exploit the other, and the more hostile they become. Perhaps the poets knew this, and really meant to say that a bad man, being without principle, is an unstable and chameleon-like being. He is a "shifty" fellow, who is perpetually "unlike" and at variance with himself, and *a fortiori* unlike and at variance with every one else. Hence the poets perhaps meant to hint that only men of

principle, the good, are really " like " one another, and that friendship can only exist between the good (213*d*–214*e*).

Yet, when we come to think of it, there is a worse difficulty to
be faced. If one thing can act on another and influence it in any
way, can the two be exactly alike ? Must there not be some unlikeness, if there is to be any interaction ? And if one party is
wholly unaffected by the other, how can the one " care for " (ἀγαπᾶν)
the other ? What " comfort " (ἐπικουρία) can the one bring to the
other ? And how can you feel friendship for that which you do not
care for ? If good men are friends, the reason must be in their goodness, not in their " likeness " (*i.e.* they must be good in *different*
ways, so that their respective goodnesses supplement each other,
214*e*–215*a*). And this, again, seems impossible. For the good man is
' sufficient for himself " in proportion as he is good. He therefore
feels no need of anything but himself. But he who feels no need
does not " care for " anything, and he who does not care for a thing
can have no affection for it. By this account there can be no friendships between the good ; being " self-sufficient," they will not miss
one another in absence or have any occasion for one another's offices
when they are together. On what ground, then, should they " set
a value " on one another (215*a*–*b*).[1]

Again we have gone off on a false track. Socrates once heard
some one say that likeness is the source of the keenest rivalry and
opposition, but extreme unlikeness the source of friendship. There
is poetic authority for this in the Hesiodic saying about " two of
a trade," and, in fact, we see that it is so. The rich and the poor,
the feeble and the strong, the ailing man and the physician, are
brought into friendly association precisely because they are unlike ;
each needs the services of the other (*e.g.* the rich man needs industrious and honest servants, the poor need an employer who
has wherewithal to pay for their industry ; the sick man needs the
physician's skill, the physician needs the fee for it). In fact, said
this speaker, the attraction of *unlikes* is the key to cosmology.[2]
Everything in nature needs to be tempered by its opposite : the

[1] Obviously we are here raising a question of vast significance. In its
extreme form it is the question whether there can be, as Christianity assumes,
a love of God for the sinner, or indeed whether God can love anything but
Himself. Socrates is raising a difficulty, but not solving it. It is true that
the better a man is, the less does the removal of friends, by accident or estrange-
ment or death, wreck his life. In that sense the good man is " sufficient to
himself."

[2] Note the way in which it is assumed throughout the dialogue that
Socrates is quite familiar with the theories of the cosmologists, and that his
young friends will recognize allusions to them. This is strictly in keeping
with the standing assumption of the *Clouds* as well as with the autobiographical
section of the *Phaedo*. The conception of φιλία in particular as " attraction
of unlike for unlike " comes from Empedocles and the Sicilian medicine which
goes back to him ; the thought that one opposite is the τροφή, " food " or
" fuel," of the other is that of Heraclitus. Heracliteanism was actually represented at Athens in the time of the Archidamian war by Cratylus ; from the
speech of Eryximachus in the *Symposium* we see that the Sicilian medical
ideas were at home there also.

hot by the cold, the dry by the moist, and so on, for everything is
" fed by " its opposite—the familiar doctrine of Heraclitus. Thus
it would be tempting to say that friendship is a case of attraction
between opposites. Yet if we say that, we shall at once fall an
easy prey to those clever men, the ἀντιλογικοί, who love to make a
man contradict himself. For they will say that hatred and love
are a pair of extreme opposites, and so are " temperance " and
profligacy, or good and evil. Our principle would thus require us
to believe that a man will generally be most attracted to the very
persons who detest him, that a remarkably temperate man will
make his bosom friend of a notorious profligate, and the like. But
manifestly these statements are not true. So once more we have
come to no result. Neither simple " likeness " nor simple " unlikeness " can be the secret of the attraction between friends (215c–216c).[1]
We may attempt a more subtle explanation. Perhaps the truth
is that in friendship one party is good, the other " neither good nor
bad," the only alternative of which we have yet taken no account.
(The suggestion is that the relation is regularly one between the
possessor of some excellence and some one who aspires to the
excellence but has not yet attained it. The friend to whom we are
drawn is what we should like to become.) We may illustrate by a
simple example from medicine. Health is a good thing, disease a
bad thing ; the human body may be said to be neutral, because it
is capable of both. Now no one cares about the doctor, so long as
he is well. But when he is afraid of being ill, he welcomes the doctor.
He does this not when he is at his last gasp, but before, when he
apprehends illness, *i.e.* when he is neither in full health nor beyond
help. We may say that this is a case in which " that which is
neither good nor bad becomes friendly to that which is good because
of the presence of what is evil " (217b). And here we must make a
careful distinction. " Some things are such as to be themselves
such as that which is present to them, others are not " (217c). Thus
if the golden locks of a boy are daubed with white paint, " whiteness " is present to them, but they are not themselves white
(since, of course, the paint can be washed off). But when the boy
has become an old man, " whiteness " will be " present " to his
hair in a different sense ; his hair will *itself* be white. (The only
object of these remarks is to warn us against supposing that when
Socrates speaks of the " presence " of what is evil to what is " neither
good nor bad," he is using the term in the sense in which it is
employed when we explain the possession of a predicate by a thing
by saying that the corresponding form is " present " to the thing.
In this sense παρουσία, " presence " of the form, is an equivalent for
μέθεξις, the " participation " of a thing in the form, as we see from
the free use of both expressions in the *Phaedo*.[2] It is assumed that

---

[1] *I.e.* it is not true either that any and every " likeness," nor yet that every
and any " unlikeness," can be the foundation of friendship.

[2] Cf. *Phaedo*, 100d, where Socrates says that we may call the relation of
form to sensible thing παρουσία or κοινωνία or " whatever you please " (εἴτε ὅπῃ

the technical language of the theory of forms is so familiar a thing that Socrates needs to warn the lads not to be misled by it : an odd representation if the whole theory had been invented by Plato after Socrates' death.)

The theory, then, works out thus. So long as a thing is not yet itself evil, the " presence " of evil makes it desire the corresponding good ; when the thing itself has become evil, it has lost both desire and affection for good. This explains why neither those who are already wise, like the gods, nor those who are simply ignorant are " lovers of wisdom " (φιλόσοφοι). " Philosophers," as we are also told by Diotima in the *Symposium*, are between the two extremes— on the way to wisdom, but only on the way. They are aware of their ignorance and anxious to get rid of it. The theory naturally appeals to the lads, since a boy's enthusiastic devotions are regularly attachments of this kind to some one older than himself whom he admires and wants to grow like (216c–218b).

Still, on reflection Socrates finds a fatal flaw in this attractive solution of his problem. If we revert to our illustration, we observe that the patient is attached to his physician " because of something " and " for the sake of something." He values the doctor *because* he is afraid of illness and *for the sake* of health, and of these disease is bad and " hateful " to him, health is dear or welcome (φίλον) and good. Thus, if we generalize the principle, we must state it more exactly than we did at first. We must say, " That which is neither good nor bad is friendly to that which is good *because* of that which is bad and hateful, and *for the sake* of that which is good and welcome." Now, passing by all merely verbal points to which exception might be taken, this statement implies that whatever is dear, or welcome, or friendly (φίλον) to us, is welcome as a *means* to something else, just as the physician's skill is welcome as a means to keeping or recovering health. But health itself is surely also welcome (φίλον). Are we to say that it too is only welcome as a means to something ? Even if we say this, sooner or later we are bound to come upon something which is dear to us simply on its own account, and is that for the sake of which all other " dear " things are dear. A father whose son has swallowed hemlock will be eager to put his hand on a jar of wine. But he only cares for the jar because it holds the wine, and he only cares about the wine because it will counteract the poison. It is his son, not a sample of Attic pottery or of a particular vintage, about whom he is really concerned. So long as a thing or person is only " dear " to us for the sake of something else, it is only a *façon de parler* to call it " dear." What is really " dear " to us is " just that upon which all our so-called affections terminate " (ἐκεῖνο αὐτὸ εἰς ὃ πᾶσαι αὗται αἱ λεγόμεναι φιλίαι τελευτῶσιν, 220b). (Thus the question about the secret sources

δὴ καὶ ὅπως† προσγενομένη). Elsewhere in the dialogue the form is said to " occupy " (κατέχειν, a military metaphor) the thing, the thing to " receive " (δέχεσθαι, again a military metaphor) or to " partake in " (μετέχειν) the form.

of affection has brought us face to face with the conception of the *summum bonum*, which is the source of all secondary and derivative goodness, 218b–220b.)

We have thus eliminated from our last statement the clause " for the sake of that which is good and welcome." Will the rest of the formula stand criticism ? Is it true that what we " care for " is " good " and that we care for it " because of " (to escape from) evil ? If the second of these statements is sound, it should follow that in a world where there were no evils, we should no longer care about anything good, any more than we should value medicine in a world where there was no disease. If this is so, then our attitude to the supreme object of all our affections is unique. We care about the secondary objects of affection " for the sake of something welcome to us " (φίλον), *i.e.* because they are means to this primary object ; but we must say of the primary object of all affection itself that we care for it " for the sake of the unwelcome " (ἐχθρόν), if we should really value it no longer in a world where there were no evils. Perhaps the question, as we put it, is a foolish one, for who can tell what might or might not happen in such a world ? But our experience of the world we live in teaches us as much as this. To feel hungry is sometimes good for us, sometimes harmful. Suppose we could eliminate all the circumstances in which being hungry is harmful, hunger would still exist, and so long as hunger existed we should " care for " the food which satisfies it. (Even in a socialist Utopia where every one was sure of sufficient food, and every one too healthy and virtuous to be greedy, men would still have " wholesome appetite " and care about their dinners.) This is enough to dispose of the theory that we only care about good as an escape from evil (220b–221c).

Thus our formula seems to have gone completely by the board, and the course of the argument has suggested a new one. It seems now that the cause of all attachment (φιλία) is desire (ἐπιθυμία), and that we must say " what a man *desires* is dear to *him* and *when* he is desiring it." (Thus we arrive at a purely relative definition of τὸ φίλον, probably intentionally modelled on the famous relativist doctrine of Protagoras that " what a man thinks true *is* true—for *him*, and so long as he thinks it so.") We may proceed to develop this thought a little farther. A creature which desires regularly desires that of which it is " deficient " (ἐνδεές). So we may say that " the deficient " (τὸ ἐνδεές) is " attached " (φίλον) to that of which it is " deficient." And deficiency means being " deprived " of something. (The " deficient " creature is " defective " ; it is without something it must have in order to be fully itself.) " Passion " (ἔρως), friendship, desire, then, are all felt for something which " belongs to one's self " (τὸ οἰκεῖον). Friends or lovers, thus, if they really are what they profess to be, are οἰκεῖοι to one another ; they " belong to " one another ; each is, as we might say, a " part of the other " in " soul, or temper or body " (κατὰ τὸ τῆς ψυχῆς ἦθος ἢ τρόπους ἢ εἶδος). A thing for which we feel affection is then something φύσει οἰκεῖον to ourselves, "our very own." It follows that since each party to the affection is thus "the very own " of the other party, affection must be reciprocal, and Socrates is careful to apply this lesson by adding that "a genuine lover " must be one who has his love reciprocated. (This is plainly intended as a comment on the current perversions of "romantic " passion. Reciprocated affection was the last thing the pervert could expect from his παιδικά, a point of which we shall hear more in the *Phaedrus*. The fashionable ἐραστής, it is meant, is not worthy of the name of a lover at all (221*d*–222*b*).)

Formally the dialogue has ended in a circle, or seems to have done so. If τὸ οἰκεῖον, "what belongs to one's self," is also τὸ ὅμοιον, "what is like " one's self, we have contradicted our earlier conclusion that friendship is not based on "likeness." If we try to escape from the contradiction by distinguishing between τὸ οἰκεῖον and τὸ ὅμοιον, it is attractive to say that all good things are οἰκεῖα to one another (in virtue of their common goodness), all bad things οἰκεῖα in virtue of their badness, and all "neutral " things again οἰκεῖα. But this would contradict our decision that friendship is impossible between the bad. Or if we identify τὸ οἰκεῖον, what is one's own, with τὸ ἀγαθόν, one's good, we should have to say that friendship is only possible between two men who are both good, and this again would contradict another of our results (222*b*–*e*).

In ending in this apparently hopeless result, the *Lysis* resembles a much more famous dialogue, the *Parmenides*. In neither case need we suppose that Plato's real intention is to leave us merely befogged. The way in which the thought that what is most near and intimate to each of us (τὸ οἰκεῖον) is the *good* is kept back to the very end of the conversation suggests that this—that man as such has such a "natural good," and that it is the one thing worth caring for in life—is the thought he means the discussion to leave in our minds. If we go back to the various proposed explanations of the secret of friendship with this thought in our minds, it may occur to us that they do not, after all, formally contradict one another. The common bond between the parties to associations which are all correctly called "friendships " may be different in different cases. Or rather, the bond between the "friends " may in every case be association in the pursuit of some "good," but goods are of very different levels of value, and "friendships " may exhibit the same variety of levels. Thus it may be that the full and perfect type of friendship can only be based on common pursuit of the true supreme good, and in that case friendship in the fullest sense will only be possible between "the good." Yet there may be associations between men founded on the common pursuit of some good inferior to the highest (*e.g.* the common pursuit of the "business advantage " of both parties, or the common pursuit of amusement or recreation). These would be "friendships " but of a lower type, and it may quite well be the case, *e.g.*, that a good man and a bad one. or even two bad men may be associated in this inferior sort of " friendship." Such, at least, are the lines on which Aristotle in the *Ethics* develops a theory of friendship in which all the conflicting points of view of our dialogue are taken up, and each is found to have its relative justification.

See further :

RITTER, C.—*Platon*, i. 284–297 (*Laches*), 343–359 (*Charmides*), 497–504 (*Lysis*).

RAEDER, H.—*Platons philosophische Entwickelung*, 95–99 (*Laches Charmides*), 153–158 (*Lysis*).

STOCK, ST. GEORGE.—*Friendship* (*Greek and Roman*) in *E.R.E.* vol. vi.

CHAPTER V

MINOR SOCRATIC DIALOGUES: *CRATYLUS*, *EUTHYDEMUS*

BOTH the dialogues to be considered in this chapter have something of the character of "occasional works." Both are strongly marked by a broad farcical humour, which is apparently rather Socratic than Platonic ; we meet it again, *e.g.*, in the comic fury of the satire in some parts of the *Republic*, but it is quite unlike the grave and gentle malice of such works as the *Parmenides* and *Sophistes*. The mirth, especially in the *Euthydemus*, has something of the rollicking extravagance of Aristophanes, and, according to the *Symposium*, there really was a side to Socrates which made him congenial company for the great comic poet. (Both men could relish wild fun, and both could enjoy a laugh at themselves.) In neither of our two dialogues is the professed main purpose directly ethical, though the Socratic convictions about the conduct of life incidentally receive an impressive exposition in the *Euthydemus*. It seems impossible to say anything more precise about the date of composition of either than that stylistic considerations show that both must be earlier than the great dramatic dialogues, *Protagoras, Symposium, Phaedo, Republic.* Since the *Cratylus* is a directly enacted drama with only three personages, while the *Euthydemus* is a reported dialogue with numerous personages and a vigorously delineated "background," this second is presumably the more mature work of the two.

Cratylus.—The personages of the dialogue other than Socrates are two, Hermogenes and Cratylus. Hermogenes is well known to us as a member of Socrates' *entourage*. Both he and Cratylus figured in the *Telauges* of Aeschines,[1] where Socrates was apparently made to criticize the squalor affected by the extreme Orphic and Pythagorist *spirituali*. We learn from Plato (*Phaedo* 59b) that Hermogenes was present at the death of Socrates. Xenophon mentions him several times and professes to owe some of his information to him. He was a base-born brother of the famous, or notorious, "millionaire" Callias, son of Hipponicus, the munificent patron of "sophists" (*Crat.* 391c), but himself poor, and apparently on no very good terms with his brother. As Callias was connected by marriage with Pericles, the appearance of him and his brother among the associates of Socrates is one of the many

---

[1] See *E.R.E.*, art. SOCRATES, and H. Dittmar's *Aeschines von Sphettus,* 213-244. He and Callias are prominent figures in Xenophon's *Symposium.*

indications that the philosopher stood in early life in close relations with the Periclean circle. Of Cratylus we apparently know only what Aristotle has told us in his *Metaphysics*,[1] that—as we could have inferred from our dialogue itself—he believed in the Heraclitean doctrine of universal " flux," and that he carried his conviction of the impermanence of everything to the length of refusing to name things, preferring to point at them with his fingers. (The use of a significant name would suggest that the thing named really had some sort of relatively permanent character.) But one may reasonably suspect the story of being no more than an invention of some wag which Aristotle has perhaps taken too seriously.[2] According to Aristotle, Plato had been " familiar " with him, and derived from him his rooted conviction that sensible things, because of their complete impermanence, cannot be the objects of scientific knowledge.

It is not clear whether Aristotle means to place this connexion of Plato with Cratylus before or after the death of Socrates, but presumably he means that it was before that event, since he says that it belonged to Plato's youth. The fact is likely enough, since Cratylus seems to have been one of Socrates' associates. (We must not suppose Aristotle to mean that when Plato associated with him he had not yet met Socrates ; the close relations of Socrates with Critias, Charmides, Adimantus, Glaucon, show that Plato must have been acquainted with him from early childhood.) We need not believe, and we can hardly believe, that the influence of Cratylus really counted for much in determining Plato's own thought ; he would not need any special master to inform him that sensible things are mutable. Most probably Aristotle, who only knew Plato in Plato's old age, has exaggerated the importance of an acquaintance which had really no great significance. In any case, the tone of the whole dialogue requires us to suppose that both Cratylus and Hermogenes are youngish men, decidedly younger than Socrates.[3] The " dramatic date " of the conversation is hardly indicated with certainty. If we may suppose, what seems to me most likely, that the " curfew regulations " in Aegina, alluded to at 433*a*, were connected with the Athenian military occupation of the island in 431, this would suggest a date not too long after the beginning of the Archidamian war, when Socrates would be in the early forties, and the other two perhaps twenty years younger.

[1] Aristotle, *Met.* 987*a* 32, 1010*a* 12.

[2] Since Cratylus appears in our dialogue as holding that many of the names by which we actually call things are not their " real names," the point of the jest may have been less recondite. It may lie in his uncertainty what the " real name " of a given thing is. A good deal of fun might obviously be got out of this, *e.g.*, in a comedy.

[3] This was certainly true of Hermogenes, since his elder brother Callias was still alive and active in public affairs at a date when Socrates, if he had still been living, would have been a centenarian. The active career of Callias hardly begins until the end of the fifth century. The youth of Cratylus is expressly remarked on by Socrates at the end of the dialogue (440*d*, ἔτι γὰρ νέος εἶ).

This is further borne out by the reference (386d) to Euthydemus as a person whose views are of interest. We shall see below that the *Euthydemus* requires to be dated at latest not after 421 or 420.[1] The ostensible subject of discussion is the origin of language. Are names significant by "nature" (φύσει), in virtue of some intrinsic appropriateness of the verbal sign to the thing signified, or only significant "by convention" (νόμῳ), *i.e.* arbitrary imposition? Cratylus takes the first view; there is a natural "rightness" of names which is one and the same for every one, Greek or barbarian (383b). If you call a thing by any other name than its own intrinsically "right" name, you are not naming it at all, even though you are using for it the word which every one else uses. Hermogenes is on the side of "convention" or arbitrary imposition; he holds that whatever we are accustomed to call anything is, for that reason, the name of the thing. The dispute is referred to Socrates, who is careful to explain that he cannot decide the question with expert knowledge, as he has never attended the expensive fifty-drachma lecture of Prodicus on the right use of language; he can only contribute the suggestions of his native mother-wit (384b).[2]

The issue under consideration is thus only one aspect of the famous "sophistic" antithesis between "nature" and "social usage" which we know to have been the great controversial issue of the Periclean age. The fancy that if we can only discover the original names of things, our discovery will throw a flood of light on the realities named, seems to recur periodically in the history of human thought. There are traces of it in Heraclitus and Herodotus; in the age of Pericles it was reinforced by the vogue of allegorical interpretations of Homer, which depended largely on fanciful etymologies. Much of the dialogue is taken up by a long series of such etymologies poured forth by Socrates under what he himself declares to be "possession" by some strange personality. It is

[1] Reference is made several times in the *Cratylus* to a certain Euthyphro who exhibited the phenomena of "possession" (ἐνθουσιασμός). This may be the same person who gives his name to the dialogue *Euthyphro*, and was attempting to prosecute his own father for murder in the spring of the year 399. There is no difficulty about the chronology if we suppose that at that date Euthyphro, whose manner is that of an elderly rather than a very young man, was a year or two over fifty, and his father seventy-five or more. But the identification, though accepted by eminent scholars, seems precarious. There is nothing about the religious fanatic Euthyphro to suggest that he was subject to "possession." It is true that Socrates playfully calls him a μάντις (*Euthyph.* 3e), but μαντική had many forms.

[2] It is not suggested that it was poverty which prevented Socrates from attending the lecture. It seems clear that Socrates was not really poor until his middle age. As Burnet has said, the way in which the comic poets dwelt on his poverty when they attacked him in 423, suggests that his losses were then fairly recent. In the *Protagoras*, which takes us back before the Archidamian war, he appears to have a house of his own with a courtyard, and at least one servant (310b, 311a), and speaks of himself in a way which implies that he could at need have helped to pay Protagoras on behalf of his young friend (311d, ἐγώ τε καὶ σὺ ἀργύριον ἐκείνῳ μισθὸν ἕτοιμοι ἐσόμεθα τελεῖν ὑπὲρ σοῦ). Hence the absence of any reference to poverty is perhaps an indication of "dramatic date."

plain that we are not to find the serious meaning of the dialogue
here, especially as, after delighting Cratylus by a pretended demonstration that language supports the Heraclitean philosophy, since
the names of all things good contain references to movement, and
the names of all bad things to arrest of movement, he turns round
and produces equally ingenious and far-fetched etymological
grounds for supposing that the original "giver of names" must
have held the Eleatic doctrine that motion is an illusion, since all
the names of good things appear to denote rest or stoppage of
motion. Obviously, we are to take all this as good-humoured
satire on attempts to reach a metaphysic by way of "philology";
as far as etymologies go, a little ingenuity will enable us to get
diametrically opposite results out of the same data.

The real purpose of the dialogue, so far as it has any purpose
beyond the preservation of a picture of Socrates in one of his more
whimsical moods, is to consider not the *origin* of language, but its
use and functions. If we consider the purposes which spoken
language subserves, we shall see that if it is to be adequate for those
purposes, it must conform to certain structural principles. Hence
the formula of the partisans of "convention" that the "right
name" of anything is just whatever we agree to call it, makes
language a much more arbitrary thing than it really is. A "right
name" will be a name which adequately fulfils all the uses for
which a name is required, and thus one man's or one city's vocabulary may name things more rightly, because more adequately,
than that of another. But so long as the purpose for which names
are required is adequately discharged by any vocabulary, things
will be rightly "named" in the vocabulary. The names for
things will not have the same syllables and letters in Greek and in
a "barbarian" language, but if the purposes for which speech is
required are equally well achieved in both languages, both names
will be equally "true" names for things. So the partisans of
φύσις, who hold, like Cratylus, that there is one particular combination of sounds which is the one and only "right name" of a
given thing, are also only partly right. They are right in thinking
that the right assignment of names is not arbitrary, but depends on
principles of some kind, and that a nomenclature which "every one
agrees in using" may, for all that, be a bad one; they are wrong in
thinking that if a given succession of sounds is a "right name" for
a certain thing, no other such combination can be its "right name."
The *Cratylus* is thus not so much concerned with the "origin" of
language, as with the principles of philosophical and scientific
nomenclature, though it contains many incidental sound observations about those analogies between the different movements of
articulation and natural processes which seem to underlie the
"onomatopoeic" element in language, as well as about the various
influences which lead to linguistic change.

Hermogenes, at the outset, adopts an extreme form of the view
that language is wholly arbitrary. If I like to call a thing by a

certain name that *is* its name for me, even in the case of my inverting
the usage of every one else. Thus, if I call "horse" what every
one else calls "man," "horse" really is my private name, the
name in my private language (ἰδίᾳ, 385a) for that being, as truly as
"man" is its name "in the language of the public" (δημοσίᾳ).
Now this assertion raises a very large question. A name is a part,
an ultimate part, of a λόγος or statement. Statements may be true
or they may be false ; they are true if they speak of realities (ὄντα)
as they really are, false if they speak of them otherwise. But if a
whole "discourse" or "statement" may be either true or false,
we must say the same about its parts. Every part of a true statement must be true, and thus, since there are true and false λόγοι,
there must be true and false names (385c). This looks like a fallacy,
but we shall see that it is not really one if we note carefully the use
Socrates makes of the distinction. His point is the sound one,
that language is a *social* activity; it is primarily an instrument of
communication. A "name" given by me privately to something
which everybody else calls differently does not discharge this
function ; it misleads, is a bad instrument for its purpose. This
is what Socrates means by calling it a "false" name. It is a
spurious substitute for the genuine article which would do the work
required.

This disposes of the suggestion of a purely "private" language
peculiar to the individual, but still it may be reasonably maintained that at any rate though the names "barbarians" give to
things are not the same as those used by Greeks, they are just as
much the "true names" of things as the Greek words (385e).
I.e. we may urge that the plurality of languages shows that language
is an arbitrary thing, though it depends on the *arbitrium* of a group,
not of a single man. But if names are arbitrary, is the reality
(οὐσία) of the things named equally arbitrary? If a thing's name
is just whatever some one likes to call it, is the thing itself just
whatever some one thinks it to be ? Protagoras actually held that
everything really is for any one just what he thinks it to be, so long
as he thinks it to be so, and Hermogenes reluctantly admits that he
sometimes feels driven to accept the view, strange as it is. However, we may perhaps dismiss it with the remark that it leaves no
room for distinguishing wiser and less wise men, since it says that
every one's beliefs are true—for him and no one else, and just as
long as he holds them. But it seems the most patent of facts that
some men are good, and therefore wise, and some wicked and therefore unwise. Yet we can hardly go to the opposite extreme with
Euthydemus, who says that all statements whatever are true, always
and "for every one." This would equally lead to the view that
there is no distinction between the virtuous and the vicious, and
consequently none between wisdom and the lack of it [1] (386d).

[1] Since, if Euthydemus is right, you can always truly predicate both virtue
and vice of any subject whatever. Formally, Protagoras says that a proposition
is true only when it is being believed by some one ; Euthydemus, that what we

Now if neither of these doctrines can be true, " objects " (τὰ πράγματα) clearly have some determinate real character of their own (οὐσίαν τίνα βέβαιον) which is independent of our "fancy"; and if this is so "activities" (πράξεις) will also have a "nature" or "reality" (φύσιν) of their own, since "activities" are one form of "object" (ἔν τι εἶδος τὼν ὄντων, 386e). Hence, if we want to perform an act, we cannot do it in any way and with any instrument we please. We must do it in the way prescribed by the nature of the object we are acting on, and with the "naturally proper" instrument (ᾧ πέφυκε). For example, in cleaving wood, if we are to succeed, we must split the wood "with the grain" and we must use a naturally suitable implement. Speaking of things and naming them is an activity (πρᾶξις), and what we have just said applies therefore to naming. If we want to name things we must name them not just as the fancy takes us, but "as the nature of the objects permits and with the instrument it permits." The instrument or tool for naming things is, of course, the name itself. We may define a name as "an instrument by which we inform one another about realities and discriminate between them " (388b–c, ὄνομα ἄρα διδασκαλικόν τί ἐστιν ὄργανον καὶ διακριτικὸν τῆς οὐσίας). In all the crafts (weaving, for example) one craftsman (e.g. the weaver) has to make a proper use of some implement which has been properly made by some other craftsman (e.g. the carpenter, who makes the wooden implements which the weaver uses). Now from our definition of a name we see at once who is the expert craftsman who "uses" names as his tools ; he is the "teacher" or "instructor" (ὁ διδασκαλικός). But who is the other expert who makes the tools which the teacher uses ? According to the very theory from which we started, they are made by νόμος, "social usage." Hence we may say that they are the manufacture of the "legislator," the institutor of social usage. And legislation is not work that anyone can do, "unskilled labour"; it is "skilled labour," work for an expert, or professor of a τέχνη. Clearly then, it is not correct to say that anyone whatever can arbitrarily give names to things (386d–389a). (Thus the result so far is that, since the function of language is the accurate communication of knowledge about things, the vocabulary of "social usage" will only be satisfactory when it supplies a nomenclature which corresponds to the real agreements and differences between the things named.)

Well, what would the expert in establishing usages have before his mind's eye in assigning names ? We may see the answer by considering the way in which the carpenter works when he makes a κερκίς for the weaver. He "keeps his eyes on" the work the κερκίς is meant to do in weaving—its function. If one of his articles breaks while he is making it, of course he makes a fresh one, and in making it he does not "fix his eye" on the spoilt and broken κερκίς but on the form (εἶδος) with an eye to which he had been

all disbelieve is as true as what we all believe. Both positions make science impossible.

making the one which broke (389*b*). It is this " model " κερκίς, kept by the carpenter before his mind's eye in making all the different wooden κερκίδες, which best deserves the name of αὐτὸ ὃ ἔστιν κερκίς, " just the κερκίς, " the κερκίς and nothing else " (*ib.*). There are three points to be got hold of here. (1) The carpenter cannot give the tools he makes for the weaver just any shape he pleases ; the shape or form of the κερκίς is determined, independently of anyone's fancy, by the work it is meant to do. (2) Strictly speaking, when the carpenter is said in common parlance to *make* a κερκίς, what he does is to put the form, which is the " natural " or " real " κερκίς, into the wood on which he is working.[1] (3) And though the shape of a κερκίς is something fixed, it will be reproduced by the carpenter in different material, according as the implement is wanted for weaving different sorts of cloth (*e.g.*, you would need the wood to be harder for work on some kinds of material than on others). We may transfer these results to the case of the " legislator " who makes names. The letters and syllables, like the wood of the carpenter, are the material into which he has to put " the real name " (ἐκεῖνο ὃ ἔστιν ὄνομα). Differences in the material will not matter, in this case any more than in the other, so long as the resulting instrument answers its purpose. This is why, though the sounds of a Greek word and those of the " barbarian " equivalent may be very different, each is a true name if it discharges the function of a name adequately (389*b*–390*a*). (It should be noted that all through this passage the technical language of the doctrine of forms is used without explanation. Plato assumes that Hermogenes and Cratylus may be counted on to know all about it. To my own mind, it is just the frequency with which this assumption is made, apparently without any consciousness that it calls for any justification, which is the strongest reason for refusing to believe that the whole doctrine was " developed " by Plato or anyone else after the death of Socrates.)

Who, then, decides whether a given piece of wood has really received the " form of κερκίς," as it should have done ? Not the expert who makes the implement (the carpenter), but the expert who will have to use it (the weaver). And this is a general rule. The man who makes an implement must " take his specifications " from the man who is to use it. Thus we arrive at a distinction

---

[1] According to the well-known statements of Aristotle (*Met.* 991*b* 6, 1080*a* 3, 1070*a* 18, *al.*), the Academy of his own day held that there are no " forms " of artificial things. No doubt the statement is true, but it has no bearing on the form of κερκίς in the *Cratylus* or that of κλίνη in *Republic* x. Aristotle is speaking of the theory as he knew it, *i.e.* after 367, and it is notorious that this version of the doctrine has to be learned from his writings, not from Plato's. The only character in the dialogues of Plato's later life who ever says anything about the doctrine is Timaeus, and he speaks pretty much as Socrates is made to do in the earlier dialogues. In the *Cratylus* there is no suggestion that the εἶδος is a sort of supra-sensible " thing." It is just a " type " to which the manufacturer's articles must conform, and its independence means simply that the structure of the κερκίς is determined by its function, independently of anyone's caprice.

afterwards explicitly formulated in the *Politicus* and reproduced as fundamental in the opening paragraphs of the *Nicomachean Ethics*, the distinction between superior and subordinate " arts," the rule being that it is the " art " which uses a product that is superior, the " art " which makes it that is subordinate.   This will apply to the case of the " legislator " who makes names.   There must be a superior expert, whose business it is to judge of the goodness of the names, namely, the expert who is to use them, and he can be no other than the expert in asking and answering questions, that is the " dialectician " or metaphysician.   The " legislator " who is to bestow names rightly must therefore work under the superintendence and to the specifications of the " dialectician," the supreme man of science.   (In other words, the test of the adequacy of language is not mere " custom," but its capacity to express the highest truth fully and accurately.)

Cratylus, then, is right in thinking that language depends on " nature," and that names can only rightly be given by a man who " fixes his eye on the real ($\phi\acute{\nu}\sigma\epsilon\iota$) name and can put its form into letters and syllables " (389*a*–390*e*).[1]   At any rate, this is how the matter looks to Socrates, though, as he had said, he cannot go on to convince Hermogenes by explaining which names are the " right " ones.   For that one must go to the professional sophists, such as Protagoras, or, since Hermogenes has no money to pay them, he might ask his brother Callias to teach him what he has learned from Protagoras on this very subject (391*a*–*c*).   Perhaps we can hardly do this, since Hermogenes has already decided against the main principle of Protagoras' book on *Truth*.   But something can be done, to make a beginning, with Homer.   He sometimes gives two names for a thing, that used by " gods " and that used by " men," and in such cases we sometimes find that the name used by the " gods " is significant (*e.g.*, we call a certain river Scamander, but the gods call it " the Yellow River," $\Xi\acute{\alpha}\nu\theta o\varsigma$).   Or again he tells us that Hector's son was called Scamandrius by the women, but Astyanax by his father and the men.   Now, on the average, the men of a society are more intelligent than their women-folk,[2] and their name for the boy is presumably his " right " name.   And,

---

[1] It is, of course, with intentional humour that Socrates forgets that Cratylus had meant something quite different when he said that names are " by nature."   Note the repeated insistence on the point that Greek has no necessary superiority over a " barbarian " language (like, *e.g.*, Persian).   The notion that " barbarians " are intrinsically inferior to Hellenes, so prominent in Isocrates and Aristotle, is foreign to the Platonic dialogues, though it is recognized as a fact that Hellenes show more aptitude than Egyptians and other peoples for science.   The all-round inferiority of the non-Hellene is not a Socratic or Platonic doctrine.   That the point should be insisted on in a discussion about language is all the more interesting since $\beta\acute{\alpha}\rho\beta\alpha\rho o\varsigma$ seems originally to have meant one who " jabbers "—like a swallow, as Clytaem-nestra says in Aeschylus.

[2] This is given as a mere statement of fact, and in a place like the Athens of the fifth century it was true.   It is not implied that it ought to be so, or need be so.   Indeed, as we shall see, Socrates held that it need not be so.

in fact, we see that it has a significance which makes it appropriate. The name means " Burgh-ward," and is therefore very suitable to the son of Hector who " warded " Troy so effectually (391a–392e).

Once started on this trail, Socrates proceeds to propound a host of derivations of names—proper names of heroes and gods, and common nouns—with the general purpose of showing that in their original form, often widely different from that to which we are accustomed, they have a " connotation " which makes them specially appropriate. There is no need to follow this part of the conversation in any detail, all the more since Socrates professes to be surprised by his own readiness and suggests that he must have been infected by an abnormal " possession " from having just left the company of the "inspired" Euthyphro (396d). We could hardly be told more plainly that the extravagances which are to follow are meant as a caricature of the guesses of " etymologists " working in the dark without any scientific foundation.[1] But, like a wise man, Socrates mixes some sense with his nonsense. Thus it is a sound principle, whatever we may think of some of the applications made of it, that proper names of men and gods are likely to have been originally significant, though their meaning has been lost through linguistic changes. It is sound sense again to say (398d) that we may often be put on the true track by considering archaic forms which are obsolete in current speech, or peculiar dialectical variants (401c). So again Socrates is quite right in calling attention to the presence of " barbarian " words in the current vocabulary (409e), though the use he makes of the fact as a convenient way out of a difficulty whenever he is at a loss is manifestly jocular (421c–d). The jocularity is even more patent when he pretends (402a) to make the sudden discovery, which he then rides to death, that the ancient names of the gods and a host of other words show that the creators of the Greek language were Heracliteans, or (409b) that the name Selene conveys the discovery, connected at Athens with the name of Anaxagoras, that the moon shines by reflected light. It is no surprise to us when, after a long interval of more serious discussion, we find him (437a ff.) expressing his doubts whether after all etymology might not be made to bear equal witness to Parmenides and his doctrine of the absolute motionlessness of the real.

We come back to seriousness at 422a with the reflection that, after all, the process of derivation cannot go on for ever. We must, in the end, arrive at a stock of primitive names, the ABC ($\sigma\tau o\iota\chi\epsilon\hat{\iota}a$) of all the rest. How are we to account for the appropriation of each of these to its *signification* ? We may do so if we reflect that language is a form of gesture. If we were all deaf and dumb we

---

[1] Probably, if only we had adequate literary records of the Periclean age we might find that a good many of the etymologies are specimens of the serious speculations of the persons satirized. Few of them are much more extravagant than, *e.g.*, the derivation of $\kappa\hat{\eta}\rho\upsilon\xi$ from $\kappa\acute{\eta}\rho$ hinted at in Euripides, *Troad.* 425.

should try to communicate information by imitating with our own
bodies the shapes and movements of the things to which we wanted
to call attention.   Now we can imitate in the same way by vocal
gestures.   If a man could reproduce the "reality" of different
things by the vocal gestures we call "letters" and "syllables," he
would be naming the various things (423a–424b).   The primitive
names may be supposed to have been produced by this method of
imitation.   We may test this suggestion and judge of the "rightness" of these primitive words by making a careful classification
of the elementary components of our speech—the vowels, consonants,
and so forth—and considering the movements by which they are
produced.   We shall ask whether there are not analogies between
these various processes and processes in nature at large, and whether
primitive names do not seem to be composed of sounds produced
by movements analogous with those of the things they signify,
allowance being made for a considerable amount of variation for
the sake of euphony and greater ease of articulation.   We might,
to be sure, save ourselves trouble by simply saying that the primitive words were invented by gods or "barbarians" of long ago,
but this would be shirking the chief problem which the scientific
expert in the theory of language has to face (425d–426b).   Socrates
therefore ventures, with misgivings, to state some of his observations on the subject.   The pages in which he does so (426b–427d)
have often been commended for their penetration, but the subject
has more interest for the student of phonetics than for the philosopher, and we need not delay over the details.   What is of real
interest to others than specialists in phonetics is the discernment
shown by the insistence on the general principle that speech is to be
regarded as a species of mimetic gesture, and the clear way in
which such vocal gesture is distinguished from direct reproduction
of natural noises and the cries of animals (423c–d).

Hitherto the conversation has been a dialogue between Socrates
and Hermogenes ; Cratylus now replaces the latter as interlocutor.
He is delighted with all that Socrates has said—no doubt because
Socrates has professed to find Heracliteanism embodied in the very
structure of language—and thinks it could hardly be bettered.   But
Socrates himself has misgivings, and would like to consult his second
thoughts.   (What the by-play here really hints is that we are
now to come to a discussion to which Plato attaches greater importance than he does to the entertaining etymological speculations
on which so much time has been spent.)

We said that name-giving is a trade, and that the workman
(δημιουργός) who makes names is the "legislator."   Now in general
there are better and worse workmen in any trade ; we should expect,
then, that there are degrees of goodness and badness in the names
made by different legislators (i.e. linguistic tradition, of which the
νομοθέτης is a personification, approximates more or less nearly,
in the case of different idioms, to the ideal of a "philosophical"
language).   Cratylus denies this, on the ground that a word either

is the right name of a certain thing, or is not that thing's name at all, but the name of something else. There cannot be any intermediate degree of " rightness " in this case. If you call a thing by the name of something else, you are not speaking of the thing in question at all; (*e.g.* to say "Hermogenes" when you meant Cratylus, is trying to say " what is not," and that is impossible). You cannot say *nothing*. Whenever you speak you must be saying *something*. Not only must you mean (λέγειν) something, but you must enunciate (φάναι) something. Hence when a man uses any but the " right name " Cratylus holds that he merely makes a senseless noise, like a " sounding brass " (ψοφεῖν ἔγωγ' ἂν φαίην τὸν τοιοῦτον, μάτην αὐτὸν ἑαυτὸν κινοῦντα, ὥσπερ ἂν εἴ τις χαλκίον κινήσειε κρούσας, 430a). In other words, you cannot make a statement which is significant and yet false. Every statement is either true or meaningless. The difficulty here suggested only seems fanciful to us, because the explanation of it given for the first time in Plato's own *Sophistes* has become part of our current thought. To say " what is not " does not mean to say what is simply meaningless, but only to say what means something *different* from the real facts of the case. Until this had been explained, there was a double difficulty for the Greek mind in understanding how it is possible to speak falsely. Partly the difficulty is due to the accident of language that the word εἶναι is ambiguous ; it means " to be " or " to exist " ; in Greek, especially in the Ionic Greek, which was the original tongue of science, it also means " to be true," as when Herodotus calls his own version of the early life of Cyrus τὸ ἐόν, " the true narrative," or Euripides in Aristophanes speaks of the story of Phaedra as an ὢν λόγος, " an over-true tale." Behind the merely verbal ambiguity there is further a metaphysical one, the confusion between " what is not " in the absolute sense of " blank nothing," and " what is not " in the merely relative sense of " what is other than " some given reality. So long as you confuse " what is not " in this relative sense with what is just nothing at all, you must hold it impossible to say significantly " what is not " (*i.e.* to make a false statement which has any meaning). This explains why, in the age of Pericles and Socrates, it should have been a fashionable trick of ἀντιλογικοί or ἐριστικοί, pretenders who made a show of intellectual brilliance by undertaking to confute and silence every one else, to argue that no statement, however absurd, if it means anything, can be false. The most violent paradoxes must be true, because they *mean* something, and therefore he who utters them is saying " what is." Plato regularly connects this theory of the impossibility of speaking falsely with the philosophy of Parmenides, and its unqualified antithesis between " what is " and mere nonentity. He means that the doctrine arises as soon as you convert what Parmenides had meant for a piece of physics into a principle of logic. Cratylus, to be sure, is a follower not of Parmenides, who regarded change of every kind as an illusion, but of Heraclitus, who thought change the fundamental reality. But he is led by a different route to the same result. Whether you start with the premise that " what is not," being just nothing at all, cannot be spoken of, or with the premise that to call a thing " out of its name " must be to speak of something else and not of the thing in question, in either case the conclusion has to be drawn that you cannot significantly say what is false, since that would be to speak of a given thing and yet not to speak of it " as it is." [1]

Though this issue of the possibility of significant false statement has been raised, we need not go to the bottom of it for our present purposes. (In fact, Plato's own logical studies had presumably not yet led him to the complete solution.) It is enough to remember that we have already agreed that a name is a " representation " (μίμημα) of that which it names. It is like a portrait, except that the portrait is a visible, the name an audible, representation. Now we might take the portrait of a woman for a portrait of a man ; we should then be connecting the portrait with the wrong original, but still it would be a portrait of *some* original. We do the same thing when we misapply a name ; it does not cease to be a name because we apply it to the wrong thing. Again, a portrait is not an exact replica. One artist seizes points which another misses, and thus there may be a better and a worse portrait, and yet both are portraits of the same original. Why may not the same thing be true of the primitive names in language ? Why may not a name be an imperfect but real " representation " of that for which it stands ? (This would explain why the primitive names in different languages may all be genuine " vocal gestures," denoting the same thing, in spite of the differences between them.) Cratylus suggests that the analogy with portraiture does not hold. A bad portrait may leave out some characteristic of its original, or put in something not present in the original, and yet be a recognizable portrait of the man. But in the case of a name, if, for example, we put in or leave out a single letter, we have not written *that* name at all.

---

[1] It has been the fashion, especially in Germany, for a generation and more, to connect the paradox about false-speaking specially with the name of Antisthenes, and to regard all the references to it in Plato as direct attacks on that rather insignificant person. This seems to me quite unhistorical. The standing assumption of Plato is that the ἀντιλογικοί are quite a numerous and fashionable body. Socrates even refers to them in the *Phaedo* (90b), where Antisthenes is supposed to be present (59b) and all possibility of an attack on his own old friend is out of the question. The one dialogue of Plato's early life in which they are singled out for special satire is the *Euthydemus*, and we see from the *Cratylus* itself that Euthydemus really was a well-known personage who held views of this kind. Isocrates too (x. 1) implies that the " eristics " who maintain the paradox are a fairly numerous body of the generation before his own. For this reason it seems to me out of the question to find attacks on Antisthenes in any of the Platonic dialogues in which Socrates is the principal figure. Whether in the later dialogues, when Socrates has fallen into the background, Plato ever criticizes Antisthenes on his own account, is another question with which we shall not be concerned until we come to deal with the *Parmenides* and *Sophistes*, though I believe we shall find reason to think that there also he has very different antagonists in view.

We may reply that it is not with quality as it is with number. Any addition or subtraction will make, *e.g.*, the number 10 another number (such as 9 or 11), but a " representation " may be like the original without reproducing it in its details. Thus the portrait-painter reproduces the outward features and complexion of his sitter, but leaves out everything else. The sitter has entrails, movement, life, thought ; the picture has none, and yet it is a picture of him. In fact, if it did reproduce the whole reality of the sitter, it would not be a portrait at all but a reduplication of the man himself. Full and complete reproduction is thus not the kind of " rightness " we require in a portrait, and we have already recognized that a name is a kind of portrait of which vocal gesture is the medium (430*a*–433*b*).

If we are agreed so far, we may now say that a well-made name must contain the " letters " which are " appropriate " to its signification ; *i.e.* those which are " like " what is signified (*i.e.* the vocal gestures which compose the name must have a natural resemblance to some feature in that which it names ; a name which contains inappropriate sounds may be still a recognizable name if some of its components are appropriate, but it will not be a well-made one). The only way of escaping our conclusions would be to fall back on the view that names are purely conventional and arbitrary. This is impossible, since in any case there must be some sort of natural appropriateness about the elementary components of vocal gesture to lead the imposers of names in the making of their first conventions, just as there must be in nature colouring materials appropriate for the reproduction of the tints of a face if there is to be such an art as portraiture. But we can see that " convention " and the arbitrary play their part in language too. Thus there is a " roughness " about the sound of the letter *r* which makes it appropriate in the name of anything hard and rough, while there is a smoothness of articulation about *l* which makes it inappropriate for the same purpose. Yet this letter actually occurs in the very word σκληρός itself, and even Cratylus must admit that " thanks to custom " he knows what the word means. It discharges its function as a name none the worse for containing an inappropriate sound (433*b*–435*b*). In particular we should find it quite impossible to show that the names of the numerals are made up of gestures naturally appropriate to signify those particular numbers. The principle of natural significance, however sound, is a most uncertain guide in etymological studies (435*b*–*c*).

We revert to a position we had laid down at the outset. The " faculty " (δύναμις) or function of a name is to convey instruction (διδάσκειν). Does this imply that a man who has knowledge of names will also have a corresponding knowledge of the realities (πράγματα) for which the names stand ? Cratylus is inclined to think so, and even to hold that the knowledge of names is the *only* way to the knowledge of things. Not only is the understanding (τὸ μανθάνειν) of words the one way to the understanding of things ; *inquiry* into language is the only road of inquiry and discovery. The one way to *discover* the truth about things is to discover the meanings of names (436*a*). But obviously this would put all science in a very unfavourable position. The study of names will only at best show what the givers of the names *supposed* to be the truth about things, and how if these name-givers were wrong in their suppositions ? Cratylus holds that we need not feel any anxiety on the point. The best proof that the " giver of names " was one who knew all about things is the consistent way in which all names support one and the same theory about things. Has not Socrates himself shown that they all point to the Heraclitean doctrine of the flux (436*c*) ? Unfortunately this is not conclusive ; if you start with false initial postulates you may be led to gravely erroneous conclusions, and yet these conclusions may be quite compatible with one another, as we see in the case of certain geometrical false demonstrations.[1] The supreme difficulty in any science is to be sure that your initial postulates themselves are true (436*c–d*). And, on second thoughts, we may doubt whether the testimony of language is quite so self-consistent as we had fancied. There are many words which seem to indicate that the " giver of names " was an Eleatic rather than an Heraclitean (437*a–c*), and it would be absurd to decide on the truth of such incompatible views by appeal to a " numerical majority " of derivations.

In any case, the view Cratylus is maintaining is self-contradictory. He holds that the inventors of the first names must have known the truth about things in order to give each its " true " name, and also that the truth about things can only be discovered by the study of names. How then did the *original* makers of names discover it ? Perhaps, says Cratylus, the first names were of a superhuman origin ; language began as a divine revelation, and its divine origin guarantees the " rightness " of the primitive names. If that is so, then both our sets of derivations cannot be sound, or, as Cratylus says, one set of words cannot be real " names " at all (438*c*). But the question is, which set—those which suggest the " flux " or those which suggest that movement is an illusion— are real names ? We cannot decide the issue by appeal to other words, for there are no other words than those employed in language. The appeal will have to be to the realities words signify, and we shall have to learn what these realities are, not from words, but "from one another and from themselves " (438*e*). Besides, even if we admit that the truth about things can be learned by studying their names, since well-made names, as we have said, are " likenesses "

---

[1] 436*d*. διαγράμματα here seems, as in some other passages in Plato and Aristotle, to mean " proofs " rather than " figures." One might illustrate the point by reference to the entertaining section of De Morgan's *Budget of Paradoxes* which deals with James Smith the circle-squarer. Mr. Smith's method of proving his thesis (that $\pi = \frac{2.5}{8}$) was to assume it as a postulate, and then show that it led to consequences compatible with itself and with one another. He forgot to ask whether it did not lead also to consequences incompatible with independently known truth.

of the things they name, it must be a nobler and more assured method to study the reality (ἀλήθεια) directly in itself, and judge of the merits of the " likeness " from our knowledge of the original than to try to discover from a mere study of the " likeness " whether it is a good one, and what it represents (439*a*). How a knowledge of realities is to be acquired it may take greater thinkers than ourselves to say, but it is satisfactory to have learned that at least we cannot acquire it by the study of names (439*b*).

Socrates keeps the point on which he wishes to insist most until the end. Whatever the opinion of the framers of language may have been, the Heraclitean doctrine of universal impermanence cannot be true. There are such things as " Beauty " and " Goodness " (αὐτὸ καλὸν καὶ αγαθόν) and other realities of that kind. Even Cratylus admits this at once. He does not extend his doctrine of impermanence to the realm of "values." Now *they* cannot be everlastingly mutable ; they are what they are once for all and always. You could not call anything " *the* so-and-so " (αὐτό, 439*d*), if it had no determinate character but were merely mutable. And the merely mutable could not be known. What is known is known as having this or that determinate character, but if the doctrine of " flux " is true, nothing ever has such determinate character. Not to mention that knowing as a subjective activity also has a determinate character, so that in a world where everything is incessantly becoming something else, there could be neither objects to be known nor the activity of knowing. But if knower (τὸ γιγνῶσκον), object known (τὸ γιγνωσκόμενον), Beauty, Good, are real, the Heraclitean doctrine cannot be true. We will not now ask which of these alternatives is the right one, but we may say that it does not *look* a sensible procedure for a man to have such confidence in names and their givers that he hands over his soul to " names " for " tendance," and asserts dogmatically that all men and all things are sick of a universal " defluxion " and as leaky as a cracked pitcher (440*a–d*). This is the issue which young men like Cratylus and Hermogenes should face seriously and courageously and not decide in a hurry (440*d*). Thus the dialogue leaves with us as the great problem, or rather the two aspects of the same great problem of all philosophy, the metaphysical problem of the reality of the forms and the moral problem of the right " tendance of the soul." [1]

Euthydemus.—The dialogue, as we have said, has more of the spirit of broad farce than any other work of Plato ; it would be possible to see in it nothing more than an entertaining satire on " eristics " who think it a fine thing to reduce every one who opens his mouth in their company to silence by taking advantage of the

---

[1] I can see no reason to fancy that the dialogue is intended as a polemic against the nominalism of Antisthenes in particular. A.'s preoccupation with names, like the choice of the themes for his extant declamations, only shows that he was influenced by the general tendencies of the " sophistic " age. I am wholly sceptical about theories which represent the Platonic Socrates as engaged in attacks on one of his own companions.

ambiguities of language. Even if this were Plato's main object, it would still be a reasonable one. An attempt to detect and expose the principal fallacies *in dictione* would be a useful contribution to the as yet only nascent study of logic. It is thus not surprising that Aristotle should have made frequent use of the dialogue in his own systematic essay on Fallacies, the *de Sophisticis Elenchis*. But the real purpose of the dialogue is more serious and proves to be a moral one, arising out of the claim of the sophists of the Periclean age to be able to " teach goodness." A man who undertakes this task must be prepared to win the adherence of a pupil by satisfying him first that " goodness," the secret of a satisfactory life, can be taught ; and next, that the speaker is one of the experts who can teach it. No one will go to school to you unless you can persuade him that you have something important to teach, and that you are competent to teach it. This accounts for the rise of a distinct branch of literature, the " protreptic " discourse, which aims at winning the hearer's assent to the idea that he must live the " philosophic " life, and encouraging his confidence that a particular teacher will show him how to do it. To this type of literature belonged, among other works, Aristotle's famous *Protrepticus* and Cicero's almost equally famous Latin imitation of it, the *Hortensius*, both now unhappily lost. The true object of the *Euthydemus* is to exhibit the directness, simplicity, and power of Socratic " protreptic," addressed to a young and impressionable mind ; the fooleries of the two sophists afford an entertaining background, without which the picture would not produce its full effect. We might suppose Plato to have felt that to a careless observer the close cross-questioning characteristic of Socrates must seem very much the same sort of thing as the futile sporting with words on which the ordinary " eristic " plumes himself. By pitting the one thing directly against the other he drives home his point that, for all their apparent minute hair-splitting, the questions of Socrates are no idle displays of ingenuity, but have the most momentous and most truly practical of all objects ; their purpose is to win a soul from evil for good.

In form the *Euthydemus* is a narrated drama. Socrates describes to his old friend Crito, with a great deal of humour, a mirthful scene in his favourite haunt, the *palaestra* near the Lyceum, at which he had been present the day before. The supposed date can only be fixed by consideration of a number of bits of internal evidence. It is, as we see from *Euthydemus*, 271c, " many years " after the foundation of Thurii (444 B.C.), and must be before the year of the great scandal about the " profanation of the mysteries," just before the sailing of the Athenian Armada for Sicily (416–5), since Axiochus of Scambonidae, father of the lad Clinias who figures as respondent, was one of the principal persons ruined by the affair.[1] A date not later than about 420, and possibly a little earlier, seems to fit all the

---

[1] For the ruin of Axiochus, the uncle of Alcibiades the person whose destruction was the main object of the raisers of the scandal, see Andocides, i. 16.

indications. The centre of attraction in the dialogue is the beautiful and modest Clinias ; it is on his person that Euthydemus, whom we have already met in the *Cratylus*, and his brother Dionysodorus, natives of Chios who had been among the original settlers of Thurii, but found themselves banished in the years of faction which followed on the foundation of the city and have since then haunted Athens and her dependencies, make the experiment of displaying a new educational discovery, a method of instantaneously " teaching goodness." Hitherto they had taught, like other professionals, the art of fence on the field and in the law-courts ; their crowning achievement is a recent invention which they are anxious to parade and Socrates to witness. It proves, in fact, to be simply " eristic," the trick of stopping a man's mouth by catching at the natural ambiguities of language. Perhaps it is an indication of date that Socrates is made to lay the stress he does on the contrast between this latest marvel and the now familiar art of effective forensic pleading which had been the thing taught by Protagoras and the earliest " sophists." The two men, however, are described as elderly, so that they will be at least as old as Socrates himself, and we must remember that though Socrates was the first Athenian to interest himself in logic, it had been founded by Zeno, who cannot at most have been more than ten years younger than Protagoras. Hence too much must not be made of this point.[1] The serious business of the dialogue is opened by Socrates in a short speech, laying down the main lines it is to follow. Clinias is a lad of great promise and illustrious connexions ; it is of the first moment that he should grow up to be a thoroughly good man. The sophists are therefore invited to prove the value of their latest discovery by convincing him " that one must give one's attention to goodness and philosophy " (275*a*). They fall to work at once by asking a series of questions so constructed that they can only be answered by " Yes " or " No," and that the respondent can be equally silenced whichever answer he gives. The first question—from its recurrence elsewhere we may infer that it was a " stock " puzzle—turns on the double sense of the word μανθάνειν, which means primarily to " learn " ; but derivatively, in colloquial language, to " understand," " take the

[1] The pair of " eristics," Euthydemus and his brother Dionysodorus, are natives of Chios who had been among the first settlers at Thurii (this is implied by the tense of ἀπῴκησαν at 271*c*), but had been exiled thence and have spent " many years " περὶ τούσδε τοὺς τόπους, *i.e.* Athens and the islands of the Aegean (271*c*). The date of the foundation of Thurii is 444. Socrates is ἤδη πρεσβύτερος (272*b*), " not exactly a young man," but no more ; this suggests an age not far off fifty, but probably something short of it. Perhaps the allusion of 272*c* to the figure he cuts among the boys in the music-class of Connus is best taken as a humorous reference to some shaft aimed at him in the *Connus* of Amipsias (exhibited in 423), and in that case, we must suppose that play to be still a recent work. Alcibiades is spoken of at 275*a* in a way which implies that he is already in the prime of manhood. 286*c* refers to Protagoras in a way which seems to mean that he is already dead. But since Plato insists that Protagoras was a generation older than Socrates (*Protag.* 317*c*) and also says that he died at about seventy (*Meno*, 91*e*), this does not take us with certainty much below the year 430.

meaning of " a statement. The eristic method of the two brothers may be reproduced in English by taking advantage of the double sense which " learning " happens to bear in our own language. Who are learners, the wise or the ignorant, *i.e.* those who already know something or those who do not ? There is here a triple *équivoque*, since the " wise " (σοφοί) may mean " clever, intelligent " pupils, as well as persons who already know the thing to be taught, and the " ignorant " (ἀμαθεῖς) may mean " the dull, stupid," as well as those who are ignorant of a given subject. The lad takes the question to mean, " Which class of boys learn what they are taught, the clever boys or the dull ones ? " and answers, " The clever." But, it is retorted, when you lads were learners in reading or music, you did not yet know these subjects and therefore were not " wise " (σοφοί) about them, and so must have been " ignorant " (ἀμαθεῖς). And yet again, in your schooldays, it was not the " dull " (ἀμαθεῖς) among you, but the quick or clever (σοφοί) who " took in " (ἐμάνθανον) what the schoolmaster dictated. *Ergo*, it is the σοφοί, not the ἀμαθεῖς who " learn." (As we might say, the dull don't get learning from their schoolmasters, but the quick (275*d*–276*c*)).

A new puzzle is now started. When a man learns something, does he learn what he knows or what he does not know ? (This again is a standing catch, intended to prove the paradox that it is impossible to learn anything, to get new knowledge.) The natural answer is that a man learns what he does not already know, since learning means getting fresh knowledge. But when a schoolmaster dictates something to you, you " learn " the sense of the passage (you take in its meaning). What he dictated is a series of " letters," but you must have " known " your letters before you could do dictation. Thus when you " learn," you must already " know " the thing you are learning. Yet, *per contra*, to learn means to get knowledge, and no one can get what he already has. *Ergo*, after all, it is what you do not know that you learn (276*e*–277*c*).

It is clear, of course, what the origin of " eristic " of this kind is. Euthydemus and his brother are borrowing and degrading the logical method of Zeno.[1] In Zeno's hands, the deduction of apparently contradictory conclusions from the same premisses had a legitimate object. The intention was to discredit the premisses themselves. And in fact, Zeno's antinomies do establish the important result that the postulates of Pythagorean mathematics are incompatible with one another and require revision (*e.g.* it is indispensable to Pythagorean geometry that every straight

---

[1] This is made especially clear twice over (275*e*, 276*e*), by the whispered remark of Dionysodorus that his brother will " catch the boy out " equally whichever way he answers the question. This construction of " antinomies," to show that the affirmation and the denial of the same proposition are equally impossible, was the special contribution of Zeno to the development of logical method. There is also probably intentional point in the way in which we are reminded of the connexion of the brothers with Thurii—the place, of all others, where they would be most certain to meet Eleatics.

line should be capable of bisection, and yet, on the Pythagorean principles, a line may contain an odd number of "points" and therefore be incapable of bisection, because you cannot "split the unit"). With eristics like Euthydemus this hunting after "antinomies," perfectly legitimate when intended as a criticism of presuppositions which lead to an "antinomy," becomes a mere delight in entrapping the respondent into contradicting himself by mere neglect to guard against ambiguity in words, and its object is not to detect error but to produce admiration for the ingenious deviser of the ambiguous formula. This is the point on which Socrates now fastens. The two "sophists" care nothing about convincing Clinias of the need for "goodness and philosophy"; their concern is merely to make a display of their own cleverness. Accordingly, Socrates interrupts the performance. He professes to think that what has gone before is not meant as any sample of the "wisdom" of the brothers. It is a mere piece of "fun," like the sportive preliminaries which precede initiation into the Corybantic rites, or, as we might say, like those popularly supposed to precede an initiation into freemasonry. So far the two great men have merely been playing a "game" with the lad, enjoying a "practical joke" at his expense; no doubt the serious part of their "protreptic" is yet to come. Before it comes, Socrates would like to show, by a conversation of his own with the boy, what, in his "foolish and amateur fashion" (ἰδιωτικῶς τε καὶ γελοίως), he supposes the drift of such exhortations must be, though, of course, he fully expects to be left in the shade by two such eminent professionals (277d–278e).

There follows at once a simple statement, in clear language such as a mere boy can follow, of the root ideas of Socratic ethics. Of course every one of us wants εὖ πράττειν, to "fare well," to "make a success of life." And equally, of course, making a success of life means having "abundance of good" (πολλὰ ἀγαθά). Now what things is it good to have? "The first man you meet" will mention some of them: wealth, health, beauty, bodily advantages in general, good birth, a position of influence and respect. But there are other good things than these, or at least other things which Socrates and Clinias regard as good: *sophrosyne*, justice, courage, wisdom. Is the list of goods now complete? Perhaps we have left out the most important of all, "good luck" (εὐτυχία), without which any other advantages may turn out to be disguised curses. And yet, on second thoughts, we have not forgotten it. For wisdom is itself εὐτυχία. Who have the best "luck" or "good fortune" in playing musical instruments, in reading and writing, in navigation, warfare, medicine? The men who know how to do these things— expert musicians, sailors, soldiers, physicians. One would, *e.g.*, think it a great piece of luck in war to be serving under a competent and not under an incompetent commander. In general, wisdom or knowledge (σοφία) leads to efficient achievement (εὐπραγία) and so to "good fortune." If we have wisdom, then

we may expect " success," " good fortune " (τὸ εὐτυχεῖν) in the
department of practice which our " wisdom " covers (278e–280a).

On reviewing these results, we see ground to criticize one of
them, the statement that we shall be happy and "make life a
success " (εὐδαιμονεῖν καὶ εὖ πράττειν) if we " have abundance of
good things." To *have* them will not benefit us unless we also *use*
them, any more than it would benefit an artisan to have the materials
and tools of his trade if he never used them. So, e.g., " wealth "
is of no benefit unless we *use* it. And it would not be enough to
say that we must not only have the various good things but use
them. We must add that, to be happy, we must use them *right*.
They are, in fact, dangerous tools ; if you use them in the wrong
way you do yourself a harm ; it would be better to leave them
alone than to use them wrongly. Now in all crafts and businesses
it is the expert's *knowledge* (ἐπιστήμη) of his craft which enables
him to use his materials and implements in the right way,
and the same holds good of health and wealth and the goods
in popular esteem generally. *Knowledge* enables us to use wealth,
health, and all other " advantages " rightly, and to achieve success
(εὐπραγία). If a man had all other possessions besides wisdom
and were not directed by " sense " (νοῦς) in his undertakings, the
less he undertook the fewer blunders he would make, and the
happier he would be. It would be happier for him to be poor than
rich, timid than courageous, sluggish and dull rather than of active
temper and quick perception, since the less he undertook the less
mischief he would do. In fact, none of the things we began by
calling good can be called unconditionally (αὐτὰ καθ' αὑτά) good.
They are better than their opposites when they are conjoined with
the wisdom to make a right use of them (φρόνησίς τε καὶ σοφία),
but worse when they are disjoined from it. It follows that, properly
speaking, there is just one thing good, wisdom, and just one bad
thing, ἀμαθία, " dullness," stupidity (280b–281e). (Compare the
precisely similar line of reasoning by which Kant reaches the conclusion that the good *will* is the only thing which is unconditionally
good, because it is the only good which cannot be misused.)

We may draw a final conclusion. We now see that since happiness depends on wisdom and knowledge, the one end after which
every man should strive is to become " as wise as possible." Hence
what we should crave to get from our parents, friends, fellow-
citizens, alien acquaintances, before everything else, is just wisdom.
One should be ready to " serve and slave " and render " any service
that is comely "[1] to any man for the sake of wisdom ; that is to say,
provided that wisdom can really be taught and does not " come by
accident " (ἀπὸ ταὐτομάτου), a difficult question which we have not

---

[1] ὁτιοῦν τῶν καλῶν ὑπηρετημάτων, 282b. The qualification is inserted because ἐρασταί have been mentioned, and Socrates wishes to guard himself
against being supposed to include chastity as one of the prices which may
be paid for " wisdom." His attitude on that point is as unqualified as Plato's
own in the *Laws*.

faced. If we may assume that wisdom can be taught, we have satisfied ourselves of the absolute necessity of pursuing it, "being philosophers " (282a–d).

Socrates has really given us so far only half of a " protreptic discourse " such as would be to his mind. He has led up to the conclusion that happiness depends on the direction of life and conduct by knowledge, but has not so far told us what knowledge in particular it is of which we cannot make an ill use. It is fundamental for his purpose that we should distinguish such knowledge from every recognized form of expert professional knowledge, and the distinction will be made later. For the present we return to the " comic relief " of the fooleries of Euthydemus and his brother, which become increasingly absurd, precisely in order that the heightened contrast of tone shall mark the second part of Socrates' discourse, when we reach it, as the most important thing in the whole dialogue. For the present he proposes that the " professionals " shall now take up the argument at this point, and decide the question whether one needs to learn every kind of " knowledge," or whether there is one special knowledge which conducts to happiness. Or, if they prefer, they may go over the ground he has already covered and do so in a less amateurish fashion. Of course they do neither ; their object is simply *épater les bourgeois*, and Dionysodorus, the older of the two, sets to work at once to administer a thoroughly sensational shock. Can Socrates and the others, who profess to feel so much affection for Clinias, be serious in saying that they are anxious that he should become " wise " ? For their language implies that he is not yet what they wish him to become. They say they want him to " be no longer what he now is "; but to wish a man to " be no longer " is to wish that he may perish—a pretty wish on the part of one's " affectionate friends " (283a–d). (Here again we are on Eleatic ground, and we see that it is not for nothing that Plato reminds us repeatedly that his two sophists had lived at Thurii. The argument that nothing can change, because that which " becomes different " is becoming " what it is not," and therefore becoming nothing at all, derives directly from Parmenides as soon as his physics are converted into logic, and, like the rest of the puzzles connected with it, only gets its solution when we come to the distinction between absolute and relative not-being introduced in the *Sophistes*. In our dialogue Plato is not seriously concerned with the solution of these difficulties ; what he is con cerned with is the futility of regarding them as a preparation for the conduct of life, and the *moral* levity of the professors who make a parade of them.) The immediate effect of the sally of Dionysodorus is to call forth from Ctesippus, an older lad deeply attached to Clinias, an angry complaint of the " falsity " of the accusation, and this gives Euthydemus an opening for airing his principal piece of " wisdom," which we have already met in the *Cratylus*—the doctrine that all statements are true, or, as he puts it now, that " it is impossible to speak falsely," for the reason that whenever you make a statement, you must either be saying " what is " or saying " what is not." In the first case, you are telling the truth, for to " say what is," is truth-speaking. As for the second case, " what is not " is just nothing at all, and no one can speak and yet say " nothing " ; whoever speaks at all is saying something (283e–284c). The regular corollary is promptly drawn that οὐκ ἔστιν ἀντιλέγειν, no man can contradict another, since there can be no contradiction unless both parties are speaking of the same " thing " (the logical subject must be the same in the two statements). But since you cannot speak of a thing " as it is not," in the case of apparent contradiction, one or both parties would have to be speaking of " what is not," and this is impossible. If the two parties are making significant statements at all, since such statements must be statements of " what is," they must be talking about two different subjects, and so there is no contradiction (285d–286c).[1]

It is characteristic of Socrates that he insists at once on calling attention to the practical bearings of this piece of logical paradox. It implies that two men cannot even think contradictory propositions ; if a false statement is impossible, mental error is impossible too, and from this it follows that no one can commit an error in *practice* (ἐξαμαρτάνειν ὅταν τι πράττῃ), and the claim of the brothers to be able to *teach* goodness must therefore be an empty one, for their teaching is superfluous.[2] Dionysodorus eludes the difficulty partly by insisting that his present assertion should be considered on its own merits independently of anything he may have said before, and partly by catching at the phrase which Socrates has used, that he cannot understand what the statement " means " (νοεῖν). How can a statement be said to " mean " anything ?[3] The conversation is rapidly degenerating into mere personalities (λοιδορία) when Socrates saves the situation by repeating his former suggestion that the eminent wits from Thurii are still only engaged on the " fun " which is to introduce their serious wisdom. They need to be pressed a little more, and we shall then get at last to the earnest. This gives him an excuse

[1] Note that at 286c Socrates describes this paradox as " stale," and ascribes it to " Protagoras and men of a still earlier date," as, in fact, it does follow from the ἄνθρωπος μέτρον doctrine. This should dispose of the fancy that Antisthenes is specially aimed at in the dialogue. The " still older " person meant is presumably Parmenides, who expressly denies that " what is not " can be spoken of or named.

[2] Exactly the same point is urged against Protagoras at *Theaetet.* 161 c–e. But in that dialogue, where Plato's main purpose is epistemological, Socrates is careful to consider whether Protagoras might not make a rejoinder to this criticism (166a–168c), and to examine the soundness of the rejoinder (171e–172b, 178a–179b).

[3] The quibble turns on the uses of the word νοεῖν, which signifies (a) to think, to intend, to purpose, (b) to mean or signify. The sophist pretends to take the expression " your words mean so-and-so," in the sense that they " intend " or " think," and asks how anything but a ψυχή can possibly " think " anything. There is the same *équivoque* in the distinction in English between " to mean " and " to mean to " say or do something.

for returning to his own specimen of serious " protreptic " at the point where he had left off.

We saw that the one thing needful for the conduct of life is knowledge. But what kind of " knowledge " ? Of course, the knowledge which will " profit " us, " useful knowledge." Now what kind of knowledge is that ? It cannot be any kind of knowledge which merely teaches us how to *produce* something without also teaching us how to *use* the thing we have produced. This enables us to dismiss at once all the specialized industrial arts, like that of the maker of musical instruments, none of which teach a man how to use the thing they have taught him to make. In particular, this consideration applies to the art of the λογοποιός, which looks so imposing. We might think that this art of composing effective speeches is just the kind of knowledge we need for the conduct of life, since it teaches us how to make the " charm " or " spell " which is potent against those most deadly of enemies, angry and prejudiced dicasteries and *ecclesiae*. Yet, after all, the important thing is to know how to *use* the " spell," but the λογοποιός only teaches you how to *make* it.[1] There might be something to say for the soldier's profession, the art of catching a human prey ; but, after all, the hunter does not know how to use the game he captures, but has to pass it on to the cook or *restaurateur* ; and in the same way the commander who " captures " a city or an army has not learned from his profession what to do with his capture when he has made it. The military art, then, is clearly not the supreme art needed for the right conduct of life (288*b*–290*d*).[2]

Incidentally we note that the claim of any of the purely speculative branches of knowledge, the mathematical sciences, has been disposed of by this criticism. The mathematicians also are, in their way, " hunters " on the trail of " realities " (τὰ ὄντα). But though their διαγράμματα (here again the word means " proofs "

---

[1] The point here, as in the *Gorgias*, which classes " rhetoric " with " swimming " as a device for preserving your life, is that the patron of the λογοποιός is normally one of the well-to-do minority of whom the Periclean democracy were naturally suspicious precisely because democracy really meant the " exploitation " of this class for the benefit of the " proletarian." From the well-to-do victim's point of view, effective public speaking is exactly what it is called here, a " spell " to put the watchful, hostile *belua* of democracy to sleep ; from the democrat's point of view, it is a trick by which the μισόδημος gulls the simple citizens into taking him for the " people's friend."

[2] Socrates is made to assert that this criticism was delivered by Clinias on his own account ; Crito thinks such a mere boy could not have shown such acuteness, and hints that the remark must really have come from Socrates himself (290*e*). This is dramatically in keeping with the picture Plato has drawn of Crito—a dull, honest man. But the real point is that the " protreptic " of Socrates is effective in the right way ; it elicits from a younger mind flashes of insight which would have been impossible but for the way in which the preceding questions have led up to them. This is the true answer to the criticism of Grote that anyone can ask puzzling questions. The peculiarity of the Socratic question is not to be puzzling, but to be enlightening.

rather than " figures ") " find " the quarry, the mathematicians do not know how to "treat " it; that task, if they have any sense, they leave to the διαλεκτικός, the critical philosopher.[1] On scrutiny, the " art " which seems to have the best claims to supremacy is the βασιλικὴ τέχνη, the " art of the king," *i.e.* statesmanship. If there is any " speciality " which can secure happiness, it should certainly be that of the man who knows how to govern and administer the community (since, of course, no one except a paradox-monger would deny that " human well-being " is what all true statesmanship takes as its end). But with this result we seem to have come round in a complete circle to the same point from which our argument set out. It is clear that statesmanship (ἡ πολιτικὴ τέχνη) is the supreme master-art; generals and other functionaries are only servants of the statesman. He *uses*, as means to his end—the well-being of the state—victory in war and all the other results which the generals and the rest *make*; and we have seen already in the *Cratylus* that the art which uses a product is always the master-art in relation to those which made the product. But the statesman too has something to produce; he uses the products of all the other " craftsmen " as means to producing something himself, and this something must be something beneficial, and therefore good. Now we had already satisfied ourselves that knowledge is the only thing which is unconditionally good. Hence, if statesmanship is really the art of the conduct of life, such results as wealth, civic independence, freedom from party strife, must be its mere by-products; its main product must be wisdom and goodness. Yet what wisdom and goodness does true statesmanship produce in those on whom it is exercised? It does not aim at making them all " good " shoemakers or " good " carpenters, or " good " at any other special calling. Apparently we must say that the knowledge which the art of the statesman produces in us is the knowledge of itself. But what use do we make of this knowledge of statesmanship? Perhaps its use is that it enables us to make other men good. But then we come back to the old question, " Good at *what*? " We seem to have reached the conclusion that happiness depends on knowing how to make other men good at knowing how to make yet other men (and so on *ad indefinitum*) good at knowing . . . no one can say precisely what (291a–292e).

[1] The point becomes clear if we think of the relation of a Pythagorean geometer to the typical διαλεκτικός Zeno. The mathematicians " track " or " hunt down " truths like the Pythagorean theorem, but they are so far from knowing what to " do with them " that it is left for a διαλεκτικός like Zeno to show that the discovery itself leads to consequences which are fatal to some of the postulates of the Pythagorean geometer (such as the incommensurability of the " side " and the " diagonal "). The last word on the question what can be " made of " the results of the sciences rests with the critical " metaphysician," who has to test the claims of these sciences to give a finally satisfactory account of " the real." Note the complete acceptance here of the " primacy of the *practical* reason," which is as characteristic of Socrates and Plato as of Kant.

The serious positive purpose of the argument, which has incidentally slipped into becoming a direct conversation between Socrates and Crito, is not hard to discover. The knowledge on which the right conduct of life and the right government of men alike depend is not knowledge of the way to meet any one particular type of situation or to discharge any one particular calling or function ; it is knowledge of good, or, to put the point in more modern phraseology, knowledge of absolute moral values. On the Socratic assumption that knowledge of this kind is always followed by corresponding action, and is therefore the only knowledge which is guaranteed against all possible misuse, the question *for what* we are to use it becomes superfluous ; we do not " use " it as a means to some ulterior end at all, we simply act it out. To put the matter in the Greek way, every " art " is an " art of opposites " ; that is, may be used for a bad as well as for a good end. The special knowledge of toxicology which makes a man a medical specialist may also make him a dangerous secret poisoner. The intimate knowledge of the Stock Exchange and share market which makes a man an excellent trustee for the fortune of his ward will also make him a particularly dangerous " fraudulent trustee " if he applies it for dishonest ends. But " knowledge of the good " is in a unique position which distinguishes it from all special professional or technical knowledge, the thing with which the " sophists " and their pupils regularly confuse it. It too, in a sense, is " of opposites, " since to know what is good involves knowing that what is incompatible with good must be evil. But, on Socratic principles, this knowledge is not a knowledge of opposites in the sense that it can be put to either of two opposite uses, a good one and a bad one. The possession of the knowledge carries along with it the possession of the " good will." We thus recover the fundamental positions of the Socratic ethics from the apparently fruitless argument. The reason why the positive result is not stated is simply that the object of Socrates' " protreptic " is not to do another man's thinking for him and present him with ready-made " results," but to stimulate him to think along the right lines for himself, so that when the " result " emerges, it comes as a personal conviction won by a genuine personal exercise of intelligence. Hence Socrates is represented as breaking off at the point we have reached, and appealing to the two distinguished strangers to help him out of the " squall " in which he seems to be threatened with shipwreck. As we should expect, they do nothing of the kind, but fall to their old trick. Socrates does not need any help, for they will prove to him that he already has the knowledge for which he is seeking. He knows some things, *ergo* he has knowledge ; but one cannot both have knowledge and not have it, *ergo* he knows everything. And so, for the matter of that, does every one else (293*a–e*). Euthydemus and his brother have, in fact, a sort of universal infallibility ; they know all trades and the answers to all the most trifling speculative questions. This, says Socrates, must be the great truth to which all that has gone before was the playful prelude.[1]

From this point onwards the dialogue becomes increasingly farcical as the two brothers go on to develop one absurdity after another, until Socrates, the only member of the company who has preserved his gravity, takes his leave of them with many ironical compliments and the advice to take care, in their own interests, not to cheapen the price of their wisdom by too many public exhibitions. There is no need to follow in detail the whole series of ludicrous paralogisms which precedes this *finale*. Aristotle found good material in it for his own study of fallacies, but Plato's object is ethical rather than logical, as has been already said.[2] The extreme absurdity of the performances by which the brothers follow up the second and more important part of the "protreptic" argument are merely meant to throw that section of the dialogue into the strongest relief.   The one comment it may be worth while to make is that the standing rule of "eristic," by which the respondent is expected to reply to each question exactly as it has been put, without raising any objection to its form or qualifying his answer by the introduction of any *distinguo*, however simple, of itself provides exceptional opportunity for the perpetration of every kind of "fallacy in the diction." From this point of view much of the dialogue might be said to be a criticism of the method of question and answer as a vehicle of philosophic thought. It is clear, and Plato may have meant to hint this, that the method is the most uncertain of weapons unless the questioner combines intelligence with absolutely good faith ; this is why it may be a powerful weapon of criticism in the hands of Socrates, but is nothing but an instrument of sophistry in those of a Euthydemus whose only object is to make men stare.

At the end of Socrates' narrative, Plato adds a sort of appendix, a page or two of direct conversation between Socrates and Crito. Crito observes that the remark had already been made to him by a certain writer of speeches for the law-courts who fancied himself a "great wit" (πάνυ σοφός), that the disgraceful scene in the Lyceum was enough to show that "philosophy" is "mere waste of time" (οὐδὲν πρᾶγμα), for the professionals who had just been making egregious fools of themselves were actually among its most eminent

---

[1] We are still dealing with the misuse of Eleatic doctrine. The proof of the infallibility of every one is made to turn on the principle of contradiction *plus* the neglect of qualifying conditions. We cannot both have knowledge and not have it ; if you know anything, you have knowledge, and therefore have all knowledge. This is just the Eleatic doctrine that there is no half-way house between "what is" and blank nonentity, transferred from physics to logic. Whenever we come on ἀντιλογικοί we are safe in looking for the influence of Zeno.

[2] Note that at 301a Socrates, without any explanation, falls into the technical language of the so-called "ideal" theory when he says that καλὰ πράγματα are different from αὐτὸ τὸ καλόν, though a certain κάλλος "is present" to them, and that this peculiar Socratic use of the word παρεῖναι is even made the subject of a jest.

living representatives. The critic who made the remark was not himself a political man, nor had he ever addressed a law-court, but had the reputation of being a skilled professional composer of speeches for litigants (304*b*–305*c*). Socrates replies that these men, who, as Prodicus once said, are on the border-line between politics and philosophy, are always jealous of the philosopher ; they think he keeps them out of rightful recognition. The truth is, that the man who tries to combine two callings is regularly inferior in both to the man who confines himself to one. *If* the philosophic life and the life of affairs are both good things, the man who tries to play both parts is certain to be inferior in each to the specialist in his own line (305*c*–306*d*).

It has naturally been suspected that there is some personal allusion underlying these remarks, and the view has often been taken that Plato is aiming a shaft on his own account at his rival Isocrates. It is true, of course, that during the lifetime of Socrates, Isocrates was known only as a λογογράφος or composer of speeches for the courts, but that some time early in the fourth century he gave up this profession for that of presiding over a regular institution for the preparation of young men of promise for a political career. It is true also that Isocrates called the kind of education he bestowed on his pupils his " philosophy," and that he affected to look down on the severely scientific studies of Plato's Academy as " useless " and unpractical. From Plato's point of view, it would be highly *à propos* to speak of Isocrates as " on the border line " between a politician and a philosopher, and inferior to each in his own department—except that one might doubt whether Plato did really think Isocrates inferior in statesmanship to the commonplace Athenian men of affairs of his own time.

Yet I think the identification quite impossible. At the date indicated by all the allusions of the *Euthydemus* Isocrates would still be no more than a lad, whereas the person spoken of by Crito is already a λογογράφος of established repute. Still less could Socrates, *at this date*, be supposed to anticipate that Isocrates would some day lay claim to the reputation of a philosopher. (The case is rather different with the express references of the *Phaedrus* to Isocrates, since, as we shall see, the date of that dialogue is supposed to be later.) We must suppose Socrates to be alluding rather to some well-known figure of the time of the Archidamian war. There is no reason why there should not have been more than one personage of the age to which Callicles and Thrasymachus belong who fancied himself as a blend of the philosophical thinker and the practical " statesman." The remains of Antiphon " the sophist," for example, suggest by their character that he might perfectly well be the person intended, and we know from a notice preserved by Xenophon [1] that he was among the acquaintances of

---

[1] Xen. *Mem.* i. 6. It is important to note, as Professor Burnet has done, that the information cannot depend on Xenophon's personal recollections, but must be taken from some source describing Socrates as he

Socrates.   It is true that there is no direct proof that he was a writer of speeches for the law-courts, but there is no reason why he may not have been.   In fact, it does not seem to me by any means established that Antiphon the " sophist " and Antiphon of Rhamnus, the famous politician and λογογράφος, are two distinct persons.[1] And I feel sure that we have no right wantonly to attribute to Plato the anachronisms which a reference to Isocrates in our dialogue would imply, nor is there, in point of fact, any real evidence that there ever was any personal ill-feeling between Isocrates and Plato.[2] The real object of the passage is probably simply to recognize the fact that to a good many persons the dialectic of Socrates must have seemed much on a par with the frivolities of Euthydemus and his brother, and to hint that, if we choose, we may discover the real difference between the two things from the dialogue itself, as we certainly can.

See further :

RITTER, C.—*Platon*, i. 450–462 (*Euthydemus*), 462–496 (*Cratylus*).
RAEDER, H.—*Platons philosophische Entwickelung*, 137–153.
STEWART, J. A.—*Plato's Doctrine of Ideas*, 34–39 (*Cratylus*.)
WARBURG, M.—*Zwei Fragen zum Kratylos*. (Berlin, 1929.)

was at the time of the Archidamian war.   This gives it all the more historical value.

[1] The question should probably be decided, if decided at all, on linguistic and stylistic grounds.   But are the remains of the " sophist " extensive enough to permit of effective comparison with those of the λογογράφος?   And to what extent should we expect to find a λογογράφος exhibiting in his compositions for the courts the peculiarities of his personal literary style?   Professor S. Luria calls my attention in particular to two articles by Bignone in the *Rendiconti del R. Istituto Lombard. di scienze*, 1919, pp. 567 f., 755 ff., as establishing the non-identity of the two men.   I regret that I have not myself seen these essays.

[2] On this point see the remarks of Burnet, *Greek Philosophy, Part I.*, 215. Isocrates may have enjoyed aiming his shafts at the Academic mathematics, but the deliberate adoption of Isocratean tricks of style in the *Sophistes* and the other later dialogues seems to show that Plato is not likely to have borne him any malice on account of his inability to appreciate science.

CHAPTER VI

SOCRATIC DIALOGUES: *GORGIAS, MENO*

THE *Gorgias* is a much longer work than any we have yet considered, and presents us with an exposition of the Socratic morality so charged with passionate feeling and expressed with such moving eloquence that it has always been a prime favourite with all lovers of great ethical literature. The moral fervour and splendour of the dialogue, however, ought not to blind us, as it has blinded most writers on Platonic chronology, to certain obvious indications that it is a youthful work, earlier in composition, perhaps, than some of those with which we have been concerned. We might have inferred as much from the mere fact that Plato has adopted the form of the direct dialogue for so considerable a work, and thus missed the chance of giving us a description of the personality of Gorgias to compare with his elaborate portrait of Protagoras. Personally, I cannot also help feeling that, with all its moral splendour, the dialogue is too long : it " drags." The Plato of the *Protagoras* or *Republic*, as I feel, would have known how to secure the same effect with less expenditure of words ; there is a diffuseness about our dialogue which betrays the hand of the prentice, though the prentice in this case is a Plato. For this reason I think it a mistake in principle to look, as some have done, for an ethical advance in doctrine as we pass from the *Protagoras* to the *Gorgias*. As we shall see when we come to deal with the *Protagoras*, the ethical doctrine of the dialogues is identical and it is inconceivable to me that any reader of literary sensibility can doubt which of the two is the product of a riper mastery of dramatic art. Beyond this general statement that the *Gorgias* must be an early work, and probably a work dating not many years after the death of Socrates, I do not think it safe to hazard any conjecture as to the date of composition.[1]

[1] We shall see when we come to deal with the *Republic* that it, and consequently any dialogues which precede it, must be dated not much later than 387, within twelve years of Socrates' death. If the *Gorgias* falls early in this period, we must place its composition quite soon after that event, while the feelings connected with it were still in their first freshness in Plato's mind. Professor Wilamowitz-Moellendorf, in his *Plato*, i. 221, ii. 94–105, makes an ingenious attempt at a more exact dating. He starts from the curious misquotation of Pindar's well-known lines about νόμος, as given by all our best MSS. at *Gorgias* 484*b* (where the text has been corrected back again in all the printed editions). He rightly, as it seems to me, holds that the misquotation is what Plato actually wrote, and then goes on (again, I believe, rightly) to infer from

It is unusually difficult to determine the date at which the conversation is supposed to be held. It has sometimes been supposed that a reference made by Socrates to some occasion when he was a member of the committee of the βουλή who had to preside over the meetings of the ἐκκλησία, and raised a laugh by his ignorance of the formalities to be observed in " putting the question " (*Gorg.* 473e), has to do with the events of the trial of the generals at Arginusae, where we know from both Plato and Xenophon that Socrates actually was one of the presiding committee. If this interpretation were certain, we should have to suppose the conversation to fall somewhere in the last year of the Peloponnesian war, when Athens was fighting with her back to the wall for her very existence. There are certainly no signs in the dialogue that this situation is presupposed ; it seems rather to be taken for granted that the political and commercial life of the city is in a normal condition. Moreover, as Burnet has said, the democracy was in no laughing mood at the trial of the generals, and we thus seem forced to suppose that the reference is to some unknown incident which happened on some former occasion when Socrates was a member of the βουλή.[1] On the other side, it would appear from the opening sentences of the dialogue that Socrates is as yet a complete stranger to Gorgias and his profession, and this suggests that Gorgias is in Athens for the first time. There seems no good reason to deny the statement of Diodorus Siculus that Gorgias visited Athens first as a member of the embassy sent thither by his native city, Leontini, in the year 427, and such a date would fit in very well with certain other indications in the work, *e.g.* the reference to the " recent " death of Pericles,[2] and the statements about the almost despotic power of the Athenian demagogue.[3] (These would suit the time when the place of Pericles was being taken by Cleon and men of his stamp to perfection.) Possibly, too, the date

Libanius' *Apology of Socrates* that the accusation of misquoting Pindar had figured in the pamphlet of Polycrates against Socrates published somewhere about 393. His final inference is that the accusation was based on this passage of the *Gorgias*, which must thus be anterior to the pamphlet of Polycrates. I hope to suggest reasons for believing that the misquotation in Plato is conscious and made for a legitimate purpose. At this point I merely wish to observe that it cannot have been the foundation of an accusation against the memory of Socrates for two conclusive reasons : (1) that in any case a misquotation in Plato would be no proof of anything against Socrates, and (2) that the person who is made by Plato to misquote Pindar is not Socrates, but Callicles, who is arguing against him. Polycrates, to judge from the line Isocrates takes with him (Isoc. xi. 1–8), was pretty much of a fool, but it is hard to believe that he could have used a misquotation put by Plato into the mouth of Callicles to damage the reputation of Socrates. At the same time, I feel no doubt that the *Gorgias* was written as early as Professor Wilamowitz holds, and most probably earlier.

[1] This is quite compatible with the statement of *Apology*, 32b 1. Socrates says there that he has been a member of the βουλή. He does not say that he had only served once in that capacity. See Burnet's note in *loc. cit.* The best historians hold that Xenophon has made a slip in saying that Socrates was the ἐπιστάτης at the famous trial.

[2] *Gorgias*, 503c.   [3] *Ibid.* 466c.

would not be too early for the allusion to the handsome Demus, the son of Plato's own stepfather Pyrilampes, as a reigning beauty, though there may be a very small anachronism here since Aristophanes first mentions the craze for Demus in the *Wasps*, which belongs to the year 422.[1] On the other side, again, we find the *Antiope* of Euripides quoted as a well-known and popular work,[2] and the date of that tragedy seems to be *c.* 408. The career of Archelaus of Macedon, again, comes in for a good deal of discussion,[3] and it has commonly been inferred from Thucydides that his reign did not begin until 414–413, though disputed successions and the simultaneous existence of several pretenders to the crown were so common in Macedonia that we cannot build very confidently on such data. It is very unfortunate that we have no independent information about Callicles of Acharnae, who appears in the dialogue as a cultivated and ambitious young man who has lately entered political life, though the mere fact that Plato specifies his deme is enough to show that he is an actual man, and not, as has been suggested, an *alias* for some one. If he really attempted to act up to the Nietzschian theories ascribed to him in the dialogue, it may not be wonderful that no record of his career has survived. In the names which Plato gives as those of his immediate associates we recognize some which were prominent in the second half of the great war, but, of course their early days would belong to its first half. On the whole, the arguments for an early dramatic date seem to preponderate, though the references to the *Antiope* and the usurpation of the Macedonian crown by Archelaus, especially the second, seem to create a little difficulty.[4]

The characters of the dialogue besides Socrates are four—Gorgias, the famous " orator " of Leontini, whose well-known rhetorical devices for adding pomp and glitter to language represent the first stage in the development of a literary prose style rising above colloquialism or bald narration of matter of fact and yet remaining prose; Polus of Agrigentum, his enthusiastic disciple and admirer; Callicles of Acharnae, of whom we only know what Plato has thought fit to tell us; and Chaerephon, the lean, impetuous, and apparently rather superstitious companion of Socrates, whom

---

[1] *Gorgias*, 481d, Aristoph. *Wasps*, 89.

[2] *Gorgias*, 484e–486d. Since Aristotle appears to have been the first person to attempt to construct a chronology of the Attic drama by making a collection of *didascaliae*, I should have attached no importance to this particular point but for the fact that if the commonly accepted view about the date of the *Antiope* is correct Plato must pretty certainly have seen the performance himself.

[3] *Ibid.* 470d–471d.

[4] The way in which Nicias is mentioned at 472a certainly seems to assume that he is living and at the very height of his prosperity. This would exclude any date much later than the sailing of the Syracusan expedition in 415. The difficulties seem to me to be created by the very wealth of topical allusions for which the dialogue is remarkable. It would be very hard, in the absence of something like the complete files of a newspaper, to make so many of these allusions without falling into a small error here or there, and there were no newspapers or gazettes at Athens.

Aristophanes finds so useful as a butt.[1] The precise scene is not indicated ; apparently it is not in the house of Callicles, who is acting as host to the distinguished visitor, but in some public place where Gorgias has been giving a display of his gifts.[2] The ostensible subject of the conversation must be carefully distinguished from the real subject. Professedly the question propounded for discussion is the new speciality which Gorgias has introduced to Athens, the art of impressive speech ; the points to be decided are whether it is really an " art " at all, and if it is, whether it is, as Gorgias claims, the queen of all other " arts." But to discover the real object of the work we need to look carefully at the general construction of the argument, and particularly at the end of the whole composition. If we do this, we find that the dialogue really consists of three successive conversations of Socrates with a single interlocutor ; it has, so to say, three scenes, each with two " actors." In the first conversation between Socrates and Gorgias the topic of conversation really is the character and worth of the " rhetorician's " art ; in the second, between Socrates and Polus, we find that the rival estimates of the worth of rhetoric depend on sharply contrasted ethical convictions about the true happiness of man. In the final conversation with Callicles, where the tone of the dialogue reaches its level of highest elevation, all secondary questions have fallen completely into the background and we are left with the direct and absolute conflict between two competing theories of life, each represented by a striking personality. The true object of the whole work thus emerges : it is to pit a typical life of devotion to the supra-personal good against the typical theory and practice of the " will to power " at its best. We are to see how the theory of the " will to power," expounded by a thoroughly capable, intelligent, and far from merely ignoble champion, like Callicles, and the " practice " of it as embodied in Periclean Imperialism look from the point of view of a Socrates, and also how the convictions and career of a Socrates look to the intelligent worshipper of " strength " ; and when we have looked at each party with the eyes of the other, we are to be the judges between them. Life and the way it should be lived, not the value of rhetoric, is the real theme, exactly as the real theme of the *Republic* is not the merits and demerits of competing political and economic systems, but " righteousness, temperance, and judgment to come." [3]

---

[1] For the leanness, cf. Aristoph. *Clouds*, 502–503 ; for the impetuousness, *Apology*, 21a, σφοδρός ἐφ᾿ ὅτι ὁρμήσειεν; for the superstition, Aristoph. *Birds*, 1553 ff., where his taste for things ghostly is burlesqued by making him the fraudulent confederate who plays the " spirits " in Socrates' *séances*.

[2] Or perhaps we are to suppose that Socrates and Callicles meet in the street, and that the scene changes to the house of Callicles after the opening courtesies.

[3] The *Gorgias* stands in sharp contrast with the greatest of the dialogues in respect of the way in which the three sections of which the argument consists are marked off, like scenes on the Greek or French stage, by the putting forward of a new respondent to bear the brunt of the argument. Where his dramatic genius is at its highest, Plato is accustomed to interweave the

Formally the dialogue opens in a familiar way. Socrates is anxious to discover the precise character of the *art* or " speciality " (τέχνη) professed by Gorgias, the art of " rhetoric." It is, as Gorgias says (449*d*), an art of " speech " or " discourse " (περὶ λόγους), and as such it makes those who possess it skilled in " speaking," and therefore, since speech is the expression of thought or intelligence, makes them intelligent (δυνατοὺς φρονεῖν, 450*a*) about something. But this is far from an adequate definition. We may say that " arts " are of two kinds : the operations of the one kind are wholly or chiefly manual, those of the other kind are purely or principally effected by λόγοι, " discourses " (450*d*), a first intimation of the distinction, which becomes fundamental in Plato's later dialogues and in the philosophy of Aristotle, between " theoretical " and " practical " sciences. Now rhetoric is not the only " art " of the second kind ; there are many others, such as theoretical and practical arithmetic (ἀριθμητική and λογιστική), geometry, medicine, and others, in which manual operations play no part or a subordinate one ; but Gorgias certainly does not mean to say that he teaches medicine or mathematics. To complete the definition we need to know what is the subject-matter with which the " discourse " of the rhetorician is concerned, as the " discourse " of the arithmetician is concerned with " the odd and even " (*i.e.* with the properties of the integer-series (451*a*–*d*)). Gorgias thinks it enough to say that the subject-matter is " the most important of human concerns " (τὰ μέγιστα τῶν ἀνθρωπείων πραγμάτων), " the supreme interests of mankind." But a statement of this kind, which attempts to define by means of a mere formula of laudation, is ambiguous, since there are different opinions on the question what is the " great concern " of man. A physician might say that it is health, an economist or a business man that it is wealth. Hence, though Gorgias may be right in his estimate of his art, the estimate itself presupposes an answer to the ethical question what is the chief good for man (452*d*). Gorgias replies that the chief good for man is ἐλευθερία, freedom, in the sense of having his own way and being able to impose his will on his fellow-citizens, and that it is rhetoric, the art of persuasive or plausible speech which produces this good (452*d*). Thus the thought is that " power " is the chief good and that rhetoric, the art of persuasion, is the supreme art, because, in the life of a city like Athens, persuasive eloquence is the great weapon by which the statesman acquires power ; the persuasive speaker gets his policy adopted by the *ecclesia*, his financial schemes by the βουλή, and successfully impeaches his opponents and defends his partisans before the *dicasteria*. The secret of a Pericles, for example, is simply his command over the resources of persuasive eloquence. Gorgias holds that he can teach this secret to a pupil, and that is why he regards his own τέχνη as the supreme achievement of the human

threads of his plot more subtly. This, again, is a fair ground for an inference about the place of the dialogue in the series of Plato's works.

intelligence.[1] It should be noted that the hint is thus given early in the dialogue that the real problem to be discussed is the ethical question, not formally reached until we come to the scene in which Callicles is the respondent, whether " power," unchecked freedom to do as one likes and to make others do as one likes, *is* the highest good. The dispute about the "merits" of the art of rhetoric is wholly subservient to this ethical purpose and is mainly introduced because, in a Greek democracy, facility and persuasiveness in speech were necessarily the chief instruments by which such "power" was to be attained.[2]

We know now what Gorgias means by "rhetoric": he means an "art" of persuasion. It is an "art" because it is, or claims to be, reducible to intelligible principles; its end or aim is to "persuade" men to accept the views of the practitioner, and so to make them consenting instruments of his will. But the definition has the fault of being too wide: it does not, in fact, state the specific differentia of the orator's accomplishment. There are other "arts," including that of the arithmetician, of which we might equally say that they are arts by which men are persuaded to accept the specialist's opinion, since they "teach" us certain truths, and he who is taught is certainly persuaded of the things taught him. We must ask then, further, what *kind* of persuasion does rhetoric employ, and about what *matters* does it produce persuasion? (454*a*). Gorgias replies that rhetoric is the kind of persuasion employed "before dicasts and mobs in general," and that it persuades about "matters of right and wrong," *i.e.* it is the art of effective public speaking on questions of morality (454*b*). This at once suggests an important distinction. Persuasion or conviction (τὸ πιστεύειν) may be produced by instruction or without it. In the first case, a man is not only persuaded to hold an opinion, he is led to *knowledge*; in the second, he is convinced but does not really *know* that his conviction is true. Now obviously a "mob" cannot be conducted to knowledge on grave and complicated issues in the short time required for the delivery of an effective speech. The orator, therefore, must be a practitioner of the mere persuasion which does not produce real knowledge. We must expect, then,

---

[1] We are certainly dealing here with a thesis actually maintained by Gorgias. For in the *Philebus*, Protarchus remarks (*Phileb.* 58*a*–*b*) that he had often heard Gorgias maintain that the art of persuasion is far superior to all others, because the man who possesses it can make every one do his will and do it voluntarily. Obviously the reference is not to the *Gorgias* itself (though 458*c* implies that an audience is present at the discussion), but to some statement actually made in a discourse of Gorgias. *Gorgias* 452*d* ff. clearly refers to the same statement and probably reproduces it with close fidelity.

[2] We might say, in fact, that the great weakness of ancient democracy was that it really meant government by irresponsible orators, as modern democracy tends to mean government by equally irresponsible "pressmen."

that such a man will not attempt to persuade his audience about matters which obviously demand special technical knowledge, such as naval and military engineering, but only about "right and wrong" (which are popularly held not to be questions for specialists). Yet, as Gorgias observes, the greatest naval and military constructions of Athens—the dockyards, the harbours, the "long walls "—were undertaken not at the instigation of engineering specialists, but at that of Themistocles and Pericles, who were eminent "orators," but not engineers. In fact, you will find that before any public audience a skilful orator will always succeed in proving more "convincing" than an "expert" who is no orator, even on questions which fall within the expert's province. The "orator" who knows nothing of medicine, for example, will always be more persuasive, even on a medical question, than the medical specialist who is no orator. In general, the man who is merely an "orator" who understands his business will be able to pass himself off before the public as a consummate authority in matters where he has no real technical knowledge at all, and this is precisely the secret of his power. (The trick is that habitually employed in our own age by the able and eloquent advocate "speaking from his brief," and the view of Gorgias amounts to holding that statesmanship is just a matter of consummate skill in speaking from a brief.) To be sure, bad men may employ this formidable weapon for the worst of ends, but that is not the fault of the teacher from whom they have learned to use it, but their own. It is as absurd to blame the teacher for a pupil's abuse of the art as it would be to hold a boxer or fencing-master responsible for a foul blow struck by one of his pupils (455a–457c). Thus we see that Gorgias makes no claim to "teach goodness." It is important that his pupils should make a right, not a wrong, use of the weapons he teaches them to use, but his concern is merely to teach the "manage" of the weapons.

There is an obvious weak point in this commendation of the orator's art, and Socrates fastens on it at once. The "orator," by Gorgias' own account, is no "expert," and the "mob" or "crowd" before whom he succeeds in silencing the real expert are not experts either. Thus, on the showing of Gorgias himself, oratory is a device by which an ignorant man persuades an audience equally ignorant with himself that he understands a question better than the expert who really knows about it. Does this apply to the moral issues with which the "orator" will be largely concerned ? Does he need to know no more about right and wrong, honour and dishonour, than about, e.g., naval engineering or medicine ? If he does need knowledge of this kind, where is he to get it, since Gorgias has explained that it is not his own business to impart it ? Gorgias, rather inconsistently, suggests that, in case of need, a pupil might incidentally get the knowledge of right and wrong from himself ; in any case, he needs to have it. The "orator" must be δίκαιος, "a moral man." (If he were not, of course, he might make the

worst use of his oratorical skill.)   But if he is " a moral man,"
he will not have the wish to do wrong.   At this rate, a true orator
would never abuse his skill, and this seems inconsistent with the
former contention that when an orator does misuse his art, the
blame lies with himself and not with his teacher (457c–461b).

So far our results have come to this : it has at least been suggested that a statesman, who owes his power in a democracy to
skill in persuasion, need not be an expert in any of the technical
arts, but does require sound moral principles, though it is not
quite clear how he is to come by them.   Here Gorgias retires from
the argument, and his place is taken by his younger disciple and
admirer Polus, who is prepared to break with conventional views
about morality, as the respectable Gorgias is not.   According to
Polus, Socrates has taken an unfair advantage of the conventional
modesty which had led Gorgias to disclaim the status of a professional teacher of right and wrong.   The disclaimer was a mere
piece of good manners, and Socrates has himself committed a
breach of manners in pretending to take it seriously.   Polus also
insists that Socrates shall play the part of " respondent " and
submit his own definition of rhetoric for examination, as Socrates,
in fact, is quite willing to do.   According to this definition, which
opens the second of the three sections of the dialogue, rhetoric is
not an " art," a matter of expert knowledge, at all.   It is a mere
empirical " knack " ($\dot{\epsilon}\mu\pi\epsilon\iota\rho\iota a$, $\tau\rho\iota\beta\acute{\eta}$), and more precisely, a
" knack of giving pleasure " (462c).   In this respect it is like
confectionery.   The confectioner pleases the palates of his customers by a clever combination of flavours, and the " orator "
in the same way " tickles the ears of the groundlings " by attractive
combinations of words and phrases.   It is meant that neither
confectionery nor oratory is really an application of rational principles ; you cannot lay down rules for either, since both are mere
tricks of gratifying the tastes of a body of patrons, and in each case
the trick depends on nothing more scientific than a tact which
cannot be taught but only picked up by long personal experience
of successes and failures.   There is thus nothing " fine " about
either ; they are both branches of a " knack " for which the proper
name is $\kappa o\lambda a\kappa\epsilon\iota a$, " humouring the moods of a patron," [1] " acting
the parasite."

We may, in fact, distinguish four species of this $\kappa o\lambda a\kappa\epsilon\iota a$,
each of which is a spurious counterfeit or " ghost " ($\epsilon\iota\delta\omega\lambda o\nu$) of a
real science or art.   We start from the now familiar Socratic con-

---

[1] The word must not be translated " flattery."   The successful demagogue
often scores his point better by "slanging " his audience than by flattering
them.   In the language of the fifth century, $\kappa\delta\lambda a\xi$ meant what the new
comedy calls $\pi a\rho\acute{a}\sigma\iota\tau os$, the " trencherman " or sycophant or toady who keeps
his place at a great man's table by compliance with his moods, like the
" hangers-on " of Gaunt House in Thackeray.   The thought of Socrates is
that the " statesman " who supposes himself to be imposing *his* will on the
" many-headed monster " is merely adroitly " pandering " to the creature's
lusts.   This is the verdict of philosophy on all successful " opportunism."

ception of the "tending" of a thing. There is a double art of tending the body, that is, of keeping it in a state of health and fitness, and a corresponding double art of tending the soul. In the case of the body, the two arts of "tending" have no common name; they are those of "gymnastic," bodily culture (which sets up the ideal of true bodily "fitness"), and medicine (whose function it is to restore the "unfit" to health). The art of "tending" the soul has a single name; it is called πολιτική, "statesmanship": but it also has two branches, legislation (νομοθετική), which sets the standard of spiritual health, and "justice" (or righteousness, δικαιοσύνη), which corrects and repairs disease in the soul. Each of these four is a genuine art; it aims at the good or true best condition of body or soul, and thus rests on a scientific knowledge of good and evil. The regulations of "gymnastic" and medicine are based on knowledge of what is wholesome for the body, those of the legislator and the judge on knowledge of what is wholesome for the soul. But each of the four arts has its counterfeit, and the counterfeit differs from the true art in taking as its standard the pleasant and not the good. Thus the confectioner is a counterfeit of the physician. The physician aims at prescribing the diet which will be wholesome for us, the confectioner at prescribing that which will please our palates. Now it is possible to know what diet is wholesome, but you can only discover what diet will please a man's palate by guesses based on long acquaintance with his moods and whims, and even when you guess right, the dishes you prepare will commonly not be good for your patron.

In the same way, κομμωτική, the "art," if you could call it so, of bodily adornment (the calling of the *friseur*, the professional beautifier, the jeweller, and many others), is a parody of the genuine art of the trainer. "Gymnastic" makes the body inherently attractive and graceful by training it in the exercises which produce genuine grace, agility, and vigour; κομμωτική mimics this real art by producing a sham grace and charm effected by the artifice of cosmetics, fashionable clothes, and the like. (Here, again, there is no real standard, nothing but the caprice of the passing "fashion.") So with the arts which have to do with the health of the soul. The sophist professes to teach goodness, but what he teaches as goodness is merely the kind of life which is likely to recommend itself to his auditors; the "orator" claims to be the physician of the disorders of the body politic, but the measures he recommends only persuade his audience because he is careful to recommend what is agreeable to their mood of the moment. Thus we may define rhetoric by saying that it is the counterfeit of one part of "politics," namely, of justice (463a–466a).[1]

Polus urges in reply that rhetoric cannot be a form of κολακεία,

---

[1] The most extravagant "public man" always insists that he is only advocating the "just rights" of his nation, or church, or class. But a "just right" in his mouth means, in fact, whatever his supporters are keenly set on demanding.

since the " hanger-on " is a disreputable character, whereas the
" orator " is the most powerful person in the community, and, it is
implied, the figure of highest consequence.   He can use his influence
to secure the banishment of anyone he pleases, to confiscate his
goods, even to procure his execution.   Thus he is virtually an
autocrat with no superior.   Socrates admits the fact, but denies the
inference that either orator or autocrat is really powerful, if by
" power " you mean anything which it is good for a man to have.
The autocrat, recognized or unrecognized, no doubt always does
" as he thinks good," but for that reason he never does " what he
wishes " (466e).   And it is not good for a man to do " as he thinks
good " if his thinking is false.   To explain the point more fully,
we may put it thus.   There are many things which we do, not for
the mere sake of doing them, but as means to something else, as
when a man drinks a disagreeable medicine at his doctor's order,
for the sake of recovering health, or follows the fatiguing and
dangerous calling of the sea with a view to making a fortune.   In
all such cases, where a thing is done as a means to some ulterior end,
it is the ulterior end, not the disagreeable or indifferent means to it,
that the man wishes for.[1]   And he wishes for the end because he
thinks it a good.   So when we put a man to death, or banish him,
or confiscate his property, we always have an ulterior end.   We only
do these things because we think they will be " useful " in view of
that end.   If the autocrat, then, is mistaken in supposing that such
steps will " be for his good," if they are really bad for him, he is
not doing " what he wished," and should not be called " powerful."
(The thought is thus that every one really wishes for good, no one
wishes for evil.   " The object of every man's desire is some *good*
to himself."   To be really powerful means to be able to get good ;
it is weakness, not power, to " do whatever you please," if the
consequence is that you reap evil and not good (466a–469e).)
  We now pass to the direct enunciation of the main ethical
doctrine of the dialogue.   This is elicited by the unmannerly
remark of Polus that, whatever Socrates may be pleased to
profess, he would certainly envy the man who could forfeit, im-
prison, or kill anyone he pleased.   Socrates replies that he would
not.   The man who inflicts such things on another, even when they
are righteously deserved, is not to be envied ; the man who inflicts
them undeservedly is miserable and pitiable.   What is more, he is
more pitiable and miserable than the unfortunate innocent victim,
since to commit injustice is much worse than to have to suffer it.
Socrates himself would, of course, like Candide in a similar case,

---

[1] Note that in the course of this argument (at 468a) Socrates talks of things
" participating " in good and " participating " in evil, using the very word
(μετέχειν) which appears in connexion with the theory of Forms as technical
for the relation between the " particular thing " and the " universal " we
predicate of it.   Since it cannot reasonably be doubted that the *Gorgias* is a
considerably earlier work than the *Phaedo*, this creates a grave difficulty for
those who suppose that the theory is an invention of Plato's own, expounded
for the first time in the *Phaedo*.

"choose neither the one nor the other," but if he had to choose, he would much rather suffer the crime than commit it (469a–c).

Polus treats this view as a ridiculous paradox. He admits that any man with a knife under his cloak might claim to be "powerful," in the sense that he can, like the autocrat, kill any one he has a mind to kill, but for one thing, the certainty of punishment. Impunity must be stipulated for as one of the conditions of "power," but a child could refute Socrates' view that it is only "better" to kill, banish, and confiscate at will when these acts are done "justly." One has only to consider the very latest example from contemporary life, that of Archelaus, who has made himself king in Macedonia. His whole career has been one of rebellion and murder, but he has gained a throne by it. By Socrates' theory he ought to be the most wretched of men, but he is, in fact, the happiest, and there is not a man in Athens, not even Socrates, who would not dearly like to change places with Archelaus (469c–471d). An appeal of this kind is, however, an *ignoratio elenchi* in the most literal sense. Even if every one but Socrates would be willing to go into the witness-box on behalf of Polus, it is possible that a solitary witness may be a witness to truth, and the testimony of numbers on the other side erroneous. Socrates will not consider his own case as established unless he can produce one solitary witness to it, the antagonist himself (472b). In other words, the appeal must be to argument and not to authority. The first step we must take is to define the issue at stake as precisely as we can. It is, in fact, the most important of all practical issues, the solution of the question, "Who is the truly happy man?" Polus maintains that a man may be happy but wicked; Socrates denies this. As a corollary, there is a secondary disagreement. Polus holds that the wicked man, to be happy, must go unpunished; Socrates, that such a man is in any case unhappy, but more unhappy if he escapes punishment than if he suffers it, and he must try to convince Polus on both points (472d–474c).

The precise point of disagreement between the opposing views now receives a still more exact definition. Polus is still so far under the influence of current moral conventions that he admits at once that to commit a wrong is more "ugly" or "disgraceful" (αἴσχιον) than to suffer one, but he declines to draw the further inference that the "uglier" thing must also be the greater evil. He distinguishes, as Socrates refuses to do, between the good (ἀγαθόν) and the "fine" or "noble" (καλόν), and consequently also between the "ugly" (αἰσχρόν) and the evil (κακόν). The task of Socrates is to show that these distinctions are unreal The argument runs as follows. When we distinguish between "fine" bodies, colours, sounds, callings (ἐπιτηδεύματα) and others which are "ugly" or "base," our standard is always either "benefit" or "pleasure." By a "fine" shape or colour or sound, we mean one which is either serviceable or immediately agreeable in contemplation or both. The same thing holds good when we speak of "fine" or "noble"

usages (νόμοι) and callings in life, or of the " beauty " of a science.[1]
We mean that the usage or business or science in question either is
highly beneficial or " creates in the disinterested spectator a pleasing
sentiment of approbation," or both, a view which delights Polus
by its apparent Hedonistic implications.   It follows that by calling
anything " ugly " or " base," we must mean that it is either dis-
serviceable, or painful, or both.   Also, that when we say " A is
finer than B," we must mean that A is either more pleasant or
more useful than B, or both more pleasant and more useful.   And
when we call A " more ugly " than B, we mean that it is either
more harmful or more painful, or both.   Now we are agreed that
the commission of wrong (τὸ ἀδικεῖν) is an " uglier " thing than the
suffering of it (τὸ ἀδικεῖσθαι), and it is certainly not the case that it is
more painful to commit the crime than to have it committed on
you.   It must follow that the commission of the wrong is the more
harmful, *i.e.* the more evil course, the worse course.   Now no one
can rationally prefer an alternative which is at once the worse
and the more " ugly " of those open to him, and Socrates has thus
established his main point out of the mouth of his antagonist
(474c–476a).   We come now to the proof of the corollary.

We begin with a consideration of general logic.   Wherever
there is an agent (ποιῶν) there is a correlative " patient "
(πάσχων), a thing or person which is acted upon.   Also the
modality of the activity gives rise to strictly correlated qualifications (πάθη) in agent and patient.   If the agent, *e.g.*, strikes a
sudden, or a severe, or a painful blow, the patient is suddenly,
severely, or painfully struck.   If the agent " cuts deep," the patient
is " deeply cut," and so forth.   Now to be punished for a crime is
to be the patient in a relation in which the inflictor of the penalty
is the agent.   Hence, if the agent inflicts the penalty deservedly or
justly, the patient undergoes it deservedly or justly.[2]   And, as
Polus does not deny, what is just is " fine," and therefore, as we
have seen, either good or pleasant.   Hence the man who is justly
punished has something good done to him (since no one will suggest
that he finds the punishment *pleasant*).   He is benefited by what
is done to him.   We may go on to specify the nature of the benefit.
Goods and evils may be classed under three heads : good or bad

---

[1] Note that the " induction " is exactly parallel with that of the famous
speech of Diotima (*Symposium*, 210a ff.), when the successive stages in the
ascent to the contemplation of Beauty are delight in one person's bodily beauty,
in bodily beauty universally, in beauty of soul and character, beauty of
occupations and usages (ἐπιτηδεύματα and νόμοι), beauty of sciences (ἐπιστῆμαι).
The more carefully the Platonic dialogues down to the *Republic* are studied,
the more of a piece we find their teaching to be, and the harder it becomes to
trace any " development " within them.

[2] Observe once more that the logical principle presupposed here of the
interconnexion between the modalities of correlates is that which is used in
the *Republic* to establish the reality of the distinction between the " parts in
the soul "(*Rep.* iv. 438b–e).   Both passages presuppose the existence of a
good deal of recognized logical doctrine as early as the time of the Archi-
damain war.

conditions of fortune (χρήματα), of body, of soul. A bad condition of fortune is poverty; of body, weakness, disease, deformity. The corresponding bad state of soul is wickedness (ἀδικία), and admittedly wickedness is the "ugliest" of the three. Yet it is certainly not more *painful* to be wicked than to be destitute or physically ill. By our preceding reasoning, therefore, it must be very much more evil or harmful. Badness of soul is thus the very greatest evil to which a man is exposed, and thus we get back to the fundamental principle of the whole Socratic ethics (476b–477e).[1]

One further step remains to be taken. There is an "art" which covers each of the three kinds of evil. Business (χρηματιστική) releases us from poverty, medicine from physical disease, "justice" administered by a competent judge from wickedness. The judge who passes sentence on the criminal is thus a physician of the soul, and his calling is a "finer" one than that of the healer of the body, because he cures a graver disease. In both cases the process of treatment is disagreeable but salutary for us. And again, in both cases, the happiest condition is to be in bodily or spiritual health, and so not to need the physician. But in both also, the man who is cured of a grave disease by a sharp treatment is much less badly off than the man who has the disease without receiving the cure. Thus a man like Archelaus who lifts himself by successful crime above all possibility of correction is like a man with a deadly disease who refuses to submit to the surgeon. The claim advanced for rhetoric, then, that it enables its possessor to "get off" when he is called to account for his misdeeds, is wholly vain. The best use a man who has fallen into crime could make of eloquence would be to expend it in denouncing himself and ensuring that he shall receive from the judge whatever chastisement may be needed to restore his soul to health. If eloquence is to be used to enable the criminal to "get off" the penalties of his misdeeds, it would be appropriate to reserve this employment of it for the case of our mortal enemies, as the deadliest injury we can inflict (477e–481b).

So far we have been concerned simply with an emphatic statement of the thesis that to do wrong is always worse than to suffer it, with the inevitable corollary that it is worse to do wrong with impunity than to be punished. With the opening of the third scene of Plato's drama we proceed to the application of these moral principles to the theory of statesmanship and government. That this application is the principal theme of the dialogue is indicated both by the fact that this part of the work is longer than both the others together, and by the introduction of a new spokesman whose case is presented with an unmistakable gusto quite absent from all that has gone before. The new speaker is a certain Callicles of Acharnae, of whom we learn little more than that he has recently begun to aspire to a prominent place in Athenian public life. He is

[1] Note the assumption of the threefold classification of goods as goods of soul, body, and "estate," as something quite familiar (*Gorg.* 477a ff.). This too, then, is clearly pre-Academic.

one of the very few characters in Plato's dialogues of whose historical reality we have no independent evidence, but it should be clear from the very vigour with which his character is drawn that he is a genuine man of flesh and blood. His intervention at once gives a more realistic touch to the dramatic picture and lifts the argument to a distinctly higher level. Polus was not only half-hearted in his professed rejection of conventional moral convictions, but also wanting in moral seriousness. He had nothing more inspiring to say in support of his eulogy of the " tyrant " than that it is a pleasant thing to be able to gratify all your passions without apprehension of consequences. Clearly, established morality is in no danger from the assaults of worldlings of this type, least of all when they are mere literary gentlemen talking for talking's sake. Callicles is quite another matter. His morality, like Nietzsche's, may be an inverted one, but it is one with which he is in downright earnest. He has a definite ideal which carries him off his feet, and, though it is a false ideal, Plato plainly means to make us feel that there is a certain largeness about it which gives it a dangerous fascination. To be fascinated by it, indeed, you need to have a certain greatness of soul ; it is notable that Callicles himself is wholly above the appeal to the mere enjoyability of being able to gratify ignoble cupidities, of which Polus had made so much. The ideal he is defending is that of the men of action for action's sake, the Napoleons and Cromwells, and it is his conviction that there is a genuine moral right on which the ideal rests. His imagination has been fascinated by the vision of a Nature whose law is that " the weakest goes to the wall," and he sees the life of human societies in the light of this vision. He is as earnest as Carlyle in his conviction that superior ability of any kind gives the moral right to use the ability according to your own judgment and without scruples. Hence he feels that in rejecting " conventionalism " in morals he is not rejecting morality itself ; he is appealing from a petty and confined morality of local human conventions to an august morality of " Nature " or " things-as-they-are." The case for the partisans of φύσις in the fifth-century dispute about φύσις and νόμος could not well be argued more persuasively, and it is Plato's purpose that it shall be argued with the maximum of persuasiveness with a view to its thorough refutation.

If Socrates is in earnest and his theory is true, Callicles says, the whole of our actual social life is organized on wrong lines ; our whole conduct is " topsy-turvy." Socrates does not deny this, but replies that he and Callicles are lovers of two very different mistresses, " philosophy " and the Athenian democracy. Socrates' mistress, " philosophy," has taught him to speak her language, and, unlike the mistress of Callicles, she always holds the same language. It is she, not her lover, whom Callicles will have to refute.[1]   Callicles

---

[1] 481d. Here comes in the humorous reference to the mortal " sweetings " of Socrates and Callicles respectively, Alcibiades and Demus, son of Pyrilampes. We know from Aristophanes (*Wasps*, 98) that Demus was the fashion-

thinks the task will not be difficult if once we make the distinction between mere "convention" and Nature, or "reality." Polus had only been silenced because he had not the courage to say what he really thought. He deferred to the tradition of the average respectable man by saying that it is "uglier" to commit a wrong than to suffer one. But this is a mere convention of weaklings, set up for their own protection. In "reality" to commit a wrong or aggression is not the "ugly" thing; the "ugly" thing is to have it committed on you. It is weaklings, slaves, persons who cannot stand up for themselves like men, who have to "put up" wrongs; the strong are aggressive and commit what the conventions of the weak call "wrongs." If we look at φύσις, "things-as-they-are," we see that the stronger animal regularly pushes the weaker aside. Human life displays the same features, if we look at it on the large scale. By what right, for example, but that of the stronger did Darius attack the Scythians or Xerxes the Greeks ? Their proceedings may have been unlawful by the standard of the self-interested conventions of the weak, but they had Nature's right—the right of the strong to impose his will on the weak—on their side ; indeed, the conqueror is acting in strict accord with "Nature's νόμος"[1] in disregarding our paltry human νόμοι. When a really strong man—in fact, the *Übermensch*—appears, he will soon tear up our "contracts" and "formulae," and prove himself what he really is "by right of nature," the master of us all, as Pindar hinted in his well-known eulogy of the piratical feat of Heracles who drove the cows of Geryones "without leave asked or price paid."[2]

able beauty at Athens in the year 422. So far the jest makes for giving the *Gorgias* a dramatic date in the Archidamian war. But the supposed relations between Socrates and Alcibiades could also be used playfully in the *Symposium*, the assumed date of which is the year 416, so that the argument is not conclusive. If Socrates is thinking of the profession of the "Paphlagonian," to the personified Attic Demus in Aristophanes (*Knights*, 732, φιλῶ σ', ὦ Δῆμ', ἐραστής τ' εἰμὶ σός), this would also make for the earlier date.

[1] *Gorg.* 483e, κατὰ νόμον γε τὸν φύσεως. The first occurrence, so far as I know, in extant literature, of the ominous phrase "law of Nature." Callicles, of course, intends the words to be paradoxical—"a convention, if you like, but Reality's convention, not a human device."

[2] *Gorg.* 484b. I agree with Wilamowitz that the misquotation by which the MSS. made Callicles credit Pindar with saying that νόμος ἄγει βιαιῶν τὸ δικαιότατον "does violence to the most righteous claim" (whereas the poet wrote δικαιῶν τὸ βιαιότατον, "makes the most high-handed action just") comes from Plato and should not be "corrected," as it has been by all the editors. (Callicles expressly says that he does not know the lines accurately.) But I doubt the cogency of the far-reaching inferences, including one as to the date of composition of the dialogue, which Wilamowitz bases on the misquotation. I should conjecture that Plato makes it quite deliberately, and that the verses had been actually quoted in this form by the champions of φύσις against νόμος in the fifth century. We must remember that in the time of Socrates there were no "official" texts at Athens, even of the Attic dramatists ; still less would it be possible to secure the text of a foreign poet against misquotation. In the *Apologia Socratis* of Libanius (fourth century A.D.) Anytus is represented as having made a point of this particular misquotation at the trial of Socrates. This probably means, as Wilamowitz holds, that the complaint occurred in the pamphlet of Polycrates against Socrates, published some

As for what Socrates has said about the lessons of philosophy, philosophy is a graceful accomplishment in a young man, but to take it in earnest in mature life is ruin. It unfits a man for the life of action, leaves him ignorant of the laws of the community, the principles of public and private business, and the real passions of his fellow-men, like Amphion in the *Antiope* of Euripides. One should cultivate philosophy up to a certain point, when one is a lad, but a grown man should lay it aside with the toys of his boyhood. It is unmanly in a man of ability and ripe years to take no part in affairs and sit whispering " with a parcel of lads in a corner." [1] Callicles pushes the point " in a spirit of friendship " ; Socrates is a man of admirable natural parts, but his way of life has left him at the mercy of anyone who wishes to do him a harm. If he were falsely accused on a capital charge, he would be quite incapable of making an effective defence—more's the pity (481c–486d). Socrates professes himself delighted to have such an opponent to deal with, a man who is at once " educated," sincere (as is shown by the fact that his professed view of the proper place of philosophy in man's life is one which Socrates knows him to hold in common with several distinguished associates), and perfectly frank in speaking his mind without any deference to the conventions. If we can convince a man with these qualities of the soundness of our view of life, there can be no reasonable doubt of its truth. But first we must be quite clear on the point that, in the doctrine of Callicles, " better " is a mere synonym of " stronger " and " worse " of " weaker." If this is granted, as it is, then, since " the many " are stronger than one man, *their* conventional usages are the usages of the stronger, that is to say, of the better, and should be regarded as the " naturally fine " (κατὰ φύσιν καλά). But *their* convention is just what Callicles has been denouncing, the convention that aggression is wrong and that to commit it is " uglier " than to suffer it. Thus the antithesis between " nature " and " convention " on which Callicles had based his argument is unsound. This, says Callicles, is mere catching at a word. He never meant by the " stronger " (κρείττους) those who are merely superior in muscle and brawn (ἰσχυρότεροι). A *canaille* of slaves would, at that rate, be stronger and better than the " strong man." By the " stronger " he really meant " the wiser " (φρονιμώτεροι), the " men of parts." " Natural right " is that " the better and wiser should rule and have the advantage over (πλέον ἔχειν) the worse " (486d–490a).

years after 399 B.C. But the complaint cannot have been based on our passage, where it is Callicles, not Socrates, who misquotes.

[1] *Gorg.* 485d 7. Plato has sometimes been thought to have fallen here into attributing his own way of life in the Academy to Socrates. But (a) it is most unlikely that the Academy existed when the *Gorgias* was written ; (b) from Plato's account it appears that most of the conversations of Socrates with his young friends *were* held " in a corner," in places like the gymnasium of the Lyceum or the *palaestra* of Taureas, so that Callicles' language is perfectly appropriate.

But what exactly may this mean ? If food and drink are to be distributed to a company of men of varying physique, and there is just one physician among them, he is certainly the " wisest " in matters of diet, and it may be reasonable that he should regulate the distribution by his orders; but is he to get the biggest ration, even if he should be the greatest invalid of the party ? Should the weaver always have the biggest and finest clothes or the maker of shoes the biggest shoes and most of them ? Naturally not ; Callicles really means that the " strong " are men with the intelligence to know how a city may be " well administered," and the daring to carry out their designs (οἳ ἂν εἰς τὰ τῆς πόλεως πράγματα φρόνιμοι ὦσι, ὄντινα ἂν τρόπον εὖ οἰκοῖτο, καὶ μὴ μόνον φρόνιμοι ἀλλὰ καὶ ἀνδρεῖοι, ἱκανοὶ ὄντες ἃ ἂν νοήσωσιν ἐπιτελεῖν, 491b). It is right that such men should be sovereign in the State and " have the advantage " (πλέον ἔχειν) of their subjects.

Should we add that the best men are also sovereigns over themselves in the popular phrase, *i.e.* can govern their own passions ? No ; for in the nature of things the great man is one who has great passions and is intelligent and daring enough to secure them full gratification. The popular commendation of temperance is a mere trick by which the weaklings of the " herd," who have not manhood enough to live the best kind of life themselves, enslave their " natural superiors " (492a). If a man is born to a throne, or has the manhood to win his way to a throne, it would be base and bad in him not to rise above the conventional " temperance " and " justice " of the herd, and reap the full benefit of his capacity for himself and his friends. In the capable, lawless self-will (τρυφὴ καὶ ἀκολασία καὶ ἐλευθερία, 492c) are virtue and happiness ; regard for the " unreal catchwords " (τὰ παρὰ φύσιν συνθήματα) of the vulgar is contemptible. Thus the ideal of Callicles, like that of Nietzsche, is the successful cultivation of the *Wille zur Macht*, and his " strong man," like Nietzsche's, is a being of the type of Caesar Borgia as conceived in popular legend.[1]

The thesis of Callicles and the moralists of the " will to power " then is that one " ought " (δεῖ) to have violent desire and gratify it to the full ; to " want nothing " is the condition of a stone. But perhaps, as Euripides said, what we call life is really death. There is a rival view, developed by a certain wise man of Italy, that the tale of those who are condemned in the underworld to draw water in leaky pitchers is an apologue descriptive of the death-in-life

---

[1] Cf. Blake, *Marriage of Heaven and Hell*: " Those who restrain Desire do so because theirs is weak enough to be restrained ; and the restrainer or Reason usurps its place and governs the unwilling. And being restrained, it by degrees becomes passive, till it is only the shadow of Desire." The recently discovered Oxyrhynchus fragments of Socrates' contemporary, Antiphon " the sophist," have revealed to us one of the quarters in which these conceptions found literary expression in the age of the Archidamian war. It is, I believe, of Antiphon among others that Plato is thinking when he makes Glaucon declare that this same theory is widely current in his own circle (*Rep.* ii. 358b).

of the service of the passions. The leaking pitcher, or sieve, is
" the part of the soul, in which our desires are " ; the more gratification you give them, the more they crave, and this impossibility
of ever contenting them shows the intrinsic absurdity of the
attempt.[1] And it is clear that if one had to fill a number of vessels
from a few scanty springs, a man who did not care whether his
vessels were sound or cracked, and who allowed a vessel to run over,
would have a very difficult task. The man who made sure that
his pitchers were sound and that none of them ran over would be
much more successful. Callicles, however, thinks this simile
misleading. When the vessel has been filled, you can get no more
enjoyment out of the process of " filling " it ; the enjoyment
($\dot{\eta}\delta o\nu\dot{\eta}$) depends on the continuance of the flow. To get it, you
must always have room for " more " to flow in (494b).[2] (Callicles
thus assumes the psycho-physical theory according to which pleasure
is or accompanies—the theory hardly distinguishes these alternatives—the " filling-up " or making good of a process of " depletion " in the organism, pain the process of " depletion " itself.
The doctrine is familiar to us from Plato's acceptance of it, so far
as the satisfaction of physical appetites are concerned, in the
Republic and *Philebus*, and Aristotle's vigorous polemic against it
in the *Nicomachean Ethics*. Plato rejects it, except for these cases,
and the rejection of it is the basis of the important distinction of the
Philebus between " pure " or " neat " and " mixed " pleasures.
It is taught more unreservedly by the Pythagorean Timaeus at
Tim. 64a–65b, and we see from Aristotle's polemic that it was fully
accepted by Speusippus and the extreme anti-Hedonists of the
Academy. Its origin is pretty clearly to be found in the medical
doctrine of Alcmaeon, according to which all disease is disturbance
of the state of $\dot{\iota}\sigma o\nu o\mu\dot{\iota}a$ ("constitutional balance") between the
hot, the cold, the moist, and the dry in the organism. The im-
mediate assumption of Callicles that $\dot{\eta}\delta o\nu\dot{\eta}$ and $\pi\lambda\dot{\eta}\rho\omega\sigma\iota\varsigma$ may

---

[1] *Gorg.* 498a–c. Note (1) that, as Burnet says, the allusion to the Italian
" sage " seems plainly meant for Philolaus or some contemporary Pythagorean ; (2) that the unexplained mention of " the part of the soul in which
the $\dot{\epsilon}\pi\iota\theta\upsilon\mu\dot{\iota}a\iota$ are " presupposes the doctrine of the " tripartite soul " more
fully explained in *Rep.* iv., which must thus be, as there is much in the
Republic itself to indicate, of Pythagorean origin, as Posidonius is known to
have asserted (Burnet, *Early Greek Philosophy*[3], 278, n. 2). It is evidence of
the same thing that the doctrine is taught also in Plato by the Italian Pythagorean Timaeus, who cannot be supposed to have learned it from Socrates
just before delivering his own discourse. (3) The tale of the cracked pitchers
is not connected by Plato with the Danaïds. His version represents it as
describing the future destiny of the " uninitiated " ; this suggests Orphic
provenance.

[2] Cf. Hobbes, *Leviathan*, c. **xi.** : " There is no such *Finis* ultimus (utmost
ayme) nor *Summum Bonum* (greatest Good) as is spoken of in the Books of
the old Morall Philosophers. Nor can a man any more live, whose Desires
are at an end, than he, whose Senses and Imaginations are at a stand. . . .
So that in the first place, I put for a generall inclination of all mankind, a
perpetuall and restlesse desire of Power after power, that ceaseth onely in
Death."

be equated shows us that this doctrine was a commonplace in cultivated circles of the age of Socrates.)

Obviously, if happiness depends on such a process of unending
" filling-up," it demands a similarly unending process of " depletion."
If water is always to be running into the pitcher, it must also be
always running out at the cracks.   Would it then be intense happiness to have a continual itch, provided one could go on endlessly
getting the gratification of chafing the itching place ?   You must
admit this if you mean to be serious with the theory.[1]   What is
more, the life of a catamite must be eminently happy, if he can only
get a perpetual series of satisfactions for his unnatural *prurigo*.   For
all his " freedom from convention," Callicles objects to this particular " transvaluation of values," but you cannot avoid it so
long as you persist in identifying good with pleasant.   To condemn
any kind of gratification, you must distinguish good from pleasant,
and this Callicles admits he cannot consistently do (495*a*).

We proceed next to consider the identification of good and bad
with pleasure and pain on its merits.   Two difficulties occur to us
at the very outset.   (*a*) Good and bad are " contraries " ;   you
cannot predicate both at once of the same subject, nor can you
deny both at once.   A man cannot have both predicates at once, nor
" get rid " of both at once.   Pleasure and pain are not opposed in
this way.   *E.g.*, when a hungry man is satisfying his hunger by a
square meal, he feels at once the pleasure of appeasing the hunger
and the painfulness of the still unappeased hunger which urges
him to eat more.   When his hunger is sated and he leaves off, the
pleasure and the pain are both at an end.   But it is just at this
point, where both the pleasure and the pain are over, that the man
reaches the good to which eating ministers, the restoration of normal
equilibrium in his organism.[2]   (*b*) Callicles himself makes a dis
tinction between " good " men and " bad " ones, the " good,"
according to him, being the intelligent and bold, the " bad " the
silly or timorous.   He must hold, therefore, that good is " present
to "[3] the former and not to the latter.   But he cannot deny that
fools and cowards feel pleasure and pain at least as keenly as the

---

[1] Dante, it may be remembered, regards such a life as a torment for the
damned, and the worst of the damned (*Inferno*, xiv. 40, xv. 131, xxix. 76 ff.).

[2] The presupposed doctrine is that explained at length in the *Philebus*,
that the satisfactions of appetite attend on the process (γένεσις) by which
a " depletion " of the organism is made good.   Thus they are (*a*) preceded
by a painful consciousness of " want " (ἔνδεια), and (*b*) are not, even while
they last, wholly pleasurable.   Their piquancy and intensely exciting character depends on the tension between satisfied want and the persistence of
still unsatisfied want.   This is why these pleasures are " mixed," not " neat "
(καθαραί).

[3] *Gorg.* 497*e*, " We call good men good in virtue of the presence of good
things " to them (ἀγαθῶν παρουσίᾳ).   παρουσία has here precisely the sense
it bears when used in connexion with the forms in the *Phaedo*.   The predicate
" good " is predicable of a certain man because he " has " goodness of some
kind or other, is " possessed of " good.   On a Hedonist theory this means that
" *X* is good " always implies " *X* is enjoying pleasure," and it is this implication Socrates is calling in question.

intelligent and daring, if not more keenly, since cowards, for example, seem to feel more distress in the face of the enemy and more delight at their disappearance than brave men do. Thus there are empirical objections to the identification of pleasure with good (495*c*–499*b*).

Callicles extricates himself for the moment in the only way possible to a Hedonist in a " fix." Like Mill, he declares it obvious that " pleasures differ in quality "; there are better pleasures and worse pleasures, and it is unfair in Socrates, as Mill said it was in his opponents, to neglect the distinction. For example, a pleasure which contributes to bodily health is good, one which is detrimental to health is bad, and the same thing is true of pains. The rule for choice is that we should choose the good pleasures and pains and avoid the bad ones. In fact, Callicles is prepared to admit now that pleasure is a *means* to good (500*a*). But the right selection of pleasures will demand a " competent expert "; not every one can be trusted to make it.

We are thus brought face to face with the final problem raised by our dialogue. Socrates and Callicles stand respectively for two antithetical ideals in life, the one for the " life of philosophy," the other for the " life of action " as followed by a man of affairs in the Athenian democracy. The choice between these competing ideals is the ultimate practical problem, and it is this issue which is to be decided by the " competent judge." The distinction we have been forced to make between the pleasant and the good shows that the qualifications of the competent judge must not be based (as Mill tries to base them) on an empirical acquaintance with the flavours of pleasure (a thing of which the empiric understands neither the character nor the cause, 501*a*), but on a true τέχνη, which knows about the *good* of the soul as medicine does about the good of the body ; in fact, Socrates means, moral science is to prescribe the soul's regimen as medicine prescribes the regimen of the body (501*b*–*c*).[1]

Now there is certainly one class of " rhetoricians," *i.e.* practitioners of the use of language to work on men's feelings and imaginations, who are empirics of the type of the confectioner, namely, the poets. Their standard is always simply the " taste " of their public. They aim at pleasing this taste, and incidentally gaining their own advantage by doing so, without troubling themselves in the least whether their productions will make any one a better man. And what is poetry, when you divest it of the addition of tune, rhythm, and metre, but rhetoric—the effective use of language ? Has the rhetoric of an Athenian politician any saner basis ? Does the politician aim at the improvement of his public, or merely at gratifying their moods (501*d*–502*e*) ?[2]

[1] Thus Socrates disposes in advance of Mill's preposterous appeal to a jury of pleasure-tasters devoid of all ethical preferences. From his point of view, to consult judges with such a " qualification " about pleasures would be like selecting medicines by the agreeableness of their tastes.

[2] The whole indictment of poetry in the *Republic* is contained in principle in what is said here about its character as a " mere mechanic " trick of pleasing

Callicles thinks that, though the suggestion of Socrates may be true about some statesmen, there are others who really are guided by regard for the good of their fellow-citizens. He could not say so much for any living man of affairs, but it is true of the great men of the past, from Themistocles to the recently dead Pericles. They *did* make Athenians " better " by their careers. Socrates will not admit this. Themistocles and the rest made Athens great, if it is greatness to gratify all your cravings and passions, good and bad alike. But the scientific practitioner in any department must have an ideal before him into accord with which he sets himself to bring the material on which he works, as, *e.g.*, the physician has an ideal standard of health which he tries to reproduce in his patients. Has there ever been a statesman in Athens who, in the same way, has had an ideal of character, " goodness of soul," and set. himself to promote it in the citizens ? The physician, unlike his counterfeit the confectioner, aims at producing in a human body a definite " order and regulation " (τάξις καὶ κόσμος) ; the statesman, if he is more than a mere unprincipled empiric, should aim at doing the same thing for the human soul. This is to say that his purpose should be to produce " temperance and justice " (σωφροσύνη καὶ δικαιοσύνη) in the souls of his public. The object of a statesman and orator *secundum artem* is the production of national character. If the ἐπιθυμίαι of the citizens, the " national " aspirations and ambitions, are unhealthy and evil, the public man who is not a mere " toady " will aim at repressing them, and so making the national soul " better " by " chastisement " (505*b-c*).

Callicles is so disgusted with this return of the argument to the apparent paradox which had led to his intervention in the discussion, that Socrates is left to act as respondent to his own questions as he draws to his formal conclusion. Good is not the same thing as pleasure ; it depends universally on " order and rightness and *art*," and shows itself in a condition of " regulation and orderliness." This means that the temperate or " disciplined " soul is the good soul, the " unchastened " (ἀκόλαστος), " undisciplined " soul is bad. The former acts " appropriately to the situation " in all the situations of life, and consequently acts well, does well, and is " happy " ; the latter, not meeting the situations of life with the appropriate responses, is not merely bad but unhappy, especially if it is not held in check by " chastisement." These are the principles on which public no less than private conduct should be organized ; the life of the " superman " or of the " superstate " is simply that of a bandit, and a bandit has the hand of gods and men against him. He does not know how to " communicate " or " go shares " (κοινωνεῖν), but all social life depends on " communica-

and amusing. That poets aim merely at pleasing the taste of an audience, good or bad, was a current view. Herodotus uses it (ii. 116) to explain why Homer adopted a " false version " of the story of Helen, Euripides (*H.F.* 1341–6) to discredit the whole poetical mythology. In the δισσοὶ λόγοι it occurs more than once as an objection to the appeal to poets on questions of morality that their standard is ἡδονά, not ἀλάθεια.

tion." Indeed the "wise" (the Pythagorean men of science) say that "communication" or "reciprocity" (κοινωνία) is the basis not only of all human affections and moral virtues, but of the whole physical order of heaven and earth. "Geometrical equality" is the great law of the universe (508a),[1] and this is why the "wise" call the universe κόσμος, "the *order* of things." In setting up πλεονεξία, "going beyond the limit," as a principle for life, Callicles has forgotten his geometry. But if these convictions are sound, we must also admit Socrates' paradox that the best use an offender can make of rhetoric is to ensure his own conviction. Callicles was right in saying that Socrates' rule of life left him at the mercy of an aggressor, but wrong in thinking the position "ugly." The "ugliness" is not in the suffering but in the perpetrating of aggression. To escape this conclusion you must show that the principle that "wickedness is the greatest of evils to its possessor" is false (509e).

To commit wrong, then, is the worst evil which can befall a man ; to have to submit to it, though a lesser evil, is also an evil. In neither case will the mere purpose to avoid the evil avail of itself to secure its end. To avoid being wronged you also need "power" or "strength." And, since we long ago agreed on the principle that wrong-doing is "involuntary," a consequence of error, you need to secure yourself against it by acquiring some "power or τέχνη, organized knowledge" (510a).[2] If you want to avoid being wronged, you must either be an "autocrat" or a friend of the sovereign body, whatever it may be (ἑταῖρος τῆς ὑπαρχούσης πολιτείας, 510a). In an autocracy this means that you must be a "creature" of the autocrat ; in a democracy, like Athens, you must make yourself a favourite with your "master" the populace, and conform yourself to its moods and prejudices. In neither case have you secured yourself against the greater evil of committing wrong. On the contrary, to be a favourite with either autocrat or populace you must sink to their moral level and sympathize with their injustices. Callicles thinks this only sensible, for the "leviathan" will kill you if you do not humour it. But this plea rests on the assumption that life at any cost and on any terms is supremely desirable, even at the cost of moral corruption. It amounts to basing the high claims made for rhetoric on the view that rhetoric is an art of saving your skin. No doubt it is ; the politician is constantly saving his skin by his plausible speech. But swimming

---

[1] ἰσότης ἡ γεωμετρική, *i.e.* *proportion*, "equality of *ratio*." It is called so, in contradistinction to "arithmetical" or absolute "equality," because of the part it plays in the geometry of "similar" figures. The "wise" meant are the Pythagoreans who were the discoverers of the various elementary "progressions," or, as the Greeks called them, ἀναλογίαι, "proportions," and gave the name κόσμος to what had before them been called οὐρανός. For the thought we might compare Kant's insistence on the principle of *Gemeinschaft* and reciprocal interconnexion in nature.

[2] Cf. *Ep.* vi, 322d, where Plato recommends Erastus and Coriscus to the "protection" of Hermias on much the grounds here spoken of.

and seamanship save your skin too, and are not thought of supreme moment for a gentleman's education. An ordinary skipper will bring you, your family, and all your belongings safe from Egypt or the Pontus, but he asks a very modest fare, and his calling is thought a very humble one. And this is as it should be, for the skipper has really done a man who is hopelessly diseased in body or soul no real service; it would be better for such a man to go to the bottom (511c–512b). So an ordinary engineer may save the lives of a whole community by the machines he builds, but a man like Callicles regards the engineer as a " base mechanic " and would not dream of intermarriage with his family. If mere life is the highest good, why should not all these " mechanics " advance the same claims which are put forward on behalf of rhetoric (512c–d)? The truth is that the important thing is not to live long, but to live well; is a man likely, or is he not, to attain that end by conforming himself to the spirit and temper of the community, e.g. of the Athenian δῆμος, as he must do if he means to be a " public man " (512e–513c)?

" Impressive, but not convincing," is the verdict of Callicles on all this. Convincing or not, however, it is plain that if we aim at a statesmanship which is more than successful " parasitism " [1] (κολακεία), a statesmanship which is a genuine art of " tendance of our fellow-citizens," our chief problem will be to promote national character; it is no true service of the State to increase its wealth or power, unless its citizens are fitted by their character to use wealth or wield power [2] (514a). On the hypothesis, then, our fitness for the statesman's calling depends on our possession of a science (ἐπιστήμη), in fact, on our knowledge of moral values. Now an expert can establish his claim to be an expert in two ways: (a) by pointing out the master from whom he has learned his knowledge, (b) by pointing to the results in which his knowledge has been embodied. If a man can satisfy neither of these tests, we cannot take his claims to be an expert seriously. No one would give an appoint-

---

[1] We might perhaps use a biological analogy to bring out better the full meaning of the distinction between the κόλαξ and the genuine " craftsman " which runs all through the dialogue. The κόλαξ or " trencherman " of social life lives, and lives, according to the vulgar estimate, well by living on his patron (whom he really depraves by " pandering " to his vices), exactly as the parasitical organism fattens itself on the tissues of its unfortunate " host." So the empiric in statesmanship, the " opportunist," makes a " good thing " for himself of depraving the national character and lowering the national ideals. The best comment on the view Socrates takes of the influence of the " orators " on national life is the humorous caricature of the same thing in the scene of Aristophanes (Knights, 725 ff.) where the sausage-seller and the Paphlagonian bid against each other for the lucrative post of pimp-in-chief to Demus. Aristophanes and Socrates agree in their estimate of the νῦν πολιτικοί.

[2] Cf. the lesson, e.g., of the Euthydemus that wealth and power are good or bad according as the " soul " which is to use them is good or bad. Note that there is once more a tacit allusion to the apologue of the " three lives." " Wealth " and " power " are the ends of the " body-loving " and " distinction-loving " lives respectively, ἐπιστήμη the end of the " philosophic " life.

ment as a public physician to a candidate who could not prove
that he had effected any cures as a private practitioner. So an
aspirant to statesmanship may fairly be expected to satisfy us
that he has "in private practice" made the souls or characters
of his fellow-men better. How do the famous public men of Athens,
from Miltiades to Pericles, stand this test (515d)? It is Socrates'
conviction that one and all fail under it. Pericles, as every one is
saying, made the Athenians worse, not better; he made them
"idle, cowardly, talkative, and greedy" (515e). The best proof
of this is the notorious fact that at the end of his career, they actually
turned on him and found him guilty of embezzlement.[1] The conviction was, to be sure, iniquitous, but whose "tendance" of the
animal *civis Atticus* had taught it these iniquitous ways? The
"tendance" of Pericles himself (516a–d). He made the animal
"wilder," and this disposes of his claim to be a statesman. The
same is true of Cimon and Miltiades: the very wrongs they ended
by suffering from the δῆμος prove that they too had made their
"cattle" worse by their treatment (516d–e).[2] None of these
famous men was even skilled in the spurious "parasitic" kind of
rhetoric—for each of them ended by displeasing the common
patron (517a).

You may say that, after all, these must have been great men,
for their "public works" (*e.g.* the creation of the Athenian navy,
the building of the walls, docks, and the like) speak for them. And
this really proves that they were, so to say, good "domestics" or
"personal servants" of Demus; they knew how to provide their
master with the things he desired. But what they did not know—
and true statesmanship consists in knowing just this—was how to
get him to desire what is really good (517b).[3] To call them statesmen is like calling a confectioner or a fancy baker a specialist in
hygiene and medicine; it is to compare a subordinate "art,"
which makes things, with the master-art which "uses" them
aright (517e–518c). If a man made that confusion, his cooks and
confectioners would soon ruin his constitution, and he would lay
the blame for his want of wholesome appetite on the inferiority of
his present cook as compared with his old one. Callicles is making

---

[1] 515e, ταυτὶ γὰρ ἔγωγε ἀκούω κτλ. Socrates means that this is the verdict
to be heard on all sides now that Pericles is dead and his dominance is at an
end. He would "hear" this, of course, from many quarters. It is, *e.g.*, the
view of Aristophanes and apparently of the contemporary comic dramatists
generally. The statement that Pericles had made Athenians "lazy and
greedy" διὰ τὴν μισθοφορίαν refers, of course, to his establishment of the
dicasts' μισθός. The picture of Philocleon and his friends in the *Wasps* is
an admirable illustration of the point.

[2] Socrates would have the Old Comedy on his side in what he says about
Pericles; the point about Miltiades and Cimon is made to show that the heroes
of Aristophanes and the anti-Pericleans are in the same condemnation.

[3] 515e, οὐδ' ἐγὼ ψέγω τούτους ὥς γε διακόνους εἶναι πόλεως. Pericles and the rest
have no claim to be "physicians of the commonwealth," but they were competent purveyors, major-domos, and butlers. So much Socrates will concede,
but no more.

precisely the same blunder. The real authors of the disorders of the " body politic " were the " statesmen " of the past who ruined the constitution of the public by filling it with " harbours and docks and such stuff, without justice and temperance." When the " cold fit " of the disorder arrives, the sufferer will lay the blame for his disorder on Alcibiades, or perhaps Callicles himself, who are at worst only minor contributors to the mischief.[1] When the public turns and rends one of its leaders in this fashion, he usually complains of its injustice. But the complaint is as ludicrous as that of the sophists who profess to teach their pupils " goodness," and then accuse them of cheating them of their fees. The very complaint shows that neither sophist nor politician can do what he professes to do ; the one cannot make his pupils " good," the other cannot promote the real good of the " people " (517b–520a). Of the two pretenders, there is a certain advantage on the side of the sophist. The art he caricatures, that of the legislator, is a nobler thing than the art of the judge, as that of the physical trainer who keeps the body fit is nobler than that of the physician who banishes disease. If either pretender really believed in himself, he would exercise his calling *gratis* ; a man who can make an individual or a people " good " has no need to take precautions against ungrateful or unfair treatment (520c–e).[2]

What, then, did Callicles mean when he recommended Socrates to take up " public life " ? Did he mean that Socrates should be a physician to the public or merely a " toady " and " body-servant " ? The truth is that Socrates himself is the only real statesman of his time, for he is the only Athenian who aims in his use of speech not at giving pleasure but at doing real good to those with whom he speaks. He may very possibly be dragged into court as a " corrupter of youth," and if that should happen, his condemnation is certain, for he would be the physician pleading against the confectioner before a jury of children of whom he had already spoken.[3] But he would die innocent of offence, and the dreadful thing is not to die, but to enter the unseen world with a soul laden with guilt (521a–522e).

[1] This allusion to a possible turning of the δῆμος against Alcibiades seems to make it clear that the supposed date of the conversation must at any rate be well before the event which fulfilled the prophecy—the scandal about the " profanation of the mysteries " in 415. Observe the contempt expressed by Callicles at 520a for the professional " teachers of goodness." This is strictly in keeping with his theories about the superman, since no one can teach you to be a superman ; you have to be born one.

[2] Is this an allusion to the anecdote told by later writers about Protagoras and his defaulting pupil ? Or, more probably, is not the story to which Plato alludes a contemporary jest into which the name of Protagoras was worked before the time of Aristotle ?

[3] We might at first be surprised to find Socrates at what seems to be an early stage in his career contemplating the possibility of prosecution for " corrupting the young." But we should compare *Apology*, 18b ff., where Socrates insists that the prejudice against him and his influence goes back to the old caricatures of the comic poets, who charged him with useless speculations and " making the worse argument appear the better."

The argument of the dialogue is now complete. We reach the climax of the Socratic ethics of the " tendance of the soul " with the declarations that statesmanship is nothing but the practice of this same " art " on the large scale, that its indispensable basis is knowledge of moral values, and that the apparent " mugwump " Socrates is in fact the one man of his age and city who is leading the real " active life," because he has himself, and tries to communicate to every one else, a moral faith and moral ideals. He alone, in a world of " opportunist " careerists, is doing work which will last, because he alone is building on a rock. What makes the *Gorgias* so important in spite of its *longueurs*, is that, more fully than any other dialogue, and with an intenser πάθος, it works out the application of the conception of " tendance of the soul " to the whole complicated business of life. Formally, the conversation is prolonged for a few pages, to give Socrates the opportunity to drive home the exceeding horror of sin by an imaginative myth of judgment after death, the earliest in order of composition of Plato's masterpieces in this kind. The basis of the story, in this case, seems more strictly Orphic and less Pythagorean than in the companion pictures of the *Republic* and *Phaedo*. The scenery, " the meadow where the three ways meet," [1] the judges before whom the dead appear, the original division of the universe into heaven, earth, and the underworld, used as the *motif* for the tale, are all familiar to us as features of the Orphic mythology. On the other hand, nothing is said of the Pythagorean reincarnation which plays so prominent a part in the eschatology of the *Republic, Phaedo*, and *Phaedrus*. This presumably means that that doctrine is no part of the serious convictions of Socrates or Plato, and this may be why Socrates expressly says at 524*b* that he accepts the present account of the judgment as true, without any warning, such as he gives in the *Phaedo*, against pressing its details.

The main thought of the myth is the impossibility of escaping the scrutiny of the eye of the divine judge. In the old days, men were judged while still in the body, and the stains and sores of the soul often escaped notice, especially when the party to be judged was a great man, who appeared with all the splendours of external pomp and circumstance. To prevent such mistakes, the judgment has now been placed after death, that the soul may appear at the tribunal naked, without the " tunic " of the body. This ensures that its destiny shall be decided by its worth, not by the station it has held on earth. We shall find Plato preaching the same doctrine of a divine judgment which neglects nothing and can make no

---

[1] The three ways are the roads which lead (*a*) from earth to " the meadow," (*b*) from the meadow to heaven, (*c*) from the meadow to hell. As usual, hell is depicted in the main as a purgatory for the not wholly depraved. A few incurables are detained there permanently as a warning to others, but these are chiefly " supermen " of the Napoleonic type. Ordinary human weakness is regarded as " curable." Not all " statesmen " take the road to destruction. Aristides " the just " is instanced as an example of a man who filled high office nobly and went " straight to heaven " (526*b*).

error, in the tenth book of the *Laws*, without any mythology at all. In the *Gorgias*, the point to notice is the tone of earnestness with which Socrates is made to profess the doctrine as his own personal faith. This representation is quite incompatible with the singular view that " the historic Socrates " was an agnostic on the problem of immortality. If Plato misrepresented his master in the matter, the misrepresentation did not begin with the *Phaedo*. He must have ended the *Gorgias* with a deliberate mystification.[1]

The Meno.—There are points of contact between the *Meno* and the *Gorgias* which make it convenient to consider them together, though the main purpose of the *Meno* connects it rather with two more mature dialogues, the *Phaedo* and the *Protagoras*, as well as with the *Apology*. The dramatic setting of the dialogue is of the simplest. It is a conversation between Socrates and the young Thessalian Meno, who is attended by at least one slave, broken by an interlude which brings on the scene the prominent politician Anytus, afterwards the instigator of the proceedings against Socrates. Where the conversation takes place we are not told, except that it is, of course, somewhere in Athens. The dramatic date can be readily fixed by reference to the facts about Meno recorded in Xenophon's *Anabasis*. Meno joined the expedition of Cyrus the younger against his brother Artaxerxes II at Colossae in the middle of March 401 B.C. (*Anab.* i. 2, 6), rendered the important service of being the first of the Greek adventurers to declare for Cyrus openly when the army had reached the Euphrates and its real objective became clear (*ibid.* i. 4, 13), and was present with

[1] I may here append a very brief statement about the conclusion which seems to me safest on the question of the dramatic date of the dialogue. As I have said, I think the tone of the reference to a possible revulsion of feeling against Alcibiades excludes any date later than about 416. The main difficulty to set against this conclusion is the free use made by both Callicles and Socrates of the *Antiope* of Euripides, which is assumed to be a familiar and popular work. The scholiast on Aristophanes' *Frogs* 53 refers to the play as " recently produced " at the time of production of the *Frogs* (405 B.C.), and implies that it was a later work than the *Andromeda* (produced in 412 along with the *Helena*, both of which are burlesqued by Aristophanes in the *Thesmophoriazusae*, a play of the year 411). Unless Plato has forgotten the real date of a play of which he probably saw the first performance, there must be some error in the scholiast's reckoning. The references to the actual state of affairs throughout the dialogue suggest that Pericles has not yet found a successor recognized as such by admirers like Callicles. The picture of the power actually wielded by the " orators " seems to me so completely in keeping with the tone of Aristophanes' *Knights* and *Wasps*, that I would suggest that the most suitable date is during the career of Cleon, somewhere about 424–422, or at most a little later. As the demagogues had been able to disgrace Pericles at the end of his life, 427 would be a possible date, but I think rather less likely. We need not suppose that Gorgias is in Athens for the first time, or that he only came there once. Andron, the best known of the associates of Callicles, is specially connected for us with the events of 411–410 ; he had been a member of the " four hundred," but, like Critias, took a prominent part in the overthrow of that body, being the proposer of the psephism which " attainted " its leading spirit, the orator Antiphon. But in the *Gorgias*, no doubt, we are to think of him as, like Callicles, only just beginning his career.

the others at the battle of Cunaxa. The rivalry between Clearchus and Meno, after the battle, led directly to the capture of the principal Greek leaders by Tissaphernes and the death of Clearchus (*ibid.* ii. 5, 27 ff.). Meno, with the rest, was sent a prisoner to the Persian court, where he was executed after a year's confinement (*ibid.* ii. 6, 29). Xenophon, who was a fervid admirer of the stupid and brutal Clearchus, gives Meno the worst of characters. One may discount a great deal of this, but the general impression that the man was a spoilt and petulant boy, only half civilized, is borne out by Plato's dialogue. Xenophon does not mention Meno's age at death, but implies that he was still a mere lad (ἔτι ὡραῖος, he says) when he was put in charge of the 1500 men he brought to the expedition. Hence we shall hardly be far wrong if we suppose his presence in Athens to be connected with the forthcoming enterprise. This means that we must date it not long before his arrival in Colossae. We must thus think of Socrates as an old man, within two or three years of seventy, and of the conversation as taking place after the restoration of the democracy in 403, when Anytus was one of the two or three most powerful and respected public men. The *Meno* then, unlike any of the dialogues we have so far considered, is dated at a time which would be compatible with supposing Plato to have been actually present at the conversation and to be describing it from his own recollections.[1] The dialogue opens with an abruptness hardly to be paralleled elsewhere in the genuine work of Plato by the direct propounding of a theme for discussion ; there are not even the ordinary formalities of salutation. May we argue that this indicates that its composition belongs to the very earliest years of Plato's literary activity ? This would be an important consideration, since, as no one denies, the whole characteristic metaphysics of the *Phaedo*, the theory of forms and the doctrine of " reminiscence," are explicitly taught in the *Meno*. In any case there ought to be no doubt that the *Meno* is a cruder and earlier work than either of the two great dramatic dialogues with which it is most intimately connected, the *Phaedo* and the *Protagoras*, and this of itself would be enough to prove that the *Phaedo* is not, as has been supposed, a first publication of an important philosophical discovery.

The question raised by Meno (70a) is one directly suggested by the activity of Protagoras and the other " teachers of goodness " (ἀρετή). Can " goodness " be taught, or, if not, can it be acquired

[1] The *only* other " Socratic " discourses for which this would be *possible*, so far as I can see, are the *Apology* (where Plato mentions his own presence). *Theaetetus* and *Euthyphro*, (?) *Philebus*. It would consequently be possible for the *Sophistes* and *Politicus* also, though the fiction by which the *Theaetetus*, with which these dialogues are especially connected, is represented as read from notes made by Euclides is probably intended to suggest that Plato is not a κωφὸν πρόσωπον in these discourses. These facts suggest that, except in the case of the *Apology*, Plato means us to think of himself as absent even in the one or two instances when he might, so far as date goes, have been present : his intention is to suppress his own personality altogether.

by "*practice*"—is it ἀσκητόν? If it can be acquired neither by instruction nor by practice, is it "naturally" inborn, or how do we come by it? This is just the point at issue between the champions of νόμος and the partisans of φύσις in the time of Socrates. (For the Socratic answer to the problem we need to go partly to the *Protagoras*, still more to the elaborate account of the training proposed for the "auxiliaries" and the "philosopher kings" of the *Republic*. Plato's own final position has to be learned from the educational sections of the *Laws*. At present it will be enough simply to state summarily the results reached in the *Republic*. There is no formal discussion of the problem in the dialogue, but the solution of it is given implicitly in the educational programme laid down in the course of books iii.–vii. Socrates' solution there depends on a *distinguo*. There are two distinct levels of "goodness," one which will be sufficient for the ordinary good citizen and even for the "auxiliaries," the executive force of society, and a higher, indispensable to the statesmen who have to direct the whole of the national life and determine its standard. For those whose business in life is to obey rules based on the ideals of the true statesman, all that is necessary is a discipline in absolute loyalty to the traditions in which the ideals are embodied, and this discipline is secured by the moulding of temper, taste, and imaginations described in *Republic* iii.–iv. Such an education, however, does not result in personal insight, but at best in loyalty to a noble rule of life taken on trust. The "goodness" of the classes who are "under authority" is thus not μαθητόν but ἀσκητόν, a result not of enlightenment but of discipline. But in the statesman who has to create the national tradition, something more is needed. He must know, as a matter of personal insight, what the true moral "values" are. The statesman is therefore required to possess a "philosophic" goodness, based on direct personal insight into the structure of the universe and man's place in that structure. Such insight can only be won by the mind which has been trained in arduous scientific thinking for itself, and is therefore "knowledge," and, like all knowledge, comes by "teaching"; but this teaching is no mere communication of "results." A man is not made a thinker of the first order by any imparting of "information," but by stimulating in him the power and the ambition to think for himself. This is why the one effective method of teaching in philosophy and science is the association of an older and a younger mind in the prosecution of an "original research.")

To return to the *Meno*. Meno's question, flung out in an airy way as though it could be disposed of in a sentence, cannot really be answered without facing one still more fundamental. We cannot expect to know how "goodness" is produced until we know what it is. And this is more than anyone at Athens, and most of all Socrates, professes to know. We are thus brought back to the problem of definition which has met us already in other dialogues (71c–d). According to Meno, this problem is no real problem at all. Gorgias could have told Socrates what goodness is, or, if Socrates has forgotten what Gorgias has to say, Meno, whose admirer Aristippus had been a patron of Gorgias, can remind him. There are a variety of "goodnesses" (ἀρεταί). The goodness of a man is to have capacity for public affairs, to be a valuable ally and a dangerous enemy, and to know how to hold his own; that of a woman is to look after "the home" and to obey her husband; and there are yet other goodnesses appropriate to a child, an elderly man, a slave, and so forth. In fact, every age of life and every social station has its own peculiar goodness (72a). (Thus we have once more the confusion of definition with enumeration.) These commonplaces, however, do not answer our question. We want to know what the οὐσία, or *essentia* of "goodness" is, and this must be something in respect of which the "goodnesses" of male and female, old and young, bond and free, do *not* differ, a "single identical pattern" (ἓν εἶδος, 72c), in virtue of which the common name ἀρετή is bestowed.[1]   Consider the analogy of health or strength. One might say, as Meno has done, that there is "health in a man" and "health in a woman," "manly strength" and "womanly strength," and that they have their differences. And Meno himself must admit that "in respect of being health" or "in respect of being strength" masculine health and strength do not differ from feminine.[2] There is a single "pattern" of health (ἓν πανταχοῦ εἶδος) in all healthy beings, and similarly with strength.   So, since we can speak of a good man and of a good woman, there must be some one "pattern" of goodness in man and woman, young and old. (In the language of to-day, "goodness" must be a *determinable*, of which the "goodness of a man," the "goodness of a woman," and the rest are the *determinants*.) We may note that this position, which arises at once from the application of the theory of forms to human conduct, is of first-

[1] The "something which is the same in all cases" and justifies the use of a common name is successively spoken of as οὐσία (what the thing is, its *quid*) (72b), as a single εἶδος, pattern (72c, d, e), as something which "pervades" all the cases, διὰ πάντων ἐστίν (74a), is the same "over them all," ἐπὶ πᾶσι ταὐτόν (75a).   All these are names for the objective reality indicated by the employment of a common predicate of many subjects, and the abundance of them presupposes the existence of an already rather elaborate logical doctrine founded on the metaphysics of forms. Linguistically, οὐσία is the most interesting of them, since in this sense it is a loan-word from Ionic science; the only familiar meaning in the Attic of the fifth century was the legal one, "estate," "property, personal or real." On the probability that the philosophical meaning of the word comes from the Pythagoreans, see Burnet's note on *Euthyphro*, 10a 7. As to εἶδος, criticism has not shaken my conviction that its philosophical use is a development from its source in Pythagorean mathematics—"regular figure."

[2] That in a sense there is male health and female health is clear from the simple fact that there are professors of and treatises on gynaecology. But the εἶδος of health, namely, that it is "equilibrium in the constituents of the organism," holds good for both sexes. The thesis that the "goodness" of a woman is the same as that of a man was ascribed to Socrates also by Aeschines in his *Aspasia*, and is thus a genuine tenet of the Socratic ethics (cf. Burnet, art. SOCRATES, in *Encyclopaedia of Religion and Ethics*, xi. 667).

rate importance for both logic and ethics. In logic it means that there is no third alternative between realism and nominalism. A universal, unambiguously employed, signifies something or it does not. If it signifies anything, that something is not an arbitrary fiction of my mind ; if it signifies nothing, there is an end of all science. Science stands or falls with " objective reference." [1] In ethics the doctrine means that there really is one moral standard for all of us, male or female, Greek or barbarian, bond or free. There really is one " eternal and immutable " morality, not a variety of independent moral standards, one perhaps for the " private man " and another for the " nation " or its politicians, or one for " the herd " and another for the " superman." The particular application of this conviction to the case of man and woman is shown to be genuinely Socratic by the fact that it not only appears in *Republic* v. as the principle on which Socrates justifies the participation of women in public life, but is also implied in the fragments of the *Aspasia* of Aeschines as his reason for asserting the capacity of women for the tasks of war and statesmanship.[2]

Meno is inclined at first to deny the position. But he has to admit that both what he regards as man's work and what he calls woman's work are only well done if they are performed with *sophrosyne* and justice, and similarly that wilfulness (ἀκολασία) and unfairness are faults alike in children and in elderly men. Thus *sophrosyne* and justice emerge as characteristic of human goodness, irrespective of age, sex, or status. There is then such a thing as a " goodness in virtue of which all human beings are good " ; can Meno remember what Gorgias supposed this goodness to be ? He suggests that it may be " capacity to command " (ἄρχειν οἷόν τ᾽ εἶναι τῶν ἀνθρώπων, 73d). But what then about a child or a slave (who, of course, show their " goodness " not by giving orders, but by obeying them) ? And again, one may give unjust commands, and this can hardly be goodness, since it is not disputed by Meno that justice is a virtue and injustice a vice. We must at least qualify the statement by saying that goodness in man is the capacity

---

[1] We could not meet the argument by falling back on Aristotle's well-known doctrine of the " analogous " employment of universals. True as that doctrine is, it remains also true that in its strict and primary (κύριον) sense the universal can still be asserted of a plurality of subjects, and to be significant must be asserted of each and all of them in the same sense. Thus, even if it be granted, that there is no one common " goodness " of all things, *e.g.* that there is no more than an analogy between the goodness of a good razor and that of a good man, the Aristotelian ethics is based on the view that there is a " human goodness " which is one and the same for all men ; there is not one goodness of Peter and a different and merely analogous goodness of Paul. Peter and Paul have to be pronounced good or bad by the *same* standard. Aristotle's attempt in the *Politics* to justify the conventional prejudice which sets up a different moral standard for the two sexes amounts to a denial of the moral unity of humanity, and contradicts the very principles on which his own ethics are constructed.

[2] See the collection of these fragments in H. Dittmar's *Aeschines von Sphettos.*

to command justly (73*d*). This at once raises the question whether commanding justly is goodness or only ἀρετή τις, *one* form of goodness; in fact, in the language of a more developed logic, whether we are not confusing a genus with one of its own species. We may illustrate the confusion by a simple example. It would be false to say that " circularity is figure " (σχῆμα), though true to say that it is *one* figure among others (73*e*). There are other figures besides circles, and Meno admits that there are " many " forms of goodness besides justice. Our attempt at definition has failed ; like the original enumeration, it has left us with *many* goodnesses instead of one (74*b*).

Perhaps we may get a hint of the kind of statement we really want if we go back to our illustration of the circle. There are many figures (σχήματα) of which the circle is only one, just as there are many colours, of which, *e.g.*, white is one among others. But we might try to define figure in a way which would express what is common to all figures, by saying, for example, that " figure is the one thing which always accompanies colour," " the sole inseparable concomitant of colour " (ὃ μόνον τῶν ὄντων τυγχάνει χρώματι ἀεὶ ἑπόμενον, 75*c*). It is true, as Meno remarks, that such a " definition " would involve the undefined term " colour." A pugnacious eristic would ignore this criticism ; he would retort that he had done his part in giving his own definition and that any amendment of it was the business of his antagonist. But we are not disputing for victory, and Socrates is ready to meet the criticism by attempting a better definition. Meno will admit that he knows what mathematicians mean by a " boundary " ; if we say then that " figure is the boundary of a solid " (στερεοῦ πέρας), the statement will hold good universally and exclusively, and not be open to the criticism that it introduces a second " unknown " (76*a*).

Meno should now attempt a similar definition of goodness, but irrelevantly insists that Socrates shall go on to define colour. This, as Socrates says, is the mere whim of a capricious " beauty," but he will comply with it. Meno at any rate will be satisfied by a definition based on the doctrine of Gorgias, which is derived from the " efflux " theory of Empedocles.[1] Assuming this theory, we may say that colour is " an efflux from surfaces which fits into the passages of the visual apparatus and is sensible " (ἀπορροὴ σχημάτων ὄψει σύμμετρος καὶ αἰσθητός, 76*d*), a definition which Meno thinks

---

[1] For the Empedoclean theory of the part played by these " effluxes " and the " passages " in the sense-organs into which they fit, see Theophrastus *de Sensu*, 7–9, and the criticism of Aristotle *de Generat.* A 324*b* 25ff., *de Sensu*, 437*b* 23ff., with the striking fragment 84 of Empedocles, quoted by Aristotle, *de Sensu*, 437*b* 26 [*R.P.* 177*b*, *c*] ; Burnet, *Early Greek Philosophy* [3], 246–249. The definition is based on the Empedoclean theory because Gorgias, as a Sicilian, is assumed to be in accord with the biological views of the founder of Sicilian medicine. Quintilian iii. 1, 8 [*R.P.* 232] gives it as the " tradition " that Gorgias had originally been a " disciple " of E. Cf. D.L. viii. 58–59. In the *Timaeus* Plato makes his spokesman, who is represented as holding the principles of the Sicilian medicine, give the same account of colours. (*Tim.* 67*c*–68*d*.)

admirable, though Socrates calls it "stagy" and says it is inferior to that just given of figure.[1]

Meno at last makes an attempt at the definition of goodness. It is "to desire the fine things and to be able to secure them" (ἐπιθυμοῦντα τῶν καλῶν δυνατὸν εἶναι πορίζεσθαι, 77b). But the statement is doubly open to criticism. (a) It implies that it is *possible* to desire what is not "fine," that is, to "desire evil." But, in fact, no one can or does desire what he knows to be evil, for that would be equivalent to the impossibility of desiring to be unhappy (77c–78b). The first clause of Meno's definition is thus superfluous, and it reduces to the statement that goodness is "ability to secure goods." (b) By "goods" he means, as he explains, such things as wealth, health, and high civic and social distinction (the ends, be it noted, of the "body-loving" and "distinction-loving" lives). But we cannot call ability to get these things by any means, fair or foul, *goodness*; it would be truer to say that the virtuous man is *in*capable of gaining fortune or position by foul means. So we have to introduce the qualification that goodness is capacity to secure good things "by righteous" or "honest" means, or something to that effect. Now righteousness, honesty, or whatever other qualifications we introduce, have already been admitted to be "parts" of goodness, so that we are in effect saying that goodness or virtue is attaining certain ends by the practice of some specific virtue (*i.e.* we introduce one or more of the determinants of a given determinable into a proposed definition of that determinable itself, and thus commit a vicious "circle," 77b–79e). We are thus no nearer to a satisfactory definition than we were before.

Meno is half inclined to lay the blame for the collapse of the argument on Socrates, who, he says, has the reputation of always being bepuzzled himself and communicating his bewilderment to others. He benumbs men's wits as the fish called νάρκη benumbs their muscles if they touch it. In any other company Meno would have plenty to say about "goodness," but in the presence of Socrates he is "paralysed." In any foreign city Socrates would run a real risk of being arrested for sorcery. Socrates has to admit the accusation, with the reservation that the comparison with the νάρκη is only apt on the assumption that the creature itself is as "numb" as its victims. The difficulties his conversation creates in others are only the reflection of those he finds in his own thinking. But if Meno will adventure on the definition of "goodness" over again, he will do his best to examine the new result (80 a–d). At this point Meno again tries to run off on an irrelevant issue. He brings up the "sophistic" puzzle which we have already met in

---

[1] Why does Socrates prefer the definition of figure to that of colour? Presumably because the second implies a detailed physical and physiological speculation which is highly problematic; the other presupposes only the principles of geometry, and geometry is an indubitable "science." The definition of colour is τραγική, "stagy," because it makes a show with grand words which are only a cover for imprecision and uncertainty.

the *Euthydemus*, that " inquiry " is impossible because you cannot inquire after something you already know, nor yet after what you do not know (since, in the second case, you would not even recognize the object you were looking for, if you should succeed in finding it). This dilemma, however, would cease to be a difficulty if there should be truth in a doctrine which Socrates has learned from " priests and priestesses who have been at the pains to understand their professional duties " and also from Pindar and other poets. The doctrine is that our soul is immortal and our present life only one episode in its history. If this is so, the soul must long ago have " learned " everything, and only needs to be " put in mind " of something it has temporarily forgotten in order to regain its knowledge by diligent following of the clue provided by " reminiscence." Learning, in fact, is just a process of " re-call " (ἀνάμνησις), and for this reason the sophistic argument to show that it is impossible to learn a new truth is a mere appeal to mental indolence (80*e*–82*a*). (As we are encountering the doctrine of " recollection " for the first time, it is worth while to note what the exact point of it is. It must be observed that it is not a theory of " innate ideas," or " innate knowledge," in the popular sense of the words. We are not supposed to bring any actual knowledge into the world ready-made with us. On the contrary, we are said to " have learned " truth but to have lost it again, and we have to recover what we have lost. The recovery requires a real and prolonged effort of steady thinking ; what " recollection," or more accurately " being reminded," does for us is to provide the starting-point for this effort. In the *Phaedo*, this is illustrated by the way in which chance " associations " will start a train of thinking, as when the sight of an absent friend's belongings or his portrait sets us thinking of the friend himself. The main emphasis thus falls not on the Orphic doctrine of pre-existence and re-incarnation, which Socrates professes to have learned from poets and priests, but on the function of sense-experience as suggestive of and pregnant with truths of an intelligible order which it does not itself adequately embody or establish. And the philosophical importance of the doctrine is not that it proves the immortality of the soul,[1] but that it shows that the acquisition of knowledge is not a matter of passively receiving " instruction," but one of following up a personal effort of thinking once started by an arresting sense-experience. But for this " suggestiveness " of sense-experience the *ignava ratio* of the eristic, " you cannot learn the truth from any teacher, because unless you know it already, you will not recognize it for the truth when he utters it," would be valid. We see, then, why both Socrates and Plato hold that " knowledge " can only be won by

---

[1] In the *Phaedo* itself the argument is found insufficient to meet the formidable difficulty raised by Cebes that even if pre-existence is true, it gives us no guarantee that we shall continue to be after the dissolution of our present body. For the illustrations from " association," see *Phaedo*, 73*c* ff.

personal participation in " research " ; it cannot simply be handed on from one man to another.[1]

An illustration of the principle that " learning " is really " being reminded of something," *i.e.* is the following up by personal effort of the suggestions of sense-experience, may now be given. Socrates calls forward the lad who is attending on Meno, after satisfying himself that the boy can understand a question in plain Greek, but has never been taught any mathematics, and undertakes to show how he can be brought to see geometrical truths for himself by merely asking appropriate questions which enable the answerer to correct his own first hasty thoughts. The point to be established is that the areas of squares are proportional to the second powers of the lengths of their sides, and in particular that the area of a square described on the diagonal of one previously described is double the area of the original figure.[2] We are to think of Socrates, of course, as drawing the requisite figure, which will be found in any commentary on the *Meno*, in the sand as he speaks. The boy's first thought is that if we want to make a square with twice the area of a given one, we must make its sides twice as long. (That is, he argues, " since $2^2 = 2 \times 2$, $4^2 = 2 \times 4$.) He is easily made to see for himself that this cannot be true (since $4 \times 4 = 16$), and amends his first answer by suggesting that the side of the second square should be to that of the first as 3 to 2 (*i.e.* he suggests that $3^2 = 8$). Again it is easy to get him to see that this is impossible (since $3 \times 3 = 9$). The length of the line we require must be greater than that of our original line, but less than half as great again ($\sqrt{2} > 1 < \frac{3}{2}$). And with a few more questions, the lad is led to see that the line we require as the base of our second square is no other than the diagonal of our original figure ($82b–85b$).[3] The point insisted on is that the lad starts with a false proposition, is led to replace it by one less erroneous, and finally by one which, so far as it goes, is true. Yet Socrates has " told " him nothing. He has merely drawn diagrams which suggest the right answers to a series of questions. The only " information " he has imparted to the slave is that a certain line is technically called by " the sophists," *i.e.* " professionals," a " diagonal." Everything else has been left to the boy to think out for himself in response to the suggestions provided by Socrates' diagrams and questions. Yet undeniably

[1] See the language on this point of Plato, *Ep.* vii. 341c. Perhaps I may refer to the statement of the theory in my little volume, *Platonism and its Influence* (Boston, U.S.A., 1925) c. 2, as well as to Burnet, *Greek Philosophy, Part I.*, pp. 220–222.

[2] The particular theorem is chosen, no doubt, because of the importance of the " side and diagonal " as the most elementary instance of a pair of " incommensurable " magnitudes.

[3] Thus, to put it arithmetically, what has been proved is that $\sqrt{2}$ lies somewhere between 1 and 1·5. In the famous passage *Rep.* 546b ff. it is made clear that Socrates, in fact, knows quite well how to construct the whole series of fractions which form the " successive convergents " to $\sqrt{2}$. For his purpose here it is enough to consider the " second convergent," $\frac{3}{2}$, and to show that this is too large a value.

the lad began by not knowing something and ended by knowing it. Thus he "brought up the knowledge from within" (ἀναλαβὼν αὐτὸς ἐξ αὑτοῦ τὴν ἐπιστήμην), and such a process is "being reminded," "recalling" something. We infer then that the slave once "had" the knowledge he had forgotten, and since he has never in this life been "taught" geometry, the "once" must have been "before he was a man,"[1] and thus we see that the soul is immortal. (Socrates, however, hastens to remark that he would not care to be too confident about anything in the theory except the main point that it proves that we can arrive at truth and thus saves us from the sloth and self-neglect which are natural consequences of the eristic *ignava ratio* (86b).[2])

We have wandered away far from our original question about the teachability of goodness, and Meno is anxious to have that answered without further digression. The humour of the situation is that this is impossible. We cannot really expect to know whether goodness or anything else can be taught unless we first know what the thing in question *is*, as we have admitted that we do not. But we may give a tentative and provisional answer to the question ἐξ ὑποθέσεως, subject to an initial postulate, *sous condition*. Only we must make another digression to explain what we mean by this restriction. If you ask a geometer whether a certain problem is soluble, he may often have to say that he does not know whether the problem has a perfectly general solution or not, but that he can give a solution for it, subject to a specified restriction. This is illustrated for us by the example of a problem about the inscription of a triangle of given area in a circle of given diameter. The geometer may be unable to say whether the inscription can be effected unless the data are further specified by some restricting condition. He will then answer that "I cannot solve your problem as it stands, but *if* the area in question satisfies the condition X, the inscription is possible."[3]   So we, in our present state of uncertainty

---

[1] The same way of speaking about our ante-natal condition as the "time when we were not yet men" is characteristic of the *Phaedo*. It implies that the true self is not, as is commonly thought, the embodied soul, but the soul *simpliciter*, the body being the instrument (ὄργανον) which the soul "uses," and the consequent definition of "man" as a "soul using a body as its instrument." Since that which "uses" an implement is always superior to the implement it uses, this definition merely embodies the Socratic conviction that the soul is the thing of supreme value in us.

[2] The caution should not be understood to mean that Socrates doubts the *fact* of immortality. His firm belief in that is the assumption of the *Phaedo* and is really presupposed by *Apolog.* 40c–41c. He means, as he says, that he will not go bail for the λόγος; it is not really a complete demonstration of pre-existence and immortality, as is frankly admitted in the *Phaedo*, though, no doubt, it suggests their possibility. The real reason why Socrates attaches so much importance to the doctrine of "reminiscence" (ἀνάμνησις) is independent of the use of it as an argument for "survival." One should be careful to bear in mind that ἀνάμνησις does not properly mean in the theory "remembering," but "being reminded of" something. Sensible experiences are always "suggesting" to us "ideal" standards which none of them actually exhibit.

[3] The precise character of the restriction imposed by the geometer in Socrates' illustration has been a matter of much dispute, which is due partly

about the true character of goodness, can only answer Meno's question *sous condition* If goodness is knowledge, *then* it is something which can be taught, *i.e.* according to the theory of learning we have just laid down, something which can be " recalled to mind " (ἀναμνηστόν, 87b) ; if goodness is anything other than knowledge, it cannot be taught. (We now see the real purpose of the introduction of the doctrine of ἀνάμνησις. The object is to show that though the " teachability " of goodness is a direct consequence of the Socratic principle that " goodness is knowledge," Socrates does not mean, as some of the " sophists " seem to have done, that a man can become good by any mere passive listening to the " instructions " of a lecturer, since no knowledge whatever is acquired in this way ; *all* " learning " is an active response of personal thought and effort to the " hints " derived from a more mature fellow-learner.)

Goodness, then, can be taught, if goodness is knowledge and not otherwise, and we are thrown back on the antecedent question whether goodness is or is not knowledge. (Thus we conform to the rule of order laid down at *Phaedo* 101c–e. We first consider what are the " consequences," συμβαίνοντα, of a " postulate " ; only when we are clear on this preliminary question do we go on to ask whether the " postulate " itself can be " justified.") To answer our new question, we have again to start with an unproved " postulate," the ὑπόθεσις that ἀρετή is a good thing. (No question arises of a " justification " of *this* ὑπόθεσις, because both Socrates and Meno accept it as common ground ; it is an ἱκανόν τι such as is spoken of in the passage of the *Phaedo* about logical method.) It follows at once that if knowledge is the only good, " goodness " or " virtue " (ἀρετή) must be knowledge ; if there are other goods besides knowledge, it is *possible* that ἀρετή may be one of these other goods (87d). Thus we find ourselves driven in the end to face the ultimate question whether knowledge is not the *only* good, or at any rate an indispensable constituent of all good. This question is now treated in the way already familiar to us. Whatever is good is " beneficial " (ὠφελιμόν), *i.e. does* us good. Now the commonly recognized goods are such things as health, physical strength, comeliness, and we may add, wealth. But none of these is " unconditionally " good ; all *may* " harm " their possessor ; they benefit him when they are rightly used but harm him when they are misused. So with the commonly recognized good characters of the " soul," of which Socrates proceeds to give a list. Courage, in the popular sense, covers " daring " or " venturesomeness " (θάρρος) of every kind. But though venturesomeness combined with sound sense (νοῦς) is beneficial, senseless daring is harmful to its possessor, and the same thing is true of σωφροσύνη, " appetitive coldness," retentive memory, and qualities of soul generally. To

to uncertainty about the technical terminology of geometers in the fifth century. For our purpose it is sufficient to grasp the main point that there are such restrictions. It is, *e.g.*, obvious that some restricting condition must connect the area of the given triangle with the radius of the given circle.
For a correct solution see A. S. L. Farquharson in *C.Q.*, xvii. 1 (Jan. 1923).

be beneficial, they must be accompanied by intelligence or under-standing (φρόνησις) ; they, too, are harmful when misused. We infer, then, that the goodness of all other good things is conditional on the " goodness of soul " of the possessor, and this again conditional on his intelligence (φρόνησις). It follows that intelligence, or some specific form of intelligence (ἤτοι σύμπασα ἤ μέρος τι), is identical with " goodness," and therefore that " men are not good by nature," *i.e.* goodness is not a matter of congenital *endowment* (as Callicles maintains in the *Gorgias* for example, 87*d*–89*a*).[1]

This last inference admits at once of empirical verification, for if goodness were congenital endowment, we could detect its presence in early life, and so we could secure a succession of true statesmen by merely selecting the properly endowed natures in early life and bringing them up " under guard," carefully isolated from all risks of contamination.[2] Yet, on second thoughts, we may see reason to distrust our identification of goodness with knowledge. If it were knowledge, surely there would be professional teachers of it and they would have " pupils." But there does not appear to be any such " profession." It is lucky for us that Anytus has just taken a seat by our side at this point of the conversation. He is the son of a worthy citizen who made a fortune by steady intelli-gence and industry ; the popular judgment is clearly that he has had an excellent early training and education, as is shown by his repeated election to high offices. His opinion on the question whether there are " teachers of goodness " ought therefore to be highly valuable (89*b*–90*b*).

(Why does Plato introduce Anytus at this particular point ? Note that he is not supposed to have heard the preceding discussion, which he would have been quite incapable of appreciating. He comes up to the bench on which Socrates and Meno are sitting, and joins them just in the nick of time, as they are beginning to consider the problem about the professional teachers of goodness. Nor is there any appearance of " irony " in what is said about him ; unlike Xenophon, Plato never suggests that Anytus had any dis-creditable private motives for supporting the prosecution of Socrates. The irony of the passage only concerns Anytus to the same degree

---

[1] Note again the exact correspondence of the Socratic argument for the identity of virtue and knowledge with Kant's argument for the thesis that the only unconditional good is the " good will." Kant's further proposal to make conformity with the bare form of a universal imperative the direct and sufficient criterion of right action might be said to be simply a reckless develop-ment of one side of the Socratic ethics, its " intellectualism," in unreal isolation from its " eudaemonism."

[2] It might be objected, is not this selection, here assumed to be impossible, actually proposed as the very foundation of the " ideal state " in the *Republic* ? The answer is No. In the *Republic* it is, of course, recognized that endowment counts for something, and therefore there is an early initial selection of pro-mising future " guardians." But educational tradition counts for much more ; hence the length at which the problem of the creation of a right educational tradition is discussed, and the provision for promotions and degradations at all stages according as the subject under education justifies or belies his early " promise."

as the whole of the Athenian public who respect and trust him. It is clearly meant that, to the measure of his intelligence, Anytus is an able and public-spirited man who deserves the trust he receives. This defect, one which he shares with the whole Athenian public, is simply that he is an *esprit borné*. He has the average Athenian democratic prejudice against men who are "too clever," the *intelligentsia*, and the average Athenian's incapacity for ever calling his own prejudices in question, and it is just because he is such a "representative man" that the public trust him. The purpose of bringing him in is clearly to make us realize the violence of the Athenian prejudice against the "intellectuals," and the inability of even a well-to-do and "educated" public man to discriminate between Socrates and the "intellectuals by profession." If Socrates could be so misconceived by the "leaders of public opinion," we understand how he came to be prosecuted without needing to impute his fate to anything worse than honest stupidity.)

If you wish a young man to learn a science such as medicine or an accomplishment such as flute-playing, to whom do you send him? You always select a teacher who claims to be a professional expert, and for that very reason charges a fee for his instructions; you would never think of putting him under a mere "amateur" who does not make a profession of imparting his own skill. It should seem, then, that statesmanship, the science of the right conduct of affairs and the right manage of life must, by parity of reasoning, be learned from the specialists who claim to have made a profession of teaching its principles, and consequently, like all professionals, charge a fee—that is, from the "sophists, as men call them." Anytus has the profoundest horror of the whole profession; they are, he says, as every one can see, mere depravers and corrupters of all who frequent their lectures. Yet it is difficult to accept this view of them. It would be a unique fact that any class should make a paying profession of visibly spoiling the materials entrusted to it.[1] In point of fact, Protagoras made a considerable fortune by the trade of "teaching goodness," and he exercised it for over forty years. Thus there was plenty of time for him to be found out in, but he never was found out, and his high reputation has survived him to this day, and he is not the only example in point.[2] Anytus is quite sure, though he is thankful he has never in his life had to do with a sophist, that the sophist is a designing scoundrel,

---

[1] *E.g.* the medical profession would not continue to provide anyone with a living wage if medical men really killed off their patients. In real life a "faculty" of Sangrados would be "found out." Anytus supposes that the "sophists" *have* been found out, and yet contrive to grow fat on their quackery.

[2] I think we are bound to take the observations about Protagoras (*Meno*, 91d–e) quite seriously. Socrates seriously means that the lifelong success of Protagoras, and the high esteem in which he was and is held, show that the democratic view that there was nothing at all in him, that he was "a palpable and mischievous impostor," is far too simple to account for the facts. Protagoras may not have been all he supposed himself to be, but there must have been *something* in him to inspire such long-continued trust and veneration.

and the society which does not make penal laws to suppress him **a**
silly dupe. But, however true his views may be—though by his
own showing he must be arriving at them by " divination "—they
are not to the point. The question is not who are the corrupters
of youth, but who are the " teachers of goodness " from whom the
young may learn the true principles of the conduct of life. Anytus
holds that we need specify no particular professional teachers ; the
conduct of life can be learned from any " decent " Athenian, and
he has learned it from his father, who learned it again from his.
It is simply a matter of imbibing an hereditary tradition—a view
illustrated in the *Protagoras* by the way in which children pick up
their mother-tongue or their father's trade without any formal
teaching or apprenticeship (*Protag.* 327e ff.). To doubt the possibility of this would amount to denying that there have been " good
men " in Athens (90c–93a).

Socrates does not deny that there are and have been at Athens
men who are " good at citizenship " (ἀγαθοὶ τὰ πολιτικά),[1] but what
he does doubt is whether such men have also been competent
teachers of the goodness they practise. The difficulty is that the
sons of these men have all proved either worthless or insignificant.
Thus they clearly did not teach their goodness themselves to their
sons, and it is notorious that even those of them who, like
Themistocles, were careful to have their sons trained in mere elegant
accomplishments, never sent them to anyone for special education
in " goodness." The obvious inference is that the " good Athenians,"
whom Anytus regards as competent teachers of goodness, do not
think themselves or anyone else competent to teach it ; they must
have supposed that goodness is not the kind of thing which can be
taught. Anytus is so chafed at having to listen to such unsparing
criticism of the eminent figures of the national history that he misses
the point and relapses into silence with an angry warning to Socrates
that the Athenian democracy is no safe abode for a man who will
not learn to bridle his tongue,[2]—a plain hint, on Plato's part, that

---

[1] It has been suggested by Th. Gomperz that these words are meant to
soften down the asperity of the declaration of the *Gorgias* that none of the
great figures of Athenian democracy was a true statesman, and even that the
chief motive of Plato in writing the *Meno* was to placate a public opinion
naturally irritated by such utterances. This seems to me hopelessly fanciful.
(*a*) There is really no " recantation " in the *Meno*. The democratic leaders
had been denied in the *Gorgias* to be statesmen on the ground that they were
empirics, whereas statesmanship is a *science*. According to the *Meno*, these
same leaders are so convinced that their own " goodness " is not teachable
that they make no attempt to get it taught to their sons. This is just the
criticism of the *Gorgias* put in other words. (*b*) In one respect the *Meno*
goes further than the *Gorgias*. That dialogue had conceded Athens at least
one genuine statesman, Aristides " the just " (*Gorgias*, 526b). In the *Meno*
Aristides figures among the rest of the famous men who must have supposed
that goodness cannot be taught, since he never had it taught to his son
(*Meno*, 94a).

[2] Hannibal Chollop's advice to Mark Tapley, " You had better crack us up,
you had," is much the same as that Anytus gives to Socrates, and in both
cases the warning is probably not meant unkindly.

it was just this sort of unsparing and impartial free speech about the democracy and its leaders which caused the mistaken but intelligible suspicion of *incivisme* to attach to the philosopher (93*b*–95*a*). That Socrates was really in the habit of employing these criticisms is clear from the fact that the very same use of the argument about statesmen and their sons occurs both in the *Protagoras* and in the *Alcibiades*.

The sophists may, in any case, be dismissed from the discussion, since Meno, on the whole, agrees with Anytus that they cannot teach goodness and thinks it a point in favour of Gorgias that he disclaimed the pretension. In fact, most men, like the poet Theognis, find themselves unable to make up their minds whether goodness is teachable or not. They say " Yes " and " No," according to their moods. Goodness is thus in a uniquely unfortunate position. The claims of the professional teachers are generally disbelieved, and the persons whose practice is generally admired cannot make up their own minds whether their specialty can be taught. It looks as though there were neither teachers nor learners of goodness, and consequently that it is not a thing which can be taught. But how, then, is it ever produced, as we must admit that it is ? On second thoughts, we see a way out of the difficulty. Knowledge is not the only thing which is beneficial in practice. A right belief ($\dot{o}\rho\theta\dot{\eta}\ \delta\dot{o}\xi a$) will direct practice as satisfactorily as genuine knowledge. A guide who had a right belief about the road to Larissa would take you there as successfully as one who really knew the way. For practical purposes, then, a right belief is as good as knowledge—but for one trifling drawback. There would be no practical difference, if you could make sure that a man will always retain his right belief. But beliefs are like the fabled statues of Daedalus, which can walk away if they are not fastened to their place. The statues are fine pieces of work, but their price is naturally low if they are loose. So a correct belief is a fine thing, if it will only stay with you, but it will not stay long unless you fasten it down $a\dot{i}\tau\dot{i}as\ \lambda o\gamma\iota\sigma\mu\hat{\omega}$ " by thinking out the reason why " of it (98*a*), and this process is what we have already called " being reminded " ($\dot{a}\nu\dot{a}\mu\nu\eta\sigma\iota s$). When we have thought out the " reason why," the belief becomes knowledge and is abiding. We may apply this distinction to the solution of our problem.

The " eminently good men " of Athens plainly do not owe their usefulness as political leaders to knowledge, for if they did, they could teach " statesmanship " to others. Themistocles and the rest were therefore not " scientific statesmen," not $\sigma o\phi o\dot{i}$ (99*b*)— the conclusion also reached in the *Gorgias*—and it is absurd to think they owed all their achievements to accident. Their successes must have been due to " correct opinions " ($\epsilon\dot{v}\delta o\xi\dot{i}a$, 99*b*). They were much on a level with givers of oracles and diviners, who often say very true things without knowing it (since the responses are delivered in a sort of temporary " frenzy "). Thus we may class together " seers," poets, and statesmen, as beings who all say and

do brilliant things without really knowing what they are saying
or doing, because they are all acting in a state of " possession,"
though Anytus, perhaps, will not like our conclusion (95*b*–99*e*).[1]
To sum up, then : goodness is neither inborn nor yet learned from
teachers, but arises from a happy irrational " divine possession "
(θείᾳ μοίρᾳ ἄνευ νοῦ), unless, indeed, there could arise a statesman
who could teach statesmanship to others. His "goodness" would
be to that of other men what substance is to shadow. We must,
however, remember that our conclusion is tentative ; we cannot
say with certainty how goodness arises until we have answered the
still outstanding question what it is. In the meanwhile Meno
would be doing Athens a service if he could make Anytus more sympathetic with our point of view (99*e*–100*c*).

The full meaning of these last remarks only comes out when we
read them in the light of the *Republic* and *Phaedo*. The " statesman who can make another a statesman " is just the philosopher-
king of the *Republic*, where the crowning achievement of the "ideal
state " is to make provision for the permanent teaching of a statesmanship which is *science*, clear intellectual insight into fundamental
moral principles, not a succession of " inspired " adventures, and
the provision takes the form of a system of thorough education in
hard scientific thinking which culminates in the direct apprehension
of " the good." In the light of this educational scheme, we can
see that the main object of the concluding argument in the *Meno*
is to distinguish between a higher and a lower kind of goodness.
The higher kind is that which the *Republic* calls the goodness of the
philosopher, and it is based upon certain and assured personal
knowledge of the true scale of goods, and is therefore " abiding."
The lower kind, which is at best a " shadow " of true goodness, is
based on " opinions " which are true, but are not knowledge, and
therefore not to be counted on as permanent ; in fact, it rests on
acceptance of a sound tradition of living which has not been converted into personal insight into the scale of goods. This is all
which is demanded in the *Republic* even of the soldiers of the
State ; their goodness is loyalty to a tradition of noble living in
which they have been brought up, but of which they have never
even asked the reason why, life by an exalted standard of "honour."
Since there are sound elements in the moral tradition of any
civilized community, it is possible for an Athenian statesman in
whom the best traditions of his city are inbred to " profit " the
State by goodness of this inferior kind, " popular goodness," as the
Phaedo calls it. But security for permanent continuance in well-
doing is only to be had when a sound traditional code of conduct
has been converted into " knowledge " by understanding of the

[1] Socrates regards the achievements of a Themistocles or a Pericles as
"wizardry," but he does not mean this as a compliment. "Possession"
was popularly regarded as a kind of disease, and we have only to go to Aristophanes to see what the current estimate of χρησμῳδοί and θεομάντεις was.
The effect of his classification is much that which might be produced to-day by
speaking together of " ventriloquists, mediums, and cabinet ministers."

" reason why," that is by personal insight into the character of good and personal understanding of the place of each of the " goods " of life in the hierarchy of good. Thus the true statesman would be the Socratic philosopher who understands the principle that the " tendance of the *soul* " is the supreme business of both individual and State, and judges soundly of the nature of the " spiritual health " at which the " tendance " aims. Of course, we readily see that " philosophic goodness," being thus identical with *knowledge* of true good, must be " teachable," if you go to work the right way, whereas a " goodness " which does not repose on apprehension of principles cannot be taught ; it can only be " imbibed " by habituation in conformity to a tradition. The vacillation of mankind in their attitude to the teachability of virtue is thus to be explained by the ambiguity of the word " goodness " ; men are dimly aware that real goodness depends on grasp of intelligible principles and thus ought to be teachable, but they confuse this real goodness with its shadow, loyalty to an established tradition *qua* established, and common experience shows that this, however it is to be secured, cannot be secured by teaching. The contributions of the dialogue to the theory of knowledge, the exposition of the doctrine of " reminiscence " and of the principles of method, with all their importance, are meant to be secondary to this main result ; the account of pre-existence and immortality, again, is strictly subordinate to the theory of ἀνάμνησις itself. It would be a complete misunderstanding to find the main purport of the dialogue in these things, though there is no reason to doubt that they were connected in the personal *Welt-Anschauung* of Socrates with his main tenet, the supreme worth of the ψυχή and its specific good, knowledge.

See further :

RITTER, C.—*Platon*, i. 391–449 (*Gorgias*), 476–484 (*Meno*).

RAEDER, H.—*Platons philosophische Entwickelung*, 111–125 (*Gorgias*), 130–137 (*Meno*).

THOMPSON, W. H.—The *Gorgias* of Plato.

NETTLESHIP, R. L.—*Plato's Conception of Goodness and the Good* (*Lectures and Remains*, i. 238–394).

DIÈS, A.—*Autour de Platon*, ii. 414–418, 462–469.

STEWART, J. A.—*Myths of Plato*, 1–76 (*Introduction*), 114–132 (*The Gorgias Myth*) ; *Plato's Doctrine of Ideas*, 24–29 (*Meno*), 29–34 (*Gorgias*).

STENZEL, J.—*Platon der Erzieher*, 147–178.

CHAPTER VII

SOCRATIC DIALOGUES : *EUTHYPHRO, APOLOGY, CRITO*

I HAVE reserved these well-known dialogues for consideration at this point for the simple reason that it is difficult to
separate them from the *Phaedo*; thus it is natural to make
the treatment of them the immediate prelude to a study of the
four great works in which Plato's dramatic genius shows itself
most perfect. I do not mean to imply that I regard the whole
series of dialogues which centre round the trial and death of Socrates
as uninterruptedly following one another in order of composition.
As I have already explained, I do not feel satisfied that we are safe
in saying more on the question than that the slighter works we are
considering must, at least in the main, be regarded as earlier than
the four great dramatic dialogues. It is possible, perhaps even
probable, that at any rate the *Apology* may have been written
before several of the works we have already dealt with, but the
probability need not affect our treatment if it is true, as the present
analysis tries to show, that there is no serious variation in the
doctrine of Plato's dialogues until we come to the series unmistakably shown by style to be later than the *Republic*. In treating of
the whole series of these " dialogues of the trial and imprisonment "
I shall avail myself fully of the commentaries of Professor Burnet
(*Euthyphro, Apology, Crito*, 1924; *Phaedo*, 1911); this will make it
possible to aim at a brevity which I should have been only too glad
to secure for some other parts of this book.

1. *Euthyphro.*—On all questions connected with the scene and
personages of the dialogue, see Burnet's *Introductory Note*, to which
I would only append the following remarks. It is not certain that
the Euthyphro of our dialogue is the person of the same name whom
we have encountered in the *Cratylus*, though this is possible. If
the two men are one and the same, we shall clearly have to think of
Euthyphro as now in middle age and his father as a man of some
seventy-five or more. To my own mind, the tone of the conversation is consistent with these suppositions and inconsistent with
regarding Euthyphro as in any sense young. (He is a familiar
figure in the *ecclesia* which he often addresses.) I fully agree with
Burnet that the supposed proceedings by Euthyphro against his
father as a murderer must be historical fact ; the situation is too
bizarre to be a natural fiction. Also I think it clear that legally

Euthyphro had no case and was probably non-suited by the *Basileus*, but I would add that in all probability Euthyphro himself counted on this issue. His object, as he explains at 4c, is to clear *himself* from the religious pollution incurred by being in any way accessory to a φόνος. If he files an information against his father, even with full knowledge that it will be dismissed on technical grounds, he has done all that a scrupulous conscience can require. Any possible " pollution " will henceforth rest not on him but on the authorities, and he would probably feel himself free for the future to live in ordinary family relations with his father. This is presumably what he wished to do. We need not suppose that he expects or desires any grave consequences to happen to the old gentleman. As to the main purpose of the dialogue, again, I think Burnet is clearly right. As both Plato and Aeschines represent, Socrates had lived in association with religious ascetics and mystics of the Orphic type ; every one also knew that he had been formally convicted of some kind of religious innovation. The natural inference would have been that he was himself a sectary much of the same type as Euthyphro, as Euthyphro seems to suppose. It was a duty of piety to his memory to make it clear that his views on religion were very different from those of a sect who found the " deep things of God " in stories like those of the binding of Cronus and the mutilation of Uranus—tales which had nothing to do with the official worship of Athens and· were repulsive to the ordinary Athenian. It is equally clear that Euthyphro is not intended, as has often been said, to represent " Athenian orthodoxy," *i.e.* the attitude of the dicasts who voted for the conviction of Socrates, since, as Burnet points out, he instinctively takes the side of Socrates as soon as he has heard the nature of the charge against him, and classes Socrates and himself together as theologians exposed to the unintelligent derision of the " vulgar." [1]

Ostensibly the problem of the dialogue is to determine the real character of ὁσιότης, "piety," or as we should probably say now, " religion," that part of right conduct which is concerned with man's duty to God. As usual, no final result is expressly arrived at, but the interest lies in the comparison of two different conceptions of what " religion " is. The conclusion to which we seem to be coming, but for an unexpected difficulty, is that religion is the " art of traffic between man and gods," or the art of receiving from the gods and giving to them (*Euthyphro*, 14d, e). On the face of it, this is a view of religion thoroughly in keeping with the more sordid side of the ancient State cultus, which was very much regulated

[1] See the full treatment of all this in Burnet, *op. cit.* pp. 2–7. As to the ordinary Athenian estimate of the Hesiodic stories about Uranus and Cronus, see Aristophanes, *Clouds*, 904, Isocrates, xi. 38–40. How far the Athenians were from taking Cronus seriously is sufficiently shown by the simple fact that κρόνος is Attic for " old Methusalem " or " Rip van Winkle." Even the allusion of Aeschylus, *Ag.* 168 ff., 'has a touch of contempt for the unnamed being who is now " down and out " (τριακτῆρος οἴχεται τυχών) and the " bully " who preceded him (παμμάχῳ θράσει βρύων).

on the *do ut des* principle. It exactly hits off, for example, the spirit of *religio* as understood in the early days of the Roman republic. Hence it is not surprising that more than one editor (Adam, Burnet) should have found the real point of the dialogue in a hint thrown out, but not followed up, a little earlier (*Euthyphro*, 13e), that religion should rather be thought of as the co-operation of man with God towards some noble result (πάγκαλον ἔργον) which is left unspecified. It is at least certain that the making of this point is one of the main objects of the discussion, and that the view is shown to arise directly out of the application to religion of the notion of " tendance " (θεραπεία), so fundamental in the Socratic ethics. But I think it would probably be mistaken to suppose that the other formula is intended to be rejected as conveying a selfish and sordid conception of religion. In the sense put upon it by ordinary Athenian practice, and apparently by Euthyphro himself, that religion consists in knowing how to perform a ritual worship which will procure tangible returns for the worshipper, the formula is, no doubt, sordid enough and wholly at variance with the conception of God and the service of God attributed to Socrates throughout the dialogues. But this interpretation is not the only one which could be put on the phrase. If we think rightly of the blessings for which it is proper to pray, it will be a worthy conception of religion that it *is* an intercourse between man and God in which we offer " acceptable sacrifice " and receive in return the true goods of soul and body.[1] And there can be no doubt both that " praying and sacrificing aright " are ὁσιότης and that ὁσιότης, since it is virtue or a part of virtue, is in the Socratic view an ἐπιστήμη or τέχνη, an application of knowledge to the regulation of practice. Plato himself, who deals with the regulation of institutional religion at length in the *Laws*, would have had nothing in principle against such a formula, rightly interpreted. The early Academy seem to have been right in including among their definitions of " piety " (εὐσέβεια) alternative formulæ which are obviously conflations of the different suggestions of our dialogue, " a faculty of the voluntary service of the gods ; right belief about honouring the gods ; the science of honouring the gods." [2] Hence I do not feel at liberty to treat the two suggestions about the nature of religion as meant to be exclusive of one another.

A very brief analysis of the argument will enable us to re-

[1] Cf. the model of an acceptable prayer offered by Socrates, *Phaedrus*, 279c, and the conception of δαίμονες as the middlemen in the " traffic between man and God " in the speech of Diotima reproduced by Socrates in *Symposium*, 202e.

[2] [Plat.] *Def.* 412e 14, δύναμις θεραπευτικὴ θεῶν ἐκούσιος· περὶ θεῶν τιμῆς ὑπόληψις ὀρθή· ἐπιστήμη περὶ θεῶν τιμῆς. Cf. the definition of ἀγνεία (*ibid.* 414a 12), τῆς θεοῦ τιμῆς κατὰ φύσιν θεραπεία, and of ὅσιον (*ibid.* 415a 9), θεράπευμα θεοῦ ἀρεστὸν θεῷ. That the Academic definitions of our Plato MSS. in the main belong to the earliest days of the Academy is shown by the frequent appeals made to them in Aristotle, especially in the *Topics*. In some cases the testimony of Aristotle enables us to refer a definition specifically to Speusippus or Xenocrates as the author.

discover in the *Euthyphro* the principal points of both ethical and metaphysical doctrine with which we are already familiar.

The act for which Euthyphro is arraigning his father, we must remember, is specifically an offence against religious law, not a civil wrong, and Euthyphro does not profess to be in any way actuated by motives of humanity or regard for civil right. He is afraid of incurring religious " pollution " by living in household relations with a " sacrilegious person," and wishes to safeguard himself. It is implied that the average Athenian, who is shocked at his procedure, is ignorant of or indifferent to the religious law in which Euthyphro considers himself an expert. Obviously, then, as a " doctor in theology " he may be presumed to know what we might call " canon law " in its entirety, not merely the paragraphs of it which deal with homicide. Hence Socrates, as a person shortly to be accused of irreligion, appeals to him as an expert for an answer to the question what " piety " (τὸ εὐσεβές) or " religious duty " (τὸ ὅσιον) is in its genuine character. There must be some one character which belongs to all action which is " *religiously* right " (ὅσιον), and an opposite character which is shown in all action which is religiously wrong. There must be a definition of " religious obligation," and we want to know what it is. It is noticeable that this common character of the " religiously right " is at the outset spoken of as a single ἰδέα (*Euthyphro*, 5*d*) and subsequently as an εἶδος (6*d*) and an οὐσία (11*a*). This is the language familiar to us as technical in the so-called Platonic " theory of Forms," but it is represented as understood at once by Euthyphro without any kind of explanation. It seems quite impossible to escape the conclusion that from the very first Plato represented Socrates as habitually using language of this kind and being readily understood by his contemporaries.[1]

Like so many of the interlocutors in these early dialogues of Plato, Euthyphro at first confuses definition with the enumeration of examples. " Religious duty " is to proceed against the party guilty of an offence against religion, whether it be a homicide or a sacrilegious theft, or any other such crime, without being deterred by any regard for the ties of blood ; to neglect this duty is " irreligious " (5*d–e*). We have the best of examples for this, that of Zeus himself who " chained " his own father. Of course, if this statement is taken to be more than a production of instances, it would be delightfully " circular," since it makes *religious* duty amount to active opposition to *irreligion*. Socrates prefers to regard the statement as a mere illustration and simply repeats his request for an account of the " one form " in virtue of which

---

[1] There is indeed an important point on which Socrates is represented as needing to explain himself in the *Phaedo* ; he has to explain at some length how the theory of Forms bears on the problem of " coming into being and passing out of being." We may readily believe that *this* would need some explaining to most persons, but the meaning of the words, ἰδέα, εἶδος, and the reality of the existence of " forms," is simply presupposed in the *Phaedo*, as elsewhere, without any explanation or justification.

all religious duties are religious. This leads to a first attempt at definition : " the religious is what is pleasing to the gods, the irreligious what is not pleasing to them " (6e). This is, in form, a good definition ; whether it is sound in substance remains to be seen. The difficulty is that, according to Euthyphro himself, dissensions and enmities exist among the gods.[1] Now it is not every disagreement which leads to quarrels and enmities. A difference of opinion about number, size, or weight is readily settled by an appeal to counting, measuring, or weighing. It is when we come to disagreement about moral questions—"right and wrong, fine and ugly, good and bad "—that it is hard to find a standard by which to settle the disagreement, and this is why it is regularly differences of this kind which lead to quarrels and factions among us [2] (7c–d). We may fairly reason that if the gods quarrel and fight, it is over the same questions ; they quarrel about right and wrong, and each party will be pleased by what it regards as right and offended by what it thinks wrong. Thus what pleases one god may offend another, and the same act will be, in that case, both religious and irreligious (8a). Cronus, for example, can hardly be supposed to approve of Euthyphro's present proceedings.

Euthyphro's way of meeting the difficulty is to commit in an undisguised form the circle already implied in his original statement. There are points, he urges, on which all the gods would agree ; they would all agree, for example, that wrongful homicide ought not to go unpunished. (Thus he suggests that the definition might run that religious acts are those which the gods approve unanimously, with the explanation that the class " acts unanimously approved by the gods " is identical with the class of rightful acts.) But the suggestion makes matters no better. No one, not even the defendant in a prosecution for homicide, ever denies that *wrongful* homicide, or any other wrongful act, ought to be punished. The issue at stake is always which of the two parties is in the wrong and what is the precise character of the wrong committed. If the

---

[1] These " wars in heaven " refer principally to the stories of the dethronement of Cronus and the Titans and the war of the gods with the giants, to which allusion has already been made. They are part of the Orphic and the Hesiodic theogonies. Socrates does not believe such stories (*Euthyphro*, 6a–c) and it is easy to show that they were not taken seriously by Athenians in general, but Euthyphro has expressly avowed his belief in them and still stranger tales (6b), and it is he who is offering the definition. Hence the objection is perfectly valid against him.

[2] The passage is noteworthy. Plato is fond of assimilating the use of a true " scale of values " to the employment of number, measure, and weight. We may fairly conjecture with Burnet that the suggestion comes from Socrates. Knowledge of good, by enabling us to estimate correctly the relative worth of different " goods," would reduce our heated quarrels about our " rights " to a problem in " moral arithmetic." There is much truth in this. In the bitterest of such quarrels both parties often sincerely wish for no more than their " fair due." The trouble is that they cannot agree on the question how much that is. Compare Leibniz's hope that a perfected " symbolic logic " would reduce all philosophical disputes to the working of a " calculation."

gods are at variance, then, their difference cannot be on the question whether a wrongful act should be punished, but on the very different question what acts are wrongful. How do we know, for example, that different gods might not be of different mind about the rightness or wrongfulness of the step Euthyphro is now taking? This, however, is only a minor difficulty. We may allow Euthyphro to put his definition in the amended form, "The religious is that which the gods approve and the irreligious that which they disapprove unanimously." But we still have to ask the graver question, "Is a religious act religious because the gods approve it, or do they approve it because it is religious?" (8*b*–10*a*).

(The question is one which has played a prominent part in ethical controversy in later days. It amounts to asking whether acts of piety, or more generally virtuous acts, derive their character of being right from the mere fact of being commanded, or are commanded because they are antecedently *intrinsically* right. Are the "commandments of God" arbitrary? Is moral obligation *created* by the imposition of a command? This is, in effect, the thesis of both Hobbes and Locke, and is what Cudworth is denying in his treatise on *Eternal and Immutable Morality*, when he sets himself to argue that acts are good or bad " by nature " and not by " mere will." The same issue reappears in a different terminology in the objection taken against Hutcheson's doctrine of an "implanted moral sense " by those who urged that on the theory in question our Creator might have given us an inverted "moral sense," and then the promotion of human misery would have been our highest duty.)[1] The point is too fine to be taken at once by a man of Euthyphro's type, and therefore has to be explained at a length which we find superfluous. The difficulty hardly exists for us, because we are accustomed from childhood to the distinction between the active and passive " voices " of a verb. In the time of Plato there was, as Burnet reminds us, no grammatical terminology; the very distinction between a verb and a noun is not *known* to have been drawn by anyone before Plato himself, and that in a late dialogue, the *Sophistes*. The point to be made is the simple one that a definition of an οὐσία cannot properly be given by means of a verb in the passive voice (Burnet, *loc. cit.*). That is, it is no answer to the question what something is, to be told what some one or something else does to it. In more scholastic terminology, a formula of this kind would be a definition by means of a mere " extrinsic denomination," and would throw no light on the *quiddity* of the *definiendum*.[2] (It must be remembered that

[1] The problem was also a prominent one in the age of Scholasticism. It is against the view that obligation is created by command that St. Thomas (*S.C.G.* iii. 122) says that fornication is not sufficiently proved to be sinful by alleging that it is an " injury to God." " For we only offend God by doing what is against our own good." It therefore still remains to show that the conduct in question is " against our own good."

[2] Of course such definitions are common enough ; *e.g.* you could not define " trustee " except by a verb in the passive voice or its equivalent. But what

in a question of moral science we are not concerned with a purely *nominal* definition, like those of mathematics, the mere interpretation of a new symbol by a combination of symbols already familiar. The definition of a *character* such as ὅσιον is inevitably a *real* definition, and this is why Socrates calls it a discourse about an οὐσία.)

The principle to be laid down is that when something happens to, or is done to, a thing there is always a correlated person or thing who is the doer. Thus if a thing is carried, or is seen, there is some one or something who carries or sees that thing. And when we use a " passive " participle or adjective to characterize anything, we do so *because* something is being done to the thing by something else. (Thus, it is meant, if a thing is being seen by some one it is a " thing seen " or *visible* (ὁρώμενον), but you could not argue that because a thing is visible some one must actually be seeing it.[1]) In other words, a passive participle or adjective of passive sense is always a *denominatio extrinseca*. Now a thing which is liked or approved (φιλούμενον) comes under this rule ; " it is not because it is a-thing-approved that some one approves it ; it is because some one actually approves it that it is a-thing-approved " (10c.) But this consideration is fatal to our proposed formula, if the formula be taken as a definition of τὸ ὅσιον. If " all the gods " approve the " religious act," that, as Euthyphro concedes at once, is because the act *is* " religious " ; its character as ὅσιον is the *cause* of their approbation. The " extrinsic denomination " thing - approved - by - the - gods, on the other hand, only belongs to τὸ ὅσιον as a consequence of the *fact* that the gods approve it. Thus the formula does not tell us what the character on the ground of which the gods approve certain acts *is* (its οὐσία), but only something which happens to these acts, namely, that the gods approve them ; it tells us an " affection " (πάθος) of the " religious," not its *quiddity* (11a).[2]

Thus we have to begin the work of looking for a definition of the " religious " over again. Our definitions keep running away from us, like the mythical statues of Daedalus, the reputed ancestor

you are really defining in this case is a relation, the relation of the trustee to the " truster." In the case of τὸ ὅσιον we are attempting to define a *quality* (πάθος), and it is no definition of this quality to say that " the gods like it."

[1] Berkeley, it is true, *seems* sometimes to be arguing as though we could infer from the fact that a thing is visible, the further fact that some one is always seeing it. But even he would hardly have argued that if a thing is eatable, some one must be eating it.

[2] It is tacitly assumed that if the gods approve *x, y, z* . . . they do so for an intelligible reason. There is some character common to *x, y, z* over and above the " extrinsic denomination " of being in fact approved, and this character is the ground of the approbation. On the use of the words οὐσία, πάθος (the most general name for anything, mode, quality, relation, etc., which can be asserted of a subject), see Burnet's notes, *loc. cit.* The way in which the terms are used without explanation implies that they are part of an already familiar logical terminology.

of Socrates.[1] Socrates must have inherited, much against his will, a double portion of his ancestor's gift, for it seems that he can bestow mobility on other men's " products " as well as on his own. But he will try to do what he can to remedy the trouble. At this point (12a) the discussion makes a fresh start—a start, we may note, due to the direct suggestion of Socrates, whose part in the dialogues is by no means so exclusively that of a mere critic of others as is sometimes fancied. What is the relation of τὸ ὅσιον (religion) to δικαιοσύνη (duty, obligation, morality in general)? We both admit that whatever is religious (ὅσιον) is " dutiful " or " right " (δίκαιον); can we convert the proposition *simpliciter* and say that whatever is right is religious? *I.e.* is all duty duty to God? Euthyphro has the difficulty which seems to beset all beginners in logic in seeing that the universal affirmative proposition does not admit of simple conversion, and the point has to be made clear to him by examples. All reverence (αἰδώς) is fear, but it is not true that all fear (*e.g.* fear of illness) is reverence. All odd integers are numbers, but all numbers are not odd. Reverence is a " part " of fear as " odd number " is of number. In the more developed logical terminology of Aristotle, the thing would, of course, be expressed by saying that reverence and odd number are *species* (εἴδη) of the *genera* fear and number, but Plato, who sits loose to terminology, except when it is needed for the purpose immediately in hand, habitually uses the word " part " (μόριον, μέρος) for what we still call the *membra dividentia* of a logical " division." When the point has been explained to him, Euthyphro at once answers that τὸ ὅσιον is only one part of τὸ δίκαιον—that is, in modern language, that duty to God is not the whole of the duty of man, but one specific branch of it. Thus, like the mass of mankind, he believes in a plurality of distinct " virtues." Man has, *e.g.*, a certain set of " duties to God," and another distinct set of duties to his fellow-men, and it would follow that you might specialize in one of these branches of duty but neglect the others. You might be strong in " religion " but weak, *e.g.*, in honesty, like the legendary Welshman who " had a wonderful gift in prayer but was an awful liar." From the Socratic point of view, this would be impossible. *All* virtue is knowledge of good, and consequently any one real virtue, if you live up to it, will prove to cover the whole of human conduct. The " content " of morality and that of religion would thus alike be the whole sphere of human conduct, and it would be quite impossible in principle to distinguish a man's " religious " from his " moral " duties. At bottom, the reason why the *Euthyphro* ends negatively is the same as that which accounts for the formally negative result of the *Laches* or *Charmides*, the fact that genuine " goodness " is a unity.

[1] For the point of the jest, see Burnet, *loc. cit.* It would be *spoilt* if there were any truth in the later story that Socrates was actually the son of a sculptor and had practised the calling himself, as any intelligent reader ought to see.

This is suggested at once for us in 12*d*. If " religion " is a " part " of morality, we must go on to ask " which " part it is ; *i.e.*, to use the technical phrase which meets us as such for the first time in the *Theaetetus*, we must ask for the " difference " which marks off " religious " duties from the rest of our duties. We may suggest that τὸ δίκαιον can be divided into two species, the " cult " or " service " (θεραπεία) of the gods and the cult or service of man ; the former will be religion (12*e*). The thought is that all morality is service, and that service falls under two mutually exclusive heads, the " service of God," and " the service of man," a view still widely popular. (From Socrates' point of view, of course, the view would be false ; you cannot serve man without in the very act serving God, nor serve God without serving man.)

To follow the argument to which this third attempt at a defini- tion gives rise, we have to remember that the word θεραπεία was in use in two special connexions. It was used of the *cult* of a deity by his worshipper (cp. our objectionable use of the phrases " divine service," " Sunday services "), or of a great man by his courtiers, and of the " tending " of men or animals by professionals such as physicians and grooms (the sense of the word from which Socrates developed his conception of the " tending of one's soul " as the supreme business of life). The problem is to determine in which, if either of these senses, religion is to be called the " service " of God. If we start with the second sense, that in which the pro- fessional trainer of hounds or oxherd may be said to " tend " or " serve " the hounds or oxen, we see that the aim of such tendance is always to make the " tended " better, to get the dogs or oxen into the pink of condition and keep them so. But we cannot suppose that religion is the service of God in this sense. No one would say that by performing his " religious duties " he " makes his gods better " (13*a–c*). We must mean " service " in the very different sense in which slaves are said to " serve " or " tend " their owner. Now the " service " of a slave consists in acting as an instrument or " understrapper " in carrying out his owner's business ; it is a form of ὑπηρετική, " co-operating as a subordinate with a superior for the achievement of some result " (13*d*).

Now we can say at once what the result to which the slave of a medical man contributes under his master's direction is ; it is the curing of the master's patients. So the slave of a builder contri- butes as a subordinate to the construction of a ship or a house. If, then, " serving God " means contributing as an underworker contributes to the business of his superior, if it is " co-operation as an instrument," what is the great work to which *we* contribute " under the gods " ? (13*e*). (No answer is given to the question in our dialogue. None could be given by a man like Euthyphro who keeps his morality and his religion in separate " water-tight com- partments," and Socrates naturally does not answer his own question. But it is not hard to discover from other dialogues what the Socratic answer would be. The great business of man, we know, is to " tend " his own soul, and so far as he can the souls of all who come into contact with him, to "make them as good as possible." We shall find him, in the *Phaedo* and elsewhere, describing this course of life as "assimilation to God" (ὁμοίωσις θεῷ). Thus we shall not go far wrong if we say that the "great and glorious work of God" is to be the source of order and good to the universe, and that we "contribute under God" to that work in the degree to which we bring order and good into the little "world" of our own personal life and that of the society to which we belong. Such an answer would, of course, presuppose the "unity of the virtues," and break down all barriers between the service of man and the service of God, morality and religion ; it would make irreligion a breach of morality and laxity of morals an offence against religion.)

Euthyphro's inability to follow the thought of Socrates throws him back on what had all along been his implied position, the position of the fanatic who divorces religion from morality. "If a man knows how to please the gods by his words of prayer and his acts of sacrifice—that is religion, and that is what makes private families and public commonwealths prosperous" (14*b*). In briefer phrase, religion is "a science of sacrificing and praying" (14*c*). (Euthyphro, of course, takes the word "science" employed by Socrates to mean simply correct knowlege of the ritual to be observed.) Now in sacrificing we give something to the gods and in prayer we ask something from them. So we may finally put Euthyphro's thought into this definition (the fourth and last of the dialogue), "Religion is the science of asking the gods for things and giving things to them" (14*d*). Now the right way of asking will be to ask for what we really need, and the right way of giving will be to give the gods what *they* want of us, and thus religion turns out to be "an art of traffic between men and gods" (ἐμπορικὴ τέχνη θεοῖς καὶ ἀνθρώποις παρ' ἀλλήλων, 14*e*). But traffic is, of course, a transaction between two parties for mutual advantages ; one "cannot be buyer and seller too." What one party to the traffic between gods and men gets out of the transaction is obvious ; the gods send us all the good things we enjoy. But what "advantage" (ὠφελία) do they get from us ? No "profit," says Euthyphro, but "honour and thanks and gratitude" (τιμή τε καὶ γέρα καὶ χάρις, 15*a*). "The religious act" thus turns out to be "that which is grateful (κεχαρισμένον) to the gods," and this brings us back to the very definition we have already had to reject, that "the religious" is τὸ τοῖς θεοῖς φίλον, "what the gods approve" (15*e*) ; so that we are no nearer knowing what religion is than when we began our discussion.

As I have said, the gentle satire on the unworthy conception of religion as a trade-enterprise carried on by God and man for their mutual benefit ought not to blind us to the fact that the definition of it as *knowing* how to ask from God and how to make a return to Him is capable of being understood in a genuinely Socratic sense. The very introduction into this formula of ἐπιστήμη as the *genus* of religion should indicate that it contains a suggestion we are meant to follow out. "Imitation," says the proverb, "is the sincerest form of flattery." And we may add that the "imitation of God" shown in a life devoted to the "tendance of the soul" is the one acceptable τιμή and the true thanksgiving for the goods we receive from God. So understood, the formula that religion is asking the right things from God and making the right return does not contradict but coincides with the other formula that it is co-operation as agents "under God" in a great and glorious "work."

2. *Apology.*—The *Apology* is too well known to require any elaborate analysis, though it must not be passed over without some remarks on points of general interest. Apart from its strictly historical interest as a professed faithful reproduction of the actual language of Socrates at the memorable trial, it has a philosophical interest as a picture of the life of "tendance of the soul" adopted with full consciousness and led at all costs to its appropriate and glorious end. What is depicted is the life of a "martyr" of the best type as seen from within by the martyr himself; the object of the picture is to make us understand why the martyr chooses such a life and why the completion of his career by the martyr's death is a *corona* and not a "disaster." In our more commonplace moods we are accustomed to think of martyrdom as a highly disagreeable duty; perhaps it must not be shirked, but we feel that, to be made tolerable to our imagination, it must be "made up" to the martyr by an "exaltation" to follow it. Plato means us rather to feel that the martyrdom is itself the "exaltation": *in cruce gaudium spiritus; ambula ubi vis . . . non invenies altiorem viam supra, nec securiorem viam infra, nisi viam sanctae crucis.* The *Apology* is the Hellenic counterpart of the second book of the *Imitatio.*

For the considerations which make it certain that in substance Plato has preserved the actual speech of Socrates (which, as he lets us know, he himself heard), see Burnet's *Introductory Note* and the works referred to there. We must, of course, understand that, like all the circulated versions of celebrated speeches (those of Aeschines and Demosthenes in the matter of the "Crown," for example), the published speech is supposed to have been "revised" in accord with the canons of prose-writing. Plato has, no doubt, done for the defence of Socrates what men like Demosthenes did for their own speeches before they gave them to the world. At the same time we clearly have no right to assume that the process of revision and polishing involves any falsification of fundamental facts. That what we possess is in substance a record of what Socrates actually said is sufficiently proved by the single consideration that, though we cannot date the circulation of the *Apology* exactly, we can at least be sure that it must have been given to the world within a few years of the actual trial, and would thus be read by numbers of persons, including both devoted admirers of the philosopher and hostile critics (and presumably even some of the judges who had sat upon the case), who would at once detect any falsification of such recent facts.[1] It should also be added that even the subtle art by which Socrates, while professing to be a mere "layman" in forensic oratory, actually makes his speech conform to precedent in its general structure, an art most readily appreciated by following Burnet's careful analysis, is certainly not a mere stylistic "improvement" by Plato. The *Gorgias* and *Phaedrus* would be mere mystifications if it were not the fact that, for all his contempt for the ideals of contemporary "rhetoric," Socrates was quite familiar with its recognized methods and principles. Indeed, the *Apology* might be said to afford an ironical illustration of the paradox of the *Gorgias* about the uses which may legitimately be made of rhetorical devices. Socrates is in the position of an accused party, and he makes a "defence" which has been felt from the time of Xenophon onward to be something very much like an avowal of guilt. This is exactly in accord with the principles of the *Gorgias*. Socrates is accused of an offence, and in the eyes of an average Athenian, though not in his own, he has done what amounts to the commission of that offence. Consequently he uses impressive eloquence, not to veil the facts but to put their reality in the clearest light. He is, and for many years has been, a "suspected character," and the whole "defence" consists in insisting on the point and explaining that the suspicion has been inevitable. Even the act of which an ordinary advocate would have made the most as evidence of "sound democratic sentiments," Socrates' defiance of the order of the "Thirty" in the affair of Leon (*Apol.* 32c–d), is deliberately introduced by a previous narrative of an event of which such an advocate would have been careful to say nothing, or as little as possible, Socrates' opposition to the δῆμος at the trial of the Arginusae generals. Thus what might have been used by a man like Lysias to make an acquittal morally certain is actually employed by Socrates as an opportunity to warn the court that they must expect from him no sacrifice of conviction to "democratic sentiments." From the point of view of a Lysias, Socrates must have been "throwing away the ace of trumps" by using the story of his defiance of the Thirty as he does.

The very singular historical circumstances of the trial of Socrates have been better explained in Professor Burnet's notes to his edition of the *Apology* and the chapter on the "Trial" in *Greek Philosophy, Part I.*, than anywhere else. I shall therefore refer the reader to those works for full discussion, contenting myself with an indication of the points which seem most important.

Though the actual prosecutor was Meletus, every one knew that the real instigator of the whole business was Anytus one of the two

[1] In particular, it is quite unthinkable that Plato should have invented the few words, addressed to friends and supporters after the court had voted the penalty of death, with which the *Apology* closes. Modern writers, who think it "impossible" that Socrates should have spoken after sentence had been pronounced, are simply transferring the procedure of a modern European court of justice to the Athens of the fifth century. For the opportunity the case would give for the making of the remarks, see Burnet, *Apology*, p. 161.

most admired and trusted leaders of the restored democracy. Since Anytus was in one and the same year assisting the prosecution of Socrates but helping the defence of Andocides on the very same charge of " irreligion," we cannot suppose motives of fanaticism to have had anything to do with his action.   We may fairly suppose that what he attributed to Socrates was the " corruption of the young men," and that this meant exercising an influence hostile to the temper of unquestioning loyalty to the democracy.   That this crime, if it is a crime, was one of which Socrates was guilty can be proved from the *Apology* itself, where his capital point is that he is ready to encounter the hostility of the πλῆθος or of any one else at the bidding of conscience.   Such criticisms of the heroes of the old democracy as we read in the *Gorgias* and *Meno* are additional evidence, though, in fact, a " practical politician " like Anytus would need no evidence beyond the notorious intimacies between the philosopher and men like Alcibiades, Critias, and Charmides. But there was a reason why Anytus could neither put his real case forward without disguise of some kind nor appear as the actual prosecutor, and this reason has rightly been insisted on by Burnet. The worst " offences " of Socrates had been committed under the old democracy and all open reference to them was banned by the Act of Oblivion forbidding all questioning of citizens for anything done before the archonship of Euclides.   Anytus had himself been one of the foremost promoters of this Act and could therefore neither himself prosecute, nor instigate anyone else to prosecute, acts covered by this amnesty.   It was necessary to put forward some further pretext for proceeding and to find a nominal prosecutor who would make the pretext the main charge in his indictment. This explains why, to judge from the *Apology*, the precise nature of the " corruption of the young " by Socrates was left so much in the dark that we only discover what is meant by reading rather carefully between the lines of the defence.   It also explains the selection of " irreligion " as the accusation to be pressed home and of Meletus as the nominal prosecutor.   Burnet is plainly right in holding that it is most improbable, since the name Meletus is a rare one, that there should have been two men of that name, one of whom prosecuted Socrates and another Andocides for the same offence in the same year.   If, as is probable, the prosecutor in both cases was the same man, and the speech " against Andocides " preserved to us under the name of Lysias that delivered by Meletus in the prosecution of Andocides—whether it is a composition of his own, or one written by Lysias to be spoken " in character," we see at once why Meletus was selected.   The speech against Andocides is that of a sincere but hopelessly crazy fanatic—the very man to make the right sort of tool for a political intrigue just because he combines absolute honesty with the simplicity of a half-wit.   Such a man would throw himself heart and soul into the prosecution of an *impie*, none the less effectively because, as is clear from the line taken by Socrates in his defence, neither he nor

anyone else knew precisely what the " impiety " consisted in.
(It is also worth notice that according to Andocides Meletus was
one of the party who executed the illegal arrest of Leon, in which
Socrates refused to be concerned, and thus, as a man who had
contracted the pollution of φόνος, ought to have been in the dock
himself on the very charge he was bringing against less guilty folk.
That Socrates disdains to make a point of this is strictly in keeping
with his character.) As to the meaning of the " impiety " charged
against Socrates, all that we learn from the *Apology* is that Socrates
regards it as having something to do with the caricatures of his
earlier scientific pursuits in the *Clouds* and other comedies, where
men of science in general are represented as having no respect for
the gods of the current official worships. No doubt this statement
is correct, as far as it goes, but there must have been something
more behind the indictment of Socrates. The fact that Andocides
was tried on the same charge about the same time for a ritual offence
and found it necessary in his defence to go into the whole old
scandal of the " mutilation of the Hermae " and the " profanation
of the mysteries " seems, as Burnet has urged, to give us the key
to the secret. Alcibiades and other prominent men among the
associates of Socrates had been deeply implicated in the affair
of the " mysteries," and this would, no doubt, be in the minds of all
the judges. Socrates makes no allusion to the matter in his defence, but this only proves what we should expect from the whole
tenour of his life, that, even in defending himself on a capital charge
he was scrupulous to observe the spirit of the law by which
offences before the archonship of Euclides had been " amnestied."
Meletus is likely to have been less cautious.

We cannot well acquit Anytus of having stooped to instigate
a proceeding in which he was ashamed to take the principal part,
and of having used a tool whom he must have despised. But this
is no more than has often been done by politicians who, as the
world goes, are counted high-minded. His object was simply to
frighten away from Athens a person whose influence he believed to
be undesirable, much as Dutch William resorted to trickery to
frighten King James out of England—an act for which he is eulogized
by Macaulay. Socrates might have preserved his life by going
away before trial, as it was customary to do when there was any
doubt about acquittal. Indeed Plato is careful to let us see that
even when the case came into court, escape would have been easy.
The verdict of guilty, even after the uncompromising speech of the
accused had been delivered, was only obtained by a small majority.
We may safely infer that an opposite verdict could pretty certainly
have been secured by a little deference to popular opinion, a little
adroit silence about one or two incidents and stress on others—
such as the excellent military record of the accused—with a few
words of regret for the past and promise of cautious behaviour in
future. Even without any of this, it is clear that if Socrates had
chosen to propose a moderate fine as a sufficient penalty, the offer

would have been accepted. (Not to mention that he could readily have escaped during his unexpected month of detention in custody, and that public opinion would not have blamed him.) The accusers had no wish to have the guilt of any man's blood at their doors ; Socrates himself forced their hand. Without any desire for a martyrdom, they had created a situation in which there must inevitably be one, unless the other party would compromise with his conscience, and a martyrdom Socrates determined they should have. This is what he means (*Apology*, 39*b*) by saying that both sides must abide by their τίμημα. Socrates holds in conscience that his conduct has been that of a public benefactor, his opponents that it amounts to crime worthy of death. They would like a confession from himself that their estimate is correct ; if by act or word he would admit this, they are willing not to inflict the penalty. They do not wish to inflict death, but they do wish for the admission that it is deserved. *If* it is deserved, says Socrates, let it be inflicted ; you shall be compelled to " have the courage of your opinions."

In dealing with the analysis of the *Apology* we have to start by understanding that the real and serious defence of Socrates, which is made to rest on his conviction of a special divine mission to his fellow-countrymen, does not begin until we reach page 28*a*. What goes before (*Apol.* 17*a*–27*e*) is introductory matter, and is concerned with two preliminary points, the explanation of the prejudices which have grown up about Socrates (18*a*–24*b*), and a proof that the accuser himself cannot say, or at any rate dares not say, what he really means by his charges (24*b*–27*e*). Throughout the whole of the preliminary pages we must expect to find abundant traces of the whimsical humour which the enemies of Socrates in Plato call his " irony " ; at every turn we have to allow for the patent fact that he is " not wholly serious " ; the actual defence of his conduct through life, when we reach it, is pure earnest. (It is important to call attention to this, since the well-known narrative of the part played by the Delphic oracle in the life of the philosopher belongs to the preliminary account of the causes of the popular misconceptions about him, and has to be taken with the same allowance for his native humour as the account of the burlesques on him by the comic poets. The claim to be conscious of a special mission, imposed not by " the gods," nor by " Apollo," but " by God," comes from the actual defence. The two things have very little to do with one another, and are treated in very different tones ; nothing but misconception can come of the attempt to confuse them. Similarly the point of the " cross-examination " of Meletus has repeatedly been missed by commentators who have not seen that the whole passage is humorous, though with a humour which is deadly for its victim.)

(*a*) *Plea for an Impartial Hearing and Explanation of the Existing Prejudices unfavourable to the Speaker.*—The speech opens in a very usual way with an apology, mainly playful, for the speaker's unacquaintance with the diction of the courts, and a request to be allowed to tell his story in his own way (17a–18a). The one piece of downright earnest in this exordium is the insistence that the supreme business of " oratory " is to tell the truth—a business in which the speaker may claim to be more than a match for his accusers. Like every one who wishes for an impartial hearing, he is first bound to remove any prejudices the audience may have conceived against him. It will not be enough to deal with the attempts the prosecution has just made to create such prejudices ; there is a more inveterate prejudice dating from old days ; the judges who are to decide the case have heard long ago that Socrates is a " clever man " who " busies himself about things aloft and under the earth, and makes the weaker cause appear the stronger "—the double accusation of being a physicist and being an " eristic," which is, in fact, made in the *Clouds* of Aristophanes. " Intellectuals " of this type are popularly suspected of disregard of the gods ; the charges were made in comedies which many of the judges must have seen a quarter of a century ago, in boyhood, when impressions are easily made ; they have never received any rejoinder; what is more, they have been repeated since of *malice prepense* [1] by a host of anonymous slanderers, and it is these vague prejudices rather than the accusations of the present prosecutors that are likely to stand in the way of a fair trial (18a–e).

The sufficient answer to all this is that Socrates is not responsible for the nonsense he is made to talk in the *Clouds*. His judges themselves must know whether they ever heard him discourse on such topics. But he is careful to add that he means no disparagement to knowledge of this kind ; if it exists.[2] Neither is it true that he has ever made a " profession " of " educating men " ; *i.e.* he is not one of the professional teachers of " goodness," though, again, he is far from disparaging so splendid a calling. If he really could " teach goodness," he says humorously, he would not, like Evenus, do it for a paltry five minae. He would know how *se faire valoir* (20b).

How then has he got the name for being " clever " or " wise " ? Here comes in the well-known tale of the Delphic oracle and its response to Chaerephon, that no man living was wiser than Socrates. Socrates says that he was at first staggered by this pronouncement, and set to work to prove Apollo of Delphi—never a *persona grata* at Athens, for excellent reasons—a liar. With this view he went round looking for a wiser man than himself in the various sections of society. He began with the " statesmen," but soon found that though they fancied themselves very wise, they certainly had no

---

[1] φθόνῳ καὶ διαβολῇ, 18d. It is implied that there was no real ill-feeling on the part of the comic poets who started these stories. They meant no more than fun. We can see for ourselves that this is true of Aristophanes.

[2] *Apol.* 19c. As Burnet points out, *loc. cit.*, what is said here is quite in keeping with the representation of the *Phaedo* that Socrates was deeply interested in all these matters in early life, until he discovered that he " had no head for them " (an expression itself to be taken playfully).

wisdom.   Next he tried the poets with much the same result.   He found that they were hopelessly incapable of explaining what they meant in their finest work ;   this showed that the poet, like a possessed person, speaks under the influence of a genius and inspiration of which he is not master.[1]   Finally, he turned to the artisans ; they were less disappointing than " statesmen " and poets, since it turned out that they did know something.   They knew their own trades.   Unfortunately they fancied that because they knew their trades, they must equally be competent to judge of the greatest questions (*e.g.*, no doubt, as Burnet has said, how to govern an empire).[2]   It seemed then as though the Delphic god was not lying after all ;   he was merely speaking in riddles, the notorious trick of his trade.   He meant to say that human wisdom is such a sorry affair that the wisest man is one who, like Socrates, knows that he does *not* know anything to boast of (*Apol.* 20a–23b).

Naturally enough, the victims of this experiment did not take it any too kindly, and the matter was made worse by the young folk, sons of wealthy and leisured citizens, who accompanied Socrates, " without any pressing on his part " (αὐτόματοι, 23c ; *i.e.*, they were not in any sense " pupils "), for the sport to be got out of the thing, and even tried to practise the trick themselves.   Their victims, of course, complain that Socrates is the ruin of the young people.   When they are asked how he ruins them, shame prevents the reply, " By exposing the ignorance of us older men," and so they fall back on the old charges against scientific men in general, the accusation of irreligion and " making the weaker case the stronger."   The present prosecutors are the mere mouthpieces of this idle talk (23c–24b).

(*b*) *Direct Reply to Meletus.*—Socrates now turns to the charges actually brought against him by the prosecution, with which he deals very curtly.   The humour of the situation is that the prosecutor cannot venture to say what he means by either of his charges without betraying the fact that, owing to the " amnesty," the matters complained of are outside the competency of the court. What he really means by the " corruption of the young " is the supposed influence of Socrates on Alcibiades, Critias, Charmides, and others who have been false to the democracy ;   the charge of irreligion is connected with the scandals of the year 415.   But to admit this would be to invite the court to dismiss the case.   Hence, when Meletus is pressed to explain what he means, he has to take refuge in puerile nonsense.   The judges could understand the situation and, no doubt, enjoy it amazingly ;   many modern commentators have been badly perplexed by the " sophistical " character of Socrates' reasoning simply because they have not set them-

---

[1] As Burnet says, *loc. cit.*, Euripides would be about the first of the " tragedians " to whom Socrates would apply his test.   We have seen already that Socrates held the " modern " view of poetry as dependent on " inspiration."

[2] Compare Mr. Chesterton's *mot* about " the authority which obviously attaches to the views of an electrical engineer " on the existence of God or the immortality of the soul.

selves to realize the difficulty of Meletus' position. They have missed the irony of Socrates' pretence that a prosecutor who is fanatically in earnest is merely playing a stupid practical joke.

Meletus professes to have detected Socrates depraving the young. If he has, clearly he must be able to say who improve them. Under pressure, Meletus has to fall back on the view that any good Athenian improves the young by his association with them (because his influence is exerted in favour of the moral tradition of society, exactly as we have found Anytus maintaining in the *Meno*, and shall find Protagoras explaining more at length in the dialogue called after him). Socrates stands alone in making young people worse by his influence on them (25*e*). Now this is contrary to all analogy ; if you consider the case of horses or other domestic animals, you find that they are improved by only a few, the professionals who understand the art of training them ; they are spoiled when entrusted to anyone else. Moreover, a man must be very dull not to see that he would be acting very much against his own good by depraving the very persons among whom he has to live. No one would do such a thing on purpose (the Socratic doctrine that " no one does evil voluntarily "). If a man makes so grave an error involuntarily, the proper course is not to prosecute him but to open his eyes to his mistake. But Meletus, by prosecuting Socrates, makes it clear that he thinks him capable of the absurdity of purposely trying to deprave the very persons whose depravity would expose him to risk of harm at their hands (25*c*–26*b*).

Again, in what particular way does Socrates " deprave " his young friends ? No open allusion to the facts really meant being permissible, Meletus has to fall back on the reply that the depravation consists in incitement to the religious offence alleged in the indictment. Socrates sets the example of irreligion (26*b*). This brings us to the consideration of this accusation on its own account. Socrates professes to be quite unable to understand what can be meant by the statement that he " does not worship the gods of the city but practises a strange religion.¹ If Meletus means any-

---

¹ As to this accusation, see Burnet, *loc. cit.* It is quite certain on linguistic grounds that the meaning of the phrase that Socrates οὐ νομίζει τοὺς θεοὺς ἣ πόλις νομίζει is that he does not conform to the *cultus*, does not " worship " the official gods, not that " he does not *believe* in their existence." Aristophanes is punning on this sense of the word νομίζειν when he makes Socrates explain to Strepsiades that ἡμῖν θεοὶ νόμισμ' οὐκ ἔστι (" the gods are not legal tender *here* "). It is certain also that in the additional clause ἕτερα δὲ δαιμόνια καινά, δαιμόνια is adjective, not substantive, and that the sense is therefore, " but practises certain other unfamiliar religious observances." The meaning of this is made clearer by comparison with the *Clouds*, where Socrates is represented as combining the functions of a scientific man with those of president of a conventicle of ascetics. It was true that the Ionian men of science used the word θεός in a wholly non-religious way for whatever they took to be the primary body (this is why in the *Clouds* Socrates swears by Respiration and Air, and prays to " the Clouds "), and also that Socrates was an associate of Orphic and Pythagorean ascetics, like Telauges in the dialogue of Aeschines called by that name, who had a religion of their own not officially recognized by the State. So far there is an intelligible basis for the

thing, he must presumably mean that Socrates is an atheist. (Meletus does not really mean this, and Socrates knows that he does not mean it. But he cannot explain what he really means without risking the collapse of his case, and Socrates is fully entitled to embarrass him for his own and the court's amusement. He despises the charge too much to take it seriously.) If this is what he means, and he dares not explain that it is not, his charge refutes itself. A man cannot be both an atheist and the votary of a " strange religion " ; to make an accusation of this kind is simply wasting the time of the court [1] (26e–27e).

(c) *The Vindication of Socrates' Life and Conduct* (28a–35d).— We come at last to Socrates' serious defence of his character, not against the frivolous charges on which he is being ostensibly tried but against grave misconceptions of old standing. He is well aware that his life is at stake, a thing which has happened to many a good man in the past and will happen again. But there is nothing dishonourable in such a situation. A man's part is to stand loyally, in the face of all risks, to the part which he has judged to be the best for himself, or to which his commander has ordered him. Socrates himself has acted on this principle in his military career, when his superior officers have commanded him to face dangers. Still more is it his duty to be loyal to the command of God which, as he is persuaded, has enjoined him to " spend his life in devotion to wisdom and in examining himself and his fellows " (28e). The real atheism would be to disobey the divine command. Disobedience would be a known evil, but the death with which he is threatened if he does not disobey may, for all he knows, be the greatest of good. Hence if he were offered acquittal on the condition of abandoning " philosophy," with certain death as the alternative, he would refuse acquittal. For God is more to be obeyed than any human law-court. For that reason, so long as life is in him, Socrates will never cease urging on every man the duty of " care for wisdom and truth and the good of his soul " and the relative unimportance of care for health or fortune. That is God's commission to him, and if Athens only knew it, his " service " (ὑπηρεσία) [2] of God is the greatest blessing that could befall the

---

reference to the δαιμόνια καινά. But it is still unexplained what ground there is for saying that Socrates does not worship the gods of the city, and it is this part of the charge on which Socrates fastens. It seems to me that Burnet is right in supposing that what is really meant is the old affair of the " profanation of the mysteries." The " psephism of Diopithes " has nothing to do with the matter. All " psephisms " before the year of Euclides were invalidated (*Andocides* i. 86).

[1] Formally, the argument is rather more elaborate. A man who concerns himself with τὰ δαιμόνια (the " supernatural," as we might say) must believe that there are δαίμονες (" supernatural beings ") ; these δαίμονες are either themselves " gods " or are the " offspring of gods," and in either case, a man who believes in them cannot be an atheist. This is pure *persiflage*, but it is as good as Meletus and his backer Anytus deserve.

[2] Compare what has been already said in connexion with the *Euthyphro* about the conception of religion as serving God in the production of a πάγκαλον ἔργον. Socrates pleads that his whole life has been dedicated to this work.

whole community (30*a*). If he "corrupts the young" at all, it must be by preaching to them his unchanging conviction that "it is not wealth which makes worth (ἀρετή), but worth makes wealth and all else good." His present speech is not made to save his own life—Anytus and Meletus may procure his death, but the really dreadful thing is not to lose your life but to *take* a life wrongfully (the thesis of the *Gorgias*)—he would save his fellow-citizens from misusing the gift God has bestowed on them, and is not likely to give them a second time, a gadfly whose buzzing prevents that high-bred but somnolent animal "the People" from drowsy sloth (30*c*–31*c*).

It may be asked why a man with such a mission has never attempted to act as a *public* monitor and adviser.[1] Well, the fact is that the "mysterious something" which has warned Socrates all his life against "unlucky" proceedings has always checked any attempt to take part in public life. *Et pour cause :* a democracy (πλῆθος) soon puts an end to anyone who defies its humours in the cause of right. Hence it was a condition of the exercise of the mission that it should be exercised on individuals, not on the multitude (31*c*–32*a*). In fact, Socrates has only twice been called upon by his mission to come into conflict with authority, once when he withstood the popular sentiment by refusing to be accessory to the unconstitutional steps taken against the generals after Arginusae, and once, more recently, when he disregarded the illegal command of the "Thirty" to arrest Leon. In both cases he ran a great personal risk, and in the second, might well have lost his life but for the downfall of the "Thirty" (32*a*–*e*). As for the charge of de-moralizing his "pupils," he has never had any "pupils," though he has never refused to communicate his convictions freely to every one (33*a*–*b*) as his mission required of him.[2] He is ready to summon the parents and elder brothers of the young men who have associated with him as witnesses that none of them have been made worse by his companionship (33*d*–34*b*).

The defence is now, in substance, concluded, and we have reached the point at which it was customary to make an appeal

[1] The implication is that a man of the remarkable gifts of Socrates, who carefully abstains from putting them openly at the service of the community, though he is believed to have employed them freely for the service of men like Alcibiades, must be a formidable anti-democratic conspirator.

[2] Note that in denying that he ever had μαθηταί, Socrates is still referring to the suspicion connected with his relations with prominent persons who are now dead. From Isocrates xi. 5, we learn that the pamphleteer Polycrates made it a principal charge that Alcibiades had been Socrates' pupil, just as Aeschines the orator (i. 173) says the same thing about Critias. Isocrates relates that Alcibiades had never been "educated" by Socrates, thus agreeing with Plato and Xenophon (*Mem.* I. 2, 12 ff.). Socrates is too scrupulously observant of the "amnesty" to explain himself, but it is Alcibiades and Critias, not younger unknown men like Plato and Aeschines of Sphettus, whom he means by his supposed "disciples." The reference to the "divine sign" at 31*c* is playful, like other allusions of the kind in Plato. The real reason why Socrates took no part in active politics is the one he goes on to give, that he knew the hopelessness of such an attempt.

to the clemency of the court for the sake of one's family and connexions. Socrates declines to follow the usual course, not because he has not dependents, friends, and relatives to whom he is bound by natural ties, but because the procedure would be unworthy of his character and an attempt to seduce the court from its duty. That would be a real "impiety." The issue must now be left in the hands of God and the judges (34*b*–35*e*).

The object of the pages which follow (36*a*–38*b*) is to explain why Socrates did not, after conviction, secure his life by proposing a moderate fine as an alternative penalty, as he clearly could have done. This must have been felt as a real difficulty by common-place persons even among the philosopher's friends, as we see from the absurd explanation given by Xenophon (*Apol.* 1–8) that Socrates deliberately provoked his own execution in order to escape the infirmities of old age. It has to be explained that his real motive was a worthy one. To propose any penalty whatever would amount to admitting guilt, and Socrates has already told the court that he regards himself as a minister of God for good to his countrymen. Hence he cannot in consistency propose any treatment for himself but that of a distinguished public benefactor, a place at the public table (σίτησις ἐν πρυτανείῳ). It should be noted that, strictly speaking, this is the τίμησις which Socrates offers as an alternative to the death-penalty demanded by the accusers. The whimsical mood has returned on him after the intense earnestness of the defence of his life and character. He urges that as he regards himself as a benefactor he can only propose the treatment of a benefactor for himself. The subsequent offer to pay the trifling sum of a mina (only raised to one of thirty minae at the urgent instance of friends) is made with the full certainty that the court, which has just heard Socrates' real opinion of his deserts, will reject it. The real issue is not whether a prophet of righteousness is a major or a minor offender, but whether he is a capital traitor or the one true "patriot," and Socrates is determined that the court shall not shirk that issue, as it would like to do. (As to the sum of thirty minae which Socrates' friends offer to pay for him, one should note (*a*) that in *Epistle* xiii. Plato, writing a generation later, mentions it to Dionysius II as a good dowry for anyone but a very rich man to give his daughter and that this estimate is borne out by a careful examination of all the references to dowries in the fourth-century orators, (*b*) that, though Plato and Apollodorus are joined with Crito as "security," the main burden of payment would, no doubt, fall on the wealthy Crito. The family of Plato are not likely to have been particularly well off just after the failure of the revolution in which its most prominent members had taken the losing side.[1] As we see from the speeches of Lysias belonging to this

---

[1] Cf. what Xenophon makes Charmides say about his own finances at *Symp.* 29 ff., where there seems to be an (anachronistic) allusion to the effects of the "Decelean" war.

period, the downfall of Athens in 404 had been followed by a wide-spread commercial crisis. Socrates' friends are making what, in the circumstances, must have been a very strenuous effort to save him. This is why they "ask for time" instead of offering to pay money down.[1])

In the concluding remarks of the speech made after the voting on the penalty, note in the first place how clearly it is recognized that Socrates has forced the issue, and that he could have secured his acquittal by simply "asking for quarter" (38d–39b). This is, of course, true of every typical martyr. Martyrdom is dying when you could escape if you would compromise a little with your conscience ; in this sense every martyr forces the issue. Anytus would rather not have killed Socrates, just as the average Roman proconsul would rather not have condemned Christians, or as Bonner (as appears even from the partial accounts of his enemies) would much rather not have sent Protestants to the stake. But it is not the business of the martyr to make things easy for the forcer of consciences.

In the impressive words of encouragement directed to his supporters (39e–41c), the important thing to note is that, contrary to the absurd opinion of many nineteenth-century writers, Socrates makes his own belief in a blessed life to come for the good perfectly plain. The best proof of this is that to which Burnet has appealed, comparison of his language with the brief and hesitating phrases in which the Attic orators are accustomed to allude to the state of the departed. In this respect the *Apology* agrees completely with the *Phaedo*, when we allow for the fact that in the former Socrates is speaking to a large audience, most of whom would not share his personal faith. No one but a convinced believer would have said half what he is made to say about his "hope" (not to mention that the "divinity" of the soul is at bottom the reason why the "tendance" of it is so much more important than that of the body, and, as Rohde long ago observed, to the Greek mind "immortality" and "divinity" are equivalents). The specific allusions of 41a to Hesiod, Musaeus, Orpheus and the Orphic judges of the dead, also make it clear that Socrates' convictions are not meant as simply inferences from "natural theology" ; we have to see in them the influence of the Orphic religion, though the *Euthyphro* and the second book of the *Republic* show that Socrates thought very poorly of the ordinary run of "professing" Orphics in his own time.

3. *Crito*.—The *Euthyphro* and *Apology* between them have made us understand what Socrates meant by religion, and why his sense of duty to God forbade him either to evade prosecution or to purchase his life by any concessions. There is still one question connected with his death to which the answer remains to be given. Owing to unexpected circumstances, a month elapsed between

---

[1] This is implied in the mention of "security" (αὐτοὶ δ' ἐγγυᾶσθαι, 38b). Socrates could clearly have paid down the "one mina" of which he had spoken.

condemnation and execution. His friends took advantage of this delay to provide means of escape ; Socrates might still have avoided drinking the hemlock if he would have walked out of his prison, but he refused. Why was this ? No one would have thought the worse of him, and there would have been no question of a compromise with the leaders of the democracy. Persons who held with Socrates himself that the whole proceedings against him had been frivolous, and that he had been condemned for an offence which he had not committed, by a court which had no competence, might fairly be puzzled to know why he thought it a duty to refuse the means of escape. This is the point to be cleared up in the *Crito*. The explanation depends on an important distinction which the ordinary man to this day finds it hard to draw. The condemnation was in point of fact, as Socrates himself insisted, iniquitous. He was quite innocent of any real impiety. But it was strictly legal, as it had been pronounced by a legitimate court after a trial conducted in accord with all the forms of law. And it is the duty of a good citizen to submit to a legal verdict, even when it is materially false. By standing a trial at all, a man " puts himself on his country," and he is not entitled to disregard the decision to which he submits himself, even if his country makes a mistake. The " country " is entitled to expect that the legally pronounced sentence of a legitimate court shall be carried into effect ; there would be an end of all " law and order " if a private man were at liberty to disregard the judgment of the courts whenever he personally believed it to be contrary to fact.

Even so, there is a further point to be considered. We have seen that, strictly speaking, the court was not competent to take account of the offences which the prosecutors really had in mind, and that Socrates shows himself aware of this in the *Apology* when he cross-examines Meletus. It might, then, be urged that if Socrates had escaped he would not have been disregarding the decision of a competent court ; is it wrong to disrespect the sentence of an *in*competent one ? Two things need to be remembered : (*a*) the court thought itself competent, and Athenian law made no provision for the quashing of its findings as *ultra vires* ; (*b*) this being so, for an individual man who had all his life set the example of strict and complete compliance with the νόμοι of the city to follow his private judgment on the question of the competency of the court would have been to stultify the professions of a lifetime. Plato himself, in the same situation, Adam says, would probably have chosen to escape. This may be, but the second consideration just mentioned would not have applied to Plato in 399. A young man of under thirty, whose most important relatives had just four years before lost their lives in the cause of " oligarchy," could not be considered as having thrown in his lot definitely with the democracy and its νόμοι ; his position would have been really different from that of an old man of the Periclean age. The argument, used by Socrates, that to have neglected the opportunity to settle elsewhere is equivalent to a compact to live by the νόμος of the city, would have been inapplicable to a younger man who, in fact, had never had the option in question.   Thus, in the last resort, there is a "subjective" and personal element in the considerations which lead Socrates to feel that he would be belying his whole past by escaping.   Plato's object is not to lay down a categorical imperative for the guidance of all the wrongfully condemned, but to throw light on the motives of an individual great man.   (Whether Plato would himself have chosen to escape, if he had been placed in the same situation *in his own seventieth year*, is another question. Much would depend on his view as to the work which might remain to him to do elsewhere.)

The dramatic *mise-en-scène* is necessarily exceedingly simple. The conversation is *tête-à-tête* between Socrates in his apartment in the prison of the Eleven and Crito, unless we count the "Laws" into whose mouths the last word of the argument is put as an unseen third party to the talk.   The time is in the "small hours" before dawn, while it is still dark.   Crito, who brings the news that the "sacred vessel" on whose return Socrates will have to die has just been sighted off Sunium, has been some time watching Socrates as he sleeps, when Socrates wakes from a strange dream and the conversation ensues.   Crito fears that Socrates, whose sentence will be executed the day after the vessel reaches port, has only one more night to live ; Socrates, on the strength of his dream, expects, as turned out to be the fact, that the boat will not make so quick a voyage and that his death will be deferred another day.   (In his interpretation he evidently takes the "fair and comely woman" of 44a for the "fetch" of the approaching vessel, and her "white garments" for its gay white sails.)   This brief introduction leads straight to the conversation in which Crito puts the case for escape, to which Socrates replies point for point. (a) The friends of Socrates will suffer in reputation if he persists in dying.   It will be supposed that they were too mean to find the money necessary for corrupting his jailers.   The answer is that "decent folk" will know better than to think anything of the sort, and what the "many" think does not matter (44c).   (b) Unfortunately it does matter what the "many" think.   The power of popular prejudice is shown only too plainly by the present position of Socrates himself.   *Answer :* the "many" are powerless to do much in the way of either good or ill, for they can neither make a man wise nor make him a fool ; hence it matters very little what they do to him (44d).   (c) Perhaps Socrates is really thinking of the interests of his friends, who will be exposed to "blackmailers" (συκοφάνται) [1] if he breaks prison, and be forced to pay these persons to hold their tongues.   He need not consider that point ; his friends are in duty bound to take the risk and, besides, these worthies

---

[1] As Burnet points out *loc. cit.*, the source of the annoyance caused by "sycophants" was the procedure of Attic law, which left it to the "common informer" (Ἀθηναίων τῷ βουλομένῳ) to institute prosecutions for offences against the "public."

are not very expensive to satisfy. If Socrates has a delicacy about exposing Crito to the risk, his "foreign" friends, Simmias, Cebes, and others, are ready to open their purses (45*a–b*).[1] He need have no difficulty in finding an abode where he will be made welcome. Crito himself has relations with powerful men in Thessaly who would honour his friend and act as his protectors (45*c*) (*d*) Besides, it is not even morally right that Socrates should throw away his life. That would be gratifying the very men who have prosecuted him. Also it would be deserting his family, and an honourable man has no right to disregard his obligations to his children. Thus refusal to escape will look like a display of unmanly cowardice in both Socrates and his friends (45*c*–46*a*).

Socrates begins his formal reply by saying that all through life it has been his principle to act on his deliberate judgment of good. He cannot feel that the judgments he expressed in his defence before the court are in any way affected by the result of the trial. If he is to take Crito's advice, he must first be convinced that there is something unsound in these principles ; it is useless to work on his imagination by setting up bugbears. The strength of Crito's case all through has lain in the appeal to "what will be thought of us." Now formerly we both held that it is not every opinion nor the opinions of every man which matter. Socrates is still of the same mind about this, and so, as he has to confess, is Crito. We should attach weight to the opinion of those who know (the φρόνιμοι), and disregard the opinion of those who do not. For example, in the matter of bodily regimen the physician and the trainer are the experts who know, and their approval or disapproval ought to count, whereas a man who followed by preference the approvals and disapprovals of the "many," who are laymen in such matters, would certainly suffer for it in bodily health. The same principle applies to matters of right and wrong, good and bad, such as the question we are now considering, whether it will be right or good for Socrates to break prison. We have not to take into account the opinions of the "many," but those of the one expert, if there is such a man, by neglecting whose advice we shall injure "that which is made better by right but depraved by wrong." (That is, the soul ; the argument is from the standing analogy between health in the body and moral goodness in the soul.)

Further, we agree that if a man has ruined his physical constitution by following the opinions of the "many" and disregarding those of the medical expert, life with a ruined physique

---

[1] The point is that "aliens" would run no risks from the συκοφάνται because they could get out of Attic territory in a few hours. The purpose for which Simmias is said to have brought money at 45*b* 4 is not to appease the συκοφάνται, from whom a Theban could suffer no trouble. From the *Phaedo*, Simmias appears to have spent the month between the trial and death of Socrates at Athens, but this need not exclude a journey to Thebes to procure money to pay the warders who were to connive at Socrates' escape. Hence, as I now see, I was wrong in my *Varia Socratica* in supposing that Meletus is one of the persons meant by the reference to blackmailers.

is not worth preserving. But " that in us, whatever it is, in which wickedness and righteousness have their seat " is not less but more precious than the body. (Much less, then, is life worth preserving if this—that is, the soul—is vitiated.) Crito has therefore raised a wrong question. We ought to ask not what " the many " will think of Socrates' behaviour or that of his friends, but what will be thought by the man who " understands " right and wrong. True, the " many " can put you to death if you disagree with them ; but then another principle which both Socrates and Crito hold as strongly since the recent trial as before it is that the all-important thing is not to live but to live a *good* life, and that living a good life means the same thing as living *aright* (δικαίως). The real question to be answered then is, " Would it be *right* for me to take my leave of this place without a public discharge ? " All the other considerations which Crito has raised are irrelevant (46b–48e).

Again, we both still retain our old conviction that to commit a wrong is, in all conditions, a bad thing for the man who commits it (the thesis of the *Gorgias*). It follows that we must hold, contrary to the opinion of the " many," that a man must never repay wrong by retaliatory wrong (ἀνταδικεῖν), and therefore that we must never repay ill-treatment by ill-treatment (ἀντικακουργεῖν κακῶς πάσχοντα). In a word, no treatment received from another ever justifies wronging him or treating him ill, though this is a conviction so opposed to the code of the " many," that those who accept and those who reject it cannot even discuss a problem of practice with one another (οὐκ ἔστι κοινὴ βουλή, 49d). Socrates and Crito can only discuss the course Socrates is to adopt because they agree about this initial principle (49a–e).

Next, ought a man, on these principles, to keep his word when he has given it (assuming that what he has promised to do is *in se* morally right),[1] or may he break it ? Of course, he must keep it. Our immediate problem, then, reduces to this. If Socrates leaves the prison without a public discharge, will he, or will he not, be wronging the very party whom he ought to be most careful not to wrong ? Will he be keeping a right and lawful pledge, or will he be violating it ? Let us consider what the Laws, or the State, might have to say if they could take us in the act of " making our lucky " (μέλλουσιν ἀποδιδράσκειν). This appeal to the personified figure of the State or the Laws is, as Burnet says, in principle a Platonic " myth." Its function is the same as that played in other dialogues by the vision of the Judgment to come. That is, it does not carry the argument further, but brings it home powerfully to the imagination. Artistically the function of the picture is to evoke a mood of ideal feeling adequate to the elevation of the ethical demands of

---

[1] δίκαια ὄντα, 49e. This is inserted to exclude a promise to do what is *impermissum in se*. Socrates' view is that a promise to do what is in itself illicit is null and void. But we see in the sequel that the tacit " compact " by which Socrates is pledged to the νόμοι or κοινόν of Athens involves nothing but what is strictly *licitum*.

Socraticism on the conscience, to arouse unconditional "reverence" for the dignity of the moral law as that which demands and justifies the philosopher's martyrdom. So far, and no further, it acts as the sight of the Crucifix does on a Christian. The conception of society implied, as something too obvious to need explanation, is the same which underlies all the versions of the doctrine of "social contract," a doctrine naturally familiar to the members of a society which knew from its own experience how legislation is made. But it gives us the fundamental truth of the theory of "contract" uncontaminated with any element of historical error about the first origins of "society." The thought is that a man who has cast in his lot with the community by accepting its "social system" all through life has tacitly bound himself to support the organization on which the social order depends, and cannot in honour go back from his pledge for the sake of his personal convenience. This is what is really meant by the much-misrepresented doctrine of "passive obedience," and it is interesting to remark that Socrates thus combines in himself the "nonconformist's" reverence for "conscience" and the "non-juror's" reverence for the "powers that be." He is the one absolutely consistent "conscientious objector" of history, because, unlike most such "objectors," he respects the conscience of τὸ κοινόν as well as his own.

The Laws might complain that Socrates would by an *évasion* be breaking his own "compact," and that without the excuse that the compact had been made under duress, or obtained by false representation or without sufficient time for consideration.[1] He has had a life of seventy years for reflection and in all this time has never attempted to adopt a new domicile, but has absented himself less than almost any other citizen from Athens. Thus he cannot plead any of the recognized excuses for regarding his assent to live under the laws of the city as anything but free and deliberate. (Of course the meaning is not that Socrates could have been "naturalized" in some other community; but he might have chosen to live as a resident alien under the protection of another society, or as a colonist at *e.g.* Amphipolis or Thurii.) The whole course of his life bears silent witness that he has accepted the system of institutions into which he had been born, and it is an integral part of the system that an Athenian citizen shall respect the decisions of the duly constituted courts. He is not at liberty to reject the jurisdiction because in his own opinion the decision of a court does him a material wrong (50c). To run away to escape the execution of the court's sentence would be following up the exalted speeches he made before the judges by the conduct of the paltriest of eloping slaves. If he does break his "compact," what good can he expect to accrue to his connexions or himself? His family and friends will certainly run the risk of

---

[1] *Force majeure*, fraudulent misrepresentation, insufficient time for consideration, are thus recognized as the three conditions which might, severally or conjointly, make a promise void.

banishment or loss of property. As for himself, suppose he makes his escape to a neighbouring city such as Thebes or Megara, which have good institutions, and where, as we know, he would find warm friends, he must be looked on by all honest citizens as an enemy, who has defied one society and may be expected to do the same by another, and thus will fairly be under the suspicion of being a " corrupter " of the young who may associate with him. If, to avoid such reproach, he takes refuge in a disorderly and lawless community, what kind of life does he propose to lead ? For very shame, he cannot continue his professions of devotion to " goodness and law " with his own conduct staring him in the face. Even in so lawless a society as that of Thessaly, he might for a while live under the protection of Crito's connexions there, and they might find the story of his successful escape from prison an excellent joke, but he must expect to hear the painful truth about his behaviour as soon as he offends anyone. Even if he escapes that disgrace by making himself a general toady, his life will be that of a " trencherman " and parasite, and what will become of all his fine professions about right and goodness ? As for the final appeal which Crito had made to his parental affections, what good will such an existence do to his children? Does he propose to bring them up as hangers-on in Thessaly ? If they are to grow up as free men and citizens at Athens, will all his friends neglect them more because he has removed to the other world than they would if he had removed to Thessaly ? Besides, the plea will be useless when life is over at last and a man has to stand before the judges of the dead. If Socrates abides execution now, he will have a good defence before that tribunal. He will appear as an innocent victim of the injustice not of law, but of individuals who have abused law for his destruction.[1] If he does not, he will have to answer for having done what lay in him to shake the authority of law itself, and must expect to have the law itself against him in the next world as well as in this. It is this appeal which rings in the ears of Socrates and makes him deaf to the voice of Crito, nor can Crito find anything to set against it. We must, therefore, be content to follow the path along which God is leading us (50a–54e).

See further :
BURNETT.—*Euthyphro, Apology, Crito.* (Oxford, 1924.)
RIDDELL.—*Apology* of Plato. (Oxford, 1867.)
BURNET.—*Early Greek Philosophy, Part I.*, Chapter IX. 180–192.
RITTER, C.—*Platon,* i. 363–390.
RITTER, C.—*Sokrates.* (Tübingen, 1931.)
TAYLOR, A. E.—*Socrates.* (London, 1932.)

---

[1] 54b. This is, in fact, the fundamental distinction on which Socrates founds his whole argument. When a man is legally but wrongly convicted of an offence he has not committed, the wrong is inflicted not by the law, but by the persons who have misused the law. Anytus, not the law, has done Socrates a wrong. But the prison-breaker is doing what he can to make the whole social system ineffective. *His* conduct is a direct challenge to the authority of law itself.

CHAPTER VIII

THE *PHAEDO*

WE are now to consider the group of four great dialogues which exhibit Plato's dramatic art at its ripest perfection. It may fairly be presumed that they all belong to one and the same period of his development as a writer, a view borne out by a cautious and sane use of the available "stylometric" evidence. Outwardly they have all the same form, that of a conversation supposed to have taken place before a numerous audience and subsequently described either by Socrates himself (*Protagoras, Republic*), or by one of the original auditors (*Phaedo, Symposium*). We have already found Plato using this difficult literary form for comparatively short dialogues (e.g. *Charmides, Euthydemus*), but it is a more arduous task to keep it up successfully throughout a work of considerable compass ; as we have seen, in the dialogues which there is other reason for thinking later than the *Republic*, it is only adopted once (in the *Parmenides*), and there is a formal explanation of its abandonment in the *Theaetetus*. This is good reason for thinking that Plato's great achievements in this kind belong neither to his more youthful nor to his later period of literary activity, but to his prime of maturity as a writer (which need not, of course, coincide with his ripest maturity as a thinker). I do not think there is any satisfactory method of dating the four dialogues themselves in the order of their composition. We may reasonably presume that the *Republic*, as the work of greatest range and compass among them, must have taken longest to write, and was the last to be completed. It also contains what looks like a concealed reference to the *Phaedo* (*Rep.* 611*b* 10), though the fact is by no means certain.[1] Now there is one consideration which perhaps allows us to fix an approximate date in Plato's life for the writing of the *Republic*. In *Ep.* vii. 326*b*, where Plato is describing the state of mind in which he paid his first visit to Italy and Sicily, he says that he had been driven to state, in a eulogy of genuine philosophy (ἐπαινῶν τὴν ὀρθὴν φιλοσοφίαν), that humanity will never escape its sufferings until either true philosophers occupy political office

---

[1] The " other arguments " (ἄλλοι λόγοι) for immortality referred to in passing *may* mean those which Plato's readers would know from the *Phaedo*, but they may equally well mean those which readers of Socratic literature would know to be current among Orphics or Pythagoreans generally. Thus the words cannot be pressed as an argument for the priority of the *Phaedo*.

or political " rulers," by some happy providence, turn to philosophy. It seems impossible not to take this as a direct allusion to *Republic* vi. 499*b*, where the same thing is said, almost in the same words, as part of a " eulogy " of true philosophy. Since Plato also says (*Ep.* vii. 324*a*) that he was about forty years old at the time of his voyage, this seems to give us 387 B.C. as an approximate date for the writing of the *Republic*, or, at least, of its central and most difficult section, and we are led to think of his dramatic activity, culminating in the four great " reported dialogues," as marking the late thirties of his life. Beyond this, so far as I can see, we have no means of going. We cannot tell, for example, whether the *Phaedo* is earlier or later than the *Symposium*, or either earlier or later than the *Protagoras*. My own reason for taking the *Phaedo* before the other two is simply that it connects outwardly with the events of Socrates' last day, and consequently illustrates the same side of his thought and character as the three dialogues we have just examined.

As in the case of these three dialogues, I must be content to a considerable extent to refer my reader to Professor Burnet's commentary for treatment of details. The scene of the conversation is laid at Phlius, where Phaedo of Elis, apparently on his way home from Athens, relates the story of the last hours of Socrates to a party of Phliasian admirers of the philosopher who have not yet had any account of the details. The one member of this party who is named is Echecrates, independently known to us as a Pythagorean. Hence Burnet is probably not far wrong in supposing the story to be told in the " meeting-house " of the local Pythagoreans. The surroundings will thus harmonize with the general tone of the conversation, in which the two principal interlocutors are also pupils of an eminent Pythagorean, Philolaus. It should be noted that these two speakers, Simmias and Cebes, are both represented as young, and that they evidently belong to the group of Pythagoreans in whom the religious side of the original movement has been completely overshadowed by the scientific. It is Socrates who has to recall them to the very conceptions which are at the root of Pythagorean religion, and persuade them that their scientific " developments " are inconsistent with the foundations of that religion. We need also to be alive in reading the *Phaedo* to two important facts which are sometimes forgotten. One is that Socrates himself is very careful to qualify his assent to the main tenet of the Orphic and Pythagorean faith, the deathlessness of the soul, by cautious reserve as to the details of the eschatology in which that faith has found expression. He is sure that he will leave this world to be with God ; he is very far from sure about the rest of the Orphic scheme of rewards and punishments. The other is that we must not take the *Phaedo* by itself for a complete expression of the whole spirit of Socraticism. It sets Socrates before us in the last hours of his life, and dwells on just the side of his thought and character which would be sure to be most prominent in the given situation, but we should misconceive his doctrine if we did not integrate the picture of the *Phaedo* with such a representation of the philosopher in the midst of life as we get, for example, in the *Protagoras*, where the underlying body of doctrine is identical but the situation wholly different and the emphasis correspondingly different. Probably the directest way to an understanding of the influence and personality of Socrates would be to read and meditate these two great dialogues together, interpreting each in the light of the other. (It is worth observing that Aristotle seems to have done something of the kind. His views about the philosophy of Socrates as a whole seem to be derived chiefly from the *Phaedo*; when he has occasion, in his own *Ethics*, to discuss the Socratic theses about the conduct of life, it is demonstrable that the unnamed source of his information is primarily the *Protagoras*.)

There can be no doubt that Plato intends the reader to take the dialogue as an accurate record of the way in which Socrates spent his last hours on earth, and the topics on which he spoke with his intimate friends in the face of imminent death. This is indicated, for example, by the care shown to give a full list of the names of the persons present. Most of these were probably still living when the *Phaedo* was circulated ; it is quite certain that this was the case with some of them, *e.g.* Euclides and Terpsion, who, as we see from the *Theaetetus*, were still alive and active thirty years later ; Phaedo, the actual narrator, who is represented in the dialogue as still a mere lad; Aeschines of Sphettus, and others. Though Plato is careful to mention and account for his own absence, it is quite certain that he must have been fully informed of the facts, since the statement that he spent some time after the death of Socrates with Euclides and Terpsion at Megara comes to us on the excellent authority of his own pupil Hermodorus. We are therefore bound to accept his account of Socrates' conduct and conversation on the last day of his life as in all essentials historical, unless we are willing to suppose him capable of a conscious and deliberate misrepresentation recognizable as such by the very persons whom he indicates as the sources of his narrative. This supposition is to my own mind quite incredible, and I shall therefore simply dismiss it, referring the reader who wishes for discussion of it to the full Introduction to Burnet's edition of the dialogue.

The purpose of the dialogue is not quite accurately described by calling it a discourse on the " immortality of the soul." To us this suggests that the main object of the reasoning is to prove the soul's endless survival, and *nothing* more. But to the Greek mind ἀθανασία or ἀφθαρσία regularly signified much the same thing as " divinity," and included the conception of ingenerability as well as of indestructibility. Accordingly, the arguments of the dialogue, whatever their worth may be, aim at showing that our souls never began to be quite as much as at proving that they will never cease to be. But neither of these positions is the main point of the reasoning. The subject of the dialogue is better indicated by the

name used by Plato himself in *Ep.* xiii. 363*a*, where it is said to be
" the discourse of Socrates about the ψυχή." The immediate and
principal object of the whole conversation is the justification of the
life of " tendance of the soul " by insisting on the *divinity* of the
human soul, and on " imitation of God " as the right and reasonable
rule of conduct ; the immunity of the soul from death is a mere
consequence, though an important consequence, of this inherent
divinity. The argument is, in the proper sense of the phrase, a *moral*
one ; the worth and dignity of the soul afford reasonable grounds
for hoping that death is, to a good man, entrance on a better life,
an " adventure " which he may face with good comfort—the
summary of the whole matter given by Socrates himself at 114*d*–115*a*.

A possible misconception which would be fatal to a real understanding of the dialogue is to look upon the members of the series
of arguments for immortality as so many independent substantive
" proofs," given by the author or the speaker as all having the same
inherent value. Any careful study will show that they are meant
to form a series of " aggressions " to the solution of a problem, each
requiring and leading up to the completer answer which follows it.
In particular, Plato is careful, by skilful use of dramatic by-play
and pauses in the conversation, to let us see what he regards as the
critical points in the argument. These pauses are principally two,
that which occurs at 88*c*–89*a*, where the narrative is interrupted
by a short dialogue between Phaedo and Echecrates, and 95*e*–100*a*,
where Socrates relates the story of his early difficulties with the
physical " philosophy " of Empedocles, Diogenes, and others. It is
evidently meant that the two outstanding difficulties which must
be faced by the philosophical defender of the doctrine of immortality
are the " epiphenomenalist " theory of consciousness and the
" mechanical theory of nature," the one represented for us in the
Phaedo by the " objection " of Simmias, and the other by that of
Cebes.

As I shall point out later on, Plato himself in the *Laws* specifies
just these theories as being at the root of all irreligious philo-
sophizing, and it would still be true to say that to-day they constitute the speculative basis for most of the current denials of human
immortality. We are thus directed to find in the *Phaedo* a statement of the position of Socrates on these two perennial issues ; for
Plato's own personal attitude towards them we need to look primarily
to the express refutation of the " unbeliever " in the tenth book of
the *Laws*. The background presupposed in one refutation is the
science of the fifth century, that of the other is the Academic science
of the fourth, but both agree in the assertions (*a*) that mental life
is not the effect of bodily causes, and that physical reality itself—
" coming into being and passing out of being "—is not explicable
in purely mechanical terms. This—apart from the impressive
picture of the fortitude of the true philosopher in the moment of
death—is the main lesson of the *Phaedo*.

The immortal narrative must be passed over in the present

connexion with just one word. It may not be superfluous to associate ourselves with Burnet's protest against the absurd charge of " hardness " as a husband which has been brought against the dying Socrates. It is clear that his wife and infant son are supposed to have spent the last night of his life with him in the prison. They are conducted home at the opening of the discourse (60a) for the reason at which Socrates himself hints later on (117d), because Xanthippe is, naturally enough, on the verge of a " nervous breakdown," and Socrates desires to spare both her and himself. The children and the " ladies of the family " reappear again at the end (116b) for a final interview in the presence of no witness but Crito, the oldest friend of the family, and we are expressly told that the interview was a lengthy one. Phaedo cannot describe this eminently private scene, because he had not witnessed it, but it is the mere fact that he was not present which has given rise to misunderstanding (assisted, perhaps, by the incapacity of modern sentimentalists to understand the reticence of all great art).

THE ARGUMENT OF THE DIALOGUE

I. STATEMENT OF THE MAIN THESIS (60b–70b)

The main issue of the dialogue is made to emerge in a simple and natural way from the remark of Socrates that the genuine " philosopher " is one who is ready and willing to die, though he would regard it as " criminal " to put an end to his own life (61c). (That is, he trusts that death is the entrance on a better state, but holds that we may not force the door ; we must wait for it to be opened to us in God's good time. The Pythagorean origin of the absolute veto on suicide is indicated by the allusion to Philolaus at 61d.) This may seem a paradox, but it is intelligible if we conceive of man as a " chattel " ($\kappa\tau\hat{\eta}\mu\alpha$) of God, just as a slave is a " chattel " of his owner, and therefore has no right to dispose of his own life, as it does not belong to him. Socrates would not like to commit himself entirely to the Orphic dogma that while we are in the body we are " in ward," *i.e.* undergoing penal servitude for ante-natal sin, but he thinks it at least adumbrates this truth that " we men are chattels of the gods " (62b),[1] and therefore may not dispose of ourselves as we please. (The kind of $\kappa\tau\hat{\eta}\mu\alpha$ (" chattel ") meant is clearly a $\delta o\hat{\upsilon}\lambda o\varsigma$, who is, as Roman lawyers put it, in the

---

[1] For the doctrine in question see in particular the important fragment of Clearchus the Peripatetic quoted by Burnet *loc. cit.* I think it clear that the $\phi\rho o\upsilon\rho\acute{a}$ means " house of detention," not " post of military duty." To the passages making for the former interpretation quoted by Burnet add Plutarch, *de sera numinis vindicta*, 554d. The $\mathring{\alpha}\pi o\delta\iota\delta\rho\acute{a}\sigma\kappa\epsilon\iota\nu$ of 62b 5 exactly suits a prisoner " breaking prison," but not a sentry leaving his post, for which we should need $\alpha\mathring{\upsilon}\tau o\mu o\lambda\epsilon\hat{\iota}\nu$. Socrates' refusal to commit himself to the " mystical " dogma is important. It makes it clear at the start that, in spite of all appearances to the contrary, it is no part of the object of the dialogue to prove " pre-existence " and " transmigration."

dominium of his owner and therefore has no " proprietary right "
in his own body.) Yet in saying this we seem to be merely replacing
one paradox by another. If we are the "chattels" of the gods,
that means that we are under the "tendance" of good and wise
owners who know what is best for us much better than we do ourselves. Death would seem to mean being released from this
tendance and left to look after ourselves. Surely a wise man
would think such an *emancipatio* a thing to be dreaded (exactly,
that is, as a shrewd slave would be very unwilling to be "freed"
from a first-rate owner and left to fend for himself (62*d*)). The
paradox would be a very real one if Socrates were not convinced
that after death one will equally be under the care of good and wise
gods, and perhaps—though of this he is not equally sure (63*c*)—in
the company of the best men of the past. This is the faith (ἐλπίς)
which gives him courage to face death, and he will try to impart
it to his friends. Thus the thing to be proved is primarily not the
" natural immortality " of the soul. A proof of immortality,
taken by itself, would not be adequate ground for facing death in
a hopeful spirit. It would be quite consistent with holding that
we only leave this world to find ourselves in a much worse one.
What is really to be proved, if possible, is that "the souls of the
just are in the hand of God" after death as much as before.
Socrates, like all great religious teachers, rests his hopes for the
unseen future in the last resort on the goodness of God, not on the
natural imperishability of the human ψυχή. (So in the *Timaeus*
(41*a*–*b*), it is the goodness of the Creator's will which guarantees the
immortality even of the " created gods," *i.e.* the stars.) What'
is to be shown, in fact, is that the faith and hope with which the
" philosopher " faces death is the logical consequence and supreme
affirmation of the principles by which he has regulated his whole
life. To lose faith when you come to die would be to contradict
the whole tenour of your past life ; for, though the world may not
know it, the life of " philosophy " itself is nothing but one long
" rehearsal " (μελέτη) [1] of dying (64*a*). Possibly, indeed, the
" world " would say that it does know this well enough ; it knows
very well that " philosophers " are " morbid " creatures who are
only half alive, and that it serves them right to eliminate them
(a plain allusion to the Aristophanic caricature of the φροντισταί as

[1] *Not* " meditation " of death. μελέτη means the repeated practice by
which we prepare ourselves for a performance. It is used of the " practising "
of a man training for an athletic contest, and again of the " learning by heart "
of such a thing as a speech which you have procured from a λογογράφος and
want to have " perfect " when the time for deliverance comes. No doubt,
then, it was also the word for an actor's " study " of his " part." (Cf. *répétition*
as used of the rehearsals of a play or a symphony in French.) The thought is
thus that " death " is like a play for which the philosopher's life has been a
daily rehearsal. His business is to be perfect in his part when the curtain
goes up. Note that, as Burnet says (*Phaedo*, 64*b* 3 n., *E.G.Ph.*³, 278 n. 1), it is
implied throughout the argument that " philosophy " has the special sense,
which is clearly Pythagorean, of devotion to science *as a way to the salvation
of the soul.*

living "ghosts"). Only the world is mistaken on one small point ;
it does not understand the sense in which the philosopher uses the
word "death," and that is what we must explain (64b). It is all
the more necessary to attend to the explanation that it is really the
key to the whole of the *Phaedo*, and that its significance has been
often misapprehended by both admirers and critics down to our
own time as completely as by the δῆμος of Thebes or Athens.[1]

To put the matter quite simply, death, as every one understands, is the "release" of the soul from the body ; in other
words, it is the achievement of the soul's independence. Now
we can see that what the philosopher has been aiming at all his
life long is just to make the soul, as completely as he can, independent of the fortunes of the body. We can see this from the
following considerations : (a) The philosopher sets no great store
on the gratifications of physical appetite, and disregards the
"tendance of the body" in general (fine clothes and foppery)
"beyond what is needful." [2] What he "tends" is the soul, and
that is why the "mass of men" think him as good as a ghost or
corpse (64c–65a). (b) In his pursuit of knowledge he finds the
limitations of the body a hindrance to him in more ways than one,
and is always doing his best to escape them. He soon discovers
the grossness and untrustworthiness of our senses, even of the two
most acute of them, sight and hearing, and tries to arrive at truth
more accurate and certain than any which the evidence of sense
could furnish. This is why he trusts to thinking rather than to
sense ; but in thinking the soul is independent of the body in a
way in which she is not independent in sensation. (This is, of course,
strictly true. Socrates would probably be thinking primarily
of the danger of trusting to a "figure" in mathematics, a danger
which will be mentioned a little further on. It is equally true that,
even in our own times, when the scientific man is so abundantly
supplied with "instruments of precision," we have always to allow
for a margin of unknown error in all conclusions depending on data
derived from sense-perception ; absolute accuracy and certainty
can only be obtained, if at all, in "pure" science which makes
no appeal to sense, even for its data.) So pleasurable or painful
excitement derived from the body also gravely interferes with the
prosecution of truth. (One is hampered in one's scientific work
when one's head aches or one's liver is out of order.) (c) The
supreme objects of our studies, "*the* right," "*the* good," "*the*
beautiful," "figure," "health," in short, *the* "reality" (οὐσία)
investigated by any science is always something which none of the

---

[1] Socrates' point is that—to use the language of Christian mystics—the
"world" confuses a dying life with a living death. The "philosopher" is
out for "dying into life" ; the world thinks he is making his existence a
death in life, but it is really the worldling who is "dead while he lives."

[2] 64e, καθ' ὅσον μὴ πολλὴ ἀνάγκη αὐτῶν. This is inserted to show that
Socrates has no sympathy with the gratuitous slovenliness of persons like the
Telauges of Aeschines' dialogue or his own companion Antisthenes. He does
not regard "dirt" as a mark of godliness.

senses perceives, and the less we depend on any of them—the less, that is, we substitute " sensing " for " thinking " in our science—the nearer we come to apprehending the object we are really studying (65*d*–66*a*).[1] Having all these considerations in mind, we may fairly take a " short cut " (ἀτραπός) to the conclusion that so long as we have the body with us it will always be a hindrance to the apprehension of " reality " (τὸ ἀληθές) as it is. At the best we lose much valuable time by being obliged to take care of the body. If it gets out of condition, our quest of " the real " (τὸ ὄν) is even more hindered. Bodily wants and the passions connected with them—which, incidentally, are the causes of business and war, the two great occupations of the " active life "—leave us hardly any opportunity or leisure for the pursuit of knowledge. And even in the scanty time we are able to devote to the things of the mind, the body and its needs are constantly " turning up " and diverting our attention. Thus the man who is really " in love with knowledge " must confess that his heart's desire is either only to be won after death, when the soul has achieved her independence of her troublesome partner, or not at all. While we are in the body, we make the nearest approach to our supreme good just in proportion as we accomplish the concentration of the soul on herself and the detachment of her attention from the body, waiting patiently until God sees fit to complete the deliverance for us. When that happens, we may hope, having become unmixed and undiluted intelligence, to apprehend undiluted reality. Meanwhile the life of thinking itself is a progressive purifying of intelligence from the alien element and a concentration of it on itself. The philosopher is the only type of man who makes it the business of his life to accomplish this purgation and concentration and so to win spiritual independence. This is why we may call his life a " rehearsal of death," and why unwillingness to complete the process would be ridiculous in him (66*c*–68*b*). The conception set before us in these pages is manifestly the Hellenic counterpart of the " mystical way " of Christianity. The underlying ideas of both conceptions are

[1] That is, the object studied by any science is always what Socrates calls an εἶδος or ἰδέα, though the technical term is not yet introduced. It is important to note the immediate and emphatic assent of Simmias to this statement (65*d*). He is clearly supposed to have learned all about the matter from his Pythagorean teachers. The examples are taken from ethics (δίκαιον, ἀγαθόν, καλόν), mathematics (μέγεθος), medicine (ὑγίεια, ἰσχύς). Of course you can see μεγέθη, but it is quite true that you cannot see μέγεθος. So you can see or draw approximately elliptical lines, but you cannot even approximately draw " the general conic " or " the curve of the third order." If you did try to draw them and relied on some characteristic of your figure as a property of the curve on no better evidence than that of your eyes, you would soon be led into error about the " reality " you are investigating. A thorough empiricist would have to go to much wilder extremes. He would, for example, have to hold that it is quite uncertain whether, if you only went on counting long enough, you might not come on two odd integers without an even one between them, or on a highest prime number, or even on an integer which is neither odd nor even. These things are actually maintained by some empiricist mathematicians, but they would be the death of ἐπιστήμη.

that there is a supreme good for man which, from its very nature, cannot be enjoyed " in this life." The best life is therefore one which is directed to fitting ourselves for the full fruition of this " eternal " good beyond the limits of our temporal existence. In both cases this means that the highest life for man while on earth is a " dying life," a process of putting off the old man with the affections and the lusts and becoming a " new creature." The constant presence of this aim makes the life of devotion to science, as conceived by Socrates and his friends, a genuine *via crucis*. And they, like the Christian mystics, conceive of the best life as one of contemplation, not of action. The ultimate aim of the " philosopher " is not to *do* things, but to enjoy the vision of a reality to which he grows like as he looks upon it, the ideal already expressed in the apologue of the " three lives " popularly ascribed to Pythagoras. We must be careful, however, to guard ourselves against two insidious misconceptions. For all the stress laid on " purification " of the mind from contact with the body, we must not suppose that Socrates is thinking of a life of mere negative abstentions.

The whole point of the insistence on unremitting preoccupation with thinking as the philosophic form of " purgation " is that the object of the renunciation of the philosopher is to make his life richer ; by " purification " from external preoccupations, his intelligence becomes more and more intense and concentrated, just as, *e.g.*, alcohol becomes more potent the more nearly your specimen is " pure " alcohol. Nor must one suppose that the contemplative life, because it is not directed ultimately on action, is one of indolence or laziness. Socrates, who claims in our dialogue to have spent his whole life " in philosophy," was busy from morning to night with his " mission." Probably, when we remember the way in which Plato in the seventh *Epistle* insists on the political character of his own original ambitions and on his lifelong conviction that the business of the philosopher among men is to be a statesman, we may infer that he would not himself at any time have subscribed to the doctrine of the *vita contemplativa* without a great deal of explanation and reservation. Even the Pythagoreans who formulated the doctrine had stood alone among the scientific schools in playing an important part, as a society, in the politics of the early fifth century. They only became a merely scientific society when their political activities had been crushed by revolution. But it may well be that the ablest men of action feel even more strongly than the rest of us that the " conduct of business," the carrying on of commerce, governing, and fighting cannot be its own justification. To be everlastingly " meddling " seems an end not worthy the dignity of human nature ; at bottom we all want not to *do* something but to *be* something. To make " doing things " your ultimate object is merely to take " Fidgety Phil who couldn't keep still " as your model of manly excellence. It has been said with truth that the great " practical reforms " which have proved of lasting value have mostly been the work of men whose hearts were all the time set on something different.

If a man, then, plays the craven when death comes, we may be sure he is no true " lover of wisdom," but a " lover of the body," which is as much as to say a man whose heart is set on wealth (a φιλοχρήματος) or on " honours " (a φιλότιμος), or both at once (68c. This direct allusion to the Pythagorean " three lives " is, of course, intentional.) On the other hand, the philosopher will be marked by eminent courage and eminent " temperance " in the popular sense in which the word means control over one's physical appetites. In fact, when we come to reflect, there is something paradoxical about the courage and temperance of the rest of mankind. They are courageous in the face of danger because courage serves to protect them against death, which they fear as the worst of evils. Thus their very valour is rooted in a sort of cowardice. (As an Indian says of the English in one of Kipling's tales, " they are not afraid to be kicked, but they are afraid to die.") And the decent (κόσμιοι) among them keep their lusts in hand because they think they will get more pleasure by doing so than by giving way, so that " slavery to pleasure " is the source of what they call their " temperance." But the truth is that real virtue is not a business of exchanging pleasures and pains against one another. Wisdom is the true " coin of the realm " for which everything else must be exchanged, and it is only when accompanied by it that our so-called " virtues " are genuine goodness (ἀληθὴς ἀρετή). Without it, the kind of goodness which is based on the " calculus of pleasure and pain " is no more than a painted show (σκιαγραφία).[1] The Orphic saying is that " many carry the narthex but few are real βάκχοι," and we might apply this to our purpose by taking the " real βάκχος," who genuinely feels the " god within," to mean the true philosopher. Of these chosen few Socrates has all his life tried to become one ; with what success he may know better in a few hours (68b–69e).[2]

II. THE ARGUMENTS FOR IMMORTALITY

In substance, what has gone before contains Socrates' vindication of his attitude in the face of death. But, as Simmias remarks, the whole vindication has tacitly assumed that there is an hereafter. Now most men find it very hard to believe that the soul

[1] 69a 6–c 3. On the text and grammar of this sentence, which have undergone much corruption, see Burnet, *loc. cit.*, where it is also pointed out that σκιαγραφία does not mean an " imperfect outline," but a stage-painting in which, *e.g.*, a flat surface is made to look like the façade of a temple. The point is not that " vulgar " goodness is " imperfect " but that it is illusory.

[2] In this context Socrates' claim can hardly be understood to mean less than that he had been a " follower of the way." We cannot well believe that Plato invented this, still less that he had anything to do with " the way " himself.

is not " dispersed like smoke " when a man dies, and Simmias
shares their difficulty. To complete his " case " Socrates must
therefore satisfy us that the soul continues to be, and to be intelligent after the death of the "man." Accordingly he now proceeds
to produce three considerations which point to that conclusion.
It is not said that they are demonstrative. Simmias had asked
only for πίστις (conviction), not for demonstration, and Socrates
professes no more than to consider whether immortality is " likely "
(εἰκός) or not. In point of fact, the first two proofs are found to
break down and the third, as Burnet observes, is said by Socrates
(107b 6) to need fuller examination. Thus it is plain that Plato
did not mean to present the arguments as absolutely probative to
his own mind. The argument he does find convincing and develops
at great length in the *Laws* is put briefly into the mouth of Socrates
in the *Phaedrus*, but no mention is made of it here.[1]

(a) THE FIRST ARGUMENT (70c–77d).—This argument itself
falls into two parts, a (70c–72e) and β (72e–77d) ; the two have to
be considered in conjunction to make anything which can be called
a proof, and what they go to prove is not " immortality " but
merely that the soul continues to be " something " after death.
It is not simply annihilated. This, of course, is only the first step
to establishing what is really in question, the persistence of intelligence beyond the grave.

(a) *First Reason for holding that the Soul is not simply annihilated at Death* (70c–72e).—There is an ancient doctrine (it is,
in fact, Orphic) of rebirth, according to which a soul which is born
into this world is one which has come back from " another world "
to which men go at death. This, if true, would establish our point.
To look at the matter from a more general point of view, we see
that the world is made up of " opposites " (ἐναντία)—such as hot,
cold ; great, small ; good, bad. Now if a thing " becomes bigger " it
must have first been " smaller," if it becomes hotter it must have
been cooler, if it becomes " better " it must have been " worse,"
and so on. So we may say universally that whatever comes to be,
comes to be " out of its opposite," and that to correspond to each
pair of opposites, there are two antithetical processes of " becoming." Hot and cold are opposites, and similarly there are the two
processes of contrasted sense, " becoming hotter," " becoming

---

[1] It is the argument from the " self-moving " character of the soul
(*Phaedrus*, 245c 5–246a 2, *Laws*, x. 893b 6–896d 4). Why is nothing said of this
argument in the *Phaedo* ? It has been suggested that the reason is that the
argument is an invention of Plato's own and that he had not thought of
it when he wrote the *Phaedo*. I do not think this likely, since the argument is
really in principle that of Alcmaeon of Crotona, and is thus much older than
Socrates (Aristotle, *de Anima*, A2. 405a 30). I should suggest a different
explanation. The argument starts from the reality of motion. But this
would have been denied by the Eleatic Euclides and Terpsion, and Socrates
wishes to base his reasoning on premises his company will admit. We
must remember also that Euclides and his friend were very probably the
persons from whom Plato derived most of his knowledge of the last hours of
Socrates

cooler." All this will apply to the case of life and death. Being alive and being dead are opposites, just as being awake and being asleep are. And we have agreed that everything comes to be " out of its opposite." The living must come from the dead, and the dead from the living, and thus here, as elsewhere, there will be two opposed processes, corresponding to the two opposed conditions of being alive and being dead. We see and have a name for one of these processes, that by which a living being becomes dead ; we call it dying. But there must, on our principle, also be an antithetic process of " coming to life " which terminates in actual birth. In fact, if the whole process were not cyclical, life would ultimately perish, and there would be only a dead universe left. Thus the drift of the argument is simply to confirm the " ancient doctrine " of rebirth by showing that it is only one case of the universal natural law of cyclical " recurrence." The illustrations from the alternation of sleep and waking seem to show that Socrates is thinking primarily of the way in which this " law of exchange " had been assumed as the fundamental principle of the philosophy of Heraclitus, with whom death and life, sleeping and waking, are explicitly co-ordinated (Her. Fr. 64, 77, 123, Bywater). But the general conception of the world as made up of " opposites " which are generated " out of one another " was, of course, a commonplace of the earliest Greek physical science (cf. Burnet, *E.G.Ph.*[3], p. 8). Socrates' Pythagorean auditors, in particular, would be at once reminded of their own table of " opposites " by reasoning of this kind.

(It is easy to see that the reasoning is neither cogent nor, if it were, probative of what we want to prove. As Aristotle was afterwards to explain more fully, the whole conception of the generation of opposite " out of " opposite is vitiated by an ambiguity in the phrase " out of." A thing which grows cool has previously been warmer, but it is not true that " heat " is a stuff or *matter* out of which " cold " is made. In Aristotelian language, the thing which grows cool has lost the " form " of " the hot " and acquired the " form " of the cold ; the original " form " has not itself been made into an " opposite " form. Again, it is simply assumed, without warrant, that cyclical alternation is the universal law of all processes. To us there is no absurdity in the view that living organisms should finally vanish, or that differences of temperature should cease to exist. If the " principle of Carnot " could be taken to be true without any restriction, we should have to regard these consequences as inevitable. For the purposes of Socrates, however, it is sufficient that the reasoning should be based on assumptions which would be granted as common ground by his audience ; it is not necessary that they should be admitted by anyone else. Still, even when his assumptions are granted, nothing follows so far beyond the bare admission that the soul which has passed from this world to the other, and will, in turn, come back from the other world to this, has some sort of reality in the interval ; it has not become a mere nothing. To admit so much would, of course, be compatible with the crudest kind of materialism, and would do nothing to justify the conviction Socrates means to defend, the belief that the soul which has won its independence has passed to a "better" life.[1] Hence the necessity for a combination of this line of reasoning with that which is next introduced.)

(β) *The Argument from the Doctrine of Reminiscence* (72e–77d).— Cebes observes that we might have reached our conclusion, independently of the doctrine of recurrence, by arguing from Socrates' habitual position that what we call "learning" a truth is really being "put in mind" of something we had forgotten. If this is true, we must at one time have known all that in this life we have to be "reminded" of. Our souls must have existed "before we were men," and presumably therefore may continue to exist when we have ceased to be men. (This argument, if sound, brings us nearer to the conclusion we want, since it goes to prove that the soul not only was "something" but was fully intelligent before it had been conjoined with the body.) The main argument for this doctrine of reminiscence, we are told, is the one already considered in the *Meno*, that a man can be made to give the true solution of a problem by merely asking him appropriate questions, as we see particularly in the case of problems of geometry.[2] The answer is produced from within, not communicated by the questioner.

---

[1] Note that Socrates himself in the end throws over the principle of universal cyclical recurrence. His "hope" is that the final destiny of the righteous soul is to be with the gods and to live endlessly "apart from the body" (114c). This would be a swallowing up of death by life just as impossible on the principle of recurrence as the universal reign of death. He is, in fact, borrowing from two pre-philosophical traditions, that of endless "reincarnation" and that of the soul as a fallen divinity destined to regain its forfeited place among the gods. These traditions are not really concordant with one another, and it is the second which really represents his personal faith.

[2] ἐάν τις ἐπὶ τὰ διαγράμματα ἄγῃ (73b) may mean literally "if one shows the man a diagram," but since διαγράμματα sometimes means simply "geometrical proofs" (e.g. Xenophon, *Mem.* iv. 7, 3, where the δυσσύνετα διαγράμματα seem to mean simply "intricate demonstrations"), probably we should not press the literal sense of the word here. It is an interesting point that though Cebes knows all about the doctrine and attaches importance to it, Simmias, who appears later on as having gone further than Cebes in dropping the religious side of Pythagoreanism, has forgotten it. I think we may infer two things from the passage. (*a*) The doctrine of reminiscence was not originated by either Socrates or Plato, since Cebes knows both what it is and what is the recognized "proof" of it. It is presumably a piece of old Pythagoreanism which the "advanced" members of the school had dropped or were dropping by the end of the fifth century. (This explains why we never hear anything about it in Plato's later writings.) (*b*) I suggest that the connexion with immortality comes about in this way. To judge from the Orphic plates found at Thurii and elsewhere, the original idea was that what the soul has to be reminded of is her divine origin and the dangers she will have to surmount on her way back to the abode of the gods. The Orphic plates are, in fact, buried with the votaries to serve them as a kind of Baedeker's guide. The conversion of this piece of primitive theology into a theory of the *a priori* character of mathematics will be part of the spiritualization of old theological traditions due to the mathematician-saint Pythagoras.

Hence the answerer is plainly in possession of the truth which the questioner elicits. Socrates points out that the conclusion might be reached by a simple consideration of what we call " association." When you see an article belonging to an intimate friend, you not only see the article, but think of the owner, and that is what we mean by saying that the coat or whatever it is, " reminds " us of its owner (" association by Contiguity "). Again, when you see a portrait, you think of or " are reminded " of the original (" association by Resemblance "). Thus you may be " reminded " of something both by what is *unlike* it (" Contiguity ") and by what is *like* it (" Resemblance "). In the second case we also note whether the likeness is complete or not (*e.g.* whether the portrait is a good one or a bad one).

Well, then, let us consider a precisely parallel case. In mathematics we are constantly talking about " equality "—not the equality of one stone to another stone, or of one wooden rod to another wooden rod, but of the " just equal " (αὐτὸ τὸ ἴσον), which is neither wood nor stone—and we know that we *mean* something by this talk. But what has put the thought of the " just equal " into our minds ? The *sight* of equal or unequal sticks, or something of the kind. And we note two things. (*a*) The " just equal " is something different from a stick or a stone which is equal to another stick or stone ; we see the sticks or stones, we do not see " mathematical equality." (*b*) And the so-called equal sticks or stones we do see are not exactly, but only approximately, equal. (Even with instruments of precision we cannot *measure* a length without having to allow for a margin of error.) Thus plainly the objects about which the mathematician reasons are not perceived by the eye or the hand ; the thought of them is *suggested* to him by the imperfect approximations he sees and touches, and this suggestion of *B* by *A* is exactly what we mean by " being reminded of *B* by *A*." But *A* cannot remind us of *B* unless we have already been acquainted with *B*. Now from the dawn of our life here, our senses have always been thus " reminding us " of something which is not directly perceptible by sense (*i.e.* perception has always carried with it estimation by an " ideal " standard). Hence our acquaintance with the standards themselves must go back to a time before our sensations began, *i.e.* to a time before our birth. We have argued the case with special reference to the objects studied by the mathematician, but it applies equally to all other " ideal standards," like those of ethics, the good, the right ; in fact, to everything which Socrates and his friends called a " form." The only alternative to supposing that we had ante-natal acquaintance with these " forms " would be to say that we acquired it *at the moment* of birth. But this is absurd, since we are quite agreed that we bring none of this knowledge into the world with us ; we have to recover it slowly enough from the hints and suggestions of the senses. We conclude then that if " the kind of being we are always talking about," that is the " forms," exist, and if they are the standard by which we interpret all our

sensations, it must be equally true that our souls also existed and
were actively intelligent before our birth (76d–e). (One should
note several things about the way in which the doctrine of the
" forms " is introduced into this argument. For one thing, we
see that there is no room in the theory for " innate ideas " in the
strict sense of the word, and that there is no question of a knowledge
acquired independently of experience. The whole point of the
argument is that we should never be " put in mind " of the " forms,"
but for the suggestion of the senses. Again, the most important
feature of the process of " being reminded " is that sense-per-
ceptions suggest standards to which they do not themselves conform. The same visual sensations which suggest the notion
" straight " to me, for example, are the foundation of the judgment
that no visible stick is perfectly straight. The " form " is thus
never contained in, or presented by, the sensible experience which
suggests it. Like the " limit " of an infinite series, it is approxi-
mated but never reached. These two considerations, taken together,
show that the theory does full justice to both parts of the Kantian
dictum that " percepts without concepts are *blind*, concepts without
percepts are empty." [1] We may also note, as Burnet has done,
that the stress laid on the point that the sensible thing always falls
short of a complete realization of the " form " means that sensible
things are being treated as " imitations " (μιμήματα) of the
" form," a view we know from Aristotle to have been Pythagorean.
It is quite untrue to say that the " imitation " formula only appears
in Plato's latest dialogues as an improvement on his earlier formula
of " participation." In the *Phaedo* itself Socrates starts with the
conception of things as " imitating " forms ; " participation "
will only turn up at a later stage in the argument.)

Simmias is particularly delighted with this argument precisely
because, as he says, it proves the ante-natal existence of the soul
to be a consequence of the doctrine of Forms, and that he regards
as the most clear and evident of all truths (77a). (This delight,
by the way, would be quite unintelligible on the theory that the
doctrine was an invention of Plato.) But, as he goes on to say
after a moment's reflection, to prove that the soul " arose " before
our birth is not to prove that it will survive death, and it is against
the fear of death that Socrates has to provide an antidote.
Formally, as Socrates says, the point would be established if we
take arguments (α) and (β) together. (β) has proved the pre-

---

[1] It is very important to remember that on the theory there are no " forms "
except those which sense-experience suggests, or, to use the language which
will meet us later in the dialogue, there are no " forms " which are not " participated in " by sensible particulars. The " forms " are not Kantian " things
in themselves." But equally the " form " is not " the sensible thing rightly
understood," for the first fact you discover about any sensible thing, when
you begin to understand it, is, in Socrates' phrase, that " this thing is trying
(βούλεται) to be so-and-so, but not succeeding" (74d). This implies a " realistic " metaphysic; from the point of view of " nominalism," " terminalism,"
or " conceptualism," the whole doctrine is nonsense.

existence of the soul, (*a*) will prove—on the assumption that the alternate cycle of birth and death is endless—that the souls of the dead must continue to exist in order that men may continue to be born. But the " child in us " which is afraid of the dark is not to be quieted so readily, and we must try the effect of a more potent " charm " on him (77*a*–78*b*).

(*b*) SECOND ARGUMENT FOR IMMORTALITY (78*b*–84*b*).—This argument goes much more to the root of the question, since it is based not on any current general philosophical formula, but on consideration of the intrinsic character of a soul. In Aristotelian language, the first proof has been " logical," the second is to be " physical." The reasoning adopted lies at the bottom of all the familiar arguments of later metaphysicians who deduce the immortality of the soul from its alleged character as a " simple substance," the " paralogism " attacked by Kant in the *Critique of Pure Reason*. The " proof," as Kant knew it from the writings of men like Wolff and Moses Mendelssohn, is a mere ghost of that offered in the *Phaedo*. Socrates' point is not. that the soul is a " simple substance,"—he had not so much as the language in which to say such a thing—but that it is, as the Orphic religion had taught, something *divine*. Its " deiformity," not its indivisibility, is what he is anxious to establish ; the indivisibility is a mere consequence. Hence he is not affected by Kant's true observation that discerption is not the only way in which a soul might perish. No doubt it might perish, as Kant said, by a steady diminution of the intensity of its vitality, *if it were not divine*,[1] but what is divine in its own nature is in no more danger of evanescence than of discerption.

Simmias had spoken of the possible " dissipation " of the soul at death. Now what sort of thing is liable to dissipation and what not ? Obviously it is the composite which, by its own nature, is liable to be dissipated ; the incomposite, if there is such a thing, should be safe from such a fate. And it is reasonable to hold that whatever maintains one and the same character in all circumstances is incomposite, what is perpetually changing its character is composite. Thus for the crude contrast between the " simple " and the composite, we substitute the more philosophical antithesis between the permanent and the mutable. (This takes us at once to ground where Kant's criticism would not affect us. If the soul is, in any sense, immutable, it is so far secured against the lowering of intensity of which Kant speaks.) In the kind of being of which we speak in our scientific studies, the being we are always trying to define—the " forms," in fact—we have a standard of the absolutely immutable. " Just straight," " just right," " just good," are once and for all exactly what they are, and are invariable.

---

[1] And yet, does not Kant's argument rest on the erroneous assumption that if a series has the lower limit o, o must actually be a *term* of the series ? But he is at least right in saying that survival as a " bare monad " would not be the kind of immortality from the thought of which any man could derive hope or comfort.

But the many things which we call by the same names as the
" forms " are in perpetual mutation. (The " good " man loses his
goodness, the " handsome " garment its beauty, and so on.) Now
these latter mutable things are all things you can touch or see or
apprehend by one or other of the senses ; the immutable " standards "
are one and all apprehensible only by thought (διανοίας λογισμῷ).
This suggests that we may recognize two types of objects, each type
having a pair of characters—the invisible and immutable, and the
visible and mutable.[1]   Also we are agreed that we have a body and
have a soul. To which of our types does each of these belong ?
Clearly the body can be seen, the soul is invisible (of course " seen "
and " unseen " are being used here *per synecdochen* for " sensed," " not
sensed," respectively). In respect of this character there can be no
doubt of the type to which each belongs. What about the other pair
of contrasted characters ? As we said before, when the soul relies
on the sense-organs in her investigations she finds the objects she
is studying perpetually shifting, and loses her own way (πλανᾶται)
among them.   When she relies on her native power of thinking
and attends to objects which are strictly determinate and unchanging, she finds her way among them without uncertainty and
confusion, and it is just this condition of the soul we call " wisdom "
or intelligence (φρόνησις).   This would indicate that the soul
herself belongs more truly to the type with which she is most at
home, the immutable, whereas the body certainly belongs to the
mutable.[2]

Again, in the partnership of soul and body, it is the soul which
is rightly master and the body servant (the thought which the
Academy crystallized in the definition of man as a soul *using* a
human body as its instrument). Now it is for the divine to command and rule, for the mortal to serve and obey ; hence it is the
soul in us which plays the divine, the body which plays the mortal
part. (This brings us at last to the point on which Socrates really
means to insist, the " deiformity " or " kinship with God " of the

[1] This is identical at bottom with Dr. Whitehead's recent distinction
between " objects " and " events," *e.g.* between " Cambridge-blue " and
" Cambridge-blue-here-and-now." Dr. Whitehead, I think, does not expressly
say that it is only events which can be " sensed," but that is really implied in
his language. I *see* " Cambridge-blue-occurring-here-and-now " ; the *object*
" Cambridge-blue," which does not " happen," is suggested to me by my sensation of what is " happening ". I *recognize* it, am " put in mind of it " by the
event which happens. Cf. *Principles of Natural Knowledge*, p. 81 : " Objects
are entities recognized as appertaining to events ; they are the recognita amid
events. Events are named after the objects involved in them."   This is
precisely the doctrine of " forms " and of " recollection."

[2] Of course it is not said that the soul is absolutely immutable. This
would not be true ; we can change even our most deeply cherished scientific
and moral convictions. But it is true that, by contrast with the body, the
soul emerges as the relatively immutable. My intellectual and moral convictions do not undergo " adaptive " modifications to a changing environment
with the readiness shown by my organism. My body, for instance, will adapt
itself to a great climatic change more readily than my mind to a society with
a different morality or religion from my own.

soul. In view of the standing Greek equation of "immortal" with "divine," the formal inference to the immortality of the soul follows as a matter of course.)

The soul, then, is relatively the permanent and divine thing in us, the body the merely human and mutable. We should therefore expect the body to be relatively perishable, the soul to be either wholly imperishable or nearly so. And yet we know that, with favourable circumstances,[1] even a dead body may be preserved from corruption for ages, and there are parts of the body which seem all but indestructible. Much more should we expect that a soul which has made itself as far as possible independent of the mutable body, and has escaped by death to the divine and invisible, will be lifted above mutability and corruption. But if a soul has all through life set its affections on bodily things and the gratifications of appetite, it may be expected to hanker after the body even when death has divorced them, and be dragged down into the cycle of births again by this hankering. We may suppose that the place in the animate system into which it is reborn is determined by the nature of its specific lusts, so that each soul's own lusts provide it with its appropriate "hell," the sensual being reborn as asses, the rapacious and unjust as beasts of prey, and so forth. The mildest fate will be that of the persons who have practised the "popular goodness" misnamed temperance and justice without "philosophy" (*i.e.* of those who have simply shaped their conduct by a respectable moral tradition without true insight into the good, or, in Kantian phrase, have lived "according to duty," though not "from duty"). These, we may suppose, are reborn as "social creatures," like bees and ants, or as men again, and they make "decent bodies" as mankind goes. The attainment of "divinity" or "deiformity" is reserved for the man who has resolutely lived the highest of the three lives, that of the "lover of wisdom," and subdued his lusts, not like the "lover of wealth" from fear of poverty, nor like the "lover of honour" from concern for his reputation, but from love of good. This explains the reason why the lover of wisdom lives hard. It is because he knows that what a man comes to feel pleasure and pain about becomes his engrossing interest. To find your joy and woe in the gratifications of the body means to come to be bound up with its fortunes, and this bars the way to deification and binds you down to the wheel of birth. It is for the sake of this supreme good, "deification," that the lover of wisdom denies "the flesh." To consent to its motions would be to act like Penelope, who unwove by night what she had spent the day in weaving. Now a man whose whole life has been an aspiration to rise above mutability to deiformity will be the last person to fear that the new and abiding

[1] The meaning of ἐν τοιαύτῃ ὥρᾳ (80c) has been much disputed. From a comparison with *Tim.* 24c 6, *Phileb.* 26b 1, *Critias*, 111e 5, I take the meaning to be "climate," though I cannot produce another example of the singular of ὥρα in that sense.

deiform self which is being built up in him will be unbuilt by the event of death.[1]

(I make no apology for having drawn freely on the characteristic language of Christian mysticism in expounding this argument. Under all the real differences due to the Christian's belief in the historical reality of the God-man, the ideal of Socrates and the Christian ideal are fundamentally identical. The central thought in both cases is that man is born a creature of temporality and mutability into a temporal and mutable environment. But, in virtue of the fact that there is a something " divine " in him, he cannot but aspire to a good which is above time and mutability, and thus the right life is, from first to last, a process by which the merely secular and temporal self is re-made in the likeness of the eternal. If we understand this, we shall be in no danger of supposing that Socrates is merely anticipating the jejune argument from the indivisibility of a " simple substance," or that the Kantian polemic against Wolffian rationalism seriously affects his reasoning. The thought is that the real nature of the soul has to be learned from a consideration of the nature of the specific " good " to which it aspires. A creature whose well-being consists in living for an " eternal " good cannot be a mere thing of time and change. In this sense, the morality of the Platonic dialogues, like all morality which can command an intelligent man's respect, is from first to last " other-worldly.")

FIRST INTERLUDE (84c–85b).—At this point the thread of the argument is broken ; a general silence ensues, but Simmias and Cebes are observed to be whispering together, as though they were not quite satisfied. Artistically the break serves the purpose of lowering the pitch of the conversation and relieving the emotional strain. It also has a logical function. Impressive as the moral argument for immortality is, there are scientific objections to it of which we have so far heard nothing, and these deserve to be carefully stated and adequately met, since we cannot be called on to accept any view of man's destiny, however attractive, which contradicts known scientific truth, nor is Socrates the man to wish, even in the immediate presence of death, to acquiesce in a faith which is not a reasonable faith. That would be simple cowardice (84e). He has just broken out into his " swan-song," and like the swans, his fellow-servants of the Delphic (? Delian) god, he sings for hope and joy, not in lamentation. He is therefore robust enough in his faith to be only too ready to hear and consider any objections.

OBJECTIONS OF SIMMIAS AND CEBES (85c–88c).—Simmias thinks, like a modern " agnostic," that certainty about our destiny may be unattainable. He would at heart like to be able to appeal to

---

[1] Like Spinoza, but without, like him, being hampered by a naturalistic metaphysic, Socrates holds that the man who lives best has the soul of which the greatest part is eternal, i.e. the more thoroughly you live the philosophic life, the less is the personality you achieve at the mercy of circumstance, even if the circumstance is the change we call death.

" revelation " (a λόγος θεῖος, 85*d*) on such a question, but agrees that, in the absence of a revelation, one should resolutely examine all human speculations on the problem, and adopt that which will stand close scrutiny best. The difficulty he feels about Socrates' reasoning is that what he has said about the soul and the body might equally be said about the " melody " of a musical instrument and the strings which make the music. The strings are visible and tangible bodies, are composite and perishable, the music is invisible, incorporeal, and " divine." But it would clearly be absurd to argue that, for this reason, the music still exists and sounds " somewhere " when the instrument is broken. Now it is " our belief " that the body is like a musical instrument whose strings are its ultimate components, the hot, cold, moist, and dry, and that the soul is the music this instrument gives out when these ' strings " are properly tuned. If. this is so, we may grant that the soul is " divine," like all beauty and proportion, but we must also grant that disease and other disturbances of the constitution of the organism break the strings of the instrument or put them out of tune, and this makes it impossible to argue that because the *débris* of the broken instrument continues to exist after the fracture, *a fortiori* the music must persist still more immutably (85*e*–86*d*).

Cebes has a different objection. He does not attach much importance to the epiphenomenalism of Simmias, but he complains that nothing has really been proved beyond " pre-existence," which has been all along regarded as guaranteed by the doctrine of "reminiscence." Even if we grant that the soul, so far from being a mere resultant of bodily causes, actually makes its own body, this only shows it to be like a weaver who makes his own cloak. In the course of his life he makes and wears out a great many cloaks, but when he dies he leaves the last cloak he has made behind him, and it would be ridiculous to argue that he cannot be dead because the cloak which he made is still here, and a man lasts longer than a cloak. So the soul might make and wear out a whole succession of bodies—indeed, if it is true that the body is always being broken down by waste of tissue and built up again by the soul, something of this sort happens daily. But even if we go so far as to assume that the soul repeatedly makes itself a new body after the death of an old one, it may be that, like the weaver, it exhausts its vigour sooner or later, and so will make a last body, after the death of which the soul will no longer exist. And we can never be sure that the building up of our present body is not the last performance of such a worn-out soul, and consequently that the death we are now awaiting may not be a complete extinction (86*e*–88*b*).

These objections, Phaedo says, struck dismay into the whole company, with the single exception of Socrates. For they appeared to dispose of the whole case for immortality, and, what was worse, they made the hearers, who had been profoundly impressed by Socrates' discourse, feel that they would never be able to put any confidence in their own judgment again, if what had seemed to be completely proved could be so easily disposed of. Plato is careful to interrupt the narrative at this point still more completely, by allowing Echecrates to add that he sympathizes with the general consternation, since he too has hitherto been strongly convinced that the soul is the " attunement " of the body and is therefore anxious to know how Socrates met the difficulty (88c–e).

The purpose of all this by-play is to call attention to the critical importance of the two problems which have just been raised. We are, in fact, at the turning-point of the discussion. The " moral " argument based on the divinity of the soul, as proved by the character of the good to which it aspires, has been stated in all its impressiveness, and we have now to consider whether " science " can invalidate it. To use Kantian language, we have seen what the demand of " practical reason " is, and the question is whether there is an insoluble conflict between this demand and the principles of the " speculative reason," as Echecrates and the auditors of Socrates fear, or, in still more familiar language, the question is whether there is or is not an ultimate discord between " religion " and " science."

As to the source and purport of the two objections it may be enough to say a very few words. That of Simmias, as is indicated by the remarks of Echecrates, is represented by Plato as based on the medical and physiological theories of the younger Pythagoreans. It is a natural development from the well-known theory of Alcmaeon that health depends on the ἰσονομίη or " constitutional balance " between the constituents of the organism. The comparison with the " attunement " of the strings of a musical instrument would be suggested at once by the Pythagorean discovery of the simple ratios corresponding to the intervals of the musical scale. From this to the conclusion that " mind " is the tune given out by the " strings " of the body, the music made by the body, is a very easy step; and since we now know that Philolaus, the teacher of Cebes and Simmias, had specially interested himself in medicine, we may make a probable conjecture that we are dealing with his doctrine (which is also that of his contemporary Empedocles, Frs. 107, 108). Since the same doctrine appears in Parmenides (Fr. 16), it was clearly making its way among the Pythagoreans by the beginning of the fifth century, though it is, of course, quite inconsistent with their religious beliefs about re-birth in animal bodies: (on all this, see E.G.Ph.[3] 295–296).

In principle the theory is exactly that of modern " epiphenomenalism," according to which " consciousness " is a mere by-product of the activities of the bodily organism, the " whistle," as Huxley said, given off by the steam as it escapes from the engine. A satisfactory refutation of it must *ipso facto* be a refutation of the whole epiphenomenalist position.

The source of the difficulty raised by Cebes is different. His allusion to the alternation of waste and repair in the organism at once suggests a Heraclitean origin ; he is thinking of the view of

Heraclitus that the apparent stability of "things" lasts just so long as the antithetical processes of the "way up" and the "way down" balance one another, and no longer. (For the evidence of Heraclitean influences on fifth-century Pythagoreanism, see *E.G.Ph.*[3] Index, *s.v.* Hippasos; *Greek Philosophy, Part I.,* 87–88.) How "modern" Cebes' point is will best be seen by reflecting that the Heraclitean theory of "exchanges" is really a dim anticipation of the modern principle of the conservation of energy. The argument is, in effect, one quite familiar in our own times. If we reject epiphenomenalism and admit interaction between mind and body, it is argued that the mind must part with "energy" in acting on the body, and Cebes, like a modern physicist appealing to the principle of Carnot, holds that this loss of energy cannot be made good indefinitely. A time will come when the effective energy of the ψυχή has been wholly dissipated. Thus his criticism, like that of Simmias, is precisely of the kind which a man of science is tempted to urge against the belief in immortality in our own day. The one difference between the two positions is that the objection of Simmias is primarily that of a biologist, the difficulty of Cebes is that of a physicist. Cebes may also be said in a way to be anticipating Kant's criticism of the argument from the "simplicity" of the soul. His conception of the soul as perishing by wearing out her stock of vitality answers pretty closely to Kant's conception of a gradual sinking of the "intensity" of "consciousness" to the zero-level.

SOLUTION OF THE SCIENTIFIC DIFFICULTIES (88*e*–102*a*).—This section of the dialogue falls into three subdivisions. There is first a preliminary discourse by Socrates intended to warn us against being disgusted with serious thinking by the occurrence of difficulties and so led into mere "irrationalism," next a discussion of the difficulty of Simmias, and then a longer treatment of the much more fundamental problem raised by Cebes, this last subdivision receiving a special narrative introduction of its own.

(*a*) *The Warning against Misology* (89*a*–91*c*).—Socrates, alone of the company, shows himself calm and even playful in the presence of the bolt—or rather bolts—just shot from the blue. The "argument," at any rate, shall be "raised again," if he can perform the miracle. But whether he succeeds or not, he would at least utter a solemn warning against "misology," irrationalism. Distrust of reason arises much in the same way as misanthropy, distrust of our fellows. The commonest cause of misanthropy is an unwise confidence based on ignorance of character. When a man has repeatedly put this ignorant confidence in the unworthy and been disillusioned, he often ends by conceiving a spite against mankind and denouncing humanity as radically vicious. But the truth is that exalted virtue and gross wickedness are both rare. What the disillusioned man ought to blame for his experience is his own blind ignorance of human nature. So if a man who has not the art of knowing a sound argument from an unsound one has found himself repeatedly misled by his blind trust in unsound " discourses," there is a real danger that he will lay the blame on the weakness of our intellectual faculties and end as a mere irrationalist.[1] To avoid this fate, when we find our most cherished convictions apparently breaking down under criticism we must lay the blame not on the inherent untrustworthiness of " discourse " but on our own rashness in committing ourselves to an uncriticized position. We will therefore reconsider our case and try to meet the objections which have been brought against us, in the spirit of men who are contending honestly for truth, not for an argumentative victory.

(β) *The Objection of Simmias removed* (91c–95a).—In the first place, it may be pointed out that the difficulty raised by Simmias is incompatible with his own professed principles. He avows himself satisfied now by what had been already said that knowledge is " reminiscence," and that, consequently, our souls existed before they wore our present bodily guise. Plainly that cannot be the case if the soul is an " epiphenomenon," the melody given out by the body, the " whistle of the engine," to recur to Huxley's version of the same doctrine. The musical instrument must pre-exist and its strings be screwed up to the right pitch before the melody can be there. We may assert either that all knowledge is " reminiscence " or that the soul is an epiphenomenon ; we must not assert both propositions at once. And Simmias himself has no doubt which of the two positions has the better claim to acceptance. The doctrine of " reminiscence " has been deduced from the " postulate " (ὑπόθεσις) of the reality of the " forms," a principle which Simmias has all through accepted as certain. The epiphenomenalist theory of the soul rests on nothing more than a plausible analogy, and we all know how deceptive such analogies can be—in geometry, for example (92d).

(There is real point in Socrates' *argumentum ad hominem*, independently of the assumption of pre-existence. We may compare the story of W. G. Ward's crushing reply to Huxley, who had just explained mental life to his own satisfaction by epiphenomenalism *plus* the laws of association, " You have forgotten *memory*," *i.e.* the fundamental fact of the *recognition* of the past as past. As Huxley had to admit, his scheme could give no account of recognition, and without presupposing recognition it would not work.)

But the epiphenomenalist theory is not merely incompatible with our unproved postulate about " forms " ; it is also demonstrably false on independent grounds. There are two things which are characteristic of every " attunement " or " melody " ; every " attunement " is completely determined by its constituents, and no " attunement " admits of degrees. If a pair of vibrating strings

---

[1] The description of the misologist would equally cover both the case of the man who ends in pure scepticism and that of the man who takes refuge in a blind faith in what he openly avows to be irrational. Socrates stands for a *fides quaerens intellectum* against both " universal doubt " and indifferentism and blind fideism or " voluntarism." Hence the partisans of the one call him a " dogmatist," those of the other an " intellectualist."

have one determinate ratio, the interval their notes make will be the fourth, and cannot possibly be anything else ; if they have another determinate ratio, the interval will be the fifth, and so on. Again, a string either is "in tune" or it is not, and there is no third alternative. Between any pair of notes there is one definite interval ; they make that interval exactly and they make no other. C and G♭, for example, make an interval as definite, though not as pleasing, as C and G. "No attunement is more or less of an attunement than any other." What inferences about the soul would follow from these two considerations, if the soul is an "attunement" ? It would follow at once from the second thesis that no one soul can be more or less of a soul than any other. But we have to reckon with the recognized fact that some souls are better or worse than others. Now there seems to be a real analogy between goodness and being "in tune," and between badness and being "out of tune." Either then we should have to express this difference by saying that one "attunement" (the good soul) *is* more "attuned" than another (the bad soul), and our own admissions forbid us to say this ; or we must say that the good soul not only is an "attunement" but *has* a second further "attunement" within itself, and this is manifestly absurd. If a soul is an "attunement," we can only say that every soul is as much an "attunement" as any other, and this amounts to saying that no one soul is morally better or worse than another, or even that all souls, since all are precise "attunements," are perfectly good. But this denial of differences of moral worth is manifestly ridiculous. The argument is, then, that epiphenomenalism is incompatible with the recognition of differences of moral worth, and that these differences are certainly real. A theory which conflicts with the first principles of ethics must be false, since these principles are certain truth.

(The argument, though stated in a way unfamiliar to us, is precisely that which weighs with men who are in earnest with ethics against a philosophy like Spinoza's. Though Spinoza does not make "consciousness" depend causally on the organism, for *practical* purposes his theory of the independent "attributes" works out in the same way as epiphenomenalism. The ψυχή, though not causally dependent on the constituents of the organism, is supposed to be *mathematically* determinable as a function of them. Consequently, just as Simmias has to allow that no "attunement" is more or less an "attunement" than any other, Spinoza holds a rigidly nominalist doctrine about "human nature." There is really no such thing as a "human nature" of which Peter or Paul is a good specimen, but Nero a very bad one. Nero is not, properly speaking, a bad specimen of a man ; he is a perfect specimen of a Nero. To say that he may be a perfect Nero, but is a very bad man, is judging by a purely arbitrary and "subjective" standard. (See *Ethics*, Part I., Appendix, Part IV., Preface.) But, if this is so, Spinoza is undertaking an impossible task in writing a treatise on the good for man and the way to obtain it.)

Again, we have to consider the consequences of the thesis that an " attunement " is a determinate function of its constituents. Given the constituents, the musical " interval " between them is also once and for all completely given. Now the most potent fact about our moral life is that it is a conflict or struggle between an element whose rightful function is to dominate and direct, and a second whose place is to obey and be directed. The soul is constantly repressing the desires for gratification of appetites connected with the body. (It is not meant, of course, that the *whole* of moral discipline consists in subduing such elementary appetites ; they are taken as examples because they are the simplest and most obvious illustration of a principle.) The moral life is a process of *subjugation* of the " flesh " and its desires to the " godly motions of the spirit." The " spirit " which dominates the " flesh " clearly cannot be itself just the " attunement " or " scale " constituted by the ingredients of the " flesh." If this were so, the state of soul at any moment should be simply the resultant and expression of our " organic " condition at that moment, and there should be no such experience as the familiar one of the division of " spirit " or " judgment " against " flesh " or " appetite." (Here, again, the criticism is conclusive for a serious moralist against all forms of epiphenomenalism. The epiphenomenalist is tied by his theory to a " one-world " interpretation of human experience ; morality presupposes a " two-world " interpretation. Its very nature is to be a " struggle " between a higher and a lower. If man were merely a creature of time, or again if he were simply eternal, the struggle could not arise ; its tremendous reality is proof that man's soul is the meeting-place of the two orders, the temporal and the eternal, and this, of itself, disposes of the *simpliste* theory of human personality as a simple function of the passing state of the " organism " or the " nervous system." The epiphenomenalist psychophysics merely ignore the most important of the " appearances " which a true account of moral personality ought to " save." Like all the arguments of the dialogue, this reasoning, of course, presupposes the objective validity of moral distinctions ; to the denier of that ὑπόθεσις it will bring no conviction.)

(γ) *The Difficulty of Cebes discussed* (95a–102a).—As has been said already, the difficulty raised by Cebes is of a much more serious kind than that of Simmias. As the subsequent history of psychology has proved, epiphenomenalism is after all a thoughtless and incoherent theory based on hopelessly misleading analogies and incompetent to take account of the obvious facts of mental life. The theory on which Cebes is relying is a very different matter ; he is appealing to the first principles of a " mechanical " philosophy of nature. Put in modern language, his contention comes to this, that the action of mind on body presupposed in ethics cannot be reconciled with the principles of natural science except by supposing that mind " expends energy " in doing its work of " direction." If this expenditure of energy goes on without compensation, a time must come when the available energy of the mind is exhausted. Thus the issue raised is at bottom that which is still with us, of the universal validity of the postulates of a mechanical interpretation of nature.

Does the guiding influence of intelligence on bodily movement come under the scope of the two great laws of the Conservation and the Degradation of Energy ? If it does, we must look with certainty to the disappearance of our personality after the lapse of some finite duration ; if it does not, the principles of mechanics are not of *universal* application. The development of Energetics in the nineteenth century has enabled us to state the problem with a precision which would have been impossible not merely to Plato, but even to Descartes or Leibniz, but in principle the problem itself has remained the same under all these developments ; Socrates in this part of the *Phaedo* is dealing with the very question which is the theme, for instance, of James Ward's *Naturalism and Agnosticism*.

The importance of the problem demands that we should formulate it with very special care. We may state it thus. Granting the " real distinction of mind from body," it is possible that in every act of intercourse with the body the mind parts with energy which it cannot recover ; if that is so, its progress to destruction begins with its very first entrance into contact with a body, and the completion of the progress is only a matter of time (95*d*). Now in discussing this problem we are driven to face a still more fundamental one, the question of " the causes of coming into being and passing out of being "(95*e*), that is, the question of the adequacy of the whole mechanical interpretation of Nature. Socrates' object is to persuade his friends that no single process in Nature is adequately explained by the mechanical interpretation. He can most readily carry them with him by first giving an account of his own personal mental history and the reasons why he gave up the mechanical philosophy in early manhood. This brings us to the

SECOND INTERLUDE (95*e*-102*a*).—*The Origin of the Socratic Method.*—(For the, to my mind, overwhelming evidence that the narrative which follows is meant by Plato as a strictly historical account of the early development of Socrates I must refer to Burnet's detailed notes in his edition of the dialogue. The main point is that the general state of scientific opinion described can be shown to be precisely that which must have existed at Athens in the middle of the fifth century, and cannot well have existed anywhere else or at any later time. The " scientific doubts " of which Socrates speaks are all connected with two special problems—the reconciliation of Milesian with Pythagorean cosmology, and the facing of the contradictions Zeno had professed to discover in the foundation of Pythagorean mathematics. It is assumed that the system of Anaxagoras is the last great novelty in physics, and there are clear references to those of Diogenes of Apollonia and of Archelaus. This fixes the date to which Plato means to take us back down to the middle of the fifth century, a consideration which disposes at once of the preposterous suggestions that the narrative is meant as a description either of Plato's own mental development or of the development of a " typical " philosopher. Of course, Plato cannot tell us at first-hand what Socrates was doing and thinking more than twenty years before his own birth, but he has, at least, taken care that his story shall be in accord with historical probabilities, and we may fairly presume that some of the information employed in constructing it came to him directly from Socrates himself. Thus we have as much evidence for its accuracy as we can have for that of any narrative of events related by a narrator born a quarter of a century after the period he is describing.[1])

The general drift of the narrative is as follows. As a young man, Socrates had felt an enthusiasm for " natural science " and made himself acquainted with the biological theories of the Milesians, the Heracliteans, Empedocles, the psychology of Alcmaeon, the flat-earth cosmologies of the Ionians and the spherical-earth cosmologies of the Italian Pythagoreans, as well as with the mathematical subtleties of Zeno about the "unit " and the nature of addition and subtraction. The result of all this eager study was to induce a state of *dubitatio de omnibus*; so far from discovering the cause of all processes, Socrates was led to feel that he did not understand the " reason why " of the simplest and most everyday occurrences. At this point he fell in with the doctrine of Anaxagoras that " mind " is the one cause of order everywhere. The doctrine appealed to him at once, from its teleological appearance. If all the arrangements in the universe are due to intelligence, that must mean that everything is " ordered as it is best it should be," and Socrates therefore hoped to find in Anaxagoras a deliverer from all scientific uncertainties. He expected him to solve all problems in cosmology, astronomy, and biology by showing what grouping of things was best, and consequently most intelligent. But when he read the work of Anaxagoras, he found that its performance did not answer to its promise. Anaxagoras made no use of his principle when he came to the details of his cosmology ; he merely fell back on the same sort of mechanical causes ("airs " and " waters ") as the rest of the cosmologists. Like them, he made the fatal mistake of confusing a cause, or *causa principalis*, with " that without which the cause would not act as a cause," *causae concomitantes* or "accessory conditions." This was much as though a man should say that the reason why Socrates is now sitting quietly awaiting death, instead of being in full flight for Thebes or Megara, is the condition of his sinews, muscles, and bones. The real reason is

---

[1] The autobiographical pages of our dialogue are thus the ancient counterpart of Descartes' *Discours de la méthode pour bien conduire sa raison* with the interesting differences, (1) that though both philosophers are concerned to simplify philosophy by getting rid of a false and artificial method, Descartes' object is to revive the very "mechanical" interpretation of nature which Socrates rejected, and (2) that Socrates left it to the piety of another to do for his mental history what Descartes did for himself.

that he judges it good to abide by the decision of a legally constituted court ; if he judged otherwise, if he thought flight the more reasonable course, his bodily mechanism would be in a very different condition. Of course, if he had not this apparatus of bones and sinews and the rest, he could not follow up his judgment, but it remains true that it is his judgment on the question which really determines whether he shall sit still or run. This is precisely what we mean by saying that Socrates acts νῷ, rationally or intelligently.

The disappointment, Socrates says, confirmed his opinion that he was " no good " (ἀφυὴς ὡς οὐδὲν χρῆμα) [1] at natural science, and must try to find some way out of his " universal doubt " by his own mother-wit, without trusting to " men of science," each of whom only seemed to be able to prove one thing—that all the others were wrong. His description of the " new method " reveals it to us at once as that which is characteristic of mathematics. It is a method of considering " things " by investigating the λόγοι or " propositions " we make about them. Its fundamental characteristic is that it is deductive. You start with the " postulate," or undemonstrated principle, which you think most satisfactory and proceed to draw out its consequences or " implications " (συμβαίνοντα), provisionally putting the consequences down as " true," and any propositions which conflict with the postulate as false (100a). Of course, as is made clear later on, a " postulate " (ὑπόθεσις) which is found to imply consequences at variance with fact or destructive of one another is taken as disproved. But the absence of contradiction from the consequences of a " postulate " is not supposed to be sufficient proof of its truth. If you are called on by an opponent who disputes your postulate to defend it, you must deduce the postulate itself from a more ultimate one, and this procedure has to be repeated until you reach a postulate which is " adequate " (101e 1), that is, which all parties to the discussion are willing to admit. (We hear more of this part of the method in *Rep.* vi. 510–511, where we discover that the ideal goal of the method is to deduce the whole of science from truths which are strictly self-evident, but nothing is said of this in the *Phaedo*.) The most important special rule of the method, however, is that, also insisted on by Descartes, that a proper order must be observed. We are not to raise the question of the truth of a " postulate " itself until we have first discovered exactly what its consequences are. The

---

[1] Of course this is said humorously. It is the man who can discourse learnedly about " airs " and " waters "—we might say about " electrons " and " electric fields "—and yet ignores the distinction between " cause " and " accessory conditions " who is really, from Socrates' point of view, ἀφυὴς ὡς οὐδὲν χρῆμα for the work of hard thinking. Later on (99c), Socrates calls the method he fell back on a δεύτερος πλοῦς, or " second-best " course. As the phrase originally refers to taking to the oars when the wind prevents using the sails, the suggestion is that Socrates' method is " second-best " rather in being slower and harder than the slap-dash dogmatism of the physicists than in leading to inferior results.

confusion of these two distinct problems is the great error of the
ἀντιλογικοί (101e). In spite of his humorous depreciation of
his proceeding as that of an amateur, Socrates has evidently, like
Descartes, reflected carefully on the nature of geometrical method,
and, like him, he is proposing to introduce the same method into
scientific inquiry in general. An illustration, he says, may be given
by considering his own familiar practice of "postulating" such
"forms" as "the good," "beauty," and the rest. He intends, in
a few minutes, to show that if this "postulate" is made, the immortality of the soul will follow as an implication (100b). (There
is no question of proving the "postulate" itself, as the whole
company are ready to concede it.) At this point we leave the
autobiographical narrative and pass to an application of the
"postulate" of "forms" to the theory of causation, which
is a necessary preliminary to the final argument for immortality
(100c–102a).

What Socrates intends to explain is what we have learned from
Aristotle to call "formal" causality, but he has no technical
terminology ready to hand and therefore makes his meaning clear
by examples. If we ask *why* something is beautiful, we may be told
in one case, "because it has a bright colour," in another "because
it has such-and-such a shape." The point that Socrates wants to
make is that such answers are insufficient. There must ultimately
be one *single* reason why we can predicate one and the same character, beauty, in all these cases. Having a bright colour cannot be
the cause of beauty, since the thing we call beautiful on the strength
of its shape may not be coloured at all; having a particular shape
cannot be *the* cause of beauty, since we pronounce things which
have not that shape to be beautiful, on the strength of their colour,
and so on. Hence Socrates says he rejects all these learned explanations and sticks to the simple one that universally the reason
why anything is beautiful is that "beauty" is "present to it,"
or that it "partakes of" beauty. The thought is that whenever
we are justified in asserting the same predicate univocally of a
plurality of logical subjects, the predicate in every case names one
and the same "character." It is these characters which Socrates
calls "forms." We might call them "universals" if we bear two
cautions carefully in mind. They are not to be supposed to be
"ideas in our minds" or anything of that sort; they are realities
of which we think. Also, as the case of "beauty" is well adapted
to show, a "form" may be "present" to a thing in very varying
degrees. A thing may be very beautiful, or it may be only very
imperfectly beautiful, and it may well be that nothing is super-
latively and completely beautiful. We should also note that the
precise character of the relation which Socrates calls "presence"
or "participation" or "communication" (κοινωνία) is nowhere
explained, and his hesitation about the name for this relation (100d)
may perhaps mean that he feels that there is an unsolved problem
involved by his "postulate." There obviously is such a problem.

We naturally ask ourselves at once what else a particular sensible thing is, besides being a complex of " forms " or " characters." As far as the *Phaedo* goes, we are not told that the thing is any more than a " bundle of universals." The attempt to say what else it is has played a prominent part in later philosophy. Plato's answer has to be collected with difficulty from Aristotle's scattered notices of his informal oral discourses. Aristotle and the mediaeval Aristotelians tried to answer the same question by their doctrine of " matter " and " form," Scotus by the difficult doctrine of *haecceitas*. But there is no evidence that Socrates had any answer to the difficulty. The immediate point is simply that if we admit the existence of " forms," we must say in every case that the " cause " or " reason " why a predicate β can be asserted of a thing a is that a corresponding " form " B " is present " to a, or that a " partakes of " the " form " B. How it has come to do so is a different question, and we must not suffer ourselves to be led away on a false trail. (The question is, *e.g.*, " Why is this thing now beautiful ? What do I mean by calling it so ? not, What had to be done to it before I could call it so ?)[1]

We might seem here to have lost sight of the insistence on teleology which had marked Socrates' comments on Anaxagoras, but there is really a close connexion between " end " and " formal cause," as Aristotle was to show at length. To say that the primary problem is always to explain what a thing is by reference to its " form " carries the implication that we have to explain the origins and rudimentary phases of things by what the things are, when they are at last there, not to explain what they are by discoursing on their origins, and this is precisely what we mean by taking a " teleological " point of view. But it would take us too far away from the *Phaedo* to discuss the full implications of such teleology.[2]

At the point we have reached, the narrative of Phaedo is once more broken in order that Echecrates, as a mathematician, may express his high approval of Socrates' doctrine of method (which, in fact, is pretty plainly inspired by the example of Zeno in his famous polemic, the point of which was to show that there must be something amiss with the " postulates " of the early Pythagorean

---

[1] The importance of Socrates' warning against substituting some other problem for that of the formal cause is well illustrated by the perpetual confusion in our own times between explaining what a thing is and theorizing about its origin. Thus we are incessantly being offered speculations about the way in which morality or religion may have originated as if they were answers to the question what art or religion or morality is.

[2] One obvious implication may just be mentioned. As the earlier stages in our own life can only be fully explained in the light of what we were then going to be, so to explain a man's life as a whole we need to know not only what he is now, but what he may yet grow to be. Thus the problem of our ultimate destiny is strictly relevant to the ethical problem proper, on what principles we ought to regulate our present conduct. It is idle to say that it " makes no difference to ethics " whether the soul is immortal. It ought to make all the difference, just as it makes all the difference to the rules of the nursery that babies do not remain babies.

geometers, since they could be shown to lead to pairs of contradictory implications). We then embark formally on the

(c) THIRD (AND FINAL) PROOF OF IMMORTALITY (102a–107b).— The "forms" had entered incidentally into both the proposed proofs which have been already examined. In this final proof we are offered a direct deduction of immortality from the fundamental postulate that the "forms" exist. This marks the argument as intended to be the climax of the whole reasoning, since the proof, if successful, must be recognized as complete by Cebes or any one else who regards the reality of the "forms" as the basis of his whole philosophy.

We have, in the first place, to stipulate for an unusual accuracy of expression which is necessary if we are to avoid fallacy. We commonly speak, for example, of one man as taller or shorter than another. We say Simmias is taller than Socrates but not so tall as Phaedo. On the face of it this looks as though we were calling Simmias at once tall and short, and therefore asserting the simultaneous presence in him of two "opposed" Forms. But all we really mean is that Simmias *happens* to be relatively taller than Socrates and shorter than Phaedo. It is not "in virtue of being Simmias" (*en sa qualité de Simmias*) that these things can be predicated of him. The distinction here taken is that between essential and accidental predication since made familiar to us all by Aristotelian logic. Or, in scholastic terminology, it is the distinction between an intrinsic and an extrinsic denomination. The point has to be made, because the force of the argument now to be produced depends on the fact that it deals entirely with *essential* predication.

This being premised, we may go on to assert (*a*) that not only will no "form," *e.g.* magnitude, combine with an opposed "form," but further, "the magnitude *in us* will never admit the small" (102d). That is, not only can we dismiss at once as false such assertions as that "virtue is vice," "unity is plurality," but we can also equally dismiss any proposition in which a subject, other than a "form," of which that form is *essentially* predicated, is qualified by a predicate opposed to that which attaches to it *essentially* in virtue of the "form" under consideration. Thus, if "shortness" were an essential predicate of Socrates, we could say that "Socrates is tall" must be false ; it is only because a given stature is an "accident" of Socrates that it is possible to say of him at one date that he is short, but at another (when he has grown) that he is "tall." (Or to take an example which perhaps illustrates the point even better, not only is it absurd to say that virtue itself is vice, it would also be absurd to say "the virtues *of the old pagans* were splendid vices," if we meant such a phrase as anything more than a rhetorical exaggeration.) When a "form" opposite to that which is *essential* to a certain thing "advances" to "occupy" the thing, the original "form" cannot subsist side by side with its rival in joint occupation of the ground. It must either "beat its retreat" (ὑπεκχωρεῖν) or be "annihilated" (ἀπολωλέναι). (The metaphors, including that indicated in the last phrase, ἀπολωλέναι, are all military.) And this statement is quite consistent with that of our first " proof " about the generation of " opposites " from one another. For we were talking then about " opposite *things* " (πράγματα), and meant that a *thing* which becomes cool must have been warm, a thing which becomes big must have been small. Now we are talking about the predicates or characters of the things, and mean that *hot* does not become *cold* nor *cold hot*. The two positions are thus fully compatible with each other (103*b*).

(β) We can make a further assertion which will conduct us straight to the conclusion we want. There are certain things which are not themselves " forms," but of which participation in a given form is an essential character. Thus fire is not " warmth " nor is snow " cold." But fire will not " admit " the form " cold," nor snow the form " warmth." Fire is never cool nor snow hot. As we said already, when " cold " attempts to " occupy " fire, or heat to " occupy " snow, an *essential* character of the thing must either " withdraw " or be " annihilated," and in either case the thing, the fire or the snow, is no longer the thing it was. But we may now add that in cases like that of fire and snow, when each of a pair of subjects has predicated of it *essentially* " participation " in a form " opposite " to one in which the other member of the pair *essentially* participates, the same thing will occur. Thus " cold " is essentially predicated of snow and " hot " of fire. And we may say not only the snow will " retire " or be " annihilated " rather than allow itself to be " occupied " by heat, but further that snow will not abide the " advance " of fire. It *melts* and ceases to be snow when you expose it to fire. (This is a case of the alternative of " annihilation." The snow, so to say, allows itself to be " cut up " in defence of its " position " when the forces of the fire make their onslaught.) So again the number " three " is not the same thing as " the odd," or " odd number," since there are many other odd numbers, but it " participates " *essentially* in the " form " odd. (It is true that " three " and the other numbers, unlike fire and snow, are also themselves spoken of freely in this and other dialogues as " forms," but Socrates makes no difficulty about treating the " participation " of a sensible thing in a " form " and the " participation " of one " form " in another as examples of the same relation. As we might put it in the terminology of modern " logistic," he does not discriminate between the relation of an individual to a class, and the relation of total inclusion between one class and another.) Consequently " whatever is occupied " by the " form " three is also " occupied " by the accompanying " form " odd ; the cardinal number of every " triplet " is an odd integer. Hence no triplet will allow itself to be " occupied " by the " form " even number. You cannot make an even triplet (*e.g.*, when a man's fourth child is born, the class " children of So-and-so " does not become an even triplet ; it ceases to be a triplet as well as to be " odd." This is an example of the alternative of " withdrawal " or "retreat," since "oddness" is not, like low or high temperature, a character which can be "destroyed." The whole "universe" might conceivably be reduced to a uniform low temperature, but not the number-series to a series with all its terms even.)

We now apply these results to the case of the soul. Life is a necessary concomitant of the presence of a soul, as illness is of the presence of fever, or heat of the presence of fire. A soul always brings life with it to any body in which it is present. Now there is an "opposite" to life, namely, death. Hence we may say that a soul will never allow itself to be occupied by the opposite of the character it always carries with itself. That is, life may be essentially predicated of the soul and therefore death can never be predicated of it. Thus the soul is, in the literal sense of the word, "undying" (ἀθάνατος); that is, the phrase "a dead soul" would be a *contradictio in adjecto*. So much has now been actually demonstrated (105*e*).

Of course this does not take us the whole of the way we wish to go. What has been "demonstrated," and would probably not be denied by anyone, is that, properly speaking, "death" is a process which belongs to the bodily organism. It is the body which dies, speaking strictly, not its "mind." But to prove that there is no such thing as a "dead soul," though there are dead bodies, does not prove that the soul continues to live after the body has died, and Socrates is well aware of this. His demonstration, on his own admission, leaves us with an alternative : since "dead" cannot be predicated of a soul, the soul must either be annihilated or must "retire" when the body dies. Socrates' faith is that the second member of the alternative is correct, but the emphatic "so much has been demonstrated" of 105*e* 8 seems to show that, when all is said, this remains for him an article of faith, not a demonstrated proposition of science. Our decision between the two alternatives will depend on the question whether the soul is not only "undying" but "imperishable" (ἀνώλεθρος). If it is, then we may safely say that what befalls it at death is merely "withdrawal elsewhere." He is not actually called on to argue this fresh point, since his auditors at once assert their conviction that if what is "undying" is not imperishable, nothing can be supposed to be so, whereas there are, in fact, imperishables, such as God, and "the form of life." Thus, in the end, the imperishability of the soul is accepted as a consequence of the standing conviction of all Greek religion that τὸ ἀθάνατον = τὸ θεῖον = τὸ ἄφθαρτον. It is the soul's "divinity" which is, in the last resort, the ground for the hope of immortality, and the divinity of the soul is a postulate of a reasonable faith which the dialogue never attempts to "demonstrate." The last word of Socrates himself on the value of his demonstration is that its "primary postulates" (*i.e.* the "forms" and the divinity of the soul) really demand further examination (107*b* 5).

THE PRACTICAL BEARING OF THE DISCUSSION (107*c*–108*c*).— This brings us to the real moral of the dialogue. As we have just seen, even if we are satisfied with the deduction of immortality from the doctrine of " forms," that doctrine itself is a postulate which is not exempt from reconsideration. But the mere admission that the hope of immortality is not irrational has a profound significance for the conduct of life. It follows that the " tendance of the soul " is incomparably the most serious of human interests, and the danger of neglecting this " tendance " the most awful to which we can expose ourselves. If death ends all, it may not matter so much what sort of soul a man has, since, in a few years, his wickedness will end with his life. But if the soul lives for ever, it takes with it into the unseen world nothing but its own intrinsic character for good or evil, and its unending future depends on that. This is really what the Orphic stories about the judgment of the dead should teach us. On the character we bring with us into the unseen world, our company there will depend, and our happiness and misery will depend on our company. As in the *Gorgias* and *Republic*, the hope of immortality is thus used for a moral purpose. The value of faith in it is that it drives home the question what manner of men we ought to be, if there is an endless future before us, and thus invests the choice for moral good and evil with an awful importance it would otherwise not have (*Phaedo* 107*c*; *Rep.* 608*b*, 621*b–d*. Plato enlarges on the same theme on his own account at *Laws*, 904*a*–905*b*). In the end, for Socrates and Plato, no less than for Kant, immortality is a postulate of the " practical " use of "reason." [1]

I do not propose to make this chapter longer by dwelling either on the impressive myth in which Plato fits an imaginative picture of the future lot of the virtuous and the vicious into a framework supplied partly by a scheme of astronomy which seems to be Pythagorean, and possibly, as the admiring comment of Simmias at 109*a* suggests, due to Philolaus, and subterranean geography which manifestly comes from Empedocles, or on the famous description of the last earthly moments of Socrates. I must be content to refer the reader to Burnet's commentary, and, for a study of the influence of the picture on later eschatology, to Professor J. A. Stewart's *Myths of Plato*. It is useless to discuss the question how much in these myths of the unseen represents a genuine " extrabelief " of either Socrates or Plato, and how much is conscious " symbolism." Probably neither philosopher could have answered the question himself. But we must bear in mind that Socrates regularly accompanies these stories with the warning (e.g. *Phaedo*, 114*d*) that no man of sense would put much confidence in the details, and that the one thing of serious moment is that we should

---

[1] If the question is asked whether the faith defended in the *Phaedo* is a belief in " personal " immortality, I can only reply that, though the language of philosophers was not to acquire a word for " personality " for many centuries, the faith of Socrates is a belief in the immortality of his ψυχή, and by his ψυχή he means the seat or *suppositum* of all we call " personal character," and nothing else. " Tendance of the soul " is precisely what we call the development of " moral personality."

live as befits men who are looking for a city that does not yet appear, and that the real object of " tending the soul " is to make us fit for citizenship in the eternal (*Phaedo*, 115*b*). From the historical point of view, the supremely interesting feature of this particular myth is that it is an attempt to get into one picture the flat earth of the old Ionian science and the spherical earth of the Pythagoreans, as Burnet notes.   This is done by imagining the sphere of the earth to be of enormous magnitude and to contain a number of shallow depressions like that of the Mediterranean   Each of these depressions will look very much like the flat earth of Anaximenes or Anaxagoras or Democritus.   As Burnet says, some such reconciliation of the two cosmographies may have suggested itself at Athens in the middle of the fifth century to some one ; it would be absurd to suppose that it could ever have been entertained by contemporaries of Plato.

See further :

BURNET.—*Plato's Phaedo* (Oxford, 1913); *Greek Philosophy, Part I.*, Chapters IX.-X.
RITTER, C.—*Platon*, i. 532–586.
RAEDER, H.—*Platons philosophische Entwickelung*, 168–181.
NATORP, P.—*Platons Ideenlehre*, 126–163.
STEWART, J. A.—*Myths of Plato*, 77–111 (*The Phaedo Myth*) ; *Plato's Doctrine of Ideas*, 39–47.

NOTE.—Plutarch's essay *de Genio Socratis* is rich in interesting traditions about Simmias and the Pythagoreans at Thebes.   It describes Pelopidas and his fellow-conspirators, who recaptured the citadel of Thebes from the Spartans in 379, as meeting for their enterprise in the house of Simmias.   Plutarch, as a Boeotian, was well informed on Theban matters and his story presumably has historical foundations.

CHAPTER IX

THE *SYMPOSIUM*

THE *Symposium* is perhaps the most brilliant of all Plato's achievements as a dramatic artist ; perhaps for that very reason, it has been worse misunderstood than any other of his writings. Even in its own day it was apparently quite mis-apprehended by Xenophon, if one may judge by the tone of the very inferior imitation of it in his own piece of the same name. Xenophon was led by the form of the dialogue to suppose that it is meant to deal with the sexual passion and to pit against it a *Symposium* of his own, which has as its climax a eulogy of the pleasures of married life. Our own and the last generation, with the poison of Romanti-cism in their veins, have gone farther and discovered that the dialogue anticipates William Blake's " prophecies " by finding the key to the universe in the fact of sex. This means that such readers have sought the teaching of the *Symposium* in the first instance in the Rabelaisian parody of a cosmogony put very appropriately into the mouth of Aristophanes. The very fact that this famous speech is given to the great γελωτοποιός should, of course, have proved to an intelligent reader that the whole tale of the bi-sexual creatures is a piece of gracious Pantagruelism, and that Plato's serious purpose must be looked for elsewhere. Similarly, it is more from the *Sym-posium* than from any other source that soul-sick " romanticists " have drawn their glorification of the very un-Platonic thing they have named " platonic love," a topic on which there is not a word in this or any other writing of Plato. We must resolutely put fancies like these out of our heads from the first if we mean to understand what the real theme of the dialogue is. We must remember that Eros, in whose honour the speeches of the dialogue are delivered, was a cosmogonic figure whose significance is hope-lessly obscured by mere identification with the principle of " sex." We must also remember that the scene is a festive one, and that the tone of most of the speeches is consequently more than half playful, and rightly so, as the gaiety of the company is meant to set off by contrast the high seriousness of the discourse of Socrates. It is there that we are to find Plato's deepest meaning, and when we come to that speech we shall find that the " love " of which he speaks the praises is one which has left sexuality far behind, an *amor mysticus* which finds its nearest modern counterpart in the writers who have employed the imagery of *Canticles* to set forth the love of the soul for its Creator.

In form the dialogue is an indirectly reported drama. The actual narrator, Apollodorus of Phalerum, a friend of Socrates (who is mentioned at *Apol.* 38*b* as one of the persons who offered to give security for a fine of thirty minae, and at *Phaedo* 117*d* as breaking into hysterical tears when Socrates drained the hemlock, and again by Xenophon as a constant attendant on the master, at *Mem.* iii. 11, 17), repeats to some friends the story of the banquet held in honour of the first tragic victory of the poet Agathon. Apollodorus is too young to have been present, but had the story direct from an eyewitness, Aristodemus, of the deme Cydathenaeum, apparently the same person as the Aristodemus whom Xenophon makes Socrates take to task (*Mem.* i. 1, 4) for his neglect of public worship. The time of narration is supposed to be " a good number of years " (172*c*) after Agathon's retirement from Athens. When that was we do not know, except that it was after the production of Aristophanes' *Thesmophoriazusae* (411) and before that of the *Frogs* (405), so that the actual narration must be supposed to be given some time in the last few years of the fifth century. The real object of introducing all these particulars seems to be to remind us that Plato himself could not have been present at the banquet, and does not therefore pretend to guarantee the historical accuracy of the narrative in detail.

It is more interesting to remark the careful way in which the spirit of the time is kept up in the account of the banquet itself. Not only is the occasion itself, the first public victory of a new poet, a festive one, but the year is one in which the temper of the Imperial city itself was exceptionally joyous and high. The date is only a few months before the sailing of the great Armada which was confidently expected to make the conquest of Sicily a mere stepping-stone to unlimited expansion, possibly to the conquest of Carthage (Thuc. vi. 15); the extraordinary tone of ὕβρις characteristic of Alcibiades in the dialogue becomes much more explicable when we remember that at the moment of speaking he was the commander-designate of such an enterprise and drunk with the ambitions Thucydides ascribes to him quite as much as with wine. We note that Aristophanes also is depicted as he must have been at the height of his powers, when the *Birds* and the *Lysistrata* were yet to be written, not as the broken man, whom Plato might have known personally, who could sink to the tiresome dirtiness of the *Ecclesiazusae*. In a few months' time the whole situation was changed by the scandal about the Hermae and the profanation of the mysteries ; Alcibiades was an exile at Sparta, bent on ruining the city which had disgraced him, and there is good reason to think that at least two other speakers in our dialogue (Eryximachus and Phaedrus) were badly implicated in the same affair.[1] For the δῆμος itself, the year may be said to have been the crisis of its fate. It had staked its all on a great aggressive bid for *Weltmacht* and the bid failed. The city never recovered the loss of men and material ;

[1] For the evidence see Burnet, *Greek Philosophy, Part I.*, 190–191.

the commander of whom she had made a deadly enemy was the man who taught the thick-witted Spartans where to deal her the wound which would, in the end, prove fatal. It is part of Plato's consummate art that he hints at nothing of this. He fixes the mood of the time and of the man of the time, " flown with insolence and wine," with complete objectivity and without after-thought, as a background to set off the figure of " philosophy " incarnated in Socrates.[1]

INTRODUCTION (*172a–178a*).—Aristodemus, then, related that, the day after Agathon's victory, he met Socrates in very unusual " festal array," on his way to Agathon's dinner-party and accepted his proposal to join him. On the way Socrates fell into one of his ecstasies and left his companion to enter Agathon's house, where he was warmly welcomed, alone. Agathon knew enough of Socrates' habits not to be startled by learning that he was standing " tranced " in the doorway of the next house. He did not make his appearance until dinner was half over, when he took his seat by Agathon in the gayest of humours. When the dinner was finished, the party resolved, on the advice of the physician Eryximachus, that there should be no enforced deep " potting " and no flute-playing. They would entertain themselves, as sensible men should, with discourses. Phaedrus, another member of the party, had often remarked on the singular fact that though so many persons and things have been made subjects of eulogy, no one has as yet made an adequate eulogy of Eros.[2] It would be a good way of spending the evening if each member of the party would deliver such a eulogy, beginning with Phaedrus, as the source of the proposal. Socrates fell in at once with the suggestion which, he declared, suited him admirably, as the " science of love " was the only science he possessed.

The main object of this little introduction is plainly to call our attention to a marked feature in the character of Socrates. He is at heart a mystic and there is something " other-worldly " about him. We shall hear a great deal more about this later on from Alcibiades when he describes Socrates' long " rapt " in the trenches before Potidaea, an experience which may have had a great significance

---

[1] I do not think it necessary, with Mr. R. G. Bury, to look for any hidden meaning in the references made by Apollodorus to a less accurate narrative of the scene given by a certain Phoenix. These touches are intended merely to suggest that the incidents had aroused a good deal of interest and been much talked about. I do not believe that there is any reason to suppose that Plato is replying to charges made in the καταγορία Σωκράτους of Polycrates anywhere in our dialogue. If he had done so, we should probably have learned something about the matter from Xenophon or from the *Apologia* of Libanius (which shows signs of a knowledge of Polycrates' pamphlet).

[2] Mr. Bury naturally reminds us that there is a chorus about Eros in the *Antigone* and another in the *Hippolytus*. But the ode of the *Antigone* (781–801) deals with the ruin and havoc Eros causes and the crimes to which he prompts even " the just." That of the *Hippolytus* (525–564) is similarly a prayer against his " tyrannical " violence. Neither can be called a eulogy. Cf. E. Bevan, *Hellenism and Christianity*, pp. 93 ff.

for his " mission." A minor experience of the same kind is introduced at the outset to prepare us for this narrative and for the high
" other-worldliness " of Socrates' own discourse on Eros. But,
as with other great mystics, Socrates' other-worldliness is compatible
with being a " man of the world " in the best sense and knowing
how to adapt himself readily to the mood of the gayest of companies. (It is worth noting that the biographers of the fervent
" ecstatic " St. Francis Xavier dwell on precisely the same combination of qualities as part of the secret of his influence over
company of every kind, and that Xavier himself, in his instructions
to his remplaçants, lays almost as much stress on the importance of
knowing how to win men by being " good company " as on that of
intense secret devotion.)

Speech of Phaedrus (178a–180b).—Phaedrus is known to us
chiefly from the part he plays in the dialogue called after him,
where he appears as an amateur of rhetoric and a fervid admirer
of the fashionable stylist of the moment, Lysias, in contradistinction
to Socrates, who regards Lysias as intellectually inferior to the, as
yet, little known Isocrates. Socrates is made to say of him there
(*Phaedrus*, 242b) that he has been the cause of more " discourses,"
either by delivering them himself or being the occasion of their
delivery by other men, than any living person, if we leave Simmias
of Thebes out of account. If we may trust the list of names inserted in Andocides i. 15, he was among the persons accused, a few
months after Agathon's dinner, of having " profaned the mysteries "
(unless, though this is not so likely, the reference is to some other
Phaedrus). In Lysias xix. 15 he is said to have fallen into poverty,
but " not through vicious courses." There is a well-known epigram
in the *Anthology*, ascribed to Plato, which makes him an ἐρώμενος of
the author, but, since Phaedrus was a man in 416 when Plato was
a small boy, this is chronologically impossible.[1]

The speech of Phaedrus is properly made jejune and commonplace, for a double reason. As a point of art, it is necessary to
begin with the relatively tame and commonplace in order to lead
up by a proper *crescendo* to the climax to be reached in the discourse
of Socrates. And the triviality and vulgar morality of the discourse is in keeping with the character of the speaker as depicted
for us in the *Phaedrus*. Phaedrus understands by Eros sexual
passion, and particularly passion of this kind between two persons
of the same sex. At Athens these relations were regarded as
disgraceful both by law[2] and, as the next speaker in our dialogue
will remind us, by general opinion, but literature shows that they

[1] Of course the Phaedrus of the epigram might be another person. But
when we find Agathon and Phaedrus figuring in an ἐρωτικὸς λόγος by Plato
and also appearing as ἐρώμενοι in epigrams ascribed to Plato, it is surely most
likely that the epigrams were composed and fathered on Plato by some later
author who had read the *Symposium* and forgotten that it is Socrates and
not Plato who poses playfully there as an ἐρωτικός.

[2] For the attitude of Attic law to παιδεραστία, the great source of information is the speech of Aeschines against Timarchus.

were in fact cultivated particularly by the " upper classes " as part of the general craze for imitation of Sparta. It is important to remember that all such aberrations were strongly disapproved by the *viri Socratici*. The present dialogue and the *Phaedrus* are complete evidence for the theory and practice of Socrates ; Plato's attitude in the *Laws* is the same. At *Laws* 636*b* it is made a special reproach to Sparta to have set an example of such " corruptions," and their complete suppression in a really moral society is taken as a matter of course at 841*d*.[1] Xenophon's attitude is the same.

The argument of the speech is that Eros is entitled to honour on two grounds—(*a*) his *noblesse*, as proved by his antiquity, and (*b*) the advantages he bestows on us. The first point is established by an appeal to Hesiod and the cosmogonists generally, who presuppose Eros—the impulse to generation—as an original first principle of the universe. It is brought in as a regular commonplace of encomiasts, who are fond of dwelling on the " pedigree " of their hero. (Socrates regarded this pride of birth as pure vanity as he tells us at *Theactet.* 175*a–b*, where he criticizes the common run of panegyrists on this ground.) The second point is supposed to be proved by the argument that " love " is the most powerful of incitements to ambition. A lover will do anything and endure anything to win the admiration of his " beloved " and avoid disgracing himself in his eyes. (Note then that Phaedrus has no conception of any " good " surpassing that of the " lover of honours.") Hence an army of " lovers," if one could be raised, would be invincible. In short, the great service which Eros renders to men is that he inspires them with μένος (" prowess "). (This was, in fact, exactly the view taken in Spartan and other Dorian communities, where " homo-sexual love " in its coarsest form was encouraged because it was believed to contribute to military " chivalry." [2]) The point is illustrated by the cases of Alcestis who died for her " love " Admetus, and Achilles who died for his " lover " Patroclus. Heaven rewarded this devotion by restoring Alcestis to life [3] and translating Achilles to the " isles of the blest." Orpheus, a mere " chicken-hearted " musician, was not allowed to recover his Eurydice, because he had not the " pluck " to die for her but sneaked down to the house of Hades without dying. In substance, then, the speech simply amounts to a defence of an unnatural practice on the plea of its military value. It is an apologia for the theory and practice of Sparta.

[1] These considerations show that we must not put a gross interpretation on the passing remark of Socrates at *Rep*. 468*c*. The reference is merely to innocent marks of affection and admiration which the younger people are to show to the brave soldier, and is half playful in tone.

[2] On this aspect of the subject see in particular the instructive article of Bethe (*Rheinisches Museum*, lxii. 438 ff.).

[3] *Symp.* 179*b*. Apart from the play of Euripides, which Phaedrus probably has in his mind, this is the first reference in extant Greek literature to the famous story.

In manner it is a poor and inadroit " encomium " of a common-place type.[1]

Speech of Pausanias (180c–185c).—Pausanias is virtually an unknown figure to us. He appears also in the *Protagoras* (the supposed date of which must be roughly some twenty years before 416), in company with Agathon, then a mere stripling, and Socrates is there made to say playfully that he should not be surprised if the pair are " lovers " (*Prot.* 315d). Xenophon has dutifully worked him in in his own imitation of the *Symposium* (viii. 32), where he is said to be the " lover of the poet Agathon " and to have " defended homo-sexual vice." [2] This, however, is merely a Platonic reminiscence. Xenophon has taken the remark of Socrates in the *Protagoras* with dull literalness and gone on to attribute to Pausanias the remark about an " army of lovers " actually made in our dialogue by Phaedrus.

The speech of Pausanias, unlike that of Phaedrus, really does attempt to take account of specifically Athenian moral sentiment, and is much more elaborately worked out in point of form. He is dissatisfied with Phaedrus on moral grounds, because he has drawn no distinction between worthy and criminal " love." The distinction is even prefigured in mythology, which recognizes a difference between a " heavenly " Aphrodite, daughter of Uranus without any mother, and a " vulgar " (πάνδημος) Aphrodite, daughter of Zeus and Dione. Since Aphrodite is the mother of Eros, we must consequently distinguish between a " heavenly " and an earthly or " vulgar " Eros. The one is admirable, the other not. In fact—so far Pausanias agrees with Socratic ethics—there is a right and a wrong in all human activities, and consequently there must be a right and a wrong way of " being in love."

The " low " form of love has two characteristics : (1) its object may be of either sex, and (2) what it loves in that object is the body rather than the soul, and this is why the vulgar lover prefers his beloved to be empty-headed (ἀνόητος) and therefore an easy quarry. The " heavenly " love is all masculine in his ccmposition. The object of this love is therefore always male and the passion is free from " grossness " (ὕβρις). It is directed not on the young and pretty but on an object just on the verge of manhood, a person whose *character* promises assured lifelong friendship.

To this distinction corresponds the apparently self-contra-dictory character of the Attic " use and wont " in respect of Eros. In some communities, such as Elis and Boeotia, the " vulgar " and the more refined Eros are both permitted, in the Ionian cities both are regarded as disgraceful. This is because Eleans and Boeotians

---

[1] Cf. Bury, *Symposium*, p. xxv. But he is unjust to the " sophists " in suggesting that it is a fair specimen of their performances, and I think he would be nearer the mark if he had said that the moral standpoint of the speech is that of an average Spartan, than he is in speaking of " the average citizen " of Athens.

[2] For another clear echo of our dialogue, cp. Xen. *op. cit.* ii, 26 with *Symp.* 198c 3. There are plenty of others.

are dull and stupid ; Ionians have been inured to slavish conformity to institutions which serve the purposes of their Persian masters. Eros, philosophy, bodily culture, are all discouraged by the Persians as influences unfavourable to acquiescence in despotism. At Athens and Sparta (this last statement can hardly be strictly true) social custom is not so simple. Use and wont are divided ; public opinion " loves a lover " and sympathizes with all his extravagances, but the young, on the other hand, are expected to resist his advances and promises, and parents and relatives take all possible care to protect their charges against them. (Just as in a " romantic " society it is thought honourable in a man to practise " gallantry," but the point of female honour to be " cruel " to the gallant.) The explanation of this apparent contradiction is that the difficulties put in the way of the " lover " are intended to make it certain that he loves with the higher and celestial kind of Eros, directed to the soul, and that the " beloved " is won not by the wealth or social position of the lover but by his genuine " goodness " and " intelligence."

In some respects the speech is morally on a higher level than that of Phaedrus. It is a real contribution to the discussion to introduce as fundamental the distinction between a noble and an ignoble " love." And Pausanias is so far following a right instinct when he makes the noble " love " independent of obvious physical prettiness and attractiveness and maintains that its object is a *consortium totius vitae* in the fullest sense of the words. So far he is in accord with the distinction we should draw ourselves between the love that is little more than a sensual weakness and the love which can lead to a " marriage of true minds." To this extent, I cannot agree with the disparaging estimate of Mr. Bury (*Symp.* xxvii). That Pausanias conceives of a *consortium totius vitae* as only possible between a younger and an older *male* is to be explained by the Attic neglect of the intellectual and moral education of the womenfolk of the citizens. There is no possibility of the " shared life " where one of the partners is an intelligent human being and the other a spoilt child or a domestic animal, and it is fair to remember this when we find Pausanias assuming that all love of women belongs to the ignoble kind. On the other hand, Pausanias' conception of the noble Eros is pitched far too low. As his inclusion of Sparta as one of the places where the distinction is recognized would be enough to show, he quite definitely means to give his approval to what Socrates and Plato, like ourselves, regard as not merely " guilty " but " unnatural," provided that it is made the basis for a permanent life of intimate devotion. The persons on whom he bestows unqualified admiration as having achieved the perfection of human excellence are just those whom Socrates is made to treat in the *Phaedrus* much as we should treat the " knight " who is spurred to chivalrous exploits by a love which, though " sinful," is not *merely* " carnal." (Unlike Socrates, Pausanias would clearly never have understood why Sir Lancelot came short in the spiritual quest of the Sangraal.) He does, indeed, expect passion to be "sanctified" by being pressed into the service of "goodness," but his conception of "goodness," if it is not as crude as that of Phaedrus, who makes it equivalent to mere "prowess," is still unspiritual. Harmodius and Aristogiton who "slew the tyrant" furnish him with his standard of "noble love" and its services to man. On the formal merit of the speech, as judged by the rules of "epidictic" introduced to Athens by Gorgias, see the remarks of Mr. Bury in his edition of the dialogue (Introduction, xxvii–xxviii).

Interlude and Speech of Eryximachus (185c–188e).—We must not forget that we are listening to the speeches delivered at a gay party by guests, many of whom are in a merely festive humour. The grave moral issues which have been raised by the magnification of Eros will receive their proper treatment when we come to the great discourse of Socrates, but before Plato can so much as introduce that, he must raise the imaginative level of the conversation to a pitch at which the first crude glorification of "passion" only survives in an undertone. Otherwise, there will be far too violent a "modulation into a different key." This function of desensualising the imaginative tone of the dialogue is to be achieved by making the speech of Socrates follow directly on one by Agathon, which is a brilliant but passionless and fanciful tissue of jewelled conceits. Even this needs to have the way prepared for it, if we are not to be conscious of too violent a change of mood. Hence the two interposed speeches of Eryximachus and Aristophanes with the little interlude which introduces them. The tone of this part of the dialogue is wholly playful, and I think it would be a mistake to regard it as anything more than a delightful specimen of "Pantagruelism." The numerous persons who are unhappily without anything of the Pantagruelist in their own composition will continue, no doubt, to look for hidden meanings in this section of the *Symposium*, as they look for them in Rabelais, and with much the same kind of success. Fortunately, we need not imitate them, any more than we need take Rabelais' book to be a disguised treatise on the "new monarchy."

It was now, we are told, the turn of Aristophanes to speak, but as he was impeded by a hiccough, the physician Eryximachus undertook to speak out of order as well as to prescribe for the poet's "passing indisposition." Hidden allusions have been suspected in this simple incident, but without reason. Aristophanes, one of the sturdy topers of the party (176b), is held up, when his turn to speak comes, by an accident which is a small joke in itself ; the medical man of the group, who also happens to be a sober soul (176c) not able to carry much liquor, gives him professional aid and fills up what would otherwise be a gap in the evening's programme. There is nothing here which calls for a "serious" explanation.

Eryximachus is presumably the same person as the Eryximachus who was implicated in the business of the "profaning of the mysteries" (Andoc. i. 35) ; at least, there was a certain Acumenus who was also among the denounced (*ibid.* i. 18), and the name is a very unusual one, so that it looks as though the denounced persons were our physician and his father. He is, we might almost say, the F.R.S. of Agathon's party, and all his behaviour is strictly in character. He announces himself from the first as a very " moderate drinker," and, as Mr. Bury observes, takes his departure later on, as soon as the scene has become one of wild revelry. His speech is carefully adapted to his character and profession. It is, in fact, under the guise of a panegyric of Eros, a little discourse on the principles of " science," especially of medical science. The scientific, and particularly the medical man, is the real repository of the secrets of love. The style of the speech is appropriately sober, free from the artifices of rhetoric and marked by a plentiful use of professional terminology. We may, with Mr. Bury, call him a " pedant," if we do him the justice to believe that the pedantry is, of course, part of the fun of the evening and is presumably intentional. The learned man is presumably amusing himself, as an eminent man of science might do to-day in an after-dinner speech, by making a little decorous " game " of his own professional occupations. I see no need to suppose that *Plato* intends any serious satire on the " science " of the speaker, especially as it represents the views of the Sicilian medical school, the very type of biology from which both Plato and Aristotle draw the biological analogies which play so large a part in their ethics.

Eryximachus opens his speech by giving emphatic assent to the distinction between a good and a bad Eros, but protests against looking for the effects of these contrasted forces exclusively in the souls of men. They can be traced everywhere in the structure of the universe, no less than in the human organism.[1] This may be illustrated from medicine. The healthy and the diseased constituents of the body have both their " cravings " ; there are wholesome appetitions and morbid appetitions. The business of medical science is to gratify the one and check the other. We might define the science as " knowledge of the body's passions for repletion and evacuation," and the man who can tell which of these " passions " are healthy and which " morbid," and can replace the morbid cravings in his patient by healthy ones, is the complete physician. The body is, in fact, composed of " opposites " which are at strife with one another, the hot, the cold, the dry, the moist, etc. ; medicine is the art which produces " love and concord " between these opposites. The task of " gymnastic," agriculture, music, is precisely similar, and this may be what Heraclitus meant by saying, " It is drawn together in being drawn apart," and talking of the " concord of opposites," though his language is inadequate, since in the establishment of " concord," the previous " opposition " is

---

[1] 186b, καὶ κατ' ἀνθρώπινα καὶ κατὰ θεῖα πράγματα, *i.e.* not only in biology but in physics. The θεῖα here gets its meaning from the habit, universal in Ionian science, of giving the name θεός or θεοί, in a purely secular sense, to the assumed primitive body or bodies.

cancelled out and disappears. In music, again, we can distinguish
the "good" and the "bad" Eros. The "good Eros" is exemplified
by those scales in which a really cultivated taste takes pleasure,
the "bad" by those which tickle the fancy of the vulgar. So in
the wider world of the physicist, a good and healthy climate is a
right and equable "temperament" (κρᾶσις) of heat and cold, rain
and dry weather, a bad climate is an instance of the "violent"
Eros ; it is an unhealthy "blend" of heat and cold, dry and wet
weather. Astronomy thus is another science of "love." So,
there is a "good" and a "bad" Eros of gods and men ; a religious
and an irreligious way of sacrificing and interpreting signs and
portents, and the professional knowledge of the priest and seer
becomes another example of the science of Erotics.

Thus the point of the speech is to insist on the cosmic significance of Eros. The underlying thought is that nature is everywhere made up of "opposites," which need to be combined or
supplemented by one another ; they may be combined either in
proportions which make for stability, and then the result is temperate climate, health,. prosperity, tranquillity, or in proportions
which lead to instability, and the result is then cataclysms of nature,
disease, misfortune, violent and unwholesome excitement. The
business of science in all cases is to discover the proportions upon
which the "good" results depend. The sources of the doctrine
are easily indicated. We detect the influence of the Heraclitean
conception of the balance of "exchanges" as the explanation of
the seeming permanences of the world-order, the Pythagorean
doctrine that all things are combinations of "opposites," and of the
special biological working out of the thought which is characteristic
of the philosophy of Empedocles, the founder of Sicilian medicine.
The general point of view, as German scholars have pointed out,
is much like that of some of the treatises of the Hippocratean
corpus, notably the περὶ διαίτης α', in which the attempt is made to
find a speculative foundation for medicine in the Heraclitean
cosmology. The only inference we are entitled to draw is that the
main ideas of Sicilian medicine could be presumed to be generally
known to cultivated persons at Athens in the last third of the fifth
century, as is, in fact, shown abundantly by the use made of
analogies based upon them all through the ethical dialogues of
Plato For the argument of the *Symposium* itself the chief function
of the speech is to divert attention from the topic of sex, as must
be done if sex itself is to be treated with the necessary philosophic
detachment in the discourse of Socrates, and to call attention to
the universal cosmic significance of the conception of the reconciliation of "opposites" in a higher "harmony." This preludes
to the discourse of Socrates, where we shall find that the principle
has actually a *supra-cosmic* significance. Meanwhile, the introduction of this thought of Eros as a "world-building" principle
provides the starting-point for the brilliant and characteristic
burlesque cosmogony put into the mouth of Aristophanes.

Speech of Aristophanes (189a–193d).—To the general reader, this is perhaps the best-known section of the whole dialogue, and one of the best-known passages in the whole of Plato. It is the more important to avoid misapprehending its purpose, which is simply humorous and dramatic. We should note that the speech itself is introduced by a thoroughly Aristophanic jest, and that the poet tells us in so many words that he means to live up to his profession by being "funny." The speech itself may be very briefly summarized. In the beginning man was a "round" creature with four arms and four legs and two faces, looking different ways, but joined at the top to make a single head. There were *three* "sexes," if we can call them so, of these creatures, the double-male, double-female, and male-female, the first derived from the sun, the second from the earth, the third from the moon, which is at once a "luminary" and an "earth." But as yet there was no sexual love and no sexual generation. The race procreated itself by a literal fertilization of the soil. These creatures were as masterful as they were strong and threatened to storm heaven or blockade it, as we learn from the old traditions about the "giants." As a measure of safety, Zeus split them longitudinally down the middle and reconstructed them so that their method of propagation should henceforth be sexual. Since then, man is only half a complete creature, and each half goes about with a passionate longing to find its complement and coalesce with it again. This longing for reunion with the lost half of one's original self is what we call "love," and until it is satisfied, none of us can attain happiness. Ordinary wedded love between man and woman is the reunion of two halves of one of the originally double-sexed creatures ; passionate attachment between two persons of the same sex is the reunion of the halves of a double-male or a double-female, as the case may be. If we continue in irreligion, it is to be feared that Zeus may split us again, and leave us to hop on one leg with one arm and half a face.

As I have said, the brilliance of this fanciful speech must not blind us to the fact that it is in the main comedy, and that the real meaning of the dialogue must not be looked for in it. Plato is careful to remind us that the speaker is a professional jester ; he is too good an artist to have made the remark without a purpose, or to have discounted the effect of the discourse of his hero Socrates by providing his dialogue with two centres of gravity. To be sure, there are touches of earnest under the mirth of his Aristophanes, as there always are under the wildest fun of the actual historical Aristophanes. There is real tenderness in Aristophanes' description of the love-lorn condition of the creature looking for its lost "half," and a real appreciation of unselfish devotion to the comrade who is one's "second self." Aristophanes shows more real feeling than any of the speakers who have been heard so far. It is also true that he is making a distant approximation to the conception, which Socrates will develop, of love as the longing of the soul for union with its true good. But the distance is even more marked

than the approximation. The goal of love, as Socrates conceives
it, is not incorporation with a mate of flesh and blood, nor even
lifelong "marriage" with a "kindred mind," but the ἱερὸς γάμος
of the soul with the "eternal wisdom" in a region "all breathing
human passion far above." The passion Aristophanes describes
is that which finds its most lapidary, perhaps its most perfect
expression in Dante's canzone *Così nel mio parlar voglio esser aspro,*
not that which animates the *Paradiso,* the "female love" which
Blake would have us give up before we can see "eternity." It is
in keeping with this that Aristophanes, like Pausanias, relegates
the love of men for women to the lowest plane, on the ground that
the woman is the "weaker vessel," the "earthy" ingredient in our
original composition, thus denying the Socratic and Platonic tenet
that "the goodness of a man and of a woman are the same," and
proves his point by the allegation (192a) that those who are sensible
of female attractions show themselves inferior in "politics." (Like
Pausanias, he has no conception of any worthier life than that of the
"lover of honours.")

We may put the discourse in its true light by a consideration
of its obvious sources. In the first place, I think it is clear that in
composing the speech Plato had in view the brilliant burlesque of
an Orphic cosmogony in Aristophanes' own *Birds* (693–703), where
also Eros is the great primitive cosmic active force. From the *Birds*
comes again the suggestion of the danger that the gods might run
if the turbulent round-bodied creatures cut off the supply of sacrifices, the very method by which the birds of the play reduce
Olympus to unconditional surrender. As for the details of the
story, I think it is clear that they are a humorous parody of
Empedocles. Creatures in whom both sexes are united figure in
his cosmology (Fr. 61), along with the "men with the heads of
oxen" and similar monsters, as appearing in the early stages of the
evolutionary cycle to which we belong, the period of the world's
history in which "strife" is steadily disintegrating the "sphere" by
dissociating the complexes into their constituent "roots." This
is enough to provide a hint for the construction of the whole narrative. We know that the theories of Empedocles became known at
Athens in the fifth century. The *Phaedo* represents Socrates and
his friends as well acquainted with them, and Aristotle tells us that
a certain Critias—we may safely identify him with Plato's great-
grandfather, the Critias of the *Timaeus* and *Critias*—had expressly
adopted one of them, the view that "we think with our blood."[1]
As the *Clouds* and *Birds* are enough to prove, Aristophanes was
fairly well at home in the doctrines of the men of science of whom
he made fun, and it is quite in keeping with Plato's dramatic
realism that he should be made to burlesque Empedocles, exactly
as he has burlesqued Diogenes and the Orphic cosmologists in his
extant comedies. It is from this humorous burlesque (carefully
"bowdlerized" to suit Christianized ethics, *bien entendu*), that the

[1] *de Anima,* 405b 6.

popular misconceptions about so-called " platonic love " seem to have taken their origin.

There are now only two members of the party who have still to speak, Agathon and Socrates. A little by-play passes (193e–194e), which has no purpose beyond that of enhancing our anticipation and making it clear that their speeches are to be the " event " of the evening. It is worth noting that Plato is ready on occasion to turn the humour against the foibles of his own hero. Socrates is allowed, after his fashion, to put an apparently simple question, simply that he may be called to order ; if he were not checked, the programme would be ruined by the substitution of a dialectical discussion for a eulogy. To be sure, when it comes to Socrates' turn to speak, he gets his way after all and we are plunged into dialectic whether we like it or not ; this is part of the fun.

The two speeches marked out as supremely important are wrought with even more art than any of those which have preceded. In form, as in matter, they exhibit the tension between opposites which is the life of a drama at its acutest pitch. Agathon is morally commonplace, cold in feeling, superficial in thought, for the lack of which he compensates by a free employment of all the artificial verbal patterns popularized by Gorgias ; his encomium is a succession of frozen conceits with no real thought behind them— *littérature* in the worst sense of the word. Socrates is, as usual, simple and direct in manner ; he begins what he has to say in the usual conversational tone of his " dialectic," though, before he has done, the elevation of his thought leads to a spontaneous elevation in style, and he ends on a note of genuine eloquence which leaves all the " fine language " of Agathon hopelessly in the shade. He is on fire with his subject, but with the clear, white-hot glow of a man whose very passion is intellectual. He thinks intensely where Agathon, and fine gentlemen like him, are content to talk prettily. And we are not allowed to forget that Agathon's profession is the " stage " ; he is the " actor," impressing an audience with emotions he simulates but does not feel ; Socrates is the genuine man who " speaks from the heart " and to the heart. (Note the adroit way in which this point is worked in at 194b.)

Speech of Agathon (194e–197e).—The whole speech is a masterly parody of the detestable " prose-poetry " of Gorgias, as will readily be seen by comparing it with the specimens of the original article which time has spared to us. It may be summarized, when divested of its verbal extravagances, as follows. Previous speakers have ignored the main point which a eulogy should make ; they have talked about the gifts of Eros to men rather than about his intrinsic qualities. It is these on which the eulogist should dwell. (1) Eros is the most beautiful of all gods ; for (a) he is the youngest of all, not the oldest as Phaedrus and his cosmologists pretend. The " wars in heaven " would never have happened if Eros had held sway then. Also he is eternally fair and young and consorts with youth, not with " crabbed age." (b) He is " soft " (ἁπαλός) and tender, and that is why he makes his dwelling in the tenderest place he can find, the soul, and only in souls whose temper is yielding (μαλακόν). (c) He is " pliant " (ὑγρὸς τὸ εἶδος), can wind his way imperceptibly in and out of the inmost recesses of the soul. (d) He is comely and lovely and bright of hue, and that is why he will not settle and gather honey from a body or soul which is " past its flower." (2) He has all the virtues : [1] (a) justice, for he neither does nor suffers violence. He cannot suffer from it, for love is unconstrained, and he never inflicts it, for all things are his willing slaves and *nemini volenti fit iniuria*. (b) Temperance, for he " masters all pleasures " (an idle verbal quibble). (c) Valour, for he can master Ares, the " warrior famoused for fights." (d) Wisdom ; he is the author of medicine, as Eryximachus had said ; he inspires poetry in the most unpoetical and must therefore be himself a supreme poet. He shows his wisdom, further, in being the contriver of all generation and the teacher of all crafts. It was love, love of the beautiful, which inspired the various gods who were their discoverers. In the beginning, when necessity held sway, heaven itself was a place of horror ; the birth of Eros has thus been the cause of all that is good in heaven and on earth. In short, Eros is the giver of peace among men, calm in air and sea, tranquil sleep which relieves our cares, mirth, jollity—and here the speech loses itself in a torrent of flowery phrases, which " bring down the house," as they were meant to do.

We see, of course, as Plato means that we shall, the barrenness of thought which all this euphuism cannot conceal. In a way, the praise of Eros, in Agathon's mouth, has " lost all its grossness," by transmutation into unmeaning prettiness, but it has incidentally lost all its reality. The discourse has all the insincerity of the conventional petrarchising sonneteer. Like the sonneteering tribe, Agathon is so intoxicated by his own fine-filed phrases, that he is evidently not at all clear which Eros he is belauding, the " heavenly " or the " vulgar." For the euphuist's purpose, this really does not matter much ; the theme of his discourse is to him no more than a peg on which to hang his garlands of language. There had been real feeling, under all the burlesque and the grossness, in the speech of Aristophanes ; from Agathon we get only " words, words, words." Socrates indicates as much in the humorous observations which introduce his own contribution to the entertainment. He really began to be afraid, as Agathon grew more and more dithyrambic, that he might be petrified and struck dumb by the " Gorgias' head." He bethought himself, now that it was too late, that he had been rash in undertaking to deliver a eulogy at all. In the simplicity of his heart, he had supposed that all he would have to do would be to say the best which could be truthfully said of his subject. But it now appears that the eulogist is expected to glorify his subject at all " costs," regardless of truth. This is more than Socrates engaged

---

[1] Note that the list of the " cardinal virtues " is taken for granted as familiar. Thus it is no discovery of Plato or of Socrates.

to do, or can do. Like Hippolytus in the play, he is "unsworn in soul," and must be allowed to deliver his speech in his own artless fashion, telling the truth and leaving the style to take care of itself, or the result may be a ridiculous collapse. And he must make one more little stipulation. Perhaps Agathon would answer one or two questions, so that Socrates may know where to make a beginning. Thus, we see, the philosopher contrives to get his way after all—we are to have "dialectic," in other words, thinking, as well as fine talking, as part of our programme (198b–199c).

Dialectical Interrogation of Agathon by Socrates (199c–201c).— The purpose of this little interlude, as Socrates had said, is to make sure that his own encomium, which was to "tell the truth," shall begin at the right starting-point. In other words, we are to be brought back to reality, of which we have steadily been losing sight. Eros, "love," "craving," is a relative term ; all Eros is Eros *of* something which is its correlate, and it is meant that this correlate is a *satisfaction*. This would be clear at once in Greek, but is a little obscured for us in English by the ambiguity of our word "love." In English there are at least three quite distinct senses of the word "love," and much loose sentimental half-thinking is due to confusion between them. If we would be accurate, we must distinguish them precisely. There is (1) "love of complacency," the emotion aroused by the simple contemplation of what we admire and approve, the "love to the agent" of which the moral-sense school speak in their accounts of moral approval. We may feel this towards a person wholly incapable of being in any way affected for good or bad by our acts or affecting us by his, as when we glow with attachment to the great and good of whom we have read in history. There is (2) "love of benevolence," which prompts us to confer kindnesses on its object or to do him services. This love we may feel to the good and the evil alike. It may show itself as active gratitude to a benefactor, as pity for the unfortunate or the sinful, and in many other guises. There is finally (3) "love of concupiscence," *desirous* love, the eager appetition of what is apprehended as our own "good." It is only this *desirous* love which can be called ἔρως in Greek.[1]

Eros, then, is always a desirous love of its object, and that object is always something not yet attained or possessed. Agathon had said that "love of things fair" has created the happiness of the gods themselves. But if Eros "wants" beauty, it must follow that

[1] Hence when Euripides says ἐρᾶτε, παῖδες, μητρός, he means a great deal more than we can express by saying "love your mother." He means that the sons of such a mother as his heroine are to be "in love" with her ; she is to be to them their true mistress and "dominant lady," as Hector in Homer is "father and mother" to Andromache. One might illustrate by saying that in Christianity God is thought of as loving all men with "love of benevolence," and the righteous with an added "love of complacency," but as loving no creature with "love of concupiscence." The good man, on the other hand, loves God with love of concupiscence, as the good for which his soul longs, and with love of complacency, but could hardly, I suppose, be said to love God with *amor benevolentiae,* since we cannot do "good turns" to our Maker.

he does not yet possess it, and therefore is *not* himself " ever fair,' and in the same way, if he " wants " good. he cannot himself *be* good.

At this point Socrates closes his conversation with Agathon and enters on his " discourse," having found the ἀρχή for it. The questioning of Agathon is no piece of mere verbal dexterity. It is indispensable that we should understand that the only Éros deserving of our praises is an *amor ascendens*, a desirous going forth of the soul in quest of a good which is above her. And this going forth must begin with the knowledge that there is *something* we want with all our hearts but have not yet got. As the old Évangelicals said, the first step towards salvation is to feel your *need* of a Saviour. " Blessed are they which *hunger* . . . for they shall be filled." The soul which is to be love's pilgrim must begin by feeling this heart-hunger, or it will never adventure the journey. This is the ἀρχή demanded by Socrates for any *hohes Lied der Liebe* which is to " tell the truth."

Speech of Socrates (201*d*–212*c*).—Though Socrates had affected to make his " dialectic " a mere preliminary to the " discourse " he was contemplating, he actually contrives to turn the discourse itself into " dialectic," genuine thinking, by putting it into the mouth of one Diotima, a priestess and prophetess of Mantinea, and relating the process of question and answer by which the prophetess had opened his own eyes to understand the true mysteries of Eros. The purpose is that his hearers shall not merely follow his words and possibly be agreeably affected by them, but shall follow his *thought*. They are to listen to the " conversation of his soul with itself." At the same time, I cannot agree with many modern scholars in regarding Diotima of Mantinea as a fictitious personage ; still less in looking for fanciful reasons for giving the particular names Plato does to the prophetess and her place of origin. The introduction of purely fictitious named personages into a discourse seems to be a literary device unknown to Plato, as has been said in an earlier chapter, and I do not believe that if he had invented Diotima he would have gone on to put into the mouth of Socrates the definite statement that she had delayed the pestilence of the early years of the Archidamian war for ten years by " offering sacrifice " at Athens. As the *Meno* has told us, Socrates did derive hints for his thought from the traditions of " priests of both sexes who have been at pains to understand the *rationale* of what they do," and the purpose of the reference to the presence of Diotima at Athens about 440 is manifestly not merely to account for Socrates' acquaintance with her, but to make the point that the mystical doctrine of the contemplative " ascent " of the soul, now to be set forth, was one on which the philosopher's mind had been brooding ever since his thirtieth year. This, if true, is very important for our understanding of the man's personality, and I, for one, cannot believe that Plato was guilty of wanton mystifications about such things. At the same time, we may be sure that in reproducing a conversation a quarter of a century old, Socrates is blending his recollections of the past with his subsequent meditations upon it, as normally happens in such cases. He sees an episode which had influenced his life profoundly in the light of all that had come out of it, much as St. Augustine in later life saw the facts of his conversion to Christianity in a changed perspective, as we are able to prove by contrasting the *Confessions* with the works composed just after the conversion.

To all intents and purposes, we shall not go wrong by treating the " speech of Diotima " as a speech of Socrates. We can best describe the purpose of the speech in the language of religion by saying that it is the narrative of the pilgrimage of a soul on the way of salvation, from the initial moment at which it feels the need of salvation to its final " consummation." In spite of all differences of precise outlook, the best comment on the whole narrative is furnished by the great writers who, in verse or prose, have described the stages of the " mystic way " by which the soul " goes out of herself," to find herself again in finding God. In substance, what Socrates is describing is the same spiritual voyage which St. John of the Cross describes, for example, in the well-known song *En una noche oscura* which opens his treatise on the *Dark Night*, and Crashaw hints at more obscurely all through his lines on *The Flaming Heart*, and Bonaventura charts for us with precision in the *Itinerarium Mentis in Deum*. The Christian writers see by a clearer light and they have an intensity which is all their own, but the journey they describe is recognizably the same—the travel of the soul from temporality to eternity. In Greek literature, the speech, I think we may fairly say, stands alone until we come to Plotinus, with whom the same spiritual adventure is the main theme of the *Enneads*. Unless we have so much of the mystic in us as to understand the view that the " noughting " and remaking of the soul is the great business of life, the discourse will have no real meaning to us ; we shall take it for a mythological *bellum somnium*. But if we do that, we shall never really understand the *Apology* and the other dialogues which deal with the doctrine of the " tendance of the soul," a simple-sounding name which conceals exactly the same conception of the attainment of " deiformity " as the real " work of man." In the *Phaedo* we have had the picture of a human soul on the very verge of attainment, at the moment when it is about to " lose itself in light." In the *Symposium* we are shown, more fully than anywhere else in Plato, the stages by which that soul has come to be what it is in the *Phaedo*. We see with Plato's eyes the interior life of the soul of Socrates.

The desirous soul, as was already said, is as yet not " fair " or " good " ; that is what it would be and will be, but is not yet. But this does not mean that it is " foul " and " wicked." There is a state intermediate between these extremes, as there is a state intermediate between sheer ignorance and completed knowledge— the state of having true beliefs without the power to give a justification of them (ἄνευ τοῦ ἔχειν λόγον δοῦναι). This may be expressed mythologically by saying that Eros is not a " god," nor yet a "mere mortal," but a δαίμων or " spirit," and a mighty one (202d–e). According to the received tradition, " spirits " stand half-way between mortality and divinity ; they convey men's prayers to the gods, and the commands, revelations, and gifts of the gods to men ; intercourse between gods and men has them as its intermediaries. Eros is one of these " spirits " (203a). His birth answers to his function. He is the child of Poros son of Metis (Abundance, son of Good Counsel), by the beggar-maid Penia (Need), conceived in heaven on the birthday of Aphrodite, and he inherits characters from both his parents. He is, like his mother, poor, uncomely, squalid, houseless, and homeless. But he has so much of the father about him that he has high desires for all that is " fair and good," courage, persistence, endless resourcefulness, and art in the pursuit of these desires. He is the greatest of " wizards and wits " (δεινὸς γόης . . . καὶ σοφιστής), he " pursues wisdom all his life long " (φιλοσοφῶν διὰ παντὸς τοῦ βίου). He is neither god nor mortal, but lives a " dying life," starving and fed, and starving for more again.[1] He is your one " philosopher " ; gods do not aspire to " wisdom," for they already have it, nor yet " fools," for they do not so much as know their need and lack of it. " Philosophers," aspirants after wisdom, of whom Eros is chief, are just those who live between these two extremes.[2] They feel the hunger for wisdom, the fairest of things, but they feel it precisely because it remains unsatisfied. The conventional representation of Eros as the " ever fair " is due to a simple confusion between the good aspired to and the aspirant after it (201e–204c).

When the thin veil of allegory is removed, we see that what is described here is simply the experience of the division of the self characteristic of man, when once he has become aware of his own rationality. Rationality is not an endowment of which man finds himself in possession ; it is an attainment incumbent on him to achieve. Spiritual manhood and freedom are the good which he must reach if he is to be happy, but they are a far-away good, and his whole life is a struggle, and a struggle with many an alternation of success and failure, to reach them. If he completely attained them, his life would become that of a god ; he would have put off temporality and put on an eternity secured against all mutability. If he does not strive to attain, he falls back into the condition of the mere animal, and becomes a thing of mere change and mutability. Hence while he is what he is, he is never at peace with himself ; that is the state into which he is trying to grow. It is true, in a deeper sense than the author of the saying meant, that *der Mensch ist etwas das überwunden werden muss* (we are only truly men in so far as we are becoming something more). (That the " temporal "

---

[1] The βίος φιλόσοφος, we might say, has as its motto *quasi morientes et ecce vivimus ; tanquam nihil habentes et omnia possidentes.*

[2] Cf. the classification of rational beings ascribed to the Pythagoreans, " gods," " men," " beings like Pythagoras " (φιλόσοφοι). Aristot. Fr. 192, Rose.

in us which has to be put off is always spoken of by Socrates as " ignorance " or " error," not as " sin," has no special significance, when we remember his conviction that the supreme function of " knowledge " is to command and direct, to order the conduct of life towards the attainment of our true *good*.)

It will be seen that Socrates is formally deferring to the dictum of Agathon about the proper disposition of the parts of an encomium. He has dealt with the question what the intrinsic character of Eros is ; he now proceeds to the question of his services to us (τίνα χρείαν ἔχει τοῖς ἀνθρώποις). What is it that, in the end, is the object of the heart's desirous longing ? Good, or—in still plainer words—happiness (εὐδαιμονία). All men wish happiness for its own sake, and all wish their happiness to be " for ever." (*Weh spricht, Vergeh ! Doch alle Lust will Ewigkeit*.) Why, then, do we not call all men lovers, since all have this desirous longing ? For the same reason that we do not call all craftsmen " makers," though they all are makers of something. Linguistic use has restricted the use of the word ποιητής (" maker ") to one species of maker, the man who fashions verse and song. So it is with the name " lover " ; all desirous longing for good or happiness is love, but in use the name " lover " is given to the person who longs earnestly after one particular species of happiness—τόκος ἐν καλῷ (" pro-creation in the beautiful ")—whether this procreation is physical or spiritual (καὶ κατὰ τὸ σῶμα καὶ κατὰ τὴν ψυχήν, 206b).

To explain the point more fully, we must know that maturity of either body or mind displays itself by the desire to procreate ; beauty attracts us and awakens and fosters the procreative impulse, ugliness inhibits it. And love, in the current restricted sense of the word, is not, as might be thought, desire of the beautiful object, but desire to impregnate it and have offspring by it (desire τῆς γεννήσεως καὶ τοῦ τόκου ἐν καλῷ). (It is meant quite strictly that physical desire for the " possession " of a beautiful woman is really at bottom a " masked " desire for offspring by a physically " fine " mother ; sexual appetite itself is not really craving for " the pleasures of intercourse with the other sex " ; it is a passion for *parenthood*.) And we readily understand why this desire for procreation should be so universal and deep-seated. It is an attempt to perpetuate one's own being " under a form of eternity," and we have just seen that the primary desire of all is desire to possess one's " good " and to possess it for ever. The organism cannot realize this desire in its own individuality, because it is in its very nature subject to death. But it can achieve an approxi-mation to eternity, if the succession of generations is kept up. Hence the vehemence of the passion for procreation and the strength of the instincts connected with mating and rearing a brood in all animals. The only way in which a thing of time can approximate to being eternal is to produce a new creature to take its place as it passes away. Even within the limits of our individual existence, the body " never continues in one stay " ; it is a scene of unending waste made good by repair. Our thoughts and emotions too do not remain selfsame through life. Even our knowledge does not "abide"; we are perpetually forgetting what we knew and having to "recover" it again by μελέτη ("study," "rehearsal"). It is only by giving birth to a new individual to take the place of the old that the mortal can "participate in deathlessness" (208b).[1]

The passion for physical parenthood, however, is the most rudimentary form in which the desirous longing for the fruition of good eternal and immutable shows itself, and the form in which Diotima is least interested. Her main purpose is to elucidate the conception of spiritual parenthood. If we turn to the life of the "love of honours"—note that this reference (208c) implies that in what has been said about the physical instincts we have been considering the "body-loving" life—the passion for "fame undying" which has led Alcestis, Achilles, Codrus, and many another to despise death and danger is just another, and more spiritualized, form of the "desirous longing for the eternal." Thus, just as the man who feels the craving for physical fatherhood is attracted by womankind and becomes "exceeding amorous," so it is with those whose souls are ripe for the procreation of spiritual issue, "wisdom and goodness generally"; the mentally, like the physically adult looks for a "fair" partner to receive and bear his offspring (209a–b). He feels the attraction of fair face and form, but what he is really seeking is the "fair and noble and highly dowered" soul behind them. If he finds what he is looking for, he freely pours forth "discourse on goodness and what manner of man the good man should be, and what conduct he should practise, and tries to educate" the chosen soul he has found. The two friends are associated in the "nurture" of the spiritual offspring to which their converse has given birth, and the tie is still more enduring than that of literal common parenthood, inasmuch as the offspring which are the pledges of it are "fairer and more deathless." Examples of such spiritual progeny are the poems of Homer and Hesiod, and still more the salutary institutions and rules of life left to succeeding ages by Lycurgus and Solon and many another statesman of Hellas or "Barbary"; some of these men have even been deified by the gratitude of later generations (209e).[2]

---

[1] This has absurdly been supposed to be inconsistent with the doctrines of the *Phaedo*, and it has even been argued that the *Symposium* must have been written before Plato discovered the doctrine of immortality expounded there. In point of fact, there is no inconsistency. According to both dialogues the "body" belongs to the "mortal" element in us, and perishes beyond recall. Hence *man*, according to the *Phaedo*, is strictly mortal; what is immortal is not the man, but the "divine" element in him, his ψυχή, as has already been explained. There is not a word in the *Symposium* to suggest that the ψυχή is perishable. Hence no inference about the priority of the one dialogue to the other can be based on comparison of their teaching.

[2] The allusion to "temples" erected to deified statesmen presumably refers to Oriental communities in which the "laws" were traditionally ascribed to remote "divine" rulers. The Greeks did not deify their legislators. At *Laws* 624a the Cretan speaker, indeed, attempts to claim Zeus as the author

The desirous longing for an eternal good, however, has far higher manifestations than these, and Diotima will not take it on her to say whether Socrates is equal to making the ascent to them, though she will describe them, and he must try to follow her.[1] (The meaning is that, so far, we have been talking only about what is possible within the limits of the two lower types of life : we have now to deal with the more arduous path to be trodden by the aspirant to the highest life of all, that of " philosophy.") He who means to pursue the business in earnest must begin in early life by being sensible to bodily beauty. If he is directed aright, he will first try to " give birth to fair discourses " in company with one comely person. But this is only the beginning. He must next learn for himself [2] to recognize the kinship of all physical beauty and become the lover of " all beautiful bodies." [3] Then he must duly recognize the superiority of beauty of soul, even where there is no outward comeliness to be an index to it. He must be " in love " with young and beautiful souls and try to bring to the birth with them " fair discourses." Next, he must learn to see beauty and comeliness as they are displayed in ἐπιτηδεύματα and νόμοι, avocations and social institutions, and perceive the community of principle which comely avocations and institutions imply. Then he must turn to " science " and its intellectual beauties, which will disclose themselves to him as a whole wide ocean of delights. Here again, he will give birth to " many a noble and imposing discourse and thought in the copious wealth of philosophy "—that is, he will enrich the " sciences " he studies with high discoveries.

of the νόμοι of Crete, but he knows, of course, that the traditional author of them was Minos, who was not a god, and so says they may " in fairness " be credited to Zeus (because, according to Homer, Minos " conversed " with Zeus).

[1] Much unfortunate nonsense has been written about the meaning of Diotima's apparent doubt whether Socrates will be able to follow her as she goes on to speak of the " full and perfect vision " (τὰ τέλεα καὶ ἐποπτικά, 210a 1). It has even been seriously argued that Plato is here guilty of the arrogance of professing that he has reached philosophical heights to which the " historical " Socrates could not ascend. Everything becomes simple if we remember that the actual person speaking is Socrates, reporting the words of Diotima, Socrates is as good as speaking of himself, and, naturally, Diotima must not say anything that would imply that he is already, at the age of thirty, assured of " final perseverance." In the *Phaedo*, speaking on the last day of his life to a group of fellow-followers of the way, Socrates can without impropriety say that he has " lived as a philosopher to the best of his power."

[2] αὐτὸν κατανοῆσαι, 210a 8. The αὐτόν seems to be emphatic. The necessity for a " director " (ὁ ἡγούμενος) is admitted for the first step of the progress only. The rest of the way must be trodden at one's own peril, by the " inner light." Yet there is a return to the conception of " combined effort " at 210e 6, ἐπὶ τὰς ἐπιστήμας ἀγαγεῖν.

[3] It is not meant that this widening of outlook must act unfavourably on personal affection. The thought is that *intelligent* delight in the beauty of one " fair body " will lead to a quickened perception of beauty in others, just as genuine appreciation of your wife's goodness or your friend's wit will make you more, and not less alive to the presence of the same qualities in others.

Even so, we have not reached the goal so far ; we are only now coming in sight of it. When a man has advanced so far on the quest he will *suddenly* descry the supreme beauty of which he has all along been in search—a beauty eternal, selfsame, and perfect, lifted above all mutability. It is no " body," nor yet even a " science " or " discourse " of which beauty could be *predicated*, but that very reality and substance of all beauty of which everything else we call beauty is a passing " participant " ; the unchanging light of which all the beauties hitherto discerned are shifting reflections (211*b*). When this light rises above his horizon, the pilgrim of Eros is at last " coming to port." The true " life for a man " is to live in the contemplation of the " sole and absolute Beauty " (θεωμένῳ αὐτὸ τὸ καλόν), by comparison with which all the " beauties " which kindle desire in mankind are so much dross. Only in intercouse with It will the soul give birth to a spiritual offspring which is no " shadow " but veritable " substance," because it is now at last " espoused " to very and substantial reality.[1] This and only this is the true achieving of " immortality." Such was the discourse of Diotima, and Socrates believes it himself and would fain persuade others that Eros (" desirous longing ") is the truest helper we can have in this quest after immortality. This is what he has to offer by way of a eulogy on the " might and manhood " of Eros (212*b–c*).[2]

The meaning of the discourse is clear enough. In the earlier stages of the " ascent " which has just been described, we recognize at once that " tendance of the soul " or care for one's " moral being " which Plato regularly makes Socrates preach to his young friends as the great business of life. That the work of " tendance of the soul " must go further than the development of ordinary good moral habits and rules, that it demands the training of the intellect by familiarity with the highest " science," and that the task of the true philosopher is, by his insight into principles, to unify the " sciences," and to bring the results of ripe philosophical thinking to bear on the whole conduct of life, is the same lesson which is taught us in the *Republic* by the scheme propounded for the education of the philosophic statesman. As in the *Republic*, the study of the separate sciences leads up to the supreme science of " dialectic " or metaphysics, in which we are confronted with the principles on which all other knowing depends, so here also Socrates describes the man who is coming in sight of his goal as descrying " one single science " of Beauty (210*d* 7). And in both cases, in the final moment of attainment, the soul is described as having got beyond " science " itself. Science here passes in the end into direct " contact," or, as the schoolmen say, " vision," an apprehen-

---

[1] *Symp.* 212*a* 4. The allusion is to the tale of Ixion and the cloud which was imposed on him in the place of Hera, and from which the Centaurs sprang. All loves but the last are, in varying degrees, illusions.

[2] 212*b*, ἐγκωμιάζων τὴν δύναμιν καὶ ἀνδρείαν τοῦ ἔρωτος. The ἀνδρεία is specified because the pilgrimage is so long and arduous that it is no easy thing to " play the man " to the end of it. It is a warfare against " flesh and blood."

sion of an object which is no longer " knowing about " it, knowing propositions which can be predicated of it, but an actual possession of and being possessed by it.   In the *Republic*, as in the *Symposium*, the thought is conveyed by language borrowed from the " holy marriage " of ancient popular religion and its survivals in mystery-cults.   Here it is " Beauty " to which the soul is mated ; in the *Republic* it is that good which, though the cause of all being and all goodness, is itself " on the other side of being." [1]

We must not, of course, especially in view of the convertibility of the terms καλόν and ἀγαθόν which is dwelt on more than once in our dialogue, be misled into doubting the absolute identity of the " form of good " of the *Republic* with the αὐτὸ τὸ καλόν of the *Symposium*.   The place assigned to both in the ascent to " being and reality " is identical, and in both cases the stress is laid on the point that when the supreme " form " is descried, its apprehension comes as a sudden " revelation," though it is not to be had without the long preliminary process of travail of thought, and that it is apprehended by " direct acquaintance," not by discursive " knowledge about " it.   It is just in this conviction that all " knowledge about " is only preparatory to a direct *scientia visionis* that Socrates reveals the fundamental agreement of his conception with that of the great mystics of all ages.   The " good " or αὐτὸ τὸ καλόν is, in fact, the *ens realissimum* of Christian philosophers, in which the very distinction between *esse* and *essentia*, *Sein* and *So-sein* falls away.   You cannot properly predicate anything of it, because it does not " participate " in good or any other " form " ; it *is* its own *So-sein*.   Consequently, the apprehension of it is strictly " incommunicable," since all communication takes the form of predication.   Either a man possesses it and is himself possessed by it, or he does not, and there is no more to be said.   This does not mean that the " most real being " is *irrational*, or that by " thinking things out " we are getting further away from it, but it does mean that we cannot " rationalize " it.   We cannot give its constituent " formula," so to say, as we could that of an ellipse or a cycloid.   You might spend eternity in trying to describe it, and all you found to say would be true and reasonable, so far as it goes, but its full secret would still elude you ; it would still be infinitely rich with undisclosed mystery.   As the Christian mystics say, God may be apprehended, but cannot be comprehended by any of His creatures.   That is why He is " on the other side of being." The " deiform " do not " think about " God, they live Him.   This does not mean that " myth " is something in its own nature superior to scientific truth, a misconception on which Professor Burnet has said all that is necessary.   *Because* " vision " is direct, the content of a " tale " or " myth " cannot really convey it.   A " tale " is as much a mere form of " knowing about " as a scientific description, and as a form of " knowing about " it is, of course, inferior.   In

[1] *Rep.* 508b 9. For the metaphor of the " holy marriage," cf. e.g. *Rep.* 490b, 496a.

fact, all the mystics insist on the point that the direct vision of supreme reality is not only incommunicable, it cannot even be recalled in memory when the moment of vision has passed. You are sure that you " saw " ; you cannot tell what you saw even to yourself. This is the real reason why, as Burnet says, Plato never uses " mythical " language about the " forms," but only about things like the soul, which he regards as half real, partly creatures of temporality and change. We should note, however, that the supreme reality which is apprehended in the culminating vision is never said in Plato to be God, but always the supreme " form." It is the *good* which is the Platonic and Socratic *ens realissimum*.

The position of God in the philosophy of both seems to me ambiguous and not fully thought out. Formally, Plato's God is described in the *Laws* as a perfectly good soul (ἀρίστη ψυχή). This ought to mean, as Burnet clearly holds it to mean, that God too is only half-real, and belongs on one side to the realm of the mutable. I confess that I do not see how to reconcile such a position with the religious insistence on the eternal and immutable character of God which meets us everywhere in Plato. We could not meet the difficulty by supposing that God is an imaginative symbol of the " good," since the whole point of Plato's Theism is, as we shall see, that it is by the agency of God that the " participation " of the creatures in the good is made possible. Thus God is not identical with the good, and it seems equally impossible to suppose that God is simply a " creature " participating in good. I can only suppose that there was a really unsolved conflict between the Platonic metaphysics and the Platonic religion. In fact, the adjustment of the two became a cardinal problem for Plotinus and the Neo-platonic succession.[1] We shall not be in a position to deal with the topic properly until we come to speak of Plato's latest written works and the " unwritten doctrines " expounded in the Academy.

Plato clearly means, in spite of Diotima's words of caution, to present Socrates in the *Symposium* as a man who has in his supreme hours attained the " vision " for himself, and for that very reason impresses his fellow-men by his whole bearing as being not of their world though he is in it. We could have inferred at least that he was steadily treading the road to " unification " with the supreme reality from the close correspondence of the description of that road by Diotima with what Plato elsewhere represents as his hero's course of life. But naturally enough, Socrates cannot be made to boast of the supreme achievement with his own lips, and this is why Alcibiades, the most brilliant living specimen of the " ambitious life," is introduced at this point. We are to gather from his famous narrative of the impression Socrates made on him in their years of close intercourse, and the hold the recollections of those years still

---

[1] The Neoplatonic way of dealing with the problem, by making " The One " the source from which νοῦς and its correlate τὰ νοητά directly emanate, definitely subordinates the " forms " to God. Through Augustine this view passed to St. Thomas and still remains part of Thomistic philosophy.

have on his conscience and imagination, what could not well be said in any other way, that Socrates has " seen," and that the vision has left its stamp on his whole converse with the world. Perhaps there is a further thought in Plato's mind. Socrates, we might say, is the man who has renounced the world to find his own eternal " life "; Alcibiades, naturally endowed with all the gifts required for " philosophy," but a prey to the lusts of the flesh and the eye and the pride of life, is the man who might have " seen " if he would, the man who has made the " great refusal " of sacrificing the reality for the shadow. He has chosen for the world and has all the world can give. We are made to look on the two types side by side, and to listen to the confession of the triumphant worldling in the full flush of triumph, that he has chosen the *worser* part. On the panegyric of Socrates by Alcibiades (215a–222b) it is not necessary to dwell here. Its importance is for the understanding of the characters of Socrates and of Alcibiades, not for any contribution it makes to our comprehension of the Socratic or the Platonic philosophy. It shows us Socrates in act following the route of the pilgrimage already described by Diotima. One should, of course, note, in order to avoid some strange misconceptions, that the famous story told by Alcibiades of his own " temptation " of Socrates (216d–219d) is meant to go back to a time when Alcibiades, who fought in the cavalry before Potidaea in 431–30, was still a mere boy, little more than a child (217b). We must date the events somewhere between 440 and 435, when Socrates would be in the earlier thirties. This being so, it is important to observe that even then his fame for wisdom was such that Alcibiades could think no price too high to pay for the benefit of " hearing all that he knew," We must also, of course, understand that Socrates is to be thought of as a man still young enough to feel the charm of beauty in its full force, and to feel it in the way characteristic of the society of his age, but too full of high thoughts to be vanquished by " the most opportune place, the strong'st suggestion his worser genius can." He moves through a brilliant and loose-living society like a Sir Galahad, not because he is not a man of genuine flesh and blood, but because his heart is engaged elsewhere, and he has none to spare for " light loves." This testimony, coming from Plato, is enough to dispose once and for all of the later gossip of Aristoxenus and the Alexandrians who collected such garbage. We must also, I think, with Burnet, recognize that the prominence given to the account of Socrates' " rapt " for four-and-twenty hours at Potidaea (220c–d) is intended to suggest that this was the outstanding " ecstasy " of his life, and left an ineffaceable mark on his whole future. It can hardly be a coincidence that the earliest " missionary " effort of Socrates related by Plato, his attempt to convert Charmides, is dated immediately after his return from the campaign of Potidaea.[1] For the rest, Socrates' remarkable power of adapting

---

[1] *Greek Philosophy, Part I.,* 130, 138–142 ; *E.R.E.* xi. 670, col. 1. Professor Burnet has fallen into an oversight in the first of these passages when he makes

himself in appearance to the tone and manner of the world, and yet contriving without any visible effort to bring with him the suggestion of being all the while in constant contact with the other " unseen " world which is at once so near and so far is one of the best-known characteristics of the greatest " contemplatives " ; the stress laid on the point helps to strengthen our conviction that we are presented with a realistic portrait of an actual man. (The same " adaptability " is noted as eminently distinctive of Xavier by his biographers. Xavier recalls Socrates too by the " gaiety " of which the biographers speak as the most striking feature of his conversation.)

On the description of the scene of revelry with which the " banquet " ends, I need only make one remark. We are told (223d) that when the new morning broke, Socrates, Aristophanes, and Agathon were the only persons in the party who were equal to continuing the conversation, and that Socrates was left by Aristodemus trying to convince the two dramatists that the man who can compose a tragedy τέχνῃ, " by his art," can also compose a comedy. Much ingenuity has been wasted on the interpretation of this remark, and it has even been supposed to be a kind of prophecy of Shakespeare's " tragi-comedies," which are neither tragedies, nor yet comedies in the sense in which we give that name to the brilliant personal burlesques of the Attic " old comedians." The real meaning lies on the surface. As we have seen, Socrates dissented from the current view that poets are σοφοί and their productions works of conscious " art." He held that they depend on " genius " or " inspiration," and cannot themselves explain their own happiest inspirations. His point is thus that the inability of Agathon to compose comedies and of Aristophanes to write tragedies, is a proof that neither of them is a σοφός, working with conscious mastery of an " art." Both are the instruments of a " genius " which masters *them*, not wielders of a tool of which they are masters. The passage should really be quoted, not as an excuse for gush about Shakespeare, but as an illustration of what Socrates says in the *Apology* about his attempts to " refute the oracle " by finding a σοφός among the poets and their failure. In fact, he fails here. His two auditors are half asleep after their night of merriment and " do not quite take the point " (οὐ σφόδρα ἑπομένους νυστάζειν, 223d 6).

See further :

    RITTER, C.—*Platon*, i. 504–531.
    RAEDER, H.—*Platons philosophische Entwickelung*, 158–168.
    NATORP, P.—*Platons Ideenlehre*, 163–174.
    BURY, R. G.—*Symposium of Plato*. (1909.)
    ROBIN, L.—Platon, *Le Banquet*. (Paris, 1929.)
    LAGERBORG, R.—*Platonische Liebe*. (Leipzig, 1926.)
    STEWART, J. A.—*The Myths of Plato*, 397–450 (*The Two Symposium Myths*) ; *Plato's Theory of Ideas*, Pt. ii.
    STENZEL, J.—*Platon der Erzieher*, 209–241.

---

the " rapt " take place at a time of " hard frost." The time was high summer (*Symp.* 220d 1).

CHAPTER X

THE *PROTAGORAS*

IF there is any Platonic dialogue which can challenge the claim of the *Symposium* to be its author's dramatic *chef d'œuvre* it is the *Protagoras*, with its brilliant full-length portrait of the famous Protagoras and its mirthful sketches of the two minor "sophists," Prodicus and Hippias. The very life-likeness of the narrative has led to grave misunderstanding of the philosophical significance of the dialogue. It has been assumed that so lively a work must be a youthful composition, and this has led to the further supposition that its teaching must be "undeveloped," as compared with that of *e.g.* the *Gorgias*. By way of providing Plato with a crude "early ethical doctrine," for the *Gorgias* to correct, it has then been discovered that the *Protagoras* teaches the Hedonism of Bentham, a misconception which makes the right understanding of its purpose wholly impossible. We shall see, as we proceed, that the dialogue does not teach Hedonism at all; what it does teach is something quite different, the Socratic thesis that "all the virtues are one thing—knowledge," and that its philosophical purpose is simply to make it clear that this thesis is the foundation of the whole Socratic criticism of life. The absurdity of regarding the dialogue as a juvenile performance is sufficiently shown by the perfect mastery of dramatic technique which distinguishes it. No beginner, however endowed with genius, produces such a masterpiece of elaborate art without earlier experiences of trial and failure. He has first to learn the use of his tools. And it is worth noting that Aristotle must have regarded the dialogue as a particularly ripe and masterly exposition of the Socratic moral theory, since he has taken directly from it his own account in the *Ethics* of the characteristic doctrines of Socrates.[1]

---

[1] *E.N.* 1116b 4, Socrates thought that courage is knowledge, a reference to the lengthy treatment of this point at *Protag.* 349d ff. (rather than, as suggested by Burnet in his commentary on the *Ethics*, to the *Laches*); 1144b 18, Socrates held that all the "virtues" are φρονήσεις (an allusion probably to the assertion of this in *Protagoras* and *Phaedo*); 1145b 23 ff., Socrates denied that there is such a state as ἀκρασία in which "passion" commits a "rape" on judgment, δεινὸν γὰρ ἐπιστήμης ἐνούσης, ὡς ᾤετο Σ., ἄλλο τι κρατεῖν καὶ περιέλκειν αὐτὴν ὡς ἀνδράποδον (a verbal allusion to *Protag.* 352c); 1147b 15, οὐδ' αὔτη (sc. ἡ κυρία ἐπιστήμη) περιέλκεται διὰ τὸ πάθος (another echo of the same passage); 1164a 24, on Protagoras' method of charging for his services, looks like a loose reminiscence of *Protag.* 328b 6–c 2; *E.N.* 1109b 6 is a plain reminiscence of *Protag.* 325d 6; *E.E.* 1229a 15 is a direct allusion to *Protag.* 360d 4, as is also 1230a 7 ff.; 1246b 34 echoes *Protag.* 352c. Though Aristotle never names the dialogue, he evidently appreciated its importance.

In form, the dialogue is once more a narrated drama, but, like the *Republic*, with a slightly less complicated formula than the *Symposium*. Socrates himself gives an unnamed friend, with whom he meets in a public place in Athens, an account of a brilliant company from whom he has only just parted. The method of indirect narration is once more necessary, because Plato wishes to impress it on us that the date of the gathering was before his own time. From the jocular opening remarks we learn that Alcibiades is only just becoming old enough to be spoken of as a " man." Since Alcibiades served at Potidaea in 431, this will take us back at least to the beginning of his " ephebate," which cannot be put later than 433, and is more naturally put at least a year or two earlier. (For it would be unreasonable to suppose that he must have been called out for a hard and distant service as soon as he had the minimum age qualification.) Thus we are at a period before the opening of the Archidamian war. This accounts for the presence, on the most friendly terms, of distinguished men belonging to states shortly to be official enemies of Athens, and for the complete absence of any hint that inter-state relations are in any way disturbed. (Hippias of Elis could hardly be made to glorify Athens as he does at 336c–338b, and to preach a homily on the " internationalism " of *Kultur* if the war-clouds were already gathering.) The time is thus the Periclean age ; Athens is at the very height of her opulence and glory, and Socrates must be thought of as a man of about thirty-five. Of the other figures in the drama, the most important, Protagoras of Abdera, is an older man. He says (317c) that he is advanced in years and might easily be the father of any one present, and subsequently (320c) alleges his superior age as a graceful excuse for conveying his views in a fable, " as a man may in talking to his juniors." Thus we are directed to think of him as a generation or so older than Socrates, and therefore a man at any rate, approaching sixty-five.[1] Prodicus and Hippias will be roughly men of Socrates' age. The scene is laid in the house of the famous " millionaire " Callias, son of Hipponicus,

[1] This would throw back the birth of Protagoras to some time not very far from 500 B.C. and make him a contemporary of Anaxagoras. The Alexandrian chronologists made him some fifteen years younger, and they have mostly been followed by modern writers. It seems to me, as to Professor Burnet, that we must accept Plato's statement. He must have known whether Protagoras really belonged to the generation before Socrates, and could have no motive for misrepresentation on such a point. All through the dialogue the advanced age of Protagoras is kept before the reader's mind, so that Plato is not simply falling into an oversight. The Alexandrians obviously depend on one of their usual arbitrary constructions. The foundation of Thurii (444) was their regular " fixed era " for events of the Periclean age, and as Protagoras was known to have had to do with legislating for Thurii, they fixed his ἀκμή to the year of its foundation. The restoration of Protagoras to his true date enables us finally to dispose of the fable of his prosecution (in 415 or in 411) for " impiety," a story which bears the marks of its futility on its face. From the references of the *Meno* we see that Protagoras must have died during the Archidamian war, and that he ended his life in high general repute.

of whom we read in the *Apology* that he had spent more money on " sophists " than any living man. He must be supposed to be quite young, since his activity as a man of affairs begins at a much later date. Aristophanes makes a topical joke about his presence at the battle of Arginusae and his renown as a lady-killer in the *Frogs* [1] (405 B.C.). In the speech of Andocides on *the Mysteries* he figures as the villain of the story, the party who, according to Andocides, is instigating the prosecution in pursuance of a personal grudge, and we hear endless scandal about his domestic affairs. From Lysias xix. (delivered between 390 and 387) we learn that the family capital, which had once been believed to amount to two hundred talents, had now shrunk to two. (We must take into account the economic revolution which followed on the collapse of Athens in 404.) We hear of Callias from time to time in the *Hellenica* of Xenophon. He was commanding the Athenian force at Corinth on the famous occasion (390 B.C.) when Iphicrates cut up the Spartan *mora* with his peltasts (*op. cit.* iv. 5, 13), and was one of the representatives of Athens at the critical congress held at Sparta early in 371, two or three months before the battle of Leuctra. Hence the agreement then concluded between the Athenian and Peloponnesian confederacies has been generally known as the " Peace of Callias." His important social position at Athens can be gauged from the facts that he held by heredity the position of " Torchbearer " in the Eleusinian mysteries and *proxenus*, or, as we might say, " Consul " for Sparta. For a proper historical appreciation of Socrates it is important to note that Plato represents him, at this early date, as associating with persons like Callias and Alcibiades, both connected with the Periclean circle, on equal terms, and being in high consideration with both them and the most eminent of the foreign " wits." [2]

We cannot rate too high the importance of the *Protagoras* as the fullest and earliest exposition of the character and aims of the sophistic " education in goodness." Nowhere else in Greek literature have we an account of the matter comparable for a moment to that which Plato has put into the mouth of Protagoras himself. There is really no reason why we should feel any distrust of the strict " historicity " of the statements. Plato stood near enough to the Periclean age to be excellently well informed of the facts. He could form his conclusions not merely from what he might be told by men of an elder generation who had known Protagoras, or actually taken his course, but from the work or works of the distinguished sophist himself. (The silly tale of their destruction is refuted not only by the way in which it is assumed in the *Theaetetus* that all the parties to that conversation are familiar with

---

[1] *Frogs*, 432. For an earlier Aristophanic allusion to Callias as a spendthrift and *coureur de femmes*, cf. *Birds*, 284–6. He had already been attacked as a " waster " and patron of sophists by Eupolis in his Κόλακες (421 B.C.).

[2] See the compliment paid him by Protagoras at 361*e*, and observe that it is assumed to be based on an acquaintance begun still earlier on a former visit of Protagoras to Athens.

them, but by the express statement of Isocrates.[1]) He stood far enough away from it to have no personal motive for misrepresentation of any kind, and, in point of fact, the personality and the ideas of Protagoras are treated all through the dialogue with respect and understanding, though we are made to see what his limitations are. His exposition of his programme is done with as much "gusto" as anything in the whole of Plato's works; so much so that some worthy modern critics have even discovered that Protagoras is the real hero of the dialogue who is meant to be commended at the expense of the *doctrinaire* Socrates. Preposterous as this exegesis is, the fact that it has been given in good faith is the best proof that the dialogue is no satirical caricature, so far as Protagoras is concerned. He is depicted as a man of high aims and sincere belief in the value of the education he gives; his one manifest foible is that he is not conscious of his own limitations, and in that respect, according to the *Apology*, he is only on a level with all the other "celebrities" of the Periclean age.

If we discount the little exchange of pleasantries between Socrates and his unnamed acquaintance (309a–310c), which merely serves the purpose of dating the interview of Socrates and Protagoras by reference to the age of Alcibiades at the time, the dialogue falls into the following main sections: (1) an introductory narrative, preparatory to the appearance of Protagoras on the scene (310a–316a); (2) a statement by Protagoras of the nature of the "goodness" he professes to be able to teach, followed by a series of "sceptical doubts" urged by Socrates against the possibility of such an education, which are, in their turn, replied to by Protagoras at great length (316b–328d); (3) an argument between Socrates and Protagoras leading up to the Socratic "paradox" of the unity of the virtues, which threatens to end in an irreconcilable disagreement (328d–334c); (4) a long interlude in which the conversation resolves itself for a time into the discussion of a moralizing poem of Simonides (334c–348c); (5) resumption of the argument begun in (3), with the further developments that the one thing to which all forms of "goodness" reduce is seen to be "knowledge," and the consequence is drawn that "all wrong-doing is error" (348c–360e); (6) a brief page of conclusion in which both parties to the discussion admit the need of further inquiry and take leave of one another with many courtesies (360e–362a). This general analysis of itself shows that the central purpose of the dialogue is to exhibit clearly the ultimate ethical presuppositions of the Socratic morality and the "sophistic" morality at its best, and to show exactly where they are in irreconcilable opposition. The one serious exegetical problem we shall have to face is that of discovering the connexion of the discussion of the poem of Simonides with what precedes and follows.

---

[1] Isoc. x. 2, νῦν δέ τίς ἐστιν οὕτως ὀψιμαθής, ὅστις οὐκ οἶδε Πρωταγόραν καὶ τοὺς κατ' ἐκεῖνον τὸν χρόνον γενομένους σοφιστάς, ὅτι καὶ τοιαῦτα καὶ πολὺ τούτων πραγματωδέστερα συγγράμματα κατέλιπον ἡμῖν;

I. INTRODUCTORY NARRATIVE (310a–316a).—The narrative is given in a tone of humour marked by touches of satire, which is directed not against Protagoras but against the excessive adulation bestowed on him by his younger admirers, and to a less degree against the self-importance of second-rate " professors " of the type of Prodicus. Its main object, however, is to insist on the great importance of education in " goodness," if such an education is to be had, and thus to raise our interest to the appropriate pitch, before Protagoras and his programme are actually put before us. Socrates has been roused from sleep in the " small hours " by his young friend Hippocrates, who has just heard of the arrival of Protagoras, and is anxious not to lose a moment in getting an introduction to him and putting himself under his tuition. As it is still too early to think of disturbing the great man, Socrates and the lad walk about for a time in the αὐλή of Socrates' house, conversing to pass the time. The drift of the conversation is that by profession Protagoras is a " sophist," but Hippocrates is not proposing to study under him in order to enter the " profession " itself ; he would be degrading himself by such a course. His object is, like that of the pupil of an ordinary schoolmaster or trainer, to get " culture " (παιδεία) as a free gentleman should. That is to say, he is about to put his " soul " into the hands of a professional " sophist " to be " tended." (The point intended is that " culture " is a much more serious thing than is commonly supposed. It really means the moulding of the " soul " for good or ill.) Hence, before we take such a risk, we ought to be quite clear on the point " what a sophist is," *i.e.* to what ends it is his profession to shape us. He is a σοφός or " wit," as his name shows,[1] but we might say as much of a painter. We want to know further on what his " wit " is exercised, of *what* accomplishment he is master. Hippocrates makes the obvious suggestion that the particular accomplishment of the sophist is the skilful use of speech—the " art " which, in fact, the pupils of Protagoras were specially anxious to learn from him. But any skilled professional can speak well and to the point about his own technicality, and in teaching us that technicality, he will make us also able to speak properly about it. Thus the all-important question is, What is it of which a " sophist " as such is by profession a teacher?—and Hippocrates cannot answer this question (312e).[2]

Clearly then, Hippocrates is taking a great risk and taking it

[1] 312c. It is assumed that the popular etymology of σοφιστής made it a derivative from σοφός and εἰδέναι, σοφιστής = ὁ τῶν σοφῶν ἱστής.

[2] Hippocrates makes the suggestion that the " sophist's " speciality is to be δεινὸς λέγειν, of course, because the special skill of which Protagoras notoriously boasted was the power to " make the weaker argument the stronger," by stating the case forcibly and plausibly. " Advocacy " is what the young men of Athens pay Protagoras to teach them. Socrates' point is that the worth of his teaching as a " culture for the soul " depends on *what* he " advocates " and teaches others to advocate. Even from the most utilitarian point of view, to be a clever advocate is not the one and only requisite for a statesman.

in the dark. He would be slow to trust the care of his body to a
particular adviser, and would do all he could to be sure of such a
man's competence before he became his patient. How much more
foolish to put that much more precious thing, his soul, into the hands
of a recently arrived foreigner, without any consultation with older
and more responsible friends and relatives, and actually without
knowing the real character of the stranger's profession ! We might
suggest that the sophist is by profession a sort of importer and
retailer (ἔμπορός τις ἢ καπηλός) of foreign articles of spiritual diet
(a suggestion taken up again with a good deal of humour in a much
later dialogue, the *Sophistes*). The " food of the spirit " is, of
course, " studies " or " sciences " (μαθήματα), and we need to
guard against the risk that the purveyor of this sustenance may
deceive us, as other vendors often do, about the quality of his
merchandise. The ordinary vendor praises the wholesomeness of
his wares, but without really knowing anything about the matter.
You would do well to take the advice of a medical man before you
patronize him. So if one could find a " physician of souls," it
would be desirable to take his advice before patronizing the spiritual
wares vended by Protagoras. This is all the more important that
you cannot carry away samples of his wares, as you might of a
food for the body, and examine them at your leisure before consuming them. " Sciences " have to be taken direct from the
vendor into the soul itself, and if they are unsound articles the
mischief is thus done at the very time of purchase. You and I,
says Socrates, are still too young [1] to judge for ourselves what is
wholesome diet for the mind. But we can, at any rate, go and
hear what Protagoras has to say about his merchandise, and take
the advice of others accordingly, before we commit ourselves
(314*b*).

We need not delay over the lively description of the scene in
the house of Callias, the crowd of visitors, and the figures of those
lesser lights Prodicus and Hippias. Some of the party must
have been mere boys ; Socrates says this, in so many words, of
Agathon, and it must be as true of Charmides, who was still a mere
lad in the year of Potidaea. Plato has been reprimanded for
making fun of the invalidism of Prodicus, but for all we know,
Prodicus may really have been a *malade imaginaire* at whom it is
quite fair to laugh. It is interesting to note that all the speakers
of the *Symposium* are present except Aristophanes, who would
be little more than a child at the supposed date of our dialogue.

---

[1] ἡμεῖς γὰρ ἔτι νέοι. Note the repeated insistence on the comparative
youth of Socrates. Plato is determined that we shall not forget the date to
which he has assigned the conversation. I should suppose that his reason is
that he knew or believed that Socrates, as a fact, did meet Protagoras at this
date, and that this was the most important occasion on which the two met,
just as he mentions in the *Phaedo* that Socrates first learned Anaxagoras'
doctrine about νοῦς from hearing some one " read aloud," as he said, " from
a book of Anaxagoras," simply in order to make the historical point that the
two men had not actually met.

(I should have mentioned in speaking of the *Symposium* that Aristophanes must be the youngest of the speakers in that dialogue, a man of about twenty-eight.)

II. THE PROGRAMME OF PROTAGORAS (316*b*–328*d*).—As soon as Protagoras makes his appearance, Socrates, who already knows him personally, opens the business on which he has come. His young, well-born, and wealthy friend Hippocrates has political aspirations which he thinks might be furthered by studying under Protagoras. But a preliminary interview is desirable. Protagoras is of the same opinion, and is glad of the chance of explaining his aims as a teacher, since the profession is one in which a man cannot be too careful of his own reputation. Men feel a natural ill-will towards a brilliant stranger when they see the young men of promise preferring his company and instructions to those of their own most eminent countrymen. This is why all the most influential " educators " have preferred to disguise their real practice, from Homer's time on, and have professed to be poets, physicians, musicians, anything but what they really are. Protagoras plumes himself on his own courage in taking the opposite course and frankly avowing that his calling is to " educate men." His boldness has proved the wiser course, for in a long professional career he has escaped all serious consequences of the popular prejudice.[1] So he has nothing to conceal and is ready to expound his aims with complete frankness. The whole company thereupon forms itself into an audience for the promised exposition.

Socrates now repeats the question he had already put to Hippocrates ; what precise benefit may be expected from study under Protagoras ? The answer Protagoras gives is that a pupil who comes to him will go away daily " better than he came," (318*a*. This establishes the formal equivalence of the notions of " educating men " and " teaching goodness.") But this statement needs to be made more precise. *Any* master of a speciality might say as much. If you studied under Zeuxippus, you would improve— in drawing, if under Orthagoras—in flute-playing. But in what will you improve daily if you study under Protagoras ? The question, says Protagoras, is rightly and fairly put, and the answer is that his pupil will daily improve, not in knowledge of astronomy or geometry (like the pupils of the polymath Hippias), but in what is the great concern of life, " prudence in the management of one's private affairs and capacity to speak and act in the affairs of the city." That is, Protagoras undertakes to teach us not how to be

[1] 316*b*–317*c*. Protagoras is, of course, speaking playfully when he suggests that Homer, Simonides, and others were really " sophists " who tried to escape unpopularity by passing themselves off for something different. But we may infer from his remarks (1) that the popular, and very natural, feeling against the professional sophist really existed in Athens in the Periclean age, and is not, as Grote supposed, an invention of Plato and the Socratic men ; (2) that Protagoras was actually the first man avowedly to practise the " educating of men " or " teaching of goodness " as a paid profession. Unless these are facts, there is no point in what Plato makes him say.

good specialists, but how to be good men, and what, to a Periclean
Athenian, is the same thing, good active citizens. He is really
claiming to be able to teach "statesmanship" (319a). (This,
of course, *was* precisely what aspiring young Athenians paid him
to teach them.)

There can be no doubt that this is the most important thing a
man could teach, if it is really true that statesmanship can be
taught. But Socrates feels a perplexity on the question whether
statesmanship *is* teachable. It is hard to disbelieve in the claims
of a famous man like Protagoras who has been pursuing his profession for so many years ; on the other hand, there are considerations which make the other way, and Socrates now proposes to
state them. We must observe that he does not undertake to prove
that statesmanship cannot be taught, nor does he commit himself
to any of the views he goes on to present. He merely urges that,
seeing the quarter from which they come, they cannot be simply
dismissed, but have to be met. The argument is one from what
Aristotle calls εἰκότα, the probabilities of the case.

The Athenians have a great name for being a "clever" people,
and it is not likely that an opinion held very strongly by such a
people should be a mere delusion. Now *the Athenian public* would
appear to hold that "goodness" cannot be taught. For it is singular
that though they will only accept public advice on what are
admittedly matters for expert knowledge from properly qualified
advisers, they listen to an opinion on the statesmanship of a proposed course of action without any such regard for qualifications.
They will listen, on a point of naval construction, to no one
who is not known either to be an expert himself or to have
studied under experts. But when the issue is one of statesmanship—that is, one of the goodness or badness, the rightfulness or
wrongfulness, of a proposed public act—they treat any one man's
opinion as equally deserving of a hearing with another's ; they
make no demand here that a man shall be an approved "expert"
or have learned from one.

And this is not merely the attitude of the "general" ; the
individuals who are regarded as our wisest and best statesmen show
by their conduct that they hold the same view. They neither
teach their own "goodness" to their sons nor procure masters of
it for them, but leave it to chance whether the young men will pick
up this goodness for themselves. The example selected, in this
instance, is that of Pericles. Thus Socrates argues the case by
appealing, in Aristotelian fashion, first to the opinion of the "many"
and then to that of the "wise," the acknowledged experts. It is
not likely that a very widespread conviction should be merely
baseless ; it is not likely that the convictions of "experts" should
be merely baseless ; it is still less likely that both parties should
be victims of the same delusion. The point is raised simply as a
difficulty ; Socrates is quite ready to listen to a proof from Protagoras that, after all, both parties are wrong. The question is thus

not whether goodness can be taught or not, but whether Protagoras can satisfy Socrates that it is teachable, in other words, whether goodness can be taught on the principles and by the methods of Protagoras.

In dealing with the reply of Protagoras, we must be careful to remember that his case is not established by the mere fact that there is a great deal of truth in what he says, so far as it goes. What is required is that he should make out sufficient justification for his claim to be able to teach statesmanship as a speciality, exactly as another man might teach geometry or medicine. If we keep this point carefully in view, it will be found that, though what Protagoras says is true enough, as a vindication of his own claim it is a complete *ignoratio elenchi*.

He begins by indicating his position by means of a fable about the culture-hero Prometheus. At the making of living creatures, Epimetheus was charged with the work of distributing the various means of success in the " struggle for existence " among them ; Prometheus was to act as supervisor and critic. Epimetheus managed the distribution so badly that when he came to deal with mankind, the various serviceable qualities had already been used up on the lower animals ; none were left for man, who would thus have been helpless and defenceless if Prometheus had not stolen from heaven fire and the knowledge of industrial arts. (In plainer words, man is not equipped for self-preservation by a system of elaborate congenital instincts, and he is handicapped also by physical inferiority : he has to depend for survival on intelligence.) In the " state of nature," however, intelligence and the possession of fire were not enough to secure men against their animal competitors ; they had further to associate themselves in " cities," and this gave occasion for all kinds of aggression on one another. (One may compare Rousseau's speculations about the opportunity given by the social impulses of mankind to the exploitation of the many by the able and unscrupulous few.) Hence Zeus intervened to preserve the human race by sending Hermes to bestow on them δίκη and αἰδώς, the sense of right and conscience. But Zeus expressly commanded that these gifts were not to be confined, like *e.g.* skill in medicine, tō a few specialists ; they were to be distributed to every one, since " political association " is impossible on any other terms (322*d*). Hence the behaviour of the Athenian *ecclesia*, which has surprised Socrates, is reasonable and right. " Political goodness " is wholly a matter of justice and " temperance," and no member of the community is a layman or outsider where justice and temperance are concerned ; every " citizen," in fact, is an expert in the virtues. This is also why we expect a man who is a layman in other accomplishments to confess the fact, and ridicule him if he pretends to an accomplishment which he does not possess. But when it comes to " justice," or " temperance," or any other " goodness of a citizen," we expect a man to pretend to it, even if he does not possess it ; hypocrisy is a tribute we expect vice to pay to virtue (323c). Similarly we may easily satisfy ourselves that the Athenian people really believe that " goodness " can and must be taught, by reflecting that they never " admonish " or " correct " those who suffer from defects which they cannot help. A man is not reprimanded or corrected for being ugly or undersized or sickly ; he is pitied. But men are properly reprimanded and punished for moral delinquencies, and the whole object is that the reprimand or punishment may be a " lesson " to the offender or to others not to offend in the future. The very existence of criminal justice is thus proof that " goodness " is held to be something which can be taught (323c–324d). (This does not mean that either Protagoras or Plato rejects the " retributive " theory of punishment. The " retributive " theory means simply that before a man can be held liable to punishment, he must by his acts have given you the *right* to punish him. You are not entitled to inflict a penalty simply because you think the suffering of it would " do the man good " ; the penalty must be preceded by the commission of an *offence*. No sane theory of the right to punish can ignore this.)

The little fable about Prometheus has already revealed Protagoras to us as a strong believer in the view that morality is dependent on νόμος, the system of conventions and traditions embodied in the " usages " of a civilized community. As we follow his explanation we shall find him laying still more stress on this point. Like Hobbes, he holds that in a " state of nature," there would be no morality to speak of, and the lack of it would make human life " poor, nasty, brutish, and short." He declares himself strongly opposed to the view of some of his rivals, that " citizen goodness " is a thing that comes by " nature," in other words, that men are born good or bad. He is wholly without any belief in the moral goodness of the unspoiled " savage " and, in fact, looks on morality as a product of civilization, a matter of imbibing a sound social tradition. Such a view would seem to suggest that, since, as we have just been told, every civilized man has to be a " specialist " in justice and temperance, there is no room and no need for the expert teacher of goodness, a conclusion which would make Protagoras' own professional activities superfluous. Hence he goes on, at once, to explain that he does not mean to deny that goodness can be taught or that there are expert teachers of it. You do not imbibe it unconsciously ; it is a thing which comes by teaching and training (323d). His position is that, in a civilized society, life is one long process of being taught goodness, and every citizen is, in his degree, an expert teacher. But there are a few exceptionally able teachers with a special vocation for their function, who do what every good citizen is doing, but do it better, and Protagoras himself is simply one of these.

In support of this view he makes an eloquent and telling speech on the educational process to which the civilized man is all through life subjected, as a consequence of the very fact that he is a member ot a society with social traditions. Even in infancy parents, nurses, servants, are all busy teaching a child by precept and example that " this is right " and " that is wrong." The elementary schoolmaster next takes up the same task. The boy's reading lessons are passages from the poets, full of sound moral instruction, and the preceptors from whom he learns to read and write and tune his lyre pay more attention to his conduct than to anything else. So the trainer in bodily exercises makes it his prime business to teach hardihood and manliness of temper, the first requisites of a future soldier. When " school days " are over, and the boy enters on manhood, the city by its laws sets before him a rule for the whole conduct of his life, and penalizes him if he does not learn from this rule how " to govern and be governed." Thus the citizen's life is one unbroken progressive process of learning goodness (325c–326e). It is this very universality of the teaching which explains the puzzle about the sons of statesmen. If any of the " accomplishments " of which Socrates had spoken, for example flute-playing, were held by some community to be so important that every citizen must acquire it, and every one was anxious to communicate his own knowledge of it to others, what would happen ? The citizens of such a community would not all be first-rate performers. Any one of them would be a much better performer than an average member of a community which did not insist on the accomplishment ; but the very universality of the instruction would lead to differences between the individual citizens, based on their more or less marked natural aptitude. Where the means of instruction were open to all, and their use compulsory for all, proficiency would be most manifestly in proportion to aptitude. If no one but the son of a musician learned music, or no one but the son of an expert in " goodness " learned goodness, we might reasonably expect that the sons of musicians would always be our most successful musicians and the sons of " good men " our best men. Just because every one " learns," this does not occur in an actual society, and Socrates' paradox is thus seen to be no paradox at all. If he would compare the worst men in a civilized society, like that of Athens, not with imaginary " noble savages," but with real savages, he would soon discover on which side the superiority lies (326e–327e). And as for his argument that there is no provision of a special class of expert teachers of goodness, we may reply that neither are there special experts to whom a child has to be sent to learn to speak its mother-tongue, or to whom the son of an artisan must be apprenticed to learn his father's business. In both cases, the child picks up the knowledge from its " social environment." Besides, there are some men, like Protagoras himself, who have a special and superior gift for teaching goodness, and their pupils do make exceptional progress (327e–328d).

The reply to Socrates' doubts looks plausible, and has apparently traversed all the points of his case. But the plausibility is, after all, only apparent. If we look more closely, we shall see that the

whole argument depends on simply identifying " goodness " with
the actual traditions of an existing civilized state.   What you do
imbibe, as Protagoras has said, from parents, servants, schoolmasters, daily intercourse with your fellow-Athenians, is nothing
but the νόμος, the social tradition, of the group in which you live.
In a different social group, at Megara for example, the same influences of the social environment would be equally powerful, but
the type of character they would tend to produce would be in
many ways different.   Thus the theory expounded by Protagoras
can only be accepted as satisfactory if one assumes, as he has tacitly
done, that morality is entirely " relative," that is, that there is no
moral standard more ultimate than the standard of respectability
current in a given society.   If this is conceded, Protagoras has
made out his main contention that " goodness " can be, and actually
is, learned as a consequence of birth into a society with a definite
tradition.   But the whole point of the Socratic identification of
morality with " knowledge " is that morality is not any more
" relative " than geometry.   The traditions of Athens are no more
an ultimate standard in matters of right and wrong than they are
in questions of mathematics.   In other words, what Protagoras
really means by " goodness," if his argument is to be conclusive,
is just the medley of uncriticized traditions which Socrates calls in
the *Phaedo* " popular goodness " and opposes to " philosophic
goodness," as the imitation to the reality.   Goodness, as Socrates
understands it, is a matter not of traditions but of insight into
principles.   Now this, to be sure, *is* " knowledge," and must therefore be capable of being taught.   But the kind of goodness Protagoras must have in mind when he says that any Athenian citizen,
as such, is a teacher of it, is something which, as his own illustration
about the boy who picks up his father's trade rather naïvely indicates, is not got by teaching of principles at all, but merely picked
up, in the main, automatically.   Without knowing it, Protagoras
has really admitted that such goodness is what the *Gorgias* had
called a mere " knack."

Hence it follows that there is a certain inconsistency between
Protagoras' main position and the vindication of his profession with
which he concludes his speech.   To make the whole speech consistent, we should have to understand him to be claiming for himself a certain exceptional ability in catching the tone of the " social
tradition " of Athens, or any other community he visits, and
communicating that tone to his pupils.   Now it would, in the
first place, be something of a paradox to maintain that a brilliant
foreigner from Abdera can so successfully take the print of the
social traditions of every community where he spends a few weeks,
that a lecture from him will impress that tone on a young man more
effectively than lifelong intercourse with a society in which it is
dominant.   It would be bad manners, at least, for a brilliant
Frenchman or American to profess that a few weeks spent in this
country had enabled him to understand the " tone and temper of

the British people " better than any of us understand it for our-selves." [1] If " goodness " is knowledge, we can understand that a Chinaman, knowing nothing of " British traditions," may have lessons of first-rate importance to impart to us in it ; the claim becomes absurd if goodness means, in us, simply thorough conformity to the traditions of British respectability. The claim to be an expert teacher of goodness is only justifiable on the Socratic view that goodness is something eternal and immutable. It is in flat contradiction with the relativism professed by Protagoras. The further development of the discussion will make it still clearer that it is bound to end in an irreconcilable divergence because, from the first, the parties to the conversation have meant different things by " goodness."

III. The Unity of the " Virtues " (328d–334c).—There is just one " little " point Socrates would like to have cleared up, before he can profess himself completely satisfied. Protagóras had specified *two* qualities as bestowed on mankind by Zeus—the sense of *right* (δίκη), and conscience (αἰδώς) ; he had gone on to mention piety and *sophrosyne* also as constituents of " goodness." Does he mean that " goodness " is an aggregate of which these characters are distinct constituents (μόρια), or are we to understand that " conscience," " sense of right," " *sophrosyne*," " piety," are synonymous ? He meant to be understood in the former sense. But did he mean that the constituents are constituents in the way in which eyes, nose, and ears are constituents of a face, or in the sense in which the smaller volumes contained in a homogeneous mass (like a lump of gold) are constituents ? *i.e.* have the different " virtues " each its own constitutive formula, or is there only one such formula ? The question is one on which a practical teacher of goodness is bound to have a definite opinion, because it has a very direct bearing on his educational methods. On the first view, a man might " specialize " in one virtue (for example, courage), while his neighbour might prefer to specialize in some other, just as one man may specialize in diseases of the respiratory organs and another in disorders of the digestive system, or as one man may become a crack oarsman, another a fast bowler. (Or again, a man might set himself to acquire " goodness " by specializing first in one of its " parts " or " branches " and then in another, like Benjamin Franklin.) But on the second view, the principle of goodness will be exactly the same in whatever relation of life it is displayed. A

---

[1] That Protagoras actually took the line here suggested seems to follow from the well-known passage of the *Theaetetus* where the question is raised how Protagoras could reconcile his doctrine of " Man the measure " with his own claim to be able to *teach* " goodness." Socrates suggests that Protagoras might have pleaded that what he does for his pupils is not to give them " truer " views—a thing impossible on the *Homo mensura* theory—but to give them " more useful " views (*Theaetetus*, 166a–168c). This amounts to the suggestion of the text, that Protagoras believes himself to have a special aptitude for appreciating the tone of the current tradition of a community and impressing it on his hearers.

man who *really* acquires one "virtue" will have to acquire all simultaneously (329e).

Protagoras at once adopts the first alternative, that which recommends itself to average common sense. For he thinks it obvious that there are many brave but licentious men, and many "fair-dealing" men (δίκαιοι), who are far from "wise." (Note the way in which the "quadrilateral" of the four great virtues is thus taken for granted by Protagoras, as by other speakers in Plato, as something already traditional.) [1]

A view of this kind implies that each form of "goodness" has a *function* (δύναμις) of its own, distinctive of it, and radically different from the function of any other form. (We have already seen that this view, widely current in ordinary society, is in sharp opposition to the Socratic theory, in which the great difficulty of defining a given "virtue" is that we regularly find ourselves driven to adopt a definition which is equally applicable to every other virtue.) We proceed to treat this position in the recognized Socratic fashion by examining its consequences. It will follow that "justice," to take an example, has a definite function, "piety" or "religion" another and a different function. Justice is not piety, and religion is not justice. But we cannot adopt the monstrous moral paradox that justice is impious, or that religion is "unjust," or wrong, though this would seem to follow from the complete disparity between the "functions" of the different virtues just asserted by Protagoras.[2] Hence Protagoras himself is driven to take back what he had just said about the radical disparity of the different forms of goodness. The matter is, after all, not so simple as all that; there is some vague and unspecified resemblance between such different "parts" of goodness as piety and justice, though we cannot say exactly what or how close the resemblance is (331e). The reference to the scale of colours or hardnesses as illustrating the point (331d) shows that the meaning is that one virtue somehow "shades off" into a different one, though you cannot say exactly where the boundary-line should be drawn, as white shades off into black through a series of intermediate grays.

To expose the looseness of this way of thinking and speaking, Socrates resorts to another simple argument. Wisdom has been included by Protagoras in his list of forms of goodness, and the contrary opposite of wisdom is ἀφροσύνη ("folly"). But *sophrosyne*

[1] It seems to me that the same allusion must underlie the curious phrase of the poem of Simonides for the Scopadae shortly to be discussed, where the "complete" good man is called "four-cornered" (τετράγωνος ἄνευ ψόγου τετυγμένος). Presumably we are dealing with a Pythagorean τετρακτύς. It should be clear, at any rate, that the "quadrilateral" is no invention of Plato, since he represents it as familiar to so many of his fifth-century characters.

[2] The reasoning (331a ff.) does not really commit the error of confounding otherness with contrary opposition. The point of the passage is actually to make the distinction, though in simple and non-technical language; the suggestion that not-just (μὴ δίκαιον) = unjust (ἄδικον) is made only that it may be at once rejected.

is also a virtue which we ascribe to men who act "rightly and beneficially." Now *sophrosyne* means by derivation moral "sanity," and *its* contrary opposite, the conduct of those who act "wrongly and harmfully," is consequently *aphrosyne* ("folly"). For it is a principle of logic, which we can illustrate by an abundance of obvious examples, that ἐν ἑνὶ ἐναντίον (every term has one and only one definite contrary). Further, what is done "in contrary senses" (ἐναντίως) must be done "by contraries," *i.e.* in virtue of contrary characters in the agents. Thus if we can oppose what is "foolishly" done to what is "sanely" or "temperately" done, we may also oppose "folly" to *sophrosyne*, temperance, moral sanity. But we have already opposed wisdom and folly as contraries. On the principle then that one term (here "folly") has one and only one contrary opposite, wisdom and *sophrosyne* must be identified. Thus either we must abandon a fundamental logical principle, or we must give up the distinction between wisdom and *sophrosyne*, as our former argument was meant to show that we must give up the distinction between justice and piety (or religion).

(The reasoning here appears at first sight to turn on a mere "accident" of language, the fact that profligacy happens to be spoken of in Greek as "folly." When we reflect on the familiarity of the corresponding expressions in all languages which have an ethical literature, we should rather infer that the fact is no accident, but valuable evidence of the truth of the main tenet of Socratic morality. The thought underlying the linguistic usage is clearly that all morally wrong action is the pursuit of something which is not what rightly informed intelligence would pronounce good, and it is always wise to pursue what is truly good and foolish to prefer anything else.)

The next step in the argument is this. We have seen ground for identifying justice with piety and wisdom with temperance or moral sanity. This leaves us, so far, with two great types of "goodness," justice, regard for right, and moral sanity. But may we not further identify these two? Can we really say of any act that it is "unjust," a violation of some one's rights, and yet that it is "morally sane" (σῶφρον) or "temperate"? As a man of high character, Protagoras says that he personally would be ashamed to make such an assertion, but he knows that the "many" would make it. We may therefore examine the assertion simply as a piece of the current ethics of respectability, to see what it is worth (333*b*–*c*).[1] We must be careful, then, to bear in mind that, from

---

[1] Observe that the highly prized virtue, courage (ἀνδρεία), seems to have fallen into the background. This is a piece of Plato's dramatic art. The identification of the other commonly recognized virtues with one another is comparatively easy. But to the popular mind there *is* something "irrational" in high courage; it "ignores" the risks which "rational calculation" would take into account. The identification of courage with knowledge will therefore be the great *crux* for a rationalist moralist. Hence the discussion of ἀνδρεία is deliberately reserved for the second half of Socrates' argument.

the present onwards, Protagoras is avowedly acting as the dialectical advocate of a current morality which he personally regards as defective. It is not Protagoras of Abdera but the current ethics of respectability, for which he consents to appear as spokesman, that is on its trial. The question is whether a man who is acting "unjustly" can be acting with *sophrosyne*. In our time, as in that of Pericles, the average man would say that this is quite possible. A man may be "temperate" enough, he may be clear of all "licentiousness," but he may be greedy or ambitious and quite unscrupulous about infringing the "rights" of other men in pursuing his greed or ambition. (Macaulay's character of Sunderland would be in point here as an illustration [1]) In fact, it is proverbial that profligacy is a vice of youth and hot blood, avarice and ambition vices of "cold" later age, and the "old young man" (like Joseph Surface) has always been specially unpopular with the ordinary satirist, who is commonly indulgent to the "rake," unless he happens to be an elderly rake. Socrates' conviction, like that of Dante, who punishes the prodigal and the miser in the same circle, is that Charles Surface and Joseph are brothers in the spirit, no less than in the flesh; the antithesis of the Sheridans and Macaulays between the "generous" and the "mean" vices, is a false one; there are *no* "generous vices," and no "milksop" virtues.

Formally, the argument is not allowed to reach a conclusion; Protagoras, finding his case hard to defend, tries to take refuge in irrelevancy by diverting attention to the theory of the "relativity" of good. Socrates has started with the linguistic identification of "temperance" with moral sanity. The man who behaves with moral sanity is the εὖ βουλευόμενος, the man who acts "with good counsel." Hence if a man can in the same act be both temperate and unjust, it must be possible to act with good counsel in violating a "right." But a man only shows himself to be acting with good counsel when he "succeeds" or "does well" by disregarding that right. Socrates is thus taking advantage of the ambiguity of the expression εὖ πράττειν, which may either mean "to act well," or simply to "succeed in doing what you are proposing to do." How he would have continued the argument is indicated by his next question, "Do you recognize the existence of *goods*?" He means, having got the admission that injustice is only "well-advised" when it is successful injustice, to argue that no injustice really does "succeed" in procuring the aggressor on another man's rights what he is really aiming at getting, real good or well-being; it is always unsuccessful because it always involves sacrificing the good of the soul to something inferior (the thesis of the *Gorgias* and of the closing pages of *Rep.* i.). But the moment he shows his hand by

and we are prepared for it by the long half-comic interlude in which the poem of Simonides is canvassed; this is Plato's way of indicating that it is the hardest and most important section of the dialogue.

[1] "He had no jovial generous vices. He cared little for wine or beauty; but he desired riches with an ungovernable and insatiable desire," etc. etc. (*History*, c. 6).

asking whether "good things" do not mean "what is beneficial to man," Protagoras tries to escape the development he foresees by delivering a wholly irrelevant homily on the thesis that what is good for one animal may be bad for another, and what is good for man taken externally as a lotion, may be very bad if taken internally, in short that nothing can be pronounced good absolutely and unconditionally. This is, of course, a direct and simple application of Protagoras' own principle of "man the measure" to ethics, and the facts to which Protagoras appeals are all real facts; only they have no bearing on the issue at stake. It is true that I may be poisoned by drinking something which would have done me good if I had used it as an embrocation, that I should damage my health if I tried to live on the diet on which a horse thrives, and so forth. It does not in the least follow that there are not "good activities of the soul," which are absolutely good in the sense that it is good that any man should exhibit them at any and every time, and that scrupulous respect for "rights" is not one of these goods, and possibly the best of them. In common fairness, we may suppose that Protagoras is alive to this, and that he is simply doing his best for his client, the ethics of the average man, by diverting the attention of the audience from the weak point of his case.[1]

IV. INTERLUDE.—*The Poem of Simonides* (334c–348a).—At this point the conversation threatens to end in a general confusion, and the interrupted argument is only resumed after a long and apparently irrelevant episode. The main reason for the introduction of the episode has already been explained. The argument for the Socratic "paradoxes" makes a severe demand on the reader's power of hard thinking, and the most difficult part of it is yet to come. The strain of attention therefore requires to be relaxed, if we are to follow Socrates to his conclusion with full understanding. Plato also wants an opportunity to produce two striking dramatic effects. He wishes to contrast the manner of the "sophist," who is highly plausible so long as he has the argument to himself, but gets into difficulty the moment he is confronted by close criticism with the manner of Socrates, who cares nothing for eloquent plausibility and everything for careful and exact thinking. And he wants to provide a part in the drama for the secondary characters, Prodicus and Hippias; they will get no chance of a "speaking part" while Protagoras and Socrates occupy the centre of the stage. Hence I think we should take the whole of this long interlude as intended mainly to be humorous "relief," a gay picture of the manners of cultivated Athenian society in the later years of the Periclean age, and not much more.

The fun opens with the humorous pretence of Socrates that, in

[1] To judge from the *Theaetetus*, Protagoras had actually made the obvious application of the *Homo mensura* doctrine to ethics for himself (Burnet, *Greek Philosophy, Part I.*, 116–7). It leads directly to that identification of "virtue" with what a respectable society actually approves which is the foundation of his explanation of his own educational theory and practice, and is common ground to "subjectivists" in ethics.

kindness to his "shortness of memory," Protagoras should curb his eloquence and make his answers to questions as brief as he can. (The self-depreciation is, of course, fun. Socrates means that he would like fewer words and more thought ; but the implied criticism has to be made with due regard for "manners.") Protagoras is a little huffed by the suggestion that the other party to the discussion should prescribe the character of his responses ; Socrates politely expresses his regret for the weakness to which he has referred, and discovers that he has an engagement elsewhere, and the party thus seems to be on the point of dissolution, when the auditors intervene to prevent such a misfortune. The point of chief interest in the general conversation thus caused is provided by the entertaining burlesque of Prodicus, the great authority on the right use of words. All he really has to say is that the audience who listen to a discussion should give a fair hearing, without fear or favour, to both parties, and assign the victory to the party who makes out the better case. But his remarks are so disfigured by the mannerism of stopping to discriminate each of the terms he uses from some other with which it might conceivably be confused, that it takes him half one of Stephanus's pages to make his remark. It is clear that the real Prodicus (who, as we must remember, actually survived the execution of Socrates, and so must have been a well-remembered figure to many of the first readers of our dialogue) must have been very much of a formal pedant in manner, or the stress laid on the point by Plato would be unintelligible. No doubt we are also to understand that the defect is being exaggerated for legitimate comic effect. But it is not likely that the exaggeration is very gross. Prodicus was trying to make a beginning with the foundations of an exact prose style, and it would be quite natural that, once impressed with the importance of distinguishing between "synonyms," he should ride his hobby to death. We know from the remains of Varro's *de lingua Latina*, from Quintilian, Aulus Gellius, and others, to what lengths the men who attempted to perform the same services for Latin were prepared to go, and it is likely that if the writings of the "sophists" had been preserved, we should have found that Prodicus was not outstripped by his Roman imitators. There is no trace of any personal malice or dislike in the entertaining sketch Plato has given us. Hippias is allowed to make a speech of about the same length, *his* main point being to mark his disagreement with the partisans of "convention," and his conviction that the whole company, in spite of the differences of "conventional" political allegiance, are all "naturally" fellow-citizens. His tone is exactly that of a cosmopolitan eighteenth-century *philosophe*. Since Xenophon (*Mem.* iv. 4) pits Hippias and Socrates against one another as champions of φύσις and νόμος respectively, this cosmopolitanism is presumably a real trait of Hippias, though we cannot be sure that Xenophon is not simply developing a hint taken from the *Protagoras* itself. But even so, his representation shows that he thought Plato's little picture true to life in its main point. None of the interveners in the general conversation shows any sense of the real bearing of the argument which has just broken down. All treat it as a mere contest of verbal skill between two parties, each of whom is " talking for victory." In the end, a heated disagreement is only avoided by the consent of Protagoras to submit to further cross-questioning, if he may first be allowed to deliver another speech. He absolutely declines Socrates' proposal to submit himself to be questioned and to give an example of what he thinks the right way to meet criticism (338*d–e*). The scene which ensues can hardly be understood as anything but broad comedy. Protagoras, having carried his point about the delivery of a set speech on a theme of his own choosing, remarks that it is an important part of " culture " to understand the poets and criticize their perform-ances, and that he will accordingly now expound and criticize a poem composed by Simonides for the Scopadae. This is a task suggested naturally by the previous course of the conversation, as the contents of the poem have to do with " goodness."

Unfortunately the poem (Fr. 3 in the *Anthology* of Hiller-Crusius, 12 of Schneidewin) has to be reconstructed from the *Protagoras* itself, and the reconstruction can be neither complete nor certain, so that we are not entitled to speak with too much confidence about the precise drift of the poet. The general sense, appropriate enough in an encomium of a half-barbaric Thessalian chief, seems to be that it is idle to expect complete and all-round " goodness " in any man ; there are difficult situations out of which no human goodness comes with credit. We must be content to call a man " good," if his general conduct shows regard for right ($\delta i\kappa a$), if he never misbehaves without highly extenuating circumstances ; absolute superiority to circumstance can only be expected in a god. The impression one gets is that one is reading a paid panegyric on a magnate against whom there is the memory of some shocking deed or deeds which the eulogist wishes to excuse or palliate by the " tyrant's plea, necessity." [1]

The point on which Protagoras fastens is this. Simonides takes occasion to comment unfavourably on the saying commonly ascribed to Pittacus that " it is hard to be good " ($\chi a\lambda\epsilon\pi\grave{o}\nu\ \dot{\epsilon}\sigma\theta\lambda\grave{o}\nu$ $\ddot{\epsilon}\mu\mu\epsilon\nu a\iota$). But he has just said the very same thing himself in almost the same words ($\ddot{a}\nu\delta\rho$' $\dot{a}\gamma a\theta\grave{o}\nu\ \mu\grave{\epsilon}\nu\ \dot{a}\lambda a\theta\acute{\epsilon}\omega s\ \gamma\epsilon\nu\acute{\epsilon}\sigma\theta a\iota\ \chi a\lambda\epsilon\pi\acute{o}\nu$). He has thus committed the absurdity of censuring Pittacus for the very sentiment he has just uttered as his own (339*d*).

Socrates now seizes the opportunity to defend the poet by the aid of Prodicus and his famous art of discriminating between words. The point, he says, is that whereas Pittacus had said that it is hard

---

[1] Simonides writes much as a poet would have to do if he were composing an ode in praise of William III and felt that he could not be silent about the murder of the De Witts and the Glencoe massacre. The apologetic tone shows that his hero had done something which was regarded by most persons as highly criminal.

to *be* (ἔμμεναι) good, Simonides says that it is hard to *become*, (γενέσθαι) good; " to be " is one thing, " to become " another, and thus there is no formal contradiction between denying that it is hard to be good and asserting that it is hard to become good. But, objects Protagoras, this distinction only makes matters worse for Simonides ; if he denies that it is hard to be good, he must mean that it is easy to possess goodness, and the common sense of all mankind is against him. Socrates is ready with a rejoinder. Possibly Simonides, like his fellow-Cean Prodicus, was a votary of precision of speech, and regarded the employment of χαλεπόν in the sense of " difficult " as a misuse of words, just as Prodicus objects to the common colloquial use of the word " awful " (δεινός) in such phrases as " awful wealth " (δεινὸς πλοῦτος), on the ground that only bad things can properly be called " awful." Let Prodicus, as a fellow-countryman, tell us what Simonides really meant by χαλεπόν. Prodicus at once says he meant κακόν (" bad ").¹ If that is so, Pittacus was, from his Lesbian ignorance of the exact meaning of a Greek word, unconsciously uttering the senseless statement that " it is bad to be good," and Simonides was right in objecting this to him. Prodicus at once accepts this explanation, but Protagoras naturally rejects it as ridiculous. " So it is," says Socrates, " and you may be sure Prodicus is only making fun of us " (341*d*).

(So far, it is clear that the whole tone of the passage about Simonides is playful. Plato is laughing, as he often does, at the fifth-century fashion of trying to extract moral principles from the remarks of poets, especially of poets with a reputation, like Simonides, for worldly wisdom and a shrewd regard for the interests of " number one." The mock-respectful discussion of another dictum of the same poet in *Republic* i. is couched in exactly the same tone. The solemn pedantry of Prodicus is a second subject of mockery. But the main stroke is aimed at the superficiality of Protagoras. With all his eloquence about the value of a critical study of " literature," his ideal of criticism is to fasten on the first and most obvious weak point, and make an end of the matter. He has shown his cleverness by catching Simonides in a verbal contradiction ; he does not see the need of an attempt to understand the drift of his poem as a whole, or to consider whether the apparent contradiction will vanish when taken in the light of the general context. We are all only too familiar with this sort of " criticism," which aims at nothing more than the commendation or censure of individual phrases, while it lets " the whole " go unregarded.)

Socrates now undertakes to propound an interpretation which will pay due regard to the meaning of the whole poem (342*a*). He introduces it by some general observations, the tone of which ought

---

¹ The suggestion is not quite so absurd as it looks, absurd as it is. χαλεπόν, in the sense " a hard thing to bear," may often be paraphrased by κακόν without injury to sense. Cf. Pindar's τερπνῶν χαλεπῶν τε κρίσις (" issues of weal and woe "), or Homer's χαλεπὸν γῆρας (*Il.* Θ 103) (" grim old age "), and the like.

to settle the question whether we are to take his exegesis in earnest or not. Crete and Sparta are really the most philosophical communities in the Greek world, and " sophists " abound there more than anywhere else; but they conceal the fact from mankind at large by passing themselves off as rough fighting-men, and by vigilantly discouraging intercourse with other cities, so that they may keep their wisdom for their own exclusive benefit. This is why the ordinary Spartan startles you from time to time by the pungency and pertinence of his " dry " and brief apophthegms. They are all the product of this unique " Spartan culture." The famous " seven sages "—the list of them given in this passage is the earliest extant—were all trained in this school, and Pittacus was one of them. Hence his saying " it is hard to be good " was much admired as a piece of this sententious " philosophy," and Simonides, being an ambitious man, wished to win a great reputation by refuting it. This is the object of his whole poem (342*a*–343*c*).

(It ought not to have to be said that this whole representation of Sparta and Crete, the least " intellectual " communities of Hellas, and the two which Socrates himself takes as his models in *Republic* viii. in describing the State which has made the mistake of " neglecting education," is furious fun. Socrates is diverting himself by his whimsical suggestions that the " laconizing " fashionables of other cities, who affect the dress and appearance of prize-fighters, are all the while imitating the wrong thing, the pretence under which the Spartans disguise their real interests, and that the " superiority of Sparta " is really based not on military prowess and success but on intellectual eminence. And if the explanation which introduces the exposition of the poem of Simonides is thus sheer fun, we are bound in common sense to expect that the exposition will turn out to be mainly fun too.)

We are now given the professed exegesis of the poem, which is only arrived at by a series of violences done to its language. Simonides must be understood as correcting the saying " it is hard to be good " by saying " no, the *truly* hard thing is not to be, but to become a thoroughly good man, though this is possible. To *be* permanently good is not hard, but absolutely impossible for a man; it is only possible to a god." A *man*, as Simonides goes on to say, cannot help proving " bad " when he is " struck down " by irretrievable misfortunes. Now no one who is already down can be struck down. Hence Simonides must mean by a " man," an " expert," a wise and good man, and his meaning is shown by the fact that he goes on to say that a man is " good " as long as he " does well " ($\pi\rho\acute{a}\xi as \ \mu\grave{e}v \ \gamma\grave{a}\rho \ e\mathring{v} \ \pi\hat{a}s \ \mathring{a}v\grave{\eta}\rho \ \mathring{a}\gamma a\theta\acute{o}s$). For the man who " does well," or " succeeds " in anything is the man who *knows* how the thing ought to be done, the man who " does ill " is always the man whose *knowledge* fails him. Simonides is thus made, by an arbitrary exegesis, to bear witness to the Socratic doctrine that " goodness " and knowledge are the same (345*b*). His meaning is that it is hard to become good but impossible for man to be permanently good, because of the limitations and imperfections of all human *knowledge*.

The rest of the poem develops the same thought. In particular, when the poet says that he will "praise and love the man who does no deed of shame willingly," (ἑκών ὅστις ἔρδῃ μηδὲν αἰσχρόν,) we are not to take his words in what seems their natural grammatical sense. The "cultured" Simonides must be supposed to know that it is a vulgar error to suppose that anyone would do evil voluntarily. Hence the ἑκών must be taken by an extravagant *hyperbaton* with the words which precede it, so that the sense is, "I *readily* praise and love the man who does no deeds of shame" (though my profession sometimes unfortunately requires me to pay *constrained* compliments to "tyrants" who have committed crimes).

Though there have been commentators who have taken Socrates' exposition of the poem as perfectly serious, the blunder ought to be impossible to any man with a sense of humour or of the necessity of maintaining a dramatic unity of spirit throughout a scene. We have been prepared for the discussion of the verses by an introductory homily on the devotion of Sparta to "culture," which is manifestly the merest playful humour; we are fairly entitled to suspect Socrates whenever we find him pretending to discover deep philosophic truth in the compositions of any "poet," and particularly in those of the poet who had become a byword for his adroit and profitable flatteries of "the great"; his purpose should be made unmistakable by the forced character of the verbal constructions he is driven to advocate. Clearly we are dealing with an amusing "skit" on the current methods of extracting any doctrine one pleases from a poet by devices which can make anything mean anything. Socrates is amusing himself by showing that, if he chooses to play at the game, he can beat the recognized champions, just as in the *Parmenides* Plato amuses himself by showing that he can, if he likes, outdo the constructors of "antinomies" in the use of their own weapons. The one thing in the whole of the "lecture" on the verses of Simonides which is not playful is Socrates' insistence on the doctrine that wrongdoing is error, and is therefore not "voluntary." Here he is in intense earnest, but the device by which he extracts the doctrine from the text of Simonides by an impossible "punctuation" is itself merely playful, just as his suggestion that what he well knew to be the "paradox" of his own theory is so universally admitted by all thinking men that it is incredible Simonides should not accept it, is equally playful. He knows that the very proposition he represents as too well known to be ignored by Simonides will be rejected as an extravagance by his audience when he comes shortly to defend it. His object in getting it into the otherwise whimsical exposition of Simonides is simply to bring back the discussion to the original issues from which it has been allowed to diverge, and he has the natural delight of a humorist in clothing his thesis in the most provocative and arresting words he can find. How far he is from expecting his excursus into literature to be taken seriously is shown by his remark that he has now discharged his part of a bargain by allowing Protagoras to deliver a second speech, and would be glad if Protagoras would honour the agreement by returning to the interrupted discussion. For his own part, he thinks it unprofitable to spend our time debating the meaning of the poets, whom we cannot call directly into court; it is much better to let them alone and try to get at truth by the direct interplay of our own thoughts (347c–348a).

V. The Main Argument Resumed.—*The Identity of Goodness with Knowledge, and its Consequences* (348c–360e).—Now that Socrates has succeeded in bringing back the conversation to the point where it had been broken off, he carefully restates the question, with a polite assurance that he is not talking for victory but honestly asking the help of Protagoras towards the clarification of his own thought. The question is whether the names of the great virtues are different names for one and the same thing (349b), or whether to each of these names there answers " a peculiar reality or object with its own special function " (ἴδιος οὐσία καὶ πρᾶγμα ἔχον ἑαυτοῦ δύναμιν, where note that the word οὐσία, exactly as in the *Euthyphro*, implies the whole of the " doctrine of forms," expounded in the *Phaedo*). Protagoras has been so far impressed by the former arguments of Socrates that he now restates his original opinion with a large modification. He admits that most of the " parts of goodness " are " fairly like one another," but holds that ἀνδρεία, valour, courage, has a distinct character of its own. This is a matter of everyday observation, for it is a manifest fact that many men are singularly brave, but have no other virtuous quality; they have no regard for rights, no religion, no command over their passions, no prudence. (The view is a familiar one; it is habitually adopted, for example, in the character-sketches of a work like Macaulay's *History*. It implies, of course, that its supporters identify ἀνδρεία with the " popular " courage which the *Phaedo* pronounces to be a counterfeit of true valiancy, mere hardihood in the face of perils.) The first point which has to be made against this position is that it rests on the false conversion of a true proposition. It amounts to identifying " the valiant " with the " confident " or " fearless " (θαρράλεοι). Now it is true that all brave men are fearless, but it is not true that all the " confident " or " fearless " are truly brave, and the two classes, therefore, cannot be identified. In the absence of a logical terminology, this point has to be made by examples. Men who have learned a " dangerous " accomplishment, such as diving, fighting in the cavalry, or the like, will be " fearless " in facing the risks they have learned to deal with, as we also call them " brave " divers or fighters But persons who have never learned to dive or to manage a horse will also sometimes be reckless in throwing themselves into the water or plunging into a charge. But this, Protagoras says, is not valour ; it is simply madness. (He means, of course, that there is no valour in taking a risk simply because you are not alive to its magnitude. True valour involves consciousness of the risk you are facing.) Protagoras accordingly points out that though he had admitted that the valiant are fearless, he had not admitted the converse, and complains that Socrates is treating him unfairly (of course, Socrates' real object was simply to lead up to the making of the distinction). It is true that fearlessness may be the effect of knowledge, but it may also be the effect of high temper (θυμός) or mere frenzy (μανία) ; hence the superior fear-lessness of the man who has learned to swim or to use his weapons is no proof that *courage* (as distinct from mere fearlessness) is the same thing as " wisdom " or knowledge (σοφία). In fact, Protag-oras holds that the fearlessness which deserves to be called valour is due not to knowledge but to something else, " nature " (φύσις) and a " thriving " or " well-fed " state of soul (εὐτροφία τῶν ψυχῶν, 351b), just as physical strength is not due to knowledge but to bodily constitution and sound nourishment.[1]

Thus the question whether valour can be shown, as Protagoras now admits that the other leading forms of " goodness " can be, to be knowledge, requires us to raise still more fundamental questions. We admit that one may live well or live ill, and that the man who lives a life of pain and misery is not living well, but the man who lives a pleasant life is. May we say then that the pleasant life is the good life, the unpleasant life the bad ? Protagoras wishes to stipulate that the pleasure must be " pleasure in fine, or noble, things " (τοῖς καλοῖς, 351c), thus anticipating Mill's " distinction of qualities " of pleasure. But might we not say that things are good just in so far as they are pleasant, and bad in so far as they are unpleasant, so that good and pleasant are synonyms ? Protagoras thinks it due to his character to maintain that this is not true ; there are bad pleasures and good pains, and there are both pleasures and pains which are neither good nor bad. But he is willing to treat the suggestion, in the Socratic manner,[2] as one for further investigation. (It is very important, then, to remark that the Hedonist identification of good with pleasant comes into the con-versation, in the first instance, as problematic ; it is to be adopted or rejected according as its implications approve themselves or do not.) And the question about the relation between pleasure

---

[1] The precise position is, and is meant to be, vague. The champion of νόμος is clearly conceding more importance to φύσις (" original temperament ") than we might have expected of him from his earlier utterances. This part of the *Protagoras* has directly suggested Aristotle's observations about the " fearlessness " produced by ἐμπειρία or by native θυμός (*E.N.* 1116b 3 ff.).

[2] 351e, ὥσπερ σὺ λέγεις, ἔφη, ἐκάστοτε, ὦ Σώκρατες, σκοπώμεθα αὐτό, κτλ. Thus Protagoras knows all about the Socratic method of " hypothesis " expounded in the *Phaedo*. We must suppose that he had learned of it on the earlier occasion when he had met Socrates and formed a high opinion of his abilities. Rightly read, the *Protagoras* confirms the *Phaedo* in a way which can hardly be accounted for except by supposing that both are portraits of the same original.

and good directly raises another fundamental issue. The popular opinion is that " knowledge " has not much influence on conduct. It is held that a man often knows quite well that something is good or evil, but acts " against his better knowledge," which is mastered by " temper," or " pleasure," or " pain," or " lust," as the case may be. But may it not be that the popular opinion is wrong, and that if a man knows good and evil, nothing will ever prevail on him to act contrary to his knowledge ? Protagoras thinks that it would only be proper in a professional teacher of goodness, like himself, to take this view, and Socrates expresses his firm conviction of its truth.[1] But, since most men think otherwise, we, who dissent from them, must give a correct analysis of the facts they have in mind when they talk of a man's judgment as " overcome " by pleasure or pain, and satisfy them that the popular analysis of these facts is inaccurate (353*a*). We might, in fact, ask the mass of men, who profess to believe that a man can be seduced by the prospect of pleasure or frightened by that of pain into doing, against his better knowledge, what he recognizes to be evil, the following questions : (*a*) When you talk of something as pleasant but evil, do you not mean simply that the pleasant thing in question leads to painful consequences, and when you call some things good but unpleasant, do you not mean that, though unpleasant for the time being, they lead to pleasurable consequences ? " The many " would readily admit this, and thus would (*b*) commit themselves to the view that good and evil are identical with pleasant and painful. In fact (*c*) they would admit that the end they always pursue is getting the " greatest possible balance of pleasure over pain " (354*c–e*). It follows at once that, on the showing of the " many " themselves, the experience which they *call* " being overcome by pleasure or by pain " is really making a false *estimate* of pleasures and pains. To be " overcome " means " to take a greater amount of evil in exchange for a smaller amount of good " (356*e*), and on the hypothesis we are examining, " good " means " pleasure " and " evil " means " pain." Errors of conduct are thus on the same level as false estimates of number, size, and weight. Now we are preserved from mistakes about number, size, weight, by the arts or sciences (τέχναι) of counting, measuring, and weighing. In the same way we need to be preserved from false estimates in moral choice by a similar art of estimating the relative *magnitudes* of " lots " of prospective goods and evils, that is to say, prospective pleasures and pains, in fact by an " hedonic calculus," which will terminate disputes. And a " calculus," of course, is " knowledge," or " science." An argument of this kind ought to reconcile the " many " themselves to the view that

---

[1] 352*d* 2-4. Note that Socrates definitely commits himself to one of the two premisses of the argument which is to follow, the proposition that no one really acts against his own knowledge of good and evil. He never commits himself to the other premiss, the Hedonistic doctrine that good is pleasure. This remains a suggestion for examination.

wrong choice, the victory of passion over knowledge as they call it, is really nothing but miscalculation, and therefore that wrong action is due to error and is always involuntary (357–358).

It is on this section of the dialogue that the notion of a Platonic "Hedonism" has been erected, with the consequence that one of two equally impossible inferences has to be made, either that there is no consistent ethical doctrine to be found in the dialogues—Plato allows himself at pleasure to argue for or against any view which interests him for the moment (the theory of Grote)—or that the *Protagoras* expresses an "early theory" which is afterwards abandoned when we come to the *Gorgias* and *Phaedo*. Careful reading will show that neither of these conceptions is justified. Neither Protagoras nor Socrates is represented as adopting the Hedonist equation of good with pleasure. The thesis which Socrates is committed to is simply that of the identity of goodness and knowledge. The further identification of good with pleasure is carefully treated, as we have seen, as one neither to be affirmed nor denied. We are concerned solely with investigating its consequences. One of these consequences would be that what is commonly called "yielding to passion against our better knowledge" is a form of intellectual error and is involuntary, since it means choosing a smaller "lot of pleasure" when you might choose a greater. (These consequences are, in fact, habitually drawn by Hedonists.) Hedonism thus is in accord with the doctrines of Socrates on one point, its reduction of wrong choice to involuntary error, and for that reason Socrates says that you can make the apparent paradoxes of his ethics acceptable to mankind at large, if you also adopt the Hedonist equation, good=pleasure. (The "many," in fact, do in *practice* accept this equation, because they are votaries of some form of the βίος φιλοχρήματος.) It does not follow that because Socrates agrees with vulgar Hedonism on the point that wrong choice is involuntary error and arises from lack of knowledge of good, that he identifies knowledge of good, as the Hedonist does, with calculation of the sizes of "lots" of pleasure and pain. All he wants to show is that even from the point of view of the persons who mistake "popular goodness" for genuine goodness, it is no paradox to say that goodness is knowledge of some sort; the Hedonist is a "rationalist" in his ethics, though his "rationalism" may not be of the right kind. That this is all that is meant is clear from the way in which Socrates is careful to insist over and over again that the appeal is being made to the standards of "the mass of mankind." We must also not forget that the appeal to the unconscious Hedonism of the average man is being made for a further special purpose. The object of convincing the average man that, on his own assumptions, goodness is a matter of right calculation, is to prepare the way for the further proof that, even on these assumptions, courage can be brought under the same principle as all the rest of "goodness." When we thus take the argument in its proper context, we see that the *Protagoras* no more teaches

Hedonism than the *Phaedo*, which also represents the morality of average men as a business of estimating pleasures and pains against one another. Rightly interpreted, *Gorgias*, *Phaedo*, *Protagoras*, are all in accord on the one doctrine to which Socrates commits himself in the present section of our dialogue, the doctrine that " goodness " is knowledge. The confusion between " knowledge of the good " and computation of pleasures and pains is given, in the *Protagoras* as in the other dialogues, for what it is, a confusion of the " average man," and for nothing more.

To come to the application to the problem about ἀνδρεία. What is it that the courageous face, but the cowardly refuse to face ? The current answer is that it is " dangers " (τὰ δεινά). But " danger " means an anticipated evil, and we have just seen that even the average man, when he comes to theorize about his own practice, holds that no one " goes to face " what he believes to be evil for him. The very fact that he chooses to face the situation shows that he regards it as the " lesser evil " to do so. The real reason, then, why some men face the risks of war but others run away, must be that the former judge that more good, which to them means more pleasure, is to be got by standing your ground than by running away ; the latter think that they will get more good, and again they mean more pleasure, by running. If we praise the one and condemn the others, we are praising a true (and also condemning a false) calculation about the " balance of pleasure over pain." The brave man of everyday life faces the present pain and peril because he has correctly calculated that endurance of it will lead to a greater balance of pleasure than flinching. Thus even the unconscious theory of the average man at bottom implies the view that courage is a matter of *knowing* what is and what is not formidable (σοφία τῶν δεινῶν καὶ μὴ δεινῶν, 360c). This is, in fact, exactly what Socrates says about " popular " courage in the *Phaedo*. (That what the " many " suppose to be knowledge of the good— namely, knowledge of the hedonic consequences of your act—is something very different from what Socrates means by knowledge of the good is true, but irrelevant to the present argument, which only aims at showing that, even if you adopt the working morality of the average man, courage stands on the same footing as the other " virtues." From his standpoint, it resolves itself, like the rest, into calculation of hedonic consequences ; from Socrates' standpoint, it and all the rest issue from knowledge of the true and eternal good.)

VI. EPILOGUE.—Our discourse has, after all, only ended by bringing us in face of the really fundamental problem, what true " goodness " *is* (360c). (This remark, again, shows that Socrates is not represented as accepting the Hedonism which he finds to be the unconscious assumption of the average man. We have seen clearly enough what " goodness " is, on that theory.) In fact, we have ended by exchanging positions in a very entertaining fashion. Protagoras, who began by being sure that goodness can be taught and that he can teach it, seems now to be equally sure that, whatever goodness is, it is not the one thing which can be taught, knowledge ; Socrates, who began by raising the doubt whether it can be taught, is now doing his best to prove that it must be knowledge and nothing else.   And here the party breaks up, with a last word of graceful compliment on the part of Protagoras.   He has often testified to his admiration of Socrates' parts and rates him far above all other persons of his years ; he would not be surprised if he should yet become famous for his " wisdom."

Of course, the apparent paradox of which Socrates speaks can be very simply explained.   What he doubted was whether the sort of " goodness " of which the public men of Athens are examples can be taught.   Since this " goodness " is just another name for " tactful management " of affairs, it obviously cannot be " taught." A man has to acquire tact by the handling of affairs and men for himself ; you cannot teach the theory of it.   But political tact is something very different from anything Socrates understood by goodness.   There is thus no real confusion or shifting of ground, so far as he is concerned.   Protagoras is in a different position. By his own showing, the " goodness " he aims at teaching is just the secret of political success, and political success really does depend on a " tact " which cannot be taught.   Hence Protagoras really does combine incompatible positions when he asserts both that " goodness " is not knowledge, and also that it can be taught. If by " goodness " we mean what Protagoras defined as " success in managing the affairs of your household and city," he is right in maintaining that goodness is not knowledge, but clearly wrong in holding that it is an " art " which he can teach.[1]

See further :

RITTER, C.—*Platon*, i. 308–342.
RAEDER, H.—*Platons philosophische Entwickelung*, 106–111.
NATORP, P.—*Platons Ideenlehre*, 10–18.
GOMPERZ, TH.—*Griechische Denker*, i. 250–264.
STEWART, J. A.—*The Myths of Plato*, 212–258 (*The Protagoras Myth*).
DITTMAR, H.—*Aeschines von Sphettus*, 186–212 (on Aeschines' dialogue *Callias*, where, however, the author's chronology of the life of Callias is wrong.   Callias had two sons, both in at least their later 'teens in 399.   *Apol.* 20a–c.)

[1] Cf. Burnet, *Early Greek Philosophy, Part I.,* 170–179.

CHAPTER XI

THE *REPUBLIC*

THE *Republic* is at once too long a work, and too well known by numerous excellent summaries and commentaries, to require or permit analysis on the scale we have found necessary in dealing with the *Phaedo* or *Protagoras*. We must be content to presume the student's acquaintance with its contents, and to offer some general considerations of the relation of its main theses to one another and to those of dialogues already examined.

To begin with, it is desirable to have a definite conception of the assumed date of the conversation and the character of the historical background presupposed. It should be clear that Athens is supposed to be still, to all appearance at any rate, at the height of her imperial splendour and strength.[1] Also, the time is apparently one of profound peace. No reference is made to military operations ; though the company consists mainly of young men of military age, no explanation of their presence at home is offered. Yet Plato's two elder brothers, Adimantus and Glaucon, who are both young men, have already distinguished themselves in a battle near Megara (368c), which can hardly be any other than that of the year 424 (Thuc. iv. 72). We have to add that the sophist Thrasymachus is assumed to be at the height of his fame, and we know that he was already prominent enough to be made the butt of a jest in the first play of Aristophanes, produced in the year 427.[2] Similarly, the tone of Socrates' initial remarks about old age as an unknown road on which he will yet have to travel shows that we are to think of him as still very far from the age (sixty) at which a man officially became a γέρων at Athens. Damonides of Oea is referred to at 400b as still alive, and since we have the evidence of Isocrates for the statement that he " educated " Pericles, we cannot suppose him to have been born much, if at all, later than the year 500. All these considerations, taken together, suggest that the supposed date of the conversation must be about the time of the

[1] This is made especially clear by the tone of the satire on democracy viii. 557 ff., where it is unmistakably the powerful, opulent, and formidable democracy of the Archidamian war that Socrates is depicting. The year 411, assumed as the dramatic date by some commentators, is about the worst of all possible choices. It is rendered impossible by the fact that in the *Republic*, Cephalus, the father of Polemarchus and Lysias, is still alive, though an old man. The date is thus before his death and the removal of his sons to Thurii, whence they returned, after a good number of years, to Athens in 411 (*Vit. Lysiae*, c. 1).

[2] Aristoph., Fr. 198.

peace of Nicias (421 B.C.) or the preceding truce of 422. It is important to remember that Athens came out of the Archidamian war, though not quite on the terms she might have got, but for the folly of the democratic leaders after Sphacteria (425), far and away the richest and most powerful of the combatant states, with the main of her empire intact. For purposes of illustration the student should read by the side of the *Republic*, the *Wasps* and *Peace* of Aristophanes, as illustrative of the conditions of the time. Socrates must be thought of as being no more than middle-aged, somewhere about fifty years old, and we must bear in mind that it was at most a couple of years before that Aristophanes had brought him on the stage in the *Clouds*. Plato himself would be a mere child of some five to seven years.

There is nothing in the dialogue to support any of the fanciful modern speculations about a possible " earlier edition " without the central books which discuss the character and education of the " philosopher-kings," or the possible existence of the first book by itself as a " dialogue of search." On the contrary, the appearances are all in favour of regarding the whole as having been planned as a whole. It is not until we come to the sixth book that we are in sight of the " goodness " which is one and the same thing with knowledge ; the goodness of the " guardians " of *Republic* ii.–iv. has been carefully marked as remaining all along at the level of " opinion." It rises no higher than loyalty to a sound national tradition taken on trust, and is thus so far on a level with the " popular " goodness of the *Phaedo*, though the tradition in this case is that of a morally sounder society than that of Athens, or of any existing Greek πόλις.[1] Hence it is inconceivable that Plato should ever have composed a *Republic* which ignored the central points of Socratic ethics. The first book, again, serves its present purpose as an introduction to the whole work perfectly. In outline, all the main ideas which underlie the description of the ideal man and the ideal society are there, the conception of the life of measure (in the argument about πλεονεξία), the thought of happiness as dependent on " function " or vocation, and the rest ; but all are stated, as they should be in an Introduction, in their abstract form ; their real significance only becomes apparent as they are clothed with concrete detail in the full-length picture of the good man and the good community. To me it is inconceivable that *Republic* i. should ever have been planned except as the introduction to a work covering the ground of the *Republic* as we have it.[2]

[1] This is why in Book IV. the virtues, as practised in the "reformed" city, are still distinguishable, so that different virtues are most specially prominent in different sections of society, and, again, why we are told at iv. 430c 3 that the account just given of courage is adequate only as a description of " citizen " courage, and may have to be revised later on. The " unity of the virtues " only emerges in *Republic* vi. when we come to discuss the character of the " philosopher-king."

[2] The only specious argument for an earlier *Urstaat* is that, at the beginning of the *Timaeus*, where Socrates is made to recapitulate the contents

It has sometimes been asked whether the *Republic* is to be regarded as a contribution to ethics or to politics. Is its subject " righteousness," or is it the " ideal state " ? The answer is that from the point of view of Socrates and Plato there is no distinction, except one of convenience, between morals and politics. The laws of right are the same for classes and cities as for individual men. But one must add that these laws are primarily laws of personal morality ; politics is founded on ethics, not ethics on politics. The primary question raised in the *Republic* and finally answered at its close is a strictly ethical one, What is the rule of right by which a man ought to regulate his life ? And it should be noted that the first simple answer offered to the question, that of Cephalus and Polemarchus, makes no reference at all to the πόλις and its νόμοι, and this, no doubt, is why it is put into the mouths of speakers who were not Athenian πολῖται but protected aliens. The political reference is brought into the dialogue in the first instance by Thrasymachus, who insists on treating morality as a mere product and reflex of the habit of obedience to a political κρεῖττον or " sovereign." Socrates finds it necessary to keep this political reference in view throughout his own argument, but he is careful to explain that the reason for studying the public life of classes and communities is simply that we see the principles of right and wrong " writ large " in them ; we study the " larger letters " in order to make out the smaller by their aid. All through, the ultimate question is that raised by Glaucon and Adimantus, what right and wrong are " in the soul of the possessor." This comes out most clearly of all in the part of the work which is written with most palpable passion, the accounts of the degenerate types of city and men. Each defective constitution is studied and the tone of public life fostered by it noted, in order that we may learn by this light to read the heart of the individual man. We see the real moral flaw in the outwardly decent man who regards becoming and remaining " well-off " as the finest thing in life, by considering the quality of national life in a merchant-city, like Carthage, where the " merchant-prince " is dominant and gives the tone to the whole community, and so on. The *Republic*, which opens with an old man's remarks about approaching death and apprehension of what may come after death, and ends with a myth of judgment, has all through for its central theme a question more intimate than that of the best form of government or the most eugenic system of propagation ; its question is, How does a man attain or forfeit eternal salvation ? For good or

of the *Republic* (*Tim.* 17a–19a), nothing is said about the philosopher-kings and their education. Nothing, however, is said about the account of the " imperfect " types of men and societies in *Republic* viii.–ix. either. The silence of the *Timaeus* about everything which follows *Republic* v. can be explained conjecturally in more ways than one. The simplest explanation is that the real purpose of the recapitulation is to serve as an introduction to the projected but unfinished *Critias*. Any explanation of the facts must remain conjectural, since Plato wrote only the opening pages of the projected *Critias*, and we do not know how he meant to develop the story.

bad, it is intensely " other-worldly." Man has a soul which can attain everlasting beatitude, and this beatitude it is the great business of life to attain. The social institutions or the education which fit him to attain it are the right institutions or education : all others are wrong. The " philosopher " is the man who has found the way which leads to this beatitude. At the same time, no man lives to himself, and the man who is advancing to beatitude himself is inevitably animated by the spirit of a missionary to the community at large. Hence the philosopher cannot be true to himself without being a philosopher-king ; he cannot win salvation without bringing it down to his society. That is how the *Republic* views the relation between ethics and statesmanship.

The fundamental issue is raised in the introductory book with great artistic skill. From the simple observations of old Cephalus about the tranquillity with which a man conscious of no undischarged obligations can look forward to whatever the unseen world may have to bring, Socrates takes the opportunity to raise the question what δικαιοσύνη, taken in the sense of the supreme rule of right—" morality " as we might say—is. What is the rule by which a man should order the whole of his life ? Before we can embark on the question seriously, we need to be satisfied that it is not already answered for us by the ordinary current moral maxims of the decent man ; that there really is a problem to be solved. Next we have to see that the theories in vogue among the superficially " enlightened," which pretend to answer the question in a revolutionary way, are hopelessly incoherent. Only when we have seen that neither current convention nor current anti-conventionalism has any solution of the problem are we in a position to raise it and answer it by the true method. Thus there are three points of view to be considered: that of the unphilosophical decent representative of current convention, sustained by Cephalus and his son Polemarchus ; that of the " new morality," represented by Thrasymachus ; and that of sober philosophical thinking, represented by Socrates.

As to the first point of view, that of decent acquiescence in a respectable convention which has never been criticized, we note, and this may serve as a corrective to exaggerations about the extent to which " the Greeks " identified morality with the νόμος of a " city," that Plato has deliberately chosen as the exponent of moral convention a representative who, as a μέτοικος, naturally makes no appeal to the " city " and its usages ; the rule of Cephalus is specially characteristic not of a πόλις but of a profession, and a profession which in all ages has enjoyed the reputation of sound and homely rectitude. The old man's morality is just that which is characteristic of the honourable merchant of all places. " Right," according to him, means " giving to every man his own, and speaking the truth," *i.e.* a man is to honour his business obligations and his word is to " be as good as his bond " ; the man who acts thus has discharged the whole duty of man. The point of the conversation

begun between Socrates and Cephalus, and continued with Polemarchus as respondent, is merely that this simple rule for business
transactions cannot be regarded as a supreme principle of morality
for two reasons. (1) There are cases where to adhere to the letter
of it would be felt at once to be a violation of the spirit of right ;
(2) if you do try to put it into the form of a universal principle by
explaining that " giving a man his own " means " treating him as
he deserves," " giving him his due," however you understand the
words " a man's due," you get again a morally *bad* principle.[1]
Against Polemarchus, who thinks that morality can be reduced to
" giving every one his due " in the sense of being a thoroughly
valuable friend to your friends and a dangerous enemy to your foes
(a working morality expressed in the " gnomic " verses of Solon
and Theognis), it has to be shown that to make such a principle
of conduct acceptable to a decent man's conscience, we must at
least take our " friends " and " foes " to mean " the good " and
" the bad " respectively, and that, even then, the principle is
condemned by the fact that it makes it one half of morality to
" do evil " to some one. The argument equally disposes incidentally
of the " sophistic " conception of " goodness " as a kind of special
accomplishment by showing : (1) that in any definite situation
in life, the " accomplishment " needed to confer the benefit demanded by that situation is some kind of skill other than " goodness " ; and (2) that all these accomplishments can be put to a
morally bad, as well as to a morally good, *use*. Virtue, for example,
will not make a man the best of all advisers about an investment,
and the knowledge which does make a man a good counsellor on
such a matter also makes him a very dangerous adviser, if he
chooses to use it for a fraudulent end. This prepares us to discover
later on that though " goodness " in the end is knowledge and
nothing but knowledge, it is something quite different from the
" arts " or " accomplishments " with which the professional
" teachers of goodness " confound it.

When we come to the anti-conventional " immoralism " of the
" enlightenment," it is important to remark that Thrasymachus
is made to overstate the position ; as Glaucon says, at the opening
of the second book, he has bungled the case. (As we know of no
reason why Plato should misrepresent a prominent man of the
preceding generation, the violence and exaggeration is presumably
a genuine characteristic of the actual Thrasymachus, and it is used

[1] The apparent triviality of the examples chosen by Socrates to illustrate
his point is only apparent. He takes simple illustrations, as Professor Burnet
has said, because the issue at stake is most readily seen in such cases. Thus,
e.g., the question whether one should return a weapon to a lunatic because it is
his raises the problem whether it is the duty of a banker to honour all the
cheques of a wealthy senile client, or of a solicitor to take his instructions for
a manifestly insane will without any warning to his family; and these are
questions of moment, not only for the casuist but for the legislator. Grotius
has to begin with precisely the same·kind of elementary example when he
wants to discuss the problems connected with international good faith in the
De iure belli et pacis.

mainly for humorous effect. Thrasymachus, like modern authors whom one could name, must not be taken to mean all he says too seriously. Bluster is a mannerism with him, as it is in fact with some successful advocates. The serious statement of the immoralist case is reserved for Glaucon.) As Thrasymachus states the case, there is really no such thing as moral obligation. What men call " right " is " the interest of the superior." (In this phrase, τὸ κρεῖττον is to be taken as neuter, and what is meant is " the sovereign " in a community.) The theory is that right or morality is a synonym for conformity to νόμος (the institutions and traditions of the community). But these institutions have been originally imposed on the community by the " sovereign " purely with a view to his own benefit, and the *only* reason why they should be respected is that the " sovereign " has the power to make you suffer if you do not respect them. Hence, unlike Hobbes, Thrasymachus feels no need to justify the absolutism of the " sovereign " by appeal to the " social contract " by which he has been invested with his sovereign powers ; since he does not regard " right " as having any meaning, he has not to show that the sovereign has any right to obedience ; it is sufficient to observe that his *power* to enforce obedience is guaranteed by the simple fact that he *is* the sovereign. Like the imaginary prehistoric kings and priests of Rousseau or Shelley, he has succeeded in imposing his will on the community and there is nothing more to be said. In practice this theory would work out exactly like that of Callicles in the *Gorgias*, but there is the important difference that, in theory, the two immoralists start from opposite assumptions. Callicles is a partisan of φύσις who honestly believes that in the " order of things " the strong man has a genuine *right* to take full advantage of his strength ; Thrasymachus is pushing the opposite view of all morality as mere "convention" to an extreme. The evidence for his theory is, in the first instance, simply the fact that all governments make "high treason," the subversion of the sovereign, the gravest crime. The first care of every government is to ensure the constitution, whatever it is, against revolution. By pure confusion of thought the safeguarding of the constitution is then identified with the safeguarding of the private interests of the particular persons who happen at any moment to be exercising the function of sovereignty. Subsequently an appeal is made to the familiar facts about the " seamy side " of political and private life, the unscrupulosity and self-seeking of politicians, and the readiness of private men to cheat one another and the community, to job for their families and the like, when the chance offers. It would be easy to show that the indictment is drawn up with careful reference to features of contemporary Athenian life, but the reasoning of Thrasymachus rests on the further assumption that the seamy side of life is its only side ; life is robbing and being robbed, cheating and being cheated, and nothing else. This is, after all, not an impartial picture even of a society groaning under the rule of a tyrant or a demagogue, and when Socrates comes to reply, he also finds no difficulty in appealing to equally " real " facts of a very different kind, *e.g.* the fact that a politician expects to get some sort of remuneration for his work, which shows that the work itself is not necessarily a " paying " thing. Even in the world as it is, the " strong man's " life is not all getting and no giving.

The fact is that Thrasymachus, like Mr. Shaw or Mr. Chesterton, has the journalist's trick of facile exaggeration. He is too good a journalist to be an *esprit juste*, and the consequence is that he lands himself in a dilemma. If his " sovereign " who has a view only to the interests of " number one " is meant to be an actual person or body of persons, it is obvious, as Socrates says, that he is not infallible. It is not true that the moral code and the institutions of any society are simply adapted to gratify the personal desires of the sovereign who, according to Thrasymachus, devises them, or to further his interests ; judged by that standard, every existing set of νόμοι is full of blunders.[1] But if you assume that the sovereign is always alive to his own interests and always embodies them in his regulations, your sovereign is a creature of theory, an " ideal," and you lay yourself open at once to the line of argument adopted by Socrates to show that his worth depends on fulfilling a social function, independently of the question whether he gets any private advantage from his position or not. The " new morality " of Thrasymachus must therefore stand or fall on its own merits as an ethical theory ; it derives no real support from his speculations about the origin of government in the strong man's " will to power."

On the argument by which Socrates meets the strictly ethical assertion that " conventional " morality is a mere expression of the low intelligence and weakness of the " herd," all I wish to remark here is that he is guided throughout by the Pythagorean analogy between tuned string, healthy body and healthy mind, which is the key to half the best thought of the Greek moralists. The immoralist's case is really disposed of in principle by the often misunderstood argument about πλεονεξία (*Rep.* i. 349*b*–350*c*). The reasoning already contains in germ the whole doctrine of the " right mean " afterwards developed in the *Philebus* and the *Ethics* of Aristotle. The point is that in all applications of intelligence to the conduct of activity of any kind, the supreme wisdom is to know just where to stop, and to stop just there and nowhere else.

---

[1] For example, on Thrasymachus' theory, the δῆμος, which is the κρεῖττον at Athens, must be supposed to have adopted the institution of ostracism in the interests of the δῆμος, as a safeguard against would-be " dictators." But in actual working the institution favours the aspirant to a dictatorship by giving him a chance to remove the natural leaders of a " constitutional opposition." The selection of magistrates by lot, again, must be supposed to have been adopted to equalize the chances of the citizens ; but, as its ancient critics said, it may work the wrong way, since it gives the μισόδημος as good a chance of office as anyone else, whereas he would be handicapped under an elective system by his known or suspected hostility to the constitution.

The "wise man," like the musician or the physician, knows what the fool or the quack never knows, "how much is enough." The mistake common to the fool in the management of life and the bungler tuning a musical instrument or treating a sick man, is that they believe in the adage that you "can't have too much of a good thing." On the strength of this misleading faith, one ruins his instrument, another kills his patient, and the third spoils his own life. There is a "just right" in all the affairs of life, and to go beyond it is to spoil your performance, and consequently to miss "happiness." Once grasped, this point leads on to the other that the "just right" in any performance means the adequate discharge of function, and that happiness, in turn, depends on discharge of function. The introduction to the *Republic* thus leads us up to precisely the teleological conception of the rule of conduct from which Butler starts in the Preface to his *Sermons*. "Happiness" depends on "conformity to *our* nature as active beings." What "active principles" that nature comprises and how they are organized into a "system" we learn in the immediately following books.

With the opening of the second book, we are introduced to the genuine version of the immoralist doctrine of which Thrasymachus had given a mere exaggeration, the theory that regard for moral rules is a *pis aller*, though one which is unfortunately unavoidable by ordinary humanity. The theory is often referred to as that of Glaucon and Adimantus, but it should be noted that Adimantus takes no part in the statement of the theory and that Glaucon, who does explain it fully, is careful to dissociate himself from it; it is given as a speculation widely current in educated circles of the time of the Archidamian war and supported by specious though, as Glaucon holds, unsound arguments. His own position is simply that of an advocate speaking from his brief. He undertakes to make an effective defence of the case which Thrasymachus had mismanaged, in order that it may really be disproved, not merely dismissed without thorough examination of its real merits. The important feature of his argument is not so much the well-known statement of the "social contract" theory of the *origin* of moral codes as the analysis of existing morality to which the historical speculation is meant to lead up. The point is that "men practise the rules of right not because they choose, but because they cannot help themselves." At heart every one is set simply on gratifying his own passions, but you will best succeed in doing this by having the fear of your fellow-men before your eyes and abstaining from aggression on them. If you get the chance to gratify your passions without moral scruples, and can be sure not to be found out and made to suffer, you would be a fool not to benefit by your opportunity. This is the point of the imaginative fiction about the "ring of Gyges." The real fact which gives the sting to the fiction is simply that we all know that there is no human virtue which would not be deteriorated by confidence of immunity from detection. None of us could safely be trusted to come through the ordeal with our characters undepraved. We are all prone to lower our standard when we believe that there is no eye, human or divine, upon us. There can be little doubt that a theory of this kind, which amounts to the view suggested as possible by Kant that no single human act has ever been done simply " from duty," was a current one in the age of Socrates, and we can even name one of the sources upon which Plato is presumably drawing. The theory attempts to combine in one formula the two rival conceptions of " nature " and " convention " as regulative of action. It amounts to saying that there is a morality of unscrupulous egoism which is that of " nature " and is practised by us all when we are safe from detection, and another and very different " morality of convention," a morality of mutual respect for " claims and counter-claims " which we are obliged to conform to, so far as our behaviour is exposed to the inspection of our fellows. This doctrine is taught in so many words in a long fragment, discovered at Oxyrhynchus, of Socrates' contemporary and rival, Antiphon the " sophist." [1] According to Antiphon, the " wise man," who means to make a success of life, will practise " conventional justice " when he believes that his conduct will be observed by others, but will fall back on " natural justice " whenever he can be sure of not being found out. This is exactly the position Glaucon means to urge in his apologue. What he wants Socrates to prove is that the conception of the two rival moralities is a false one ; that mutual respect of rights is the true morality of " nature," as much as of " convention," the course of conduct suitable to " our nature as agents." The proof is supplied in the end by the doctrine of the " parts of the soul " in *Republic* iv., exactly as Butler attempts to supply a similar proof of the same thesis by his account of the hierarchy of the " active principles " in his three *Sermons on Human Nature.*

The contribution of Adimantus to the discussion is that he places the argument for regarding respect for the rights of one's neighbour as a mere cover for self-seeking on a basis independent of all speculations about moral origins. The tone of his speech is carefully differentiated from that of Glaucon. Glaucon, as he himself admits, is simply making the ablest forensic defence he can of his case, and can jest about the gusto with which he has thrown himself into the cause of a dubious client ; Adimantus speaks from the heart in a vein of unmistakable moral indignation. He complains not of the speculations of dashing advanced thinkers, but of the low grounds on which the defence of morality is based by the very parties who might be presumed to have it most at heart. Parents who are sincerely anxious that their sons should grow up to be honest and honourable men regularly recommend virtue simply on the ground of its value as a means to worldly success and enjoyment ; they never dwell on the intrinsic worth of virtue

---

[1] *Oxyrhynchus Papyri*, XI. no. 1364.

itself. On the contrary, their habitual insistence on the hardness
of the path of virtue and the pleasantness of vicious courses suggests
that they think virtue in itself no true good. And the poets all
speak the same language. When you come to the representatives
of religion, who might be expected to take the highest line, you
find that they are worst of all. They terrify the sinner by their
stories of judgment to come, but only as a preliminary step to
assuring him that they will, for a small consideration, make his
peace with Heaven by easy ritual performances and sacraments
which involve no change of heart. The whole influence of religion
and education seems to be thrown into the scale against a genuine
inward morality, and this is a much more serious matter than the
speculations of a few clever men about the " original contract "
and the motives which prompted it. We need a new religion and a
new educational system. (We must, of course, note that the
indictment of religion is throughout aimed not at the official cultus
of the city, but at the Orphic and similar sects ; the vehemence
with which Adimantus speaks seems to indicate an intense personal
hostility to these debased " salvationists " which is presumably a
real trait of the man's character.)

The effect of the two speeches, taken in conjunction, is to impose on Socrates the task of indicating, by a sound analysis of
human nature, the real foundations of morality in the very constitution of man, and of showing how education and religion can be,
and ought to be, made allies, not enemies, of a sound morality.
This, we may say, is the simple theme of the whole of the rest of the
dialogue. Some comments may be offered on the various stages
of the demonstration. The theme has already been propounded
in the demand of Glaucon that it shall be made clear how " justice "
and " injustice " respectively affect the inner life of their possessor,
independently of any sanctions, human or divine. It is to the
answer to this question that Socrates is really addressing himself
in the picture of an ideally good man living in an ideal relation to
society, which culminates in the description, given in Books VI.–VII.,
of the philosopher-king, his functions in society, and the discipline
by which he is fitted for their discharge, as well as by the briefer
studies, in Books VIII. and IX., of increasing degeneration from
the true type of manhood. The answer to Adimantus, so far as his
indictment of education is concerned, has to be found in the account
of the training of the young into worthy moral character by a right
appeal, through literature and art, to the imagination (Books III.–IV.);
his attack on immoral religion may be said to be the direct occasioin
both of the regulation of early " nursery tales " with which Socrates
opens his scheme of reform in Book II., and of the magnificent
myth of judgment with which the dialogue closes, itself a specimen
of the way in which the religious imagination may be made the most
potent reinforcement of a noble rule of life. In dealing with the
details of the positive contributions of the dialogue to both politics
and religion, it is necessary to observe some caution, if we are to

avoid specious misunderstandings. We must remember all through that the political problem of the right organization of a state is avowedly introduced not on its own account, but because we see human virtue and vice " writ large " in the conduct of a state or a political party, and may thus detect in the community the real moral significance of much that would escape our notice if we only studied humanity in the individual.[1] Hence we shall probably be misunderstanding if we imagine, as has sometimes been imagined, that either Socrates or Plato is seriously proposing a detailed new constitution for Athens, and still more if we imagine that either would have approved of the introduction of the new constitution by revolution into a society wholly unprepared to receive it. The most we are entitled to say about any of the detailed proposals of the *Republic* is that Plato presents them as what, according to Socrates, is most in accord with the moral nature of man, and may therefore be expected to be approximately realized in a thoroughly sound condition of society.

(1) In the impressive picture given in Books II.–IV. of the working of the principle of specialization of function according to vocation, which will ultimately turn out to be the foundation of all " justice," there are one or two points which have perhaps not received sufficient attention, and may therefore be briefly noted.

I think it is clear that we must not take the description of the three successive stages through which Socrates' community passes as meant to convey any speculation about the beginnings of civilization. The " first city " is already on the right side of the line which separates civilization from barbarism. Its inhabitants are already agriculturists, permanently cultivating a fixed territory ; they are at home in the working of metals, and in some respects they exhibit an advance in economic organization on the Athens of the Periclean age. (Thus they have their clothes made by a distinct class of artisans, not woven in the house by the women of the family, as was still largely the custom at Athens.) The notion that we are reading a satire on Antisthenes and the " return to nature " is merely ludicrous. What is really described is, in the main, the condition of a normal πόλις where the citizens are farming-folk. To me it seems clear that, so far as Plato has any particular historical development before his mind, he is thinking of what Athens itself had been before the period of victory and expansion which made her an imperial city and the centre of a world-wide sea-borne commerce. (This is suggested almost irresistibly by the assumption that even the " first city," like Athens, requires to import a good many of its necessaries from elsewhere,

---

[1] For example, punctuality is what is commonly considered a " minor social virtue." A man is not thought much the worse of, if he is always late at an appointment. But when we see how the issue of a campaign or even of a war may be affected, if expected reinforcements arrive just a little too late, we are reminded that it is a dangerous thing to call any virtue a " minor " one. The contemplation of the " large letters " teaches us not to despise " minute particulars."

and consequently contains merchants and sailors, and is already producing for the foreign market.)   In the description of the steps by which this little society expands and becomes a city with a multitude of artificial wants, and trades which minister to them, thus acquiring a " superfluous population " which must somehow be provided for, we can hardly see anything but a conscious reflection of the actual expansion of Attica under Cimon and Pericles.

(2) We must, of course, note that not all the artificial wants which arise in the city as it becomes " luxurious " are meant to be condemned.   Even the demand for delicacies for the table is an indication that the standard of living is rising, and all social students know that a rise in this standard is by no means an entirely unwholesome thing.   It is more significant that one of the chief features of the development is the growth of professions like those of the actor and the *impresario*.   People are beginning to feel the need of amusement, and this means, of course, that they are becoming conscious that they have minds, which need to be fed no less than their bodies.   Presumably the reason why Socrates could not look for " justice " in the community of farmers, but has to wait for the " luxurious city " to come into existence and be reformed, is precisely that the members of the first society would hardly be alive to the fact that they have souls at all ; they could not feel the need for a daily supply of any bread but that which perishes ; they have no " social problem."

(3) It has been asked why, when over-population leads to an acute social problem, aggressive warfare rather than colonization should be assumed as the only way out of the difficulty.   The answer, of course, is simple.   In the first place, peaceful colonization of derelict territories had never been a feasible procedure for a Greek city.   The founders of the ancient and famous cities we call the " Greek colonies " had regularly had to wrest their sites from previous occupants not much inferior to themselves in " culture."   There was no America or Australia in the Mediterranean basin.   And in the second, Socrates knows his countrymen and is well aware that a Greek " surplus population " would not be likely to transport itself across the seas in quest of a new home so long as there was a fair chance of a successful inroad on its neighbours.   He is, as he says, not discussing the morality of the proceeding ;   he is merely noting that it is what the city would, in fact, do.   (In *theory*, to be sure, it was a commonplace that an aggressive war of expansion is not a *iustum bellum*.)   And the point he wishes to insist on is the perfectly sound one, that the experience of having to make common sacrifices and face common dangers in war, just or unjust (but when did any nation throw its soul into the prosecution of a war which it seriously believed to be unjust ?), does more to generate self-devotion in citizens than any other.   War gives the social reformer his chance, for the double reason that it produces the temper which is willing to live hard, make sacrifices, and submit to discipline, and, when it is hard contested and

the issue doubtful, it makes the necessity for sacrifice and submission pressing and patent. We who have lived through the events of 1914–1918 should be able to understand this from our own experience.

(4) It is unhappily customary to make two bad mistakes about the nature of the reconstituted social structure which, in Socrates' narrative, emerges from the experience provided by a great war. It is called a " system of caste," and the matter is then made worse by calling the δημιουργοί who form the third of Socrates' social classes, " the working class," or " the industrial class." The immediate consequence is that the social and political theory of the *Republic* suffers a complete travesty, due to the unconscious influence of ideas derived from our experience of modern " industrialism." To guard against misconceptions of this kind, we must, in the first place, be clear on the point that there is no system of " caste " in the *Republic*. The characteristic of " caste " is that one is born into it, and that once born into a caste it is impossible to rise above it. You may forfeit your caste in various ways, as a Brahmin does by crossing the seas, but no one can become a Brahmin if he is not born one. Now Socrates believes, rightly or wrongly, that heredity is a powerful force in the intellectual and moral sphere ; as a general rule, a man will find his natural place in the " class " to which his parents belong (all the more, no doubt, as procreation is to be placed under careful " eugenic " regulations). But the rule has its notable exceptions : there are those who prove quite unfitted for the work of the class into which they are born, and those who show themselves qualified to take their place in a higher class. Hence it is part of Socrates' idea that the early life of the individual shall be under close and constant surveillance, and subjected to repeated tests of character and intelligence. There is to be every opportunity for the discovery and degradation of the unworthy and the promotion of the worthy; no one is to be ensured by the accident of birth in a particular social status, and no one is to be excluded by it from rising to the highest eminence. This qualification of the principle of heredity by the antithetic principle of the " open career " for ability and character is absolutely destructive of " caste." The philosopher-kings or the soldiers of the Socratic state are no more a " caste " than Napoleon's marshals. And, in the second place, the δημιουργοί do not correspond to what we call the " artisan " or " working " class, *i.e.* to wage-earners or persons who maintain themselves by selling their labour. They include our wage-earners, but they also include the great bulk of what we should call the civilian population, independently of economic status. The thought underlying the distinction of the three classes has primarily nothing to do with economic status. It is simply that in any full-grown society, you may distinguish three types of social service. There is a small section which serves the community directly by directing its public life, making rules and regulations and controlling policy. These are the " complete " or " full-grown " guardians. There is necessarily

an executive arm, whose business it is to support the directive action of the first class by the necessary physical force against enemies from without and malcontents and offenders from within, the army and police. It is this body which Socrates calls by the name· ἐπίκουροι, and it should be noted that he selects the word not merely for the appropriateness of its literal sense ("helpers," "auxiliaries"), but because it was, as we can see e.g. from Herodotus, the technical name for the trained professional body-guard of monarchs, and therefore indicates the important point that the "executive" of the Socratic State is a carefully trained professional fighting force, not an amateur constabulary or militia. The associations of the word are the same as those of such an English expression as "the Guards," and Socrates does not scruple to apply to his ἐπίκουροι the opprobrious name by which such permanent professional soldiers were called in Greek democracies, which objected on principle to their existence. They are, like the Ionian and Carian soldiers of an Amasis, μισθωτοί ("mercenaries"),[1] except for two considerations—that they are citizens, not aliens, and that the only μισθός they get is their "keep." These two classes are distinguished by the fact that they are the only direct "servants of the public." What remains is the whole bulk of the "civilian population," with the exception of the "guardians"— every one who does not directly serve the public either as a states-man or as a soldier or policeman. Thus the δημιουργοί include not only all the so-called "working class," but the whole body of professional men, and the whole class of employers of labour. Since the two superior classes are expressly forbidden to have any kind of property, personally or as classes, it follows that the whole "capital" of the State is in the hands of the δημιουργοί. A "merchant prince," under such a classification, is just as much one of the "industrials" as his clerks and office-boys. Much purely perverse criticism of the scheme would have been obviated if this simple consideration had been duly kept in mind.

(5) An immediate consequence is that, in spite of all that has been said about the "socialism" or "communism" of the Republic, there is really neither socialism nor communism to be found in the work. The current confusions on the point are probably due mainly to the mistaken notion that the emphatic demand of Book IV.[2] for the banishment of "wealth" and "penury" from society must be the proposal of a communist, or at least of a socialist. This assumption is, on the face of it, absurd. The point made in Book IV. is simply that a man's character and work in life will be spoiled equally by the possession of irresponsible wealth, with no adequate social duties attached to it, and by a penury which breaks his spirit and forces him to do bad and scamped work in order to keep himself alive. A man may be aware of these dangers without adopting either the socialist or the communist theory of the right economic organization of society. In point of fact,

[1] Rep. iv. 419a–420a.　　　　[2] Rep. iv. 421d ff.

nothing much is said in the book about the economic organization of the only class who have any economic function at all, the δημιουργοί, but the implication of what is said is that there are differences of wealth among them, and that the " means of production and distribution " are individually owned and operated. In Book VIII. it is carefully indicated that one of the first signs of the degeneration of the ideal State into a " timocracy " is the acquisition of real and personal property by the two superior classes (they " appropriate lands and houses," (viii. 547b)), but nothing is said of the first introduction of private property among the δημιουργοί, who thus must be presumed to have enjoyed it all along. There are other more general considerations which point to the same conclusion. For one thing, both pure communism and " State monopoly " of the means of production are so alien to the system of a Greek πόλις— the " State ownership" of the silver mines at Laurium was an exception at Athens—that Socrates could not be presumed to be contemplating either, unless he expressly explained himself. For another, it is clear that agriculture is the assumed economic foundation of the life of his city, and agriculture is just the pursuit to which a " socialistic " economic system is least easy of application. Collectivism is historically an ideal of the " proletariat " of great towns ; the farmer has always been tenacious of the very different ideal of peasant ownership. And it is noticeable that in the *Laws* Plato declares himself for peasant ownership in its extreme form. The citizens there not merely own their " holdings " but own them as their inalienable patrimonies, and " common cultivation " is expressly forbidden (v. 740a–b). We may fairly take it that if he had intended to represent his master as advocating views of a radically different type, he would have made the point unmistakable. Hence, it seems to me that we must recognize that the economic organization of the ideal city of the *Republic* is definitely " individualistic." Yet we must not suppose that Plato is in any sense putting Socrates forward as a conscious " anti-socialist." The real object of the one restriction of ownership on which the dialogue insists as fundamental, the prohibition of all property to the direct servants of the State, is not economic. The purpose is the same as that of the still more emphatic prohibition of family life, the elimination of the conflict between public duty and personal interest. What Socrates wants, as Bosanquet has said, is simply to divorce political power from financial influence. Wealth is to have no political influence in his society ; it is " plutocracy," not individual ownership, which he is determined to suppress. His rulers are much more in the position of a mediaeval military monastic order than in that of a collectivist bureaucracy.

(6) It may not be unnecessary to remark that, as there is no socialism, there is also no " community of women " in the *Republic*. If the reader will take the trouble to work out the consequences of the regulations prescribed for the mating of the guardians, he will find that the impulses of sex and the family affections connected with

them are subjected to much severer restraint than any which has ever been adopted by a Christian society. It is plain that the governing classes, to whom the regulations are meant to apply, are expected to find no gratification for the sexual impulses except on the solemn occasions when they are called on to beget offspring for the State. The extension of the duties of the " guardian " to both sexes of itself carries the consequence that these occasions arise only at long intervals ; and the self-denial implied in the acceptance of such a rule of life might prove to be even severer than that imposed on the monk by his vow of chastity, for the very reason that the inhibition has to be broken through at the time when the State so commands. Indeed, the overwhelming probability is that if any society should attempt to enforce on any part of itself regulations of the kind proposed in the *Republic*, the attempt would fail just because of their intolerable severity. No actual ruling class would be likely to consent to the absolute elimination of the affections of the family circle from its own life, even if it were prepared to reduce the gratification of the physical impulses of sex to the contemplated minimum. The true criticism on the whole treatment of sex in the *Republic* is that, like all non-Christian moralists, rigourist or relaxed, Socrates very much *under*estimates the significance of sex for the whole of the spiritual life. Whatever we may think on this point, it is important to remember that at any rate the general principles which underlie the treatment of the position of women in *Republic* v. are no personal " development " of Plato's ; they belong to the actual Socrates. Aeschines, in the remains of his *Aspasia*, agrees with Plato in representing the philosopher as insisting that " the goodness of a woman is the same as that of a man," and illustrating the thesis by the political abilities of Aspasia and the military achievements of the Persian " Amazon " Rhodogyne.[1] Hence the thought that the duties of statesmanship and warfare should be extended to women must be regarded as strictly Socratic, and the rest of the proposals of *Republic* v. are no more than necessary consequences of this position. If they are to be rejected, we must refute the assumption on which they are based, that the distinction of sex is one which only affects the individual in respect to the part to be played in contributing to procreation and the rearing of a new generation ; we must be prepared to hold that the difference goes deeper and modifies the whole spiritual life profoundly.

(7) There are one or two remarks which may be made about the plan of moral and religious training laid down in Books II. and III., as supplementary to the many excellent studies of this part of the dialogue already in existence. We note that in the proposed purification of the stories by which religious impressions are to be communicated to the very young, it is not merely, nor even mainly, the Homeric mythology to which exception is taken. The crowning offenders are Hesiod and the other theogonists who have related

[1] See the fragments of the *Aspasia* collated in H. Dittmar's *Aeschines von Sphettos*, 275-283.

stories of the violent subversion of older dynasties of gods by younger. This would, of course, include the Orphicists ; Socrates has not forgotten that it was they against whom the denunciation of Adimantus had been more specially directed. It is even more instructive to observe that the attack on tragedy as propagating false religious conceptions is directly aimed at Aeschylus, who has often been mistaken in modern times for an exponent of the religion of simple-minded Athenians. This means two things. It means that to the Periclean age, even as late as the time of the peace of Nicias, Aeschylus was still the great representative of tragedy, in spite of the popularity and renown of Sophocles, who was clearly thought of, as he is thought of in Aristophanes' *Frogs*, as a follower, though a worthy follower, of the great originator of tragedy. If Sophocles had in his own day already been recognized as " the mellow glory of the Attic stage," it would be a mystery why nothing is said of the very unsatisfactory part played by the gods in such a work as the *King Oedipus*. It also means that Socrates is alive to the fact that Aeschylus is no old-fashioned, simple-minded worshipper of Apollo of Delphi, or the Olympians generally. In fact, a " blasphemy " against Apollo is precisely one of the counts brought against him. If it is " atheism " to represent the Olympians as practising a questionable morality, Aeschylus, in spite of Dr. Verrall, is just as much an " atheist " as Euripides, and Socrates rightly makes the point.[1]

(8) Most of the specific criticisms contained in the discussion of the educational employment of poetry and music are, naturally enough, negative. Socrates clearly holds quite strongly that the tendency of the art of his own time is to a love of a relaxed and formless complexity and variety for its own sake, and he thinks it necessary, in the interests of character, as well as of taste, to revert to austerer and more " classical " standards. It is important to remember that these strictures are put into the mouth of Socrates, speaking not later than the peace of Nicias.

We must not, then, suppose that they are aimed at *epigoni* of a later generation. It is not the floridity of Timotheus or Agathon which is the object of attack, but the art of the Periclean age. We are only throwing dust in our own eyes if we suppose that Socrates wants merely to repress the cheap music-hall and the garish melodrama, or the equivalents of freak movements like *Dada*. He is seriously proposing to censure just what we consider the imperishable contributions of Athens to the art and literature of the world, because he holds that they have tendencies which are

---

[1] It would be singularly unlikely that Aeschylus, who had fought at Marathon, should feel any particular devotion to a god who had " medized " all through the Persian wars. That he felt none is surely proved by the part Apollo is made to play all through the Orestean trilogy. The so-called *naïveté* of Aeschylus, like that of Herodotus, is a product of consummate art. In one important passage where the poet really is expressing personal religious conviction he is at pains to tell us that " popular orthodoxy " is against him (*Agam.* 757, δίχα δ᾽ ἄλλων μονόφρων εἰμί).

unfavourable to the highest development of moral personality. The magnitude of the sacrifice is the true measure of the value he ascribes to the end for which he purposes to make it. We shall not appreciate his position unless we understand quite clearly that he is in downright earnest with the consideration that the connexion between aesthetic taste and morality is so close that whatever tends to ennoble our aesthetic taste directly tends to elevate our character, and whatever tends to foster a " taste " for the debased in art tends equally to deprave a man's whole moral being. Whether we share this conviction or not, the recognition that Socrates holds it with as little qualification as Ruskin is the key to the understanding of the whole discussion of early education. We are allowed also to see incidentally that the suggested reforms in " musical " education are not meant to be limited to the censure of what is debased. It is meant that the young " guardian " is to be subjected from the first to the positive influences of lofty art of every description. (Painting, embroidery, architecture, and certain " minor arts "—one naturally thinks of the characteristic Athenian art of pottery as an example—are expressly specified, *Republic* iii. 401*a* ff.) The growing boy or girl is to live in an environment of beauty, and the appreciation of the beauty of the environment is expected to lead insensibly to appreciation of whatever is morally lovely and of good report in conduct and character. To Socrates' mind the moral employment of such epithets as " fair," " foul," " graceful," " graceless," is no mere metaphor, but a genuine analogy based on the fact that all sensible beauty is itself the expression and shadow of an inward beauty of character.[1]

(9) Since the whole of the early education contemplated in the *Republic* is based on an appeal to taste and imagination, it follows that, as Socrates is careful to insist, the " goodness " it produces, though it will be quite sufficient for every class except the statesmen, is not the true and philosophic goodness of which the *Phaedo* speaks. As we are carefully reminded, the self-devotion of even the fighting force of the reformed city is founded on " opinion," not on knowledge ; their virtue is absolute loyalty to a sound tradition which they have imbibed from their " social environment," not loyalty to the claims of a *summum bonum* grasped by personal insight. Thus the virtue described and analysed in Book IV. is still " popular virtue " ; its superiority over the goodness of the average Athenian, the respectability we have heard Protagoras preaching, is due simply to the superiority of the " social tradition " of the Socratic city over that of Periclean democracy. There is thus a double reason

---

[1] Besides painting, embroidery, and architecture, the *Republic* (*l.c.*) mentions weaving, the manufacture of all " vessels " or " furniture " (σκευῶν), and appears to allude to gardening. There would be plenty of room in Socrates' city for the arts of design, if there is not much left for the poet and dramatist. It is an interesting question whether Socrates may not be right in what is his evident conviction that the greatest art does require a certain austerity and severe restriction in the matter of its vehicles of expression. I suggest the question without wishing to answer it.

why we are bound to regard the picture of philosophers and their
philosophic virtue drawn in the central books as an essential part of
the argument, and to reject any speculations which treat this part
of the *Republic* as an afterthought. The account of that supreme
goodness which is indistinguishable from knowledge is absolutely
necessary in any presentation of Socratic ethics. And again, since
the statesmen of the *Republic* have to control and conserve the
national traditions, they must have a goodness which is not simply
the product of those conditions themselves. There would be no
point in subjecting the good soldier to the control of a higher
authority if the loyalty to established tradition which is the
soldier's point of honour were the highest moral principle attainable.
In a *Republic* without the central books, Sparta would have to
figure not as an example of the second-best, but as the ideal community itself, whereas the whole point of the description of the
" timocracy " in Book VIII. is that a State like Sparta, where the
qualities of the mere soldier and sportsman are regarded as a moral
ideal, has taken the first fatal step towards complete moral anarchy
and, in the ordinary course of things, must be expected to take those
which follow in due succession.

Recognition that the whole account of the virtues given in *Republic* iv. is thus provisional should save us from attaching too much
importance to the famous doctrine of the " three parts " of the soul.
We must be careful to understand that this doctrine does not profess
to be original nor to be a piece of scientific psychology. We have
already found it presupposed as something known in educated
circles in the *Gorgias* and *Phaedo*, and have seen reason to think
that it is Pythagorean in origin, as Posidonius is known to have
maintained,[1] and directly connected with the theory of the " three
lives." This means that we are to take it primarily as a working
account of " active principles," or " springs of action," which sufficiently describes the leading types of " goodness," as goodness can
be exhibited in any form short of the highest. The scheme will
thus be excellently applicable to the goodness of the ἐπίκουροι,
for their life is still a form, though the worthiest form, of the
φιλότιμος βίος. Loyalty to " honour," " chivalry," " ambition "
(though a wholly unselfish ambition), is the utmost we demand of
them ; the life of duty remains for the best of them a struggle
between a " higher " and a " lower," though a struggle in which
the " higher " regularly wins, and this justifies our recognition of a
plurality of " parts of the soul " in them. It will be characteristic
of their experience that there should be conflicts of " desire " with
the tradition of loyalty, and that chivalrous sentiment should be
required to act as the reinforcement of loyalty to tradition in the
conflict. But the familiar Socratic doctrine is that the " philosopher " who has directly gazed for himself on that supreme good
of which the *Symposium* has told us, necessarily desires the good
he has beheld ; to him " disobedience to the heavenly vision "

[1] Burnet, *Early Greek Philosophy*[3], 296 n. 2.

would be impossible, exactly as in Christian theology sinful volition is held to be impossible to the saints who actually enjoy the beatific vision of God. Hence it must follow that, as a description of the moral life of the philosopher, the doctrine of the distinct " parts " of the soul becomes increasingly impossible as he makes progress towards the goal at which his activity is consciously directed. This is why the last word of Socrates on the doctrine is to remind us that it may be necessary to revise it when we have grasped the truth of the " divinity " of the soul (*Rep*. x. 611*b* ff.), and why we are told, when it is first introduced, that we must not expect to arrive at exact and certain truth by the line of inquiry we are now pursuing (iv. 435*d*).[1] I do not think it needful to say more about the doctrine here, than to utter a word of warning against two possible misunderstandings. We must avoid every temptation to find a parallel between the " parts " or " figures " in the soul and the modern doctrine of the " three aspects " of a complete " mental process " (cognition, conation, feeling). Plato is not talking about " aspects " of this kind, but about rival springs of action, and the doctrine, as presented in the *Republic*, has no reference to anything but action and " *active* principles," or " determining motives." Also we must not make the blunder of trying to identify the θυμοειδές with " will." From the Socratic point of view, *will* cannot be distinguished from the *judgment* " this is good," and this judgment is always, of course, a deliverance of the λογιστικόν. But the λογιστικόν may pronounce a true judgment, or it may be led into a false one under the influence of present appetite or of anger or ambition, or again, it may only be saved from false judgment because the " sense of honour " comes into collision with the promptings of appetite. To look in the scheme of the *Republic* for some *facultas electiva*, intervening between the formation of a judgment of " practical thinking " and the ensuing action, would be to misunderstand its whole character.

(10) We see then why there can never have been a " first *Republic*," including the " guardians " and the scheme for their early education, but without the philosopher-king and his training in hard scientific thinking. The philosopher-king is doubly demanded as the only adequate embodiment of the Socratic conception of goodness, and also as the authority whose personal insight into good creates the public tradition by which the rest of society is to live. To do full justice to the conception we must not forget that Socrates' statesmen are expected to combine two

---

[1] The suggestion is that in the man who achieves his eternal salvation, the elements of " mettle " and " concupiscence " are, so to say, transubstantiated, swallowed up in intellect. (Of course this " intellect " would not be a " cold, neutral " apprehension of truth, but an intellect on fire with intellectual " passion," a white-hot intelligence.) The same suggestion is made more openly in the *Timaeus* (69*c* ff.). Since we cannot suppose the Pythagorean Timaeus to have learned about the " tripartite soul " for the first time from the conversation of Socrates two days before, the fact that he makes a point of the doctrine indicates that Plato regards it as Pythagorean.

characters which are not often united. They are to be original scientific thinkers of the first order, but equally, they are to be " saints." In the account of the character which will be demanded of them and the natural endowments it presupposes, we hear, indeed, of the qualifications we also should demand of a scientific genius—intellectual quickness, retentive memory and the like—but we hear as much, if not more, of what we should regard as moral qualifications for sainthood, which may be wanting to a man without impairing his eminence in science. How serious Socrates is with this side of the matter is shown by the fact that his philosophers are to be selected exclusively from the best specimens of young people who have come out pre-eminently successful from the hard discipline by which the fighting-force is made. The " auxiliary " himself, as described in the earlier books, is expected to have all the moral elevation of Wordsworth's " Happy Warrior," and the " Happy Warrior " is, in turn, only the raw material out of which years of hard intellectual labour will make the philosophic states- man. If we lose sight of either half of this ideal we shall form a sadly defective notion of what the *Republic* means by a " philo- sopher." By thinking only of the sainthood, we might come to imagine that the philosopher is a kind of Yogi, bent on a selfish absorption into the divine calm of the Absolute ; it would then be a mystery why he is to be trained for his vocation by years of severe mathematical study, and again why, when he has at last descried the vision of the good, he should at once be made to devote all his powers, throughout the prime of his life, to the work of government. If we think only of the science, and say merely that what is aimed at is that the highest intellectual attainments shall be employed in the business of governing the world, we shall be forgetting that many of the most eminent men of science would have been dis- qualified for the supreme position in Socrates' city by defects of character. From the point of view of intellectual eminence we could think, perhaps, of no names so illustrious as those of Galileo and Newton. But it may be taken as certain that both would, by the Socratic standard, be relegated to the class of δημιουργοί. The moral cheapness of the one man's character, the vein of small egotism in the other's, would debar them from being so much as ἐπίκουροι. What we need to understand clearly is that Socrates holds firmly to two positions at once—the position that only a moral hero or saint is fit to be a supreme ruler of men, and the further position that discipline in sheer hard thinking, which can only be won by personal service of science, is the immediate and indis- pensable path to the direct vision of good which makes the saint or hero. We are clearly here on Pythagorean ground. The under- lying thought is just that which seems to have been distinctive of Pythagoras, the thought that " salvation " or " purification " of the soul is to be achieved by science (μαθήματα), not by a ritual of ceremonial holiness ; the philosopher-kings embody the same ideal which had inspired the Pythagorean communities when they set to work to capture the government of the cities of *Magna Graecia*. There is no reason to doubt that the actual Socrates, whose standing complaint against Athenian democracy in the dialogues is that it has no respect, in matters of right and wrong, for the authority of the "man who knows," shared these ideas. They are avowed by Plato himself in his correspondence, where they figure as the true explanation of his apparently Quixotic attempt to make Dionysius II into a possible constitutional monarch by an education in mathematics. No doubt Plato and his friends were expecting from science something more than it has to give, but, as Professor Burnet has said, their proceedings are unintelligible unless we understand that the expectation was passionately sincere.

How preoccupation with science was expected to ennoble character (provided that only the right type of person is allowed to meddle with it), we see most readily by comparing the courage pronounced in Book IV. to be all that is wanted of the ἐπίκουροι with the still higher type of courage declared in Book VI. to be part of the character of the philosopher. The "courage" demanded of the good soldier, in whose make-up θυμός plays the leading part, was defined as steadfast loyalty in the face of perils and seductions to the right *opinions* inculcated in him by education. Its foundation is thus allegiance to a code of honour held with such passion that no fear of pain or death and no bait that can be offered to cupidity is able to overcome it. Clearly a courage like this will carry a man "over the top," make him volunteer for a desperate enterprise, or win him a V.C. But there are situations in life which make a demand for a still higher degree of fortitude. It is matter of experience that a V.C. may not be equal to the task of duty imposed, for example, on a priest whose business it is to tend daily the last hours of the victims of some foul pestilence in a plague-smitten city. Or again a brave soldier, who will face deadly peril when his "blood is up" and the eyes of his comrades and his commander are on him, may not have the nerve of the scientific man who will quietly inoculate himself with some loathsome disorder to study its symptoms, or try the effects of some new and powerful anæsthetic upon himself, in order to decide on its possible utility in medicine. This is the sort of courage of which Socrates speaks as only possible to a man who "knows" the relative insignificance of the duration of any individual personal life from his habitual "contemplation of all time and all existence." We should, probably, prefer, both in the case of the priest and in the case of the man of science, to speak of "faith," but the point is that, in both cases, the agent is inspired by an absolutely assured personal conviction about the universal order and his own place in it. Without this absolute assurance of conviction, one is never wholly free from liability to illusion about one's own personal importance, and so never quite a free man. Because Socrates holds that the sciences form a ladder which leads up in the end to the vision of the

" Good " as the clue to the whole scheme of existence, he looks to science, as its supreme service, to make us thus at last completely free men. From this point of view, clearly in the soul of the man who " knows," the " parts " (μόρια) or " figures " (εἴδη) which have been distinguishable at a lower level of moral development will be finally fused. His life will have only one spring of action or active principle, his vision of the supreme good itself. The forms of virtue, at its highest level, will therefore lose their distinction. It might be possible for the average good civilian, or even for the good soldier of the State, to be characterized by one form of good-ness more than by another. This is what is meant by the assign-ment of different virtues as characteristic to different sections of the community. It is not meant that so long as the shop-keeper or the farmer is " temperate," it does not matter whether he is a coward. He could not be a good man at all, if he were that, and a society in which no one had any courage except the members of the army and police would be morally in a bad way. But fighting is not the civilian's trade. He will be none the less a valuable member of society as a shop-keeper or a farmer because he has not been trained to show all the pluck and presence of mind which would win a D.S.O. or a V.C., though the State would succumb in the hour of peril if its fighting-arm had no more martial courage than the average civilian. But if a man is inspired in all the acts of his life by the vision of the supreme good, he will be equal to all the emergencies of life alike ; in having one virtue, he will neces-sarily have all. Substitute for " the good " God, and the principle of the unity of the virtues takes on the familiar form *Ama et fac quod vis.*

(11) The conception of science as the road to vision of the good leads us at once to consideration of the central metaphysical doctrine of the *Republic*, the doctrine of the " Form of Good " (ἰδέα τἀγαθοῦ). As is usual when the forms are mentioned in a Platonic dialogue, their reality is neither explained nor proved. It is taken for granted that the company in the house of Polemarchus, or at least Glaucon and Adimantus who conduct the discussion with Socrates, know quite well what the theory means and will not dispute its truth. It is assumed also as known to every one that the mathematical sciences are concerned with forms ; forms are the objects which we get to know from mathematics, though the mathematician leads us up to acquaintance with them by starting from the sensible " figures " which he employs as helps to our imagination. So far, we are told nothing we have not learned from the *Phaedo*. But there are two points of the first importance on which the *Republic* adds to that dialogue. (*a*) We now hear of a certain supreme " form," the " Good " or " Form of Good," which is the supreme object of the philosopher's study. We learn that, over and beyond the recognized mathematical studies, there is a still more ultimate discipline, " dialectic," and that it is the function of " dialectic " to lead directly to this vision of the " good." Further, we are told

that this " good " is something Socrates cannot describe ; it is not
" reality or being," but " on the other side " of both, though it is
the source of all the reality (ἀλήθεια) and being (οὐσία) of everything. (b) The procedure of the mathematical sciences is criticized
and contrasted with that of " dialectic," with a view to explaining
just why the ideal of science is realized in dialectic and in dialectic
alone. Both points call for some special consideration.

(a) THE *FORMS* (ἰδέαι) IN THE *REPUBLIC*.—From the *Phaedo*,
among other dialogues, we gather that there is a form corresponding
to each " universal " predicate which can be significantly affirmed
of a variety of logical subjects. The same thing is explicitly said
in the *Republic* (vi. 507b, x. 596a) ; in the latter place the " form
of bed (κλίνη) or table " (τράπεζα) is given as an example. (This
seems at variance with the well-known statement of Aristotle
that " we "—*i.e.* the Platonists—deny that there are " forms " of
artificial things,[1] but we must remember that Aristotle is speaking
of the doctrine as elaborated in the Academy, not of the position
ascribed to Socrates in the dialogues.) But in the *Republic* we
learn that there is a " Form of Good " which is to the objects of
knowledge and to knowing itself what the sun is to visible objects
and to sight. This is then further explained by saying that the
sun both makes the colours we see and supplies the eye with the
source of all its seeing. In the same way, the " good " supplies
the objects of scientific knowledge with their being (οὐσία) and
renders them knowable. And as the sun is neither the colours
we see nor the eye which sees them, so the " good " is something
even more exalted than " being." [2] Later on, we find that the
sciences form a hierarchy which has its culmination in the actual
apprehension of this transcendent " good." [3] Now, since it is
assumed in the *Republic* that scientific knowledge is knowledge of
forms, the objects which are thus said to derive their being from
" the good " must clearly mean the whole body of the forms.
The " good " thus holds a pre-eminence among forms, and strictly
speaking, it might be doubtful whether we ought to call it a " form "
any more than we can call the sun a colour. At least, all the other
forms must be manifestations or expressions of it. In the *Phaedo*
nothing was said which would warrant this treatment of the forms
as a hierarchy or ordered series with a first member of such a unique

[1] *Metaphysics*, A. 991b 6, M. 1080a 6.
[2] *Rep.* vi. 508b–509b. For the full understanding of the analogy with the
sun it is necessary to understand the theory of colour-vision implied, which is
fully expounded in the *Timaeus*. A colour is itself a kind of " flame "
(*Timaeus*, 67c ff.), and the immediate organ of the sight by which it is apprehended is also itself a fire, like that of the sun, which is contained in the eye
and issues forth from it in the act of vision (*ibid.* 45b ff.). Thus the sun, as the
source of light, actually is also the source both of colour and of colour-vision.
The well-known Neoplatonist formula that νοῦς and τὰ νοητά taken together
as inseparable proceed immediately from the supreme reality " the One " is
a perfectly correct transcript of the doctrine of the *Republic* into the terminology of technical metaphysics.
[3] *Rep.* vii. 532a.

character ; they appeared rather to be a vast plurality of which all the members stand on the same footing. Hence it is intelligible that the view should have been taken that the " good " of the *Republic* represents a Platonic development going far beyond anything we can attribute to Socrates himself. I think, however, that we must be careful not to exaggerate on this point. There can, at least, be no doubt that the " form of good " is identical with the supreme Beauty, the vision of which is represented in the *Symposium* as the goal of the pilgrimage of the philosophic lover. Hence, though it is true that the name " form of good " occurs nowhere but in the central section of the *Republic*, it would not be true to say that the object named does not appear in the *Symposium* with much the same character. Again, though the *Phaedo* does not name the " form of good," the phrase εἶδος τἀγαθοῦ is verbally no more than a periphrase for τὸ ἀγαθόν (" the good "), just as similar periphrases occur constantly with the words φύσις, δύναμις, in Plato.[1] And it is in the *Phaedo* itself that we are told of Socrates' conviction that the ἀγαθὸν καὶ δέον (the " good and the ought ") is the principle which " holds everything together," and thus the cause of all order in the universe.[2] The statements of the *Republic* merely make the implications of this passage of the *Phaedo* a little more explicit. If the good is the universal cause, it obviously must have just the character the *Republic* ascribes to it. Hence Professor Burnet seems to be right in holding that what is said of the " form of good " is strictly within the limits of Socratism, and that this explains the point of contact between Socrates and an Eleatic like Euclides of Megara.[3] That Socrates finds himself unable to speak of this form of good except negatively, and that he can only characterize it positively by an imperfect analogy, is inevitable from the nature of the case. The same thing may be seen in any philosophy which does not simply deny or ignore the " Absolute " or supreme source of all reality. Because this source is *ex hypothesi* a *source* of all reality, you are bound to insist that it transcends, and is thus " wholly other " than, every particular real thing ; every predicate you affirm of it belongs properly to some of its effects in contradistinction from others and can therefore only be asserted of the supreme source " analogically " and with the warning that the analogy is imperfect and would mislead if pressed unduly. At the same time, because it is the source of all *reality*, every predicate which expresses a " positive perfection " must, in its degree, characterize the source of all " perfections " and must be ascribed to it " analogically." All we gain by knowledge of the " detail " of the universe must add to and enrich our conception

---

[1] To take the first examples which come to hand : *Phaedo*, 98a 2, αἰτίας ἄλλο εἶδος=another cause ; *Phaedrus*, 246d 6, ἡ πτεροῦ δύναμις=" a wing " ; *Timaeus*, 70d 8, τὴν τοῦ σώματος φύσιν=the body.

[2] The physicists are accused (*Phaed.* 99c 5) of falsely thinking that τὸ ἀγαθὸν καὶ δέον συνδεῖ καὶ συνέχει οὐδέν. As one might say, " they forget that obligation is the ligature " which connects all things.

[3] *Greek Philosophy, Part I.,* 168-170.

of the source of reality, and yet we can never " comprehend " or completely " rationalize " that source. It remains, when all is said, an unexhausted and surprising " mystery." Hence the necessity Christian theology has always felt itself under of incorporating the profound agnosticism of the " negative way," or " way of remotion," in itself and the grotesque aberrations into which it has always fallen in the hands of second-rate theologians who have attempted to know God as one may know the " general conic." Hence also the tension between the affirmative and the negative moments in a metaphysic like that of Mr. Bradley. Hence equally the inevitable failure of " positive science " to complete its task of explaining everything. To explain everything would mean to get completely rid of all elements of " bare fact," to deduce the whole detail of existence from a body of " laws," perhaps from a single " law," in themselves (or itself) " evident to the intellect," as Descartes tried to deduce physics from geometry, because geometry appeared to him to involve no postulates which are not immediately " evident " as true. In fact, we only " rationalize " nature, in the sense of eliminating " bare fact " for which no explanation is forthcoming, at one point by reintroducing it somewhere else, as M. Meyerson has insisted in his series of illuminating works on the philosophy of the sciences. And it is just because science is under this restriction that its interest is perennial ; if we could ever expect to " complete " it, we should have to anticipate a time when it would no longer interest us. Science is eternally progressive just because it is always tentative.[1]

The language used in the *Republic* of the " Form of Good," as the last paragraph has suggested, at once raises the question whether or not this form can be identified with God, of whom language of the same kind is used by Christian theologians and philosophers. We cannot answer this important question correctly except by making a *distinctio* sometimes forgotten. If the question means " is the Form of Good another name for *the God recognized in the Platonic* philosophy ? " the answer must be definitely No, for the reason given by Burnet, that the good is a form, whereas God is not a form but a " soul," the supremely good soul. When we come to deal with the *Laws*, we shall see the importance for Plato's own thought of this distinction. It is just because his God is not a form that God can play the part the Platonic philosophy assigns to Him. But if we mean " is the Good spoken of in the *Republic* identical with what Christian divines and philosophers have meant

---

[1] The last word on the question whether the philosophy of the *Republic* and the dialogues generally is " rationalism " or not is briefly this. If we could fully comprehend " the good " we should see directly that it is through and through intelligible, and the *only* object which is wholly and perfectly intelligible ; as we never can comprehend it completely, there is, in fact, always something mysterious, not yet understood, about it. It is free from all self-contradiction, but it always contains " surprises " for us. We can " see into it " to some extent, and it is the philosopher's duty to see further and further into it ; but you will never " see through it."

by God ? " the answer must be modified. In one most important respect it is. The distinguishing characteristic of the " Form of Good " is that it is the transcendent source of all the reality and intelligibility of everything other than itself. Thus it is exactly what is meant in Christian philosophy by the *ens realissimum*, and is rightly regarded as distinct from and transcendent of the whole system of its effects or manifestations. And, as in the *ens realissimum* of Christian philosophers, so in the " Form of Good " the distinction, valid everywhere else, between *essentia* and *esse*, *So-Sein* and *Sein*, falls away. In other language, it transcends the distinction, too often treated as absolute, between value and existence. It is the supreme value and the source of all other value, and at the same time it is, though " beyond being," the source of all existence. This explains why, when a man at last comes in sight of it at the culmination of his studies in " dialectic," it is supposed to be grasped by direct vision, and for that reason is strictly " ineffable." Neither Plato nor anyone else could tell another man what the good is, because it can only be apprehended by the most incommunicable and intimate personal insight. Thus, as it seems to me, metaphysically the Form of Good is what Christian philosophy has meant by God, and nothing else. From the Christian standpoint, the one comment which would suggest itself is that since, on Socrates' own showing, the distinction between *essence* and *existence* falls away in the good, it should not properly be called one of the forms at all, and hence Socrates and Plato are not fully alive to the significance of their own thought when they speak of a " God " who is a ψυχή and thus on a lower level of " reality " than the good. Their form of theism is only necessitated because, in fact though not in words, they are still haunted by a feeling that the good is, after all, a " value " or an *essentia*, and needs some intermediate link to connect it up with the hierarchy of " realities " or " existents." On this point the last word of Greek constructive thought was said not by Plato but by Plotinus and Proclus. (Of course, also, we must remember that a specifically Christian philosophy is determined in its attitude towards the theistic problem by the fact that Christianity is an *historical* religion. It starts with the *fact* of the " Word made flesh," itself a coalescence of existence and value, and to preserve its Christian character, it is bound to be true to that starting-point in its whole metaphysical construction.)

(*b*) THE CRITICISM OF THE SCIENCES.—In studying the criticism Socrates passes upon the sciences and his theory about their limitations, we must not be misled by the fact that he deals throughout only with the various branches of mathematics as recognized in the fifth century. This was inevitable because he had before him no other examples of systematic and organized knowledge. In principle what he has to say is readily applicable to the whole great body of more " concrete " sciences which has grown up since his own day. If we speak of his comments as a criticism on the mathematical method, we must understand the phrase "mathematical method " in the same wide sense in which it is to be understood in reading Descartes, as meaning simply the method which aims at knowing exactly what its initial assumptions mean, and at deducing their implications exactly and in the right order. This is the method of all genuine science whatsoever ; there is nothing in it, as Descartes rightly insisted, which involves any restriction to the special subject-matter, " number and quantity " (and, in fact, pure mathematics themselves have long ago outgrown the restriction). The point of the criticisms is that the μαθήματα themselves do not and cannot succeed in being absolutely true to the ideal of method they set before themselves. This is why we find that if we are to pursue the path of science to the end, we are driven to recognize the reality of " dialectic " as the crowning science of all sciences, and to demand that the existing μαθήματα shall themselves be reconstituted on a more certain basis by the light of the dialectician's results. The recognition of this necessity may well belong to the actual Socrates, since the most sensational thing in the whole history of fifth-century science had been the demonstration by the dialectician Zeno that the postulates of mathematics, as hitherto prosecuted by the Pythagoreans, contradict one another.[1] To save mathematical science in the face of Zeno's arguments it became necessary in the fourth century to reconstruct the whole system, and the reconstruction is preserved for us in the *Elements* of Euclid.   The men by whom the actual reconstruction was done, Eudoxus, Theaetetus, and their companions, so far as they are known to us, were all associates of Plato himself in the Academy, and it is quite certain that this revision of the accepted first principles of mathematics was one of the chief problems to which the school devoted itself.   In the *Republic*, which is concerned with the fifth century, we naturally hear nothing about the way in which the difficulty was subsequently met, but we are allowed to hear of the imminent need that the work should be done.

The main thought is quite simple.   In all the sciences the objects we are really studying are objects which we have to think but cannot see or perceive by any of our senses.   Yet the sciences throughout direct attention to these objects, which are, in fact, forms, by appealing in the first instance to sense.   The geometer draws a figure which he calls a " square " and a line which he calls

---

[1] To take one of the simplest examples : you cannot advance a step in elementary geometry without recognizing that any terminated straight line can be bisected, and there is no doubt that the Pythagorean geometers made the assumption.   But it is also one of their assumptions that points are " *units* having position."   If this is so, since a " unit " cannot be split, when I " bisect AB at C " ; C cannot be a " point of AB," and, in fact, cannot be a " point " at all.   Thus one at least of the assumptions, " a straight line can be bisected at " a point," " a point is a unit having position," must be false. But the Pythagorean geometer cannot see his way to do without either.   All Zeno's " antinomies " are of this type.

its "diagonal." But when he demonstrates a proposition about the square and its diagonal, the objects of which he is speaking are not this visible figure and this visible line but *the* square and *the* diagonal, and these, of course, we do not see except "with the mind's eye" (vi. 510*d–e*). (It would not even be true to say, like Berkeley, that what he is talking about is *this* visible figure *and* an indefinite plurality of others which are "like" it, for the simple reason that we can construct no visible figure at all which exactly answers to his definition of a "square.") Further, all through his reasoning the geometer or arithmetician depends on certain "postulates" (ὑποθέσεις) of which he "gives no account" (λόγος), such as the "postulate" that every number is either odd or even, or that there are just three kinds of angle. It is meant that these postulates are neither immediately self-evident, nor is any proof given of them. They are "synthetic" in Kant's sense of the word, and they are assumed without proof (vi. 510*c–d*). Thus there are two initial restrictions on the thinking of the mathematicians, as represented by the existing state of their science. They depend upon sensible things like diagrams as sources of suggestion, though not as the objects of their demonstrations. What cannot be "illustrated" or "represented" to the eye falls outside the scope of their science. And they make no attempt to reach real self-evidence in their initial postulates. They show that their theorems follow by logical necessity from a group of unproved premises, but they do not undertake to show that there is any necessity to admit these premises themselves. Thus the whole body of conclusions is left, so to say, hanging in the air. The geometer's "results" in the end rest on a tacit agreement (ὁμολογία) between himself and his pupil or reader that the question whether his assumptions are justifiable shall not be asked. In strictness we cannot call the results "knowledge" so long as the assumptions from which they have been deduced are thus left unexamined (vii. 533*c*).[1]

This suggests to us at once the possibility and necessity of a higher and more rigorous science, "dialectic." Such a science would differ from the sciences in vogue in two ways : (1) it would treat the initial postulates of the sciences as mere starting-points to be used for the discovery of some more ultimate premises which are not "postulated," but strictly self-luminous and evident (ἀνυπόθετα), a real "principle of everything," and when it had

---

[1] We may readily supply further examples in illustration of the two points on which Socrates dwells. Thus the notion that the visible diagram is either the object about which the geometer reasons, or at any rate, a necessary source of suggestion, is dispelled by the elementary consideration that *e.g.* a work on Conics commonly begins with propositions about the properties of the " general conic." But you cannot draw even a rough diagram of a " general conic." So the other point is well illustrated by the labour spent for centuries on trying to show that what we now know to be the arbitrary Euclidean postulate of parallels (that non-intersecting straight lines in the same plane are equidistant) is a necessity of thought.

discovered such a principle (or principles), it would then deduce the consequences which follow; (2) and in this movement no appeal would be made to sensible aids to the imagination, the double process of ascent to the " starting-point of everything " and descent again from it would advance from " forms by means of forms to forms and terminate upon them " (vi. 511b–c). In fact, we may even say that " dialectic " would " destroy " (ἀναιρεῖν) the postu-lates of the existing sciences (τὰς ὑποθέσεις ἀναιροῦσα, vii. 533c), that is, it would deprive them of the character of ultimate postu-lates by showing that—so far as they are not actually false, as they may turn out to be—they are consequences of still more ultimate truths.

In this account of the aims of dialectic we recognize at once the method described in the *Phaedo* as that of σκέψις ἐν λόγοις on which Socrates had fallen back after his disillusionment about Anaxagoras. Only here the special emphasis is thrown on just that side of the dialectic method which the immediate purposes of the *Phaedo* permitted us to dismiss in a single sentence. We are contemplating the procedure there said to be necessary if anyone disputes an initial " postulate." In that case, the *Phaedo* told us, our " postulate " will require to be itself deduced as a consequence from one more ultimate, and the process will have to be repeated until we come to a postulate which all parties are content to accept. In the last resort this would, of course, involve deduction from some principle which can be seen to possess unquestionable internal necessity. Thus, so far, the *Republic* agrees exactly with the *Phaedo* about the task of " dialectic," except that it lays special stress on just that part of it which had not to be taken into account in the *Phaedo* because the company there were all willing to admit the doctrine of forms as a " postulate " without demanding any justification of it. It is clear from the *Republic* that *if* a disputant should refuse to make this admission, the theory of forms itself would require to be examined in the same way in which the postu-lates of the mathematician *von Fach* are to be investigated. In the one passage of the dialogues where any such examination is made, it is not put into the mouth of Socrates but into that of the Pythagorean Timaeus (*Tim.* 51b 7 ff.).

Though Socrates naturally confines himself to criticisms of the sciences which had attained some degree of organization in his own day, it is obvious that they would apply with equal force to any others. Physics, chemistry, biology, economics are all full of undefined " primitive notions " and undemonstrated assumptions, and it is part of the work of the students of these sciences themselves to make a steady effort to ascertain just what their untested pre-suppositions are, and to consider how far they are really required, and how far they form a consistent system. The progress made by pure mathematics in the last half-century has largely consisted in a more accurate and complete statement of the " primitive notions " and " indemonstrable postulates " of the science and the elimination of numerous conscious or tacit " postulates " as actually false. Thus, for example, the process by which the Infinitesimal Calculus has been purged of bad logic and false assumptions, or the development of " non-Euclidean geometry," is an excellent illustration of the self-criticism and self-correction of thought which Socrates and Plato call " dialectic." Socrates' complaint (vii. 533c) about the mathematician who gives the name of science to a procedure in which the starting-point is something one does not know, and the conclusion and the intermediate steps " combinations of things one does not know," would be a perfectly correct description of the contents of any average text-book of the Calculus in vogue seventy years ago. And it is manifest that the same sort of scrutiny is required by such notions as " force," " acceleration," " atomicity," " evolution," " price." They are all inevitably in practical use long before the sciences which employ them have formulated any very precise account of their meaning, and the progress of science as science (as distinct from its application to " commerce ") consists very largely in the steady correction of our first crude attempts to explain what we mean by them. The physicist of to-day may, like Democritus, make the " atomic structure of matter " a foundation-stone of his science, but he means by his " atom " something Democritus would not have recognized as " atomic " at all. Similarly we all talk of the " evolution " of species, but the view that new species originate by sudden and considerable " mutations," if established, would change the whole character of the special " Darwinian " postulate about the character of the process ; it would involve exactly what Socrates means by a " destruction " of the postulate. Thus, so far, we may say that what the *Republic* calls " dialectic " is, in principle, simply the rigorous and unremitting task of steady scrutiny of the indefinables and indemonstrables of the sciences, and that, in particular, his ideal, so far as the sciences with which he is directly concerned goes, is just that reduction of mathematics to rigorous deduction from expressly formulated logical premises by exactly specified logical methods of which the work of Peano, Frege, Whitehead, and Russell has given us a magnificent example.

But the " reduction of all pure mathematics to logic " is only a part, and not the most important part, of what the *Republic* understands by " dialectic." Such a unification of the sciences as the *Republic* contemplates would require a combination of the reduction of mathematics to logic with the Cartesian reduction of the natural sciences to geometry. When the task was finished, no proposition asserting " matter of fact," devoid of internal necessity, should appear anywhere among the premises from which our conclusions are ultimately drawn. The first principles to which the dialectician traces back all our knowledge ought to exhibit a self-evident *necessity*, so that science would end by transforming all " truths of fact " into what Leibniz called " truths of reason." This involves a still more significant extension of the range of

" science." It implies that in a completed philosophy the distinctions between value and fact, *essentia* and *esse*, *So-sein and Sein* are transcended. The man who has attained "wisdom" would see that the reason why anything is, and the reason why it is *what* it is, are both to be found in the character of an *ens realissimum* of which it is self-evident that it is and that it is what it is, a self-explanatory "supreme being." This is why dialectic is said to culminate in direct apprehension of "the good" as the source of both existence and character. The thought is that all science in the end can be transformed into a sort of "algebra," but an algebra which is, as Burnet says, *teleological*. The demand for such a science is, in fact, already contained by implication in the remark of Socrates in the *Phaedo* that he hoped to find in Anaxagoras a solution of the problem of the shape and position of the earth based on proof that " it is best " that it should have just that shape and position and no other (*Phaedo* 97*d–e*). When a modern biologist explains the structure of an organism by the notion of "adaptation" to its environment he is thus using on a small scale the principle which the *Republic* would make the supreme universal principle of all scientific explanation whatsoever. Only, of course, the biological conception of "adaptation" stops short with a relative best; the particular environment of a particular species is taken as (relatively) constant and independent; the "best" realized in the development of the species is adequate adaptation to that given environment. When the principle is made universal, the "best" becomes an *ethical* and absolute best, since no place is left for an "environment" of everything. The "goodness of God," or its equivalent, takes the place of the fixed "environment" as that to which the structure of things is conceived as "adapted."

We need not suppose that Plato imagined this programme for the completion of science as capable of actual execution by human beings. We have learned from the *Symposium* that "philosophy" itself is a life of progress, it is not those who are already in possession of "wisdom," but those who are endeavouring after it, who philosophize. The *Timaeus* reminds us with almost wearisome repetition that, in physical science in particular, all our results are inevitably provisional, the best we can reach with our present lights, and that we must be prepared to see them all superseded or modified. One of the standing contrasts between Plato and his great disciple Aristotle is just that this sense of the provisionality and progressiveness of science is so prominent in the one and so absent from the other. Plato never assumes, as Aristotle was so apt to assume, that he can do the world's scientific thinking for it once for all. This apparent finality, which made Aristotle so attractive to the thinkers of the thirteenth century, who were just recovering the thought of "Nature" as a field for study on her own account, makes the real value of Aristotle's science rather difficult for us to appreciate to-day. Plato was far too true to the Socratic conception of the insignificance of human knowledge by comparison with the vastness of the scientific problem to fall into the vein of cheap and easy dogmatism. But though the final " rationalization " of things may be an unattainable goal, there is no reason why we should not try to get as near to the goal as we can. If we cannot expel the element of " brute fact " for which we can see no reason from science, we may try, and we ought to try, to reduce it to a minimum. We cannot completely " mathematize " human knowledge, but the more we can mathematize it, the better. We shall see, when we come to speak of Plato's oral teaching in the Academy, how earnestly he set himself to carry out the programme by getting behind the mere assumption of the forms as the last word in philosophy, and deducing the forms themselves from the " good."

(c) It should be unnecessary to dwell on the point that, with all his devotion to this demand for a critical metaphysic of the sciences, Plato is no champion of a mere *vita contemplativa* divorced from practical social activity. One could not even say that he, like Kant, conceives of " speculative " and " practical " reason as active in two distinct spheres of which one is subordinated to the other. To his mind, the two spheres are inseparable. The unification of science is only possible to one who is illuminated by the vision of the Good which is the principle of the unification, and the Good is only seen by the man who *lives* it. Hence the demand that the " philosopher " shall devote the best years of his working life to the arduous practice of governing, in all its details great or small, is only the other side of the conviction that without the " heroic " character no one will ever rise to the supreme rank in science itself. The " philosopher " is necessarily a missionary and a sort of lesser Providence to mankind because, on Socratic principles, the " Good " cannot be seen without drawing all who see it into its service. The " philosophers' " social activity is all the more effective that it is not pursued directly for its own sake, in the spirit of the well-meaning but tiresome persons of our own day who take up " social work " as they might take up typewriting or civil engineering, but issues naturally and inevitably, as a sort of " by-product," from their aspiration after something else, just as the " great inventions " of modern times regularly issue from the discoveries of men who were not thinking at all of the applications of science to convenience and commerce, or as art, literature, social life have all owed an incalculable debt to St. Francis and his " little brethren," who never gave a thought to any of them.

(12) This desultory chapter may be brought to an end by a few remarks on the impressive picture of *Republic* viii.–ix. about the stages of progressive degeneration through which personal and national character pass as the true ideal of life falls more completely out of view. It should be obvious that the primary interest of these sketches is throughout ethical, not political. The " imperfect " constitutions are examined in order to throw light on the different phases of personal human sinfulness, not in the interests of a theory

of political institutions. We see the sinfulness of even " honourable " ambition or " business principles," when they are made the
mainspring of a man's life, more clearly by considering the type
of national character exhibited by a community in which these
motives determine the character of national life. Socrates is still
adhering to his declared purpose of using the " larger letters "
to decipher the smaller. In the sketches themselves, Socrates is
all through " drawing with his eye on the object." We are told
in so many words that Sparta has furnished the model for the
picture of the second-best society, where education is neglected and
the highest moral ideal is to display the character of a good fighting-
man and sportsman, *i.e.* the society in which " honourable ambition,"
the pursuit of the *cursus honorum*, is thought the supreme virtue.
As mankind go, a community of this kind is not a bad one ; it is
morally in a much healthier state than a society where every one
regards " getting rich " as the great aim in life, and the " merchant
prince " is the national hero. Rome, in its better days, would be
an example of the kind of society intended, no less than Sparta.
The point of Socrates' criticism is that when " ambition " becomes
master instead of servant, it is not likely to remain " honourable "
ambition, ambition to " serve." From the first, the ambition of
the " timocratic " State has not been aspiration to be pre-eminent
in the best things ; at their best, the Spartans made a very poor
contribution to the positive pursuit of the highest life. When
they were not at their best, their " ambition " took the form of
mere devotion to military success ; and at their worst, they were
mere aspirants to the exercise of power and the accumulation of
the wealth to be got by " empire," as the " timocratic man," in
his old age, degenerates into the kind of character who is greedy
of the power money will give him. It ought to have been impossible to find any idealization of Sparta in the picture. As I have
written elsewhere, it would be truer to say that in the *Republic*
we discern the shadows of the third-century ephors and of Nabis
behind the " respectable " figure of Agesilaus.

It is generally admitted that the picture of the " democratic "
city where every one does as he pleases, and the most typical of
citizens is the gifted amateur who plays, as the mood takes him,
at every kind of life from that of the voluptuary to that of the
ascetic—a sort of Goethe, in fact—is a humorous satire on Athenian
life and manners. Of course we should be alive to the further point
that the satire would be wholly beside the mark if directed against
the drab and decent *bourgeois* Athens of Plato's manhood. The
burlesque is aimed directly against the Imperial democracy of the
spacious days of Pericles when Athens was a busy home of world-
commerce and the " new learning." If we read the description
side by side with the famous Funeral Oration in Thucydides, we
shall see at once that the very notes of Athenian life which Pericles
there selects as evidence of its superiority are carefully dwelt upon
by Socrates for the opposite purpose of proving that, for all its

surface brilliancy, such a life is at bottom so diseased that society is on the verge of complete collapse. I, at least, cannot avoid the conviction that Socrates sees in just what must have been the great charm of Athens for men like Sophocles, Protagoras, Herodotus—its apparently inexhaustible variety and freshness—the unmistakable "symptoms of the end." [1] (Perhaps he was not very far wrong. What would probably have been the issue of the Periclean age if Alcibiades, the incarnation of its energy and versatility, had returned triumphant from the subjugation of Sicily ? One may " hazard a wide solution.")

We are given no hint of the source from which the picture of the intermediate society, where wealth is the great title to admiration and "merchant princes" control the national destiny, is taken. But I do not doubt that we can name the State which Plato has in mind. When we remember that, as we see from allusions in the *Laws* and in Aristotle's *Politics*,[2] there were just three cities whose constitutions impressed Greek thinkers by their appearance of being framed on definite principles—Sparta, Crete, and Carthage. I think it may safely be assumed that Carthage has supplied the hints for the Venice or Amsterdam of the *Republic*, just as we may presume that Socrates has the Carthaginians more than anyone else in mind in the earlier passage where he remarks on the exceptional aptitude of " Phoenicians " for commerce. The subsequent history of Carthage during the first two Punic wars affords an interesting commentary on what is said about the internal dissensions which paralyse the " oligarchical city." On the concluding argument, by which the life of respect for right is pronounced far superior in happiness to the life of sating one's cupidities and ambitions,[3] there is no need to say much. The reasoning is that we have already met in the *Gorgias*, and turns on the application of the medical formula of " depletion and recovery from depletion " to the moral life. The " passions," like the physical appetites of hunger and thirst, are capable of no permanent and progressive satisfaction. You feed full to-day, but to-morrow finds you as hungry again as though to-day had never been. What you mistake for happiness has been only the temporary arrest of a " depletion." On the other hand, what you gain in knowledge

---

[1] Cf. V. Soloviev's saying that " visible and accelerated progress is a symptom of the end."

[2] Arist. *Politics*, B 11 (1272*b* 24 ff. ; note that Aristotle too comments on the "plutocracy" of the Carthaginian scheme, and plutocracy is what is meant by " oligarchy " in the *Republic*). For a reference to Carthage in the *Laws*, see *Laws*, 674*a*, written, no doubt, after Plato's association with affairs in Sicily had made Carthage very much of an actuality to him. Commerce made Carthage an object of interest to Athens in the Periclean age (Aristoph. *Knights*, 174), and it has been plausibly suggested that the great plague of the third year of the Archidamian war was brought to Athens from Carthage by infected merchandise.

[3] *Republic*, ix. 583*b* ff. Cf.
      " ' Mete unto wombe and wombe eek unto mete,
      Shall God destroyen bothe,' as Paulus seith."

and goodness is not won to-day to be " excreted " by the time to-morrow is upon you. It is permanently acquired. It is not with character and intellect as it is with bodily health, which is a mere balance between antithetic processes of waste and repair ; character and intellect are κτήματα ἐς αἰεί. This is the reason for the distinction between the " false " pleasures of sensuality and ambition and the "true" pleasures of the philosophic life. The former are "false," not in the sense that they are not really felt, but in the sense that they are not what they promise to be. " Alle Lust will Ewigkeit," but no *Ewigkeit* is to be got out of the βίος φιλοσώματος or the βίος φιλότιμος, a truth which no special pleading for Hedonism can explain away. I will add one final caution against possible misinterpretation. Plato credits the " three lives " with distinctive pleasures, much as Mill talks of a distinction of " higher " and " lower " in pleasure.[1] But he gives a rational reason for his preference of the " philosopher's " pleasure where Mill gives an absurd one. Mill tries to persuade his readers that a jury of pleasure-tasters devoid of all moral principle would be unanimous in preferring the philosopher's pleasures, or, alternatively, that the dissentients may be disabled as no genuine connoisseurs.[2] Plato gives the right reason for the preference, that the issue is one which must be decided by " intelligence," and it is just intelligence which the philosopher has and his rivals have not. This is what John Grote also meant when he said that Mill's argument is based on a misconception of our reason for attaching weight to the philosopher's verdict. We go to him not as Mill assumes, for *evidence*, but for *authority*.[3]

See further :

NETTLESHIP, R. L.—"Lectures on the *Republic* of Plato " (vol. ii. of *Philosophical Remains*) ; *Plato's Conception of Goodness and the Good* ; *The Theory of Education in Plato's Republic* in *Hellenica* ², 61–165.

NATORP, P.—*Platons Ideenlehre*, 175–215.

RITTER, C.—*Platon*, ii. 3–39, 554–641 *al.* ; *Platons Staat, Darstellung des Inhalts.* (Stuttgart, 1909.)

RAEDER, H.—*Platons philosophische Entwickelung*, 181–245.

BARKER, E.—*Greek Political Theory : Plato and his Predecessors*, 145–268.

STEWART, J. A.—*Myths of Plato*, 133–172 (*Myth of Er*), 471–474 (*Myth of the Earth-born*) ; *Plato's Doctrine of Ideas*, 47–62.

SHOREY, P.—*Plato's Republic.* (London and New York, Vol. I. 1930, Vol. II. 1935.)

DIÈS, A.—*Introduction* to the edition of the dialogue in the *Collection des Universités de France.* (Paris, 1932.)

---

[1] *Republic*, 582a–e.

[2] Mill's plea is a perfect example of the kind of argument the Greeks called a λόγος ἀντιστρέφων, i.e. one which makes for neither party, because it can be equally well applied by the other. If the sage disables the judgment of the profligate on the plea that he must have lost the taste for the " higher pleasures " before he can prefer the lower, the profligate can equally retort on the sage with the adage about sour grapes. " You have taken to philosophy," he may say, " because you are physically too old to enjoy debauchery."

[3] *Examination of the Utilitarian Philosophy*, p. 47.

CHAPTER XII

THE *PHAEDRUS*[1]

THE *Phaedrus* presents a double difficulty to the student of Plato's work as a whole. What is its proper place in the series of the dialogues ? And what is its purpose ? Is it, as it professes to be, a discussion of the principles upon which " rhetoric " (prose style) may be made into a " science," or is its real subject Eros ? Is Plato primarily concerned with the question of the use and abuse of sexual passion, or are the speeches Socrates delivers on this topic merely examples of the right and the wrong use of persuasive eloquence ?

The first question, on examination, proves capable of being narrowed down to one which we may regard as of minor importance. No serious student of Platonic style now defends the singular theory of some critics in classical antiquity that the prominence of Eros in the dialogue and the loaded rhetoric of Socrates' encomium on him prove the work to be a youthful writing, perhaps the earliest of all the dialogues.[2] It is matter of common agreement that, on stylistic grounds, the dialogue cannot be placed earlier than those works of Plato's maturity as a writer with which we have been dealing in the last four chapters ; it cannot be far removed from the great quadrilateral in point of date. But there still remains the question whether it may be earlier than some of these four, or whether it is later than all of them. In particular, we have to ask whether the *Phaedrus* is earlier or later than the *Republic*. Arguments from stylometry cannot be wholly trusted in this case, since it is manifest that many of the peculiarities of language are due to deliberate imitation. On the whole, the stylometrists appear to be satisfied that the *Phaedrus* is the later of the two works, and this view is plausibly supported by the contention urged by H. Raeder, that some of the details of the mythical part of the dialogue are hardly intelligible except on the assumption that its readers would be familiar with *Republic* v. and the concluding myth of *Republic* x. I do not myself find the argument conclusive.[3] On the other hand,

---

[1] On the problems connected with the dialogue, see *inter cetera* Thompson, *Phaedrus*, Introduction ; C. Ritter, *Platon*, i. 256 ; H. Raeder, *Platons philosophische Entwickelung*, 245 ff.

[2] Diogenes Laertius (iii, 25) mentions the theory ; Olympiodorus repeats the story as a fact.

[3] Raeder sees in the mention of the " journey of a thousand years " on which the soul enters after each incarnation (*Phaedrus*, 249a) a reference to the fuller explanation in the *Republic* (615a). This is inconclusive, since the

as we shall see in the next chapter, there is convincing reason for thinking that the *Theaetetus*, which pretty certainly opens the group of dialogues of Plato's later life, was not written until about twenty years after the *Republic* and its immediate fellows, and it is perhaps hard to believe that so great a writer as Plato was absolutely silent through so long a period. Hence I have nothing to set against the conclusions of recent eminent scholars on the point, and would merely remark that the priority of the *Republic* is not absolutely demonstrable, and also that, in view of the difference in spirit between *Republic* and *Theaetetus*, we must fairly suppose the *Phaedrus*, if the composition falls in the interval between those two dialogues, to have been written early rather than late in the interval.

The other problem is more difficult, and I would recommend the reader to suspend his judgment on it until he has followed our analysis of the dialogue. My own opinion is on the side of those who regard the right use of " rhetoric " as the main topic, for the following simple reason. In Socrates, with whom the " tendance of the soul " was the great business of life, it is quite intelligible that a discussion of the use of rhetoric or anything else should be found to lead up to the great issues of conduct. If the real subject of the *Phaedrus* were sexual love, it is hard to see how its elaborate discussion of the possibility of applying a scientific psychology of the emotions to the creation of a genuine art of persuasion, or its examination of the defects of Lysias as a writer, can be anything but the purest irrelevance.

In structure the dialogue is of the simplest type. Socrates falls in with Phaedrus who is, under medical advice, taking a constitutional in the country outside the city walls, and, for the sake of his company, joins him, departing for once from his preference for the streets of the town. He soon persuades Phaedrus to sit down by the bank of the Ilissus under the shade of a plane tree ; the conversation which ensues takes place here and is strictly *tête-à-tête*. As for the supposed date of the conversation, it can be approximately fixed by the opening sentences. Lysias, who figures as a mere lad in the *Republic*, is now at the height of his fame as a writer of λόγοι (228*a*), and is living at Athens (227*b*). We may add the further detail that Polemarchus is also alive and, according to Socrates, " has betaken himself to philosophy " (257*b*), also that Isocrates, though still young, is already rivalling Lysias in his profession ; Socrates anticipates that he may either throw Lysias and all former professors of it into the shade, or even aspire to a still higher calling,

period seems in both cases to be taken over from current Orphic mythology. So the reference to the " lots " which play a part in assigning a new body to the soul (*Phaedrus*,249*b*) need not be to *Republic* 617*d*, since the κλῆροι appear to be Orphic (Burnet, *Early Greek Philosophy*[3], 190 n. 3). Still less convincing is the argument that the *Phaedrus* tacitly presupposes the doctrine of the " parts of the soul " expounded in *Republic* iv., since this is equally true of the *Gorgias*, as we have seen, and the doctrine appears to be a piece of fifth-century Pythagoreanism. Raeder's other arguments are complicated by the assumption that the dialogue contains a polemic against Isocrates. On this *vide infra*.

for " there really is philosophy in him " (279*a*). The conversation thus falls at some date between 411, when Polemarchus and Lysias returned to Athens from Thurii, and the year of anarchy, 404–3, when Polemarchus fell a victim to the " Thirty." The tradition was that Isocrates was some seven years older than Plato, so that his birth would fall about 435 B.C. ; as he survived the battle of Chaeronea (338 B.C.), he cannot well have been born much if any earlier ; hence he would be about twenty-four in 411 and thirty-one in the " year of anarchy." A date intermediate between 411 and 404 is thus required by the supposed facts. We note then that Phaedrus must now be between five and twelve years older than when we met him in the *Symposium* ; no lad (for he figured in the *Protagoras*), but a man at least approaching forty[1] ; Socrates is a γέρων, a man of at least sixty and perhaps more.

When Socrates falls in with Phaedrus, the time of day is already close on noon (this explains why the pair so soon take rest under the plane-tree). Phaedrus has spent the early morning listening to a brilliant and paradoxical λόγος—we should call it an essay—by Lysias in defence of the thesis that a lad should be kinder to a wooer who is not " in love " than to one who is. He has the written text with him, and Socrates professes to believe that he is taking his solitary stroll for the express purpose of getting it by heart. The main point of the short and playful conversation between Socrates and Phaedrus as they make their way to the place they have chosen for their *siesta* (227–230) is to pitch the ethical key for what is to follow. Socrates is not interested in the " rationaliza-tion of myths," like that of Boreas and Orithyia, because he is pre-occupied with a graver problem, that of learning to " know him-self " ; he is indifferent to the charms of the country, because the trees, unlike the men he meets in the streets, can " teach him nothing " that bears on this supreme topic, the moral being of man. These remarks prepare us for the moral earnestness with which the merits of Lysias's essay and the possibilities of rhetoric are to be treated in the body of the dialogue.

THE ESSAY OF LYSIAS (230*e*–234*c*).—It has been disputed whether the discourse Phaedrus proceeds to read is an authentic composition of Lysias or a brilliant imitation of his style by Plato himself. There is no evidence either way, but for my own part, I feel that we must agree with those scholars, including Lysias' latest editor, Hude, who regard the essay as genuine. No one doubts Plato's ability to compose a λόγος for Lysias with perfect fidelity to the style of the supposed author. But, since the dialogue ends with severe and formal censure of Lysias, founded on a search-ing criticism of the λόγος, I find it difficult to believe that the document is an invention. It would be self-stultifying to publish a severe criticism of a well-known author based on an imitation of him which the critic had composed for his own purposes and could

[1] The same point is taken by Parmentier, *Bulletin de l'association Guillaume Budé*, No. 10, p. 4.

not expect readers to take as authentic.   One might as well suppose that Berkeley could have made the point he wants to make in *Alciphron* about the false glitter and shallowness of Shaftesbury by composing an imitation of the *Characteristics*.   Plato's purpose, like Berkeley's, demands that the attack should be made on work which is both genuine and admired by the circles whose literary and moral false taste is to be exposed.   Hude seems to me fully justified in printing the discourse as part of his text of *Lysias*.

The thesis of Lysias, we must remember, would be an offensive paradox even to the section of Athenian society which practised " unnatural " aberrations.   The fashionable theory was that the relations in question are ennobled when they are inspired by genuine " romantic " attachment, but not otherwise, as is taken for granted by the encomiasts of them in the *Symposium*.   To suffer the advances of an ἐραστής from calculations of advantage was regarded as the basest thing a Greek lad could do.   For a modern parallel to the paradox we might imagine a clever essay written to show that Tom Jones's conduct towards Lady Bellaston is morally more innocent than his affair with Molly Seagrim.   We must not suppose that Lysias intends his argument to be taken seriously.   He simply means to exhibit his cleverness by showing how good a case he can make out for the worst conduct, much as a clever writer to-day might amuse himself and his readers by an essay on the moral elevation of a bomb-throwing " Communist."   But there are theses which cannot be defended and arguments which cannot be employed, even in jest, without revealing deep-seated moral depravity or insensibility ;   the kind of cleverness which sustains such theses by the use of such arguments is a real moral danger to the community and requires to be countered, as it is by Socrates, with better morality and superior wit.

The discourse may be summarized very briefly ;   it is throughout an appeal to considerations of " utility " in the most sordid sense of the word.   One is likely to make one's price much more effectively out of a suitor who is a cold sensualist.   Romantic love has its fits of repentance and its lovers' quarrels ;   it changes its object, and when it does so, it passes into hate and scorn.   It imperils reputation, since the romantic suitor " blabs " of his success, while the business-like sensualist knows how to hold his tongue.   The " lover " is notoriously jealous and tries to monopolize his beloved ;   the cool sensualist does not object to going shares with rivals recommended by their wealth or other qualities.[1]   The " lover " is attracted by physical charm before he has considered the suitability of the connexion in other respects ;   the man who is not " in love " chooses carefully.   The lover's judgment is blinded by his passion, and this makes him the worst of confidants and advisers. He flatters one's weaknesses and quarrels with one's better qualities. On all these grounds it is absurd to expect solid and lasting advantage from one's complaisances towards him. (Manifestly such a

[1] Like our own Charles II, to take an actual example.

discourse, apart from the moral turpitude which pervades it, is really a failure, considered merely as a defence of its thesis. Lysias gives a number of excellent reasons for thinking that it is bad to " grant favours to a lover " ; he has given no reason for thinking that it may not be as bad, or worse, to grant them to a sensual " man of the world." The speech is thus, judged by any reasonable standard, bad rhetoric, as well as bad ethics, a point which Socrates will not be slow to make.)

Socrates professes at first to have paid no attention to the matter of the discourse. He was attending wholly to its stylistic qualities, and these even Lysias himself could hardly approve, since it was full of empty repetition and tautology. The mere recollection of what poets like Sappho and Anacreon have said about love would enable a man to make a much better speech on the same theme. Lysias has in fact shown no " invention " in his essay ; he has merely dwelt on one obvious point, the " blindness " and irrationality of the lover's passion," a point no one could miss. The whole merit of his performance, if it has any, must be looked for in the arrangement (διάθεσις) of this commonplace material. Phaedrus himself admits this (236a–b), but challenges Socrates, if he can, to treat the same theme (ὑπόθεσις), the admitted " madness " of the lover's passion, better than Lysias has done. Socrates accepts the challenge, with a prayer to the Muses to make up for his well-known ignorance by the aid of their " inspiration." With this preface he makes a rival speech on the theme, only carefully introducing one slight but significant modification. The supposed speaker, in his discourse, is to be not a cold-blooded sensualist making a disgraceful " business proposition," but a " lover " astute enough to cloak his passion under an *appearance* of indifference. (This gives Socrates a double advantage over Lysias. He safeguards his own character by abstaining from even a playful defence of a morally disgraceful thesis, and he leaves himself free, if he pleases, to urge subsequently that the apparent reasonability of the speech is only the simulated rationality of a madman, since the client into whose mouth it is put is really inspired all the time by " romantic " unreason.)

FIRST SPEECH OF SOCRATES.—Thesis : *It is Bad to Listen to the Blandishments of a " Lover "* (237b–241d).—The first requisite for all sound deliberation is to *know* the real character of the object about which we are deliberating. Since the question is whether one should yield to a lover, we must start by understanding what " love " is, and what it aims at, and whether it is for our good or for our harm. " Love " is, of course, a desire or craving for something. Now there are two principal types of desire—the " inborn " craving for the *pleasant*, and the desire for the " best," which is not inborn, but has to be acquired, and is based on judgment (δόξα)— and there is often a clash between the two. The victory of judgment (δόξα) in this conflict over appetitive craving is what we call *sophrosyne* ; the victory of appetite over our judgment of good we call "lust" or "passion" (ὕβρις). "Love" (ἔρως, sexual passion) is one special variety of ὕβρις or "lust." It is the prevalence of violent desire for the pleasant uninformed by rational judgment of good, when aroused by physical beauty (238c). The question before us, then, is whether it is for the benefit or for the hurt of the party who has aroused such a passion to gratify it. And here, Socrates says, he will give the rein to an almost "poetical" eloquence with which he feels himself inspired beyond his ordinary, perhaps by the surroundings in which he is speaking. (The artificial graces of Lysias are to be met by the "unstudied eloquence" of the "heart.")

The "lover," being a slave to his pleasures, will, of course, desire his beloved to be the pliant minister to them, and will hate everything which makes him less subservient, and gives him any kind of personal independence. Now wisdom, valour, even ready wit and eloquence themselves, tend to give one an independent personality, and for that reason a "lover" will object to them in the object of his passion. His jealousy will prompt him to exclude the beloved from all intercourse which would "make a man" of him, and above all from "divine philosophy." The last thing he will desire is that his "minion's" charm for himself should be endangered by the acquisition of intelligent and manly qualities of soul. In the next place, he will resent the acquisition of hardy and manly physical qualities such as make one of worth in "war and other necessities"; he will deliberately, for his own pleasure, try to keep the ἐρώμενος to a soft and effeminate course of life. Finally, he will be anxious to isolate his victim from all the influences of family affections; he will object to his having any financial independence, or to his marrying and forming a family of his own, since he resents whatever tends to emancipate the victim from the position of mere minister to his own selfish pleasure. Thus the "lover" is an enemy to the good alike of the victim's soul, of his body, and of his estate. (We see that Socrates' pretence of being carried out of himself on a flood of "inspired" eloquence must not be taken too seriously. He is deliberately observing the rules of arrangement which Lysias had neglected. His theme is nominally that of Lysias, the jealous and petulant selfishness of the "lover." But he has carefully articulated his argument and avoided vain repetition by grouping the effects of the lover's jealousy on his victim under the heads of mind, body, estate. This has given him further the opening for lifting the whole argument to a worthier moral level by insisting on the supreme importance of the moral goods which are jeopardized by complaisance. Considered simply as an example of effective pleading, Socrates' speech has thus stylistic advantages over that of Lysias which far outweigh his neglect of the verbal graces and prettinesses of the other.)

The speech ends with a further consideration. Connexion with an ἐραστής has been shown to be productive of evil to mind, body, and fortune. We may add, as a minor point, that besides being " harmful," it is also not even pleasant. Association with a flatterer or a kept mistress is also hurtful, but the palliative can be urged that, at any rate, these are " pleasant vices." But in the connexion of the ἐραστής with his victim, the victim does not even get the pleasure ; such as it is, it is all on the side of the other party ; the victim's position is intolerable, and he only sustains it on the strength of promises of solid advantages, which the " lover" will not implement, when once he has had his wicked will and sated himself. The " love " of the ἐραστής is thus the proverbial love of the wolf for the lamb.

Even Phaedrus can see that this discourse, though it gives good reasons against bestowing favours on a " lover," does nothing to advance the plea of the suitor who is not " in love." Socrates, who, of course, did not mean to act as advocate for such a client, suggests that it would be enough to add that such a person is in all respects the very opposite of the lover whose faults we have exposed. He is about to take his leave of Phaedrus with this remark, when " the divine sign " checks him. He professes to understand this as a warning that, since Eros is a god, he has committed an impiety by denouncing him and must purge himself of his contempt by a palinode, as Stesichorus did when he had blasphemed Helen. If a real gentleman had overheard either the speech of Lysias or that which Socrates has just delivered, he would have imagined that he was listening to persons brought up among " common sailors," incapable of understanding what a free man means by " love." Thus the point of the " palinode " is to be that it is a recantation of the identification of ἔρως with a brutal physical appetite (241d–243e).[1]

SECOND SPEECH OF SOCRATES (244a–256e).—*The True Psychology of Love.*—The ground on which we have so far maintained that it is better to associate with one who is not in love than with a " lover " is that the lover is " beside himself " (μαίνεται), but the man who is not in love retains his sanity, and sanity is better than " madness." This is the proposition we are now to recant. It would be true if there were only one kind of frenzy, common madness. But there is an inspired " frenzy " which is productive of good we could not equally obtain in a state of sanity and control of ourselves. One of its forms is *prophecy* ; the priestess of Delphi, who predicts in a state of " exaltation," is far superior as a prophet to diviners who predict the future by calculations based on the flight of birds and similar omens ; a second form is the " exaltation " of the authors of " purifications " and " initiations," " founders of

[1] The definition of ἔρως from which the speech of Socrates started was correct in the sense that it is a true definition of what Lysias had called ἔρως in formulating his thesis. Hence it was rightly adopted also by Socrates for the immediate purpose of showing how the same thesis might have been treated with less superficiality and without idle repetition. But, as we shall see, it is not in fact an adequate account of even guilty and degraded *human* " love," to call it a craving for a certain physical " exoneration." (Even an unholy love—if it is " love " at all—is the pollution of a high sacrament.)

religions " as we should say ; a third is the inspiration of the poet. No one who attempts to compose poetry in a state of " sanity " by rules of art ever achieves anything great (244a–245e). The madness of the lover, as we shall find, is a fourth form of this divine " frenzy " which is so much wiser than the wisdom of the world.[1] We intend to show, that, if the lover is mad, his madness is an inspiration from heaven and may be a great blessing. To prove this we must lay down the principles of a sound psychology ; we must see what is the nature, and what the actions and passions of the soul.

In the first place, the soul is immortal (245c), a statement which means to a Greek that it is divine. The proof of this is that whatever is always in motion is immortal, and the soul is always in motion. The minor premiss of this syllogism is again proved thus. The soul is the source and initiator of its own motions ; its motions are not communicated from without, but spontaneously originated from within. Thus they were never started by anything else, and, as the soul itself is the first fountain of them, they can never come to an end. If the soul could come to an end, there would be an end of nature and becoming universally (245e)—a statement which implies that souls are the *only* things which can move from within, and so the only possible sources of movement. The soul may thus be rigorously defined as " that which moves itself " (246a).[2] But

---

[1] To appreciate this doctrine aright, we must neither forget the habitual " irony " of Socrates nor exaggerate it. The key to his meaning is given by his well-known theory about the poets. He found the poets unable to explain in bald prose what they meant by their finest passages, or how they came by them. Hence he classes them among the persons who think they have a knowledge which they really have not. They are not alive, whatever they may suppose, to the full significance of their best work. He does not, of course, mean to suggest either that the great things in Sophocles or Euripides are not really great, or that great poetry may be nonsense. It means more than the poet himself in his " uninspired " hours could tell you, and this shows that some influence which the poet cannot wholly control has been speaking through him. In the same way, though it is part of his irony to dwell on the alleged benefits conferred on men by the trance-utterances of the Pythia or the " purifications " devised by abnormal and eccentric " religious geniuses," it is quite consistent with his habitual attitude to " things divine " that he should suppose a higher power to use such vehicles for revealing the future, and admit the real healing effects of some " initiations " and " purifications " on the body and mind. The great defect he finds in poetry as in μαντική is just that the spirits of the prophets are *not* subject to the prophets. Hence you cannot depend on the Pythia's predictions, and hence also the great poet is apt to decline into bathos or nonsense as much as the Shadwell to deviate (occasionally) into sense.

[2] This argument, in an expanded form, is reproduced in the *Laws*, as we shall see, and treated there as the sufficient proof both of the existence of God and of the immortality of the soul. Unlike the arguments of the *Phaedo* it has no special connexion with the theory of the forms. But it would be rash to say that its introduction shows that we are dealing with a post-Socratic development of Plato's own thought, since in principle the argument is that of Alcmaeon of Crotona that the soul is immortal because it " is like immortal things, and is like them in the point that it is always in motion " (Aristot. *de Anima.* 405a 30). Hence the argument must have been well known to

what is the character of this " self-moving " source of all movement ? For our purposes, we may content ourselves with an
analogy. It is like a charioteer with a pair of winged steeds,
forming a single living whole.[1] In the case of the gods, driver and
horses are all as good as they can possibly be ; in the human soul,
the driver has to manage two horses of different strain, and this is
what makes his task so difficult. While the horses keep their wings,
they travel round the circuit of heaven and the soul " administers "
the Cosmos. But they may lose their wings and fall to earth ; the
soul then acquires an earthly body which seems to be able to move
itself (though it is really moved by the soul within it), and it is this
complex of body and soul which we call the mortal " animal."
By analogy we come commonly to think of God (falsely) as a being
with a soul and body which are never separated by death (246*d*).

(We see at once that we are dealing in a parable with the " three
parts " of the soul ; the driver is judgment, the two horses are
" honour " or " mettle " and " appetite." If we press the details,
they imply that all three " parts " are present not only in the soul
which has not yet put on the garment of the flesh, but in the gods,
who are never embodied at all. This would be quite at variance
with the hints of the *Republic* and the express teaching of the
Timaeus. But it is not really permissible to extract metaphysics
from mythical details which are necessitated by simple regard
for the coherency of the pictorial representation.)

The myth proceeds to describe the life of all souls under the
image of a great festal procession. The souls progress, under the
leadership of the gods, round the whole compass of the heavens,
maintaining the universal order of things. The goal of the whole
pilgrimage is reached by an ascent to a region outside the whole
heaven, " the plain of reality," where the procession pauses and
enjoys a Sabbath rest in the contemplation of " bodiless reality,
without figure, colour, or tangible quality " (in other words the
forms) ; this is the true home of souls, and the source of their
spiritual food. Thus the thought is that it is in the strength of this
pure contemplation that gods and men alike execute the practical
task of establishing and maintaining natural and moral order in the
realm of mutability and becoming. Like Moses they make everything after the pattern they have seen " in the mount." The gods,
of course, achieve this " steep ascent of heaven " with complete
success ; they actually conduct their living chariots out of the
whole region of " nature " to the goal outside it. With men it is
otherwise. The best of them only succeed for a time in getting
their heads above the visible region, and attaining a glimpse of

Socrates, who alludes to the views of Alcmaeon about the brain as familiar to
himself in the autobiographical narrative of the *Phaedo*.

[1] *Phaedrus* 246*a*, ἐοικέτω δὴ συμφύτῳ δυνάμει ὑποπτέρου ζεύγους τε καὶ ἡνιόχου.
συμφύτῳ here should mean, as the word regularly does in Plato, literally *con-
cretae*, " grown together into one." It is inserted in order to insist on the
unity of the individual mind. We are to think of the driver and his horses as
a single organism.

what lies wholly beyond it, and then redescend. The worse are thrown into complete confusion by the restiveness of the horse of inferior strain and the unskilfulness of the horseman. Their horses lose their wings, and horses and horseman sink to earth, not to regain their old place until the wings of the soul have grown afresh. The magnitude of the fall is shown by the kind of life which the now incarnate soul leads in the body. Those who have " seen most " become philosophers, lovers of beauty, musical men or lovers ; then follow in descending order, law-abiding kings and soldiers, men of affairs and business, athletes and physicians, prophets and " initiators," poets and artists, mechanics and farmers, professional sophists and demagogues, tyrants. The rule which applies to all is that after each life a man receives the rewards of the deeds done in the body. None may recover his wings and return to the place from which he fell until ten thousand years are over, except one who chooses to live the life of the " philosopher or philosophic lover " three times in succession. For such a man the ten thousand years are reduced to three thousand.[1] For others the scheme includes, like that of the *Republic*, reincarnations in animal as well as in human bodies, but no soul can finally recover its wings after such a degradation until it has once more been reincarnated in human form, for the recovery of the soul's wings is only effected by *recollection* of the things of which the soul caught a glimpse when it was following the great procession of the gods, and it is only man to whom the experiences of sense suggest these recollections. A man in whom these recollections are being awakened is popularly thought " distracted," from his loss of interest in the things other men take seriously, but he is really " inspired " (ἐνθουσιάζων).[2]

Now our sensible experiences only suggest few and faint images of righteousness and temperance and the other forms, but beauty is much more impressively adumbrated in sense-experience, and the effect of the experience in awakening "recollection" is therefore exceptionally startling. In the soul which has all but lost the impression of heavenly beauty, the effect of its earthly adumbration is to provoke "brutal" appetite (τετράποδος νόμον, 250e) for intercourse with the beautiful body. But in a soul fresh from deep contemplation of spiritual beauty, the sight of earthly beauty

---

[1] Thus the scheme is the same as that of the myth of Er in the *Republic*. The assumption is that the normal extreme limit of human life is a hundred years. Reincarnations take place once in a thousand years in order that the rewards and punishments at the end of each incarnation may be on a tenfold scale. The privilege of escape from the wheel after three incarnations and the hope that in general it will be achieved after ten, are not mentioned in the *Republic*, but I suspect Orphic origin for part at any rate of this. Empedocles fixes the soul's period of exile from heaven at 30,000 " seasons " (Fr. 115, R.P., 181), and we may suspect that he is reckoning three ὥραι to the year, ἔαρ, θέρος, χειμών. On the details of the *Phaedrus* myth the student should consult the full commentary in Stewart's *Myths of Plato*.

[2] Cf. Browning's *Epistle of Karshish* with its treatment of Lazarus as " the madman," or St. Paul's language about the " foolishness " of the Cross.

arouses religious awe and worship ; the soul's wings begin to sprout, and this process, like the getting of teeth, is a mingled one of uneasiness with intervals of relief, pain in the absence of the beloved, rest and pleasure in his company. Hence the lover gladly forsakes all other society, neglects his property, and throws convention to the wind, so long as he can win the society in which he is getting his heart's desire. Men call this " being in love " ; it is really growing one's spiritual wings again (250d–252c). What sort of person will provoke this passion is a matter of the lover's peculiar temperament. In the best type of man the qualities which awaken it are " love of wisdom " and a " commanding personality " (252e) ; others are attracted by different gifts. In every case the " lover " aims at moulding the being he " idolizes " into the more and more perfect image of the " god " whom both serve, and the affection between them grows with every fresh step of the process (252c–253c).

But we must remember what we said about the difference in strain between the horses of the human soul. The better horse is modest and chivalrous, a " thorough-bred " ; the worse horse is a " bolter." So when the charioteer is wrapt in the contemplation of the beloved, the better horse modestly holds himself in, but the worse " bolts," in spite of rein and whip, from lust after carnal delight. The worse horse may be often " pulled to his haunches," but he persists in his struggles, and the time of really fierce temptation comes when the passion which began on one side is reciprocated on the other. If the temptation is successfully resisted, the pair have won one out of the three " Olympic victories " necessary to release them from incarnation in the flesh. Henceforward they have mastered the evil in themselves and won their freedom. But if their lives are directed only to the second-best, " honour," in the place of the first-best, " wisdom," the evil horse may get his way in an unguarded moment, and then there will be other such moments in their lives, though not many, as their conduct has not commended itself to their " whole souls." Their attachment will be real, but not so real as that of the pair who have won the mastery over themselves. At death, they are still " wingless " though " desirous to be winged," and even this is a gain. It is at least a beginning of the journey heavenwords, and the rest will come (253a–256d).[1]

This, then, is what association with a true lover may bestow ; intimate relations with the man who is " not in love " lead to a meanness of soul, falsely taken for a virtue, and a nine-thousand-years' period of " folly," spent on and under the earth. May Eros accept this recantation, grant Socrates not to lose his " skill in matters of love," and punish Lysias by converting him, as his

---

[1] The power and insight with which this account of the conflict between the spirit and the flesh is written should not mislead us into supposing that it must be concealed autobiography. Comparison with what Alcibiades says in the *Symposium* about the relations between himself as a boy and Socrates suggests that the model for Plato's picture of the lover who has come through the severest temptation unsmirched is to be found in Socrates and his behaviour to the beautiful and petulant boy.

brother Polemarchus has already been converted, to philosophy [1] (256e–257b).

Phaedrus is delighted with the fine speech to which he has just listened. Lysias himself could hardly match it. Perhaps he would not try ; he is a touchy man and was recently gravely offended by a politician who had called him a mere " writer of speeches " in depreciation. But, says Socrates, politicians who affect to despise " discourse-writing " are only disguising envy under the mask of contempt. They are vain enough of the decrees they propose and carry, and what is a decree but the record of a " discourse " to which the author has prefixed the names of its admirers, " the council " or " the people " ? And how much vainer a man is when his " discourses " are preserved in perpetuity as the " laws " of a State. Clearly, if there is any discredit it is not in composing discourses, but in composing them ill. And this raises the whole question, what is *good* writing ? (258d). This is the sort of problem which it gives an educated man real pleasure to discuss. If we neglect it and prefer to sleep out the warm noon-tide, the cicadae over our heads may carry our bad report to their patrons the Muses.[2] Accordingly, we now find ourselves launched on a serious inquiry into the problem of *style*. What is a good style ?

THE PRINCIPLES OF STYLE (259e–278b).—(Nominally the question under discussion is that of the canons of a sound *rhetoric*, but we shall see that it rapidly expands into a consideration of the character of " style " in literature in general. A speaker or writer has a case of which he wishes to convince his hearer or reader. The question is what principles may be laid down for the presentation of this case in the way which will be most effective. Thus the considerations urged by Socrates bear as much on the written exposition of a subject in an essay or a treatise as upon the spoken presentation of it to an audience. The reason for approaching the topic primarily from the side of spoken discourse is simply that, in the age of Socrates, there was no serious prose literature in existence. The one still extant prose work of importance of an earlier date than the supposed conversation between Socrates and Phaedrus was the book of Herodotus. The " pre-Socratic philosophers " had, indeed, attempted to state their views about φύσις in a sort of prose ; the Periclean age saw the first written manuals of " rhetoric " and medicine, and the first written discussions of ethical and political problems. But the writers of τέχναι made no pretensions to style, and their compositions were not regarded as " literature." Literary prose, as a vehicle for the artistic expression of reflection upon life, was the creation of Isocrates,

---

[1] The point of the remark about Polemarchus is unknown. Had he, as would be quite possible, fallen in with some belated survivor of the downfall of the Pythagoreans during his years in Italy ? *E.g.* with Philolaus ?

[2] Note the allusion in 259d to the saying familiar from the *Phaedo* that philosophy is the μεγίστη μουσική. It is assumed that the saying is already current ; hence we cannot be far wrong in supposing that its origin was Pythagorean

and at the assumed date of the conversation, Isocrates is still simply a composer of speeches to be delivered in the law-courts.)

It would seem obvious that the first prerequisite of a really good " discourse " is that the deliverer of it should know the truth about his subject. Yet the accepted view is that this is unnecessary. To compose a telling speech you need not know what are the δίκαια, the " rights and wrongs of the case " ; you need only know what the audience who are to decide the issue *think* right and wrong. You win your case by appeal to the " prejudices of your hearers." But this view will not bear examination. It would be a comic situation if Phaedrus, being under the impression that the word " horse " means a donkey, should be persuaded by a discourse on the usefulness of the horse in war to provide himself with a donkey [1] against his next campaign. It would be worse than comical if a public man with a persuasive tongue confused evil with good and led the community to embark on a policy based on the confusion. This would not be statesmanship, but the reverse of it. Possibly, however, the professors of rhetoric might reply that they do not claim for their art that it can teach us the principles of good and evil, but simply that even if you know these principles, you will not be able to turn your knowledge to account in practice unless you also follow their precepts.[2] Thus sound knowledge of good and evil would be an indispensable prerequisite for statesmanship, but mastery of the technical rules of rhetoric would be necessary for the statesman who needs to convince the public. So far as it goes this is a fair defence of rhetoric,—on one condition. The condition is that the rules in question form a real τέχνη or " art," the application of real scientific knowledge to practice. But there is a view that they are nothing of the kind ; " persuasion " is a mere empirical " knack " (τριβή) for which no rules can be laid down, and there is no " art of speaking " distinct from the knowledge of the true facts about the subject-matter of the discourses. This view demands consideration (259e–261a).

May we not define rhetoric as verbal " sorcery " (ψυχαγωγία) [3] whether practised in the courts, in other public gatherings, or in private life, and whether the issues on which it is employed are grave or trivial ? The writers on the subject, it is true, generally confine the sphere of the art to public discourses before law-courts and popular assemblies ; but they forget that such a restriction would amount to excluding Zeno and his paradoxes from considera-

---

[1] The implication is that Phaedrus is still a rich man ; he would have to serve in the cavalry, if called out, and thus belongs to the class of πεντακοσιο-μέδιμνοι or that of ἱππῆς.

[2] This, we may remind ourselves, is actually the view taken by Gorgias in the dialogue called after him. He disclaims any pretence to be able to " teach goodness."

[3] The word should be understood in its literal sense of " spirit-raising." The eloquent speaker deals with the ψυχαί of the audience as the sorcerer does with the ghosts he raises and lays ; he puts a " spell " on you. So we hear in our modern slang of " wizards " and " spell-binders " in public life.

tion. This would be a bad mistake. Zeno, like the speakers in the courts or the *ecclesia*, is a controversialist. Just as a skilled political or forensic pleader can make us think the same course or the same case just or unjust at his pleasure, Zeno makes us accept or deny the same proposition in the mathematics as he pleases. Rhetoric is thus universally skill in controversy. Success in it depends on ability to establish resemblances or similarities and to expose resemblances which have been tacitly presupposed by the antagonist [1] (261*e*). Now we are most readily led astray in cases where the dissimilarity between two things is apparently slight, and therefore a man who wants to confuse others but avoid being misled himself, as the controversialist does, needs to *know* what are the real similarities and dissimilarities between things, and this makes it ridiculous to talk of an " art of discourse " which can be divorced from " knowledge of the real " (262*c*). We may illustrate the point from the discourse of Lysias with which we have been concerned. Lysias is discussing the question whether a " lover " is a blessing or a curse. Now " love " is not, like " iron " or " silver," a word with a definite and undisputed meaning. Different persons understand very different things by the name. It is idle to ask whether a " lover " is a blessing or not, unless we begin by defining " love." Lysias never explains what he means ; in his opening sentence he introduces the word " lover " without any explanation. The ambiguity thus introduced into his speech is definitely an offence against art, a violation of a law of good style. He begins where he ought to have ended.[2] Socrates was better inspired by the local deities, since he opened his speech by the required definition.

A second grave fault in style is that there is no recognizable order in the discourse of Lysias. It is not the consistent development of a theme and has no organic structure. There is no discoverable reason why the various points of the speech might not have been made in a wholly different order. But a good discourse ought to have a definite organic structure, just like a living creature. There should be a definite plan underlying it which would be ruined if you inverted the order of its paragraphs.[3] Here again the discourse with which the Nymphs inspired Socrates presents an instructive contrast. It began by saying what " love " is, a kind of " madness " or " frenzy." Next it distinguished two main types of

---

[1] Cf. the appeals to " precedents " which are so common a feature of both forensic and political oratory. The παράδειγμα which Aristotle calls a " rhetorician's form of induction " (*Analyt. Post.* A, 71*a* 9) is just the " appeal to precedent."

[2] The right order of thought would be to say first what the passion " love " is, then to consider how it will affect the man who is dominated by it, and last of all to ask whether these effects will make him a better influence in a lad's life than the man who is not " in love." Lysias *begins* with this last question, and never raises the others.

[3] Socrates puts his finger on the defect which, above all others, is the most glaring fault of the bad stylist, neglect of the logical sequence of the parts of his essay or the chapters of his book.

madness, that due to human disease and that due to divinely sent " exaltation " above everyday " conventionalities." Then it went on to make a further subdivision of divine " exaltation " itself, and so to distinguish the " exaltation " of the lover from that of the " seer," the " poet," and the founder of a religion, and ended with an imaginative hymn in praise of Eros (264b–265c). Much of what we said was, perhaps, sportive, but there are two points about the method we followed which are of serious importance. When any subject is to be expounded, it is vitally important to define it, and to define it one must be able to " collect " its *disiecta membra* into a single " pattern " (ἰδέα), as we did when we reduced all the manifestations of " love " under the one head of " distraction " (παράνοια). But it is no less important, when we have got our single " pattern," to " divide " it again rightly into sub-patterns, like a skilful carver who disjoints an animal at the proper articula-tions. This was what we tried to do when we went on to distin-guish a " sinister," or left-hand and a " right-hand " distraction, and then carefully subdivided both again along the proper lines, so that we were left with a " sinister " love which we were entitled to denounce and a clearly discriminated " right-hand " or " divine " love which was eulogized as the source of the greatest blessings. (It was just this process of first " collecting " the definition and then making a scientific subdivision of the *definitum* on a proper *funda-mentum divisionis* which enabled us to give a rational justification for our answer and our approbation.) Socrates is devoted to this method of combined " composition " and " division," and is ready to follow the steps of the " dialectician " who possesses it, as those of a god. Thus we are brought to the conclusion that " dialectic is philosophy " in the wide sense in which that word means the capacity for seeing the real affinities in things, and so grouping them in well-defined *genera* ; and detecting the differences which mark off different *species* within the *genus*, is the first requisite of a masterly style. To be a true stylist, you must have a clear view of your subject as a whole, and be able to articulate it aright (265c–266a).

Phaedrus agrees that this is a good account of " dialectic," and that Socrates has a correct conception of a " scientific style." But Thrasymachus and the other teachers of prose style have not the qualities we have described. What they mean by " rhetorical style " is something different. They mean, in fact, the arrangement of the parts of a " discourse " on a certain model which they pre-scribe, but which has nothing to do with the kind of logical structure just described. To use technical terms, they say, *e.g.*, that a good speech must have its *exordium* (προοίμιον) ; then you must go on to the *narration* (διήγησις), which relates what you allege to be the facts of the case; next to the production of the *depositions* (μαρτυρίαι) of witnesses; then to a consideration of the *presumptions* (τεκμήρια) and plausibilities (εἰκότα) ; and there are many other subdivisions. (The precise meaning of the technical terms is in many cases uncertain, since some of them were not preserved in the later manuals of the art, and even of those which are preserved, we cannot be certain that they already had their later meanings as early as the fifth century. The reader may consult the notes in Thompson's edition of the dialogue.) Gorgias and his master Tisias insist on the importance of a dexterous art of exaggeration and extenuation; Polus and Protagoras before him on grace and appropriateness of verbal phrasing. We need not follow them into all these details, but we must test the worth of their theory of style as a whole ; perhaps its texture will look very loose if we view it in a clear light (266c–268a).

Suppose a man claimed to be a physician on the ground that he knew recipes for raising and lowering the body's temperature, producing a vomit and an evacuation and the like, would specialists like our friend Eryximachus admit his claim ? If he did not know also in what patients, when, and with what violence to produce these effects, they would say at once that he did not know medicine. So Sophocles or Euripides would say to anyone who knew how to make single speeches effectively but not how to construct an artistic whole out of them, " You may understand the preliminaries to play-making, but you don't know how to make a *play*." So Pericles, we may be sure, would have told us urbanely that a man who has learned the devices of the textbooks has only learned the preliminaries to " rhetoric." The art consists in knowing how and when to use the various devices to effect ($\pi\iota\theta\alpha\nu\hat{\omega}\varsigma$) and to make your discourse into a real *whole* (268a–269c).[1]

Admittedly *this* cannot be learned from any of the law-books : how then should a man set himself to acquire a really persuasive style ? To begin with, he must have a natural *gift* of expression, or he will be wasting time in trying to cultivate a barren soil. If he has the natural gift, its cultivation demands both knowledge and practice ($\mu\epsilon\lambda\acute{\epsilon}\tau\eta$), and is thus not wholly a matter of " art." In so far as it does depend on knowledge and thus is an " art," Lysias and Thrasymachus have misconceived the kind of knowledge required. What it is may be suggested to us by the facts about Pericles, the most effective of all our great orators. Over and above his natural gift of speech ($\pi\rho\grave{\sigma}\varsigma$ $\tau\hat{\omega}$ $\epsilon\acute{\nu}\phi\nu\grave{\eta}\varsigma$ $\epsilon\check{\iota}\nu\alpha\iota$, 270a), Pericles had the advantage of early association with Anaxagoras. This gave him a certain largeness of mental outlook which makes itself felt in his political oratory.[2] The great stylist, in fact, needs

---

[1] Note that Euripides is definitely associated here with Sophocles (268c). Both are assumed to be living and accessible. Hence we should date the conversation before the final departure of Euripides from Athens (408 or 407). The reference to Eryximachus and his father (268a) shows that if they are the persons of the same names who were implicated in the scandal of 415, it had not such serious consequences for them as it had for some of their circle.

[2] Of course, the allusion is half playful. The suggestion is that Pericles turned to account in practical statesmanship the Anaxagorean physical speculations about the sovereignty of $\nu\sigma\hat{\upsilon}\varsigma$; he made *mens agitat molem* into a political principle (270a 5).

to build on the same foundations as the great physician. If a man is to be more than a mere empiric in medicine, as we may see from the teaching of Hippocrates, he needs a scientific knowledge of the body, which can hardly be acquired without a knowledge of " nature " as a whole. He must know whether the human body is composed of one single ingredient or of many, and, in either case, he must further know how the substance or substances composing the human body are affected by each and all of the substances which medicine employs in its pharmacopoeia. Without this scientific basis, medicine would be a mere " fumbling in the dark." [1] The same thing is true of the " orator." He is trying to produce healthy convictions in the minds of his audience by discourses exactly as the physician produces healthy conditions in their bodies by his prescriptions. Hence anyone who undertakes to teach the art of persuasion needs first of all to have a thoroughly scientific knowledge of the *mind*. He must know what are *its* components and exactly how each type of discourse will affect them. In a word, he must have a sound psychology of human nature. Thus he must understand what different temperaments there are among his auditors, what different types of " discourses " there are, and why such and such a type of " discourse " appeals to such and such a temperament. And this is not all. The effective speaker, like the successful physician, must have skill in diagnosis. He must be able in practice to judge rapidly and surely of the temperament of an actual audience and the type of appeal which will go home to them. Only when he has thus diagnosed his hearers' temperaments and decided on the right kind of appeal to make will he be in a position to apply the rules given in the hand-books for producing the kind of effect which will be opportune (269*d*–272*b*).

The road to oratorical success we have described is, no doubt, a long and difficult one ; but can the writers of the handbooks really show us an easier short cut ? We know that, as has been already mentioned, they often say the " speaker " or " stylist " need not concern himself with realities or " truths " ; he need only aim at being plausible, and, indeed, should often prefer plausibility to truth. Thus if he is employed in a case where a plucky little man has beaten a stronger but cowardly man, he would, speaking

---

[1] Plato is thinking mainly of the doctrine of the four fundamental " humours " (blood, phlegm, red bile, black bile) on which the Coan school of medicine built up its humoral pathology, and is arguing that the physician must have a scientific knowledge of the action of each substance in the pharmacopoeia on each of these " humours." The counterpart would be a scientific knowledge of the " active principles," as Butler calls them, in the human mind and the way in which each may be stimulated or inhibited by the appropriate type of verbal appeal. The particular Hippocratean work alluded to is, perhaps, the περὶ φύσιος ἀνθρώπου, where the humoral pathology is expressly expounded. But see the discussion of Diés, *Autour de Platon*, 30 ff. The sure and rapid gauging of the temper of the audience, on which he rightly insists as all-important, is just the sort of thing of which there can be no τέχνη. No rules can be given for it ; it is a matter of αἴσθησις (271*e*).

for the defence, dwell on the improbability that the small man should have attacked a bigger man, or, if he spoke for the prosecution, he would try to suggest that there had been a concerted assault by several assailants.   In either case, the real facts of the situation are just what the clever advocate would take care to keep dark. But we must retort once more that one can only judge of the " plausibilities " in proportion as one knows the real facts.   (The advocate may rely on distortion of the facts, but he must know what they are if he is to distort them in a really plausible way.) So we adhere to our view that it is a long and a hard task to acquire the art of a persuasive style.   The time and labour required would be disproportionate if one's object were merely to make an impression on one's fellow-mortals, and not, as it ought to be, to make our words, like our deeds, acceptable to God.   (That would, of course, be the aim of a true statesman, who employs his knowledge of human temperaments and the way in which they may be appealed to, to enlist his fellow-citizens in the prosecution of good and the avoidance of evil.)   This is, in substance, all we have to say about the principles of an *art* of style.   It must be based on a masterly knowledge of the subject-matter dealt with and an equally masterly knowledge of the psychology of the hearers (or readers) addressed, combined wtih a natural gift of language (272c–274b).

We may now turn to the question, suggested by the sneer of the unnamed politician about Lysias (257c), whether it is a proper thing to perpetuate one's discourses in writing.   Socrates professes to have heard a story—Phaedrus prefers to think that he is inventing it—that, in the old days when Egypt was governed by gods, the god Thoth invented the art of writing and recommended it to Amon,[1] who then ruled at Thebes, as a device which would make the Egyptians wiser and improve their memories.   Amon reproved him, on the ground that written records tend to make us neglect the cultivation of memory by making it unnecessary, and to fill men with an empty conceit of their own wisdom.   They think they know a great deal which they have merely read without understanding and without any abiding effect on their minds.   The art of writing does not act as a substitute for memory ; it merely provides us with *memoranda*—convenient means of *refreshing* our memory from time to time.   A book is like a picture.   The figures of the picture may actually " look alive," but they cannot speak. So the words and sentences in a written book look full of wisdom, but if you question the book about its meaning, you can get no reply. A " discourse," once written down, comes into the hands of the unintelligent, as well as of the intelligent, and is exposed to misinterpretation.   If it is to be rightly understood, it needs the living voice of the author to explain and defend it.   Thus the written discourse is at best a lifeless image of the living thought which is

---

[1] Plato calls him Thamus, but the mention of Thebes shows what Egyptian god he has in mind.   Is the name Thamus, which has perplexed the commentators, due to a presumably wilful confusion with the Syrian Thammuz ?

written " in the soul of him who understands it." A gardener may, for amusement, force flowers in a " garden of Adonis," [1] but he takes care to sow the seeds of crops about which he is in earnest in the appropriate soil and to wait months for their maturing. So the man who is in earnest about raising the fruit of righteousness and goodness will not trust to forcing it by writing his deepest convictions in ink ; he will trust to the slow and steady cultivation of them in his own soul, and in those of others with whom he is in constant personal contact. When he commits his thoughts to writing, it will be partly as a *memorandum* against the " forgetfulness of his old age," partly because such literature affords a worthy form of entertainment in our hours of relaxation. So we may tell Lysias—and we might say the same thing to Homer and the poets, or to Solon and the " composers " of laws—that if any of them has really understood what his " works " can effect and what they cannot, and how secondary a place they hold by comparison with his living thought—such a man has a claim to a very different name from that of λογογράφος ; he is a true " philosopher." But if he really has nothing better to give mankind than the painfully elaborated phrases and clauses of his writings, he deserves to be called a mere poet or speech-writer or " law-writer." [2] The man ought always to be greater than his book or poem or code (274*b*–278*e*).

This conviction that a man's personality ought to be greater than his literary " work," and, in particular, that the true philosopher is a great personality whose very deepest thoughts are those which he cannot set down " in black and white," was one Plato held strongly and retained to the end of his life.[3] It explains why he never attempted to put in writing any of his own profoundest metaphysical speculations. They were the fruit of a " way of life," and, to be understood, pre-supposed the living of the same life on the part of the recipient. To record them for the world at large would have been merely to court dangerous misunderstanding. Even so, Carlyle, as the jest has it, wrote thirty-seven volumes to persuade the world that silence is golden. Naturally he could not tell us the secret of the " golden silence." That could only be told to a man with the soul of a second Carlyle, and such a man would discover the secret without needing to read the thirty-seven volumes.

[1] As we should say, " in a hot-house." The *horti Adonidis* were pots in which flowers were rapidly forced, to die again equally rapidly.

[2] νομογράφον (278*e* 2) cannot mean " writer of music." The word appears to be used nowhere else in literature. Here it obviously means a " code-maker," and the point is that if a man like Solon really exhausted all his wisdom in the mere excogitation of the clauses of a code of laws, so that in personal intercourse he merely talked his own code, as some writers are said to talk their own books, he deserves to be spoken of with disparagement. The word is invented to convey the same sort of depreciation as λογογράφος.

[3] Compare the insistence on the point in *Ep.* vii. 341*c*–342*a*, 343*e*–344*d*, where the imagery and language seem directly reminiscent of our dialogue.

Epilogue (278c–279c).—Has Socrates any message for his friend Isocrates, the younger rival of Lysias? He can only conjecture what the young man's development will be, but he believes that Isocrates has better natural endowments and a nobler temper of soul than Lysias. Probably, if he continues in his present profession, he will out-distance all rivals and competitors, and it may be that he will be led " by a diviner impulse " to still higher things, for there really is a " strain of philosophy " in him.

Nothing remains now but that Socrates should take leave of the spot where he has spent his hour of *siesta* with a brief prayer to Pan and its other tutelary spirits. His prayer is that " he may become fair in the inward man, and that the outer man may be conformable to the inward; that he may regard wisdom as the true riches and that his wealth may be such as none but the temperate can carry." Thus the prayer is for good of mind, body, and fortune, and is worded in a way to remind us of the Socratic estimate of the relative importance of the three.

There is no real need to enter into the idle questions which have been raised about the significance of the allusions to Isocrates. What is said is strictly true and appropriate to the assumed situation. Isocrates certainly had greater parts than Lysias and stood on a higher intellectual and moral level. He showed his superiority in parts by becoming the real creator of literary prose style, and his superiority in character by deserting " speech-writing " for the foundation of a school for the training of the young for public life. However defective Plato may have thought the training he gave, the simple fact that it was based on a generous Pan-Hellenism, and that Isocrates was the recognized mouthpiece of this Pan-Hellenism among the publicists of his age, fully explains Plato's ascribing to Socrates the remark, quite likely enough to have been actually made, that there was a strain of philosophy in the man. There can be no doubt about the historical fact of the influence of Socrates on Isocrates.[1] As to the alleged " feud " between Isocrates and Plato, of which much has been made by some modern writers, there is really no evidence for it. The frequent expressions in Isocrates' writings depreciatory of " science " and " eristic " as a propaedeutic for the statesman are, indeed, pretty clearly meant specially for the Academy, but the attempts to find sarcastic rejoinders in Plato to these little acerbities have not really been successful, and the ingenuity devoted to these attempts seems to me to have been simply wasted. After all, Plato and Isocrates had a good deal in common in their views on practical politics, and they were neither Alexandrian *literati* nor German Professors. We in this country can quite understand how two eminent men can differ in their

[1] On this see Burnet, *Greek Philosophy, Part I.*, 215–219; " Socratic Doctrine of the Soul," in *Proceedings of the British Academy*, 1915–16, p. 235 ff. So the point of Isocrates' comments on the attack on Socrates by Polycrates is that Socrates was as absurd a theme for invective as Busiris for eulogy. Polycrates showed his silliness by denouncing a man of exemplary virtue no less than by eulogizing a monster (Isocr. xi. 4).

philosophical programmes without becoming personal enemies, or how the bigger man of the two can afford to take an occasional " rap over the knuckles " from the lesser in good part. (No one supposes, for example, that Shakespeare's relations with Ben Jonson were disturbed by Ben's occasional quips.) Hence I cannot but agree with Professor Burnet in thinking that the tradition followed by Cicero, which represents Plato and Isocrates as being on personally friendly terms, is likely to be the true one.[1]

In taking leave of the *Phaedrus*, we may note that while it supplements the *Gorgias* in its conclusions about the value of " style," it modifies nothing that was said in the earlier dialogue. The moral condemnation pronounced on the use of eloquent speech to pervert facts and produce false impressions remains the same. So does the verdict that the sort of thing the professional teachers from Tisias to Thrasymachus profess to expound is not a science but a mere " trick " or " knack " (and therefore cannot be conveyed, as they professed to convey it, by " lessons "). In adding that a thorough knowledge of a subject-matter and a sound knowledge of the psychology of the public addressed furnish a really scientific basis for a worthy and effective style, Plato is saying nothing inconsistent with the results of the *Gorgias*. There is thus no sufficient ground for thinking that the teaching of the *Phaedrus* represents a later " development " from the more " Socratic " position of the *Gorgias*. Socrates cannot have lived in the Athens of the Archidamian war and the subsequent twenty years without having had occasion to turn his thoughts to the problem of the value of " rhetorical " style, and there is no reason why he should not actually have reached the conclusions of the *Phaedrus*, though naturally we cannot *prove* that he had.

See further :

THOMPSON, W. H.—Plato's *Phaedrus*.

ROBIN, L.—*Phèdre* (*Collection des Universités de France*, Paris, 1933).

RITTER, C.—*Platon*, ii. 39–62 ; *Platons Dialog Phaidros*², pp. 1–28a.

RAEDER, H.—*Platons philosophische Entwickelung*, 245–279.

NATORP.—*Platons Ideenlehre*, 52–87.

STEWART, J. A.—*Myths of Plato*, 306–396 (*Phaedrus Myth*) ; *Plato's Doctrine of Ideas*, 62–65 and Part II.

DIÈS, A.—*Autour de Platon II*, 400–449.

---

[1] Cicero, *Orator*, xiii. 42, " me autem qui Isocratem non diligunt una cum Socrate et Platone errare patiantur." Cf. Diogenes Laert. III., 8, where we are told that the Peripatetic Praxiphanes wrote a dialogue in which Isocrates figured as the guest of Plato. The theory of a rivalry has no ancient tradition behind it. This is the more significant that the rivalry between Aristotle and the school of Isocrates is quite well attested (Cicero, *de Oratore*, iii. 35, 141, *Orator*, xix. 62). I should suppose that Plato's purpose in ending the dialogue with a marked compliment to Isocrates is to show that it is *not* meant as a polemic against him.

CHAPTER XIII

THE *THEAETETUS*

IT seems possible to date the composition of the *Theaetetus* more precisely than that of any other Platonic dialogue. For the main discussion is introduced by a short preliminary conversation between the Megarians, Euclides and Terpsion, whom we met in the *Phaedo* as members of the inner Socratic circle. Terpsion relates that he has just met Theaetetus of Athens, who is being conveyed home from the Athenian camp at Corinth after a battle, wounded and suffering severely from dysentery. The thought of the loss such a man will be to the world reminds Euclides that Socrates had once met Theaetetus, just before his own death, and had prophesied a distinguished future for the lad. Euclides professes to have heard all about this from Socrates himself; he was so struck that he at once wrote out *memoranda* of what Socrates had told him, and afterwards corrected and enlarged them with the help of Socrates himself.

Since much stress is laid on the point that Theaetetus, who is called a distinguished " man " by Terpsion (142*b*) was a mere " lad " in the year 399, it is clear that the battle from which Theaetetus, as the whole tone of the Prologue implies, was carried home to die, must fall a good while later. As Dr. Eva Sachs has shown,[1] the known engagement which best satisfies the implied conditions is that of the year 369, in which Epaminondas broke through the Athenian and Spartan lines on Mt. Oneion.[2] Manifestly the dialogue was written as a tribute to the memory of Theaetetus, shortly after his death, which Euclides and Terpsion regard as certainly impending. This brings us to 368 or the beginning of 367 as the date of its completion. Thus, as Burnet points out, it must have been finished on the very eve of Plato's departure from Athens to throw himself into his great political adventure at Syracuse, and probably with full consciousness that he was, for the time, about to abandon the studious life for that of affairs.

Several points in the introduction call for remark. (1) When Euclides explains that, to avoid tediousness, he has adopted the

[1] In her dissertation *de Theaeteto Atheniensi* (Berlin, 1914), which finally disposes of Natorp's singular theory that the dialogue is a juvenile work.
[2] Xenophon, *Hellenica*, vii. 1, 41 ; Bury, *History of Greece*, p. 608. The engagement appears to have been a trivial one, but even trivial engagements involve casualties. Theaetetus apparently owed his death more to dysentery than to his wounds (142*b*)

directly dramatic form of narration (143*b–c*), we must, of course understand that this is really Plato's explanation of his abandonment of the method adopted in all the great dialogues of his literary prime (except the *Phaedrus*). Henceforth, with a possible exception for the *Parmenides*, we shall find him returning to the simply dramatic method of his earliest writings.[1] This is, no doubt, because in these later works the old interest in reproducing a living picture of Socrates and his contemporaries has at last yielded pretty completely to the more philosophical interest of developing the subject-matter. The *Theaetetus* is the latest dialogue in which the personality of Socrates is made prominent. (2) The stress laid on the prophetic insight shown by Socrates in his estimate of the lad Theaetetus seems unintelligible, unless we are to take the meeting of the lad and the old philosopher, and the forecast made by the latter, as genuine historical facts. They are just the sort of facts which might properly be made the most of in a work meant as a " tribute " to the memory of Theaetetus. (3) Euclides' account of the way in which he worked up his narrative, with the help of Socrates himself, may be a fiction, but Plato evidently thought it a natural fiction. We may fairly infer that admirers of Socrates actually took down such notes of striking conversations, and that Plato himself may have used such records, made by himself or others, as material for his Socratic dialogues. In the present case, by appealing to the record of Euclides he contrives to let us know that he was not himself actually present when Socrates met Theaetetus, though we might otherwise have expected him to be there. Possibly this is explained by the illness which also kept him away from the death-scene of the Master a few weeks later. (4) The introduction of Euclides and Terpsion into the narrative, like the preoccupation with the personality of Parmenides and Zeno in the *Parmenides*, and the appearance of a " visitor from Elea " as chief speaker in the two later dialogues, which are made to continue the conversation of the *Theaetetus*, shows that we have reached a period in Plato's life when his special interest is to define his attitude towards the Megarian developments of Eleaticism. This is a matter which will call for consideration more particularly when we go on to deal with the *Parmenides* and *Sophistes*. We shall find Plato in these dialogues taking up an attitude of decided hostility to the one-sided intellectualism of the school as tending to pervert philosophy into a mere barren sporting with " abstractions." The same attitude is shown in our dialogue by the emphatic recognition of the contribution of sensation to real knowledge. By virtually dedicating the dialogue to his old friend Euclides,[2]

---

[1] On the question whether the *Parmenides* is earlier or later than the *Theaetetus*, see the next chapter. In any case, they must be nearly contemporary. Probably the difficulty of keeping up the indirect method in the *Parmenides* was the immediate occasion for its abandonment.

[2] Euclides can hardly be assumed to have died in the interval between 369 and 367. That would be too much of a coincidence.

Plato gives us to understand that his growing dissatisfaction with the contemporary "Megarians" implies no change in his sentiments towards the founder of the school, an old and faithful member of the group who had been lifelong admirers of Socrates.

The main conversation is dated very shortly before the famous trial of 399, as we see from the concluding sentence (210*d*), where Socrates explains that he has to attend at the offce of the "king," to put in his answer to the indictment of Meletus. The parties present, besides Socrates, are the Pythagorean geometer Theodorus, the lad Theaetetus, his companion the younger Socrates (147*d*), who is a "mute personage," and possibly one or two other unnamed lads. The scene is an unnamed *palaestra* (144*c*), possibly that in the Lyceum. We learn in the course of the dialogue that Theodorus comes from Cyrene, and that he is a friend and admirer of the now deceased Protagoras, though he professes to be strictly a mathematician, wholly unversed in the methods and terminology of contemporary Athenian "philosophy" (146*b*, 165*a*). That he belonged to the Pythagorean order is indicated by the appearance of his name in the list of Pythagoreans given by Iamblichus (*Vit. Pythag.* xxxvi. 267). A notice preserved by Proclus in his commentary on the First Book of Euclid's *Elements* (Friedlein, p. 66) shows that Eudemus in his History of Mathematics ranked Theodorus with Hippocrates of Chios as one of the greatest of fifth-century geometers. Xenophon (*Mem.* iv. 2, 10) mentions him in a way which implies that Socrates knew him, though this may be only Xenophon's inference from our dialogue. Theaetetus, it is important to remember, was a member of Plato's Academy and one of the very first mathematicians of the fourth century. Eudemus, as we see from Proclus (*loc. cit.*), named him along with Archytas and Leodamas as one of the three prominent geometers of the fourth century. From notices in the Scholia to Euclid's *Elements* and elsewhere, we gather that he was one of the first mathematicians to begin the systematic study of the types of "quadratic surd" worked out to its completion in Euclid's Tenth Book, and he is still more often referred to as the geometer who completed the theory of the "regular solids," by adding to the three known to the Pythagoreans (tetrahedron, cube, dodecahedron) the remaining two (octahedron, icosahedron).[1]

Though the dramatic power of the *Theaetetus* is still remarkable, it has features which show that we are near the point at which

[1] There is a little difficulty here. The meaning of the statement must be that the fifth-century geometers already knew the constructions for the inscription of three of the figures in the sphere : Theaetetus added the constructions for the remaining two and thus completed the doctrine of Euclid, *Elements*, xiii. But Plato definitely attributes to the Pythagorean Timaeus a knowledge of all five regular solids (and this is why these solids were known in antiquity as the "figures of Plato"). Careful reading, however, will show that Timaeus is never allowed to *mention* the inscribing of the octahedron and icosahedron in the sphere, as he does that of the tetrahedron and icosahedron and dodecahedron. This seems to me confirmation of the tradition that these constructions were unknown in the fifth century.

dialogue will become a mere conventional form for what is in reality an essay on a set theme. The theme is propounded at the beginning of the discussion and is then pursued, except for one remarkable digression, owned to be such by the author himself, with a system and strictness we have not yet met in any of the major dialogues. The Socratic cross-questioning is becoming a conscious pursuit of the " critical " method, brought to bear on a single determinate problem. This makes the analysis of the dialogue unusually easy to follow.

INTRODUCTION (143*d*–151*e*)

The problem to be discussed is still made to arise, in the fashion of the *Protagoras* or *Republic*, apparently almost by accident. In the old way, Socrates is made to speak of his interest in the young and to ask Theodorus whether any of the lads of Athens have struck him as showing remarkable promise. Theodorus says that there is one whose remarkable combination of quick intelligence, perseverance, and modesty afford grounds for hoping very great things of him, Theaetetus. It is curious that this remarkable boy has a quaint physical resemblance to Socrates himself. This gives Socrates his opening. He calls Theaetetus out of the group of lads who are anointing themselves after their exercises and begins a conversation with him. Theodorus, he says, has just made a remark about our facial resemblance. As Theodorus is not a portrait-painter, such a remark from him is not very important. But as he is an eminent man of science, his opinion about our mental endowments carries weight. Hence Socrates would be glad to discover whether the lad's mental gifts really bear out the very high commendation they have just received. He will put this to the test by asking a question. Theaetetus is learning geometry and other things from Theodorus. Now to learn means to be acquiring knowledge. But what exactly is knowledge ? Can Theaetetus offer any answer to this question, one which has often perplexed Socrates himself ? The lad begins, as Plato so often makes an interlocutor do, by an enumeration. Geometry and the other things taught by Theodorus are knowledge ; so is shoe-making or carpentry.

Of course, as Socrates points out, this is no answer to the question. To answer the question what knowledge is by saying that shoemaking is knowledge only amounts to saying that *knowing* how to make shoes is knowledge. Knowing how to make furniture is also knowledge. Our problem is to say what we mean by the " knowing " which appears as a " determinable " in both these statements. Theaetetus seizes the point at once, since it makes the problem under consideration the same in type with a mathematical one which he and the younger Socrates have just solved. That problem was to find a common formula for what we call, in our modern terminology, " quadratic surds," or " irrational square roots." As stated by Theaetetus, the question is treated, exactly as it is in Euclid, as one about " lines " (γραμμαί). You cannot construct a straight line commensurable with your unit of length, such that the square upon it is 3 or 5 or 7 or 11 or 13 or 17 times the area of the square on the unit line. But you can devise a general formula for all these cases as follows. We may divide the integers into two classes: those which are the product of two equal factors (4, 9, 16, etc.), and those which are not (e.g. 6, 8). We may then call the first class " square " and the second " oblong " numbers. This enables us to make a correlated division of all terminated straight lines. If the area of the square described on such a straight line can be represented, in terms of the area of the square on a unit line by a number which is the product of two equal factors, we call the line in question a " length " (μῆκος); if this area is represented by a number which is not the product of two equal factors, we call the corresponding line a " power." Lines of the first class are all commensurable with one another, since they are all " measured " by our standard unit of length; lines of the second class have *no* common measure, but the areas of the squares on them have (e.g. √3 and √5 have no common measure, but an area of 3 square feet and one of 5 square feet have one, namely, the square on a line 1 foot long). This is why the lines of the second class are called " powers "; they are not themselves commensurable with one another but their " second powers " are commensurable.[1] Thus, since every terminated straight line under consideration belongs to one and only one of these two classes, Theaetetus has succeeded, by the use of dichotomy, in strictly defining the class which we should call " quadratic surds " (148b).

Socrates is delighted with this achievement, and only wishes Theaetetus to apply the same ability to determining the class of " sciences " or " knowledges," by bringing them all under one common determinable (148d). Theaetetus is eager to solve the problem, but does not feel equal to the task, though he cannot persuade himself to let it drop from his mind. This shows that Theaetetus is " pregnant " with a thought which he cannot successfully bring to the birth. Now Socrates, like his mother, practises the obstetric art, not, like her, on the bodies of women, but on the souls of men. He has no spiritual offspring of his own to bear, as midwives are no longer fruitful when they enter on their profession.[2] But he has great skill in assisting at the birth of a younger man's thoughts, and in discerning whether they are healthy and well formed or

---

[1] The use of the word δύναμις in this sense of " quadratic surd " was presumably an experiment in language which did not perpetuate itself. The name for the " quadratic surds " which became technical in the Academy and has passed thence into Euclid and later mathematics generally, is εὐθεῖαι δυνάμει σύμμετροι, straight lines whose squares have a common measure (Eucl. *Elements*, x. Def. 3).

[2] Note that it is implied in the comparison that Socrates had not always been spiritually " past procreation," any more than his own mother had always been barren.

sickly and misshapen. This discernment is the more necessary that the offspring of the mind, unlike that of the body, are sometimes mere fantastic " ghosts " (εἴδωλα) of thoughts.[1] Socrates is like his mother in another respect. Midwives are excellent match-makers, since their professional skill makes them good judges of the physical suitability of a couple to one another. So Socrates has often judged shrewdly that some of the young men who have frequented his company are not really " pregnant " with thoughts at present, and in such cases he has found mates for them in whose society they have ceased to be barren, such as Prodicus.[2] He has now an occasion for the practice of his gift. He will help Theaetetus' spiritual first-born into the world, and then we will try it, to see whether it is a genuine thought or a mere " changeling " (149*e*–151*d*).

FIRST DEFINITION OF KNOWLEDGE (151*e*–186*e*)

KNOWLEDGE AND SENSATION : THE THEORY STATED (151*e*–160*d*).—With this encouragement Theaetetus attempts a first definition. A man who knows a thing " perceives " the thing he knows (as our own proverb says, " seeing is believing "). So we may say, as a first suggestion, that " knowledge (ἐπιστήμη) is just perception " (αἴσθησις).[3] This would seem to be only another way of saying what Protagoras expressed by the formula that " man is the measure." Theaetetus, who has often read Protagoras (152*a*), agrees with Socrates that Protagoras meant by this that " what *appears* to me, *is* to me ; what *appears* to you, *is* to you." In fact, " I perceive this " = " this appears to me " = " this *is* so to me " (152*b*). " Sense " (αἴσθησις) is thus always apprehension

---

[1] The suggestion is that if—as is not the case—a woman sometimes gave birth to a real child and sometimes to a " changeling," the midwife's task would become even more responsible than it is. She would have to decide in a given case whether the offspring should be cast away. The passage lends no support to the erroneous popular theory of infanticide as a feature of Athenian life.

[2] The transparent irony of this passage has actually been missed by some of the zealots for the " sophists." It is the minds which Socrates judges to be barren, the persons on whom his own endeavours would be thrown away, *i.e.* the second-rate, whom he hands over to Prodicus and his likes. That the conception of the obstetrics of the soul is a genuine Socratic fancy is shown by the allusion in Aristophanes' *Clouds*, 137 ff.

[3] I render αἴσθησις in this statement by " perception," rather than by " sensation," since it is not clear to me that Theaetetus is at first using the word with the specific meaning of discernment by *sense*. Until Socrates leads him to make his statement more precise, he seems to me to be employing αἰσθάνεσθαι, in the fashion of the pre-Socratics, for direct apprehension of any kind, whether sensuous or not. What a man is directly apprehending he is sure of (ἐπίσταται). For this sense of ἐπίστασθαι cf. Heraclit. Fr. 35 (Bywater), τοῦτον ἐπίστανται πλεῖστα εἰδέναι, " they *feel sure* he—sc. Hesiod—was so wise." That αἴσθησις is meant at first to include *all* immediate conviction is shown by the introduction of the argument about numerical propositions, 154*c* ff.

of something which *is* (τοῦ ὄντος), and is infallible, and therefore is the same thing as *certain* knowledge (ἐπιστήμη) (152c).

We should note very carefully exactly what is the theory here ascribed to Protagoras. (That the interpretation of his *dictum* is the correct interpretation, or at least that supposed by his readers at large to be correct, is clear, since it is assumed that all the parties to the conversation are quite familiar with the context of the saying, and not one of them suggests that there can be any mistake about its meaning.) The view Plato ascribes to Protagoras is *not* " subjectivism." It is not suggested that " what appears to me " is a " mental modification " of myself. The theory is strictly realistic ; it is assumed that " what appears to me " is never a " mere appearance," but always " that which is," " reality." But Protagoras denies that there is a *common* real world which can be known by two percipients. Reality itself is individual in the sense that I live in a private world known only to me, you in another private world known only to you. Thus if I say the wind is unpleasantly hot and you that it is disagreeably chilly, we both speak the truth, for each of us is speaking of a " real " wind, but of a " real " wind which belongs to that private world to which he, and only he, has access. No two of these private worlds have a single constituent in common, and that is precisely why it can be held that each of us is infallible about his own private world. Protagoras is not denying the genuine " objectivity " of each man's private world ; his equation of " appears to me " with " is, *is real*, to me " is meant to insist on this objectivity. But he denies the reality of the " common environment " presupposed by " intra-subjective intercourse." His thesis is strictly metaphysical, not psychological.

But now, how if Protagoras really meant something more elaborate than this, and explained his meaning more fully to his intimates " in secret," though he gave the world at large only this one hint of it ? There is a " far from contemptible " (οὐ φαῦλος) view which we might regard as implied by the Protagorean dictum, and it is as follows.[1] *All* truth is strictly relative. Nothing, *e.g.*, is big or hot " absolutely," but only " big " or " hot " relatively to some *standard* of comparison. If you selected your standard differently, the same thing could truly be said to be " small " or " cold," relatively to the new standard. This applies even to existential propositions. You cannot say absolutely " this *is*," any more than you can say " this is so." You can only say " this is, is real " relatively to something else. For the very word " is " is a misnomer. The things we speak of as " existing " are really events which " *happen* " as a consequence of movements ; movement is the only thing which is ultimately real in the universe, as

---

[1] *Theaet.* 152c–d. Since Socrates suggests that this doctrine was only told by Protagoras to his followers "in a mystery," *sub sigillo* (ἐν ἀποῤῥήτῳ), clearly nothing of the kind can have been found in his book. The suggestion is that if you think out all that is really implied in the *Homo mensura* formula, you will be led to the metaphysical theory now to be expounded.

all the " wise," with the solitary exception of Parmenides, seem to have held from time immemorial. All life, bodily or mental, is movement and activity; cessation of movement is lethargy, stagnation, death (152c–153d). Now apply this to the case of anything we perceive by sense, *e.g.* a white expanse. We must not say that the white we see is " in " a body outside our own, nor yet that it is " in " our own eye. It is not anywhere. The truth is that what we call our " eye " and what we call the " outside world " are simply two sets of motions. When they come into contact and interfere with one another, something " happens " (γίγνεται) momentarily as a consequence of this interference, and this something is the colour, which is thus neither " within " us nor " without " us, but is just the joint product of *two* factors, the system of motions which are outside the organism and the system of motions which are the eye[1] (153e). This explains at once why each of us lives in a strictly private world. Any change in either of the causal factors, the " motions " in the larger world and the " motions " in the organism, may affect their joint product, and therefore a man and a dog will not see the same colours, nor a man in health the same colours as a man out of health. If the perceived quality, " hot," " white," or what not, were simply an affection of " that by which we measure or apprehend," *i.e.* of our own organism or " sensibility," it ought not to be modified by changes in anything else (as, in fact, it is by, *e.g.*, variations in illumination) ;[2] if it were simply a character of " that which is measured or apprehended " (the external object), it should similarly be unaffected by changes internal to the organism (but, in fact, it is affected by them). The facts thus show that the perceived world is a function of two variables, *my* special organism and its environment ; hence it is *necessarily* a " private " world (154b).

Before we can judge such a theory on its merits we need a further clarification of our thoughts. On the " private-world " theory, six dice will not only " appear " but " be " at once " many " and " few ": " many," if a group of four is my standard of comparison, " few " if my standard is a dozen. Reflection on such cases leads us irresistibly to make three affirmations which seem to be self-evident and yet not all mutually compatible : (1) nothing can become greater in bulk or number except by being augmented

---

[1] We shall see later on that this is not a complete account of the matter. The " product " of the two motions is itself a motion, and this motion has *two* aspects. The " seeing eye " is as much a momentary event as the seen colour. As to the terminology of 153e, the *active* motion (τὸ προσβάλλον) must be conceived as that of the eye's own " visual ray " issuing out of the eyeball ; the *passive* (τὸ προσβαλλόμενον) is what we commonly call the " external " object on which this supposed visual ray impinges. *We* should think more naturally of reflected light striking on the retina as the προσβάλλον, but Plato always presupposes the Empedoclean conception of seeing as effected by a " searchlight " thrown out by the eye into the world around us.

[2] In 154b, τὸ παραμετρούμενον is simply a paraphrase for αἴσθησις. Socrates inserts the παραμετρούμενον simply to echo the curious use of the word μέτρον in the formula of Protagoras.

(αὐξηθέν); (2) that to which nothing has been added and from which nothing has been subtracted has been neither augmented nor diminished ; (3) what once *was* not but now *is* must have " come to be " in the interval (*i.e.* there has been a transitional process of " coming into being," 155*b*).[1]

Yet the case of the dice, or the case in which Socrates is one year taller than Theaetetus but the next shorter, seems to create a difficulty. In this last case, Theaetetus has grown, but Socrates has neither grown nor shrunk. He *is* now, what he was *not* last year, " shorter," and yet there has been no process of " coming to be shorter." How are we to explain the paradox? We cannot explain it at all to a corporealist who denies the reality of acts and processes and the invisible generally. But it might be explained by the theory of certain more refined (κομψότεροι) persons, whose secret Socrates offers to disclose (156*a*). Their theory is this. As has been already suggested, the only reality is motion. There are two types of motion, the active and the passive. The mutual friction or interference (τρῖψις) of an active and a passive motion regularly gives rise to a *twin* product, " sense "+" sensible quality," and neither of these is ever to be found without its " twin." And this twin product is itself, again, a pair of movements, though of movements more rapid than those which gave rise to it. Thus, to apply the theory to the case of vision, you have first two " slower " causative " movements " (the " active " movement *here* is supposed to be the " event " which is the visual apparatus, the " passive " is the event we call the environment) ; when there is an " interference " of these two motions, in that very process there emerge two correlated " quicker " movements, neither of which ever exists without the other,[2] " vision in act " and " seen colour." Thus the couple " seeing eye " and " colour seen " are themselves a dual more " rapid " event produced as an effect by the mutual interference of the two " slower " causal movements. It follows that all predication is strictly relative. The " causal " motions themselves are strictly relative to one another, each is " active " or " passive " only in relation to its correlate ; and similarly in the " effect," the seen colour is seen only by *this* " seeing eye," and this " seeing eye " sees only *this* colour. " Being " is thus a strictly relative term. To speak accurately, we ought never to say " *x* is," but " *x* is, relatively to *y* " ; if we omit the qualification, it is only because of an inveterate linguistic bad habit. Socrates does not

---

[1] Note that we have here in outline the fundamental thought of the Aristotelian doctrine about " generation " and " corruption." The ἀπορίαι connected with the problem are one of the topics of the *Parmenides* (155*e*–157*b*).

[2] Thus the theory is closely analogous to Aristotle's doctrine that in actual perception the αἴσθησις and the αἰσθητόν are, while the perception lasts, one and the same. The important difference is that in the account given here, *both* the αἰσθητόν and the αἰσθανόμενον only exist actually during the process of perception ; apart from the process, " eye " and " colour " only are " potentially." On Aristotle's theory, this is true of the " seeing eye," but not of the seen colour.

commit himself to this theory of "absolute becoming," any more than to any other, but he has stated it because we cannot dispose of the assertion that " is " = " appears to me " without deciding this still more fundamental question (158*d*).

We note that the difference between the Protagorean formula and the doctrine now given as that of certain unnamed "fine wits " is that the first is a piece of " epistemology," the second is ontology, and professes to give the grounds for the individualistic or " solipsist ' epistemology. The proposition that *my* perceived world only exists *for* me, and that it is meaningless to ask whether your " world " and " mine " can contain one and the same object, is only one special consequence of the much more far-reaching doctrine that " is " itself has no meaning unless one adds the qualification " relatively to." It is now being asserted not merely that perceived qualities only exist " for " the percipient who is aware of them, and he is only " percipient " of just these qualities, but that the correlated active and passive " slower " movements, thing and environment, only *are* relatively to one another. (Thus, *e.g.*, the statement that a particle *A* exists would actually *mean* that *A* interacts in a certain way with *B* and *C*, and so on for *B* and *C* themselves.) This is why the doctrine described here cannot be disposed of in the summary way in which Mr. Bradley has disposed of the " phenomenalism " of many modern scientific men in *Appearance and Reality*. The persons of whom Mr. Bradley is thinking have really not got behind the restricted doctrine of the " relativity " of perceived quality to percipient. At the back of their minds there is still the notion that both percipient and perceived quality are effects of something which, though not itself perceived, *is*, or is real in an absolute sense, and thus they are easily convicted of inconsistency with themselves. But the theory we are now dealing with asserts that the " slower motions," assumed by the victims of Mr. Bradley's dialectic to be simply " real," are *themselves* purely relative, each such " active " motion being relative to a specific " passive " motion and *vice versa*. It is thus not open to the criticism that it regards anything whatever, perceptible or imperceptible, as simply real ; " this is real " is, on this view, always an incomplete statement which, as it stands, is strictly devoid of significance.

It is not clear from what quarter Socrates is supposed to have learned the theory. He is clearly not inventing it, since he represents it as the " secret " of certain refined wits. Nor do I think it likely that Plato has devised the whole thing for himself simply as a metaphysic which might be urged, and in fact would have to be urged, by a far-seeing defender of the Protagorean formula. The insistence on motion as the only reality at once suggests a Heraclitean influence, and the elaborate kinematic working out of the thought further suggests that the κομψοί of whom Socrates is thinking are persons with a strong mathematical interest. If we had more information than we have about the curious blend of

Heracliteanism and Pythagorean mathematics represented in our tradition by the stories told of the mysterious Hippasus, we might be able to say something more definite. From Plato's own point of view, the theory would be perfectly acceptable as an account of "pure" sensation; but we must remember that, as it is part of the object of the dialogue to show, no piece of knowledge, not even the crudest statement about present fact, ever is a *mere* deliverance of sensation.

With this general metaphysical theory as a presupposition, we could now dispose of the superficial objection to Protagoras that some "appearances"—those of dreams, delirium, fever—are deceptive. The world of the sleeper or the fever-patient is as real to him, while his dream or fever lasts, as the world of the man awake and in health is to him. And it is not true to say that there is any conflict between the way in which the world appears *to one and the same percipient*, according as he is awake or asleep, ill or well. On the theory, the "twin-product," sensation + sensed quality is a function of the complex, organism + environment. But it is an immediate consequence that, since a sleeping or delirious organism is different from a waking or healthy organism, the result of interaction with environment must be different. Socrates asleep is different from Socrates awake in important organic respects, and, on the theory we are considering there is no "self" or "percipient" but the organism as it is at the moment. Thus the *sensa* of Socrates asleep are real relatively to Socrates asleep, exactly as those of Socrates awake are real relatively to Socrates awake, and it would be abandoning the whole theory of the relativity of "being" to judge of the reality of the *sensa* of Socrates asleep by reference to those of Socrates awake (157e–160c). The *sensa* of any percipient organism at any moment are relative to the state of that organism at that moment, and to nothing else, just as that organism at that moment is relative to those *sensa* and to nothing else. (The *esse* of the organism at the moment *t*, we may say, is to perceive the *sensa* it perceives at that moment; the *esse* of those *sensa* is to be perceived by it at that moment; neither organism nor *sensa* have any further reality.) Consequently the "world" of any percipient at any moment is private to *that* percipient and that moment. "My perception is inerrant, for it is relative to my world (ἐμὴ οὐσία) at that moment."[1] Thus the theory we have stated justifies the Heracliteans in saying that all is motion, Protagoras in saying that "man" is the measure, and Theaetetus in saying that sense is knowledge (160d–e).

---

[1] 160c, ἀληθὴς ἄρα ἐμοὶ ἡ ἐμὴ αἴσθησις—τῆς γὰρ ἐμῆς οὐσίας ἀεί ἐστιν, where note (a) that ἀεί means not "always" but "at each moment," "at a given moment," and (b) that ἡ ἐμὴ οὐσία does not mean "my own being," as though the thought were that what I perceive is a "subjective" πάθος or state of my own body or mind, but "the reality which is mine," a real world of objects which is my own *private* world. The crux of the whole theory is that it is an attempt to insist at once on the *objectivity* of the world I perceive and on its purely private character.

THE THEORY EXAMINED.—*First Criticism* (160e–165e).—The thought of which Theaetetus was in labour has now been fairly brought into the world, Our next task is to consider whether it is a genuine piece of thinking or only a " changeling." To give the lad breathing-time for recollection, Theodorus partially takes his place as respondent while Socrates raises a number of critical doubts. (*a*) How does Protagoras justify his selection of man in particular as the " measure " ? The theory would equally warrant the statement that any creature—a pig, a baboon, or a tadpole—is the " measure," provided only that it is sentient. (*b*) If each of us is the " measure " of reality and unreality in his own world, where has Protagoras any advantage over his pupils ? How can he claim to correct a pupil's views about the reality of a world which, on the theory, is private to the pupil and relative to the pupil as its " measure " ? (The very attempt implies, contrary to the theory, that there is a " world " of some kind common to Protagoras and the pupil, and that Protagoras is a better " measure " of it than the other.) Was the professional career of Protagoras a prolonged practical joke ? Protagoras might, however, fairly say that this sort of " criticism " is mere caricature.[1] We must examine the proposed identification of sense-perception with knowledge in dead earnest. So we go on to ask (*c*) whether when we *hear* foreigners speaking their own language we also *know* " what they are saying," or whether when a person who cannot read *sees* a written page he *knows* what is written on it. The only possible answer is that in such a case one does know what one actually hears or sees, the pitch of the syllables or the shape and colour of the letters, but one does not know the *meaning* of the foreign vocables or the written words. (Thus the formula knowing = perceiving by the senses will not cover the case of knowing the meaning of such symbols ; their meaning can neither be heard nor seen.) (*d*) Suppose a man has seen something and then shuts his eyes, but still remembers what he saw. He no longer sees it, but can we say that he does not *know* what he has seen and still remembers ? There is real point in these questions, but we must take care not to " crow " over Protagoras and his theory prematurely. If he were alive, he would probably have known how to make a telling rejoinder to such cavils. As he is dead and has no one to represent him, we must try to act as his advocates ourselves, and to plead the cause as effectively as we can (164e–165a).[2] If we are to press mere verbal points, any

---

[1] *Theaet.* 162*d–e*. This might be, but need not be, a hint that there had been attempts to discredit the formula of Protagoras by caricatures of this kind. But I think it very rash to indulge in conjectures about Antisthenes—to whom I can discover no certain allusions in Plato—as the author of the arguments. The ἀντιλογικοί were a fairly numerous class, and we may suppose that many of them exercised their wit on so tempting a theme. Protagoras would have an easy retort to the first of the four objections. A tadpole is quite a good " measure " of the " world " with which the tadpole has to concern itself.

[2] The personification of the " discourse " of Protagoras as an " orphan " whose natural guardians are neglecting their duties lends no colour to the silly

ἀντιλογικός could quite easily make many more formidable than those we have made ourselves, without ever coming to close quarters with Protagoras' real thought.

SOCRATES' PROPOSED DEFENCE OF PROTAGORAS (166a–168c).— Protagoras might fairly say that he would not have been affected by the question about memory which puzzled a lad like Theaetetus. He would have exposed the absurdity of talking about memory as if it meant the " persistence " of the state of the organism in which it was at the moment of stimulation. He would have insisted on the point that, according to his theory, each of us is not one percipient but a different percipient with every change in the state of his organism. And he would have urged that it is for his opponent to refute him directly by proving *either that a man's " senses "* (αἰσθήσεις) *are not private to himself, or, alternatively, that, granting this position, the sense-object which " appears " or " is " need not be private.*[1]

Meanwhile, the thesis of Protagoras remains untouched. Each percipient has his own strictly personal and private world ; it is not merely his " apparent " world, but a real, though private, world. And yet there is a difference between the wise man and his neighbours, a *practical* difference. The wise man is one who can influence another so that the other man's private world, which appears and really is bad, is made to appear and be good (166d). Thus the abnormal perceptions of the diseased organism are as much a disclosure of reality as the normal perceptions of the healthy. The physician does not attempt to argue the patient into denying their reality. He subjects the patient to a regimen which brings his perceptions into accord with those of his fellow-men, and thus makes them " wholesome " or " useful," whereas they were, before treatment, dangerous and unwholesome. So the " sophist," who is the physician of the soul, aims not at giving a pupil " truer views " —that would be impossible, if the pupil is the " measure " of his own real world—but at giving him " better " and more wholesome views of life (166d–167c). The defence made by Socrates for Protagoras thus amounts to crediting him with a " pragmatist " view. Any one belief, actually held, is as " true " as any other, but some sensations and some ways of thinking are " better," that is, " more useful in practice " than others. It is implied, though not actually said, that the " useful " way of perceiving and thinking is that

legend about the prosecution of Protagoras and the destruction of his book. Socrates is merely jesting over the reluctance of Theodorus to commit himself to a "non-professional" controversy. Theodorus is called the natural guardian of the orphan simply because he professes to be an old friend and admirer of its author. The image, of course, implies that the book of Protagoras had *not* been destroyed, but had survived its " father." Only, no one will venture on an " official " defence of it.

[1] *Theaet.* 166c. In this alternative, the first position, that each man's αἰσθήσεις are " private," cannot be contested. I see with my own eyes, and no other man can see with them, any more than I can see with his eyes. Thus the issue between realism and " absolute phenomenalism " is rightly made to be just whether two men, each using his own private senses, can perceive an object which is " common " to both of them.

which agrees with the perception and thought of your " social environment," since it is only such agreement which makes concerted action possible. To be gravely " eccentric " in your perceptions or your moral convictions puts you into the class of the insane and makes practical co-operation with your neighbours impossible. The root of the matter is that, though the notion of a " common " natural or moral world is, strictly speaking, a fiction, it is a fiction which is necessary to life. The practical urgencies of life require that my private world and your private world should not be very dissimilar. If they are sufficiently alike, by a useful fiction we can act " as if " we had a common world ; where the divergence is too great to admit of this fiction, when I call black what you call white, one of us needs a physician for the body or the soul. By altering the state of the percipient, the physician, according to the Protagorean theory itself, necessarily also alters the character of his " world."

Since Socrates offers this interpretation as a substitute for an " official " exegesis, it is clear that it cannot have been given by Protagoras himself ; since it is welcomed by Protagoras' old admirer Theodorus, we may infer that it is offered as a fair and honest attempt to explain what Protagoras meant, on the assumption that he was a man of intelligence and that his doctrine was intended to be compatible with his claims for himself as a practical teacher. So far as I can see, it is not only offered in good faith, but is about the best defence which can be made for the view that the " common " world is strictly the *creation* of the " intersubjective intercourse " on which all practical co-operation depends. Against modern statements of pragmatism it has the advantage that it does not attempt the task of equating " true " with " practically useful " ; it simply sets aside the distinction between " true " and " false " as irrelevant to human life, and *replaces* it by the obviously relevant distinction between " useful " and " harmful." Our attention is thus concentrated on the fundamental question whether the abolition of the distinction of true from false really leaves this all-important practical distinction between useful and harmful standing or not. This ultimate issue is so serious that we cannot allow the case for the pragmatist to be prejudiced by being left to the championship of a boy, even if he is, like Theaetetus, a boy of genius ; Theodorus must take the defence on himself (168c–169e).[1]

[1] It may be advisable to warn some readers again against the really wanton attempt to find a hidden attack on Antisthenes in the pleasantries interchanged between Socrates and Theodorus at 169b. Theodorus compares Socrates with Antaeus, who compelled every one to wrestle with him, merely because Socrates is so insistent on dragging Theodorus himself into a philosophical argument he would rather decline. This leads naturally to the mention of Heracles as the person who finally vanquished Antaeus. It is needless to look for any more recondite reason for the allusion. And it is still more needless to suppose that when Socrates speaks of the numerous Heracleses with whom he has had stiff " bouts," he is thinking of his own friend and companion. It is to be hoped that we shall hear less in the future of the imaginary " feud " of Plato with Antisthenes since Wilamowitz has uttered his timely protest against this *Antisthenes-Legende*.

SECOND EXAMINATION OF THE PROTAGOREAN THESIS (169*d*–172*c*, 176*c*–179*b*).—The task now before us is to examine the " pragmatist " philosophy on its own merits. The examination falls into two sections, between which the famous panegyric on the life of devotion to " useless science " is inserted, admittedly as a digression. It strikes us at once, as a common experience, that every one knows there are some things about which he thinks himself wiser than others and other things about which he thinks others wiser than himself (170*a*–*b*). Every one admits that there are things about which he is ignorant and incompetent and needs to be taught or directed. And by " wisdom " and " ignorance " men suppose themselves to mean true and false belief (δόξα) respectively. According to the thesis of Protagoras, this belief that some of my beliefs are true and others false, being one of my beliefs, must be true. It must be true, since it is a belief, that there are things of which a given man is *not* the " measure." This is a direct consequence of Protagoras' own principle, and yet it contradicts that principle. And the worst of it is that if there is one point on which every one, even those who would most readily concede that any one man's sensations are just as veridical as any other's, is agreed, it is that when you come to the question what is wholesome or hurtful, each of us is not equally the " measure " for himself. That is just why we need the expert physician (171*e*). So in moral matters, even those who hold that there is no common standard of right and wrong, but that " right " means simply for any community what that community agrees in approving, never think that " expediency " is a purely relative matter. No one holds that the expedient is what a given community thinks expedient, though many persons hold that right is just whatever the community happens to think right. Every one holds that there is a *common* standard of expediency (172*b*). These considerations are meant to lead up to the conclusion that the plausible " pragmatist " substitution of the " useful " for the " true " as the criterion of value in beliefs fails at its central point. It refutes itself by presupposing that the value of the belief " this is useful " itself must be estimated by reference to a standard of " truth." " It is true that this practice is useful " cannot simply mean " it is useful to believe that this practice is useful." The full development of the thought is postponed for a moment by the introduction of the eulogy of the contemplative life.

DIGRESSION.—*The Contemplative Life* (172*c*–176*c*).—How far the pragmatist criterion is from being self-evident or universally accepted we may see by contrasting the whole attitude towards life of the philosopher or true man of science with that of the " man of affairs," and the man of law. The former is free where the latter is a slave,[1] as we can see by comparing the style of their " discourses."

---

[1] *Theaet.* 172*d*. The distinctive mark of the " free man " is that all his time is σχολή, " leisure," " free time," " his own time." The " life of business " is not " free " because in business a man's time is not " his own " ; it is engrossed

The one can follow up his thoughts wherever they lead ; time is no object to him, and the length of an argument no obstacle, so long as it leads him to the " reality." The other has to plead with a time-limit and under a double control. He must speak " to his brief "— his opponent will take care of that—and he must adapt himself to the prejudices of his "lord and master," the court, or he may have to pay dear for it, and thus cannot afford to have a single-minded eye to simple truth. The other is free, as we are at this moment, to follow up any line of thought which seems promising ; he is the master, not the slave, of his " case." Hence the violent contrast between the whole characters of the typical thinker and the typical " practical man." The former, in an extreme case, barely knows where the law-courts and places of public assembly are, or what is being done in them ; he belongs to no political "club," and cares as little about the social as about the serious side of such institutions. He knows nothing of the current political and social gossip, and is not even alive to his own deficiency. You might say that, while his body is here in Athens, his mind freely roams over the universe as its domain. When he is dragged down into the world of petty local affairs, proceeded against in the courts for example, he is lost in such a strange situation, and the practical man sets him down as an absent-minded fool. He cannot make a telling invective because he is quite unaware of the personal scandals which furnish the appropriate matter. He is equally ineffective in eulogy, since the topics of the ordinary eulogy, the subject's illustrious descent and splendid wealth, are unimpressive to him. The biggest estate seems a little thing to one who is accustomed to think in terms of the spaces of astronomy, and the finest pedigree laughable to one who knows how many kings and how many beggars there must be in every genealogy, if we could only trace it back through unrecorded generations. Hence the popular contempt of him as a man who is so wrapt up in his star-gazing that he cannot see what is under his nose.

But from the philosopher's point of view, the brilliant practical man is equally absurd. Take him away from the field of small personal concerns and set him to think about the ultimate issues of life, what are right and wrong, what are human happiness and misery, and how is the one to be found and the other shunned—in a word, take him out of the realm of the temporal into the eternal, and he is helpless in " discourse," for all his forensic " acumen."

This conflict between opposing standards of valuation is inherent in " mortality," and that is the very reason why the man who means to be happy must make it his supreme aim to " escape " from mortality. The only way of escape is " to become assimilated

by the demands of those whom he serves—his customers, patrons, clients, " the public." The thought reappears in Aristotle's *Ethics* and *Politics*, where the best life for man is identified with the " noble use of leisure," and the standard in education is made fitness to prepare the recipient to make this right use of his " leisure."

to God as wholly as may be," to exchange temporality for eternity. And "assimilation" means becoming "righteous and pious and wise." The difficulty is to convince men that the real reason for this pursuit of goodness is not the advantage of a reputation for goodness, but the fact that goodness and wisdom make us like God and therefore constitute real "manhood," and confer the only real happiness.

The whole passage recalls, and is obviously meant to recall, the spiritual mood and even the phraseology of the *Gorgias* and *Phaedo* But its connexion with the present argument is loose, and hardly amounts to more than this, that the worldly man's estimate of the philosopher and the philosopher's estimate of him furnish the best proof that there is no single accepted standard of valuation. The most natural way of accounting for the presence of the digression is that of Burnet, that it is an expression of the mood in which Plato is contemplating his own coming absorption in the necessarily largely uncongenial mundane life of the Syracusan court. The ideal of the world-renouncing pure "scientist" had never been his own; his early ambitions had been definitely political, and his mature conviction was that the gifts of the philosopher ought to be consecrated to the work of practical administration, but we can readily understand that he would have a keen sense of the sacrifice he was making to public duty and the pettiness of the personalities and problems with which he was now called to mix himself up.[1] It would be a bad mistake, though the mistake has been made, to find in so splendid a passage a polemic against the aims of his older rival Isocrates. Whatever the limitations of Isocrates were, Plato must have sympathized with his attempt to give his pupils at least a broader and nobler outlook on the problems of public life than that of the mere party-man of a little Greek πόλις ; the whole picture of the "man of affairs" who is pitted against the philosopher suggests in its details an admirer of Antiphon or Thrasymachus rather than a figure from the school of Isocrates, the last place where the cult of "successful unrighteousness" would be likely to be in favour.

Second Criticism of the Protagorean Thesis concluded (176c–179b).—To return. We had just said that though the thinkers who identify reality with change and those who teach that "what appears to anyone is for him the reality," are ready enough to extend these formulae to right and wrong, no one seriously contends that what a city agrees to regard as *good* or *useful* must really be so, so long as the agreement continues. Every one recognizes that what is really good or profitable is so independently of the beliefs which may be entertained about it. Now this suggests a generalization of the problem raised by the saying of Protagoras. When a city makes regulations to ensure good or advantage, it is acting with a view to the *future*. So we may ask, granting that the *Homo mensura* formula is valid for convictions about the present,

[1] *Greek Philosophy, Part I.* pp. 244–5.

is it also valid for convictions about the future? If a man feels hot, he *is* hot. *Soit;* but if a man believes that he is going to have a fever with a " temperature," while his physician denies it, what then ? In such a case the physician's forecast is certainly a better " measure " of what is going to be the layman's " reality " than the layman's opinion. So the best " measure " of the sweetness or dryness of next autumn's vintage is the husbandman ; a skilled cook's judgment about the enjoyment a company will receive from the dishes he has prepared is sounder than their own. Protagoras would be a better judge than one of us about the effect of a speech one of us was going to deliver. Generally, whenever a future issue is in question, the specialist will be the best " measure " of other men's experiences as well as his own. The *Homo mensura* formula thus is invalid in all cases where there is a reference to *future* experiences. And this rids us of the doctrine that any and every belief is true, which is, moreover, self-refuting, since it implies its own contradictory. But we have still to examine the metaphysical theory which is the foundation of the dictum that *actual present* sensation and the judgments (δόξαι) based on it are always true.

Final Refutation of the Identification of Knowledge with Sense-perception (179d–186e).—The complete examination of the theory that actual present sense-perception is knowledge demands a consideration of the already mentioned metaphysical theory that nothing is real but movement. We cannot get any coherent statement of the grounds for this theory from its official representatives, the Heracliteans, who disdain connected exposition and affect to speak in cryptic aphorisms ; we must try what we can make of the doctrine for ourselves (179e–180c). We must remember, too, that Melissus and Parmenides maintain the very opposite—that what is is one and unmoving. A complete examination would involve studying the views both of the " men of flux " (the ῥέοντες) and of the " faction of the one-and-all " (the τοῦ ὅλου στασιῶται) ; it might end by carrying us over into one of the camps, or by leaving us in the comically persumptuous position of standing alone against both parties. Still we must make the venture, and we will begin by considering the Heraclitean view (180c–181b).

Everything is always in motion : what is the precise sense of this ? There are two easily distinguishable types of " motion ": (*a*) one which includes translation and rotation, which we will call *locomotion* (φορά) ; (*b*) another illustrated by the transition from youth to age, from black to white, from hard to soft ; we will call it *alteration* (ἀλλοίωσις). Is it meant, then, that everything is at every moment changing both its position and its quality, or only that each thing is at every moment exhibiting one or other of these changes ? If the statement that there is *no* rest or stability in the world at all is meant strictly, we must take the former interpretation. Nothing ever keeps the same quality for the tiniest interval, any more than it retains the same position (181e). Otherwise there would be some sort of stability about things.

Let us bear this in mind and remember also the further details, which are part of this same theory, of the way in which the mutual interference of two of the "slower" motions gives rise to the twin effect sensation + sensible quality. The theory was that when two such "slower" motions meet, the result is a *definite* process of sensation + a definite sensible quality, *e.g.* a "seeing of white"+ "white seen." But if nothing has any permanency, there is no such definite process of seeing white, and no such definite white seen. The process of seeing white itself is at any moment turning into some other process, and the white seen is turning into some other quality. We must not even speak of "colour-vision" and "colour," since both process and quality are always turning into something else. It will be no more true to say at any moment that a man is seeing or having sensation of some other kind than that he is not having it, and therefore, if sensing is knowing, it will never be more true to say that a man is knowing than to say that he is not knowing. The safest answer to any question would be to say, "It is so and it is not so," but even this is more than we should be really warranted in saying, since the very word "so" implies a determination which, on the theory, never exists (183*b*). These considerations dispose finally of both statements: that every one is the "measure," and that knowledge is sensation. Both must be false, if the theory of absolute "fluidity" on which they themselves rest is to be upheld. Theaetetus would like to proceed now to consider the rival Eleatic theory that "nothing happens," there is no "fluidity" at all. But his wishes must not be indulged. Socrates met Parmenides, who was then an old man, in his own youth and was powerfully impressed by his "noble depth."[1] If we discussed his view, we should very likely misunderstand it, the examination would have to be very long and searching, and we should be diverted from our present task, which is to practise "spiritual obstetrics" on Theaetetus (184*b*).

Socrates now enters on a line of thought which is by far the most important contribution the dialogue has as yet made to the solution of its problem. He calls attention to the, so far neglected, distinction between sensation and thought, or judgment. We can point out the bodily instruments which a man uses in seeing, hearing, touching. He sees with his eyes, hears with his ears, and so forth. Or to be still more accurate, since it is always the man, that is his ψυχή, which sees and hears, we should do well to say rather that he sees and hears *through* his eyes and ears (184*d*).[2]

---

[1] *Theaet.* 183*e*. There is a similar reference to this encounter at *Soph.* 217*c*, and the *Parmenides* professes to be a third-hand report of it. It seems to me that the emphatic way in which the impression made on the youthful Socrates is insisted on in both references shows us that Plato wishes us to regard the meeting as a real fact, and there is no reason why it should not be one (see Burnet, *E.G.Ph.*[3], p. 168, n. 3).

[2] The point of the distinction here made between that *with* which (ᾧ) and that *through* which (δἰ οὖ) we see and hear can be better expressed in English differently. It might be made by objecting to the accuracy of the expressions

Eyes, ears, and the rest of the body are not the agents in perception but the *implements* (ὄργανα) of it—the first appearance of the word " organ " in this sense. For each " implement " there is what Aristotle was later to call its " proper " (ἴδιον) sensible. None can do the work of another. Colour can only be taken in by the channel of the eye, sound through the ear. But if a man is *thinking* about two such sensibles of different senses, comparing and discriminating them, or counting them as " two," pronouncing them like or unlike, asserting that they are " really there," the soul is considering the matter " by herself " (αὐτὴ δι᾿ αὑτῆς) without the employment of a bodily " implement " (185d).[1] If we try to make a list of the determinations of an object which are thus made " without any bodily organ," we have to reckon among them not only " reality " (οὐσία), number, sameness, difference, likeness and unlikeness, but good and bad, right and wrong (186a). Thus the ultimate categories of value, like those of " fact," are apprehended by thought, not by sense. In fact, they are asserted as the result of reflection, comparison, and discrimination : this explains why animals are as capable of sensation as men, and babies as adults (186c), but sound convictions about " reality and value " (οὐσία and ὠφέλεια) are only attained by us with time and pains and education. Now we cannot have knowledge without apprehension of a " reality " (οὐσία) which is known. Hence it follows that " knowledge " is not to be sought for in the affections of our sensibility (τοῖς παθήμασι) but in the mind's reflection upon them (ἐν τῷ περὶ ἐκείνων συλλογισμῷ, 186d). And this finally proves that knowledge is *not* the same thing as sensation (*ibid. b*).

SECOND DEFINITION. KNOWLEDGE IS TRUE JUDGMENT
(187b–200c)

The common name for the process of reflection, comparison, and discrimination to which the occurrence of our sensations gives rise is " belief " or " judgment " (δόξα, τὸ δοξάζειν). The word δόξα is being used here in a way characteristic of Plato's later dialogues. In his earlier writing δόξα had commonly been thought of as contrasted with ἐπιστήμη ; it had meant " belief," with the implication that the belief is a mistaken one, or at any rate a doubtful one ; in our dialogue, and henceforward, the meaning is judgment, intellectual conviction in general, without any suggestion of disparagement. This is one of the many indications that a chief

---

" the eye sees," " the ear hears," and the like, on the ground that they obscure the point that both seeing and hearing are functions of a unitary central consciousness. This is what Socrates means by saying that there are not a group of αἰσθήσεις seated inside a man, like the warriors in the fabled " wooden horse " of Troy.

[1] It does not occur to Socrates to consider the view, afterwards taken by Aristotle, that some at any rate of the functions enumerated here might be discharged by a " common sensorium " (κοινὸν αἰσθητήριον), placed by Aristotle in the heart.

difference between mature Platonism and the Socraticism out of
which it developed is that the former attributes a decidedly higher
value to beliefs which do not reach the level of demonstrated
" science," that is, to our " empirical knowledge " of the sensible
world. We must not suggest that judgment is knowledge, since
there are such things as false judgments. But we may take it as
an amended definition that knowledge is *true* judgment (187*b*).

If we are to examine the truth of this statement, we must begin
by considering the difficulty suggested by the old arguments which
have been used to show that a false judgment is impossible. The
old argument, which we have met in the *Euthydemus*, was that either
you know what you are judging about or you do not. If you do
know, you cannot judge falsely; and if you do not, you cannot
make any judgment at all, because your mind is a mere blank
about that of which you " know nothing." The point has now
to be considered elaborately with a view to discovering the specific
character of *true* judgments. If a man knows *both* A and B, it
would seem that he cannot mistake one for the other ; if he knows
A but not B, how can he compare A with the merely unknown ?
If *both* A and B are unknown, is not the impossibility of a confusion
even greater (188*a–c*). Perhaps we may avoid these difficulties
if we say that a false judgment is a belief in " what is not " (188*d*),
thus avoiding all reference to " knowing " in our definition.[1] But
the " unreal " (τὸ μὴ ὄν), it may be said, is just nothing at all, and
you can no more think and yet think nothing than you can see and
yet see nothing. To think or believe is always to think or believe
something ; to think nothing is all one with not thinking at all.
(Just as Parmenides had long ago declared that " what is not " can
neither be thought nor spoken of.) This consideration leads us
to try a third explanation of what we mean by a false judgment.
We mean thinking that one reality (one ὄν) is some *other* reality,
thinking that something is *other* than it is (ἀλλοδοξία) ; false
thinking is thus the mental confusion of one reality with another
(189*c*), *e.g.* thinking that " fair is foul and foul is fair." In the
Sophistes we shall find that this is the true account of the matter
and can be successfully defended against the Eleatic dialectic.
But the defence will depend on recognizing that the Eleatic metaphysic itself requires a grave modification ; there is a sense in
which " the unreal " can be both thought and spoken of. In our
dialogue Socrates is not allowed to probe the question to the bottom ;
he has already explained that he is not prepared at present to
examine Eleaticism as a metaphysical theory. He contents himself therefore with raising the question within what limits the
" confusion " of one reality with another would seem to be possible.

[1] The difficulty it is intended to avoid by the new formulation arises from
the ambiguity of the word εἰδέναι, which may mean either " to be acquainted
with " or " to know *about*." It is suggested in effect that we may eliminate
the ambiguity by recourse to metaphysics ; we will say that false belief is
belief in something " unreal " (in a μὴ ὄν). But, as we shall see, this at
once raises the Eleatic problem how it is possible to think the " unreal " at all.

To understand the very possibility of such a confusion, we must begin by recognizing that thinking is a kind of argument (λόγος) in which the mind carries on a debate within itself, asking itself a question and answering its own query. The judgment, once formulated, is the verdict or conclusion which puts an end to this internal dispute (190a). In what conditions is it possible for this verdict to involve " confusion " of one thing with another ? At first sight, the old dilemma about the impossibility of confusing a thing you " know " either with something else which you " know " or with something you do not " know " appears equally formidable when you substitute the word " believe " or " think " for " know " (190b–191a). But we seem to have been wrong in admitting the premisses of the dilemma. Clearly a man who " knows " Socrates might mistake an " unknown " stranger for Socrates, if he saw the stranger in the distance. The hard and fast distinction between " what I know " and " what I do not know " is false to fact and rests on the deliberate ignoring of the consideration that there is such a thing as " learning," " getting to know " something one did not know before (191c). Let us consider the nature of this process.

We may represent the process figuratively thus. There is something in each of us like a wax block prepared to receive the " impressions " of signets of all kinds ; the quality of the wax is very different in different persons. We may regard sensation as a process in which an object stamps an impression of itself on the wax (the whole of the traditional language about " impressions " and " ideas " is ultimately derived from this passage).[1] How definite this impress is and how long it will remain undeformed depends on the original quality of the wax. So long as the impress remains, we may say that a man has memory and knowledge (191d). Now consider the case of a man who " knows " the impresses left on the block, and at the same time is attending to his present sensations. We may say that the confusion with which we have identified error can only arise in one specific way. If I " know both Theodorus and Theaetetus and am simply thinking about one of them, I cannot confuse him with the other. If I " know " only one of them, I cannot confuse him in thought with the other, who is wholly unknown to me. If I neither " know " nor am

[1] In particular, the Aristotelian description of perception as a process in which the soul " receives the forms of *sensibilia* without their matter, as the wax receives the shape of the iron signet-ring without the metal," is seen at once to be directly based on the simile of the wax block, which is consequently the far-away source of the whole mediaeval doctrine of " sensible " and " intelligible " *species*. Note that the suggested theory is a psychologizing version of the doctrine that " knowledge is recollection." The first stamping of the wax with a wholly novel pattern gives " acquaintance " ; ἐπιστήμη arises when the wax is stamped with the pattern a second time and the pattern is " recognized " as already familiar. The whole argument would have been easier to follow if Attic, like Ionic, had possessed the word εἴδησις, which might then have been specialized to mean " acquaintance." Plato can discriminate οἶδα from ἐπίσταμαι, but he has no verbal noun which stands to οἶδα as ἐπιστήμη to ἐπίσταμαι.

actually seeing either, confusion of thought is impossible. It can only come in in one case ; when I " know " both parties, and so have the " impressions " made by past perception of both still remaining in the waxen block, but also am actually seeing both or one of the two, I may try to " fit " the new " impression " or " impressions " into the old " imprints," and may fit them into the wrong ones. That is, I may make an error in *recognition*, like that of the man who tries to put his foot into the wrong shoe. Thus " false judgment " will depend on mistaken *recognition*, and consequently will only be possible when there is a misinterpretation of an actually present sensation. Such misinterpretation may be caused by any of the defects of memory symbolized by the various defects which make a given block of wax unsuitable to receive a clear-cut impression, or to retain it permanently, or to receive many such distinct impressions without crowding and superposition of one on another. The result is that error cannot arise in sensation taken by itself, nor in thought taken by itself, but only " in the conjunction of sensation with thought " (195*d*). *I.e.* a false judgment is always a misinterpretation of present sensation, from which it would seem that true judgment, which the definition under consideration identifies with knowledge, is always the correct interpretation of present sensation by thought.

On reflection, however, this theory proves to be unsatisfactory in spite of its attractiveness. For it is not the fact that all error is misinterpretation of present sensation. A man may falsely think that $7+5 = 11$, and most men do make arithmetical errors of this kind in operating with big numbers. And they do not make such mistakes only when they are counting things present to their senses, but when they are simply thinking of numbers and numerical relations. Thus error (and by consequence true judgment) cannot be restricted to the interpretation of present sensations. There may be false (and also true) judgments where the " sensible " does not figure as a constituent of the judgment at all (195*d*–196*b*). Thus our simile of the waxen block has not done what we hoped it would for us. (It has the merit of taking into account the *facts* of learning and forgetting, ignored in the crude old argument against the possibility of " false beliefs," but it leaves the possibility of sheer *intellectual* error where it found it.[1])

To cover the case of purely intellectual error we must amend our account of ἀλλοδοξία, and this may be done if we borrow a hint from a current statement about knowledge. (It is true that a mere " disputant for victory " would deny our right to use any such statement while we are still in quest of a definition of knowledge, but the fault, if it is one, is inevitable, and we have committed

---

[1] The one criticism I should feel inclined to pass on Burnet's analysis of the dialogue (*Greek Philosophy, Part I.*, 237-253) is that he seems to make Plato into a Kantian by ascribing to him the view that all knowledge contains as a *constituent* a factor supplied by the " manifold of sense." This seems to me to miss the point of the illustration from false judgments in arithmetic.

it already every time we have used such phrases as " we know that . . .," " we understand that . . .," and the like.) Knowing is commonly said to be the " having " of knowledge (197*b*). But we might improve on this statement by distinguishing " possession " and " having." A man may " possess " or " own " a cloak without actually " having it on." So possibly a man may " possess " knowledge without " having " it. In fact, we may distinguish " possession " from " having in *use*." A man who has caught and caged a multitude of wild birds " possesses " them all, but may not actually have any one of them in hand, though he can " put his hand " on one when he wants it (197*c*). Let us then introduce a new simile. The mind is like an aviary ; when we are babies the aviary is empty (Locke's " empty cabinet ") ; each new piece of knowledge we acquire is like a wild bird caught and caged. But actual knowing is like putting our hand on the bird we want and taking it out of the cage. Now a man may put his hand on the wrong bird instead of the one he wants, since the captured birds are alive and can fly about in the cage. So we may " possess " a certain knowledge, and yet when we want to use it, we may not be able to recapture it, we may capture the wrong piece of knowledge, and this will be the case of the man who makes a false judgment (197*d*–199*c*).

Clearly the new suggestion has advanced the argument. As Socrates says, the distinction between knowledge in possession and knowledge in use has relieved us of the old difficulty that false judgment seems to involve both knowing and not knowing the same thing ; there is no difficulty in admitting that a man " possesses " what he cannot lay his hand on. We may add (1) that a comparison of " beliefs " with living creatures is psychologically much sounder than the old comparison with " impresses " made once for all on a block of wax ; judgment is a living process, not the mere retention of a stamp left on the mind once for all ; (2) that the distinction made here is the starting-point for the more extended antithesis of " potentiality " and " actuality "[1] in which Aristotle was to find the universal explanation of movement and becoming ; (3) that the formula no longer requires us to confine the possibility of error to the interpretation of present sensation.

But there is still a grave unsolved difficulty. Error is now said to be due to a wrong " use " of knowledge which we already have in possession. If this is so, a man's knowledge is the direct source of his false judgments ; he only confuses *A* with *B* because he possesses " knowledge " of them both. At this rate, might we not equally say that error may be the cause of knowledge, or blindness of vision ? (This difficulty is perhaps not meant to be taken wholly

[1] That the distinction between the actual and the potential is primarily due to the Academy seems to be further indicated by its appearance as something needing no explanation in Aristotle's *Protrepticus* (Fr. 52, Rose), which is shown by the considerable remaining fragments of it to have been an eloquent exposition of Platonism and was probably written during Plato's lifetime (Jaeger, *Aristoteles*, c. 4).

seriously. It is true that the more you " know," in the sense of " having the knowledge in possession," the graver are the errors to which you are exposed. As Mr. Chesterton says somewhere, " a man must know a great deal to be always wrong." Really grave error is regularly due to the misuse of wide knowledge. But the point is not really examined. Socrates' object is simply to prelude to a much more real difficulty.)

Theaetetus suggests that we might elude this difficulty by modifying our image. We might say that there are " ignorances " as well as " pieces of knowledge " in the aviary, and that the man who makes a false judgment is putting his hand on an " ignorance." But if that is so, since he really believes his false judgment, he must suppose the " ignorance " to be a piece of knowledge. And this gives an opening to the eristic for raising the old problem once more. Can a man who knows what knowledge and ignorance are confuse one with the other ? And if he does not know what both are, how can he confuse something he knows with something of which he is quite unaware, or one thing of which he is unaware with another of which he is equally unaware ? If we try to meet our opponent by suggesting that there is a " knowledge of the difference between knowledge and ignorance " which is a sort of knowledge of the second order, and that false judgment arises from inability to put one's hand on *this* knowledge, we shall clearly be involved in an impossible " infinite regress " (200c). Thus the point which Socrates is labouring is the sound one that it is impossible to have a psychological *criterion* of true and false beliefs.

Independently of this impossibility of a criterion, there is an obvious objection to the identification of knowledge with a " true belief." A man may be induced to hold a belief which in fact is true not by *proof* but by *persuasive* dexterous special pleading.[1] Thus the court which is led by clever advocacy to find a man guilty of an act of dishonesty cannot be said to know that he has committed the crime ; to know that, they would require to have seen the act committed. But if the man had really committed the act, the court has a " true belief " about him. This proves beyond all dispute that there is true belief which is not knowledge. The importance of the point may become plainer if we put it in a rather more modern way, What the illustration shows is that there is a real and significant difference between " historical " and " scientific " truths. History is not, and never can be, a department of " demonstrative science."

THIRD DEFINITION. KNOWLEDGE IS " TRUE JUDGMENT
ACCOMPANIED BY DISCOURSE " (201*d*–210*d*)

Possibly the difficulty just raised may be turned. As Theaetetus says, he had forgotten to specify that a true judgment, to be

---

[1] The same point reappears at *Timaeus* 51*e*, where it is put into the mouth of Timaeus of Locri. Presumably it is not specially Socratic nor Platonic.

knowledge, must be accompanied by "discourse" (λόγος). If there are any objects of which there is no "discourse," they will not be objects of *knowledge,* though we may have true judgment about them. At least, so Theaetetus has heard from some one whom he does not name. The point of the correction is to distinguish between "*simple* apprehension" and apprehension attended by "discourse," and to deny the name "knowledge" to simple apprehension. Thus the passage is the source of the familiar Aristotelian and mediaeval doctrine that the "complex enunciation," or proposition, is the unit of knowledge, as well as of the notion of "thought" as "discursive." We note also, at once, that the theory suggested has a remarkable *prima facie* resemblance to that put forward by Socrates himself in the *Meno,* where it was said that "beliefs" are converted into knowledge when they are "secured" αἰτίας λογισμῷ, by a "computation oi the grounds" for them. In our dialogue, Socrates says that he too has a dream to tell. He seems to have heard "in a dream" that there are certain *elementa* (στοιχεῖα) which are the ABC of nature, all other things being "syllables," complexes of these "letters." The "letters" can be simply apprehended and named, but we can *say* nothing about them, can predicate nothing of them, since to attribute any predicate to them would be admitting complexity in them (contrary to the hypothesis). The complexes composed of these letters have a λόγος, since you can analyse the complex back into its simple constituents, just as you can spell a syllable. The complexes then are "knowable and rational" (ῥητά), but their elements are not; they have to be seized by direct simple apprehension (are αἰσθητά). Knowledge, "*grounded* belief," is always of the complex. Probably this theory is the same as that of which Theaetetus had heard (201*d*–202*c*). We are not told anything of the authorship of this interesting theory, which has its counterparts in our own day, though it is plain that it is not being invented by Plato. Where it comes from we can only guess. The atomists have been thought of, but without much probability. The question which Socrates goes on to raise, whether a "syllable" is nothing but its components or a new unity, would have no significance for persons who disbelieved in the reality of all "composition," and is not a natural criticism to address to them. It would be more reasonable to think of the doctrine of Empedocles, which admits of genuine "chemical" composition. From his point of view, the "four roots" correspond exactly to the ABC of the book of Nature, bone, flesh, and other tissues to "syllables," and organisms composed of these tissues to complete words. But the employment of the epithet ῥηταί ("expressible") to describe the "syllables" of Nature's language suggests also mathematical connexions of some kind. Thus I should be inclined to attribute the theory to some Pythagorean of the type who were trying in the later part of the fifth century to find room within their own doctrine for the "four roots" and the Empedoclean biology.[1] But why is Socrates said only to have heard of the theory " in a dream " ? Possibly because the person who is responsible for it had only produced it after the death of Socrates, or because it only became known at Athens after that date, and therefore some apology has to be offered for making Socrates speak of it. Hence, when we remember the precisely parallel doctrine attributed by Theophrastus to the Pythagorean Ecphantus of Syracuse, it is natural to suspect with Burnet that the reference is to him.[2]

The analogy from letters and syllables is specious, but we must examine it more closely. It is true that the first syllable of Socrates' name, the syllable So, has a certain λόγος. You can say that it is S and o—the letter S has no such λόγος. You can make statements about it, e.g. that it is a "hissing" sound, but you cannot explain the sound by analysing it into components. But now arises a difficult question. Is the syllable So simply the sounds or signs S and o, taken in that order, or is it a new unity of a type different from that of its "component" sounds or symbols? If you take the first view, that So is just " S and o," then it seems ridiculous to say that a man can "know" "S and o," and yet neither know S nor know o. On the second view, So is itself a unity, and has not really S and o as "constituent" parts. Hence the syllable should, like the single letter, be an object of simple apprehension, and therefore, on the proposed definition, not an object of knowledge (202d–205e). Besides, the experience of our own early schooldays seems to show that we learned to recognize syllables simply by learning to recognize the letters of which they are composed; this tells forcibly against the view that "syllables" can be known when their component "letters" are not known (206a–c).

Apart from the question of the soundness of this analogy from letters and syllables, what may we suppose to be meant by λόγος ("discourse") in the statement that knowledge is "a true judgment accompanied by discourse"? Three, and only three, possible meanings occur to us. (a) "Discourse" may mean actual uttered speech made up of nouns and verbs. This, however, cannot be the meaning intended, for any true judgment can be expressed in speech, even if it is not entitled to rank as knowledge (206d). (b) Or the meaning might be a complete enumeration of the component "parts" of the thing thought about. Hesiod says that a hundred planks go to a waggon. You and I cannot name more than a few of them: is it meant, then, that we have only a "true judgment" about a waggon, but should know what a waggon is, if we could name all the hundred? The objection to this interpretation is that we cannot say that a man really knows a complex unless he can recognize its components not merely as components of that

---

[1] Philolaus is now known to have been a Pythagorean of this type (Burnet, E.G.Ph.³, 277 ff.), and it is just this combination of Pythagorean mathematics with the biology and medicine of Empedocles which is expounded at length in Plato's Timaeus.

[2] For the doctrine of Ecphantus see Diels, Fr. d. Vors.³, i. 340–341. The historical reality of E. is, as Diels says, guaranteed by the fact that our notices of him come from Theophrastus, who could not well have been mistaken on the point. Whether he belongs to the fifth or the fourth century is not clear

complex, but when they recur in another setting. *E.g.*, we should not say that a man " knew " how to spell the syllable *The*, if he wrote it correctly in spelling the name of Theaetetus but wrongly when he had to spell the name Theodorus. And a man *might* be liable to make the same sort of blunder about each of the remaining syllables, and yet might spell the one name Theaetetus right. Thus he would have enumerated all its letters correctly and yet would have mere " right judgment," not knowledge (208*b*). (*c*) Or was it meant that a true judgment about a thing becomes knowledge when you add to it the discourse which indicates the character which distinguishes that thing from every other thing ? Is knowledge a true judgment accompanied by a statement of the *differentia* (διαφορά, διαφορότης) of the subject of the judgment ?[1] This account looks as though it ought to be true, but when you examine it closely it is as perplexing as theatrical stage-paintings seen from close quarters. How can I have a " true judgment " about Theaetetus at all, if I am not alive to the distinctive individual characters which mark off Theaetetus from every one else ? If I am unaware of them, how can my judgment be said to be about Theaetetus rather than about Theodorus or any man you please ? Thus it would seem that to make a true judgment about Theaetetus, I must already have the *differentia* of Theaetetus in mind. Then what is added when this true judgment is converted into knowledge by the addition of the " discourse " of the *differentia* ? It cannot be meant that we are to add a " true judgment " of the *differentia* to our existing true judgment, for we must clearly have possessed that in order to make a true judgment about Theaetetus. And to say that what is meant is that we reach knowledge when we not merely think but actually *know* the *differentia* amounts to the circular definition that " knowledge is true judgment *plus* knowledge of the *differentia* " (208*c*–210*e*).

Thus our dialogue of search ends formally with a negative conclusion. Three suggestions have been made and all found untenable. Theaetetus has no further suggestion of which to be delivered. If he should ever find himself pregnant with any further suggestions in future, we must examine them in the same fashion. It is not the function of Socrates to make any positive contribution to knowledge, and besides it is time that he went to the " king's " office to make his formal reply to the indictment preferred by Meletus (210*b*–*d*).

The *Theaetetus* has thus been true to type as a Socratic dialogue in ending with no avowed results. But negatively we have reached a series of results of the highest importance. We have disposed of the identification of knowledge with sensation or any form of simple apprehension. We have also seen that pure relativism is untenable alike in the theory of knowledge and in metaphysics. It may be added that it has been at least forcibly suggested by the tenour of the whole argument that all the proposed definitions have failed precisely because each of them has attempted to provide a *psychological* criterion of knowledge, and no such psychological criterion is possible. The most important positive

---

[1] The first occurrence of the word in the sense which Aristotle was to stereotype as a technicality of logic.

result of the discussion is probably the recognition that the discovery of the great categories both of existence and value is the work of thought, " the soul by herself without any instrument." We may note also the appearance for the first time of a whole series of technical terms of the first importance : " quality " (ποιότης), " organ " of perception (ὄργανον), " criterion " (κριτήριον), " differentia " (διαφορά, διαφορότης). Also we see the very fundamental problems connected with the notion of " simple apprehension " and the difference between " acquaintance " and " knowledge about " coming into prominence and receiving illustration, though without the formulation of a definite result.

Possibly the most striking feature of the whole dialogue is its silence on a matter about which we should have expected to hear something. Plato has written a long and elaborate discussion of knowledge without making a single reference to the doctrine of forms, though we might have thought it almost impossible for him to keep it out of the argument against relativism. A similar silence may be said to occur in all the dialogues we still have to examine. The forms are mentioned only in two of them : the *Parmenides*, where the doctrine is said to be that of Socrates in his early years and is criticized by Parmenides and Zeno, and the *Timaeus*, where it is put into the mouth of a fifth-century Pythagorean. I do not see how to account for these facts on the view that Plato had himself originated the doctrine and regarded it as his special contribution to philosophy. If we trust his own accounts of the matter, we shall find it most natural to suppose that in the earlier dialogues, which speak of the forms, Plato has not yet developed a doctrine which he feels to be specifically his own ; he is reproducing the common inheritance of Socratic men. If that is so, the silence about the forms in the *Theaetetus* may mean either that when he wrote that dialogue he was feeling the necessity for a " Platonic " doctrine which had not yet been definitely worked out, or else that he *had* already arrived at the results Aristotle always assumes to be the Platonic teaching, and felt that they were so definitely his own that dramatic versimilitude would be outraged by putting them into the mouth of Socrates.

See further :

BURNET.—*Greek Philosophy, Part I.*, 234–253.
CAMPBELL, L.—*The Theaetetus of Plato*. (Oxford, 1883.)
RITTER, C.—*Platon*, ii. 96–120 ; *Gedankengang und Grundanschauungen von Platos Theätet* in appendix to *Untersuchungen ueber Platon*. (Stuttgart, 1888.)
RAEDER, H.—*Platons philosophische Entwickelung*, 279–297.
DIELS, H.—*Elementum*. (Leipzig, 1899.)
DIÈS, A.—*Autour de Platon*, 450–452.
STEWART, J. A.—*Plato's Doctrine of Ideas*, 65–68.
NATORP, P.—*Platons Ideenlehre*, 88–116.
SACHS, E.—*de Theaeteto Atheniensi* (1914).

CHAPTER XIV

THE *PARMENIDES*

IT is most probable that the *Parmenides* and the *Theaetetus* were composed almost simultaneously. The *Parmenides* cannot well be a decidedly earlier work than the other, since it exhibits the same interest in Eleaticism and its great founder Parmenides ; it cannot well be later, since it is the best example in Plato of that cumbrousness of the indirectly reported dialogue form which is mentioned in the *Theaetetus* as the reason for return to the simpler type of the earliest dialogues. Indeed, it may well be that it was just the difficulty of keeping up in the *Parmenides* the fiction that the whole is recited by a speaker to whom it had been formerly recited by a second person, who in his turn had heard it from a third, which led Plato to renounce this type of composition for the future. It had been useful so long as his purpose had been largely dramatic, but was found to be worse than useless for works in which the main interest lies in the analysis and criticism of ideas.

The dialogue has always been regarded as an exceptionally puzzling one, and the most divergent views have been held about its main purpose. Yet if we attend to certain plain hints, given by Plato himself, we may find that his object is indicated with unusual clearness. The general scheme of the dialogue is this. It falls into two parts of unequal length. In the first and briefer part (126a–135c) Socrates is represented as a very young man expounding his newly formulated theory of the " participation " of sensible things in forms to the great Parmenides and his famous scholar Zeno ; Parmenides subjects the theory to a series of criticisms which look annihilating and to which Socrates offers no reply. Still he maintains that philosophy cannot dispense with the conception of the forms. The weakness of Socrates is that, being very young, he is attempting to philosophize without a sufficient logical discipline in considering all the consequences which follow from the acceptance or denial of a fundamental " hypothesis." In the second part of the dialogue (136a–166c), Parmenides illustrates the kind of logical discipline he has in mind by taking for examination his own thesis that " Reality is One " or that " Things are a Unity." He apparently shows in a series of antithetical " antinomies " that whether this thesis is affirmed or denied, the consequence is that a host of pairs of contradictory statements may *either* be simultaneously affirmed *or* simultaneously denied. In either case, of course, the principle of Contradiction has been violated. The dialogue ends without a word of comment on this portentous result.

Now it is quite certain that Plato never dreamed of denying the law of Contradiction ; Aristotle would certainly have said something on the point if that had been so.[1] We get a clue to Plato's real drift when he makes Parmenides say (135*d*) that the method of which he is about to give an example is that of Zeno, the inventor of " antinomies." This remark is clearly meant to send us back to the earlier sentences (128 *c–d*) in which Zeno has been made to explain the real intention of his own famous puzzles. His purpose, he says, was simply to retort on opponents who said that the Parmenidean doctrine " reality is one " leads to paradoxical conclusions by showing that their rival " hypothesis " that " reality is many " leads to still worse paradoxes. If we interpret the *Parmenides*, as we clearly ought to do, in the light of these broad hints, we shall see that it is constructed on the same pattern as the paradoxes of Zeno. A series of attempts to show that the Socratic " hypothesis " of forms leads to impossible results is retorted upon by an elaborate attempt to show that the Eleatic hypothesis is in still worse case. It is not safe even to mention it, for whether you assert it or deny it, in either case a clever formal logician can compel you to admit either that all assertions whatsoever are true or alternatively that they are all false.

It follows then that the objections urged against the doctrine of sensible things as " partaking of " forms are not Plato's own, and are not meant as a serious criticism by himself either of Socrates or of his own earlier theories. They correspond to the objections against Parmenides which Zeno had in view in composing his own work. In other words, we are directed to regard these criticisms as coming from opponents of the theory of " participation." And since Plato's imitation of the Zenonian method takes the form of raising still worse puzzles about the consequences of the Eleatic doctrine, it is clear who these opponents must be. We must look for them among the formal logicians of the school of Megara who were the continuators of Eleaticism. It is in strict keeping with this interpretation that the main point of the objections made by Parmenides to Socrates is not to raise difficulties about the reality of the forms. *That* he seems to concede. What he criticizes is

---

[1] Cf. Aristot. *Met.* 1005*b* 25, where it is mentioned that " some persons " suppose Heraclitus to deny the principle of contradiction, " but it does not follow necessarily that a man means what he says." *Ibid.* 1007*b* 22, the " argument of Protagoras " would lead to the denial of the principle, as is argued at length at 1009*a* 6 ff. Heraclitus and Protagoras are the only eminent men named in the course of the argument, and of them Aristotle only says that by pressing, in one case, the thinker's mere words and, in the other, the consequence of his thesis, you could reach this result. He means that neither really intended to reject this " most certain of all principles." If he supposed the antinomies of the *Parmenides* to be meant seriously, he would have been bound to refer to the point in this context.

the view of Socrates that sensible things "partake" of the forms, and so have a kind of secondary reality. This is exactly as it should be if the critics Plato has in view are the Eleatics of Megara. From their point of view, the great fault of the doctrine expounded in the *Phaedo, Republic,* and other dialogues is that it allows any kind of reality at all to the objects of sense. Plato does not, in the dialogue, offer any answer to these extreme "idealists"; he simply sets himself to show that two can play at the game of abstract formal logic, and that he can, if he pleases, play the game better than its professed champions. Their own methods may be applied to their own fundamental doctrine; let them see how they will like the result.

If this is the right way to understand the dialogue, and Plato seems to tell us that it is, it follows that the *Parmenides* is, all through, an elaborate *jeu d'esprit*, and that all interpretations based on taking it for anything else (including an earlier one by the present writer), are mistaken in principle. It equally follows that the ironical spirit of the work must not be forgotten in dealing with isolated passages. *E.g.*, when Parmenides gravely censures Socrates for refusing to believe in forms of mud and dirt, and says that he will get the better of such a prejudice when he grows older and more philosophical (130*e*), we must understand the remark to be a piece of polite irony. In Parmenides' mouth, it can only mean that a man who is going to admit any kind of reality in sensible things ought to be prepared to "go the whole hog," and nothing more. Presumably the remark is a reproduction of actual Megarian criticism. It tells us nothing of *Plato's* own thought. More than any other Platonic work of any considerable compass, the *Parmenides* bears throughout the stamp of being an "occasional' composition. Its purpose is to "have some fun" with Monists who regard the sensible as illusion, and very little more.

There are several interesting points to be noted in connexion with the introductory narrative. The otherwise unknown speaker, Cephalus, who recites the dialogue, is a citizen of Clazomenae, the native town of Anaxagoras. It is not said where he is speaking or to whom, but apparently the scene is in one of the Ionian cities. The assumption is that he had gone to Athens expressly to learn the true story of the meeting between Socrates and the great Eleatics from the only surviving person who could relate it, Plato's own half-brother Antiphon, son of Perictione by her second husband, the well-known statesman Pyrilampes. Antiphon could tell the tale accurately because he had often heard it when he was younger, from Pythodorus. (The person meant is the well-known Pythodorus, son of Isolochus, prominent in the Archidamian war, whom the writer of the *Alcibiades I* names as an actual pupil of Zeno.) Pythodorus had been the host of Parmenides and Zeno on their visit to Athens at the time of the great Panathenaea in a year when Socrates was still "very young." It follows from all this that we are to suppose the meeting of Socrates with the Eleatic philosophers to have taken place about 450 B.C., nearly a quarter of a century before Plato's own birth. The visit of Cephalus and his friends to Antiphon must be supposed, as Proclus said, to be after the death of Socrates. The recital of Antiphon was needed precisely because all the persons who had been present at the original meeting were dead.

Why does Plato make this unparalleled assumption that a conversation of Socrates is being repeated outside Athens, after Socrates' death and a good half-century after the holding of the conversation ? Clearly, by insisting on the early date of the conversation, and the fact that no one is living who could check the third-hand report of what passed, he frees himself from responsibility for the strict accuracy of his narrative. If we find the conversation so à propos to present-day Megarianism, well, we only know what Socrates and Parmenides said from a second-hand story told by Antiphon, a younger man than Plato himself, and who will go bail for Antiphon ? I think it ought also to be said that the tale of the anxiety of the Ionian philosophers to hear Antiphon's story justifies an inference. Why the Ionians of Asia Minor should feel this interest is obvious. They would be members of the school founded in Ionia by Anaxagoras on his removal from Athens ; Socrates, the favourite pupil of Anaxagoras' successor Archelaus, would in any case be an object of interest to such a group. That Plato thinks it a plausible fiction that their interest should lead them to visit Athens in order to gather a true account of events fifty years old seems only explicable on the supposition that the encounter of Socrates with the great Eleatics was a real historical fact and, for philosophical circles, a memorable one, as an encounter between two great chess-players or gamblers is memorable for persons interested in chess or gaming.

The situation at the opening of the conversation is this. Zeno has just been reading aloud his famous work containing the antinomies for which he is still remembered. Socrates fastens on one of them, an argument which has not survived and of which the precise sense is uncertain, to the effect that " if things are many, they must be like and must also be unlike, but this is absurd," as an example of the rest. He proposes to regard the whole work as intended to establish the thesis of Parmenides by disproving its contradictory. Parmenides says " reality is one," Zeno that " reality is not many." Zeno accepts the statement with the minor correction that his object was not to prove the Parmenidean thesis, but simply to silence its critics by showing that their own rival " hypothesis " has even more impossible consequences than those they urge against Parmenides (127d–128e). Socrates then suggests that if we will only accept the doctrine of forms and the participation of things in forms, there is really no paradox in saying that the same " things " may " partake " at once of the form of likeness and of that of unlikeness, and so be at once like and unlike. But it would be a real and intolerable paradox (τέρας) to hold that unlikeness can be predicated of the form of likeness or likeness of the form of unlike. So it is intelligible enough that a sensible thing, my body, for example, should be *one* body out of the six or seven human bodies present in this room and also have *many* members. But it would be quite another thing to hold that *Unity* is many or *Plurality* one (129*a*–130*a*). Parmenides and Zeno are both impressed by the ability of Socrates, and Parmenides at once asks him whether the theory is original. " Did you make this distinction between forms and things which partake of them αὐτός ? "—" for yourself," " out of your own head " (130*b*) ? Parmenides asks the question, as Proclus says, because it might be that Socrates had " heard of " some such distinction from some one else. The noticeable thing is that it is not the doctrine that there are " intelligible " forms which strikes Parmenides as novel ; the original point which impresses him is that Socrates holds that the things we see and handle " participate in " the forms. None of the difficulties he intends to raise arises from the belief that there are forms ; the difficulties all concern the relation of " participation " by which the sensible thing is connected with a form. It is the reality of the " phenomenal " world which he, as an Eleatic, finds a stumbling-block. The conclusion to which his criticism is meant to conduct us is the double one (*a*) that unless we admit the reality of the forms, there is an end of all philosophy; if we do admit it, the form cannot be " present in " sensible things, and these must therefore be simply unreal (135*a*–*c*).[1] This is precisely the position of Euclides and his friends, who taught that " reality is one ; the ' other ' is unreal " (Aristocles *ap.* Euseb. *P.E.* xiv. 17, R.P. 289). Hence we shall expect to find that the arguments urged against Socrates by Parmenides are theirs also.

I may summarize these arguments the more briefly that they are admirably dealt with by Professor Burnet in *Greek Philosophy, Part I.*, 253–264, and other writers on the philosophy of Plato. I have attempted a complete discussion of their weight and derivation elsewhere in " Parmenides, Zeno, and Socrates," *Philosophical Studies*, pp. 28–90, whither I may refer a reader desirous of further information.

Parmenides begins by raising the question what precisely is the content of the world of forms. Socrates professes himself certain that there are forms corresponding to the fundamental notions of *ethics*—Right (δίκαιον), Good (αγαθόν), Noble (καλόν) ; he is doubtful about forms of organisms and physical things (Man, Fire, Water) ; in the case of such things as mud, dirt, hair—*i.e.*

---

[1] This is, in fact, the position of the historical Parmenides himself. His " one " is, no doubt, corporeal; it is a solid homogeneous sphere. But our eyes and ears do not show us anything of the kind. Hence the apparent " things " which they disclose to us must be pure illusion. Though the " one " is corporeal, we only apprehend it by *thinking*. Its sole reality is deduced by Parmenides from what he regards as the postulates of coherent thought.

sensible things which do not appear to have a recognizable type of structure—he is inclined to think that there are no forms. In these cases there is no reality beyond "what we see." But he is not quite sure that consistency would not demand forms of these too, though he is afraid the admission might lead him into "abysmal nonsense" (130 b–d). What he means by this "nonsense" we can see, as Burnet suggests, by the notices preserved to us of the arbitrary fashion in which the Pythagorean Eurytus attempted to assign "numbers" to man, horse, and other things. The main point is, that though Socrates is not certain about the contents of the system of forms, the forms of which he is most certain are those which correspond to our ethical ideals. (Since we can define these as the mathematician defines his "figures," they must have the same kind of reality as that the geometer ascribes to his figures.)

The theory then is that all the "particulars" of which a common predicate is affirmed owe their possession of that predicate to their "participation" in the corresponding form, and Parmenides sets himself to show that, however we understand this relation of "participation," we are led to consequences which are logically absurd. This is exactly the line of reasoning adopted by Zeno for the confutation of the Pythagorean mathematicians who assume that "reality is many." The argument may be analysed as follows: (a) If a form is "in" each of a number of things, either the whole of it is "in" each of them, or only part of it is "in" each. In the first case the form itself being as a whole "in" each of several separate things is "outside" itself (i.e. it is, after all, many and not one, contrary to the Socratic thesis of its unity). In the second case, the form is divisible (μεριστόν), and thus becomes many by division just as, on the alternative view, it becomes many by multiplication; the whole form is thus "in" no one of the things called after it, and thus they are not really entitled to the "common name" (131a–e). Thus we have an apparent reductio ad absurdum of the "hypothesis" of "participation"; it permits of only two alternative interpretations and you are led, by a slightly different route, to the same denial of the hypothesis itself, whichever alternative you adopt. The hypothesis is thus "self-refuting." (The precise meaning of the reasoning by which the second of the alternatives is refuted in the special case of the form "magnitude" is obscure, but seems to be this. If you say that one thing is bigger than another in virtue of the presence in it of a "part" of the form of "magnitude," less than the whole of the form, you are maintaining in effect that there is such a relation as "not quite bigger than." Thus you are committed to holding that, e.g., if A and B are segments of a straight line, the relation between them may be that A is "not quite longer" than, or "nearly longer" than B, and this is manifestly nonsense. So, in the case of the form of "smallness," you are committed to the view that it would be significant to say that "A is nearly smaller than B, but not quite smaller." But this is senseless. Either *A* is quite smaller than *B* or it is not smaller at all. If there is *any* departure from strict equality, either *A* is definitely greater than *B* or it is definitely less than *B*, a perfectly valid argument against the notion of strictly " infinitesimal " differences, which is exactly on a par with the argument of Zeno against the view of the point as a " vanishing " magnitude.) We note, of course, that the reasoning is not directed against the reality of forms, but against the assumption that a form can be " in " or " present to " something which is not a form.

(*b*) The reason and the only reason for Socrates' doctrine is the assumption that when several things have a common predicate, it is assumed that there is a single determinate reality (the form) denoted by this predicate. But it ought to follow that, since the common predicate can be affirmed of the form itself, there must be a second form " present " alike to the first form and the things which " participate " in it, and similarly, by the same reason, a third, and so on *in indefinitum*. Thus there must be no one single form of, *e.g.*, magnitude, but a simply infinite series of forms of magnitude ; thus, once more, the Socratic theory is shown to be self-refuting, and again it is the asserted " presence " of forms to things which has created the difficulty (132*a–b*).

In strict logic this reasoning is not conclusive, since it turns on a confusion between a predication and the assertion of an identity. *E.g.* David and Jonathan are a *pair* of friends, Orestes and Pylades are another pair. Both pairs have something in common, the cardinal number 2, which is *the* number of the members of each. But the number 2 is not itself a pair ; it *is* a number, and cannot be said to *have* a number. Since Plato's object is merely to rehearse the objections of Eleatics to the Socratic doctrine in order to over-trump them by showing that their own methods can be turned with even more effect against their own theories, we need not suppose that he was unaware of this logical flaw, though he has no occasion to expose it. He had already made Socrates himself in the *Republic* (597*c*) remark in passing that if you once surrender the absolute unity of the form by admitting that there can be two forms of the same thing, you are committed to the " infinite regress." We may reasonably infer that this kind of reasoning was already current in Socrates' own lifetime, not invented for the first time after his death by Eleatic critics of the positions ascribed to him in the Platonic dialogues. Hence I think it unlikely that this particular difficulty has anything to do with the difficulty urged, as Alexander of Aphrodisias tells us, by Polyxenus the Megarian against the doctrine of " participation." As I understand the statements of Alexander, the point of Polyxenus was that on the Platonic theory there ought to be not only visible men, like Socrates and Plato, and a form of man, but also a " third " man, intermediate between the two, exactly as, on the Platonic theory itself, there are certain " mathematical objects " intermediate between the form of circularity and the visible diagram drawn on a black-board.¹ I think also that when Aristotle talks of the "third man" as a difficulty to which the doctrine of forms leads us,² he is always intending to refer to this last-mentioned argument and not, as is commonly supposed, to the "indefinite regress." I have tried to argue the point fully in the essay already referred to (*Philosophical Studies*, pp. 52–69).

Zeno, and Socrates, pp. 255–270).

(c) At this point Socrates suggests a way of escape from the difficulty about the unity of the form. How if a form is really a "thought" (νόημα) and therefore is not "in" things at all, but "in our minds" (ἐν ψυχαῖς)? We could then maintain its unity without exposing ourselves to either of the lines of argument (a) and (b). Parmenides, however, has a reply based on the principle which is employed in his own poem as the foundation of his criticism of all his precursors. You cannot think without thinking of *something*—that is, of something *real* (to think of nothing would be equivalent to not thinking at all) ; this something is some *one determinate* thing which "that thought thinks, as being there in all the instances." In other words, what the thought thinks is always a form. (*E.g.*, when you think of Socrates, Plato, and Aristotle, you think some *definite* predicate about them, such as, *e.g.*, that they are all *men*, and thus we are back at our old position. You are thinking of *man* as a form " present " to the three.) What then, on this view that a form is a thought, can the " presence " of the form to the thing mean ? Does it mean that a thing is a complex of thoughts and that everything thinks ? Or would you admit that there are " thoughts which do not think " ? (132*b*–*c*).

Once more, the difficulty is one not about the reality of the form but about the possibility of the " presence " of it to something

¹ Thus we can distinguish (1) *the* circle of which we give the equation in analytical geometry, (2) the terrestrial equator, (3) the black line on a terrestrial globe which stands for the equator. (1) is the form, (2) is an invisible perfect " instance " of the form, (3) a visible and imperfect embodiment of the form. On Polyxenus see *Early Greek Philosophy, Part I.*, pp. 254, 259–260. It has been suggested that the difficulties urged by Parmenides were originally raised against Plato himself by his pupil Aristotle, and that it is in acknowledgment of this that the Aristotle who was afterwards one of the " Thirty " figures as a character in the dialogue and is made the respondent throughout the second part. The fancy must be rejected for the following reasons : (1) Aristotle only entered the Academy in the year 367, the very year of Plato's departure for Syracuse, as a mere lad. It may even be doubted whether he can have held any personal intercourse with Plato until after the end of Plato's first visit to Dionysius II ; (2) the one real point of contact between the Aristotelian criticism of Plato and the *Parmenides* is the supposed identity of the τρίτος ἄνθρωπος with the argument from the " regress." If the two are not identical, this point of contact disappears. Even if they are, the very fact that Aristotle refers to the argument by such a nickname indicates that it was something already familiar. (3) As has been finally established by Jaeger in his *Aristoteles*, Aristotle's divergence from the Academy on the doctrine of forms was first indicated in the work περὶ φιλοσοφίας shortly after Plato's death. His earlier works, so far as we know them (*Eudemus, Protrepticus*), are wholly Platonic in spirit.

² *Met.* 990*b* 15 ff. = 1079*a* 11 ff., 1039*a* 2 ff., 1059*b* 8 ff. ; *S.E.* 178*b* 36.

which is not a form. Socrates has just suggested that the form
or univeraal may be just a "thought in our minds," a *way of
looking at* things. The theory is, in fact, that historically known to
us as Nominalism, though Conceptualism would be a better name
for it. It treats a "significant universal" simply as a point of
view from which the mind contrives to look at a plurality of things
with a single glance. We find it convenient, as making for
"economy of mental effort," to look at Socrates, Plato, Aristotle,
all together as "instances of the universal *man*"; according to the
theory, the employment of this common name "man" only expresses the fact that we have effected this economy and nothing
more ; what is common to Socrates, Plato, Aristotle, is simply that
we have succeeded in viewing them together and have therefore
given them the common name. Parmenides' objection is, in
principle, that the name remains insignificant unless there really is
a "common nature" which justifies the common name. But if
the common "nature" is a "thought in our minds," then the
things which are said to have this common nature must be just
complexes of thoughts, and we shall have to say that everything
whatever thinks, or, alternatively, since in any case a thing is assumed
to be a complex of forms, and forms have been declared to be
thoughts, that there are "thoughts which do not think" (ἀνόητα
νοήματα). The suggested Conceptualism, it should be noted, would
be just as fatal to Aristotelianism as to Platonism. On the Aristotelian view, though there are no universals *ante res*, there are
universals *in rebus*, and it is only because there are universals *in
rebus* that there are also universals in the *intellectus* of the scientific
thinker. As against the Conceptualism which, like that of Mach
or Karl Pearson, denies that universals exist at all except *in in-
tellectu*, where they are merely labour-saving devices, "conceptual
shorthand," the rejoinder of Parmenides seems decisive. As to
the source of this Conceptualism, it is not easy to say anything
with confidence. The best suggestion known to me is that made
ad loc. by Grote,[1] who calls attention to a statement of Simplicius
(commenting on Arist. *Cat. 8b* 25) that the "school of Eretria"
maintained that "qualities" are ψιλαὶ ἔννοιαι, "mere thoughts,"
"mere notions." Since Menedemus of Eretria and his followers
were famous formal logicians and agreed with the Eleatics of
Megara in objecting to negative predication (Diog. Laert. ii. 135),
it seems to me that Grote is probably on the right track, and that
we are still dealing with a criticism on the theory of forms derived
from Eleatic sources.

(*d*) Socrates next falls back on what Aristotle regarded as the
Pythagorean formula for the relation between form and thing.
The form is an archetype or model (παράδειγμα), the other things
called by its name are likenesses (ὁμοιώματα) of it, so that the
relation between sensible thing and form is that the "thing" is a

[1] Grote, *Plato and the other Companions of Socrates* (ed. 1885), vol. iii.
74 n. 2.

" copy " of the form. (This would, apparently, save the unity of
the form by suggesting that there may be many "imitations " of
one form just as there may be many copies of the same original.)
Parmenides again argues that the theory refutes itself. For
" resemblance " is a symmetrical relation. If A is like B, B is also
like A. It follows that the form must be like the things which
" resemble it." And, since the theory itself explains the likeness
of one thing to another by the existence of a common archetype
of both, we must account for the likeness of form to " thing "
by postulating a more ultimate archetype of both, and so on *in
indefinitum* (132d–133a).

As before, the difficulty really arises from a fallacy. As Proclus
rightly says, the relation of copy to original is not simply one of
likeness. (It is in fact a relation of resemblance+derivation, and
this relation is not symmetrical. My reflection in the glass is a
reflection of my face, but my face is not a reflection of it.) It
should be specially remarked that the suggestion that the relation
between form and " thing " is one of " likeness " is not offered as
an alternative to the doctrine of " participation," but as a further
specification of its precise meaning (132d 3, ἡ μέθεξις αὕτη . . . τῶν
εἰδῶν οὐκ ἄλλη τις ἢ εἰκασθῆναι αὐτοῖς), and that Parmenides meets
both formulae with precisely the same objection that they appear
to involve the " indefinite regress."

(e) The gravest difficulty of all has yet to be faced. It is that
the recognition of two " worlds," presupposed by Socrates, a world
of forms and an " other " world of " things " which somehow
" partake " of the forms, leads direct to complete scepticism (133a–
135c). For the world of which each of us is a member is *ex hypothesi*
not the world of forms, but the " other " world (since it had been
observed at the outset that each of us is *a man*, none of us is the
" form of man "). Consequently the relations between forms
will belong exclusively to the world or system of related forms ;
corresponding relations of which " we " are terms will belong to
" our world " and will have their correlates within " our world."
There will be a relation between " master " as such and " servant "
as such, and the terms of this will be the form of master and the
form of servant. But each of us will be master or servant to
another man, and the relation between this pair will fall outside
the world of forms ; it will connect one man with another man, not
with a form. So the correlate of the form of knowledge will be
Reality as such. But the correlate of our knowledge will be such
reality as the objects of our world possess. And it is admitted that
" our " knowledge is not the form of knowledge (that is, the knowledge we have is partial and imperfect). Its counterpart therefore
is not the completely real. We are precluded from knowing what
real good is, for the counterpart of a merely relative and partial
knowledge must be a relative and partial reality. And we may
invert the argument with even more startling results. God, at
any rate, might be supposed to possess " absolute " or " perfect "

knowledge. But, by our previous reasoning, it follows that God knows nothing of our imperfectly real world. And in the same way, we may deny the rule of God over us, on the ground that the correlate of human subject is human superior. In a word, the consequence of a theory of two distinct " worlds " or " orders " will be that every relation falls wholly within one of the two ; there can be no relation connecting a member of the one world with a member of the other. (In the mouth of an Eleatic, of course, this means that one of the two " worlds " is an illusion, and that one is the supposed " sensible world." Parmenides, who wrote the words ταὐτὸ γὰρ ἔστι νοεῖν τε καὶ εἶναι (" it is the same thing which can be thought of and can be "), has no intention of surrendering the " intelligible " world, and any interpretation of the *Parmenides* which assumes that its object is to discredit the reality of the intelligible is necessarily false).

Yet to deny the reality of forms is destructive of thought itself, since it amounts to a denial of the possibility of definite knowledge. If Socrates has been badly perplexed by the discussion which has just been closed, it is because, in his zeal, he has attempted to enunciate his doctrine about forms without a sufficient preparatory discipline in arid and apparently " useless " formal logic. The kind of discipline required may be exemplified by Zeno's famous antinomies, but needs to go even beyond them. Zeno had attempted to prove the thesis that " reality is many " self-refuting by showing that it can be made to lead to pairs of contradictory conclusions. For a really searching investigation it is not enough to ask what follows from the assertion of a thesis, but also what follows from the denial of it. *E.g.* Zeno should have asked not merely, " If things are many, what can be asserted about the many things, and what about the unit, and about the relation of the two ? " but also, " If things are not many, what follows about plurality, the unit, and their relations ? " (It was not enough to argue that the consequences of Pluralism are self-contradictory ; the same issue should have been raised about the consequences of denying Pluralism.) Complete investigation of any proposed philosophical principle demands this twofold consideration of the implications both of its assertion and of its denial (135*b*–136*c*).

In these remarks, which effect a transition to the second half of the dialogue, there are two interesting implications. If Parmenides ascribes the helplessness of the young Socrates in face of the difficulties just raised to want of training in formal logic, we may infer that the suggestion is that the apparently formidable arguments are themselves fallacious and would be seen to be so by a more practised logician. That is, the fault of Plato's Megarian critics is not that they are logicians, but that they are not logical enough. If we are only thorough enough with our logic, the alleged logical objections to the metaphysic of forms will vanish of themselves. It seems further to be meant that the particular fault of these logicians is one-sidedness. They scrutinize the consequences of the

Socratic and Platonic assertion of the "participation" of sensible things in forms, but they forget to consider whether the denial of the assertion may not involve worŝe antinomies than those they have detected in the Platonic dialogues. Plato is, in fact, suggesting that he knows how to play the game of formal logic according to the rules even better than the famous professionals themselves. Beyond these significant hints that what we need is not less but more logic, the dialogue provides no solution of the problem it has raised.

In the second part of the dialogue Parmenides consents to give an elaborate example of the kind of logical method he has been recommending, choosing as the respondent to his questions the youngest member of the party, Aristoteles, on the ground that his very youth will be a guarantee that his answers will be given without *finesse* of any kind. The thesis selected for examination is, naturally enough, Parmenides' own principle that "reality is one." (136c–137c. It is significant that he speaks of the whole proceeding as an elaborate "game" (παιδιά), a plain hint that the antinomies now to follow are not to be taken quite seriously, and that we must not be surprised if there is a touch of conscious "sophistry" about some of them. In fact, it is incredible that Plato should not have known that some of them are pure fallacies. But, as his purpose is simply to show that the methods of his critics can be made to recoil on themselves, it is strictly fair that he should play their game by their own rules. Any kind of reasoning they permit themselves is equally permissible in a "skit" upon them.)

According to the programme already laid down by Parmenides, we should expect to find him raising four problems: (1) if the real is one, what can be asserted about this one real? (2) if the real is one, what can be said about "the many"? (3) if the real is not one, what can be said about the one? (4) if the real is not one, what can be said about the many? But by a further refinement, each of these questions is raised twice over, the purpose being to show that on either assumption (that the real is one or that it is not one) you can make it appear at pleasure either that contradictory predicates can be both affirmed or both denied alike of the one and of the many. Thus we get altogether eight arguments forming four "antinomies"—two in which the subject of both thesis and antithesis is the one, and two in which it is the many. The issue is that the apparent dilemma to which Socrates had been reduced at the end of the first part of the dialogue, that knowledge of the real is equally impossible with or without his theory about forms and "participation," is more than matched by the dilemma offered to the Eleatics, and maliciously offered through the mouth of their own founder Parmenides professing to be applying their own peculiar method, that, whether you accept or reject their Monism, you must either simultaneously assert or simultaneously deny both members of an indefinite series of contradictory pairs of propositions.

The formal arrangement of the eight " hypotheses " is this :

A {
   I. *If the real is one,* nothing whatever can be asserted of it (137c–142a).

   II. *If the real is one,* everything can be asserted of it (142b–157c).[1]
}

B {
   III. *If the real is one,* everything can be asserted of " things other than the one " (157b–159b).

   IV. *If the real is one* nothing can be asserted of " things other than the one " (159b–160b).
}

C {
   V. *If the one is unreal,* everything can be asserted of it (160b–163b).

   VI *If the one is unreal,* nothing at all can be asserted of it (163b–164b).
}

D {
   VII. *If the one is unreal,* everything can be asserted about " things other than the one " (164b–165e).

   VIII. *If the one is unreal,* nothing can be asserted about anything (165e–166c).
}

It would be taking Plato's metaphysical jest too gravely to make a minute examination of all the details of these bewildering arguments. It will be sufficient to point out the peculiar character of the dialectical method employed and to summarize the results. The peculiarities of the method are dictated by the consideration that it is avowedly a parody of that of Zeno. Now Zeno's special trick of fence, a perfectly legitimate one, was to turn one-half of the assumed "_postulates_" of his opponents against the other half. This is the secret, for example, of the famous " paradoxes " about motion. The double assumption of the geometers whom Zeno is criticizing is that (*a*) any finite segment of a straight line can be bisected, (*b*) such a segment is a path between two end-points which are finite minima of magnitude. The geometers cannot give up (*a*) without ruining their whole scientific edifice ; they cannot give up (*b*) without destroying the parallelism between geometry and arithmetic which is part of their system. Zeno turns (*a*) against (*b*). From (*a*) it follows at once that there must be an endless series of points intermediate between any two given " end-points," and this is fatal to the view that the point has a finite magnitude. His reasoning silences his opponents because they are not prepared to surrender (*a*) by admitting the existence of " indivisible lines," nor yet to give up (*b*) by regarding the point as a geometrical zero. In exactly the same way, the " hypothesis " of the Eleatics—" if It is one " or " if there is One "—as *they* understand it, really covers two assumptions—(*a*) unity is real, (*b*) reality is unity; Plato's trick is to play off one of these assumptions against the other. This will come out more clearly if we compare the main positions of the antithetical members of each " antinomy."

A. I. " It is one ; " therefore, " it " is not many, and therefore is not a whole and has no parts. *Ergo* it has neither beginning,

---

[1] The main argument ends at 155e 3. What follows down to 157b 5 is an appended special development which would, in a modern writing, be relegated to a note.

middle, nor last part. *Ergo* it is unbounded (ἄπειρον) and has no figure (σχῆμα). " It " has no place, since it cannot be " in " anything. *Ergo* " it " cannot *change* its place, nor can it change its quality without ceasing to be one. Thus " it " cannot move. Nor yet can it be " at rest," since we have seen that it cannot be " in " any place at all, and therefore not " in the same place where it was." It cannot be identical with or other than anything. For it cannot be identical with anything but itself, nor yet different from itself. Nor can it be different from something " other " than itself. If it were, it would be different from the other in virtue of some point of difference ; thus it would have two characters at once : it would be one and also " different " from something in some specific way. That is, it would " be " two things at once, whereas, by hypothesis, it is one and only one. So again, it cannot be identical with itself. For " to be one " and " to be identical with " are not the same. Once more, if " it " were " identical with itself," it would have two characters, unity and identity, and so would be two and not one. For similar reasons, " it " can neither be like nor unlike itself or anything else. Again, it can be neither equal nor unequal to itself or to anything else. For terms are equal when they are of " the same measures " (τῶν αὐτῶν μέτρων, 140*b*). And " it," as we have seen, cannot be " the same " with anything in any respect and yet remain one. Nor can it be unequal to anything. That would mean that it has " more " or " fewer " measures than something, and therefore that it has parts.

So it can have no temporal predicates. It cannot be contemporary with, nor more nor less ancient than itself or anything else (the reasoning being exactly like that just used about equality and inequality). It cannot, then, be in time at all. For we may say of whatever occupies time, but of nothing else, that (*a*) it is at any moment " becoming older " than itself and also " becoming younger " than itself ; and (*b*) that its existence fills just the duration it does, and neither more nor less, and so it is " simultaneous with," " of the same age as " itself. Since neither statement can be made about the one, it cannot be " in time." Therefore, we must not say of it, " it was," " it became," " it will be," " it will come to be," since all these expressions involve reference to past or future, that is, to time. But the very word " is " or " comes to be " also involves a reference to time, to present time. And therefore we may not say of " it " that " it is " or " it becomes," since " it " is not in time at all. But if we cannot say " is " of the one, we cannot ascribe being to it. It must be nonexistent. And if it is non-existent, it cannot even be one, for to be one, it would have to be. But what is nothing at all can neither be named, spoken of, thought of, known, nor perceived by the senses. Thus we actually deduce from the proposition " it is one " the conclusion that nothing whatsoever can be thought or said about " it."

It has been asked what the " it " presupposed as the subject of the thesis " it is one " is. The answer, as the character of the reasoning shows, is " anything whatever which is conceived to be a mere undifferentiated unity admitting no plurality whatsoever." The argument is that *all* affirmation implies plurality of some kind, possibility of distinguishing. If there is anything which is such a mere undifferentiated unity that there are no distinctions within it, you cannot even affirm of it that it is one. It is the " hypothesis " of the Eleatics that their " One," which is the only thing there is, is just such a bare unit, and this hypothesis is self-refuting. We note then, that in I., in the hypothesis " if there is one," the emphasis falls on the unity of reality, not on the reality of unity. The assumption is that " what is is one," not that " something which is one is." The work of turning that part of the Eleatic " hypothesis " against the other is undertaken in II.

II. If the one *is* (ἓν εἰ ἔστιν), it " partakes of " being. It has *two* distinct characters; it *is*, and it is *one*. Thus it has " parts " (or, as we should say, distinct " aspects "). Unity and existence are *parts*, or constituents of " the existing one," which is therefore a *whole*. And each of these " parts," on inspection, is found to have itself the same two " parts." Each *is* a constituent of the " existing one " and each is *one* such constituent. The " existing " one " is thus an infinite manifold (ἄπειρον πλῆθος). Again, unity is different from existence, and difference is itself something different from both existence and unity. Here then are several terms—unity, existence, difference—which can be grouped into pairs. Each pair has a number—the number 2. We have thus established the existence of the numbers 1 and 2, and the addition of 1 and 2 establishes the existence of 3. We can then go on, by addition and multiplication, to establish the existence of the whole integer-series as a direct consequence of the existence of " the one." Being thus has an infinite plurality of parts, and each of these parts is *one* part ; there are as many units as there are " parts " of being. Thus not only " being " but " unity " itself turns out to be infinitely many.

Since parts are parts of a *whole*, they are contained by the whole and thus have a bound (πέρας). The " existing one," then, is not only indefinitely many or boundless, but is also bounded, and therefore has first, last, and intermediate parts—beginning, middle, and end. Thus it has a *shape* or *form* (σχῆμα) of some kind. It is " in " itself, for all the parts are in the whole, and " the one " is at once " all the parts " and " the whole." But equally the whole is not *in* the parts, either singly or taken together. To be in them all, it would have to be in each singly, and that is impossible. But it must be somewhere, if it is anything, and, as it cannot be " in itself," it must be " in " something else. Thus, considered as " all the parts," it is in itself ; considered as " the whole," it is in something not itself. Since it is " in itself " and so in *one* place (ἓν ἑνί) it is at rest ; but since it is " always in something else," it cannot be at rest, and so is moving. The one is neither a part of itself nor related to itself as whole to part, nor different from itself ; hence it is *identical* with itself. But, as we said, it is also outside itself, and therefore *different* from itself. Of course, also it is *different* from the things which are other than itself. But it is also *identical* with these other things. For there can be no difference in what is " the same." Hence " difference " can never be " in " *anything*, for, if it were so for the smallest fraction of a moment, it would be, for that time, " in the same thing." Hence the things which are not the one are not different from the one. Nor do they " partake " of it ; for then they would not be " not one," but, " in a sense, one." So they are not a whole of which the one is a part. And they are not parts of the one. The only possibility left is that they are *identical* with the one.

The one is different from other things, and they are neither more nor less different from it, but to a " like " degree. Thus the one and other things are *alike* because different. But if difference implies likeness, identity will imply unlikeness, and the one and other things have just been shown to be identical. Therefore, because identical, they are *unlike*. And yet again, in so far as two terms have the same predicate they are alike, and in so far as they have different predicates they are unlike. So the one and other things will be alike because identical, and unlike because different. And since the one has been shown to be both identical with and different from itself, it must be both like and unlike itself.

Since the one is both " in " itself and " in " other things, it will have *contact* with itself and with them. But things which are in contact must occupy adjoining regions (ἐφεξῆς κεῖσθαι), and that which is *one* cannot occupy two adjoining regions. Hence the one is not in contact with itself. But once more, nothing has contact with itself, and if there are to be *n* contacts, there must be $n+1$ things in contact. Now the " things other than the one " cannot have any number, since what has a number " partakes of unity." There can therefore be no contact between the one and other things, since contact implies number.

Again, the one is at once equal to and unequal to itself and to " other things." (*a*) If *a* is > *b*, this means that the form of μέγεθος is in *a* relatively to *b*, and the form of σμικρότης in *b* relatively to *a* ; if *a* is to be absolutely small or large, this means that the form σμικρότης or μέγεθος is " in " *a*. But neither μέγεθος nor σμικρότης can be " in " the one as a whole or in any part of it. For if σμικρότης is in the one as a whole it is equal with the one, and if it " envelops " it it is greater than the one ; in either case the form σμικρότης would be " doing the function " of the different form ἰσότης or μέγεθος. And the same reasoning applies if we suppose σμικρότης to be in any one part of the one. We may argue in the same way, *mutatis mutandis*, about μέγεθος. Thus σμικρότης and μέγεθος cannot be " in " anything whatever, and it follows that nothing, except the form of μέγεθος, can be " greater than " anything, and nothing except the form of σμικρότης " less than " anything.

Hence neither the one nor what is other than the one can be greater or smaller than the other, and therefore they must be equal. For the same reason, the one can be neither greater nor smaller than itself, and is therefore equal to itself. (*b*) Since the one is " in " itself, it contains and is contained by itself, and thus must be, as container greater, as contained less than, itself. Further, there is nothing outside the one and things other than the one. And whatever is must be somewhere, and consequently the one and " the others " must be in each other reciprocally, and therefore each of these terms is at once greater and less than the other. And therefore also the one will be metrically of " equal," " more numerous," " fewer " measures, and so numerically equal with, higher and lower than, itself and " the others."

Once more, " if there is one," the one *is*. And *is* expresses *present* participation of being. Hence the one is " in time." And time " goes on " (πορεύεται). Hence the one is always *getting* older than itself as time goes on, and therefore, since " older " always has " younger " as its correlate, it is always *getting* younger than itself also. And at any moment in this process, it *is* both older and younger than itself. And yet it fills the same duration as itself, neither more nor less, and so neither is nor grows older nor younger than itself. Again, before there can be several things, there must be one to start with. Hence the " one " must have come to be before " the others "; it must be more ancient than " the other things." Yet we proved that the one has " parts," beginning, middle, end. Its beginning must have come to be before itself; the one itself will not be there until its end also comes to be. Thus the one is the last thing to come to be; everything else is more ancient than the one. But, after all, each " part " of the one is *one* part, and thus whenever anything comes to be, the one comes to be, and the one thus comes to be contemporaneously with everything else. Next, if one thing is older or younger than another, the interval in age between the two never grows greater or less. So we may say that the one *is* more ancient or more recent than other things, but never *grows* more ancient or more recent. And yet, though the one has been " in being " (γέγονε) longer than " the others," the difference between their respective ages is steadily being relatively diminished as time goes on, and we may therefore say that, in so far as the one is more ancient than " the others," it steadily becomes less ancient relatively to them, and they more ancient relatively to it. But, in so far as it is less ancient than " the others," it is steadily growing, relatively to them, older, and they, relatively to it, younger. And finally, in so far as a time-interval remains the interval it is, the one is neither becoming more nor becoming less ancient than anything else.

In conclusion, the one, " partaking of time," has past, present, future. It was, is, will be, was becoming, is becoming, will become. It stands, has stood, will stand, in various relations. There can be knowledge of it, belief about it, perception of it, and therefore it can be named, described, and, generally, everything which was denied in I. must be affirmed.

Appendix (155e–157b).—The one, then, both is and is not, and its being is " in time." It is during some intervals, during others it is not, since it cannot be said to be and not to be *at once*. It must pass through transitions from being to not-being and from not-being to being. It undergoes aggregation and disgregation, assimilation and dissimilation, augmentation and diminution. It begins to move and ceases to move. So these reversals of the sense of a process must also be " in time." And yet they cannot be " in time " ; the reversal must be strictly *instantaneous*, occupying no time, however paradoxical we may find the conception of an instant (τὸ ἐξαίφνης) which is strictly without duration. *At* the instant of the reversal of sense, *both* members of a pair of antithetic processes must be denied of the one. At such an instant, it is not " coming to be " nor yet " passing away," neither being aggregated nor being disgregated, neither being assimilated nor dissimilated. As with states, so with processes ; both members of an antithesis must be asserted of the one and both must be denied.

Perhaps the most striking feature of this argument to our own minds is this introduction at its close of the notion of an unextended " instant." Plato is plainly stating exactly the paradoxes which beset the founders of the Calculus when they took the notion of the " infinitesimal " seriously and mistakenly supposed that the Calculus really deals either with infinitesimal increments or with ratios between infinitesimals. But the subtlety of some parts of the long development must not blind us to the fact that most of the reasoning throughout II. is purely sophistical and much of it clearly consciously sophistical, and that the fallacies committed are mostly of a very obvious kind, such as equivocation between " each " and " all collectively." Plato can and does, in this very dialogue, when it suits his purpose, expose the very confusions in question and therefore must not be supposed to be serious when he commits them. It is enough for his purpose to perplex the " eristics " by availing himself of fallacies of the kind which they habitually commit in their own argumentation. His parody of their *elenchus* is also an exposure of it. The one important point to keep in mind is that the conclusions to which he is led by his application of the Eleatic methods to the Eleatic " hypothesis " are not meant to be asserted as his own. They are simply what happens to the " hypothesis " if you make the Eleatic criticize himself by his own methods. If we wish to know what Plato himself thought of the Eleatic thesis, we must turn from the *Parmenides* to the *Sophistes*, where he is really criticizing it by the rules of a logic which is his own. For the present it is enough to remark that, just as in I., the emphasis was laid on the *unity* of " what is," with the consequence that being itself has to be denied of it, so in II. the emphasis is laid on its reality, with the consequence that the unity of the one has to be simultaneously affirmed and denied. So far, and no further, the paradoxes of the *Parmenides* prelude to the positive results of the *Sophistes*.

III. If the one is, what of " other things " ? Since they are " other " things, they are not the one ; yet they must " partake of " it. For they must have parts (if they had not, they would be just " the one "), and therefore parts of *one* complete whole. And each of these parts must again be itself *one* definite part of the *one* whole. The " other things " are therefore a manifold or aggregate (πλείω). They must be a numerically *infinite* manifold, since each " part " *participates* in unity and therefore is not itself, in its own nature, one. And yet, in the act of participating in unity, each part is " bounded " or " limited " or " determinate " relatively to the whole and to any other part ; " something arises in it " which constitutes a bound (πέρας). The " other things " are thus at once infinitely numerous and also bounded. In so far as all are " unlimited," each is *like* every other, and again each is like every other in exhibiting " limit." But in so far as each is at once unlimited and limited, each is *unlike* itself and the rest, and by similar reasoning we may show that all the antithetical pairs of predicates canvassed in I. and II. may be both affirmed and denied of the " other " things.

IV. But let us consider the same question once more. " The one " and " the others " form a complete disjunction. Neither is the other, and there is no *tertium quid*. They are thus completely " separated " (χωρίς). And what is strictly one can have no " parts." From these two premisses it follows that neither the one as a whole, nor a " part " of it, can be in " the others." They cannot participate in it in any sense. There is no unity in them, and therefore they are not even a manifold (πολλά), and have no number. They are, after all, not " both like and unlike " one another ; if they were, each of them would have in it *two* opposed forms, and would thus " partake of two," whereas we have just seen that none of them can even " partake of one," and therefore we must also deny that *either* member of the alternative " like-unlike " can be asserted of " the others." The same kind of reasoning will show that no predicates at all can be asserted of them.

III. and IV. thus answer in inverted order to I. and II. In III., as in II., the emphasis falls on the reality of the Eleatic ὂν ἕν, in IV. as in I., on its unity. III. proves for τὰ ἄλλα what II. had proved for τὸ ἕν. IV. undertakes to prove of them what I. had established for τὸ ἕν. The total result of I.–IV. is summed up for us at 160*b* 2 : " If the one is, the one is everything and is nothing at all, relatively alike to itself and to ' the others.' "

V. We come to the second half of the complete dialectical investigation proposed at 136*a–b*. *If the one is not, what follows ?* When a man says " if the one is not," or " if magnitude is not," or generally " if *x* is not," he is making an intelligible supposition. Whether we say that " the one " is or that it is not, we mean the same thing by " one " in both cases, and we mean something definite. So we may put our question in the form, "If the one *is* not, what must be true of it?" (τί χρὴ εἶναι). It must be knowable, or the statement " there is no one," " the one does not exist," would have no sense. "The others" must be *different* from it, and it from them. Thus we must be able to call the one " that " or " this " and to ascribe *relations* to it. We must not say that it *is*, but we are bound to say that it " partakes of " many things (has many predicates). It is *unlike* anything else, but *like itself*. It is not *equal* to τὰ ἄλλα, for then it would be *like* them; hence it is *unequal* to them, and therefore has magnitude, is greater and less. But whatever is greater than *x* and less than *y* is equal to something. Thus the *one* must, after all, be *equal* to something. It must also have *being* of some kind (μετέχειν πῃ οὐσίας), because we can ascribe *true* predicates to it, just as " what is " must partake of not-being, since it " is not " whatever can be truly denied of it, so " what is not " must in a sense be, since " it is " whatever can be significantly predicated of it. And since the " non-existent one " thus both is and is not, it must pass from one of these conditions to the other and so change. It must exhibit motion. But again, it is nowhere, and thus cannot change its place, nor rotate, nor suffer change in quality (for if it did, it could no longer be "the one"). Thus it has no motion, and so is at rest. But it is also moving and therefore does change in quality, for whatever has moved " is no longer *as* it was but otherwise." The one, then, alters and does not alter, and so at once " comes to be " and " passes away " and does neither. Everything can be affirmed of it and everything denied. (Thus V. corresponds to II. ; all that had been proved of the one in II. on the assumption that the one *is*, is proved of it in V. on the assumption that it is *not*.)

VI. And yet again, " if the one is not," that means that being is wholly denied of it. The denial is absolute and must be understood without qualification. If the one is not, it cannot come to *be*, nor pass out of *being*, since it can neither get nor lose what is, *ex hypothesi*, wholly foreign to it. Neither can it *alter* in any way, for the same reason, and therefore it cannot *move*. Nor can it be at rest, for to be at rest is to *be* " in the same place " at successive times. It can have no predicates or relations, for if it had any, it would *be* whatever you truly assert of it. Hence it cannot be known, thought of, perceived, spoken of, or named. (Thus what was proved about the one in I. on the assumption that it exists, is now proved on the assumption that it does not exist. In either case nothing can be affirmed or denied of it.)

VII. " *If the one is not*," *what must be said of* " *the others* " ?— They must be " other than " and therefore *different* (ἕτερα) from something or we could not call them " the others." As there is no " one " from which they could differ, they must be different from one another. They must also be different infinite *assemblages* (ὄγκοι), not different *units*, since, *ex hypothesi*, there is no unit

Each of them must be an infinite assemblage, different from the rest of these assemblages, which falsely *seems* on a distant view to be one single thing. Since each such assemblage *seems* to be one thing, there will seem to be a definite number of them, and there will *seem* to be a *least* among them, though this again will seem to be many and numerous by comparison with its own components. Each assemblage will be bounded by others (will have a πέρας), but will have in itself neither first term, middle, nor last term (*i.e.* each assemblage will be an infinite series without end-terms, and every component of it will be another assemblage of the same type). Thus each will *seem* to be both bounded and unbounded, to be like or unlike any other, according as we take a distant or a near view of it. (In general, all that III. had said of τὰ ἄλλα will *appear* to be true of them.)

VIII. And yet, to go over the ground for a last time, " if there is no one," τὰ ἄλλα obviously cannot be one. And they cannot be many, for then each of the many would be one. They must be zeros, and no multitude can be constructed out of zeros. And they do not even *seem* to be one or to be many. By hypothesis, "the unit " is just nothing at all, and hence nothing can even seem to be a unit ; *a fortiori* nothing can seem to be *many*, a collection of units. By carrying the thought out it would follow that τὰ ἄλλα have none of the positive or negative determinations we have ascribed to them, and do not even seem to have any. *Nothing* can be thought or said of them, (a conclusion which answers to that drawn in IV.). Thus we may summarize the result of our whole series of antinomies by saying that " whether the one is or is not, it and ' the others ' alike, are and seem to be, and also are not and do not seem to be, all sorts of things (πάντα), relatively both to themselves and to one another " (166c 2).

In the four discussions which take for their point of departure the non-existence of the " one " or " unit," even more obviously than in those which have preceded, the ultimate source of our perplexities is the ambiguity of the word " is." We get contradictory results according as " is " is taken to be the symbol of predication (Peano's ε), or that of *existence* (Peano's ∃).[1] Many of the inferences turn simply on this confusion of a predication with what we now call an " existential proposition." It is legitimate parody to employ this fallacy, because, as we can see from the remains of the poem of Parmenides, the whole point of Eleaticism lies in ignoring the distinction. To make it clear, and to show that Eleaticism had ignored it, is, in fact, the main purpose of Plato's *Sophistes*. So long as he is merely undertaking to show that the Eleatic logic would be even more damaging to the Eleatic " postulate " than to the Socratic postulate of μέθεξις, he is fully entitled

---

[1] There is, of course, a further confusion of both with the symbol of *identity* (=). The poposition *A is an a* is treated on occasion as implying both *A exists* and *A is identical with a.* (Not to mention the further refinement that *existence* also appears to be itself a *vox equivoca.*)

to avail himself of the double-edged tools of his opponents. It does not follow that Plato himself was not alive to the ambiguity when he wrote the *Parmenides* and only discovered it in the interval between the composition of that dialogue and of the *Sophistes*. The presumption from the skilful way in which he makes or ignores the distinction in the *Parmenides* just as it suits his immediate purpose is that his own logical doctrine is already complete in his own mind ; the parody of Megarian dialectic probably serves a double purpose. It provides a highly enjoyable philosophical jest, and also provokes the thoughtful mind, by the manifest impossibility of the conclusions reached, to reflections which may prompt the reader to discover the sources of the trouble for himself, without waiting to have them explained to him by Plato. More than any other dialogue the *Parmenides* has the appearance of being written for a rather circumscribed group of readers ; it was presumably meant to amuse the literary circles but to fructify in the students of the Academy.

See further :

BURNET.—*Greek Philosophy, Part I.*, 253–272.
RITTER, C.—*Platon*, ii. 63–96 ; *Platons Dialoge*, 1–24. (Stuttgart, 1903.)
RAEDER, H.—*Platons philosophische Entwickelung*, 297–317.
NATORP, P.—*Platons Ideenlehre*, 215–217.
APELT, O.—*Beiträge zur Geschichte der griechischen Philosophie*, 3–66. (Leipzig, 1891.)
STEWART, J. A.—*Plato's Doctrine of Ideas*, 68–84.
STALLBAUM, G.—*Platonis Parmenides*. (Leipzig, 1848.)
WADDELL, W.—*The " Parmenides " of Plato*. (Glasgow, 1894.)
WAHL, J.—*Étude sur le Parménide de Platon*. (Paris 1926.)
DIÈS, A.—*Platon, Parmenide*, vi.–xix., 1–53. (Paris, 1923.)
ROBIN, L.—*Platon*, 119–140.
HARDIE, W. F. R.—*A Study in Plato*. (Oxford, 1936.)
TAYLOR, A. E.—*Parmenides Zeno and Socrates* (*Philosophical Studies*, London, 1934, pp. 28–90).
TAYLOR, A. E.—*Plato's Parmenides*. (Oxford, 1934.)
LEE, H. P. D.—*Zeno of Elea*. (Cambridge, 1936.)
TANNERY, P.—*Pour l'Histoire de la Science Hellène* (ed. 2, by A. Diès, Paris, 1930, c. x. *Zénon d'Elée*).

CHAPTER XV

SOPHISTES–POLITICUS

THE dialogues which we have still to consider all reveal themselves, by steady approximation to the style characteristic of the *Laws*, as belonging to the latest period of Plato's activity as a writer. In particular they all agree linguistically in the adoption of a number of the stylistic graces of Isocrates, particularly the artificial avoidance of *hiatus*, a thing quite new in the prose of Plato. They also agree, as regards their form, in two important respects. All of them are formal expositions of doctrine by a leading character speaking with authority ; the part of the other speakers is merely to assent, and there is no longer any thoroughly dramatic eliciting of truth from the clash of mind with mind ; in every case, except that of the *Philebus* where there is a good reason for the exception, Socrates is allowed to fall into the background, and in the *Laws* he is absent. To account for so marked a change in manner even from the *Theaetetus* and *Parmenides*, it seems necessary to suppose a reasonably long interval of interruption in Plato's literary activity, and if, as we have seen reason to think, the *Theaetetus* was composed just before Plato's visit to Syracuse in the year 367, we can account for the interruption by the known facts of his life. From 367 down to at least 361–360, the year of Plato's second and longer sojourn with Dionysius II and his final resolution to take no further direct part in the affairs of Syracuse, he must have been too fully occupied in other ways to have much time for composition. We must probably, therefore, think of this whole group of latest dialogues as written in the thirteen last years of Plato's life, 360–348/7. Since the *Sophistes* and *Politicus* attach themselves outwardly to the *Theaetetus*, and the former, in fact, contains the critical examination of Eleatic principles which that dialogue had half promised, it is reasonable to hold, as most recent critics do, that the *Sophistes* opens the series. The curious state of the text of the *Laws*—it is not permissible to account for it by the arbitrary assumption that our MSS. are less trustworthy for the *Laws* than for other works—seems to show that the work had never received the author's final revision. Thus Plato's activity as a writer has no assignable *terminus ad quem* earlier than his death. Beyond this, we have no special evidence by which to date the composition of the individual dialogues. The main thing which is clear about the whole group is that Plato felt that the logical, cosmological, and juristic matter with which they deal could not be handled by Socrates without a gross violation of historical truth; hence the selection of other characters to play the principal part, except in the *Philebus*, which deals with the same ethical problems we have already met in the *Gorgias* and *Republic* as the " speciality " of Socrates.[1]

In a biography of Plato it would be necessary to dwell at some length on the precise character of his experiences at Syracuse, as illustrated by his extant correspondence with Dionysius and Dion. I must be content to refer the reader for all details to the excellent accounts of Grote[2] and E. Meyer,[3] and the shorter narrative of Professor Burnet.[4] The chief points which have to be borne in mind are these. Plato's interposition in Syracusan affairs had from the first a very practical object. The immediate political necessity was to secure the future of Greek civilization in Sicily and the West against the double peril that the work of Dionysius I might be undone by the aggressions of Carthage, or that, under a successor unequal to the position, the Oscans or Samnites whom that vigorous ruler had employed might usurp the sovereignty of Syracuse for themselves. The project of Dion and Plato was clearly that Dionysius II should first be educated into statesmanship himself, and should then use his position to convert the real though informal " tyranny " at Syracuse into a constitutional monarchy embracing the cities which Dionysius I had subdued, and strong enough to hold both the Carthaginians and the Italians at bay. The hope of making a scientific statesman out of Dionysius II appears not to have survived Plato's experiences of 367/6, and, indeed, had always, according to *Epistle* vii., been a very remote hope; the more modest anticipation that the personal feud between Dionysius and Dion might be accommodated and that constitutional monarchy might at least get its chance, though an imperfect chance, took Plato back once more to Syracuse in 361. It even outlasted his final disillusionment about Dionysius, as we see from the fact that most of the correspondence with that monarch belongs to the time after Plato's last departure from Syracuse. For the years between 367/6 and 361/360 we have only one contemporary document (*Epistle* xiii.). The suspicions which have been felt about the letter have been based entirely on its contents; linguistically it is above suspicion. One or two of the objections commonly raised are curiously captious. It is said, absurdly enough, that the reference to Plato's mother as still living, and to the existence of four

---

[1] The *Sophistes* and *Politicus* would have to be dated earlier if E. Meyer and others were justified in identifying them with the διαιρέσεις spoken of in *Ep.* xiii. as sent with that letter to Dionysius (*i.e.* in 366 or at latest 365). But the way in which these διαιρέσεις are mentioned (*op. cit.* 360*b*) should show that the reference is not to works of Plato, but to *specimens* or *samples* of " divisions " (πέμπω σοι τῶν διαιρεσέων—partitive genitive).

[2] *History of Greece*, chapters lxxxiv.–lxxxv.

[3] *Geschichte des Altertums*, v. 497–528.

[4] *Greek Philosophy, Part I.*, 294–301.

great-nieces whom he, as their most well-to-do kinsman, may be legally required to portion, are ludicrous. Yet it is a fact that old ladies do sometimes live to be centenarians, especially when they belong to families of marked longevity, and that elderly men some-times have a number of young nieces. Plato has even been thought incapable of estimating the expense of his mother's anticipated death and funeral at ten minae, on the ground that in the *Laws* he limits such expenses to one mina ; as though Plato and his mother were living in the Cretan colony for which the *Laws* professes to legislate.

Read without misconceptions of this kind, the document is a natural one enough, and highly creditable to the writer. Apart from references to certain small commissions undertaken by Plato at the request of Dionysius, and from an introduction to him of Helicon, who had studied under Eudoxus and Polyxenus as well as in the school of Isocrates, as a man who could be serviceable to him in his studies,[1] the writer is chiefly concerned with a friendly settling of accounts, such as was inevitable in the situation. Plato must have been put to considerable expense and inconvenience in removing himself for months to Syracuse ; he is anxious to be as little beholden to Dionysius in return as possible, but thinks it reasonable that he should receive what assistance he may need in meeting the impending expense of burying his mother and portioning the eldest of his grand-nieces, who is on the point of marrying her uncle Speusippus.[2] Dionysius had also undertaken to defray the expenses of his voyage to Syracuse.

Apart from this settlement of accounts between the parties, the letter deals with two other matters. Dionysius had employed Plato's offices in attempting to obtain a credit on the Aeginetan banker Andromedes, who declined to make any advance, on the ground that he had found it difficult to recover advances made to Dionysius I. Application in another quarter was more successful, and Plato takes the opportunity to administer a courteous homily to the young king on the importance of prompt discharge of money obligations and attention to one's accounts. The details of the transaction in question are only hinted at, but it can hardly have been concerned simply with the personal settlement between Dionysius and Plato. More probably Dionysius wanted a credit for his own purposes, and found it difficult to obtain one from bankers who had known his father as an unsatisfactory customer. This would explain the emphasis laid in the letter on the necessity to a monarch of a good financial reputation.

[1] Helicon would thus represent at once the political ideas of Isocrates, the mathematics of Eudoxus and the formal logic of Megara.

[2] The request is not, as often supposed, for portions for all the nieces. Plato asks to be helped, if necessary, to portion the eldest niece, now on the point of marrying. He mentions the portioning of the others, one of whom is an infant, simply as possible future contingencies. The dowry he thinks necessary, thirty minae, is not, as some have supposed, a large one, but, as the letter says, a " moderate " or " middle-class " portion, as will be seen by reference to contemporary speeches for the courts which deal with these matters.

There is also a cryptic reference to the relations between Dionysius and Dion, who was at the moment living in a sort of real, but not technical, banishment at Athens. The writer says that he has not actually approached Dion about a certain matter, but his judgment is that he would take the business very ill, if it were proposed ; in general, Dion's attitude to Dionysius is reasonably amicable. Probably the matter, about which Dionysius had clearly asked for a confidential opinion, may be his own desire that Dion should dissolve his marriage with Arete, aunt of Dionysius. This would be a way of showing that he had no sinister designs on the " tyranny " of Syracuse, and, in fact, when Dionysius became more suspicious, the marriage was forcibly dissolved without Dion's consent. We may fairly take it that Dionysius would have preferred a " parting by mutual consent " and had asked Plato's opinion on the matter. If so, Plato's reply amounts to a tactful disapproval of the project. There is nothing discreditable to him either in his being consulted or in the response that the suggestion of such an arrangement would gravely embitter Dion's feelings.[1]

SOPHISTES-POLITICUS

Though the main interest of the *Sophistes* is logical, that of the *Politicus* political, outwardly the two form a single whole, and both are externally linked more loosely with the *Theaetetus*. The assumption is that we are still in the spring of the year 399. The personages of the *Theaetetus* have reassembled, as had been suggested in the last words of that dialogue (210*d* 3), but Theodorus has brought a friend with him, an Eleatic pupil of Parmenides and Zeno, who is—the words imply that one would not have expected it —a really profound " philosopher." After a brief initial conversation this Eleatic visitor takes the conduct of the conversation into his own hands ; Socrates and Theodorus relapse into what is all but unbroken silence. The Eleatic remains throughout anonymous, and in this respect stands alone among the characters in Plato, but for the other example of the Athenian who plays the leading part in the *Laws*. We could hardly be told more plainly that these two personages are purely fictitious ; the object of the fiction seems to be that, as they have no historical character to sustain, they may be used freely as simple mouthpieces for the views of their creator. No one doubts that this is the case with the Athenian of the *Laws*. We are not entitled to say that he is meant precisely as a portrait of Plato by himself, but he is certainly meant to represent the ethics and politics of the Academy. Our Eleatic, too, turns out to be a respectful but exceedingly outspoken critic of the main thesis of his nominal teacher, Parmenides. The suggestion plainly

[1] There is no question of a private plot between Plato and Dionysius against Dion's family happiness. The dissolution of a " royal " marriage, if that is really the matter in question, is an " affair of state," and it would be quite proper in a young monarch to ask confidential advice on such a point. Plato's answer is plainly meant as a strong dissuasive.

is that, in spite of all divergences, it is Plato, and not the professed Eleatics of Megara, who is the true spiritual heir of Parmenides. One of the objects of the *Sophistes* in particular is to justify this claim.

Formally there is a further link between the *Sophistes* and the *Politicus*. The question propounded at the opening of the *Sophistes* is whether sophist, statesman, philosopher, are three different names for the same person, or three names for two types of person, or names for three different types.[1] The answer of the " Eleatic " is that the three characters are all distinct. The object of the two dialogues is ostensibly to prove this by defining first the sophist and then the statesman ; both definitions are obtained by elaborate and repeated use of the characteristically Academic method of subdivision of a genus (εἶδος) into its constituent species. The method itself has consequently to be explained and illustrated by simple and half-playful examples. Incidentally this explains what might at first seem a strange feature of the *Politicus*. We can understand the silence of Socrates in the *Sophistes*, where the logical matter of the discussion takes us far away from the circle of ideas commonly represented by Plato as familiar to him. But the problems of politics are precisely those in which the Socrates of the *Gorgias* and *Republic* had been peculiarly interested, and we might have expected that here he would be given his old part of chief speaker. What makes this impossible is not so much the particular character of the results arrived at, though they do depart to a marked degree from the uncompromising " idealism " of the *Republic*, but the necessity of employing the precisely formulated " method of division." The peculiarity of both dialogues is that each has thus a double function. Each has certain definite results to be arrived at ; each is meant, at the same time, independently of its special conclusions, to be an elaborate exercise in the careful employment of logical method. As far as " results " go, we might say that the object of the one is to explain the true character of a significant negative proposition, of the other to justify " constitutionalism " in politics. But we must not allow ourselves to forget that both have further the common purpose of presenting us with an " essay in philosophical and scientific method." Hence the chief speaker in both must be a logician ; it is because the speaker is a " formal logician," with a sounder logic than that of the Eleatics of Megara, that he is represented as the true continuator of Parmenides and

---

[1] Thus the question arises, Did Plato intend to devote a further dialogue to the character of the " philosopher," and if he did, must we suppose that he abandoned his design, or are we to identify the *Philosopher* with some existing dialogue ? In antiquity some persons thought of the *Epinomis* (D.L. *Vit. Plat.* 60 ; so, doubtfully, Raeder, *Platons philosophische Entwickelung*, 354). Moderns have thought of the *Parmenides* (Stallbaum, at one time, Zeller), *Phaedo* (Schleiermacher), *Republic* vi.–vii. (Spengel), *Symposium* (Schleiermacher). Chronological reasons, even if there were no others, make all these suggestions impossible except the first. This also seems excluded by the impossibility of regarding the *Epinomis* as anything but a part of the *Laws*.

Zeno. The true cure for the "antinomies" of the "eristic" is not to desert logic for some method more "varied and flexible," but to be *more* in earnest with it.

1. THE *SOPHISTES*.—The opening words of the dialogue show us how keenly Plato feels that the Megarian formal logic is a departure from the genuine Socratic spirit of pursuit of real truth. He is greatly relieved to learn that the Eleatic friend of Theodorus is a "truly philosophic soul"; from his antecedents he had expected rather to find in him a θεὸς ἐλεγκτικός, a "fiend" in constructing dilemmas, (like those of the *Parmenides*). But the true philosopher is not always easy to recognize; he is taken sometimes for a sophist, sometimes for a statesman, and sometimes for a downright madman. Now this raises the question whether the philosopher, the sophist, the statesman, are three distinct characters, or two, or possibly are all the same. The genuine Eleatic tradition is that they are three distinct types, though it is hard to define the precise differences between them (217*b*). The Eleatic undertakes, if Theaetetus will act as respondent, to attempt a precise delineation of one of the three types, the sophist, though he warns his audience that the discussion will be long and tedious, a distinct hint that the name "sophist" will be found to stand for something less readily recognizable than the familiar type of the fifth-century teacher of "goodness." We discover, as the dialogue proceeds, that the persons meant are, in fact, the Megarian pedants of an uncritical formal logic. They are "sophists," not genuine philosophers, precisely because they have never subjected the principles on which their own logic rests to a thorough critical scrutiny. (In fact, they are "dogmatists" in Kant's sense of the word.) This special use of the word σοφιστής is a real innovation in terminology, though its adoption by Aristotle, who regarded his Megarian opponents as conscious tricksters, has given rise to the modern conception of sophistry as the deliberate abuse of logic. The length of the discussion is due to the difficulty of analysing so elusive a thing as the spirit of uncritical logical formalism.

Illustration of Method (218*d*–221*c*).—Our problem, then, is to frame a satisfactory definition, and it is to be solved by a method characteristic of Plato and the Academy, the method of accurate logical *division* of a genus into its constituent species. As this method was definitely a creation of Plato and his immediate followers, it is necessary to explain and illustrate it for the reader by applying it to a simple and familiar case; Plato chooses that of the *angler*. Of course, as Burnet has said, the example is half-playful; the very baldness of the illustration chosen is an advantage since the simplest and most obvious illustrations are the best for the purpose of setting the principle of the procedure in the clearest light. In practice the use of the method in the Academy led to results of great importance. Thus the tenth book of Euclid's *Elements*, that great repertory of demonstrated propositions about "quadratic surds," is at bottom concerned with the attempt to make a systematic classification of such expressions. The vast zoological work of Aristotle, again, belongs mainly to the years before he had finally separated himself from the Academy, and thus has to be taken in connexion with the similar, though no doubt inferior, work in the same field of Speusippus and other Academics, and their starting-point, as we can see from the remaining fragments of the book of Speusippus on *Homologies*, was the search for a satisfactory classificatory system. The *Laws* again offers us repeated examples of the importance of the same problem in the field of jurisprudence and political theory. The services rendered to science by Plato's elaboration of the method of division have to be measured by results of this kind, not by the easy examples furnished to the " general reader " in the *Sophistes* and *Politicus*.

In principle the procedure is this. If we wish to define a species *x*, we begin by taking some wider and familiar class *a* of which *x* is clearly one subdivision. We then devise a division of the whole class *a* into two mutually exclusive sub-classes *b* and *c*, distinguished by the fact that *b* possesses, while *c* lacks, some characteristic *β* which we know to be found in *x*. We call *b* the right-hand, *c* the left-hand, division of *a*. We now leave the left-hand division *c* out of consideration, and proceed to subdivide the right-hand division *b* on the same principle as before, and this process is repeated until we come to a right-hand " division " which we see on inspection to coincide with *x*. If we now assign the original wider class *a* and enumerate in order the successive characters by which each of the successive right-hand divisions has been marked off, we have a complete characterization of *x* ; *x* has been defined. The Aristotelian rule of definition by " genus and difference, or differences " is simply the condensation of this Academic method into a formula ; a still more exact reproduction of it has been given in our own times in W. E. Johnson's account of the progressive determination of a " determinable " (*Logic*, i. xi). It is, of course, presupposed that we are already adequately acquainted with the " determinable " or " genus " *a* itself, and that, at each step in its further determination, we have the " gumption " to select as the character constitutive of the new " right-hand " division one which is *relevant* to the specification of *x* and also itself admits of further " division " ; finally that we recognize the point at which the process can stop because *x* has now been sufficiently specified. The satisfaction of these conditions depends on our native acumen and our acquaintance with the subject-matter, and no rules can be given for it, precisely as no rules can be given for the discovery of a promising explanatory hypothesis. The method, like all scientific methods, will not work *in vacuo*. This is what Aristotle seems to ignore in his depreciatory remarks about the " method of divisions " (*Analyt. Prior.* A 46a 31 ff.). He complains that the method involves a *petitio principii*. From *man is an animal, an animal either is mortal or is immortal*, it does not follow that *man is mortal*, but only that *man either is mortal or is immortal*; and so with the other successive steps of the division, so that nothing is really *proved* when the division has reached its end.   As a criticism of Plato, the complaint misses its mark.   When we are told in the *Sophistes* that hunters capture their prey either by snaring or by wounding, and that the angler is a hunter who makes his capture by wounding, we are presumed to know from our acquaintance with the facts of life that a rod and line are not a snare ; there is no intention to *prove* the point by making the division.   We are as much entitled to draw on our general stock of information for guidance as we are to go to the same source for our information that the Duke of Wellington is a man when we infer his mortality from the admitted mortality of men.   Neither the syllogism nor any other formal logical device can enable us to dispense with first-hand acquaintance with facts.   Possibly some members of the Academy may have overlooked this limitation in their enthusiasm for their own method, but Aristotle seems equally to be forgetting for the moment that his own method of syllogism is subject to precisely the same conditions.

DEFINITION OF THE SOPHIST (221c–237a)

The actual " division " by which the definition of angling is obtained need not detain us long.   So far as it is anything more than a simple illustration of the method to be adopted in characterizing the sophist, its further point lies in the playful suggestion of certain unpleasing features which we shall rediscover in the sophist himself, who is also, among other things, a kind of " angler."   The division itself may be graphically represented by the following tree :

```
        Arts
         ∧
of making   of acquiring
             ∧
of acquiring   of capture
by consent
                 ∧
    of open   of stealthy capture
    capture    =hunting
                   ∧
        of lifeless   of living
          things       things
                     ∧
          of terrestrial   of animals which
            animals        live in a fluid
                        ∧
            of birds   of fishes
                          ∧
        fishing by nets   fishing by striking
                            ∧
                by night   by daylight
                             ∧
                  by a stroke   by a stroke
                  from above    from below
                                = angling.
```

By a summing up of the " differences " constitutive of the successive " right-hand " divisions we get the definition that angling is an art of acquiring by stealthy capture creatures which inhabit the water, the capture being made by daylight, by a stroke delivered from below. We might, of course, have carried the division further, but our acquaintance with the facts makes this superfluous. It is a linguistic fact that we give the name *angling* to every procedure which has the characteristics enumerated and to no other.

We now proceed to apply this method several times over to the sophist. (Thus Plato is fully alive to the point that the same species may be determined by the division of different *genera*, the same term may have more than one adequate definition ; relevancy to the purpose in hand will be the principle which guides us in the selection of a *genus* to be divided. Each of the successive divisions is meant to throw some one characteristic of the sophist into strong relief.)

(*a*) We might follow the precise example we have just chosen down to the point where we divided the art of hunting living things, and then turn our attention to the left-hand division of this. For the sophist is a hunter of " civilized living beings," that is, of men. He hunts them, not like kings, pirates, and kidnappers, by violence, but by the arts of persuasion. Persuasion may be practised in public, or, as the sophist practises it, on individuals. And the persuading may be done by one who *gives* a present (the lover), or by one who *takes* a fee. And the fee may be taken for making one's self agreeable and amusing (as in the case of the κόλαξ or " parasite ") or got by promising to impart " goodness." This gives us a possible definition of the sophist as a professional of the art of hunting rich young men individually for a cash payment, on the pretence of educating them (223*b*). Thus the points brought out are the sophist's commercialism, the unreality of his " wisdom," and his suspicious family likeness to the " parasite."

(*b*) The sophist, however, has more guises than one. We might detect him again if we started by dividing the left-hand branch of the art of acquisition, namely, acquisition by exchange, and then subdivided exchange into exchange of presents and exchange of commodities (ἀλλακτική). Exchange of commodities again includes the transactions of the man who sells his own produce and those of the middleman who sells that of others. And middlemen may be engaged either in the home retail traffic (καπηλική) or in inter-state trade (ἐμπορική). One branch of such inter-state trade is traffic in mental wares (ψυχεμπορική), serious or trifling. Under this head falls inter-state traffic in sciences (μαθήματα), and one form of this traffic is the selling of scientific knowledge of " goodness." This enables us to define the sophist again as a retail exporter of the knowledge of goodness (224*d*), though we must add that he sometimes retails his merchandise in the home market, and occasionally even manufactures some of it himself. As before,

stress is laid on the commercialism of this peddling of spiritual
wares for a living, and a new point is introduced by the suggestion
that the "ideas" which the sophist sells are usually not his own,
but come to him "second-hand."

(c) Yet again, we might diverge from our original division at a
different point. We spoke of an art of acquisition by open capture.
We may, if we please, divide this into two branches, competition
and combat. (Plato is thinking of competition for prizes in the
great games, at the Dionysia, and the like.) And combat may be
physical or mental; the latter being contention, of which "discourses" (λόγοι) are the weapons. When the "discourses"
employed are question and answer, we call this sort of contention
disputation, and disputation about right and wrong (περὶ δικαίων
αὐτῶν καὶ ἀδίκων) carried on under regular rules of the game is
what we call eristic. When eristic is practised for gain, it is
sophistry. Thus the sophist now appears as a man who makes
a paying business of contentious disputation about right and
wrong (226a). He invents insincere paradoxes about morality
for gain.

(d) We have not done with him even now. Making an entirely
new start, we observe that there are a host of familiar occupations
which are all alike in being ways of *separating* different materials
from one another. Now some of these separate like from like,
others aim at separating a better from a worse, and all these we may
group together under the common rubric of purifying or refining.
Purification or refining, again, may be either of the body or of the
soul. And purification of the soul itself may be of two kinds,
since there are two "vices" which affect the soul: spiritual disease
and spiritual deformity (αἶσχος), villainy, "wickedness" as it is
commonly called, and mere ignorance (ἄγνοια). The soul is
purified from wickedness by justice, "the art of discipline"; from
ignorance by teaching (διδασκαλική). But there are different
kinds of ignorance and correspondingly different kinds of teaching.
The worst form of ignorance is the self-conceit which believes itself
to know what it does not know; the teaching which purifies from
this is what we mean by παιδεία, "education," "culture," and all
other teaching is merely subservient to it (229d). There are, again,
two forms of παιδεία. There is the old-fashioned method of the
père de famille who relies for success on rebuke, mingled with exhortation; this we may call *admonition* (νουθετητική). But some
of us are convinced by reflection that all error is involuntary,
and that no one can be expected to "learn better" until he has
been convinced that as yet he does not know. They adopt the
milder method of trying to convince the man who has a false conceit
of his wisdom by asking questions which lead him to discover
his ignorance for himself and to feel the longing for knowledge
(230b-e). We cannot well give the name sophist to those who
practise this kind of teaching (which is, in fact, the familiar "obstetric" of Socrates); the title would perhaps be too high an

honour for them.[1] There is a certain resemblance between the eristic and these dialecticians, but it is such a resemblance as that of the wolf to the high-bred dog. Still, for the sake of argument, let us waive this scruple and define the sophist once more as a professional of the art of purifying the soul from its false conceit of wisdom (231b). (Here, of course, it at last becomes clear what quarry Plato is hunting. The definitions already suggested would cover Protagoras and his rivals ; the specialization of the sophists' method to " contention by question and answer " definitely indicates that the persons meant are inferior imitators of the Socratic dialectic who abuse its resources for a purpose which Plato regards as at bottom commercial.)

(e) We have still not gone quite to the root of the matter. The sophist has exhibited the guises successively of : (1) a paid hunter of rich youths ; (2) an exporter of spiritual lore ; (3) a retailer of such lore in the home market ; (4) a small manufacturer of it ; (5) an " athlete " of controversy ; (6) a " refiner " of convictions which are hostile to knowledge (though his title to this last distinction is not uncontested). To penetrate deeper we must ask what one calling there is which can masquerade in all these guises (233a). The answer is suggested by the consideration that, as we have seen, the sophist is, among other things, an ἀντιλογικός, a pitter of discourse against discourse, a contradiction-monger. He undertakes to discover antinomies everywhere—in divinity, in nature, in morals and politics—and writes books explaining how the specialist in all these departments can be reduced to silence. Now obviously one man cannot really be an " expert " in all knowledge. The secret or miracle (θαῦμα) of sophistry lies in contriving to *appear* to be such a universal expert. A clever illusionist might delude children into the belief that he can *make* anything and everything by showing them *pictures* of all sorts of things at a sufficient distance. (If a child were young enough, it would, *e.g.*, take the men and horses in a cinema picture for real animals.) Why then should there not be an analogous art of illusion by means of discourses which imposes " imitations " of truth on the youthful mind ? May we not say that at bottom the sophist is an " imitator " and

[1] 231a 3, μὴ μεῖζον αὐτοῖς προσάπτωμεν γέρας. Ostensibly the remark is ironical. Socrates, for example, who made it a point in his defence that he had never professed to be able to " educate men," would say that he had never aspired to so fine a name as σοφιστής. But the suggestion is intended that the practitioner of the Socratic method is the " philosopher " whom it is the nominal purpose of the dialogue to distinguish from the sophist. φιλόσοφος, as we have learned from the *Symposium*, is a less assuming *designation* than σοφός (or its equivalent σοφιστής), but the character is the loftier. (Campbell's interpretation *in loc. cit.* that " the sophist seems scarce worthy of so high a dignity " seems to me to miss the irony and to be grammatically impossible.) The connexion of 231a with what follows in 231b is simply that the speaker proposes, for the time being, to disregard the scruple he has just raised and to define the sophist in terms which are really applicable only to the true dialectician. This is, as we are to see, irony. He professes for the moment to take the eristic at his own valuation. The expression ἢ γένει γενναία σοφιστική (231b 7), which has been oddly misunderstood, is meant merely to point the irony.

"illusionist" (γόης) or "wizard" (θαυματοποιός, 235b). This yields
us a new "division." The sophist's "illusionism" is clearly a
branch of εἰδωλοποιική, the art of making images. But there are
two kinds of "images." Some are "likenesses" (εἰκόνες), exact
reproductions of an original in all its proportions and colouring.
But in some cases, as in that of the makers of "colossal"
figures, the artist has to distort the real proportions to get a result
which will look right when seen from below ; [1] we may call his product
a "phantasm" (a deceptive reproduction), to distinguish it from
an exact likeness. The question then arises whether the sophist's
product is a "likeness" or a "phantasm" of truth. If we say
that it is a "phantasm," a distorted reproduction of a reality, we
commit ourselves to the view that there are such things as *false*
appearances, *false* discourses, *false* beliefs. We are assuming that
there can be an "*unreal* something," that "what is not" can be.[2]
This has always been felt to be a paradox, ever since Parmenides
called attention to the difficulty, and we must therefore examine
the question to the bottom (237a–b). This leads us straight up to
what, though formally a digression, is materially the main topic
of the dialogue.

Criticism of Eleaticism (237b–249d).—The difficulty must first
be fairly stated. If we say seriously "*x* is not," it seems clear that
the subject of the statement *x* cannot be anything that *is* (an ὄν),
and therefore cannot be a "somewhat" (τὶ), since "somewhat"
always means *a* "being," *an* "existent." Hence he who speaks of
"what is not" seems to be speaking about "nothing." Yet can
we say that he is "saying nothing" (making an "unmeaning
noise," 237e) ? This is bad, but there is worse behind. If we are
to talk about "non-entity" at all, we must do so either in the
singular (μὴ ὄν) or in the plural (μὴ ὄντα). But mere non-entity
can have no predicates, and so neither unity nor plurality can be
significantly asserted of it. Hence it seems we can neither think
nor speak of it at all (238c). Yet in the very act of saying that "*it*
is unthinkable," by using the word "it" we are talking of non-
entity as though it were *one* thing (239a). It seems then that we
must say nothing whatever about "what is not," and this ruins
our attempt to characterize the sophist as an artist in illusion.
He would argue that an illusion is "what is not," and therefore
that "maker of an illusion" is a meaningless sound. Unless the
sophist really "takes us in" by producing a false belief in us,
there is no illusion, and if he succeeds for a moment in producing
the illusion, a false belief must be *something* real ; but, as we have
just seen, that is what the sophist will not admit. He will say that

[1] Plato's example (235e) is that in the case of the colossal work of art, the
upper parts (the head of the statue, the capital of the column, etc.) must be
made larger in proportion than it really should be if it is to look duly pro-
portioned when seen from the ground.

[2] And if you try to get over the difficulty by saying that the illusion is really
something, it *is* a "real illusion," he will merely reply that "real illusion" =
"real unreality" (240b).

in calling a belief "false" we are involving ourselves in the contradictions we have just exposed. If we are to defend ourselves against this attack, we shall have, with all respect, to correct the fundamental principle of the great Parmenides, to say that "what is not in a way *is*, and what is, also, in a sense is *not* (241d)." If the Eleatic principle "what is is, what is not is not " is maintained in all its rigour, there can be no such thing as a "likeness" or "image," and no "false beliefs."

We may say that Parmenides and all the early thinkers have dealt with the problem too light-heartedly, almost as though they were merely "telling a fairy-tale" (μῦθον, 242c). Some of them have said that what is is three things (?Pherecydes); another (?Archelaus),[1] that it is two, *e.g.* the hot and the cold, or the moist and the dry; Xenophanes, and our own school of Elea, that it is one. Heraclitus and Empedocles say that it is both one and many: the "austerer" Heraclitus that it is both at once, the "laxer" Empedocles that it is each by turns. Every one of them is too anxious to get on with his story to trouble himself about our ability to follow him (242c–243a). But if we look into the matter, these different statements about what is are just as puzzling as we have found the current statements about what is not. We have to ask what these thinkers really meant by *being* (243d). When a man says, *e.g.*, that "the hot and the cold are" and are all that there is, he says of each of them that *it is*, and thus he means by "being" something, and one something, which is different both from "being hot" and from "being cold" (243d–e) (he is making a "synthetic" judgment). So the Eleatic who says that "there is just *one* thing," can hardly mean that "one" and "being" are just two equivalent names for the same thing; if he means what he says, he cannot well admit that there are names, since no name is a name for itself (244b–d). Parmenides complicates matters still more when he talks of "what is" as a *whole*. He implies that it has parts, but how can this be if it is "just one"? If "wholeness" is a character of the one, then there are two significant terms, "one" and "whole," and not merely one; if "wholeness" is a significant term but "what is" is *not* a whole, it is *not* something, and so there *is* something wanting in "what is." If "wholeness" means nothing at all, there is the additional complication that "what is" cannot even come to be, for "whatever has come to be in every case has come to be as a *whole*."[2] Thus we see that the theory of those who

---

[1] Or is the reference to some Pythagorean cosmology? In any case, the "opposites" are those which play the chief part in the various Ionian cosmologies.

[2] τὸ γενόμενον ἀεὶ γέγονεν ὅλον, 245d 4. The meaning is that a γένεσις or process of "being evolved" is, at any moment of its duration, unfinished, a process to a goal not yet reached. So long as the process is still going on, that of which it is the "evolution" is not yet there. When it is there, the process is over and complete. That process is *finished*. This is the principle used by Aristotle in *N.E.* x. to prove that a feeling of pleasure is not a γένεσις. Note the way in which this short section of the *Sophistes* assumes and recapitulates the difficulties already developed in the second part of the *Parmenides*.

draw this precise and fine line of distinction between " what is " and " what is not " involves difficulties about being quite as serious as any of those raised by the Eleatics about " what is not " (245e).

To complete our survey of the difficulties about being, let us consider what " the other side " [1] have to say about it. This " other side " falls into two main sections who are at loggerheads with one another, like the giants with the gods in the old tale. The " giants " insist that nothing is but what can be laid hold of and felt ; " being " and " body " are the same thing. The other party maintain that real being consists of " intelligible bodiless forms," and that the bodies which their opponents regard as the only being are " becoming," not " being." We need not say much about the thesis of the " materialists," but we may imagine them to be at any rate so far better than they actually are as to deign to answer our questions civilly. We will then ask them whether there *is* not such a thing as a soul; whether some souls are not righteous and wise, others wicked and foolish. If they say Yes, as they must, we shall ask whether this does not imply that wisdom and the other " virtues " are something, and whether they are anything that can be seen or handled. Even if they try to save themselves by saying that the soul is a kind of body, they will hardly venture to say that wisdom is a body, nor yet to say that it is nothing at all, though a genuine and persistent materialist would have to take this second alternative. We shall have gained our point with any of them who will admit that anything whatever can be and yet not be a body. To put it most simply, we shall ask them to admit no more than this, that anything which has any " power," however slight, of acting or being acted upon, certainly is—in fact, that " what is " is δύναμις (" force "), active or passive (245e–247e).

It is not clear precisely what persons are meant by the " giants " of materialism. They are certainly not atomists, as has sometimes been fancied. The atomists who insisted on the reality of the ἀναφὴς φύσις (*vacuum*) cannot be classed among persons who say that only what can be seen and felt is. Nor could Theaetetus say, as he does (246b), that he has met " lots " of these men ; he would not meet many disciples of Leucippus, to say nothing of Democritus, in the Athens of 399 B.C. It seems to me most probable that Plato has in view the crass unthinking corporealism of the " average man," rather than the doctrine of any particular " school." We must also be careful not to make the mistake of taking the proposed definition of " being " as " force " for one seriously intended by Plato. It is given simply as one which the materialist could be led to concede if he were willing to reflect, and we are warned that, on further consideration, we might think better of it.

---

[1] τοὺς ἄλλως λέγοντας, 245e 8. Since they are opposed to the διακριβολογούμενοι ὄντος τε πέρι καὶ μή, *i.e.* the Eleatics, this " other side " must be pluralists of various kinds ; the men of Megara cannot be included among them, as they were always regarded in antiquity as Eleatics of a kind, and are, of course, among the διακριβολογούμενοι περὶ ὄντος. This point is important.

The point is simply that the " materialist " who uses the notion of a " force " has already surrendered his materialism.

We have now to consider the view of the " friends of forms," the immaterialists already referred to. They hold that " becoming " and " being " are sharply contra-distinguished. Our body is in touch with " becoming " through sense-perception ; our mind in touch with real and unchanging " being " through thought (248a). We have to ask them what they mean by " being in touch with " (τὸ κοινωνεῖν). Do they mean " acting or being acted on by a force " ? Theaetetus may not be able to say, but the Eleatic speaker is familiar with the persons who are being criticized, and consequently knows that they would reject the statement. So far from accepting the identification of being with " the power to act or be acted on," they would say that both action and passion belong to the realm of " becoming " ; " being " neither acts nor is acted on.[1] But we shall then ask them whether they do not admit that " being " is known by the mind, and whether " being known " is not " being acted on " and knowing, acting. To be consistent, they will have to deny both statements. If " being " is acted on in being known, it πάσχει (" has something done to it "), and therefore is " moved," and it is not true that being is simply " quiescent " (ἠρεμοῦν, 248e).

We cannot seriously think that " what utterly is," the perfectly real, neither thinks nor lives, or that it thinks but does not live. If it thinks and is alive, it must have a soul, and if it has a soul, it cannot stand everlastingly still ; it must have movement. If mind is to be real, there must be both motion and variety and also rest and uniformity in things (248e–249d).

It has been a much-discussed question who are the thinkers to whom the dialogue ascribes the doctrine just criticized. From the statement of their theory, it is clear that they are extreme dualists, who regard " being " and " becoming " as absolutely sundered. They then identify " becoming " with the sensible world, and consequently hold that the sensible world has no real existence. To put the same thing from the epistemological stand-point, they deny that sensation has *any* cognitive value, or plays any part in the apprehension of truth. This shows that the reference cannot be to the type of theory ascribed to Socrates in the *Phaedo* and *Republic*. The whole point of the doctrine of " participation " of sensible things in forms was just to break down the absolute severance between a real world of " being " and an illusory world of " becoming," by ascribing a partial and secondary reality to the sensible. So the doctrine of " recollection " was intended to assign sensation a genuine, if a humble, part in the process of reaching truth ; sensation is, on that theory, just what " suggests " or " calls into our minds " the thought of the forms. *A fortiori*,

---

[1] 248c 7–9. The view suggested is that acting and being acted on, both involve process and change : hence neither can be found in the realm of eternal and changeless being.

if the criticism is not aimed at Socrates, it is not directed against Plato's " earlier self " or disciples, if there were any, who retained a doctrine which Plato had once held, but had outgrown.   Nor, again, can the persons meant be Euclides and his friends at Megara. They were strict rationalistic monists who did not admit the existence of even an " illusory " world of " becoming," and regarded themselves as Eleatics, whereas the " friends of forms " are one of two groups who have both been carefully distinguished at 245e from the Eleatic monists.   The one hint of their identity is given by the Eleatic visitor when he says (248b) that Theaetetus probably will not know their views, but he is acquainted with them himself διὰ συνήθειαν, because he has lived with the men in question.   As the speaker is certainly an Italian Eleatic—he refers to his own personal recollections of Parmenides (237a)—we must plainly look to Italy for these rationalistic dualists.   Hence Proclus is pretty likely to be right when he says that the persons meant are " wise men in Italy " whom he also calls Pythagoreans, especially, as Burnet remarks, since he makes the statement without any discussion as though it were the recognized traditional interpretation.[1]   The Pythagorean formula that " things *are* numbers " would readily lend itself to development along these lines.

The Meaning of Significant Denial.—The Platonic Categories (249e–259e).—So far we have reached the result that though movement and rest are contraries, both of them certainly *are*.   There *is* movement and there *is* rest, and when I say " rest *is*," I do not mean that rest is motion, nor when I say that " motion *is*," do I mean that motion is rest.   Motion, rest, being, are all distinct, and being embraces both of the others ; though it is neither of them.   It thus seems as difficult to say what " being " is the name for, as we found it to say what " what is not " is the name for.   If we can answer the one question we shall probably find that we have learned how to answer the other [2] (250e–251a).

Every one knows that we are always making assertions about, *e.g.*, a man, in which we do not confine ourselves to the statement that " a man is a man," but say something further about his complexion, his shape, size, good or bad qualities, and the like, and in all these cases we are saying that a man is not one thing only, but at the same time many (not merely a man, but ruddy, tall, lanky, patient, etc.).   Raw lads and men who have begun their thinking too late in life [3] fasten eagerly on such " synthetic " propositions,

[1] Proclus in *Parmen.*, p. 562 Stallbaum (Cousin, iv. 149) ; *Greek Philosophy, Part I.*, 91 n. 1, 280.

[2] This means, to use language more familiar to ourselves, that if we can solve the question, What is implied by an affirmative " synthetic " proposition ? the answer will also solve the problem about significant denial.   The upshot of the whole discussion is to be a general theory of the conditions of significant non-identical assertion.

[3] I can see no allusion to Antisthenes in the use of the adjective ὀψιμαθής (251b 6).   There is no reason why he should be dragged into the discussion, and, as he had been a pupil of Gorgias (D. L. vi. 1), the epithet ὀψιμαθής is really not quite applicable to him.

and declare them to be absurd, on the ground that they all imply that one can be many and many one. They plume themselves on the discovery that only identical propositions can be true. This is the thesis we have really to combat (251c–d).

If we consider the three concepts being, rest, motion, there are just three logical possibilities : (a) that they all " partake in " one another, *i.e.* any one can be predicated of any other ; (b) that none of them can be conjoined with any other, *i.e.* none can be predicated of another ; (c) that *some* of them can be predicated of (" partake in ") others. We can reject (b) at once, since it would forbid us to say both that there is motion and that there is rest. This would make an end of the views alike of Heracliteans, Eleatics, " friends of forms," as well as of all the physicists who account for things as due to the aggregation and disgregation of " elements," whether infinite in number (Anaxagoras) or finite (Empedocles). The theory is actually self-refuting, since you cannot state it without using such words and phrases as " is," " apart from everything else," " by itself," and the like (252c). You cannot even deny the possibility of " synthetic judgments " except by making such a judgment. The proposition " only identical propositions are true " is not itself an identity ; (a) is an even more absurd theory, since it would require us to affirm that rest is motion and motion rest (252d). Thus the only possible alternative is (c) that some " concepts " will " combine " and others will not (252e), just as some letters can be combined to form syllables, others cannot.

This illustration suggests a further point of supreme importance. Vowels hold a " favoured position " among the elementary sounds of language. Every syllable must contain a vowel, and the vowels are thus the " connecting links " which make syllabic composition possible. There is a special art (τέχνη), that of the " teacher of letters," which considers what combinations of consonants by the help of a vowel are possible and what are not, just as another art, music, considers what combinations of notes of different pitch will make a tune and what will not.[1] So there clearly must be a science which considers what " concepts " will " blend " so as to give rise to " discourses " (λόγοι) and what will not, and again whether there is a class of concepts which, like the vowels in spelling, make all combinations possible, and another class which gives rise to distinctions (253c). Thus logic is here, for the first time in literature, contemplated as an autonomous science with the task of ascertaining the supreme principles of affirmative and negative propositions (the combinations and " separations "). But this task of dividing things rightly according to their " kinds," detecting one " form " (ἰδέα) where it is disguised by complication with others, and distinguishing several which form a single complex, is precisely that of " dialectic." Thus we have unexpectedly identified the true philosopher before

---

[1] The reference is, of course, to permissible and unpermitted melodic intervals, not to the construction of " chords." Thus the parallel between γραμματική and μουσική is kept exact.

we have come to an end with our identification of the sophist.
The philosopher is the dialectician who knows how to find the many
in the one and the one in the many (253a–e). We had already been
told much the same thing by Socrates in the *Phaedrus*, but there is
an important point in which the problem now under discussion
marks a great advance on the theories ascribed to Socrates in the
earlier dialogues.   In them, the combinations or complications
considered seem always to be the " things " of the everyday world
of sense.   The sensible " thing " had been treated in the *Phaedo*
and *Republic* as a sort of complex " partaking " at once in a plurality
of forms—in fact, as a bundle of " universals."   Each form had
been spoken of as something independent of every other, and the
only " combination " of several forms contemplated had been their
simultaneous   " presence "   in   the   same   αἰσθητόν.   Or, to put
the same thing from the opposite point of view, the question had
never been raised, what constitutes the *particularity* of the particular thing.   Plato is now raising a different issue.   We are to see
that forms *as such* can " combine," so that you can predicate one
" universal " of another, and it is the special function of the new
science Plato is contemplating to specify the lines on which such
combination is possible.   The doctrine of forms as known to us
from the " Socratic " dialogues throws no light on this problem,
and this, no doubt, is why it is never referred to in our dialogue.
It is not that it is disavowed, or even called in question, but that it is
simply not relevant to the issues which Plato now finds himself
called on to face.   We might, perhaps, say that the language of
the *Phaedrus* about the dialectician's task of seeing the one in the
many and the many in the one, if followed up, raises precisely
the same question.   But the *Phaedrus* is, to all appearance, one of
the very latest " Socratic " dialogues, and Plato is probably there
on the verge of straining the limits of historical accuracy.

We cannot now work out the whole inquiry into the " communion " between forms, but we may deal with it for the special
case of a few of the most important and all-pervading.   As we have
said, " being," " motion," " rest," are three of these *universalissima*
or μέγιστα γένη.   Two of them—rest and motion—refuse to combine.   But the third will combine with both of the two, since both
motion and rest *are*.   Moreover, each of the three is distinct or
different (ἕτερον) from the other two, but identical with itself.
And difference and identity, again, are neither motion nor rest.
Nor is either of them the same as " being."   We ascribe being alike
to motion and to rest, but this is not to assert that motion is identical
with rest.   For " different from " is always a relative term, whereas
being has an absolute sense.[1]   Thus we have five, not merely

---

[1] 255d 3–7.   The meaning is, that I cannot intelligibly say " *x* is different "
without specifying some *y* from which *x* differs.   But I can intelligibly say
not only that " *x* is a *z*," but that " *x* is," " there is an *x*."   To this absolute sense
of " is " there is no corresponding sense of " is different."   See Campbell's
note, *loc. cit.*

three, Forms (εἴδη, γένη, both words are used interchangeably) to consider — being, motion, rest, identity, difference. *Difference* manifestly pervades all the others, for each of them is different from the rest, and so " partakes of the form of different " (254*b*–255*e*).

Let us now consider the relations between these five all-pervading forms. (It is never said that the list of the *universalia universalissima* is complete, though later Platonists, like Plotinus in *Ennead* vi. 1–3, treat them as a complete list of Platonic " highest universals," or categories.) Motion is not rest, nor rest motion. But both *are* and are identical with themselves, and thus " partake " (μετέχει) of being and identity, and also, since each is different from the other, of difference. Thus we can say, *e.g.*, that motion is— it is *motion*; but also is *not*—it is *not* rest. But in just the same way we can say that motion " partakes of " being and so *is*— there is such a thing as motion; but motion is not identical with being, and in that sense we may say that it is *not*, *i.e.* it is not-being. The same line of thought shows that " not-being " may be asserted of all the five forms already enumerated, even of being itself, since each of them is different from any of the others, and thus is *not* any of the others (255*e*–257*a*).

Now these considerations enable us to dismiss the difficulties which have been raised about " not-being." When we say that something " is not so-and-so," by the not-being here asserted we do not mean the " opposite " (ἐναντίον) of what is but only something different from what is. " *A* is not *x* " does not mean that *A* is nothing at all, but only that it is something other than anything which is *x* (257*b*–*c*). Not-beautiful, for example, is the name not of nothing but of all the things other than the things which are beautiful. And the things which are not-beautiful *are* just as truly as those which are beautiful. The " not-large " *is*, every whit as much as the " large," the " not-right " as much as the " right." In making a denial we are not asserting an antithesis between nothing and something, but an opposition of something and something else different from it (258*b*). We may say, then, that " not-being " is as real and has as definite a character as being. This is our answer to Parmenides. We have not merely succeeded in doing what he forbade, asserting significantly that " what is not, is "; we have actually discovered *what* it is. It is " the different " (τὸ θάτερον), and since everything is different from all other things, we may say boldly that " not-being " is thoroughly real (ὄντως ὄν, 257*b*–258*e*). Henceforth we shall not give ourselves any further concern about the alleged paradox that " what is not " is that unthinkable thing " the absurd," the " opposite " of what is. It is childishly easy to see that any thing is different from other things and so may be said to be " what is not "; the true difficulty is to determine the precise limits of the identity and difference to be found among things (259*d*).

Application of our Result to the Problem of " False Opinion " : Final Definition of the Sophist (260a–268c).—Our identification of

" not-being " with difference shows that " not-being " itself is a pervasive and categorial feature in things. We have now to consider whether this pervasive characteristic can " combine " with discourse and belief (δόξα). If it cannot, if we cannot say or think " what is not," falsehood of speech or thought will not be possible, and consequently there will be no such thing as error or illusory belief, and no " resemblances," " likenesses," or " phantasms," all of which *seem* to be what they are not. The sophist's last retreat will be to the position that at any rate discourse and belief will not " blend " with " what is not " : there is no such " complex " as utterance of or belief in what is not, and therefore no such art as the fabrication of " phantasms." This is the position from which we have now to dislodge him (261*a*). Let us begin by an analysis of discourse. Just as not all combinations of letters yield a syllable, not all complexes of forms a concept, so not all combinations of words yield a significant discourse. The words of a language fall in the main into two great classes: nouns (ὀνόματα) and verbs (ῥήματα). The verbs are vocal symbols of actions (πράξεις), the nouns are the names of the agents in these actions. A string of verbs, *e.g.* " walks, runs, sleeps," is not a λόγος or significant statement, neither is a string of nouns, *e.g.* " lion, deer, horse." The simplest discourse, the unit in discourse, is the complex of a noun and a verb, *e.g.* " a man learns." Here not only is something *named*, but something is signified (262*d*). Further, a discourse or statement must be " of " or " about " something and it must have a certain " quality," must be ποιός τις. Thus, take the two statements, " Theaetetus is sitting down," " Theaetetus, to whom I am now speaking, is flying." The " quality " of the first statement is that it is *true*, of the second that it is *false*, for Theaetetus is not at this moment flying but sitting [1] (263*b*). And both the statements are *about* Theaetetus, the false statement no less than the true. A statement which was not about (or " of ") some subject would not be a statement at all (263*c*). Thus some complexes of nouns and verbs are false. Now thinking is an internal conversation in which the mind asks itself a question ; belief or judgment (δόξα) is the statement, affirmative or negative, in which the mind answers its own question, without audible words. Sometimes the internal conversation is accompanied by sensation, and then we call it " fantasy " (*i.e.* when the debate of the mind is started by the attempt to interpret a present sensation). Hence, from the possibility of false statement or discourse follows the equal possibility of false belief or judgment and false " phantasy " (erroneous interpretation of sensation,

[1] I cannot agree here with Burnet (*Greek Philosophy, Part I.*, 287 n.) that what is meant by the *quality* of propositions is *tense*. It is clear from 263*b* 2–3 that the speaker means " truth-value," as has usually been supposed. His point is that the two statements about Theaetetus have *opposed* " quality " ; but both of them have the *same* tense. For a similar reference to " true " and " false " as the " qualities " of propositions, which Burnet has overlooked, see *Philebus*, 37*b* 10–*c*2.

264*a-b*). A false belief that Theaetetus is now flying is not a belief about nothing at all but a belief about Theaetetus which asserts of him that he is performing a definite πρᾶξις different from that which he is in fact performing. This disposes of the old objection to our assumption that there are "images" and "phantasms," and so we may go back to our attempt to define sophistry as a branch of the art of making images (264*c*). We now proceed to divide the making of images more carefully.

We said that we could divide it into the making of accurate likenesses (εἰκόνες) and the making of inaccurate images (φαντάσματα), both of which are forms of "imitation." Let us reconsider this more in detail. The making of imitations is a branch of creative art, as distinguished from the arts of acquisition, as we said long ago. We may now divide creative art into divine creative art and human creative art. The difference is that God (not, as the thoughtless say, unintelligent "nature") creates all real things without any pre-existing material (πρότερον οὐκ ὄντα, 265*c*) [1]; man's "creating" only originates fresh combinations of materials thus created by God. Next we may take a new principle of division, and subdivide both divine and human creation into creation of actualities and creation of images.[2] The images created by God are such things as dreams, shadows thrown by a light, reflections in a polished surface ; those created by man are pictures of things made by man (houses, etc.), and the like. Here we bring in again our former and now justified subdivision of images. Man-made "images" are either accurate *likenesses* or phantasms. Phantasms again are of two kinds: those produced by tools of some kind (like the painter's brush), and those for which the producer acts as his own tool, as when another man (*e.g.* an actor) imitates the physical bearing or the tone of voice of Theaetetus by his own facial gestures and his own voice, and this kind of imitation is what we call *mimicry* (μίμησις). Mimicry, again, is twofold. A man may know what he is mimicking or he may not know it. Many persons who have no knowledge of the true figure (σχῆμα) of justice or goodness generally try to make their speech and action exhibit the appearance of what they fancy to be goodness and justice, and some of them succeed in conveying the impression they are aiming at. This is a plain case of mimicry by a man who does not know (267*d*). There is no recognized name for this specific "mimicry by the man who does not know," so we coin one for the moment and call it δοξομιμητική

---

[1] The language, perhaps, must not be unduly pressed, but it proves at least that the idea of "creation *ex nihilo*" was quite intelligible to Plato.

[2] The language of 266*a* 1 about the division in πλάτος presupposes this diagram :

Divine creation of actualities.	Human creation of actualities.
Divine creation of images.	Human creation of images.

("counterfeiting"). But there are also two varieties of the art of counterfeiting. The maker of the sham may honestly believe that he knows the reality which, in fact, he does not know. Or he may have an uneasy suspicion all the time that he does not really know what he poses as knowing (268*a*). In the second case he is an "ironical imitator," a conscious "humbug," as well as a mere counterfeiter—in fact, an impostor. The professional sophist has had too much practice in "discourse" to be a mere honest pretender ; he must have his suspicions of the unsoundness of his own "discourse," and thus his "art" falls under the head of conscious counterfeiting—imposture or charlatanism. Only one further distinction remains. The charlatan may practise his imposture in lengthy discourses before a public audience, or he may employ brief discourses with an individual in which he tries to make his interlocutor contradict himself. The one type of impostor is the δημολογικός, the dishonest "spell-binder" passing himself off for a statesman ; the other is the sophist who counterfeits the "wise man," more than half knowing himself to be a fraud (268*c*).

One closing remark may be made on the main result of the whole dialogue. Plato's solution of the old puzzle about "what is not" and the later paradox, grafted on it, of the impossibility of error, turns, as we see, on distinguishing what we should call the use of "is" as the logical *copula*, or sign of assertion, from the existential sense of "is." To us the distinction may seem almost trivial, but it only seems so because the work of making it has been done so thoroughly, once for all, in the *Sophistes*. Though Plato lets us see that he thought the ordinary Megarian a good deal of a conscious impostor, the difficulty about the possibility of error and of significant denial was a perfectly serious one with its originators and remained so until the ambiguity had been thoroughly cleared up. It is impossible to overestimate the service to both logic and metaphysics rendered by Plato's painstaking and searching examination. We shall realize the magnitude of the issue better if we are careful to remember that, as Plato himself knew, the problem is at bottom one which affects *all* assertion. His point is that *all* significant propositions are "synthetic," in the sense that they are more than assertions of the equivalence of two sets of verbal symbols, and that they are all "functions" of an "argument" which is "not null." This would be a mere paradox if there were no other sense of "is" than the existential. We can see that a completed logic would have to carry the work of distinction further than it is carried in the dialogue. Notably the "is" which asserts the identity of the object denoted by two different descriptions (*e.g.* "the victor at Pharsalia is the consul of the year 59 B.C.") needs to be distinguished both from the "copula" and the existential "is." But the first step and the hardest to take is the recognition of the "copula" and its functions for what they are. Since the *Sophistes* takes this step for the first time, it is not too much to say that it definitely originates scientific logic.

2. THE *POLITICUS*.—We must deal much more briefly with the application of the method of division to the definition of the states-man. We may be content, now that we have grasped the principle of the method, to concentrate our attention in the main on the solid result it is used to establish. Plato's real purpose in the dialogue is much less merely to continue his lesson in logical method than to deal with a fundamental problem in the theory of government on which men's minds even now continue to be divided. The issue is whether, as the actual world goes, " personal rule " or impersonal " constitutionalism " is the better for mankind, and Plato means to decide definitely for constitutionalism and, in particular, to commend " limited monarchy." His reading of the facts of the political situation is that monarchy has to be revived, as it was in fact revived by Philip, Alexander, and their successors, but that whether it is to be a great blessing or a great curse will depend on the question whether it is revived as constitutional monarchy or as irresponsible autocracy. Democracy, with all the defects it has shown at Athens, is the most tolerable form of government where there is no fixed "law of the constitu-tion," autocracy the most intolerable ; where there is such a fixed law, a monarch is a better head of the executive and administrative than either a select " oligarchy " or a " town's meeting."

In form, the dialogue is a continuation of the *Sophistes*, with one change in *personnel*. Theaetetus is present as a silent character, but, to save him from undue fatigue, his place as respondent is taken by his companion, a lad named Socrates, who has been present without speaking through the *Theaetetus* and *Sophistes*. (The great Socrates, as in the *Sophistes*, is completely silent but for one or two opening remarks.) The " younger " Socrates has been introduced by one phrase in the *Theaetetus* ($147d$ 1) as studying mathematics in company with Theodorus and Theaetetus. He is known to have been an original member of the Academy. There is one further reference to him in a letter belonging to the later years of Plato's life, usually condemned by the editors as spurious, though for no obvious reasons (*Ep.* x. 358e). We learn there only that he is in poor health at the time of writing. Aristotle mentions him once (*Met. B* 1036b 25) in a way which shows that he belonged to the Academic group reproached elsewhere by Aristotle for their " pam-mathematicism." [1] I think it all but certain that it is he, not the

---

[1] The statement of Aristotle is that " the younger Socrates " used to regard the " material " constituent in the human organism as falling completely outside the definition of man, exactly as the bronze of which a disc is made falls outside the definition of circle. Aristotle's own view is that there is a difference in this respect between a " physical " and a mathematical definition. It is indispensable to mention in the " physical" definition the fact that the material constituents in which the formula is embodied are such-and-such. (Just as it would be no adequate definition of water to say that it is " two units of something with one of another " : you must specify that the two units are units of *hydrogen*, and the one a unit of *oxygen*.)

great philosopher, to whom Aristotle's practice has given a spurious immortality as a " logical example." [1]

The dialogue begins (257a–267c) with an attempt to characterize the science or art (τέχνη, ἐπιστήμη) of the king or statesman (πολιτική, βασιλική) by assigning it a place in the classification of the sciences. Some " sciences " merely provide us with knowledge, others, including all the industrial arts, produce results embodied in material objects (σώματα). So we begin by dividing sciences into the practical (πρακτικαί) and the purely cognitive (γνωστικαί). The science of the statesman involves little or nothing in the way of manual activity ; it consists wholly or mainly in mental insight. Thus we class it as *cognitive* (259c). But there are two kinds of cognitive sciences. Some of them are concerned merely with apprehending truths, and may be called *critical* (arithmetic is an example) ; others issue directions or orders for the right performance of actions, and may be called *directive* (ἐπιτακτικαί), and the science of the statesman is of this kind (260c). Again, some of the arts which direct merely pass on instructions which do not originate with the practitioner (as a " herald " communicates the directions of his commander), others give *sovereign* directions, are sovereignly directive (αὐτεπιτακτικαί, 260e). Among these we may distinguish those which have the sovereign direction of the production of living beings from those which are concerned with the production of lifeless things (like the science of the master-builder). This puts the king, or statesman, in the class of persons exercising sovereign control over the production and nurture (τροφή) of animals. Next, there is a distinction between the groom, who exercises this calling on a single animal, and the herdsman who practises it upon a whole herd or flock ; the statesman, like the latter, has a flock or herd to deal with (261d.).

We are thus on the point of identifying the ruler with the shepherd of a human flock (a metaphor as familiar to the Greeks from their recollections of Homer as it is to us from the language of Old Testament prophecy). But it would be a violation of the rules of method to divide " herds " at once into herds of men and herds of other animals. We must observe the rule that a division must proceed in regular order from the highest to the lowest classes, not make sudden leaps. It is unscientific to single out mankind as one class and to throw all the rest of the animal world, irrespective of all differences of structure, into the one ill-constituted group " other animals," just as it would be unscientific to divide mankind into Greeks and " barbarians " (262d) or integers into " the number 10,000 " and " all other numbers." A reflective crane might be

[1] This seems to be proved by the illustration of *Topics* 160b 28 ff., where it is supposed that " if Socrates is sitting, he is writing." Obviously the allusion is to a scene in the lecture-room ; Socrates is one of the audience and it is wrongly inferred that he must be taking notes of the lecture. So the common examples, " S. is λευκός (pale)," " is μουσικός," are not naturally understood of the famous Socrates. He is not likely to have been " pallid " ; it is impossible to see an allusion to the *Phaedo* in his " sitting " and his " music."

supposed just as reasonably to divide animals into " cranes " and " brutes " (263d). We must take care to avoid constituting *infimae species* so long as our division permits of being continued. Animals may be divided into the " wild " and the " domesticated " (τιθασόν, 264a), domesticated animals into the aquatic and the terrestrial (the tame fishes of Egypt belong to the one class; our familiar domestic quadrupeds, domesticated geese, and the like to the other). The terrestrial, again, are either birds which fly or beasts which walk. From this point we may proceed by either of two alternative routes, a longer or a shorter, to the same result. The longer route is to divide " gregarious domesticated beasts " into the horned and the hornless, the hornless once more into those which can be " crossed " and those which cannot, and the last group into quadruped and biped (266b) (or, alternatively, we might have divided the hornless class into those with undivided and those with divided hoof). A division like this has a comic side to it ; it ranks that most dignified of beings, a king, much on a level with a swine-herd. But science has no concern with our conventions about dignity, and is anxious only to get at the true facts (266d). The shorter procedure would be to divide " gregarious domestic animals " into quadrupeds and bipeds. Since observation teaches us that man is the only wingless biped, we might then divide the bipeds into winged and wingless, with the same result as before (266e).

The effect of our division then is to define the statesman as a kind of herdsman of gregarious animals, with a trade of the same kind as the cow-keeper or the pig-drover, except that his herd consists of unusually " kittle " beasts. But there is a difficulty of which such a definition takes no account. In the case of the statesman there are a goodly number of rivals who might challenge this description. Farmers, corn-dealers, physicians, professors of " gymnastic," might all urge that the definition " raiser of the human herd " applies to themselves as much as to the ruler. This difficulty does not arise in the other analogous cases of the shepherd, ox-herd, swine-herd, because every one of them is at once breeder, feeder, and physician of his herd. As this is not the case with the ruler of men, there must be something faulty about the classification we have followed ; our business is next to see where the error has come in. We may get a hint from a tale we all heard as children, the story that the sun reversed his daily path in horror when Thyestes started the series of crimes which disgraced the line of Pelops by stealing the " golden lamb " (268e).

The imaginative myth which now follows (268e–274e) is built up on the basis of ideas of which we may find traces in the early cosmogonists, combined with fancies known to have been specially affected by the Pythagoreans. From the cosmogonists we have the notion of a past " golden age " before Zeus had dethroned Cronus ; many of the details about this age of gold seem to be " Hesiodic." The conception of the life of the universe as an alternation of half-cycles with opposite senses is most familiar to us from the fragments of Empedocles ; the thought of the world as a ship sailing over the stormy waters of the ἄπειρον is specifically Pythagorean,[1] though, no doubt, both Empedocles and the Pythagoreans were availing themselves of the suggestions of pre-scientific cosmologists. Thus dramatic propriety is observed by making the Eleatic visitor utilize for his story precisely the materials which would be specially familiar to a native of Magna Graecia. The tale is told simply to make an immediate point. It is wrong on principle to take any part of it as scientific cosmology meant seriously by Plato, and to attempt, like Adam, the impossible task of fitting the story into that of the *Timaeus*. In outline the story runs as follows. The tale of the sun's return on his track, like much of the existing mythology, is a fragment of a very ancient tradition about the transition from the age of Cronus to the age of Zeus. The whole may be reconstructed thus. Only God has complete immortality. The universe as a whole, being corporeal, cannot be quite immutable, but makes the nearest approximation it can to immutability by alternately revolving round the same axis in opposite senses. There are periods when God himself is at the helm of the world-ship with his hand on the rudder, and there are alternate periods when he "retires" to his look-out (περιωπή, 272e) and leaves the ship to follow its own course. The immediate result is a complete reversal of sense of all biological as well as cosmological processes. Life runs backward, in "looking-glass" fashion. The reversal of sense is attended by gigantic cosmic catastrophes, but when the first confusion is over, the ship settles down once more to a uniform course, though with a reversed sense ; at first the regularity of its processes is almost as complete as when God was steering. But as time goes on, the world "forgets God its Maker," and the irregularities due to the "lusts" inherent in its bodily frame accumulate ; all regularity is on the point of vanishing, the ship nearly founders in the "sea" of the "infinite," when God puts his hand to the tiller again, and once more reverses the sense of the cosmic movements.

The stories of the golden age, when men lived peacefully, without agriculture, clothes, or laws, are reminiscences of the condition of the world "under Cronus," when God was actually steering the ship, and acting literally as the "shepherd" of mankind, with departmental gods under him as "deputy shepherds." Our own age, that of Zeus, belongs to the period when the world is left to itself,

---

[1] For the "world-ship" see *E.G.Ph.*[3] 294, with notes *in loc. cit.* On the whole "myth" cf. Stewart, *The Myths of Plato*, 173–211 ; Adam, *Republic of Plato*, ii. 295 ff. As to the "sea," see *Politicus*, 273e 1, where the true reading is not τόπον, as given by MSS. and editors, but πόντον. This is not a conjecture of Stallbaum, but the best authenticated text, as it is the only reading recognized by Proclus, who frequently refers to the passage. The variant τόπον is senseless, but may be ancient, since it appears at Plotinus, *Enn.* i. 8, 13, ἐν τῷ τῆς ἀνομοιότητος τόπῳ—a passage where the metaphor of the ship is missing. Unless, indeed, Plotinus also wrote πόντῳ, as is just possible.

and is separated from the " golden age " by the catastrophic reversal of all motions. At this reversal the gods withdrew from their immediate direction of the human flock. Mankind were left naked, needy, uncontrolled ; all *our* arts of industry and government have been slowly acquired in the gradual conquest of nature. (The " noble savage " is thus not a figure in *our* history ; he belongs to a world where men are born as full-grown out of the earth and " live backwards.") [1]

Were the men of the golden age really happier than ourselves who belong to the " iron time " ? It depends on the use they made of their immunity from the struggle with nature for physical existence. If they used their freedom from the cares of life to glean wisdom from the beasts and one another, no doubt they were happier. If they used it merely to fill themselves with meat and drink, and to tell idle stories to the beasts and one another, we know what to think about that kind of life (272c).

The moral of the story is that our attempt to define the statesman as the " shepherd of men " has involved two errors—one serious, the other comparatively light. The serious error is that we have confused the work of a statesman in our historical world with that of one of the gods of the "age of Cronus." They actually " fed " their flock ; the statesman of the historical world does not. The minor fault was that we said truly that the statesman is a *ruler*, but made no attempt to specify the kind of " rule " he exercises. We ought to have reserved the work of " feeding and breeding " the flock for a god ; of the statesman, who is a man among men, we should have said more modestly that his business is the " tendance " (ἐπιμέλεια, θεραπεία) of the flock (275b–276b). (The object of the remark is to eliminate the " superman " from serious political theory, and so to strike at the root of the worship of the " man who can," the autocrat or dictator paternally managing the rest of mankind without the need of direction or control by law.) If we had made this clear, we should not have found the provision-dealers and others claiming that our description was as applicable to them as to the statesman. As to the other fault, it arises from overlooking an important step in our division. We forgot that the " feeding," or, as we now propose to say, the " tendance," may be either forced on the flock (βίαιον) or freely accepted by them (ἑκούσιον). This is what makes all the difference between the true " king " and the " tyrant " or " usurper." The " tyrant "

---

[1] The humorous zest of the description of life in the days when it began with old age and ended with babyhood ought of itself to prevent us from taking the story seriously. The cosmological story of Timaeus is given, not indeed as science, but as a " *likely* story," and Plato is careful, for that reason, to allow no such extravagances in it. We may reasonably infer that Plato regards the whole conception of the happiness of the alleged " state of nature " as a mere unhistorical fancy. In the real world to which we belong, man has painfully fought his way up out of hunger, nakedness, and savagery. The " state of nature " dreamed of by sentimentalists belongs to the unhistorical world where animals talk. Adam (*loc. cit.*) is an example of the danger of reading Plato without a sense of humour.

forces his tendance on his subjects: the "king" is the freely accepted ruler of freemen, a "free tender of free bipeds" (276e).

Yet we must not be too much in a hurry to accept this as an adequate account of statesmanship. We have, it may be, drawn the outline of our portrait of the statesman correctly, but we still have to get the colouring of the picture right (277a–c). To explain what we mean by this, we shall do well to illustrate our point by a familiar example. And before we do this, we may even illustrate the use of examples by a preliminary example. This preliminary example shall be taken from the way in which small children are taught their letters. At first they may be given a set of very simple syllables which they soon read off exactly. But they still make mistakes in recognizing these very same combinations when they meet with them elsewhere. We correct their mistakes by making them compare the combinations they have misread with the standard alphabet or syllabary they have already mastered. This is their exemplar; the purpose of repeatedly referring them back to it is to make them able to detect unerringly any combination given them when they meet with it again in a new setting. This is the function of every example (277c–278d).

Now for our example of the kind of discrimination which will be necessary, if we are to distinguish the statesman's "tendance" of the community from all cognate or analogous occupations. We may take it from the humble industry of weaving woollen garments. If we set to work to distinguish the weaver's industry from every other, a series of obvious "divisions"—we need not repeat them, though Plato gives them—soon leads us to the result that it is the industry of fashioning defences against climate and weather by the intertexture of wools (279b–280d). But this statement, though true, is not sufficiently precise. If we described the weaver as occupied with the "tendance" of clothes, wool-carders, fullers, stitchers, and others, to say nothing of the makers of the implements they all use, might put in a claim to be called "weavers." If we are to avoid this difficulty, we must, in the first place, distinguish carefully between the art which actually makes a thing, and those which only contribute in a subsidiary way to its production —the principal and the subordinate arts (281d–e). Next, among principal "arts" concerned with clothes, we must set aside those which have to do with cleansing, repairing, and adorning the material; this is "tendance of clothes," but not the kind of tendance exercised by the weaver (282c). Next, if we consider the work of actually making the clothes, which we will call "working in wool" (ταλασιουργική), we can divide it into two kinds, each of which may be subdivided again. Part of the work consists in separation of the composite (the carding of the wool is an illustration); part consists in combining the separate into one. And this work of combining may take either of two forms, twisting or interlacing (282d). Both the warp and the woof of the intended web are made by twisting (or spinning), the one being spun closer and the other less close ; the weaving is the subsequent interlacing of the threads of warp and woof to make the web (283a). We might, of course, have made so simple a statement without going through the tedious series of divisions which have led up to it. They might be thought superfluous and unduly prolix. This leads us into a digression on the true standard of proportion in discourse generally (283c).

We may distinguish two kinds of measurement (μετρητική) and two standards of measure—one extrinsic and relative, the other intrinsic and absolute (the actual names are mine, not Plato's). We may measure things as great and small simply by reference to one another, or by reference to the standard of τὸ μέτριον, the *right* amount, or, as it is also expressed, in words meant to sound paradoxical, κατὰ τὴν τῆς γενέσεως ἀναγκαίαν οὐσίαν (" by the standard of the being which is indispensable to the production," 283d). (The meaning is, to take a simple example, that a tea-spoonful of a liquid may be " very little " by comparison with a bucketful ; but it is dreadfully "too much," a dreadful " over-dose," if the liquid contains a concentrated poison, medicinal in minute doses.) The arts and their products, for example both statesmanship and the art of weaving, of which we have just spoken, are constantly employing this standard of the " just proportionate " in estimating excess and defect ; it is by adhering to it that " all good things " are produced and preserved. To demonstrate the reality of this intrinsic standard of measurement might prove as long a business as we found it to demonstrate the reality of " what is not," and, as we do not wish to be led too far away from our immediate topic, it is sufficient for our purpose to point out that unless we recognize it we shall have to deny the very possibility of applying science to the regulation of action (284a–d). (This thought of a " just right mean " and its significance for action will meet us again still more prominently in the *Philebus*. From the use made of it in the *Ethics* it has come to be spoken of familiarly as the Aristotelian principle of the Mean. In justice to both Aristotle and Plato it is necessary to point out that the whole doctrine is Platonic, and that Aristotle never makes any claim to its author-ship, though he is careful to call attention, throughout the *Ethics*, to the points on which he believes himself to be correcting Plato and the Academy.)

Thus the sciences generally fell into two classes—those which measure numbers, lengths, areas, velocities, etc., against one another, and those which take as the standard of their measure-ments the right mean (μέτριον), the appropriate (πρέπον), the seasonable (καιρός), the *morally* necessary (δέον). The saying that " all science is measurement " is only true on the condition that we remember this distinction between two kinds of measure-ment. {Thus Plato combines the view that " science is measure-ment " with strict adherence to the principle of the absoluteness of moral and aesthetic *values*.) As an illustration of the point, we cannot answer the question whether the disquisitions of the present conversation or of yesterday's are "excessively long" except by considering that our *primary* object has not been to define the weaver's work or even the statesman's, but to train our souls in the accurate apprehension of the most important realities—those which are incorporeal and unseen. If this purpose could not have been equally effected by a quicker method, our longest digressions cannot be said to have been "too long" (284*e*–287*b*).

We now return to the main argument. The example has impressed it on us that in defining a science it is indispensable to discriminate it from others which are (*a*) subsidiary to it; (*b*) analogous, but not identical with it. We must try to make this double discrimination for the case of the statesman (287*b*–305*d*).

Arts or callings subsidiary to a principal "art" will, with a little forcing, come under one of the following heads:

1. Those which make the *instruments* used by the principal art as its implements;
2. Those which make *vessels* for the safe keeping of products of all kinds;
3. Those which make stands and vehicles (ὀχήματα);
4. Those which make coverings and defences of all kinds;
5. Those which ornament and embellish a product, and make it tasteful—arts of "play";
6. Those which fabricate what the principal art uses as its "raw material";
7. Those which provide nutriment of all kinds (287*c*–289*c*).

If we add one other branch of art, "the rearing of herds," already often mentioned, this classification will cover all our "property" (κτήματα), except slaves and personal servants (*i.e.* except those human "chattels" who directly assist a man, in a subordinate way, in the actual *living* of his life). (The thought is that the only piece of "property" which cannot be reckoned, roughly speaking, under the head of "implements" or "provisions," is the "chattel" who is also your *assistant* in the work of living. You could not well apply to the services of your confidential clerk—who at Athens would have been your "property"—the formula that his business is to make, or to take care of, that which you *use*. He really is, in his degree, contributing to the actual "tendance" of your soul.) Thus there is the same sort of analogy between the work of the king and that of a personal servant or slave as between the work of the weaver and that of the carder or spinner. The person whom it would be most excusable to mistake for the king—the irony is characteristically Platonic—is the "menial" (289*c*). For all his pomp and circumstance, the king really is very much like a "menial servant."

We should expect, then, that the most plausible false pretender to the functions of the king would be some class of menials. On inspection we find, however, that most menials never dream of advancing such pretensions. If we extend the range of the term to include all who render " personal services," we may bring seers (μάντεις) and priests under it ; both seer and priest are " messengers " or " errand-runners " of a sort (290c–d). Now we are getting on the track of the pretender we wish to detect. Seers and priests are persons of self-importance and " prestige," as we see from many examples, particularly from that of Egypt, where it is a rule that the king *must* be a priest. But the pretender whom it is hardest to distinguish from the true statesman or king is a rather different creature, who, like the sophist, has many disguises, and may, in fact, be said to be the greatest " wizard " (γόης) and sophist of all (291c). What he really is we may discover from the following considerations.

There are three well-known types of government : monarchy (the rule of a single person), oligarchy (rule by a small select group), democracy (rule by the general citizen body). But we may add that the first two have two forms, so that the whole number of types should be reckoned as five. The single person may rule in accord with law and with the consent of the ruled,[1] or he may rule by mere force, without law ; in the first case we call him a monarch, in the second a " tyrant " (dictator, usurper). So the rule of the few, based on law, is aristocracy ; the lawless rule of the few by mere force is oligarchy. Democracy commonly retains the name whether it is based on law or on mere force (291d–292a). This is the current popular classification of forms of government. (It is, in fact, that regularly insisted on by Isocrates, a good representative of " popular culture.") But is the classification really scientific ? We have already seen that kingship or ruling is a directive science. The one relevant distinction between claimants to be rulers is therefore their possession or want of this science, not the distinctions between rule by the rich and rule by the poor, rule by fewer or more persons, on which the current classification is founded (292c). Now real knowledge of the science of ruling men is a very rare thing —rarer even than first-rate knowledge of draughts, though even that is rare enough. The number of genuine statesmen must be exceedingly few (293a). Those few, because they have scientific knowledge of principles, will be true kings or statesmen, whether they exercise their profession with the popular consent or not, with a written law as a control or not, just as the man who knows the science of medicine is the true physician whether his patients like his treatment, whether he follows the prescriptions of a textbook, or not (293a–b). In any case, he, and only he, does the work of the physician, preserves the bodily health of the patients he " tends." So the one ideally right form of statesmanship is rule by the man who has true scientific knowledge about the " tendance of the soul,"

---

[1] It is assumed that government resting on a law of the constitution is the same thing as government by consent of the governed. This is in accord with the current view that νόμος ἰς συνθήκη πολιτῶν (" the convention of the citizens "). It is not meant that anything like the original formal " social compact " has ever passed.

and makes the souls of the citizens healthy, be his methods what
they may (293*e*).

Yet it is a hard saying that it is indifferent whether government
is carried on by law or without it, and our position requires further
examination.   Legislation is, in a sense, part of the work of a statesman, and yet the ideally best thing would be the supremacy not
of the laws but of the embodied wisdom of the true king.   For
no law can be trusted to produce the best effects in every case ;
this is impossible, since the law cannot take account of the infinite
variations of individual character, situation, and circumstance.
Any law will give rise to "hard cases" (294*b–c*).   Why, then,
is legislation indispensable ?   Because it is impossible for the
ruler, who is a man with the limitations of humanity, to give individual direction in each of the countless cases which have to be
considered.   He has to fall back on giving general directions which
will suit the "average" man and the "average" situation (295*a*).

Now suppose that, over and beyond this, any practitioner of a
directive science, *e.g.* a physician, were compelled to absent himself
from his patients for long and frequent intervals, how would he
meet the risk of their forgetting his directions ?   He would provide
them with written memoranda of the regimen they were to follow
in his absence ; but if he came back sooner than he had expected,
he would have no scruple about changing these written regulations
if the case demanded it.   So the true statesman, if he could return
after an absence, would have no scruple in modifying his institutions
and regulations for similar reasons, nor a second true statesman in
changing those of a first (295*e*).   It is popularly said that an innovation in the laws is permissible if the proposer can *persuade* the
city to adopt it, but not otherwise.   Yet we should not say that a
medical man who insisted on breaking through a written rule of
treatment when he thought it necessary to do so had committed a
fault in medical treatment because the patient had objected to the
departure from the "books" ; so if a statesman makes the citizens
better men by forcing them to innovate on their written and inherited laws, we must not say that he has committed a fault in *his*
science, a "crime" or a "wrong" (296*c*).   Nor does a man's claim
to make such innovations depend on superior wealth ; the one and
only relevant qualification is his wisdom and goodness.   If he has
these qualifications, he is entitled to save the "vessel of the State"
as his goodness and wisdom direct, just as an actual pilot shapes his
course by his living "art," not by a written rule.   The wise ruler
has only one rule which is inviolable, the rule of doing what is wise
and right (τὸ μετὰ νοῦ καὶ τέχνης δικαιότατον, 297*b*).   The one
perfect "form of government" would be government by the living
insight of such an ideal ruler ; all others are mere imperfect
"imitations," of varying degrees of merit.

In the absence of such an ideal ruler, that is, in the actual
circumstances of human life, the best course is the very one we have
just pronounced absurd where the ideal ruler is presupposed.   The

laws ought to be absolutely sovereign, and violation of them should be a capital crime in a public man (297e). We may illustrate the point by recurring to the examples of the navigator and the physician. It is quite true that the competent navigator or physician frequently puts us to grave inconvenience and discomfort, and actually expects to be paid for doing so. But if this led us to make a rule that no one should practise these callings αὐτοκράτωρ (with full authority), but that anyone who pleased might follow them on the condition of always adhering to regulations approved by a public assembly of laymen, we should get very strange results, and still stranger, if we further went on to appoint our practitioners annually by lot or by a property qualification, and required them, at the end of the year, under heavy penalties, to satisfy a court that they had infringed none of the regulations (298a–299b). If we went on the further length of enacting that anyone who made a new discovery in these or any other of the practical sciences might be prosecuted as a traitor and " corrupter of youth," and put to death if convicted, there would soon be an end of science and of life itself (299b–e). But the case would be even worse if the courts entrusted with the enforcement of the supposed regulations were not expected to follow any regulations themselves, but were free to give their verdicts as personal considerations prompted (300a). After all, there was some experience (πεῖρα) which suggested these rules, and some intelligence employed in getting them generally accepted ; they were not the expression of mere individual greed or vanity or caprice.

The laws are at least an approximate " imitation " of the principles on which the living ideal " king " would act. As we said, such a man would refuse to be bound by formulae when they do not really apply. In this one respect of departing from formula and precedent, the politicians who disregard the law are like the true statesman. But, since they are by hypothesis ignorant of the principles of statesmanship, they imitate his " innovations " badly they depart from law and precedent in the wrong cases and for wrong reasons. In any community where the ruler is not the ideal scientific statesman, and that means in every society where the " sovereign " is a body of several men, and most, if not all, when he is one man, the law ought to be absolutely paramount (301a). (This means that we must eliminate from " practical politics " the " rule of the saints " at which the Pythagorean brotherhood had aimed in the cities of Magna Graecia. The infallible ruler would be a god or a superman. Supermen are not found in the historical world ; there, the sovereignty of law is the *succedaneum* for an actual theocracy, as is further explained in the fourth book of the *Laws*.)

These considerations explain why in actual fact we find five, not merely three, distinguishable forms of government. When the " well-to-do " govern with strict regard for law we have aristocracy ; when they disregard law, oligarchy. One person ruling with reverence for law is so near an imitation of the ideal statesman that we give him the same name of king. When he "pretends to act, like the true statesman, always for the best, unhampered by regulations," but is really inspired by ignorance and lust, we call him a tyrant. Democracy receives one and the same name, whether it rests on a fundamental law or not. Since the perfect scientific statesman is not met in actual life, and his place has to be taken by very imperfect laws which must not be contravened, it is not surprising that the public life of states should be as unsatisfactory as it is ; the real marvel is that some of them exhibit as much vitality and permanence as they do (302a).

It is an important, if not strictly relevant, question which of these various constitutions is least unsatisfactory. We may say at once that monarchy, the rule of a single person, is the best of all, if it is strictly subject to good fundamental laws ; in the form of sheer personal rule without laws, "tyranny," it is worst of all. As for the "rule of a few," it is "middling"; the rule of the multitude, from the inevitable subdivision of the sovereign power, is weakest of all for good or evil. Thus, where there is a fundamental law, monarchy is the best constitution, aristocracy the second, democracy the worst ; where caprice rules instead of law, democracy is least bad, oligarchy worse, despotism worst of all. (There is likely to be more "fundamental decency" in a big crowd than in a little "ring," and least of all in an uncontrolled autocrat, 302b–303b.)

We can now at last say who are the serious pretenders to the name of the statesman or king, from whom it is so important to discriminate him. They are the men of affairs in the imperfect constitutions, who delude themselves and their admirers into false belief in their practical wisdom ; they call themselves πολιτικοί (statesmen), but are really στασιαστικοί (party politicians). These are the supreme "wizards" and "sophists" of the world (303c).

We have now, so to say, purged away all the dross from our concept of statesmanship ; only good ore is left. But as "adamant," itself a precious thing, is separated from gold in the last stages of the process of refining, so we have still to distinguish statesmanship from the tasks of the soldier, the judge, the preacher of righteousness who "persuades men" into goodness by the noble use of eloquence. Reflection satisfies us that the business of the statesman is not to persuade or to win battles, but to decide whether persuasion or enforcement shall be adopted, whether war shall be made or not. So his business is not to administer the laws but to make the laws which the courts then administer. Each of the callings just mentioned has charge of one action, the proper performance of which is its contribution to the "tendance" of the city ; the statesman's superior function is to control and co-ordinate all these inferior activities (303d–305e). His task is to weave together all classes in the State into the one fabric of the life of the whole.

Just as a web is made by the intertexture of the stiffer threads of the warp and the softer of the woof, so the garment of national life or character has corresponding components : there are the harder and sturdier and the softer and gentler temperaments, as material. Speaking generally, there are two main types of temperament—the adventurous, keen, and masculine, and the quiet and gentle. The very " virtues " of the two are, in a way, opposed ; that of the one is valour, that of the other modesty and orderliness (σωφροσύνη). And either, carried to the extreme and untempered by the other, degenerates, the one into harshness, violence, and fury, the other into softness and sloth. If the life of a society permanently takes its tone from the predominance of the softer type, it begins by being unambitious, peaceful, and neighbourly, but there is the risk that, for sheer want of grit and backbone, the city will end by being enslaved ; where the adventurous, ambitious type prevail, the same result is likely to follow from the hostilities in which such a society is sure to be entangled by its aggressiveness (308a). The task of true statesmanship is just to weave these two contrasted strains well and deftly together. The true statesman would begin by a careful testing of the temperaments in the State ; he would then demand that the educator should train the characters of the young, so as to make them into the right kind of material from which to weave the fabric of a sound public life, as the weaver of cloth looks to the carder and others to provide him with properly prepared yarn (308d). Thoroughly intractable temperaments would be excluded by death and banishment, or at least reduced to the status of slavery (309a).

The statesman then proceeds to give instruction for the interweaving of the threads he has selected, the characters who can be trained into the combination of valour with *sophrosyne*. He will regard as the threads of his warp the temperaments in which the original bias is to action and adventure, as the threads of the woof the tamer and quieter. The actual weaving of the two together is a double process ; the " everlasting " in the souls of the citizens will be knit by a " divine " bond, the merely " animal " by a " human." The " divine " bond is constituted by " true and assured beliefs " about good and right, bad and wrong. These the statesman will look to the educator to provide. The effect of such an education is to make the naturally daring soul gentler by teaching it respect for the rights of others, and to develop the natural orderliness of the quiet and unambitious into *sophrosyne* and wisdom. This education, which corrects the bias of each type, is the " divine " bond which most effectively produces unity of life and character, but it will only produce its full effect in the finest souls. The " human " and inferior way of producing unity in the society is to take care that marriages are contracted on the right principles.

At present, to say nothing of marriages based on equality in fortune or rank, the tendency is for persons of the same type of temperament to mate with one another, the adventurous with the adventurous, the quiet with the quiet. But this is a false principle, and militates against real unity of spirit in the community. The right principle would be that persons in whom either bias is present should be mated with partners of the other bias. This would not only prevent the society from falling outwardly into two groups without close relations, but would lead to a cancelling out of one-sided bias in the children of the marriage, and so make for the permanent continuance of the type of citizen whom we must have if the community is to endure. The main necessity is to provide by the right kind of education that both " temperamental " types shall have the same convictions about good and evil ; if this is once attained, the further unification of the community by proper regulations about marriage and the like is an easy task (309*b*–311*a*). When the fabric has been thus duly woven, it only remains for the statesman to constitute the officials necessary for the administration. Where a single official is required, he will take care to select one who exhibits the union of the two strains of temperament of which we have spoken. Where a board has to be constituted, he will see that both types are properly represented, so that the energy and vigour of one part of its members tempers and is tempered by the gentleness and caution of the other part (311*a*–*b*). This is how the science of the statesman directs and controls the construction of the most glorious of all fabrics, the garment of a righteous and happy national life.

It will be observed that the dialogue is peculiarly rich, apart from its immediate political teaching, in ideas which have passed over into the substance of Aristotelian ethics. Thus, in addition to the conception of the " intrinsic " standard of the Right Mean, we may mention the distinction between Cognitive and Practical Science, which corresponds to Aristotle's fundamental distinction between Theoretical and Practical Philosophy ;[1] the conception of the relation of a " directive," or, as Aristotle says, " architectonic " science to its subordinate disciplines, together with the specification of the two marks of the " directive " science—that it *uses* what its subordinate disciplines *make*, and that it superintends and regulates their practitioners ; the conception of the science of the statesman—Politics—as being, in virtue of its concern with the production of the good life for the community, *the* single supreme directive practical science ; the insistence upon education, which provides the statesman with his proximate raw material, men and women with the right type of character, as the most important of all the disciplines subservient to statesmanship. All these conceptions happen to be more familiar to us from the *Ethics* and *Politics* than from the *Politicus*, but it is from the *Politicus* that

---

[1] There is the difference that Aristotle, unlike Plato, insists that Politics is a *practical* science. This is a mere verbal difference. Plato's reason for calling it cognitive is that, though it deals with πράξεις, its work is not *manipulative*, but the giving of *directions*, an intellectual task. Aristotle's real reason for denying Politics the name of " theoretical" science is that he is preoccupied, in a way in which Plato is not, by his distinction between necessary and contingent subject-matter.

Aristotle took them, as is shown by the frequency with which he echoes his master's phraseology and repeats his illustrations.

See further:

BURNET.—*Greek Philosophy, Part I.*, 273–301; *Platonism* (1928), c.5.

RITTER, C.—*Platon*, ii. 120–165, 185–258, 642–657; *Platons Dialoge*, 25–67; *Neue Untersuchungen ueber Platon*, 1–94.

RAEDER, H.—*Platons philosophische Entwickelung*, 317–354.

NATORP, P.—*Platons Ideenlehre*, 271–296, 331–338.

APELT, O.—*Platonische Aufsätze*, 238–290. (1912.)

APELT, O.—*Platonis Sophista*. (Leipzig, 1897.)

STEWART, J. A.—*Plato's Doctrine of Ideas*, 84–91; *Myths of Plato*, 173–211 (*The Politicus Myth*).

DIÈS, A.—*Autour de Platon*, ii., 352–399, 450–522.

BARKER, E.—*Greek Political Theory : Plato and his Predecessors*, 276–291.

CAMPBELL, L.—*Sophistes and Politicus of Plato*. (Oxford, 1867.)

DIÈS, A.—*Platon, Le Sophiste* (Paris, 1925) and *Platon, Politique* (Paris, 1935).

CORNFORD, F. H.—*Plato's Theory of Knowledge*. (Translation of *Theactetus* and *Sophistes* with Commentary, London, 1935.)

STENZEL, J.—*Zahl und Gestalt bei Platon und Aristoteles*, 10–23, 126–133. (Leipzig, 1924.)

And for the history of Plato's relations with Dion and Dionysius II, the full treatment in

MEYER, E.—*Geschichte des Altertums*, v. 497–528.

IN the *Philebus* we are once more dealing with "practice," and more specifically with "individual" morality. The dialogue is a straightforward discussion of the question whether the " good for man " can be identified either with pleasure or with the life of thought. Socrates once more takes the part of chief speaker, a place given him in no other dialogue later than the *Theaetetus*. The explanation of this is no doubt, as Burnet has said, that the subject-matter, the application of Pythagorean " categories " to problems of conduct, is precisely that which Plato represents as having always been his chief interest. I think it significant that, as we shall see, all through the discussion the " categories " with which Socrates works are the Pythagorean concepts of the Unbounded, the Limit, and their synthesis. We know from Aristotle that one of the characteristic divergences of Plato from the Pythagoreans was that he substituted for their antithesis of the Boundless and the Limit that of the Boundless, conceived as " unbounded in both directions " (the Great-and-Small), and the *One*.[1] (On the Pythagorean view, the One, or Unit, was the simplest synthesis of the Boundless with Limit.) It is clear, since Aristotle never hints at any change in Plato's teaching, that the doctrine he calls Platonic must have been taught in the Academy as early as his own arrival there in 367 ; the *Philebus* is certainly one of the latest works of Plato's life, and must have been written years after 367, but it still uses the Pythagorean, not the Platonic, antithesis. I can see no explanation except the simple one that for the purposes of the discussion the Pythagorean categories are satisfactory, and that Plato is unwilling to make Socrates expound what he knows to be a novelty of his own.

There are no data for determining the relative dates of composition of *Philebus, Timaeus, Laws*. Presumably the composition of the *Laws* was going on when the other two were written. The dramatic date of the conversation cannot be fixed, except that from *Philebus* 58a 7 we see that it is later than the first visit of Gorgias to Athens ; the scene is also left unspecified, though it is, no doubt, " somewhere in (or about) " Athens. The two young men who figure as interlocutors, Protarchus and Philebus, are entirely

---

[1] *Met.* A 987b 25, τὸ δ' ἀντὶ τοῦ ἀπείρου ὡς ἑνὸς δυάδα ποιῆσαι καὶ τὸ ἄπειρον ἐκ μεγάλου καὶ μικροῦ, τοῦτ' ἴδιον.

unknown to us.[1] Socrates addresses the former as " son of Callias," but the name Callias was a common one, and we cannot say what Callias is meant, except that it cannot be Socrates' acquaintance Callias the " millionaire," whose children were mere boys at the time of Socrates' trial (*Apol.* 20a).

If we know so little about the date of the dialogue, we seem able to say much more definitely than for most of the dialogues what were the circumstances which occasioned its composition. The object of the discussion is to examine two rival theses about the " good ": (a) that it is pleasure (ἡδονή), (b) that it is " thinking " τὸ φρονεῖν, τὸ νοεῖν. The way in which the theses are formulated at the outset (11b) suggests at once that we are dealing with a *quaestio disputata* within a regular philosophical school. When we find that the purpose of the dialogue is to criticize both, to dismiss both as inadequate, and to suggest a *via media*, the impression naturally arises that Plato, as head of the Academy, is acting as " moderator " in a dispute within his own school. The evidence of Aristotle's *Nicomachean Ethics* seems to convert the possibility into a certainty. As is well known, Aristotle there deals twice over with the problem of the relation between good and pleasure. In the discussion of the seventh book, he starts with an anti-Hedonist thesis that pleasure is not good at all, examines the arguments adduced by its defenders, and urges that they are so inconclusive that they do not even prove that pleasure is not the supreme good. The arguments are all taken from Platonic dialogues, including the *Philebus* itself, but employed to prove something different from the conclusions drawn in Plato. Since one of these is that " pleasure must be bad, because it hinders thought "—a misrepresentation of the argument of *Phaedo* 66a ff.—the persons who advanced them clearly held that the good is " thinking " (τὸ φρονεῖν), the thesis pitted against the identification of good with pleasure at the opening of our dialogue. Aristotle incidentally mentions among their arguments the contention that pleasure cannot be the good because pleasure and pain are both bad things which a wise man avoids, and names the author of the doctrine, Speusippus.[2] In the second discussion of the subject, he also tells us who the person who identified " the good " with pleasure was ; it was the famous

---

[1] It is assumed that there is also a considerable number of young men who form a silent audience (16a 4). Socrates is even said to be granting the party a συνουσία (19c 5), a word which has the suggestion of a formal " lecture " or *conférence*. It is clear, in spite of the opposite view of some editors, that Philebus, who is almost silent throughout the dialogue, is a mere lad, much more immature in mind than Protarchus. This explains the touch of petulance about his declaration (12a) that nothing will ever persuade him out of his Hedonism. His worship of ἡδονή is just a boy's zest for the *joie de vivre*.

[2] *E.N.* 1153b 5. Speusippus argued that the badness of pain does not prove the goodness of pleasure ; both are opposed to the " good," as " the greater " and " the less " are both opposed to " the equal." *I.e.* the good condition is absence of both pleasurable and painful excitement. Hence the point that " the good man pursues not the pleasant but the painless " (*E.N.* 1152b 15) will be part of his argument.

mathematician Eudoxus, and his argument was precisely that which is hinted at in the opening words of the *Philebus* (11b 5) and alluded to again at its close (67b 1), that pleasure is the one end which *all* living things instinctively and spontaneously pursue.[1] These references seem to make it certain that the issue discussed in the dialogue is one which had actually divided the members of the Academy, the question what is really meant by the Platonic " Form of Good." One party thinks that it means pleasure, the other that it means thought.[2] The attitude taken by Plato in the dialogue to this discussion is, to all intents and purposes, precisely that of the "moderator" in the schools of the Middle Ages "determining" a *quaestio disputata*. The arguments produced by both parties are reviewed and weighed, and the balance is struck between the disputants. It is decided that the issue shall be narrowed down to a consideration of the " good for *man* " in particular. When the question has thus been delimited, it is "determined" by the answer that neither pleasure alone nor thought alone is the " good " or best life for men ; the best life must include both thought and grateful feeling ; but of the two, thought is the "predominant partner." This is, in fact, the conclusion to which the discussion is made to lead ; it is also the verdict given on the same issue in Aristotle's *Ethics*, which owe more of their inspiration to the *Philebus* than to any other Platonic dialogue.

THE QUESTION PROPOUNDED (11a–20b).—What is "the good"? Philebus has an answer to this question : "pleasure, joy, delight," this is the good for all living creatures. Socrates disputes this : "thought, intelligence, memory, true judgment," are better than pleasure "for all who can share in them" (11b). Thus Philebus originally makes an assertion not simply about the good for *man* in particular, but about good universal, "the" good. Socrates commits himself to no assertion about good universal, but asserts that for an intelligent being, like man, there is something better than pleasure, namely, the exercise of intelligence. If we are to decide between those conflicting views, we must at least agree on the sense to be put on the phrase, "the good for man." We may take it that both of us mean by this phrase "a condition and state (ἕξις καὶ διάθεσις) of soul which can make any man's life *happy*" (11d).[3] The question is whether pleasure, or again, thought, or possibly something better than either, is that "state and condition."

[1] *E.N.* 1172b 9–15.

[2] Few scholars would now make the old mistake, which unfortunately persists in some of the best expositions of the dialogue, of supposing the Hedonists and anti-Hedonists aimed at to be Cyrenaics and Cynics respectively.

[3] This is the definition of Aristotle also, except that Aristotle holds that the true genus of happiness is not ἕξις (state) but ἐνέργεια (activity). This is a valuable correction of the language of the Academy, but no more than a correction of their language. Aristotle never suggests that Plato, or any member of the Academy, *meant* that the " good " is a mere passive state. He blames their *terminology* for not marking the difference between such a " state " and an " activity."

In this last case, we should have to say that neither pleasant feeling nor thought is, by itself, the good for man, but we should still have to say that whichever of the two is most akin to the complete good for man is the better of them (11*e*). (These remarks foreshadow the coming conclusion that the "good for man" includes both components, but that thought is the more valuable of the two.)

Now "pleasure" is a word with many shades of meaning. A "life of pleasure" often means a vicious life, yet we say that the continent man finds his very continence pleasant ; we talk of the "pleasures" of folly and extravagant day-dreams, but we also say that the "thinking man" finds his thinking pleasant. Thus there may be pleasures of many kinds, and we have no right to assume that *all* must be good (12*d*). You may say, as the Hedonist does, that the difference of which Socrates speaks is a difference in the *sources* from which pleasure is derived, not in the pleasure yielded, but this would be evading the real issue. All pleasant experiences agree in being pleasant, just as all coloured surfaces agree in being coloured. But there are more or less marked colour-contrasts also. Why then may there not be pleasure-contrasts within the *genus* pleasure ? If there are, this will be a reason for hesitating to ascribe the predicate *good* to all pleasures.

"Pleasure is good" is, in fact, a synthetic proposition (13*a*), and therefore we cannot assume the impossibility of regarding some pleasures as good, but others as bad. They are all, of course, pleasant, but pleasantness might be present both in good and in bad experiences. Similarly, if we consider the rival thesis, that thought is "the good," we can see that it is one thing to make the analytic propositions "science is science," "knowledge is knowledge," another to say that "science (or knowledge) is *good*." If there are a plurality of "sciences," or other activities of intellect, some of them may conceivably be good, others bad (14*a*). Thus we see that our present discussion raises the old and eternally recurring problem of the one and the many (14*c*).

One form of this problem may now be regarded as long ago disposed of, the ancient difficulty of the possession of many qualities or parts by the same individual (14*d–e*). This was the form in which the problem had arisen, *e.g.* in the *Phaedo* ; presumably Plato means that the solution given there is sufficient to dispose of the question. The case which still needs investigation is that in which the " one " is not a thing which comes into or passes out of being, but belongs to the non-phenomenal order. This case gives rise to three questions : (*a*) whether there really are such non-phenomenal " units " ; (*b*) how we are to reconcile their *unity* with their reality or *being* ;[1] (*c*) how we can think of such units as being at

---

[1] *Phileb.* 15*b* 2–4. The wording of this second question is a little obscure, but the meaning seems to be made plain if we read the words in the light of the " antinomies " of the *Parmenides*. When we try to think of an ὃν ἕν, a *real* unit, we seem driven either to deny its unity in order to maintain its reality, or to deny its reality in order to save its unity. This is also how Burnet takes the words (*Greek Philosophy, Part I.*, 326, n. 2).

once one and many. (This last question is manifestly the same which has met us in the *Sophistes*, the problem of the " communion " of a form itself with other forms.)   These are the problems which still give rise to vehement discussion (15*a–c*).

We certainly cannot evade these problems ; they are perpetually turning up in all our " discourses," and we must meet them as best we can (15*d–16b*).   There is no better way of dealing with them than that of which Socrates has always been a lover.   (Compare the way in which he speaks in the *Phaedrus* of his reverence for the true dialectician who knows how to " divide " a subject rightly.) There was long ago a Prometheus—Pythagoras is the person meant —who revealed the art by which such problems may be treated. His followers have handed down to us the tradition that " whatever is at any time said to be " is composed of the constituents limit and the unlimited.   No matter what subject we study, we can find these elements in it.   We can always find a single form (the allusion is to the Pythagorean doctrine that the " unit " is the first combination of limit and unlimited)—and on inspection we shall, with care, be able to discover two, or three, or some other number of definite further forms included in it.   We should next take each of these forms and look for a definite number of forms included in them, and continue this process as long as fresh forms are to be found.   It is only when we can no longer repeat the process that we should let things " go to infinity."   In this way, the only way worthy of a dialectician, we shall discover not only that every form is at once one and infinitely many, but also *how* many it is (16*c–17a*). (That is, we must not be content to say, for example, that animal, or anything else, is one kind and also that there are an indefinite number of animals ; we must attempt to make a logical division which will show us exactly what and how many *species* of animals we can distinguish.   It is only when we have reached an *infima species* incapable of further logical subdivision that we may consider the indefinite multiplicity of individuals.   So long as you can go on with the logical division, each genus has not an indefinite plurality but a determinate number of constituents.)   Thus the grammarian must not say that articulate sound is in a sense one, and yet that there are " any number " of different articulate sounds ; he must know how many distinct sounds his alphabet has to represent.   To do this he has to divide articulate sounds into vowels and consonants, and the consonants again into " stops " and " sonants."   It is only if he finds that these classes cannot be subdivided into sub-classes that he may then *enumerate* the individual vowels, stops, or sonants.   Thus definite number (the number of the constituent species and sub-species) is everywhere the intermediate link between the one genus and its indefinitely numerous members (17*b–18d*).

We must apply this consideration of method to our special moral problem.   Before we can decide whether *all* pleasure or *all* thinking is good or not, we must know not only that pleasure is one and knowledge one, and again that there are " ever so many " pleasures and forms of knowledge, but also *how* many there are. The question is, in fact, whether we can discover distinct " forms " or " kinds " (εἴδη) of pleasure or of thinking, and how many (19*b*). But this is a long and perplexing inquiry, and Protarchus would be glad if Socrates could find some way of deciding the immediate question whether thinking is better than pleasure without raising this more fundamental issue (20*a–b*).

PRELIMINARY DELIMITATION OF THE PROBLEM.—*Neither Pleasure nor Thought alone is the Good for Man* (20*c–22c*).—Socrates, as we shall see, has no serious intention of allowing the question whether there are " kinds " of pleasure to be shirked. But we can get rid of one of the issues raised without going so deep into the matter. He seems to remember hearing—perhaps in a dream—that " the good " is neither pleasure nor thought, but something better than both. If that should be true, we can, at any rate, dispose of the doctrine that pleasure is *the* good, and we can deal with this point without going into the question about " kinds " of pleasure (20*c*), if we can agree on certain " notes " [1] characteristic of the supreme good and find that pleasures do not exhibit these notes. Obviously it is a note of *the* good that it is something " finished " or " complete " (τέλεον), and consequently that it is " sufficient " (ἱκανόν), and finally, therefore, that it is the one thing and the whole of the thing at which any creature which apprehends it ever aims, the whole and complete fulfilment of desire (20*d*).[2] We may thus make it a criterion of the good for man that it is what any one of us who knows what it is would choose in preference to anything else, and would be completely satisfied by. Judged by this criterion, neither pleasure nor " thought " can be that good. Even a professed Hedonist would not choose by preference a life simply made up of moments of intense pleasurable feeling and nothing else. He would want to be aware that he *is* feeling pleasure in the present, to remember that he has felt it in the past, and to anticipate that he will feel it in the future. Thus he would demand intellectual activity as well as feeling to make him happy ; a life all feeling would be that of an oyster rather than of a man. The same thing is true about a life which is all thinking and no feeling. No *man* would choose a life of mere intellectual activity entirely neutral in feeling-tone. Any man would prefer a " mixed " life, which contains both " thought " and pleasant feeling. The " mixed life " is thus better for *man* than the unmixed. A life of " unmixed " feeling would only be " complete " and " sufficient " for a brute, or perhaps a plant ; a life of " unmixed " intellect may perhaps be suitable to

---

[1] I use the word much as Newman uses it when he talks of the " notes " of the true Church.

[2] These same notes are adopted by Aristotle from the dialogue as the characters which must be exhibited by the " good for man " (*N.E.* 1097*a* 25 ff.). The λόγος of which it is there said that it " comes to the same thing " as Aristotle's own is the Academic theory of the " good for man," as given in the *Philebus*.

God, but not to man. The good for man must exhibit both factors. But the real problem of our dialogue still remains. Does the "mixed life" owe its goodness primarily to the presence of thought in it, or to the presence of pleasant feeling? Which is preponderantly the *cause* of its goodness? Socrates must not expect to be "let off" this discussion, and to deal with it we shall require to follow a long and difficult line of thought. This brings us to the main argument of the dialogue.

THE RELATIVE SIGNIFICANCE AND PLACE OF PLEASURE AND THOUGHT IN THE GOOD FOR MAN (*23c–66d*).—*Formal Character of Each* (*23c–30e*).—Anything which is actual can be placed in one of four classes: (*a*) infinite or unbounded (τὸ ἄπειρον); (*b*) limit (πέρας); (*c*) the "mixture" or combination of both these constituents; (*d*) the *cause* which brings them together (*23c–e*). To explain a little more precisely: "temperature," or, in the Greek phrase, "hotter and colder," is an example of what we mean by (*a*). We can call it "infinite" or "boundless" because anything can always be made hotter or colder than it is; there is no temperature which is the maximum or minimum conceivable, and again, if you have two different degrees of temperature, you can insert between them an endless number of intermediate temperatures different from both. Since temperature may be increased or diminished, we may also call it a "great and small" or "a less and more" (a μέγα καὶ μικρόν), and this, as we know from Aristotle, was Plato's own name for what the Pythagoreans, whose language Socrates is using in our dialogue, called the ἄπειρον. And what we can say about temperature, we can equally say about everything which allows of indefinite variation in magnitude or in degree, admits of "more and less," or such qualifications as "intense," "slight." We may thus class together all that admits of such variation under one single head as the "infinite" (*24e*). The "infinite" is thus what we should call quality with a continuous range.

By the "limit," again, as a single "form" we mean whatever does not admit "the more and the less," but admits such predicates as "the equal," "the double," in a word, whatever is "as an integer to an integer or a measure to a measure" (*25b*). The limit (πέρας) means thus precise mathematical determination, number, ratio, measure. (The last is added to cover the case of "surd" ratios, like that of 1 : √2 or side of square : diagonal.)

The "mixed" class, or "mixture of the two," means a precise and definitely determined magnitude or intensity of any quality. (Thus, *e.g.*, temperature is an ἄπειρον, 20° is a πέρας, a temperature *of* 20° C. is an instance of the "mixture"; rainfall is an ἄπειρον, 6 is a πέρας, but a rainfall *of* 6 inches is a μεικτόν, and so on.) The introduction of determination into a "more and less" is precisely what we call a γένεσις, or process of becoming (*25e*). (*E.g.*, to raise water to a temperature of 100° C. is the "process" of making it boil, it is also the introduction of the "limit" 100° into the ἄπειρον, temperature.)

Now we note that health in the body, proper attunement in music, beauty and proportion in a body or a face, good climate, and the like, all depend on the production of definite " limit " or ratio in an ἄπειρον of some kind ; departure from this proper ratio produces disease, false intervals in music, ugliness, bad climate. And the same thing holds about goodness in the soul (26*b* 6). The point to be made is thus that the right or sound or good state of anything is marked by definite proportion and " limit " ; there may be infinitely numerous divergences from this one right proportion or equilibrium, but they are all in varying degrees bad. This is what is meant by calling the development which leads up to and stops at the production of the right proportion a γένεσις εἰς οὐσίαν, a development leading to a stable *being* (26*d*). The point is that the physician producing health in his patient, for example, may do so by steadily increasing the proportion of the " dry," or again of the " moist," in the invalid, but he does not aim at increasing this beyond limits. There is a definite ratio of the " hot " to the " cold," or of the " moist " to the " dry," which is characteristic of health. When the γένεσις set up by the physician's treatment has secured this ratio, he dismisses the patient. Health once attained, you don't make the man healthier *in indefinitum* by passing further and further beyond the " limit " ; you would only give him a new disease instead of the old one. This explains why we shall be told directly that all the good things in life belong to this class of the " mixed."

As for the " cause," we mean by it the agent which sets up such a process as we have described, τὸ ποιοῦν (26*e*). We have therefore to distinguish it both from that which it produces, the process or γένεσις, and that which " subserves it for the process," the " matter " of the process. The process we have already referred to our third class ; the " matter " of the process is just the factors which are brought into combination, the unlimited and limit. This is why we had to add the fourth class to the other three. We note here that the account of the " mixed " class is the direct source of the " right mean " in Aristotle's *Ethics*. " Moral " goodness, according to Aristotle's familiar account in *E.N.* ii., is a fixed and habitual right " mean " or proportion in our appetitions and tempers, and the process of becoming good is one of " qualifying " them, *i.e.* training them to exhibit just the proportion demanded by the " right rule " (ὀρθὸς λόγος).[1] Thus it is just such a process of γένεσις εἰς οὐσίαν as has just been described, the ἄπειρον in the case being the indefinite degrees of frequency and intensity which tempers and appetitions admit, and the πέρας the *exact* degree demanded by the " right rule."

---

[1] The ὀρθὸς λόγος itself is Platonic too, and appears to come from *Laws*, 659*d*, where education is said to be the " drawing and attracting of children to the right discourse (ὀρθὸς λόγος) uttered by the law." That Aristotle was influenced by this passage is shown by his allusion to it as excellently said by Plato at *E.N.* 1104*b* 12.

Now let us apply what we have just said to our particular problem. We see that the " mixed life," including both intellectual activity and agreeable feeling, on the face of it, falls in our third class, because it has these two distinct factors. (It is intended to hint at the result to be established later, that the two factors need to be combined according to definite law and proportion.) But what about the life of pleasure recommended by Philebus, which consisted in having as much pleasure and as intense pleasure as you can get ? Pleasure, and again pain, clearly belong to the class of the " infinite," since neither, in its own nature, has a minimum or a maximum (27e). Philebus thinks that it is this impossibility of ever exhausting the possibilities of pleasure which makes it so good. But you might also say that it is the same impossibility of exhausting those of pain which makes pain so bad (28a). Hence it is clear that the mere indefinite range of pleasure is no proof of its goodness. What, again, about the " intelligence " (νοῦς), knowledge, wisdom, preferred by Socrates ? Into what class does this fall ? (28a). We are agreed to reject the theory that the course of the universe is random (εἰκῇ, 28d), and to agree with the traditional belief that it is directed by a supreme wisdom (φρόνησις) and intelligence (νοῦς) in every particular. Now when we look at our own constitution, we see that the materials of which our body is made are only small parcels of the great cosmic masses of similar materials, and that these constituents are found in a much higher degree of purity from other ingredients elsewhere in the universe than in our bodies. The " fire " in us [1] is small in bulk and " impure " in substance by comparison with the fire in the sun. And again the " fire " or " water " in us is fed and kept up by that in the larger world (29c). And generally our little body is fed by the mass of body without us (29e). By analogy, we may infer that since there is soul in us, it too comes from a greater and brighter soul in the universe. Also, we see in our own case that when things are amiss with the body, it is the intelligence, resident in the soul, which re-establishes order by means of the medical art. So we may reasonably hold that in the universe at large, the same holds good. The order in it is due to intelligence (νοῦς), and intelligence is only found in souls. So we may hold that there are superhuman souls, and that it is their intelligence which is the cause of cosmic order (30d). And we may answer the question now before us by saying that νοῦς (intelligence) belongs to the fourth of our classes, the class of " the cause of the mixture " (30e).[2]

---

[1] Plato may be thinking, e.g., of the " animal heat " of the organism and its dependence on a proper supply of solar warmth, but more probably his allusion is to the theory, adopted in the Republic and Timaeus, that the immediate organ of vision is itself a ray of light issuing from the eye, and is itself derived from the sun's light.

[2] I have given the general sense of the passage from 30a 8 to 30e 3 without going into the question of precise reading and interpretation of particular phrases. I think Plato clearly means to identify νοῦς with the " cause of the mixture." This is not inconsistent with his view that the good for man is not

There has been a great deal of discussion on the point of the place to be assigned to the forms, as we know them from earlier dialogues, in the classification of the *Philebus*.[1] No one has imagined that they could be reckoned as examples of the ἄπειρον, but different scholars have placed them in each of the other three classes. I do not propose to spend much time on the problem, since it seems plain that the fourfold classification has been devised with a view to a problem where the forms are not specially relevant, and the true solution is thus that they find *no* place in this classification. We must not look for them in the class of the "cause," since *cause* has been explicitly equated with *agent*, and it is quite certain that the forms of the *Phaedo* and *Republic* are not agents. (At least, we could only ascribe agency to the "Form of Good," and that, as Socrates' difficulty in speaking of it shows, holds a unique place in the scheme.) Limit, again, has been defined in a way which shows that it means specifically mathematical ratio. Hence, though, in a way, the forms may be said, as defining and determining the character of the sensibles which "partake" them, to function as "limits," they must not be identified with the πέρας of this dialogue. Again, though this is a matter which must not be discussed until we reach our final chapter, it is plain from Aristotle's allusions [2] that, according to the doctrine taught in the Academy as early as 367–6, the forms, "man," "animal," and the rest actually contain two factors, a "great-and-small" and a limiting factor, "the one" or "unit." So far they resemble the "mixed class" of our dialogue, and Professor H. Jackson did right to call attention to this. But all the examples of the "mixed" class in the *Philebus* are taken from the world of "events," and the forms clearly are not "mixtures" of that kind. Not to dwell on the further point that the πέρας of the *Philebus* stands for *any* definite ratio, whereas the πέρας element in the forms, according to Aristotle, was the "one," and the "one" in the *Philebus* is only spoken of as equivalent to any *genus* regarded as a single whole. It is clear that the line of thought which leads to the classification in the *Philebus* brings us nearer to what Aristotle knew as the central doctrine of Platonism than anything else in Plato's writings. But it seems equally clear that Plato's final thought is not disclosed even here. From his own language in *Epistle* vii. we may infer that he never intended the reading of a written work to do more than supply hints which might put a really original mind in the position to discover his thought after a great deal of hard personal thinking, and that he did not expect even as much as this apart

νοῦς. It is clear from the *Republic* (506b) that the general question whether the good can be knowledge or pleasure is older than the speculations of Speusippus and Eudoxus. What is distinctive in the *Philebus* is the appeal to psychology as relevant to the issue.

[1] See Burnet, *Greek Philosophy, Part I.*, 332 ; R. G. Bury, *Philebus*, pp. lxiv–lxxiv ; H. Jackson, *Journal of Philology*, **x.** 253 ff. ; Raeder, *Platons philosophische Entwickelung*, 370 ff.

[2] Cf., *e.g.*, Aristot. *Met.* 987b 18–27.

from the actual daily contact of the student's living mind with his own.[1]   Hence I shall defer anything I have to say about the central mystery of the Platonic philosophy for consideration in a final chapter.   Provisionally, I will merely say what is quite obvious, that, viewed in their relation to the things which "partake" of them, the forms, as we have so far met with them, act as an element of "limit" and determination, but that, as the recognition in the *Sophistes* of a "communion" of forms, as such, with one another shows, this is quite consistent with the view that a form which functions as a "limit" should itself also be analysable into a combination of an "unlimited" and a "limit."

THE PSYCHOLOGY OF PLEASURE AND PAIN (31*a*–53*c*).—We have seen to what class pleasure and pain themselves belong; they are ἄπειρα.   We must next consider "that in which they arise" (the subject of them), and the πάθος, or state of things, which gives rise to them, in other words, the actual conditions of their occurrence.   To begin with pleasure.   "That in which pleasure (or pain) arises" is always a living creature, the creature which feels the pleasure (or pain), and as such it belongs to the "class of the mixture," since its organism is a complex of a plurality of ingredients (31*c*).   The way in which they arise, the πάθη which occasion them, are that "when the attunement (that is, the proper balance between the ingredients of the organism) in an animal is disturbed, pain is felt, and when it is restored after disturbance, pleasure is felt." Disturbance of organic equilibrium is attended by pain, restoration of the equilibrium by pleasure (31*d*–*e*).   Thus when the body is unduly heated or chilled, we have a λύσις τῆς φύσεως or disturbance of the normal organic equilibrium, and it is painful; the antithetic process of recovering the normal temperature, which is a return to the οὐσία (the "natural state"), is pleasant.   This defines for us one kind or form (εἶδος) of pleasure, namely, the agreeable processes of return to the normal condition of the organism after disturbance, or, as the defenders of the same type of theory in modern times usually say, the process of recovery from organic waste (22*a*–*b*).[2]   Next, there is a second "form" or "kind" of pleasure which depends on processes purely mental, and is not attended by either disturbance or recovery of the balance in the organism.   A simple example is that the mental anticipation of a painful disturbance of the organic balance is itself painful, the expectation of the agreeable antithetic recovery from disturbance is itself pleasant, and in these cases there is no actual accompanying organic process, the pleasure and pain belong in a special way to "the soul by herself" (32*c*).   These are the two distinct εἴδη of pleasure and pain it is necessary to begin by discriminating, if

[1] *Ep.* vii. 340*c*–*e*, 341*c*–*e*, 343*e*–344*d*.

[2] Like Aristotle, Plato confines the waste-and-repair, or depletion-repletion theory of pain and pleasure to the case of pains and pleasures connected with the body and its needs. He does not regard it as applicable to pain and pleasure generally. For a criticism of this type of theory, when extended to all pains and pleasures, see Stout's *Analytic Psychology*, ii. c. 12.

we are to judge soundly on the question whether all pleasures are good.

Next, if there are antithetic processes of disturbance and recovery of the organic balance, and these are respectively painful and pleasant, there must also be an intermediate case, that in which the balance is maintained without deflection in either direction, and this, on our theory, must be neutral in respect of feeling-tone, neither pleasant nor painful (32e). This would be the condition, so far as feeling-tone is concerned, of the life of thought unmixed with pleasure or pain already spoken of, and there is no impossibility in the notion that there might be such a life, a life of permanent maintenance of equilibrium. Very possibly it is the life appropriate to a god (33b) and so the best of all. But we are discussing a different matter, the part which thought and pleasant feeling should play in the life of men like ourselves (for whom such an existence without any rhythmic alternation is out of the question). For our purposes, we must pursue the psychology of the second class of pleasures and pains further. They are all dependent on *memory* (since, of course, without memory we could have no anticipations), and this makes it necessary to explain briefly what memory is and what sensation itself is. We may say that some bodily processes die away before they can reach the soul, but others penetrate to the soul : the first we may call unconscious ; the second are conscious. This enables us to define sensation as a movement (κίνησις) which affects the body and soul together (κοινῇ, 34a). Memory (*i.e.* *primary* memory) is the retention (σωτηρία) of sensation as thus defined (*ibid.*) ; and, finally, recollection (ἀνάμνησις) is the recovery (reproduction) by the soul " by herself " of a lost memory or sensation (34b–c). These considerations will make it clearer what we mean by a " purely mental " pleasure, and also throw light on the nature of desire (ἐπιθυμία, 34e). To understand what desire is, we may consider it in its simplest form, such as hunger or thirst. A thirsty man desires, or lusts after drink. To speak more precisely, the thirsty man is in a state of depletion, his organism has been depleted of its normal supply of liquid, What he really desires is not simply " drink," but to be " filled up " with the liquid he will drink. (He desires not the water, but the drinking of it.) Thus he actually is in one state (a state of depletion), but desires the antithetic state (the corresponding repletion). To desire to drink the thirsty man must " apprehend " (ἐφάπτεσθαι) repletion. He does not " apprehend " it with his body. That is just what is undergoing the unnatural depletion, and it cannot be passing through two antithetic processes at once. Thus it must be with his soul that he " apprehends " the repletion he lusts after. The importance of the example is that it shows that (in spite of popular language), there is really no such state as a " bodily " desire or lust. All desiring is a state of soul (35c), since desire is endeavour towards the opposite of the present state of the organism, and it is in virtue of memory that this " opposite " is apprehended.

These considerations show that all impulse and desire belong to the soul.

They also suggest an important problem. When a man is actually in a state of pain due to organic "depletion," but remembers and thinks of the pleasant experiences which would remove the depletion, can we say that his condition is either purely painful or wholly pleasant? If he despaired of ever realizing the anticipation of "filling up," no doubt, he would be doubly wretched, but suppose he is feeling the painful depletion but expecting the repletion (like a really hungry man who expects to be fed)? The anticipation that his want will be removed is pleasant, but the felt want must surely be painful, and thus it appears that we must say that, in the case assumed, the experience is a mixed one, pleasurable and painful at once (36b).

(The conception of "mixed" states which are half pleasant, half painful, is so characteristic of Plato and so important in itself that it cannot be passed over without some comment. Hedonists naturally refuse to accept it, since it is quite inconsistent with the treatment of pain as equivalent to subtraction of pleasure which lies at the root of the Hedonic calculus. They have, accordingly, to explain the facts to which Plato appeals in one or other of two ways. They have to hold that the total feeling-tone of any moment of life is either simply pleasant or simply painful. It is then open to them either to interpret the facts about still unsatisfied craving by holding that the experience is one of rapid alternation between pleasure and pain, or by holding that it is, according to circumstances, one of a low degree of pleasure, or one of pain, though of a moderate degree of pain. Neither view seems to me to be in accord with fact. When I am genuinely and acutely thirsty, e.g. in the course of a long tramp in hot weather, but confidently anticipating arrival at a place of refreshment in an hour's time, it is not the fact that I oscillate rapidly between pure misery and pure delight according as my attention is directed to my present condition or to the condition I anticipate ; nor yet is it true that I am continuously feeling a qualified pleasure or a qualified pain. I certainly feel the tension between the pleasant anticipation and the actual pang of thirst in a single pulse of experience. And there is no real difficulty in understanding why this is so, if we remember that the physical correlate of my mental condition is made up of a great complex of neural excitations. No one of the constituent neural excitations can have two antithetic senses at once, but the complex may perfectly well contain elements with opposite senses. Hence it seems to me that Plato's doctrine of "mixed states," which coincides with the standing thought of great poets about the "unrest which men miscall delight," is strictly true to the facts of common experience, and that the criticisms levelled against it are all based on false simplification of the facts.)

TRUE AND FALSE PLEASURE (36c–53c).—We have thus distinguished two "kinds" of pleasures: (a) those directly due to an

actual organic process of recovery of equilibrium or repair of waste ;
(*b*) those dependent on mental anticipation, where no such actual
organic process is taking place. The recognition of this second
class at once suggests a further question of first-rate ethical importance : Can we admit of a second and different distinction of
pleasures (and pains) as true and false, real and merely apparent ?
(36*c*). In other words, when we come to the *valuation* of pleasures
as ingredients in the good for man, must we make any deduction
for the " illusoriness " of some of them ? This is the vital distinction for the Platonic ethics ; it is to lead up to and justify it
that the whole psychological discussion has been introduced.
Protarchus denies the validity of the distinction. Beliefs or judgments can be true or false, but not feelings (36*d*). Hedonists, like
Grote, have naturally taken his side and argued that Socrates is
merely in the wrong in making the distinction. For, it is argued,
a pleasure or a pain is exactly what it is felt to be ; its *esse* is simply
the fact of its being felt. If I feel pleased or pained, I am having
pleasure or pain ; if I feel greatly pleased, I am having a great
pleasure ; the pleasure always exists when it is felt, and it is
always just as great as it is felt to be. This reasoning, however,
is irrelevant to Socrates' contention. He is not asking whether I
am pleased when I *feel* pleased, or greatly pleased when I *feel* greatly
pleased ; he is asking whether I am always pleased when I *think*
I am pleased, or intensely pleased when I *think* I am intensely
pleased, and this is a perfectly reasonable question, and, as he
says, one which needs careful examination. To put it simply,
the issue is this : Is the excitement in an exciting experience a
true measure of its pleasantness ?[1] May not the excitingness of
an experience lead to an over-estimate of its pleasantness ? To
answer this question, we need to make a considerable apparent
digression.

There is such a process as judging, and such a process as feeling
pleased. When we judge, we make a judgment about something,
and when we feel pleased, we are pleased with something. And a
judgment does not cease to be an actual judgment because it is
false ; similarly a false feeling of pleasure would still be an actual
feeling of pleasure (37*b*). (This last remark, of itself, shows that
Plato has no intention of denying that a " false " pleasure is a
pleasure ; it is its worth, not its actuality, which is in question.)
The question is whether pleasure and pain, like judgment, permit
of the qualifications true and false. They certainly permit of some
qualifications, such as " great," " small," " intense"; and Protarchus

[1] The question is vital, since the " intensity " regarded by all Hedonists
as a dimension of pleasure or pain is primarily a character of the situation by
which we are pleased or pained. We can only measure the intensity of the
pleasantness or painfulness by measuring the intensity of an objective feature
of the situation, and this makes it all-important to know whether such
a measurement can be implicitly trusted. For example, the satisfaction of
the impulses of sex is normally an intense organic excitement, but is its
pleasantness equally intense ?

allows that they may permit of the further qualification " bad."
But he denies that a pleasure can be said, like a judgment, to be
" erroneous " or false (37e) ; if, as often happens, a false belief
yields us pleasure, the falsity belongs to the belief, not to the
pleasure.

Let us look at the facts.   Pleasure and pain sometimes accompany true beliefs or judgments, sometimes false.   Now these beliefs
may be regarded as answers given by the soul to questions which
she has put to herself ; sometimes the answer is right, sometimes
it is wrong.   We have, so to say, a scribe and a painter within our
souls.   The interpretation of present sensation by the aid of
memory involved in all perception is the work of the scribe writing
" discourses " in the soul ;   the painter (imagination) designs
illustrations (εἰκόνες) to the scribe's text (39a–c), and his pictures
may be called true or false " imaginings " according to the truth or
falsity of the " discourse " they illustrate.   These discourses and
pictures concern the future as well as the present or the past ; we
are all through life full of " fancies " (ἐλπίδες) about the future, and
when we anticipate pleasure or pain to come, we take an " anticipatory " pleasure or pain, which has already been classed as strictly
" mental " in entertaining such expectations (39d–e).   This is
true of good and bad men alike, but, since the good are " dear to
God," their pleasant anticipations are commonly fulfilled, those of
the bad are not (40a–b).   (The good man gets pleasure in anticipating
sequences which are in accord with the order God maintains in the
world ;   the bad man gets his pleasure from day-dreams of sudden
enrichment and other events which do not come about in the
" world as God made it.")   Thus the bad man's pleasure in his
anticipations is as actual as the good man's, but the good man, as a
rule, gets the pleasure which he anticipates, the bad man does not.
This affords one sense in which the bad man may be said to have
false, or unreal, pleasures ; he derives present pleasure from anticipations which will not be realized, and this pleasure may rightly be
said to be deceptive, a *caricature* of true pleasure, and the same
argument will apply to pains due to anticipation (40c) as well as
to emotions—fear, anger, and the like—generally (40e).   Like beliefs,
all these states may have a foundation in reality or may have none.
Now the goodness of a belief lies in its truth, and its badness in its
falsity ;   only true beliefs are good, and only false beliefs are bad.
(For, of course, the *raison d'être* of a belief is that it should be true ;
that is what every belief aims at being.)   May we not say then
that the badness of bad pleasures—Protarchus has allowed that
there are such states—is simply falsity and nothing else ? a bad
pleasure means a " false " or " deceptive " pleasure.

Protarchus is unconvinced.   There may be " wicked " (πονηραί)
pleasures or pains, but pleasures and pains are not made wicked
by being " false."   We will, however, reserve the consideration
of wicked or sinful pleasures for a moment, and call attention to
a second sense in which it might be possible to speak of many

pleasures as " false " (41a–b). Consider once more the case already mentioned of unsatisfied appetite, where the soul is craving for the removal of a state of painful organic want now present in the body. In this case we simultaneously apprehend the present painful want and the pleasant anticipated reaction against it. " The body supplies us with a certain feeling, and the soul desires the opposite condition " (41c). And both pleasure and pain admit of " the more and the less." Hence the problem constantly arises how to estimate the painfulness of the present state against the pleasurableness of the desired " opposite condition " (or, again, the pleasureableness of the present state against the painfulness of the " opposite "). In making such estimates we are always liable to errors of perspective ; the anticipated " opposite " is over-estimated by contrast. We expect the coming pleasure to be greater than it will really prove to be, by contrast with the present pain, and an expected pain is over-estimated in the same way by contrast with present pleasure (41e–42c). There is thus an element of illusion in all such cases, which must be allowed for before our estimate of anticipated pleasure or pain can be admitted as correct.

The illusion is still more marked in other cases. As we said before, disturbance of the organic balance is painful, restoration of the balance is pleasant. But suppose the organism is undergoing neither process. It is true that many of the wise deny that this case actually occurs ; they say that " everything is always flowing either up or down," or, in Leibniz's phrase, that the " pendulum never is at rest." But they must concede at least that we are not always *conscious* of its oscillations. Small oscillations either way are " infinitesimal." It is only considerable oscillations which are attended by pleasure and pain (43c). Thus we have to admit the possibility of a life which is neither pleasant nor painful, but just painless. There are persons who actually say that this painless life is the " most pleasant " of all (44a). But this statement cannot be strictly true. To feel no pain is manifestly not the same thing as to feel pleasure, though this is the thesis of the real " enemies of Philebus," th∴ downright anti-Hedonists. These anti-Hedonists are eminent scientific persons, who maintain that there really is no such thing as a pleasure and that the experience Philebus and his friends call pleasure is merely " relief from pain " (44c).[1] Though we cannot accept this doctrine, which is really due to the scorn of fastidious souls for vulgar pleasures, it will yield us a useful hint towards the discovery of the kind of pleasures which deserve to be called " true " (44d). Their thought is this. If we want to

---

[1] *Phileb.* 44b 9, καὶ μάλα δεινοὺς λεγομένους τὰ περὶ φύσιν. The words are enough to prove that neither Antisthenes nor Diogenes is meant. They could not be called δεινοὶ περὶ φύσιν. But the phrase exactly fits the anti-Hedonists of the Academy—Speusippus, Xenocrates, and their followers. The reference is probably rather to their views about forms and numbers, discussed in Aristotle's *Metaphysics*, than to such things as the works of Speusippus on zoological classification. It is meant that they are διαλεκτικοί.

understand any "form" or quality, we do well to study it in its extreme and most marked manifestations. So, if we want to know what pleasure really is, we ought to start by considering the most vehement and violent pleasures. But these—this is given as the reasoning of the anti-Hedonists—are the pleasures connected with the body (45a). Now such pleasures are found in their most exciting degree not in health, but in disease. The delight of refreshing thirst with a cool draught, for example, is much more intense when one is suffering the heat of a raging fever than at another time, because the preceding want (ἔνδεια) or craving is so much more violent. We are not arguing, of course, that pleasures are more *numerous* in disease than in health ; our point is that they are more violent and exciting (45c). And so the life of "sin" (ὕβρις) is marked by violent and exciting pleasures which make a man "beside himself" ; the life of virtue by moderate pleasures, regulated by the rule of "nothing too much" (45d–e). The most exciting and violent pleasures, as well as the most violent pains, are to be found in the diseased or bad body or soul.

Now let us consider one or two examples of these exciting experiences. A man who has an itching spot on his body gets great enjoyment from scratching or chafing it ; but, of course, he is only stimulated to do so by the irritation of the itching. This is typical of a host of experiences which language calls "bitter-sweet." They depend on a tension between antithetic processes ; these processes may be both bodily, or one may be bodily and the other purely mental, or both may be mental. In all cases the violently exciting character of the experience depends on the tension. There must be a highly painful factor in order that the rebound may be intensely pleasant (46b–c). (Thus the difference between this case and that of the "illusions of perspective" already mentioned is that the element of contrast and antithetical tension is now an ingredient in the actual concrete single experience.) The point, then, is that in such a "mixed" experience, there may be an exact balance of pleasurable and painful ingredients, so that, exciting as it is, its "net pleasure value" would be nil, or pleasure may predominate, or pain may predominate. But in no case is the "pleasure value" simply measured by the intensity of the excitement, and the "ticklish" person, for example, who gets so excited when he is tickled that he says he is "dying with pleasure," is not really getting anything like the "quantity of pleasure" he supposes. For the intensity of the excitement is due to the simultaneous contrast between the fully stimulated region of the skin and a neighbouring region which is uneasily aching for similar stimulation, 46d–47b). Here is a plain case where a man's own estimate of the pleasure he is getting is erroneous. The cases of tension already mentioned, where the antithesis is between the actual condition of the body and a mentally anticipated "opposite" condition, may, of course, give rise to the same "mixture" of pleasure with pain and the same errors in estimation (47c).

There is still a third case where both factors in the tension belong to the soul. There are a whole range of painfully toned emotions—anger, fear, malice, and others—and we know, and the poets constantly tell us that, though they are painfully toned, to give them full expression may be pleasant. To let yourself go, when you are angry, Homer says, is sweeter than honey (47*d–e*), and it is possible to revel in lamentation. So people in the theatre enjoy a sensational tragedy which sets them crying for the distresses of the hero (48*a*). Our feelings, when we see a comedy, are a still subtler example of a "mixed" state, half painful, half pleasant. This leads Plato to indulge in an acute psychological analysis of the emotion aroused by comedy. We have just spoken of φθόνος (*malice*) as an unpleasantly toned emotion, and yet by malice we mean " being *pleased* by the misfortunes of our neighbour " (48*b*). Now ignorance and folly are certainly misfortunes. But what is it which amuses us in a "comic situation"? A certain kind of badness (πονηρία) in the comic character, namely, want of " self-knowledge." (It is the discrepancy between his real character or situation and his own estimate of them which makes him " comic.") "Ignorance of self " may be : (1) ignorance of one's financial position, as when a man fancies himself richer than he is; (2) ignorance of one's physical defects, as when a man has an empty conceit of his beauty or strength; (3) ignorance of the state of one's soul, especially a false conceit of one's own wisdom (49*a*). All these states are bad, but we may make a distinction. They may be accompanied with feebleness or they may not. In the former case a man's vain conceit of self does not lead to any serious harm to anyone, and is merely " funny " ; in the latter it is not funny, but dangerous. It is the "harmless self-conceit " of the hero which we find comic and laugh at (49*a–c*).

Now to explain why the feeling this spectacle rouses in the audience is "mixed." It might seem that it is wrong to enjoy the misfortunes of our friends ; yet we do find self-conceit in persons we like " funny," when, as has just been explained, it is quite harmless. (The connexion with comedy, I take it, is that, if we are to enjoy a comedy, we must feel that we " like " the person who is being exposed, for all his failings. If we could not find him likeable, the comedy would cease to be comic, as *Tartuffe* does, for the simple reason that we detest Tartuffe seriously.) Thus our sense of the " comic " is a kind of *malice* (φθόνος), and this is, in its nature, a painful emotion ; yet our laughter shows that we are enjoying the experience, which must therefore be a " mixed " one (49*e*–50*a*). (The observation appears true and subtle ; when, for example, we see Malvolio on the stage, there is an element of the painful in our mirth. It is, in a way, humiliating to see another man " make such a fool of himself." If the absurdity were carried a little further, or the exhibition of it a little more prolonged, the painful would distinctly predominate. Even as it is, we can detect its presence by a careful examination of our feelings.) Now this

is true also of the " tragedy and comedy " of actual life ; the situations of real life are constantly provoking emotional reactions in
which the painful and the pleasing are blended, no less than the
situations in a stage-play.   We may take it as certain then that the
fusing of the pleasant and the painful in a single experience occurs
where the sources of both factors lie in the soul, no less than where
the source of one or both is in the body (50b–e).

   We may now consider the question what experiences are purely
pleasant without any admixture of painfulness. On our general
theory of the connexion of feeling-tone with organic process, we can
see at once that in any case where a " subliminal " or unconscious
process of " depletion " is followed by a conscious process of " repletion," there will be an experience which is wholly pleasant.
This may explain the case of the pure aesthetic pleasure we get
from the contemplation of pattern (σχήματα), colour (χρώματα), tone
(φθόγγοι), and the great majority of odours (51a–b).[1]   These
pleasures are not preceded by a painful sense of craving, like those
of the satisfaction of hunger or thirst, and do not owe any part of
their apparent intensity to contrast ; they are " pure," in the sense
of being pleasant through and through, without any admixture of
painfulness. We may suppose that they correspond to processes
of organic repletion after depletion, but that the depletion has been
insensible.[2] We must note, however, that we are not referring
here to pleasure got by seeing " patterns " which are likenesses of
animals or the like, where the pleasure arises from our perception
of the resemblance of the copy to the original, but strictly to the
pleasure we take in geometrical form as such, and the same remark
applies to the pleasantness of colours and sounds, and still more to
odours (51c–e).[3]

   Again the " intellectual pleasure " which we get from the
" sciences " (μαθήματα) is of this " unmixed " kind.   There is
no felt pain antecedent to it ; merely not to possess geometrical
knowledge, for example, is not painful as hunger is painful; and
again, the process of forgetting something we have learned is not
attended by pain. Of course it may be disagreeable to find that we
have forgotten something which it would now be advantageous to
know, but the process of forgetting itself is not painful, as the
process of growing hungry again, after we have eaten, is (52a–b).

   [1] He says " most " odours, of course, to exclude the case of those, e.g., of
articles of food, or those which indicate to the male animal the proximity of
a female.   The pleasantness of these would depend on a previous sense of unsatisfied want.

   [2] Timaeus expressly teaches that this is the case (Tim. 64a–65b).

   [3] I do not take this to mean that Plato regards the pleasure we get from
seeing the " faithfulness " of a picture to its original as aesthetically illegitimate.
His purpose is simply to exclude from the list of unmixed pleasures any which
depend on a previous sense of want for their existence or their intensity. Thus
the degree of pleasure got from contemplating a " nude " clearly may be
affected by unsatisfied sexual desire in the beholder ; the pleasure with which
we hear the sound of a beloved voice will often depend for its intensity on a pre-
existing longing to hear that voice again.

By comparison of these now discriminated types of pleasures, we can see that the "mixed" type, which depend on antecedent painful craving, are marked by violence and "want of measure," and exhibit the fluctuations of the "more and less"; the "unmixed" type, on the other hand, exhibit "restriction by measure," are "moderate in intensity" (52c). But we may make a further distinction between the two types. They differ in "truth" or "genuineness" (ἀλήθεια). Just as a small expanse of white colour, for example, if it is a pure white, with no admixture, is more truly white than a vast expanse which is not equally pure, so even a "small" pleasure which is pleasure through and through, is more truly pleasure, deserves that name better, than a "big" pleasure which is mixed throughout with its opposite, pain (52d–53c). *I.e.* the highly exciting experiences which are commonly reckoned the "greatest pleasures," since their exciting character actually depends on tension and contrast with a painful factor equally indispensable to the effect, are not the "truest to type." It is the "moderate" pleasures, preceded by no painful craving and independent of internal tension, which are pleasant through and through, and thus deserve the name of pleasures most completely. It is in this sense that Plato speaks of this class as "true," of the others as "false" or "deceptive" pleasures. The first are what they are taken to be; the others are, to a large extent, something different from what men take them to be.

THE METAPHYSICS OF PLEASURE.—*Can it be an End?* (53c–55c).— We may remind ourselves of a second doctrine of the "wits" (κομψοί), which we shall find suggestive. They say that pleasure is always a "process of becoming" (γένεσις); that it has *no* stable and determinate *being* (οὐσία, 53c). That is, the theory is that pleasure is an accompaniment of transitions, incompleted developments. It is felt while the development is going on, but falls away when the definite and permanent goal of the "evolution" is reached. We must not be misled into identifying the "wits" of this passage with the third-century Cyrenaics who called pleasure a "gentle motion," nor have we any right to ascribe their doctrine by anticipation to the elder Aristippus. We meet it again in Aristotle's *Ethics*, where one of the string of arguments against the goodness of pleasure, all taken from recognizable passages in Plato, is said (1152*b* 13) to be that "every pleasure is a sensible transition (or development) into a natural condition" (γένεσις εἰς φύσιν αἰσθητή), an obvious allusion to the section of the *Philebus* we are now considering. We may take this as an indication that the κομψοί to whom the doctrine is due are the anti-Hedonist party in the Academy, a view which, as we shall see, is borne out by the language of Aristotle in dismissing their doctrine. The thought arises by a natural, though illegitimate, extension of the depletion-repletion formula to cover all cases of pleasures. On this theory, the good, healthy, or normal state is, of course, that of balance or equilibrium; pain and pleasure are both felt only when there is a departure from this ideal condition—pain while the process of depletion is going on, pleasure while that of repletion, restoration of the balance, is happening. The natural end or goal of this "repletion" is the establishment of an equilibrium, and the best that could befall a man is that the equilibrium, once restored, should be permanent. But, on this theory, pleasure is only felt during the "filling-up" by which we approach this best condition. When we have reached it and are steadily persisting in it, there is no longer any process of "filling-up," and consequently no pleasure. Pleasure attends our progress to the "good," but not our fruition of it; that will be the "neutral condition," painless but not pleasurable. This is what is meant by the view that pleasure is always "becoming," never is "being."

We can now express this thought in a general formula. The end or goal is always of more worth and dignity than the means or road to it. The means is "for the sake of" the end, not the end for the sake of the means. And a process which culminates in the establishment of a permanent condition is to that condition as means to end. Thus the processes of shipbuilding and all the appliances and raw material they employ are "for the sake of" what comes out of them, the vessel. (*E.g.* the naval architect's skill, his implements, the timbers of which he makes the vessel, all of them only have worth because the vessel itself has worth—in this case, an "economic" worth (54*c*).[1]) If pleasure is a "becoming," then it must be relative to an end in which it culminates, must be the coming-to-be of *something*. That something will be in the μοίρᾳ or category of the *good*, *i.e.* will have "intrinsic value." But the end and the process by which it is reached are never in the same category, and therefore, on the hypothesis, pleasure will not be a good. The "wits" from whom we have borrowed this suggestion will therefore think it ridiculous to say that life is not worth having without pleasure. This would amount to saying that life is worth having when it is an alternation of aspiring after a good we have not yet attained and losing one we have attained, but not when it is the fruition of present good (54*c*–55*a*).

We note that Socrates is not made to accept the doctrine that pleasure is only felt in the *transition* from an "unnatural" to the "normal state" as his own. He clearly does not accept it without reserve (as Spinoza does in his definitions of *laetitia* and *tristitia*, *Ethics*, iii. Appendix, def. 2, 3). He cannot do so because he holds, as we shall see, that some pleasures, the "pure" or "unmixed" class, are themselves good, whereas the theory under criticism, as he is careful to point out, compels us to hold that *no* pleasure is good, since no pleasure, according to it, can be an end. The criticism of Aristotle on the theory is based on the same conviction of the

---

[1] The φάρμακα of 54*c* 1 are, of course, the paints employed for coating the sides of the vessel, etc. So the ὕλη mentioned along with the "tools" does not mean "raw material" in general, but the "timber" from which the planks of the ship are made.

goodness of these unmixed pleasures, and is one of the most valuable things in the *Ethics*. As he points out, even the pleasures of " repletion " cannot be proved not to be good, or even *the* good, by this line of reasoning. For what gives rise to the feeling of pleasure which accompanies return to the " normal state " after disturbance, is not the process of return itself, but the successful reassertion of the activities of the organism which were not affected by the disturbance. The " filling-up " only gives rise to the pleasure *accidentally* because it is attended with removal of an inhibition. The thought is that the feeling-tone of normal organic life is itself pleasant. A disturbance of the " balance " partially inhibits function. Recovery from the inhibition is pleasant because it is the successful reassertion of a normal activity which has persisted, though under inhibition, all through the antecedent " depletion." Hence we need to correct the proposed definition of pleasure as " sensible transition to a natural state " into " unimpeded exercise of a natural activity." The pleasure-giving process is not a " coming-to-be " (γένεσις) but the discharge in act (ἐνέργεια) of an already developed function.[1] The insistence on the difference between the two kinds of process, " coming-to-be " and " activity," is a correction of first-rate importance in the Academic terminology. We need not suppose that Aristotle is correcting Plato's views about the worth of pleasures, which, in fact, agree with his own. It is Speusippus and Xenocrates, not Plato, whose anti-Hedonism he is criticizing, though he rightly notes that the want of a word like his own ἐνέργεια makes it easy for the Academic to employ this unconvincing argument against the goodness of pleasures.

We may add the further consideration that it is a paradox to hold that all goods are mental, that pleasant feeling is the only mental good, and, by consequence, that, *e.g.*, beauty and strength, valour, temperance, intelligence, have no inherent value, and that a man's intrinsic worth depends on the question how much pleasure he is feeling (55*b*). This, we see, is a valid argument against the Hedonist, independently of the worth of the contention that all pleasure is a γένεσις.

THE INTELLECTUAL VALUES (55*c*–59*d*).—We have seen that there are two types of pleasures, the " pure " and the " mixed," and we shall expect to find that they have different values for human life. We must now consider intellectual activities and their worth in the same way. As with pleasures, so with forms of knowledge, we have to discover which are " truest to type," most fully deserving to be called knowledge. We may begin by dividing " knowledges " or " sciences " into those which have to do with *making* things, the " industrial " arts (χειροτεχνικαὶ ἐπιστῆμαι), and those which are περὶ παιδείαν καὶ τροφήν, have to do with the cultivation of the soul itself, the " cultural " arts and sciences. (This is, in effect, the Aristotelian distinction between " theory " and " practice.") We may begin by considering the " industrial,"

---

[1] *E.N.* 1153*a* 7–14

manual, or operative arts themselves, and ask whether some of them do not contain more, others less, of genuine knowledge, so that we can introduce again the distinction between " purer " and " more mixed " forms of knowledge. We see at once that if we eliminated from the industrial arts all that they derive from the exact knowledge of number, measure, weight, very little which we can call knowledge would be left. What these arts contain beyond the application of number, weight, and measure is little more than empirical guess-work. We see the presence of this empirical factor in such callings as those of the musician (who has largely to depend on his " ear "), the practising physician, the soldier ; we might fairly say that there is more genuine science in the builder's business than in any of these professions, because he is so much more concerned with the exact processes of measuring, so dependent at every point on his implements of precision, plumb-line, compass, and the rest. So we will divide these crafts into a more exact and scientific class of which building is the type, and a less exact, of which music is typical (55c–56c). (The notion of " exact " science seems to be definitely formulated here for the first time in literature ; the thought is that of Kant, that every branch of knowledge contains just as much science as it contains mathematics.)

Again, if we consider the " exact " sciences themselves, we have to make a similar distinction. There are two " arithmetics " : that of the " many," and the much more scientific arithmetic of the " philosopher." The former operates with " concrete " and very unequal units, such as one man, one army, one ox, and disregards the fact that the men, oxen, armies, counted may be unequal ; the other operates with units which are absolutely and in every way equal—in fact, with *numbers*, not with numbered *things*. So there are two forms of " mensuration " : the loose measurement of the architect or the retail trader, and the accurate measurement of the geometer and calculator.[1] Thus one " knowledge," no less than one pleasure, may be " purer," truer to type, than another. The " exact " forms of knowledge which are concerned with number, measure, weight, are much more exact and " truer " than all others, and the " philosopher's " or " theorist's " arithmetic and geometry are much more exact and true than those of the mechanician or engineer (56d–57e). And we cannot, without blushing, deny that dialectic, whose business it is to study the absolutely real and the eternal, must insist on a still more rigid standard of exactness and truth than any other kind of knowledge. It must be still more intolerant of mere approximation than any other science. Gorgias, to be sure, used to claim the first place among the sciences for rhetoric, on the ground that it can secure

---

[1] The simple man who undertook to settle the value of π by fitting a string round a disc, unrolling it, and measuring it with a measuring-stick was confusing the " tradesman's " mensuration, which is always rough approximation, with the geometer's, which must be accurate within a known and very precise " standard of approximation."

the voluntary services of the professionals of all the rest. We need not quarrel with him about this. Our question is not what "art" has the highest prestige or the greatest utility-value, but simply which sets up the most severe standard of truth and accuracy, and there can be no doubt about the claims of dialectic in this particular. Most of the "arts" are content to build on δόξαι, contested beliefs, and even the cosmologists confine their attention to "actual fact," what "happens"; absolutely *exact* knowledge of actual fact is never to be had; there is always an element of the incalculable and contingent about it. The knowledge which is through and through knowledge must therefore be "abstract"; that is the price it pays for its exactness. It must be concerned with the non-temporal (57*d*–59*d*).

THE FORMAL STRUCTURE OF THE GOOD LIFE (59*e*–66*d*).—The best life for men, we saw, must be a blend of two constituents—intelligent activity and pleasant feeling. We have now examined each genus of the two apart, and distinguished in each a variety which is truer, and one which is less true, to type. We have now to consider on what principle the two ingredients should be blended. What will be the formula which appears as the πέρας in this "mixture"? Our task is like that of the man who mixes the ingredients of a sweet drink; pleasure is the honey for our mixture, intelligent thought the water; the problem is to mingle them in just the right proportion (61*c*). It would be rash to assume that we shall succeed in doing this by simply blending every form of pleasure with every form of "thought"; we need to proceed more cautiously. It will be prudent to begin by considering first those pleasures and those forms of knowledge which we have found to be most genuine, most true to type (ἀληθέστατα); if we find that the blend does not completely satisfy our original condition that the "good" must be "sufficient," *all* a man's life requires, we can then consider admitting the inferior pleasures and arts into the mixture (61*e*). There can be no dispute about stipulating that the good is to include all knowledge of the "truer" type, the exact knowledge of the timeless things; we shall certainly require for the best life a knowledge of "righteousness itself" and the intelligence to use the knowledge, and the same considerations will apply to all such knowledge of the "absolute." But will this be enough for the purposes of life? If a man is to live a life among men, he must have some at least of the inferior knowledge which is inexact. A man who knew only the "absolute" and exact lines and circles of the geometer, but knew nothing of the rough approximations to them with which life presents us, would not even know how to find his way home. (As we might say, a chemical balance is a beautiful thing, but it won't do to weigh your butter and cheese in.) So the intervals we make on our musical instruments are only approximations, they are not "true"; but a man must be conversant with them, as well as with the mathematical theory of harmonics, unless he is to go through life with none but the "unheard" melodies for his companions. In fact, we may reasonably let in the whole crowd of second-class knowledges; some of them we really need if we are to live as men among men, and none of them will do us any harm, if we have the superior knowledge too, and so are not in danger of mistaking the rough approximation for something better (62a–d).

Thus we have let all the " water " go into the bowl in which the draught of " happiness " is to be brewed. We must now consider what we are to do with the " honey." Here, again, it will be safer to consider the " unmixed " pleasures first and the " mixed," which, as we have seen, are not wholly true to type, afterwards. It is clear that we shall not be able to let in all this second class without reflection. If there are any of them which are " unavoidable " (ἀναγκαῖαι, sc. such as arise directly from the functions of sound and healthy life themselves), they must, of course, be admitted. But whether we can admit all the rest depends on the question whether all pleasures, like all knowledges, are profitable, or, at worst, harmless (63a). To decide this question we may ask the pleasures themselves whether they would prefer to keep house with all wisdom and knowledge, or by themselves. We may be sure (since we have seen that the best life is the " mixed " one) that the pleasures would reply that it is not good to live alone, and that the best companion with whom to keep house would be " knowledge of all things and in especial of ourselves " (63c).

Now we put the same question to the various knowledges. " Do you need the company of pleasure ? "   " In particular, do you need, over and above our class of true pleasures, the company of the intense and violent pleasures ? " Knowledge would say that, so far from desiring these exciting pleasures, she finds them a perpetual hindrance ; they vex the souls in which she has taken up her abode with mad frenzies, and destroy her offspring by producing forgetfulness and neglect. She would claim kinship with Socrates' class of " true " and " unmixed " pleasures ; of the rest— those which are " mixed " satisfactions—she would accept such as accompany health and a sober mind and any form of goodness, but reject those of " folly and badness " in general, as obviously unfit to find a place in such a " blend " as we are contemplating (63d–64a).[1] There is only one further ingredient for which we must stipulate—ἀλήθεια, " truth," " reality," " genuineness." If this is left out, the result of the blending itself will not be real or genuine. (The bearing of this remark is a little obscure, but it is probably meant to lead up to the next stage of the argument, the consideration of the relative importance to be laid on the different constituents of the " mixed life " for man and the assigning of the first place in it to its rational structure, the last, to the " harmless " pleasures.)

We have now tracked down the good, so to say, to its very

---

[1] Thus a place would be found in the " good for man " for all the pleasure which attends the healthy and morally virtuous satisfactions of " bodily appetite." It is not expected that the best man shall not enjoy his dinner when he is hungry. But dinners are not things he cares supremely about.

doors. It only remains to discriminate the relative values of its various ingredients and so to answer the question we have been considering so long, whether intelligence or pleasure is more akin to the principle or cause which makes the good life so satisfactory to us all (64c). We may say at once that what makes any mixture or blend a good one is *measure* and *proportion* (μέτρον, ἡ τοῦ συμμέτρου φύσις). Neglect of the rule of due proportion makes a " mixture " unstable and vitiates the components. Where the rule is neglected, you get not a genuine " mixture " but a mere " mess." The good is thus a form of the beautiful (καλόν), for measure and proportion are the secret of all beauty (64c–e). We may thus take measure or proportion (συμμετρία), beauty, and truth (or reality, ἀλήθεια) as three " forms " (ἰδέαι) or " notes " found in the good and say that the goodness of our " mixture " is due to the presence of this trinity in unity (65c). Our business is now to confront first intelligence and then pleasure successively with these three distinguishable but inseparable notes of the good. Let us begin with the note of ἀλήθεια (truth, genuineness). Pleasure is the " hollowest " (ἀλαζονίστατον) of all things, *i.e.* it promises to be so much more satisfactory than it proves to be ; the illusoriness of the " pleasures of sex " is a notorious case in point. Intelligence (νοῦς) is either the same thing as ἀλήθεια, or, at any rate, it is the most " genuine " thing in the world (the least illusory, 65c–d). Next, as to the note of " measure " : pleasure notoriously tends to wild excess ; there is nothing more " measured " than intelligence and science (65d). And finally, as to beauty. There is no uncomeliness (οὐδὲν αἰσχρόν) in wisdom and intelligence, but the intensest pleasures are so unseemly that we think the spectacle of a man who is indulging in them is either ridiculous or disgraceful. We are actually ashamed to see such a sight, and think that it ought to be covered by darkness (66a).

We may now draw our conclusion. Pleasure is neither the best nor the second-best thing. We must give the first place to " measure the measured, that which is 'in place' " (τὸ καίριον) ;[1] the second to proportion, beauty, completeness (τὸ σύμμετρον καὶ καλὸν καὶ τὸ τέλεον καὶ ἱκανόν) ; the third to intelligence and wisdom (νοῦς καὶ φρόνησις) ; the fourth to " sciences and arts and true convictions " (ἐπιστῆμαι καὶ τέχναι καὶ δόξαι ὀρθαί) ; the fifth to the class of pleasures, whether involving actual sensation or not, which have no pain mixed with them (the " pure " pleasures of the discussion) : we stop short, like Orpheus, with the sixth " generation " (66a–d).[2]

---

[1] The concluding words of 66a 8 are the worst textual crux in Plato. The mischief is in the ἀίδιον. Burnet's suggestion τὴν ἄ (=πρώτην) ἰδέαν is highly attractive, or conceivably we might read αἰτίαν, rendering, " you may say that . . . the cause has been hunted down in the region of μέτρον. M. Diès holds that W supports a variant ὁπόσα τοιαῦτα, χρὴ νομίζειν τινὰ ἥδιον ἡρῆσθαι. But is ἥδιον quite in place *here* ?

[2] This might mean that the moderate satisfactions of appetite, which we expect to find in the sixth place, are excluded from the " good " (on the

(For the precise meaning of this enumeration I would refer the reader to Appendix B in Mr. R. G. Bury's edition of the dialogue. I understand the passage in a way which is, I suppose, much the same as Mr. Bury's. Measure, proportion, rational structure are mentioned first because they have a cosmic significance ; they are found in the " great world " without, no less than in the lesser world of man's soul, and they are the " notes " of good, wherever found. Then ἐπιστῆμαι and " pure " pleasures are mentioned, in that order, because they are the two aspects in which rational structure and law show themselves in *human* mental life, and ἐπιστῆμαι are put first, because we have just seen that intelligence is " more akin to " rational structure, reveals it more manifestly and clearly than feeling. There is no question of introducing into the good for man any *constituents* beyond the two which have been contemplated all along, intellectual activity and grateful feeling.)

FORMAL EPILOGUE TO THE DISCUSSION (66d–67b).—Philebus had originally said that the good for us is the plenitude of pleasure (ἡδονὴ πᾶσα καὶ παντελής), Socrates that "intelligence" (νοῦς) is at any rate (γε) a far better thing for man's life than pleasure. We long ago convinced ourselves that neither can be the whole of human good, since neither would be " all-satisfying," apart from the other. But our investigation has shown us that " intelligence " is at any rate infinitely (μυρίῳ) more closely related to the " victor " (the " mixed life " which proved to be the best of all for a man) than pleasure. (The point is that though the best life includes both elements, it is the element of rationality which gives it its specific character. A man is not a creature who uses an intellect to contrive ingenious devices for getting pleasures, but a creature who finds it pleasant to practise intellectual activities. Hume's view that in action reason " is and ought to be the slave of the passions " just inverts the true relation. *Human* " passions " should be the servants of intelligence.) Pleasure is not the good, even though all the horses and oxen of the world should say it is, with the assent of the " many " who think the " lusts of beasts " better evidence than the discourses of philosophers (67b).

The last sentence obviously alludes, in its reference to the θηρίων ἔρωτας, to the argument of Eudoxus, afterwards adopted by Epicurus, that pleasure must be " the good " because it is that which " all living creatures " pursue when left to themselves (*E.N.* x. 1172b 9 ff.). The supposed unmannerly reference to Aristippus in the remark about the " horses " (ἵπποι) is a mere unhistorical fancy. Even if Aristippus had been aimed at in the criticism of Hedonism, such an allusion would be impossible, for the simple reason that the leading anti-Hedonist of the Academy, Speusippus,

ground that they are not actually good but merely harmless). As they were admitted at 63ε, however, the meaning may be that the " sixth degree " is actually counted in as the lowest and last. This makes the allusion to " Orpheus " (Fr. 14, Kern) more apt. The theogonic poet quoted must have described his " sixth generation " of deities as well as the preceding five.

whose views we have found Plato expressly reproducing in two places, had a " horse " in his name too.

See further :

BURNET.—*Greek Philosophy, Part I.*, 324–332.
RITTER, C.—*Platon*, ii. 165–258, 497–554 ; *Platons Dialoge*, 68–97 ; *Neue Untersuchungen ueber Platon*, 95–173.
RAEDER, H.—*Platons philosophische Entwickelung*, 357–374.
NATORP, P.—*Platons Ideenlehre*, 296–331.
NETTLESHIP, R. L.—*Plato's Conception of Goodness and the Good*. (Works, i. 307–336.)
BAEUMKER, C.—*Das Problem der Materie in der griechischen Philosophie*, 193–196. (1890.)
POSTE, E.—*The " Philebus " of Plato*. (Oxford, 1860.)
BURY, R. G.—*The " Philebus " of Plato*. (Cambridge, 1897.)
DIÈS, A.—*Autour de Platon*, ii., 385–399.
STEWART, J. A.—*Plato's Doctrine of Ideas*, 92–100.
ROBIN, L.—*Platon*, c. iv.

CHAPTER XVII

TIMAEUS AND CRITIAS

THE *Timaeus* stands alone among the Platonic dialogues in being devoted to cosmology and natural science. Owing to the fact that the first two-thirds of it were continuously preserved through the " dark ages " in the Latin version and with the commentary of Chalcidius, it was the one Greek philosophical work of the best age with which the west of Europe was well acquainted before the recovery of Aristotle's metaphysical and physical writings in the thirteenth century ; it thus furnished the earlier Middle Ages with their standing general scheme of the natural world. In the present volume it is impossible to deal with the contents of the dialogue in any detail ; I have tried to perform the task in my *Commentary on Plato's Timaeus* (Oxford, 1928), with which the later commentary of Professor Cornford (*Plato's Cosmology*, London, 1937) should be compared.

The date of composition cannot be precisely determined. There is no external evidence, and the internal evidence of style only serves to show that the dialogue belongs to the last period of Plato's authorship ; thus we must place the composition at some time after the *Sophistes*, *i.e.* within the years 360–347. It is quite uncertain, so far as I can see, whether we should regard the *Timaeus* or the *Philebus* as the later work. As to the date of the imagined conversation I think it is possible to be more precise. We have to consider (*a*) the internal evidence of the *Timaeus* itself, (*b*) the evidence supplied by the *Republic*. (*a*) The interlocutors in the dialogue are Socrates, Timaeus, Critias, and Hermocrates. Of Timaeus nothing is known except what we learn from Plato, that he is a Locrian from South Italy, with a career of eminence in both science and politics behind him (20*a*). From the fact that the doctrine he is made to expound is recognizably a version of Pythagoreanism in which the biology and medicine of Empedocles is grafted on the original Pythagorean mathematics, we can really have no doubt that he is meant to be a Pythagorean of the same type as the more famous Philolaus. This suggests that he is at least as old a man as Socrates, and that we may perhaps connect what we are told of the magistracies he has filled with the facts about Pythagorean political ascendancy in Magna Graecia in the first half of the fifth century.[1] Hermocrates is plainly the famous

[1] I cannot agree with those who dispute Plato's intention to represent Timaeus as a Pythagorean. Everything in his doctrine can be traced back

Syracusan best known by the prominent part he played in the defence of Syracuse against the Athenian Armada of 415. Socrates implies (20a) that Hermocrates is still a man with his career before him, and bases his estimate of him on the general report. This shows that Hermocrates is a stranger at Athens and indicates that the conversation is presumably to be dated not too long after the " pan-Sicilian Congress " at Gela in 425, where Hermocrates seems to have first made his reputation (Thuc. iv. 58).[1] Critias is certainly not, as all writers before Professor Burnet have assumed, Critias the so-called " oligarch " who figured in the usurping government of 404-3. He has already distinguished himself in science and politics (20a), and he refers pointedly to his own extreme old age and the way in which he remembers the distant events of his childhood, though he can hardly recollect what he has been told yesterday (26b). He also says that his great-grandfather was a friend and connexion of Solon (20e), and that he himself, as a boy of ten years old, used to sing the verses of Solon, which were then a " novelty " (21b). All this shows that the Critias meant is the grandfather of the " oligarch," Plato's own great-grandfather. Even so we have to suppose him, at the date of the dialogue, to be extremely old. (b) The *Timaeus* unmistakably announces itself as in a way a continuation of the *Republic*. Socrates opens the dialogue by recalling the main heads of what he had said " yesterday " to the present company (17a–19a), and the recapitulation coincides exactly with the contents of *Republic* i.–v. Thus we seem directed to date the discourse of Timaeus two days after the conversation in the house of Polemarchus.[2] If we were right in our view of the dramatic date of the *Republic*, this brings us to the time of the peace of Nicias or very shortly before it, the year 422 or 421. Such a date fits all the indications of the *Timaeus* itself. It enables

to Pythagorean sources except the use of the four Empedoclean " roots " and the equally Empedoclean sense-physiology and medicine, a point which I have tried to establish in detail elsewhere. For the evidence that Philolaus similarly combined Pythagorean mathematics with Empedoclean biology, see Burnet, *E.G.Ph.*[2] 278–279, *Greek Philosophy, Part I.*, 88–89. I have tried to add something to the evidence elsewhere. The name is not given as that of a Locrian by Iamblichus in his catalogue, but he mentions a Timaeus among the Crotoniates, and again (unless it is the same man) among the Parians, who precede the Locrians immediately in his list. This looks as though the name had been displaced by a copyist. Plato's avoidance of the name of Pythagoras is a standing habit; it, no doubt, has to do with the disrepute into which the word was brought by the more superstitious members of the order.

[1] It is impossible to imagine the meeting as taking place *after* the dispatch of the Athenian fleet to Syracuse. As we know from Xenophon and Diodorus, Hermocrates was serving against Athens in the East from 413 until his descent on Sicily in 409 or 408. We cannot suppose that he would be likely to choose Athens as a place to visit in this interval, or that he could meet Socrates there on friendly terms, still less that Socrates would contrast him, at that date, as a man with a career to make, with Timaeus and Critias as men whose distinction has been already achieved.

[2] It is, however, suggested that the present discourse is held during the Panathenaea, which do not fall even within two months of the day mentioned in the *Republic* (the feast of Bendis). This secures us against connecting the two dialogues too closely.

us to understand that the boyhood of old Critias would fall immediately after the expulsion of the Pisistratidae from Athens, and we can guess why the poems of Solon would be likely to be popular and " novel " at that date.   (Pisistratus and his sons are not likely to have encouraged the singing of them.)   It also gives us a reason for the presence of a distinguished public man from Locri and another from Syracuse.   Only a year or two before the peace the Athenians had sent envoys on a tour of the South Italian cities, including Locri, for the express purpose of forming a league to keep the power of Syracuse in check.   A general pacification would, of course, leave a good deal to be " redd up " in the western Mediterranean. We may be sure that Timaeus did not come to Athens expressly to talk to Socrates about the creation of the world.   We see also why Hermocrates is known to Socrates only by reports of his abilities and education.   And it is significant that, if we are right, the date at which Socrates is represented as listening with keen interest to a cosmological lecture is only a year or two after the burlesque of him in the *Clouds*.   This is a much more appropriate dramatic date than one later in his life.   Hence I feel little doubt that it is right.

The dialogue falls into three distinct parts : (*a*) introductory recapitulation of the contents of *Republic* i.–v. by Socrates (17*a*– 19*b*), with expression of a strong desire to see the doctrine there laid down embodied in a dramatic story of concrete achievements (19*b*–20*c*) ; (*b*) relation by Critias of the alleged heroic exploit of Athens in resisting and defeating the kings of Atlantis (20*c*–26*d*) ; (*c*) the cosmological discourse of Timaeus, which extends unbroken, but for an occasional word of assent from Socrates, to the end of the dialogue (27*c*–92*c*).   We may consider these divisions in their order.

(*a*) *Introduction* (17*a*–20*c*).—There is not much on which we need make any comment.   It is useless to speculate on the identity of the unnamed person who has been kept away from the conversation by indisposition and whom Timaeus agrees to replace as speaker. As Timaeus takes his place, we are no doubt to understand that he belongs to the same group of " Italian " philosophers   Philolaus, as Burnet suggests, would suit the part, or we might perhaps even think of Empedocles.   Plato is merely intending a graceful expression of the debt of his dialogue to fifth-century " Italians." The most striking feature of the recapitulation of the *Republic* is that it covers only the ground of Books I.–V.   Nothing is said of the philosopher-kings and their education in mathematics and dialectic, of the Form of Good, or of the contents of *Republic* viii.–x. I suggest that the most likely explanation of this silence is that which is also the simplest.   Just so much of the *Republic*, and no more, is recalled as will be an appropriate basis for the story of the Athenian victory over Atlantis.   Plato is quite alive to the fact that the philosopher-king is an " ideal " which has never been realized, and therefore abstains from an attempt to exhibit a society of philosopher-kings in action. It is more credible that there should be an actual society at the level of that described in *Republic* i.–v., and he feels himself equal to the vivid imaginative delineation of its performances.

The remarks with which Socrates closes his recapitulation are interesting as showing that Plato fully understood that his own hero had his definite limitations. Socrates, as he says, can give us a picture of the really healthy society, but he cannot " make the figures move." He cannot tell an actual story of the behaviour of such a society in a life-like way, and the reason is that he has not enough personal experience of the work of the active statesman. He remains, after all, something of the theorist and *doctrinaire* (19*b–e*). This was, in fact, true of Socrates, and it helps to explain the fact that his influence on many of his associates was not wholly beneficial. Association with him in early life was not an unmixed good for the average lad ; so far, there was just a slight basis of foundation for the distrust with which practical workers of the democratic constitution, like Anytus, regarded him.

(*b*) *The Story of Atlantis* (20*c*–25*d*).—The story told by Critias is to the effect that nine thousand years before the time of Solon Athens had enjoyed just such institutions as those described in *Republic* i.–v. Her soil was then wonderfully rich and fertile, as it had not suffered from the denudation which has since reduced the district of Attica to a rocky skeleton. The prehistoric Athenians, strong only in public spirit and sound *moral*, encountered and defeated the federated kings of Atlantis, an island lying in the Atlantic outside the Straits of Gibraltar, who had already successfully overrun all Europe as far as Italy, and all Africa as far as the Egyptian border. Afterwards both the prehistoric Athenian victors and the island Atlantis were overwhelmed in a single day and night of earthquake and inundation. The story only survived in the records of Egypt, where Solon heard it when on his travels.

It should be clear that this whole tale is Plato's own invention. He could not tell us so much more plainly than he does in the *Critias* (113*b*), when he makes Critias appeal to the testimony of " family papers " as his sole evidence for the narrative. Not only the existence of the island-kingdom, but the statement that Solon had ever contemplated a poem on the subject is represented as a " family tradition " ; in other words, nothing was ever really known of any such intention. It is not hard to see what the materials for the tale are. The alleged shallowness of the sea just outside the " pillars of Heracles," and perhaps tales of Carthaginian sailors about islands in the Atlantic, are the foundation for the story of the lost island ; the account of its destruction is manifestly based on the facts of the great earthquake and tidal wave of the year 373 which ravaged the Achaean coast. The main conception of the successful conflict of a small and patriotic nation in arms against an invader with vast material resources and immense superiority in the art of military engineering—a point on which the *Critias* lays great stress—is clearly suggested by the actual facts of the Athenian resistance to Darius and Xerxes. Plato has projected the events of the Persian wars backwards, magnified their scale, and thus made the moral, that numbers, wealth, and engineering skill are no match for the national spirit of a free people, the more obvious to the dull. Strictly speaking, the whole narrative has no logical connexion with the special theme of the *Timaeus*. Its real function is to serve as a prelude to the *Critias*, where the narrative now briefly summarized was to be told with full detail. As Critias puts it, at the end of his story (27a–b), the division of labour between speakers is to be that Timaeus shall now describe the formation of the world and of man, as its closing " work," Socrates is then to be understood to have explained how man is educated, and it is left for Critias to describe the heroic achievements of the men whose production has been dealt with by Timaeus and their education discussed by Socrates. Thus the *logical* order of the three dialogues would have been *Timaeus, Republic, Critias*. The express allusion in this passage to the contribution of Socrates seems to show that this definitely means the *Republic*, the only Platonic work where Socrates expressly discusses the question of educational method. From the absence of any reference to a discourse of Hermocrates, and the difficulty of seeing what has been left for him to discourse upon, I should infer that it was never Plato's intention to carry the scheme beyond the *Critias*. Hermocrates, the youngest member of the group, was probably to be a listener, not a speaker.

(c) *The Discourse of Timaeus* (27c–92c).—The lecture which Timaeus now delivers covers the whole ground of natural knowledge from astronomy to pathology and psychophysics. It will be impossible to deal with more than its most outstanding features. It starts with two fundamental positions : (a) that the sensible world, being sensible, " becomes," or, as we might say, is a world of " happenings " or " events " ; (b) that whatever " becomes " has a cause, by which Timaeus means that it is the product of an *agent* (28a–c). The " artisan " or " craftsman " (δημιουργός) who makes the world thus comes into the story, and it is assumed that this maker is God. Now a craftsman always works with a model or archetype before him, and so we must ask whether the model on which the world has been made is itself something that has " become " or something eternal. Since the maker is the best of all causes and the thing he makes the best of all effects, clearly the model of which the sensible world is a " copy " or " likeness " (εἰκών) is eternal (29a). (In more modern language, it is meant that the natural world is not constituted by " events " only, but by events and the objects (in Professor Whitehead's sense) situated in the events, and this is why it is intelligible and can be known.) This leads us to lay down an important canon of the degree of truth to be expected in natural science. Discourse about the fixed and unchanging archetype, or model, can be exact and final ; it has the definitiveness of its object : discourse about its sensible copy, which is continually varying and changing, can only be approximate. Hence in natural science, we have no right to demand more than " likely stories," *i.e.* in metaphysics and mathematics there can be finality ; in the natural sciences we have to be content with approximate and tentative results, though our business is to make our approximations as accurate as we can (29*b–d*). In other words, physical science is progressive in a sense in which metaphysics and mathematics are not. (Newton's gravitation formula may be a "first approximation" on which later physicists can improve ; such a formula as $\cos \theta = \frac{1}{2}(e^{\theta i} + e^{-\theta i})$ is no "first approximation" and there is no improving on it.) This principle, that a proposition of physics is always "approximate," and that none is therefore beyond the possibility of correction, is one so important that Timaeus is careful to call repeated attention to it in connexion with the special scientific hypotheses he propounds to explain special groups of facts. A simple modern illustration would be the consideration that all actual measurements of physical magnitudes are approximate, and that no determination of such a magnitude by experimental methods can be trusted, unless it is accompanied by a statement of the "probable error." When we are told that all our natural knowledge is only a "likely story," it is not meant that we may substitute fairy tales for science ; what is meant is that while we must make our results as precise as we can, we must remember that they are all liable to improvement. Our best measurements may be superseded ; our most satisfactory explanatory hypotheses may always have to be modified in the light of overlooked or freshly discovered facts. What Timaeus is really trying to formulate is no fairy tale but, as we shall see, a geometrical science of nature.

Next we may ask ourselves *why* the Maker produced a world at all. He was perfectly good, and for that very reason did not want to keep his goodness to himself, but to make something like himself. So he took over the whole of the "visible," which was in a condition of chaotic disorder, and made it into an ordered system, since order is *better* than chaos. For the same reason, he put *mind* (νοῦς) into it, and, as mind can only exist in a soul (ψυχή), he gave it a soul, and thus the sensible world became "by the providence of God, a living being with soul and mind" (30*b*). The model in the likeness of which he made it was, of course, a νοητόν or "intelligible," something complete and whole (τέλεον), and something living. The sensible world, then, is the sensible embodiment of a living creature or organism (ζῷον) of which all other living creatures are parts. And there is only one "world" of sense (as against the Milesian tradition of the "innumerable" worlds). For the model is one, and a *perfect* copy of it will reproduce its uniqueness (30*c*–31*b*).

Thus, in the scheme of Timaeus, we see that the "efficient cause" of the world is thought of definitely as a "personal" God, and this "creator" or "maker" is, strictly speaking, the only God, in our sense of the word, the dialogue recognizes.   Later on we shall find the *name* θεός given both to the world itself as a whole and to certain parts or denizens of it, but this must not mislead us.   These θεοί are all " created " ; their *raison d'être* is the will of the δημιουργός (29e, 41b), who is thus distinguished from them as God is from " creatures " in Christian theology.   The *formal* cause of the world, however, is not God but the " intelligible living creature," the αὐτὸ ὃ ἔστι ζῷον, which God contemplates as the model for his work. The language used about this model shows that we are to think of it as a form, the " form " of an organism of which all other organisms are parts.   It thus has the peculiarity that there is only *one* unique " sensible " which " partakes " of it.

It may naturally be asked how much of this can be conceived to be serious Platonic teaching and how much is mere imaginative symbolism ?   No one, of course, could answer the question precisely ; possibly Plato himself could not have made a hard-and-fast distinction between philosophical content and mythical form.   But one or two points are important.   It would stultify the whole story to follow the example of some interpreters, who wish to find something like the philosophy of Spinoza in Plato, by making the " artisan " a mythical symbol of his " model," the νοητὸν ζῷον. This may or may not be good philosophy and theology, but it is not the thought of Plato, as we shall see more clearly when we come to deal with the doctrine of God in the *Laws*.   God and the forms have to be kept distinct in Plato for the reason that the activity of God as producing a world " like " the forms is the one explanation Plato ever offers of the way in which the " participation " of things in forms is effected.   If " God " simply meant the same thing as the forms, or as a supreme form, it would remain a mystery why there should be anything but the forms, why there should be any " becoming " at all.   How far the explanation that God " makes " a world on the model of the forms was taken by Plato to be a literal statement of truth is a question that may be left to anyone who is bold enough to pronounce exactly how literally Leibniz intended his similar language about God's " choice of the best " as the reason why the actual world is actual.   The one thing which is clear from the *Laws* is that God, in Plato, is a " soul," not a form.

A more legitimate question is whether God in the *Timaeus* is quite all we mean by a " creator."   Are we to take seriously the representation, which runs through the dialogue, of God's action as the imposing of order on a pre-existing chaos ?   Does Plato mean that the world was formed out of pre-existing materials ? On this point we find a discrepancy of interpretation springing up in the first generation of the Academy itself.   Aristotle, as is well known, insists on finding in the *Timaeus* the doctrine that the world is γεννητός (" had a beginning "), and is severely critical of this error, as he regards it.   On the other hand, the Platonists for the most part — the Neoplatonists unanimously — adopt the view, originally propounded by Xenocrates, that the representation of the world as having a beginning is adopted simply " for convenience of exposition " (διδασκαλίας χάριν), as a geometer talks of " drawing " a line, when all that he does is to point out that the existence of the line is *already* implied by our initial postulates.[1] Thus, on their view, the account of the world, or rather its constit-uents, as they were before God began his work, is merely a picture of the sort of thing you would have left on your hands if you tried to do what you never can do successfully, to think away all traces of the order and structure in which God's authorship of things reveals itself. The only two Platonists who are known to have taken Aristotle's view on this question are Plutarch and Atticus, a writer of the Antonine age. It is significant that their attempt to take the words of Timaeus literally gets them into very grave difficulties. Since the undoubted Platonic doctrine, expounded most fully in the *Laws*, is that " soul " is the cause of all movements, Plutarch finds himself bound to discover in the *Laws* the doctrine that there is an " evil " world-soul, which he supposes to have animated the original chaos. Though this discovery has been followed in modern times by such scholars as Zeller, it is certainly a mere "mare's nest." The words of the *Laws* say no more than that, since there is disorder in the world as well as order, there must be some soul or souls other than God to cause the disorder.[2] And we may be sure that Aristotle would never have been silent about a doctrine which would be, to him, sheer blasphemy, if he had known of it as a Platonic theory.

If we look at the text of the *Timaeus*, we shall see that at any rate Plato does not mean to say that there ever was a *time* before God constructed the world, since he tells us, as Aristotle allows,[3] that time and the world "began" together, God, in fact, making both of them. Thus the language which seems to imply a primi-tive state of pure chaos cannot be meant seriously, and so far Xenocrates seems to be right in his interpretation. (This would leave it a logical possibility that the series of events had a first member, and that the interval between the first member and the event which is my writing of these words, is a finite number of years, but I do not think any scholar acquainted with Greek thought is likely to suppose Plato to be contemplating this alternative.) Again, as will be clearer from what we shall have to say later on about the use of the notion of "necessity," it seems plain that the

[1] For Aristotle's interpretation, see *Physics*, 251*b* 17, *de Caelo*, 280*a* 30, *Metaph.* 1072*a* 1. Since he comments on the fact that the dialogue makes time and the world begin together, he is presumably alive to the point that Timaeus does not ascribe a beginning to nature in the usual sense of that phrase. For the explanation of Xenocrates, see Plutarch, *de Animae Pro-creatione in Timaeo*, 1013*a–b*, where it is admitted that on this point the Academy in general followed Xenocrates.

[2] *Laws*, x. 896*e*, where all that is said is that, since there is disorder and " dysteleology " in the world, the perfectly good soul cannot be the only soul there is ; there must be *one or more* faulty souls. Neither Plutarch nor Zeller had any right to manufacture an " evil world-soul " out of this straightforward rejection of Pantheism.

[3] *Physics*, 251*b* 17, *Metaph.* 1072*a* 1.

Timaeus knows of no external limitation imposed on God's will by conditions independent of God himself. The "maker's" goodness is the whole and complete explanation of the very existence of the natural world. This should justify us in saying that the "Demiurge" really is thought of as a Creator in the full sense of the word. Probably Xenocrates may also have been right in taking the dialogue to imply the "eternity of the world" in the sense in which that phrase is commonly, but inaccurately, used, that the order of events never had a first member. It still remains true that, in Plato's own more accurate terminology, the world is a γεγονός, "something that has become," not ἀΐδιον, eternal. Even if there never was a first event, everything sensible has "emerged" as the result of a process; in the Platonic conception the world is always "in evolution," even if the evolution never began and will never come to an end. This is why the world, unlike God, has a *history*. It is always getting itself made ; there is never a point at which it is full-made.

The story of the making we cannot here follow far into its details. Since natural things can be seen and grasped, fire (light) and earth must be among their constituents. To combine two such terms in a stable way, there must be a "mean" between them. But fire and earth are volumes and have three dimensions. Hence you cannot insert a single mean proportional between them, but need two.[1] This need is met by air and water. Fire is to air what air is to water and water to earth. This playful application of the doctrine of the geometrical mean effects a transition from Pythagorean mathematics to the four "roots" of Empedocles. We shall see shortly that for Timaeus they are not "elements" (31*b*–32*c*). God used up the whole of these materials in making the world. It excretes nothing and assimilates nothing, and this secures it against age or disease. Its form was appropriately made spherical, since the sphere has the greatest volume of all bodies with the same perimeter, and is therefore the right figure for that which is to contain everything. It was given no sense-organs, since there is nothing outside itself to be apprehended, no digestive organs, as there is nothing it can take in as food, and no organs of locomotion, for it has nowhere to travel. It needed no hands, for there is nothing for it to grasp or repel. Being alive, however, it moves with the most uniform of all motions, uniform rotation on its own axis. Finally, we must add that it was animated all through with a ψυχή, and this was the generation of a "blessed god" (32*c*–34*b*).

We have begun, however, at the wrong end. We should have described first the fashioning of the world's soul, since soul takes precedence of body in order of "production" as well as of worth

---

[1] The allusion is to the famous problem of the "duplication of the cube," connected by later anecdote with Plato's own name. The meaning of Timaeus is clearly that no one rational "mean" can be inserted between two integers, when each is the product of three *prime* factors and no more.

(since, on Plato's view, soul initiates all movements). The world's soul has three constituents: (*a*) a *Being* which is intermediate between that which is *always* "self-same" and that which "becomes and is divisible" in bodies; (*b*) a similarly "intermediate" kind of *Sameness*, and (*c*) of *Otherness*. God thus makes the soul as a *tertium quid* between the eternal and the temporal.[1] Next he "divided" the result in accord with the intervals of a musical scale which Timaeus describes.[2] (Apparently we are to imagine a long ribbon with intervals marked on it at distances corresponding to the numbers indicated by the directions for making the notes of the scale.) Next, the ribbon was split longitudinally into two halves, which were laid cross-wise, thus +. Then each ribbon was bent into a circle so as to give two circles, in planes at right angles to one another, with double contact, like the equator and a meridian on a sphere. The outermost of these circles was called that of the Same, the innermost that of the Other. The circle of the Same was made to revolve "to the right," that of the "Other" was subdivided into seven concentric circles at unequal distances from one another, which were made to revolve with unequal velocities "to the left" (34*c*–36*d*). We learn a little later that the inclination of the two circles was made oblique (39*a*), so that they turn out in the end to stand for the sidereal equator and the ecliptic, their revolutions being the (apparent) diurnal revolution of the "starry heavens" and the orbits of the sun and the planets in the Zodiac respectively. It must be carefully noted that nothing is said of "spheres," and, again, that as usual in the classical period, the *orbit* of a heavenly body is thought of as itself revolving, like a cart-wheel, and carrying round the body which is set in it. We have heard now of the orbits of the whole and of the seven planets, but so far nothing has been said about any *bodies* which, as we should say, "revolve in" these orbits. We are now at last (36*e*) told that the creator finally constructed the body of the world "within" its soul and adapted the two; this begins the "unceasing and reasonable life" of the κόσμος as an organism. The circle of the Same and the Other, being circles primarily "in the soul" of the world, have an epistemological as well as an astronomical significance. Their absolutely uniform revolutions symbolize—perhaps *Timaeus* means that they actually embody—

---

[1] I have adopted the exegesis given by Mr. Cornford in *Plato's Cosmology* as convincing, and modified these sentences accordingly.

[2] For the construction of this scale—its compass is four octaves and a sixth —see *Tim.* 35*b*–36*b*. Modern editors and translators in general have, in my opinion all been led into errors by exaggerated deference to Boeckh, who, in his turn, has been misled by an erroneous statement in *Timaeus Locrus* about the sum of the terms of the progression. That Boeckh and his followers, at least, must be wrong seems to be shown by their twice introducing into *their* scale the interval called the ἀποτομή or major semitone. As Proclus says, the silence of Timaeus shows that he does not intend to admit this interval, but only the minor semitone, or λεῖμμα, which he is careful to describe.

in the one case, science of the eternal and unchanging, in the other true conviction (δόξα) about the temporal (37a–c). (We must remember that the cosmic animal is a rational animal.)

The creator next proposed tc make his work even more like the model on which he had designed it. He could not make it, like its model, eternal (ἀΐδιος) (since nothing sensible can be so), but he made it as nearly eternal as he could. He devised a " moving image of eternity," which he called *time*. Time is to eternity as number is to unity; its absolutely uniform flow is an imperfect mirroring of the self-sameness of eternity, and time is the characteristic form of the sensible. We try to speak of the eternal as that which " was and is and is to be." But strictly, what is eternal simply " is "; we must not say that it " was " or " will be," for such language can only be used properly of what " happens." So again we say that the past *is* past, the future *is* to come, the non-existent *is* non-existent. But all such language, which ascribes *being* to what is mere " becoming " and even to " what is not," is unscientific [1] (37c–38b). The true state of the case is that the model eternally is, its sensible embodiment has been going on and will be going on all through time (38c). If there is to be time, there must be perceptible bodies with uniform movements to serve as measures of it, and so God devised the sun and the other " planets " and put them into the orbits provided for them by the splitting of the circle of the Other. Their order, reckoning outwards from the earth, is Moon, Sun, Hesperus, the " star of Hermes," then the three " outer" planets, for which no names are given here. The sun, Hesperus, and the " star of Hermes " have the same " period," but the two latter are in an unexplained way opposed to the sun, so that they are always catching him up and being caught up by him. The details about the apparent behaviour of the others would require more time than we can spare for their description. The important points to remember are that their velocities are different, that each of them has two motions, one communicated to it by the outermost circle, that of the Same (which revolves from E. to W. with a period of twenty-four hours), another, oblique to this, and with a longer period (the planet's " year "), from W. to E. The result is that the actual visible movements are complicated " corkscrews " (ἕλικες). Men ought to understand, as they do not, that the components of the movements of all are perpetually uniform and regular, and are " time " just as much as a lunar month, or a solar year. There is a great period, the longest of all, at the completion of which all the planets are once more, relatively to the sidereal heavens and to one another, in the same positions. " To enable them to see their way " round these circuits, a great

[1] Timaeus, we see, is not allowed to show any consciousness of the important logical results Plato had reached in the *Sophistes*. This is presumably because his discourse must be kept within limits imposed by the assumption that he is a fifth-century Pythagorean. All through the dialogue we need to remember that the speaker is not Plato, and that Plato need not be supposed to regard his utterances as a complete exposition of his own convictions.

light (the sun) was kindled in the circle next but one to the earth (37*c*–39*d*).[1]

God had now to make the various lesser animals which were to inhabit the different regions of the universe. This was done by reproducing the various forms of organism mind discovers in the form of " living being." Of these there are four, each inhabiting its own region : gods who live in the sky, winged creatures who inhabit the air, aquatic creatures, and land-animals. The " gods " were made approximately of pure fire, given spherical form, distri-buted over the heaven which revolves with the circle of the Same, and given a double movement—motion with the circle of the Same (*i.e.* a diurnal revolution), and an axial revolution of their own. (Thus the " gods " of Timaeus are simply the stars. We gather that they are self-luminous, since they are made of fire, and from com-parison of the mention of their axial rotations, with the absence of any corresponding statement about the planets, we may (perhaps ?) infer that the *planets* are not supposed to have any such rotations.) As for the earth, our mother, God made it for " a guardian and artificer of night and day, swinging (ἰλλομένην) on the path about the axis of the universe " (τὴν περὶ τὸν διὰ παντὸς πόλον τεταμένον, 40*b*). To describe the system further would be impossible without an actual visible model, and is irrelevant (39*e*–40*d*).

Full discussion of this astronomical passage is impossible here, but the following points should be noted. (*a*) There is no reference to the famous theory devised by Eudoxus within the Academy itself, which analyses the apparent movements of the heavenly bodies into combinations of axial rotations of imaginary " spheres," with a common centre at the centre of the earth. Timaeus never speaks of " spheres," but, in the language originated by Anaxi-mander, of " circles," conceived to turn round like a wheel spun about its centre. And though one of the motions of each true " star " is said to be " controlled by " the circle of the Same (40*b*), this motion is expressly ascribed to the star itself, not to an outer-most " sphere." Presumably the mere fact that Timaeus is a fifth-century astronomer, speaking many years before the origina-tion of Eudoxus' hypothesis, sufficiently explains this. (*b*) The stars are not thought of, after Aristotle's fashion, as made of a superior and " celestial " stuff. They are made of " fire," the finest quality of fire, but still the same fire to be found in ourselves and bodies round us. We cannot too carefully remember that the fateful distinction between " celestial matter " and " elementary matter " was unknown to Greek science until Aristotle introduced it as a direct consequence of his hypostatization of the purely mathematical spheres of Eudoxus into physical globes. (*c*) It is worth while also to observe the complete freedom of the whole theory from any traces of the planetary astrology which was, later on, to infest the minds of the Hellenistic age. The position of

---

[1] *I.e.*, *all* the planets shine by reflected solar light, as Empedocles had taught for the case of the moon.

the planets in the theory is a very humble one. They are not called " gods," as the stars are, and the natural interpretation of Timaeus' language is that they are not supposed to have any " souls " of their own, but merely to be directed by the soul of the κόσμος. They serve as timepieces, and that, so far, is all. The remark of Timaeus (40*d*) that though their movements are all calculable, their occultations, reappearances, and conjunctions frighten " those who cannot do a sum," and are supposed to be portents, is probably meant to deride the astrological superstitions of the East, and it is amusing to note that the negative in the phrase " who cannot do a sum," preserved in A, and guaranteed by the version of Cicero, has been dropped in our other best MSS. and marked for deletion by the *diorthotes* of A. In the age of our copyists, it was assumed that it is just the astronomer, who can do the sum, who is frightened by the appearances he foresees ! (*d*) As to the astronomical theory itself, it agrees with that of Eudoxus in being one of a " double " planetary motion. Each planet is assumed to have a " proper motion " through the zodiac from W. to E., and, over and above this, to be affected by the diurnal revolution from E. to W., with the result that it is brought daily back almost, but not quite, to the position it had twenty-four hours earlier. Thus, in this view, the moon, which most successfully resists the " diurnal revolution," is the swiftest of the planets, Saturn the slowest, since the moon succeeds in getting round the zodiac in a month, Saturn takes about thirty years. Both theories thus contradict the older view, traceable back to Anaximander, that *all* revolutions are in the same sense. If this were so, we should have to say that the moon is left farthest behind, Saturn lags least behind the diurnal revolution.[1] Since the double revolution theory is expressly employed in the myth of Er (*Rep.* 617*a*), it is pretty clearly of Pythagorean origin, and may be as old as Pythagoras himself, though this is uncertain.

(*e*) A much more important question is suggested by the remarks about the earth. Does Timaeus mean to ascribe a motion to the earth, or does he not ? In the middle of the last century there was a sharp controversy on the point between Grote, who found the motion of the earth in the dialogue, and Boeckh, who denied it. On one point Boeckh was clearly right. Timaeus cannot mean, as Grote thought, to give the earth an axial rotation with a period of twenty-four hours, since this would conflict with his own express attribution of this period to the " circle of the Same " at 39*c*. If the stars were revolving round us once in twenty-four hours and the earth rotating in the opposite sense with the same period, manifestly the interval between two successive transits of the same star over the meridian would not be twenty-four hours but twelve, and we cannot suppose, as Grote suggested, that Plato may have forgotten so obvious a point. On the other hand, though nearly all later editors have followed Boeckh, it is equally plain that he must be wrong in making the earth of Timaeus motionless. His inter-

[1] On all this see Burnet, *E.G.Ph.*³ 110–111.

pretation is overthrown at once by restoration of the correct text of the passage (τὴν περὶ τὸν διὰ παντός, κτλ). The τήν here can only mean τὴν ὁδόν or τὴν περίοδον, and is an accusative of the path traversed. Also the verb used, ἰλλομένην, is notoriously a verb of motion, and we have to add that Aristotle twice over, commenting on the passage, expressly interprets it as asserting a movement of some kind. He does not even produce any argument to show that this is what is meant, but assumes that no one will dispute the point. Hence I think we may feel fairly sure that it was the accepted exegesis of the first generation of the Academy.[1] It follows that Timaeus regards the centre of the universe as empty and ascribes to the earth a "to-and-fro" movement about it. This oscillatory motion we must pretty certainly take to be recti-linear, not circular or cycloidal like the movement of a pendulum-bob. This will explain why Aristotle, discussing the motion of the earth in *de Caelo*, B 13, distinguishes the view of Pythagoreans and certain unnamed other persons, that the earth revolves "*round* the centre," from that of the *Timaeus*, that it moves "*at* the centre."

The interpretation just given follows Professor Burnet, who is at least certainly right in insisting that the word used by Timaeus of the earth (ἰλλομένην) must stand, as Aristotle said, for a notion of some sort. Mr. Cornford has since developed a very different, and attractive explanation, according to which the meaning is that the earth, situated at the centre of the universe, has a diurnal rotation in the opposite sense to that of the "circle of the same" and thus exactly compensating it (*op. cit.*, pp. 120–124). Attrac-tive as this view is, I still doubt whether it could have been ex-pected to be divined by a reader with nothing before him but the bare statement that the earth ἴλλεται, "winds" or "curls," and have therefore hesitated to adapt my text to it, though I am not confident that it may not be right after all. But it is conceivable that Timaeus may be supposed to hold that some sort of "slide" of the earth would explain one or both of two "appearances," (*a*) the inequality of the "seasons" into which the year is divided by the equinoxes and solstices, (*b*) the notorious fact that though the sun and moon are "in conjunction" every lunar month, a solar eclipse is not regularly observed at each conjunction. But I give this avowedly as a guess.[2]

---

[1] For Aristotle's interpretation, see *de Caelo*, B 293*b* 30 ff., and cf. *ibid.* 296*a* 26. The important point is that the grammar of the passage in the *Timaeus* demands a verb of motion, and that Aristotle expressly explains the word by adding καὶ κινεῖσθαι. That he should be mistaken, or speaking with *mala fides*, on such a point seems incredible. Cf. Burnet, *Greek Philosophy, Part I.*, 348 and notes. The summary to D.L. (iii., 75) also ascribes a motion to the earth, though wrong about its nature (κινεῖσθαι περὶ τὸ μέσον).

[2] On the anomaly of the seasons, see Theo Smyrnaeus, p. 153 (Hiller), and on the Metonic cycle the passages quoted in Diels, *Fragmente der Vorsok-ratiker*³, i. 29, 9 (*s.v.* Oinopides). For the problem raised by the comparative rarity of visible eclipses of the sun, see *Placita*, ii. 29 (the explanation ascribed to the Pythagoreans and to Anaxagoras). I suspect that Timaeus may intend his sliding motion to explain why we do not see an eclipse of the sun

It is, in any case, improbable that the vague expression put into the mouth of Timaeus is meant to disclose Plato's full doctrine. Theophrastus, as Plutarch has told us, related that "in his old age" Plato repented of having placed the earth at the "centre," which should have been reserved for a "worthier body."[1] In the chapter of the *de Caelo* already referred to, Aristotle, after mentioning that some of the Pythagoreans held that the earth is a planet revolving round a central luminary, adds that "many others too might accept the view that the centre should not be assigned to the earth, for they think (οἴονται) that the most honourable region should belong to the most honourable body, and that fire is more honourable than earth, and the boundary than the intermediate. Now circumference and centre are boundaries ; so on the strength of these considerations they *think* that not the earth, but rather fire, is situated at the centre of the sphere " (*op. cit.* 293a 27–35). Aristotle does not say who these persons are, except that they are not the Pythagoreans of whom he had begun by speaking. Yet he must be speaking of actual persons, since he twice uses the phrase " they think." From what Plutarch has told us on the authority of Theophrastus, it seems to me certain that the unnamed " some " mean here, as so often in Aristotle, Plato and his followers. In that case, we have the evidence not only of Theophrastus, though that would be sufficient, but of Aristotle, that Plato " in his old age " regarded the earth as a planet revolving along with the rest round a central luminary, a view quite unlike that expounded by Timaeus. This is borne out by the evidence of an important passage in the *Laws* (821e–822c) where the Athenian speaker speaks of it as a truth which he has only recently learned that every planet has one and *only* one path (οὐ πολλὰς ἀλλὰ μίαν ἀεί). This can have only one meaning, that the speaker intends to deny the doctrine of the double or composite motion on which Timaeus insists. He must mean that the diurnal revolution is not communicated to the planets, and so is not a component of their motions ; each planet has only its " proper " movement through the Zodiac. Since the appearances which prompted the double motion theory still have to be accounted for, we are driven to suppose that the " diurnal revolution " must be intended to be regarded as only apparent, being really due to a motion of the earth. The implication is that the earth is a planet revolving round an invisible central luminary in a period of twenty-four hours, as the moon is supposed to revolve round the same body in a lunar month, or the sun in a year. A little more light is thrown on the matter by a sentence of the *Epinomis*, a dialogue which is generally " athetized " on extremely inadequate grounds, but admitted to have been at any

at every new moon, nor an eclipse of the moon at every full moon, by suggesting that on most of these occasions the earth happens to be a little " out of the centre."

[1] Plutarch, *Quaest. Platon.* 1006c, *Vit. Numae,* c. 11. See on this evidence Burnet, *Greek Philosophy, Part I.,* 347.

rate composed immediately after Plato's death by a disciple for circulation along with the *Laws*, and is therefore, in any case, likely to be faithful to the master's teaching. We are there told (*Epin.* 987*b*) that the various planets revolve in one sense and with different periods; the outermost circle revolves—we are not told with what period—in the opposite sense, " carrying the others with it, as it might seem to men who know little of such things." [1] This is, of course, only an urbane way of saying that it does not " carry the others " with it, another denial of the double motion theory of Timaeus. Presumably the reason why the period of this revolution is not stated is that, now that the twenty-four hours' period has been given to the earth, there is no reason to suppose that we know what the period of revolution of the " outermost circle " is. It must have a movement, because the world has a ψυχή ; that Plato supposes its revolution to explain any particular appearance is very unlikely. We can only say that, since the periods of the planets become steadily longer as we advance farther from the " centre," the period of the outermost circle is presumably a very long one.[2]

Plato's own doctrine would seem, thus, to be neither that of the motionless earth, nor that of Timaeus, nor the full-blown Copernicanism which some modern admirers have read into him. He appears to attribute one motion only to the earth, a motion of revolution round an invisible centre (not round the sun), with a period of twenty-four hours. The important point is not that he has a well-worked-out hypothesis, but that his scientific instinct has seized the fundamental point that a true mechanic of the heavens must start with a revolving earth ; this, no doubt, is his reason for dissatisfaction with the scheme of Eudoxus, beautiful as it is. Another inference of first-rate importance is this. We clearly have no right to assume that the view ascribed to Plato by Theophrastus and apparently presupposed in the *Laws* was arrived at after the completion of the *Timaeus*. We have seen that the *Timaeus* and the *Laws* must have been in progress simultaneously. And it is hardly credible that if Plato had suddenly made so

---

[1] *Epin.*, *l.c.*, ἄγων τοὺς ἄλλους, ὥς γε ἀνθρώποις φαίνοιτ᾽ ἂν ὀλίγα τούτων εἰδόσιν. If it only " appears so " to the " beginner," of course it is not so. Burnet's insertion of οὐκ before ἄγων only makes the meaning needlessly plain at the expense of Plato's little jest at the blunder of disciples like Aristotle, who had committed themselves to the Eudoxian view. There seems to be a deliberate rejoinder in Aristot. *Met.* 1073*b* 8, ὅτι μὲν οὖν πλείους τῶν φερομένων αἱ φοραὶ φανερὸν τοῖς καὶ μετρίως ἡμμένοις· πλείους γὰρ ἕκαστον φέρεται μιᾶς τῶν πλανωμένων ἄστρων—just what the *Laws* denies.

[2] This interpretation of the testimony of Theophrastus is that of Schiaparelli, C. Ritter, and Burnet. However we understand his evidence, it is far too weighty to be simply set aside, nor do I think Mr. Cornford's ingenious attempt to minimize its significance (*Plato's Cosmology*, p. 128) happy. I think it more likely that Plato has deliberately chosen for his fifth-century astronomer phraseology which, except that it ascribes movement of some kind to the earth, is left studiously vague.

startling a change in his doctrine during the time when Aristotle
was a member of the Academy, Aristotle should have told us nothing
about the fact.   It would have been " grist to his mill " if he could
have urged against the doctrine of a moving earth that Plato had
been forced to hold two inconsistent theories about its motion
in the course of a few years.   Presumably, then, Plato held astronomical views more developed than those which he has ascribed
to Timaeus at the very time he was writing the dialogue.   This
should help us to appreciate Plato's real regard for historical
verisimilitude and make us on our guard against over-readiness to
suppose that all the theories of his Pythagorean are such as he
would find himself satisfied with.

Timaeus next adds that the Creator further made a number of
created gods who, unlike the stars, only show themselves when
they choose, Oceanus, Tethys, Phorcys, Cronus, Rhea, and their
offspring.   We have no evidence for the existence of these beings
except that of persons who claim to be their descendants, but we
may fairly suppose these persons to know their own pedigrees
(40d–e).   This is, of course, satire, not, as has been sometimes supposed, a concession for safety's sake to the religion of the State.
Most of the figures named belong to the cosmogonies of poets like
Orpheus and Hesiod, not to the Attic cultus, and the ironical
remark that a man must always be believed about his own family-
tree is aimed at poets like Orpheus and Musaeus.   Timaeus, as a
scientific Pythagorean, has his own reasons for not wishing to be
confounded with the Orphics.   The Creator now addresses the
created gods, explaining that whatever is his own immediate work
is imperishable.   Hence for the making of creatures which are to
be perishable, he will employ these created gods as his intermediaries
(41a–d).   He then himself makes immortal souls, in the same
number as the stars, of the " seconds " and " thirds " of the mixture
from which he has made the souls of the world and the stars.   Each
soul is conducted to its star and made to take a perspective view
of the universe and its structure.   It is then explained to the souls
that in due process of time they are all to be born as men in the
various " instruments of time " (i.e. the planets).[1]   If they live
well in the body, they will return to their native stars ; if less well,
they will have to be reincarnated in the bodies of women ; if that
lesson is insufficient, they will be reborn as various brutes, and
will never return to their " star " until they have first climbed up
the scale from brute to man again.[2]   The souls are then sown, like
seeds, in the various planets, while the created gods fashion bodies

[1] The souls sown in the planets are not, of course, to be future inhabitants
of the earth.   They are to inhabit the planets where they are " sown."
Timaeus is alluding to the Pythagorean belief that there are men and animals
in the planets as well as on earth.

[2] The connexion of a soul with its " star " has nothing to do with either
planetary or zodiacal astrology.   The thought is simply that there is a correspondence one-to-one between the " gods " and the human denizens of the
universe.

for them and any additions to their souls which may be required for their life in the body (41e–42d).

We are next told something of the way in which this work was done, but the story is only given in outline, with the necessary warning that, since it has to do with the mutable, it can only be tentative (42e–47e). In making the human body, the gods first constructed the head as a suitable dwelling-place for the immortal soul, which, of course, like the soul of the κόσμος, contains the two circles of the Same and the Other. (This means that Timaeus rightly accepts the discovery of Alcmaeon of Crotona that the brain is the central organ in the sensory-motor system.) The skull was therefore made spherical, as the body of the κόσμος is spherical. The trunk and the limbs were added for the safety and convenience of the head (44c–45b). The organ of sight was then constructed. It is literally a ray of sunlight dwelling within the body and issuing out through the pupil. We thus see by an actual long-distance contact of this ray, which is a real, though temporary, member of the body, with the visible object—the theory explained by Empedocles in verses cited by Aristotle. To this account of vision Timaeus appends an explanation of sleep as produced by an equable diffusion of this internal " fire " when darkness prevents its issuing out to join its kindred fire outside us, and a brief account of mirror-vision (45b–46c). His main points at present are, however, of a different kind. He dwells on the thought that the effect of the conjunction of the soul with a body which is always " flowing," giving off waste material and taking in fresh, is to throw the movements of the " circles " in the soul into complete disorder. The movement of the circle of the Same is temporarily arrested, and that of the circle of the Other rendered irregular. Hence the thoughtlessness and confused perception and fancy of our infancy and childhood. It is only when the " flow " of the body becomes less turbid, as waste and repair come to balance one another in adult life, that the movements of the " circles " recover from the init al disturbance of birth, and men come to discretion and intelligence, and then only with the aid of " right education " (43a–44c). Also, we must be careful to remember the distinction between true causes and mere subsidiary causes (συναίτια). Any account we give of the mechanism of vision, or any other function, is a mere statement about the subsidiary or instrumental cause. The true cause, in every case, is to be sought in the good or end a function subserves. Thus the real end for which we have been given eyes, is that the spectacle of the heavenly motions may lead us to note the uniformity and regularity of days, nights, months, and years, and that reflection on this uniformity may lead us to science and philosophy, and so make the revolutions of the " circles in the head " themselves regular and uniform. And the same thing is true of hearing ; its real purpose is not that we may learn to tune the strings of a lyre, but that we may learn to make our own thinking and living a spiritual melody (46c–47e).

We next come to one of the most important and character-istic sections of the discourse—an outline of the principles of a geometrical science of nature. So far we have been talking about the work done by Intelligence in the construction of the sensible world. But this world is a " mixed " product, born of Intelligence (νοῦς) and Necessity (ἀνάγκη), and we must now describe the con-tribution of Necessity to the whole. The relation between In-telligence and Necessity, which is also called the " errant " or " irregular " cause (πλανωμένη αἰτία), is that " for the most part " Intelligence is superior (ἄρχων, 48a), Necessity is servant, or slave, but a willing slave ; Intelligence " persuades " (πείθει) Necessity. The special reason given for now studying the working of Necessity is that, unless we do so, we can give no account of the origin of the " four roots " of Empedocles, the " stuff " we have so far been assuming as there for God to form a world of.   Hitherto no one has explained the structure of these bodies ; they have been treated as the ABC (στοιχεῖα, *elementa*, 48b) of things, though, as we shall see, they do not even deserve to be called syllables. We are now to analyse them back into something very much more primitive, and we are carefully reminded again that, from the nature of the case, our analysis can at best be tentative and " likely."

The sections which are now to follow are marked by Timaeus as the most original and important part of his whole cosmology. We shall see that they serve to connect the two main currents of scientific thought, the biological and the mathematical, by providing a geometrical construction for the " corpuscles " of the four " elements " which the biologist Empedocles had treated as the " simples " of his system. The four types of body thus con-structed are then, in the Empedoclean fashion, treated as the immediate units from which the various tissues and secretions of the living body are formed by chemical composition. The result is thus that Timaeus, in the spirit of Descartes, offers us an anatomy and physiology in which the organism appears as an elaborate kinematical system ; natural science is thus reduced in principle, as Descartes and Spinoza held it ought to be, to geometry.   Plato is not, of course, very strictly committed by the details of speculations which he repeatedly says are provisional, but it is clear that he is in sympathy with the general attitude known to-day in biology as mechanistic. The human organism, as he conceives it, is a machine directed and controlled by mind or intelligence, but the machine itself is made of the same ultimate constituents as other machines and the workings of it follow the same laws as those of the rest.

It is important, if we are to approach the exposition in the right spirit, to understand what is meant by the initial distinction between the part of Intelligence and that of Necessity in the cosmic system. We must be careful not to confuse the " necessity " of which Plato is speaking with the principle of order and law. Law and order are precisely the features of the world which he assigns to intelligence as their source ; we are carefully told that necessity

is something disorderly and irregular, the πλανωμένη αἰτία, a
name probably derived, as Burnet has suggested,[1] from the use
of the disrespectful name πλανῆται, " tramps," " vagabonds," for
the heavenly bodies which seem at first sight to roam about the
sky with no settled abode. Thus the Necessity of the *Timaeus* is
something quite different from the Necessity of the myth of Er,
or of the Stoics, which are personifications of the principle of rational
law and order. On the other hand, Necessity is plainly not meant
to be an independent, evil principle, for it is plastic to intelligence ;
mind " for the most part " is said to " persuade it " ; its function
is to be instrumental to the purposes of νοῦς.[2] The reason for
introducing it into the story seems to be simply that it is impossible
in science to resolve physical reality into a complex of rational laws
without remainder. In the real world there is always, over and
above " law," a factor of the " simply given " or " brute fact," not
accounted for and to be accepted simply as given. It is the business
of science never to acquiesce in the merely given, to seek to " explain " it as the consequence, in virtue of rational law, of some
simpler initial " given." But, however far science may carry this
procedure, it is always forced to retain *some* element of brute fact,
the merely given, in its account of things. It is the presence in
nature of this element of the given, this surd or irrational as it
has sometimes been called, which Timaeus appears to be personi-
fying in his language about Necessity. That " mind persuades
necessity " is just an imaginative way of saying that by the analysis
of the given datum we always can rationalize it further ; we never
come to a point at which the possibility of " explanation " actually
ceases. But the " irrational " is always there, in the sense that
explanation always leaves behind it a remainder which is the " not
yet explained." When we have followed the exposition a little
further, we shall discover that in the last resort this element of the
irreducible and given turns out to be exactly what Professor Alexander has called the " restlessness of space-time." But, unlike
Professor Alexander, Plato does not believe that the restlessness of
space-time is enough to account for its elaboration into more and
more rationally articulated systems ; left to itself, it would be

[1] *Greek Philosophy, Part I.,* 341-346. The " necessity " of the *Timaeus*
is not " uniform sequence." So far as sequences are " uniform," the uniformity is due to the " persuasion " of necessity by νοῦς ; that is, the uniformity is an effect and sign of the presence of rational purpose. It is the
exceptional departures, the " sports " in nature, which we are to account for
by the presence of a πλανωμένη αἰτία. More generally, " necessity " explains
why the course of actual fact only conforms *approximately* to the formulae of
kinematics. The " necessity " of the dialogue is thus precisely what Aristotle
has taught us to call " contingency."

[2] This excludes the superficial identification of " necessity " with an evil
" material principle." The doctrine that " matter " is the source of evil is
wholly un-Platonic. Historically, of course, the ἀνάγκη of Timaeus connects
directly with the ἄπειρον of early Pythagoreanism. It is the element of
indetermination in events, the element which a Spinozistic conception of the
universe persists in ignoring.

merely restless ; order and structure are the work of the mind of God, in whose hands necessity is plastic.

We find, then, that we need to revise our first account of the sensible world. We had already spoken of two things which need to be carefully discriminated, the intelligible archetype and its visible copy. We have now to take into account a third concept which we shall find obscure enough, that of the " receptacle " (ὑποδοχή) or "matrix" (ἐκμαγεῖον) in which "becoming" goes on. This receptacle or matrix of process cannot be fire or water or any of the things which the earliest philosophers had selected as the primary "boundless." Experience shows that these are constantly passing into one another ; there is now fire where there was water, or water where there was fire. The various bodies are mutable and impermanent ; what remains permanent under all the variations is the region or room or place where they arise and vanish. This is there and self-same under all the processes of change, and has no form or structure of its own, precisely because it is its indifference to all which makes the appearance of all within it possible. We find it hard to apprehend, because it cannot be discerned by sense ; it must be thought of, but can only be thought of by a sort of " bastard reflection " (λογισμῷ τινι νόθῳ, 52b), *i.e.* by systematic negation, the denying of one definite determination after another. It is, in fact, " place " (χώρα). We may, incidentally, remind ourselves that each of our three principles is apprehended in a special way. We can satisfy ourselves of the reality of the forms by considering that if there were only sensible objects, science and true belief would be the same ; whereas it is clear they are not. Science can only be acquired by learning (διδαχή) a true belief may be produced by " persuasion," appeal to our emotions ; what we know can always be justified to the intellect (τὸ μὲν ἀεὶ μετ᾽ ἀληθοῦς λόγου), a true belief not always ; we cannot be argued out of the one, we can be persuaded out of the other. Since science and true belief thus differ, their objects must be different.[1] (Thus Timaeus has nothing to say in the one passage in which he discusses the forms which differs from the presentation of them in the *Phaedo*.) Sensible things we apprehend, of course, by sight and the rest of our senses ; " place," as we have just said, by a curious kind of thinking (48e–52c).

If we try to picture the condition of things " before " the introduction of ordered structure, we have to think of the " receptacle "

---

[1] There is an almost absolute equivalence of Timaeus' analysis with that of Whitehead in his *Principles of Natural Knowledge*, and *Concept of Nature*. Whitehead's " objects " have exactly the formal character of the ἰδέαι; his account of the " ingredience of objects into events " corresponds almost verbally with that given by Timaeus of the determination of the various regions of the " receptacle " by the " ingress " and " egress " of the impresses of the forms. The " receptacle " itself only differs from " passage " in being called " space " and not " space-time." If we try to picture " passage " as it would be if there were only " events " and no " objects " ingredient in them, we get precisely the sort of account Timaeus gives of the condition of the " receptacle " before God introduced order and structure into it.

or *matrix* just described as *place* as agitated everywhere by irregular disturbances, random vibratory movements, and exhibiting in various regions mere rude incipient "traces" (ἴχνη) of the definite structure we know as characteristic of the various forms of body. (Thus its general character is exactly that of the "boundless" of Anaximander, agitated by the "eternal motion," before the "opposites" have been "sifted out" and a κόσμος formed. This is, in fact, pretty clearly the historical starting-point from which Pythagorean cosmology had taken its departure).[1] The first step God takes towards introducing determination and order into this indeterminate "happening" is the construction of bodies of definite geometrical structure. This brings us to the doctrine of the geometrical structure of the "corpuscles" of the "four roots" which Empedoclean biology wrongly treats as simple ultimates. The construction is effected by making a correspondence between the "four roots" and the originally Pythagorean doctrine of the regular solids which can be inscribed in the sphere (53c–56c). There are five and only five distinct types of regular solid, and four of them can be built up geometrically by starting with two ultimate simple types of triangle, which are the most beautiful, and therefore the most appropriate, of all. These two triangles are the ultimate "elements" of the *Timaeus*. One of them is the isosceles right-angled triangle, called by the Pythagoreans the "half-square"; the other is the triangle which can be obtained by dividing the equilateral triangle into six smaller triangles by drawing the perpendiculars from the angular points on the opposite sides, or less symmetrically, by dividing the equilateral triangle into two by a single such perpendicular. (Hence the Pythagorean name for it, the "half-triangle.") Timaeus does not explain what the peculiar beauty of these triangles is, but we know independently that it lies in the fact that the ratios of the angles of the two triangles are the simplest possible. Those of the "half-square" have the ratios $1 : 1 : 2$, those of the "half-triangle" the ratios $1 : 2 : 3$. From the former, by a symmetrical arrangement of four such triangles about a centre of position we get the square, and from a proper arrangement of six square faces, the *cube*. A similar symmetrical arrangement of six triangles of the second type gives us the equilateral triangle, and there are three regular solids which can be made with equilateral triangles as their faces—the *tetrahedron*, the *octahedron*, the *icosahedron*. For physical reasons, we take the cube as the form appropriate to a corpuscle of earth, the tetrahedron as that of a particle of fire, the other two as the forms of the particles of air and water respectively. There is still a fifth regular solid, the dodecahedron, which has twelve pentagons as its faces; but this can be constructed from neither of the elementary triangles, and has a different part to play. God employed it (55b) "for the whole, adorning it with constellations." (This

---

[1] For the historical connexion of Pythagorean cosmology with the scheme of Anaximander see *E.G.Ph.*[3] 108 ff., *Greek Philosophy, Part I.*, c. 2.

out the celestial sphere for purposes of astronomical description by
dividing it into twelve pentagonal regions, exactly as a leather ball
is made by stitching together twelve pentagonal pieces of leather.[1])
It follows from the theory that a corpuscle of one of the " roots "
can only be broken up along the edges of the triangles from which
it has been built up. Hence, since earth is formed from a special
type of triangle, it cannot be " transmutable " with any of the other
three, but they are all transmutable with one another. Timaeus
then proceeds to give a number of equations which determine the
equivalences between the corpuscles of these "roots." Into the
physical difficulties created by this table of equivalences we cannot
enter here. It must be enough to have seen that the general programme contemplated is precisely that reduction of all physics to
applied geometry and nothing else which is equally characteristic
of Descartes.

We next have an attempt to specify the most important
" varieties " of each of the four types of body and the " chemical
compounds " they form with one another, and to account for the
sensible qualities of all these bodies by reference to their geometrical structure, which must be passed over here (58c–68d). Its
most interesting feature is a long psycho-physical account of the
conditions of pleasure-pain (64a–65b), in terms of the depletion-
repletion formula. The " unmixed " pleasures of sense are brought
under the formula by the hypothesis that they are sudden and
appreciable " repletions " of a " depletion " which has been too
gentle and gradual to be propagated to the " seat of consciousness."

With the next section of the dialogue we pass definitely from
physics to anatomy, physiology, and medicine (69a–87b). Again,
it must be sufficient in this volume to pass over the details lightly.
The main point is that the organism has been constructed throughout to minister to the soul.   To fit the soul for its embodied life it
had to receive two temporary and inferior additions, the " spirited "
and " concupiscent " " parts " or " forms " already familiar to us
from the *Republic*.   Each of these has a central " organ " or " seat,"
just as the " rational " part has its seat in the brain ; " spirit " is
lodged in the thorax, " appetite " in the lower region of the trunk,
beneath the diaphragm (69a–70e). In connexion with this least
orderly and disciplined element in the soul, the liver has a specially
important part to play. It is the source of visions and bad dreams

---

[1] The whole of this construction is Pythagorean in origin, as we see by
comparison with the valuable fragment preserved at the end of the *Theolo-
gumena Arithmetica* from the work of Speusippus on *Pythagorean Numbers*
(Speusippus, Fr. 4; Diels, *Fragmente d. Vorsokr.*[3] i. p. 303 ff.), where the relations
silently presupposed by Timaeus between the angles of the " half-square "
and " half-triangle " are explained in full. The one point where Timaeus may
be going beyond results reached by the Pythagoreans is in his tacit assumption
that all his five solids and no others can be inscribed in the sphere. Note
that he makes a point of it that Socrates and the others are *mathematicians*,
and so will follow him easily (53c 1).

of all kinds, and the utterances of the " possessed," " seers," and the like are really due to a disordered liver. They can be interpreted by spokesmen (προφῆται), who are themselves not in the state of " possession," and thus given a salutary moral influence (71a–72b). The details of the anatomy and physiology have more interest for the historian of these sciences than for the student of philosophy, especially since they are all given as tentative and liable to revision. The most prominent feature of the section is the elaborate attempt (77b–79e, 80d–81e) to account (of course in a fanciful way) for respiration, the systole and diastole of the heart, digestion, all together as one vast rhythmical mechanical process with the double purpose of maintaining the vital heat of the organism and distributing nourishment through the blood to the various tissues.

The physiology is followed up by a section on pathology which makes a curious attempt at a classification of the various known diseases (82a–86a). The theory could only be properly discussed in connexion with what we know of other fifth- and fourth-century speculations on the same subject from the Hippocratean *corpus* and other sources. Its most outstanding feature is that it departs wholly from the lines of the Hippocratean " humoral pathology " by treating " phlegm " and " bile " not as ingredients of the organism in its normal state but as unwholesome morbid secretions. I have tried elsewhere to show reasons for supposing that Plato is deriving the doctrine from Philistion of Locri, with whom, as we see from the *Epistles*, he had made acquaintance at Syracuse, and that in its main outlines it is in general accord with what we know to have been the medical theory of Philolaus, though there are points of difference. If this is so, we can understand why this particular medical theory should be expounded by the Locrian Timaeus. In any case, we must not suppose that Plato has invented an amateur pathology of his own and is teaching it dogmatically. He will simply be following what he regards as respectable specialist authority.

The pathology of the body leads up to the pathology of the soul (86b–87b), and this to some regulations of physical and mental hygiene (87e–90d). Undesirable moral propensities are due very largely to physical constitutional defects ; *e.g.* undue propensity to sexual irregularities is largely of physiological origin. The other chief cause of " badness " is education in bad social traditions. Hence Timaeus infers—not quite consistently with his own earlier insistence on personal responsibility—that those who begot and educated the transgressor are really more to blame than the transgressor himself. We must remember that he is, among other things, a medical man, and that " the profession " are prone to views of this kind. Plato may well be treating his speaker with a certain touch of irony when he makes the moral theory of Timaeus a little inconsistent with his mental pathology.

In laying down rules of hygiene, the supreme object we should aim at is the correction of any disproportion between the body and the soul which animates it. This disproportion is dangerous to both body and soul. The soul which is too big for its " pigmy body " actually wears the body out, as we see in the case of so many keen political and scientific controversialists ; when the body is too robust for its soul, a man too often makes the soul dull and slow by ministering to the body's clamant appetites. The rule should be that neither body nor soul should be exercised exclusively. The student must take care to attend to his physical condition, or he will suffer for it in soul as well as body. The best kind of " motion " by which to exercise the body is active muscular exertion, and the next best easy rhythmical passive motion, like swinging, riding in a carriage, being rowed on the water. The worst kind, which may only be resorted to in case of absolute necessity, is the violent production of intestinal motions by drugs and purges (87c–89d).

A still more important topic is the hygiene of the mind which is to rule and direct the movements of the body. Timaeus cannot relevantly enter on a systematic discussion of the principles of education, but he lays down the general principle that our intelligence is the divine thing in us, and the real " guardian spirit " (δαίμων) of each of us. It has been truly said that man, whose divine part resides in the head, is like a tree with its root not in the earth, but in the sky (90a). The rule of healthy living for the soul is that this divine thing in us should " think thoughts immortal and divine," and that the merely human " parts " of the soul should " worship " and " tend " it. The true " tendance " of any creature consists in providing it with its appropriate food and " exercise " (κινήσεις, 90c), and the " exercise " appropriate to the rational soul is thus " the thoughts and revolutions of the whole." The end of life is to correct the " revolutions in the head " and bring them once more into correspondence with the " tunes and revolutions " of the world-soul, in whose image they were made at first (90a–d).

The story closes with a development which should not be taken as seriously as has been done by some interpreters. Timaeus, we remember, had incorporated in his narrative the old fancy that the first men were directly sprung from the soil. Hence his physiology has taken no account of the reproductive system. This, we are now told, was only wanted in the second generation, when the second-best of the original " men " came to be reborn as women. He gives an unmistakably playful account of the modifications which had to be introduced into the physiological scheme to suit the new situation (90e–91d), and then adds more briefly that the lower animals in general were also derived by degeneration from the original human pattern, the deformation being greater or less as the souls which were to tenant the various bodies had fallen more or less short of virtue and wisdom in their first life (91d–92b). Nothing is said here of the hell and purgatory of the eschatological myths of the *Gorgias, Phaedo, Republic*. Presumably the scientific Pythagoreans of the middle of the fifth century regarded them as no more than edifying mythology, exactly as the author of the so-called *Timaeus Locrus* regards Timaeus' own statements about metamorphosis. We should pretty certainly be wrong if we took this part of the discourse as a serious speculation on the part of Plato about a possible evolution *à rebours*. Timaeus himself is probably meant to be less than half in earnest ; as in the tale of Aristophanes in the *Symposium*, we are really dealing with a playful imitation of the speculation of Empedocles about the "whole-natured" and double-sexed forms with which evolution in the "period of strife" began. What Plato himself thinks of all this is sufficiently indicated when we are told in the *Politicus* that the "earth-born" men and the "age of Cronus" do not belong to our "half of the cycle," *i.e.* they belong to fairy-tale, not to history.

Here our story comes at last to an end. We have now told the whole tale of the birth of this sensible world, "a visible living creature, modelled on that which is intelligible, a god displayed to sense" (92c).[1]

The *Critias* calls for no special consideration. Its declared purpose is to relate in detail the story of the defeat of the Atlantid kings, of which Critias had given the bare outline in the *Timaeus*. It remains, however, a bare fragment. Critias describes the topography of Attica and Athens as they were before the process of denudation which has reduced the country to a mere rocky skeleton (109b–111d), and the happy condition of the inhabitants (111e–112e). He then gives a much longer account of the island of Atlantis and its kings, the descendants of the god Posidon, their institutions, and their wonderful engineering works (118a–120d), and is about to relate how their hearts were lifted up with pride in their wealth and power, and how Zeus resolved to bring them into judgment, when the fragment breaks off, just as Zeus is about to declare his purpose to the assembled gods. The chief things which call for notice are the clear-headed way in which Plato has grasped the effects of gradual geological denudation on Attica,[2] and the special stress he lays on the marvellous skill of the Atlantids in naval engineering. The description may have been inspired by a re-collection of what had actually been effected at Syracuse,[3] but the

---

[1] εἰκὼν τοῦ νοητοῦ, θεὸς αἰσθητός. In this sentence νοητοῦ must not be taken, against all the rules of grammar, as masculine agreeing with an "understood" θεοῦ, since the word θεός has not yet occurred in the sentence. νοητοῦ is neuter, and we must either understand ζῴου from the preceding ζῷον, or possibly take τὸ νοητόν substantively. The *v.l.* ποιητοῦ found in A is inferior to the vulgate, which is also the better supported reading, as it occurs in both F and Y.

[2] But it is said (Rivaud, *Timée*, p. 239) that much of the denudation of Attica ascribed by Plato to the natural cataclysm mentioned at *Timaeus* 25d and *Critias* 112a is actually the work of man.

[3] Plato is thinking also, perhaps, of the conversion of the Piraeus into a great naval harbour, but the immediate source of the description is probably what he had seen himself at Syracuse.

works ascribed to the mythical kings more than sustain comparison with the greatest achievements of Roman architects and engineers. The whole account illustrates Plato's exceptional knowledge of the technical arts and his high estimate of their possibilities. We may be sure that, if the story had been completed, one of its main points would have been the triumph of patriotism and sound *moral* over technical skill.

The conception of the " purpose of Zeus " seems to be an echo from epic poetry. It is hardly a mere accident that the last complete sentence of the fragment recalls the version of the Trojan story given in the *Cypria*, where the origin of the great war is traced to the plan of Zeus for the prevention of over-population. There may be some significance in the fact that Zeus is said to summon the divine council to his " most honourable abode " in the centre of the universe.[1] Since one of the names given by those Pythagoreans who believed in a " central fire " to this luminary was Διὸς φυλακή, this looks as though Critias meant to hint at that astronomical doctrine. Timaeus, as we have seen, makes the " centre " empty.

See further :

BURNET.—*Greek Philosophy, Part I.*, 335–349 ; *Platonism* (1928), c.7.

RITTER, C.—*Platon*, ii., 258–287 al. ; *Platons Dialoge*, 98–158 ; *Neue Untersuchungen über Platon*, 174–182.

LEVI, A.—*Il Concetto del Tempo nella Filosofia di Platone*. (Turin, N.D.)

STEWART, J. A.—*Plato's Doctrine of Ideas*, 101–105 ; *Myths of Plato*, 259–297 (*The Timaeus*), 457–469.

DIÈS, A.—*Autour de Platon*, ii., 522–603.

TAYLOR, A. E.—*A Commentary on Plato's Timaeus*. (Oxford, 1928) ; *Plato, Timaeus and Critias* (translated) (1929).

RIVAUD, A.—*Platon, Timée, Critias*. (Paris, 1925.)

FRIEDLANDER, P.—*Platon ; Eidos, Paideia, Dialogos* (1928). *Excursus II.* (on the city of Atlantis).

RAEDER, H.—*Platons philosophische Entwickelung*, 374–394.

NATORP, P.—*Platons Ideenlehre*, 338–358.

BAEUMKER, C.—*Das Problem der Materie in der griechischen Philosophie*, 115–188.

MARTIN, T. H.—*Études sur le Timée de Platon*. (Paris, 1841.)

ROBIN, L.—*Études sur la signification et la place de la physique dans la philosophie de Platon*. (Paris, 1919.)

ROBIN, L.—*Platon*, c. v.

CORNFORD, F. M.—*Plato's Cosmology* (*Timaeus* translated with commentary, Cambridge, 1937).

---

[1] *Critias* 121c 2–4. The sentence adds to the case for my view that the astronomy of Timaeus is not Plato's own.

CHAPTER XVIII

THE *LAWS* AND *EPINOMIS*

THE *Laws* is not only the longest of all Plato's writings ; it also contains his latest and ripest thought on the subjects which he had all through his life most at heart—ethics, education, and jurisprudence. Plato's services to the theory of education, in particular, have usually been grossly underrated, from an inexcusable neglect of the very thorough treatment given to it in what he probably himself regarded as his most important work. His theology, again, has often been misconceived in modern times, because the tenth book of the *Laws* is the only place in his works where it is systematically expounded. This neglect of so noble a work is perhaps to be explained by two considerations. In one respect the *Laws* makes a greater demand on the reader than any other Platonic writing. The dramatic element is reduced to a minimum ; if one does not care for the subject-matter of the book, there is little in its manner to attract. To all intents and purposes, the work is a monologue, interrupted only by formulae of assent or requests for further explanation. Further, the purpose of the whole is severely practical, and will not appeal to a reader who cares more for metaphysics and science than for morals and politics. More than any other work of Plato, the *Laws* stands in direct relation to the political life of the age in which it was composed and is meant to satisfy a pressing felt need.

In the last twenty years of Plato's life it was becoming more and more obvious that the old city-states which had been the centres of Hellenic spiritual life had had their day. Athens herself had become a second-rate power ever since the collapse of the great Syracusan expedition, as Plato knew only too well. Sparta, to whom the hegemony had passed at the end of the Decelean war, had proved wholly unfitted for such a post, and had been crushed, in a way from which she never recovered, by the brilliant successes of Epaminondas, which made Thebes for a few years a power of the first order. Meanwhile the very existence of Hellenic civilization was endangered by the encroachments of Persia in the East and Carthage in the West. It was clear that if civilization of the Hellenic type was to hold its own, none of the older city-states was in a condition to become its centre. We know now that the historical solution of the problem was to be provided by the rise of the Macedonian monarchy and the achievements of Philip and Alexander.

But the work of Philip was only in the beginning in Plato's last years; his appearance south of Thermopylae as the ally of Thebes against Phocis, the first manifest sign that a new power had succeeded to the hegemony of the Hellenic states, did not take place until the year after Plato's death. In the meantime, the most striking feature of the situation was the founding of new cities or the revival of old ones. Epaminondas' foundation of Megalopolis as a centre for Arcadia is a good example of the one process, his restoration of Messene an equally good example of the other; and it is pertinent to remember that, according to Greek ideas, the first thing to be done in such a situation was to provide the new or revived community with a complete constitution and fundamental law. It was naturally the practice to call in the aid of experts in " politics " as advisers in the task. In the fifth century, Pericles had employed Protagoras in this way, to give advice on the laws to be made for Thurii; in the fourth, the Academy was constantly being asked, as a recognized society of experts in jurisprudence, to do the same sort of work. Plato himself is said to have been requested to legislate for Megalopolis, and, though he declined, work of the same kind was done by his associates for many foundations.[1] Hence it was eminently desirable that men contemplating the probability of being called on to " legislate," should be provided with an example of the way in which the work should be gone about, and the *Laws* is meant to furnish just such an example. The assumed situation is that a new city is to be founded, and that an Athenian is invited to lend his assistance in the work. The particular situation assumed, of a city to be founded in Crete on the site of a prehistoric town, is presumably fictitious, especially if, as Wilamowitz has asserted, the topographical details show that Plato was not really acquainted with actual Cretan conditions; a fictitious situation will serve as well as a real one to illustrate the principles which have to be enforced.

The date of composition of the work cannot be very precisely fixed. But we may readily fix a *terminus a quo*. One of the chief principles on which Plato insists is that the legislator has not really done his work when he has merely enunciated an enactment and provided it with a " sanction " in the form of a penalty for non-observance. This is like the method of an empiric " slave " doctor, treating other slaves; he merely orders a prescription to be followed under the threat of consequences if it is neglected. A great physician treating an intelligent freeman tries to enlist his patient in the work of the cure by explaining to him the principles on which the treatment rests. In the same way, a legislator should try to enlist

[1] See the list of active " law-givers " among Plato's pupils in Plutarch (*Adv. Colotem,* 1126c–d). " Plato sent Aristonymus to the Arcadians, Phormio to Elis, Menedemus to Pyrrha. Eudoxus and Aristotle wrote laws for Cnidus and Stagirus. Alexander asked Xenocrates for advice about kingship; the man who was sent to Alexander by the Greek inhabitants of Asia and did most to incite him to undertake his war on the barbarians was Delius of Ephesus, an associate of Plato." Cf. D.L. iii., 23, for the request from Megalopolis.

the sympathies of decent men on the side of the law by prefixing to his whole legislation and to the several main divisions of it "proems" or "preambles" explaining the aims of the legislation and the reasons why its enactments are what they are, and why the penalties for transgression are what they are (*Laws* 719e–722a). Now in *Epistle* iii. 316a, Plato refers to himself as having been occupied with Dionysius at Syracuse upon "preludes" or "preambles" to the laws to be given to the cities they were proposing to form into a constitutional monarchy. Thus we may reasonably infer that the conception of legislation characteristic of the *Laws* was suggested by Plato's personal experience of the Syracusan situation. The occasion to which *Epistle* iii. refers is probably that of Plato's last visit to Syracuse in 361/60, though it may conceivably be that of the visit of 367/6. In either case, it is unlikely that Plato would have the leisure to plan a work of the scope of our *Laws* before 360, when his direct connexion with the affairs of Syracuse was over. Such a work would necessarily involve a great deal of thought and time and may well have occupied Plato more or less continuously for the remaining years of his life, though the one actual allusion to a dateable event seems to be the mention (638b) of a victory of Dionysius II over the Locrians, probably to be assigned to the year 356.

The *personnel* of the dialogue, if we can call it one, is exceedingly simple. There are three characters—an Athenian, left anonymous, who is the main speaker, and two minor characters, Megillus, a Spartan, and Clinias, a Cretan. All of them are old men ; of the Athenian we learn that he has astronomical and mathematical knowledge, is regarded by the others as a highly suitable person to give advice on matters of jurisprudence and political science, and that he has had personal experience of association with a " tyrant " (711a). Thus his intellectual qualifications are those of a member of the Academy, and his personal experiences are modelled on Plato's own, and to that extent we may fairly take him as standing for Plato, though we have no reason to suppose that he is drawn with any deliberate intention of self-portraiture. All we learn of the others is that the Spartan belongs to a family in which the office of *proxenus* of Athens is hereditary, and that the Cretan is connected by blood with the famous medicine-man Epimenides (642b, d). This is meant to account for the unusual readiness of both to learn from an Athenian. When the work opens we find the three old men engaged in a general conversation about the merits and purpose of the institutions of the traditional legislators of Sparta and Cnossus, Lycurgus and Minos. They propose to continue their conversation as they walk to the cave of Dicte, the legendary birth-place of Zeus. The full situation is only disclosed at the end of the third book (702b–d). It then appears that the Cretans have re-solved to resettle the site of a decayed city ; the making of the necessary arrangements has been left to the citizens of Cnossus, who have devolved it upon a commission of ten. Clinias, the head of this commission, proposes to take the Athenian and Spartan into consultation as advisers about the legislation and the constitution generally. We have already incidentally heard that the time of the year is midsummer, so that the long day will suffice for a full discussion.

The argument of the first three books may be regarded as introductory. Plato winds his way very gradually into his subject, advancing almost imperceptibly from a problem of ethics, through educational theory, to the consideration of strictly political and juristic matter, and does not reveal his full purpose until the preparatory positions have been thoroughly secured. This method is very characteristic, and it is unfortunate that some modern readers should have appreciated it so little as to speculate about the possibility that the whole arrangement is due to the piecing together of disconnected papers by an editor. I trust that the brief analysis which follows will reveal the real march of the argument as far too carefully studied to be the result of a well-meant blunder.

(Book I.) What is the central purpose of the institutions of Lycurgus and Minos ? The Spartan and Cretan agree that their law-givers have discovered the fundamental truth that, under all disguises, the brute hard fact about the life of a city is that it is a " war to the knife " with all rivals ; almost in Hobbes's phrase, independent cities are in a state of nature towards one another, and the state of nature is a state of real but undeclared war (πόλεμος ἀκήρυκτος). Hence the supreme good for a city is victory in this unremitting warfare, and the business of a citizen is to be, before everything, a combatant. All the institutions of Sparta and Crete are therefore rightly directed towards producing the one great virtue, efficiency in warfare, ἀνδρεία, valour. The Athenian dissents entirely from this ethic of warfare. The supreme victory for any community or any man is not victory over the foe without, but victory over self, that is, the conquest of the worser elements in the community or the individual soul by the better. And this victory is not complete when the better elements coerce or expel the worse ; it is only complete when subjugation is followed by reconciliation and harmony. Peace, not war, between the components of community or individual soul is the best state; it is with a view to peace that a good legislator must make his enactments. From this point of view, wisdom, *sophrosyne*, justice, are the supreme virtues ; mere martial valour will rank only fourth (631c). Now when we consider the Spartan system of training we see that all its peculiarities—the common meals of coarse fare, the bodily exercises and hunting, and the rough discipline in general —aim only at fostering the one virtue we have just ranked lowest among the four of the familiar quadrilateral. And, what is more, they aim at teaching only the easier and less valuable half of the one virtue.

True " manliness " or valour does not consist simply in the power to face danger, pain, and weariness ; it means also being able

to face the seductions of pleasure without giving in to them, and
this is the finer half of the virtue and the harder to learn. But
Megillus himself cannot point to any training provided by the
Spartan system in this part of valour (634*b*). The explanation is
that the only way to learn to get the better of temptation is to be
made to face it and overcome it. The Spartans act on this principle when they teach the young to face peril and pain bravely by
exposing them to them. They avoid making them learn to face
and overcome the seductions of pleasure. Indeed, the perverse
sexual practices which are fostered by the " barrack-room " life
of Sparta have given her a universal bad name (636*b*) no less than
the relaxed manners of her women (637*c*).

A chance remark of Megillus in reply to these criticisms provides
the material for the rest of the discussion of Book I. He regards it
as highly creditable to Sparta that its pleasures are so few ; a wine-
party, for example, is an unheard-of thing (637*a*). This leads the
Athenian into a long discussion of the practice of μέθη, the *convivial*
use of wine. (As a mere drink with meals wine was used sparingly
at Sparta, as everywhere else in Greece, for the simple reason that
the water is bad.) Some communities wholly prohibit the practice,
others allow anyone who pleases to indulge in it as much as he
pleases and whenever he likes. Both, the Athenian thinks, are
mistaken. A Spartan may urge that the Spartans beat the " wet "
forces in the field whenever they meet them, but we cannot generalize
by enumeration from a few instances. The issue of numberless
engagements goes unrecorded, and we can point to examples on
the other side, such as the victory of the toping Syracusans over
the abstemious Locrians. If we are to judge of wine-drinking or
any other practice we must see what can be made of it under proper
regulation. Now under two important conditions—(*a*) that the
party is presided over by a sober man who is not himself giving way
to the merriment, and (*b*) that this president is a man of more years
and experience than the rest of the party—such a gathering might
have valuable social uses. *In vino veritas* is true in the sense that
when a man is warmed with wine, he shows himself for what he is
without disguise. He blurts out thoughts which he would normally
keep to himself, and exhibits tempers he would normally hide. If
there were a drug which would gradually produce groundless fear
and apprehension, as there is not, it would enable us to make a very
safe and easy test of a man's courage. We could make him take
deeper and deeper draughts of it, and watch his success in mastering
his pathological alarms. We should thus be able to do without
risk what, in fact, we can only do by exposing a man to actual risk,
distinguish the more from the less valiant. Wine does give us
such a test of a man's *sophrosyne*. We can see who forgets himself
least and keeps his modesty best under the artificial removal of
restraints produced by the wine-cup, and, if the party is rightly
conducted, there is no danger that the application of the test will
have serious consequences ; the subject will be a little noisy and

silly for the time, and that is all.   It is much better to learn a man's
weakness from such a slight exposure than to have to discover it
from his exposure to a grave temptation to unlawful love or the like.
The practice might thus be of great value to the magistrate who
wants to know what citizens he can safely trust to come well out
of positions where there is opportunity for gratifying the desire for
unrighteous pleasures.   And to the members of the party, of course,
learning to " drink their wine like gentlemen " does afford a very
real drill in learning to say " no " at the right time.   On these
grounds the Athenian advocates the strictly regulated permission
to drink wine convivially.   If there is to be no regulation of such
parties, he would like to see wine absolutely prohibited to the young
of both sexes, soldiers in the field, servants, magistrates during
their tenure of office, sea-captains, jurymen and counsellors when
acting in that capacity, and " any person immediately contemplating
the procreation of children " (674a–b).   No doubt the main reason
for the discussion is that it serves to illustrate the great principles
that the better half of valour is mastery over one's desires, and that
the true way to master temptation is to stand up to it, not to make
its occurrence artificially impossible.

(Book II.)   The sentence just quoted does not occur until the
end of the second book, but before we reach it, Plato has ingeniously
made the problem of the right use of wine lead up to that of the use
of music and poetry as a vehicle of early moral education.   There
is still a further valuable social service which may be derived from
a proper use of wine, but before we can say what this service is,
we must ask the question what right education is.   To answer this,
we reflect that a child's first experience in life is acquaintance with
pleasure and pain (653a), and that an education in character begins
with learning to feel pleasure and pain about the right things
(*ibid. b*).   To understand how this education is to be got, we consider
that a young creature cannot keep still ; it is always jumping and
shouting (*ibid. d*).   In man, by the gift of God, these boundings and
shoutings can be transformed into tuneful and rhythmical singing
and dancing, and it is with this transformation that education
begins (654a).   Thus, by a liberal interpretation, the whole of the
early moral training of the young, which is to begin as soon as they
are sensible to melody and rhythm, can be brought under the rubric
of education in the " choric " art, the art of song accompanied by
the lyre and by the movements of an appropriate *ballet d'action*.
The connexion of the discussion with the previous problem of the
right use of wine is effected by a playful artifice very characteristic
of Plato.   It is at first assumed that, since the community as a
whole must take its part in the worship of the Muses, there will be
three choirs at our musical festivals—one of the boys and girls, a
second of the younger, and a third of the older, men.   But old men
who are " stiff in the joints " and past the feelings of frolic will
naturally not find it easy to recapture the youthful spirit of gaiety
which will make it natural for them to sing and dance before a

public audience. If they do not enter thoroughly into the spirit of the thing, there will be an awkwardness and constraint about their contribution which is specially out of place in a festival of the deities of graceful achievement. The concession to them of a proper use of wine would provide just the requisite means of recovering for the time the *abandon* of youth, and would be appropriate, when we remember that Dionysus, one of the gods who are patrons of song and dance, is also the giver of wine. As the argument develops, we discover that we are not to take the description of the functions of this " choir of Dionysus " quite literally. What they are really to do is to select the words and music for the songs of younger persons. They are, in fact, to be compilers of the official anthology, and the use of wine is to assist them in this task. The besetting fault of compilers of anthologies for the young is that they make their selections much too " grown-up." The middle-aged compiler's taste is not a safe guide. Plato thinks that if he came to his work warmed with a few glasses of a generous wine, he would be more likely to escape this commonly recognized danger and to make a wiser selection.

The details of the book cannot be discussed here, but it should be noted that while the treatment proceeds on the same main principles as those laid down for the employment of music in the schoolroom in *Republic* iii., the whole discussion is much richer in psychological insight ; no account of Plato's views about the moral influence of music on character can possibly afford to neglect *Laws* ii., though many professed accounts commit the fault. For the general theory of moral education, the most significant utterances are the declaration, emphatically commended by Aristotle, that the whole problem is to teach the young to " feel pleasure and pain " rightly (653*b*) and that " rightly " means " in accord with the rightly uttered discourse of the law" (659*d*, πρὸς τὸν ὑπὸ τοῦ νόμου λόγον ὀρθὸν εἰρημένον),[1] a sentence which seems to be the source from which the expression ὀρθὸς λόγος has got into the *Ethics* of Aristotle. We may also note the vigour of the protest against the view that " the tastes of the audience " are the standard of excellence in art (658*e*–659*c*), and the allusion to the example of Egypt as proof that it is possible to establish permanent canons of aesthetic taste (656*d*, *e*).[2]

With Book III., we enter on the main problem of political science, what a " city " is, and how it arises. To illustrate the way in

[1] The whole sentence should be familiar to every one who wants to appreciate Plato's educational theory ; " education (παιδεία) is the drawing and guiding (ὁλκή τε καὶ ἀγωγή) of children towards the discourse rightly uttered by the law and assented to as truly right by the best and oldest men, on the strength of their experience." The *immediate* point is that sound musical education must accustom the young from the first to *enjoy* what is really good, so that " young and old alike " have the *same* tastes in music.

[2] Note that Plato does not, as is often said, express any approval of the actual " stereotyped " Egyptian art. He merely appeals to the fact that Egyptian art has remained stationary as a proof that permanent standards are possible.

which historical development of institutions is conditioned, we imagine what would happen if a natural cataclysm destroyed the whole of a community with the exception of a few shepherds and goat-herds who escaped by the very fact that they occupied a remote and inaccessible position. They would be the rudest members of their society, and thus all the arts of civilization would be temporarily lost. It would be only very gradually that the chief industrial arts and the arts of letters would be recovered. The survivors would at first live in isolated family groups in out-of-the-way places, with little or no means of intercommunication, and hardly any implements of industry. In the main, when they began to recover communication with one another, they would live, after the fashion of nomads, on the produce of their herds, without accumulating "portable property," and hence without strife and greed (679a–e). Their rule of life would be "patriarchal," each head of a house making regulations for his own household, as Homer has correctly assumed in his account of the pastoral Cyclopes (680b).

In course of time, men would pass from this "nomad life" to agriculture, and the inhabiting of some sort of "city." These settlements would naturally be made first of all in the uplands, and agriculture would bring along with it the first rude attempts at "enclosures" (681a). For defence against dangers, families would coalesce in large "houses" (like the "long houses" of the North American Indians). This would, in time, lead to an *Ausgleich* of rules of life. The "large house" would develop a rule of life out of the various rules each family group brought with it into the settlement, and we might call this the first rude beginning of legislation (*ibid. b–c*). So we should find the first beginnings of sovereignty at the same stage in the appearance of a sort of "aristocracy" of headmen, who see that the rule of life is duly observed (681d). When the memory of the cataclysm had sufficiently died out, a further step would be taken. Men would venture to come down into the plains and build cities on a larger scale, like Homer's Ilios (682a). With this development we find ourselves in an age of rich and powerful monarchs who can engage in serious hostilities. (It will be noted with how sure an eye Plato discerns the general character of the Greek "Middle Ages," as they are depicted for us in the *Iliad*, which he rightly regards as historical in its representation of the old days of "chivalry.")

The traditional story of the disasters of the return from Troy and of the Dorian conquest of the Peloponnese also has a lesson for us. The narrative of the conflicts between the returning warriors and the new generation, and of the Dorian invasion, throw light on the way in which a "world-war" changes the face of history (682d ff.). The main point, made at considerable length, is that the Dorian invaders, if they had only been wise in their generation, had the opportunity of establishing a State which could have held its own against all the Oriental monarchies, since they found

themselves in occupation of a new territory, had no ancient traditions or vested interests to hamper them, and so had a free hand for
legislation. They must have misused their opportunity, for, though
tradition says that they set up a federation of three States—Sparta,
Argos, Messene—pledged to mutual support, two of the three were in
course of time reduced to subjection or impotence by the third,
and it is only in part, and in the one city of Sparta, that the old
rule of life, which dates from the conquest and was, in fact, dictated
by the position of the Dorians as invaders in the midst of an alien
and hostile population, has lasted on. The great mistake made at
the conquest was that, though the three kingdoms tried to ensure
the permanency of their institutions by a compact that if any attempt
at innovation was made in any one of the three States, the other
two would help to suppress it, they did not understand the all-
important principle that (691c–d) the permanent well-being of any
State demands the *division* of the sovereign power between several
parties. Concentration of the plenitude of sovereignty in the
same hands is fatal. If Sparta has retained much of the old institutions it is because the " division of power " has preserved her.
Providence gave an opening for this, when circumstances led to
the division of the kingship between two houses ; the wisdom of
an ancient statesman—this certainly means Lycurgus—carried the
principle further, by dividing sovereignty between the kings and
the γερουσία ; the process was afterwards completed by the institution of the ephors. Hence the Spartan constitution is, as
Plato holds that a stable constitution always ought to be, a mixed
one (691e–692c).
   We learn the same lesson from the history of Persia and that of
Athens. The principle is that, in the last resort, there are two
" matrices " of constitutions—personal rule (monarchy), and
democracy (popular rule, 693d). In a sound constitution both
need to be blended. This was the case with the Persians under
Cyrus, as well as with the Athenians of the same time. But in
Persia, the element of popular control has disappeared, and government has become capricious autocracy, with the result that Persia
is now only formidable on "paper," since there is no real loyalty
in the subject. At Athens, respect for personal character and
authority has been lost in a complete reign of the mob. The cause,
in both cases, has been the same, ignorance of the true principles
of education. Since the great Darius, every Persian prince has
been " born in the purple " and brought up by women and eunuchs,
who ruin him by gratifying all his caprices. At Athens, the mischief began when the uneducated learned to think their own opinion
about music and drama as good as that of the educated, and the
same delusion soon spread to political matters ; the Athens of today is not really a " democracy " but a " theatrocracy " of ignorant
sensation-lovers (694a–701d). In Persia, no one is taught how to
command, and in Athens no one learns how to obey. The lesson
of history for the intending legislator is thus that every wholesome

government must rest on a "division of sovereignty"; it must combine the "popular" element with "something of personal authority," or, as Plato puts it, must unite "monarchy" and "freedom." There must be somewhere a seat of authority, but authority must not degenerate into regimentation; there must be ἐλευθερία, the freedom of the individual, but not a freedom which is anarchical.

It is a good corrective to some popular misconceptions of Plato, to note the judicious way in which he employs poetry and tradition as the basis for his tentative reconstruction of pre-history, and the moderation and sobriety of the lessons he draws from history. In the main, his conception of the stages by which men pass through the nomad to the agricultural state, and from the life of the family group to that of the "city," agrees with Aristotle's, and I might suggest that the well-known account of the "household" and "village" as the precursors of the "city" in the *Politics* is consciously inspired by the more detailed picture of *Laws* iii. In one respect, Plato is more "modern" than Aristotle or any other ancient ; he, like ourselves, has a vivid sense of the enormous lapses of time and the numerous changes which must have gone to the making of society before our records begin. Alone among the Greeks, he has a genuine sense of the recency of the "historical" period of human life, and the importance of pre-history. For the theory of politics, the great feature of the book is the clear and definite enunciation of the principle of the "division of sovereign power." Lord Acton once wrote, improving on Dr. Johnson, that the first Whig was not the devil, but St. Thomas. It might be even truer to say, neither St. Thomas nor the devil, but Plato.

The third book of the *Laws* ends with the statement that Clinias and his friend are actually engaged in a visit to the site of the proposed new city, and an invitation to the Athenian to assist them by continuing his discourse on legislation as they walk. In Book IV. Plato proceeds at once to give us a lesson in practical constitution-making. The very first requisite is to be well informed about the topography, climate, economic resources of the State for which we are to legislate, and the character of its inhabitants. The constitution and legislation must, of course, be adapted to all these conditions ; Plato is no builder of Utopias, but an extremely practical thinker. In the present case, he assumes that the territory of the imagined city is varied : it contains arable, pasture, woodland, and the like, in reasonable quantity, but it is not extremely fertile. In situation, the city is some miles from the sea, though there is a spot in its territory which would make a good harbour. It has no very near neighbours. These conditions are assumed, because without them some of the features Plato regards as most desirable in national life could not be secured. He wants his territory to be varied in order that it may be as nearly as possible self-supporting and independent of imports ; he wants it not to be over-fertile, mainly in order to exclude the rise of production for the foreign market, and for much the same reasons he is glad that it should not have easy access to the sea, the great highway of commerce. His objection is to the influx of large bodies of aliens engaged in trade, whose presence would be a menace to the stability of national traditions of life. (There is to be no Peiraeeus.) And he wants to exclude a big export trade also, because he does not wish the spirit of the community to be commercialized. A further danger is that, as in the case of Athens herself, the development of a sea-borne commerce will lead to the growth of a navy, and with it to the growth of aggressive " imperialism." This explains the motive for the long passage in which it is argued that, contrary to the general opinion, the rise of Athens as a sea-power has been her chief misfortune (705*d*-707*d*). This was also the opinion of Isocrates, and seems to be true, in spite of the customary glorification of Themistocles and Pericles. It was the spirit of commercialistic imperialism which led directly to the attempt of Alcibiades and his admirers to create an Athenian empire in the western Mediterranean, and it was this adventure which irretrievably ruined the Periclean democracy.[1] The history of Athens explains why Plato wishes a morally healthy society to be agrarian rather than industrial, just as Ruskin, Carlyle, and Morris all wished the same thing for England. The composition of the prospective inhabitants by invitation of settlers from all over Crete and from the Peloponnese is intended to provide another advantage. As the citizens come from different quarters, they will have different original traditions, and this will mean that a legislator will not have the same dead weight of unintelligent conservatism to contend against (708*d*).

Now what would be the most favourable opportunity for the creation of a thoroughly sound system of laws and institutions ? Though the remark seems paradoxical, the best chance would be offered by the co-operation of a thoroughly wise statesman with a " tyrant," but the tyrant would have to be young, intelligent, and endowed with unusual moral nobility (709*e*). The thought is that in this case the statesman would have the freest hand. He would need only to convert the autocrat to his plans, and the rest of society would follow suit, partly from loyalty, partly because the autocrat has the requisite force to constrain the malcontent. He must be young as well as intelligent, of course, if he is to be won to such an undertaking : an older man would be less easily impressed. He must have moral nobility, because he will be called on to sacrifice his own position as autocrat, if the combination of authority with " freedom " is to be effected. It is improbable that there should ever be such a conjuncture as the association in one age and place of a supreme statesman with a young autocrat of such unusual qualifications, but we cannot say that the thing is impossible (711*d*). So we may imagine that the condition has been realized and proceed

[1] Of course it was not the fault of the Athenians that they were a naval power. They had to be one, just because, like ourselves, they needed to import their wheat. But the necessity of possessing a powerful fleet inevitably led to the temptation to use it for purposes of selfish aggrandizement.

to consider what institutions the statesman with such a force at his disposal would be likely to recommend.[1]

If a man with a genius for statesmanship ever got this favourable opportunity of carrying his conceptions out in practice, he would, in accord with the principles already laid down, take care not to establish an " unmixed " constitution of any of the three types familiar in the Greek world. That would be to create a sovereignty of a favoured person or class over a subject class or classes. In a true " constitution " the sovereign is not class-interest, but God, and the voice by which God makes His commands known is the law. Hence the fundamental principle of good government is that the sovereign shall be not a person or a class, but impersonal law (713e). In such a society the posts of authority will be awarded for superiority not in birth, or wealth, or strength, but in whole-hearted service to law. Its point of honour will be loyalty to the laws. The Athenian accordingly imagines himself to be in the position of a legislator speaking in the presence of the whole body of intending citizens, and proceeds to begin an address to them on the majesty of law (715e–718a) ; the opening words of this speech are, perhaps, the one " text " quoted more frequently than any other by the Platonists of later antiquity. God eternally pursues the " even tenour of his way," and Justice attends Him ; he who would be happy must follow in their train with a " humbled and disciplined " spirit (ταπεινὸς καὶ κεκοσμημένος). To follow God means to be like God, who is the true " measure of all things " (716c). We are like God so far as we follow the life of right measure.

In the life of measure reverence (τιμή) must be meted out to its various recipients in the right order, first to the gods of the upper world and our city, next to those of the underworld, then to " spirits and heroes," then to ancestors and dead parents, and last to our living parents ; in honouring these last, we must remember that to support them with our substance is the least office, to minister to them with our bodies something more, to give them the affection and devotion of the soul the great thing. We cannot do too much for them while we have them with us ; when they die, the most modest funeral is the most decent and honourable. At this point the discourse on the duties of life breaks off, to be resumed again in the following book. The reason for the interruption is that the speaker recollects that there are two possible types of law, a brief one and a longer. The brief type of law is that in common vogue. It consists of a command or prohibition accompanied by a " sanction " in the form of a penalty threatened for non-compliance.

[1] Why does not Plato suggest that the supremely wise statesman should himself be born heir to the throne ? Presumably because wisdom in states-manship only comes with years and experience. But an experienced monarch of advanced years would have neither the enthusiasm nor the entire freedom from self-interest demanded of the autocrat who is to employ his position to suppress himself. Hence the wisdom must be that of a man who has not to struggle with the insidious temptations of self-interest, the enthusiasm that of a man who has not lost the first flush of youth.

The wise legislator will not, however, wish to overawe the subject into obedience by mere threats. He would prefer to enlist the feelings of the subjects in favour of his regulations as far as he can, leaving only the worst kind of citizen to be merely coerced. If we look at the practice of physicians of the body, we shall see that there are two types among them. There are the mere empirics, usually themselves slaves with slaves for their patients, who give a prescription magisterially with a threat that things will go ill with the patient if he disregards it. There are the eminent physicians, educated men with educated men for their patients ; they explain to the patient the nature of their treatment and the purpose of their regulations and do all they can to get him to help in effecting the cure. It is their method the legislator should adopt. He should therefore prefix to his whole legislation and to the principal sections of it " preambles " explaining the purpose of his regulations and the reasons why such-and-such penalties are proper for neglect of them, and so win the sympathies of the society for whom he legislates (719e–720e). Thus, in enacting that a man shall marry before he reaches a given age or be subject to fine or loss of civil rights (ἀτιμία), he would dwell on the reason for the law, namely, that it aims at securing such immortality as is possible for the race,[1] and the reason for selecting just this " sanction," namely, that the man who shirks the duty to save himself expense shall be visited in his pocket, and that the man who has done nothing to leave a younger generation behind him shall not share in the honours we expect to be shown by the younger generation to their parents (721a–d). We may therefore regard the interrupted discourse on the beings entitled to reverence and the respective degrees in which they are entitled to it, as the opening of a general preamble to our whole legislation.

Book V. in its opening pages contains the continuation of the great preamble (726–734d). From reverence to parents, we proceed to the reverence or respect due to ourselves and our fellows. The rule of self-reverence is that the soul is more than the body and the body than possessions. A man must prize his soul more than his body and his body more than his " goods." We dishonour our own soul when we put bodily vigour and health or power or riches before wisdom and virtue, or when we gratify unworthy caprice or passion. We dishonour the body when we prefer wealth to health. Plato's view is that extraordinary beauty or robustness or wealth are bad for the soul, generally speaking, no less than extraordinary ugliness, deformity, ill-health, penury. The first breeds vanity, the second gross lusts, the third idleness and luxury. In respect of advantages both of body and of fortune,

---

[1] This thought, which had already appeared in the *Symposium*, has no bearing on the doctrine of the immortality of the *soul*. It is the *man*—the complex of soul and body—of whom Plato says that survival in his descendants is the nearest approximation he can make to deathlessness. The ψυχή divorced from the body is not ἄνθρωπος but just ψυχή, a " spirit."

the middle condition is preferable to an extreme. The main rules for right relations with others are that (1) in our relations with friends and fellow-citizens, we should rate the benefits we receive from them at a higher rate than they themselves do, the services we render them at a lower; (2) in relations to the alien, especially to the suppliant, we ought to be specially careful to be on our best behaviour, for nothing is so odious to man and God as taking advantage of those who are defenceless (726–730a).

Next follows an exhortation as to the spirit in which a man should conduct himself in matters where the law can lay down no specific commands or prohibitions. The supreme demand on a man is for ἀλήθεια (" genuineness ") in all the relations of life—in fact, for " loyalty." A man who is not " true and loyal " is wholly untrustworthy; want of loyalty makes friendship and all the happiness of life impossible. We must lay it down that in this, and in all points of virtue, it is good to practise them yourself, better to go further and to bring the misdeeds of others to the knowledge of the authorities, best of all, actually to assist them in chastising the misdoer. We must add that rivalry in goodness of all kinds is the one form of emulation we should encourage in all our citizens, as it is the one kind of rivalry which aims not at en-grossing a good to one's self, but at communicating it as widely as possible. To the faults of others a good man should be merciful, whenever they are remediable, since he knows that " no one is bad on purpose "; he will only let his anger have its course with the incorrigible. A man must beware, too, of the deadly fault of im-proper partiality to one's self. And he must repress all tendency to unrestrained emotionalism (726b–732d).

We must not forget that it is men, not gods, whom we are trying to enlist on the side of virtue. We must therefore make allowance for the universal human desire for a pleasant existence. We cannot expect men regularly to choose the noble life unless they are per-suaded that it is also the pleasant. Its nobility has already been argued; Plato now proceeds to contend that, even by the rules of a Hedonic calculus, if you only state the rules correctly and work the sum right, the morally best life will be found to be also the pleasantest. The rules are that we wish to have pleasure, and not to have pain; we do not wish for a neutral condition, but we prefer it to pain. We choose a pain attended by an overbalance of pleasure, and refuse a pleasure attended by an overbalance of pain; to an exact balance of pleasure and pain we are indifferent. We have to take into account as " dimensions " of pleasure and pain " number " and " size "—i.e. frequency and duration and intensity. We wish to have a life in which, when attention has been given to all these " dimensions," the balance works out on the side of pleasure; not to have one in which the balance is on the side of pain. The life in which the balance is zero is preferable to that in which there is a balance of pain. If we consider four pairs of lives, correspond-ing to the four currently recognized virtues and their contrary vices—the life of the temperate and that of the profligate, the life of the wise man and that of the fool, the life of the brave man and that of the coward, the morally "healthy" and the morally "morbid" life—we find that in the first member of each pair there is less excitement than in the second ; the pleasures and pains are both less intense, but at the same time these pleasures are more frequent and more lasting than the pains, whereas, in the second members of the pairs, the pains are more numerous and lasting than the pleasures. Thus, in each case, the balance is on the side of pleasure in the first member of the pair, on the side of pain in the second. This is Plato's proof that, if the calculation is fairly worked, the better life proves to be also the pleasanter. Its moral superiority, we must remember, is not identified with nor inferred from its greater pleasantness, but is taken to have been already established independently (732*e*–734*e*). This brings us to the end of our general prelude to the legislation.

There is still one more matter to be dealt with before proceeding to the legislation in detail—the creation of the necessary magistracies. The magistrates are, so to say, the warp, the rest of the citizens the woof, of the fabric we have to weave. The warp must have the stronger and tougher constitution, must be made of those elements of the population who have most strength of character and are least pliable. We begin by laying it down (737*c*) that the size of the community, the number of households, must be kept permanent. (We want to exclude the social revolutions which would be produced by either marked decline or marked increase in population.) We require to have just such a population as our territory will support in industry and sobriety, neither more nor fewer. If the population grows beyond this limit, it will begin to expand at the cost of wrong to its neighbours ; if it falls below it, it will not be adequate to its own defence. The actual number of households will depend on the size of the territory, but, for purposes of illustration (737*e*), we may imagine it fixed at 5040, a number which recommends itself by the fact that it is divisible by all the integers up to 10. This is convenient, since there may be practical reasons for wishing to divide the inhabitants into administrative groups for various purposes.[1]

We may say at once that the very best and happiest of all societies would be one where there was no "private" interest, where even wives and children were "common," and the word "my own" never heard (739*c*). What we are describing now is a

---

[1] 5040 = 7 ! (the continued product of the integers from 1 to 7). Plato has chosen it because, since 7 is the highest prime number less than 10, and the numbers 8, 9, 10 are each products of a pair of factors of which each is less than 7, 7 ! will obviously be divisible by every integer up to 10. It will also be divisible by 12 (2 × 6) ; and this is a great convenience, since 12 is the number of months in the year. Ritter's note on the passage rightly points out that the reason for choosing such a number is strictly practical ; it prevents any difficulty in determining the precise quota a particular subdivision of the population ought to contribute to the revenue or the defences.

society which is to come nearest to this ideal, an ideal only possible perhaps to beings who are more than men (θεοὶ ἢ παῖδες θεῶν, 739d).[1] For this " second city " we must lay it down that the land is not to be cultivated in common ; there are to be private estates and houses, as a concession to human weakness, but the owner of a patrimony must always regard it as belonging to the " city " as much as to himself. It will be an obligation of religion that the number of " hearths " is always to be the same. A patrimony is always to descend undivided to one son, chosen by his father, who will keep up the household worship. Daughters are to be provided for by marriage, and, to ensure their marriage, there will be a law against giving or receiving dowries (742c). A man's remaining sons will be provided for by encouraging adoption on the part of the childless or those who have been bereaved of their sons. Plato is thus aware that his scheme demands that the normal family shall be one of two children. Tendency to over-population will be counteracted by " moral suasion " (740d), or, in the last resort, by sending out colonies. (Apparently no " artificial " methods of birth-control are contemplated.) Unavoidable depopulation by epidemics and the like can be met, though reluctantly, by inviting new settlers.

It will, unfortunately, be impossible to prevent economic inequalities altogether, but they may be kept within bounds, and both penury and irresponsible wealth excluded by the following regulations. The patrimonies should be, as nearly as possible, of equal value (737c) ; to secure that they remain inalienable in the same family, a careful survey of the whole territory will be made and preserved in the public archives (741c). To keep out the taint of commercialism, the State will have its own currency, value-less outside its own territory, and it will be a crime in a citizen to own the coined money of a foreign city (742a).[2] There shall be no lending of money on interest, and no credit (742c). The reason for this is simply that we do not wish to encourage a man to live on the automatic return of investments ; we want him to be a farmer living by the labour of his own hands. Accumulation will be checked by the establishment of four economic classes, the poorest possessing nothing beyond their patrimony, the richest being allowed to possess no more than four times the yield of the patri-mony. Any further increase of wealth will be escheated to the State (744d–745a). Thus wealth will have some weight, as well as character and birth, in the distribution of offices. This is re-grettable, but it is a condition we cannot wholly exclude (744b).

[1] Plato still adheres to the moral ideal of the *Republic*, though he seems definitely to be saying that it cannot be actually embodied in flesh and blood. It may be doubted whether he had ever thought otherwise. At any rate, he now regards a system of peasant-proprietorship with inalienable patrimonies as the society in which ordinary men and women will be likely to show most of the spirit of devotion to the " common " good.

[2] A regulation based on the Spartan practice, which is proposed also by Fichte in his *Geschlossener Handelsstaat*.

The community will be divided into twelve " tribes," [1] care being taken that the total property of the tribes is approximately equal and that their holdings are equalized. Each patrimony will be divided into a half situated nearer to and one situated farther from the town, which must have a central position, and we should be careful to see that this division is fairly made, so that, *e.g.*, a man who has the advantage of having half his estate close to the town shall have the other half on the outskirts of the State (745*b–e*). In connexion with the topic of subdivisions and measurements, Plato shows his practical interest in small matters by expressly insisting on the importance of a rigid standardization of the currency and of all weights and measures (746*e*),[2] the object being, of course, to suppress the possibility of small dishonest gains. It is an unphilosophical prejudice to suppose that the eye of the law should be blind to such things. Arithmetic is of the highest value, provided it is pursued in a spirit untainted by the commercialism of Phoenicians and Egyptians (747*a–c*).

Book VI. brings us at last to the appointment of the various magistrates and administrative boards. We must be content here to describe the most important of these and the method by which they are constituted, as illustrative of Plato's insight into the practical business of " representation." The most important ordinary magistracy is that of the νομοφύλακες or guardians of the constitution, a body of thirty-seven men of approved character and intelligence, who must be at least 50 years old at appointment, and must retire at the age of 70. Their functions are to watch over the interests of the laws in general and, in particular, to take charge of the register of properties, and penalize and " blacklist " any citizen guilty of fraudulent concealment of income. They figure also as the presiding magistrates in connexion with the trial of grave offences of various kinds. They are to be elected by votes given in writing and signed with the voter's name (as a precaution against an irresponsible vote), and the election has several stages, by which the three hundred names first selected are finally reduced to thirty-seven (three for each " tribe " with an odd man to prevent an equal division of opinions).

The ordinary great council, the " representative chamber " of the society, is elected on a plan ingeniously contrived to eliminate extreme " class-consciousness " and to make wire-pulling and cabal impossible. It is ultimately to consist of 360 members, ninety from each of the four property-classes, but the selection has several stages and is spread over a week. In the first instance 360 representatives of each class are chosen, the voting covering four days.

[1] The number is selected for the practical convenience that it makes it easy for an office or duty to rotate through all the tribes in the course of a year. The official year is to have 365, not 360, days—a reform never adopted by any actual Greek " city " until a later date (828*b*).

[2] Ritter, *ad loc.*, rightly calls attention to the point that Plato is here, for the first time, pointing out the necessity of regulations of this kind, which were unknown in Hellenic practice.

Citizens of the two richest classes are obliged under a penalty to vote for the representatives of all four classes. The citizens of the third and fourth classes are compelled only to vote on the first two days, and may or may not vote on the second two, as they please. (The thought is that they would mostly abstain, since they have already lost two days from their working week, and will not wish to lose two more. Thus, as the poorer citizens will be the most numerous, the representatives of the two richer classes will be elected by a vote in which the poorer classes will have most influence ; those of the poorer classes will mainly be chosen by the votes of the richer. This means that the names selected will be those of moderate men from all classes ; neither a Coriolanus nor a Cade will stand much chance of election. This secures that the whole body shall be public-spirited, fair-minded, and likely to co-operate harmoniously.) In the second stage of the process, the number of names is reduced to one-half by a vote which must be compulsorily exercised by all citizens. (An extremist who might slip through the first election would thus very probably be eliminated at this stage, and, as the voting is compulsory for every one, the danger that the richer classes might make the representation of the poorer a farce by inducing their poorer fellow-citizens to abstain from voting for the members of their own class is also reduced to a minimum.) Finally, the numbers are again reduced to one-half by the use of the lot. (This would be a final precaution against electioneering jobbery.) The council thus appointed holds office for the year, one-twelfth of it forming a committee which exercises the main functions of sovereignty for each month.

The chief criticism a modern thinker would be likely to pass on the scheme would probably be that it runs the risk of making the extremist all the more dangerous by leaving him no chance of airing his grievances in the " council of the nation." But it might be said that we are learning by experience how hard it is for the same body to combine the functions of a " safety-valve " and a really effective national council.

The most important office in a Platonic community is, as we should expect, that of the Minister of Education. The well-being of the community depends directly on the character of the education given to successive generations, and the overseer of education should therefore be the best and most illustrious man in the community, as holding its most responsible post. He must be a man of over fifty, with children of his own, and should be elected for a period of five years out of the body of the νομοφύλακες by the votes of the other magistrates (765d–766b). The " President of the Board of Education " is thus the " premier " in Plato's commonwealth.

If the life of the society is to be thoroughly sound from a moral point of view, we must first ensure that the tone of family life itself is sound. Marriage must be regarded as a solemn duty to society ; selfish neglect to discharge that duty, as we have already learned, will be penalized. Extravagant expenditure on wedding festivities must be discountenanced. The peace of the household also demands that we lay down a right rule for the treatment of servants. A master must, for his own sake as well as for his servant's, make it a rule to be even more scrupulously fair in his treatment of his slaves than he is in his behaviour to his equals (777*d*). But he should be strictly just, without compromising his position as master by improper familiarities. His word must be law to his slave, and he must punish all disobedience. When our young people have been married, we must see to it that they begin their married life on the right lines. We must not let them think they can spend these early days, before children have yet come, just as they please, as a sort of honeymoon. The young husband must, for example, take his place at the public table with his fellow-citizens, exactly as he has been used to do (780*b*). And, though this is a thing which has not been attempted even at Sparta, women, no less than men, must be taught to live under the eye of the society to which they belong. They are frailer than men, and need even more to be safeguarded by the knowledge that their conduct is open to public censure. They, too, must have their common table, and we should not listen to the complaints always raised against the moral reformer who claims the right to regulate " private affairs " (780*d*–781*d*). The three keenest of human appetites are those of hunger, thirst, sex, and the rudiments of civilized existence are only made possible by the proper regulation of all three (782*d*–783*b*). When man and woman have been married, they must think it their bounden duty to present the city with worthy offspring. There should be a board of ladies, appointed by the authorities, to supervise the behaviour of married couples in this respect and advise them. This committee will have a general control over married people for ten years after marriage, and it will treat its duties from both a eugenic and a moral point of view. If a marriage remains childless, they will arrange for its dissolution on equitable terms after the ten years. They and the νομοφύλακες will act as conciliators in conjugal disputes, and there will be penalties for parties who are intractable to their remonstrances. They will also see that violations of conjugal fidelity are chastised, where they are too grave to be winked at. It need not be said that a careful register of births and deaths must be kept ; without it we could not secure observance of the regulations about the proper age qualifications for marriage, public office, or military service. Men must marry between 30 and 35, girls between 16 and 20.[1] A man may not be appointed to an office under 30, nor a woman under 40. The period of liability for military service will be for a man from 20 to 60 (the Athenian rule) ; if women are given any " war work," it should be after they have borne their children and before they have reached 50 (783*d*–785*h*)

---

[1] Later on (833*d*) the minimum age of the girls at marriage is reckoned at 18 ; we must remember that the *Laws* has not received its final revision by the author.

The seventh book of the *Laws* contains Plato's most important and detailed scheme for a universal education. The principles are at bottom those already familiar to us from the *Republic*, but the treatment is much more detailed, and in some respects the level of the demands has risen. There must be systematic organization from the first, since if we leave anything to the caprice of the individual householder, we shall not secure the community of spirit and character we need in the State. And we cannot take the matter in hand too early. It is just when the child's body and mind are most plastic that most enduring harm can be done by wrong treatment. We ought, therefore, to begin the task even before a child's birth, An expectant mother must take such exercise as is required in the interests of her unborn child (789*d*). When the child is born, we must see that, even before it can walk, its nurse gives it the exercise and air which is good for it, and particularly, that it is not allowed to injure itself by walking too early (789*e*). A baby should live, as nearly as possible, as though it were always at sea ; it should be dandled and danced about and sung to (790*c–e*) to keep it from being frightened. This is a first preparation for the development of a brave and steadfast character. And care must be taken to keep the baby in a placid mood ; it is a bad moral beginning for it to be allowed to become fretful or passionate (791*d–*793*d*). When the child is 3 or older, we can begin to correct it judiciously, and it will take to playing games. It is best to leave children to invent their own games, but from the age of 3 to 6 they should be brought together daily in the various temples to play under the supervision of ladies appointed by the authorities, who will thus have the opportunity of seeing that the nurses really bring up their charges in the way the State expects of them (793*d–*794*c*). At the age of 6, lessons will begin in earnest, and with them the segregation of the girls from the boys. The boys should be taught to ride and use bow, sling, and dart, and it would be well for the girls to learn the same things, or at any rate, the use of these weapons (794*c–d*). Care should be taken to train the children to be ambidextrous. That this is possible we see from the indifference with which the Scythians use either hand to hold the bow, and it is of great practical importance to have two " right hands " (794*d–*795*d*). Taking " gymnastic " and " music " as the names for the training of body and mind respectively, we may divide the former into two branches, dancing and wrestling. For educational purposes, " trick " wrestling is useless ; only the stand-up sort which is also good training for warfare is to be practised (796*a–b*) [1] ; the dancing to be specially commended is similarly the dance in armour, which affords a good preliminary training against the years of military education (796*b–d*).

" Music " requires a fuller treatment. We must remind our-

[1] Plato has no use for fancy wrestling and boxing, and would clearly have thought ju-jitsu unseemly. He condemns in so many words the art of Antaeus, who was fabled to vanquish an opponent by sinking to the ground.

selves once more of the great practical importance of the subject. It is important that there should be no needless innovations in the " play " of a society, for innovations in play lead on to innovations in what is supposed to be earnest, and all departure from an established " regimen " is attended with risk to the health of a society, just as it is dangerous for an organism (797a–798d). Music, as we have so often said, " imitates " or " reproduces " types of moods and characters, and, since we wish the national ideal of character to be kept constant, we shall need to keep the standards of this imitation constant too. The Egyptians set us an example in this ; each type of permitted musical form is consecrated by them to the cultus of a god, and innovation thus becomes sacrilege, and we ought to require that the example shall be followed in our city, singular as it seems to a Greek. To see that it is observed should be one of the functions of our board of νομοφύλακες (799a–800b). They will not allow the festivals of the gods to be polluted by choruses declaiming blasphemies and wailing in a way only seemly for the performer of a dirge (800c–e). (This is meant to exclude tragic " choruses " and tragedy itself along with them.) Our poets must feel that their work is prayer, and that the first rule for it is that of εὐφημία, reverent reticency ; the second that they do not know themselves how to " ask aright " and must learn from the law what are the true blessings for which men should pray (801a–c). The poets, then, must submit to a censure and circulate no composition which has not the *imprimatur* of the νομοφύλακες (801d). It will be the business of the State to compile a suitable anthology of verse which meets our requirements ; the compilers, besides being men of sound taste, must have reached the mature age of 50. In this way we may hope to imbue our young people from the first with the right taste for high austere art (802a–d). There should, of course, be a distinction between the songs learned by boys and by girls ; the tone of the former must be lofty and manly, of the latter, sedate and pure (802e).

We proceed with the details of the education to be reared on this basis of a sound taste which is at once aesthetic and moral. We have, so to say, laid the keel of the vessel and have now to design the ribs. We may feel, perhaps, that the voyage of life is not so serious an affair as it seems. Perhaps we are only playthings for God, but even if that is so, we must " play the game " well, not in the inverted fashion of mankind at large, who fancy that war is the business of life, peace only the play. The truth is that it is peace which is " real " and " earnest," for it is only in peace that we can pursue *education*, the most serious affair of life (803a–804c).

To return to our subject. We shall need schools for the teaching of the things we have spoken of, with proper buildings and grounds. And the teachers in these schools will have to receive salaries, and therefore must be foreigners. All the children must attend school (φοιτᾶν) daily ; this must not be left to parental caprice. This applies to girls as well as to boys ; they must even learn to ride and shoot, or the State will be deprived of the services it has a right to expect at need from the one-half of its citizens (804e–805b).

It is important to note the magnitude of the proposal made here. As Professor Burnet points out, what is being conceived for the first time is the " secondary school," a permanent establishment for the higher education of boys and girls by specially competent teachers duly organized and paid. (The impossibility of maintaining such an institution without salaries is the reason why, in accord with Hellenic sentiment, it is assumed that they must all be non-citizens.) The " grammar school " meets us as an actual institution in the Macedonian age ; it is presumable that it owes its existence to the influence exerted in that age by members of the Academy as the recognized experts in education and jurisprudence. The old practice of the Periclean age had been that " higher education " of all kinds was got from attending the lectures of sophists, each with his speciality. Plato's new idea is the systematization of secondary education by co-ordinating the specialists in single institutions.

We need not be afraid of the criticism that our views on the education of women are paradoxical. We see that women can share the labours of men by the example of Thrace and other districts where they do agricultural work, though at Athens they are expected to do nothing but sit indoors, mind the store-closet, and spin and weave. At Sparta a middle course is followed ; the girls learn to wrestle, and they do no house-work, but they are not expected to be capable of doing anything for the national defence. With all courtesy to a Spartan hearer, we must confess that we cannot be satisfied with such a compromise ; the women should at least be able, in case of need, to scare away raiders from the city (806b).[1]

The scheme we have adopted for our community makes it certain that our citizens will not have to labour long hours for the means of existence ; they will have abundant leisure, and they must not waste it in fattening themselves like cattle, but use it in setting themselves to live the most strenuous of all lives, that which aims at goodness of mind and body. They will have to be up betimes, before all the servants, and to prevent waste of the precious hours in sleep, it will be enjoined that public as well as household business shall be transacted in the early morning. Sleeping long and late is as bad for the body as for the mind (806d–808c). It follows that the boys must be taken to school at daybreak, and both the servants who conduct them there and the schoolmasters must pay the closest attention to their *moral*, for a boy, just because he has a " spring of intelligence " in him, which does not as yet run clear, is the most unruly of all animals. As to the subjects of

---

[1] There is a clear allusion to the fact dwelt on by Aristotle (*Pol.* B 1269b 37), that the panicky behaviour of the Spartan women when Epaminondas was threatening an assault on the city proved that the famous training in rough exercises had no effect in making them braver than women anywhere else.

education at school, we have already spoken of the principles on which songs and poems should be selected, but it will be more difficult to select suitable prose. Of course enough arithmetic must be learned for the purposes of daily life, enough elementary astronomy to understand the Calendar (809c–d), and enough of music to know how to tune one's lyre. This will suffice until a boy is 16 years old, if we allow three years (from 10 to 13) for reading and writing and three more for the study of the lyre, taking care that the sharp boys are not permitted to push on too fast nor the dull to lag behind (810a). The one serious problem at this stage is the selection of prose reading. We may certainly let the boys read sound works on morals and law (811c–e), but there is a difficulty about other kinds of prose, and too wide reading would not be good for boys (811b).[1] The supervision of the whole system will be in the hands of the Minister of Education, assisted by the advice of experts chosen by himself (813c). It must be understood that there will be paid expert teachers of all the exercises we have prescribed for the training of the body; there will be women as well as men among these teachers, and girls as well as boys will receive the training, so that they may be capable of defending themselves in necessity (814a).

There are still three " branches of knowledge " (μαθήματα) which any free man should possess—arithmetic, geometry, astronomy (817e). Only a few young people are capable of high proficiency in them, but all must study them " so far as is truly necessary " (818b). But how far is that ? At least as far as the Egyptians succeed in carrying large classes of young people. They have a method of teaching them to deal with fractions and to find the divisors of numbers by means of games in which garlands and other objects have to be divided among a given number of persons,[2] or boxers to be paired. The study of this sort of problem can readily be made to lead up to the recognition that there are " incommensurable " lengths, areas, and volumes, a subject on which Greeks, even Greeks who dabble in mathematics, are disgracefully ignorant (820b), but we must not let our young people share such ignorance. Similarly our secondary education in astronomy must correct the really " impious " mistake of current Greek astronomy, which ascribes irregular movements to the heavenly bodies, and leads to calling the swiftest of them the slowest. We must make it clear that every so-called " planet " has a strictly regular motion and only *one* such motion (822a).[3]

---

[1] The point of this is that what prose literature there was in Plato's time consisted for the most part of the works of the Ionian men of science and of technical works on medicine and rhetoric. For reasons which will become apparent when we speak of Plato's theology, he regards books on science as dangerous reading for the boys and girls.

[2] Two problems seem to be contemplated, the discovery of the factors of composite numbers and the handling of fractions. On the Egyptian problems in question see Burnet, *E.G.Ph.*[3] 18–19.

[3] τὴν αὐτὴν γὰρ αὐτῶν ὁδὸν ἕκαστον καὶ οὐ πολλὰς μίαν ἀεὶ κύκλῳ διεξέρχεται. This clearly means not only that the real motion of a planet is regular, but that it

It might seem in place here to add something about the value of hunting as a pursuit for the young. But we must lay it down once for all that we cannot be expected to deal with the whole of such problems in a law. The details must be left to the really competent Minister of Education to regulate by his personal judgment (822d–823d). For us it is enough to say that we mean only to encourage the sort of hunting which contributes to make good men. We do not wish our citizens to take to the sea, so we shall discourage sea-fishing ; for stronger reasons, we object to raiding and capturing men, and to any kind of chase which depends on mere cunning. Hence we should discourage the mere netting and snaring of any kind of creature, retaining only " the hunting of quadrupeds with horses and dogs and one's own body," as a training in endurance and courage (824a).

The contents of Books VIII. and IX. must be dealt with very summarily. Provision is made, as would be the case in any actual Greek " legislation," first of all for the cultus of the State, every month of the year and every day of the month being provided with its appropriate worship ; the object is simply to place the whole daily life of the whole community under the " religious sanction " (828). Since there will be " gymnastic " and musical " contests " as part of this regular worship, Plato then goes on to lay down regulations for the regular monthly exercises of the citizen militia, as well as for the " contests " which will mark special festivals. The latter are meant to correspond to the pan-Hellenic games of actual life, but the programme of " events " is revised. Competition is to be in exercises of strength and endurance which have a real military value, particularly in rapid evolutions in complete accoutrement, and the mimic warfare is to reproduce its model as closely as possible ; there must be a spice of real danger about it. The girls and women must share in all this, so far as their physique permits, but we cannot make detailed regulations on this point in advance (829–835d).

This raises an important ethical question. Is there not a real danger that the very free association of young people of both sexes in pursuits of this kind, and their abundant leisure from " work," may lead to a relaxed sexual morality ? Plato thinks not, if we can only establish the right social tradition in such matters, which is that " homo-sexual " relations of all kinds must be reprobated as unnatural and that the normal sexual appetite is to find no gratification outside the bounds of lawful matrimony. This demand may strike most persons as Utopian, and as an attempt to suppress " love." But we must not be misled by equivocal terms. " Love of good-will " is one thing, love of carnal appetite quite another ; the suppression of the second in no way militates against

is not composite. The object is thus to deny all theories, like that of Eudoxus, which ascribe to a planet a double motion in opposite senses. I still think that this must be meant, in spite of the dissent of Professor Storey and Professor Cornford.

the cultivation of the first.[1] That the standard of continence proposed can be attained is proved by the lifelong abstinence of well-known athletes, and surely our citizens can do to obtain a spiritual crown what boxers will do for an Olympic garland.[2] That carnal appetite can be effectually restrained by moral and religious sanctions we see from the complete suppression of incestuous desire in the lives of civilized societies, which is effected simply by the tradition that incest is shameful. So our standard will be found practicable when once it has been consecrated by the sanctions of a social tradition (835*d*–842*a*). If we should find it beyond our power to secure absolute conformity to this rule, we shall at least demand that " unnatural " passion shall be wholly suppressed and that more normal irregularities shall be visited by disgrace if detected.

The speaker now turns to a consideration of regulations necessary for the pursuit of agriculture, the economic foundation of his contemplated society. Under this caption we have proposals for dealing with such matters as encroachments on boundaries, diversion of watercourses, ownership of stray animals, regulation of the market,[3] and the like. In matters like these, there are many already existing good rules which we shall do well to follow (843*e*), a significant hint that many of the regulations proposed are simply based on the actual code of Attica. The student of Plato's political philosophy need not delay over such details, though they have a double interest for the historian of law and custom. They throw a great deal of light on questions of Attic law, and they provide the starting-point for the casuistry by which Roman lawyers and, in modern times, publicists like Grotius and Pufendorf have laboured to arrive at the principles of a satisfactory law of property. It is not surprising that Plato's actual examples recur, for example, in the *Institutes* of Justinian and the *de Jure Belli et Pacis*. The discussion of the regulation of the market leads naturally to consideration of the conditions on which aliens may be allowed to enter the society and practise industry (850*b*–*d*). They are to be subjected to no poll-tax, but they must have an industry by which to support themselves, must conform to the rules of the

---

[1] *Loc. cit.* 837*b*–*d*. This is a criticism of the current theory of many Greek societies—not of Athens—according to which " unnatural " attachments are of great value for military purposes because of the mutual devotion they inspire, the theory presupposed by the institution, *e.g.*, of the Theban ἱερὸς λόχος. The *Phaedrus* had already denied the fact of the " devotion " ; the *Laws* exposes the verbal equivocation by which the practice is defended. (For such a defence, cf. the speech of Phaedrus in the *Symposium*, 178*e*.)

[2] *Loc. cit.* 839*e*–840*c*. The reasoning is familiar to us from the Pauline parallel, 1 Cor. ix. 23–27. The standard here set up is no novelty of Plato's last years ; the demands made on the guardians of the *Republic* would be even more rigorous.

[3] The important points in connexion with the market are that (1) all transactions must be on the basis of immediate payment, (2) there is to be no " higgling " about prices. The seller must have a fixed price and must take neither more nor less. Like Ruskin, Plato is not so anxious to prevent a seller from asking too much as to keep him from palming off bad wares at a pretended " sacrifice " (*loc. cit.* 849*a*–850*a*).

State, and should normally be expected to depart again after twenty years' residence (*i.e.* they are not to acquire a "right of settlement ").

We come now to criminal jurisprudence, with an apology for the necessity of admitting that there will be any crime to be legislated against in a rightly constituted society. The crimes first considered are, in the order of their gravity, sacrilege, treason, parricide. These are "capital" crimes, and it is best for a citizen who commits them that he should be allowed to live no longer, but we must lay it down once for all that the capital sentence must not include the penalizing of his innocent family by the confiscation of property, and that they are not to be regarded as tainted in their honour by his offence. Similar crimes in an alien or a slave will be more mildly visited by whipping and expulsion from the country. In general, Plato allows himself a freer use of corporeal chastisements than modern legislators, since he does not accept the "humanitarian" estimate of physical pain nor the view that its infliction is peculiarly degrading. These capital crimes are to be tried before a court composed of the νομοφύλακες and a number of the magistrates of the preceding year,[1] and the proceedings must be spread over three days.

We must insist, however, that in our State criminal jurisprudence takes a scientific account of the psychology of the offender (857c–d). Current opinion on this matter, as shown by the practice of existing societies, is in a state of confusion. Justice is held to be a "fine " thing (καλόν), but the just chastisement inflicted on a criminal is regarded as a disgrace to him (859d–860b). Yet to be consistent, we ought to hold that if it is "fine " to do what is just, it is also "fine " to get what is just done to you.[2] The secret of the current confusion is that actual jurisprudence assumes that men are bad and do wrong "voluntarily," hence the one great distinction recognized by actual law is the distinction between voluntary and involuntary transgression. But we must adhere to the philosophical principle so familiar to us from earlier dialogues that "all wrongdoing is involuntary " (860d), and therefore we cannot make the distinction between voluntary and involuntary the basis of our penal code (861d). The distinction we really need is a different one, that of βλάβη, the causing of hurt or loss, from ἀδικία, the violation of a right. In inflicting penalties, the proper question is not whether the act committed was voluntary or not, but whether the person on whom it was inflicted received mere loss or hurt, or was further injured in his rights. The proper thing to say about a man who has caused an unintended loss or hurt to another is not,

---

[1] 855c ff. The constitution of the court is thus suggested by that of the Attic Areopagus. Plato is careful to avoid the miscarriage of justice attending on the Athenian practice of allowing a capital case to come before an irresponsible body of ordinary citizens chosen by lot, from whom there was no appeal.

[2] The thought is the old one of the *Gorgias*. It is good for the offender's soul to receive the penalty, and since the suffering is good for him it cannot be αἰσχρόν. The "disgrace " lies not in the punishment but in the crime.

as current jurisprudence says, that he has done an " involuntary wrong," but that he has not committed a wrong at all, but only caused a loss or hurt (861*e*–862*c*). It is this distinction between causing loss and infringing a right which we really need to make fundamental in assessing penalties. Thus the important distinction between the causing of detriment and the infraction of a right, with the consequent distinction between an action for damages and a criminal prosecution, is introduced into legal theory for the first time in *Laws* ix. The courts can make mere damage good by the award of *compensation* for it, but contravention of a right must further be met by the imposition of a *penalty* intended to make the offender's soul better (862*c*–*e*). If we doubt whether wrongdoing is really involuntary, we need only remember what its causes are—temper, (θυμός), lust for pleasure, ignorance (863*a*–864*b*).

Plato now applies these principles to the construction of a penal code. We have to distinguish violation of rights from the mere causation of damage, and in the case of the former, we must distinguish between violence and craft. Regulations are then laid down for the cases of homicide, suicide, maiming, wounding with intent to kill, minor assaults, the object being to give a specimen of a logically constructed criminal code. The penalties will depend not only on the main distinction already laid down, but on the status of the parties, whether citizens, aliens, or slaves. The details must be passed over here. What inevitably impresses a modern reader most unfavourably is the special severity with which injuries committed by a slave on free persons are treated. This is, however, a direct consequence of the recognition of the servile status, which gives these crimes something of the character of mutiny.

Book X. introduces us to one of the most important developments of Platonism, its theology. Plato appears as at once the creator of natural theology and the first thinker to propose that false theological belief—as distinguished from insults to an established worship—should be treated as a crime against the State and repressed by the civil magistrate. He is convinced that there are certain truths about God which can be strictly demonstrated, and that the denial of these leads directly to practical bad living. Hence the denial of these truths is a grave offence against the social order and must be punished as such, the principle upon which the Roman Church still maintains that it is the duty of the magistrate to suppress heretical pravity. Historically we have here the foundation of natural or philosophical theology, The name we owe to the famous Roman antiquarian, M. Terentius Varro, who distinguished three kinds of theology, or " discourses about gods,"— the poetical, consisting simply of the myths related by the poets; the civil, which means knowledge of the Calendar of the State's cultus and is the creation of the " legislator "; and the natural or philosophic, the doctrine about things divine taught by philosophers as an integral part of their account of φύσις, *natura*, reality. The first, according to a view as old as Herodotus, is the mere invention of poets who aim only at interesting and amusing; the second has been manufactured by the authorities with a view to social utility; the third, and only the third, claims to be part of the truth about things.[1] We must, of course, be careful to remember that the epithet " natural," as originally applied to this kind of theology, conveys no contrast with a " revealed " or " historical " theology; it means neither more nor less than " scientific."

The three heresies Plato regards as morally pernicious are, in the order of their moral turpitude: (*a*) atheism, the belief that there are no gods at all, the least offensive of the three ; (*b*) Epicureanism, as we may call it by a convenient anachronism, the doctrine that God, or the gods, are indifferent to human conduct ; (*c*) worst of all, the doctrine that an impenitent offender can escape God's judgment by gifts and offerings. It is morally less harmful to believe that there is no God than to believe in a careless God, and it is better to believe in a careless God than in a venal one. Against these three heresies Plato holds that he can prove the existence of a God or gods, the reality of providential and moral government of the world and man, and the impossibility of bribing the divine justice.

(*a*) *Atheism.*—Atheism is treated by Plato as identical with the doctrine that the world and its contents, souls included, are the product of unintelligent motions of corporeal elements. Against this theory, he undertakes to demonstrate that all corporeal movements are, in the last resort, causally dependent on " motions " of soul, wishes, plans, purposes, and that the world is therefore the work of a soul or souls, and further that these souls are good, and that there is one ἀρίστη ψυχή, " perfectly good soul," at their head. Thus the demonstration of the being of God serves also, in principle, as a proof of the indestructibility of the soul, a doctrine which has to be introduced in refuting the two graver heresies. He indicates that atheism as an opinion has two chief sources—the corporealism of the early Ionian men of science, who account for the order of nature on purely " mechanical " principles without ascribing anything to conscious plan or design (889*a*–*d*), and the sophistic theory of the purely conventional and relative character of moral distinctions (889*e*–890*a*). If these two doctrines are combined, atheism is the result. It has to be shown, as against this atheism, that the motions of body are actually all caused by prior " movements " of soul, so that τέχνη, conscious design, purpose, is the parent of τύχη, not τύχη of τέχνη, as the proverb says (892*b*). Or, more briefly, mind, not bodies, is " what is there to begin with " (892*c*).[2]

---

[1] See for Varro's doctrine on this point Augustine, *de Civitate Dei*, vi. 5.

[2] 892c, γένεσιν τὴν περὶ τὰ πρῶτα = τὴν τῶν πρώτων γένεσιν = τὸ τῶν πρώτων γένος = τὸ πρῶτον. That γένεσις here is equivalent to γένος is clear from the context.

The proof turns on an analysis of the notion of κίνησις, motion or process (893*b*–894*e*). Ten senses of the word are enumerated. The first five are different forms of actual physical motion : (1) revolution in a circular orbit, (2) rectilinear motion, (3) rolling, (4) aggregation, (5) disgregation. Then follow three " ideal " motions : (6) the " fluxion " of a point which " generates " a line, (7) the fluxion of the line which generates a surface, (8) the fluxion of a surface which generates a solid. These distinctions are merely preliminary to that which is essential for the purposes of our proof. All motions belong to one of two classes : (9) *communicated* motion, " the movement which can only move other things," or (10) spontaneous motion, the " movement which can move itself " (894*b*). And it is argued that causally communicated motion always presupposes spontaneous motion as its source (894*c*–895*b*). Now when we see anything which exhibits spontaneous, or internally initiated, motion, we call it *alive*, ἔμψυχον ; we say that there is ψυχή in the thing. ψυχή, in fact, is the *name* which language gives to " the motion which can move itself." Thus, " soul " is the name, or *definiendum*, of which the " discourse " (λόγος), " movement which can move itself," is the *definition*. The name and the discourse are therefore equivalent, and it follows that the movements of soul, " tempers and wishes and calculations, true beliefs, interests (ἐπιμέλειαι), and memories," are actually the source and cause of all physical movement, since no physical movement is spontaneous (896*d*). This constitutes the proof that soul or mind is the cause of cosmic movement. So far the argument is an elaboration of that which has been given more briefly in the *Phaedrus* for the immortality of the soul.

Next, there must be more than one soul which is the cause of cosmic movements (*i.e.* Plato's theology is theistic, not pantheistic). There *must* be at least two such souls and there *may* be more. For there is disorder and irregularity in nature as well as order and regularity, hence the " best soul " clearly cannot be the only source of motion in the universe ; since order has the upper hand, God, the " best soul," is clearly the supreme cause, but there must be other souls which are not wholly good (896*e*–898*d*). (It must be carefully noted that there is no trace in the language of the doctrine of a " bad world-soul " read into the *Laws* in ancient times by Plutarch and Atticus, and in modern times by Zeller and others. The point is not that there are *two* souls responsible for the universe, but that there are at least two ; the " best soul " is not the only soul there is, but we are at liberty to suppose as many inferior souls as the appearances seem to require.)

If we are not to misunderstand Plato's whole conception we must note the following points carefully. (1) Evil, no less than

since the criticism made on the old physicists is that they regard such things as " fire " and " air," *i.e.* their primary bodies, as the γένεσις περὶ τὰ πρῶτα. For this use of γένεσις see Ast, *Lexicon Platonicum*, s.v., who, however, wrongly places the passage under a different heading.

good, is expressly said to be due to " soul," being identified with disorderly motion.   Hence the doctrine of " matter " as intrinsically evil, and the source of evil, which figures in the popular Platonism of later times, is wholly un-Platonic.   (2) God (or the gods) is quite definitely declared to be a ψυχή, and we are told that this means that the universe is a result of τέχνη, design.   Plato thus definitely believes in a divine purposive activity—in other words, in what is really meant by the " personality " of God.   " Pantheism," which repudiates the notion of conscious creative design, would be only another form of the very doctrine Plato identifies with atheism. (3) God is a soul, not a form.   The movement which can move itself is the highest type of agent known to Plato, and the fundamental difference in theology between Plato and Aristotle is just that Aristotle insists on getting behind it to a still more divine source of movement, an " unmoved " mover.   We have to think of Plato's God as contemplating the forms and reproducing them in the order of the sensible world.   Plato's last word on the old question of the *Phaedo*, " what is the cause of the presence of a form to a sensible thing ? " is that God is the cause.   Being perfectly wise and good, God makes the sensible order after the pattern of the forms he contemplates.   (4) The argument disregards the question, never felt by a Greek to be very important, whether there is only one God or many.   But the very phrase " best soul " shows that there is one such soul which is supreme.   This, no doubt, is the soul responsible for the one movement which, from the point of view of Plato's astronomy, presents no irregularity or anomaly at all, the movement of the " outermost heaven."   This soul would be God in a special sense.   How it is related to that which it moves Plato does not tell us, though he suggests alternative views (899*a*). (5) What are the irregularities which, to his mind, prove that not all cosmic motions are due to a single divine soul ?   We may reasonably conjecture that they are, in the first place, the various apparent anomalies in the motions of the planets.   These anomalies are not ultimate, but they at least require us to analyse the appearances into combinations of several movements, and this would suggest, as it does to Aristotle, the plurality of " movers."   But I think something further is meant.   The course of nature on the whole, by its regular periodicities, favours the development of intellectual and moral civilization.   Yet there are natural " catastrophes " which are adverse to this development, inundations, successions of barren or pestilential seasons, volcanic eruptions, and the like, and these exceptions to the rule have to be referred to the agency of souls of some kind ; clearly these souls must be thought of as at least partly irrational and evil.   Whatever we may think of a Theism of this kind, it seems to me plain that we can find no other doctrine in Plato without doing violence to his language, and we should take note that, though religious faith in God was, of course, no novelty, Theism as a doctrine professing to be capable of scientific demonstration is introduced into philosophy for the first time in this section of the *Laws*. Plato is the creator of " philosophical Theism."

The refutation of the two other heresies now becomes a simple matter.

(*b*) *Epicureanism* (899*d*–905*d*).—The belief that though there are gods they are indifferent to our conduct is suggested by the spectacle of successful lifelong iniquity, but it is really no more than a nightmare or bad dream (900*b*). If the gods pay no attention to our conduct, the reason must be either that they are unable to regulate everything or that they regard man and man's doings as trifles, and neglect the control of these small matters either because they think them insignificant or because they are " too fine " to attend to them. We may dismiss the suggestion of lack of power at once ; it is easier in action to handle small affairs than to handle great, though it is the minute things which it is hardest to perceive accurately. As to the other suggestions, all competent practitioners of medicine, engineering, and the other arts, especially that of the statesman, know that no one ever succeeds in the main of any enterprise if he neglects what appear to be " small details," and we cannot suppose that the " best " soul is more ignorant than a human practitioner, even if it were certain, as it is not, that human conduct is a " trifle " from God's point of view. To suppose that God neglects us because He is too indolent or fastidious to attend to us, would amount to saying that the " best soul " is cowardly or " work-shy," and this is no better than blasphemy. Nor is it true that the regulation of human destiny in accord with moral law would involve en lless " interference " with the machinery of things. The result is secured from the first by a law of singular simplicity, the law that " like finds its like," souls, like liquids, " find their level." A man " gravitates " towards the society of his mental and moral likes, and thus, through the endless succession of lives, he always " does and has done to him " what it is fitting that such a man should do or have done to him (904*e*). That is the " justice of God " from which no man can escape in life or death.

We may dispose of (*c*) the doctrine that God can be bribed to wink at sin even more summarily (905*e*–907*d*). For our argument has justified the old belief that we are the " chattels " or " flock " (κτήματα) of the gods. If they wink at the conduct of human " beasts of prey," they are behaving like shepherds or watch-dogs who allow the wolf to rend the flock on condition of sharing in the plunder. A blasphemy like this is more fittingly met by honest indignation than by argument or gentle remonstrance.

We now come to the penalties for the publication of these various heresies. The overt maintenance of any of them ought to be brought at once to the notice of the magistrates, who are to bring the case before the proper court. If a magistrate neglects to act, he must himself become liable to prosecution for " impiety." In the case of each class of offenders we must distinguish between two degrees of guilt—that of the heretic who is otherwise morally blameless, and that of the worse offender who adds practical evil-living to his heresy. For the morally inoffensive heretic the penalty, on conviction, will in every case include at least five years of imprisonment in the " House of Correction," where he will see no one but members of the " nocturnal council," who are to visit him from time to time and to reason with him on the error of his ways (909*a*). A second conviction is to be followed by death.[1] The worst offenders are those who add to the speculative belief that the gods are indifferent or venal the still graver crime of trading on the superstition of their neighbours for their own profit or aggrandisement, by founding immoral cults. They are to be imprisoned for life in " penal servitude " in the most desolate region of the country, visited by no citizen whatever, and cast out unburied at death, in fact, treated as " dead in law " from the moment of conviction. But their innocent families must not suffer for their offence, and should be treated as wards of the State [2] (909*c*).

Plato is so much in earnest with this horror of immoral superstition that he ends by proposing to suppress all shrines and sacrifices except those belonging to the public worship of the city. No one may be permitted to have a private " chapel " or " oratory " or to sacrifice except at the public altars and with the established ritual. His motive is not so much the economic one of preventing the locking-up of wealth in the " dead hand," as the moral one of protecting society against the insidious lowering of the ethical and religious standard.

The discourse now proceeds to deal with legislation for the security of private property and trade, particularly with the regulations necessary to prevent dishonesty in buying and selling, and in executing or paying for " piece-work." Then follow regulations about wills, the guardianship of orphans, the conditions on which a son may be disinherited, and the enforcement of the claims of parents on their children. Penalties are enjoined for vendors of philtres and sorcerers, with the remark that the last-named offence

[1] We may suppose that the term of imprisonment would be longer for the two graver heresies. The length of the term and the rule of seclusion are meant, of course, to give full opportunity for a genuine conversion and to prevent the contamination of the rest of the community. Death is the penalty for a second conviction, because the offender is presumed to have shown himself " incurable," and death is better for such a man. On the composition of the " nocturnal council " see below.

[2] The simple atheist apparently runs no risk of this severer penalty, since his heresy is not one on which an hypocritical " priestcraft " can be grafted. It may be remarked here that by demanding a grading of prisons into (1) a house of detention for persons awaiting trial, (2) a house of correction for the reclaimable, (3) a house of punishment for the irreclaimable, Plato has anticipated an important reform never fully carried out in our own administration until quite recent times.

might be ignored in a society of perfectly rational persons, but must be treated as serious in a community where the current belief in the sorcerer's powers makes him mischievous (933*b*). We then have a paragraph dealing with larceny and robbery and another on the necessity of enforcing proper supervision of the insane and mentally deficient. Begging must be strictly suppressed, but it will be the duty of the State to see that no one, not even a slave, who is unemployed through no fault of his own is allowed to starve (936*b*). Rules are laid down about the admission of evidence in courts of law and the penalties of perjury. Litigiousness, a common Athenian failing, should be checked by penalizing the vexatious prosecutor ; if his motive was gain, the penalty should be death.[1] The abuse of the profession of λογογράφος is to be met by making the σύνδικος in a vexatious suit liable to the same penalties as his principal (938*a–c*).

These matters of private law must not detain us here, though Plato's treatment of them has the double interest of being founded largely on Attic practice, which he is trying to amend where it seems defective, and of having exercised a considerable indirect influence on the development of Roman law.[2] With Book XII. we return to the sphere of public law and the law of the constitution. Peculation or embezzlement of the public funds, an offence regularly charged on every Attic politician by his enemies, is unpardonable and in a citizen must always be visited with death, irrespective of the magnitude of his defalcation (942*a*). In military matters everything depends on discipline and strict fidelity to orders ; this must therefore be enforced in all the exercises which have been enjoined as the standing military training. Cowardice in the face of the enemy is to be punished by loss of all citizen-rights as well as by a heavy fine (944*e*–945*a*).

To ensure that the magistrates do their duty, Plato adopts the Attic practice of requiring every magistrate at the end of his term of office to submit to a εὔθυνα or audit, and gives special care to the appointment of the board of *corregidors* (εὔθυνοι) charged with the holding of the audit. The members of the board must be over 50 years old, and are to be chosen by the following method. There is a vote by universal suffrage, each citizen voting for only one candidate. This process is to be repeated until the number of names not eliminated is reduced to three. Twelve such officials are to be appointed in the first instance. As soon as the three oldest members of the board reach the age of 75 they retire, and in future there will be an annual election of three new

---

[1] The severe penalty is due to the heinousness of the attempt to make the court of justice itself accessory to the infliction of a wrong. The abuses Plato has in view are specifically Athenian, and would not be likely to be common in the sort of society for which he is ostensibly legislating.

[2] See Burnet, *Greek Philosophy, Part I.*, p. 304. The Academy was the first permanent and organized school of law as well as of mathematics. The two studies are really connected by the importance for both of " clear and distinct ideas."

members (946c).[1] Arrangements are made, however, for an appeal against the findings of the board, and any member whose action is quashed is to lose his post (948a). This board of *corregidors* is the highest ordinary court of justice, and it is interesting to see that Plato provides for appeals from its verdicts.

It would be inconsistent with the whole spirit of the legislation to permit citizens to withdraw themselves from the life of the State at their choice. Travel abroad must therefore always receive the sanction of the authorities, and this sanction will only be given in the case of persons over 40 (950d). It is desirable that older men of sound character should visit other States with a view to learning how the customs of our own society may be improved by judicious imitation of those of others. The traveller should, on his return, make a report on his observations to the " nocturnal council," a sort of extraordinary Committee of Public Safety, which is to be in perpetual session and is charged with a general supervision over the public welfare. We have heard of this body before in connexion with the proceedings against heresy, and are now told how it is constituted. Its members are the εὔθυνοι,[2] the ten senior νομοφύλακες, the minister and ex-ministers of Education, and ten co-opted younger men between the ages of 30 and 40. It gets its name from the regulation that its daily sessions are to be held before daybreak. One of its chief functions is to foster sound scientific research (952a). There will be a similar careful control of the temporary admission of foreign visitors to our own community. Special encouragement will be given to responsible persons from abroad whose object is to impart or acquire lessons in true statesmanship. They will be honoured " guests of the nation " (953d).

It is not enough to have made a good constitution and code for our society ; there is need for constant vigilance to preserve our institutions from degeneration (960d). This vigilance will be exercised by the " nocturnal council," which may fairly be called the " brain " of our whole system (961d). To discharge its functions it will need to have a thorough understanding of the end to which social life is directed, the development of " goodness " in all its four great forms. This means that its members will require very much more in the way of education than anything we have yet provided (965b). If they are really to understand what goodness is, they must be able to " see the one in the many " (965c), to appreciate and realize the great truth of the unity of all virtues (*ibid. d–e*). In fact, they must have a genuine knowledge of God and the ways of

----

[1] It is clear that the details of the plan would need more adjustment before it would work in practice. Perhaps it is tacitly assumed that most of the original twelve εὔθυνοι would be nearer 75 than 50, and that the three oldest retire in each subsequent year.

[2] The actual words are (951d) τῶν ἱερέων τῶν τὰ ἀριστεῖα εἰληφότων ; that this means the εὔθυνοι is shown by comparison with 947a. In the recapitulation at 961a–b the composition of the council is apparently slightly different. The two passages would, no doubt, have been better adjusted on a final revision of the text.

God (966c) ; they must not be content, as the average citizen may be, with a mere faith based on the tradition of the society (*ib.*). (In other words, they must thoroughly understand the natural theology already laid down in Book X.). We have seen that scientific astronomy, with its doctrine of the regularity and order of the celestial motions, is a chief foundation of the whole Platonic *apologia* for an ethical Theism. Hence a thorough knowledge of astronomy will be indispensable for the men who are the intellect of the State. It is a common, but wholly mistaken, opinion that such science makes men " infidels." When astronomical knowledge is combined with insight into the true nature of the soul as the one source of movement, it leads direct to piety. Hence no one will be qualified to serve on the nocturnal council unless he is a trained mathematician and astronomer and has also rightly grasped the principle of the causal priority of soul in the scheme of things. There remains the task of determining what other studies are implicitly demanded by our programme (966c–969d).

It is sometimes said that in the *Laws* astronomy has taken the place formerly given to dialectic as the supreme science, and that this indicates a growing uncertainty in Plato's own mind about the possibility of metaphysics. This is a complete misinterpretation of the concluding section of the *Laws*. The intellectual quality demanded in the members of the supreme council, that they should be able to see the " one in the many " is precisely the character always ascribed in the dialogues to the dialectician. And we note that astronomical science is only one-half of the qualification laid down. It must be accompanied by a right understanding of the doctrine of the place of ψυχή in the universe, the doctrine which, more than any other, lies at the root of Platonic metaphysics. Though the name " dialectic " is not used, the demand for the thing remains unabated.[1]

THE *EPINOMIS*.—There is no real division between the *Epinomis* and the *Laws*, and the former is sometimes actually quoted by later writers as the " thirteenth " book of the *Laws*, though the *Epinomis* was already reckoned as a distinct work by Aristophanes of Byzantium.[2] There is no real ancient evidence against the authenticity of the dialogue. Diogenes Laertius (iii. 1, 37) says that " some " ascribed it to the Academic Philippus of Opus, but, as he has just told the story that Philippus " transcribed " the *Laws* " from the wax," he presumably only means that he was said to have done the same for the *Epinomis*. Proclus, who disliked the work, wished to reject it, but, as he merely offers two very bad arguments for his view, he presumably knew of no Academic tradition

---

[1] The *name* is avoided, presumably, as specially characteristic of Socrates, who is absent from the dialogue. The word is carefully avoided also in the *Timaeus* for the same reason.

[2] He made the (spurious) *Minos*, the *Laws*, and the *Epinomis* one of his " trilogies " (Diog. Laert. iii. 1, 62).

in its favour.[1] I can detect no linguistic difference whatever between the style of *Epinomis* and *Laws*, and the very fact that the *Laws* have manifestly not received even the trifling editorial revision which would have removed small verbal inaccuracies and contradictions makes it incredible to me that Plato's immediate disciples should have issued as his the work of one of themselves. Hence I am confident that the current suspicion of the dialogue is no more than a prejudice really due to the now exploded early nineteenth-century attacks on the genuineness of the *Laws* themselves.[2] In any case, we have to recognize that the work was known to Aristotle, who has a curious allusion to it at *Metaphysics* 1073b 9.[3] I feel justified, therefore, in regarding the *Epinomis* as Plato's, and holding that it was intended as an integral part of the *magnum opus* of his last years.

The immediate purpose of the dialogue is to discuss the question left unanswered in *Laws* xii., of the complete scientific curriculum necessary for the members of the " nocturnal council ": What studies will lead to σοφία (973b) ? We must recognize that σοφία, in any case, is only attainable by a select few, and with difficulty (973c ff.), and that most of the so-called ἐπιστῆμαι do not help us to it (974d). Thus we may exclude all the arts and sciences which simply contribute to material civilization or to amusement (974e–975d), as well as those of war, medicine, navigation, and rhetoric, and still more unhesitatingly the mere art of acquiring and retaining multifarious information, which many confuse with σοφία (975e–976c). We ought to give the name σοφία only to studies which make a man a wise and good citizen, capable of exercising or obeying righteous rule. Now there is a branch of science which, more than any others, has this tendency and may be said to be a gift of a god to man, being in fact the gift of Heaven (οὐρανός) itself. This gift is the knowledge of *number*, which brings all other good things

---

[1] His arguments are given in the *Prolegomena to the Philosophy of Plato*, apparently by Olympiodorus (*Platonis Opera*, C. F. Hermann, vi. 218). They are (1) that Plato would not have gone on to write another dialogue, leaving the *Laws* unrevised, (2) that motion from W. to E. is called in the *Epinomis* " to the right " (*Epin.* 987b), whereas in the dialogues (*Timaeus*, 36c) it is called " to the left." But (1) assumes that the *Epinomis* is really meant to be " another dialogue," and (2) overlooks the point that the *Laws* use the same language as the *Epinomis* (760d 2). The really significant thing is that Proclus makes no appeal to testimony.

[2] See the good defence of the *Epinomis* in Raeder, *Platons philosophische Entwickelung*, 413 ff. Stenzel (*Zahl und Gestalt*, 103 n. 4) rightly declines to commit himself to rejection. The " demonstration " of the spuriousness of the *Epinomis* by F. Müller (*Stilistische Untersuchung der Epinomis des Philippos von Opus*, 1927) leaves me still unconvinced.

[3] It is said there that it is obvious τοῖς καὶ μετρίως ἡμμένοις, that the motions of the planets are composite, a fairly clear retort to *Epin.* 987b 9, where the theory that the " diurnal revolution " is a component of the planetary orbits is said to be " what might seem true " ἀνθρώποις ὀλίγα τούτων εἰδόσιν. Jaeger (*Aristoteles*, 146, 153 ff.) has called attention to the connexion between the *Epinomis* and Aristotle's περὶ φιλοσοφίας, but regards the former as an Academic rejoinder to the latter.

along with itself (977*b*).[1] Without knowledge of number we should be unintelligent and unmoral (977*c–e*). How divine a thing it is we see from the consideration that where there is number there is order; where there is no number, there is nothing but confusion, formlessness, disorder (977*e*–978*b*). To be able to count is the prerogative which marks men off from the animals. We learn to count up to fifteen by simply studying the daily changes in the face of the moon as she rounds to the full; a much bigger problem is set us when we go on to compare the period of the moon with that of the sun, as the agriculturist must. In our own recent discussion it was easy enough to see that a man ought to have goodness of soul, as well as of body, and that to have this he must be " wise." The difficult question was what kind of knowledge this all-important " wisdom " is. What we have just said suggests the answer (978*b*–979*d*).

Perhaps we may not discover a single " wisdom " which covers the whole ground. In that case, we must try to enumerate the various branches of wisdom and say what they are (980*a*). We may go back to our thought that the best way a man can spend his life is to spend it in praising and honouring God. Let us then, to the praise of God, construct an improved " theogony," holding fast to the natural theology we have laid down, and particularly to the principle of the causal priority of soul over body (980*b*–981*b*). An " animal," we know, is a soul conjoined with a body. There are five regular solids, and we may recognize five corresponding forms of body—earth, water, air, fire, and aether [2]—and five corresponding kinds of animal, each with its special habitat. The body of each kind of animal is a compound in which the " element " that forms its habitat is predominant. Hence the two most conspicuously visible classes of living beings are those which live on the earth, of whom man specially interests us, and those which have bodies made chiefly of fire and are gods, the stars and planets. Their bodies are more beautiful than ours, and more lasting, being either deathless or of age-long vitality. A comparison of the restless and disorderly movements of man with the majestically orderly movements of the heavenly bodies is enough to show that their souls equally surpass man's in intelligence. If they, unlike us, never deviate from one path, it is because their motion exhibits the necessity imposed by rational pursuit of the best (982*b*). Their real bulk, as science can demonstrate, is enormous, and there is

---

[1] Number is the gift of " Uranus," because, as Plato holds, the science of it has been developed in the interest of learning to number and compute days, months, and years. Cf. *Timaeus*, 38*c*, 39*b*.

[2] The corpuscular theory of the *Timaeus* is here implied, with the addition that, to get something to correspond with the dodecahedron, the αἰθήρ, the clear blue of the upper air, is recognized as a fifth " body." This πεμπτὸν σῶμα (whence the name *quinta essentia*) is identical with Aristotle's πρῶτον σῶμα, or " celestial matter." But, unlike Aristotle, Plato does not regard it as the "matter" of the heavenly bodies; they are made mainly of fire, as *Timaeus* had taught.

only one answer to the question how such masses can be made to revolve endlessly in the same orbits ; it is that the masses are alive, and that it is God who has conjoined their ψυχαί with these vast bodies (983*b–e*). Either they are themselves gods, or they are images of gods wrought by the gods themselves (984*a*), and therefore more to be held in honour than any images of man's making. We may suppose that the intervening regions of aether, air, water, are also inhabited by appropriate denizens. A man may give what account he pleases of Zeus and Hera and the rest of the traditional pantheon, but we must insist on the superior dignity of the visible gods, the heavenly bodies. Air and aether will have denizens with transparent bodies and therefore invisible to us ; we may suppose that they are a hierarchy of " spirits " (δαίμονες), who act as unseen intermediaries between gods and men, favouring the good and warring against the bad (984*d*–985*b*). There may be similar semi-divine denizens of the water of whom men get occasional glimpses. The current worships have been largely prompted by real or imagined appearances of such beings, and a wise law-giver will not wantonly interfere with them. Men cannot have real knowledge about such things (985*d*). But the neglect of Greeks to pay proper honour to the heavenly bodies, the gods whom we all do see, is quite inexcusable. They should be honoured not merely by feasts of the Calendar, but by setting ourselves to get a scientific knowledge of their motions and periods (985*e*).[1]

This means that we must master the science of the revolutions of the stars and planets. At present we have not so much as names for the planets, though they are called the stars of several gods, a nomenclature which has come to us from Syria (986*e*–987*d*).[2] It is the general rule that whatever Greeks borrow from barbarians they improve upon (987*e*). Every man who is a Greek should therefore recognize the duty of prosecuting astronomy in a scientific spirit, and cast off the superstitious fear of prying into divine matters. God knows our ignorance and desires to teach us (987*d*–988*e*).

The study we need to lead us to true piety, the greatest of the virtues, is thus astronomy, knowledge of the true orbits and periods of the heavenly bodies, pursued in the spirit of pure science, not in that of Hesiod's farmer's calendar (990*a*). But since such a study is concerned with the difficult task of the computation of the relative periods of sun, moon, and planets (and thus has to reckon with

[1] The irony of the whole passage about the supposed denizens of aether, air, and water and the popular cults of such beings must not be overlooked. We have been told (980*c*) that the whole account is a " theogony," though, as is added at 988*c*, a less objectionable one than those of the old poets, and that knowledge on such matters is impossible. All that is really serious is the insistence on the necessity of giving the first place in the popular cult to the heavenly bodies and recognizing the study of astronomy as the right way to worship them. The rest is a concession to the maxim that harmless popular rites are not to be disturbed. Timaeus had taken the same line (*supra*, p. 452).

[2] The names " star of Aphrodite," " of Ares," " of Zeus," " of Cronus," from which our designations are derived, appear for the first time in literature in this passage. " Star of Hermes " is first found in *Timaeus*, 38*d*.

highly complicated arithmetical problems), it must have as its foundation a thoroughly scientific theory of number. This includes not only a scientific doctrine of whole numbers ("the odd and even," 990c), but two other studies, commonly called by the misleading names geometry and stereometry. Geometry is really arithmetic, a study of *numbers* " which are in themselves dissimilar, but are assimilated by reference to surfaces," and stereometry is similarly the study of another class of numbers which become similar when raised to the third power. Also we need to study for its physical importance the theory of progressions. The geometrical series 1, 2, 4, 8 reveals to us the principle on which the magnitude of length, area, and volume are interconnected; in the arithmetical progression 6, 9, 12 and the harmonic progression 6, 8, 12 we have the secret of music, since the two means 9 and 8 correspond to the two great intervals within the octave, the fifth and the fourth. Thus we might say that consideration of the ratio 2 : 1, its powers, and the means between its terms, discloses the supreme secret of nature (990a–991b). And besides we must add to this study of a scientific arithmetic which has been extended to cover geometry plane and solid, as the completion of the whole curriculum, insight into the absolute unity of principle which runs through the whole of exact science and makes it one (991c–e).[1] (Thus once more dialectic, the synoptic apprehension of the principles which pervade all science and the whole of the *scibile*, reappears as the foundation of statesmanship.)

Without this scientific knowledge, a city will never be governed with true statesmanship, and human life will never be truly happy. The wisest man is the man who has attained all this knowledge; we may feel confident that when death translates him from the sensible region, he will finally achieve the complete unification of the self, and his lot, wherever it may be cast, will be truly blessed. As we said before, the attainment is only possible for the few, but we must insist that our supreme governors at least shall devote themselves to it (992a–d). Thus the *Epinomis* ends by the unqualified reassertion of the old demand that statesmanship and science shall be combined in the same persons.

[1] The text of 990c 5–991b 4, the most important mathematical passage in the Platonic *corpus*, is unfortunately uncertain, in part probably corrupted, in part also possibly never reduced to grammatical form by the writer, but the sense is clear. The point of chief significance is the revolutionary demand that quadratic and cubic " surds " shall be recognized as *numbers* in opposition to the traditional view that there are "irrational" magnitudes (lengths, areas, volumes), but no " irrational " numbers. The meaning of the rest is that the succession of the " powers " 2^1, 2^2, 2^3, is the most elementary example of the principle that similar areas have the duplicate and similar volumes the triplicate ratios of the corresponding " sides," and that the ratios corresponding to the fourth and fifth in the scale respectively, the ἐπίτριτος and ἡμιόλιος λόγος, are also the harmonic and arithmetic means between 1 and 2 (Plato selects 6 and 12 as surrogates for 1 and 2 in this illustration because he wishes the two " means " to be whole numbers.) Stenzel comes near explaining the passage correctly (*Zahl u. Gestalt*, 98 ff.).

See further :

BURNET.—*Greek Philosophy, Part I.*, 301–312 *al.*
RITTER, C.—*Platon*, ii. 657–796 *al.* ; *Platons Gesetze, Kommentar zum griechischen Text* (Leipzig, 1896) ; *Platos Gesetze, Darstellung des Inhalts* (Leipzig, 1896).
A. E. TAYLOR.—*The Laws of Plato translated into English.* (London, 1934.)
RAEDER, H.—*Platons philosophische Entwickelung*, 395–419.
NATORP, P.—*Platons Ideenlehre*, 358–365.
BARKER, E.—*Greek Political Theory : Plato and his Predecessors*, 292–380.
JAEGER, W.—*Aristoteles*, 125–170.
MÜLLER, F.—*Statistische Untersuchung der Epinomis des Philippos von Opus* (1927).
HARWARD, J.—*The Epinomis of Plato.* Translated with *Introduction and Notes.* (Oxford, 1928.)
And for the problems presented by the *Epistles :*
FRIEDLÄNDER, P.—*Platon : Eidos, Paideia, Dialogos* (1928).
EGERMANN, FR.—*Die platonischen Briefe VII und VIII*, (Vienna, 1928.)
SOUILHÉ, J.—*Platon, Lettres.* (Paris, 1926.)
NOVOTNÝ, F.—*Platonis Epistulae.* (Brno, 1930.)
HARWARD, J.—*The Platonic Epistles.* (Cambridge, 1932.)

CHAPTER XIX

PLATO IN THE ACADEMY—FORMS AND NUMBERS

TO us Plato is first and foremost a great writer, but from his own point of view, books and the study of them are a secondary interest with the "philosopher"; what counts as supreme is a life spent in the organized prosecution of discovery (τὸ συζῆν). There can be no doubt that Plato thought his work as the organizer of the Academy much more important than the writing of dialogues. Since Aristotle commonly refers to the teaching given in the Academy as Plato's "unwritten doctrine" (ἄγραφα δόγματα), we may be reasonably sure that Plato did not even prepare a MS. of his discourses. This explains why there were several different versions in the next generation of the famous lecture on "the Good," which seems to have contained Plato's most explicit account of his own philosophy. We are told that several of the hearers, including Aristotle, Xenocrates, and Heraclides of Pontus, all published their notes of it, and the obvious implication is that there was no "author's MS." to publish. Consequently we have to discover Plato's ultimate metaphysical positions indirectly from references to them in Aristotle, supplemented by occasional brief excerpts, preserved by later Aristotelian commentators, from the statements of Academic contemporaries of Aristotle, like Xenocrates and Hermodorus. This creates a serious difficulty. When it is a mere question of what Plato *said*, the testimony of Aristotle is surely unimpeachable; but when we go on to ask what Plato *meant*, the case is different. Aristotle's references are all polemical, and Aristotle is a controversialist who is not unduly anxious to be "sympathetic." Unfortunately, too, mathematics, the science specially important for its influence on Plato's thought, is the one science where Aristotle shows himself least at home. Thus there is always the possibility that his criticisms may rest on misunderstanding. And the misunderstandings may not even originate with him. The criticism of Plato all through the *Metaphysics* seems to be subsidiary to Aristotle's standing polemic against Xenocrates, the contemporary head of the Academy. Hence it is possible that much of the criticism of *Metaphysics* M–N, the most sustained anti-Academic polemic in Aristotle, may be directed rather against Academic misinterpretation of Plato than against Plato himself.

In a necessarily brief statement our safest course is to deal only with views expressly attributed by Aristotle to Plato, and with them only so far as their meaning seems to be beyond reasonable doubt. This is, at any rate, all I can attempt in the space at my disposal. But we must carefully avoid the nineteenth-century mistake of treating the statements described by Aristotle under the name of the "doctrine" (πραγματεία) of Plato as a sort of senile dotage. Aristotle definitely identifies Platonism with these doctrines and never even hints that he knew of any other Platonism, though he does occasionally remark that the dialogues differ from the "unwritten" discourses. It seems to follow that the theories called Plato's by Aristotle must have been formulated as early as 367 B.C., the year of Aristotle's entry into the Academy, and, quite possibly, even earlier.

When we turn to these Aristotelian statements we find that, for the most part, they amount to a version of the theory of forms with a very individual character, and of a much more developed type than anything the dialogues have ascribed to Socrates. There are also one or two other notices of specific peculiarities of Plato's doctrines, all concerned with points of mathematics, and it is with some of these I propose to begin, as they may help us to understand the point of view from which the doctrine of forms as known to Aristotle was formulated.

We must remember that though mathematics was by no means the only science cultivated in the Academy, it was that which appealed most to Plato himself, and that in which the Academy exercised the most thoroughgoing influence on later developments. All the chief writers of geometrical textbooks known to us between the foundation of the Academy and the rise of the scientific schools of Alexandria belong to the Academy. In Plato's own lifetime, Theaetetus had completed the edifice of elementary solid geometry, by discovering the inscription of the octahedron and icosahedron in the sphere. He and Eudoxus and others had laid the foundations of the doctrine of quadratic surds as worked out in the tenth book of Euclid's *Elements*; Eudoxus had invented the method of approximating to the lengths and areas of curves by exhaustion (the ancient equivalent of the Integral Calculus), and had recast the whole doctrine of ratio and proportion in the form in which we now have it in Euclid's fifth book, for the purpose of making it applicable to "incommensurables." We naturally expect to find traces in Plato's doctrine of this special preoccupation with the philosophy of mathematics which is characteristic of the work of the school.[1]

To understand the motives which were prompting the Academy to a reconstruction of the philosophy of mathematics, we must go

[1] For an account of the Academic work in mathematics I may refer the reader to any of the standard works on the history of mathematics, *e.g.* Zeuthen, *Histoire des mathématiques dans l'antiquité et le moyen âge* (Fr. tr., Paris, 1902), or, for a still briefer account, Heiberg, *Mathematics in Classical Antiquity* (Eng. tr., Oxford, 1922). The ancient notices are chiefly preserved in the second prologue to Proclus' *Commentary on Euclid* i., and in the scholia to Euclid.

back to the age of Zeno. In the Pythagorean mathematics of the fifth century there were two serious logical flaws. One was that in treating geometry as an application of arithmetic, the Pythagoreans had made the point correspond to the number 1, as is indicated in the traditional definition of the point, often mentioned by Aristotle, that it is μονὰς ἔχουσα θέσιν, "a 1 with position." The identification implies the view that a point is a minimum volume, and was ruined by Zeno's acute argumentation from the possibility of unending bisection of the straight line and the impossibility of making a line longer or a volume bigger by adding a point to it. There are just two ways of meeting the difficulty : one is to evade it, by severing geometry from its dependence on arithmetic, as Euclid does; the other is that actually hinted at by Zeno's own language and definitely adopted by modern philosophical mathematicians, of making the point correspond to 0 and regarding 0, not 1, as the first of the integers.[1] It was towards this view that Plato was feeling his way, as we shall see immediately. The other great trouble was the discovery that there are "incommensurables" or "surds," e.g. that the ratio of the length of the side of a square to its diagonal is not that of "integer to integer." Here, again, two ways of meeting a difficulty fatal to the old philosophy of mathematics as it stood are possible. One is again to surrender the parallelism between geometry and arithmetic by admitting the existence of surd geometrical magnitudes, but denying that there are "surd" numbers. This is the position taken by Aristotle in express words and tacitly by later mathematicians like Euclid, who always represents an "incommensurable" by a line or an area. The other is that of modern rationalistic mathematics, to revise the conception of number itself, so that it becomes possible to define "irrational" numbers of various kinds and to formulate laws for their addition and multiplication in terms of the already known arithmetic of integers. The problem has only been satisfactorily solved in the work of the last half-century, but, as we saw in dealing with the *Epinomis*, this was the line which already commended itself to Plato. Geometry and "stereometry" are, according to him, really the arithmetic of the quadratic and cubic "surds," as plane geometry has been said in our own time to be simply the "algebra of complex numbers." In this way the parallelism of geometry with arithmetic is preserved by a revised and enlarged conception of arithmetic itself.[2]

With these considerations in mind, we can readily understand certain statements which Aristotle makes about mathematical views of Plato. There are three such statements which we may at once elucidate. (*a*) Plato stated that the "point" was a

[1] Cf. the definition of the integer-series in Frege's *Grundgesetze der Arithmetik* which is, put into words, "the integers are the successors of 0."

[2] For a real comprehension of Plato's thought it is indispensable to have a grasp of the modern logic of arithmetic. I would recommend as sufficient (but also necessary) such an exposition as that given in chap. i. (Real Variables) of Professor G. H. Hardy's *Pure Mathematics*.

" fiction of the geometers," and spoke, instead, of the " starting-point of the line " (*Met*. A 992*a* 20). This means, of course, that Plato rejected the conception of a point as a minimum of volume, or " unit." It has no magnitude of its own but is " the beginning " of the straight line which has such a magnitude (its length). In other words, what corresponds in arithmetic to the point is not 1 but 0, if only Greek arithmeticians had possessed a word or symbol for 0. The underlying thought is that which reappears in later Greek Platonists when they speak of a line as the " fluxion " (ῥύσις) of a point, in the very terminology Newton was later to introduce into English. We are on the track of the ideas and terminology of the inventors of what we call the Differential Calculus. It is true, of course, that this notion of an " infinitesimal " which is not quite nothing nor quite something, but a nothing in the act of turning into something, involves a logical paradox and that it has only been finally disposed of by the purification of mathematical logic, which has eliminated " infinitesimals " from the so-called Infinitesimal Calculus. But the Calculus had to be there first before its purification from bad logic could be possible, and it is hard to see how it could ever have been originated without this defective but useful conception. (*b*) (*Met. ibid.* 22) Plato " often used to assume his indivisible lines " (πολλάκις ἐτίθει τὰς ἀτόμους γραμμάς). Aristotle, who apparently distinguishes this point from the one he has just mentioned, does not explain its meaning. In the textually badly corrupt Peripatetic tract *de Lineis insecabilibus*, which appears to be a polemic of an Aristotelian of the first genera-tion against Xenocrates, the " indivisible line " is regarded as a minimum length, and it is urged that there are insuperable geo-metrical difficulties about such a conception, as, in fact, there are. What Plato may have meant by the expression we can only con-jecture. As a conjecture I offer the suggestion that his intention is precisely to deny the conception attributed to some Academic, apparently Xenocrates, by the Peripatetic tract. A line, however short, is " indivisible " in the sense that you cannot divide it into elements which are not themselves lines—in other words, it is a " continuum." The point makes a straight or curved line not by addition or summation, but by " flowing " ; a straight or other line is not made of points in the way in which a wall is made of bricks laid end to end.[1] (*c*) Plato said that " there is a first 2 and a first 3, and the numbers are not addible to one another " (*Met.* M 1083*a* 32, the one statement about numbers which is definitely attributed to Plato by name in the last two books of the *Metaphysics*). A similar point is made about the Academy gener-ally in the *Ethics* (*E.N.* 1096*a* 17 ff.), where we are told that they held that there is no form (ἰδέα) of number, because " in numbers

---

[1] Cf. the observations of Stenzel, *Zahl u. Gestalt*, 89 ff. The technical expressions ῥεῖν, ῥύσις, the source of Newton's language about " fluents " and their " fluxions," come from the accounts of the doctrine in the Aristo-telian commentators and were presumably coined by the Academy.

there is a before and an after," *i.e.* because numbers form a *series*. The meaning of these statements seems not to have been clear to Aristotle, but is manifest to anyone who has learned to think of number *en mathématicien*. The sense is that the series of numbers is not made by adding " units " together. *E.g.* we say that $3+1=4$, but we do not mean that 3 is three " units " or that 4 is 3 *and* 1 ; 4 is not four 1's, or a 3 and a 1, it is *one* 4. What we really *add* together is not numbers but aggregates or collections. Thus it is true that if you have a group of *n* things and another group of *m* things, and form the two into one group, the new group contains $m+n$ things, but it is not true that the *number* $m+n$ contains a number *m* and a number *n*. The importance of this view is that it leads to revision of the whole conception of number. The fifth-century theory, still represented by Euclid's definition of ἀριθμός (*Elements* vii. def. 2) is that a " number " is πλῆθος μονάδων, a " collection of 1's." On the new view, the only really sound one, no number is a " collection " ; the statement that $3=2+1$, which is the definition of 3, does not mean that 3 is " a 2 and a 1," but that 3 is the term of the integer-series which comes " next after " 2.

This explains why there is no form of number. The reason is that each " number " is itself a form, as was really implied in the *Phaedo* itself when Socrates spoke of " the number 2 " and " the number 3 " as instances of what he meant by a form. Hence the ordered series of integers is not *a* form, it is a series of forms. The point may be grasped if we remember that in our own philosophy of mathematics we do not find it possible to define " number " or even " integer " ; all that we can do is to define the *series* of integers or the series, *e.g.*, of " real " numbers, and to define individual numbers. I can define " the integer series " as a series of a certain type with a certain first term, and I can define " the integer " $n+1$ by saying that it is the number of that series which is next after *n*, but I cannot really define " integer." Aristotle is never tired of arguing against Plato that there is no number except what Aristotle calls " mathematical " number, or alternatively " number made of 1's " (μοναδικὸς ἀριθμός) ; but the simple truth is that *no* " number " is " made of 1's," and that it is precisely what Aristotle calls " mathematical " number which has no existence except in his imagination. Plato may well have been led to this denial that numbers are " addible " by his recog-nition that " surds " like $\sqrt{2}$, $\sqrt[3]{2}$, must be admitted into arithmetic as numbers, since it is evident that no process of " adding 1 to 1 " could ever yield such numbers as these.[1] Thus this doctrine, also, may well be connected with the fact that the " real " numbers form a *continuum*. But it is important to be clear on the point that the principle that number is not really generated by addition of 1's

[1] This is the consideration made prominent in the treatment of the doctrine by M. Milhaud in *Les Philosophes-géomètres de la Grèce*, a work really indispensable to the student of Plato. But, as we shall see immediately, it is not the whole, nor the most important part, of Plato's doctrine.

applies equally to the numbers of the integer-series, which is not a continuum.

This brings us to the consideration of Aristotle's account of Plato's theory of forms. According to the *Metaphysics*,[1] Plato actually called the forms numbers, and maintained that each form or number has two constituents, the One, which Aristotle regards as the formal constituent, and something called the " great-and-small " or "the indeterminate duality " (ἀόριστος δυάς), which Aristotle treats as a material constituent. In other words, a number is something which arises from the determination of a determinable, (the great-and-small), by the One. Since the forms are the causes of all other things, these constituents of the forms are the ultimate constituents of everything, and this is what is meant by the statement that other things " participate " in the forms.[2] Aristotle remarks on the theory that it is of the same type as the Pythagorean doctrine that "things are numbers," or are " imitations of numbers," but differs from that view by substituting the " duality " of the " great-and-small " for the " indefinite " (ἄπειρον) as one constituent of numbers, and also by maintaining that " mathematicals " (τὰ μαθηματικά) are intermediate between numbers and sensible things, whereas the Pythagoreans said that the numbers *are* the things.[3] He seems also to connect this theory with the special point in respect of which he holds Plato and the Pythagoreans inferior to Socrates, namely, that they " separated " (ἐχώρισαν) the " universals " or forms from " things " as Socrates had not done.[4]

It is plain from the explanations attempted by the later commentators on Aristotle that the chief source from which the doctrine alluded to in the *Metaphysics* was known in antiquity was the reports of the auditors of Plato's famous lecture on "the Good." As we do not possess these reports and cannot be sure how far the statements of Peripatetic commentators on Aristotle about them can be trusted, we need to be cautious in our interpretation. But there are certain points on which we can be reasonably certain. It is quite clear from the whole character of Aristotle's polemic against " ideal numbers," that the numbers which Plato declared

---

[1] *Met.* A 987b 18–25.

[2] The simple meaning of this is that, as we have been told by Timaeus, all the characters of " things " depend on the geometrical structure of their particles, and thus, in the end, on the structure of the " triangles " into which the faces of these particles can be resolved. And a triangle is determined again by three " numbers," those which give the lengths of its sides.

[3] *Met.* A 987b 25–28. Oddly enough, he does not mention the much more important point that the One is made by Plato the formal constituent in a number, whereas the Pythagoreans taught that " the unit " is the first *product* of the combination of *their* two constituent factors, πέρας and ἄπειρον, though he had correctly stated this doctrine just before, *Met.* A 986a 19.

[4] *Met.* M 1078b 30. Plato is not named in this passage, but a comparison of the criticism passed immediately below (1078b 34 ff.) with that made on Plato at A 990b 2 ff., shows that Aristotle regards the charge of making the " separation " as applicable to him.

to be forms are just the integers and nothing else, and also that the doctrine does not mean that it is denied that " man," " horse," and the like are forms, but that " the form of man " and the like are now held to be themselves in some sense " numbers." Hence Aristotle can raise the difficulty whether the " units " which make up the number which is the form of man or horse are the same as those which are found in the form of animal, or those of the form of man the same as those of the form of horse (*Met.* 1081a 9, 1082a 18, 1084a 13). It also looks as though Aristotle meant to ascribe to Plato, as well as to the Pythagoreans, the view that the integer-series is a succession of repetitions of the numbers up to 10, so that the Form-numbers would be, in a special sense, the first ten natural numbers. (*E.g. Met.* 1084a 12, though the allusion there might be rather to a theory of the Pythagoreans and Speusippus than to a personal view of Plato.) It seems clear, at any rate, that the key to the doctrine, if we could recover it, would be found in a theory of the character of the series of integers up to 10.

To some extent, at least, it seems possible to recover this key. We have to begin by understanding what is meant by speaking of one constituent of a number as the " great-and-small " and by calling this an " indeterminate duality." Even without the help of the commentators on Aristotle, the *Philebus* would enable us to give a reasonable answer to this question. We saw there that " that which admits of more and less indefinitely " was Plato's description of what we call a " continuum," though the number-series itself does not figure among the examples of continua given in the dialogue. This enables us to see at once why Plato spoke of what the Pythagoreans had called the " unlimited " (ἄπειρον) as a " great-and-small " or a " duality." It is a duality because it can be varied indefinitely in either of two directions. Probably the commentators are right in connecting this with the more specific view that you can equally reach plurality, starting from unity, by multiplication or by division, *e.g.* when you divide a given class regarded as a whole into sub-classes, you have two or more more determinate forms within the original γένος. This indicates a direct connexion between the theory of number ascribed to Plato by Aristotle and the preoccupation with the problem of the subdivision of forms in the later dialogues on which Stenzel has done well to insist, though he has allowed himself to neglect too much the specifically mathematical problem. We can also see, I think, why the other constituent of a number should be said to be "the one," and why the " unit " is no longer regarded, in Pythagorean fashion, as a " blend " of " limit " with the " unlimited," but as itself the "limit." Here, again, we have a point of contact with the theory of logical " division." As the *Philebus* had taught us, we may arrive at a " form " in either of two ways ; we may start with several different εἴδη as many and seek to reduce them to unity by showing that they are all special determinations of a more general " form," or again we may start with the more general " form " and discover more specific "forms" within it; whichever route we follow, we presuppose as already familiar the notions of a form and of forms in the plural. "A" and "some" will be ultimate indefinables.[1]

In the case of numbers it is easy to see how the conception, already implied in the *Epinomis*, of a "continuum" of "real" numbers leads to the Platonic formulas. If we wish to discover a number whose product by itself is 2, it is easy to show that we can make steady approximation to such a number by constructing the endless "continued fraction":

$$1 + \cfrac{1}{2 + \cfrac{1}{2 + \cfrac{1}{2 + \cfrac{1}{2 + \dots}}}}$$

By stopping off the fraction at successive stages, we get a number of values 1, $1 + \dfrac{1}{2}$, $1 + \dfrac{1}{2 + \dfrac{1}{2}}$, etc., with the following peculiarities. The values are alternatively less and greater than $\sqrt{2}$, and each value differs from $\sqrt{2}$ less than the preceding value; by carrying the fraction far enough, we can get a fraction a/b such that a^2/b^2 differs from 2 by less than any magnitude we please to assign. This is what we mean by saying that $\sqrt{2}$ is the limiting value to which the fraction "converges" when it is continued "to infinity." Now in forming the successive approximate values, or "convergents," we are making closer and closer approximation to the precise determination of an "infinite great-and-small." It is "infinite" because however many steps you have taken, you never reach a fraction which, when multiplied by itself, gives exactly 2 as the product, though you are getting nearer to such a result at each step. It is "great-and-small," because the successive approximations are alternatively too small and too large. $\sqrt{2}$ is, so to say, gradually pegged down between a "too much" and a "too little," which are coming closer together all the time. I choose this particular example because this method of finding the value of what we call $\sqrt{2}$ was pretty certainly known to Plato.[2]

[1] We must, of course, distinguish carefully between the notion of "a" and that of "the integer 1." The latter is definable exactly as any other integer is. 1 is the number of any group x which satisfies the conditions that (a) there is an a which is an x; (b) "b is an x" implies "b is identical with a." This distinction is not yet clearly recognized in the Platonic formula.

[2] The denominators and numerators of the successive "convergents" are the series called in Greek respectively the πλευρικοί and the διαμετρικοὶ ἀριθμοί. The rule for finding any number of them is given by Theon of Smyrna (p. 43–44, Hiller). The geometrical construction by which the rule was discovered is given by Proclus (*Comm. in Rempubl.* ii. 24, 27–29, Kroll). The source of both Theon and Proclus appears to be the Peripatetic Adrastus in his commentary on the *Timaeus* (Kroll, *op. cit.* ii. 393 ff.). Plato himself alludes to the πλευρικοί and διαμετρικοὶ ἀριθμοί at *Rep.* 546c 5.

The same point might be similarly illustrated by the definitions given by modern mathematicians of the "real numbers." The definitions are to a certain point arbitrary, but they all turn on the notion of a "section." *E.g.* we cannot find a rational fraction the "square" of which is exactly 2. But we *can* divide all rational fractions into two classes, those of which the "squares" are less than 2 and those of which the "squares" are not less than 2. We see at once that the first of these sets has no highest term, the second no lowest, and that no fraction can belong either to both sets or to neither set ; thus our "section" is unambiguous, *i.e.* every fraction falls into one and only one of the two sets thus constituted. We may then define the "square root of 2" either as this "section" itself, or, if we prefer it, as the set of "fractions whose squares are less (or, if we like, greater) than 2." Here again, the notion of a "section" of the rational fractions exhibits the Platonic characters. It involves a "duality," or "great-and-small," the two sets, one of which has all its terms less than, the other all greater than, a specified value, and the duality is "indefinite" because one of the sets has no highest term, the other no lowest. The section is a determination of the "great-and-small" of the fractions by the "one" precisely because it makes an unambiguous "cut" just where it does. Other cuts can be made at other places in the series, and each will define a different "real number."[1]

It is clear, however, that we have not yet exhausted the meaning of Plato's doctrine. From Aristotle's polemic we see that the Platonic analysis was not meant to apply simply to the case of the "irrationals" which Plato was the first to recognize as *numbers*. The theory also involves a doctrine of the structure of the integer-series itself, since it is clear that the numbers with which the forms are identified are, as Aristotle always assumes, the integers. The integers themselves, then, have the "great-and-small" and the "one" as their constituents. How is this to be understood?

---

[1] Cf. G. H. Hardy, *Pure Mathematics*[2], p. 14. The "rational fractions" are, to be sure, not a continuum, but they satisfy the only condition for a continuum known in Plato's time, that between any two a third can always be inserted. Stenzel rightly dwells on the connexion of the "duality" with "convergence," but misses the illustration from the πλευρικοί and διαμετρικοί ἀριθμοί (*Zahl u. Gestalt*, 59). The endlessness of the "continued fraction" makes it clear why the "great-and-small" was identified with the "non-being" of which we read in the *Sophistes* (Aristot. *Physics*, A 192a 6 ff.). The meaning of what is said about geometry, plane and solid, in the *Epinomis* will thus be, that the real scientific problem is to obtain a series of "approximations," within a "standard" which we can make as narrow as we please, to the various quadratic and cubic surds. In doing so, we are discovering the ratios of the "sides" or "edges" of the various regular polygons and solids to one another. We discover, *e.g.*, exactly how long—within a known "standard"—a line must be if the area of the square or volume of the cube on it is to be 2, 3, 5 . . . times a given area and volume; and since all rectilinear areas and volumes can be expressed as those of squares and cubes, this solves the question of the surveyor and the "stereometer." It is precisely with such metrical problems, relating to the "regular solids," that Euclid's Book XIII. is concerned, a safe indication of its Academic *provenance*.

The difficulty is that the integers do not form a continuum, even in the sense in which continuity means no more than infinite divisibility, *i.e.* the possibility of inserting a third term between any two given terms of the series. For each integer is "next after" another.

How, then, does Plato suppose the series of integers to be constructed? I doubt if the notices preserved to us enable us to answer the question finally. What is clear is that Plato rightly rejects the view retained by Aristotle, that an integer is a collection of "1's," and that the series is thus constructed by additions of 1 to itself. 2 is not "1 and 1" but "the number next after 1." (This ought to be plain from the simple consideration of the way in which we learn to count. We do not count, "one, one, one, one, . . ." but "one, two, three . . .") But when we ask in what way the "duality" comes in in constructing the series of integers, we are puzzled by the confusion which seems to run through Aristotle and his commentators between the "indeterminate duality" or "great-and-small" and the *number* 2. If it were only in the polemic of Aristotle that this confusion were found, we might conceivably dismiss it as a mere misunderstanding, but it appears to have occurred also in the Academic reports of Plato's doctrine. The complete study of the problem would require a long discussion of the mass of material collected and examined by M. Robin in his volume *La Théorie platonicienne*. Here it must be enough to remark that the following points seem to be quite certain. (1) The "dyad" was called δυοποιός, because it "doubles" everything it "lays hold of." There is no doubt that the "dyad" meant is the "great-and-small," but "it also seems clear that there is a confusion, perhaps from the very first, with the αὐτὸ ὃ ἔστι δυάς, the number 2, and that the function of the "dyad" within the integer-series is thought of as being to produce the series of "powers" of 2 by repeated multiplication, 1×2, 1×2×2, 1×2×2×2, and so forth (cf. *Epinomis* 991a 1–4).[1] (2) The "one," we are told, puts a stop to the "indeterminateness" of the "great-and-small" by "equalizing" or "stabilizing" it (τῷ ἰσάζειν).[2] This, I suggest, as my conjectural explanation of an obscure expression, means that each odd number is the arithmetical mean between the preceding and following even numbers, and so "halves their difference." Each odd number will be got by halving "the sum of two even" numbers. Thus the order of the "decade" will be, 1, 2, 4, 8; 3 (which equalizes 2 and 4); 6 (double of 3); 5, 7 (which "equalize" 4 and 6, and 6 and 8); 10 (double of 5); 9 (which equalizes 8 and 10).[3] Cp. Aristotle's

[1] Cf. Aristot. *Met.* 1084a 5, 1091a 12, 1082a 14, 987b 33.

[2] Plutarch, *de Anim. procreat.* 1012d, reporting the explanation of Xenocrates, ἐκ δὲ τούτων γένεσθαι τὸν ἀριθμὸν τοῦ ἑνὸς ὁρίζοντος τὸ πλῆθος, Aristot. *Met. M.* 1083b 23, 29, where the "unit" is said to arise from the "equalizing" of the "dyad" of the great-and-small.

[3] See Robin, *La Théorie platonicienne*, p. 449. The mathematical reader will see at once a certain analogy between this procedure and the "quadrilateral construction" of von Staudt.

use of the "arithmetical mean" as an "equalizer," *E.N.* 1132*a* 1 ff. If this was the construction, it must be pronounced very faulty. Not only does it involve the confusions of "a" with 1 and of "plurality" with 2, but it involves obtaining the terms of the series in an unnatural order and using more than one principle of construction where one is sufficient. (The one really satisfactory way of defining the integers is to proceed by "mathematical induction," *i.e.* to define each in terms of its immediate precursor. This is readily done in the following way. When we have defined the integer *n*, we can go on to define *n* + 1 by the statement that *n* + 1 is the number of members of a group satisfying the conditions (*a*) that it contains a group with *n* members, (*b*) that it contains a member *a* which is not a member of this group; (*c*) that it does not contain any member which is neither *a* nor a member of the group of *n* members already mentioned.)

If, as seems probable, Plato's conception has these defects, we must not be surprised. He probably started with the right conviction that what we should call the notion of a "section" is necessary for the definition of the "irrationals," and went on to extend the conception to cover the case of the integers. What could not be expected of the first thinker who had formed the notion of a "real" number is the recognition that integers, rational fractions, real numbers, do not form a single series, in other words that the "integer," 2, the "rational number" 2/1, and the "real number 2" are all distinct. In the logical construction of the types of number, we need three distinct steps: the rules for defining the successive integers, the derivation of the rational numbers from the integers, and the derivation of the "continuum" of the real numbers from the series of rational numbers. These, however, are matters on which mathematical philosophers have only reached clear comprehension in very recent times. The important point is that Plato should have grasped the necessity of enlarging the traditional conception of number and of strictly defining numbers of all kinds.[1]

What are the "mathematicals" which Plato distinguished from his numbers or forms? Aristotle tells us that they differ from forms in the fact that they are many, whereas the form is one, and from sensible things by being eternal (*Met.* A 987*b* 15). It is to be noted that he does not call them "mathematical numbers,"

[1] Stenzel, *Zahl u. Gestalt*, 31, gives a different construction, but without justifying it. I venture to think he has been misled by an anxiety to discover Plato's number theory directly in the *Philebus*, where it could not have been introduced without the dramatic absurdity of putting it into the mouth of Socrates. In the main, I hope I am in accord with Burnet, *Greek Philosophy, Part I.*, 320 ff. But I should say that I can make nothing of n. 2 to p. 320, which manifestly is a *non-sens*. It appears to be a *partially* correct explanation of something Aristotle tells us about the Pythagoreans, which has got into its present place by some inadvertence. How *can* "the one" be the terms of the series $\sqrt{2}, \sqrt{6}, \sqrt{12} \ldots$?

but τὰ μαθηματικά, and that he never appears to ascribe to *Plato* the recognition of "mathematical *number*." The meaning seems to me to be best shown by two passages in the Aristotelian *corpus*. At *Metaphysics* K 1059b 2 ff., it is made an objection to the theory of forms that just as the μαθηματικά are intermediate between the form and sensible things, so there ought to be—on the theory—something intermediate between such a form as man or horse and visible men and horses (though we see that there is not). This implies that the "mathematicals" are something quite familiar. I would couple with this *de Anima* A 404b 19, where we are told that in τὰ περὶ φιλοσοφίας λεγόμενα Plato said that the form of animal is composed of the one and "the first length, breadth, and depth." The form of animal is, according to the *Timaeus*, the archetype on which the sensible world is constructed, that is, it is the *res extensa*, the subject-matter of geometry, and Aristotle's meaning is thus that this *res extensa* is constituted by the three dimensions of length, breadth, and depth. These *correspond*, as the context of the passage in the *de Anima* makes clear, to the numbers 2, 3, 4 (the line being determined by two points, the plane by three, three-dimensional space by four). Thus Plato's construction recalls the Pythagorean tetractys of the numbers 1, 2, 3, 4. But he spoke not of numbers, but of the first "length, breadth, depth." This seems to mean that though, as the *Epinomis* says, plane and solid geometry may be identified with the study of certain kinds of number, lengths, areas, volumes are not identical with numbers. The study of number provides the key to all these relations, and yet they are not themselves numbers, and the significance of number is not exhausted by its geometrical applications.

So we, too, are familiar with analytical geometry in which we study the properties of curves and surfaces by means of numerical equations. All the properties of the curves and surfaces can be discovered from these equations, but the application of equations is not confined to geometry or geometrical physics ; the same methods, for example, play a prominent part in the study of economics, as when we plot out curves to show the effects of modifications of duties on the " volume " of foreign trade. In a word, I take it, the " mathematicals " are what the geometer studies.

We may now perhaps be in a position to see what is meant by the statement that the constituents of the forms are the constituents of everything. The things of the sensible world, as we have learned from the *Philebus*, are one and all in " becoming " ; they are events or processes tending to the realization of a definite law and this law, Plato thinks, can be expressed in numerical form. Because these things are always " in the making," they do not exhibit permanent and absolute conformity to law of structure ; if once they were " made " and finished, they would be the perfect embodiment of law of structure. And because the stuff of things is extension itself, the law thus realized would be geometrical and therefore, as we should say, be expressible in the form of an equation or equations. This is what Plato means at bottom in his own philosophy by the " participation " of the sensible in forms and by the doctrine that the στοιχεῖα of number are the στοιχεῖα of everything. (I abstain from commenting on the further numerous passages in Aristotle where the question of the relation of the ἀρχαί of geometry to those of arithmetic is raised, since these seem to form part of the polemic against Speusippus and Xenocrates, and it is not clear to me how far any of the views canvassed are meant to be directly ascribed to Plato.)

Aristotle seems, as I said, to connect his complaint about the Academic " separation " (χωρισμός) between forms and sensible things specially with the doctrine we have just been discussing. He is commonly taken to mean no more than that the Platonic form is a sort of " double " of the sensible thing, supposed to be in some " intelligible world," wholly sundered from the real world of actual life. It is hard to suppose that he could put such an interpretation on a theory which according to himself makes the στοιχεῖα of number the στοιχεῖα of everything. Hence I think Stenzel[1] is on the right track in looking for a more definite meaning in the Aristotelian criticism, and that he has rightly indicated the direction in which we should look. As he points out, one of Aristotle's chief difficulties about the " numbers " is that he holds that if " animal " is one number and " man " is another, we have to face the question whether the " units " in " animal " are part of the " units " which constitute " man " or not ; (e.g. if you said " animal " is 2, " man " is 4, since $2 \times 2 = 4$, " man " would seem to be the same thing as " animal " taken twice over). The complaint, as Stenzel says, is not that an εἶδος is treated as something distinct from a sensible individual, but that the more universal εἴδη, the γένη as Aristotle calls them, are thought of as though they had a being distinct from that of the ἄτομον εἶδος or *infima species*. Aristotle's point is that " animal," for example, has no being except as " horse," " man," " dog," or one of the other species which can no longer be divided into sub-species. This would be, in effect, a criticism on the method of division as practised in the *Sophistes*, where it is made a rule that in summing up the result of the division into a definition, all the intermediate *differentiae* which have been employed must be recapitulated. This is a procedure condemned by Aristotle's own doctrine that a definition need only state genus and specific difference ; the specific difference includes in itself all the intermediate differences. Hence, according to Stenzel, the χωρισμός of which Aristotle complains is that the Platonic account of " division " as

---

[1] See Stenzel, *Zahl u. Gestalt*, 133 ff., with the Aristotelian texts discussed there. The all-important passage is *Met.* Z 1037b 8–1038a 35. Aristotle urges that if, *e.g.*, you first divide animals into footed animals and animals without feet, and then divide the former into bipeds and others, the Platonic rule would require you to say that man is a " two-footed footed animal." But the determination " footed " only exists actually as contained in the more specific determinations " two-footed," " four-footed." The same problem recurs in *Met.* H 6, 1045a 7 ff.

the instrument of definition is fatal to the unity of the *definiendum*,[1] and, since the process is a direct outcome of the doctrine of μέθεξις, the defect is one which requires the doctrine of μέθεξις itself to be revised. (Thus Aristotle's rejection of the Platonic doctrine of forms would at bottom be based on rejection of the logical tenet that the relation of species to genus is identical with that of individual to species.) Whether this interesting interpretation is sound is, however, a question for the student of Aristotelianism rather than for an expositor of Plato.[2]

See further :

BURNET.—*Greek Philosophy, Part I.*, 312–324 ; *Platonism,* c. 5, 2, 7.

NATORP, P.—*Platons Ideenlehre*, 366–436.

BAEUMKER, C.—*Das Problem der Materie in der griechischen Philosophie*, 196–209.

STENZEL, J.—*Zahl und Gestalt bei Platon und Aristoteles.* (1924.)

ROBIN, L.—*La Théorie platonicienne des idées et des nombres après Aristote.* (Paris, 1908.)

MILHAUD, G.—*Les Philosophes-géomètres de la Grèce, Platon et ses prédécesseurs.* (Paris, 1900.)

TAYLOR, A. E.—*Philosophical Studies*, pp. 91–150.

THOMPSON, D'ARCY W.—" Excess and Defect " in MIND, N.S., 149.

---

[1] *Zahl u. Gestalt*, 126 ff.

[2] It seems clear that a definitive interpretation of Plato's main thought must start with a thorough study of the material collected in M. Robin's great work *La Théorie platonicienne*. It is time that we should make an end of the pretence of understanding Plato by ignoring the evidence or by arbitrarily reading into him the views of our own favourite modern metaphysicians. In this brief chapter I have only been able to hint at the interpretation the material suggests to myself. These hints I have tried to develop briefly in a notice of Stenzel's book in *Gnomon*, ii. 7 (July 1926), and more fully in an essay in MIND, " Forms and Numbers," with reference to the Aristotelian evidence. (See the reference given above.)

ADDENDA

P. 21, l. 18 ff. It seems necessary, in view of some criticisms, to say expressly that I regard the date 387 B.C. as a mere convenient " approximation," not as the known precise date of the founding of the Academy. And, of course, my language about the long interruption in Plato's literary activity must be understood with the qualifications (1) that I expressly decline to commit myself to an opinion about the relative order of composition of *Republic, Phaedo, Symposium,* and (2) that I never meant to exclude the possibility of a minor " occasional " violation of silence. On my own view the *Menexenus* would have to be dated c. 380–379. Understood in this " common-sense " way, the view that " roughly speaking " the dialogues earlier than the *Parmenides* and *Theaetetus* were written before the foundation of the Academy still seems to me as probable as it did to Burnet.

P. 207, l. 26 ff. The reality of Plato's own personal faith in immortality is surely put beyond doubt by the words of Ep. vii. 335*a*, " one must put genuine faith in the ancient sacred sayings which indicate that our soul is immortal, has to face a judge, and pays the gravest penalties when one has left the body," etc. (πείθεσθαι δὲ ὄντως ἀεὶ χρὴ τοῖς παλαιοῖς τε καὶ ἱεροῖς λόγοις, οἱ δὴ μηνύουσιν ἡμῖν ἀθάνατον ψυχὴν εἶναι δικαστάς τε ἴσχειν καὶ τίνειν τὰς μεγίστας τιμωρίας ὅταν τις ἀπαλλαχθῇ τοῦ σώματος).

P. 263, par. 2. It should be noted that the Glaucon of the *Symposium* is not Plato's brother, who figures in the *Republic*, since (*Symp.* 173*a*) he, like Plato himself, was a mere παῖς at the date of Agathon's party.

P. 263, par. 2. Professor Burnet, in the posthumous volume of lectures on *Platonism* delivered at the University of California, expresses the opinion that the *Republic* and consequently the *Timaeus* are to be given a dramatic date anterior to the Archidamian War (*Platonism*, pp. 25–26). This would, so far as I can see, be *possible* but for one consideration. It would compel us to hold that Perictione, since she was the mother of two sons who are young men before 431, was *at the very least* over a hundred years old in 366, when *Ep.* xiii refers to her as still living. This is just possible, but hardly likely, and since I am as convinced as Burnet himself of the genuineness of *Ep.* xiii., I would rather not follow him on this point.

P. 278, n. 1. Xenophon also (*Symp.* ii. 9) ascribes to Socrates the thesis that " woman's *nature* is not inferior to man's " (ἡ γυναικεία φύσις οὐδὲν χείρων τῆς τοῦ ἀνδρὸς οὖσα τυγχάνει), though she is not his equal in physical strength and intelligence (γνώμης τε καὶ ἰσχύος δεῖται). But he may be dependent on Plato or Aeschines, or on both.

P. 309, n. 1. Aeschines also in his *Alcibiades* ascribed the " erotic " temperament to Socrates, with special reference to his affection for Alcibiades. (ἐγὼ δὲ διὰ τὸν ἔρωτα ὃν ἐτύγχανον ἐρῶν ᾿Αλκιβιάδου οὐδὲν διάφορον τῶν Βακχῶν ἐπεπόνθειν. Fr. 11, Dittmar.   This evidence seems to me to make nonsense of all the inferences about the personality of Plato which have been drawn from the *Phaedrus* and *Symposium*.

P. 450.   In *Platonism* (1928), p. 106, Burnet now says that " it can be proved " that Plato " discovered the heliocentric system " in astronomy.   The evidence offered is simply the statement of Theophrastus discussed in our text.   I do not understand how Burnet reconciles this view with his own defence of the *Epinomis*, in which the sun is still expressly treated as a " planet " (986b–987d).   I am wholly in accord with Burnet about the genuineness of the *Epinomis* and *therefore* am compelled to dissent from his attribution of " Copernicanism " to Plato.

P. 472, l. 20.   But it should be remembered, as Mr. Lorimer reminds me, that Aristotle does once observe (*Pol.* 1329b 25) that the various arts of civilized life must have been discovered " often, or rather an indefinite number of times in the course of ages," and " Ocellus Lucanus " (c. 3) that " Hellas has often been barbarian, and will often be so again."

P. 516, l. 4.   That is, Aristotle's great difficulty with the theory of " forms," as it seems to me, is not so much that there should be a " form " of *man*, " besides " Socrates and Coriscus, as that there should be a " form " of *animal*, " besides " horse, and dog and man.   *That* is what he is specially anxious to deny.

CHRONOLOGICAL TABLE

428-7. Plato born (Ol. 88, 1). Fourth year of Archidamian War; year following death of Pericles. Revolt and subjugation of Mytilene. Capture of Plataea by Peloponnesians. *Hippolytus* of Euripides.

427. Gorgias at Athens as envoy from Leontini. Aristophanes' first comedy (Δαιταλῆς) produced.

425. Tribute of Athenian allies raised. Capture of Sphacteria. Pan-Sicilian congress at Gela. *Acharnians* of Aristophanes performed. (?) *Hecuba* of Euripides.

424. Athenian defeat at Delium (Pyrilampes wounded.) Brasidas in the north. Loss of Amphipolis and banishment of Thucydides. Battle outside Megara. *Knights* of Aristophanes.

423. Year's truce with Sparta. Revolt of Scione. *Clouds* of Aristophanes. *Connus* of Amipsias.

422. Death of Brasidas and Cleon before Amphipolis. (?) Socrates serves in this campaign. *Wasps* of Aristophanes.

421. Peace of Nicias ; Scione captured and inhabitants massacred. *Peace* of Aristophanes.

418. Battle of Mantinea ; Laches killed. διοικισμός of Arcadians by Sparta.

416. Melos captured by Athenians and inhabitants massacred. Tragic victory of Agathon.

415. Mutilation of Hermae and "profanation of mysteries." Despatch of Syracusan expedition under Alcibiades, Nicias and Lamachus ; recall and disgrace of Alcibiades. *Troades* of Euripides.

414. *Birds* of Aristophanes.

413. Final ruin of Syracusan expedition ; deaths of Nicias and Demosthenes. Decelea occupied by Spartans. (?) *Electra* of Euripides. (?) *Iphigenia in Tauris.*

411. Revolution of the "four hundred." Return of Polemarchus and Lysias from Thurii. *Thesmophoriazusae* and *Lysistrata* of Aristophanes.

410. Battle of Cyzicus. *Philoctetes* of Sophocles (410–9).

409. Carthaginian invasion of Sicily ; Selinus and Himera destroyed.

408. Hermocrates in Sicily. *Orestes* of Euripides.

407. Battle of Notium. Return of Alcibiades to Athens. Hermocrates killed in street-fighting at Syracuse.

406. Battle of Arginusae. Trial and condemnation of generals ; protest of Socrates. Deaths of Euripides and Sophocles.

405. Battle of Aegospotami. Dionysius I becomes "tyrant" at Syracuse.

404. End of Peloponnesian War ; Athens surrenders to Lysander. Appointment of the " Thirty " ; murder of Polemarchus. Affair of Leon of Salamis (404–3).

403. Fall of " Thirty " ; deaths of Critias and Charmides. Restoration of democracy at Athens.

401. Expedition of Cyrus and battle of Cunaxa.

399. Trials of Andocides and Socrates for impiety and death of Socrates in archonship of Laches.

395–87. Corinthian War. Rebuilding of Athenian Long Walls (395–393). Pamphlet of Polycrates against Socrates (c. 392–390). *Ecclesiazusae* of Aristophanes. Destruction of Spartan *mora* by Iphicrates (?392 or 390).

c. 388. First visit of Plato to Sicily and Italy at age of 40. Traditional date of capture of Rome by Gauls.

387. Corinthian War ended by " King's Peace." *Approximate* date of foundation of Academy.

385. Birth of Aristotle at Stagirus.

382 Spartan seizure of citadel of Thebes and political murder of Ismenias.

380. *Panegyricus* of Isocrates.

379–8. Spartan garrison expelled at Thebes by Pelopidas and his associates. Raid of Spartan Sphodrias on Piraeus.

378. Alliance of Athens and Thebes. Second Athenian League founded.

373. Great tidal wave and earthquake on the Achaean coast.

371. " Peace of Callias " between Sparta and Athens. Spartan power broken by Epaminondas at Leuctra. Liberation of Messene and foundation of Megalopolis follow in the next year or two.

369. Spartan lines on Mt. Oneion broken by Epaminondas. (Theaetetus probably wounded in this campaign.)

367. Death of Dionysius I. Plato summoned to Syracuse by Dion. Aristotle enters Academy. Traditional date of "Licinian rogations " and defeat of Gauls by Camillus at Alba.

362. Battle of Mantinea ; Epaminondas killed.

361–60. Third visit of Plato to Sicily. Traditional date of penetration of Gauls into Campania.

357. Capture of Syracuse by Dion.

c. 356. Birth of Alexander the Great at Pella.

354. Murder of Dion by Callippus. Plato's VII *Epistle*. Earliest extant speech of Demosthenes (on the *Symmories*.)

353. Overthrow of Callippus. Plato's VIII *Epistle*.

351. *First Philippic* of Demosthenes.

349–8. *Olynthiacs* of Demosthenes. Capture of Olynthus by Philip (348).

347 Death of Plato.

346. Peace of Philocrates. Philip acts as general in the " Sacred War " against the Phocians, becomes a member of the Amphictionic Council and presides at the Pythian games. Temporary restoration of Dionysius II at Syracuse.

344–3. Dionysius finally overthrown by Timoleon. Aristotle (343–2) at Pella as tutor to Alexander.

APPENDIX

THE PLATONIC APOCRYPHA

In using the name *Apocrypha* as a convenient collective designation for those items contained in our Plato MSS. of which it is reasonably certain that they have no real claim to Platonic authorship, I make no gratuitous assumption of fraudulence in their writers or worthlessness in their contents. Apart from the collection of *Definitions*, which has its own special character, the *Apocrypha* seem to be undiguised imitations of Platonic " discourses of Socrates," and most of them to be the work of the early Academy ; the attribution to Plato has arisen naturally and by accident. The works in question fall into three classes : (*A*) items actually included in the canon of Thrasylus ; (*B*) the collection of ὅροι or definitions, which falls outside the division into "tetralogies"; (*C*) νοθευόμενοι, dialogues recognized in antiquity as spurious.

A. Dialogues included in the " tetralogies," but certainly, or all but certainly, spurious.

Of these there are seven : *Alcibiades I, Alcibiades II, Hipparchus, Amatores* (the whole of the fourth "tetralogy"), *Theages* ("tetralogy " V), *Clitophon* ("tetralogy" VIII), *Minos* ("tetralogy" IX). All were clearly regarded as genuine by Dercylides and Thrasylus. The only fact known about their earlier history is that Aristophanes of Byzantium had included the *Minos* in one of his "trilogies" along with the *Laws* and *Epinomis* (D.L. iii. 62). Since we never hear of Dercylides or Thrasylus as *introducing* any items into the Platonic canon, it seems reasonable to infer that the whole group were already accepted by the Alexandrian scholars of the third century B.C. and that the composition of all must therefore be dated earlier still. None of the group is certainly quoted by Aristotle, or even Cicero,[1] but this proves nothing since none contains anything which makes any difference to the interpretation of Plato's thought. As I shall try to show, the linguistic evidence is also decidedly against a late date in almost every case ; the Greek with which these dialogues present us is recognizably that of the fourth century.[2] It follows that we should assign their composition,

---

[1] The allusion of Cicero, *Tusculans*, iii. xxxiv. 77, is certainly, that of *de Oratore*, ii. 8 almost certainly, not to *Alcibiades I*, but to the *Alcibiades* of Aeschines of Sphettus.

[2] The statement perhaps needs a little qualification in the case of *Alcibiades II*, as will be pointed out later.

speaking roughly, to the half-century between Plato's death and
the opening of the third century, while one or two may quite
possibly have been written even within Plato's lifetime.   I shall
also try to show that the thought is quite Platonic, though the
way in which it is presented is not altogether that of the Master.
My own conclusion is that the whole group is the work of Platonists
of the first two or three generations, intending to expound Academic ideas by " discourses of Socrates." This thesis cannot be
formally demonstrated, but seems more probable than either the
extreme view of Grote, who accepted the whole group as Platonic,
or the rival extreme view which would bring some of the items well
within the Alexandrian period.

Alcibiades I.   This is in compass and worth the most important
member of the group, as it contains an excellent general summary of the Socratic-Platonic doctrines of the scale of goods and
the " tendance " of the soul.   The Platonic authorship has been
defended by Grote, Stallbaum, C. F. Hermann, J. Adam and
recently M. Croiset and P. Friedländer ; Jowett included a version
in his English translation of Plato.   For my own part I feel reluctantly forced to decide for rejection on the following grounds.
(1) Close verbal study seems to show that in language the manner
is that of the later Plato,[1] whereas the thought is that of Plato's
earliest ethical dialogues, and the exposition, at points, so unskilled
that a resolute defender is almost bound to regard the dialogue as
one of the earliest of all.   (2) It seems incredible that Plato, who has
given us such vivid portraits of Alcibiades in the *Protagoras* and
Symposium, should ever have treated his personality in the colourless
fashion of this dialogue.   (3) It should be still more incredible
that Plato, with his known views on the worth of " text-books,"
should have composed what is, to all intents, a kind of hand-book
to ethics.   The work has the qualities of an excellent manual,
and this is the strongest reason for denying its authenticity.   I
agree, then, with those who hold that *Alcibiades I* is a careful
exposition of ethics by an early Academic, written well before
300 B.C., and possibly, though perhaps not very probably, even
before the death of Plato.   I should say with Stallbaum that it
contains nothing actually *unworthy* of Plato, but I am equally
satisfied that it contains echoes of Plato which are not in the manner

---

[1] On this question see C. Ritter, *Untersuchungen über Plato*, 89–90 ;
Raeder, *Platons philosophische Entwickelung*, 24–25 ; Lutoslawski, *Origin
and Growth of Plato's Logic*, 197–198.   I would add that comparison with
the remains of the *Alcibiades* of Aeschines and that of Antisthenes shows
that our dialogue is almost certainly dependent on the former, and possibly
also on the latter.   Use of these sources in this way is barely credible in
Plato.   Also, Socrates is represented (103c) as posing as the tongue-tied
" lover " of Alcibiades, whereas according to Plato in the *Symposium* it was
rather Alcibiades who posed as the " beloved " of Socrates.   For further
discussion, and for evidence that *Alcibiades I* depends also on Xenophon,
see H. Dittmar, *Aeschines von Sphettos*, 163–177.

of a writer who is echoing himself. In particular, the closing words (135e) [1] can hardly be anything but an allusion to Plato's description (*Rep.* 491 ff.) of the corruption of the young man of genius by the blandishments of that supreme sophist, the "public," a passage itself perhaps inspired by the tragic career of Alcibiades. There are other similar disguised quotations, as we shall see.

The writer's purpose is to expound the thoughts that the one thing needful for true success in life is self-knowledge, that this means knowledge of what is good and bad for our *souls*, and that such knowledge is different in kind from all specialism. Alcibiades is drawn as a young man of boundless ambition just about to enter on public life. (The date assumed is the end of his "ephebate," before the outbreak of the Archidamian War. Pericles is at the head of affairs, 104*b*.) Socrates, who has long admired the wonderful boy from a distance, is now allowed by his "sign" to express his admiration for the first time.[2] He knows that A. is ambitious to become the first statesman of Europe and Asia, and can help him to realize the dream if A. will only answer his questions (103*a*–106*b*).[3] To succeed as a statesman, A. must be a good adviser and so must have knowledge which his neighbours have not, and this knowledge must come to him either as a personal discovery or by learning from others. But none of the things A. has "learned" are matters considered by sovereign assemblies, and in the matters which such an assembly does consider there are experts who would be much better counsellors than A. His boasted "advantages" of person, rank, wealth, are irrelevant. On what topics, then, would he be a competent adviser of the public ? He says, "On the conduct of their own affairs, *e.g.* the making of war and peace." Yet it is the *expert* we need to advise us whether it is *better* to make war, on whom, and for how long. Our standard of the "better" is supplied by the expert's τέχνη. Now, what τέχνη is the relevant one in these questions of state ? When we declare war, we always do so on the plea that our *rights* have been infringed. Has A., then, ever learned "justice," the knowledge of rights and wrongs ? He has never received instruction in it, nor can he have discovered it for himself. To do that he would need first to look for it, and to look for it he must be first awake to his ignorance of it. But from his childhood he has always been wrangling with his companions

---

[1] ὀρρωδῶ δέ, οὔ τι τῇ σῇ φύσει ἀπιστῶν ἀλλὰ τὴν τῆς πόλεως ὁρῶν ῥώμην, μὴ ἐμοῦ τε καὶ σοῦ κρατήσῃ.

[2] 103*a*. The representation that S. has not spoken a word to the lad for years seems an un-Platonic exaggeration. Contrast the representation in the *Protagoras* which depicts a scene from the same period of the philosopher's life.

[3] This self-confidence, again, is not in keeping with Plato's conception of Socrates ; it looks to be borrowed from the Socrates of Xenophon. It is definitely "un-Platonic" that Socrates boasts (124*c*) of having God for his "guardian," with reference, as we see by a comparison with 103*a* 5, to the "divine sign." God and the "sign" are never confused in this way in any certainly genuine work of Plato.

about his "rights," as if he already knew what they are (106*c*–110*d*). And he certainly cannot have "picked up" knowledge of right and wrong from the "many" at large, as he has done the use of his mother-tongue.[1] The "many" all *agree* about the meaning of vernacular words, and this is why one can learn the language from them. Where their views are at hopeless variance, they cannot be our teachers, and there is nothing about which they are more at variance than their "rights" and "wrongs." A. then is proposing to teach others what it is not possible that he knows himself (110*e*–113*a*).

But, says A., the politician need not know what is right ; he need only know what is *expedient*. Well, if A. thinks he knows what the expedient is, let him answer one question : Is the expedient always the same as the right or is it not ? A. thinks not, but Socrates is confident that he can prove the contradictory (114*d*). The proof turns on establishing the equations καλόν = ἀγαθόν, αἰσχρόν = κακόν (114*d*–116*b*).[2] He who acts "finely" also "does well," *i.e.* is in possession of *good*,[3] and the good for us = the expedient for us. He then who advises as expedient what is wrong is a bad adviser. If A. hesitates whether to admit or to deny this, his very hesitation is a sign that he is becoming conscious of his ignorance about the most important of all subjects (117*a*). He is suffering from virulent ἀμαθία, the common malady of "public men" (118*b*). Pericles, indeed, is said to have "learned" wisdom from Anaxagoras and Damon. But since he never imparted "wisdom" to anyone, we may fairly doubt whether he had it.[4] A. might reply that if all our public men are "laymen," he need not be more than a layman himself to compete with them. But the real antagonists for whom an Athenian statesman needs to be more than a match are foreign powers, the Spartan and Persian kings. Both have the advantage of A. alike in descent, in careful preparatory training for their office,[5] in wealth and resources.[6]

---

[1] An echo of *Protagoras*, 327*e* ?

[2] Cf. *Gorgias*, 474*c*.

[3] Cf. *Rep.*, 353*e* ff.

[4] Cf. *Protagoras*, 319*e*, *Meno*, 94*b* (both echoed by *Alc. I*, 118*e*).

[5] The starting-point for the long and over-coloured picture of the education of a Persian king (which must be meant ironically) seems to be Aeschines, Fr. 8 (Dittmar), where Socrates ironically argues that Themistocles must have practised "tendance of himself" before venturing to match himself with Xerxes. The development of this hint in our dialogue seems to reflect Xenophon's romance of the *Education of Cyrus* (itself possibly influenced by the *Cyrus* of Antisthenes). Plato's view (*Laws*, 684) is that no Persian prince ever receives any "education" at all. So far I should accept the conclusions of H. Dittmar, but I am wholly sceptical of his further theory that the real object of *Alc. I* is to discountenance the preference of Eastern theosophy, represented by Zoroaster, to Hellenic philosophy.

[6] Note that the statements of the dialogue about the wealth of Sparta would only be true for the period between the surrender of Athens to Lysander and the battle of Leuctra. They are not true for the supposed date of the conversation.

If one is to compete with such rivals, the first lesson to be learned must be "knowledge of self" (the lesson of not underrating your opponent.)

How, then, must we set to work on the "care" (ἐπιμέλεια) of ourselves? We wish to be as good as possible at the goodness of a καλὸς κἀγαθός, that is, of a φρόνιμος, a man of sound judgement in all things. About *what* things do the καλοὶ κἀγαθοί, the "virtuous", show this sound judgment? A. says, in capacity to command "men who associate with one another to transact the business of civic life" (125c), or more briefly, "men sharing in the constitutional rights and functions of citizenship" (125d). The statesman's τέχνη is εὐβουλία, "excellence in counsel respecting the conduct and safety of the State." This safety depends on the existence of φιλία, or more precisely, ὁμόνοια, "oneness of mind" between the citizens; not the "oneness of mind" secured by the arts of number, weight and measure, but the kind of "oneness of mind" which makes men agree "in a house" and is the basis of family affection. Such agreement implies that both parties to it *have* a "mind of their own," and so differs from any arrangement by which one party leaves a matter of which he is himself wholly ignorant to the sole discretion of the other. *That* is not what is meant when justice is said to be "minding your own business and leaving others to mind theirs" (127d). (The exposition at this point shows traces of a confusion one would not expect in Plato.)

Again (the transition is oddly abrupt), what is "care for a man's self"? With some needless elaboration, we reach the result that to care for a thing means to make it better, and that we cannot tell what will make a thing better unless we know what the thing *is*. So our question becomes "What *is* the self?" (128a). It is argued at length that an *agent* is never identical with the tools he *uses*. All of us are constantly using our hands, eyes, members generally, as tools. The body is thus an *instrument* used, and therefore cannot be the *agent* who uses the instrument. The real self, the agent which "uses" and "commands" the body, must be the ψυχή, and the true definition of man is that he is a "soul *using* a body"[1] (130c.) "Know thyself," then, means "know thy ψυχή"; sophrosyne, the true self-knowledge, must be different from any of the "arts" which "tend" our bodies or our possessions. And to be in love with another's body is not to be in love with *him*. (His body is not really his "person.")

The great business of life is "self-knowledge," the "care" of ourselves (132c).[2] Now the eye can see itself only by looking at its reflection. So the soul can "see itself" only by either gazing at another man's soul, particularly at "that region of it where the

---

[1] In refutation of the allegation that this definition, always insisted on by the Neo-Platonists, is "not platonic," Raeder properly refers to *Phaedo*, 115c–d.

[2] Cf. the reference to ἐπιμέλεια of the self in Aeschines, Fr. **8**.

goodness of a soul is to be found," or contemplating God, a mirror of perfection brighter than any human soul.[1] We get to know ourselves truly by knowing God (133c). Until we know ourselves, we cannot know what is good for ourselves, for other men, for the State. Without such knowledge, a man's career will be disastrous to himself and the public (134a). Thus, the true prosperity of a city depends not on its navy, but on its virtue (134b).[2] The states-man must impart *goodness* to his countrymen, and he cannot impart what he has not. It must be his first concern to get good-ness by "looking to God." Freedom, the power to make one's will supreme, is a bad thing for the ignorant; it leads them to disease, shipwreck, moral ruin. Until one has acquired goodness, servitude to a better, not being " one's own master," is the condition which befits one.

Alcibiades II. A poor production, stamped as not Plato's by its style, by manifest imitations of *Alcibiades I*, and, as has generally been admitted since Boeckh, by a definite allusion to one of the Stoic " paradoxes." [3]

The subject is *Prayer*. The writer seems to take his cue either from the passage of the *Memorabilia* where Xenophon, who *may* himself be thinking of the closing words of the *Phaedrus*, says that Socrates " used to ask the gods simply to give him good things, since they know best what things are good," and thought it perverse to pray " for gold or silver, or a tyranny, and things of that kind," [4] or possibly from *Laws*, 689c–e, where the speaker expresses the same view. A. is about to pray. Now, some prayers are granted, others are not. So a man should be careful not to ask what is bad for him; his god might happen to be in a giving mood and take him at his word, as happened to Oedipus.[5] A. says, Oedipus was notoriously " a mere lunatic." This raises a problem. " Lunatic " is the contrary of " sane." But mankind may be divided into two classes which allow of no *tertium quid*, the φρόνιμοι, men of sound judgement, and the ἄφρονες, men of unsound judgement. On the

---

[1] The argument presupposes the doctrine of the *Laws* which identifies God with the ἀρίστη ψυχή.

[2] A plain allusion to the language of *Gorgias*, 519a, a passage which seems to be in the writer's mind all through his own account of " *sophrosyne* and justice."

[3] On these points see Stallbaum's *Introduction* to his Commentary on the dialogue, and for remarks on the language, C. Ritter (*Untersuchungen*, 88–89), who accepts Stallbaum's objections to several words and phrases, but owns that the dialogue would not be condemned by his own stylometric tests— a significant confession.

[4] Xenophon, *Mem.* i. iii. 2, ηὔχετο δὲ πρὸς τοὺς θεοὺς ἁπλῶς τἀγαθὰ διδόναι, ὡς τοὺς θεοὺς κάλλιστα εἰδότας ὁποῖα ἀγαθά ἐστι. This perhaps explains why the dialogue was attributed by some persons to Xenophon (Athenaeus, 506e), with whose manner it has no affinity.

[5] Who prayed that his sons might divide their inheritance by the sword. The writer follows the version of the story which accounts for the imprecation as due to mere insanity. Cf. Frs. 2 and 3 of the *Thebais*, often regarded in antiquity as " Homeric."

principle that "one term has one, and only one, opposite," it looks as though this means that *all* men, except the few φρόνιμοι, are lunatics. But this thesis can hardly be sound ; if all men were lunatics, we could not mix with them, as we do, with safety to life and limb. (Thus the writer knows, and goes out of his way to attack, the Stoic tenet that πᾶς ἄφρων μαίνεται, every one but the ideal "sage " is out of his wits.) We may urge that there are many bodily ailments, many trades ; but no invalid has all the diseases, no tradesman follows all the trades, at once. So there are many degrees of " want of sense," from mere dullness to stark lunacy, and so lack of judgement must not be equated with lunacy (138a–140d).

The φρόνιμοι are those who know "what is proper to do and say." The ἄφρονες do not know this, and so unintentionally do and say what they should not. Oedipus does not stand alone in this. If a god appeared to Alcibiades himself and offered to make him autocrat of Athens, or Hellas, or Europe, A. would probably think he was offered a great boon. Yet the power and splendour of the position would be no true boon to one who had not the *knowledge* how to use it. A tyranny may prove fatal to the recipient, as was the case with the murderer of Archelaus ; he was himself murdered after a reign of three days.[1] Many Athenian citizens have been undone by attaining high office ; children may prove a curse to those who have prayed for them. The poet who asks Zeus simply to give him what is good and withhold what is bad, even if he asks it, speaks like a wise man (140e–143a). *What* ignorance is thus shown to be so bad for us ? Some ignorance may be better for us than knowledge. If A.—the example is un-Platonic in its bad taste—formed a murderous design on his guardian Pericles, it would be *better* that he should lose the power of recognizing Pericles when he meets him. Knowledge of other things, not accompanied by knowledge of good, is most often harmful. It is better not to know *how* to do a thing, unless you also know whether it is *good* to do that thing. Mere professional skill does not make men φρόνιμοι ; the national life of a society of " professional experts " destitute of the knowledge of *good* would not be admirable (143b–146b). Most men have not the knowledge which would tell them whether what they do " skilfully " (προχείρως) is really beneficial. So it is better that the " many " should neither have nor fancy themselves to have a professional skill which they would be sure to misuse. Hence the importance of knowledge of good in private and public life. If it is wanting, the fresher the breezes of fortune blow, the graver the peril. Homer hinted at this when he said of Margites that he " knew a lot of things, but knew them all *badly* " (143b–147e).[2]

---

[1] This is a bad anachronism, since Archelaus was killed in 399, some years after the death of Alcibiades, who is a mere boy in the dialogue.

[2] πόλλ' ἠπίστατο ἔργα, κακῶς δ' ἠπίστατο πάντα. The forced interpretation of κακῶς as " to his own hurt " looks like an imitation of the whimsicalities of Socrates' exposition of Simonides in the *Protagoras*.

A. now thinks that he would not jump blindly at the offer of a " tyranny," and approves the wisdom of the unnamed poet whom Socrates had quoted. The Spartans, Socrates adds, show a like wisdom. Their only public prayer is a brief petition for καλά ἐπ' ἀγαθοῖς, the *honestum et bonum*. There is a tale that the Athenians once asked the oracle of Ammon why Heaven favours the Spartans who, in spite of their wealth, are niggardly with sacrifices, more than the liberal Athenians.[1] The oracle answered that the Spartan εὐφημία—by which it presumably meant the decency of the prayer just mentioned—is more pleasing than all burnt-offerings. In the same spirit the gods rejected the costly offerings of Priam. They are not to be bribed, and they look at our souls, not our gifts (148e–150b).

A. would do well, then, to postpone his prayer until he has learned to pray aright. But who will teach him ? " Your sincere well-wisher," says Socrates, " but there is a mist which must first be removed from your soul." A. rewards these words of encouragement by " crowning " Socrates with the garland he had meant to wear while praying, and Socrates fatuously accepts the compliment. (A tasteless reminiscence of the Platonic playful " crowning " of Socrates by the drunken Alcibiades, *Sympos.* 213d–e.)

The very poor dialogue is dependent on, and therefore later than, *Alcibiades I*. Besides the echoes already mentioned, we note that the μαινόμενον ἄνθρωπον of 138a 6, said of Oedipus, is a verbal imitation of the use of the same phrase, "a mere lunatic," with reference to Alcibiades' own brother at *Alc. I*, 118e 4. The ill-managed fiction of the god who offers A. the " tyranny " of Athens, Hellas, or Europe, is founded on what is said more naturally of A.'s own day-dreams at *Alc. I*, 105b–c.

It is still more significant that the discussion of the Stoic " paradox " is forcibly dragged into the argument at its very opening. Oedipus is mentioned merely to give an opening for the remark that he was " crazy," and the nominal main argument is kept standing still while Socrates goes off at a tangent to discuss the irrelevant question whether all unwise persons are " crazy " too. The writer thus betrays the fact that his real concern is to attack the Stoics. This shows that he is not writing before some date when Stoicism was already in existence, *i.e.* not before the early decades of the third century. In the time of Arcesilaus, president of the Academy from 276 to 241 B.C., anti-Stoic polemic became the main business of the school. It does not *necessarily* follow that the polemic may not have begun rather earlier.

Linguistic considerations do not take us far. Stallbaum produces a respectable " haul " of alleged non-Platonic words and phrases, but forgets that many of these may only go to show that the writer was a poor stylist, without throwing any light on his

---

[1] The reference to Spartan wealth is another anachronism, taken pretty obviously from *Alc. I*.

date, while, in one or two cases, the text is not certainly sound. No great weight can be attached to his point that the use of the word μεγαλόψυχος at 140c for a " megalomaniac " is singular. This might well be a polite euphemism—it is given as one—in any age. It is urged that the plural οὐδένες is found twice (148c, e). But the same *form* occurs also in Plato (*Euthydemus*, 305d, *Timaeus*, 20b, *Ep.* vii. 344a) and in Isocrates, and I take its double appearance in a single half-page of *Alc. II* to be due to conscious imitation. The forms ἀποκριθῆναι (149a), οἴδαμεν (141e, 142d) are definitely not classical Attic,[1] but the majority of the Academy were never Athenians. Aristotle, for example, was an Ionian and constantly betrays the fact by his vocabulary. Too much has been made of the employment (140a, 150c) of τυχόν in the adverbial sense of " perhaps." This is not usual in good classical Attic, but there is at least one example in Isocrates.[2] By comparison with such early specimens of the κοινή as the extant remains of Epicurus, *Alc. II* might almost be called Attic. Hence I think it should not be confidently dated too late in the third century. It may belong to any time soon after the first rise of Stoicism.

Amatores (or *Rivales*. The title is Ἐρασταί in the famous MSS. BT, Ἀντερασταί in the margin of B).

The scena is the school of the reading-master Dionysius, said by Diogenes and others (D.L. iii. 5) to have been Plato's own first teacher. Two boys are disputing, apparently on a point of geometry. Socrates is told by the " lover " of one of them that they are " chattering philosophy " about "things on high " (τὰ μετέωρα). The tone of the remark leads him to ask whether philosophy is a thing to be ashamed of. The " lover's " rival is surprised that Socrates should act so much out of character as to put this question to a man who leads the life of a voracious and sleepy athlete. This new speaker is a votary of " music," as the other is of " gymnastic." His opinion is that philosophy is so divine a thing that a man must be less than human if he disprizes it. But what *is* this " philosophy " ? " What Solon meant when he spoke of ' learning something fresh every day of one's life '."[3] Yet, is it so clear that philosophy is simply identical with multifarious learning ?[4] We are used to think that philosophy is for the soul what exercise is for the body. If so, " polymathy " must be the mental counterpart of πολυπονία, excessive exertion, and it may be doubted whether this latter is a good thing. The cultivated " lover " feels bound,

---

[1] The first may be a vulgarism, the second is Ionic. Yet before the time of the New Comedy οἶδας is found once in Euripides, once (probably) in Xenophon ; οἴδαμεν once in Antiphon (the orator), once (probably) in Xenophon.

[2] *Isocr.* iv. 171, τυχὸν μὲν γὰρ ἄν τι συνεπέραναν. Cf. Xenoph., *Anab.* vi. 1, 20, νομίζων . . . τυχὸν δὲ καὶ ἀγαθοῦ τινος ἂν αἴτιος τῇ στρατιᾷ γενέσθαι.

[3] Solon, Fr. 2, γηράσκω δ' αἰεὶ πολλὰ διδασκόμενος.

[4] πολυμαθία (133c). The allusion is to Heraclitus, Fr. 16 (Bywater), πολυμαθίη νόον οὐ διδάσκει.

as a fair-minded man, to allow that πολυπονία may be good, though
the admission goes against his personal bias. His "athletic"
rival takes a different view. As all experts know, it is "moderate"
exertion which keeps the body fit; even a hog has the sense to
understand that. In that case, may we not argue by analogy that
it is not excessive but moderate "studies" (μαθήματα) that are
good for the soul? This question leads straight up to another:
Who is the expert who determines what is the right measure in the
matter of studies?

Again, what studies would a true lover of wisdom regard as
most important? The "musician" says, "Those which will win
you the highest reputation." A philosopher should be at home in
the "theorick" of *all* the professions, or at least, of those which
are in high consideration, though he should not stoop to meddle
with their manual part. He should know them as the "master-
builder"[1] knows his business (135b–c). But can a man be really
proficient in the theory of two professions at once? Only if we
concede that the philosopher need not have the "finished" knowledge of a great specialist, but such an amateur's knowledge as will
enable him to follow the discourse of the specialist intelligently
and form a sound judgement on it. That means, says Socrates,
the philosopher is to the great specialist what a "pentathlist" is
to a first-rate boxer or wrestler. He is not supreme in any one
speciality, but a good second-rate man in several (136a). As he is
not subdued to any speciality, he is not circumscribed by any.[2]
But what is the *good* of his philosophy? We do not want to trust
a second-rate physician when we are ill, nor a second-rate navigator
when we are in danger on the sea. If the philosopher is first-rate
at nothing, life has no place for him; this seems fatal to the conception of him as an all-round "intelligent amateur" (137b).

Let us make a fresh start. In the case of our domestic animals,
there are two sides to the professions which "tend" them. The
expert *knows* a good horse or dog from a bad one better than other
men; he also "disciplines," or "corrects" (κολάζει), the animals
under his care. What "art" similarly "corrects" human beings?
Justice, the "art" of the dicast; hence we should presume that
the practitioners of this art also *know* a good man from a bad one.
The layman in the art is ignorant even of himself, does not know
the true state of his own soul. This is why we say that he has not
sophrosyne; by consequence, to have *sophrosyne* will mean to be a
practitioner of the art we have just called justice, the art of true
self-knowledge. We call this art *sophrosyne* because it teaches us
to *know* ourselves, and also justice, because it teaches us to "correct" what we discover to be amiss (138b). Since the life of society

---

[1] A tell-tale allusion to *Politicus*, 259e ff. ?

[2] This reminds one of the unnamed person described at the end of the
Euthydemus as being on the border-line between politics and philosophy (see
supra, p. 101). I suspect the writer means to recall that passage.

is kept sound by the employment of this " correction," we may also call this same self-knowledge " politics," the art of the statesman, or, when it is practised by one man for the whole community, the art of the king, or even of the autocrat (τύραννος). It is the same art which is exercised on a smaller scale in regulating a household. So we may say that the " master," the householder, the statesman, the king, the autocrat are all specialists in an " art " whose true name is indifferently *sophrosyne* or justice. The expert in this art is the person whose discourse a philosopher must be able to follow, and on whose results he must be able to pass a sound judgement (138*d*). What is more, the philosopher ought to be himself a first-rate practitioner of it (ib. *e*), and this disposes of the attempt to identify the philosopher with the all-round connoisseur.

The purpose of the little work is clearly to set the Platonic conception of philosophy as the knowledge of the good, with its corollary, the identification of the true philosopher and the true king, in sharp contrast with the shallower conception of philosophy as " general culture." The great representative of *this* view of philosophy in Attic literature is Isocrates,[1] and I think the 'Ερασταί may fairly be described as a pleasing essay on the superiority of the philosophy of the Academy to the thing called by the same name in the school of Isocrates. This may have some bearing on the date of the composition. The tension between Isocrates and the Academy seems to have reached its maximum in the last years of Plato's life, when Aristotle was coming into prominence as a rival teacher of " rhetoric." It is natural to regard our dialogue as a contribution to the Academic side of the controversy, a view borne out by the complete absence of all linguistic traces of later date. The explicit recognition of the " tyrant " as a practitioner of " *sophrosyne* and justice " indicates a more favourable view of " personal rule " than anything to be found in Plato. Unless it is to be taken as mere irony, it seems to imply that the writer regards an autocracy as a *fait accompli* of which he definitely approves. He also retains the demand that the philosopher ought to be himself a " ruler," disregarding the modified view of the *Laws*, where the philosopher acts as the sovereign's adviser and coadjutor. May we infer that he is unacquainted with the *Laws* and therefore presumably writing before their circulation ?[2] The facts would,

---

[1] Burnet, *Greek Philosophy, Part I*, 215.

[2] See the remarks of Jaeger, *Aristoteles*, 53–60, on the relation between Aristotle's *Protrepticus* and [Isocr.] I. The *Panathenaicus* of Isocrates is a contribution to the controversy ; the " sophists " of whom he complains there as rivals and critics are unmistakably the Academy. I suggest that the 'Ερασταί belongs somehow to the same " war of pamphlets." There is a remark ascribed (D.L. ix. 37) to Thrasylus that εἴπερ οἱ 'Αντερασταὶ Πλάτωνός εἰσι, the " lover " to whom Socrates makes the suggestion that the philosopher is a kind of " pentathlist," must be Democritus. This, as it stands, is nonsense. Perhaps Thrasylus really said, what is true, that Democritus was the kind of " all-round man " whom Socrates has in view. I think with

I think, fall into line if we supposed the writer to be connected with the Academic group formed, at the end of Plato's life, at Assos under the protection of the converted " tyrant " Hermias of Atarneus.   I offer this suggestion for whatever it may be worth.

Theages.   The main object of the work seems to be to relate a number of anecdotes about Socrates' " sign." Theages, son of Demodocus (perhaps the general of the year 425–4 mentioned at Thuc. iv. 75), is twice named in Plato (*Apol.* 33*d*, *Rep.* 496*b*). From these references we learn that he suffered from delicate health and was dead in 399.   According to the *Republic*, he might have been lost to philosophy but for the invalidism which kept him out of public life.   In the *Theages* he is a mere lad whose future destination is giving his father some anxiety.   There is no indication of dramatic date except that in 127*e*, apparently verbally echoed from *Apol.* 19*e*.   Prodicus, Polus and Gorgias are all assumed to be present in Athens.   The piece can hardly be said to have an argument.   Demodocus thinks that nothing would prepare his son for a great career so well as association with Socrates. But, says S., my young friends do not always benefit by my society ; everything depends on the " divinity."   My " sign " sometimes interferes, and it is always lost labour to disregard it.   Charmides neglected my advice not to train for the foot-race at Nemea and had reason to be sorry for it.   Timarchus insisted on leaving a dinner-party to keep an engagement in defiance of the " sign." The " engagement " was, in fact, to assist in an assassination, and Timarchus afterwards confessed, on the way to execution, that he had done wrong to disregard my warnings.   The " sign " also predicted the great public disaster at Syracuse.   Aristides, grandson of the great Aristides, made famous progress while he was with me, but, in a short absence, forgot all he had learned, though Thucydides (the grandson of Pericles' opponent) was associating with me to his great advantage.   Aristides explained that he had never directly learned anything from me, but found his own intelligence mysteriously aided by being in the same room with me.

All through this conversation there are recognizable borrowings from the Platonic dialogues.   The " sign " is described (128*d*) in the actual words of *Apol.* 31*d* ; the statement that it warned S. that some lads would not benefit by his company is taken from *Theaetet.* 151*a*, and the anecdote about the boys Aristides and Thucydides has been constructed by combining that passage with the *Laches*, where these two lads are introduced to S. by their fathers.   There is an allusion to the usurpation of Archelaus (124*d*) which verbally reproduces *Gorg.* 470*d*.   Theages, like the young

Grote that the words εἴπερ κτλ. need not indicate any doubt of the genuineness of the dialogue.   They may quite well mean, " Since, as every one knows, the work is Plato's."   The object may be to argue that Plato has made Socrates allude to Democritus.   This would be a retort to the charge that Plato ignores Democritus out of envy (D.L. iii. 25).

Alcibiades of *Alc. I*, would like to be a τύραννος, " and so, I am sure,"
he says, " would you, or any one else " (125e). All these passages
are ultimately borrowings from *Gorg.* 469c. There is one glaring
anachronism, a reference to the mission of Thrasylus to Ionia in
the year 409.[1] Since the *Republic* manifestly speaks of Theages
as a grown man, the reference to the Sicilian disaster is probably
a second. The curious theory of 129e ff. that the " sign " could
infect the associates of S. with intelligence is unlike anything in
Plato, but we may take it as indicating Academic authorship that,
in spite of its wonderful stories, the *Theages* agrees with Plato against
Xenophon that the " sign " gave no positive recommendations
(128d).

Stallbaum[2] had a theory which would bring the *Theages* down
to a very late date. He argues that the opening for its composition
was provided by the words of *Theaetet.* 150d, where Socrates says
that those of his young friends " to whom God permits it " (οἶσπερ ἂν ὁ
θεὸς παρείκῃ) make great progress. Our writer wrongly supposed
that " God " here means the " sign," which has nothing to do with
the matter. This shows that he was influenced by the Stoic faith
in prophecies, divination and omens. We know from Cicero[3] that
Antipater of Sidon, a Stoic of *c.* 150 B.C., related curious tales about
the " divination " of Socrates, and may infer that the stories of
the *Theages* come from him. Hence the work is not earlier than
150 B.C. Stallbaum reinforces this argument by producing a
longish list of suspicious words and phrases.

I see no force in this reasoning, which starts with a bad blunder.
Stallbaum has forgotten the statement of the *Theaetetus* (151a)
about the warnings of the " sign " which is our author's real starting-
point. There is no misunderstanding of the *Theaetetus* in the
Theages. Also it is antecedently just as likely that the *Theages*
is one of the sources from which Antipater " collected " his tales
as that it is drawing on him. In fact, a Stoic would not be likely
to be satisfied with Plato's account of the merely inhibitory
character of the " sign." Xenophon's version of the matter,
which makes the " sign " give positive guidance, is much more
in keeping with Stoic theories about " the divinity." Hence I
hold that the fidelity of the *Theages* to Plato on this point is definite
evidence *against* the presence of Stoic influence. The linguistic
arguments are also nugatory. Some of the expressions to which
Stallbaum took objection are actually Platonic, others are mere
examples of a slightly turgid diction.[4] On the evidence I think it

---

[1] For this mission see Xenoph., *Hellenica*, i. 2, 1.

[2] See his *Introduction* and *Commentary*.

[3] Cicero, *de Divinatione*, I. liv. 123, permulta collecta sunt ab Antipatro
quae mirabiliter a Socrate divinata sunt.

[4] He objects to βιῶναι, though Plato has ἐβίωσαν, βιῷ, βιῴη, and even βιώσας ;
to τεκμαίρεσθαι ἀπό τινος εἴς τι (a phrase directly imitated from *Theaetet.* 206b 7) ;
to ποιοῦμαι δεινὸς εἶναι, an odd expression but paralleled, *perhaps*, *Rep.* 581d
10 (where the τι οἰώμεθα of editors is a correction of the MSS. ποιώμεθα.)

most probable that the dialogue is the work of an Academic of the last third of the fourth century, a man of the type of Xenocrates, (president of the Academy 339–314 B.C.). Xenocrates was notoriously interested in " daemons " and seems to have been the original authority, or one of them, for the later Platonist lore on the subject. The *Theages* is the very sort of thing we might expect from his circle.[1] Its chief interest for us lies in the probability that some of its anecdotes *may* have come down from men who had actually seen Socrates, and thus *may* reflect the impression his oddities made on contemporaries. Perhaps it is un-Platonic that the *Theages* represents the δαιμόνιον σημεῖον as leading Socrates to check the acts of other persons. There is no parallel for this in any certainly genuine dialogue.

Hipparchus. By general admission the language and diction of the dialogue are excellent fourth-century Attic, not to be really discriminated from the authentic work of Plato. This should put Stallbaum's view that it is a clever late imitation out of court. That might have been *possible* after the rise of " Atticism," but not earlier. I shall discuss Boeckh's unlucky speculation on the authorship later on.

Socrates and an unnamed friend [2] are considering the question what avarice (or greed, τὸ φιλοκερδές) is and who is the avaricious or greedy man (the φιλοκερδής). The first and obvious answer is " A greedy man is one who is not above making a profit from an unworthy source " (ἀπὸ τῶν μηδενὸς ἀξίων). But a man who expects to make a profit from what he *knows* to be worthless must surely be silly, whereas we think of the greedy not as silly, but as " cunning knaves," " slaves of gain " who know the baseness of the source and yet are not ashamed to make the profit. Here there is a difficulty. He who knows when and where it is " worth while " to plant a tree, or perform any other operation, is always some kind of expert. And an expert would *not* expect to make a profit out

---

(And in the *Theages* it is quite possible that we ought to read προσποιοῦμαι.) He objects to the use of προσαγορεύειν in the sense of " to name," which is justified by parallels at *Sophist.* 251a, *Polit.* 291e, *Phileb.* 12c, 54a, and the phrase ἅρματα κυβερνᾶν, a mere piece of " Gorgianism " with a close parallel in *Laws*, 641a 2. The only really suspicious *word* in his list is ἰδιολογεῖσθαι, apparently used nowhere else before Philo Judaeus. But as the noun ἰδιολογία occurs in Epicurus, three centuries before Philo, the suspicion does not amount to much. Ritter (*Untersuchungen*, 94) finds the mannerisms in agreement with Plato's earlier style, though inconceivable in a dialogue later than the *Theaetetus*, on which the *Theages* is dependent.

[1] See also H. Brünnecke, *de Alcibiade II, qui fertur Platonis* (Göttingen, 1912), 113. H. Dittmar (*Aeschines von Sphettos*, 64) thinks of Heraclides of Pontus and his friends, which comes to much the same thing.

[2] This is not in Plato's manner. Apart from the purposely anonymous chief speakers in the *Sophistes-Politicus* and *Laws*, he only introduces unnamed ἑταῖροι as persons to whom Socrates reports the conversation (e.g. in the *Protagoras*), never as interlocutors in the dialogue proper. It is also not his practice to name a dialogue after a character who is not an interlocutor, though Aeschines seems to have done this in his *Miltiades*.

of worthless material or by using worthless instruments, as we may readily convince ourselves by taking simple examples. This disposes of the suggestion that *cleverness* is part of the definition of the φιλοκερδής. We try a second formula : the greedy are those who are insatiably eager for *petty* profits. (The emphasis now falls on the paltriness of the gain.) Still, they cannot be supposed to *know* how petty the profit is. Also, *ex hyp.* they are *eager* for the gain. Gain is the " opposite " of detriment, detriment is always an evil and *therefore* men are made worse by it, *therefore* it is always an evil (227a, a singular argument in a circle). Gain, then, being the " opposite " of something which is *always* an evil, must always be a good. A man who loves gain is one who loves " good," as we all do. With the first definition it would seem that no one could be greedy, with the second that everyone must be greedy. If we try a third suggestion, that the greedy man is one who is not " above " making gain from sources to which the respectable (οἱ χρηστοί, 227d) will not stoop, it may still be replied that if it is true (a) that to make a gain is to be benefited (ὠφελεῖσθαι), and (b) that all men desire good, it must follow that the " respectable " are as much " fond of *all* gain " as others. And it would not help us to say that they do not desire to gain by that which will do them harm, or to make a " wicked " gain. For to be harmed = to suffer loss of some kind, and it is meaningless to talk of losing by a gain ; and if gain is *always* good, how can there be any " wicked " gain ?

Here the friend complains that Socrates is " gulling " him. But that, says S., would be a shocking act and would violate the precept of that good and wise man Hipparchus, the eldest of the Pisistratids. He introduced Homer's poetry to Athens, regulated its recitation, patronized Anacreon and Simonides, all out of zeal for improving his fellow-citizens. For the country-folk he set up Hermae by the roads engraved with maxims intended to surpass the wisdom of the famous Delphian inscriptions. One of these maxims was *MH ΦIΛON EΞAΠATA,* " never gull a friend." *After* the murder of this great and good man, his brother Hippias ruled like a tyrant, but so long as he lived, Athens enjoyed a golden age. The true story of his death is that Harmodius murdered him from jealousy because Aristogiton preferred the wisdom of Hipparchus to his own.[1]

To return : we cannot give up any of our theses, but perhaps we might *qualify* one of them, the thesis that gain is always good. Perhaps some gain may be bad. But at least, gain is always gain, as a man, good or bad, is always a man. In a definition we should

---

[1] The story makes a deliberate point of contradicting the facts in every possible detail. It is thus certainly not meant to be taken seriously, but should be regarded as a not quite successful attempt to recapture the " irony " of Plato's Socrates. Stallbaum's denunciation of the *homuncio* who could make such a string of blunders is wasted. So is the labour of those who have gone to the passage for light on the " Homeric problem." The dialogue gets its name from this intercalated piece of awkward pleasantry.

indicate the common character of all gain, as we do that of all
" meats," wholesome or not, when we call them " solid nutriment "
(ξηρὰ τροφή). We might try, as a last attempt, the definition that
gain is " anything acquired at no outlay, or an outlay less than
what accrues from it." But we reflect that one might acquire
an illness, not only at no expense, but by being feasted at another's
expense, and yet this would not be a gain. If we add the qualification that the thing acquired must be a good, we shall be thrown back
on a difficulty which has already given us trouble. And the words
" with no outlay, etc." also have their difficulties.[1] To make their
meaning clear, we need to introduce the notions of *value* (ἀξία 231d)
and a *standard* of value. The profitable = the valuable, and the
valuable = that of which the possession, or ownership, is valuable.
But this seems to mean just the " beneficial " or " good." We
have ended by equating " gain " with " good " a second time and
are thus baffled by the plain fact that there appear to be " wicked "
gains which good men do not desire, and by the notorious common
employment of φιλοκερδής as a term of reproach.

The thoughts of the trifle are, all through, as Platonic as its
language, and, apart from the one awkward " circle " in the reasoning, the main argument seems to me worthy of Plato in his more
youthful vein. The interest shown in economic facts is thoroughly
intelligent. The real evidence of non-Platonic authorship is, to
my mind, the anonymity of the interlocutor and the inferiority and
irrelevant length of what is meant to be the humorous interlude
about Hipparchus. The dialogue should be assigned to an Academic
of the earliest period with an excellent style and an intelligent
interest in economics.[2]

Clitophon. The work is no more than a brief fragment, but
raises interesting questions. Clitophon, a minor character in the
Republic,[3] is conversing with Socrates, who has been told that he is
a great admirer of Thrasymachus, but inclined to be critical of
Socrates himself. Clitophon explains his real position. He holds
that as long as S. confines himself to preaching the need for " learning justice " his discourse is most awakening. He is convincing,

---

[1] The point is that you might, *e.g.*, exchange gold for twice or four times
its weight in silver and yet lose by the transaction, though you acquire a
greater weight of metal (since the ratio of the value of gold to that of silver
is 12 : 1).

[2] It stands " stylometric " tests well. C. Ritter (*Untersuchungen*, 91)
thinks—or thought—its genuineness an open question. I agree with him
that the writer has " learned more than his style " from Plato, and am content
to believe that his work may actually have been read by Plato.

[3] He is mentioned there at 327b in a way which suggests that he has
come to the party in company with Thrasymachus. At 340a–b he says a
few words urging that Thrasymachus shall be allowed " fair play." Presumably he is the Clitophon mentioned by Aristotle, Ἀθηναίων Πολιτεία, 34,
as one of the more moderate supporters of the establishment of the 400 in 411
B.C., whose object was to return to the institutions of Clisthenes. Aristotle
classes him with Theramenes, Archinus and Anytus.

again, when he is exposing the error of the belief that injustice is ever " voluntary," [1] and the folly of trying to use what you have not yet learned how to use, or insisting that if a man does not know how to " use " his ψυχή, he would be better dead, or under the control of another who has this knowledge, which is the " art of the statesman." [2] (That is, Cl. accepts the whole of the theoretical Socratic ethics.) But when one has been converted to the necessity of " learning justice " and is anxious to set about the task, Socrates fails one. We may illustrate the nature of the failure thus. A medical man can do two things with his knowledge. He can make another man a medical specialist by imparting it ; over and above this, he can *cure* a patient. Socrates should not merely tell us that by " learning justice " we shall become specialists in the subject ; he should also explain what justice produces, as medicine produces health in the patient (409b). We want to know what " health of soul " is. Some say that the *product* of justice is the *expedient* (συμφέρον), some that it is the *right* (δίκαιον), some that it is the *profitable* (λυσιτελοῦν), or the *beneficial* (ὠφελιμόν). None of these answers—they are taken from *Rep.* 336c–d where Thrasymachus says he will not be fobbed off with any of them as a definition —are very enlightening. An associate of S. has said that justice produces *friendship* (φιλία) in *cities*. But he went on to say that some φιλίαι, those with boys or animals, are not good. True φιλία is ὁμόνοια, the concord of two minds, and ὁμόνοια is a *science* (ἐπιστήμη). The argument went no further, because no one could explain what it is about which all just men are " of one mind." Clitophon referred the question to Socrates, who told him that justice makes us able to " do good to our friends and harm to our enemies." Yet, on being pressed, S. admitted that a " just " man will do no harm to any one.[3] It looks, then, as though one of two things must be true. Either Socrates has the same limitations as a man who can speak eloquently in praise of a science in which he is himself only a layman, or, more probably, Socrates did not choose to explain himself fully. Clitophon is sure he needs a physician of the soul, but, unless S. can do more for him than he has so far done, he will be left to fall into the hands of Thrasymachus or another for practical treatment (410a–e).

It is not quite clear to what conclusion the writer is leading up, but it should be plain that the apparent commendation of Thrasymachus at the expense of Socrates is ironical. Clitophon's point is that unless Socrates can do more for him than simply preach on the

---

[1] 407d–e, where the allusion is to the treatment of this topic in the *Protagoras*.

[2] 407e ff. The allusions seem to be to the " protreptic " discourse of Socrates in the *Euthydemus* ; 408b 3 seems to refer to the simile of the mutineers in the *Republic* itself (488a ff.).

[3] The allusion is to *Rep.* 332a–d, but there it is Polemarchus who offers the definition and Socrates who criticizes it on the very ground mentioned by Clitophon.

necessity of " tending " the soul, he is in the position of a sick man
in danger of falling into the hands of a confident " quack." I
suspect that if the writer had gone on with his argument, Socrates
would have been made to explain why the physician of the soul
cannot simply give his " patient " a set of rules for moral regimen,
why, in fact, morality is not a professional specialism. Such an
argument would furnish a sound Academic commentary on the
discourse between Socrates and Polemarchus in *Rep*. I. We might
understand the piece better and, perhaps, discover something about
its origin, if we could be sure how to interpret the reference to the
ἑταῖρος of Socrates who maintained that " justice " produces ὁμόνοια
in cities and that ὁμόνοια is a science.[1] Since the passage cannot be
explained out of the *Republic* itself, we clearly have here an allusion
to some actual controversy [2]; the very irrelevance of the thesis
to its immediate context shows that the point is one to which the
writer attaches importance. That this writer is not Plato seems
to be proved by his manifest dependence on *Republic, Euthydemus,
Protagoras*. There would, so far as I can see, be no linguistic difficulty in admitting Plato's authorship. Hence I should ascribe
the piece to some fourth-century Academic.[3]

Minos. Like the *Hipparchus*, this dialogue gets its name from the
introduction of an historical narrative ; the respondent is anonymous.
The question discussed is the nature of *law*, and the point is to be
made that it is not of the *essentia* of law to be a *command*. A law is
the *discovery* (ἐζεύρεσις) of a truth,—the view common to all champions
of " eternal and immutable " morality. The piece opens, in an
un-Platonic way, by a direct question from Socrates, " What is
law ? " (The abruptness seems to be copied from the opening of
the *Meno*, but there the abrupt question is put into the mouth of
Meno and is dramatically appropriate.) The answer given is that
" the law " is a collective name for τὰ νομιζόμενα, the aggregate of
" usages." But this is like saying that sight (ὄψις) is the aggregate
of visibles (ὁρώμενα). The statement, that is, tells us nothing about
the *formal* character of the " legal " as such. A new definition is

---

[1] That justice produces φιλία and ὁμόνοια is said at *Rep*. 351d by Socrates
himself.

[2] The question in what " goodness " makes men of one mind is, as we
saw, raised in *Alc. I*., but the allusion cannot well be to that dialogue as Adam
thought, since there is nothing there about the φιλίαι of " boys and animals."
H. Dittmar suggests Aristippus as the ἑταῖρος of S. intended. It seems
improbable, however, that he wrote any Σωκρατικοὶ λόγοι. I fancy the
guess is based on the fact that the ἑταῖρος is said to be κομψός and the mistaken identification of the κομψοί of the *Philebus* with Cyrenaics. φιλία was
a standing topic with writers from the Academy ; Speusippus, Xenocrates,
Aristotle all treated of it.

[3] See C. Ritter, *Untersuchungen*, 93, who finds the language closely akin
to that of the latest Platonic dialogues. Perhaps there may be an allusion
to the view that ὁμόνοια is an ἐπιστήμη in Aristotle's remark that agreement
about astronomy is not ὁμόνοια since the sphere of " concord" is τὰ πρακτά
(of which there is no ἐπιστήμη, E.N. 1167a 25). E.E. 1236b 2 ff., which has
some remarks about φιλίαι with θηρία, may allude to the same discussion.

offered : a law is δόγμα πόλεως, a pronouncement of the community. (*I.e.* it is the *authority* of the " sovereign " which gives to " use " the formal character of law—the view of Hobbes and Austin.) S. treats this statement as equivalent to saying that a law is an *opinion* (δόξα) of the community, and, in spite of the contemptuous comments of Stallbaum, the equation is a sound one. On the proposed definition, a law *is* an embodied "judgement" of society, or its representative, the "sovereign." But we also hold that οἱ νόμιμοι, "respecters of law," and they only, are δίκαιοι and that δικαιοσύνη, regard for right, is good and preserves society ; its contrary, ἀνομία, disregard for law, is bad, and destroys society. Now a given enactment may be a "bad law." But how can a bad δόγμα πόλεως really be law, if law is what really exalts a nation ? It is suggested that we should define law as a *sound* judgement (χρηστὴ δόξα) of society. But here *sound* is a mere synonym for *true*, and truths are not manufactured but *discovered*. It seems, then, that formally a law is ἐξεύρεσις τοῦ ὄντος, a *discovery* about (moral) *reality*. This is the main point of the *Minos*, and it is a perfectly just one.[1]

What are we to say about the notorious divergences between the laws of different communities or different generations ? One thing is clear ; no society ever fancies that right can really be wrong. A law not based on reality (τὸ ὄν) is an *error* about τὸ νόμιμον. (It may be accepted as law, but it *ought* not to be so accepted.) And we see from the examples of medicine, agriculture and other arts that the laws of an art are the regulations of the ἐπιστήμων, the man who has expert knowledge about some region of τὸ ὄν. So the true "laws" of civic life are the directions given by "kings" and good men (the experts in *moral* knowledge), and therefore will not vary ; a mistaken direction has no right to be called "law."

Now, who knows how to "distribute" (διανεῖμαι) seeds to different soils properly ? The farmer who knows his business. The physician's "distributions" of food and exercise are the right distributions for the body, the shepherd's distributions the right ones for the flock. Whose distributions are the right ones for men's *souls*? Those of the *king* who knows his business.[2] In ancient days, there were such "divinely" wise experts in kingship, of whom Minos of Crete was one. The current story is that he

---

[1] Cf. Sir F. Pollock, *Spinoza*,[2] 304, "Law is not law merely because the State enforces it ; the State enforces it because it is law," and the definition in the *Institutes*, iurisprudentia est divinarum et humanarum rerum notitia, iusti atque iniusti scientia.

[2] There is here a conflation of the language of the *Politicus* about the king as tender of the human herd with that of *Laws*, 713c–714a, where νόμος, "law," is playfully derived from νέμειν in the sense *to divide, distribute, assign*, and law is said to be the "assignment" (διανομή) made by νοῦς. The allusion to this passage explains the awkward double use of νομεύς in the *Minos* as covering at once the meanings *herdsman* and *dispenser*.

was a savage tyrant, though his brother Rhadamanthys is proverbial for righteousness.   This is a mere calumny of Attic poets
on a successful antagonist of Athens.   Homer and Hesiod speak
very differently.   Homer says that Minos used to "converse"
with Zeus every ninth year.[1]   Zeus was a superlative sophist and
Minos his pupil.   Rhadamanthys was not taught by Minos the
whole art of royalty, but only how to do the "understrapper's"
share of the work.[2]   He and Talus—the iron man of the tale—
policed Crete under Minos.   Now what does the wise king "distribute" to souls as the wise trainer "distributes" food and
exercise to bodies?   If we find ourselves unable to say, we must
confess that this inability to say what is good or bad for our souls
is disgraceful.   (Thus we end with the familiar point that a man's
first duty is to get knowledge of good, to "tend" his soul.)

The thought of the *Minos* is Platonic; not so Platonic is the eulogy
of Minos, of whose institution the *Laws* speaks with some severity.[3]
Since the use of the *Laws* is unmistakable, the date of composition must be after Plato's death.   This disposes of the unhappy
suggestion of Boeckh that the *Hipparchus* and *Minos*, with two
of the νοθευόμενοι (*de Iusto, de Virtute*), are the work of the cobbler
Simon, who was believed in later antiquity to have circulated
"notes" (ὑπομνήματα) of conversations held in his shop by Socrates
(D.L. ii, 128).   The language is really open to no exceptions.[4]
Stallbaum's theory that the work is an Alexandrian forgery is
excluded by the known fact that Aristophanes of Byzantium placed
it in one of his "trilogies."   The right inference is not Stallbaum's,
that Aristophanes brought the work into the Platonic canon, but that
he found it there.   The language points to a date after the death
of Plato, but still in the fourth century.   Aristophanes and Thrasylus both evidently regarded the *Minos* as a kind of "introduction"
to the *Laws*.   The discrepancy between its estimate of Minos and
Cretan institutions and that of *Laws, I.* shows that the piece can
hardly have been intended so.

I subjoin here some brief notes on the contents of those among

---

[1] An allusion to *Laws*, 624*a–b*, where Homer's obscure phrase ἐννέωρος
βασιλευτής is explained in the same way.

[2] The distinction between the king and his "underling," as Boeckh and
Stallbaum saw, comes from the *Politicus*.   The explanation given of the
bad repute of Minos is strictly true, in spite of Stallbaum's ridicule.   The
venom of the *Attic* versions of the legends about him and his family (Pasiphae,
Phaedra, the Minotaur) is accounted for by the hostile relations between
Attica and the prehistoric rulers of Cnossus.   To the Athenian ear the name
Minos suggested "chains and slavery."

[3] At *Laws*, 630*d*, the Cretan complains τὸν νομοθέτην ἡμῶν ἀποβάλλομεν εἰς
τοὺς πόρρω νομοθέτας.

[4] See C. Ritter, *Untersuchungen*, 92–93, though he holds that the *style* is
more like that of the *Gorgias* than of any other dialogue.   Stallbaum took
offence at the use of ἁρμόττειν = *convenire*, to be fitting, at 314*e*, as only
found elsewhere in *Ep.* viii. 356*d*.   But the author of *Ep.* viii. *was* Plato,
and our writer is imitating him.

the *Epistles* of which I have given no account in the body of this book.

I. By an unknown and turgid writer to an unknown recipient, who seems to be, virtually at least, an autocrat. The writer has long held the highest ἀρχαί in " your city," and has had to shoulder the odium of false steps taken against his advice. He has now been dismissed with contumely, and so washes his hands of the " city " and returns an insultingly small sum of money sent him for his present expenses. The situation answers to none in the life of Plato, nor, so far as one can see, in that of Dion, to whom Ficinus wished to transfer the authorship. Yet the style seems fourth-century, and its total unlikeness to that of all the other *Epistles* shows that we can hardly be dealing with a deliberate forgery meant to pass as Plato's. If the "city" is Syracuse, the writer might be a Syracusan who has been sent into actual or virtual banishment and therefore poses as no longer a citizen. But why does he write in Attic ? Or is our text a transcription into Attic ? (I have sometimes thought of the historian Philistus— who had been sent into virtual exile at Adria by Dionysius I but returned at his death and was the chief opponent of Dion—as a possible author.[1])

V. *Plato to Perdiccas of Macedonia.* A letter recommending Euphraeus of Oreus as a political adviser. Constitutions, like animals, have their distinctive " notes " ; Euphraeus is skilled in the knowledge of these, and would not be likely to recommend measures "out of tune" with monarchy. An unfriendly critic might discount the recommendation by urging that its author has not even caught the "note" of the democracy in which he lives. But the truth is that " Plato was born too late in the day " for his country to listen to advice which he would have rejoiced to give. Objections to the letter will be found in the works of C. Ritter and R. Hackforth,[2] but seem to me trivial. I cannot think Plato, who wrote the *Politicus* and played the part he did at Syracuse, would have thought it unreasonable to give advice to a Macedonian king, and the influence of Euphraeus with Perdiccas is attested as a fact. (Athenaeus 506e.) The attacks on the very intelligible language about the " notes " of different constitutions seem to rest on the arbitrary assumption that the writer must be recalling and mis-understanding the words of *Rep.* 493a–b about the cries of the demo-cratic *belua*. Ritter can urge nothing against the language, which he regards as very much like that of *Ep.* iv. ; he gives away his whole case, to my mind, by suggesting that v. is a genuine letter

---

[1] The same suggestion is thrown out by L. A. Post, *Thirteen Epistles of Plato*, 130, but rejected on the ground that the writer appears not to be a citizen of Syracuse. As explained above, I think this inconclusive. But why should Philistus write in Attic ?

[2] C. Ritter, *Neue Untersuchungen*, 327–398. R. Hackforth, *Authorship of the Platonic Epistles*, 73–75.

of Speusippus. (*I.e.* his real reason for denying it to Plato is that he cannot rid his mind of the notion that Plato must have been "above" corresponding with a Macedonian king. I think Plato understood the political situation better than this.) The letter, if genuine, falls some time in the reign of Perdiccas (365–360 B.C.).

VI. *Plato to Hermias, Erastus and Coriscus.* The two young Academics (Coriscus is Aristotle's friend whose name figures so often in his "logical examples") are introduced to Hermias, who had made himself "tyrant" of Atarneus and was soon to be the patron of Aristotle, as well as the first martyr in the Hellenic "forward movement" against Persia. He needs confidants of high character; the two young men have character and intelligence, but need an ἀμυντικὴ δύναμις, a "protector," whom they can find in him. The writer hopes that his letter will lay the foundation for an intimate friendship. We are not likely to hear any more of the "spuriousness" of vi. since the vigorous defence of it by Wilamowitz in his *Platon* and the throwing of a flood of light on the philosophical and political importance of the "Asiatic branch" of the Academy at Assos by Jaeger.[1] The letter is valuable as showing that the foundation of the "colony" at Assos was undertaken in Plato's lifetime and on his initiative. The letter must belong to the last years of his life.

IX. *Plato to Archytas.* Archytas has complained of the heavy burdens and anxieties of public life. He should remember that our country and our family have both as much claim on our thought and our time as our personal concerns.[2] A promise is made to care for a young man named Echecrates, from regard to Archytas no less than on his own and his father's account. No one has alleged anything suspicious in the language of ix. The difficulty which has been made about the youth of Echecrates arises from the assumption that he is the man of that name who appears in the *Phaedo.* Archer-Hind rightly called attention in his edition of the dialogue to the mention of an Echecrates of Tarentum, the city of Archytas, in Iamblichus's list of Pythagoreans. The date of the letter cannot be fixed. Plato and Archytas were already friends in 367 B.C. (*Ep.* vii. 338a) and we do not know how much earlier.

X. *Plato to Aristodorus.* A mere note commending the loyalty of the recipient to Dion and expressing the conviction that "loyalty, fidelity, honesty" (τὸ βέβαιον καὶ τὸ πιστὸν καὶ ὑγιές) are the true "philosophy." There are no materials for judgement either way, but, as Ritter says, the tone "seems genuine." And why should one forge such a note?

XI. *Plato to Leodamas.* A meeting would be desirable, but

---

[1] Jaeger, *Aristoteles,* 112–124, 303–305.
[2] Cicero quotes the sentiment with approval, *de Finibus,* II., xiv. 45: ut ad Archytam scripsit Plato, non sibi se soli natum meminerit, sed patriae, sed suis, ut perexigua pars ipsi relinquatur.

L. cannot contrive a visit to Athens and Plato is not equal to a journey which would probably bear no fruit. He might have sent Socrates, *i.e.* the Academic of that name who figures in the *Politicus* —but he is ill. One hint may be given to L. in connection with the colony he is projecting. A sound public life requires an authority which can exercise vigilant supervision of daily life. Such an authority can only be created if there is an adequate supply of persons fit to undertake the charge. It is useless to dream of setting up such a body if its members would first have to be educated for the position. The date of the letter, if genuine, is probably about 360 B.C.[1] That Leodamas, a mathematician and member of the Academy,[2] as well as a statesman, should have consulted Plato about the founding of a " city " and received an answer is in keeping with all we know of the interests and position of the Academy in Plato's advanced age. C. Ritter, who finds linguistic affinities between xi., ii. and xiii., has only rather pointless objections to urge. He thinks that the precise character of the " illness " of Socrates would not be given in a genuine letter. But surely we all, even if we are philosophers, do give such information to friends at a distance, and there is real point in making it plain that the illness is not "diplomatic." Ritter also thinks the reason given for Plato's unwillingness to face the journey himself "unworthy." (It seems to be a polite way of saying that he is too old.) Finally, it is "not Platonic " to say that when a situation is desperate, one can only " pray " for better things. But why not ? Plato says the very thing at *Ep.* vii. 331*d*. And the way in which the younger Socrates is mentioned is far too natural for the Hellenistic forger.[3]

XII. *Plato to Archytas.* A note acknowledging the receipt of certain " papers " (ὑπομνήματα) and expressing admiration of their author as fully worthy of his legendary ancestors. The writer sends certain unrevised " papers " of his own in return. Our chief MSS. append a note that the authenticity of this letter was disputed,— when or why is not known. C. Ritter inclines to attribute it to the author of ii., vi. and xiii. (that is, as I hold, to Plato). The strongest argument on the other side is its apparent connection with the pretended letter from Archytas to Plato prefixed to *Ocellus* (or *Occelus*) *the Lucanian on the Eternity of the Cosmos.*[4] If this were genuine, xii. would be Plato's reply to Archytas, and the " papers " sent to Plato would have to be identified with " Ocellus." There is no doubt that " Ocellus " is a fabrication of the first or second century B.C. or that the " letter of Archytas " is part of the fabrica-

---

[1] Post, *op. cit.*, 37.

[2] Proclus in *Euclid. I.* (Friedlein), 66, 212.

[3] A forger, even if he knew of the younger Socrates, would have been afraid to make his document look suspicious to the purchaser by a reference which would seem like a bad chronological blunder about the great Socrates.

[4] The fiction is that " Ocellus " is an ancient Pythagorean of the sixth century, whose work has just been unearthed after long concealment.

tion. Hence Zeller suggested the now widely accepted view that
Ep. xii. is also the work of the same hand. This plausible view has,
to my thinking, one fault. It assumes that the fabricator had the
wit and sense to avoid introducing into Plato's " reply " a single
word which would definitely identify the " papers " spoken of
with " Ocellus." Of course the introduction of such language is
just the way in which the ordinary fabricator " gives himself away,"
but the cleverness of avoiding the blunder seems to me a little too
clever for the sort of persons who " faked " Pythagorean remains.
I think it possible, then, that *Ep.* xii. *may* be a genuine note from
Plato to Archytas about matters otherwise unknown, and that
its existence *may* have suggested to the fabricator of " Ocellus "
the basis of his romance.[1] But appearances are certainly strongly
against xii. I take no account of the few additional " letters "
which figure in the *Life* of Plato in Diogenes. They were never
included in the " canon," or in any known Platonic MS. It was a
mistake in principle on the part of C. F. Hermann to prejudice the
case for the collection of the " thirteen epistles " by printing these
items in his edition of Plato.[2]

B. The *Ὅροι.*

This is a collection of definitions of terms of natural and moral
science. The total number of terms defined is 184, but a good
number of them receive two or more alternative definitions. In
the " canon " the collection was definitely marked off from the
genuine work of Plato by exclusion from the " tetralogies." Since
our collection was thus known to Dercylides and Thrasylus, it must
be older than the Christian era. I do not know that there is any
further evidence to show when or where it was made. The genuineness of the contents as old Academic work is fairly guaranteed
by two considerations. Many of the definitions are simply extracted
from the dialogues ; others are quoted and criticized by Aristotle,
whose *Topics*, in particular, are rich in allusions of this kind. I
think it will be found that there are no signs of Stoic influence,
and this suggests that the collection, or a larger one of which it
is what remains, goes back to a time before the *rapprochement*
between Academicism and Stoicism under Antiochus of Ascalon
in the second quarter of the first century B.C. There seems also
to be no serious trace of Aristotelian influence. No use is made
of the great Aristotelian *passe-partout* ἐνέργεια ; the genus of εὐδαιμονία
is actually given (412*d*) as δύναμις ; the Aristotelian distinction

---

[1] Since Zeller, the fabrication of " Ocellus " and the correspondence
connected with it has usually been assigned to the first century B.C. The
latest editor, R. Harder, argues strongly for an earlier date in the *second*
century (Harder, *Ocellus Lucanus*, 149 ff.).

[2] On the *Epistles* generally see also the *Introduction* to J. Souilhé's edition
of them in the *Collection des Universités de France*. But the conclusions
reached there seem to me vitiated by a violent animus against admitting
authenticity.

between σοφία and ἐπιστήμη, the speculative, and φρόνησις, the practical exercise of intelligence, has not affected the terminology. On the other side, ὄρεξις, Aristotle's technical word for "conation," unknown elsewhere in the Platonic *corpus*, occurs twice, in the definitions of *wish* (413c) and of *philosophy* (414b). The statement that νόησις is ἀρχὴ ἐπιστήμης (414a) and the definition of δεινότης (413c) also sound Aristotelian. But these are trifles when set against the absence of the distinction between ἐπιστήμη and φρόνησις. On the whole I believe we should be reasonably safe in saying that the collection fairly represents Academic terminology as it was in the time of Xenocrates and Aristotle. Since we know that Speusippus was keenly interested in terminology, and that a collection of ὅροι was included among his works (D.L. iv. 5), we may infer that he is likely to be the ultimate source of much of our document. The *Divisions* of Xenocrates (D.L. iv. 13) are also likely to have contributed. As Aristotle quotes and criticizes Academic definitions not found in the collection, it is clear that we possess only an extract from more copious materials.

C. νοθευόμενοι.

de Justo. A conversation between Socrates and an unnamed friend on the nature of τὸ δίκαιον. Justice, the art of the judge (δικαστής), like counting, measuring, weighing, is an art of *distinguishing*. It distinguishes the rightful from the wrongful. A given act, *e.g.* the utterance of a false statement, may be sometimes right, sometimes wrong: right when it is done "in the appropriate situation" (ἐν δέοντι), wrong in all other cases. It is *knowledge* which enables a man to recognize the appropriate occasion. Wrongdoing, then, is due to ignorance, and so is involuntary.

de Virtute. This conversation also is held by Socrates with a friend who is anonymous in most of the MSS. In the Vatican MS. called by Burnet O he has a name, Hippotrophus. The piece is thus presumably that mentioned by Diogenes Laertius under the alternative names *Midon* and *Hippotrophus*. It has the same type as the last. The question is whether "goodness" can be taught. In both pieces Socrates is made, as in the *Minos*, to originate the problem. The example of the various "arts" is used to show that if you would acquire special knowledge, you must put yourself under a specialist's tuition. But "goodness" apparently cannot be acquired thus, since Themistocles, Aristides, Thucydides, Pericles were all unable to impart it to their sons. Again "goodness" does not seem to come "by nature." If it did, we might have specialists in human nature, as we have fanciers of dogs and horses, and they would be able to tell us which young persons have the qualities that will repay careful training. "Goodness," then, like prophecy, seems to depend on an incalculable "divine" inspiration.

Boeckh, as we have said, regarded these trifles as the genuine work of an acquaintance of Socrates, the cobbler Simon.[1] They cannot be that for several reasons. For (1) they are slavishly close imitations, often reproducing whole sentences of Plato's text. Thus the argument about the parallel between " justice " and the arts of number and measure in the *de Iusto* has been directly copied, as Stallbaum said, from *Euthyphr. 7b* ff.   The *de Virtute* is largely made up of similar " liftings " from the *Meno* and *Protagoras*. (2) The discourses ascribed to the cobbler Simon must have been shorter even than our two νοθευόμενοι, for there were thirty-three of them in a single roll (D.L. ii. 122).   (3) The work ascribed to Simon was almost certainly a forgery.   (The learned Stoic Panaetius said that the only certainly genuine dialogues by " Socratic men " were those of Plato, Xenophon, Antisthenes, Aeschines ; those ascribed to Euclides and Phaedo were doubtful, all others spurious.   D.L. ii. 64.)   In fact, it is hard to doubt that we are dealing with late exercises in imitation of Plato's style, " atticizing " copies of a classic.   The purity of the language is partly explained by this, partly by the presence of *verbatim* extracts.

Demodocus.   This hardly even pretends to be a dialogue.   It is a direct harangue of Socrates to an audience which includes Demodocus (? the father of Theages).   The style is halting to the verge of inarticulateness.   The drift, obscured by verbiage, is that Socrates has been asked to advise the audience on some decision they are about to take.   The request implies that there is a " science of giving advice."   Either the present audience possess this science or they do not.   If they all possess it, there is nothing to discuss ; if none of them possess it, discussion is waste of time.   If one or two possess it, why do not they advise the others ?   Where is the use of listening to rival counsellors, or of taking a vote when their counsel has been heard ?   How can persons who do not know for themselves which is the advisable course vote to any purpose on the advices of rival counsellors ?   Socrates will certainly not advise such a set of fools.

At this point the shambling speech ends.   What follows seems to be a detached set of anecdotes, having nothing in common with what has gone before, except that Socrates is apparently the narrator, and that each anecdote embodies a rather puerile dilemma.

(*a*) I once heard a man blame his friend for accepting the story of the plaintiff in a suit without troubling to hear the other side. This, he said, was unfair and a violation of the dicast's oath.   The friend retorted that if you cannot tell whether one man is speaking the truth, you will be still more at a loss if there are two speakers with different stories.   If they should both tell the same story, why need you listen to it twice ?

(*b*) A man is reproached by a friend to whom he has refused

---

[1] For a statement of Boeckh's case see his essay *In Platonis qui vulgo fertur Minoem* (Halle, 1806).   It is fairly met and disproved by Stallbaum in the introduction to his own commentary on the *Minos*.

a loan. A bystander comments, "Your rebuff is your own fault.
For a *fault* means a failure to effect one's purpose, and you have
failed to effect yours. Also, if your request was an improper one,
it is a fault to have made it ; if it was proper, it is a fault not to
have made it successfully. Also, you have not gone to work the
right way, or you would not have been refused ; *ergo*, you have
made a fault." A second bystander urged that any man may
fairly complain if one whom he has helped refuses to help him in
turn. But the first speaker said, "The man either is able to do
what you ask, or he is not. If he is not, you should not make so
unreasonable a request ; if he is, how is it you did not succeed
with him ? " "Well, a man at least expects better treatment
for the future if he remonstrates." "Not if the remonstrance is
as groundless as it is in this case."

(*c*) A man is blamed for giving ready credence to the random
utterances of irresponsible persons. Why ? Because he believes
the tale of "anyone and everyone" without investigation. But
would it not be an equal fault to believe the tales of your most
particular intimates without examination ? If a speaker is an
intimate of *A* and a stranger to *B*, will *A* be right in believing his
tale and *B* equally right in disbelieving the same story ? If the
same tale is told you by an intimate and a stranger, must it not
be equally credible on the lips of both ?

The shambling and helpless style of these anecdotes shows
that they come from the same hand as the foolish harangue to
Demodocus. The writer must have been a person of low intelligence, with no power of expression and a taste for futile "eristic."
I doubt whether his scraps were meant to form a connected whole.

Sisyphus. Socrates is in conversation with a Pharsalian of
the singular name of Sisyphus,[1] whom he expected to have seen
the day before among the audience at an *epidexis* or show-speech.
Sisyphus explains that he was kept away by "our rulers," who
commanded his presence at an important consultation.[2] But what
is consultation (τὸ βουλεύεσθαι) ? A process of inquiry (τὸ ζητεῖν).
Inquiring is trying to get fuller knowledge of something of which
we have some preliminary notion, but not full knowledge. It is
the presence in us of ignorance which makes this process difficult.
But men do not "consult" about what lies beyond the range of their
knowledge ; hence the business of yesterday should have been
called an *inquiry* into the interests of Pharsalus. Why did not
the inquirers take the course of "learning" the truth from some

[1] Presumably the Sisyphus of Pharsalus mentioned also by Theopompus,
Fr. 19 (*ap.* Athenaeus, 252*f*). Sisyphus was perhaps a "nickname."
Xenophon (*Hellenica*, iii. 1, 8) says that the Spartan commander Dercylidas
was called so for his "artfulness." Athenaeus (500*b*), quoting from Ephorus,
gives the *sobriquet* in his case as σκύφος, an obvious corruption (CK for
CIC).

[2] Then is Socrates supposed to be in Thessaly, or were the "government
offices" of Pharsalus at Athens ?

one who already knew it, rather than the inferior course of trying to puzzle it out for themselves ? And can there really be a difference between better and worse advice ? Advice always has reference to the future, the future is what " has not happened " and therefore has no determinate character (οὐδὲ φύσιν ἔχει οὐδεμίαν). One guess about it cannot well be better or worse than any other.

The writer is perhaps the same man as the author of the *Demodocus* ; he has the same foible for childish eristic, the same interest in the alleged puzzle about " deliberation " and the same helplessness of style, though the *Sisyphus* is not quite so helpless as the *Demodocus*. He has read the *Meno* [1] and he has one real point, though he does not know how to manage it. He is playing with the conception of the future as something which is, as yet, nothing at all,[2] and therefore not a subject for rational consideration. Possibly he is thinking of the Cyrenaic doctrine that the future, being unreal, is " nothing to us," [3] and trying to " expose " it ?

Eryxias. This is a much more serious production than any of the four just examined. The writer has provided a definite audience, scene and date. Socrates is talking in the portico of Zeus Eleutherius [4] with Critias (the " oligarch "), Eryxias and Erasistratus, nephew of Phaeax (the contemporary and rival of Alcibiades). The date is supposed to be between the Peace of Nicias and the determination taken in 416 by Athens to attack Syracuse, as we see from the opening remarks made by Erasistratus on the necessity of taking a firm line with that " wasp's nest." The subject of the discussion, which is made to arise quite naturally, is the nature and worth of πλοῦτος, " capital," as we should say. Erasistratus holds that " the richest man is he who owns what is worth most." If so, may not a poor man in lusty health be said to be richer than an opulent invalid with whom he would never dream of changing places ? And there may be things of higher worth than health. It is evident, also, that the thing of highest worth is happiness (εὐδαιμονία). It should follow that the richest of men are the " wise and good," because they do not impair their happiness by making false steps in life : " the man who knows what is good is the only real capitalist,"—a clear allusion to the Stoic paradox, *solus sapiens dives*. Eryxias objects that a man might be as wise as Nestor and yet in want of the bare necessaries of life. Still, says S., such a man's wisdom might have a high value in exchange in any district where it was esteemed. A man

---

[1] As we see not only from his reference to the old eristic quibble about τὸ ζητεῖν, but from his allusion to " inquiring " into the ratio of " diagonal " to " side," to which he adds the later problem of the " duplication of the cube."

[2] The view adopted by Dr. C. D. Broad, *Scientific Thought*, 66 ff.

[3] Cf. the saying ascribed to Aristippus, μόνον ἡμέτερον εἶναι τὸ παρόν, μήτε δὲ τὸ φθάνον μήτε τὸ προσδοκώμενον· τὸ μὲν γὰρ ἀπολωλέναι, τὸ δὲ ἄδηλον εἶναι εἰ πάρεσται, R.P. 267.

[4] For which see Pausanias, i. 3, 2. It is also the scene of the *Theages*.

who understood the direction of life might make capital of his knowledge, if he chose. Eryxias treats this as a verbal quibble, and this leads to a dispute between him and Critias in which S. acts as seconder to Eryxias. Leaving on one side the verbal paradox that the wise man is the true capitalist, we may more profitably ask what ways of acquiring wealth are honourable, and whether wealth itself is or is not good. Eryxias thinks it is, Critias that it is not, since *for some persons*, those whose wealth leads them to perpetrate follies or crimes, wealth is so clearly not good ; but what is not good for *everyone* is not properly called a good. That argument, says S., is a mere borrowing from Prodicus, who had publicly defended the thesis that everything is good for the man who knows how to *use* it, bad for the man who does not, but had been silenced and put to shame by a mere lad. The lad's counter-argument was that only a fool expects to get as answers to prayer things he might learn from a teacher, or find out for himself. Pro-dicus, like other men, asks in his prayers that " his lot may be good " : on his own theory this amounts to praying that he may himself *become* good, and also, according to his own theories, good-ness is something a man can learn from a teacher. Critias is borrowing the argument of Prodicus, and if he is not hooted down, that is only because reasoning which would be seen to be bad in a " sophist " imposes on hearers who respect Critias as a gentleman and man of the world.

Here S. directs attention to the original and still more funda-mental question what wealth *is*. You may say, " abundance of χρήματα, means." But what are means ? It is argued, with a little needless display of general information, that means are " possessions which are of *use* to us." Hence a cartload of Car-thaginian currency would not be " means " at Athens, where it will not exchange for anything. Coin is popularly confused with wealth simply because it exchanges freely for clothes and all other com-modities. Now a professional man can exchange his professional services for commodities, and thus ἐπιστῆμαι, knowledge of pro-fessions, seems to be one form of capital. Again an article is only capital to one who knows how to use it, and the καλοὶ κἀγαθοί are the persons who know how to make the right use of everything. Thus there is a sense in which to make a man wiser is to make him richer. Critias still protests that possessions are not wealth, but the argument is continued. In any trade, a man's capital clearly includes not only his materials but his implements, and sometimes also appliances for making those implements. If a man were once fully equipped with all that his body requires, money and such things would be useless to him. Again, since to learn you must be able to hear, the money a man pays his doctor for taking care of his hearing is actually useful as a means to " goodness." This money may have been made in a " base " calling, and thus a " base " thing *may* be useful for good. We are almost tempted to say that, since a man can only become wise, healthy, good, if he has previously been ignorant, unwell, bad, ignorance, disease, vice are conditions *sine quibus non* of their opposites, and therefore useful, and ought, by consequence, to be called wealth. But apart from this paradox, we may ask ourselves one question, " When is a man happier and better, when he has the most or when he has the least numerous and expensive wants ? " Since this amounts to asking whether a man is happier in disease or in health, the question answers itself. The rich, who have many and expensive wants, are not the truly happy.

I think it clear that the purpose of the dialogue, which is very interesting for its economic theses, is to canvass the Stoic doctrine that wisdom, virtue, wealth are identical, and that the sage is the only " capitalist." This is the thesis which Eryxias treats as idle playing with words and Socrates " side-tracks," in order to discuss the more than verbal question whether riches are good or bad. It is part of the anti-Stoic polemic that S. supports Eryxias against Critias who denies that " property " is wealth. The author means to protest against " pulpit declamation " which amounts to nothing but words and to replace it by the dispassionate Academic view that wealth and wisdom are different things, the one at the bottom, the other at the top of the scale of good. The Greek of the dialogue is not the Attic of Plato, yet it is hardly the vulgar κοινή. I should conjecture that the work belongs to the beginnings of the Academic polemic against Stoicism, in the early decades of the third century. The writer seems to have drawn some of his material from the *Callias* of Aeschines,[1] in which the wealth of the famous " millionaire " family was a prominent topic and Prodicus received some notice. Suidas ascribes an *Eryxias* to Aeschines himself, but there seems to be no other evidence for the existence of such a work. Presumably our *Eryxias* is meant, and Suidas has made a mistake about its authorship.

Axiochus. In style this dialogue is far inferior to the *Eryxias.* The language is a vulgar κοινή, full of non-Attic words and phrases. The *mise-en-scène* shows complete ignorance of the personages of Plato's dialogues. The principal figure, apart from Socrates, is Axiochus of Scambonidae, the uncle of Alcibiades. The supposed date is fixed by a reference to the trial of the generals after Arginusae (368*d*) as not earlier than 405, and Axiochus represents himself as having supported the protest of Socrates against the unconstitutionality of the proceedings. The writer has forgotten that Axiochus was, next to Alcibiades, the chief victim of the scandals of 415 and shared the capital sentence.[2] In the opening

---

[1] See H. Dittmar, *Aeschines von Sphettos*, 198–199, who, however, perhaps mistakes a probability for a demonstration.

[2] Andocides, i. 16, Agariste, wife of Alcmeonides and widow of Damon, gave information against Alcibiades, Axiochus and Adimantus, καὶ ἔφυγον οὗτοι πάντες ἐπὶ ταύτῃ τῇ μηνύσει. Alcibiades afterwards had his hour of

scene (364a) Damon is mentioned as the music-master of Axiochus' son Clinias (the Clinias of the *Euthydemus*), and Socrates sees the two " running towards him," though Damon, a contemporary of Anaxagoras, would have been almost a centenarian if he had been living at the supposed date.   The scheme of the dialogue is simple. Axiochus has been seized by a severe " fit " and apprehends death ; Socrates is called in to " console " him.   He does this by the arguments that (1) death is utter unconsciousness and after it there are no more pains to fear ; (2) life in the body is one unbroken scene of anxiety and suffering, so that it is a positive good to have done with it.   This second point, intended to rule out the possible rejoinder to (1) that even if death brings no posthumous disagree-ables with it, it is still dreadful because it puts an end to the *joie de vivre*, is argued at length in a speech professedly taken from the eminently wise Prodicus.   (3) A further argument, also ascribed to Prodicus, is the dilemma, " death matters neither to the living nor to the dead ; while we live, *death* is not there, and when we have died, *we* are not there."   Axiochus rejects these " consola-tions " scornfully.   They are the " superficial twaddle " which is coming into vogue just now with empty-headed lads.   It all sounds fine, but when one is face-to-face with death it proves idle bravado (369d).   In the remainder of the dialogue Socrates drops the pre-tence of holding the views of Prodicus and discovers himself as a convinced believer in the blessed immortality of the soul.   This, he says, is proved (1) by the achievements of man in his ascent from barbarism to civilization, (2) and particularly by his great intellectual triumph, his creation of astronomy, the science which reveals to us the *magnalia Dei*.   Man could not have done all this, " were there not indeed the breath of God in his soul."   This message goes home to the heart of Axiochus, who feels himself now delivered from his terrors.   Socrates then completes his good work by relating a myth, in the Orphic style, of the blessedness of souls in the next life, professing to have learned it from a Persian *magus*.   The myth leaves Axiochus actually " in love " with death.

I feel personally convinced that Immisch is right in the view taken of the purpose of the dialogue in his edition of it.[1]   As he points out, the third of the pretended " consolations " produced by Socrates is the familiar Epicurean dilemma, " death is nothing to us, for while we are, death is not, and when death is, we are not." [2]   This is the argument of which Axiochus speaks with marked contempt as superficial " twaddle " momentarily fashion-

triumph and restoration, but he had been banished again before 405 and all his connections were then in the worst odour.   The alleged " support " given to Socrates is unknown to the historians, and the reference to πρόεδροι in the *ecclesia* (368e) seems to show ignorance of the fifth-century method and procedure.

[1] O. Immisch, *Philologische Studien zu Plato. Erster Heft. Axiochus*, Leipzig, 1896.

[2] Epicurus, *Ep.* iii. 125 (Bailey), Lucretius iii. 830.

able with mere boys. Immisch seems also to have shown that there are numerous distinctively Epicurean turns of speech throughout the so-called discourse of Prodicus on the misery of existence. Hence I cannot reject his conclusion that the dialogue is a piece of anti-Epicurean polemic, intended to contrast the Platonic with the Epicurean answer to the perennial question *What may I hope for?* and to insinuate that the "wisdom" of Epicurus is not even original. It is a mere revival of the ideas of a second-rate sophist, and a "doctrine of despair" into the bargain. It is natural, though not absolutely necessary, to draw Immisch's further conclusion that, in the writer's day, Epicureanism was just beginning to be in vogue among *fin-de-siècle* youths. In that case we must date the composition as early as somewhere *c.* 305–300 B.C., since Epicurus established himself at Athens in 307/6. Other scholars, such as Wilamowitz and H. Dittmar, reject this date as too early, but, though I do not want to be over-confident, I suspect they may be ascribing to "lateness" faults of style and vocabulary which may only mean that the writer is neither an Athenian [1] nor a person with a literary sense. I see no need to suppose a date later than the time of Epicurus, whose Greek is much of the same stamp. There was an earlier *Axiochus* by Aeschines of Sphettus of which all that is known is that, as we learn from Athenaeus, it painted an unfavourable picture of the debauched life of Alcibiades, and presumably of his uncle also. It can hardly have supplied our author with material.[2]

It is hardly necessary to say anything of the little trifle, not contained in our Plato MSS., called the *Alcyon* and attributed, in MSS., variously to Plato or to Lucian. (It is commonly included in printed texts of Lucian ; the only recent editor of Plato to print it is C. F. Hermann.) This piece of silly prettiness is certainly neither Plato's nor Lucian's ; since it was already known to Favorinus of Arles,[3] it must be the work of some Atticist earlier than Lucian. It describes Socrates and Chaerephon as walking by the Bay of Phalerum, where they hear the cry of the (mythical) halcyon. Socrates relates the legend that the bird is a transformed woman, argues that, since God's power is incomprehensibly great, we must not be too ready to reject such "miracles," and commends the story for its moral of wifely devotion.

Diogenes Laertius (iii. 62) gives the following list of νοθευόμενοι : *Midon* or *Hippotrophus, Eryxias* or *Erasistratus, Alcyon,* [a corrupt

---

[1] The attempt to argue from 365*e*, 368*d* that the writer must be an Athenian because he makes his characters talk of *their* national heroes as they naturally would, does not deeply impress me.

[2] On the *Axiochus* of Aeschines see H. Dittmar, *Aeschines von Sphettos,* 159–163.

[3] Favorinus ascribed it to a certain Leon (D.L. iii. 62). Athenaeus (516*c*) calls the author " Leon the Academic," on the authority of Nicias of Nicaea. If this means the fourth-century mathematician Leon, the ascription is most improbable.

word], *Sisyphus, Axiochus, Phaeaces, Demodocus, Chelidon, Hebdome, Epimenides.* The only " work " we possess not included in this list is the *de Iusto.* This is absent, unless it is covered by the corrupt entry ἀκεφάλοις or ἀκέφαλοι or ἀκέφαλος ἤ (Schanz, ἤ), before the *Sisyphus.* As there was a dialogue *Cephalus* ascribed to Speusippus (D.L. iv. 4), the reference of Diogenes may be to that, as the Basle editors of the *Vita Platonis* suggest. Athenaeus (506*d*), apparently following Hegesander of Delphi, the author of a foolish diatribe against Plato, refers to an otherwise unknown *Cimon*, alleged to contain invectives against Themistocles, Myronides, Alcibiades and Cimon himself. Some of the statements made in this attack on Plato are so absurd that one may wonder whether the *Cimon* ever existed, except in the imagination of a careless scribbler.

There still survives in Syriac a translation of a " Socratic " dialogue, *Herostrophos* [1] dealing with the soul. The text was published by Lagarde in his *Analecta Syriaca* (1858) ; there is a German version with a discussion of *provenance* by V. Ryssel in *Rheinisches Museum,* N.F. xlviii. 175-196, on which the following remarks are based. The dialogue is shown by its vocabulary and other peculiarities to be a genuine version of a Greek original ; the translator, according to Ryssel, was the priest and physician Sergius of Rāsain, a student of Aristotle who died at Constantinople soon after 536 A.D. The name of the interlocutor Herostrophos appears to be a miswriting of Aristippus. (He is represented as a stranger attracted to Socrates by his reputation for wisdom, exactly as Aeschines of Sphettus (D.L. ii. 65) related that Aristippus was drawn to Athens κατὰ κλέος Σωκράτους. The two names, as written in Syriac, only differ by a single letter.) The problem to which he desires an answer is that of the fate of the soul at death. Does it perish with the body, enter a new body, or die for a time and revive again with the same body ? (The last alternative seems to be suggested by the Christian dogma of the " resurrection of the flesh," but might allude only to the Pythagorean and Stoic conception of " cyclical recurrence " ?) I do not myself understand the confused reply of Socrates. He seems to be combining insistence on the thought that the soul is imperishable and immutable with the notion that it has fire as its chief component, and the suggestion of an analogy between death and sunset. As the sun rises again to-morrow, so the soul reappears again with a new body after the death of the present body. It does not appear that the lost Greek original was ever taken by anyone for a work of Plato, and I find it hard to believe that it is not influenced by Stoicism. This might account for the apparent materialism and also for the suggestion of the reappearance of the same body, if this is not actually a borrowing from Christianity.

[1] My attention was first drawn to the point by Mr. W. L. Lorimer of St. Andrews University.

The *Anthology* contains a number of epigrams ascribed to Plato (though, in one or two cases, to other authors also). The fact of the ascription does not prove authenticity. On the other side, the manner and diction of Greek epigram is so stereotyped that it would probably be impossible to prove any of these compositions spurious on linguistic grounds. The collection will be found most conveniently in Hiller-Crusius, *Anthologia Lyrica*,[3] *Pt. I*. The items which, if genuine, would throw some light on Plato's personality are 1, the well-known couplet on Agathon, translated by Shelley; 8, the lines on Alexis and Phaedrus; 14, 15, two famous couplets on a beautiful boy, *perhaps* called Aster; 7, a fine epigram commemorative of Dion. 1 and 8, at any rate, if genuine, would prove Plato to have had the " erotic " temperament. To my own mind, the occurrence of the names Agathon and Phaedrus is proof of spuriousness. The author clearly has in his mind the parts taken by Agathon the poet and Phaedrus of Myrrhinus in Plato's great ἐρωτικὸς λόγος the *Symposium*, and has forgotten that both were grown men when Plato was under twelve. I see no reason why most of the other epigrams should not be Plato's, except that there is no particular reason why they must be. Even the lines on Dion, though worthy of Plato, can hardly be said to contain anything which might not be said by any other good epigrammatist. And it is, perhaps, hardly likely that Plato, writing after he was seventy about his devotion to a friend who had lived to be over fifty, would use the word ἔρως to describe the attachment. I fear we must be content to say that though some of the verses may be Plato's, none need be so.

A more interesting personal document is Plato's Will (D.L. iii. 41–43). The probability is that this and the Wills of Aristotle and Theophrastus are genuine. The Academy would have legal reasons for safeguarding the document, just as a society to-day preserves its charter of incorporation or its title-deeds. The Will runs thus: " Plato leaves possessions and devises them as hereunder. The property at Iphistiadae bounded on the N. by the road from the shrine at Cephisia, on the S. by the shrine of Heracles at Iphistiadae, on the E. by the land of Archestratus of Phrearria, on the W. by the land of Philippus of Chollidae, shall be neither sold nor alienated, but secured in every way to the boy Adimantus.[1] The property at Iresidae purchased from Callimachus and bounded on the N. by the land of Eurymedon of Myrrhinus, on the S. by the land of Demostratus of Xypate, on the E. by the land of the said Eurymedon, on the W. by the Cephisus.[2] . . . *Item*, three *minae* of silver. *Item*, a silver goblet, weight 165 dr. *Item*, a cup, weight 45 dr. *Item*, a gold finger-ring and earring, com-

---

[1] Presumably a descendant (? grandson) of Plato's eldest brother.

[2] There is no statement about the way in which this property is devised. Either the text is defective or we must understand that this property also is part of the settlement on Adimantus.

bined weight 4½ dr. Euclides the stone-cutter owes me three *minae*. I give Artemis her freedom. I leave the following household slaves, Tychon, Bictas, Apollonides, Dionysius. Also the household furniture specified in the annexed schedule of which Demetrius has the duplicate. I leave no unpaid debts. I appoint as executors Leosthenes, Speusippus, Demetrius, Hegias, Eurymedon, Callimachus, Theopompus."

By comparison with the similar wills of Aristotle and Theophrastus we can see that Plato was by no means in affluent circumstances.

See further on the works dealt work above :

SHOREY, P.—*What Plato Said* (pp. 415–444, " Doubtful and Spurious Dialogues ").

SOUILHÉ, J.—*Platon, Dialogues Suspects* (Paris, 1930. The author tends to accept the *Clitophon*, and *Alcibiades* I) : *Platon, Dialogues Apocryphes*. (Paris, 1930.)

FRIEDLÄNDER, P.—*Die Platonischen Schriften* (Berlin and Leipzig, 1930), pp. 117–127 (on *Hipparchus*), 147–155 (on *Theages*), 233–245 (on *Alcibiades* I). All these are accepted.

INDEXES

I. INDEX OF PROPER NAMES

(This index makes no pretensions to be exhaustive, but it is trusted that it will be found sufficient)

Academy (the), 5–7, 21, 286, 290, 318, 343 n., 375, 378, 393, 409 ff., 417, 464, 503 ff., 529, 531, 544
Acton, Lord, 472
Adam, J., 396 n., 397 n., 522
Addison, J., 5
Adimantus, 2, 263, 271
Adrastus, 510 n.
Aeschines (orator), 156, 165 n., 212 n.
Aeschines (of Sphettus), 35 n., 132 n., 133 n., 143, 147, 163 n., 278, 517 n., 521 n., 522 n., 525 n., 534 n., 550, 553
Aeschylus, 147 n., 279
Agathon, 210 ff., 221, 240, 554
Alcibiades, 13, 44, 91 n., 116 n., 127, 158, 161, 165 n., 210, 233, 236, 309 n., 473, 512–14, 550
Alcmaeon, 120, 184 n., 194, 306 n., 453
Alexander (Aphrodisiensis), 355
Alexander, S., 455
Amipsias, 58, 91 n.
Anaxagoras, 83, 199, 201, 208, 212, 214, 294, 314, 352, 387, 449 n., 524, 551
Anaximander, 447–448, 457
Andocides, 158, 237, 550 n.
Antiochus (of Ascalon), 544
Antipater (of Sidon), 533
Antiphon (orator), 101–102
Antiphon (son of Pyrilampes), 351
Antiphon (sophist), 101–102, 119 n., 2/1, 336
Antisthenes, 35 n., 86 n., 89 n., 96 n., 180 n., 273, 331 n., 333 n., 386 n., 423 n., 522 n.
Anytus, 117 n., 130, 140, 158, 167, 173 n.
Apollodorus (of Phalerum), 210
Arcesilaus, 12 n., 528
Archelaus (of Macedon), 105, 113, 527

Archelaus (philosopher), 199, 383
Archer-Hind, R. D., 542
Archytas, 6, 8, 322, 542, 543
Aristarchus (of Samos), 449
Aristides, 57, 128, 142 n.
Aristippus (of Cyrene), 427, 434, 548 n., 553
Aristocles (Peripatetic), 353
Ariston, 1, 2
Aristophanes (Byz.), 11, 497
Aristophanes (Com.), 2 n., 51 n., 58, 75, 85, 105, 116 n., 125 n., 129 n., 161, 163 n., 209, 210, 219, 220, 234, 240–241, 263 n., 264, 325 n., 461
Aristotle, 3, 6, 10, 13, 14, 17, 26, 32 n., 35, 41, 61, 64, 76, 81 n., 82 n., 90, 105 n., 120, 148 n., 176, 185, 203, 235, 258 n., 269, 286, 297 n., 312 n., 328 n., 334 n., 341 n., 345, 347 n., 350 n., 356, 376–378, 393, 406, 408 ff., 413 n., 415, 417, 423 n., 427, 443, 447–449, 450 n., 469, 472, 484 n., 492, 503 ff., 536 n., 538 n., 544, 555, al.
Aristoxenus, 1 n., 283
Aspasia, 13, 41, 42, 278
Athenaeus, 541, 547 n., 553
Atticus, 443
Augustine, St., 28 n., 225, 232 n., 263, 490 n.
Axiochus, 90, 550 ff.

Bentley, R., 16 n.
Berkeley, G., 152 n.
Bethe, E., 213 n.
Bevan, E., 211 n.
Bignone, E., 102 n.
Blake, W., 119 n., 209, 220
Blass, F., 16 n.
Boeckh, A., 445 n., 448, 540, 545–546
Bois-Reymond, E. du, 57
Bonaventura, St., 225

557

II. INDEX OF SUBJECTS

(The list is unavoidably far from exhaustive)

A CATALOG OF SELECTED
DOVER BOOKS
IN ALL FIELDS OF INTEREST

A CATALOG OF SELECTED DOVER
BOOKS IN ALL FIELDS OF INTEREST

CONCERNING THE SPIRITUAL IN ART, Wassily Kandinsky. Pioneering work by father of abstract art. Thoughts on color theory, nature of art. Analysis of earlier masters. 12 illustrations. 80pp. of text. 5⅜ x 8½.   23411-8 Pa. $4.95

ANIMALS: 1,419 Copyright-Free Illustrations of Mammals, Birds, Fish, Insects, etc., Jim Harter (ed.). Clear wood engravings present, in extremely lifelike poses, over 1,000 species of animals. One of the most extensive pictorial sourcebooks of its kind. Captions. Index. 284pp. 9 x 12.   23766-4 Pa. $14.95

CELTIC ART: The Methods of Construction, George Bain. Simple geometric techniques for making Celtic interlacements, spirals, Kells-type initials, animals, humans, etc. Over 500 illustrations. 160pp. 9 x 12. (Available in U.S. only.)   22923-8 Pa. $9.95

AN ATLAS OF ANATOMY FOR ARTISTS, Fritz Schider. Most thorough reference work on art anatomy in the world. Hundreds of illustrations, including selections from works by Vesalius, Leonardo, Goya, Ingres, Michelangelo, others. 593 illustrations. 192pp. 7⅛ x 10¼.   20241-0 Pa. $9.95

CELTIC HAND STROKE-BY-STROKE (Irish Half-Uncial from "The Book of Kells"): An Arthur Baker Calligraphy Manual, Arthur Baker. Complete guide to creating each letter of the alphabet in distinctive Celtic manner. Covers hand position, strokes, pens, inks, paper, more. Illustrated. 48pp. 8¼ x 11.   24336-2 Pa. $3.95

EASY ORIGAMI, John Montroll. Charming collection of 32 projects (hat, cup, pelican, piano, swan, many more) specially designed for the novice origami hobbyist. Clearly illustrated easy-to-follow instructions insure that even beginning papercrafters will achieve successful results. 48pp. 8¼ x 11.   27298-2 Pa. $3.50

THE COMPLETE BOOK OF BIRDHOUSE CONSTRUCTION FOR WOOD-WORKERS, Scott D. Campbell. Detailed instructions, illustrations, tables. Also data on bird habitat and instinct patterns. Bibliography. 3 tables. 63 illustrations in 15 figures. 48pp. 5¼ x 8½.   24407-5 Pa. $2.50

BLOOMINGDALE'S ILLUSTRATED 1886 CATALOG: Fashions, Dry Goods and Housewares, Bloomingdale Brothers. Famed merchants' extremely rare catalog depicting about 1,700 products: clothing, housewares, firearms, dry goods, jewelry, more. Invaluable for dating, identifying vintage items. Also, copyright-free graphics for artists, designers. Co-published with Henry Ford Museum & Greenfield Village. 160pp. 8¼ x 11.   25780-0 Pa. $12.95

HISTORIC COSTUME IN PICTURES, Braun & Schneider. Over 1,450 costumed figures in clearly detailed engravings–from dawn of civilization to end of 19th century. Captions. Many folk costumes. 256pp. 8⅜ x 11¾.   23150-X Pa. $12.95

STICKLEY CRAFTSMAN FURNITURE CATALOGS, Gustav Stickley and L. & J. G. Stickley. Beautiful, functional furniture in two authentic catalogs from 1910. 594 illustrations, including 277 photos, show settles, rockers, armchairs, reclining chairs, bookcases, desks, tables. 183pp. 6½ x 9¼. 23838-5 Pa. $11.95

AMERICAN LOCOMOTIVES IN HISTORIC PHOTOGRAPHS: 1858 to 1949, Ron Ziel (ed.). A rare collection of 126 meticulously detailed official photographs, called "builder portraits," of American locomotives that majestically chronicle the rise of steam locomotive power in America. Introduction. Detailed captions. xi+ 129pp. 9 x 12. 27393-8 Pa. $13.95

AMERICA'S LIGHTHOUSES: An Illustrated History, Francis Ross Holland, Jr. Delightfully written, profusely illustrated fact-filled survey of over 200 American lighthouses since 1716. History, anecdotes, technological advances, more. 240pp. 8 x 10¾. 25576-X Pa. $12.95

TOWARDS A NEW ARCHITECTURE, Le Corbusier. Pioneering manifesto by founder of "International School." Technical and aesthetic theories, views of industry, economics, relation of form to function, "mass-production split" and much more. Profusely illustrated. 320pp. 6⅛ x 9¼. (Available in U.S. only.) 25023-7 Pa. $10.95

HOW THE OTHER HALF LIVES, Jacob Riis. Famous journalistic record, exposing poverty and degradation of New York slums around 1900, by major social reformer. 100 striking and influential photographs. 233pp. 10 x 7⅞. 22012-5 Pa. $11.95

FRUIT KEY AND TWIG KEY TO TREES AND SHRUBS, William M. Harlow. One of the handiest and most widely used identification aids. Fruit key covers 120 deciduous and evergreen species; twig key 160 deciduous species. Easily used. Over 300 photographs. 126pp. 5⅜ x 8½. 20511-8 Pa. $3.95

COMMON BIRD SONGS, Dr. Donald J. Borror. Songs of 60 most common U.S. birds: robins, sparrows, cardinals, bluejays, finches, more–arranged in order of increasing complexity. Up to 9 variations of songs of each species. Cassette and manual 99911-4 $8.95

ORCHIDS AS HOUSE PLANTS, Rebecca Tyson Northen. Grow cattleyas and many other kinds of orchids–in a window, in a case, or under artificial light. 63 illustrations. 148pp. 5⅜ x 8½. 23261-1 Pa. $7.95

MONSTER MAZES, Dave Phillips. Masterful mazes at four levels of difficulty. Avoid deadly perils and evil creatures to find magical treasures. Solutions for all 32 exciting illustrated puzzles. 48pp. 8¼ x 11. 26005-4 Pa. $2.95

MOZART'S DON GIOVANNI (DOVER OPERA LIBRETTO SERIES), Wolfgang Amadeus Mozart. Introduced and translated by Ellen H. Bleiler. Standard Italian libretto, with complete English translation. Convenient and thoroughly portable–an ideal companion for reading along with a recording or the performance itself. Introduction. List of characters. Plot summary. 121pp. 5¼ x 8½. 24944-1 Pa. $3.95

TECHNICAL MANUAL AND DICTIONARY OF CLASSICAL BALLET, Gail Grant. Defines, explains, comments on steps, movements, poses and concepts. 15-page pictorial section. Basic book for student, viewer. 127pp. 5⅜ x 8½. 21843-0 Pa. $4.95

THE CLARINET AND CLARINET PLAYING, David Pino. Lively, comprehensive work features suggestions about technique, musicianship, and musical interpretation, as well as guidelines for teaching, making your own reeds, and preparing for public performance. Includes an intriguing look at clarinet history. "A godsend," *The Clarinet,* Journal of the International Clarinet Society. Appendixes. 7 illus. 320pp. 5⅜ x 8½. 40270-3 Pa. $9.95

HOLLYWOOD GLAMOR PORTRAITS, John Kobal (ed.). 145 photos from 1926-49. Harlow, Gable, Bogart, Bacall; 94 stars in all. Full background on photographers, technical aspects. 160pp. 8⅜ x 11¼. 23352-9 Pa. $12.95

THE ANNOTATED CASEY AT THE BAT: A Collection of Ballads about the Mighty Casey/Third, Revised Edition, Martin Gardner (ed.). Amusing sequels and parodies of one of America's best-loved poems: Casey's Revenge, Why Casey Whiffed, Casey's Sister at the Bat, others. 256pp. 5⅜ x 8½. 28598-7 Pa. $8.95

THE RAVEN AND OTHER FAVORITE POEMS, Edgar Allan Poe. Over 40 of the author's most memorable poems: "The Bells," "Ulalume," "Israfel," "To Helen," "The Conqueror Worm," "Eldorado," "Annabel Lee," many more. Alphabetic lists of titles and first lines. 64pp. 5$^{3}/_{16}$ x 8¼. 26685-0 Pa. $1.00

PERSONAL MEMOIRS OF U. S. GRANT, Ulysses Simpson Grant. Intelligent, deeply moving firsthand account of Civil War campaigns, considered by many the finest military memoirs ever written. Includes letters, historic photographs, maps and more. 528pp. 6⅛ x 9¼. 28587-1 Pa. $12.95

ANCIENT EGYPTIAN MATERIALS AND INDUSTRIES, A. Lucas and J. Harris. Fascinating, comprehensive, thoroughly documented text describes this ancient civilization's vast resources and the processes that incorporated them in daily life, including the use of animal products, building materials, cosmetics, perfumes and incense, fibers, glazed ware, glass and its manufacture, materials used in the mummification process, and much more. 544pp. 6⅛ x 9¼. (Available in U.S. only.) 40446-3 Pa. $16.95

RUSSIAN STORIES/PYCCKNE PACCKA3bl: A Dual-Language Book, edited by Gleb Struve. Twelve tales by such masters as Chekhov, Tolstoy, Dostoevsky, Pushkin, others. Excellent word-for-word English translations on facing pages, plus teaching and study aids, Russian/English vocabulary, biographical/critical introductions, more. 416pp. 5⅜ x 8½. 26244-8 Pa. $9.95

PHILADELPHIA THEN AND NOW: 60 Sites Photographed in the Past and Present, Kenneth Finkel and Susan Oyama. Rare photographs of City Hall, Logan Square, Independence Hall, Betsy Ross House, other landmarks juxtaposed with contemporary views. Captures changing face of historic city. Introduction. Captions. 128pp. 8¼ x 11. 25790-8 Pa. $9.95

AIA ARCHITECTURAL GUIDE TO NASSAU AND SUFFOLK COUNTIES, LONG ISLAND, The American Institute of Architects, Long Island Chapter, and the Society for the Preservation of Long Island Antiquities. Comprehensive, well-researched and generously illustrated volume brings to life over three centuries of Long Island's great architectural heritage. More than 240 photographs with authoritative, extensively detailed captions. 176pp. 8¼ x 11. 26946-9 Pa. $14.95

NORTH AMERICAN INDIAN LIFE: Customs and Traditions of 23 Tribes, Elsie Clews Parsons (ed.). 27 fictionalized essays by noted anthropologists examine religion, customs, government, additional facets of life among the Winnebago, Crow, Zuni, Eskimo, other tribes. 480pp. 6⅛ x 9¼. 27377-6 Pa. $10.95

FRANK LLOYD WRIGHT'S DANA HOUSE, Donald Hoffmann. Pictorial essay of residential masterpiece with over 160 interior and exterior photos, plans, elevations, sketches and studies. 128pp. 9¼ x 10¾. 29120-0 Pa. $14.95

THE MALE AND FEMALE FIGURE IN MOTION: 60 Classic Photographic Sequences, Eadweard Muybridge. 60 true-action photographs of men and women walking, running, climbing, bending, turning, etc., reproduced from rare 19th-century masterpiece. vi + 121pp. 9 x 12. 24745-7 Pa. $12.95

1001 QUESTIONS ANSWERED ABOUT THE SEASHORE, N. J. Berrill and Jacquelyn Berrill. Queries answered about dolphins, sea snails, sponges, starfish, fishes, shore birds, many others. Covers appearance, breeding, growth, feeding, much more. 305pp. 5¼ x 8¼. 23366-9 Pa. $9.95

ATTRACTING BIRDS TO YOUR YARD, William J. Weber. Easy-to-follow guide offers advice on how to attract the greatest diversity of birds: birdhouses, feeders, water and waterers, much more. 96pp. 5³⁄₁₆ x 8¼. 28927-3 Pa. $2.50

MEDICINAL AND OTHER USES OF NORTH AMERICAN PLANTS: A Historical Survey with Special Reference to the Eastern Indian Tribes, Charlotte Erichsen-Brown. Chronological historical citations document 500 years of usage of plants, trees, shrubs native to eastern Canada, northeastern U.S. Also complete identifying information. 343 illustrations. 544pp. 6½ x 9¼. 25951-X Pa. $12.95

STORYBOOK MAZES, Dave Phillips. 23 stories and mazes on two-page spreads: Wizard of Oz, Treasure Island, Robin Hood, etc. Solutions. 64pp. 8¼ x 11.
23628-5 Pa. $2.95

AMERICAN NEGRO SONGS: 230 Folk Songs and Spirituals, Religious and Secular, John W. Work. This authoritative study traces the African influences of songs sung and played by black Americans at work, in church, and as entertainment. The author discusses the lyric significance of such songs as "Swing Low, Sweet Chariot," "John Henry," and others and offers the words and music for 230 songs. Bibliography. Index of Song Titles. 272pp. 6½ x 9¼. 40271-1 Pa. $10.95

MOVIE-STAR PORTRAITS OF THE FORTIES, John Kobal (ed.). 163 glamor, studio photos of 106 stars of the 1940s: Rita Hayworth, Ava Gardner, Marlon Brando, Clark Gable, many more. 176pp. 8⅜ x 11¼. 23546-7 Pa. $14.95

BENCHLEY LOST AND FOUND, Robert Benchley. Finest humor from early 30s, about pet peeves, child psychologists, post office and others. Mostly unavailable elsewhere. 73 illustrations by Peter Arno and others. 183pp. 5⅜ x 8½. 22410-4 Pa. $6.95

YEKL and THE IMPORTED BRIDEGROOM AND OTHER STORIES OF YIDDISH NEW YORK, Abraham Cahan. Film Hester Street based on *Yekl* (1896). Novel, other stories among first about Jewish immigrants on N.Y.'s East Side. 240pp. 5⅜ x 8½. 22427-9 Pa. $7.95

SELECTED POEMS, Walt Whitman. Generous sampling from *Leaves of Grass*. Twenty-four poems include "I Hear America Singing," "Song of the Open Road," "I Sing the Body Electric," "When Lilacs Last in the Dooryard Bloom'd," "O Captain! My Captain!"–all reprinted from an authoritative edition. Lists of titles and first lines. 128pp. 5³⁄₁₆ x 8¼. 26878-0 Pa. $1.00

THE BEST TALES OF HOFFMANN, E. T. A. Hoffmann. 10 of Hoffmann's most important stories: "Nutcracker and the King of Mice," "The Golden Flowerpot," etc. 458pp. 5⅜ x 8½. 21793-0 Pa. $9.95

FROM FETISH TO GOD IN ANCIENT EGYPT, E. A. Wallis Budge. Rich detailed survey of Egyptian conception of "God" and gods, magic, cult of animals, Osiris, more. Also, superb English translations of hymns and legends. 240 illustrations. 545pp. 5⅜ x 8½. 25803-3 Pa. $13.95

FRENCH STORIES/CONTES FRANÇAIS: A Dual-Language Book, Wallace Fowlie. Ten stories by French masters, Voltaire to Camus: "Micromegas" by Voltaire; "The Atheist's Mass" by Balzac; "Minuet" by de Maupassant; "The Guest" by Camus, six more. Excellent English translations on facing pages. Also French-English vocabulary list, exercises, more. 352pp. 5⅜ x 8½. 26443-2 Pa. $9.95

CHICAGO AT THE TURN OF THE CENTURY IN PHOTOGRAPHS: 122 Historic Views from the Collections of the Chicago Historical Society, Larry A. Viskochil. Rare large-format prints offer detailed views of City Hall, State Street, the Loop, Hull House, Union Station, many other landmarks, circa 1904-1913. Introduction. Captions. Maps. 144pp. 9⅜ x 12¼. 24656-6 Pa. $12.95

OLD BROOKLYN IN EARLY PHOTOGRAPHS, 1865-1929, William Lee Younger. Luna Park, Gravesend race track, construction of Grand Army Plaza, moving of Hotel Brighton, etc. 157 previously unpublished photographs. 165pp. 8⅞ x 11¾. 23587-4 Pa. $13.95

THE MYTHS OF THE NORTH AMERICAN INDIANS, Lewis Spence. Rich anthology of the myths and legends of the Algonquins, Iroquois, Pawnees and Sioux, prefaced by an extensive historical and ethnological commentary. 36 illustrations. 480pp. 5⅜ x 8½. 25967-6 Pa. $10.95

AN ENCYCLOPEDIA OF BATTLES: Accounts of Over 1,560 Battles from 1479 B.C. to the Present, David Eggenberger. Essential details of every major battle in recorded history from the first battle of Megiddo in 1479 B.C. to Grenada in 1984. List of Battle Maps. New Appendix covering the years 1967-1984. Index. 99 illustrations. 544pp. 6½ x 9¼. 24913-1 Pa. $16.95

SAILING ALONE AROUND THE WORLD, Captain Joshua Slocum. First man to sail around the world, alone, in small boat. One of great feats of seamanship told in delightful manner. 67 illustrations. 294pp. 5⅜ x 8½. 20326-3 Pa. $6.95

ANARCHISM AND OTHER ESSAYS, Emma Goldman. Powerful, penetrating, prophetic essays on direct action, role of minorities, prison reform, puritan hypocrisy, violence, etc. 271pp. 5⅜ x 8½. 22484-8 Pa. $8.95

MYTHS OF THE HINDUS AND BUDDHISTS, Ananda K. Coomaraswamy and Sister Nivedita. Great stories of the epics; deeds of Krishna, Shiva, taken from puranas, Vedas, folk tales; etc. 32 illustrations. 400pp. 5⅜ x 8½. 21759-0 Pa. $12.95

THE TRAUMA OF BIRTH, Otto Rank. Rank's controversial thesis that anxiety neurosis is caused by profound psychological trauma which occurs at birth. 256pp. 5⅜ x 8½. 27974-X Pa. $7.95

A THEOLOGICO-POLITICAL TREATISE, Benedict Spinoza. Also contains unfinished Political Treatise. Great classic on religious liberty, theory of government on common consent. R. Elwes translation. Total of 421pp. 5⅜ x 8½. 20249-6 Pa. $10.95

MY BONDAGE AND MY FREEDOM, Frederick Douglass. Born a slave, Douglass became outspoken force in antislavery movement. The best of Douglass' autobiographies. Graphic description of slave life. 464pp. 5⅜ x 8½. 22457-0 Pa. $8.95

FOLLOWING THE EQUATOR: A Journey Around the World, Mark Twain. Fascinating humorous account of 1897 voyage to Hawaii, Australia, India, New Zealand, etc. Ironic, bemused reports on peoples, customs, climate, flora and fauna, politics, much more. 197 illustrations. 720pp. 5⅜ x 8½. 26113-1 Pa. $15.95

THE PEOPLE CALLED SHAKERS, Edward D. Andrews. Definitive study of Shakers: origins, beliefs, practices, dances, social organization, furniture and crafts, etc. 33 illustrations. 351pp. 5⅜ x 8½. 21081-2 Pa. $12.95

THE MYTHS OF GREECE AND ROME, H. A. Guerber. A classic of mythology, generously illustrated, long prized for its simple, graphic, accurate retelling of the principal myths of Greece and Rome, and for its commentary on their origins and significance. With 64 illustrations by Michelangelo, Raphael, Titian, Rubens, Canova, Bernini and others. 480pp. 5⅜ x 8½. 27584-1 Pa. $10.95

PSYCHOLOGY OF MUSIC, Carl E. Seashore. Classic work discusses music as a medium from psychological viewpoint. Clear treatment of physical acoustics, auditory apparatus, sound perception, development of musical skills, nature of musical feeling, host of other topics. 88 figures. 408pp. 5⅜ x 8½. 21851-1 Pa. $11.95

THE PHILOSOPHY OF HISTORY, Georg W. Hegel. Great classic of Western thought develops concept that history is not chance but rational process, the evolution of freedom. 457pp. 5⅜ x 8½. 20112-0 Pa. $9.95

THE BOOK OF TEA, Kakuzo Okakura. Minor classic of the Orient: entertaining, charming explanation, interpretation of traditional Japanese culture in terms of tea ceremony. 94pp. 5⅜ x 8½. 20070-1 Pa. $3.95

LIFE IN ANCIENT EGYPT, Adolf Erman. Fullest, most thorough, detailed older account with much not in more recent books, domestic life, religion, magic, medicine, commerce, much more. Many illustrations reproduce tomb paintings, carvings, hieroglyphs, etc. 597pp. 5⅜ x 8½. 22632-8 Pa. $12.95

SUNDIALS, Their Theory and Construction, Albert Waugh. Far and away the best, most thorough coverage of ideas, mathematics concerned, types, construction, adjusting anywhere. Simple, nontechnical treatment allows even children to build several of these dials. Over 100 illustrations. 230pp. 5⅜ x 8½. 22947-5 Pa. $8.95

THEORETICAL HYDRODYNAMICS, L. M. Milne-Thomson. Classic exposition of the mathematical theory of fluid motion, applicable to both hydrodynamics and aerodynamics. Over 600 exercises. 768pp. 6⅛ x 9¼. 68970-0 Pa. $20.95

SONGS OF EXPERIENCE: Facsimile Reproduction with 26 Plates in Full Color, William Blake. 26 full-color plates from a rare 1826 edition. Includes "TheTyger," "London," "Holy Thursday," and other poems. Printed text of poems. 48pp. 5¼ x 7. 24636-1 Pa. $4.95

OLD-TIME VIGNETTES IN FULL COLOR, Carol Belanger Grafton (ed.). Over 390 charming, often sentimental illustrations, selected from archives of Victorian graphics—pretty women posing, children playing, food, flowers, kittens and puppies, smiling cherubs, birds and butterflies, much more. All copyright-free. 48pp. 9¼ x 12¼. 27269-9 Pa. $9.95

PERSPECTIVE FOR ARTISTS, Rex Vicat Cole. Depth, perspective of sky and sea, shadows, much more, not usually covered. 391 diagrams, 81 reproductions of drawings and paintings. 279pp. 5⅜ x 8½. 22487-2 Pa. $9.95

DRAWING THE LIVING FIGURE, Joseph Sheppard. Innovative approach to artistic anatomy focuses on specifics of surface anatomy, rather than muscles and bones. Over 170 drawings of live models in front, back and side views, and in widely varying poses. Accompanying diagrams. 177 illustrations. Introduction. Index. 144pp. 8⅜ x11¼. 26723-7 Pa. $9.95

GOTHIC AND OLD ENGLISH ALPHABETS: 100 Complete Fonts, Dan X. Solo. Add power, elegance to posters, signs, other graphics with 100 stunning copyright-free alphabets: Blackstone, Dolbey, Germania, 97 more—including many lower-case, numerals, punctuation marks. 104pp. 8⅛ x 11. 24695-7 Pa. $9.95

HOW TO DO BEADWORK, Mary White. Fundamental book on craft from simple projects to five-bead chains and woven works. 106 illustrations. 142pp. 5⅜ x 8. 20697-1 Pa. $5.95

THE BOOK OF WOOD CARVING, Charles Marshall Sayers. Finest book for beginners discusses fundamentals and offers 34 designs. "Absolutely first rate . . . well thought out and well executed."—E. J. Tangerman. 118pp. 7¾ x 10⅝. 23654-4 Pa. $7.95

ILLUSTRATED CATALOG OF CIVIL WAR MILITARY GOODS: Union Army Weapons, Insignia, Uniform Accessories, and Other Equipment, Schuyler, Hartley, and Graham. Rare, profusely illustrated 1846 catalog includes Union Army uniform and dress regulations, arms and ammunition, coats, insignia, flags, swords, rifles, etc. 226 illustrations. 160pp. 9 x 12. 24939-5 Pa. $12.95

WOMEN'S FASHIONS OF THE EARLY 1900s: An Unabridged Republication of "New York Fashions, 1909," National Cloak & Suit Co. Rare catalog of mail-order fashions documents women's and children's clothing styles shortly after the turn of the century. Captions offer full descriptions, prices. Invaluable resource for fashion, costume historians. Approximately 725 illustrations. 128pp. 8⅜ x 11¼. 27276-1 Pa. $12.95

THE 1912 AND 1915 GUSTAV STICKLEY FURNITURE CATALOGS, Gustav Stickley. With over 200 detailed illustrations and descriptions, these two catalogs are essential reading and reference materials and identification guides for Stickley furniture. Captions cite materials, dimensions and prices. 112pp. 6½ x 9¼. 26676-1 Pa. $9.95

EARLY AMERICAN LOCOMOTIVES, John H. White, Jr. Finest locomotive engravings from early 19th century: historical (1804–74), main-line (after 1870), special, foreign, etc. 147 plates. 142pp. 11⅜ x 8¼. 22772-3 Pa. $12.95

THE TALL SHIPS OF TODAY IN PHOTOGRAPHS, Frank O. Braynard. Lavishly illustrated tribute to nearly 100 majestic contemporary sailing vessels: Amerigo Vespucci, Clearwater, Constitution, Eagle, Mayflower, Sea Cloud, Victory, many more. Authoritative captions provide statistics, background on each ship. 190 black-and-white photographs and illustrations. Introduction. 128pp. 8⅞ x 11¾. 27163-3 Pa. $14.95

LITTLE BOOK OF EARLY AMERICAN CRAFTS AND TRADES, Peter Stockham (ed.). 1807 children's book explains crafts and trades: baker, hatter, cooper, potter, and many others. 23 copperplate illustrations. 140pp. 4⅝ x 6.
23336-7 Pa. $4.95

VICTORIAN FASHIONS AND COSTUMES FROM HARPER'S BAZAR, 1867–1898, Stella Blum (ed.). Day costumes, evening wear, sports clothes, shoes, hats, other accessories in over 1,000 detailed engravings. 320pp. 9⅜ x 12¼.
22990-4 Pa. $16.95

GUSTAV STICKLEY, THE CRAFTSMAN, Mary Ann Smith. Superb study surveys broad scope of Stickley's achievement, especially in architecture. Design philosophy, rise and fall of the Craftsman empire, descriptions and floor plans for many Craftsman houses, more. 86 black-and-white halftones. 31 line illustrations. Introduction 208pp. 6½ x 9¼. 27210-9 Pa. $9.95

THE LONG ISLAND RAIL ROAD IN EARLY PHOTOGRAPHS, Ron Ziel. Over 220 rare photos, informative text document origin (1844) and development of rail service on Long Island. Vintage views of early trains, locomotives, stations, passengers, crews, much more. Captions. 8⅞ x 11¾. 26301-0 Pa. $14.95

VOYAGE OF THE LIBERDADE, Joshua Slocum. Great 19th-century mariner's thrilling, first-hand account of the wreck of his ship off South America, the 35-foot boat he built from the wreckage, and its remarkable voyage home. 128pp. 5⅜ x 8½.
40022-0 Pa. $5.95

TEN BOOKS ON ARCHITECTURE, Vitruvius. The most important book ever written on architecture. Early Roman aesthetics, technology, classical orders, site selection, all other aspects. Morgan translation. 331pp. 5⅜ x 8½. 20645-9 Pa. $9.95

THE HUMAN FIGURE IN MOTION, Eadweard Muybridge. More than 4,500 stopped-action photos, in action series, showing undraped men, women, children jumping, lying down, throwing, sitting, wrestling, carrying, etc. 390pp. 7⅞ x 10⅝.
20204-6 Clothbd. $29.95

TREES OF THE EASTERN AND CENTRAL UNITED STATES AND CANADA, William M. Harlow. Best one-volume guide to 140 trees. Full descriptions, woodlore, range, etc. Over 600 illustrations. Handy size. 288pp. 4½ x 6⅜.
20395-6 Pa. $6.95

SONGS OF WESTERN BIRDS, Dr. Donald J. Borror. Complete song and call repertoire of 60 western species, including flycatchers, juncoes, cactus wrens, many more–includes fully illustrated booklet. Cassette and manual 99913-0 $8.95

GROWING AND USING HERBS AND SPICES, Milo Miloradovich. Versatile handbook provides all the information needed for cultivation and use of all the herbs and spices available in North America. 4 illustrations. Index. Glossary. 236pp. 5⅜ x 8½.
25058-X Pa. $7.95

BIG BOOK OF MAZES AND LABYRINTHS, Walter Shepherd. 50 mazes and labyrinths in all–classical, solid, ripple, and more–in one great volume. Perfect inexpensive puzzler for clever youngsters. Full solutions. 112pp. 8⅛ x 11.
22951-3 Pa. $5.95

PIANO TUNING, J. Cree Fischer. Clearest, best book for beginner, amateur. Simple repairs, raising dropped notes, tuning by easy method of flattened fifths. No previous skills needed. 4 illustrations. 201pp. 5⅜ x 8½. 23267-0 Pa. $6.95

HINTS TO SINGERS, Lillian Nordica. Selecting the right teacher, developing confidence, overcoming stage fright, and many other important skills receive thoughtful discussion in this indispensible guide, written by a world-famous diva of four decades' experience. 96pp. 5³/₈ x 8¹/₂. 40094-8 Pa. $4.95

THE COMPLETE NONSENSE OF EDWARD LEAR, Edward Lear. All nonsense limericks, zany alphabets, Owl and Pussycat, songs, nonsense botany, etc., illustrated by Lear. Total of 320pp. 5⅜ x 8½. (Available in U.S. only.) 20167-8 Pa. $7.95

VICTORIAN PARLOUR POETRY: An Annotated Anthology, Michael R. Turner. 117 gems by Longfellow, Tennyson, Browning, many lesser-known poets. "The Village Blacksmith," "Curfew Must Not Ring Tonight," "Only a Baby Small," dozens more, often difficult to find elsewhere. Index of poets, titles, first lines. xxiii + 325pp. 5⅜ x 8¼. 27044-0 Pa. $12.95

DUBLINERS, James Joyce. Fifteen stories offer vivid, tightly focused observations of the lives of Dublin's poorer classes. At least one, "The Dead," is considered a masterpiece. Reprinted complete and unabridged from standard edition. 160pp. 5³⁄₁₆ x 8¼. 26870-5 Pa. $1.50

GREAT WEIRD TALES: 14 Stories by Lovecraft, Blackwood, Machen and Others, S. T. Joshi (ed.). 14 spellbinding tales, including "The Sin Eater," by Fiona McLeod, "The Eye Above the Mantel," by Frank Belknap Long, as well as renowned works by R. H. Barlow, Lord Dunsany, Arthur Machen, W. C. Morrow and eight other masters of the genre. 256pp. 5⅜ x 8½. (Available in U.S. only.) 40436-6 Pa. $8.95

THE BOOK OF THE SACRED MAGIC OF ABRAMELIN THE MAGE, translated by S. MacGregor Mathers. Medieval manuscript of ceremonial magic. Basic document in Aleister Crowley, Golden Dawn groups. 268pp. 5⅜ x 8½. 23211-5 Pa. $9.95

NEW RUSSIAN-ENGLISH AND ENGLISH-RUSSIAN DICTIONARY, M. A. O'Brien. This is a remarkably handy Russian dictionary, containing a surprising amount of information, including over 70,000 entries. 366pp. 4½ x 6⅛. 20208-9 Pa. $10.95

HISTORIC HOMES OF THE AMERICAN PRESIDENTS, Second, Revised Edition, Irvin Haas. A traveler's guide to American Presidential homes, most open to the public, depicting and describing homes occupied by every American President from George Washington to George Bush. With visiting hours, admission charges, travel routes. 175 photographs. Index. 160pp. 8¼ x 11. 26751-2 Pa. $13.95

NEW YORK IN THE FORTIES, Andreas Feininger. 162 brilliant photographs by the well-known photographer, formerly with *Life* magazine. Commuters, shoppers, Times Square at night, much else from city at its peak. Captions by John von Hartz. 181pp. 9¼ x 10¾. 23585-8 Pa. $13.95

INDIAN SIGN LANGUAGE, William Tomkins. Over 525 signs developed by Sioux and other tribes. Written instructions and diagrams. Also 290 pictographs. 111pp. 6⅛ x 9¼. 22029-X Pa. $3.95

ANATOMY: A Complete Guide for Artists, Joseph Sheppard. A master of figure drawing shows artists how to render human anatomy convincingly. Over 460 illustrations. 224pp. 8⅜ x 11¼. 27279-6 Pa. $11.95

MEDIEVAL CALLIGRAPHY: Its History and Technique, Marc Drogin. Spirited history, comprehensive instruction manual covers 13 styles (ca. 4th century through 15th). Excellent photographs; directions for duplicating medieval techniques with modern tools. 224pp. 8⅜ x 11¼. 26142-5 Pa. $12.95

DRIED FLOWERS: How to Prepare Them, Sarah Whitlock and Martha Rankin. Complete instructions on how to use silica gel, meal and borax, perlite aggregate, sand and borax, glycerine and water to create attractive permanent flower arrangements. 12 illustrations. 32pp. 5⅜ x 8½. 21802-3 Pa. $1.00

EASY-TO-MAKE BIRD FEEDERS FOR WOODWORKERS, Scott D. Campbell. Detailed, simple-to-use guide for designing, constructing, caring for and using feeders. Text, illustrations for 12 classic and contemporary designs. 96pp. 5⅜ x 8½. 25847-5 Pa. $3.95

SCOTTISH WONDER TALES FROM MYTH AND LEGEND, Donald A. Mackenzie. 16 lively tales tell of giants rumbling down mountainsides, of a magic wand that turns stone pillars into warriors, of gods and goddesses, evil hags, powerful forces and more. 240pp. 5⅜ x 8½. 29677-6 Pa. $6.95

THE HISTORY OF UNDERCLOTHES, C. Willett Cunnington and Phyllis Cunnington. Fascinating, well-documented survey covering six centuries of English undergarments, enhanced with over 100 illustrations: 12th-century laced-up bodice, footed long drawers (1795), 19th-century bustles, 19th-century corsets for men, Victorian "bust improvers," much more. 272pp. 5⅜ x 8¼. 27124-2 Pa. $9.95

ARTS AND CRAFTS FURNITURE: The Complete Brooks Catalog of 1912, Brooks Manufacturing Co. Photos and detailed descriptions of more than 150 now very collectible furniture designs from the Arts and Crafts movement depict davenports, settees, buffets, desks, tables, chairs, bedsteads, dressers and more, all built of solid, quarter-sawed oak. Invaluable for students and enthusiasts of antiques, Americana and the decorative arts. 80pp. 6½ x 9¼. 27471-3 Pa. $8.95

WILBUR AND ORVILLE: A Biography of the Wright Brothers, Fred Howard. Definitive, crisply written study tells the full story of the brothers' lives and work. A vividly written biography, unparalleled in scope and color, that also captures the spirit of an extraordinary era. 560pp. 6⅛ x 9¼. 40297-5 Pa. $17.95

THE ARTS OF THE SAILOR: Knotting, Splicing and Ropework, Hervey Garrett Smith. Indispensable shipboard reference covers tools, basic knots and useful hitches; handsewing and canvas work, more. Over 100 illustrations. Delightful reading for sea lovers. 256pp. 5⅜ x 8½. 26440-8 Pa. $8.95

FRANK LLOYD WRIGHT'S FALLINGWATER: The House and Its History, Second, Revised Edition, Donald Hoffmann. A total revision–both in text and illustrations–of the standard document on Fallingwater, the boldest, most personal architectural statement of Wright's mature years, updated with valuable new material from the recently opened Frank Lloyd Wright Archives. "Fascinating"–*The New York Times*. 116 illustrations. 128pp. 9¼ x 10¾. 27430-6 Pa. $12.95

PHOTOGRAPHIC SKETCHBOOK OF THE CIVIL WAR, Alexander Gardner. 100 photos taken on field during the Civil War. Famous shots of Manassas Harper's Ferry, Lincoln, Richmond, slave pens, etc. 244pp. 10⅝ x 8¼.   22731-6 Pa. $10.95

FIVE ACRES AND INDEPENDENCE, Maurice G. Kains. Great back-to-the-land classic explains basics of self-sufficient farming. The one book to get. 95 illustrations. 397pp. 5⅜ x 8½.   20974-1 Pa. $7.95

SONGS OF EASTERN BIRDS, Dr. Donald J. Borror. Songs and calls of 60 species most common to eastern U.S.: warblers, woodpeckers, flycatchers, thrushes, larks, many more in high-quality recording.   Cassette and manual 99912-2 $9.95

A MODERN HERBAL, Margaret Grieve. Much the fullest, most exact, most useful compilation of herbal material. Gigantic alphabetical encyclopedia, from aconite to zedoary, gives botanical information, medical properties, folklore, economic uses, much else. Indispensable to serious reader. 161 illustrations. 888pp. 6½ x 9¼. 2-vol. set. (Available in U.S. only.)   Vol. I: 22798-7 Pa. $10.95
Vol. II: 22799-5 Pa. $10.95

HIDDEN TREASURE MAZE BOOK, Dave Phillips. Solve 34 challenging mazes accompanied by heroic tales of adventure. Evil dragons, people-eating plants, bloodthirsty giants, many more dangerous adversaries lurk at every twist and turn. 34 mazes, stories, solutions. 48pp. 8¼ x 11.   24566-7 Pa. $2.95

LETTERS OF W. A. MOZART, Wolfgang A. Mozart. Remarkable letters show bawdy wit, humor, imagination, musical insights, contemporary musical world; includes some letters from Leopold Mozart. 276pp. 5⅜ x 8½.   22859-2 Pa. $9.95

BASIC PRINCIPLES OF CLASSICAL BALLET, Agrippina Vaganova. Great Russian theoretician, teacher explains methods for teaching classical ballet. 118 illustrations. 175pp. 5⅜ x 8½.   22036-2 Pa. $6.95

THE JUMPING FROG, Mark Twain. Revenge edition. The original story of The Celebrated Jumping Frog of Calaveras County, a hapless French translation, and Twain's hilarious "retranslation" from the French. 12 illustrations. 66pp. 5⅜ x 8½.
22686-7 Pa. $4.95

BEST REMEMBERED POEMS, Martin Gardner (ed.). The 126 poems in this superb collection of 19th- and 20th-century British and American verse range from Shelley's "To a Skylark" to the impassioned "Renascence" of Edna St. Vincent Millay and to Edward Lear's whimsical "The Owl and the Pussycat." 224pp. 5⅜ x 8½.
27165-X Pa. $5.95

COMPLETE SONNETS, William Shakespeare. Over 150 exquisite poems deal with love, friendship, the tyranny of time, beauty's evanescence, death and other themes in language of remarkable power, precision and beauty. Glossary of archaic terms. 80pp. 5³⁄₁₆ x 8¼.   26686-9 Pa. $1.00

THE BATTLES THAT CHANGED HISTORY, Fletcher Pratt. Eminent historian profiles 16 crucial conflicts, ancient to modern, that changed the course of civilization. 352pp. 5⅜ x 8½.   41129-X Pa. $9.95

THE WIT AND HUMOR OF OSCAR WILDE, Alvin Redman (ed.). More than 1,000 ripostes, paradoxes, wisecracks: Work is the curse of the drinking classes; I can resist everything except temptation; etc. 258pp. 5⅜ x 8½. 20602-5 Pa. $6.95

SHAKESPEARE LEXICON AND QUOTATION DICTIONARY, Alexander Schmidt. Full definitions, locations, shades of meaning in every word in plays and poems. More than 50,000 exact quotations. 1,485pp. 6½ x 9¼. 2-vol. set.
Vol. 1: 22726-X Pa. $17.95
Vol. 2: 22727-8 Pa. $17.95

SELECTED POEMS, Emily Dickinson. Over 100 best-known, best-loved poems by one of America's foremost poets, reprinted from authoritative early editions. No comparable edition at this price. Index of first lines. 64pp. 5³⁄₁₆ x 8¼.
26466-1 Pa. $1.00

THE INSIDIOUS DR. FU-MANCHU, Sax Rohmer. The first of the popular mystery series introduces a pair of English detectives to their archnemesis, the diabolical Dr. Fu-Manchu. Flavorful atmosphere, fast-paced action, and colorful characters enliven this classic of the genre. 208pp. 5³⁄₁₆ x 8¼. 29898-1 Pa. $2.00

THE MALLEUS MALEFICARUM OF KRAMER AND SPRENGER, translated by Montague Summers. Full text of most important witchhunter's "bible," used by both Catholics and Protestants. 278pp. 6⅝ x 10. 22802-9 Pa. $12.95

SPANISH STORIES/CUENTOS ESPAÑOLES: A Dual-Language Book, Angel Flores (ed.). Unique format offers 13 great stories in Spanish by Cervantes, Borges, others. Faithful English translations on facing pages. 352pp. 5⅜ x 8½.
25399-6 Pa. $9.95

GARDEN CITY, LONG ISLAND, IN EARLY PHOTOGRAPHS, 1869–1919, Mildred H. Smith. Handsome treasury of 118 vintage pictures, accompanied by carefully researched captions, document the Garden City Hotel fire (1899), the Vanderbilt Cup Race (1908), the first airmail flight departing from the Nassau Boulevard Aerodrome (1911), and much more. 96pp. 8⁷⁄₈ x 11³⁄₄. 40669-5 Pa. $12.95

OLD QUEENS, N.Y., IN EARLY PHOTOGRAPHS, Vincent F. Seyfried and William Asadorian. Over 160 rare photographs of Maspeth, Jamaica, Jackson Heights, and other areas. Vintage views of DeWitt Clinton mansion, 1939 World's Fair and more. Captions. 192pp. 8⅞ x 11. 26358-4 Pa. $14.95

CAPTURED BY THE INDIANS: 15 Firsthand Accounts, 1750-1870, Frederick Drimmer. Astounding true historical accounts of grisly torture, bloody conflicts, relentless pursuits, miraculous escapes and more, by people who lived to tell the tale. 384pp. 5⅜ x 8½. 24901-8 Pa. $9.95

THE WORLD'S GREAT SPEECHES (Fourth Enlarged Edition), Lewis Copeland, Lawrence W. Lamm, and Stephen J. McKenna. Nearly 300 speeches provide public speakers with a wealth of updated quotes and inspiration–from Pericles' funeral oration and William Jennings Bryan's "Cross of Gold Speech" to Malcolm X's powerful words on the Black Revolution and Earl of Spenser's tribute to his sister, Diana, Princess of Wales. 944pp. 5⅜ x 8⅜. 40903-1 Pa. $15.95

THE BOOK OF THE SWORD, Sir Richard F. Burton. Great Victorian scholar/adventurer's eloquent, erudite history of the "queen of weapons"–from prehistory to early Roman Empire. Evolution and development of early swords, variations (sabre, broadsword, cutlass, scimitar, etc.), much more. 336pp. 6⅛ x 9¼.
25434-8 Pa. $9.95

AUTOBIOGRAPHY: The Story of My Experiments with Truth, Mohandas K. Gandhi. Boyhood, legal studies, purification, the growth of the Satyagraha (nonviolent protest) movement. Critical, inspiring work of the man responsible for the freedom of India. 480pp. 5⅜ x 8½. (Available in U.S. only.) 24593-4 Pa. $9.95

CELTIC MYTHS AND LEGENDS, T. W. Rolleston. Masterful retelling of Irish and Welsh stories and tales. Cuchulain, King Arthur, Deirdre, the Grail, many more. First paperback edition. 58 full-page illustrations. 512pp. 5⅜ x 8½. 26507-2 Pa. $9.95

THE PRINCIPLES OF PSYCHOLOGY, William James. Famous long course complete, unabridged. Stream of thought, time perception, memory, experimental methods; great work decades ahead of its time. 94 figures. 1,391pp. 5⅜ x 8½. 2-vol. set.
Vol. I: 20381-6 Pa. $14.95
Vol. II: 20382-4 Pa. $16.95

THE WORLD AS WILL AND REPRESENTATION, Arthur Schopenhauer. Definitive English translation of Schopenhauer's life work, correcting more than 1,000 errors, omissions in earlier translations. Translated by E. F. J. Payne. Total of 1,269pp. 5⅜ x 8½. 2-vol. set.
Vol. 1: 21761-2 Pa. $12.95
Vol. 2: 21762-0 Pa. $12.95

MAGIC AND MYSTERY IN TIBET, Madame Alexandra David-Neel. Experiences among lamas, magicians, sages, sorcerers, Bonpa wizards. A true psychic discovery. 32 illustrations. 321pp. 5⅜ x 8½. (Available in U.S. only.) 22682-4 Pa. $9.95

THE EGYPTIAN BOOK OF THE DEAD, E. A. Wallis Budge. Complete reproduction of Ani's papyrus, finest ever found. Full hieroglyphic text, interlinear transliteration, word-for-word translation, smooth translation. 533pp. 6½ x 9¼.
21866-X Pa. $12.95

MATHEMATICS FOR THE NONMATHEMATICIAN, Morris Kline. Detailed, college-level treatment of mathematics in cultural and historical context, with numerous exercises. Recommended Reading Lists. Tables. Numerous figures. 641pp. 5⅜ x 8½.
24823-2 Pa. $11.95

PROBABILISTIC METHODS IN THE THEORY OF STRUCTURES, Isaac Elishakoff. Well-written introduction covers the elements of the theory of probability from two or more random variables, the reliability of such multivariable structures, the theory of random function, Monte Carlo methods of treating problems incapable of exact solution, and more. Examples. 502pp. 5³/₈ x 8¹/₂. 40691-1 Pa. $16.95

THE RIME OF THE ANCIENT MARINER, Gustave Doré, S. T. Coleridge. Doré's finest work; 34 plates capture moods, subtleties of poem. Flawless full-size reproductions printed on facing pages with authoritative text of poem. "Beautiful. Simply beautiful."—*Publisher's Weekly.* 77pp. 9¼ x 12. 22305-1 Pa. $7.95

NORTH AMERICAN INDIAN DESIGNS FOR ARTISTS AND CRAFTSPEOPLE, Eva Wilson. Over 360 authentic copyright-free designs adapted from Navajo blankets, Hopi pottery, Sioux buffalo hides, more. Geometrics, symbolic figures, plant and animal motifs, etc. 128pp. 8⅜ x 11. (Not for sale in the United Kingdom.) 25341-4 Pa. $9.95

SCULPTURE: Principles and Practice, Louis Slobodkin. Step-by-step approach to clay, plaster, metals, stone; classical and modern. 253 drawings, photos. 255pp. 8⅛ x 11.
22960-2 Pa. $11.95

THE INFLUENCE OF SEA POWER UPON HISTORY, 1660–1783, A. T. Mahan. Influential classic of naval history and tactics still used as text in war colleges. First paperback edition. 4 maps. 24 battle plans. 640pp. 5⅜ x 8½. 25509-3 Pa. $14.95

THE STORY OF THE TITANIC AS TOLD BY ITS SURVIVORS, Jack Winocour (ed.). What it was really like. Panic, despair, shocking inefficiency, and a little heroism. More thrilling than any fictional account. 26 illustrations. 320pp. 5⅜ x 8½. 20610-6 Pa. $8.95

FAIRY AND FOLK TALES OF THE IRISH PEASANTRY, William Butler Yeats (ed.). Treasury of 64 tales from the twilight world of Celtic myth and legend: "The Soul Cages," "The Kildare Pooka," "King O'Toole and his Goose," many more. Introduction and Notes by W. B. Yeats. 352pp. 5⅜ x 8½. 26941-8 Pa. $8.95

BUDDHIST MAHAYANA TEXTS, E. B. Cowell and others (eds.). Superb, accurate translations of basic documents in Mahayana Buddhism, highly important in history of religions. The Buddha-karita of Asvaghosha, Larger Sukhavativyuha, more. 448pp. 5⅜ x 8½. 25552-2 Pa. $12.95

ONE TWO THREE . . . INFINITY: Facts and Speculations of Science, George Gamow. Great physicist's fascinating, readable overview of contemporary science: number theory, relativity, fourth dimension, entropy, genes, atomic structure, much more. 128 illustrations. Index. 352pp. 5⅜ x 8½. 25664-2 Pa. $9.95

EXPERIMENTATION AND MEASUREMENT, W. J. Youden. Introductory manual explains laws of measurement in simple terms and offers tips for achieving accuracy and minimizing errors. Mathematics of measurement, use of instruments, experimenting with machines. 1994 edition. Foreword. Preface. Introduction. Epilogue. Selected Readings. Glossary. Index. Tables and figures. 128pp. 5³/₈ x 8¹/₂. 40451-X Pa. $6.95

DALÍ ON MODERN ART: The Cuckolds of Antiquated Modern Art, Salvador Dalí. Influential painter skewers modern art and its practitioners. Outrageous evaluations of Picasso, Cézanne, Turner, more. 15 renderings of paintings discussed. 44 calligraphic decorations by Dalí. 96pp. 5⅜ x 8½. (Available in U.S. only.) 29220-7 Pa. $5.95

ANTIQUE PLAYING CARDS: A Pictorial History, Henry René D'Allemagne. Over 900 elaborate, decorative images from rare playing cards (14th–20th centuries): Bacchus, death, dancing dogs, hunting scenes, royal coats of arms, players cheating, much more. 96pp. 9¼ x 12¼. 29265-7 Pa. $12.95

MAKING FURNITURE MASTERPIECES: 30 Projects with Measured Drawings, Franklin H. Gottshall. Step-by-step instructions, illustrations for constructing handsome, useful pieces, among them a Sheraton desk, Chippendale chair, Spanish desk, Queen Anne table and a William and Mary dressing mirror. 224pp. 8⅛ x 11¼. 29338-6 Pa. $16.95

THE FOSSIL BOOK: A Record of Prehistoric Life, Patricia V. Rich et al. Profusely illustrated definitive guide covers everything from single-celled organisms and dinosaurs to birds and mammals and the interplay between climate and man. Over 1,500 illustrations. 760pp. 7½ x 10⅛. 29371-8 Pa. $29.95

Prices subject to change without notice.

Available at your book dealer or write for free catalog to Dept. GI, Dover Publications, Inc., 31 East 2nd St., Mineola, N.Y. 11501. Dover publishes more than 500 books each year on science, elementary and advanced mathematics, biology, music, art, literary history, social sciences and other areas.

NATIONAL and REGIONAL INTERESTS in the NORTH

NATIONAL and REGIONAL INTERESTS in the NORTH

Third National Workshop on People, Resources, and the Environment North of 60°

Yellowknife, Northwest Territories
1-3 June 1983

Canadian Arctic Resources Committee
46 Elgin Street, Room 11
Ottawa, Ontario K1P 5K6

Canadian Cataloguing in Publication Data
National Workshop on People, Resources and the
Environment North of 60° (3rd: 1983: Yellowknife, N.W.T.)

NATIONAL and REGIONAL INTERESTS in the NORTH
ISBN 0-919996-18-3

1. Natural resources–Canada, Northern–Congresses.
2. Land-use–Canada, Northern–Planning–Congresses.
I. Canadian Arctic Resources Committee.
II. Title.
HC117. N5N38 1984 333.7'09719 C84-090123-2

CARC 1984 Publishing Programme
Danna Leaman, Publications Manager
Anne Kneif, Production Manager

Dr Maurice Haycock's oil sketch of Fort Conger,
Northwest Territories, is reproduced on the cover
with the artist's kind permission.

Cover design: Anne Kneif
Film separation: Herzig Somerville Limited
Typesetting and printing: M.O.M. Printing
Binding: D. Gratton Règleurs et Relieurs Inc.
Printed and bound in Canada

To Douglas Pimlott

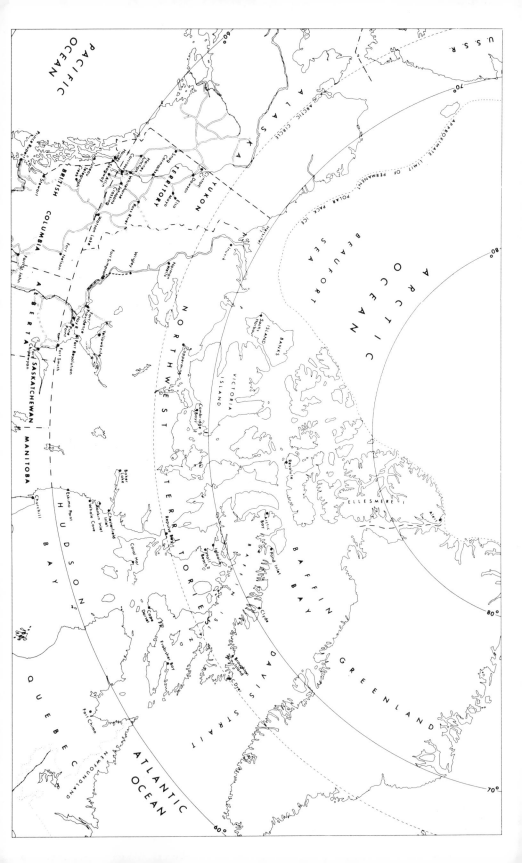

Contents

IV   CONCLUDING PLENARY SESSION

APPENDICES

xii

Introduction

Profound social, economic, and political change has occurred in the North in the last decade. During the 1970s, resource management issues in northern Canada were focused on ways to mitigate the social and environmental impacts of proposed megaprojects. In the 1980s, the emphasis is on the role of northerners in formulating and implementing policies for managing northern resources. Through constitutional reform, land-claims negotiations, and increasingly assertive territorial legislatures, northerners are insisting on greater control over northern resources. In the last decade Canadians sought to answer *how* to manage development of northern resources; in the present one we shall debate *who* will have that responsibility.

The Canadian Arctic Resources Committee (CARC) held its First National Workshop on People, Resources, and the Environment North of 60° in 1972 and its Second National Workshop in 1978. These workshops sought more enlightened and more creative approaches to northern development through the direct involvement of those interested in and affected by development decisions.* The 1972 workshop was CARC's first opportunity to bring together many persons with widely different knowledge of and concerns about the legal, environmental, and social implications of resource development in the North. At the Second National Workshop, CARC reported the results of its three-year Northern Resource and Land Use Policy Study and invited advice on future research needs from the workshop participants.

CARC's Third National Workshop, the first to be held north of 60°, was convened in Yellowknife, Northwest Territories, in June 1983. The theme of the workshop was the national and regional interests in resource management in the North. As the trustee of most of the land and resources north of 60°, the Government of Canada must act to serve the interests of northern peoples and northern governments as well as the interests of all Canadians. Northerners are calling for greater control over resource management, but the federal government continues to look to northern wealth as a way to speed the nation's economic recovery from the economic

---

* The proceedings of CARC's First National Workshop are published in *Arctic Alternatives*, Douglas H. Pimlott, Kitson M. Vincent, and Christine E. McKnight, eds (Ottawa: Canadian Arctic Resources Committee, 1973). The results of the Northern Resource and Land Use Policy Study and the proceedings of the Second National Workshop are published in *Northern Transitions*, volume 1, Everett B. Peterson and Janet B. Wright, eds, and volume 2, Robert F. Keith and Janet B. Wright, eds (Ottawa: Canadian Arctic Resources Committee, 1978).

recession and to ensure its future prosperity. Thus many Canadians often assume that these regional and national interests are so competitive as to be irreconcilable.

The goal of the Third National Workshop was to explore policy alternatives for resource management that accommodate the growing demands of northerners in a way that respects the interests of all Canadians in the development of these resources. The workshop brought together nearly 300 individuals representing many sectors of Canadian society— northerners and southerners, native and non-native persons, public servants and private citizens, industrialists, conservationists, and academics. These participants defended their own interests in resource development in the North, but many also proposed ways to shift the present balance of control so that the interests of northerners might be represented more fairly. The members of a large Alaskan delegation added an international point of view to the discussion by reminding Canadians of their obligations to the circumpolar and international communities. Many of those who participated in the workshop live north of 60°, and these individuals spoke of their unique experiences and concerns as northerners.

The workshop's opening plenary session featured addresses by John Parker, Commissioner of the Northwest Territories; the Honourable Chris Pearson, Leader of the Yukon Territorial Government; and the Honourable Richard Nerysoo, Minister of Renewable Resources, Government of the Northwest Territories, and now government leader. They emphasized the desire of northerners to assume responsibility for their present and future well-being through greater control over lands and resources, the need for the federal government to state clearly the national interest in northern Canada, and the difficulty of finding a fair balance between national and regional interests in the absence of this clear statement. The speakers' remarks and a transcript of the discussion that followed are included in part I of these proceedings.

The special plenary session on native land claims dealt with the federal government's policy for accepting and negotiating aboriginal peoples' claims to lands and resources. Panel members and participants provided vivid examples of the power of the federal government to give priority to what it perceives to be the national interest over the interests of northern peoples, their governments, and organizations. The panel responded to questions on the policy and the process of negotiating these claims and included Robert Overvold, Chief Negotiator for the Dene Nation; Clovis Demers, Executive Director of the Office of Native Claims, Department of Indian Affairs and Northern Development; and Robert Mitchell, former Chief Federal Negotiator for the Tungavik Federation of Nunavut claim. The federal land-claims policy *In All Fairness*, two background papers commenting on it, and a transcript of the discussion are included in part II of this volume.

In the context of the overall theme of national and regional interests, CARC identified eight topics of resource policy and management currently important in the North: natural resource jurisdiction and political development, regional planning and land-use planning, conservation of environmentally significant areas, mineral development, renewable resources management, inland water resources, ocean management, and development in the Beaufort Sea region. Participants were invited to attend one of the eight working groups to discuss these topics, and to address four questions:

- What are the national and regional interests in the policy or management topic addressed by the working group?
- What are the conflicts and compatibilities between these interests?
- Which of the conflicts identified can be resolved through research and discussion and which are more difficult to reconcile?
- What research is needed now and what policy and institutional initiatives will help to reconcile conflicts and improve the management of northern resources?

Background papers commissioned by CARC, opinion papers submitted by participants, and final reports from each of the eight working groups are included in part III of this volume.

Natural resource jurisdiction and political development were the concerns central to the question of how to manage northern resources. Division of the Northwest Territories into at least two political units is being discussed actively by the federal government, the territorial government, and native organizations. Yukoners, too, are pressing for greater political autonomy—the Government of the Yukon hopes to achieve provincehood within the next few years. Both territorial governments have expanded their involvement in renewable and non-renewable resource management and quickly are becoming capable of exercising additional responsibilities. Moreover, forthcoming land-claims settlements are likely to result in land ownership and resource management by native northerners.

The allocation of resources among competing users is the process that will have the greatest influence on how northern resources are used and managed. The federal government has prepared a policy for regional and land-use planning in the North to guide the process of resource allocation, but this policy has not yet been implemented. A federal policy for northern mineral development is being prepared and will be announced in 1984. CARC and other groups and individuals concerned about the impacts of development and other uses of resources have called for federal policies on the protection of environmentally significant areas and the conservation of renewable wildlife and water resources.

Canada's ability to achieve a fair balance of national, regional, and even international interests is likely to be tested most rigorously in the Arctic Ocean, especially in the Beaufort Sea region. The scale of offshore hydrocarbon exploration, production, and transportation, ownership of offshore resources, the rights of aboriginal peoples to offshore resources, and Canadian sovereignty in arctic waters are among the many issues that Canadians, especially northern Canadians, will need to resolve in the next decade.

The concluding plenary session of the Third National Workshop (part IV in this volume) attempted to draw out themes common to the working group discussions to construct a coherent picture of the interests and conflicts in northern resource development. In summarizing these themes, George Francis, Professor in Man-Environment Studies at the University of Waterloo, identified political development of northern governments as the greatest influence on all other policies and programmes in the North: "New structures for governance . . . will determine the acceptability and the outcome of whatever gets proposed for resource management." John Bayly, a lawyer from Yellowknife, summarized the answers of the working groups to the questions posed by CARC, and stressed the importance of "a northern perspective" in the search for solutions to northern problems.

The need of northerners to have a greater role in deciding when, where, and how development will occur was the interest expressed most successfully at CARC's Third National Workshop and most eloquently by northerners themselves. "There is much more involved than merely benefits or jobs," Robert MacQuarrie, MLA for Yellowknife Centre, told the participants. "We need a measure of control; we need resource revenue sharing to ensure that we are not looked upon as welfare recipients relying merely on handouts from the Government of Canada, and eventually we need ownership of sufficient resources to ensure that the peoples of the North can live in dignity and in equality with the other peoples of Canada."

CARC's purpose is to promote a rational approach to northern resource management and development—an approach that balances development that is economically wise with the protection of the environment, the social and cultural well-being of northerners, and the right of all citizens to participate in the decisions that affect these lands and resources. Our national workshops serve to identify the weights and counter-weights in such a balance. They do not provide a blueprint for northern development, nor are they just gatherings that allow individuals to exchange ideas. Each workshop lays the foundation for the next five years of CARC's policy research. Our research programmes currently underway— Conservation and the North in a Decade of Uncertainty, the Northern Decisions Study, and the Arctic Ocean Programme—will consider the need to reconcile and integrate conflicting northern policies with political development.

The workshops also offer a challenge to participants and to those who seek information or answers in these proceedings. CARC hoped that the process of identifying the national and regional interests in northern resource development and discussing the conflicts between them, in the non-adversarial setting of the workshop, would stimulate the imagination and sensibility needed to seek compromise and accommodation. The challenge to policy makers and private citizens alike is to find ways and means to articulate clearly what northern Canada should be like in the future and to make the policies and plans, as well as the compromises, needed to achieve that vision. The days have passed when the federal government can do what it wishes in the North in "the national interest," simultaneously overruling the concerns of territorial governments, native organizations, and other northerners. A northern development policy in the 1980s can be implemented effectively only if it has the support of those who live north of 60°.

CARC is grateful to those organizations that supported the workshop and made it possible to bring nearly 300 persons together to discuss the North in the North. We are particularly indebted to the individuals who gave freely of their time and energy to participate in The Third National Workshop on People, Resources, and the Environment North of 60°.

Everett B. Peterson
Chairman
Canadian Arctic Resources Committee

I
OPENING
PLENARY SESSION

Opening Plenary Session

Chairman's Opening Remarks

Alastair Lucas
Chairman
Canadian Arctic Resources Committee

On behalf of the Canadian Arctic Resources Committee (CARC), I should like to welcome all of you to this Third National Workshop on People, Resources, and the Environment North of 60°. Two previous workshops took place, the first in 1972 in Ottawa and the second in 1978 in Edmonton.

In 1972, the situation was considerably different from that in which we find ourselves today. Major development in the North—oil and gas exploration and, particularly, pipelines seemed imminent and yet it was obvious that large gaps existed in information on the implications of those development proposals for the peoples, the environment, and the regional and national economies. In particular, in the early 1970s, institutions and decision-making processes either were not in place or were simply inadequate to ensure that all interests were represented properly and were considered properly in development decisions. The means for providing information on those issues to the public and for ensuring open debate on them were lacking. When I use the term "public" here I refer to native northerners and northerners generally, as well as to the Canadian public.

By 1978 and the Second National Workshop, things were very different: the boom was on. Major pipeline approvals had been granted. Looking back, it seems hard to imagine the optimism, the enthusiasm that existed in 1978. Major oil, gas, and mineral explorations had been approved; land-claims settlement processes were moving into high gear; increasing attention was being focused on the offshore for exploration, development, and transportation. An array of megaprojects was on the horizon in oil and gas, mining, and water resources.

All of the interests in 1978 were very concerned about the pace of the development that seemed about to be unleashed on the North and about the social, environmental, and economic implications of those developments. There was a tone of urgency, almost of desperation, in the discussions that took place at that Second National Workshop.

In 1983, the situation is very different again. The major factor with which we have to deal is the uncertain economic situation in the North and in Canada generally. Megaprojects, in effect, have disappeared from our view. Planning horizons have retreated steadily. It is in this context and against this background that the theme of national and regional interests was chosen for the Third National Workshop.

This theme of national versus regional interests is obviously not something new, but it is something that now deserves particular emphasis. The recession has given us a pause in the frantic pace of development that was building in the late 1970s and early in this decade. It has given us an opportunity for reflection and for careful evaluation and consideration of the social, environmental, and economic implications of northern development. It is an opportunity for all of the interests concerned with northern development to present their views and have them tested in a more relaxed atmosphere than that which existed in 1978.

This workshop is intended to provide an independent forum for this discussion, an opportunity for all interests to consider, to discuss, and to develop recommendations on today's northern resource issues. These issues include, but certainly are not limited to, those topics that have been identified for the working groups: natural resource jurisdiction and political development, regional planning and land-use planning, conservation of environmentally significant areas, mineral development, renewable resources management, inland water resources, ocean management, and development in the Beaufort Sea region.

It will be your participation—informed, honest, and sensitive participation—in these working groups that will make them effective, that will make them work, and that will cause us to come away from the workshop with the kind of comment that is useful and that will make this a worthwhile exercise.

Keynote Address

John Parker
Commissioner
Government of the Northwest Territories

The participants at this workshop represent broad-ranging interests and are from many disciplines. Some of the most knowledgeable and experienced individuals, in all aspects of resource development, are represented here.

The theme for the workshop is particularly appropriate for the 1980s. The 1970s were taken up with concerns over possible megaprojects and ways to mitigate their effects. Megaprojects, as our chairman has mentioned, by and large have fallen by the wayside. The effect with which we must now contend is lack of employment—employment that had been anticipated through the development of megaprojects. As an interesting aside, when the Norman Wells field expansion and pipeline project was being considered, it was considered a small project in light of the megaprojects that were being considered at that time. It has now become one of Canada's megaprojects.

The 1980s must look to the role of northern peoples in, and their relationship to, the resource industries, not just as employees but as policy formulators, as government leaders, as businessmen, as tradesmen, and as professionals. Resource development will take place. We may influence the scale, the timing, and we may affect the location of projects through various tradeoffs, but if the national interest calls for resource development, it will indeed take place.

In looking at the objectives that have been set for this workshop, I note that one is the identification of perceptions of interest and the associated problem areas. I note that we are seeking a balance of national and regional interests. That is rather like threading a needle with a large piece of wet sinew. It may not be impossible, but it is certainly difficult.

In setting policies, in setting initiatives, I beg you to listen carefully to northern peoples, and then, having listened to them and having understood what they are saying, to try to set realistic objectives that will indeed balance the various competing interests. During this workshop you will hear some of the policy initiatives and objectives of the Government of the Northwest Territories (GNWT) as they relate to the workshop's theme. That, of course, will give you the opportunity to judge whether or not our territorial objectives are realistic.

Just to mention one or two of the directions in which the GNWT is headed: in addition to the balance required between national and regional interests, our government must seek and maintain a balance between development of renewable and non-renewable resources—a very difficult job at times. To further this particular aim, the GNWT has formed an interdepartmental task force to prepare a comprehensive renewable resource strategy. In other words, we are paying close attention to renewable resources, particularly in the light of development of non-renewable resources. The Government of the Northwest Territories has played a leading role in the development of an acceptable system for land-use planning. We have concerns about our rivers, water levels, and maintenance of wetlands and deltas, and at least as many concerns about the jurisdiction over those waters. That is a jurisdictional nightmare, because waters come from three provinces into the North. The GNWT is also addressing the problem of compensation for trappers and hunters when their areas are being used by resource developers, and has produced a resource development policy that is very important for northerners.

I mentioned the need for employment of northern peoples. The mining and oil and gas sectors in the Northwest Territories (N.W.T.) now provide between 3000 and 3500 jobs—45 per cent of the total industrial employment. There are examples, and I think good examples, of native groups and corporations taking part as entrepreneurs in resource development activities. If the economic and environmental conditions are acceptable, these groups are satisfied to participate, in fact, even eager to do so.

The GNWT had an excellent example of co-operation and good corporate statesmanship in the matter of the clearing of the right of way for the Norman Wells pipeline by Interprovincial Pipe Line Ltd. Northern companies, contractors, and workers were engaged in that operation, which was carried off on schedule last winter, to the great benefit of the persons along that route.

The territorial labour force grew by 76 per cent in ten years from 1971 to 1981, whereas the labour force in the fishing, trapping, and forestry sectors declined during that decade by at least 30 per cent. It is estimated that 585 workers will join the labour force in the Northwest Territories each year over the next several years. Clearly, we must be able to provide employment. Many of the jobs and opportunities for local companies can, and must, come from work in the non-renewable resource sector. One of the challenges for this workshop is to recommend sensible safeguards under which exploration, development, and production of our resources can take place.

CARC claims that its purpose is to promote a balanced approach to resource management. Environmental sensitivity and respect for rights of northerners are mentioned. I would add a third consideration—recognition of economic realities. If the economic realities are considered together with the environmental sensitivity and the respect for the rights of northern peoples, success will be assured.

Discussion

Chairman's Introductions

Robert MacQuarrie
Member of the Legislative Assembly
for Yellowknife Centre

The panelists this morning are the Honourable Christopher Pearson and the Honourable Richard Nerysoo. Christopher Pearson was elected to the Yukon legislature and became the government leader in 1978. He was re-elected, with his government, in 1982. In addition to being the government leader, Mr Pearson holds several other portfolios including Economic Development, Finance, and Governmental Relations. He is also responsible for the executive council office in the Public Service Commission.

Richard Nerysoo was elected a member of the Legislative Assembly for the Northwest Territories for the constituency of Mackenzie Delta in 1979. He was chosen as a minister and assumed responsibility for the Renewable Resources portfolio, but also holds responsibility for the Energy, Mines and Resources Secretariat.

Panelist's Remarks

The Honourable Christopher Pearson
Leader
Yukon Territorial Government

Mr Chairman, Mr Nerysoo, ladies and gentlemen: The development of a fair and intelligent balance between the national and regional interests in resource management is of special concern to the peoples of the Yukon. The size of our delegation at this workshop demonstrates the extent of that concern and, I hope, indicates that we are committed to the development of such a balance.

The Yukon government feels that its interests in resource management and, indeed, in almost all of the issues affecting us, have never been considered effectively by the federal government or, for that matter, by Canadians in general. There are many reasons for this, one being that the Government of Canada has been unable, for almost a century, to determine with any degree of confidence exactly what is in the national interest in northern Canada. Another is that the government and other Canadians have been unable to appreciate and to understand that there is no such

7

thing as "the North"; that Canada north of 60° is made up of at least two completely different political, geographic, cultural, and economic regions, each with its own characteristics, requirements, and capabilities. As a result of this lack of understanding, policies are developed and implemented that are meant to serve the needs of both regions but that, in reality, serve the needs of neither. This inability to recognize basic differences between the two territories has led to the Yukon's economic and political underdevelopment and is largely responsible for the degree of federal–territorial conflict that exists today. One of our goals during this workshop is to help you to appreciate the differences that do exist and to help you to understand that each region must be discussed on the basis of those differences.

The position of the Yukon government with respect to resource management is, simply, that Yukoners deserve the same rights and responsibilities as other Canadians to develop and to protect their vast resources. The Yukon needs to develop those resources to create an economy that will allow it eventually to become a full and responsible member of the Canadian federation. At the same time, Yukoners recognize and appreciate, more than anyone else, that it is also their responsibility to protect and to preserve their natural heritage. The environment has shaped the character of Yukon society and is of paramount significance to all of us. It is, and always will be, a major component of the tourism industry and is vital to the cultural life and heritage of our native peoples. Yukoners also understand that natural resources are part of the national trust and that their exploitation and preservation must be accomplished with that in mind.

Yukoners have a clear perception of how the balance between regional and national interests and between exploitation and preservation should be struck. Unfortunately, these balances are not seen as readily by those outside the Yukon. Some special-interest groups feel that the Yukon should be spared all resource exploitation and that the preservation of the environment should be of principal concern. On the other hand, some demand that Yukoners be given the right to determine how the Yukon's resources should be used. When the Government of the Yukon determines that a resource development project is in the best interest of the peoples who elected that government, however, the interest groups object that such development is not in the national, or even regional, interest. The federal Department of Fisheries and Oceans, for example, has determined that it is in the national interest to protect every grayling in every Yukon stream. The federal Department of Energy, Mines and Resources, on the other hand, promotes the development of mines and the exploitation of oil and gas reserves as being in the national interest. The Department of Indian

Affairs and Northern Development, with its multiplicity of responsibilities, is faced with threats to its dominance of the Yukon from all sides; it vacillates and fails to make any logical decisions with respect to the balance required.

This is the situation of the Yukon today and under which it has laboured for years. The Yukon cannot stand still; it must either move forward with the rest of Canada or it must decline, to the detriment of all concerned. For the Yukon to assume its rightful position in Canada, the conflict over the balance to be accorded to national and regional interests in resource management must be resolved. Before that resolution can occur, however, there must be a recognition by all parties that the resources of the Yukon must be developed and conserved, first for the benefit of Yukoners and then for the benefit of the nation as a whole. It must also be recognized that the Yukon has the responsibility and the capability to manage those resources and that, ultimately, the control of those resources should rest with the territorial government. It must also be recognized and agreed that the Yukon's ultimate goal is to become an equal partner in Canada, with the same rights and responsibilities enjoyed by other jurisdictions. Finally, the Yukon must be considered a distinct and separate region of Canada.

Over the past few years, some progress has been made toward the resolution of the conflicts. The federal government is beginning to realize that "the North" is not a homogeneous entity and that each region must be treated on the basis of its particular characteristics. Recently some movement has occurred toward the resolution of the land-use planning conflict, with Canada accepting (at least in part) the legitimate rights of the Yukon to share, on an equal basis, the responsibility for land-use planning. We are hopeful that progress in this matter will result in a similar level of co-operation in resolving the conflicts associated with land ownership, jurisdiction over resources, and resource revenue sharing.

Although work will continue on addressing each of these issues, the effective and long-term co-operation required to resolve the conflicts completely cannot occur until a process is in place that has as its ultimate goal the granting of full responsible government to the Yukon. Such a process would provide the basic framework upon which the Yukon and Canada could build to ensure the long-term political, economic, and social viability of the territory. This process would provide some substance for the federal government's long-standing statements respecting its goal of self-government for the Yukon and would, without question, allow Yukon peoples to plan for its future more effectively. Also it would provide basic guidelines for the transfer or, initially at least, for the sharing of responsibility for the management of the Yukon's resources. Finally, the development of such a process would provide the opportunity to define and reach agreement on the balance required between regional and national interests in the Yukon.

We are prepared to work co-operatively with the Government of Canada to develop that process. Furthermore, we continue to be prepared to discuss ways in which to resolve all of the outstanding resource conflicts. What is required is for the Government of Canada to recognize the basic rights of Yukoners to plan their own future and to become full, equal, and responsible citizens of Canada. Without this basic and fundamental understanding of the Yukon's rights and desires as a free and distinct region of Canada, conflicts cannot, and will not, be resolved to anyone's satisfaction.

The Yukon has for too long remained an underdeveloped, "third-world" region of Canada. Its peoples have struggled long and hard for the few rights that they have gained. It is essential to the Yukon's survival that steps be taken now to resolve the conflicts that have plagued us for decades. A failure on the part of all concerned to recognize and to appreciate the need for action will result in the worsening of these conflicts and in the creation of new ones of an even more serious nature—conflicts that could have detrimental implications for the future of Canada as a whole.

The representatives of the Yukon have not appeared at this workshop to continue the confrontation that has existed. We are here to listen to advice and to seek ways of resolving our conflicts through co-operation and understanding. Above all, we are here to help you gain a truer appreciation of the Yukon's goals, objectives, responsibilities, and capabilities. The peoples of the Yukon have never been more concerned about their future than they are today. The pressures being placed upon us from all sides are extreme and we require your support, confidence, and understanding if we are to deal successfully with those pressures and eventually take our rightful place in Canadian society.

Panelist's Remarks

The Honourable Richard Nerysoo
Minister for Energy, Mines and Resources
Minister of Renewable Resources
Government of the Northwest Territories

I am honoured to have been requested to address this opening session of the workshop jointly with my distinguished colleague, the Honourable Christopher Pearson, Yukon Government Leader. As representatives of the public in the North, both Mr Pearson and I must be aware of, and appreciate, divergent points of view on issues under discussion. The theme of this workshop, the interplay of regional and national interests in resource management in the North, implies that same requirement—to appreciate and to accommodate differing points of view in reaching final decisions. It is possible to blend and to accommodate divergent interests effectively, but achieving this blend is not easy. It takes commitment and discipline to treat both sides of a situation equitably and to change existing attitudes so that the benefits of taking a balanced approach are recognized and supported.

The theme to be discussed over the next two and one-half days, I suggest, is not *whether* it is possible to achieve effective interplay of regional and national interests in resource management, but rather, *how* this interplay can best be achieved to reflect fairly both regional and national interests in the management of northern resources. Many of the major issues that face the Government of the Northwest Territories (GNWT) have a common thread and seem to hinge on the question of the relative roles of regional and national interests.

My dual portfolios and the theme of the workshop have something in common: each implies a range of options and potential conflicts; resource development versus resource conservation on the one hand, and regional versus national interests on the other. My experience, however, indicates that the most appropriate and workable solutions seldom fall totally at either extreme, but instead are a careful and conscious blending of the optimum aspects of each to achieve the best fit. I suspect it is so with regional and national interests. Gone are the days when decisions were made based on only one point of view and dutifully carried out or followed by those affected by, but not consulted in, that decision. We are all better educated now, not only as individuals but also as a society. We recognize that decisions on resource development affect us and, therefore, we legitimately claim a role in those decisions, no matter what the scale, whether they concern the location of the town road or the routing of a super-tanker corridor. If these local concerns are ignored in the decision-making process, then the result is a bad decision because it creates unnecessary conflict and ignores useful, positive input. As the old adage goes: If you are not part of the solution, you are part of the problem.

The territorial government's goal is to ensure a range and balance of input into decisions appropriate to the issues under consideration. The location of a road in a northern community is primarily the concern of community residents, whereas the routing of a super-tanker corridor is primarily of national interest because its effects often reach far beyond the specific location of the corridor. The GNWT's role is to ensure that the interests of this region are expressed logically and are given full consideration in all decisions on the management and development of northern resources.

It is easy to articulate the regional interests; however, national interests in the North tend to be, with few exceptions, undefined. An exception is the National Energy Program. There is no national, much less northern, development policy or strategy to guide decisions on resource management. Without this national direction, tradeoffs between the regional and national interests are difficult to make because they lack an overall framework as a guide.

Constitutional development and resource management are two fundamental issues facing the Northwest Territories today: the residents of the N.W.T. are Canadians living in a democracy. They should be able to enjoy the rights and responsibilities that provincial residents take for granted—the right to manage provincial affairs through responsible government and all that it entails.

The Department of Indian Affairs and Northern Development is charged by Canada with fostering the development of responsible government in the N.W.T. This process, however, is painfully slow. The federal government is committed to devolution of responsibility and authority over resource management to the GNWT. Devolution will increase as the GNWT's capability to understand and deal effectively and equitably with the complex issues also grows. I am sure that the Government of Canada realizes that furthering the development of responsible government in the N.W.T. will result in a greater role and stake in resource management for the territories and, therefore, a greater tendency to encourage and to reap the benefits of resource development. The GNWT must be able to participate with Canada as a full partner or it will be reluctant to participate at all, for otherwise there is no net benefit in participation. A basic principle that must be accepted is that the GNWT is not a special-interest group; it is a legitimate government.

Every person and activity in the N.W.T. is affected by resource development. The GNWT has the responsibility to deal with many of the effects of that development, but is allowed little effective input in the development decisions. Decisions on resource development issues that affect primarily the North would be more effective if they reflected strong northern input. Those decisions, however, must be made through existing and evolving northern mechanisms, which must not be bypassed. If the GNWT could influence the type of resource developments before they occur and the terms and conditions under which they are carried out, then the effects of that development on the North also could be influenced. This would ensure better, more effective development—development that is responsive to national and regional concerns as well as to those of industry.

Authority and responsibility over the N.W.T. is split between the federal government and an elected territorial legislative assembly. Resources and revenues from resource development are controlled federally, but the responsibility for meeting the social and economic needs of the North rests with the territorial government. The GNWT has no direct access to revenues that result from the development of northern resources, yet it must ensure that effective programmes are in place to cope with the changes brought about by development.

The need to ensure better decisions that are more responsive to northern concerns has led to the realization that the N.W.T. requires its own policy framework to deal effectively with, and influence, those resource development issues within its mandate. The policy has to be comprehensive enough to accommodate and to guide further the GNWT's actions in all aspects of resource management and development. It has to be able to accommodate existing federal, territorial, private, and public authorities and responsibilities, yet be able to change as the territories evolve. The vehicle chosen to fill this requirement is the Resource Development Policy.

The Resource Development Policy is based on the principle that the GNWT will support a development when its overall economic, social, and environmental implications are judged to result in a net benefit to the peoples of the N.W.T.—when the regional interests are seen to be served. This policy and its guidelines should be viewed as an aid to improve resource development rather than as a burden—an aid to industry and an aid to the federal government. The intent is not to duplicate information or actions currently required of industry by other levels of government or the federal review processes. Instead, it will enable the GNWT to fulfil its responsibilities effectively by addressing resource development issues that are of major and primary concern in the North.

The first provision allows the designation and ranking of development impact zones. A zone is a community, group of communities, or geographic area that is likely to experience extraordinary changes as a result of resource development.

The second provision is a territorial assessment and review process. The assessment and review of a project will result in a set of terms and conditions under which the project will receive the government's support. Once the proponent agrees to meet those terms and conditions, a development certificate will be issued—the equivalent of the government's approval in principle.

The policy's third provision spells out requirements for monitoring resource development activities to ensure that terms and conditions are being fulfilled and that appropriate changes are made to improve the project's effectiveness and acceptability.

In conclusion, the policy will enable the GNWT to make decisions on the broad spectrum of resource development issues within its mandate, in a comprehensive and integrated manner. It will allow for more-effective planning for resource development with the joint participation of the public, industry, and all levels of government. I am hopeful that this will result in better, more responsive, resource development.

A great deal of effort has been put into the policy so that it enables the GNWT to meet its present obligations, allows enough flexibility to accommodate new requirements that will come with political evolution, and yet respects and aids the federal government in making final decisions on resource development. It also ensures that those final decisions benefit from the comprehensive regional input that will be co-ordinated by the GNWT.

We anticipate that the lessons learned, and the approach taken, in dealing with the resource management and constitutional development issues will be built upon, and used to guide, other government thrusts; these include, first, the establishment of a resource revenue sharing and management agreement with the federal government. The GNWT has taken the first step by developing a position paper and is now waiting for a response from the federal government.

A second thrust is the development of means to ensure direct input and greater influence in the decisions of the Canada Oil and Gas Lands Administration (COGLA) that affect the N.W.T. At present, the GNWT has no direct input into COGLA. Its views are articulated through DIAND. This situation is unsatisfactory, and proposed mechanisms to ensure more direct input into COGLA and its decisions are being developed by the GNWT.

A third thrust is the development of means to ensure an effective and influential role for the GNWT in river basin and other similar resource planning. Hydro-electric development proposals outside the N.W.T. will affect the territories. The authorities and responsibilities to deal effectively with multijurisdictional issues are yet to be finalized. The GNWT must ensure that it has a role in the decision-making structures that will result so that it can represent N.W.T. regional interests.

A fourth thrust is the continuation and successful resolution of work undertaken jointly with the Government of the Yukon on resource developments occurring on our common border, where a number of mining projects already exist and more are proposed. These projects affect both territories, and therefore require a co-ordinated approach if optimum decisions are to result. Progress is being made on the development of mechanisms and procedures for achieving this co-ordinated approach.

Effective and workable decisions require that regional and national interests be considered together to arrive at a mutual best fit. The GNWT, as the government in the N.W.T., has the responsibility to ensure that those regional interests are articulated as clearly and effectively as possible.

Christopher Pearson: I want to emphasize that in speaking of the differences between the two territories, and the necessity for everyone to recognize that those differences are there, we in the Yukon are not trying to separate ourselves from the Northwest Territories and the peoples of the Northwest Territories. We have a very close affinity for the peoples of the Northwest Territories. I think that we, better than any other Canadians, understand the concerns and the problems that they face daily.

The major difference is the make-up of the two territories. The lifestyles in a lot of cases are different. The problems that they have in the Northwest Territories are not the same problems that we have in the Yukon. In the Yukon, we have far more industry, far more of our peoples live in communities—larger communities than in the Northwest Territories. We are connected by a road system in the Yukon that has no comparison in the Northwest Territories. There is also a difference with the political system in the two territories.

Professor Robert Page, Environmental Centre, Trent University, Peterborough, Ontario: I was wondering if I might provoke some of those differences, just for a moment, by asking our two panelists specifically about their attitudes to the proposals for Stokes Point.

Christopher Pearson: The Government of the Yukon has taken the stand that it will support a development at Stokes Point, provided that the restrictions are put on it that we have outlined to the Government of Canada. Those restrictions deal primarily with the Porcupine caribou herd and with the construction of a road. There was a proposal put forward originally by Gulf Canada Resources Inc. that proposed the construction of a road to a gravel pit. We cannot abide that kind of development at Stokes Point. It has been our assessment, however, that there can be some onshore development at Stokes Point that everyone could live with. We have supported the development of Stokes Point provided that our concerns, primarily environmental concerns, are met.

Richard Nerysoo: We have taken a somewhat different position in that we are not in support of the idea of harbour development at Stokes Point. Our arguments are very much different from those of the Yukon.

We already have a harbour that has been developed in the Northwest Territories—McKinley Bay. We also have the smaller harbour at Tuktoyaktuk. We want to use those existing harbours for, of course, economic purposes. We have had development in our particular area and we think we can address the issue of, at least, an interim harbour. Until we make a final decision on a long-term development plan, we can use those we have.

That does not mean we are going to oppose the Yukon totally in its decision to develop its area of the North Slope, for that is primarily the responsibility of the government and peoples of the Yukon.

Robert Page: Do you see the Stokes Point proposals as part of a wider package toward a development corridor for the Yukon through to the coast?

Christopher Pearson: I believe that someday—and it might be a long time yet—there will be a corridor to the Beaufort Sea. I also believe that someday there will be a pipeline along the Alaska Highway. I believe that someday there will also be a pipeline along the Mackenzie River. That is where the resources are and someday Canada is going to have to get at those resources and get them out.

Whether Stokes Point goes ahead at this particular time and whether, in fact, it is the beginning of that corridor, I do not think has any bearing on the corridor in the future. I think we have to look at the Stokes Point development that Gulf Canada Resources is proposing now as something strictly for the convenience of Gulf. We understand what the N.W.T. has said; if we had been asked whether McKinley Bay should have been dredged, we probably would have said "No, do it some place else," too. In fact, we looked at that as an alternative. Could we or should we be saying to Gulf, "No, use one of the other ports that are already there." We are also interested in economic development in the Yukon and, the fact of the matter is, if Stokes Point is developed, we will be able to tax it, and that becomes an economic benefit.

Nancy MacPherson, President, Yukon Conservation Society: One of Christopher Pearson's comments was that often the conservation efforts of the Yukon government are not noticed by those outside the territory. Well, they are not noticed by those inside the territory very much either. Although I can appreciate the principle of balancing exploitation and preservation, we seem to be hearing a great deal about the long list of support that the Yukon government is giving to the exploitation of resources. I am wondering if Mr Pearson could give us a comparable list of efforts that the Yukon government is giving to conservation and preservation efforts.

Christopher Pearson: We have a real concern about the conservation of the Yukon Territory. The suggestion that our only interest is in development is erroneous. Yukoners live in the territory because they like it the way it is, but there has to be a realization that there is going to be development. We have to make sure that the development goes on in a balanced manner. There cannot be development and no conservation nor can there be all conservation and no development. If the latter occurs, many individuals will not live in the Yukon; they will move.

Nancy MacPherson: I am just asking you to fill out the other side of the balance sheet. We know what your position is on development in the Beaufort region; we know what your position is on placer mining; we know what your position is on many other developments. Can you give us a list of four or five conservation efforts that the Yukon government has undertaken in the last several years?

Christopher Pearson: Well, we have an act in place with respect to territorial parks, which was passed in spite of the federal government. We have requested the establishment of territorial parks, for conservation purposes, from the Government of Canada.

The wildlife branch in the Department of Renewable Resources is devoted to conservation and has existed for a long time. We established the Department of Renewable Resources.

Nancy MacPherson: So, in fact, you cannot give us a list of announcements on conservation areas or anything like that?

Christopher Pearson: Well, I do not know what you are looking for.

Nancy MacPherson: I was just interested in some more specific information on territorial parks. We are certainly aware that the GNWT has set aside and has promoted specific areas for conservation purposes. I am just asking Mr Pearson to be a little more specific because we do not hear of these areas in the Yukon.

Christopher Pearson: The Northern Resources Policy recommends very strongly the establishment of a national park in the northern Yukon. It also states very clearly that we want to declare Herschel Island a territorial park.

Nancy MacPherson: How can you support a port at Stokes Point within the withdrawn lands and, at the same time, support the area for preservation? That is what you have done if your position is both for preservation of the withdrawn lands and in support of a port.

Christopher Pearson: Yes, but we did not withdraw the lands.

Nancy MacPherson: But you just said you supported the withdrawal.

Christopher Pearson: No, I did not. The national park does not encompass Stokes Point, nor should it. The withdrawn lands are not ours. We did not withdraw the lands; the federal government withdrew the lands. It has had them withdrawn for years, as it has withdrawn most of the territories from development. Specifically, the North Slope is a very fragile area. The area we are talking about has been used before. It is an abandoned DEW-line site and I suspect that any environmental damage that is going to be done to Stokes Point has already been done. Our caveat with the minister of Indian Affairs and Northern Development is that the damaged area is not going to be increased by the development that Gulf wants to do. We did not agree with the first proposal. We would agree with the revised proposal given the caveats that we have put on it.

Lindsay Staples, National Parks Association, Yukon Conservation Society: Speaking on behalf of the National Parks Association, we would welcome the opportunity to review your parks systems policy and look forward to the date upon which it will be released. It has been around for some time now. We have certainly expressed an interest in it and would welcome the opportunity to get a copy in the mail.

Your government has made a number of references to opportunities for Yukoners to address their concerns about the northern Yukon. The *Northern Yukon Resource Management Model* was a government-created model. It was created internally. In the assembly several months ago, in response to a question regarding public hearings for Yukoners with respect to development on the North Slope, you indicated that when a development proposal was forthcoming, we would see some form of public review or a chance for Yukoners to speak out. In the Yukon's position on the COPE agreement in principle, you also suggest that Yukoners will have an opportunity to speak out about concerns over the North Slope. When, in fact, will Yukoners have this opportunity?

Christopher Pearson: Well, with respect to the Committee for Original Peoples' Entitlement (COPE) and the North Slope of the Yukon, I think Yukoners have spoken out twice—in 1978 and in 1982. In fact, COPE was a plank in our election platform. We were opposed to COPE and to COPE's agreement in principle.

I have not suggested that there is going to be any public input into any decision with respect to COPE because it is not our decision to make. It is the decision of the Government of Canada and it is going to be the result of negotiations. I believe what I said was that given a land-claims agreement in principle in the Yukon, then certainly there is going to be public input because that is when we are going to need it. It is going to have to be determined by the peoples of the territory whether they enter into the final agreement. This is the same process that COPE is going through in the Northwest Territories.

The development of the North Slope and public input is a very difficult thing. There is a time constraint; there has been a time constraint; and there was a time constraint on Gulf's application to the minister. Once again, it is not our government but the federal government that makes the decision with respect to the North Slope. Hearings will not be held unless the minister of Indian Affairs and Northern Development decides they are going to be held.

Lindsay Staples: I submit respectfully that public consultation is more than an election once every four years. I am interested in your perception of the differences between the Yukon and the Northwest Territories, and how they affect land-use planning, for instance.

Christopher Pearson: I think the major difference is the political evolution of the two territories. Five years ago, the Yukon was 75 years ahead of the Northwest Territories with respect to political evolution. Today it is not far ahead. I think that is good for the Northwest Territories because the political evolution may even be different from now on. In the Yukon, we do not have the problem of division that has to be addressed in this territory. Once that occurs, there will not be as many differences between whatever the western portion of the Northwest Territories ends up being and the Yukon.

The make-up of the peoples in the two territories is entirely different. The percentage of aboriginal peoples in the Northwest Territories differs dramatically from the percentage in the Yukon, and is reflected in its legislature. It is reflected in every decision that is made by the Government of the Northwest Territories and by the Government of the Yukon.

Cindy Gilday, Dene Nation: Mr Pearson, when you refer to the Yukoners, I presume you are talking about native peoples as well. I want to know if they share your view on development of the North Slope of the Yukon.

Christopher Pearson: Only the residents of Old Crow have expressed any opinion. They are divided. Those who work on the North Slope for any of the proponents are in favour of development on the North Slope. Others in Old Crow are very concerned. Their concern is not the development; their concern is what is going to happen to the Porcupine caribou herd. We have been able to ascertain that, given the constraints that we are insisting be imposed, the development will not affect the herd. There is a large number of residents of Old Crow who are opposed to development at Stokes Point. Sometimes these decisions have to be made in spite of opposition, however.

Jean Morisset, Université du Québec à Montréal: I address my question to Mr Pearson because he has said things like "we Yukoners." You know that the borders of the Yukon were established by the federal government rather than by the peoples who consider themselves Yukoners. Therefore, do you acknowledge that you are a product of Ottawa?

Christopher Pearson: We are a colony of the federal government, and so is the Northwest Territories. That is why it is very important to the country and to us that whatever we do, we do right. We do not want to make the same mistakes in building the Yukon that were made in Ontario or Québec. I am sure there were a lot of mistakes made, particularly with respect to the environment. A lot of places, if they had thought of the environment 100 years ago, would have done things differently. Now, I hope, we can learn from those mistakes. That is why we are here; we want advice. We do not always follow it, because we demand the right to make our own decisions, but we want the advice. We want to know what mistakes were made in Toronto and we shall try to avoid those mistakes.

Jean Morisset: You say that the Yukon is a colony of Canada, which means that without Canada it would not exist. The native peoples do exist without Canada.

Christopher Pearson: But we are Canadian, too. We are second-class Canadians at this time, but we are Canadians.

Gregg Sheehy, Canadian Nature Federation: There seems to be a lot of possible benefits to going to McKinley Bay. I wonder what the N.W.T. government may be doing to promote that site and possible alternatives—perhaps offshore alternatives—to meet Gulf's needs?

Richard Nerysoo: We are promoting McKinley Bay. That is the site we have suggested, at least upon an interim basis, that Gulf establish as a temporary base. Gulf has already established, as you are probably aware, a base at Tuktoyaktuk, where it has already built permanent facilities. The idea, I hope, would be to ensure that whatever is required now can be dealt with at McKinley Bay and at Tuktoyaktuk. Any other future developments or long-term developments, I think, require a bit more work by ourselves here, the federal government, and the Yukon government to see what would be the best solution to resolve the issue of a major harbour. We are concerned about the idea of an offshore base. That could become quite dangerous, particularly if you are looking at a time period when you have ice, ice floes, and that sort of thing.

We are prepared to promote McKinley Bay. I think, however, the most important element has to do with whether or not the peoples of the Northwest Territories—in particular those who are affected in the Mackenzie River Delta and Beaufort rim communities—can make a decision supporting the government, saying, "Yes, we agree," rather than saying, "No, we do not agree." There is no other solution on the table.

Nancy Russell LeBlond, President, Arctic International Wildlife Range Society: The northern Yukon was withdrawn in 1978 for a national wilderness park and other conservation initiatives. Much attention has been focused recently on a national wilderness park to the west of the Babbage River. What is the territorial government's position on the rest of the withdrawn lands?

Christopher Pearson: Our position is enunciated in the Northern Resources Policy. We support not a wilderness park, but a national park in the western portion of the North Slope. We do not think that there is any other thing that could be better done than to have a national park there. Our problem has always been one of access. Given that the whole North Slope is withdrawn and made a wilderness park, whatever that might be (by the way, we have never been able to ascertain what a wilderness park is as opposed to a national park), we are concerned about access. We think that access should be controlled very rigidly and closely.

Nancy Russell LeBlond: Are you suggesting that you would not support any conservation initiatives on the eastern half?

Christopher Pearson: No, not at all. In fact, what we are saying is that the whole area is very vulnerable to environmental damage; it is very fragile. We are concerned that there be some access, but that it also be controlled and limited. We are talking about an access corridor through the North Slope to the Beaufort Sea because we think that, at some point, that is going to be not only in the interest of Yukoners but also in the national interest.

Nancy Russell Leblond: I should like to know both governments' positions on either an informal international caribou agreement with the United States or a formal treaty.

Richard Nerysoo: I think that we have to determine first what we are going to do as Canadians. It is most important that we have an internal agreement prior to international discussions. We cannot talk to the Government of the United States when we do not even have a resolution, or at least an agreement, in place in Canada. Are we prepared to address that particular question in Canada? If you ask me, as a representative of the Government of the Northwest Territories, yes, we are prepared to work on it. Anytime that the Government of the Yukon and the federal government choose to sit down with us we are prepared to discuss that item. In fact, as a member of the legislative assembly for the communities that are affected directly—Fort McPherson and Aklavik because of their use of that particular herd—I have a direct interest in ensuring that some resolution occurs.

Howard Tracey, Minister of Renewable Resources, Yukon Territorial Government: We have proposed in our *Northern Yukon Resource Management Model* that the eastern half of the North Slope remain in the condition that it is in today and that it be planned jointly with the federal government and with the Indian people involved. That includes COPE and the Council for Yukon Indians. In fact, we are very close to having an agreement with the federal government regarding land-use planning. That is one of the considerations being looked at so that land will be planned before any use is made of it.

I have had discussions with the State of Alaska and the previous commissioner of Fish and Game in Alaska. The deputy commissioner is here today and I shall be discussing it with him. We are also discussing other subjects, such as salmon, but an informal agreement with the State of Alaska is something that we hope to arrive at within the very near future.

I should also like to enumerate four areas where we have been involved in conservation in the territory:

1. We withdrew an eight-km corridor along the Dempster Highway for resource management. That study has been going on now for about four years. We are almost at the point where we will have public participation to decide what our management plan will be for the Dempster corridor.
2. I have just signed an agreement with the federal government regarding heritage rivers so that we can protect our heritage rivers in the Yukon Territory.
3. We have established wildlife quotas on certain species that we feel are endangered.
4. We have reserved historic sites, such as Fort Selkirk. We have asked the federal government for about 26 reserves in the Yukon Territory; we have not to this date been granted any. We have ongoing archaeological studies in the territory every year.

Jim Maxwell, Department of the Environment: Both panelists used the term "development" and the term "conservation." My understanding of the way those words were used is that they are opposing forces, with the implication that conservation is essentially preservation and protection of resources or the environment. I feel that that is a very restrictive meaning and I am sure that the gentlemen do not restrict their concerns and the activities they think of as conservation just to preservation and protection.

Conservation has been defined in many ways, but one of the neatest ways, I think, is "wise use." That implies human activity interacting with the environment, in which we all operate both as physical, biological beings and as thinking peoples in societies. It implies that we make use of what is there. It talks, though, of sustainable use, sensible use of non-renewable resources. Conservation is a philosophy that should be an integral part of all the things we do in development. So they really are not opposing forces.

We should be in a bad state if the only conservation practised were that restricted to the special areas called national parks, or provincial parks, or other such protected areas, because they account for a very small proportion of our territory. If we gave no heed at all to conservation practices and principles in other parts of our land, we would be in deep trouble. In fact, we have made many bad mistakes but, when we look at developed areas in southern Canada, western Europe, or the United States, we find that some of the best conservation practices take place through multiple use of privately owned lands. I hope that we can get away from this concept of opposing forces all the time—developers on one side, conservationists on the other. It really does waste a lot of energy.

Christopher Pearson: I agree with everything you have said. There has to be co-operation. All of us must practise conservation every day of our lives in this country or we really are in trouble. I should very much like to see the day when the conflict is over, because I believe very strongly that there can be co-operation. Conflict does not work.

Richard Nerysoo: The comments are legitimate. It is easy to say we can have those types of perceptions or ideas being addressed by governments. When one is talking about conservation, and about the idea of renewable resource management in particular, however, those persons who are involved with environment or animals have a tendency to focus their attention on trying to manage human use of wildlife or the environment. The most important element should be how to use the resources that are there. We cannot really address the idea of integrating renewable resource use and non-renewable resource use without having limits, or at least guidelines as to what will be a policy. That is one of the reasons the Government of the Northwest Territories is looking at a renewable resource policy so that we can identify how we are going to use our renewable resources in conjunction with developing our non-renewable resources.

Dennis Bevington, Slave River Basin Coalition, Fort Smith, N.W.T.: I suppose our region is one of the primary examples of the development impact zone group. This public process—public participation in resource development issues—is a policy that has been outlined for us by the territorial government. We are wondering whether we still have room to develop the potential the group will have for decision making. Also, we are wondering if the groups can be designated more proactively than reactively in terms of land-use planning, on an ongoing basis for the region.

Richard Nerysoo: I think if the Government of the Northwest Territories did not agree that public participation should occur in making a decision, then the idea of development impact zones would not have come into being. The idea is that the zone group is, in fact, to be an advisory group to me, as minister, in making a decision. Usually, any recommendations are made to the bureaucracy, then the bureaucracy makes the decisions about what will be directed to the minister. In this case, there is direct access to the minister. Individuals, ministers in particular, have a wide variety of concerns they have to take into consideration as well as the issues that are being addressed by a particular development impact zone group. I think that the zones and the zone groups can play a major role in those decisions. I hope that they do not suggest that the body become a major decision-making body. That is something that has to be worked out between the minister and the zone groups.

Dennis Bevington: I think the development impact zone group is an excellent start on community participation and public participation in decisions that are going to affect the public. This is an ongoing process. That is what I was hoping you would establish with us.

Richard Nerysoo: Certainly it is an ongoing process. I do not want to stop tomorrow after recommendations are made. There is a certain responsibility that one has, as a minister, to the public: I want to hear what the general public has to say about decisions. There will be pros and cons to any decision, and all the recommendations that are put forward by the zone group may not necessarily be things that I agree with now; however, they may be part of the planning process.

II
LAND CLAIMS
PLENARY SESSION

Land Claims Plenary Session

Chairman's Opening Remarks

Ronald L. Doering
Kelly, Doering and Morrow
Barristers and Solicitors

Welcome to the Third National Workshop's plenary session on the federal land-claims policy. I am going to rely on the group here to determine the range of subjects we talk about; we will get out of this session what we collectively put into it. The subject of tonight's session is very timely. It has now been ten years since the federal government decided to negotiate settlements of claims based on aboriginal title. Its position prior to 1974 was to do nothing about aboriginal claims because they were not subject to clear definition; hence there was an attempt to pretend the issue was not there. Following the Calder decision, the government issued a press release announcing a policy designed to change its approach to land claims and to attempt to negotiate, in good faith, modern-day treaties with native claimants who had never released their aboriginal title by treaty. In effect, the policy was designed to negotiate a settlement of claims wherein native peoples would have their aboriginal title extinguished in return for land, money, and other consideration.

This autumn will be the third anniversary of the most recent government policy on comprehensive land claims. Comprehensive land claims relate to areas where there are no treaties in existence; that is, most of Canada north of 60°. The new policy developed a far more comprehensive system for such claims. The federal government is just beginning actively to assess the efficacy of the policy.

All of us here welcome this opportunity to take part, right at the beginning, in this appraisal of what is clearly a very important policy for all Canadians. Tonight we are going to assess the strengths and weaknesses of the current policy. Our objective is to analyse the policy from the perspective of how it has actually worked. Those of us who have been watching the claims process through the years will have an opportunity to express, to this group and to the federal government, our thoughts on the claims policy and the claims process.

To give us a little focus, we might want to consider these questions: Has there been real progress in the last two or three years? If there has not, why not? It may be that there is simply a lack of will to settle on the part of the native claimants or of the federal government. It may be that there is something fundamentally wrong with the process. Perhaps we made some fundamental design errors when we set it up. Or perhaps it is just that the claims are far more complex than most persons ever realized, and it is simply going to take a lot more time than we thought to work out these complicated modern-day treaties.

We are very lucky to have here three men who have had experience with the claims process. First, **Bob Overvold**, the chief negotiator for the Dene Nation, who is actively involved in the process, was negotiating last month, and presumably will be negotiating next month. Secondly, we have **Clovis Demers**, Executive Director of the Office of Native Claims, Department of Indian Affairs and Northern Development (DIAND). In the last three years, he has had a very significant role in formulating and developing the claims policy and trying to make it work. Finally, we have **Bob Mitchell**, the former chief federal negotiator on the Inuit Tapirisat of Canada (ITC) claim, now called the Tungavik Federation of Nunavut (TFN) claim. He was in that position for about a year and had what appeared to be some preliminary success on that claim.

Discussion

Chairman: To give you a couple of moments to formulate your thoughts, perhaps I could start. During the last day and a half I took part in a working group on natural resource jurisdiction and political development. One of the recurring issues was the relationship of the claims process to the Nunavut proposal, or to the political development issues. Native peoples expressed some concern about the efficacy of the policy. They took the position that it is too one-sided, that there is too much duress involved. Without asking you to comment on that specific issue, I am wondering whether you think that the federal government is satisfied with the efficacy of the policy at this stage.

Clovis Demers: We in the Office of Native Claims (ONC) and the government have not yet really looked at what has happened since the policy has been reformulated. We certainly have a feeling that things are not going as fast as we would like them to go. Whether they can go faster is another question. As far as the fundamentals of the policy are concerned, for the time being, we think it is workable. We are getting into an evaluation exercise sometime during the summer, the purpose of which will be to conclude either that it is good or bad, or that some parts are good and some parts are bad, and some changes are required, either to the policy or to the process. There could be, and ought to be, ways of improving the process and speeding it up. Currently, the negotiating teams for the federal government are made up of representatives of several departments that are the most directly interested. This causes some difficulties; how to ensure that departments look at the claims process and the claims policy positively; how they should come out with ideas in their own areas. The ONC has difficulty in its role as co-ordinator or main negotiator in getting changes, new ideas, and innovative ways of doing things from the various departments and in bringing them to the table. So, I am not satisfied with the way the process is working internally.

Dave Porter, Yukon Indian Development Corporation: Claims in the Yukon are currently under negotiation, and there is some speculation that the process could very well conclude in the near future. Part of the problem with the process as it has related to the negotiations in the Yukon all along has been the inability of the government to come forward with concrete policy for constitutional development and non-renewable resources—two areas that are seen as essential not only to any final resolution of the claims, but also to a successful claims process.

The minister of Indian Affairs and Northern Development, in his speech to the Yukon Legislative Assembly in January 1983, stated that he envisaged a tripartite process to address the constitutional issue. He has committed himself further in letters to the chairman of the Council for Yukon Indians (CYI), Harry Allen, and has indicated that the process will be parallel to the claims process and will involve as its principal negotiators the Yukon Territorial Government (YTG), the federal government, and CYI.

Mr Demers, as a result of the YTG boycott and the subsequent negotiations between the YTG and the federal government, did the federal government, in effect, give any ground to the YTG in respect to the commitment it has made in the tripartite process respecting constitutional talks? Is it still the position of the federal government that those tripartite talks will take place with CYI as a full participant? Can you indicate when that process will begin?

Secondly, on the question of resources, CYI has for many years been pushing for a statement of policy. Whenever the issue has been brought to the negotiating table, the federal negotiator has stated consistently that he is unable to deal with the question because of a lack of mandate. It is

certainly a question that deserves the attention of, and ultimately a decision from, the federal Cabinet. Can you indicate to us where the federal
Cabinet is on that policy question? Has DIAND brought forward any
documents requesting a decision? If not, where is the process at, and when
will it take place?

Clovis Demers: There are some comments I can make, but I am not going
to comment on the Cabinet process. I am certainly not in a position to
indicate whether or not a document has been, or will be, prepared and sent
to Cabinet.

The question of resource development or resource-related revenues for
claimants has arisen from the beginning. It is one where the negotiator in
each individual case has to refer back to the minister, or ministers, when a
decision needs to be made. The position of the federal government regarding resource revenues has been, up to now, that there is no exclusion of the
notion of participation in resource revenues in the area. The difficulty the
government has, and the difficulty the negotiating process runs into, is in
defining how this is done. I think there is a general acceptance on the part
of government and on the part of the ministers that for a claimant group to
have a stake in the development of the area is in everybody's interest.

Difficulty arises with the notion either of ownership of the resource or
of sharing the royalties, both of which are very closely tied to the political
evolution of the North. Because of this, I think we are forced gradually to
address this issue in a too-fragmented way. We address it when it arises
with CYI. We address it when it arises with another group. Certainly some
clarification has yet to be brought into the government's thinking on this
subject.

With regard to the tripartite process and constitutional development
in the North, that issue has also been central to our dealings with CYI,
particularly over the last three, four, or five months. I should like to quote
my minister on the subject, because I do not want to go further than, or to
stop short of, what he said, but I was not there when he made a statement to
the press around 12 May. The only answer I can give you is that the
minister has given assurances that he has not sold out anything to the YTG
in recent months in arriving at an arrangement to get the negotiations back
on the rails. Because I do not have the wording of the minister's statement, I
am not in a position to be more specific.

Dave Porter: With respect to the government's inability to come forward
with a concrete policy prior to the conclusion of the talks to at least an
agreement-in-principle stage, can Mr Demers tell me if it is the government's intention, through the agreement in principle, legally to articulate

a recognition that aboriginal rights do in fact contain rights tied to the resource question, and do mean that aboriginal peoples have the right to participate in the constitutional development of the Yukon? Will there be some language to that effect in the agreement in principle?

Clovis Demers: I do not think so. The agreements in principle that have been initialled or signed do not address those issues directly. I do not think it is the intention of the government to do so, but I am not one of the negotiators. I do not see it happening that way.

Dave Porter: Would the agreement in principle have a linkage to the constitutional process that would, in effect, guarantee the aboriginal peoples participation in those negotiations? In other words, suppose we have an agreement in principle on fishing, hunting, and all of the subjects that the parties have agreed to discuss to the agreement-in-principle stage, but the government states that it is not able to render a Cabinet decision for many aspects, possibly the constitutional question. However, the government then commits itself to a process to negotiate an arrangement with respect to the management and ownership of resources in the Yukon with the aboriginal peoples in the constitutional forum. Is there now thinking within the federal government that that is an option on which it could proceed?

Clovis Demers: We would consider proceeding on that if it were very much a demand on the part of CYI. If at the negotiating table in the course of the next month or two months, because we are coming very close to the end, CYI comes up with a demand of that order we will have to look at it. I cannot say what the government position will be, but as far as I know our negotiators do not intend, and I certainly do not intend, to offer to go into that in the claims agreement.

Jean Morisset,Département de géographie,Université du Québec à Montréal: [How can the federal government pretend that there are aboriginal rights and that it will deal with those aboriginal rights without acknowledging or admitting that there ought to be an ethnic-based province, an aboriginal province?] Translation.

Clovis Demers: [The question of a province or of a particular political regime in the North is not necessarily linked to the settlement of the claim based on aboriginal title. Thinking of the COPE discussions, the CYI discussions, and the way the TFN discussions are moving, it is entirely possible to negotiate a claims settlement in good faith, based on aboriginal rights, and to leave the question of the political regime in that area to be discussed and resolved in another forum with the participation of non-natives as well as natives.] Translation.

Jean Morisset: [You have answered in part, but only to the extent that you recognize a thing such as aboriginal rights. You are implementing a particular statute through which you conserve a federation and eventually it will certainly be necessary that aboriginal rights must be extended throughout the two territories and then we will need a structure that applies equally to a territory south of 60°.] Translation.

Clovis Demers: [I think it is political evolution that you are talking about. That could happen, that is going to happen. To what extent it will happen, I do not know, but solutions will have to be found concurrently with land claims. The settlement of claims is a contract between a group of natives and one or, in most cases, two governments that deal with economic, social, and cultural factors and the question of local government. And for the moment it seems evident that it is possible to proceed toward the solution of the questions in the framework of claims without really becoming preoccupied with the long-term evolution, in the very long term, in the North as in the South. I think that these are two things that certainly are related, but one advances while the other is not really affected.] Translation.

Chairman: Clovis, do you have an opinion about whether a claims settlement or Nunavut has to come first? Do you have a feeling about the order of the two processes, which are combined but really not dealt with together?

Clovis Demers: I certainly agree that the claims should be resolved first. The claims resolution process is a very complex one. It involves a long process of identification and clarification of rights before and after settlement. It involves setting up corporations, and setting up structures that will take care of the claims benefits. I hope we can get that done before we get into drawing lines on a map between Nunavut and whatever will be next to it and before northerners start setting up their own structures. If we had to wait for this to happen, I would venture to say that we would not have a claims settlement for a good part of the next 20–25 years. The claims settlement is possible to attain in the very near future, and I am talking in terms of two years. I think that two years is a likely period of time for the eastern Arctic claim to be resolved, cleaned up, and legislated—perhaps not completed to legislation but certainly completed to the final agreement stage.

The process of claims negotiation does not, of course, prevent the peoples in the area from starting to work on their own structures, but imagine what would happen if we had suddenly to start from scratch with a new territorial political structure. We should be delayed considerably.

Chairman: If the claim has to be settled before Nunavut—and that is certainly the statement that Mr Munro made on 11 May—do you see the other claims in the valley, such as the Dene–Métis claim, being settled too, before there is a division in the new government?

Clovis Demers: I have never thought about that. I do not know. I have no answer for that.

Peter Burnet, Executive Director, CARC: Mr Demers, the current policy, *In All Fairness*, clearly presupposes an end to or an extinguishment of aboriginal rights in the legal common law sense as decided by the courts. In fact, the document says that the thrust of this policy is to exchange undefined aboriginal land rights for concrete rights and benefits. As you know, a couple of years ago these rights were recognized and affirmed in the Constitution. There is now an elaborate process to refine further and to define those rights in the Constitution. I am wondering whether it is still the policy that there must be an extinguishment of these aboriginal land rights and, if it is, how you would go about accomplishing it in light of the Constitution.

Clovis Demers: Obviously, whatever comes out of a claims settlement cannot do what the Constitution says should not be done or will not be done. I should point out that *In All Fairness* was published before all of this happened. First, we will have to revise our terminology, and then see how the two mesh. They have to mesh. The native peoples now have a guarantee in the Constitution and whatever is said in the claims policy will have to be adjusted to it. We are asking our lawyers to give us some options as to how this is done, but I do not have the answer at this time.

Peter Burnet: Mr Mitchell, Mr Demers said earlier that there was going to be a thorough review of the land-claims policy. On the basis of your experience of negotiating for that great unwieldy institution called the federal government, do you have any comments as to the direction that review should take?

Land Claims Plenary Session

Bob Mitchell: Generally, I agree with and I respect the policy position that the federal government took some ten years ago and the policy position it has maintained since. Compared with any other country having an aboriginal population, Canada ranks far ahead in policy. The Canadian government is to be commended for that.

I had more than a year of direct experience negotiating with the ITC team, now called the TFN team—the Inuit of the central and eastern Arctic. During that time at the bargaining table, we dealt with, and disposed of, two rather large items on our agenda.

The first had to do with interim measures that would go into effect pending the settlement of an agreement in principle, in fact, pending a final settlement of the land claim. The second had to do with wildlife harvesting rights and wildlife management. It was there that I saw something missing in the translation of the policy as enunciated by the minister and the prime minister to the actual positions taken at the bargaining table. I think that to a large extent land-claims negotiations and settlements involve the sharing of power—indeed, in some cases, the transfer of power—from the government to the aboriginal group. Before these land-claims negotiations began, the government had substantial control with respect to wildlife management, land use and land management, resource development, economic development, social development, and cultural questions. ITC was asking for a share of that control, a meaningful participation in it. I found, particularly in negotiating on wildlife management, which is so crucial to the life of Inuit, that Inuit were not at all content, not at all satisfied, with the government's offer that they be allowed to sit on advisory boards to the various ministers concerned. They responded that they had experience with advisory boards. Their experience had not been good; they were not impressed; and they just were not prepared to settle for a solely advisory status. They wanted a more meaningful role. We agreed in principle that they ought to have a meaningful role, but subject to the overriding principle that government—federal or territorial—is ultimately responsible for wildlife management and because government is ultimately responsible, it has to retain the final decision-making authority.

We were able to negotiate an agreement in principle, subject to approval, on the basis of those two principles. We ran into great difficulty when some of the departments involved in wildlife management were simply not prepared to share any significant amount of control with the aboriginal group. For that reason, the agreement in principle that we negotiated some year and a half ago still awaits ratification by the federal government.

I will be more specific. In connection with the wildlife agreement, after having offered the advisory board and having that rebuffed at the table, the government introduced the prospect that we would agree to an advisory board with more teeth, whose recommendations were more than merely "advisory." It was one thing to introduce that; it was quite another to put any flesh on the principle. Clearly, if we were going to settle that issue, we had to move in that direction.

The discussion then became: What did we mean by teeth? What sort of mechanisms could be set up that would make the board's role more than merely advisory? That took us directly into the question of the willingness of the departments to allow Inuit to participate meaningfully in decision making. It was very tough. We eventually came up with a plan whereby a wildlife management board composed of representatives of Inuit and of government, four from each, would have a mandate including all questions related to the management of wildlife. That board would be supported by staff and would have access to all the data that it would need to make decisions. Its decisions would be communicated to the minister responsible. If the minister took no action on the decision, the decision would become binding after a certain period of time. If the minister took exception to the decision, he could disallow it and send it back to the board with his reasons. The board would then have an opportunity to reconsider the question and, if it was so inclined, to amend its decision. Finally, if the minister remained unsatisfied with the amended decision, he could do what he wanted. After all, he is the ultimate authority in our system, and I think properly so.

That idea gained a measure of acceptance at senior levels of the federal bureaucracy, sufficient acceptance for me to conclude an agreement on the basis of it; however, the departments concerned, two in particular, were just not going to live with it. The basis for not living with it was simply that it diminished the power of their ministers.

As I said at the outset, I regard negotiations in many areas of land claims as a question of sharing control. That cannot happen, at least not easily, from the government's point of view if there are departments that absolutely refuse to share any of the control. I am not tarring all federal departments with that brush, and certainly not departments of the territorial government, because the territorial government has a very progressive position on this question. A couple of the federal departments, however, just dug in their heels and refused, and said, "no way, we are not going to go along with this." Their position is totally inconsistent with the concept enunciated by the government ten years ago and restated in *In All Fairness*. I think that concept involves a sharing of control, a sharing of power, and that it is absolutely incumbent upon the bureaucracies involved to understand and to accept that sharing is an integral part of the land-claims policy. Until they do, I believe that the land-claims process is going to have difficulties, and, indeed, may not work.

Clovis Demers: I do not intend to go into the details of the agreement itself. It is a fact that it has not been ratified yet by the federal government. Bob seems to suggest that essentially it is a problem of the bureaucracy, that there is a system in place that prevents things that should happen from happening, and that system is made up of bureaucrats.

There is certainly some resistance on the part of the bureaucracy. Bureaucracy is by nature conservative, and once it has found ways of doing things it is not naturally inclined to invent new ways of doing the same things. But the problems are not just in the bureaucracy. There is a position in the government with regard to participation in decision making. This is the position that was approved by Cabinet and that you find in *In All Fairness*; it is one of participation and an advisory role. I think it is quite clear in that document.

There is a whole range possible under the notion of "advisory." You can have an advisory committee that just rubber stamps or meets once every year and makes declarations. You can also have advisory committees that have "teeth."

The resistance to change (and I acknowledge there is resistance) is not always an issue of simple refusal to look at new ways of doing things. There is a problem of attitudinal change. It is very important for government, as a government, for bureaucracy as a bureaucracy, to change its attitudes. We do have to change that and that is a long process. The question of ministerial jurisdiction is very important. Ministers are accountable to Parliament for what they do, and when they see that they will be less able to do the things that they are supposed to do, they resist the change.

There is also the argument that ministers and departments come up with regarding precedents elsewhere. If you do this with TFN in the North, what does that mean in the South or somewhere else in the North?

Finally, there is the question of workability, or practicability. What does it mean in practical terms to set up this board here, or that board there, and to overlap between two or three boards that were there already? The bureaucracy, and the ministers, have to look at this. Sometimes it may seem simple on paper. You can set up a series of boards and you can tell everybody how the boards should work. Nevertheless, the person who will be responsible somewhere for making part of it work has to ask: "What does that mean in practical terms? How long will decisions take to be made through that process?"

Willie Joe, Council for Yukon Indians: There is an element that I think we should point out in reference to the claims settlement in relationship to the Yukon and to the nature of land selection. In 1980, the Council for Yukon Indians advanced a position on resource issues to the Government of Canada, to which we have not received a response. More recently, we followed it up with meetings in Ottawa with various officials, Clovis [Demers] being one of them, requesting a response, and I think they are coming close to it, given Clovis' remarks earlier. What Dave [Porter] did not clarify earlier was that lands selected in the Yukon in regard to our claim were not selected on the basis of sub-surface riches. The lands selected represent maybe five per cent of the total surface lands in the Yukon. If we have selected lands all sitting on gold mines, we are fortunate, but it is a shot in the dark. The public, the Yukon Territorial Government, the Government of Canada, and other Indian associations that are involved in negotiations need to take this view into account.

I would like to pose a question related to advance payments, for which we have been asking for the last couple of years from the federal government. I read in the government's document that it has been giving our neighbours advance payments for becoming involved in business developments and a number of other activities such as oil and gas developments. We in the Yukon have been posturing in that direction, and wish to take part in these riches that we are supposed to have. We continually are told that, "I am sorry but we just do not have the mandate to deal with that matter." I am referring to our specific requests for some up-front monies in the neighbourhood of 15 to 25 million dollars to become involved in setting up and getting our development corporation off the ground, getting involved in various developments in the Yukon.

Clovis Demers: COPE (Committee for Original Peoples' Entitlement) got an advance of several million dollars several years ago. It has all been paid. I do not know whether the amount is public; I do not dare say it. COPE got a pretty good advance on its settlement and it is making good use of it, I am told.

An advance is not something that the government refuses to consider in principle. I think you have had indications that if you came up with a proposal it would be looked at. That is very definitely a decision for Cabinet to make, however, and I know that you are taking the normal means of getting it before the minister. In principle, it is possible; whether or not it happens is something that Cabinet will have to decide.

Bob Overvold: I think the question that Willie [Joe] asked is a good example of what we are discussing: the effectiveness of the government's policy *vis-à-vis* comprehensive claims. Today I skimmed over John

Merritt's paper on behalf of TFN [included in this volume] in which he essentially dismisses the federal policy as "chronic ambiguity." I think his view is fairly reflective of the views of other native groups. I should like to focus on that policy. In regard to your question, however, we have not dealt substantively with the matter of asking for up-front money to get into economic development activities. We did explore that concept in a very general way, and the federal negotiator, David Osborn, indicated that the government was very reluctant. It was done with COPE, but the government would be very reluctant to do it with other groups. The government would prefer to have benefits go out to a claimant group after a final agreement. You are right. I think that is an example of how the government will do one thing for one group but tell the other group that such a thing is out of the question.

If you get to the meat of the matter, these negotiations (whether with the Dene, the Métis, CYI, Inuit, or Inuvialuit) are over the matter of land and resources. They always have been, in terms of both the government's approach and the native claimant groups' approach. The government's position, and it has stated it over and over in policy documents and at the negotiating table, is that it sees negotiations as the exchanging of aboriginal title to the land in return for specific benefits. Someone said earlier that even that is a bit ambiguous. On one hand, through the constitutional negotiations, the government is trying to define those rights and, on the other hand, at the negotiating table, it is trying to extinguish them. Another observation is that the public sees this process as carrying on, and on, and on. Not long ago we had a negotiating session in Fort McPherson and even amongst our clientele it was said that some are just getting "land-claims tired." They do not see the process coming to an end; it seems to go on and on.

I think that is precisely because the policy is not very clear. The government wants to remove what it perceives as a cloud to government title to the land and, by and large, the native groups are also trying to get some form of interest in the land recognized. The objectives are often diametrically opposed, and on certain issues, especially land and resources, these negotiations are not going to come to a head unless the policy is changed. The government has told the Dene and the Métis that its legal position is that our aboriginal title has been extinguished by treaties 8 and 11. It is pretending that we still have title, however, and that is why it is negotiating with us. If we do reach an agreement, then we will pretend to extinguish it again. Mr Demers, can you clarify how the Dene and the Métis fit into the government's approach to other claimant groups?

Clovis Demers: We do not pretend anything. Our position is that the title has been extinguished, but we also say that the benefits that the treaty implied were not all delivered, and that it is unfinished business. In fact, we are using the same instrument with you as we use for other groups whose title, according to us, has not been extinguished. We do it because we want to finish business that was begun in 1920. The Dene–Métis claim is unique in a number of ways, and this is one element of its uniqueness. It is also unique in the sense that there are really two submissions, one from the Métis and one from the Dene. They were submitted separately, but our position is that they should lead to one settlement to avoid the divisiveness that would occur otherwise.

Bob Overvold: As I said, the nuts and bolts of what the native groups expect to get out of the settlement is an interest in the land and the resources. If you look at the claims policy as you can see it in *In All Fairness*, and as you can take it from other claims that have been advanced, such as COPE's, it deals with a number of things. When it deals with land and resources, however, it is not very clear at all. The government, on one hand, says that native groups can negotiate an interest in sub-surface resources, but only to a point. If you negotiate some form of revenue sharing—some form of royalty payments to yourselves—it cannot be ongoing. It cannot go on for the next hundred or thousand years.

On the other hand, the native groups have always said that they are not trying to negotiate and to reach a settlement for this generation, but for future generations. It would be asinine for any native group to negotiate a settlement that would benefit this generation only, leaving nothing for future generations. The policy of the government is to give some interest in land and resources only for the present generation. It is in this area that I think there is the most need for a more progressive policy from the government. If the government is reviewing the comprehensive-claims policy and what it thinks is possible in terms of native groups' negotiating an interest in sub-surface resources, does Mr Demers see or anticipate a change in this area, so that native peoples can negotiate an ongoing interest in sub-surface resources?

Clovis Demers: I know that the question is going to be debated in light of representations made by the various groups. I know that it will be looked at with great interest. It will be looked at in the context of what it will do; how it compares; how it relates to the question of resource ownership by territorial and provincial governments. What will come out of that I do not know. I have no way of knowing.

One element of the policy as it now stands is the requirement that the cost of the claims settlement be finite. This is where, in fact, the policy is incompatible with the idea of an unending share of the resources. This element of the policy is clear and has been put there by Cabinet as something that was essential. Whether or not that will be reviewed I do not know. We do hope that whatever comes out of a settlement will benefit future generations. We are not taking the attitude, "Let's give them a cheque and things are over with; we won't hear about them." It is not going to happen like that, and the government does not want it to happen in that manner. The financial component of the settlement is meant to do just what you, Bob, want it to do, to be invested in the area or elsewhere for future generations. I think this is what is happening, what will happen, what could happen in future settlements.

Murray Coolican, President, Peters, Coolican & Associates: As an observer of the land-claims process over the last few years, I am struck by a number of examples. I think the story that Mr Mitchell described is as good as any. It is said often that the policy of the government is more evident in what it does than in what it says it will do. I cannot help making the comment that it appears that the policy of the government is not to settle the claims, but to drag on the negotiations for as long as possible until either the native peoples lose patience and will accept anything, or other Canadians lose patience and demand a legislated settlement rather than a negotiated settlement or insist that there be no settlement at all.

There are many instances where it appears that the government does not have the will to come to an agreement. If a government negotiator takes a position and then the government does not have the discipline to get the agreement approved—or, in the example of COPE, bureaucrats change, politicians change, circumstances change, and therefore an agreement signed 14 months earlier is no longer appropriate—I think the essential problem is the lack of political will to settle. That means to me that the government's policy is not to settle but to drag out the negotiations for as long as possible.

Clovis Demers: The chief federal negotiator represents the government. When he goes to the table and makes an offer, it is incumbent on him to ensure that he has his principals behind him. I am not saying that Bob Mitchell did not. A chief negotiator must be able to take risks; a good negotiator sticks his neck out. His problem is how far out, and he has to sense that. He has to do his homework and do his lobbying. Nevertheless, he does represent the government. He is not there as a mediator; he is not there as a facilitator; he represents the government.

With regard to the objective being to drag on, I can understand that this is the impression that one gets from the outside. The government side of the negotiating process is a very heavy unwieldy machine, and, as I said, it has some difficulty changing attitudes. But there are two parties to the negotiations. I think that sometimes the other side is not prepared to come up with a clear position either. It has to do its homework itself. I find it a bit odd that if things drag on it has to be because of the federal government. It is not always because of the federal government.

Bob Mitchell: Before I get to that, I think that the federal government clearly did not know how complicated the process was until it was deeply into it. When Mr Munro asked me to negotiate the ITC claim I thought it would take about a year, but 16 months later I had just scratched the surface of it. Based on the progress that I made, I think that claim will be five or six years in negotiation. I introduce that number without having considered it in detail, but, clearly, the government just did not know the size of the task that it was handing to its negotiators. The machinery is very cumbersome. The government wants to settle these claims very, very badly, but it is a debate as to whether it is prepared to make the moves that are necessary in order to settle. It is my experience that the will is there to settle, but that it is just a much more complex question than had been anticipated when the policy was laid down.

If the process drags on too long and the native groups, the government officials, and Canadians in general lose patience with it, then I fear the possibility of an Alaskan-type resolution to the problem, a legislated solution. I know that there are persons around the government apparatus who have that point of view. They are not anywhere near the decision-making process now, but I believe that possibility lurks in the wings if the negotiating process does not work out. As far as my neck is concerned, well, who knows. Clovis and I are not going to get into a public debate about whether or not I had the proper mandate, but I know that both he and I remain hopeful that the agreement will be ratified.

Clovis Demers: I admire somebody who has the guts to go out and take risks, and I never fought with Bob during the 16 months we were together. He made me nervous sometimes, but I think it takes a lot of courage because you have that big machine behind you. You have six, seven, eight departments that have a direct interest, and you are not sure where they are coming out on various issues. If every two or three days or even every two or three weeks you could talk to all of these ministers, perhaps the situation would be different, but you cannot. They are busy doing something else. There is a lot of risk involved, and it is a pretty rough job.

Land Claims Plenary Session

Settling claims is really putting in place a new relationship between two parties that, in the past, have had a rather simple relationship. One told the other what to do, and when and how to do it. What you end up with is very different. The federal government is going to be the federal government next year and 10 years from now and 15 years from now, but it is probably not going to be smaller or simpler. There are complex, Byzantine hoops we have to go through to get a decision made.

That is the nature of the beast, so that is what we have to work with and that is what the other party has to work with. It is never going to be easy. Until about two or three years ago we just did not know how complicated it was. We had no idea how complicated it would be to get our act together within the federal government, or how complicated it would be for the other party to get its act together (because it does have its problems) and then to bring these together and to arrive at an agreement that is supposed to last forever—particularly now that agreements will be protected in the Constitution.

Murray Coolican: I am hearing that it is not the government's policy to drag on the claims but that it is the process of government, for the most part (there are from time to time problems on the native side), that causes the claims to drag on, and on, and on. Whether it is intentional or not, the native peoples are left with the effect that the process is dragging on. They do not have the patience or the staying power. They cannot run up deficits the way the federal government can. They do not have the pool of talent that is available to the federal government to keep changing bureaucrats, negotiators, and politicians. The native participants often remain the same. Dave Porter has been around this for a long, long time; Harry Allen has been around it for a long, long time; Sam Raddi and Peter Green have been; and the same for the Dene. They are the same persons who have to keep at it. Mr Demers, you were not there a number of years ago; it was someone else before you. There was someone before Bob Mitchell, and there will be someone after him. You are able to bring in fresh troops. I think that the deck is rather stacked against the native peoples.

You mentioned the courage and the risk taking of the federal negotiator, standing out there with that big machine behind him ready to snap his head off. To put this into perspective, we should think about the risk that the native peoples' negotiators are taking. They are making a decision for the generations that came before them and the generations that will come after, decisions that are a lot more important, I suggest, to the native peoples than the decisions made by the federal government will be to the government and to the peoples of Canada. I think that the risk that they are taking is far, far greater.

Judy Rowell, Environmental Adviser, Labrador Inuit Association: Mr Demers, I have a question that relates to your comment about DIAND's review of the comprehensive land-claims policy. The Labrador Inuit Association (LIA) has formally notified your minister that it is ready to negotiate. The Government of Newfoundland also has informed the federal government that it is ready to negotiate. LIA cannot get on the negotiating list, however, because of the criterion of having just six groups on the list at once. We are told by your department that another group cannot get onto that list until one of the six claims being negotiated is completed. Is the eligibility criterion for getting on the short list going to be part of the review of your policy, and are you going to continue to stay with the short-list concept?

Clovis Demers: The LIA claim was accepted by the federal government six or seven years ago. It has been a frustrating experience for LIA, I know, that although it tells us that it could be ready to start at three months' notice, we have to say, "Sorry, but we don't have the resources to get the LIA claim to negotiation." It is a fact that we are under instructions from Cabinet to stay with the six claims that we are negotiating and we do not get the resources to extend that to a seventh or an eighth group. Whether or not this policy will change depends on the decision of Cabinet.

In British Columbia about a month ago, our minister expressed his frustration about not being able to deal with more than the six groups; and I think he implied that he would like to be able to go beyond the sixth. It is not a question of eligibility criteria. I know the LIA claim and the LIA team quite well, and I know the team is prepared. I know it is ready and it could probably get into negotiations very effectively, very fast.

The Government of Newfoundland has said that it is prepared to negotiate. As you are probably aware, however, the Newfoundland government insists on discussions or negotiations between it and the federal government prior to the negotiations with LIA, to establish respective responsibilities. Our position has always been that we are not going to sign something with the Province of Newfoundland and go together to LIA; we want a tripartite process. We are now in discussions with the Government of Newfoundland to try to determine how far the province is ready to go, and where it is prepared to contribute, so that we can determine what we should contribute. There is work being done there in preparation for an eventual start of the negotiations. I cannot tell you whether shortly, or in the next month, or before the review is completed, the government will agree to extend the negotiations to more than six.

Land Claims Plenary Session

Judy Rowell: Can you tell me whether the department is considering developing some kind of priority rating for the teams that are standing in the wings? Because even when one claim is completed, there is no guarantee as to who is next in line. Even a priority rating would be of some assistance.

Clovis Demers: There are not many groups who are ready and willing to begin right now. There is LIA, one or two, perhaps three, groups in B.C., and that is about it. So currently there are perhaps three or four groups at the most in the wings. If we had authority to go to a seventh one today, the decision on which one would be very much a political decision, in my view.

Nigel Bankes, Canadian Institute of Resources Law, The University of Calgary: In 1973, the federal government agreed to negotiate aboriginal claims, as we all know. At that time, it said that the negotiations process was being undertaken simply as a matter of policy and not as a matter of legal obligation. We have now had a Charter of Rights and the Constitution, and I wonder, Mr Demers, if the federal government now considers that it is under a legal obligation to negotiate those claims.

My second question relates to how the federal government views the purpose of claims negotiations. I think there are probably at least two ways of looking at this. On the one hand, the federal government may be taking what I regard as a minimalist view: in other words, trying to settle the claims, obtain security of title for those interests out there, at the lowest price it can possibly obtain. It simply wants to settle as quickly and as cheaply as possible. On the other hand, maybe it is making a realistic determination of what it considers to be the needs of aboriginal groups to further their own economic and social self-determination. We have heard tonight that the federal government does consider that it is negotiating a settlement not only for present but also for future generations. We have also heard that the federal government has to consider when it is settling one claim what the effect is going to be on the other claim. I would like to quote from the paper "Perspectives on Native Land Claims Policy" [in this volume]: "Claims settlement proceedings are also complicated from time to time by a considerable gap between the declared expectations of some native groups and the limits that have been set by the federal government regarding economic benefits and other matters." How are those limits arrived at by the federal government? Are they a realistic determination of what the federal government considers, in a paternalistic way, to be the needs of aboriginal groups both now and in the future? Or are they determined by reference to figures plucked from the air, or to past settlements such as the James Bay and Québec settlement?

Clovis Demers: To your first question, the government does not believe that it is under a legal obligation to negotiate the claims. Whether or not the events of the last six months have changed that, I do not know. I would need to have advice from our legal counsel, but currently the position has not changed.

There are, as you put it, two purposes to negotiating the claims. One is to remove the cloud, and allow for orderly development that is not going to be incompatible with the interests of the natives in that area. The second purpose, of course, is to ensure some economic and social benefits, and the self-development of the native population. The object is not to settle as cheaply as possible. As you realize, our minister has a mandate to look after the interests of the aboriginal peoples—the Indians, Inuit, and Inuvialuit—and the cheapest settlement would not be in the best interests of the native peoples. So he and his colleagues have to balance what the group wants and needs on the one hand, and what the government can afford on the other. It is very much a question of what the government can afford, in terms of both economic or financial cost and other costs. Those limits are set as we move into each claim; a balance is struck between what the government can afford and what is required on the other side.

Nigel Bankes: I am somewhat surprised that the Office of Native Claims does not have a legal opinion from the Department of Justice on the question of whether the constitutional developments have changed anything in the nature of the legal obligation of the federal government to settle claims. My second point relates to something that was mentioned earlier with respect to the Treaty 11 area. If, in fact, there is no legal obligation to settle claims, I wonder why the federal government is negotiating on that particular claim after having stated that it will negotiate settlements only where the native interest in the land is considered not to have been resolved previously. Does the federal government take a different position with respect to the rights of the Dene and the Métis of the Northwest Territories from the position that it takes with respect to Indians in Vancouver?

Clovis Demers: No. On the last point, I said, and I repeat, that the government considers that the process, which was begun in the 1920s, has never been completed. Part of the deal when the treaties were signed was that land would be provided to the Dene Nation. That was never done, and I take it there are other elements of the treaty that have never been fulfilled. That is what we are doing now.

Willie Joe: I want to raise an item that deviates somewhat from the claims matter. It deals with the type of treatment that we receive from the Yukon Territorial Government (YTG) in regard to existing programmes and policies. The treatment that I refer to is strictly in reference to the economic development agreement programme that is currently under negotiation between the territorial and federal governments. Your policy here reads: "Unless agreed to by the parties, proposed settlements will not diminish the eligibility of beneficiaries to current and future programs." In my opinion, the YTG has taken this matter into its own hands and, in effect, is almost penalizing Yukon Indians because they are receiving a claims settlement.

I make reference to this because I have been, literally, just short of knocking down doors to get into negotiations on an economic development agreement. Both governments make reference to government-to-government agreements. That makes a third government very attractive to Indian people. We busted our asses just recently salvaging the one-government system in the Yukon. It became a very tenuous issue, where many of our chiefs in the Yukon were seriously considering opting out of the one-government system and going to a two-government system. Now there appears another possibility on the horizon. We find that there is a third option of an integrated or hybrid government system that could work, although it is very much still in the offing for us. Nevertheless, it is a very attractive option. As I understand that the YTG is the Government of Canada's partner at the negotiating table, there needs to be some political discipline provided to your partners. They need to understand clearly that in the balance lies the overall claims agreement and the potential for CYI to walk away and say, "Okay, fine, if you wish to talk government to government we shall form our own government so we can talk government to government." There needs to be more bending of policies here; there needs to be more recognition. If I read this document correctly, it says that there needs to be give on all sides. So far, I think Indians have given, and given, and given. Governments need now to open their policies and to make them more available to us so that we can provide ways and means of giving you other avenues of making government-to-Indian agreements.

It is very real. We are real. We are a legal entity. We are an economic force. We are a political force. We have to be dealt with; we cannot be ignored. When the YTG says, "our native people," to whom is it referring? We are Indian people in the Yukon; we are a very unique people. I do not wish to be like Chris Pearson. That is assimilating. I would not mind integrating; I will live next door to him. You people have to sit in a back room somewhere and hammer these things out so that there is more political discipline on the part of the YTG.

Don Gamble, Consultant: I am very suspicious when a government official says that the reason there is some difficulty is things are so complicated, and they are very intricate, and they involve many parties. This is meant to be an excuse for why something cannot get done, and it is meant to be a legitimate excuse. It is a self-created problem. It has nothing to do with the parties outside the bureaucracy; it is just a justification for doing nothing. Surely it is obvious after the discussions we have had here, even if one had known nothing else about the issue of aboriginal rights in Canada, that there has to be legislation. We do not have to legislate the claim, but we do have to legislate the process.

In other words, we have to pick up on exactly what Mr Demers has said and we have to legislate it out of existence. If the national interest dictates that we have to prepare special legislation to create a special agency to build a pipeline to carry American gas from Alaska across Canada to American consumers, and if that is enough reason to create a special agency within government to discipline the bureaucracy and to expedite decision making, then surely we can prepare the same kind of thing to settle native claims. I invite the views of everybody on the panel as to whether or not the problem really can be solved best by the government legislating the process within which it will settle native claims quickly and expeditiously in the national interest so that we can start doing things in this country without wallowing in the bureaucratic self-pity that we hear from persons like Mr Demers.

Bob Mitchell: It is not a bad idea that a special agency be created for that purpose by Parliament. I am not optimistic that the present process can yield agreements. It just takes too long and it is just too complex from the government's point of view. So I vote yes.

Bob Overvold: It is not a new idea. It is something we talked about four years ago when dealing with the Office of Native Claims. That particular branch was set up in DIAND to expedite the resolution of claims, but it turned out to be no better, and certainly quite a bit worse, than a lot of other government departments. I agree with Don Gamble. The process itself is the main stumbling block, and his idea is a great one. I think, however, that the native groups should have a say as to what the terms of reference or criteria are going to be for that agency.

Clovis Demers: I should like to hear more about Mr Gamble's proposal. What does he have in mind: a kind of commission with an arbitration role or with decision-making powers that would be binding on the parties?

Land Claims Plenary Session

Don Gamble: This idea has been discussed with many persons before, senior officials in government, even politicians, at various stages. Everybody seems to agree that it is the way to go, that it is the only way to get out of the mess we are in. What I cannot figure out is where the button is that one has to push to get it going. My experience in the North, at least here in the Northwest Territories, suggests that there would be agreement to this approach right across the various interest groups. I encourage you, if it has not occurred to you before, to pursue this idea.

Randy Ames, Tungavik Federation of Nunavut: "Land claims" is a term that is used pretty loosely to refer to the resolution of aboriginal claims, aboriginal rights. It appears to be pretty comprehensive in nature in as much as it deals with land, economic benefits, social provisions, and so on. In the case of Inuit, however, I think the term "land claims" is somewhat inappropriate because Inuit are a maritime people in focus and they have a great interest in offshore matters. I have read *In All Fairness*, and there does not appear to be any statement in it concerning negotiation of aboriginal rights for the offshore. I should like to know, if there is a federal policy on this, what is it? If there is not a policy, why not, and when will there be one?

Clovis Demers: You are right, there is no mention of the offshore in *In All Fairness*. The issue is arising in the discussions with TFN. Certainly the question of the use of the sea ice, and of harvesting offshore, is negotiable. I think we have made clear, however, that the question of non-renewable resources offshore is something that the federal government is not prepared to negotiate at this time. These two points are quite clear now.

Randy Ames: Is that not somewhat inconsistent with the policy dealing with non-renewable terrestrial resources?

Clovis Demers: The policy with regard to sub-surface resources under land is that the issue is negotiable. Sub-surface title is something that the government is prepared to consider and in fact has agreed to in other claims. Perhaps in your view it would be logical to do the same thing under the sea, but the government is not prepared to do that.

Randy Ames: What about management responsibilities for offshore matters that go beyond wildlife issues?

Clovis Demers: We should like to know what that involves. I am not familiar with the discussions, if there have been discussions, on that subject up to now, but I should like to know what is involved before responding.

50

Peter Burnet: The federal government's policy, I believe, is still that there is not the legal obligation to settle these claims. It is more a moral obligation. In fact, the policy is entitled *In All Fairness.* In 1973, the government decided to negotiate claims on the basis of fairness, and for no reason other than fairness and social policy. Just by chance, however, the James Bay Cree and Inuit got an injunction that year to stop the James Bay project, and the Calder case gave the federal government quite a fright. I submit that the government's approach is based clearly on the fact that there is an ill-defined but outstanding right that aboriginal peoples have that is supposed to be negotiated into certain rights and benefits. Now, in light of the fact that the government's policy is that there is not a legal obligation to settle these claims, and in light of the fact that it is also the policy that development can proceed in tandem, I am wondering what possible impetus there is to settle these claims on the part of the federal government. Mr Demers mentioned fairness. I used to practise law and whenever I was involved in a dispute on behalf of a client, I would appeal to the fairness of the other lawyer or the fairness of the other person. They were often very fair persons, but that never seemed to resolve the dispute. What did resolve the dispute was my informing them that they would be in court if they did not come to some kind of a conclusion.

It is federal government policy that if the aboriginal peoples move to go to court to enforce their claims, all funding would be cut off. There would be no more support for the aboriginal organizations supporting their claims. In light of the policy that funding would be cut off if they go to court, that development can proceed, and that there is no legal obligation to negotiate, is there any reason to assume there is any impetus to government to settle on anything other than the lowest common denominator of acceptable positions among as many as 15 government departments, several of which are renowned for their hostility to giving any special treatment to aboriginal claims? In your experience at the negotiating table, did you ever sense that there was any impetus on government's part to settle beyond the basic minimum?

Bob Overvold: None whatsoever.

Bob Mitchell: How do I follow an answer like that? Certainly, from the government's perspective, there is nothing hanging in the balance that has a clock ticking against some sort of deadline. There is a lack of urgency. When you are in negotiations without a deadline it can be a protracted discussion. Part of the problem here is that there is no deadline. I think Clovis recognizes that. It is just one of the things he has to live with in his job. I do not know where that impetus can come from. I do not know what could happen that would create that sort of deadline.

Land Claims Plenary Session

Peter Burnet: May I suggest, just for consideration, that it would be a good recommendation for the federal government to change its policy and allow the aboriginal peoples to go to court to enforce their claims without cutting off their funding?

Bob Mitchell: Perhaps, but I am not sure that would create enough pressure.

Clovis Demers: I am not too sure what Mr Burnet means by cutting all funding if the parties go to court. The funding that is provided is very specifically intended for negotiations. If there are negotiations, the funding is there. If negotiations break off, then eventually the funding for negotiations will cease. There is no doubt about that.

I think you are referring to cases that have occurred, particularly in the South, where requests have been received from native groups for litigation funding. DIAND's policy regarding litigation funding is quite restrictive. The government will fund certain types of litigation that affect a large sector of the native population, that will clarify issues of importance to more than one person or one group. We feel that the courts are probably going to be more amenable to requests for injunctions in the future, following the Constitutional Conference and the whole process that has been going on. So there is some hidden impetus there. We have seen signals in British Columbia, for example, where a judge will take a chance and really lean on the side of the native claimant. Then there is the political impetus. In some, but not all, parts of Canada there is support by non-native sectors for resolving the claims. Representations are made to government for ministers to get going and to do something about it. Groups like CARC, and events like this workshop, are certainly part of a political process that pushes in that direction. I am not saying that it is a major subject of discussion in the livingrooms of Toronto or Vancouver, but there are groups across the land that push government into doing something.

Bob Mitchell: Regarding the tendency for the government position to be the lowest common denominator of the different positions of the many departments or agencies, that is a very difficult problem for the Office of Native Claims to cope with. It has a responsibility to canvass these departments; it has the responsibility to co-ordinate a position from all of these other positions; and at least during the time I was with ONC, it had no very effective mechanism to break through the very reactionary positions of some of the departments. We had a paper on constraints on land selection that would make land selection practically meaningless in the Arctic. You would have the land, but everybody in the world could come along and trample all over it and you could not do much about it. I exaggerate for the sake of making a point: the tendency to have to accept the lowest common denominator must be a difficult problem for the ONC. It certainly was when I was there.

Gina Blondin, Dene Nation: Mr Demers, you said that the negotiations taking place in the Mackenzie Valley are unique because of the existence of treaties 8 and 11, and because your government is negotiating currently with the Dene and the Métis in the valley. At the same time, you also let it slip out that the process begun in 1920 has not been completed. Your words were "the provisions of the treaties have not been implemented adequately." You suggested that there is unfinished business. To me, that is how you are interpreting the current negotiations. I wonder, Mr Overvold, whether this is your understanding of what the Dene negotiations are all about? Mr Demers, I wonder if you could tell me exactly what you mean by your statement that elements of the treaties are just being fulfilled?

Bob Overvold: We do not accept that interpretation. We do not believe that the government is just trying to be fair with us in fulfilling those treaties. If that were the case, the government would be dealing with the specific bands and implementing the one-square-mile-of-land allotment per family. If that were the case, the government would not have accepted a claim from the Métis Association in 1977. The federal government is negotiating with us because we have aboriginal title to the land up here. It is on that basis and that basis only.

Clovis Demers: I will not argue the question of what we are negotiating, why we are negotiating, or on what basis. I just want to point out that we entered the negotiations with the Dene and the Métis with all options open. We are dealing with them in the same manner as we are with other groups for a number of reasons. The minister of Indian Affairs and Northern Development of six or seven years ago agreed to deal with this claim as with any other claims up North. To me, the important issue is that there are none of the elements that we are prepared to negotiate with, say, COPE or CYI that we are not prepared to negotiate with the Dene and the Métis. Even though we may start from two different positions, I think we both understand the process and the ultimate result of the process.

Willie Joe: The potential for governments to cut off funding in relationship to claims does not give very much autonomy to Indian groups to prepare themselves for that possible date. The Government of Canada has decided unilaterally that Indian groups across Canada should have to pay for the settling of their claims. Their claims are based on settlement of grievances that have taken place over hundreds of years in some instances, not by their own doing. It is a question of morality. The Government of Canada should pay the price for the entire activity. The reasoning behind that, of course, is quite simple. It would also give the government more impetus to settle the claims more expediently.

Clovis Demers: Willie Joe says that the groups pay for their negotiations; this is quite true. The claims funding, or at least the funding during negotiations, is an advance on the settlement. I know, however, that CYI, like other groups, has excellent negotiators and that somewhere in the course of the process a good part of their expenditures must be built in.

Andrew Thompson, Westwater Research Centre: Notwithstanding that treaties 8 and 11 extinguished land claims, the Métis and the Dene are being treated on the same basis as the others. That is very reassuring. The implication, however, is that somehow or other this is out of the goodness of somebody's heart.

We seem to forget our history. If one were to look at the case Paulette (#1) in the decision of Mr Justice Morrow, one would see that evidence was introduced to support the caveat in his opinion, although the case had a different result in other courts because of different grounds. So Justice Morrow's decision is where it stands at the moment. The findings were that treaties 8 and 11 were fraught with forgery, fraud, and misrepresentation in their negotiation; that the treaties were breached by Canada (this is in the decision of the Supreme Court of Canada in *Regina* v. *Sikyea*, and by the meeting of the Migratory Birds Convention; that the treaties had never been implemented because they provided for an allocation of 160 acres (64.750 ha) of land to each family of six, which would mean 160 acres along the north coast; and that they were totally inappropriate and were entered into only because of the pressures of oil development. Norman Wells, you see, goes back to 1924. It was the first Norman Wells discovery and the impending nature of production there that brought about the 1920 treaty.

In the 1950s the Canadian government appointed a commission to study why treaties 8 and 11 had not been implemented, and what should be done about it. If you want to examine the record, you will see the same conclusions about the way in which those treaties were negotiated and their totally inappropriate nature. All I can say as a lawyer is that if treaties were treated like other commitments we undertake, treaties 8 and 11 are not worth the paper they are written on in any legal sense.

Mike Holloway, Friends of the Earth, Alaska: The peoples of Alaska look upon the failure of land claims in Canada really as a failure of the Trudeau government, which they see as stagnant on many levels and offering a free-for-all for rampant bureaucracy. We are most disappointed in this unfortunate situation you have here in Canada, where land claims keep being set back and delayed, and delayed, and delayed, mainly because we all have an interest in the Arctic and the development of the arctic environment in a safe and rational way. We see the Government of Canada proceeding in quite a reckless way in the development of the Arctic, endangering the Arctic Ocean, and endangering arctic cultures. It is reckless especially in the way in which it proceeds without consulting the native peoples.

It is to the credit of Inuit people that they have organized the Inuit Circumpolar Conference and now they, not Canada, are the leaders in environmental protection in the Arctic. They are proceeding swiftly to develop an international arctic policy by which all countries will one day agree to the same environmental regime, by which they will proceed safely with the development of the Arctic and the industrialization of arctic countries. They have achieved their status at the United Nations to pursue that, and they will certainly use that leverage to embarrass the Canadian government to act more swiftly to that end.

Cindy Gilday, Dene Nation: Because you are in Denendeh, I cannot let you leave without having heard from a Dene person. You have heard from consultants, lawyers, and bureaucrats about how frustrating the whole process is; you can imagine how the Dene people who live on the land feel.

I was talking to an old man last summer in the Fort McPherson Assembly. He told me he had been going to these meetings for ten years hoping that some of the questions would be resolved. He said he was so tired he did not know whether he would come back to another meeting. A month ago he was at a meeting in Fort Franklin, and at that meeting the message was very, very clear. This man is very old so he does not have any concerns for his own future. He said, "We want land, not money. Control over our land is what we want." During the course of this workshop, I have talked to different persons, and they are asking if the federal government is really serious about negotiating. Is it negotiating at all? Someone suggested that it is a process of duress and intimidation. Someone else said we will get the least at the table of negotiations.

Why call them "negotiations" when the land-claims office has produced a paper that says exactly what we are going to get? The federal government has told us what we are going to get—no control over the little pieces of land that we are going to get, because it has land-use planning machinery in gear, and that machinery is not going to go away. One little phrase pops up in every major policy. It says that this "will not prejudice the land-claims settlement." What does that mean? Does that mean that the whole programme of land-use planning is going to be dismantled if the Dene do not want it within that certain area? You can bet your bottom dollar that it is not going to be dismantled, because Cabinet is giving the department money for that programme. I am just indicating how frustrating it is for the Dene when that little phrase seems to be an excuse on everyone's part to run over our traplines while everybody else is making plans for our land. We just stand by and wait for the bureaucrats and for the minister, or for the departments to decide whether they should listen to the minister. The minister has no control over his department. It is a frustrating thing for a lot of the Dene up here: waiting. We are playing a waiting game.

In All Fairness: A Native Claims Policy, Comprehensive Claims

**Department of Indian Affairs
and Northern Development**

Foreword

For some years now, the Government of Canada has been engaged in attempting to resolve what have come to be known as Comprehensive Native Land Claims, through a negotiation process. There has been moderate success but much more remains to be done. The purpose of this book is to set out for the consideration of all Canadians what the government proposes as the way forward.

I say *all* Canadians advisedly: I hope this book will be looked at by Natives and non-Natives, by northerners and southerners, by those among us who seek to conserve and by those among us who seek to develop.

What this statement contains above all, in this time of political uncertainty and general financial restraint, is a formal re-affirmation of a commitment: that commitment is to bring to a full and satisfactory conclusion, the resolution of Native land claims.

All Canadians would agree that claims have been left unresolved for too long. My wish is that this book will give all interested persons an idea of the depth of my personal commitment as well as the government's to endorsing, developing and implementing the policy initiated by one of my predecessors, the Honourable Jean Chrétien.

Essentially what is being addressed here are claims based on the concept of "aboriginal title"—their history, current activities surrounding them, and our proposals for dealing with them in the future. While this statement is concerned with claims of this nature it does not preclude government consideration of claims relating to historic loss of lands by particular bands or groups of bands. Indeed, the government, in consultation with Indian organizations across Canada, is currently reviewing its policy with respect to specific claims over a wide spectrum of historic grievances—unfulfilled treaty obligations, administration of Indian assets under the Indian Act and other matters requiring attention. A further statement on government intentions in the area of specific claims will be issued upon completion of that review process.

I ask for the support and understanding of all Canadians: individuals, associations and special interest groups of all kinds. At a time when our country is struggling to redefine itself, to determine what kind of a future we want for everyone in this land, we must in all fairness pay particular attention to the needs and aspirations of Native people without whose good faith and support we cannot fulfill the promise that is Canada.

The Hon. John C. Munro, M.P., P.C.
Minister of Indian Affairs and Northern Development

Part One

Introduction

Indian and Inuit people through their associations have presented formal land claims to the Government of Canada for large areas of the country. In response to their claims, the government has three major objectives:

1. To respond to the call for recognition of Native land rights by negotiating fair and equitable settlements;
2. To ensure that settlement of these claims will allow Native people to live in the way they wish;
3. That the terms of settlement of these claims will respect the rights of all other people.

The present policy statement is meant to elaborate the Government of Canada's commitment to the Native people of Canada in the resolution of these claims. Comprehensive land claims relate to the traditional use and occupancy and the special relationships that Native people have had with the land since time immemorial.

By negotiating comprehensive land claims settlements with Native people, the government intends that all aspects of aboriginal land rights are addressed on a local and regional basis. These aspects run the gamut of hunting, fishing and trapping, which are as much cultural as economic activities, to those more personal and communal ways of expression such as arts, crafts, language and customs. They also include provisions for meaningful participation in contemporary society and economic development on Native lands.

Native groups have been demanding recognition for particular rights and the federal government has said that it is prepared to work with Native people after patriation to determine appropriate definitions of these rights. The government has also stated that patriation of the Constitution will in no way affect any existing rights and any rights and freedoms that may be acquired by way of a land claims settlement. Negotiations are already underway with some native groups to settle their land claims and others will begin in the very near future.

It is intended that these settlements will do much in the way of helping to protect and promote Indian and Inuit peoples' sense of identity. This identity goes far beyond the basic human needs of food, clothing and shelter. The Canadian government wishes to see its original people obtain satisfaction and from this blossom socially, culturally and economically.

Recently greater attention has been given to land claims. The various demands for natural resources, vast amounts of which have been discovered in some of the areas being claimed, have pressed Native people to present their formal land claims to the government. This is not to say that the first and only reason for settling claims is development, because the government has accepted claims for negotiation in areas where development is not imminent. Rather, it is a matter of policy that the government is willing to negotiate settlements. Since 1973, the federal government has operated under a policy that acknowledges Native interests in certain land areas claimed and that allows for the negotiation of settlements for claims where these interests can be shown not to have been previously resolved.

Development has only served to make the settlement of these claims more urgent to some native groups. The government recognizes the urgency to settle land claims as quickly and effectively as possible in order that the interests of Native people be protected in the wake of development, in a way that offers them a choice of lifestyles.

When working to protect Native interests, respect for the rights of other Canadians must be maintained during the negotiation process and in the terms of settlement. It serves no just purpose if the terms of settlement ignore or arbitrarily infringe upon the rights of other citizens. Just as much as this policy addresses the land rights issues of Native people, it also respects the rights of all other Canadians.

What follows in this book, then, is an attempt to give a context in which to understand what has happened so far, and to give some indication as to how the Government of Canada intends to proceed in the years to come in relation to the question of comprehensive land claims.

Early Policy

It is important to know something of how successive regimes have dealt with comprehensive claims historically, in order to understand how procedures for the future have evolved.

The best known expression of British colonial policy towards Indians is to be found in the Royal Proclamation of 1763:

> ... We do further declare it to be Our Royal Will and Pleasure, for the present as aforesaid, to reserve under Our Sovereignty, Protection and Dominion for the Use of the said Indians, all the Lands and Territories not included within the Limits of Our said Three New Governments, or within the Limits of the Territory granted to the Hudson's Bay Company, as also all the Lands and Territories lying to the Westward of the Sources of the Rivers which fall into the Sea from the West and North West, as aforesaid:
>
> and We do hereby strictly forbid, on Pain of Our Displeasure, all Our loving Subjects from making any Purchases or Settlements whatever, or taking Possession of any of the Lands above reserved, without Our especial Leave and Licence for that Purpose first obtained.

This proclamation acknowledged the Native peoples' interest in the land they inhabited and it was a matter of policy that this interest be dealt with so that orderly settlement could be provided for. This was illustrated by the Robinson treaties as well as others.

Following Confederation, this was the policy adopted by the Government of Canada; the result was a series of formal treaties or agreements—in Ontario, the Prairie Provinces, the Mackenzie Valley and the north-eastern part of British Columbia. By and large, these early agreements addressed themselves to matters of land (reserves), cash annuities, education and the granting of hunting privileges.

In the 1920s most of the unsettled areas in which future development or settlement was anticipated had been covered by treaty or other arrangements. Because this process was not completed, Indians and Inuit in the areas not covered were forced to press their claims through submissions to the federal Parliament, through the courts and through personal intervention.

It should not surprise anyone that this situation was not satisfactory.

Recent History

Prior to 1973 the government held that aboriginal title claims were not susceptible to easy or simple categorization; that such claims represented, for historical and geographical reasons, such a bewildering and confusing array of concepts as to make it extremely difficult to either the courts of the land or the government of the day to deal with them in a way that satisfied anyone. Consequently, it was decided such claims could not be recognized.

However, by early 1973 the whole question of claims based on aboriginal title again became a central issue; the decision of the Supreme Court of Canada in the Calder Case, an action concerning the right of assertion of Native title by the Nishga Indians of British Columbia, established the pressing importance of this matter. Six of the judges acknowledged the existence of aboriginal title. The court itself, however, while dismissing the claim on a technicality, split evenly (three–three) on the matter raised: did the native or aboriginal title still apply or had it lapsed? At the same time, the Cree of James Bay and the Inuit of Arctic Québec were trying to protect their position in the face of the James Bay Hydro Electric project.

It is from these actions that the current method of dealing with Native claims emerged.

A policy statement in 1973 covered two areas of contention. The first was concerned with the government's lawful obligations to Indian people. By this was meant the questions arising from the grievances that Indian people might have about fulfillment of existing treaties or the actual administration of lands and other assets under the various Indian Acts.

The policy statement acknowledged another factor that needed to be dealt with. Because of historical reasons—continuing use and occupancy of traditional lands—there were areas in which Native people clearly still had aboriginal interests. Furthermore these interests had not been dealt with by treaty nor did any specific legislation exist that took precedence over these interests. Since any settlement of claims based on these criteria could include a variety of terms such as protection of hunting, fishing and trapping, land title, money, as well as other rights and benefits, in exchange for a release of the general and undefined Native title, such claims came to be called comprehensive claims.

In short, the statement indicated two new approaches in respect to comprehensive claims. The first was that the federal government was prepared to accept land claims based on traditional use and occupancy and second, that although any acceptance of such a claim would not be an admission of legal liability, the federal government was willing to negotiate settlements of such claims.

The 1973 Policy Implemented

Several Native groups have entered into negotiations with federal, provincial and territorial governments. Two final agreements which are consistent with this policy have been reached, with the full participation of the Province of Québec; one with the Cree and Inuit of James Bay in 1975, the other with the Naskapis of Schefferville in 1978. In the Western Arctic Region of the Northwest Territories, an agreement in principle was negotiated and signed in October of 1978 with the Committee for Original Peoples' Entitlement (COPE) representing the Inuvialuit of the Western Arctic Region. Currently in the Yukon, the Council for Yukon Indians (CYI) and the federal government, with the full participation of the Government of the Yukon Territory, is in the process of agreeing in principle on a negotiated settlement. The Inuit Tapirisat of Canada (ITC) representing the Inuit of the Central and Eastern Arctic, are presently at the negotiating table with the federal and territorial governments. In addition, negotiations commenced recently with representatives of the Dene and Métis of the Mackenzie Valley and the Nishga Tribal Council in British Columbia.

Several other native groups are in different stages of preparation for negotiations. These include the Labrador Inuit Association and the Naskapi Montagnais–Innu Association in Labrador; *le Conseil Attikamek–Montagnais* on the north shore of the St. Lawrence river in Québec; Kitwancool, Kitamaat Village, Gitksan–Carrier Tribal Council, and the Association of United Tahltans from British Columbia.

The claims presented by all of the above have been accepted for negotiation by the Minister on behalf of the Government of Canada. A word is in order, therefore, about how these claims are treated.

The Office of Native Claims (ONC) was established in 1974 to represent the Minister of Indian Affairs and Northern Development and the federal government, for the purposes of settling comprehensive claims and specific claims through the negotiation of agreements. Comprehensive claims submitted to ONC are carefully analyzed in terms of both their historical accuracy and legal merit, the latter being done by the Department of Justice. Claimant groups are required to provide as much information and documentation as possible in support of their claim.

Meetings are held where necessary in order to clarify any points that seem subject to misinterpretation. Finally, the documents are sent to the Minister of Indian Affairs and Northern Development for his formal response on behalf of the Government of Canada. If the claim is denied the claimant group is given a full explanation for the decision. If accepted, the Office of Native Claims is authorized to initiate negotiations for a settlement under the direction of the Minister. In certain instances, the Minister may appoint a negotiator from outside the Public Service to lead the negotiations.

Funding for researching, developing and negotiating Native claims is provided by other sections of the Department in the form of contributions and loans. Where the grounds of a claim have still to be established, contributions may be made to help with the process. Loans are made to claimants whose claims are accepted for negotiation, for the purpose of further developing their positions and the actual conduct of negotiations. Once the claim is settled, these loans are repayable as a first charge against monetary compensation that may be granted.

The status of the comprehensive claims already on record are outlined in an Appendix to this document. It will be seen that some claims have only recently been presented and accepted for negotiation.

A description of the objectives we hope to achieve in the negotiating process and some of the steps we think necessary to improve this important function will be found in the second part of this book.

Part Two

Future Treatment

The following pages contain what the federal government considers to be the essential factors necessary for the achievement of comprehensive land claims settlements. Very careful consideration was given to each of the principles discussed but was not limited to these alone. These considerations have evolved from past experience in the area of land claims negotiations, here in Canada and in other countries, as well as from views expressed over the years by Native people in Canada.

Basic Guidelines

When a land claim is accepted for negotiation, the government requires that the negotiation process and settlement formula be thorough so that the claim cannot arise again in the future. In other words, any land claims settlement will be final. The negotiations are designed to deal with non-political matters arising from the notion of aboriginal land rights such as, lands, cash compensation, wildlife rights, and may include self-government on a local basis.

The thrust of this policy is to exchange undefined aboriginal land rights for concrete rights and benefits. The settlement legislation will guarantee these rights and benefits.

Alternatives Considered

When the federal government was reviewing its policy on comprehensive native land claims, it looked at the experience of some other countries such as Australia, the United States, New Zealand and Greenland to see how they approached settlement of claims. Two in particular, the United States and Australia, were more thoroughly studied because in both cases major settlements of aboriginal claims have been achieved and because there are many similarities to our own situation. The Alaska Native Claims Settlement Act of 1971 was passed in favour of the first inhabitants of that state; in Australia's northern Territory, the Australian Aboriginal Land Rights (Northern Territory) Act was passed in 1976.

In both cases, although processes other than direct negotiations were employed, Native people had a marked input into the settlements and on what forms they should take. In Alaska, for example, hearings were held before a Congressional committee and representation was made on behalf of Native people. In Australia, a government-appointed Lands Commission, charged with preparing legislation, heard testimony from different aboriginal tribes. The outcome in both cases was that land and other benefits were provided to the Native groups despite pressure from other interests. In neither case were the demands of the Native groups fully met, however, and whether such a model of settlement is to be preferred to negotiated settlement remains to be seen.

Further alternatives considered by the government included arbitration, mediation and the courts. There are drawbacks to all three approaches.

For example, while a court may be able to render a judgement on, say, the status of lands, it is unable to grant land as compensation or to formulate particular schemes that would meet the needs of the plaintiff. In general, it can be said that the courts have not been found by the Native peoples to be the best instrument by which to pursue claims.

There are a number of compelling advantages to the negotiation process, as the federal government sees it. The format permits Natives not only to express their opinions and state their grievances, but it further allows them to participate in the formulation of the terms of their own settlement. When a settlement is reached, after mutual agreement between the parties, a claim then can be dealt with once and for all. Once this is achieved, the claim is nullified.

Thus the negotiation process is seen by the Canadian government as the best means of meeting the legitimate concerns of the Native people in the area of comprehensive claims. It is a process which allows a good deal of elasticity in approach to the concerns of the Native people; it is at once an expression and mutual appreciation of the rights and values of all parties in Canada. And an important factor that cannot be discounted—the government is fully committed to its success.

Benefits

Lands

Lands selected by Natives for their continuing use should be traditional land that they currently use and occupy; but persons of non-Native origin who have acquired for various purposes, rights in the land in the area claimed, are equally deserving of consideration. Their rights and interests must be dealt with equitably.

Other basic access rights must be taken into consideration: rights of access such as transportation routes within and through a settlement area; rights of way for necessary government purposes; rights of access to holders of subsurface rights for exploration, development and production of resources, subject to fair compensation as mutually agreed either through negotiation or arbitration.

Similarly, special protection must be ensured against unlimited expropriation powers in the case of lands granted in settlement. Meaningful and influential Native involvement in land management and planning decisions on Crown lands could be initiated and strengthened by providing membership on those appropriate boards and committees whose decisions affect the lives of their communities.

Where Natives use land lying in more than one jurisdiction, and in the event that this use cannot be continued through mutual agreement among the competing parties, compensation must be paid or specific wildlife harvesting rights granted, subject to the general public laws existing within the area in dispute.

Even where jurisdictions are not at issue, some lands are used by more than one native group. Where this sort of overlapping exists and where there appears to be no ready agreement among the different users, some appropriate and timely means must be found to resolve the differences. Until this is done, no land in these areas will be granted.

Again, the motive for approaching land selection in this way is to protect the rights of Canadians, Native and non-Native alike, who might be affected by the settlement. Furthermore, it is designed to encourage Native people to participate actively in the fair and equitable negotiations that surround these decisions.

Wildlife

In addition to dealing with the protection of their rights to hunt, fish and trap, the settlements should provide for the involvement of Native people in a much wider spectrum of activities affecting the whole area of wildlife. This could include, for example, fuller participation in wildlife management, such as making recommendations to the government on the establishment and maintenance of wildlife quotas or providing advice on the formulation of management policies and other related matters.

Generally, the settlements may provide for prescribed preferential rights to wildlife on Crown lands. Exclusive rights would be limited to fee simple or the equivalent Native lands or to specified species elsewhere. All areas, whether they include those for exclusive Native use or shared by the general public will continue to be subject to the existing general laws as they apply to hunting, fishing and trapping; they will be further subject to present and future sound conservation policies and public safety measures.

In any event, the settlements will clearly define the terms on which Native people will have access to wildlife resources on Crown lands. Any exceptions to the laws that generally apply to these areas will be clearly outlined, again taking into consideration any rights acquired by non-Native users.

Subsurface Rights

The federal government is prepared to include subsurface rights in comprehensive land claim settlements in certain cases. The motive for granting such rights is to provide Native people with the opportunity and the incentive to participate in resource development. Granting subsurface rights close to communities and in critical wildlife habitat areas would be a protective measure designed to eliminate any possibility of granting resource development rights to any prospective developer in conflict with the wishes of a local community.

Monetary Compensation

This can take various forms including cash, government bonds and other forms of debentures.

But no matter how these capital transfers take place, the amounts negotiated must be specific and finite. As to when payments should be made, negotiations would be tailored to meet the needs of various Native groups and government.

Other Provisions

Corporate Structures

One of the mutual goals of comprehensive land claims settlements is to give the beneficiaries control over their own affairs. With this in mind, the government recognizes that Native-controlled mechanisms will be established to facilitate the lasting participation of all the beneficiaries of the settlement. These devices will primarily be designed, staffed, and their decisions implemented by Native people; they should protect and enhance their assets through sound management practices.

Taxation

All compensation monies to be paid under proposed settlements will be regarded as capital transfers and will be exempt from all taxation.

However, incomes derived from such compensation shall be subject to the usual provisions of the Income Tax Act.

Except in relation to municipal services, unimproved lands may also be protected from property taxation.

Programs

Unless agreed to by the parties, proposed settlements will not diminish the eligibility of beneficiaries to current and future programs. Access to such programs will be in accordance with the current approved criteria.

It is not intended that new indeterminate programs geared solely to Natives be provided by the federal government in settlements. Nevertheless, it is possible to refocus normal government resources to enhance the efficiency of existing programs and to achieve mutually agreed upon ends.

Procedures

Process

Current practices in relation to determining the validity of claims will continue to be used.

Those potential claimant groups requiring assistance in the preparation of a claim will be given straightforward indications of the many aspects of settlement that may need to be considered and upon which the government is prepared to proceed.

Negotiations with a group will occur only if and when their claim has been accepted. Negotiations will then take place only with those persons who have been duly mandated to represent the claimant groups.

Claimant groups should have enough money to develop and negotiate their claims, however, the spending restraints of government and their limits will be kept in mind.

Negotiations concerning claims North of 60° will be bilateral between the claimant groups and the federal government leading to federally legislated settlements. However, provision will be made for the territorial governments to be involved in the negotiations under the leadership of the federal government.

Where claims fall in provincial areas of jurisdiction and in those cases where provincial interests and responsibilities are affected, provinces must be involved in claims negotiations in order to arrive at fully equitable settlements.

Eligibility

Those who benefit from the settlements must be Canadian citizens of Native descent from the claimed area, as defined by mutually agreed criteria. Examples in the past of such criteria have included such conditions as: percentage of Native blood, persons adopted by Natives according to traditional customs, and, where cases merit, people who are considered Native by a determination of a majority of the Native community.

In short, conditions for eligibility are negotiable. Persons living in the area of negotiated settlements who have already benefitted under a previous settlement with the Government of Canada are not eligible for benefits under another one.

Persons who are not subject to the Indian Act in no way become subject to the Act by virtue of a land claims settlement.

Appendix

To date, success in the settlement of comprehensive claims has been limited to the *James Bay and Northern Québec Agreement of 1975* and the supplementary *Northeastern Québec Agreement of 1978*. These agreements, which are currently being implemented pursuant to Québec and federal legislation, provided for the ownership of land; exclusive hunting, fishing and trapping rights; substantial participatory roles in the management of local and regional governments; financial compensation, control over education and social and economic benefits.

An Agreement-in-Principle, signed in 1978 with the Committee for Original Peoples' Entitlement (COPE), representing approximately 2,500 Inuit of the Western Arctic region was to have had a final agreement by October 31, 1979. Negotiations were delayed as a result of the 1979 general election, but the way was cleared for intensive discussions with the appointment of a new chief government negotiator in June 1980. After several months of unsuccessful negotiations, meetings were suspended in December 1980. It is hoped that negotiations translating the Agreement-in-Principle into a Final Agreement will resume in the near future.

In the Yukon, as a result of fresh initiatives, including the appointment of a new chief government negotiator, in May 1980, considerable progress is being made in the negotiations with the Council for Yukon Indians (CYI) which represents 5,000–6,000 Status and non-Status Indians. The goal here is to finalize an Agreement-in-Principle by the summer of 1982.

In 1977 the Inuit Tapirisat of Canada (ITC) submitted, on behalf of some 13,500 Inuit in the Central and Eastern Arctic of the Northwest Territories, a proposal for a new territory of Nunavut, to encompass all lands north of the treeline. The proposal contained provisions respecting land, wildlife, compensation and other elements of a claim. Until late 1980 little progress was made, since government policy distinguished between the process of constitutional change and the negotiated settlement of a claim. Late in 1979, the ITC agreed to separate the claims and constitutional processes; and in August 1980, a chief government negotiator—a new position—was appointed to conduct negotiation of the claims elements. Negotiation from late 1980 until late October 1981 has resulted in the initialing, in Frobisher Bay, of an agreement-in-principle on wildlife harvesting rights. Negotiations on the claims elements continue, in tandem with efforts on both sides to resolve the question of political development.

The Dene Nation and the Métis Association of the Mackenzie Valley, NWT presented separate claims in 1976 and 1977 respectively, but since the two claims did not reflect the actual degree of mutual interest among the native population, negotiation did not commence, and loan funding for research and development pertaining to claims was suspended by government between October 1978 and April 1980.

In April 1980 funding was resumed on the understanding that the Dene Nation would represent all the native beneficiaries during negotiation of the claims. In April 1981, a chief government negotiator was appointed and several negotiation sessions have been held to clarify principles.

In British Columbia, the potential for negotiating the Nishga claim is tenuous due primarily to the apprehension with which the provincial government approaches the possibility of unextinguished Native title within the province, and the doubt which the province has as to whether it should accept any responsibility to compensate Native people for the loss of use and occupancy of traditional lands. Nevertheless in June of this year a fulltime chief government negotiator was appointed by the Minister to negotiate a settlement and the province has agreed to participate in the negotiations. Preliminary negotiations with the Nishga Tribal Council got underway earlier this fall.

The federal government has also accepted claims for negotiation from, the Association of United Tahltans, the Gitksan–Carrier Tribal Council, the Kitwancool Band and the Kitamaat Village Council. These claims will be negotiated once the implications of the Nishga claim negotiations are apparent. Claims from the Nuu-Chah-Nulth, Haida and Heiltsuk are presently under review.

Claims on behalf of Naskapi–Montagnais Indians and the Inuit in Labrador were accepted for negotiation by the federal government in 1978. The Province of Newfoundland confirmed its willingness to participate in tripartite negotiations of these claims in September 1980. Bilateral discussions are planned to clarify the role and responsibilities that each government will assume in these negotiations.

The claim of *le Conseil Attikamek–Montagnais*, representing Montagnais and Attikamek bands living on the north shores of the St. Lawrence and St. Maurice rivers, was accepted by the federal government in October 1979, and has been met by a willingness to participate in negotiations by the provincial government. The claim will be negotiated in a tripartite forum. *Le Conseil Attikamek–Montagnais* is currently completing its research with the view to entering early negotiations.

Reprinted with kind permission of the Department of Indian Affairs and Northern Development.

Background Paper

A Review of Federal Land-claims Policy

John Merritt
Tungavik Federation of Nunavut

I have been employed by Inuit Tapirisat of Canada and, more recently, by the Tungavik Federation of Nunavut (TFN), since 1979. During that time, I have acquired some experience in aboriginal rights negotiations, both as a co-ordinator of the research programme and, since April 1981, as a member of the TFN negotiating team.

Because negotiations are underway between TFN and the federal government, this panel discussion is both timely and pertinent. For obvious reasons, the topic is sensitive. I have, tried however, to write this background paper as candidly as possible. I shall qualify my comments by explaining that I do not now live, nor have I ever lived, in Nunavut.

Like everyone, I am a product of my culture and my experience. The values that have shaped me are those rooted in white, middle-class, urban, southern Canada. Four years of employment with Inuit organizations have given me some insight into a world different from my own, but I am drawing upon my own culture and experience in writing this paper. I do not view this as a limitation, because they are the values that have generated the federal land-claims policy.

The following represents my own views and not necessarily those of TFN.

The Substance of Federal Land-claims Policy

The policy in effect today is the public statement on comprehensive land-claims policy published by the Department of Indian Affairs and Northern Development (DIAND) in 1981 under the title *In All Fairness* [reproduced in this volume]. The booklet was published mainly as a response to media speculation, fuelled by a leaked Cabinet document, about the directions of

71

land-claims policy. Considering the relatively recent date of this publication, combined with the knowledge that it was published to dampen speculation by offering a clear outline of the federal government's policy, its use as a reference point is both pertinent and fair. Unfortunately, the policy it depicts is described best by the term "chronic ambiguity."

To most Canadians, the demands and dilemmas of aboriginal peoples seem complicated and confusing. Undoubtedly, these demands and dilemmas seem complicated and confusing also to many in the federal government. These issues will become even more unmanageable, however, if those in government fail to identify basic elements of policy. The Canadian public, regardless of its knowledge of or interest in aboriginal peoples, is entitled to read a statement of government policy and understand two things: Why does the federal government feel obliged to be involved in comprehensive land-claims negotiations at all, and what does the federal government expect comprehensive land-claims settlements to accomplish? On both questions, *In All Fairness* is vague.

Careful perusal of *In All Fairness* might lead the reader to think there are two reasons for land-claims negotiations. Both reasons emerge so cautiously and so obliquely, however, that the public is left with impressions rather than conclusions.

Why Land Claims?

The first reason for land claims is an appeal to the conscience:

> we must in all fairness pay particular attention to the needs and aspirations of Native people without whose good faith and support we cannot fulfill the promise that is Canada.[1]

Sadly, this vague and banal statement is the only concrete reminder of the moral issues that must be considered when examining the relationship between an aboriginal people living in its ancestral homeland and a more powerful, more aggressive culture that has definite designs for the future of that homeland. *In All Fairness* is not cluttered with unpleasant accounts of the one-sided early treaty-making process, or by grim socio-economic statistics. Past federal government policy has led to some alarming results for aboriginal peoples, and sobering consequences for Canadian taxpayers. Yet, although morality is softly stated as a rationale to justify negotiations, stronger notions of right and wrong explain the government's position to defend third-party rights:

It serves no just purpose if the terms of settlement ignore or arbitrarily infringe upon the rights of other citizens. Just as much as this policy addresses the land rights issues of Native people, it also respects the rights of all other Canadians.[2]

The second reason for the federal government to negotiate comprehensive land-claims settlements emerges just as cautiously and obliquely. *In All Fairness* refers to the incentive of removing any legal uncertainty caused by an unextinguished aboriginal title. This motivation is phrased in a way that attempts to avoid any admission that an unextinguished title is an interest in land enforceable against the Crown by aboriginal title holders. Although aboriginal title is not acknowledged to be of any practical legal significance, *In All Fairness* emphasizes the desirability of securing settlements in areas that are experiencing, or are ripe for, development. The implication, of course, is that an unextinguished title might prove bad for business; settlements eliminating that title should be good for business.

Whither Land Claims?

The second question about federal land-claims policy is this: What are settlements expected to do? It would be reasonable to expect any comprehensive statement of claims policy to address this question explicitly, but it is neither raised nor answered. Rather, various platitudes are offered. For example:

> It is intended that these settlements will do much in the way of helping to protect and promote Indian and Inuit peoples' sense of identity. This identity goes far beyond the basic human needs of food, clothing and shelter. The Canadian government wishes to see its original people obtain satisfaction and from this blossom socially, culturally and economically.[3]

This exhortation to successful gardening is meaningless. It is unsupported by any cogent pronouncements as to what the federal government views as the guiding principles in negotiations or the objectives of settlements.

What essential interests does the federal government believe it must protect? What does the federal government see as the tests against which any settlement should be judged for its effectiveness or failure?

All of these matters are glaringly absent from discussion. Their absence is felt more as a result of these self-satisfied words:

> There has been moderate success but much more remains to be done. The purpose of this book is to set out for the consideration of all Canadians what the government proposes as the way forward.[4]

Having described the track record as a "moderate success," without identifying either the features of the past that are judged as successful or the criteria by which the term "moderate success" has been earned, *In All Fairness* avoids the need to describe the contents of future settlements by prescribing more of the same. This represents little more than an ode to inertia.

In its remorseless avoidance of basic concepts, *In All Fairness* does not supply a ready checklist of the objectives against which any settlement should be judged. A coherent policy statement requires a checklist, which should identify at least four types of objectives. These may be classified broadly as legal, political, social, and economic.

Legal Objectives

It is within the legal objectives of a settlement that, to many aboriginal peoples, land-claims policy achieves its clearest and most offensive form. Federal policy views a successful agreement as one that at least eliminates any possibility of an aboriginal interest in land surviving the agreement. As it is expressed in *In All Fairness*, this desire for finality goes well beyond the kind of legal certainty that would exchange aboriginal title for benefits under the settlement. *In All Fairness* is hostile to any features of a settlement that would allow for renegotiation and adjustment over time. For example, the notion of finality is interpreted during negotiations to reject demands for royalties flowing to aboriginal peoples over time. Rights such as royalties are viewed as offensive because their precise costs cannot be calculated in accordance with the achievement of once-and-for-all finality. Finality is the one objective of settlements that the federal government is certainly enthusiastic about:

> What this statement contains above all, in this time of political uncertainty and general financial restraint, is a formal re-affirmation of a commitment: that commitment is to bring to a full and satisfactory conclusion, the resolution of Native land claims.[5]

For the word "resolution," read "end." In a policy statement that is otherwise almost totally silent on what objectives land-claims settlements are supposed to realize, the notion of finality achieves prominence on its own. *In All Fairness* evinces a determination to achieve fixed and final settlements whatever their workability.

Political Development

Land-claims policy on the political content of settlements is clearly contradictory. *In All Fairness* states that a major objective of the federal government's land-claims policy is, "To ensure that settlement of these claims will allow Native people to live in the way they wish."[6] Although weakly expressed, this sentiment is consistent with the principle that aboriginal peoples should be able to determine their own collective future. This principle, however, is qualified by a subsequent statement:

> The negotiations are designed to deal with non-political matters arising from the notion of aboriginal land rights such as, lands, cash compensation, wildlife rights, and may include self-government on a local basis.[7]

In one breath, negotiation on political issues is ruled out. In the next, negotiation on local self-government is conceded. Apparently, the policy is not against political change *per se* through land-claims negotiations, but is opposed to political change of more than local significance. Because there is no rationale for this distinction, it is easy to conclude that aboriginal peoples can negotiate practically anything in land-claims discussions, as long as the total does not add up to much.

The confusion about topics of political significance in settlements is rendered complete by the following statement dealing with land and resources:

> Meaningful and influential Native involvement in land management and planning decisions on Crown lands could be initiated and strengthened by providing membership on those appropriate boards and committees whose decisions affect the lives of their communities.[8]

This statement appears to concede that aboriginal peoples should be guaranteed representation on bodies of public administration that make decisions about land and resource management. In a broad sense, this principle could logically extend to representation on bodies carrying out certain legislative functions. At the very least, this statement could be understood to invite negotiations toward guaranteed aboriginal representation on established or new administrative agencies with the responsibility for making decisions—decision making in the sense commonly used in administrative law.

In practice, negotiations on a guaranteed role for aboriginal peoples in administrative agencies have proved to be anything but straightforward. In negotiations between TFN and the federal government, for example, a host of reasons has been supplied by government negotiators for denying Inuit decision-making roles. Arguments have been made for the need to protect sovereignty, the Crown prerogative, ministerial discretion, and so forth. Nevertheless, TFN negotiators have never been provided with a clear understanding of what, if any, "political" or "quasi-political" topics the federal government will negotiate, and what kind of "decision-making" roles it is prepared to see Inuit play.

In the general confusion about government policy, one point is clear: the federal government is willing to negotiate a role for aboriginal peoples in virtually any vehicle of public administration, provided that the role is purely advisory in nature.

Confining aboriginal peoples to advisory roles has an obvious attractiveness to those in government with a preference for the status quo. This preference does not come, however, from a clearly identified policy. Nor does it even appear to be consistent with the faint promises held out in *In All Fairness*.

Social and Economic Objectives

Little is stated directly in *In All Fairness* about the social and economic objectives of land-claims settlements. What is stated is couched in the most amorphous terms.

Close examination of indirect references to the social and economic features of land-claims settlements reveals that federal policy favours a limited and retrospective view of the social and economic interests of aboriginal peoples. There is an assumption that the objective of land-claims settlements is to define rights and benefits for native peoples in the context of "traditional" economic priorities, "traditional" lifestyles, "traditional" values:

> By negotiating comprehensive land claims settlements with
> Native people, the government intends that all aspects of aborig-
> inal land rights are addressed on a local and regional basis. These
> aspects run the gamut of hunting, fishing and trapping, which

are as much cultural as economic activities, to those more personal and communal ways of expression such as arts, crafts, language and customs. They also include provisions for meaningful participation in contemporary society and economic development on Native lands.[9]

Note the emphasis on wildlife harvesting and cottage industries. Note the reference, by contradistinction, to "contemporary society." It is assumed that aboriginal peoples face two choices: join "contemporary society" or cling to the static manifestations of a spent way of life.

Consistent with this thinking, *In All Fairness* espouses a carry-on-camping approach to the social and economic contents of settlements. Settlement benefits are seen as a buffer between a "traditional" and, presumably, unsustainable way of life, and full integration into mainstream culture. This is clear in the sections of the policy document that are concerned with "development," a term used primarily to refer to the extraction of non-renewable resources:

> The government recognizes the urgency to settle land claims as quickly and effectively as possible in order that the interests of Native people be protected in the wake of development, in a way that offers them a choice of lifestyles.[10]

It is anticipated that aboriginal peoples will always find themselves in the "wake" of development. The possibility that a land-claims settlement could allow aboriginal peoples to be pioneers or partners in "development," is ignored.

At one point, *In all Fairness* contemplates that aboriginal peoples may be involved in development of resources other than hunting and crafts, because the policy allows for ownership of mineral rights through settlements:

> The federal government is prepared to include subsurface rights in comprehensive land claim settlements in certain cases. The motive for granting such rights is to provide Native people with the opportunity and the incentive to participate in resource development.[11]

This statement is qualified immediately, however, by the suggestion that there are two future parts to the motive. The first is to afford a measure of protection to wildlife harvesting activities; and the second is to delineate pockets of land where aboriginal peoples can subsist without intrusion by the powerful economic forces of development:

> Granting subsurface rights close to communities and in critical wildlife habitat areas would be a protective measure designed to eliminate any possibility of granting resource development rights to any prospective developer in conflict with the wishes of a local community.[12]

The primary rationale for supplying aboriginal peoples with limited mineral rights is to minimize disturbance from development activities sponsored by others. The creation of a more diversified economic base for aboriginal peoples is incidental. The policy speaks of commitment toward settlements that "allow Native people to live in the way they wish," but this objective is restricted in two ways. First, there is an unwillingness to acknowledge that aboriginal peoples must be expected to play a major role in the institutions and processes of public decision making. Secondly, the distinctive identity referred to in *In All Fairness* seems to be seen in the context of an ephemeral cultural idiosyncrasy rather than a collective political will. Distinctiveness seems to be viewed in the limited sense of crafts and folklore.

It is difficult to see what tools of social development the federal government is prepared to concede to aboriginal peoples. Presumably, advisory committees on matters of wildlife and culture are always acceptable, but the ability to control matters such as education or the design and administration of economic development programmes is always viewed with suspicion. Anything in between disappears into policy fog.

The lack of clarity becomes most telling in the area of economics. *In All Fairness* offers no idea of what economic rights and benefits, whether they be land title, cash, or whatever else, are to accomplish. Against what standards is the average Canadian expected to judge whether the economic provisions of a settlement are adequate or inadequate? What is the logic behind aboriginal peoples owning a given amount of land under a given form of title? What is the rationale behind a compensation figure that works out to be a given number of dollars per beneficiary?

Designing a federal policy that permits aboriginal peoples an acceptable degree of autonomy in the control of social programmes is not an easy task; surely, however, members of the Canadian public are entitled to hope for more concrete objectives with respect to "hard" economic issues.

The Advantages of Ambiguity

An examination of *In All Fairness* and of positions expressed by negotiators for the government does not provide any reason to believe that negotiations toward settlements are being shaped by a lucid set of overall economic objectives. Indeed, discussions with public servants most involved with carrying out land-claims policy sometimes lead to the conclusion that the lack of economic objectives in settlements is not only admitted, but celebrated.

Some public servants believe that a federal policy that avoids hard statements of purpose and intent provides a number of tactical advantages. The major advantage is to sidestep those elements of the Canadian public opposed to special status or special rights for aboriginal peoples, even if such status and rights have been recognized throughout Canada's constitutional and political history and, for some purposes, by the courts of common law. Another advantage is to play down the economic motives behind the insistence on extinguishment of aboriginal title, which, for obvious reasons, has always been anathema to aboriginal title holders. A further advantage is that it is more difficult to judge any particular settlement if clear objectives are not stated.

All these advantages have contributed to an approach that can be described by a term sometimes used by military planners—"flexible response." In this posture of "flexible response," the aboriginal parties to negotiations become accustomed to hearing terms such as "non-starters," and references to "facts of life" when they present demands that conflict with their government counterparts' perceptions of political reality. In practice, the emphasis on "flexibility" leads to unhappy results. If the entire process of negotiations unfolds with the parties having only the haziest grasp of their objectives, it is almost inconceivable that coherent or satisfactory results can be obtained. Social engineering in search of a direction must be treated with suspicion.

It is naïve to think that ambiguity or absence of policy about the objectives of settlements, particularly their economic aspects, is likely to have anything but a negative effect on public opinion. Ambiguity can, perhaps, deflect hostile public comment during negotiations; it would be difficult, for example, to launch into histrionics on the strength of a statement as cautious in its content as the following:

> Native groups have been demanding recognition for particular rights and the federal government has said that it is prepared to work with Native people after patriation to determine appropriate definitions of these rights.[13]

Statements like this may reduce the immediate opportunities for criticism by those already out of sympathy for aboriginal peoples, but they will do nothing to win long-term public awareness and support.

The public servants who must negotiate on the basis of policy often fill in the gaps out of sheer necessity. The flexibility of *In All Fairness* provides too much opportunity for bureaucrats to shape land-claims policy without requisite direction from the federal Cabinet collectively and ministers individually and without a focused public debate.

The issue of aboriginal rights is not simple. The federal politicians who have become closely involved over the last ten years or so have not enhanced their political prospects in the process. The likelihood that the complexity of the issues will increase over time warrants pronouncements of policy that are precise enough to allow, at best, tangible progress and, at the minimum, informed public discussion.

The Consequences of "Flexible Response"

The most disappointing feature of the doctrine of "flexible response" is not its theoretical flaws, but its practical, if inevitable, results. Obviously, the results of negotiations vary from one aboriginal group to another and, accordingly, the disappointments of aboriginal peoples have also varied. It is possible to generalize that the disappointments suffered by the aboriginal parties to negotiations have focused on the two distinct, but inter-related, aspects of negotiations on land and resources.

First, there is an unwillingness to provide proprietary rights that would ensure active and effective participation by aboriginal peoples in the development of the non-renewable resource potential of the areas, including some parts of the offshore, that make up their homelands. Secondly, although a number of indications suggest that federal land-claims policy might accommodate a genuine decision-making role for aboriginal peoples with respect to wildlife management, in practice, involvement of aboriginal peoples in the management of land and resources, particularly non-renewable resources, will be confined to the barest of advisory roles.

I use the expression "barest of advisory roles" deliberately and, I think, justifiably. For example, negotiations have taken place between TFN and federal government representatives about the environmental and socio-economic implications of major development proposals. Government representatives have agreed to establish an impact review agency made up of individuals nominated in part by federal and territorial governments and in part by Inuit. Government representatives have agreed further to the general proposition that major development proponents should be obligated to negotiate agreements with Inuit aimed at mitigating any harmful effects of development and at supplying some spin-off benefits such as employment and training.

Unfortunately, the land-claims policy is interpreted to prevent Inuit from having any confidence in the results. Government negotiators will not entertain the creation of a joint Inuit–government impact review agency that is capable of making decisions that can be enforced. They refuse to discuss the vesting of decision-making powers in this organization, although decisions could be overturned by federal ministers when they are contrary to stated government policies. Instead, the role of the agency must be limited to making recommendations. These recommendations, moreover, are expected to compete with, rather than replace or streamline, a host of others emanating from existing organizations. Adding another toothless actor to the development approvals process is not likely to be a particularly happy event for either Inuit or industry. In addition, when government negotiators argue that aboriginal peoples should be content with an agency that may influence events only through persuasion, they also reject the possibility of the agency being equipped with well-defined investigative powers.

On the question of management of land and resources, particularly non-renewable resources, the federal government policy provides for the illusion of power sharing without any substance. A flexible federal policy on the economic aspects of settlements does not result in bold and innovative ways of ensuring that aboriginal peoples will participate as vital partners in the development of their homelands. There is an unconscious reliance on the precedents offered in the sad history of treaty making, whereby aboriginal peoples were given hunting rights over large areas, ownership of a fraction of traditional hunting grounds, and cash payments. In exchange, aboriginal peoples extinguished their interests in all remaining resource wealth in the treaty areas.

Stripped of its more sophisticated packaging, current federal policy is not appreciably more rational or far-sighted than the negotiations on the economic elements of the treaties. For example, in the North there are only two primary economic endeavours available for the future: harvesting wildlife and the exploitation of non-renewable resources.

Government policy, as it is interpreted by federal negotiators, makes it very unlikely that aboriginal peoples will gain a major role in developing non-renewable resources in the North. This exclusion is accomplished by:

- rejecting sub-surface title in the hands of aboriginal peoples or confining sub-surface title to small areas of limited mineral potential

- rejecting royalty rights to all lands covered by a land-claims settlement, even where aboriginal parties may be willing to talk about capping formulae in the event of unexpectedly generous royalty-derived revenues
- insisting that sub-surface interests held by third parties be accommodated beyond any legal obligations to do so.

Aboriginal peoples also are denied a share of the non-renewable resource wealth of the North because capital transfers to beneficiaries must be finite in amount and fixed in duration. At a time when the existing federal deficit is enormous—and is likely to remain so for some time—it is astonishing that federal policy suggests that the only key to economic self-sufficiency lies in coaxing a huge cash settlement out of the current generation of Canadian taxpayers.

There is little in the federal land-claims policy to prevent aboriginal peoples who negotiate settlements today from becoming beggars in their own homelands tomorrow. The policy creates this risk even where the non-renewable resource base is sufficiently rich and accessible to generate abundant and enduring revenues, both public and private.

Some sectors of industry and the Canadian public might be indifferent to this possibility. But if federal land-claims policy does not promote direct participation by aboriginal peoples in the long-term development of non-renewable resources, what incentives will exist for them to welcome non-renewable resource development in their homelands? What chance is there for the secure political and social climates sought by business to exist?

A Proposal for Reform

Legal and political objectives are inextricably linked. Present federal land-claims policy insists that settlements must achieve "finality." At the same time, the political context and content of land-claims settlements are the subjects of confused, but generally hostile, comment.

The political content of settlements can be viewed in one of two ways. According to one viewpoint, aboriginal peoples can hope only to express their collective identity through pursuit of traditional, but receding, forms of livelihood—primarily wildlife harvesting—and through the equally receding forms of cultural expression that are bound up in traditional livelihood. Alternatively, aboriginal peoples can maintain their vibrant collective identity indefinitely, provided that they are conceded the institutions and tools that allow the past to survive in the present and future.

We must ask to which viewpoint the federal government subscribes. Absolute finality can be consistent only with the first approach, but that will revive the 1969 "White Paper on Indian Policy", which set the assimilation of aboriginal peoples as its main goal.[14] The federal government's desire that land-claims settlements lead to greater legal clarity of native rights and benefits, particularly for private investors, is reasonable. It is impossible, however, to design a settlement compatible with the evolution of a distinctive people when the commitment to the principle of finality assumes the status of holy writ. A land-claims settlement then becomes no more than a real estate transaction.

The second approach is more consistent with developments in the Canadian Constitution that have been witnessed for the last few years. It provides aboriginal peoples with appropriate tools to maintain their cohesive and distinct identity in ways that may vary in form or character, but that find common ground in their ability to adjust to change. Because the political relationship between the federal government and aboriginal peoples has evolved in the setting of the Canadian Constitution to permit an open discussion of the concept of self-government, it is imperative that federal land-claims policy acknowledges that settlements have to be sufficiently dynamic to secure the following results.

First, a settlement should be sufficiently broad in its scope to allow more-specific negotiations, involving developers and the representatives of aboriginal peoples, when any development is proposed on a scale that would inevitably affect the collective well-being of the aboriginal peoples in question. Negotiations should be circumscribed by general provisions of land-claims settlements, but they should provide the aboriginal peoples with a sufficiently strong position to shape results. Mandatory arbitration is preferable to litigation in the event of disputes during such negotiations, and certainly preferable to unfettered government discretion. Provisions that allow effective, but broadly predictable, negotiations on specific developments in the future would modify the principle of finality by offering some potential for dealing with unforeseeable events.

Secondly, federal land-claims policy should clearly identify the role that the federal government is prepared to guarantee aboriginal peoples for their participation in land and resource management. Identification of these roles should be accompanied by reference to the relevant constitutional and political constraints. For example, it would probably seem reasonable to many Canadians for federal policy to guarantee aboriginal peoples' participation on administrative agencies that make land management decisions, provided the major decisions struck are subject to a reasonable process of political review and modification. On the other hand, many Canadians may feel it is less than reasonable to expect aboriginal peoples to believe that the barest of advisory roles will lead to satisfactory results. Federal claims policy could vitiate some of the risks of once-and-for-all-time settlements through involving aboriginal peoples in decisions attending the management of resources.

Thirdly, and perhaps most important, the policy must clearly identify the objectives of settlements. A clear statement of objectives would supply future generations with tests to measure the fairness and adequacy of results. Aboriginal peoples would then be in a stronger position to argue for political remedies to unsatisfactory settlements. Identification of objectives also might result in greater creativity in the search for more-effective mechanisms for legal enforcement of settlements.

The need for clear identification of objectives is most relevant to the social and economic aspects of settlements. Identifying social objectives for any particular aboriginal people is likely to be an extremely subjective process; federal responsiveness to aboriginal demands for a greater role in decision making, however, could be an effective way for specific social objectives to be realized.

The federal land-claims policy should indicate that the primary objective of the economic aspects of settlements is to supply aboriginal peoples with the reasonable likelihood of meeting their economic needs over time. Cash compensation may be necessary to provide aboriginal peoples with seed capital and with some funding in the event that resources at hand cannot be developed to provide sufficient economic activity. A combination of money and minimal land title, however, cannot provide any degree of assurance that aboriginal peoples will receive a share of the benefits of the development of their homelands commensurate to their needs.

The geological roulette of "land selection," as envisioned for the North by federal policy, is especially chancy as a means of supplying assurances that basic economic needs will be met. The provisions of settlements should be styled so that the aboriginal peoples have a first call on the resource wealth, both renewable and non-renewable, of their homelands to meet their economic needs. Although it is difficult to quantify economic needs, comparative references to national levels of material well-being are available.

The recent Canada–Nova Scotia agreement on offshore oil and gas provides a useful example.[15] The federal government has acknowledged that the legitimate special interests of Nova Scotians should be translated into a first claim on the oil and gas wealth of the offshore region. The motivating objective is to provide Nova Scotians with a standard of well-being approximate to the national level. The arrangements for royalty splitting and equity participation in the areas covered by the agreement could be particularly appropriate to land-claims settlements.

Such arrangements deliver tangible benefits only if development proceeds. Incorporated into land-claims policy, such approaches would have the added advantage of overcoming the concerns of those who believe that aboriginal peoples are philosophically indisposed toward all forms of non-renewable resource development.

It is, arguably, more appropriate for the economic needs of aboriginal peoples to be realized through exploitation of resources at hand rather than through reliance on short-term transfusions of money from the taxpayers of the entire country.

The Process of Negotiations

The best way to improve the process of negotiations is to strengthen the substance of policy. A number of secondary observations can also be made:

- The appointment of federal negotiators from outside the public service represents a step forward taken by the present minister of Indian Affairs and Northern Development.
- An outside negotiator should be given the financial resources to hire his or her own personnel.
- Outside negotiators should have the confidence of the aboriginal group and of a wide spectrum of parliamentarians and senior public servants. Consideration should be given to having a candidate negotiator appear before the House of Commons Standing Committee on Indian Affairs and Northern Development.
- An outside negotiator should be prepared both to engage in negotiations and to play an active role in raising public interest in, and awareness of, land claims.
- An outside negotiator should have a close working relationship with the minister of Indian Affairs and Northern Development and considerable latitude to meet with other ministers or senior public servants outside the Department of Indian Affairs and Northern Development.
- Negotiations should be followed closely by central agencies of the federal government, particularly those with responsibilities for the ongoing involvement of aboriginal peoples in constitutional discussions.

I should like to close by suggesting an initial step that could be taken toward an improved federal land-claims policy. Aboriginal peoples should be invited to help draft a revised federal policy statement. At a time when most Canadians realize that it is absurd to consider the constitutional rights of aboriginal peoples without inviting their representatives to the table, it is odd that the federal government continues to act on a policy that was developed without the involvement, and in many ways against the wishes, of the aboriginal peoples affected.

Endnotes

1. Department of Indian Affairs and Northern Development, *In All Fairness: A Native Claims Policy, Comprehensive Claims* (Ottawa: DIAND, 1981), p. 4.

2. Ibid., p. 8.

3. Ibid., p. 7.

4. Ibid., p. 3.

5. Ibid.

6. Ibid., p. 7.

7. Ibid., p. 19.

8. Ibid., p. 23.

9. Ibid., p. 7.

10. Ibid., p. 8.

11. Ibid., p. 24.

12. Ibid.

13. Ibid., p. 7.

14. Department of Indian Affairs and Northern Development, *Statement of the Government of Canada on Indian Policy* (Ottawa: DIAND, 1969).

15. Agreement between the Government of Canada and the Government of Nova Scotia on Offshore Oil and Gas Resource Management and Revenue Sharing, Department of Energy, Mines and Resources, 2 March 1982.

Background Paper

Perspectives on Native Land-claims Policy

Office of Native Claims
Department of Indian Affairs
and Northern Development
As presented by Clovis Demers

Federal Native Claims Policy

Historical Perspective

Native land claims find their roots deep in Canadian history. Settlement by Europeans brought with it not only a territorial loss but, in many cases, the loss of a way of life that depended upon the free and unfettered use of the land. The underlying grievance arising from this historical fact has resulted in a series of policy responses by the federal government going back more than 200 years.

Clearly, the federal government had military and commercial reasons for reaching initial accommodation with the native peoples, but a feeling of moral obligation to treat them fairly was also discernable from an early date. Under these circumstances a policy was established, as reflected in the Royal Proclamation of 1763, of assuming that native peoples had an interest in the land that had to be dealt with before non-native settlement could take place. In the words of the proclamation, which, constitutionally speaking, marked the beginning of the British regime in Canada:

> it is just and reasonable, and essential to our Interest, and the security of our Colonies, that the several Nations or Tribes of Indians with whom We are connected, and who live under our protection, should not be molested or disturbed in the Possession of such Parts of Our Dominions and Territories as, not having been ceded to or purchased by Us, are reserved to them or any of them, as their Hunting Grounds. . . .[1]

Translated into practice, the policy resulted in the making of agreements, or treaties as they were afterwards called, with the various Indian tribes. The practice originated in Upper Canada and was designed to enable lands to be allotted to settlers. In return for their aboriginal title, the Indians were provided with various forms of compensation including land (reserves); cash; annuities; schools; and hunting, fishing, and trapping rights within the areas ceded.

The policy adopted by the British Crown was also followed closely by the federal government after Confederation. Consider, for example, the words from the address to the Queen from the Canadian Senate and House of Commons of 1867 relating to the surrender by the Hudson's Bay Company of lands to Canada:

> And furthermore that, upon the transference of the territories in question to the Canadian Government, the claims of the Indian tribes to compensation for lands required for purposes of settlement will be considered and settled in conformity with the equitable principles which have uniformly governed the British Crown in its dealings with the aborigines.[2]

Consider also the following extract from a speech given by the Governor General, Earl of Dufferin, in 1876 in reference to the troubled situation of Indian rights in British Columbia:

> Most unfortunately, as I think, there has been an initial error ever since Sir James Douglas quitted office in the Government of British Columbia neglecting to recognize what is known as the Indian title. In Canada this has always been done; no Government, whether provincial or central, has failed to acknowledge that the original title to the land existed in the Indian tribes and communities that hunted or wandered over them.[3]

By the 1920s, likely areas of settlement or development as then foreseen had been covered by the treaties except for the greater part of British Columbia, where the provincial government consistently denied existence of an aboriginal interest. Other regions not covered by treaties or where the aboriginal title had not otherwise been dealt with through colonial legislation or Crown proclamation included the Yukon, most of the Northwest Territories, northern Québec, and Labrador. Although little attention was given to completing normal arrangements in these regions, Indians in British Columbia and elsewhere continued over the years to press for settlement through claims submissions, court action, and political lobbying.

In early 1973, the aboriginal native claims issue was brought sharply into focus by the Supreme Court decision in the Calder case (the British Columbia Nishga assertion of native title). Although dismissing the case on a technicality, the court split three-three on the substantive issue of whether the aboriginal or native title continued to exist or whether it had been extinguished. A re-examination of policy by the government at that time led to the statement made by the minister of Indian Affairs and Northern Development on 8 August 1973, in which the government outlined its willingness to negotiate settlements with native groups in those areas of Canada where native rights based on traditional use and occupancy of the land had not been dealt with by treaty or superseded by law. Because of the broad nature of the native demands associated with these claims—land, money, access to resources, and other benefits—they came to be known as "comprehensive claims."

Besides claims settlements in northern Québec and an agreement in principle with the Inuvialuit of the western Arctic, substantial progress was generally lacking in the implementation of the 1973 policy. The two federal elections in 1979 and 1980 gave cause for reflection on government directions. Consequently, an extensive policy review was carried out by the government during the latter part of 1980, taking into account the need for a clearer sense of direction, as well as the views and concerns of the native peoples. Although the government reaffirmed its commitment to the equitable settlement of comprehensive claims through negotiation, it did so within the framework of newly enunciated guidelines.[4] It is within this framework that claims negotiations are now proceeding.

Existing Policy Guidelines

The comprehensive claims policy guidelines adopted by the federal government pursuant to its 1980 review are outlined in the following summary:

General

— Comprehensive claims are to be based on traditional use and occupancy of the land.

— The government will negotiate settlements only where the native interest in the land is considered not to have been resolved previously.

— Claims settlements are intended to protect and to promote the Indian and Inuit peoples' sense of identity while providing for meaningful participation in contemporary society and economic development on native lands.

— Constitutional development cannot be decided within the claims negotiating forum because all citizens affected must be involved, but settlements may include self-government on a local basis.
— Respect for the rights of other Canadians must be maintained during the negotiation process and in the terms of settlements.
— The government requires that the negotiation process and settlement formula be thorough so that the claim will not arise again in the future; any land-claims settlement will be final.
— The thrust of the policy is to exchange undefined aboriginal land rights for concrete rights and benefits.

Benefits

In addition to any provisions for local self-government, settlement benefits and rights may include lands, limited sub-surface rights, wildlife rights, and monetary compensation:

— Lands selected by claimants should be traditional land that they currently use and occupy.
— In the case of overlapping claims where there appears to be no ready agreement among competing native claimants, no land will be granted in the disputed area until appropriate means are found to resolve the differences; e.g., an objective fact-finding process.
— There should be meaningful and influential native involvement in land management and planning decisions with respect to Crown lands in claims areas.
— Limited amounts of sub-surface rights may be included in claims settlements both as a protective measure where settlement lands are close to communities or in critical wildlife habitat areas, and to provide beneficiaries with the opportunity and incentive to participate in resource development.
— Settlements may provide for prescribed preferential wildlife harvesting rights on Crown lands with exclusive harvesting rights limited to native lands or specified species elsewhere; sound conservation practices and public safety measures are to apply.
— Settlements should also provide for native participation in wildlife management; e.g., advising on the formulation of management policies.

— Monetary compensation may take various forms including cash, government bonds, and other forms of debentures.
— Amounts negotiated must be specific and finite, and payment schedules must be tailored to meet the needs and interests of both the claimants and the government.

Other Areas

Policy guidelines have also been adopted with respect to eligibility to benefit from settlement, the establishment of native corporate structures to manage the proceeds of settlement, taxation of settlement benefits, and access to social and other programmes:

— Those who are eligible to benefit from settlements must be Canadian citizens of native descent from the claimed area, as defined by mutually agreed criteria.
— Persons who have already benefitted under a previous settlement with the Government of Canada are not eligible for benefits under another settlement.
— Native-controlled corporations should be established to manage the proceeds of settlements under sound management practices, giving beneficiaries control over their own affairs.
— Compensation monies paid under settlements are regarded as capital transfers exempt from taxation; unimproved settlement lands are also protected from property taxation except in relation to municipal services.
— Unless agreed to by the parties, settlements will not diminish the eligibility of beneficiaries to current and future programmes of general application.
— Refocusing of normal programme resources to achieve mutually agreed upon ends should be pursued rather than the creation of new indeterminate government programmes.

Claims Process

Government Representation

As well as developing guiding principles for furthering the claims-settlement process, the federal government took the initiative in 1980 to appoint chief negotiators from outside the public service. These persons, calling upon a variety of background and experience, have each been able to bring a fresh and objective perspective to the negotiating table. While their negotiating skills are necessarily of a high order, they are also chosen for their sensitivity to native needs and aspirations. They have direct access to the minister of Indian Affairs and Northern Development on a continuing basis and are otherwise able to remain in continuing contact with federal decision-making authority. A list of current chief negotiators for the government with brief biographical notes is provided in Appendix A.

The chief negotiators for the government are each supported by a compact group organized within the Office of Native Claims in the Department of Indian Affairs and Northern Development (DIAND). As part of their responsibilities for the management of the federal negotiating teams, these groups provide research, analytical, and co-ordinating services and give back-up assistance during negotiations. Various departments are drawn into the preparation and presentation of positions as required: Justice; Environment; Fisheries and Oceans; Energy, Mines and Resources; Finance; Privy Council Office; Federal–Provincial Relations Office; and others. By mutual agreement, the territorial governments are involved actively in negotiations of claims north of 60° as part of the federal teams. Their involvement is particularly important because many of the settlements' provisions will fall within areas of territorial jurisdiction, requiring legislation and implementation by the governments concerned.

Funding of Native Claims

Funding for native claims research, development, and negotiations is provided by DIAND through the Research Branch, Corporate Policy, in the forms of contributions and loans. Contributions are made in cases where the claim has not yet been accepted for negotiation by the government, for purposes of researching, developing, and presenting the claim. Interest-free loans are made in cases where a claim has been accepted by the minister of Indian Affairs and Northern Development, for purposes of further development of the claim, preparation of negotiating positions, and actual negotiation of the claim. Interest-bearing loans are made in cases where an agreement in principle has been signed and ratified, for purposes of negotiation of the final agreement. Loans are repayable as a first charge against claim settlements. Total contributions and loans for comprehensive-claims purposes as of 31 March 1983 had amounted to $27.6 million and $56 million, respectively. For claims north of 60°, contributions had amounted to $1.63 million, with loans in the order of $27.1 million.

Settlement Stages

The settlement process normally follows a series of stages beginning with agreements in principle in which accord is reached on the general terms of settlement. This is followed by a final agreement between representatives of the parties in which all provisions of the settlement are spelled out in detail. Ratification is achieved by the claimants through referendums held in the native communities, whereas government approval is provided by Cabinet. The final stage in the settlement process is the passage of legislation by Parliament and by provincial or territorial legislatures, where concerned, giving effect to the settlement. Implementation rests with the government agencies—federal, territorial, or provincial—responsible for the administration of the various aspects of the legislation and with the beneficiaries, according to the terms of the settlement.

Description of Events—1973-1983

Pre-1980 Period

The period between 1973, when the government adopted a policy of negotiating settlements of comprehensive claims, and 1980, when it undertook a review of that policy, was characterized by exploration by both claimants and the federal government of the potential nature and limits of settlements. Of the 20 claims submitted in this period, only 6 were submitted prior to 1977. These were from groups that had been preparing their positions for a number of years. Indeed, those not covered by settlements made in 1975 and 1978 with the Crees, Inuit, and Naskapis of northern Québec subsequently resubmitted their claims in new forms after varying periods of reconsideration. Those who submitted their claims after 1976 also did so on essentially general grounds requiring periods of rethinking and clarification both internally and in discussions with government representatives. Although the Committee for Original Peoples' Entitlement (COPE), representing the Inuvialuit of the western Arctic, did succeed in presenting a fully developed claim, the general picture was one of continued uncertainty of what was both desirable and attainable. Recognizing this, the federal government decided that there was need for a thorough review of the comprehensive-claims policy including the establishment of settlement guidelines to which all parties could relate.

Post-1980 Period

The guidelines arising from the 1980 policy review find their rationale in some seven years of exploration and testing—exploration and testing not only between claimant groups and government but also within claimant groups and within government. Therefore, in reaffirming its commitment in 1981 to negotiating the settlements of comprehensive claims, the federal government did so with a clearer view of what was at issue and of what should be the limits of settlements, taking into account both native aspirations and regional and national interests. It also determined that increased resources would be required by both claimant groups and government if claims preparation and negotiation were to be sustained at a level permitting successful resolution. Such resources have been provided to the extent that claims negotiations are fully underway throughout the North. Moreover, although final agreements are still to be achieved, real progress has been made in both the Yukon and Northwest Territories.

Perspectives on each of the northern claims are provided in the following summaries.

Council for Yukon Indians Claim

The Council for Yukon Indians (CYI), representing all people of Yukon native ancestry (about 5500), was formed in 1974. It united the Yukon Native Brotherhood and the Yukon Association for non-status Indians for the purpose of negotiating their claim, originally entitled *Together Today for Our Children Tomorrow* and submitted to the federal government on 14 February 1973.[5] Between 1974 and 1979, a number of attempts were made at reaching negotiated settlement of the claim, but agreement fell short of achievement in each case. In 1980, a new initiative was undertaken with the appointment of Mr Dennis O'Connor, former magistrate of the Yukon Territory, as chief government negotiator for the claim. Negotiations led by Mr O'Connor began in June 1980.

Approval of an agreement in principle with respect to providing interim benefits to Yukon Indian elders, whose participation in a final settlement might be diminished because of their advanced years, was announced on 23 January 1981. Also, preliminary accord has been reached on the majority of claim matters, including eligibility and enrolment; Yukon Indian rights to wildlife harvesting; the provision, delivery, and funding of programmes to beneficiaries; economic and corporate structures; financial compensation and settlement land selection; and local government matters for six communities. Matters respecting sub-surface rights and economic opportunities, as well as completion of community land selections, require further work.

On 13 December 1982, the Yukon Territorial Government (YTG) withdrew from claims negotiations, attaching certain conditions that would have to be met before it would return to the negotiations. The items included matters associated with post-settlement financing by, and the transfer of lands to, the territorial government. Those matters have now been worked out, and the YTG has indicated that it is prepared to return to the negotiating table.

In the meantime, the federal government and the Council for Yukon Indians have resumed negotiations to maintain momentum and to continue to make progress toward an overall agreement in principle.

Dene-Métis Claim

There are about 8000 status Indians descended from the several Dene tribes and about 5000 non-status Indian and Métis in the Mackenzie Valley area. In 1899, the Indians signed Treaty 8, followed by Treaty 11 in 1921. Half-breed settlements were entered into by the Métis through scrip commissions operating parallel to the treaty commissions. The Dene Nation considers the treaties to be treaties of peace and friendship and not surrenders of land. The federal government, although maintaining that the treaties effected a surrender of title, has agreed to enter into a comprehensive package settlement on the grounds that the provisions of the treaties have not been implemented adequately.

In 1976, the Dene submitted their claim, followed by the Métis claim in 1977. Because the two groups live in the same area, the government has maintained that both of these claims must be embodied in a single settlement. The two organizations split over political development issues, however. In an attempt to initiate formal negotiations with the two groups, the government advanced proposals for settlement in 1978. When no progress occurred, the funding of claims was suspended until the two groups could agree on a joint negotiating mechanism. Funding was restored in April 1980 and, one year later, Mr David Osborn was appointed chief government negotiator.

In July 1981, to allay native concerns, the government announced a two-year moratorium on the Norman Wells pipeline and expansion project. Negotiations proceeded and progress was made toward clarifying principles. Periodically, negotiations stalled due to internal difficulties between the claimant groups respecting eligibility and funding. However, once the two organizations hired external negotiators, considerable progress was made.

In December 1982, a document on process describing the principles under which negotiations were to be conducted was signed in Edmonton.

On 17 February 1983, an Interim Agreement on Eligibility and Enrollment was initialled in Ottawa. Recent negotiations have focused on an attempt to resolve overlapping interests with the neighbouring Committee for Original Peoples' Entitlement (COPE) group and on Dene proposals for participation in development of the Norman Wells oilfield. Further negotiations are anticipated on land and resources.

Committee for Original Peoples' Entitlement Claim

The Committee for Original Peoples' Entitlement (COPE), representing about 2500 Inuvialuit residing in six communities in the Western Arctic Region and originally part of the general Inuit claim, submitted its own claim in May 1977 in light of anticipated imminent pipeline construction in its area of interest. An agreement in principle was signed by COPE and the federal government on 31 October 1978, involving land, wildlife, financial compensation, eligibility, corporate structures, and economic and other measures. In May 1979, agreement was reached on 85 per cent of the remaining lands over which COPE would have surface rights. Negotiations toward a final agreement were interrupted during the federal elections of May 1979 and February 1980 and the ensuing government's review of claims policy.

Preparation for resumption of negotiations proceeded until December 1980 when COPE talks broke down over disagreement regarding the negotiating process and guidelines designed to clarify the government's position on certain areas of concern.

Several attempts made during 1981 to resume active negotiations were unsuccessful. In April and May 1982, representatives of COPE discussed with department officials a possible framework for the resumption of negotiations. Subsequently, in October, Mr Simon Reisman was appointed chief government negotiator. Pre-negotiation meetings resulted, in November 1982, in an *aide-mémoire* that identified the major elements requiring negotiation.

Formal negotiations with COPE commenced on 20 January 1983. Extensive discussion and clarification have taken place on contentious issues relating to the agreement in principle. Although no agreement has been signed to date, substantial progress has been made in reaching an understanding of the respective positions of COPE and the federal government on the main issues and in the discussion of possible compromises, including resolution of overlapping interests with neighbouring claimants.

Tungavik Federation of Nunavut Claim

The Inuit claim in the central and eastern Arctic, now being negotiated by the Tungavik Federation of Nunavut (TFN), has undergone a series of revisions since it was presented originally by Inuit Tapirisat of Canada (ITC). First presented in February 1976, the claim was withdrawn in September for revision following further consultation with communities in the N.W.T. The claim was then re-submitted in December 1977 by a new Inuit Land Claims Commission in the form of 11 general principles. Five negotiating sessions were held with federal representatives between May 1978 and February 1979, at which time the ITC Board of Directors abolished the Land Claims Commission because of lack of progress. A particular difficulty was the Inuit insistence upon guarantees of a new territory and of a general freeze on development as a pre-condition to consideration of other elements.

In May 1979, negotiations resumed with regional associations. Further progress was interrupted in September 1979 when ITC presented a position paper, *Political Development in Nunavut,* and the new ITC executive undertook a review of its land-claims stance and negotiating structures. ITC completed its review in December 1979 and announced a new negotiating structure, but resumption of negotiations was delayed because of the federal election in February 1980.

In August 1980, a chief government negotiator was appointed from outside the public service in the person of Mr Robert Mitchell. A fact-finding meeting was held in November 1980, followed by a series of formal negotiating sessions during 1981 that culminated in initialling of wildlife provisions of an agreement in principle in October 1981 in Frobisher Bay. That document, describing the powers and duties of a joint Inuit-government advisory board on wildlife management and outlining the specific harvesting rights Inuit would enjoy, is under review by federal departments concerned. In the areas of land and resources, negotiations are continuing with the federal government, represented by Mr Thomas Molloy, who was appointed new chief government negotiator in March 1982. Agreements were initialled in Cambridge Bay in April 1983 on the purposes and principles of land selection. Intensive negotiating sessions are scheduled until September 1983.

Claims in the Provinces

Given the context of the workshop for which this paper has been prepared, its focus in terms of the status and outlook for comprehensive claims is north of 60°. At this point, however, a word may be added regarding comprehensive claims in the provinces to round out the national, as well as the regional, perspective.

Comprehensive-claims negotiations in the provinces require provincial government involvement because many elements of the claims such as land and natural resources pertain to provincial jurisdiction. Negotiations in these areas, therefore, depend largely on provincial policies and positions. In 1976, the Government of British Columbia agreed to participate in discussions leading toward settlement of the claim of the Nishga Tribal Council, but deferred its participation indefinitely on other comprehensive claims. The provincial government has taken the position that its involvement in the Nishga claim reflects its desire to improve the delivery of programmes and services to Indians rather than its recognition of any historical justification for comprehensive land claims in the province. The type of settlement that would result from the Nishga negotiations is seen by the provincial government as a pathfinder for the settlement of other comprehensive claims in B.C. Nevertheless, several additional claims have been accepted for negotiation by the federal government, with claimants having been advised that such negotiations are subject to the participation of the provincial government. Meanwhile, discussions between the federal and provincial governments are being pursued at both the ministerial and official levels with the objective of seeking agreement on common ground that can form a firm basis for tripartite negotiations with native claimant groups. Experience gained to date in the Nishga claim is being taken into account in this regard.

Bilateral discussions are also taking place between the federal government and the Government of Newfoundland on identifying the roles and responsibilities of each government in respect to the pending negotiations of Inuit and Naskapi–Montagnais claims in Labrador. In Québec, the provincial government has agreed to participate with the federal government in a negotiated settlement with the *Conseil Attikamek–Montagnais du Québec* and the two governments have agreed recently with the claimants on the negotiating process.

Looking Ahead

In implementing its comprehensive-claims policy in the days ahead, the federal government must be conscious of factors that both constrain and facilitate the implementation of that policy. It must be particularly conscious of the views and aspirations of the native peoples, not only in regard to claims settlements as such, but also in regard to other major areas that interface with or impinge upon claims and their settlements. The government must also be aware of third-party views and concerns and of broader regional and national interests. The following overview is concerned primarily with the situation north of 60°, although parallels in many of the areas covered can be found with regard to provincially located claims.

Constraints on Settlements

A number of constraints on claims settlements are apparent from a review of the policy guidelines previously outlined in this paper. Thus, claimants must show traditional use and occupancy of the land being claimed and settlements must take into account the legitimate interests of others in the land. Generally speaking, title will be conveyed to claimants in regard to surface rights only, although limited sub-surface rights may be granted, largely as a protective measure for native communities. With regard to wildlife harvesting rights, conservation and public safety measures are to apply. Monetary compensation must be both specific and finite—there can be, for example, no unlimited resource revenue-sharing agreements. Persons who have already benefitted under a Canadian comprehensive-claims settlement cannot benefit from another, and so on.

The above-noted types of constraints are part of the equation that must be worked out between claimants and government, and experience to date shows that they do not pose insurmountable barriers to settlement. Of more serious concern at this time are the conflicting interests that native peoples have among themselves. Indeed, the problem of overlapping claims is one of the most serious impediments to early settlements that natives and the federal government now face in the North. The overlap problem has been prominent in the COPE claim, for example, with both the Dene and the Métis claiming a competing interest with the Inuvialuit in the Mackenzie River Delta. In the eastern area of the COPE claim, the Tungavik Federation of Nunavut alleges overlapping interests in areas that COPE has requested as land selection and in other areas for the traditional harvesting of game. There also exists overlapping of traditional and current interest in lands between the Yukon Indians and Indians and other native groups normally resident outside the Yukon, such as the Association of United Tahltans in B.C. Although it is anxious that the native groups do all they can to settle their competing claims between themselves and is prepared to assist the proceedings, the federal government is taking steps to employ a fact-finding process, in conjunction with the claimants, that will promote resolution of the overlap problem in the Mackenzie Valley and elsewhere.

Claims settlement proceedings are also complicated from time to time by a considerable gap between the declared expectations of some native groups and the limits that have been set by the federal government regarding economic benefits and other matters. As well, the prospect of claims settlements implies a new way of thinking and a new way of doing things for those on both sides of the negotiating table. This process of attitudinal change takes effort and it takes time. Negotiations are further complicated by changes in leadership among the claimant groups. New leaders can bring new priorities and new demands. There have been a number of changes in leadership in recent years; as a result, in some cases, negotiations have had to start again or at least to pause and take a few steps backward before going on. The outlook now, however, is for firmer and more consistent positions generally throughout the North.

The proceedings are also made more complex by the fact that the territorial governments have an interest in the results. The governments of the Northwest Territories and the Yukon are concerned about the effect of land-claims settlements on their jurisdictions, particularly in view of their growing interest in further devolution of authority. The federal government has recognized these concerns by including representatives of the territorial governments on the federal negotiation teams and, although problems remain, it is optimistic that where differences exist they can be settled.

Interface with Political Evolution

Native groups in the North, including both Inuit and Dene, have periodically pressed to have the native claims forum accepted as a vehicle for political evolution. The Inuit proposal for a separate "Nunavut" ("our land") territory in the eastern part of the N.W.T., first put forward as a claim in 1976, remains as a cornerstone of the Inuit position. They have since agreed, however, to pursue the proposal outside the claims forum *per se*.

In 1981, the Dene released a paper entitled *Denendeh, Our Land: Public Government for the People of the North*.[6] This followed earlier proposals for political self-determination that had been included in the Dene claim. The Dene have since indicated, however, that they are prepared to pursue their land claims and political aspirations in separate forums.

COPE, the Métis, and CYI, although looking for some assurance of equitable political representation in terms of regional government or other avenues, have been generally satisfied to pursue such arrangements outside the claims forum.

In the N.W.T., the question of constitutional development is now being pursued by all parties through the Constitutional Alliance and two regional forums.

With regard to division of the N.W.T., the federal government is concerned that a consensus be reached among northerners on such issues as boundaries and distribution of powers before a final decision is made on division. Such consensus cannot be reached within a claims forum that by definition excludes non-native northerners. The government has also stated that division is contingent on the settlement of claims; i.e., that such settlement must come first and will necessarily require intensive and specialized effort. In this sense, the settlement of claims is one of the engines behind political evolution in the North. Moreover, the smooth functioning of whatever form of government evolves will be enhanced if native claims are settled equitably and will help to provide the stimulus for building a stronger economic base in the native communities.

Interface with Economic Development

Native peoples in the North are determined not only that they shall have a voice in what is happening on the economic development front but also that they shall have the opportunity to participate in whatever development is taking place. Moreover, they are fully aware that claims settlements are a principal means through which such influence and participation shall be effected. This situation is especially so in terms of meaningful and influential involvement in land management and planning to be provided for in the settlements and also through the provision of capital funds for investment and the control of considerable areas of land. Indeed, all of the claimant groups in the North are making plans to become major players in resource development or are already taking advantage of claims-related loans to begin engaging in investment and business enterprises in mining, tourism, and other areas. In view of this situation, it behooves industry to become more knowledgeable about native claims policy and settlements and for native groups to help in developing rapport with industry.

The native peoples are not about to trade economic development at the price of destroying their homelands, cultures, and lifestyles, however. This is why they are concerned about environmental protection and the wisdom of sound land management and planning. This is also why they wish to see wildlife managed properly and adequately and why they want to be closely involved in such management. In short, this is why they insist that claims settlements shall provide for both economic development opportunities and the preservation of traditional pursuits according to their own choices.

It is clear that the major development projects of the North are, for the most part, related to the production and distribution of oil and gas. Moreover, all comprehensive claims in the two territories relate in some way to regions involved in the development or transportation of hydrocarbons. A number of projects for the development and transportation of hydrocarbons could, for example, affect the COPE claim in the western Arctic. These include proposals for hydrocarbon development in the Beaufort region, natural gas pipelines via the Mackenzie Valley and Polar Gas "Y" routes, and tanker traffic in the Beaufort Sea. The claimants have expressed interest in the prospect of benefits that may accrue to them as a result of such proposals. Indeed, they have already entered into service contracts and leasing arrangements with some developers. At the same time, to minimize the effects on the environment, on the local communities, and on wildlife harvests, the claimants are seeking guarantees of a participatory role in their area through the settlement of their claim.

Some of these major hydrocarbon development and transportation proposals would also significantly affect the TFN claim area. These include the proposal for the Polar Gas "Y" pipeline and various proposals for shipment of oil and gas by tanker through the Northwest Passage. TFN has indicated that it is not opposed to development *per se*. It is, however, deeply concerned that the development and transportation of hydrocarbons will have significant adverse effects on communities, on the environment, and on harvesting activities, particularly in coastal and offshore areas. Like COPE, it is seeking guarantees of a participatory role with respect to environmental protection and social impacts.

As well, the government recognizes a relationship between hydrocarbon development and land claims in the Mackenzie Valley. In July 1981, the Honourable John Munro announced a two-year delay in construction for the expansion of the Norman Wells oilfield and a delay of two and one half years on pipelaying for the associated pipeline. Coincidentally, a two-year delay of exploration activity by Petro-Canada was imposed in the Mackenzie Valley. These initiatives demonstrate the federal government's commitment to negotiated land-claims settlements. The government is also providing $20 million over five years to provide native peoples with opportunities for training, business ventures, and planning activities associated with the Norman Wells project. Included in this package is $1.5 million for a joint venture between the developer and native organizations. The government's conviction is that exploration for and development of hydrocarbons can occur prior to claims settlements without unduly prejudicing the negotiating process.

As negotiations on the CYI claim have proceeded with respect to the various Yukon native communities, provision has been made for accommodation of future pipeline construction. In regard to the Alaska Highway gas pipeline corridor, the government position is that the native peoples may select land within the corridor, subject to the final right of way of the pipeline.

Conclusion

Clearly, the federal government has made a deep political commitment to the resolution of comprehensive claims. Such commitment was strengthened with the 1983 Constitutional Accord,[7] in which it was agreed that treaty rights recognized under section 35 of the Constitution would include rights that now exist by way of land-claims agreements or that may be so acquired. Moreover, section 25 of the Constitution, as proclaimed in 1982, had already gone far in recognizing land-claims settlements by anticipating their attainment.[8] It was also made abundantly clear in the 1981 policy statement *In All Fairness* that the federal government was committed to "bring to a full and satisfactory conclusion, the resolution of Native land claims."

The outlook for comprehensive claims in the North as elsewhere is, in terms of federal political will, therefore promising. It is important, however, that claimant groups seize the opportunity now to do all they can to achieve settlement while the will is there. This does not mean giving way on all points on all fronts at all times. It does mean, however, that compromise must be present on both native and government sides, including both federal and territorial levels. It also means that native claimants must be willing to clear up differences they have between themselves on overlapping interests and give full support to fact-finding or other intervention processes to which they agree.

Regarding public support for claims settlements, which has generally been present in the past, much will depend on the ability of government and native claimants to achieve, as soon as possible, equitable settlements, settlements that are fair not only to the native peoples but also to industry, to other residents in claims areas, and to the national interest as a whole.

Appendix A
Chief Negotiators

Dennis O'Connor: Yukon Indian Land Claim

Currently with the Toronto law firm of Borden and Elliot, and appointed Queen's Counsel in 1980, Dennis O'Connor was designated chief negotiator on 23 May 1980. A former professor of law at the University of Western Ontario, and consultant for the federal Department of Justice, Mr O'Connor has served as deputy magistrate in the N.W.T., provincial judge in B.C., and magistrate in the Yukon Territory.

Simon Reisman: COPE Land Claim

An economist and a former deputy minister of the federal Department of Finance, Mr Reisman was appointed chief negotiator on 22 October 1982. In 30 years of public service, Mr Reisman held a number of executive positions, including those of secretary to the Treasury Board and deputy minister of Industry, where he was principal negotiator of the Canada–U.S. Automotive Agreement of 1964. Mr Reisman also has the distinction of being an officer of the Order of Canada, and in 1974 he received the Governor General's Outstanding Public Service Award. Now active in the private sector as president of Reiscar Ltd. and chairman of Reisman and Grandy Ltd., Mr Reisman is a member of the boards of numerous Canadian companies.

David Osborn: Dene-Métis Land Claim

A member of the bars of Ontario and Saskatchewan, and a specialist in litigation, David Osborn was appointed chief negotiator on 21 April 1981. Mr Osborn has served as partner in the Saskatoon law firm of Lamarsh and Company; assistant professor in the School of Business Administration, University of Western Ontario; executive director of the Canadian Bar Association; and as general counsel for the Canadian Radio-Television and Telecommunications Commission. He is now a partner in the Ottawa law firm of Johnston and Buchan.

William Thomas Molloy: Tungavik Federation of Nunavut Land Claim

A Saskatoon lawyer specializing in labour relations, Tom Molloy was appointed chief negotiator on 12 March 1982. Mr Molloy is senior partner of the law firm of MacDermid and Company, and is a director of Air Canada, Develcon Electronics Ltd., and Bridge City Mortgage Corporation. A former governor of Hockey Canada, and a member of the Canadian Order of the Knights of Malta, Mr Molloy has been recognized officially by the City of Saskatoon for his service to numerous civic organizations.

Anthony Price: *Conseil Attikamek-Montagnais* Land Claim

A Québec City lawyer who has worked in both the private and public sectors, Mr Price was appointed chief negotiator on 4 March 1982. A former founding partner of the legal firm Letourneau, Stein, Amyot, with which he practised 12 years, Mr Price has founded various businesses in the province of Québec, including Whale River Outfitters Limited, an outfitter operating in northern Québec, and Musée du Fort, an electronic sound and light presentation of the military history of Québec. Mr Price spent 12 years working initially as a director of the Canadian Bilateral Aid Program in Morocco, and later in Senegal and Kenya as regional director for the International Development Research Centre of Ottawa.

John Bene: Nishga Land Claim

A retired B.C. businessman and international consultant, Mr Bene was appointed chief negotiator on 26 June 1981. Mr Bene, a graduate in mechanical and electrical engineering, founded, designed, and operated Pacific Veneer Co. Ltd. of New Westminster from 1938 to 1943, and then established and headed as president, until 1968, the company now known as Weldwood of Canada Ltd. A director of both companies, Mr Bene served in the same capacity with the Bank of British Columbia and Champion International (U.S.A.). In the public sector, Mr Bene served as special adviser to the president of the Canadian International Development Agency (CIDA), and later assumed the post of director general of the Special Advisors Branch. Joining the International Development Research Centre in 1975, he became senior adviser to the president and also served as governor on the first board of this institution. Since returning to Vancouver in 1980, Mr Bene has led CIDA missions to India and Guyana. Mr Bene is an honorary lecturer in the Faculty of Forestry at the University of British Columbia.

Endnotes

1. Royal Proclamation of 1763, quoted in Peter A. Cumming and Neil H. Mickenberg, eds, *Native Rights in Canada*, second edition (Toronto: The Indian-Eskimo Association of Canada & General Publishing, 1972), p. 291.

2. Address to Her Majesty from the Senate and House of Commons, December 1867, quoted in Peter A. Cumming and Neil N. Mickenberg, eds, *Native Rights in Canada*, op. cit., p. 73.

3. Earl of Dufferin, Governor General of Canada, 1876, quoted in Peter A. Cumming and Neil N. Mickenberg, eds, *Native Rights in Canada*, op. cit., p. 187.

4. See Department of Indian Affairs and Northern Development, *In All Fairness: A Native Claims Policy, Comprehensive Claims* (Ottawa: DIAND, 1981).

5. Council for Yukon Indians, *Together Today for Our Children Tomorrow* (Whitehorse: Council for Yukon Indians, 1973).

6. *Denendeh, Our Land: Public Government for the People of the North* (Yellowknife: The Dene Nation and Métis Association of the N.W.T., 1981).

7. Constitutional Accord on Aboriginal Rights, First Ministers' Conference on Aboriginal Constitutional Matters, Ottawa, 15-16 March 1983, Schedule, p. 1.

8. Constitution Act, 1982, s. 25.

III
THE WORKING GROUPS

Natural Resource Jurisdiction and Political Development

Chairman: Andrew Thompson

Introduction

Political development—the transfer of control over northern resources to northern peoples and institutions—was the theme central to the Third National Workshop. Each of the plenary sessions and eight working groups addressed the policy and institutional changes needed to achieve a fair and more harmonious balance between national and regional interests in northern resources. The specific purpose of this working group on natural resource jurisdiction and political development was to consider and analyse how and when the devolution of control over northern lands and resources could occur, particularly devolution to northern public governments.

The current policy of the federal government for negotiating native land claims and the process of defining aboriginal peoples' rights in Canada's new Constitution both promise a recognized role for northern aboriginal peoples in the management of their lands and resources. The governments of the Yukon and Northwest Territories long have demanded, and have begun to assume, a greater degree of control over lands and resources within their jurisdictions. The Government of the Yukon is calling upon the federal government to grant the territory provincial status. The federal government's decision in late 1982 to approve in principle the division of the Northwest Territories into at least two new territories—Nunavut in the north-east and a second territory in the west—has made possible a third federal–territorial discussion on the transfer of legal and administrative jurisdiction over non-renewable resources to the North. Formal negotiations have not yet begun, but the federal government's funding of the Western Constitutional Forum and Nunavut Constitutional Forum has put devolution on the national political agenda.

The Working Groups

The working group included:

Chairman: **Andrew Thompson**
Westwater Research Centre
University of British Columbia

Rapporteur: **Jeffrey Gilmour**
Department of Justice
Government of the Northwest Territories
Yellowknife, N.W.T.

Invited Participants:

Ron Doering
Kelly, Doering & Morrow
Ottawa, Ontario

Joe Jack
AMAX Northwest Mining Co. Ltd.
Whitehorse, Yukon

Peter Jull
Ottawa, Ontario

Robert MacQuarrie
Member of the Legislative Assembly
Government of the Northwest Territories
Yellowknife, N.W.T.

Jean Morisset
Département de géographie
Université du Québec à Montréal

Bill Musgrove
Northern Policy Directorate
Department of Indian Affairs and Northern Development
Government of Canada
Ottawa, Ontario

Dwight Noseworthy
Committee for Aboriginal Rights and Constitutional Development
Government of the Northwest Territories
Yellowknife, N.W.T.

110

Chris Pearson
Government Leader
Government of the Yukon
Whitehorse, Yukon

Dave Porter
Yukon Indian Development Corporation
Whitehorse, Yukon

Jeff Richstone
Inuit Committee on National Issues
Ottawa, Ontario

James Ross
Dene Nation
Yellowknife, N.W.T.

Al Zariwny
Energy, Mines and Resources Secretariat
Government of the Northwest Territories
Yellowknife, N.W.T.

Background documents used in the working group, in addition to those published in these proceedings, included:

DIAND. *In All Fairness: A Native Claims Policy, Comprehensive Claims.* Ottawa: DIAND, 1981.

Energy and Resource Development Secretariat. "Resource Development Policy." Yellowknife: Government of the Northwest Territories, March 1983.

Nunavut Constitutional Forum. *Nunavut.* 10 March 1983.

Working Group Report

Natural Resource Jurisdiction and Political Development

As the theme for its discussion, the working group on natural resource jurisdiction and political development adopted the question: Who gets what, when, and how? The working group developed the agenda outlined below.

Who

- Who are the interests in the Northwest Territories and the Yukon and what are their perceptions?
- What is the national interest in natural resource jurisdiction?
- What are the international obligations, constraints, and opportunities?
- What are the perceptions of industry and developers?

What

- What are the existing natural resource mandates for ownership, revenue, and regulatory control?
- What are the transferable elements of federal and territorial institutions? What do the Northwest Territories and the Yukon want? Why is natural resource control essential to political development?
- Are there regions within regions (the Western Arctic Regional Municipality (WARM), for example)?
- How does the offshore differ?
- Are the arctic islands a special case?

When

- When must each event in the sequence take place?

How

- How are the processes of aboriginal rights under the Constitution, land claims, territorial political development, land-use planning, and formula financing and revenue sharing to be integrated?
- How may development proceed without prejudice to land claims, and what policy should guide development in the interim?

- What are the implications of dividing the Northwest Territories (will there be further divisions creating more, and smaller, jurisdictions)?
- What are the strategies for accomplishing changes?
- Will land alienation and control be achieved through bridging institutions such as the proposed Nunavut land authority, the proposed Mackenzie Valley planning authority, or the proposed Yukon tripartite resources corporation?
- Are there knowledge gaps?

Discussion of Agenda Items

There appeared to be consensus among the participants on some fundamental questions: first, that federal ownership of most resources north of 60° is a significant factor; secondly, that northerners must have a degree of ownership and control if there is to be genuine political development; thirdly, that the current federal–territorial relationship is a colonial one; and finally, that many persons perceive Canada's North as a treasure trove.

The political development of the western provinces between 1870 (when the Province of Manitoba was created) and 1930 (when resource ownership was transferred to the western provinces) suggests the future likely for political development of the North. The move of the northern territories toward provincial status and jurisdiction over natural resources is similar to that of the western provinces, but there is an element present now that was absent formerly: in an age of energy crises the federal government may perceive its jurisdiction over oil and gas in the North as fundamental to the national interest.

In addition to energy security, the size, cost, and complexity of northern energy projects will make the federal government reluctant to surrender jurisdiction over natural resources to the territories.

The working group participants disagreed on the legitimacy of continued federal control in the interest of national energy security. Some felt that even if a substantial transfer of ownership and control occurs, the federal government will retain extensive jurisdiction over shipping, navigation, communications, fisheries, and other resource uses. Others felt that these national interests in the North would not require jurisdictional arrangements in the North different from those existing in southern Canada.

Transfer of Control

Transfer of control is a process that can be staged:
First stage—management and regulation
Second stage—revenue sharing
Third stage—provincial status and ownership.

In practice, the territories already exercise control in some areas that legally are still under federal jurisdiction. *Control* rather than *ownership* is the central issue. Were the territories to control the rate, sites, and manner of development, leaving formal constitutional questions aside for the time being, practical progress would be made in achieving territorial goals. Mr Munro's speech to the N.W.T. legislative assembly on 11 May 1983 indicated flexibility in the federal approach to power sharing (see pp. 133-140 in this volume).

On the question of how current processes—particularly land claims and political development—are to be integrated, the national talks on constitutional rights of aboriginal peoples were suggested as a means for integration. The agenda for these talks is not restricted, the participants are powerful, and the process is public.

Bridging mechanisms were discussed by comparing the experience of devolution of control over offshore resources from Denmark to Greenland with recent transfers of authority from the Government of Canada to the Government of Nova Scotia.* Greenland can veto policy and project decisions of the Government of Denmark; in Nova Scotia the provincial government does not have the power to veto federal decisions, but it can delay them 3 to 18 months, depending on the resources in question. The working group also discussed the proposal for a tripartite resources corporation consisting of the federal government, the provincial government, and the aboriginal peoples.

Conclusions and Recommendations

The working group on natural resource jurisdiction and political development produced the following consensus statement:

> Democratic political rights are an important component of the fundamental human rights of Canadians. These rights should apply equally to all citizens. A primary expression of these rights

*[Canada-Nova Scotia Agreement Relating to Oil and Gas Resource Management and Revenue Sharing]

Natural Resource Jurisdiction and Political Development

in Canada has been the right of persons in a region to have their government attain provincial-like powers and jurisdictions, control over natural resources and land being of fundamental importance.

This working group reports to the plenary session of the CARC Third National Workshop, in its consensus statement, that it calls on the existing federal and provincial governments in Canada to support the evolution of the territories north of 60° to provincial status in the near future and to protect effectively aboriginal rights in the transfer of powers to the new provincial governments of the North.

Background Paper

Natural Resource Jurisdiction and Political Development in the North: The Case of Nunavut

Ronald L. Doering
Kelly, Doering & Morrow
Barristers & Solicitors

Introduction

Political development issues in Canada's North are very complex, and perhaps the most controversial issue involves the matter of jurisdiction over natural resources. On the one hand, the federal government continues to see the lands north of 60° as Canada lands, and the transfer of jurisdiction over the resources of these lands as either non-negotiable or, at best, an issue to be considered only after several years when the population might warrant a meaningful discussion of provincial status. On the other hand, northerners want a greater degree of self-government now and see a share of natural resource revenues and a gradual transfer of jurisdiction as essential to their ability to become more self-sufficient and less financially dependent on the federal government.

Although the scope of legislative powers enjoyed by a territorial legislature is generally equal to that of the provinces, three critical differences remain: first, territorial laws can be overridden by federal legislation; secondly, territorial legislatures cannot amend their own constitutions; and thirdly, and most pertinent here, the ownership of public lands and resources is not vested in the territorial governments and, with the exception of game, there is no legislative power to deal with them. It is this ownership and management of land and resources that is today the main source of federal power in the North and that enables the federal government to regulate nearly every aspect of its economic development.

The law, then, accords with the northern perception that the North is a colony of the South, that northern lands and resources are "owned" by someone else, and that now, and for the foreseeable future, northern resources will be controlled by, and their associated wealth flow to, the federal government in the South so long as the present legal regime remains.[1] Out of this perception have arisen continuing demands for greater degrees of self-government and a share of resource revenues until provincehood is attained, when, it is assumed, both resources and their jurisdiction would be transferred.

These demands are two of the prime forces behind the proposal by Inuit of Canada's North to divide the Northwest Territories and to create a separate territory north and east of the tree-line to be called Nunavut ("our land"). This concept is central to the land claim presented by Inuit Tapirisat of Canada (ITC). Inuit do not want to have their aboriginal title to much of Canada's North extinguished in return for a chunk of land and a sum of money: they believe that their economic future and cultural identity can be protected only if they have some control over the government of their area and if they share in the management and the resources of their lands. The Nunavut concept therefore proposes a political development that represents a direct challenge to the existing land and resources regime. The challenge requires a comprehensive federal response, especially now that a coalition of Inuit and eastern Arctic residents called the Nunavut Constitutional Forum (NCF) has developed a formal proposal for a gradual devolution of control over some of these natural resources and for a sharing of the revenues that they generate.

Political Development: The Federal Position

Until May 1983, the most recent detailed public statement of the federal government's policy for northern ,constitutional development was set out in a paper entitled "Political Development in the Northwest Territories" (the PMO paper) published by the Office of the Prime Minister on 3 August 1977, concurrently with the prime minister's announcement that the Honourable Charles M. Drury had been appointed as Special Representative for Constitutional Development in the Northwest Territories.

On the matter of development of non-renewable resources, the PMO paper clearly stated that the "national interest dictates that the Federal Government maintain its ownership and control of the potentially significant non-renewable resources in the Northwest Territories."[2] The paper also accepted in a general way the principle "that such revenue-sharing should occur, as the result of claims settlements and through government-to-government agreements."[3]

Natural Resource Jurisdiction and Political Development

Perhaps the PMO paper was more generous on the matter of transferring ownership and control than is the current policy, when it stated:

> the Government contemplates that the ownership and control of renewable resources and of some lands will be transferred to the Territorial Government (any reference to "Territorial Government" in the future should be read as including the possibility of more than one such government in case the Northwest Territories may be divided) on the one hand, and under claims settlements to northern native groups, on the other.[4]

The most recent and, in some respects, most complete indication of the federal position on political development in the North is found in a speech given by John Munro to the Northwest Territories Legislative Assembly in Yellowknife on 11 May 1983. After firmly reiterating his earlier pre-condition for division—northern agreement on a boundary and settlement of claims—Mr Munro made a broad commitment to devolution of powers and acceptance of northern decisions. His speech marked a definite willingness to accept the growing regional interest, so long as that interest did not collide too seriously with perceived federal interests:

> the federal government's choice was the choice of northerners, as expressed in a plebiscite as well as in many of the submissions made to us in the months leading up to November. In addition, the decisions about when and how division might occur are yours to consider with a minimum of guidance from us. Devolution of program responsibilities to you, the elected representatives of the territorial government, and development of political institutions that are accountable and responsive to the needs of northerners are objectives we share.[5]

The speech made clear that the federal position on natural resources, however, was not something on which the government was going to be soft:

> The federal government decided in November that retaining federal ownership and control over non-renewable resources was in the national interest. However, there are aspects of resource development, particularly in the environmental and socio-economic areas, which must be dealt with, at least in part, locally.[6]

119

It is clear that resource ownership and jurisdiction are not negotiable in the federal position. Although the federal government may be willing to accept a gradual devolution of programme responsibility in some areas, it does not appear to contemplate any transfer of ownership or control of natural resources at this time.

Political Development: The Northern Position

Prepared for, discussed at, and approved by its annual general meeting in Igloolik, 3–7 September 1979, the ITC report *Political Development in Nunavut* represented the first comprehensive Inuit proposal for political development in Canada's North. With the earlier appointment of a new commissioner and with elections in October 1979, observers saw that Canada's North was beginning a new chapter in its political development. In his interesting short history of Nunavut, entitled *Nunavut*, Peter Jull described that time:

> A new era had begun and the new north had been recognised . . . .
> The change was complete the following month. In October, 1979, elections in which the native movement for the first time endorsed participation, returned a new type of Legislative Assembly, one full of young and energetic native leaders and younger, more open-minded whites. This new Legislative Assembly lost no time in reversing and discarding many of the actions and positions of its predecessor.[7]

The main points of *Political Development in Nunavut* can be summarized easily:

1. The Northwest Territories would be divided, and the area north of the tree-line would become a new territory called Nunavut.
2. The Nunavut Territory would have powers roughly equivalent to the powers of the existing N.W.T.
3. Nunavut would acquire provincial-type powers over a 15-year transition period, becoming a province at that time.
4. The federal government would be asked to make a commitment to Nunavut before a land-claims settlement was concluded.

5. With respect to land and resources, Inuit of Nunavut would hope to exercise some control through participation in administrative agencies, through the Nunavut government and local and regional governments, and through the ownership of large amounts of land, which they would acquire through a settlement. They also recommended a revised and more comprehensive (albeit vaguely described) planning process in which Inuit could participate significantly.

Recognizing the short-term need for continued financial assistance, the ITC report concluded that:

> In the long-term, ITC is confident that development of the resource base would not only allow Nunavut the degree of self-sufficiency engaged [*sic*] by most Canadian provinces but would also allow Nunavut to make material contributions to Confederation beyond its demographic weight.[8]

Political Development In Nunavut was the main subject of the N.W.T. Legislative Assembly at its session held at Frobisher Bay in October 1980. During that session the leader of the assembly's Committee on Unity reported that the committee "has not been able to find a consensus, or even, at the moment, to see the opportunity for consensus, favouring the continuing existence of this territory as a single jurisdiction."[9] Following the recommendations of the committee, the assembly endorsed the concept of division and called for a referendum on the question to be held two years later to allow enough time for study and debate.

In April 1982, the plebiscite was duly held on the question of dividing the N.W.T. to create Nunavut. In the eastern Arctic, where the majority of Inuit live, 80 per cent of the votes were cast for Nunavut in a voter turnout higher than in any previous national, territorial, or local election. The vote was not as high in the western Arctic, but the overall result of the plebiscite favoured division. Soon after, the N.W.T. Legislative Assembly voted 19-0 in favour of division.

The Legislative Assembly and the Inuit organizations then created the Nunavut Constitutional Forum (NCF), consisting of two Nunavut MLAs, ministers Kane Tologanak and Dennis Patterson, ITC president John Amagoalik, and Committee for Original Peoples' Entitlement (COPE) president Peter Green. Long-time Nunavut advocate Peter Jull was named research director. The forum was to be the umbrella group working on the details of a Nunavut constitution, conducting research on outstanding issues, and working with the communities on a programme of public consultation and information leading to the establishment of Nunavut. A similar forum, known as the Western Constitutional Forum, was created in the western portion of the N.W.T., and the two worked together for particular purposes as the Constitutional Alliance.

On 26 November 1982, John Munro, the minister of Indian Affairs and Northern Development, addressed the Legislative Assembly of the N.W.T. and announced the federal government's position on Nunavut: "Nunavut was acceptable subject to several conditions, the most important of which were that land claims be settled, and that northerners involved agree on the boundaries of the new territory and remain constant in their commitment to such a territory."[10] The speech signalled an important new willingness to allow northerners involved to take a more creative role in the key decisions involving political development. Mr. Munro told the assembly:

> just as you and your forefathers have made this the place it is today, you will decide what it will be tomorrow ... I have endorsed the principles for which you have fought so hard. Now it is up to you to make choices—choices that best meet the needs and aspirations of the people you represent.[11]

The following week the Constitutional Alliance visited Ottawa and held meetings with ministers, with M.P.s of all parties, and with the press to express its views and to seek support for northern political change.

> Official Ottawa was surprised by the degree of unanimity and co-operation among the Alliance principals representing, as they did, all peoples and major elective bodies in the NWT. A subject of particular concern to the Alliance was the lack of reference in the government announcement to any sharing of resources revenues with territorial governments. However, government ministers did say that Ottawa would be flexible in its considera-tion of political development and did not have a set of rigid guidelines which had to be fulfilled.[12]

The NCF Proposal on Land and Resources

Since its creation, NCF has adopted a number of tentative working posi-tions and, on 27 April 1983, it announced a set of general working princi-ples with respect to land and resources. These principles are to be set out in a discussion paper, which is to be circulated for public discussion during the summer of 1983 [*Building Nunavut*, reproduced in this volume]. The public discussion process is intended to culminate in a constitutional convention to be held in the autumn of 1983.

NCF tries to be realistic in recognizing that provincial status is some years away, but it asserts in unequivocal terms that Canada's northern territories are provinces-in-waiting and that the issue is not whether, but when, to transfer jurisdiction over natural resources.

The first principle accepted by NCF is that (pending provincial status to be granted in the years ahead) the legal title to public lands in Nunavut will continue to belong to Her Majesty in right of Canada. However, using a concept employed in the Northwest Territories Act, and subject to exceptions, NCF proposes that the right to the beneficial use and enjoyment, and to the proceeds thereof, of all lands in Nunavut (surface and sub-surface) belonging to Her Majesty would be appropriated to the Nunavut territory to be administered by the commissioner-in-assembly. As the lands would be held by, and in the name of, the commissioner, all public lands in Nunavut would effectively become commissioner's lands, as they are known in the Northwest Territories Act. The exceptions relate to certain specific federal uses such as for military lands, parks, and airports.

With respect to all minerals (except oil and gas), the federal government would continue to administer the existing legislative regime for an additional number of years. In effect, the NCF proposal would have the federal government act as trustee for Nunavut; and revenues from mineral development would go to Nunavut. The Nunavut government, during this period, would prepare for the assumption of control by developing its own capabilities in administration. At the end of the period, which would presumably involve a degree of "phasing-in," federal trusteeship would terminate, and the Nunavut government would exercise full control.

With respect to oil and gas, NCF accepts that the federal government would maintain its current beneficial use and enjoyment and its current exclusive legislative jurisdiction. The proposed Nunavut Constitution Act, however, would be accompanied by a federal–Nunavut agreement with respect to oil and gas giving Nunavut a share of managerial responsibilities, a share of revenues, and a share of equity–participation options. NCF proposes that the revenue sharing be based on the precedent already established in the Canada–Nova Scotia offshore agreement. The rationale for this position is clearly set out in the NCF discussion paper:

> Simply put, a Nunavut without access to, and a stake in, lands and resources revenues would not only be crippled but continued conflict over development policies and projects would be

ensured. After all, projects would entail costs but no visible benefits for the Nunavut authorities, with no incentive to adopt
serious development policies. A Nunavut government must share
in lands and resources revenues as a fundamental element of
political responsibility.[13]

Under the NCF proposal, federal laws of general application with
respect to natural resources that apply in the provinces would continue to
apply. For example, the National Energy Board Act would continue to
operate as before. The interim transfer of the beneficial use and enjoyment
and the eventual transfer of resources and jurisdiction would be effected,
according to the NCF proposal, without prejudice to third-party interests,
including aboriginal rights. The proposal therefore allows Inuit of the
eastern Arctic to continue to negotiate a settlement of their claim in a
separate forum, and basically to remain unfettered by the land and resources regime to be developed for the public government of Nunavut. Indeed,
the NCF proposal specifically accepts that the land-claims settlement
would take priority over the legislation creating the Nunavut government.
Acceptance of this land and resources regime would appear to confirm an
analysis contained in an NCF working paper that suggests that, under
existing structures, the issues of land claims and political development
cannot be dealt with together but, at best, can only be co-ordinated.[14]

Natural Resource Jurisdiction and Political Development: Some Issues

Resource Revenue Sharing

Under the current legal regime, the federal government owns all natural
resources in the territories and therefore collects all revenues that are
generated from the resources. Royalties, participating interests, back-in
interests, lease and permit fees, special oil and gas levies, and corporate
income taxes are some of the ways that the federal government currently
collects resource revenues. By comparison, the territorial government is
limited to a small part of corporate income tax and some small revenues
from property and business taxes collected by N.W.T. municipalities.

Northerners, through NCF, place a great deal of importance on
obtaining all revenues from minerals and an agreement to share in

revenues from oil and gas. These revenues are seen as their means of obtaining greater financial independence and, hence, greater political independence.

The federal government's position is to deny any transfer of jurisdiction or revenues at this time—a policy motivated by a number of factors. Some federal officials defend the position by explaining that these Canada lands and their resources are for all Canadians. Each Canadian "owns" his or her per capita share of Canada lands. According to this point of view, the N.W.T. is analogous to offshore lands in that currently no province or "incipient province" has any jurisdiction. There is no regional interest, only a national interest. Accordingly, the federal government is seen as the trustee and steward of northern resources for all Canadians.

Northerners, on the other hand, believe that they are the residents of "provinces-in-waiting" and that a transfer of resource ownership and jurisdiction is simply a question of "when." This fundamentally different perception of the future political development of the N.W.T. accounts for the directly opposing views on resource revenue sharing. Until one of the parties dramatically alters its position, their agreement on many other issues will not be achieved. Drury recommended a gradual devolution of resource jurisdiction. The ITC proposal demands it. The NCF position paper assumes it. The former Conservative government promised it. The current federal government "contemplates" it.

One aspect of the debate that tends to confuse it unnecessarily is the absence of a clear factual base. For example, NCF has developed a position that would give it revenues from mining activities. Yet the extent of these potential revenues is not known. When this information was sought, Dr D.D. Brown (Head, Mining Resources, DIAND) indicated to me that figures on revenues from mining contracts in the Northwest Territories had never been released to the public because "they are so changeable from year to year." Even without the information, the current level of mining activities permits speculation that net revenues might be very modest and certainly would represent only a very small fraction of the transfer payments now made from the federal government to the N.W.T.

The subject is even more confused in the matter of oil and gas. Gross revenues for oil and gas in 1981 were $12 million. Administration costs were about $1.5 million. Does that mean that net revenues were about $10.5 million? Federal officials are quick to point out that the answer must include consideration of the fact that, during the same year, between $300 million and $400 million was "spent" in the N.W.T. by the federal government in oil and gas exploration because of the "tax expenditures" under the Petroleum Incentives Program. The federal government will argue that, before any resource revenues are shared with the N.W.T., these huge sums would have to be recouped.

Furthermore, even if the N.W.T. had received all revenues from resources in 1981, they would have amounted to less than five per cent of direct federal expenditures, as the federal government now transfers in excess of $400 million per year (over $8000 per capita). The N.W.T. could expand tax bases now available but, in gross terms, they would still represent only a small percentage of current federal transfers.

The matter is further complicated by the fact that most oil and gas development is offshore; it is unlikely that the federal government will be willing to grant to Nunavut revenue-sharing concessions, which it does not permit for the provinces. Unless major new mining or onshore hydro-carbon developments emerge in the next few years, Nunavut cannot expect to rely on resource revenues to provide its residents with financial independence from the federal government for some time to come, even if it obtains a generous share of resource revenues.

The fact that current revenues are so insignificant does not mean that NCF should abandon the claim for sharing. Presumably, the federal government would not spend between $300 million and $400 million on exploration each year unless it believed that potential revenues are enormous. If Nunavut had a share in these revenues, then its interest might more clearly reflect the federal interest. This subject needs a great deal more study and attention, and simple factual information like the size of federal revenues from mining in the N.W.T. should not only be readily available but also be released. The Nova Scotian formula may be a useful precedent, but it will have to be studied fully because it may be difficult to apply to a situation in which a territory is heavily reliant on federal funds for its financial base.

The Native Claims Issue

The NCF position on lands and resources leaves Inuit land-claims negotiations unfettered, and accepts the paramouncy of any claims settlement; it recognizes that the issues are being dealt with in separate forums and with separate players. On the northerners' side, claims are ethnic-based and are the responsibility of the Inuit organization (the Tungavik Federation of Nunavut (TFN), a member organization of ITC, is negotiating a land-claim settlement on behalf of Inuit of the eastern Arctic). Nunavut is a matter of public government involving native and non-native northerners in NCF. On the side of the federal government, the claim is negotiated by a chief federal negotiator from outside the public service directly representing the minister of Indian Affairs and Northern Development and supported by DIAND's Office of Native Claims. Questions of political development cannot be negotiated in the claims forum; although the prime minister's office retains the ultimate prerogative for government organization, the day-to-day responsibility for Nunavut is now to be lodged with a constitutional group in the northern programme section of DIAND.

Although the two processes are separate, each will have to deal with many of the same issues, and a good deal of goodwill and discipline on both sides will be required if the processes are to be co-ordinated. The relationship between claims and political development raises very complex questions. For example, if the federal government is going to yield somewhere on natural resources, should it do so in the claims process or should it make concessions to Nunavut? Should Inuit devote the bulk of their time and resources to Nunavut or to the claims process? How can the COPE agreement in principle be accommodated in a Nunavut constitution before the TFN negotiations are completed? If the finalization of the claim and the creation of Nunavut cannot be achieved at the same time, which should come first? Many of the players are currently the same and a good deal of co-ordination and overlap occurs; but are the interests of Nunavut and TFN opposing to the extent that they will eventually conflict? Should a claims settlement accord to Inuit special representation on Nunavut administrative agencies? These and many other very difficult questions confront government and native politicians and require a great deal of study by both sides.

The recent problems experienced in trying to obtain federal government ratification of the wildlife agreement in principle illustrate how difficult it is going to be for Inuit to obtain concessions on natural resources from the federal government. If the federal government cannot develop a process and position that permit it to accept Inuit making decisions on wildlife matters (with a ministerial veto), then it is unlikely that the more financially significant jurisdiction over non-renewable resources is going to be transferred, even in part, in the claims process.

The controversy over the wildlife agreement illustrates how difficult it is to obtain a unified federal position when there are so many central agencies and departments that can influence policy. In the case of the wildlife agreement, one department—Fisheries and Oceans—appears to have been able to veto a position accepted by many other departments. Because of the nature of the departments (there are many little "Ottawas"), the claims process will work only if there is a great deal of leadership among the departments and very firm political will. This, however, may not exist. There may not be a strong federal commitment to a timely resolution of claims if the recent remarks of Clovis Demers, Executive

Director of the Office of Native Claims, are indicative of government thinking. In an interview with Mr Demers, a European journalist provided a rare insight into the current attitude of senior bureaucrats—an attitude that perhaps reflects the position of their political masters. Mr Demers conceded that the government is not pressured to settle the TFN claim because there are no pressing development proposals in the area, no political pressure, and therefore the government can negotiate "with some serenity" for two years. There is refreshing honesty in these remarks. Most official statements speak of the urgent need to reach a just settlement.[15]

Recent problems experienced with the claims process may encourage Inuit to put more of their effort into the Nunavut process. In the next few months, it will be interesting to observe whether the federal government will provide signals to indicate whether Nunavut will be allowed to proceed at a faster pace than the claims negotiations. The lack of progress on the land claims will continue to exert pressures on the existing TFN leadership and plays into the hands of other Inuit leaders who advocate a quick settlement for land and money. Government delay tactics may not be as inadvertent as is often assumed; a change in Inuit leadership could pave the way for a land and money settlement and ease pressure for power sharing.

Part of the official federal policy in the 1970s involved an interesting "Catch-22" situation that no doubt served well the government's objective of temporizing: policies on political development in the North could proceed only when land claims were resolved; land claims could be resolved only with clarification of policies for political development. As recently as 11 May 1983, the federal position required settlement of land claims before Nunavut could be granted and yet, although the NCF position provides some flexibility, the official position of Inuit is still that they must have Nunavut in place, or ready to be put in place, before they will settle land claims. Can both positions be accommodated?

Nunavut Jurisdiction to Regulate Environmental and Socio-economic Aspects of Resource Developments

Unlike the resource revenue sharing and native claims issues, this matter may be capable of early resolution if the parties can consolidate their thinking and devote time, attention, and resources to developing a common position. In the final analysis, Nunavut involves a claim not only for a sharing of revenues but also for a sharing of power. NCF demands a sharing of the responsibility for regulating the environmental and socio-economic aspects of major resource developments. This is one area where the federal government recently has expressed a willingness to concede a sharing of jurisdiction. In his speech on 11 May 1983, Mr Munro agreed that environmental and socio-economic aspects of resource development must be dealt with locally. Here, the federal government seems to recognize a legitimate regional interest and to be willing to negotiate a role for Nunavut. NCF has not developed a detailed position on this issue but, in light of the minister's comments, it should give this a high priority.

It may be that the recently released N.W.T. paper entitled "Resource Development Policy" provides a useful system for adoption by Nunavut.[16] This policy sets out various criteria for designating areas to be called "development impact zones." Proposed resource developments in these areas would be subject to intensive assessment and review to determine their "overall economic, social and environmental implications."[17] The policy identifies nine principles to be used in the evaluation of the implications of resource development projects to determine if they would provide a "net benefit" to the local residents.[18]

Under the proposed Territorial Assessment and Review Process, "proponents of resource development projects will need to consult with the Government of the Northwest Territories and the communities before options concerning the nature, pace and scale of the project are closed. Identification and resolution of identified adverse impacts will need to be carried out in advance of project implementation" before major resource developers are given a "development certificate" that will permit them to proceed.[19] These certificates may set out a number of terms and conditions.

The policy also creates an elaborate monitoring process. Developers may have to have their certificates renewed, and they will be subject to periodic evaluation and continuing detailed scrutiny. Although resource industries may be concerned about this further level of government regulation, at least they will know that if they comply with the N.W.T. policy, they will be able to proceed to the federal level of review having convinced the Government of the Northwest Territories of their projects' merits.

It is too early to know how this policy will fit in with federal impact assessments, but the overall scheme provides a useful precedent for Nunavut. Some system of entrenching these powers in the Nunavut constitution should be explored. If Nunavut were accorded jurisdiction to impose such a system on developers (with the circumstances for a federal override clearly set out in advance), then Nunavut could be in a position to exercise very significant control to maximize the net benefits for its residents.

Conclusion

The Nunavut proposal for a sharing of aspects of natural resource jurisdiction involves complex issues that are central to the development of policies for the political development of Canada's North. The sharing of both resources and power is possible in a federal system, but negotiations will be difficult. Important progress in many matters has been achieved in recent months—progress that makes the prospects for some compromises far better than they were even a year or two ago.

The future negotiations between northerners and the federal government will be long and hard, however, as illustrated by this discussion of the difficult issues surrounding the jurisdiction of natural resources. The negotiations will involve complex dynamics of give and take and compromise. Politicians and their bureaucrats on both sides will have to be patient, and to remind themselves that politics is "the art of the possible." As Canadians, we often pride ourselves on the genius and flexibility of our Constitution. Nunavut involves an interesting test of Canada's federal system and its political leaders because it requires a fine balancing of federal and regional interests in a context and an environment perhaps even more complex than those that were encountered by our fathers of Confederation.

Endnotes

1. This perception has been heightened by the debate that surrounded Bill C-48 and by the initial dropping of native rights from the Constitution. For the purposes of this paper, natural resources do not include renewable resources because the issues are quite different from those raised by non-renewable resources.

2. Office of the Prime Minister, "Political Development in the Northwest Territories," in *Northern Transitions*, volume 2, *Second National Workshop on People, Resources, and the Environment North of 60°*, R.F. Keith and J.B. Wright, eds (Ottawa: Canadian Arctic Resources Committee, 1978), p. 278.

3. Ibid.

4. Ibid.

5. See this volume, p. 133.

6. Ibid.

7. Peter Jull, *Nunavut* (Yellowknife: Nunavut Constitutional Forum and Government of the Northwest Territories, 1983), p. 43.

8. Inuit Tapirisat of Canada, *Political Development in Nunavut* (Ottawa: Inuit Tapirisat of Canada, 1979), p. 36.

9. Legislative Assembly of the N.W.T., "Report of the Special Committee on Unity to the 3rd Session of the 9th Assembly at Frobisher Bay, October 22, 1980," *Debates: Official Report*, 3rd Session, 9th Assembly.

10. Peter Jull, *Nunavut*, p. 59. See above, note 7.

11. John Munro, Address to the Legislative Assembly, 26 November 1982, Yellowknife, N.W.T.

12. Peter Jull, *Nunavut*, p. 59. See above, note 7.

13. See this volume, p.160.

14. Ronald L. Doering, *Nunavut and Land Claims: Options for a Public Land Regime* (Ottawa: Nunavut Constitutional Forum, n.d.).

15. "Inuit Not in Strong Negotiating Position," *Nunavut Newsletter* (Ottawa: The Nunavut Land Claims Project, 1982), p. 11.

16. Government of the Northwest Territories, "Resource Development Policy" (Yellowknife: Energy and Resource Development Secretariat, GNWT, 1983), p. 19.

17. Ibid., p. 2.

18. Ibid., p. 5.

19. Ibid., p. 3.

Notes for an Address

The Honourable John C. Munro, P.C., M.P.
Minister of Indian Affairs and Northern Development
Legislative Assembly
Yellowknife, N.W.T.
11 May 1983

Introduction

It has now been nearly six months since I last addressed this assembly. That is about the right amount of time, it seems to me, because the message I brought to you in November warranted a good deal of reflection. It would have been premature of me to intrude before now on the discussions that northerners have been having about their constitutional development. Now, after these months of deliberation, you have invited me again and I am glad to be here.

As you recall, in November I announced how the federal government sees responsible and accountable government evolving in the Northwest Territories. The elements of Cabinet's decisions, of course, included acceptance of the possibility that the Northwest Territories might be divided along new geopolitical boundaries. I therefore described certain conditions under which the federal government would want to see division occur. Those conditions were intended to guarantee the kinds of institutions and relationships which members of this assembly have endorsed.

I said then, and perhaps should repeat, that the federal government's choice was the choice of northerners, as expressed in a plebiscite as well as in many of the submissions made to us in the months leading up to November. In addition, the decisions about when and how division might occur are yours to consider with a minimum of guidance from us. Devolution of program responsibilities to you, the elected representatives of the territorial government, and development of political institutions that are accountable and responsive to the needs of northerners are objectives which we share.

From where I sit in Ottawa and from the accounts of others, I judge reaction in the North to have been generally positive and supportive. There was some initial uncertainty expressed; that was natural, given the

133

implications of such an announcement. I would be pleased to hear from any of you as the opportunities arise, in order to sharpen my own impressions of how this approach has been received.

Let me say, however, that we followed your reactions with great interest. James Wah-Shee remarked that the news I brought was "encouraging." He said the policy I outlined "goes a long way toward meeting the goals and aspirations of northern people." Dennis Patterson said the announcement "lifted the spirits" of the people of the eastern Arctic, while George Braden said he was "generally quite pleased" because the announcement included many of the suggestions of the territorial government.

I find these and other remarks I've heard not only encouraging, but reassuring that we are at last on the path toward a future that the people of this territory want for themselves. It is a future, I might add, which will be consistent with our country's broader objectives.

An additional word or two is in order at this point in view of constitutional developments that have occurred nationally since we last met. The mid-March First Ministers' Conference was a significant turning point for the Canadian Confederation. Its focus was on aboriginal and treaty rights, and these matters are of no small significance to the North. Northern political development, in the terms I used to describe it in November, is also linked to the ongoing national process. These two processes are therefore related and mutually supportive. There are obviously opportunities for new departures here in the North that do not exist in the provinces. Conversely, the national process may have implications for the kind of government and public institutions that evolve in the North.

I would like to commend the representatives of this government and other northerners for their able and useful contributions at the First Ministers' Conference. You are aware that the agenda for the ongoing national process also includes an item dealing with the repeal of Section 42 of the *Constitution Act*—that section which, among other things, provides for the extension of existing provinces into the territories and the establishment of new provinces. Yukon and the Northwest Territories are assured as well that the prime minister will invite their representatives to participate in discussions on any agenda item at the next Constitutional Conference that, in the prime minister's opinion, directly affects the territories.

The First Ministers' Conference lent clarity and strength to the process of negotiating land claims. It will result in an amendment to the *Constitution Act* providing for the inclusion under "Treaty Rights" of rights that now exist by way of land claims agreements or that may be acquired in future agreements. The settlement of comprehensive native land claims is a condition of division, as you know, so the linkage between all three of these processes is important.

That perhaps will help to clarify for you the important relationships between things that are happening on the national front while you in the North are working out your own approach to division and responsible government.

Developments since November

Among the reasons why the federal government established the constitutional development framework embodied in my November announcement was the one I mentioned earlier: division, essentially, is the way northerners wanted to go. Within this framework the federal government will encourage and support the process of constitutional development in the Northwest Territories.

The Ninth Assembly has confronted important issues during its life and has dramatically altered the speed and direction of political evolution in the North. Innovative measures have been taken to create a blueprint for political change.

Some of your more impressive achievements, in my view, include: reaching a preliminary consensus on division and then holding a plebiscite; giving support and direction to the work of the constitutional alliance; moving toward a unique form of "ministerial" government—as a prelude to full responsible government—with elected members taking on more and more executive responsibilities; selecting one of your number as leader of the elected executive; and still another important measure was the creation of the Special Committee on Education, which produced a set of recommendations for the improvement of the education system in the Northwest Territories. Finally, this assembly is to be commended for its efforts to have aboriginal rights entrenched in the Canadian Constitution.

You will recall that in March responsibility for the departments of Information and Public Works was transferred to elected members of the Executive Committee. This brought two key government functions under people who are directly accountable to the taxpayers of the Northwest Territories. Today I am pleased to announce further steps in the steady progress we are making toward the goal of responsible government in the North.

Following the next territorial election, the deputy commissioner will no longer be required as a member of the Executive Committee. Arrangements will have to be made to ensure that there is continuity during any absence of the commissioner, but it is the intention of the federal government that the position of a federally appointed deputy commissioner, as an active feature of northern politics, will cease to exist.

The role of the commissioner has changed significantly over recent years. But I must stress that he will still have an important role to play over the coming years. The commissioner represents and is symbolic of the national interest. He also acts as a direct link and avenue of communication between the federal and territorial levels of government.

Until such time as claims are settled and the political arrangements in the Northwest Territories are both clarified and well-supported by northerners, the commissioner will continue to be an important stabilizing influence.

Another area in which the federal government is already working to fulfill the promise of the November announcement is the development of a formula-based approach to territorial financing. I would expect such an arrangement to provide, on the one hand, an incentive for increased territorial fiscal responsibility and, on the other hand, a more predictable base for your fiscal planning. This development will eventually be coupled with a mechanism to provide a measure of discretionary revenues.

Officials in my department are consulting with their colleagues in other federal agencies, exploring ways to achieve these objectives. I am committed to vesting accountability for the financial activities of northern government *in* northern governments. I look forward to the day when the principles of territorial financing are brought into line with the constitutional principle of responsible government. To that end, and as a further strengthening of the role and responsibilities of elected representatives, I shall be directing the commissioner to relinquish his role as chairman of the Financial Management Board.

Encouraging progress has also been made in negotiation of comprehensive claims. Two documents to guide the process of land selection were recently initialled by the Tungavik Federation of Nunavut and federal negotiators at Cambridge Bay. Negotiations with respect to the COPE claim are proceeding, and a final agreement appears to be in sight. Finally, on the Dene and Métis claim, an interim agreement on eligibility has been initialled. I look forward to the day when all three claims are settled and the appropriate legislation is put in place to give effect and protection to these negotiated settlements.

Division

A difficult challenge for northerners will be to reach a consensus among themselves on division, and to come to an agreement with the federal government on how to define new boundaries and on the distribution of powers within the territories.

Both the federal and territorial governments have long recognized the necessity for bringing territorial public administration closer to the people it serves. Great distances are just one factor in this equation. So are the geographic, cultural and economic distinctions between the Eastern and Western Arctic and the Mackenzie Valley. Another reason, quite simply, is that it was time to move. Northerners were becoming anxious for, if not insistent on, change—while a new, restless generation was eager to assume greater responsibility and accountability.

So the decision was taken under the following conditions:

- that northerners reach a consensus among themselves, and agreement with the federal government
- that all comprehensive land claims be settled
- that the majority of Northwest Territories residents continue to support division.

There have already been important developments on the questions of the structure of and distribution of powers among northern governments. I would like to commend the Nunavut Constitutional Forum for having introduced draft proposals for a Nunavut constitution. They are clearly the product of a good deal of thinking and an attempt to deal with the aspirations of the people of the Arctic while ensuring moderation and compromise. I look forward to seeing the results of similar efforts by the Western Constitutional Forum. This can only help facilitate the negotiations with the federal government that will eventually take place.

Since November the Northwest Territories Constitutional Alliance has been building toward a consensus among the people of the Northwest Territories on the location of the boundary, and the two parties in the alliance are already debating the issues. While they have not yet reached agreement, they are working hard at it, which is what counts most at this stage. Some concessions on all sides will be necessary to achieve consensus and, as you know, division can only take place once there is such consensus. That is something that only northerners can work out for themselves.

The federal role will be to help where we can. Today I bring you news of one tangible contribution we have arranged—federal funding of the operations of the Constitutional Alliance to ensure that they are able to get the job done. Federal funds will total $2 207 500, granted directly to the two forums in response to the needs they have identified to us.

This year $2 115 500 will be made available, $799 500 to the Nunavut Forum and $1 316 000 to the Western Forum; a further $92 000 will be available to the Western Forum in 1984-85. The major portion of the money will be available for the early stages of public consultation and discussion. The alliance will then be able to call on the final $515 000 ($250 000 for the Nunavut Forum and $265 000 for the Western Forum) once the two groups have reached agreement on the boundary and the distribution of powers among levels of government, and are ready to proceed with ratification.

While I know that the Nunavut Forum is hoping to have its constitutional proposals ratified this fall, I must caution against one forum moving ahead too quickly. The question of the boundary will have to be resolved before either ratification or negotiations with the federal government can take place.

In the interests of building a framework for the negotiation process that will eventually ensue with the federal government, I have instructed federal representatives to make themselves available to attend meetings of the two constitutional forums and the Constitutional Alliance. There is no advantage in allowing surprises to occur or unrealistic expectations to develop. I am therefore prepared to have federal officials meet informally with the forums to provide tentative reactions to proposals that are under review.

Principles of Public Government in the North

In its decision on division, the federal government made it clear that provincial status was not a realistic option at this time. But despite this limitation, there is a range of options open to you.

A set of constitutional principles will help determine what options are best suited to northern interests. If there is agreement on the principles, both within the North and with the federal government, it will be easier for us to agree on the kind of government that should be put in place in the North.

The following principles may help you work toward consensus and eventual agreement with the federal government.

First is the principle of federalism. This principle establishes that matters which are primarily territorial or local should be controlled at these levels, while matters which are primarily national should be controlled federally. Where a matter has both a territorial and a national aspect, jurisdiction should be shared.

By its very nature, the federalism principle is flexible. It allows the federal government to share some of its powers through mechanisms such as delegation and joint decision making. This flexibility is especially useful where the national interest is concerned.

The federal government decided in November that retaining federal ownership and control over non-renewable resources was in the national interest. However, there are aspects of resource development, particularly in the environmental and socio-economic areas, which must be dealt with, at least in part, locally.

Joint decision-making might apply to some aspects of resource development. There are already precedents to be found for such an approach. The federal government, the government of the Northwest Territories and the native organizations have recently negotiated a set of principles that will govern the land-use planning process.

These principles call for a northern process of consultation and decision-making in conjunction with the federal government. The principles that have been agreed to will ensure that the planning process is sensitive to, and consistent with, the full range of northern interests and objectives.

The second principle is that constitutional developments in the North should be consistent with the national Constitution. Our Constitution sets out clear areas of federal and provincial responsibility. Constitutional proposals should take into account the division of powers that is already in place. The *Constitution Act, 1982*, also provides protection for individual rights in the *Charter of Rights and Freedoms*. Northern constitutional proposals must be consistent with the rights guaranteed in the *Charter*.

The third principle that I wish to discuss is the importance of protection of the rights of aboriginal peoples in the North. While land claims agreements and the entrenchment of aboriginal rights in the *Constitution Act, 1982*, will provide a significant protection to aboriginal peoples, consideration might also be given to other measures that will protect and enhance aboriginal rights and culture. For example, a reasonable residency requirement, that is consistent with constitutional standards, might be one way of approaching this concern.

The fourth principle is a practical one relating to the size and cost of northern government. There should not be too much government in the North. The goals of responsive and accountable government are not necessarily advanced by increasing the size, complexity and levels of government. Northerners should also keep an eye on the cost of implementing their proposals for constitutional change. There are substantial costs associated with the choice of a boundary, implementation of division and constitutional development which will have to be assumed by both the federal and territorial governments.

Conclusion

The federal government has ongoing national responsibilities in the political, social, environmental, cultural and economic areas. It must ensure that appropriate policies and standards are in place. However, having these responsibilities does not necessarily require continuing federal control. If northerners are able to maintain and develop these standards, then delegation or devolution of authority may be appropriate.

You and the people you represent certainly have equal responsibilities. You are the ones who can best work out the necessary balance of the unique aspirations and needs of all the people of the Northwest Territories. You are the ones who must communicate that understanding to the federal government and Canadians as a whole. And you are the ones we count on to negotiate with us in a spirit of flexibility and compromise that will let us all build a country we can pass with pride to future generations.

The contributions that you have already made to this process give me great faith in our ability to work together toward this goal. The complexities of the task ahead of us seem to me to be a small price to pay for the satisfaction we will all be able to take in the creative solutions we will find. We are making history together.

Reprinted with kind permission of the Department of Indian Affairs and Northern Development.

Building Nunavut

A working document with a proposal
for an Arctic Constitution
Nunavut Constitutional Forum
1983

Message to the Reader

This booklet is a unique invitation to you to join in the building of
Nunavut. As representatives of all the people of Nunavut, we have developed the proposals contained on the following pages for a constitution
for a Nunavut government. We want all our people to think about them
and discuss them, and then through community meetings, radio, TV and
newspaper discussions, and a constitutional assembly to meet later in 1983,
to approve the final form. Then we will take the work we have done
together and ask the Canadian government to make our new constitution a
formal law of Canada and help us create our new government.

Nunavut is "public government". That is, it is a government for all
the people who live in the area embraced by Nunavut whether they were
born in Igloolik or Trois Rivieres, Lloydminster or Yellowknife. Nunavut
is not a government only for Inuit, but a government firmly founded on the
Canadian political tradition of public services and the power of participation for all people who live in a geographical area.

A special feature of Nunavut is that land claims settlement acts will
form important parts of the total "constitution". These settlements—i.e.
the COPE and Nunavut claims now being negotiated—provide specific
guarantees for Inuit in respect of certain of their vital interests and are a
means of confirming economic and cultural rights inadequately recognised in law before now. (See the second and third paragraphs of the
chapter, Land, Resources and Environment, for further discussion of this.)
However, in terms of the overall government of Nunavut and the activities
carried out by provincial and territorial governments elsewhere in Canada,
these are strictly public and non-ethnic, open to Nunavut residents of all
languages and races.

On November 26, 1982, the Canadian government announced that it
agreed that Nunavut could be created. Several conditions were made at that
time, but in discussions since then we have been assured by Cabinet
ministers that there is considerable flexibility in Ottawa's position. We
think that in this booklet of proposals, plus any revisions agreed to over the
next months of discussion within Nunavut, the Canadian government will

find answers to the important questions of principle which must be the starting point of any work on Nunavut.

For the northern reader in Nunavut, this booklet sets out things he or she knows well and relates them to the structures and ideas of the Canadian political vocabulary.

For the southern reader, he or she will learn something about the problems and needs of Nunavut, and probably be surprised that we have so little power now to look after the ordinary matters of our lives.

For all readers we think you will see that we are making reasonable proposals which can be discussed in more detail when we sit down to write the Nunavut Act. We also think that there is enough detail that you will see the shape of what we want Nunavut to be. For the present we want agreement on that shape and those proposals; then we can do the further work needed to establish the government and administration of Nunavut.

A constitution is more than one or two documents. It may include many elements which are not in the Nunavut Act itself, and in the proposals which follow there are many questions which will have to be worked out and agreed to outside that Act. However, we are including all that we are because we think it important that everyone feel comfortable, and see the whole picture.

Nevertheless, some people may feel that there is not enough detail, or that things here are not concrete enough. That is the problem with constitutions. They do not put a seal in anyone's pot on Sunday, nor help bring medical services to people who are sick. They do not say how things are going to be, but rather who will be able to make things happen and what are the limits on their power to do so. Then the people we elect to a Nunavut legislative assembly will actually do the work. Throughout this booklet you will see that we want those people to be as free as possible to do things, and we try to avoid putting too many limits on them in advance.

There is no magic in a constitution, but there can be no power for the people of Nunavut without one. The sooner we agree on what we want, the sooner we can seek agreement with the government of Canada to create our Nunavut government. Then all these years of argument and frustration will be over, and we will be able to get on with the simple human right to run our own lives in our own way.

John Amagoalik
Peter Green
Agnes Semmler
Dennis Patterson
Kane Tologanak
Bob Kadlun

Designing Nunavut

An earlier publication of the Nunavut Constitutional Forum (NCF) outlined the history of the idea of Nunavut. To the people who live in southern Canada, Nunavut may be a new concept. But to those of us who live in Nunavut, geography, climate, history, language, culture, economics and the way we live have made us a natural region with a clear community of interests for as long as anyone can remember. Now the time has come for us to talk about how we can organise ourselves to look after important subjects in our lives by creating our own Nunavut government.

In Canada there are two main types of government. The federal government in Ottawa looks after certain subjects in all parts of Canada. These include old age pensions, the armed forces, relations with other countries, unemployment insurance, air transport, weather forecasting and icebreaking ships.

The other type of government is a provincial government, like the governments of Alberta or Quebec. These governments look after education, liquor administration, licenses for cars and trucks, regional and local government, lands and resources and many other things. The Government of the Northwest Territories is similar to a provincial government, but different. The NWT government does not yet have control of lands or resources, and is a government which can only decide things when Ottawa allows it to do so. In a province, the government can do what it wants according to its constitution, and if Ottawa tries to interfere the province can go to a court and stop it. Also, of course, Ottawa can go to court to stop provinces from doing things which are not allowed by the Constitution—for instance, a province would not be allowed to print its own dollar bills.

Each of the two governments—provincial and federal—has full power within its own list of powers. In other words, Canadians in southern Canada have two powerful votes: they can vote for the federal government, just as in Nunavut we elected Peter Ittinuar to look after our federal interest, and they can vote for a provincial government that has real power to do things. In the north, however, we do not have a provincial-type government with real power. Creating Nunavut is an important step for our people because through Nunavut we will at least have a government interested as its whole and only job in solving the problems of Nunavut. Also, the federal government is giving more power to the Northwest Territories every year and a Nunavut government would receive the same benefits.

The most important question to be decided before Nunavut becomes a reality is the division of powers between Ottawa and Nunavut. Drawing a line on a map and calling a new territory Nunavut has no meaning unless the people of Nunavut have enough powers to run their lives and to control important matters which affect them. These powers have to be suited to the needs of Nunavut and not just to the theories of political scientists in southern Canadian universities.

At the same time, Nunavut is and will remain part of Canada. Unless its powers and structures are clearly practical within the Canadian political system, it will not be possible for Nunavut to grow stronger and serve its peoples, or help them become fully involved in the opportunities of Canada. The people of Nunavut also have responsibilities within Canada, and they must take those responsibilities for the benefit of all Canadians. If the people of Nunavut allowed outsiders to destroy the environment of Nunavut, for instance, Canada would lose its international prestige as a responsible country, just as Inuit would lose their economic base. The people of Nunavut receive many benefits from living in Canada, and they give much to Canada in return. This proper balance between local and national interest is the heart of the Canadian political system, and we must ensure that it develops into a strong bond between partners in the relations of the Nunavut and Canadian governments.

Canadians have always let a few people in governments write their constitutions in the past. But the best constitutions are those which are written through a public process which allows everybody to take part and to understand what is being done. Only in that way can people really believe in the laws and governments which they live with. In 1980 Canadians began to take part in rewriting their national constitution, and the results have been worthwhile. But even that work is limited to a few subjects. Now in Nunavut we have the chance to write a whole constitution.

During the First Ministers Conference on the Constitution, March, 1983, Inuit presented a short paper on self-government. They listed various principles, and these may be worth restating here:

"1. the maximum Inuit design and management of public services which affect them, including participation in programs and policymaking which significantly affect their regions;
2. genuine political representation in provincial and territorial legislatures and the federal Parliament, and in official bodies which make decisions affecting Inuit;
3. recognition of the Inuit use and occupation of lands, waters and resources which are the underpinning of the Inuit economy and way of life, and the establishment of clear Inuit rights in respect of these so that Inuit may ensure their own collective survival;

4. access to adequate revenues to enable public bodies in the Inuit homeland to carry out their tasks;
5. access to an economic base for the future, and protection of existing economic resources (e.g. wildlife);
6. structures of government and other public institutions in the Inuit homeland which reflect and provide for the special needs and circumstances of Inuit and their culture, and with full protection for an inclusion of the rights and aspirations of non-Inuit residents in the area."

Many people at the conference were impressed with the reasonableness of these Inuit ideas, and they also read a small brochure describing the work of the Nunavut Constitutional Forum. The idea that Inuit should have a government which safeguards and reflects their culture and traditions does not upset southern Canadians, and the clear Inuit commitment to a pluralistic society in Nunavut is reassuring to those who talk about the danger of ethnically-based jurisdictions. Prime Minister Trudeau in his opening remarks at the First Ministers Conference talked largely about the problems and opportunities of native self-government in Canada, and much of the second day of the meeting was devoted to questions of self-government. The provincial governments began to warm up to the idea when they understood what was being proposed.

But Nunavut is not an ethnic government. It is public government within the Canadian tradition. Canadian federalism was designed to accommodate regional diversity, specific cultural traditions and the political rights of minority groups or regions. In Nunavut that philosophical federalism can reach its finest flower.

Boundaries

The questions of the boundaries of new territories in the north has become a controversial issue, though not in Nunavut. The Nunavut Constitutional Forum takes the view that the people and communities have the right to choose where they wish to live. The plebiscite of April 14, 1982, showed clearly where most communities wished to stand in relation to Nunavut. However, in the Western and Central Arctic there was some uncertainty revealed in the voting. The heads of organisations representing the Inuit of those areas, and an NWT cabinet minister elected in the Central Arctic, are members of the Nunavut Constitutional Forum and have fully participated in shaping its policies.

We take for granted that our proposals for a Nunavut government will be of interest to the people of Coppermine, Cambridge Bay, Holman Island, Sachs Harbour, Paulatuk, Tuktoyaktuk and Aklavik. That has been the basis of our planning.

We have, nevertheless, suggested a process for resolution of boundary questions. First of all, we would propose that the Inuit, Dene and Metis organisations meet to discuss the aboriginal land use element of a political boundary. We would, simultaneously, ask a researcher to prepare some materials on the boundary issue in the form of a report to the Constitutional Alliance which includes both the Western and Nunavut Constitutional Forums. This report would be discussed by the Alliance. With that report and this booklet as resource tools, we would propose that the communities where there is doubt about boundaries be given the opportunity to choose. Following the expression of those community choices, the Constitutional Alliance would meet again to deliberate on the exact location of a boundary.

If after that process agreement had not been reached, then the Nunavut Constitutional Forum would agree to appoint a boundary commission and to abide by its conclusions.

Preamble

Many constitutions and other important laws throughout the world have a preamble setting out the hopes and ideals behind the law. For instance, in Quebec some of the laws which give Inuit rights, powers and structures under the James Bay and Northern Quebec Agreement have a preamble first to explain that the survival of Inuit society is the goal. In some countries like the United States, a constitutional preamble is an important statement of what the people believe, learned by schoolchildren and recited at public ceremonies.

Nunavut will not only be a provincial-type government, but also the homeland of the distinct and ancient Inuit culture. It has a special role in protecting the heritage of all Inuit because it will be a government with the powers and resources to do so. To remind people, both the people of Nunavut and the people of all Canada, of this special fact, and in order to reach them and share with them these traditional values, a preamble to the Nunavut constitution may be helpful.

The international Inuit elders conference taking place in Frobisher Bay in July 1983, as part of the Inuit Circumpolar Conference will be an unprecedented opportunity to consult with wise and respected leaders from many Inuit regions on what might be included in a preamble.

It is recommended that during the summer of 1983 an Inuktitut preamble with English and French translations be prepared by an Inuk language specialist, in consultation with respected persons from the regions of Nunavut, for discussion and adoption at the Nunavut Constitutional Convention.

The Division of Powers

Canadian federalism has experienced a much more flexible division of powers than is often recognised. All senior students may know of sections 91 and 92 of the national constitution with their lists of federal and provincial powers. But the actual distribution of powers is more complex. What is more, arrangements have varied as different parts of what is now Canada have entered Confederation. The last entrant, Newfoundland, had remarkably different arrangements in respect of aboriginal peoples, for instance, than any other part of the country. At the time of becoming provinces, some areas did so with particular arrangements, such as the building of a railroad.

The Nunavut Constitutional Forum has adopted a flexible approach for several reasons. Rather than try to obtain clear and specific legislative authority in all matters, it has seemed more useful in some areas to consider ways in which Nunavut can develop expertise and share authority with federal authorities. The fact that there are no clear guidelines for the territorial form of government in Canada has also argued for a use of shared powers. At the same time, there is clearly a minimum "critical mass" of powers below which Nunavut is no more than a legal fiction like the old District of Franklin. It is essential that the government and people of Nunavut acquire enough powers and responsibilities through the various forms of agreement, devolved authorities, administrative delegations, etc. that political participation for Nunavut residents is meaningful and not simply a public relations deception.

We believe that by entering into serious discussion with the federal government on the basis that *political development* rather than *administrative reorganisation* is the key to the Nunavut project, the proposals contained in this discussion paper will satisfy the need of Nunavut at this time.

Fiscal Relations

There is no more fundamental test of political development than the ability of the authorities created to determine their spending and raise their revenues. This subject is discussed elsewhere in this paper (notably under Lands, Resources and Environment; Offshore; and Social Policy). The principles that the Nunavut authorities have access to revenues, have choices to make regarding the trade-offs between, say, a development project and the hospital its taxes might buy, and have to account to their electors, are essential. It is on this general subject that the Drury report is particularly helpful, bringing as it does the experience of a long-time senior official, Parliamentarian and Treasury Board president to bear on the problem of finance and political responsibility.

In the background study paper, *Nunavut Financial Perspectives*, by S.M. Malone, the Nunavut Constitutional Forum has a detailed discussion of the various considerations involved in financing a Nunavut government. It is not our purpose to repeat complex and technical arguments here. The principles, however, are important. These are that Nunavut residents, like other Canadians, should have both opportunities and responsibilities, and should be involved as quickly as possible in the general processes of Canadian public finance. We welcome the announcement of the federal government on November 26, 1982, that block funding for territorial governments will be adopted; this is a most important step in extending real responsibility to the north.

Nunavut Bill of Rights

Most modern constitutions include charters or bills of rights for the protection of all persons permanently or temporarily resident within their borders. Provincial and federal governments in Canada have recently provided such protections, and the new Canadian constitution includes a Charter of Rights. In proposing a Nunavut government, Inuit have always stated clearly that strong guarantees for the rights of the non-Inuit minority would be provided. A bill of rights entrenched in the Nunavut constitution would be the most forceful and visible way to meet that commitment.

Much experience in Canada and other countries with the protection of human rights has been gained in recent years. The relatively new area of provisions protecting the equal status of women, for instance, is one which has been strongly supported by Inuit in the revision of Canada's constitution. Some areas such as language rights are proposed for special protection in other sections of the Nunavut constitution. Because we are writing a new constitution now, the people of Nunavut have an opportunity to provide the most up-to-date bill of rights in Canada.

In Nunavut, the existence of a unique but unwritten code of Inuit customary law requires particular protection, and is further dealt with in the section of this discussion paper relating to the administration of justice.

The Nunavut Constitutional Forum is preparing a paper which will contain a proposed bill of rights. This will be published and circulated for discussion in the Nunavut communities as soon as possible.

It is recommended that a Nunavut bill of rights be entrenched in the Nunavut constitution with the power to take precedence over any other legislation unless a specific Nunavut law provides an exception, and to include rights in the categories of fundamental rights and freedoms, legal rights, social and economic rights, political rights and cultural rights.

Structures and Symbols

The particular forms by which the Nunavut government will be known—its flag, coat of arms, etc.—and the manner of organising itself should be decided by the Nunavut assembly when it has been elected and first meets. For instance, the assembly may prefer to call itself by a name other than Legislative Assembly—perhaps a name like Tungavik. It would be a mistake to try and make these decisions in advance.

However, certain matters must be decided in advance. A first question may be the role of the Commissioner. The Commissioner as representative of the Government of Canada will play a very special role in the creation of Nunavut. He or she will organise the new Nunavut administration and have strong powers to direct the staff and programs during the first months and years of the Nunavut government. This is essential because the people of Nunavut must have continued government services through the change of administration. But equally, it is important that a strong personality not centralise so much power in the Commissioner's office that it becomes the centre of authority in Nunavut and stands in the way of the elected Nunavut politicians.

The Working Groups

Therefore, *it is recommended that the Commissioner of Nunavut be chosen in consultation with the first elected Nunavut "MLAs" and before the first session of the Nunavut legislative assembly, and that the Commissioner's instructions from the Government of Canada contain clear guidelines for the performance of duties consonant with the maximum self-government of Nunavut vesting the elected assembly of Nunavut.*

Whether or not the Nunavut constitution should specify the system of cabinet government or remain silent as in other Canadian constitutions should be discussed at the Nunavut Constitutional Convention. However, it seems clear that the role of the Commissioner should not be written into the Nunavut constitution with more powers than would be the case of a provincial Lieutenant-Governor.

The other main question which must be resolved for a Nunavut constitution is the size and composition of the Nunavut elected assembly. An assembly of twenty-five (25) members would provide enough politicians to handle the various committees of the assembly and, most important, would give the people of Nunavut from the beginning a close relationship to their representatives. One of the main arguments for Nunavut has been the need for responsive politics. In the first years of a Nunavut government the elected members will have, in addition to their normal duties, a unique role in shaping Nunavut structures in close consultation with the people.

It is recommended that the first Nunavut assembly consist of 25 elected members.

Nunavut is a diverse area where Inuit peoples have made historical adaptations to particular circumstances, albeit within the larger framework of a common culture and environment. It is important that a regional balance be maintained in the political structure, and four regions—the Beaufort Sea (western arctic), Kitikmeot (central arctic), Keewatin and Baffin—have developed their own organisations and administrations.

At the same time, fairness requires that significant population growth in one or other area be reflected in political representation.

It is recommended that the first Nunavut assembly consist of four members from each of the four Nunavut regions, with the further nine seats allocated on the basis of population, and that this formula be the basis for future expansion of the assembly, i.e., preserving a basic equivalence in representation among the four regions.

A further question about political representation must be considered. There are many precedents in Canadian provinces and the national Parliament for the representation needs of rural areas and special regions. The

Belcher Islands in Hudson Bay, though part of the Baffin region, have unique conditions by virtue of location and culture and should be guaranteed a seat in any Nunavut assembly. The smaller communities of Nunavut are those in which the Inuit traditions and culture are strongest, and it may be that in accordance with Canadian and many international precedents, these communities should have relatively stronger representation than new and rapidly growing centres. This is a complex question and will become more so with resources development which may create new and large communities.

It is recommended that the first Nunavut assembly establish a committee to study the balance between the political representation of large and smaller communities, and recommend further provision for the Nunavut constitution to elaborate the electoral representation formula within the overall guidelines set out above.

A particular problem in Nunavut, and in the north generally, is the tremendously large proportion of the population which is transient or short-term. There may be implications for voter eligibility legislation arising from the new constitutional Charter of Rights, although a precedent which the Nunavut Constitutional Forum endorses is that of a three-year residency requirement for voting. (This three-year measure was used in the plebiscite in the NWT on division—the Nunavut issue—in 1982.) After considerable discussion, we have agreed that *the question of residency requirements for voting raise legal and political questions of concern to all northerners and therefore the Western Constitutional Forum and the Nunavut Constitutional Forum should undertake a joint study of this matter in order to bring a firm recommendation to the Nunavut constitutional convention.*

On other issues it was agreed that the usual Canadian practices should be followed, i.e.:

— *that there should be a Public Service Commission for Nunavut;*
— *that there should be a Nunavut auditing function of the usual Auditor-General type;*
— *that the executive committee or cabinet of Nunavut should contain a maximum of seven members, and be responsible to the legislative assembly;*
— *that the Nunavut constitutional act should instruct the Nunavut legislative assembly to adopt conflict of interest legislation for its members;*
— *that the Commissioner be instructed in his terms of reference from the Government of Canada to accept the advice of the Nunavut executive committee;*
— *and that an independent judiciary be established in Nunavut.*

Language

Language is the essence of culture. The Inuit majority in Nunavut has long suffered for the fact that government administration has been inaccessible to them because it is conducted in English and French. The Inuit language, Inuktitut, is a strong and rich language whose development has been actively encouraged in recent years by both territorial and federal governments in Canada. As the language used by Inuit in their daily lives, and one increasingly attuned to northern administrative and political forms, Inuktitut must be fully protected and enhanced by the Nunavut constitution. Perhaps there is no more fundamental goal of a Nunavut government, nor one more essential to guarantee the survival and unique contribution of Inuit in Canada.

At the same time, official status for Inuktitut will hasten the full participation by Inuit in employment opportunities in Nunavut. Within the administration, the use of Inuktitut will testify to the unique cultural nature of Nunavut and will encourage other residents of Nunavut to learn the language of the majority and thereby contribute to more harmonious race relations. Something of a red herring was recently introduced by a Toronto newspaper report in which the capacity of Inuktitut as a language of public affairs was questioned. Both the expertise of Canadian Inuit working in the language field and the experience of Greenland where Inuktitut is the main language of government and daily life assert that Inuktitut, like any other language, can perform the tasks which confront its speakers.

Equally, Inuit as a language minority in Canada are sensitive to the important steps taken by the Canadian government in recent times to secure the rights of French-speaking Canadians. Inuit want no second-class citizens in Nunavut, least of all those who are hindered in their participation in society by virtue of culture and ethnic background.

Accordingly, *it is recommended that Inuktitut be an official language of Nunavut and that all public services be available in Inuktitut, and that public bodies including courts and the legislature operate in Inuktitut as freely as in English;*

that French and English enjoy equal status as official Nunavut languages wherever numbers of one or other national official language group warrants, including as a language of education;

that Inuktitut be a language of instruction in the Nunavut schools at all levels as soon as practicable;

that the first Nunavut assembly appoint a Commissioner of Nunavut Languages to recommend and report regularly to the Nunavut assembly on implementation of the above provisions;

that Inuktitut versions of all Nunavut laws be published and have full official status;
and that all the above provisions be written into the Nunavut constitution.

Culture

Culture and its preservation is of particular interest to minorities. After all, a majority can securely assume that its values will be reflected in public decisions and structures. Although Inuit are a majority in Nunavut, they, like Quebecois, are a minority in a country dominated by another culture.

It has seemed to the Nunavut Constitutional Forum most useful to deal with culture under particular headings such as language, education, communications, cultural property, science and research and the administration of justice. The various cultural institutions and organisations in Nunavut, many of them already supported and encouraged by federal and territorial governments, will presumably be of special interest to the Nunavut legislative assembly which may likely wish to develop special relationships with them.

Communications

The long-standing problem of communications in Canada's north has taken a startling turn in recent years. Despite great distances, limited transportation modes and difficult climate, Inuit organisations in cooperation with the federal and NWT governments have opened up whole new approaches to communication. Most dramatic of these have been the development of Inuit broadcasting services, in both television and radio, at network and community levels. More quiet but nonetheless vital efforts have included the development of interpreter and translation systems, means of distributing news of government decisions and various efforts to develop the print media.

However, it is the telecommunications field in which Inuit have developed some particularly new approaches. Indeed, foreign countries have begun to take an interest in this developmental work and the opportunities of the export of Canadian Inuit expertise, technology and methodology are growing. The early days of federal government satellite interest saw many Ottawa officials talking of the potential for the north, and that day has dawned quickly. Many problems remain, but there are few fields more active in joint Inuit–government cooperation.

These developments are, of course, much more than technical and organisational. They have to do with the role of communications in situations where economic underdevelopment, social uncertainty and cultural retention are important issues. Communications is a tool for the social, economic and political development of a society. There has been much interest shown by international aid and development authorities in pioneer work of the Inuit Broadcasting Corporation and its applications in foreign Third World contexts. Politically, too, the broadcast media have enabled Inuit scattered in small villages distant from capitals to follow and participate in the Canadian constitutional debates with a sophistication and effectiveness which has startled southern governments.

Nevertheless, the present Inuit communications system though quite unique is still in a developmental stage. There is a very special relationship between Inuit groups and the federal communications authorities and agencies. Equally, the federal–provincial discussions of communications remain in a state of some uncertainty. Therefore, *it is recommended that the Nunavut Constitutional Forum cooperate with the Inuit Broadcasting Corporation to develop with the federal government a plan for the good order and strengthening of communications in Nunavut, both in relation to broadcasting and other telecommunications questions, and that any powers needed for a Nunavut constitution be identified before the holding of the Nunavut constitutional convention.*

Cultural Property

The protection of cultural property such as archeological sites and artifacts has been discussed to some extent in Inuit land claims negotiations. The role of a Nunavut government may require further discussion for that reason. Also, it may be that existing bodies such as the Inuit Cultural Institute and regional Inuit organisations already experienced in this subject should develop a specific relationship with the Nunavut government with respect to the protection and preservation of cultural property.

A particular concern must be the removal from Nunavut of cultural property, especially art and artifacts. As the custodian of a particular culture, that of Inuit, the Nunavut government bears a special responsibility in this matter. There are many precedents for management of cultural property around the world, and like Egypt, the Inuit homeland feeds a considerable collection of study centres and museums in Canada and abroad. The interests of all parties would be best served by a predictable and efficient management regime.

It is recommended that the Nunavut constitution be equipped with powers to safeguard cultural property to the fullest possible extent.

Education

Along with language guarantees, education is the key to cultural survival. As such, the education system must be a particular item for attention in a Nunavut constitution. The recent report on education in the Northwest Territories was developed in large part by elected Nunavut members and the recommendations in that report should provide a basis for action in Nunavut.

It is recommended that the reforming work in education led by Nunavut members of the NWT Legislative Assembly be consolidated for the benefit of Nunavut with the requisite powers specified in a Nunavut constitution, and that specific attention be given to the authority under which new and unique institutions of higher education would be established.

Science and Research

The arctic has been the scene of many types of research for a long time. The extent to which research is a major activity in the north has been the subject of many northern jokes. But too often research has been conducted with little regard for the needs and sensitivities of the people of Nunavut. Often this work has had little or no direct benefit to the people, and has not had its results communicated to them. Meanwhile, it has been used and been seen to be used by interests at odds with the values of Nunavut residents. This is not a new problem and, indeed, it has been given much thought by a minority of federal and academic scientists and researchers dedicated to the arctic. The time has come to build on the lessons learned and to facilitate a set of standards and procedures conducive to the needs of all parties.

Clearly a great deal of research done in the arctic is of value to the people of Nunavut, to all Canadians and to the world community in general. For that reason it deserves public monitoring and support. It should also be conducted under conditions which provide the maximum benefits for Nunavut. Such benefits may be economic, employment or educational.

It is therefore recommended that the Nunavut constitution specify the powers needed by a Nunavut administration to play as strong a role as possible in the design, management and communication of research in Nunavut.

Western Arctic Regional Municipality (WARM)

The Western Arctic Regional Municipality (WARM) is a structure long sought by the Inuvialuit of the Mackenzie Delta and Beaufort Sea areas. The unique needs of the region, both cultural and in terms of the fast-moving hydrocarbon development both on- and off-shore, have led the Inuvialuit to a considerable political development process in their region. This has included community consultations, negotiations with the federal government in respect of land claims and the drafting of specific plans in cooperation with the NWT government, all serving to elaborate the WARM concept of public government.

Inuvialuit have made clear that for them the coming of Nunavut includes the establishment of WARM from Day One. This concept and the reasons for it were welcomed by the Nunavut Constitutional Forum at a meeting in Tuktoyaktuk in January, 1983.

Recommendations

1. *That the Nunavut constitution provide for and entrench the Western Arctic Regional Municipality (WARM).*
2. *Flowing from the work of Inuvialuit over many years, that WARM be delegated primary responsibility in their region for:*
   — *education;*
   — *policing;*
   — *health services;*
   — *economic development;*
   — *wildlife management;*
   — *representation of regional interests within Nunavut;*
   or other responsibilities which may be delegated by the Nunavut or federal governments to WARM.

This does not necessarily imply that a WARM administration would create its own education services in all areas, for instance, but only that the development of regional programs would be decided upon at the regional level. Programs might be purchased from the Nunavut administration, or varied, or developed uniquely as in the matter, say, of the teaching of Inuvialuktun, the regional dialect of Inuktitut. The essence of the proposal as developed in the western arctic region is that in certain subject matters, the locus of choice and authority rest within communities and regions in order that the first line of defense in dealing with the social impacts of massive Beaufort Sea development be most responsive.

Regional Government

The regions other than the Delta/Beaufort Sea region may not wish at this time to commit themselves to a regional government structure. Indeed, the Nunavut proposal of 1979 envisioned that regional government might await some years of study before enactment. Important principles of "top down" vs. "grass roots" approaches require much discussion. The experience and future of the Regional Councils must be considered fully in this context. It would be simpler to create a Nunavut government and then work out the forms which local and regional governments might take, for which reason the Nunavut Constitutional Forum proposes to make no detailed recommendations on the subject at this time.

Administration of Justice

The administration of justice in Canada is a responsibility shared by different levels of government. For instance, criminal justice is a federal responsibility while family law would become a Nunavut responsibility. It is important that an administrative framework for justice matters be developed with due regard to the cultural traditions and needs of the Nunavut people as has been begun by leading figures like Judge Sissons and Judge Morrow in the Northwest Territories over many years.

Inuit turn to the formal justice system much less often than other people, preferring their own traditional methods of working out disputes within their social system. Many constitutions around the world recognize customary law and it is proposed that Nunavut should also. Much work needs to be done on this subject and the Nunavut Constitutional Forum has arranged for a study to be done on the various questions involved. For instance, key questions relate to the relative jurisdiction of customary law, methods of interpretation as well as entrenched specific provisions. Questions like the recognition of Inuit adoptions have long posed unnecessary hardship for Inuit faced with the general Canadian legal system and clearly a Nunavut constitution must accommodate the needs of the people of Nunavut.

There are many complex issues which may require considerable discussion such as the codification and administration of Inuit customary law; alternative court systems such as aboriginal courts, family courts, etc.; methods for the resolution of disputes through alternative means; the possible role of quasi-judicial or administrative tribunals; and the process of appointing judges and other officials. As well, policing and diversion programs, social and legal counselling and all manner of rehabilitation programs must be provided for.

The implications of national constitutional amendments affecting aboriginal rights must also be provided for, even though these rights are only beginning to be defined through national negotiations. This along with the Inuit customary law issue, raises many questions about the required preparation of the Nunavut courts and legal profession.

Although these are very difficult and, to some extent, speculative questions, provision must now be made at least on an interim basis for their resolution. Therefore, *it is recommended that the Nunavut Constitutional Forum continue to study the application of Inuit customary law in Nunavut, propose specific provisions for a Nunavut constitution and, with the results of that work, plan further for the overall administration of justice within Nunavut.*

Lands, Resources and Environment

The subject of lands, resources and the environment, including the marine environment (see separate section on Offshore) is the most likely to be disputed by northern residents and southern governments in any discussion of a division of powers. But the basic principles are simple and clear enough, so it may be useful to begin by considering them.

The first fact which the predominantly Inuit population of Nunavut would wish to point out is that when Canada was settled, in the south, the Europeans brought with them from overseas land and resource ownership and management concepts and applied them. This provided a basis for the orderly development of the settlers' economy and society, but simply left out the aboriginal people. For that reason the Canadian society is now engaged in a painful rethinking of official policies through the national constitutional discussions between aboriginal peoples and governments.

In the arctic or Nunavut area the situation was somewhat different. There was little settlement, and hence little need for the settlers to apply their familiar ideas from Europe or southern Canada. But at the same time, the fact that Inuit had been using the lands and waters for as long as memory was ignored. Today there is the bizarre situation where Inuit through land claims talks are "proving" that they are who they say they are and live where they say they live and, therefore, have some stake in the lands and resources they have always used and occupied. The normalisation of Inuit rights to lands and resources is clearly a first obligation of any government in Nunavut or any area where Inuit live. This fact, happily, has gained some recognition in the revised Canadian constitution, and Nunavut will be glad to lead the way. Therefore, *any land and resources policies in Nunavut must defer to the prior rights recognized through land claims settlements negotiated by Inuit, whether those settlements are reached before or after the establishment of a Nunavut government. At the same time, other interests which may have been acquired by third parties must be protected.* Inuit, having had their rights overlooked by others in the past, have no desire to cast any doubt upon the legitimate interests acquired by others in the region.

Secondly, the lands and resources of the northern territories are, for some purposes, called Canada Lands by the federal government. They are, for these purposes, considered to be equivalent to the offshore seabed in the Atlantic or Pacific Oceans. Of course the people of the provinces adjacent to those offshore lands are considered to have significant rights to their benefits and development, and the federal government is now working out agreements to that end. But in the north there are no agreements in progress, and the people who live on top of lands they have known for many centuries, and who use waters to feed their families as they have for as long as anyone knows, are forgotten. This situation is clearly not satisfactory, let alone logical or just. Therefore, *the interest of the people of Nunavut in the lands and waters which are their environment and their economic base must be recognised in any regimes established for the management and use of those lands and waters, and the right of the people of Nunavut to participate in relevant decisions and benefits.*

Thirdly, Inuit have always had a belief in use and sharing of resources, rather than in exclusive individual ownership. The laws and public policies of Canada are based on European land ownership concepts and so Inuit must have as much protection as other Canadians. But common sense as well as tradition dictates that in the arctic environment of Nunavut collective interest should be acknowledged and that planning for various uses should be a fundamental part of any land and resources regimes. The people of Nunavut are ready to share with all Canadians, provided that such sharing is subject to agreed upon principles and formulae. Sometimes it is said that joint planning is just a new way of taking something that belongs to someone else. However, the people of Nunavut recognise that all over Canada and the world the sensitivity to resources and the renewable environment squandered in the race for industrialisation has led to a new desire to conserve and to take more care for the future. There is no principle upon which Inuit as a society founded on an ancient renewable resource economy could be more in agreement. Therefore, *it is recognised that a legitimate inter-dependence on interests between Nunavut and national and international society expressed through the Government of Canada exists in respect of lands and resources, and that cooperative planning and accommodation of each other's interests is necessary.*

Fourthly, lands and resources are the main and almost the only major economic base for Nunavut. There can be no real political development in

Nunavut unless decisions respecting public revenues and public expenditures are related through the medium of accountable decision-makers. Simply put, a Nunavut without access to, and a stake in, lands and resources revenues would not only be crippled but continued conflict over development policies and projects would be ensured. After all, projects would entail costs but no visible benefits for the Nunavut authorities, with no incentive to adopt serious development policies. *A Nunavut government must share in lands and resources revenues as a fundamental element of political responsibility.*

These straightforward but essential principles can lead to a great many scenarios for a division of powers. The Nunavut Constitutional Forum believes that a particularly useful concept is that of "beneficial use and enjoyment", a term already used in legislation applied to the territories. This would provide the federal government with continued title to lands and resources until such time as that might be transferred as part of an eventual northern provincehood arrangement. But it would provide flexibility in developing agreements, sharing formulae, etc., by which Nunavut's government could work with Ottawa to provide sound and accepted northern development. The precedent for "Commissioner's Lands" is a useful one and lands and resources could be transferred to Nunavut as Commissioner's Lands subject to whatever exceptions might be required for federal purposes (including military bases, airports, parks, bird sanctuaries, coast guard facilities, etc.).

Two exceptions which are proposed by the Nunavut Constitutional Forum itself concern mining and oil and gas development. It is recommended that mining jurisdiction be transferred to Nunavut over a period of time, with the federal government acting as trustee in the interim while a Nunavut administration is prepared. It is essential that any such moves ensure continuity for the sake of industry confidence and planning, and that the ground be well prepared. The territorial government already has responsibility for mining safety, and the range of responsibilities would be widened.

With respect to oil and gas, it is proposed that the federal government continue to have control, but that an agreement such as that negotiated between Ottawa and Nova Scotia give Nunavut particular responsibilities, a share of revenues and equity participation options as now provided under the Canada Oil and Gas Act. Few Canadians would insist that the licensing and supervision of sports camps on northern lands seriously involve the national interest; on the other hand, the large operations and great potential revenue flow of hydrocarbon development are clearly of another order, with clear implications for all Canadians.

It is therefore recommended that Ottawa hold title for Nunavut lands and resources but extend beneficial use and enjoyment to a Nunavut government subject to whatever exceptions may be required;
that responsibility for minerals and mining be transferred over time to a Nunavut government with the federal government acting as trustee in the meantime; and
that oil and gas remain a federal responsibility but by federal–Nunavut agreement a Nunavut government accept certain responsibilities and share in revenues and other features now contemplated by the Canada Oil and Gas Act.

Offshore

Nunavut is a vast area with all but one or two communities located on seacoasts. Nunavut is a land of islands and straits, bays and fjords, where the life of the people is dominated by concerns with the living food species in the seas, navigation and marine transport and the threat of pollution from an advancing industrial and shipping technology. No other area of Canada is so totally dependent on and conditioned by the sea. But at present the people of Nunavut have no legislative or administrative means to protect their marine heritage, and no-one else has many either.

In Canada matters of the offshore are largely vested in the powers and administration of the federal government. Political and economic disputes are raging between the levels of government in southern Canada for control of offshore areas. But all governments agree that the people and regions affected by offshore development must have a strong voice in the management of these matters, and significant benefits from developments. The people of Nunavut must have a government which, on their behalf, can ensure that they have adequate protection from the hazards and impacts of offshore development, related employment opportunities, a revenue share from the offshore for the maintenance of their public services and a role in the management of the living species which are the mainstay of the traditional Nunavut economy.

At the same time, the people of Nunavut recognise that the reality of these questions is more important than the symbols of power. The federal government has expertise and services which Nunavut could not expect to develop for many years. Nunavut seeks a fair share in decision-making and benefits, but is not seeking outright control or ownership. The recent agreement between the federal government and the Province of Nova Scotia provides a workable basis for the sharing of responsibilities in offshore areas. Inuit and other Nunavut residents have too often had to resort to strong interventions against projects in regulatory board hearings in order to protect what few rights they have had. It is in everyone's interest that a suitable agreement between Nunavut and the federal government be achieved so that northern development can proceed on a sound basis without constant conflict.

The Nunavut Constitutional Forum is publishing a paper shortly on offshore questions because of their importance and complexity. But one important element of our proposal is that the concept of shore-fast ice zones, or "fast ice" as it is commonly known, be developed as a management and legal tool. Each year the shore-fast ice covers the Northwest Passage and forms along the arctic coasts. This zone is an extension of the land as far as Inuit are concerned, and they use it to travel (being usually smoother than overland movement), for camping and for the hunting of sea mammals on which they depend. In other words, the fast ice area is virtually synonymous with the Inuit use area. (It is also this area which is the main "impact zone" for development.) This may be an important consideration for legal argumentation by Canada of traditional use and occupancy of the arctic in international disputes.

It is recommended that a Nunavut government have particular powers in relation to the fast ice zone, its management, exploitation within it and benefits from its development, and that
a functional division of powers respecting the offshore be worked out with the federal government taking into consideration the marine nature of Nunavut, the revenue requirements of a Nunavut government, the dependence of Inuit on the arctic seas and the health of the marine environment, and the employment and economic benefits which could accrue to the people of Nunavut from offshore development.

Social Policy

Social policy is a matter familiar to all northern residents. As in Greenland, Inuit have received most governmental attention in relation to social programs be they medical or welfare assistance, educational and statistical experiments. However, it is not an easy subject for constitutional precedents because Canadian constitutions were written before social policy was a matter of public responsibility.

The whole Nunavut proposal is a social policy proposal. The medical staff of the federal government, over many years of observation and close attention to the needs of individuals in Nunavut, concluded that social problems were largely the root of health problems, and that the root of social problems was the powerlessness of the people. Canadian psychiatric journals have detailed the impacts of government "modernisation" policies on northern residents, for instance, and arrived at alarming conclusions. Danish doctors and social scientists have arrived at similar conclusions about Greenland and, indeed, this played no small part in the development of official Danish attitudes in favour of Greenland's political development.

Indeed, the main federal consideration for many years in favour of greater self-management and self-government by Canadian native peoples has been the failure of programs designed by outsiders and the persistent social problems experienced by native people.

Just as the regaining of control by Nunavut residents over decision-making in important areas of their lives is the key element of Nunavut "social policy", so may one expect that many programs will be adapted or totally changed to better meet the needs and cultural values of the people. Inuit differ from other Canadians in their sense of what is public business and what is properly dealt with through the traditional social order of extended families and other relationships, and have different notions of need and sharing. Much of this social structure is invisible to outsiders who, in most cases, have devised the social programs on southern models. Nevertheless, Inuit have always been quick to praise the pioneering work of the federal government in universal social programs like old age pensions and to give full credit for many other social policy initiatives over the years.

In recent years the apparently novel means by which communities like Igloolik have dealt with liquor regulation and television reception have been widely publicised in southern Canada. But on any such major community issues, it is not surprising that Inuit may find means unfamiliar to southern Canadians to deal with them. The Inuit residents of the arctic have been fighting a rearguard action against the adverse impacts of industrialisation and infrastructure development so rapid that it has threatened to upset their whole society. It is important that they have all possible means to deal with such matters.

As with so much else in Canada, the social policy situation is caught up in intergovernmental financing. In the arrangements to be worked out for the financing of Nunavut, a number of special factors must be taken into account. Certain social services are of very high cost—e.g. health services—and the needs of the population may be substantially greater per capita than in the south. Furthermore, some social policy areas such as housing must be a special public responsibility because of arctic economics, social needs, climate and high birth rate.

Nunavut has certain unique social characteristics in another way. The non-Inuit population is often transient. That is, southern workers and professionals spend short periods in the north, for the most part. This population, however, has public needs like all other people.

This problem of population influxes, movements and new communities is not to be taken lightly. The relative impact in the north is much greater than in the south because the proportion of transients is much greater. But even provinces like Newfoundland and British Columbia have struggled with special plans and measures to deal with offshore and Alaska pipeline projects although the dislocations are much smaller. Elsewhere in the circumpolar world, small populations of Europeans in Iceland and Shetland have defended societies similar to Nunavut, unique in both culture and renewable resource economies, by "quarantining" operations bases of outsiders. In Greenland a system of labour permits provides the government with an effective demographic policy tool. None of these societies wishes to see its fundamental character altered, nor its social fabric torn apart. Surely these are not unreasonable goals. The new constitutional Charter of Rights, however, makes the possibility of certain types of measures highly questionable. This area clearly needs more study and cooperation between northern territorial and federal governments.

A related but more positive requirement exists for good order in labour matters. And the fullest possible development of Nunavut manpower to fill the jobs which the north offers is a social imperative of the highest order, for reasons of social harmony and stability as much as of the needs of individuals.

It is recommended that a Nunavut government have all the powers in social policy of any Canadian provincial jurisdiction, with special and early attention to powers in respect of health services, housing, manpower, labour relations and social services;

that federal–Nunavut financing arrangements take into account the special costs associated with social program needs in the region;

that the Nunavut Constitutional Forum and the federal government explore ways in which the question of demographic policy and impact may be addressed in both a program and legal framework compatible with Inuit and Canadian values of fairness, and meanwhile that any development project approvals by the federal government include measures designed to protect the social and cultural character of existing Nunavut communities;

and that given the importance of the federal government as an employer in Nunavut, Ottawa join with Nunavut in manpower training and development efforts on an urgent basis.

Intergovernmental Relations

This is a very technical subject and one that is hard to explain easily. Most matters affecting a Nunavut government concern problems that the people of Nunavut experience in their daily lives. But intergovernmental relations concern how governments work together to solve problems which require the cooperation or money or powers of another government. For that reason, these are powers which are not so much seen by ordinary people as ones used by their governments to carry out the needs which the people have. If the people of Nunavut are to have the full benefits of Canadian life, they need a Nunavut government which can work for them to get the best possible benefits from the federal government in Ottawa, and in cooperation with other governments in the provinces.

Also, many big questions in Canada are solved by conferences of the federal and provincial and territorial governments. If the voice of the people of Nunavut is not heard in these meetings, decisions about the Canadian economy or social policy or the constitution or the money available to a Nunavut government from Ottawa for various programs like health care, decisions would be made without anyone in the south knowing about the problems of Nunavut. It is very important, therefore, that the government of Nunavut be able to take part in those meetings.

The problem is well expressed by Prime Minister Trudeau in his opening remarks to the First Ministers Conference on the Constitution, March, 1983. In establishing new governments, he says, there "will be the constant requirement to deal promptly and effectively with interactions among the various governments functioning within their respective spheres of jurisdiction".

A similar view was expressed in the Drury report, going further to suggest ways in which the federal government could accommodate a "government-to-government" relationship which would be consistent with the maturing of the territorial form of government. It has become clear in the development of the Nunavut proposals how vital this matter is. In any number of areas such as marine transport, search and rescue, etc., important questions for Nunavut communities were found to lie within federal jurisdiction. Indeed, the ability of Nunavut to function efficiently as a full part of Canada depends in a fundamental way on the ability of its government to deal with issues of importance to the population such as transportation and communications policies, and this can only be done through intergovernmental work. In many cases assistance could be provided to federal agencies and departments in the course of their work by a Nunavut government. But the existence of Nunavut would provide the opportunity for the people of Nunavut to work with the resources and conviction of a genuine arctic government to make their case in Ottawa. They would thereby participate more fully and effectively in the national life.

In the period during which Ottawa works with Nunavut to set up the new government, an important point should be kept in mind. Nunavut is a government, and in our political system the question of division of powers is central. It is important that in reviewing the accommodations and adjustments which would be made by federal agencies and departments for new governments in the north, the essential question is political balance and viability rather than the administrative traditions of one party to the discussions. The question of territorial relations with provincial governments has long been a thorny one for Ottawa, though in practice less so for provinces. While the federal government has a strict set of guidelines for territorial participation in intergovernmental activities, in fact the territorial governments have developed more relaxed conventions over many years and these are quite well accepted by provincial governments. These contacts have provided useful experience and information for territorial politicians and officials, and it may be argued that given the provincial type work of the territorial governments, this has been a valuable process of "growing up". What is more, the NWT government already participates in its own right in most federal–provincial meetings of ministers, with the notable exception of Ministers of Finance meetings. Given the attention of the nation to the socio-economic and other issues raised by aboriginal peoples, and the problems of rural and remote areas faced with large-scale resources development, territorial governments have a great deal of insight and experience to contribute to intergovernmental forums, a fact not lost on some participants at those meetings. The anomaly became most noticeable when the territorial governments had to be invited to the recent First Ministers Conference because their aboriginal populations, the majority of the NWT, were already seated at the table.

It would seem desirable to recognise the usefulness of intergovernmental contact as a learning tool for northern territories. The role of the federal Department of Indian and Northern Affairs has been a remarkable one, and having had those friends at court, especially so many of them with former experience working with the people of Nunavut, is something which everyone in Nunavut appreciates. But without suggesting that the role be altered, it does seem that the new Nunavut government should relate to federal departments and agencies on a government-to-government basis. Although such a revision is not usual, perhaps, in a constitutional document, its importance here may require a reference in the Nunavut constitution.

It is recommended that consideration be given to specifying in the Nunavut constitution the right of a Nunavut territorial government to conduct normal "government to government" working relations with federal, provincial and other territorial governments in Canada;
and that federal guidelines for territorial participation in federal-provincial meetings be brought up to date and recognise that growing self-government in northern Canada makes those limitations anomalous and inappropriate.

International Relations

International relations are one of the most important activities carried out by the government of a country. It is essential that in order to defend itself and promote its interests in the world, a country speak with a single voice on major issues. That is the job of the federal government and, in particular, the federal Department of External Affairs. Nevertheless, a country like Canada has great variety within its borders. The Canadian federal government has been imaginative in assisting various groups to represent themselves abroad, as well as using the special skills and resources they may have to serve the interests of all Canadians.

For instance, Canada has included Inuit in delegations to international conferences on whaling so that they could make sure that Inuit interests were considered, as well as to give the Canadian government representatives advice on technical matters which whale-hunters know best. Also, Inuit have represented Canada at United Nations organisation (e.g. UNESCO) meetings on northern peoples and their languages. As well, the Government of the Northwest Territories has sponsored many international exchanges, especially with the Inuit country of Greenland, in order for people of common culture and background to learn from each other's experience. There are many precedents for Inuit and for a new Nunavut government, in other words, to contribute to Canadian activities abroad and to carry on some international work related to their special interests.

Inuit were one people who now live in several countries whose borders were established only recently. Canadian Inuit wish to maintain contact with other Inuit just as English-speaking and French-speaking people live in more than one country and have such contact. English- and French-speaking people enjoy and are enriched by this contact without in the least wishing to change their citizenship or become part of one of those other countries. Inuit feel the same way. Already the Canadian government has provided assistance in fields like communication technology, language development and education so that Inuit could cooperate with other

Inuit. The importance of getting all the ideas possible for a Nunavut government from such contacts is obvious as we set about developing new language and school programs, and many community-based social and cultural programs to serve a largely Inuit population in Nunavut.

Through the work on the Canadian constitution, federal officials have begun to meet with Inuit to discuss how the Canadian government and Inuit can cooperate better on a wide range of issues such as international management of the arctic environment and its living species, arctic economic cooperation, travel and cultural exchanges. Inuit of Greenland, Alaska and Canada have formed the Inuit Circumpolar Conference (ICC) and this organisation is dedicated to bringing Inuit together to work on common problems. The federal government has been providing various forms of assistance to Canadian Inuit working with the ICC. But this work is new and there is much to be done. Clearly a government with the skills, organisation and resources which a Nunavut government will have should play a special role in such work.

There are broader considerations. Canadian Inuit, by virtue of their language and arctic environment, have a unique perspective on circumpolar affairs. This has been noted by distinguished writers on international relations at Queen's and Toronto universities, commentators who have suggested that Canada actively encourage and assist Inuit to work with other arctic countries like Greenland. They see that just as Canada has a growing need to strengthen its international circumpolar relationships, Inuit could perform a particular mission on behalf of all Canadians in this regard. The remarkably similar circumstances and shared perceptions of the small societies, both aboriginal and European-descended, in the North Atlantic area make Inuit an invaluable window for Canada on that increasingly important part of the world. The Canadian government would surely find another government, the Nunavut government, a particularly appropriate partner in such enterprises.

What is at issue, then, is not only the advantages Nunavut could gain from international contacts relating to its special cultural, social and geographic character. In addition, the people of Nunavut have much to offer the whole of Canada and could do so in an organised and effective way through their Nunavut government. A reference to Nunavut's ability to play such a role would be a useful addition to a Nunavut constitution.

It is recommended that the Nunavut government be recognised as having legitimate interests in various international matters and that a Nunavut constitution specify that in cooperation with the Government of Canada it may undertake such international activities as may be agreed from time to time with that Government.

A Capital for Nunavut

Few questions are likely to be debated as eagerly as the choice of a community for the capital of Nunavut. Many communities may wish to have the honour of being the Nunavut capital, while others may resist a mushroom growth. The federal government in its acceptance of Nunavut on November 26, 1982, specified the location of a capital as an important issue.

When the Northwest Territories capital of Yellowknife was chosen, the reasons were primarily practical ones of Yellowknife's large size and many facilities. A similar argument could make Frobisher Bay or Rankin Inlet the Nunavut capital. However, such a question would best be decided by the people of Nunavut. The administrative offices which Nunavut would take over from the present Northwest Territories government are widely scattered, and to develop any capital will take time for practical reasons. Phase-in times and the attention given to continuity of services will, in practice, reduce the importance of time and capacity factors, leaving cost and intangible issues as the crucial ones.

The NCF also debated the possibility of a small capital with a minimum amount of facilities and services, and with various departments/agencies located in several different Nunavut communities. This would have the advantage of not subjecting one community to tremendous growth with its attendant problems and at the same time providing the economic benefits of government employment to other communities. There may also be disadvantages in coordination, communication and planning from having staff spread over great distances. However, it is an option worth seriously considering.

Premature debate on a capital site would distract attention from the more important questions of a Nunavut constitution. For this reason, *it is recommended that the choice of a Nunavut capital be deferred for now and that the Nunavut constitutional convention propose a means of selecting the site as a final item on its agenda.*

Next Steps

Much work remains to be done. The precise definition of a Nunavut government's powers requires discussion at the political level with the federal government. In some cases active cooperation with Ottawa is needed to carry out Nunavut's proposed powers, and in others a fundamental understanding on a division of federal and Nunavut responsibilities. This will take time and it would be useful to begin clarifying the issues at once. The Nunavut Constitutional Forum has, in addition to its elected leaders, access to a considerable number of staff and advisers who can be drawn on for assistance in such work.

Also, there are the practical questions of the establishment of a new administration. That is the next major phase of the building of Nunavut and the NWT government has already begun working on that through other channels. The Legislative Assembly Special Committee on Division has prepared the ground in a detailed and thoughtful study of the practical physical requirements of the splitting of an existing administration. The Constitutional Alliance which joins the Nunavut Constitutional Forum with the Western Constitutional Forum has made its case on common issues in Ottawa. The public servants of the NWT government are to be thanked and congratulated for the way in which they have carried out the government's commitment to division and prepared the way, despite the obvious uncertainty it creates for their own immediate working environment.

Most importantly, of course, the next steps are in the hands of the people of Nunavut. It is their advice and response to this booklet—that is, of you and every reader—and their continued participation in the process of building Nunavut that will make or break this process of creation.

If you wish to make comments or seek further information, please write to:

Nunavut Constitutional Forum
The Honourable Dennis Patterson,
Associate Minister,
Aboriginal Rights and Constitutional Development,
Government of the N.W.T.,
Box 1320,
Yellowknife, N.W.T. X1A 2L9
or

Mr. John Amagoalik,
President,
Inuit Tapirisat of Canada,
Box 716,
Frobisher Bay, N.W.T. X0A 0H0
or

Mr. Peter Green,
President,
Committee for Original Peoples' Entitlement,
Box 2000,
Inuvik, N.W.T. X0E 0T0

Reprinted with kind permission of Nunavut Constitutional Forum.

Position Paper

Submission on a Non-renewable Resource Policy

Council for Yukon Indians
May 1983

Introduction

One of the few major outstanding matters yet to be resolved in land-claims negotiations is the future disposition, management, and beneficial use of non-renewable resources in the Yukon. It is widely recognized north of 60° that reserves of natural resources are the key to constitutional and economic development. All major northern organizations, native and non-native alike, aspire to securing some control over, and greater benefits from, resource developments as an essential prerequisite to financial autonomy and self-sufficiency.

The proposals as to how these objectives may best be achieved vary between groups. Some espouse royalties on revenue with some input in planning; others seek provincial status. The approach of the Council for Yukon Indians (CYI) differs from most in that we came to the clear realization that a resource agreement cannot be negotiated if it is in conflict with the legitimate interests of the federal and territorial governments, Yukoners, or the resource industry, all of whom have interests that must be respected. We have developed our own proposals in strict accordance with this belief.

Although we do not think that provincial status is the answer for the Yukon just now, we recognize the continuing need for private-sector industry, and, at the same time, we believe that Yukoners, both native and non-native, have interests that are not being met. Our proposals satisfy all of these factors.

At this point it is appropriate only to outline briefly the evolution of CYI's policies concerning non-renewable resources and related issues. Over the past decade, CYI opted for a strategy whereby a settlement of land claims would involve extremely large land selections (50 000 square miles [129 000 km²]) by the Yukon Indian people, title to all sub-surface resources on Indian lands, and a substantial royalty accruing to Yukon Indians from any resource development on non-Indian lands. The Yukon Indian people also sought significant participation in a proposed body that would manage development activities on non-Indian lands.

In the spring and summer of 1980, however, CYI decided that the foregoing position, if adhered to, would protract the negotiations considerably and, ultimately, might be unachievable. CYI decided, therefore, to modify the position by degree, rather than by direction, and thus reduced the magnitude of the proposed demands, although their basic nature remained unchanged. After having taken another hard look, CYI identified a number of fundamental problems that suggested there was a need to discard the resource proposals and to develop totally new policies. In essence, there were three basic flaws in the old proposals. First, they would have generated stiff, perhaps even irreconcilable, opposition from both industry and non-native Yukoners. Secondly, they did not reflect the existence of a strategically important national interest in Yukon resources. Finally, in so far as Indian sub-surface holdings might never be developed due to a lack of interest on the part of private industry and a lack of capital on the part of the Indian people, the proposals ultimately might not have been in the best interests of the Yukon Indian people.

Instead, CYI decided to develop new proposals based upon four principles that CYI considers absolutely essential: first, that the management and development of non-renewable resources impinges on almost every aspect of life in the Yukon, on the lives of individual Yukoners, and on the political, economic, and social structure of the territory, both now and in the future.

Secondly, existing arrangements for control of non-renewable resources and for revenue-sharing arrangements between Canada and the peoples of the Yukon are not structured in such a way as to promote the efficient, timely development of northern resources.

Thirdly, current arrangements must be modified substantially to offer Yukoners, including the Yukon Indian people, the real opportunity to participate in the management and development of the Yukon's non-renewable resources.

Finally, the Yukon's reserves of non-renewable resources are of strategic national significance by virtue of their variety, quantity, and quality, and their status as strategic national reserves clearly precludes the attainment in the Yukon of the type of rights and responsibilities enjoyed by the provinces with regard to resources.

In accordance with these principles, CYI designed, in the autumn of 1980, resource policies that have remained intact until today.

CYI's Resource Policy Proposal

CYI's resource policy contains two highly interdependent components, one addressing oil and gas, and one addressing minerals.

Oil and Gas

With respect to oil and gas, CYI recommends that the federal government negotiate with the Yukon an arrangement based upon the agreement signed by the governments of Canada and Nova Scotia on 2 March 1982. This agreement established the province's management and revenue-sharing role with respect to oil and gas activities in Canada's offshore adjacent to the Nova Scotian coast.

Using the Nova Scotian model and taking into account the unique social, political, and economic aspects of the Yukon Territory, CYI proposes an agreement that would include five features:

1. The Yukon, and the Yukon Indian people as a discrete group, would receive 100 per cent of all public revenues (except corporate income tax) from oil and gas production occurring both in the Yukon and in Canada's offshore adjacent to the Yukon coast.
2. The Yukon would continue to receive 100 per cent of the above revenues up to a point to be determined through negotiation. Upon reaching this level the revenues accruing to the Yukon would begin to decline gradually, and eventually to disappear, whereas the share accruing to Canada would increase correspondingly.
3. Native and non-native Yukoners would enjoy a preferential opportunity to purchase a portion of the federal "carried interest" in oil and gas development. The total amount available for purchase would equal 50 per cent of the carried interest in gas, and 25 per cent of the carried interest in oil.
4. Native and non-native Yukoners also would enjoy a preferential opportunity to purchase up to 50 per cent equity in any system for the transmission of oil or gas occupying a Yukon land corridor.
5. A management regime for oil and gas exploration and development activity would be established and structured in such a fashion as to allow for meaningful participation by Yukoners.

Mining

In the mining component of the resource policy, CYI recommends the creation of a corporate entity, which, with the assistance of certain restricted preferential rights, would be expected gradually to assume a major role in the Yukon mining industry. The Yukon Resources Corporation, as it is called, would have five salient features:

1. The corporation would enjoy a once-only right to purchase equity in all new mineral developments, i.e., those properties not in production at the time of the agreement in principle.
2. The time frame in which the corporation could exercise its right to acquire equity would be restricted and tied to the level of expenditures made on a given mineral property. For example, as was the case in Saskatchewan until recently, the corporation could be made either to exercise or to forego its option to buy in prior to the interest holder spending $10 000 on his property in any given year. This would not apply to small placer operations.
3. Although the maximum level of equity available for purchase by the corporation would be fixed through negotiations, CYI believes that the figure should be less than 50 per cent.
4. With respect to existing mineral operations and leased properties, the corporation would enjoy no special rights whatsoever.
5. The federal government would establish a development fund, which could be drawn upon by the corporation for the purchase of equity. The monies drawn from the fund would be repayable from Yukon Indian revenues generated by oil and gas production. The initial operations and management funds required for the operation of the corporation would come from the settlement of land claims.

Rationale

In reviewing and contemplating CYI's resource policy proposals, governments, industry, and the public should consider first that the oil and gas and mining components of the proposal are interdependent. The prospect of receiving oil and gas revenues in the future allows CYI to reduce considerably the special rights required to ensure the long-term viability of the mining corporation.

Secondly, the oil and gas component is not structured so as to exist in perpetuity. Instead, it is designed to provide Yukoners with a clearly finite flow of guaranteed revenues and the means to acquire, through purchase, a longer lasting flow of revenue.

Thirdly, the resource revenues accruing to the Yukon would be reinvested in the Yukon in community and infrastructure improvements, in new resource development opportunities, in manpower training, and in other social programmes. Thus, the revenues would be used to enhance, from the perspective of both the investor and resident, the quality of life in the Yukon.

Fourthly, while neither impairing nor jeopardizing the strategic national interest in northern resources, CYI proposals clearly would satisfy the major aspirations adhered to by both native and non-native Yukoners; for the objectives of the CYI proposals are that Yukoners should have a reasonable share of the revenues and some input on decisions respecting the nature and pace of development.

Finally, if accepted, the resource policy proposals would guarantee, to the extent possible, that the land-claims settlement would succeed, thus allowing the Yukon Indian people to sever their ties with the Department of Indian Affairs and Northern Development and enter the mainstream of Yukon society.

Regional Planning and Land-use Planning

Chairman: Alistair Crerar

Introduction

For many years southern Canadians have considered the hydrocarbons, minerals, wildlife, and waters of northern Canada to be national resources. Recently there has been much competition for the use of these resources. Conflicts have arisen not only between those who wish to develop non-renewable resources, but also between developers, hunters and trappers, a growing northern tourism industry, and others—including southern Canadians—who advocate resource conservation and protection of the environment. Most of these groups have recognized the need for a system of land-use planning to resolve these conflicts.

In July 1981 the federal Cabinet approved a northern land-use planning policy; in October 1982 the Department of Indian Affairs and Northern Development (DIAND) published a draft strategy to implement the policy. The two territorial governments, native organizations, and some industry groups rejected the proposed planning structures and processes because they gave too little control to northerners and left too much decision-making power with the federal government. When the Third National Workshop convened, representatives of the territorial and federal governments and native organizations were negotiating to increase northern representation on the proposed planning structures. Northerners were seeking to ensure that planning is conducted in the North with the primary aim of benefiting northerners.

Experience in southern Canada, Alaska, and other jurisdictions shows that the *process* of land-use planning is as important as the *product* if it is to direct and improve the manner in which land and resources are used. The chief tasks of the working group on regional planning and land-use planning were to identify the political and jurisdictional questions raised by the proposed land-use planning policy and to suggest how the process of planning can be co-ordinated with political and constitutional development and settlements of aboriginal land claims in the North.

177

The Working Groups

The working group included:

Chairman: **Alistair Crerar**
Environment Council of Alberta
Edmonton, Alberta

Rapporteur: **Maggie Jones**
Ryerson Polytechnical Institute
Toronto, Ontario

Invited Participants:

Shehla Anjum
North Slope Borough
Barrow, Alaska

Ed Caldwell
Esso Resources Canada Ltd.
Calgary, Alberta

Yvon Dubé
Northern Affairs Program
Department of Indian Affairs and Northern Development
Government of Canada
Ottawa, Ontario

Mary Jane Goulet
Dene Nation
Yellowknife, N.W.T.

A. Hodgson
Department of Renewable Resources
Government of the Yukon
Whitehorse, Yukon

Ron Livingston
Department of Renewable Resources
Government of the Northwest Territories
Yellowknife, N.W.T.

Andrew Macpherson
Department of the Environment
Government of Canada
Edmonton, Alberta

Jennifer Mauro
Mackenzie Delta Dene Regional Council
Whitehorse, Yukon

Bill Rees
School of Community and Regional Planning
University of British Columbia

Nigel Richardson
N.H. Richardson Consulting
Toronto, Ontario

Graham Smith
Department of Geography
Wilfrid Laurier University
Waterloo, Ontario

Lindsay Staples
Yukon Conservation Society
Whitehorse, Yukon

Dietmar Tramm
Council for Yukon Indians
Whitehorse, Yukon

Background documents used in the working group, in addition to those published in these proceedings, included:

Council for Yukon Indians. *Land Use Planning, Environmental Assessment and Land Ownership in Yukon: A Discussion Paper.* Whitehorse: CYI, August 1982.

DIAND. "Northern Land Use Planning," a Discussion Paper. July 1981.

DIAND. *Land Use Planning in Northern Canada,* draft. Ottawa: DIAND, 14 October 1982.

The Working Groups

Dubé, Yvon. "The Wonders and Pitfalls of Land Use Planning in the Northern Regions of Canada." Northern Affairs Program, DIAND, unpublished.

Government of the Yukon. *Land: A Yukon Resource, A Land Use Policy.* Whitehorse: Government of the Yukon, April 1982.

Land Planning Act (Bill No. 14). Legislative Assembly of the Yukon Territory, 2nd Session, 25th Legislature, 1982.

Working Group Report

Regional Planning and Land-use Planning

When the working group on regional planning and land-use planning met, negotiations on a strategy for implementing the federal government's northern land-use planning policy were underway between the federal and territorial governments. The working group, therefore, was a forum in which the various interest groups restated their positions on and frustrations with the progress of these negotiations.

The two territorial governments have different approaches to implementing the federal land-use planning policy for northern Canada. In the Northwest Territories the three major native organizations—the Tungavik Federation of Nunavut, the Métis Association of the Northwest Territories, and the Dene Nation—have agreed on a definition of land-use planning and on a set of eight principles to guide its implementation. A primary objective of the Government of the Northwest Territories is to share authority for decision making with the federal government.

The Yukon Territorial Government (YTG) is negotiating with the Department of Indian Affairs and Northern Development (DIAND) as an equal partner to develop a co-operative approach to land-use planning. A major goal of the YTG is provincial status through the transfer of resources, resource management, and land from federal to territorial jurisdiction. The division of responsibilities for land-use planning is, therefore, an important step toward achieving that goal.

The approaches of the two territorial governments differ also in the degree to which native northerners have been consulted and are to be included in the land-use planning process. The Yukon Territorial Government views the native peoples' role in planning as one that is subsidiary to the role of the federal and territorial governments. In the N.W.T. the native groups have been accepted as having an interest and a role equal to the territorial and federal governments. In neither case, however, are the native groups satisfied with the nature and extent of participation provided for in the planning process.

From the representatives of industry, the working group heard a plea for a simple process and structure for land-use planning that recognizes today's economic realities.

The role of the communities in the proposed planning process is not yet clearly defined because senior government officials have approached the process from the top downward. Government officials seem unwilling to define local roles and responsibilities and identify planning priorities. The lack of a clear role is causing concern in the communities, particularly in those anticipating development. The land-use planning process will be meaningless if the communities directly affected by the plans are not involved. Until now, participation in planning and development decisions by northerners has been to react to decisions made by others. The working group participants agreed that northern residents must have an active role in making planning decisions. The participants also agreed that land-claims settlements must take priority over the land-use planning exercise.

The Process

The *process* of planning is as important as, if not more important than, the final *product*—the land-use plan. The working group therefore chose to discuss the process and the decision-making structure.

The concept of, and the need for, land-use planning is supported by virtually all groups concerned with the North. The objectives of all levels of government, as well as those of local, regional, and national interests, can be served by land-use planning. The compatibility between these interests, however, does not extend beyond this agreement. Each interest group has a different interpretation of the planning process and of its own role and others' roles within this process. For example, all agree that public participation is an essential component of the planning process, but disagree on the point at which it should become part of the process. Their views differ also on whether the public is to play a responsible, decision-making role or merely an advisory role. Conflicts such as these were identified as the working group discussed a planning model that attempts to place each component of the planning process within a planning structure.

The working group used as a model the planning structure proposed by Rees (See Figure 1, p. 217, in William E. Rees, "Northern Land-use Planning: In Search of a Policy," pp. 199–233 in this volume). This structure was neither an ideal nor a product of consensus, but it provided an opportunity to identify the conflicts that will arise in attempting to satisfy the objectives of different groups in an actual planning exercise. In discussing the model, the participants attempted to reconcile the accepted need for local participation and endorsement with their desire for explicit policy direction from senior government officials. Without such direction, it will be difficult for all interests to participate in the planning process.

Conclusions and Recommendations

The experience and practice of planning can reduce the conflicts among competing interest groups. Experience and action, rather than more rhetoric, are needed.

One or more land-use planning pilot projects should be implemented immediately to provide a working situation in which different ways to resolve conflicts can be tested. These pilot projects should be monitored and reviewed carefully to identify the extent to which they can resolve conflicts and produce decisions and direction that will meet the objectives of local and other interests.

A single planning structure is not likely to be sufficiently flexible to work in all regions of the North.

Information collection and research are important to the land-use planning process, although they alone will not reduce conflicts. Each project will require new data and research, much of which will be generated during the planning process.

A large burden has been placed on land-use planning. The planning process is expected to facilitate constitutional reform and the transfer of land resources in the territories. It is perceived as a tool for preserving land for traditional pursuits and also for facilitating industrial development. As a result, land-use planning will be a complex task requiring much time, money, expertise, tolerance, patience, and goodwill.

Land Use Planning
Northwest Territories
Basis of Agreement

Draft Proposal
21 March 1983

Indian and Northern Affairs
Government of Canada
Department of Renewable Resources
Government of the Northwest Territories
Yellowknife, N.W.T.

1. Introduction

The need for land use planning in the North is unquestioned. Support to develop and implement a land use planning process has come from the Government of Canada, the Government of the Northwest Territories, the Native Organizations, the public, and special interest groups.

• The intent of this paper is to reach agreement and a common position on the part of all parties to cooperate, participate and implement a practical and effective system of land use planning.

• On February 16, 1983, the joint Federal–Territorial announcement confirmed that both Governments had reached agreement on principles, and a process for involving Native organizations and other participants. Both Governments are committed to land use planning, and seek the involvement of Native organizations in this process. It is intended that this will be a joint undertaking and a cooperative effort, involving public participation.

• This paper recognizes the interests, concerns, roles and responsibilities of the major parties that would be involved. It identifies primary considerations, defines what is meant by land use planning and land use plans, and briefly describes the system and process to achieve these results.

- The important role of the Government of the Northwest Territories is reflected throughout the process outlined. Its political and jurisdictional responsibilities, its special interests, and its concerns for representation and accountability to Northern residents, are fully respected.

- The rights, concerns, and aspirations of Native peoples are understood. Their agreement to participate in this process is sought: planning will not prejudice a fair and equitable settlement of land claims.

- Land use planning is a major initiative and an important tool in resource management. This offers a unique opportunity and challenge to work together towards implementing a successful land use planning program in the Northwest Territories.

2. Scope and Objectives

A common understanding of what is meant by land use planning, the scope, and what is intended under this particular program, is fundamental. This section, therefore, provides a definition for these purposes.

- Land use planning has, as its primary focus, land, land use and resources. It will concentrate on capability, use, and management of land resources. The purpose is to plan ahead and to anticipate, resolve and minimize competing demands or land use conflicts, to optimize allocation or best use of resource lands, and to ensure integrated management of resources. In so doing, social and economic factors and implications will receive attention, insofar as they relate to the focus of land use planning.

- Land use planning in the Northwest Territories would be based upon the current constitutional and legal authorities or allocation of responsibilities for land and resources.

- The interests of Native peoples and other Northern residents must be represented. Public participation and review are important elements of the land use process.

- Land use planning involves establishing a framework of goals, objectives and guidelines relating to land use, land disposition, and resource management, and serves as a frame of reference for decisions and activities affecting resource use. This would allow decisions to be made in an orderly, rational and open manner.

• Land use planning provides the spatial and temporal framework that guides land and other resource use activities within established policy guidelines. The products, or land use plans, are documents including statements of goals, objectives, policies and guidelines, with descriptive physical or geographic plans, relating to the use of land and resources. It serves as a vehicle for implementing, facilitating, coordinating and integrating the delivery of various programs. Both Governments, in keeping with respective mandates, would administer programs in harmony with the final plan to achieve the results intended.

• Special legislation for the land use planning process does not presently exist and is not essential to initiating the process at this time. The emerging nature and as yet undefined expression of the planning process makes consideration of effective legislation difficult. Once plans are approved, implementation and monitoring mechanisms will serve to ensure that compliance occurs.

3. Primary Considerations

Agreement, cooperation and participation are essential to successful land use planning. The planning system described, and the roles and responsibilities of government, are founded on due recognition of the current constitutional and legal allocation of authorities accorded each government but also flexible to allow transfer to proceed as constitutional evolution occurs.

The following considerations serve as the basis for agreement between the Federal Government and the Government of the Northwest Territories:

3.1 General:

• Land use planning goals and objectives will be determined by the Government of Canada and the Government of the Northwest Territories, with full involvement of Northern Native Organizations.

• Land use planning activity must be conducted and based in the North and is the responsibility of both Governments.

• Land use plans must be prepared through a procedure providing roles for government, Native people, and the public.

- Northern land use plans should be jointly approved by the Federal and Territorial Governments.

- The implementation of land use plans is the responsibility of all Governments involved.

- Land use planning should relate to other levels of planning, policies and programs in the North.

- Land use planning will be without prejudice to ongoing Land Claims negotiations.

- Land use planning will be directed toward the best use and management of resources.

3.2 Native Organizations:

- Native people have a special interest in land due to traditional occupancy and use, for historical, cultural and economic reasons.

- Native people will have both a role in forming and interpreting land use planning policy guidelines.

- Negotiations towards fair and just settlement of land claims are underway, and planning is not intended to interfere with this process.

- It is understood that the land use planning process implemented might have to be modified or superseded according to provisions of land claim settlements.

3.3 The Public:

- Public input and participation in land use planning is essential.

- Northern residents, industry, and special interest groups, will have formal and informal opportunities for public input and review.

4. Land Use Planning System

4.1 Overview:

• The Minister of the Department of Indian Affairs and Northern Development and the Minister of the Department of Renewable Resources, representing the Government of the Northwest Territories, will receive advice from a Joint Advisory Committee including Federal, Territorial and Native representation.

• This Committee will advise the Ministers on policies, priorities, planning, and related matters.

• An independent Commission, or Commissions, will be appointed.

• The Commission, or Commissions, will receive terms of reference from the Ministers, and will guide the planning process to ensure public participation and continuity.

• Interdisciplinary planning teams, under a Director of Planning, will prepare plans for the Commission(s).

• An Intergovernmental Committee will facilitate and support these planning efforts.

• The Minister of Indian and Northern Affairs and the Minister of Renewable Resources will receive the plan and recommendations from the Commission(s).

• Both Governments will jointly approve the plans, and these plans will be implemented according to their respective mandates.

• The system should be flexible and dynamic.

4.2 Political Authorities:

• The Minister of DIAND, on behalf of the Federal Cabinet, and the Minister of Renewable Resources (assigned responsibility for land use planning) on behalf of the Executive Committee, will jointly issue to a Commission(s) Terms of Reference, including a statement of policy, guidelines, goals and objectives as a basis for proceeding towards the establishment of a plan.

- Once the Commission(s) has completed its tasks, it will transmit the land use plan for a given area with recommendations to both Ministers.

- The Ministers will jointly discuss the proposed plan, in the context of public policy.

- Upon concluding discussions, the Minister of DIAND will seek Cabinet commitment and approval; the Minister of Renewable Resources will seek commitment and approval of Executive Committee.

- The joint commitment and approval sought is the collective determination to ensure that policies, guidelines and programs which fall under the respective jurisdictions of all the various Ministers, will conform with the goals, objectives and policy guidelines outlined in the Plan.

- Once approved, plans would be implemented on the basis of jurisdictional responsibility.

4.3 Advisory Committee:

The Advisory Committee will have a crucial role in advising both governments on the essential areas of policy, planning and priorities.

- The Advisory Committee will provide advice to the Minister of Indian and Northern Affairs and the Minister of Renewable Resources representing the Government of the Northwest Territories.

- Representation will include senior officials of major departments of the Federal and Territorial Governments with mandates in land, land use or resource management.

- Members will also include native representatives of the four major native groups.

- The Advisory Committee will include as Chairman, the Assistant Deputy Minister of the Northern Affairs Program of DIAND, and as Vice-Chairman, the Deputy Minister of Renewable Resources of the Northwest Territories.

- The Committee will provide advice on planning goals, objectives, policies, variables and priorities; Regional Planning Area Priorities; Terms of Reference for Commissions and planning areas, considering boundaries, general purpose and reason for the plan, goals, people to be served, primary clients, traditional users, and time frames; and related matters.

- It will review and analyse plans for consistency with policies, goals and objectives, and will provide recommendations.

- It will play an essential role in ensuring that plans are carried out or implemented, in an effective, timely and coordinated manner.

4.4 Land Use Planning Commissions:

The Land Use Planning Commissions are central to the land use planning process. They would be entrusted with responsibilities relating to plan development, ensuring public participation, providing recommendations on plans, and monitoring implementation.

- Options for consideration include the following:

  — a single Commission for the NWT with a standing body of seven or eight members;

  — a single Commission, with a core for consistency and continuity, but different native representatives, depending upon the planning area;

  — three separate Commissions, considering native interests and land claims areas;

  — other variations.

- A single Commission might consist of seven to eight members. The Chairman and members would be appointed by the Minister of Indian Affairs and Northern Development. Two members would be appointed on the advice of the Territorial Executive Committee, three or four on the advice of the Native Associations or Community, and two others appointed by the Minister of DIAND. (Public Servants would not be eligible.)

- It is suggested that one Commission be established initially, to deal with one priority area.

- The Commission will receive broad Terms of Reference from the Ministers for the planning area and preparation of the Plan.

- The Commission would refine and provide precise Terms of Reference for the planning study, overall direction, and guidance, and ensure appropriate public inputs.

- The Commission would receive the draft plan prepared by the planning team, analyse it, and provide recommendations for subsequent activities.

- Once the draft plan is acceptable, the Commission would sponsor public meetings or hearings to discuss, review and receive comments and recommendations, and will ensure that appropriate modifications are made.

- The Commission would transmit the plan and recommendations to both Ministers.

- The Commission would assist in monitoring plan implementation.

- The Commission would be involved again, if the need for changes arises, with respect to the plan or amendments.

- The Commission could also be used as a public review panel for projects which may not appear to conform to the plan.

4.5 Northern Director of Planning:

- A Northern Director of land use planning will be charged with the responsibility for the preparation of plans, under the direction of the Commission. Precise terms of reference and instructions will be provided by the Commission.

- The Director will act as a focal point and will fulfill crucial functions of *linkage* between the Commission, the Intergovernmental Committee, the Land Use Planning Office, and the planning teams.

- The Director will act as a planning advisor to the Commission and Chairman of the Intergovernmental Committee.

- The Director will be in charge of a Land Use Planning Office, with planning resources at his disposal.

4.6 NWT Intergovernmental Committee:

An Intergovernmental Committee will be established.

• The Director of Planning will chair this Committee and coordinate activities.

• This committee will be composed of senior officials with responsibilities for managing programs relating to land use planning.

• It would provide support and assistance to the Director of Planning, through coordinating related government activities; advising on planning requirements; identifying resourcing requirements; providing information and technical assistance; conducting special projects; and aiding in plan implementation and monitoring; etc.

4.7 Land Use Planning Office:

• A small Land Use Planning Office will be established in Yellowknife by DIAND, including a staff of planners, other specialists, and technical and administrative support services.

• This office, headed by the Director of Planning, will provide services to the Commission for preparing plans, according to the precise terms of reference provided.

• Other Federal Departments, Territorial Departments and Native Organizations participating would also contribute additional staff resources, other inputs, and advice.

• Interdisciplinary planning teams would be formed to prepare plans. The Director of Planning would coordinate activities and direct team leaders and staff throughout the various stages of plan preparation.

5. Roles and Responsibilities of the Government of Canada and the Government of the Northwest Territories

In July, 1981, the Federal Cabinet endorsed a Land Use Policy.

The basis of agreement proposed, the roles and responsibilities of the Government of Canada and the Government of the Northwest Territories, and land use planning, are founded on, and will be based on, due recognition of the current constitutional and legal allocation of authorities accorded each government.

The roles and responsibilities of the Government of Canada and the Government of the Northwest Territories are briefly summarized in sections following. Legislation should be consulted for further details.

5.1 Government of Canada:

• The duties, powers and functions of the Minister of DIAND, on behalf of Canada, derive from the Department of Indian Affairs and Northern Development Act. National interests, Northern interests, and Northern economic development, are areas of primary concern.

• A statement of government policy has guided Northern development over the past decade, with considerable emphasis on the needs of Northern People. Native claim negotiations is another area of major importance.

• The objective of the Northern Affairs Program is to advance the social, cultural, political and economic development of the Northwest Territories, in conjunction with the Territorial Government, and through the coordination of activities of Federal departments and agencies, with special emphasis on the needs of native northerners and the protection of the northern environment. Land use planning, environmental management and conservation strategy are among recent initiatives.

• DIAND has a major role to play in land use planning. DIAND is entrusted with the "control, management and administration" of most lands in the Northwest Territories, and the co-ordination of all Federal policies and programs in the North. It has a specific legislative mandate in resource development under a number of acts, chief among which are the Territorial Lands Act and Regulations, the Public Lands Grant Act, the

Northern Inland Waters Act, Arctic Waters Pollution Prevention Act, Canada Oil and Gas Act, and the Mining Regulations. The legal and administrative control exercised by the Minister of DIAND covers onshore and seafloor lands.

• Many other Federal Departments (e.g., Environment Canada; Energy, Mines and Resources; Fisheries and Oceans) also have special mandates and responsibilities, and should be involved in the process. DIAND has the mandate to coordinate these activities with respect to planning.

5.2 Government of the Northwest Territories:

• The Government of the Northwest Territories is politically accountable to the residents of the Northwest Territories, and has a role in the development and implementation of land use plans. The primary focus relates to northern socio-economic concerns, local matters and management of certain renewable resources.

• Through the Northwest Territories Act, the Government of the Northwest Territories has responsibilities in the area of economic and social development to which land use is critical. Specific resource management mandates include wildlife, agriculture and Territorial Parks. The Government of the Northwest Territories also has various legislative powers and existing ordinances which deal with lands, taxation and zoning. It also established environmental assessment and review capabilities and implemented a Resource Development Policy.

Press Release
5 May 1983

Tungavik Federation of Nunavut
Dene Nation
Métis Association of the Northwest Territories

A joint statement of principles, presented by representatives of the three major Native organizations, to guide the land use planning process in the Northwest Territories, was accepted today by the Federal and Territorial governments.

The document, which was accepted in its entirety, was prepared jointly by members of the Tungavik Federation of Nunavut, the Métis Association of the Northwest Territories and the Dene Nation, who were also represented by the Mackenzie Delta Regional Council.

The agreement, which is the first of its kind between the three Native groups, spells out the basis on which they agree to become involved in the land use planning initiative begun by the Federal Government two years ago.

The joint statement of principles was accepted following a two day meeting held in Yellowknife. That meeting was the first time that the Native organizations were given the opportunity to sit with government officials as a group to discuss the issue of land use planning.

Final acceptance of the agreement is conditional pending approval by the principals of all the parties involved.

Representatives of the Native organizations and government at the meeting also agreed to appoint members to an interim working group which will prepare a submission to Cabinet to acquire funding and policy approval for land use planning in the Northwest Territories.

Representatives of the Tungavik Federation of Nunavut, the Dene Nation, the Delta Regional Council and the Métis Association will recommend to their principals that these organizations participate in a process of land use planning for the Northwest Territories. It must be recognized that the long-term future of land use planning is a topic of both priority and substance in aboriginal rights negotiations. It is further recognized that long-term land use planning will likely emerge in different forms in various parts of the existing Northwest Territories as a consequence of aboriginal rights negotiations and constitutional development. A general approach for planning which must be discussed is outlined in the draft proposal, "Land Use Planning of the Northwest Territories: Basis of Agreement" dated March 21, 1983. Ongoing participation by these organizations with the governments of Canada and the Northwest Territories *is conditional* on the incorporation into the planning process of the following:

1. Man is a functional part of a dynamic biophysical environment and land use cannot be planned and managed without reference to the human community. Accordingly, social, cultural and economic endeavors of the human community must be central to land use planning and implementation.

2. The primary purpose for land use planning in the N.W.T. must be to protect and promote the existing and future well-being of the permanent residents and communities of the N.W.T. taking into account the interests of all Canadians. Special attention shall be devoted to protecting and promoting the existing and future well-being of the aboriginal peoples and their land interests as they define them.

3. The planning process must ensure land use plans reflect the priorities and values of the residents of the planning regions.

4. The plans will provide for the conservation, development and utilization of land, resources, inland waters and the offshore.

5. To be effective the public planning process must provide an opportunity for the active and informed participation and support of the residents affected by the plan. Such participation will be promoted through means including: ready access to all relevant information, widespread dissemination of relevant materials, appropriate and realistic schedules, recruitment and training of local residents to participate in comprehensive land use planning.

6. The planning process must be systematic and must be integrated with all other planning processes and operations.

7. It is acknowledged that an effective land planning process requires the active participation of the Government of Canada, the Government of the Northwest Territories, and regional and territorial organizations representing aboriginal people.

8. It is recognized that the funding and other resources shall be made available for the system and be provided equitably to allow each of the major participants referred to in paragraph 7 to participate effectively.

Background Paper

Northern Land-use Planning: In Search of a Policy

William E. Rees, Ph.D.
School of Community and Regional Planning
University of British Columbia

In October 1982, the Department of Indian Affairs and Northern Development (DIAND) circulated to a privileged few a draft of a policy document entitled *Land Use Planning in Northern Canada*.[1] This deceptively heavy document was the culmination of three years' gestation within the mother department, and its release was well attended by a veritable coterie of anything-but-disinterested midwives. Indeed, an atmosphere of palpable anxiety permeated the crowded delivery room: government agencies, private corporations, native organizations, and public-interest groups were all aware of the potential effects of land-use planning in the North. Simply put, a robust programme could well transform permanently the context for resource and related socio-economic development north of 60°.

Within days of the document's release, however, anxious anticipation had given way to resigned disappointment. It became clear that the new policy had come into the world with severe functional handicaps. Consequently, northern organizations from native groups to territorial governments were forced to reject DIAND's proposal in a rare display of near unanimity.[2]

None of these organizations was opposed to the principle of land-use planning. On the contrary, most had long pressed for more rational approaches to the development of land and resources in the North, and remained strongly supportive of DIAND's initiative. The problem lay in the specific structure proposed for *Land Use Planning in Northern Canada*. Most observers saw the programme as cumbersome yet incomplete; sweeping in effect, yet politically unbalanced—in a word, unworkable. In the ensuing weeks, other federal departments and southern-based interest groups also expressed varying degrees of reservation about the long-awaited policy.[3] DIAND planners had hoped to have their final text ready for approval in January 1983. Instead, in mid-February, they found themselves at the bargaining table, negotiating a fresh approach with the Government of the Northwest Territories (GNWT).

The purpose of this paper is to outline some of the essential require-ments for land-use planning in the North and to compare them with the product of DIAND's recent prolonged labour. This comparison should explain why *Land Use Planning in Northern Canada* succumbed so early to the rough and tumble of northern political ecology, and should provide some direction for future initiatives. Before contemplating these complex questions, however, we should be clear about the focus of this discussion.

What Is "Planning"?

Definitions of planning can be deceptively simple. Indeed, almost any form of planning can be described neatly as a deliberate process by which someone makes considered choices about the use of resources, to achieve specified objectives over some delimited period in the future.

Making choices implies that there are alternatives among which to choose. How quickly simplicity dissolves. Experience shows that some feasible options may not be readily apparent at the outset. Any credible planning process must therefore devote considerable energy to the identifi-cation and evaluation of possible alternatives. This activity is essential because certain planning decisions, particularly those respecting non-renewable or ecologically sensitive resources, may forever close the door on other potentially superior alternatives.

Thus the whole point of rational planning is to aid the decision maker in making the best choice on behalf of a specified client group. The "best choice" is usually defined as the one most likely to maximize, or at least to optimize, the flow of future benefits to that group. However, a problem emerges because of the pluralistic nature of society and the necessity of choosing amongst options preferred by different social groups. As empha-sized in a following section, this reality has important implications for institutional design in planning, and the criteria on which decisions are based.

Private versus Public Planning

This seems an appropriate point at which to draw a distinction between planning in the private and public sectors. Generally speaking, private planners are able to make decisions in their own best interests, usually concerning a relatively narrow range of investment options. The overrid-ing (and perfectly legitimate) goal is to maximize return on investment (i.e., profit) for themselves and their corporate shareholders.

Planning in the public sector, however, is much more complicated, particularly in a democratic society. In theory, politicians and public servants do not operate on their own behalf, but rather in the public interest. In most circumstances, however, there is not one but a diversity of "public interests," and thus there is not likely to be a natural consensus on the appropriate goals or values to pursue through planning decisions.

This reality imposes special obligations on public-sector planners. First, it significantly increases the range of policy options that they should identify and consider. At the same time, it creates an inevitable dilemma. Public planners and politicians must choose from an array of alternatives that not only may differ widely in world view while appearing equally valid to a disinterested observer, but also may be mutually exclusive.

Consequently, not all segments of society necessarily benefit equally from decisions respecting the development of public resources. Indeed, there is ample evidence that some groups low on the societal totem pole are further disadvantaged by the indirect consequences of major industrial developments, such as local inflation or pollution, occurring in their home regions.

Secondly, public planners thus have a major responsibility to strive toward distributive equity in the development of public lands and associated resources. For large projects, this responsibility requires that they develop and implement integrated programmes across a spectrum of related policy areas. It also necessitates careful attention to institutional design for planning within the development region. The planning system must operate fairly, and be responsive to local values and priorities. For example, at the economic level, one objective should be to ensure the distribution and retention of significant benefits within the development region. Not everyone can expect to benefit from a particular resource development; however, it is surely incumbent upon public planners to ensure that no one is left worse off as a result of such planning decisions.

However reasonable and desirable these social objectives may seem, they are also the source of significant political conflict. Private corporations are often involved in the development of public resources under permit or licence agreements, which creates tensions between private and public priorities. Thus, government policy aimed at maximizing the benefits of resource development to society at large may well mean lower profit margins to the corporate sector than would be the case if the decisions were strictly private.

Recognition of the difficult tradeoffs that must be made in planning underscores the importance of structuring the process to take full account of the range of interests affected.

Planning as Process

> . . . planning is not an activity resulting in products called plans:
> it is a continuous process, whereby the process itself—namely
> that of aborting the plans—is the pay off . . . .[4]

This quotation addresses a fundamental contradiction within much so-called planning activity. As part of the century-old legacy of urban master planning, planners still act as if the world can be represented as a kaleidoscopic, but frozen, image. Too often, planning consists of using yesterday's data today, to project a static picture of how planners would like things to look tomorrow, which then becomes "the plan."

The problem, of course, is that the real world is increasingly dynamic. In these economically turbulent times, the socio-political climate is in a state of constant flux along with the aspirations and priorities of all groups in society. Consequently, even so-called "scientific forecasting," which lies at the heart of much corporate and public planning, has become a hazardous occupation. Planners who operate too much in this mode get their comeuppance when the future arrives bearing scant resemblance to the product of their patient labours.

An unfortunate by-product of this state of affairs derives from our adversarial and relentlessly unforgiving political system. Constrained never to admit to error, politicians and public servants exhibit fierce loyalty to plans and programmes that ordinary folk can readily see have long since gone awry.

The much-ballyhooed National Energy Program (NEP) of 1980 provides a dramatic contemporary illustration, and one with serious consequences for northern resource development and planning. Major components of the NEP depended on the assumption that the sky-rocketing energy prices of the 1970s could be projected through the 1980s. Within months of the NEP's publication, however, crude petroleum prices on world markets had stabilized, and have subsequently fallen, which has dramatically diminished the short-term economic feasibility of marketing Canada's frontier hydrocarbon resources.

All this discussion may seem to render planning a frustrating, if not futile, exercise, but this is not the intent. What the constancy of change does imply for planning is a shift in emphasis from the product (the plan) to the process itself. In any complex planning activity, some important variables, usually among those governed by local factors, may be well known, predictable, and even under the control of decision makers. Other key variables will be independent of local conditions and may influence massively the policy emphasis required to achieve planning objectives.

The process of planning must therefore be structured so that it is able to "track" variation in key variables, which is essential if the process is to be responsive to change through programme adjustments within the planning region. Thus, the plan itself must be seen as a dynamic entity, and planning as a continuous process.

If, by definition, planning is never complete, then the successful planning process will rest on a firm foundation of mechanisms for both feedback and monitoring. The plan must reflect both the current state of driving variables and the results of its own implementation. A plan that is not in touch with the present objectives and priorities of the client group or groups is at best irrelevant, and at worst an impediment to community welfare.

The Role of Land-use Planning

Land-use planning is a special variation on the overall theme, but all the general characteristics of planning already discussed apply nevertheless. Essentially, land-use planning implies making deliberate choices about the allocation of public land and resources among competing uses.

Consider the array of possible choices that might require attention in a typical land-use planning exercise. There might be: alternative feasible uses for the same parcel(s) of land; alternative acceptable sites for a given land use; alternatives pertaining to the scale, pace, and timing of chosen developments, each of which would affect traditional land uses differently; and alternative policy programmes with the same (or different) socio-economic objectives, each with differing implications for land-use. In making such choices, land-use planning in the public sector must be particularly sensitive to the spectrum of values and interests affected by land-use decisions. Many land uses simply exclude any others, and the negative consequences of such decisions may be irreversible.

Thus, land-use planning is neither an isolated activity nor an end in itself. One could well argue that land use, whether planned or not, is invariably a reflection of a *de facto* social and economic policy and priorities. At the very least then, land-use planning should be seen as a policy tool—a means of achieving wider societal goals.

In ideal circumstances, land-use planning will be an integrated component of a more comprehensive planning process. In the latter context, land allocation and use provide the spatial and temporal framework for the implementation of overall development policy. It becomes the geographic expression of regional, social, and economic objectives, which may explain some of the excitement among those who have long awaited the introduction of land-use planning north of 60°.

Special Circumstances

Land-use planning in Canada's vast northern regions presents both opportunities and problems not found in quite the same form elsewhere. Consider that in most settled regions any large tract of land has usually been divided into numerous small parcels. Ownership of these parcels, and the legal rights attached thereto, is distributed among a diverse group of individuals and corporations who may have very different ideas concerning the future use of their lands. These differences complicate any large-scale planning enterprise that seeks to co-ordinate or to regulate the development of those lands for the greater public good.

In the northern territories, however, almost all land outside the municipalities is effectively under the ownership and control of a single entity, namely, DIAND. That department is charged with co-ordinating the activities of other federal departments, and regulating the land-use activities of the private sector in the best interests of Canada as a whole. Moreover, DIAND has a special mandate to protect, and to advance the interests of, the aboriginal inhabitants of the lands under its charge. These unique responsibilities, and the concentration of authority, present DIAND with an enviable opportunity to implement a simple, effective process for land-use planning north of 60°.

The breadth of this mandate, however, creates special problems. The department's enormous power, and the inherent conflicts among the interests it is supposed to represent, place extraordinary demands for exemplary conduct upon public servants and the minister of Indian Affairs and Northern Development.

The major issues stem from the long-standing relationship that exists between the metropolitan South where most Canadians live, and what they perceive as their northern resource hinterland. Many southern Canadians believe that their best interests are served through the rapid development of the hydrocarbon, mineral, and other non-renewable resources of the far North. Certainly, significant economic rewards and less tangible benefits (such as security of energy supply) might eventually result from this approach. On the other hand, although most of the benefits of large-scale development in the North flow south, the North, and particularly native communities, will bear the brunt of the negative environmental and socio-economic effects of that same development. Such geographic variation in the distribution of benefits and non-monetary costs of development sets up an internal north–south colonial axis within Canada.

Underlying this dilemma is the fact that ownership of the land in question is still very much in dispute. Most of the land of the present northern territories was never the subject of treaties between British authorities and the aboriginal peoples who had occupied it for thousands of years. Canadian courts agree that native peoples have certain aboriginal rights to the land, but that these rights remain ill-defined. Although several native land claims are being negotiated currently, there are not yet any formal agreements that would allow native northerners to be full beneficiaries of northern development, and that would truly legitimize the southern non-native presence in the North.

Non-natives too long have abrogated their moral responsibility to settle these matters with native northerners. Meanwhile, as a matter of policy, development proceeds apace, on a scale that may forever compromise the rights of native northerners, and that may deny the opportunity to all northerners to participate as full partners in the development of the land they call their own. Can any Canadian argue credibly that perpetuation of this situation is truly in the national interest?

The acceptability of any programme for northern land-use planning will depend on the degree to which it reflects these socio-political realities. Any approach that patently favoured alleged southern interests and corporate objectives would be rejected across the North (and by many southerners) on the grounds that it would merely entrench the north–south colonial axis, through a crude form of majority rule. Similarly, a system wholly oriented to northern interests would be politically unrealistic and grossly unfair to what are, after all, legitimate southern interests in the North. What is required, therefore, is an approach structured to ensure full and fair consideration of all legitimate interests and accountable to those who will be affected most directly by decisions made. It also must be capable of full integration with any land management systems developed for Inuit and Indian lands as ultimately determined through claims negotiations. Only when such a system is in place will DIAND finally have assumed the burden of special responsibilities that weighs on public-sector planning in the North.

DIAND's Approach to Land-use Planning in Northern Canada

With *Land Use Planning in Northern Canada*, DIAND hoped to advance "an organized process for determining the uses of land and related resources, based on co-operative decision making by governments, groups and individuals, according to their various needs and desires and to the limitations imposed by the environment."[5] The document seemed to recognize clearly the need for northern involvement, and for effective participation by local residents in the preparation of plans:

> The primary responsibility for preparing Northern Land Use Plans will rest with Northerners. Public involvement will be encouraged . . . in whatever ways are found most appropriate to meet land-use planning regional characteristics and differences.[6]

Given appropriate institutional and procedural arrangements, the degree of northern control and the flexibility in response to local conditions implicit in this statement would be a major credit to the proposed planning programme.

The planning process itself would be organized around the preparation of land-use plans (texts, charts, graphs, tables, and maps) on the basis of regions or land-use planning areas.[7] Accordingly, the department divided the whole of the Yukon and Northwest Territories into six proposed northern land-use planning regions. Each region is composed of several so-called northern land-use planning units, of which there are 50 in total. The boundaries of these units are based on natural features. DIAND considered natural boundaries as "the most appropriate basis for land use planning, and preferable to any . . . administrative boundaries which have been developed for the North."[8]

The department recognized, however, that land-use issues may not conform geographically to the proposed boundaries for the planning regions. The intent, therefore, was to combine relevant adjacent planning units to delimit a northern land-use planning area for the purposes of actual planning, and "some of these may overlap Land Use Planning Region boundaries."[9]

On Form and Function

DIAND proposed that a northern land-use planning policy committee be established for each land-use planning area. These committees would include officials from both federal and territorial governments, as well as from local native organizations. The principal function of the committees would be to recommend "broad policy objectives and priorities" and to establish the "time-frame" for planning in their respective areas.[10]

The actual "definition and conduct of planning" would be coordinated by a northern land-use planning commission, appointed by the minister of Indian Affairs and Northern Development, for each designated planning area. Representation on these commissions would be expanded beyond that of the policy committees to include affected municipalities, community organizations, "and/or other groups with an interest in the Land Use Planning Area."[11] The commissions' responsibilities would include setting the terms of reference, directing the planning, and submitting a draft plan to the minister of Indian Affairs and Northern Development for approval.

Finally, DIAND proposed that the technical task of preparing a northern land-use plan fall to a so-called area planning team, which would form the operational arm of each commission. Each team would include professionals and experts drawn from DIAND, and presumably from other government departments at both the federal and territorial levels. DIAND also expects the "full participation" of native and special-interest groups, and residents of the northern land-use planning area. "Such a broad involvement is essential to sound land use planning."[12]

DIAND's proposal provided few details on the process by which land-use plans were to be prepared and, indeed, only really outlined how the process was expected to end. Naturally enough, "Once a draft Northern Land Use Plan has been prepared . . ., the . . . Commission will forward its recommendations to the Minister of DIAND."[13] The minister then chooses "from among the alternatives recommended,"[14] and approves the northern land-use plan. Most remarkably, however, a "Northern Land Use Planning Commission will be disbanded after the Minister of DIAND has approved its Northern Land Use Plan."[15] The one thing clear from this, then, is that the process for land-use planning in northern Canada was expected to be product-oriented, that is, committed to the production of final master plans.

The document is equally sparse in its description of the implementation stage. In the absence of a legislated mandate, or similar policy commitment, DIAND can only expect "government agencies at all levels to adjust plans, programs, legislation and regulations as required to implement an approved Northern Land Use Plan."[16] In short, "implementing, monitoring and reviewing the Northern Land Use Plan . . . will rest with the various groups involved with the Land Use Planning Area . . . ."[17] Any revision of the plan that might be required over time is also left vaguely to "the appropriate groups involved with the Land Use Planning Area after consultation with each other."[18] There is no further suggestion of the mechanisms or procedures required to facilitate these essential tasks.

Critical Analysis of *Land Use Planning in Northern Canada*

DIAND is to be commended for its expressed intention to develop a policy for northern land-use planning, and for the effort that has gone into the programme so far. Several strengths of the department's proposal are particularly noteworthy. These include: the recognition of both a general policy and an area-specific planning function, and their institutional separation; the acknowledgement of the need for representation from both governments and appropriate client groups at each level of systems organization; the attempt to economize through central co-ordination and the use of existing manpower and expertise in the preparation of plans.

On the other hand, *Land Use Planning in Northern Canada* has serious flaws at several levels, and these weaknesses must be addressed openly if an alternative acceptable to all key participants is ever to emerge. The department's recent document was only a draft, and substantial changes may be wrought through continuing negotiations. Many issues will continue to be the subject of intense debate, however, and are likely to remain unresolved in any final policy statement on northern land-use planning.

Ideological Roots

DIAND's proposal for land-use planning is very revealing of the department's pro-development bias. Although ostensibly advancing a programme and "organized process for determining the uses of land and related resources,"[19] *Land Use Planning in Northern Canada* makes clear that there will be no serious re-evaluation of established directions and *de facto* policies for northern development. There will be no freeze on current development plans: "Ongoing projects will be integrated smoothly" or "adapted to the land use planning process in an efficient manner."[20] Even native claims negotiations would proceed "concurrently" with land-use planning (i.e., before settlement) "to ensure avoidance of unnecessary delays . . . ."[21] In short, everything seems geared toward ensuring that "existing schedules are met."[22] Taken together, these quotations lead to the unavoidable conclusion that the federal government does not intend public land-use planning to have a significant effect on the status quo respecting land use and its regulation in the North.

A similar conclusion can be reached from the explicit reaffirmation of existing power relationships respecting land and resources in the North. *Land Use Planning in Northern Canada* boldly states that "The primary responsibility for preparing Northern Land Use Plans will rest with Northerners,"[23] yet northerners are given little decision-making authority in the development or implementation of such plans. The minister would provide the terms of reference and planning priorities, would appoint the policy committees and the planning commissions, would choose the desired alternative, and then would approve his own choice. As one native representative at a recent *ad hoc* meeting on northern land-use planning noted, the proposed policy seems to be yet another example of northerners having to "jig to the minister's fiddle."

Such self-contradiction springs directly from contemporary political reality, and is a reflection of the north–south colonial axis within Canada. One need seek no further to explain the universal rejection of the policy north of 60°.

Conceptual Concerns

Several conceptual problems emerge from the geographical framework suggested by DIAND for land-use planning in northern Canada, i.e., the proposed northern land-use regions, areas, and units. The document notes, laudably, that the boundaries of planning units would not conform to existing administrative areas. However, why is the emphasis exclusively on biophysical features in determining planning unit boundaries? What of the distribution of cultural and language groups, to say nothing of economic land-use patterns, in the North? What about those geographic regions that have already emerged as natural laboratories for testing various recommended principles and mechanisms for northern land-use planning? For example, the Lancaster Sound region, which is already the subject of an intensive exercise in the collection of regional data, is split up among three of the suggested land-use planning regions, and no fewer than six planning units. To be fair, the document does suggest that northern land-use planning areas may, in practice, overlap several northern land-use planning regions, but this raises the question of the functional utility of such predetermined units in the first place.

DIAND's preoccupation with the biophysical also overshadows socio-economic considerations at the substantive level. The latter are to be included in the field work, but only "to the extent appropriate for land use planning."[24] A generous interpretation of this condition is that the present document is merely naïve in its separation of land-use planning from socio-economic issues. On the other hand, because planning must reflect *someone's* values, the built-in biases may exist to ensure the continued dominance of southern socio-economic interests. In short, it is only the consideration of northern social and economic concerns that is to be limited.

Institutions and the Planning Process

The few details presented on administrative arrangements for land-use planning in northern Canada suggest that the proposed structures would be cumbersome and partially redundant. For example, it is not at all clear why a policy committee and a planning commission are required for each designated planning area. Moreover, one can only guess at the intended working relationship between such entities.

A simpler but related concern is whether there are sufficient qualified personnel in the North to populate the several anticipated committees and commissions, however short-lived, given the existing duties and responsibilities involved. Disclaimers aside, DIAND's suggested structures would seem to invite the creation of a greater and more confused bureaucratic entanglement.

Despite the potential proliferation of planning organizations, DIAND is ambiguous about the role they will play in the decision-making process. What is clear is that land-use planning is explicitly "not intended to replace any existing planning mechanisms. . . ."[25] Indeed, the proposed policy does not actually require anyone to do anything! As noted above, DIAND merely expects other departments "to adjust plans, programs, legislation and regulations as required to implement an approved Northern Land Use Plan."[26]

A land-use planning programme based on co-operative voluntarism might have merit in circumstances where participating agencies and groups share the same values and objectives and are motivated by strong and coherent policy directives. This mode of implementation is hopelessly naïve, however, given the reality of competing departmental mandates, the absence of integrated policy, and the legacy of inter- and intra-cultural conflicts over the use of resources in northern development. Does DIAND really expect that the Department of Energy, Mines and Resources, for example, will now press to amend the Canada Oil and Gas Act so that the mandate of the Canada Oil and Gas Lands Administration would be subordinate to the weightless land-use plans that would emerge from this process? Significantly, DIAND does not even hint at how its own planning-related instruments, such as the Territorial Land Use Regulations, are to be integrated with the land-use planning system. The net effect of these structural shortcomings is to call into question DIAND's commitment to genuine land-use planning.

Nor does *Land Use Planning in Northern Canada* instil much confidence at the procedural level. Of prime concern, DIAND's approach would be entirely product-oriented, with scant attention to the nature of "planning as process." The proposed thrust of activity is toward the production of master plans for each planning area, followed by dissolution of the planning commissions, i.e., by the dismantling of the process itself. A cursory examination of the effect of global economic uncertainty on many northern megaprojects in the past year alone should illustrate why this approach would be unworkable.

At the planning area level, public involvement and participation must surely be the key to popular confidence in, and acceptance of, any land-use plans. However, *Land Use Planning in Northern Canada* merely states that such involvement will be "encouraged" and will be included in whatever way is "most appropriate"[27] to a given planning area. What precisely do these statements mean? Does DIAND distinguish between "informing" and "involving" the public? What institutional arrangements for public input would be deemed appropriate, and to whom? Who has responsibility for choosing and organizing these mechanisms for public involvement? There is also a question of the appropriate role of public involvement. Should communities have an opportunity to form a consensus on what plans should be advanced to the minister for approval? Can they appeal his decision? The draft policy addresses none of these major concerns.

In a similar vein, confidence in planning depends on the existence of clearly stipulated procedures for periodic review and updating of plans. Moreover, fair procedures must be spelled out to enable affected parties to appeal decisions made by implementing agencies in conformity with, or in spite of, the plan. Apart from vague references to consultation among "appropriate groups involved" and "new Commissions,"[28] the document is silent on these critical elements.

In the final analysis, if successful land-use planning requires a firm policy commitment, authoritative and visible institutional structures, clear lines of responsibility, and fair and unambiguous operating procedures, DIAND's offering is a frail façade. All these essential requirements are missing from the present draft of *Land Use Planning in Northern Canada*.

Alternative Directions

The Present Impediment

The question naturally arises as to why "[the government] should go to the trouble of forming intentions which fail to convey anything, which will have no weight a moment after they are formed . . . ."[29]

The Working Groups

Why has DIAND devoted so much time and effort since 1980 to the formulation of noble intentions that, on examination, "fail to convey anything"? The department has been under intense pressure from various sectors of society since the early 1970s to improve the administration of northern lands and resources. This pressure increased greatly with the National Energy Program of 1980, which promoted northern energy-related megaprojects as the engine for northern development and, indeed, for the economic development of all Canada in the 1980s. Whole regions of the North, previously untrammelled, would now be propelled into industrialization. DIAND's own reviews of government capability to plan or to regulate that development showed the department's resources and efforts to be woefully inadequate. Thus, there is no question both within and outside the department concerning the need for land-use policy and planning north of 60°.

At the same time, several additional factors combined to ensure that any land-use planning policy would be firmly rooted in Ottawa, and unlikely seriously to challenge the status quo. First, having made energy and northern development the cornerstone of national economic policy, the federal government would require the strongest voice in planning and related regulatory mechanisms. Secondly, although DIAND's mandate reflects a plurality of interests, the established development orientation of the northern programme dominated any internal departmental debate on the role of land-use planning. Thirdly, maintaining firm control over production of petroleum and gas from the territories would increase the federal government's leverage in pricing, taxation, and revenue-sharing negotiations with energy-producing provinces and would lessen national dependence on the existing producers. Fourthly, with the recession of 1982, the federal government has become increasingly desperate for new sources of income to relieve the growing federal deficit (to say nothing of having to justify the enormous public investment in northern oil and gas exploration). This need reinforces its desire to maintain a firm grip on any regulatory innovation with the potential to moderate the nature and pace of northern development. Its enthusiasm for any scheme that might question the distribution of future economic rents from northern resource development is also dampened. Lastly, DIAND lacked in-house experience and expertise in land-use planning. With its technocratic orientation, the department had no sense of planning as a political and social learning process.

Overriding all these factors is the reality that, under the Department of Indian Affairs and Northern Development Act, the department has a mandate for the "control, management and administration" of almost all lands, and the responsibility to co-ordinate the programmes of other federal departments in the northern territories. History yields few examples of bureaucracies that willingly preside over the dissipation of their own decision-making powers. Thus, despite promises of rapid devolution, so long as DIAND has the legal authority to do so it is likely to continue to impose its own solutions.

A Spectrum of Alternative Arrangements

Institutional arrangements for controlling land use in North America generally can be placed in one of three overlapping categories: the multi-purpose unitary bureaucracy, the single-purpose commission, and concurrent regulatory agencies. Table 1 compares and contrasts the important characteristics of these common organizational patterns.

At one extreme is the large efficiency-oriented unitary bureaucracy, which is the general model of highly centralized control, and which is probably the commonest form of land-use administration. Unitary bureaucracies operate as if on behalf of an assumed homogeneous majority in society — a singular public interest. Accordingly, their operational style is centralized, closed, and generally unresponsive to social forces outside the organization's boundaries. Although often comprehensive, plans produced by such agencies lean toward static solutions (master plans) based on the assumption of long-term social and environmental stability.

In simple terms, this approach holds that the welfare of society as a whole is more important than minority preferences; that is, the total costs of land-use decisions to whomever incurs them should be less than the benefits to whomever receives those. Unfortunately, the situation frequently arises where the costs of public decision making are systematically borne by groups different from those receiving the benefits. Thus, in circumstances where there is no societal agreement or natural consensus, "government operates collectively on the basis of constitutionally legitimized coercion . . .," and "prohibitive problems of representation arise."[30]

At the other extreme is an admittedly more complex form of land-use control, a system of concurrent agencies or specialized jurisdictions. When purposefully designed, this form recognizes explicitly that there is a diversity of public interests, and different scales of land-use problems that are beyond the comprehension of a single bureaucracy. Here the fundamental decision rule is based on a doctrine of institutional fairness, including recognition that what is fair and appropriate for one region or group of persons may be unacceptable to another. Due process replaces majority rule as the principal criterion for fairness, and generally implies negotiated agreements where the potential for mutual gain exists. The underlying

Table 1
Approaches to Land-use Planning and Control

Characteristics	Organizational Form		
	Multipurpose Unitary Bureaucracy	Single-purpose Commission	Concurrent Regulatory Agencies
Administrative structure	Unitary hierarchy and jurisdiction over multiple functions	Internal agency hierarchy	Interagency network; multiple jurisdictions
Implicit social assumptions	Homogeneous stable majority; static environment	Stable social diversity; variable environment	Social pluralism; complex dynamic environment
Decision rules	Welfare at large and bureaucratic efficiency	Balanced welfare	Institutional and procedural fairness and social effectiveness
Type of expertise	Professional bureaucrats with general expertise; oriented to technical and factual analysis	Technical staff and limited competencies; reliance on special-interest groups and expert witnesses	Specialized professionals and multiple competencies; wide representation of interests within bureaucracies and many channels to external sources
Decision-making mode	Non-consultative bureaucratic; reliance on professional judgement and internal accountability; centralized	Variable efforts to reconcile technical and value differences; centralized tendency	Explicitly consultative: negotiation and bargaining toward consensus; location-specific and non-centralized
Planning style	Synoptic "once and for all" solutions; product-oriented	Variable	Incremental or continuous; adaptive; process-oriented
Public involvement	Few opportunities; values and politics left to politicians	Public hearings and like modes of public involvement are common; recognition of political conflict over values as central to its role	Multiple forums for public input (each agency has its constituency); open consideration of competing agency mandates and public values

Modified from H.L. Boschken, *Land Use Conflicts: Organizational Design and Resource Management* (Chicago: University of Chicago Press, 1982), Table 1, p. 43.

assumption is that fair procedures can lead to a proportionate distribution of both costs and benefits amongst all affected parties, "as in a positive sum game."[31]

As might be expected, this form of administrative structure is characterized by maximum public access, and by multiple forums for deliberation. Planning is characterized by continuous incremental adjustment in recognition of a complex and fluctuating socio-economic environment.

A single-purpose land-use planning commission is a variable form, generally lying between the preceding extremes, but having a logic similar to the unitary bureaucracy. The doctrine of the welfare of society as a whole, however, is conditioned by the recognition of the need to achieve greater balance among perceived societal interests. Given their narrow substantive focus and expertise, typical land-use commissions rely on interest groups, consultants, and interventions by line agencies to raise awareness of values and issues in conflict (e.g., through public hearings).

Although more politically visible than a unitary bureaucracy, a special commission often has exclusive authority over all areas of its mandate. When its powers supersede those of line resource agencies, its operational style is inclined toward that of a unitary bureaucracy within its inclusive geographic jurisdiction.

The purpose in outlining these alternative institutional arrangements for land-use planning is not to endorse any one of them, but rather to abolish the notion of universal solutions, and to make the case that institutional design for land-use planning should be based on the specific circumstances. A unitary bureaucracy may work well under conditions of stability and minimal contention of interests, but may be overwhelmed in a complex and unstable setting characterized by socio-cultural diversity.[32] The same is true for a land-use commission operating with a centre–periphery orientation. A system of concurrent agencies, on the other hand, might be cumbersome and redundant under conditions of stability and homogeneity, but is appropriate, and even necessary, in situations where uncertainty and diversity prevail.

DIAND is a textbook example of a multipurpose unitary bureaucracy with a centralist approach to implementing its mandate. On the basis of the preceding discussion, it is easy to see that *Land Use Planning in Northern Canada* would be overwhelmed in the culturally diverse, politically volatile environment of the northern territories today. The department's traditional organizational form is simply inappropriate to the nature of the task at hand.

The central question for institutional design therefore remains: given the fact of DIAND's unitary centralist orientation, what structure would be responsive to the plurality of interests that are supposed to be accommodated through the department's mandate? Is it possible to move toward the development of consensus-building procedures within the framework of a unitary bureaucracy?

A Model for Northern Land-use Planning

As an alternative to DIAND's October 1982 proposal for northern land-use planning, the model outlined in Figure 1 accepts existing institutional realities without implying permanence thereof. Indeed, one expects continued evolution of government organization in the North with increasing political maturity.

This alternative framework is based on a series of related premises or assumptions. First, the local (or regional) planning area is seen as the critical locus of significant human relationships. Secondly, human security, dignity, and well-being are associated with the degree of control that local persons are able to exercise over their own affairs. Thirdly, so long as higher (e.g., national) interests have been articulated clearly and explained satisfactorily, local persons will be more disposed to accept them as a negotiable framework within which to express their own values and priorities. Finally, if a locally based planning process is able adequately to reflect the objectives of the central bureaucracy, the latter authorities should not be much concerned about the details of the final plan.

The proposed model addresses the issues of conflicting local and national interests through institutional design for enhanced procedural fairness. It recognizes that broad policy directives and terms of reference for land-use planning will originate largely from the top downward. Within that framework, however, an effective role in land-use decision making is delegated to a local (or regional) area planning body. Thus, representatives of local interests assume significant responsibility for formulating land-use plans for their own areas with the full technical support of professional planners. This involvement should enhance local participation and increase the contribution to the overall development of planning policy and process from the bottom upward.

At its higher levels (commissions and above), the proposed structure retains the characteristics of a unitary bureaucracy. At the local level, however, the representative council, community organizations, and multi-disciplinary planning team should be able to account adequately for affected interests.

An Alternative Approach to Northern
Land-use Planning:
Organizational Flowchart

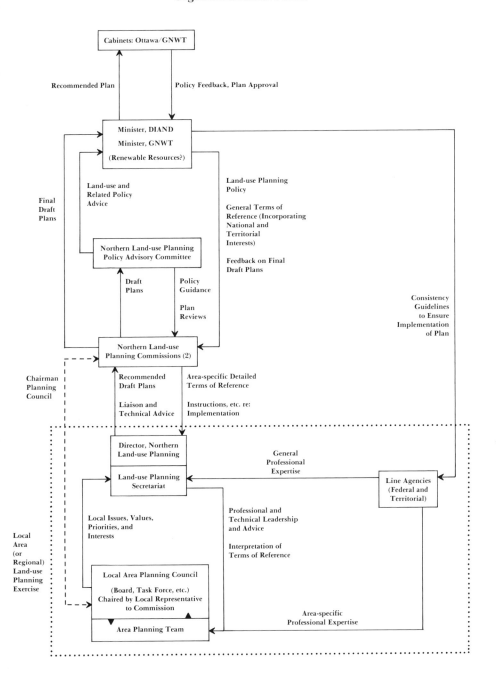

Figure 1

The Political Level

The minister of Indian Affairs and Northern Development representing Canada, and the minister of Renewable Resources, Government of Northwest Territories (GNWT), would be responsible jointly for political guidance over northern land-use planning.

Specifically, this would involve:

- receiving policy advice on land-use planning
- issuing broad policy statements on northern land-use planning, and identifying federal and territorial interests and priorities
- providing general terms of reference for area-specific planning exercises incorporating federal and territorial objectives
- receiving the final draft of recommended land-use plans
- seeking endorsement of plans from their respective Cabinets and approving the plans
- issuing "statements of commitment" with respect to approved plans, which would provide consistency guidelines to line agencies, thus enforcing compliance with local area land-use plans.

This recommended structure differs from DIAND's proposal in that approval and acceptance of final land-use plans are shared between the federal government and the GNWT.

The Policy Level

At present there is little co-ordination by senior governments of policy and programme development across the spectrum of policy areas related to land-use planning. There are, as yet, no satisfactory answers to such questions as: How can land-use planning be used to help achieve stated social and economic policy objectives? or What is the appropriate relationship of land-use planning to more comprehensive regional planning in the North?

Indeed, there is little in the way of explicit policy that addresses the compound resource that is land itself. Such traditional instruments as the Territorial Land Use Regulations respond to private development initiatives only. Conservation zones, habitat management reserves, heritage use areas, and similar designations merit serious policy consideration in their own right. Where are the proactive policy statements on land values and uses that now often seem relegated to areas "left over" after development?

The Northern Land-use Policy Advisory Committees

The present model suggests that a single permanent land-use advisory committee with adequate staff support is required to serve this function adequately. This single committee is in contrast to the multiple temporary committees suggested by DIAND's approach. Alternatively, conditions may be sufficiently different to warrant such a committee for each territory.

The northern land-use policy advisory committee would:

- advise the two ministers on broad areas of policy, such as energy, conservation, and socio-economic development, in terms of their relationship to land-use planning
- provide specific advice on land-use policy and priorities respecting ongoing planning exercises
- review plans and planning procedures to provide feedback to operational levels on the efficiency and effectiveness of the process.

This policy advisory committee should include senior officials of relevant federal and territorial departments, and representatives appointed by the native organizations. It would be chaired by the assistant deputy minister, Northern Affairs, DIAND, and co-chaired by the deputy minister, Renewable Resources, GNWT.

The Northern Land-use Planning Commissions

Again in contrast to DIAND's proposal, the present model recommends a single, permanent Northern Land-use Planning Commission for each territory. Numerical representation on the commissions should be negotiated by the two levels of government and the principal native organizations. Appointees should be citizens (i.e., not public servants) nominated by the participating governments and organizations.

The commissions' primary responsibilities would be to interpret competing objectives, priorities, and values; to guide the overall planning process; and to monitor implementation of the approved plans. Specifically, the commissions would:

- provide an additional source of advice on policy to the ministers
- recommend initiation of area planning exercises and the establishment of local area planning bodies as necessary

- refine general terms of reference and policy guidelines received from the ministers responsible and issue area-specific terms of reference to local area planning bodies
- review initial draft plans, prepare deficiency comments, etc.
- approve revised plans and transmit these to the ministers
- oversee implementation of ministerially approved plans
- recall a local area planning body as necessary to revise and update existing plans.

A single permanent commission has the virtue of maintaining continuity and accumulating experience and expertise. Moreover, consideration should be given to a commission of both permanent and temporary members. The ministers would appoint a temporary member from any local area currently involved in a land-use planning exercise. This local appointee might also serve as chairman of the local area planning body to enhance liaison between planning areas and the central commission.

The Land-use Planning Secretariat

This secretariat would be the working arm of the land-use planning commission, consisting of a small number of professional planners and planning technicians headed by a director of northern land-use planning.[33] The planning staff would:

- provide technical and professional support and advice to the commission
- co-ordinate additional technical input from existing line agencies from the federal and territorial governments
- provide professional planning skills and technical competence to local area planning bodies
- prepare the actual local area plans and related documents for the commission's iterative discussion and approval process.

Planning Area Level

Land-use plans would be prepared for land-use planning areas defined geographically on the basis of a combination of relevant biophysical and socio-economic factors, and of perceived land-use conflicts. The structure illustrated in Figure 1 is designed to maximize both participation and representation at the local level from the inception of the planning process. It involves the establishment of a local area planning council assisted by a professional and technical area planning team.[34]

Local Area Planning Council

Members of the local area planning council would be nominated by representative local interests and appointed by the ministers. Appropriate candidates might be the local leaders of native organizations, chairmen of hunters' and trappers' associations, the mayors of local communities, and representatives of the private sector with significant local operations. The chairman of an area planning council, or similar local planning body, would be chosen by its members, and might also be appointed by the ministers as a temporary representative to the northern land-use planning commission. This would enhance communication between the operational or planning area level and the central authority.

In some circumstances it might be possible to capitalize on existing organizations. For example, many of the issues to be dealt with by the newly formed development impact zone (DIZ) groups have significant implications for land use. Given the limited expertise at the local level, it would be redundant to set up a separate land-use planning body if, through modest adjustments in membership and mandate, a single local organization could serve both overlapping purposes. Participation on such a hybrid area planning council would hardly demand more time of members than involvement on either body alone.

The role of the council would be to identify local land-use issues, values, priorities, and conflicts through public meetings, internal debate, etc. and to articulate these for inclusion in the area plan. In this task the council would be paralleling, at the local level, the function of the commission at the territorial and national levels. The area planning council, working with the area planning team, would also be responsible for integrating its own land-use priorities with those of the central authorities, and for proposing adjustments and compromise. Finally, the council would approve the draft area land-use plan prior to its submission to the commission. Once the plan had been adopted by the ministers, the council could be adjourned, but as a locally based entity would be available for recall as necessary.

Area Planning Team

The area planning team would consist of a planner as team leader and technicians provided by the land-use planning secretariat. The team would be augmented by personnel and resources as required from government and private agencies with operations at the local level. The role of the planning team would be to interpret the area-specific terms of reference (incorporating national and territorial interests) to the local representatives, to help specify local interests, and to develop and prepare a plan on behalf of the council and the commission.

The director of northern land-use planning would be an ex-officio member of all such area planning teams to facilitate his role as co-ordinator of northern land-use planning.

Considerable conflict is anticipated among the interests represented on an area planning council (or similar body), and between the council and various government agencies. Ideally, however, these entities will be able to develop a consensus-based land-use plan through negotiation. Indeed, the probability of this may be enhanced by experimenting with giving all members equivalent power (e.g., a qualified veto) or requiring that only a single consensus plan (or consensual alternatives) be advanced for commission and ministerial consideration. (To have the ministers choose from among alternatives backed by different local interests would undermine the central premises of the whole process.)

In the case of intractable disputes, of course, the land-use planning commission might have to require the director of planning to oversee the preparation of a local area plan without the consensus of the area planning council. This remedy, however undesirable, would be no worse than the approach envisaged by the existing proposal.

Some Advantages of the Proposed Framework

Successful operation of the suggested approach would have several advantages over the northern land-use planning proposed by DIAND in October 1982. First, planning would in fact be done in the North, and much of it at the local level by northerners. Participants, their client groups, and home communities are more likely to "own" and support a local area land-use plan in which they have participated themselves than one imposed by itinerant technicians. Greater local responsibility also implies greater local accountability, and reduces political tensions between local areas and the central bureaucracies.

Secondly, a locally based area planning council could be readily recalled as required for the plan revision or updating of the plan and hearing of appeals, etc. In some areas, routine, regular meetings might be required to monitor implementation of the plan, and for plan revision. Participants in this continuing process would be well informed, having had the advantage of actually living with the results of their initial endeavours.

Thirdly, there would also be continuity among planning secretariat staff. Northern land-use planning would be enhanced by the cumulative experience of planners through their participation in a variety of local planning situations. Lastly, similar continuity and parallel benefits would obtain among permanent members of the single northern land-use planning commission.

Variations on a Theme

The institutional model described here, and in Figure 1, represents a median case in a spectrum of many possible configurations. Simpler circumstances exist in certain remote regions where some land-use planning is needed to accommodate specific developments, but where neither the scale of development nor local concern warrants establishment of any formal local planning body. Here an area planning team, working under the direction of a central commission and meeting informally with local interests as required, could prepare the plan.

At the other extreme, some planning areas, such as the Beaufort Sea or Lancaster Sound regions, may be so large and complex as to deserve special treatment. It might even be necessary and desirable to establish a permanent regionally based (i.e., local) planning commission or similar authority. In these circumstances, the organization's membership and operations would reflect local, territorial, and national interests; in other words, it could combine the roles of the area planning council and central commission described in the basic model. Clearly, if such fully integrated land-use planning bodies were eventually established for each development region in the North, there would be no need for the central commission.

Two points should be made here. First, the institutional arrangements for planning should reflect the circumstances to which they are applied, and hence may vary between regions. Secondly, mechanisms for planning should be permitted to evolve over time as circumstances change.

In the latter context it is important that central governments recognize the value of participation in planning as a social learning process. A local area planning council might start off in a purely advisory capacity. With increased experience it would gradually assume the greater decision-making role implied by the basic model. Eventually, if local circumstances warrant, it could be reconstructed as a fully fledged regional planning commission.

In the final analysis, then, DIAND and the territorial governments should be encouraged to experiment with various alternatives to match the variable circumstances of potential planning areas across the North. The success of any planning process will depend upon whether the persons most directly affected can either identify with the plan or, at least, feel that they have been given a fair hearing. Failure "on the ground" guarantees collapse of the whole system, no matter how elegantly structured it may be higher up.

A Final Word

A pragmatist's definition of policy might be, "what gets done, not what gets said." Whatever the stated policy of the governments in question, industrial and industry-related uses of land will increase dramatically across the North in the coming decades. The question, then, is whether the emerging pattern will be the deliberate product of an articulated policy process or merely the haphazard result of "what got done."

In this light, Canadians would do well to reflect on what is truly at stake in the challenge of northern development. A mere half of one per cent of the world's population, we claim sovereignty over a vastly disproportionate segment of the earth's surface. Moreover, our northland represents one of the largest unindustrialized tracts of land remaining on the only planet most of us will ever know.

The resources of the Canadian North represent an unparalleled opportunity for economic growth and social development. As a nation, however, we have been slow to recognize the responsibility we have as citizens of the global village to do the job right. In both symbol and substance, Canada's arctic realm is also a world heritage zone. We have a duty to protect the biophysical environment from careless destruction; we have an obligation to respect the aspirations of northern peoples whose cultures are older than our own. Despite these responsibilities we seem, so far, committed to repeating much of the history of tawdry development in the South. Any ennobling vision we might possess of our northern destiny is clouded by jurisdictional disputes and political expedience derived from economic greed.

A central premise of this paper is that although northern development may be inevitable, the particular form it takes is a matter of public choice and political will. As emphasized throughout, land-use planning is among the potentially most powerful tools for the exercise of that will. The design of the necessary policies, institutions, and procedures therefore merits the hard work and frustration it will inevitably entail.

It is sobering to realize that the present generation of Canadians is uniquely positioned to set the pattern that will dominate northern development for decades to come. The eventual outcome of our deliberations and actions is a matter for pure speculation. Certainly, however, the sensitivity with which we approach this enormous challenge will be a measure, in the eyes of the world, of our national character and our stature as an advanced society.

Acknowledgement

I should like to thank Nigel Richardson for his helpful critical reading of the original version of this paper. Its remaining weaknesses are, however, my sole responsibility.

Endnotes

1. DIAND, *Land Use Planning in Northern Canada*, draft (Ottawa: DIAND, 14 October 1982).

2. Native groups included the Committee for Original Peoples' Entitlement, the Dene Nation, and Inuit Tapirisat of Canada. These organizations and the Government of the Northwest Territories pressed to open negotiations with DIAND to reach a consensus on principles for land-use planning. The Yukon Territorial Government moved affirmatively by passing its own Land Planning Act late in 1982.

3. The Canadian Arctic Resources Committee circulated a detailed and much-cited critique in December 1982. *Comments on Land Use Planning in Northern Canada* (Ottawa: CARC, 1982).

4. S. Beer, *The Heart of Enterprise* (New York: John Wiley & Sons, 1979), p. 338.

5. DIAND, *Land Use Planning in Northern Canada*, p. 6.

6. Ibid., pp. 7–8.

7. Ibid., p. 8.

8. Ibid., p. 15.

9. Ibid.

10. Ibid., p. 17.

11. Ibid., p. 18.

12. Ibid., p. 19.

13. Ibid., p. 20.

14. Ibid., p. 21.

15. Ibid.

16. Ibid.

17. Ibid.

18. Ibid., p. 22.

19. Ibid., p. 6.

20. Ibid., p. 7.

21. Ibid., p. 10.

22. Ibid., p. 7.

23. Ibid.

24. Ibid.

25. Ibid., p. 6.

26. Ibid., p. 21.

27. Ibid., p. 8.

28. Ibid., p. 22.

29. A. Coddington. "Consistency and Commitment in the Realization of Extended Plans," *Environment and Planning* 10:869–878 (1978), p. 877.

30. H. L. Boschken, *Land Use Conflicts: Organizational Design and Resource Management* (Chicago: University of Chicago Press, 1982), p. 27.

31. Ibid, p. 28. It is worth noting that access to, control over, or ownership of land-related resources can be a key to an effective participation in planning

negotiations. These factors provide leverage to the owners in bargaining with other interests, and a means to engage in joint ventures, to collect economic rents, and to otherwise share in the economic benefits of development. Settlement of native land claims and the development of other land-related schemes to increase the bargaining power and effective participation by the territorial governments and northern communities in general is imperative as the land-use planning process evolves.

32. Ibid., p. 44.

33. DIAND's proposal implies that the director of land-use planning would report to DIAND. This would place him and his staff in the conflicting position of being responsible to both the commission(s) and the department. Richardson has discussed this problem and suggested instead that the commission be given the authority and resources to hire its own planning directors and support staff. (N. Richardson, *Land Use Planning in Northern Canada—The Proposed Planning System: Description and Commentary*, A Working Paper (Yellowknife: GNWT, January 1983).)

34. The term "council" is used here as a matter of convenience to denote a local planning body that is more than a mere advisory committee. Other names and arrangements might be appropriate in certain circumstances.

Addendum
The World after October 1982

Two important documents pertaining to northern land-use planning have been circulated in the months since the release of DIAND's policy document in October 1982:

1. *Land Use Planning Northwest Territories: Basis of Agreement*
   Draft proposal, 21 March 1983
   Indian and Northern Affairs, Government of Canada;
   Department of Renewable Resources, Government of the Northwest Territories
2. *Press Release*, 5 May 1983
   A joint statement of principles presented by representatives of the major native organizations, to guide the land-use planning process in the Northwest Territories, was accepted by the federal and territorial governments.

Basis of Agreement

The *Basis of Agreement* of March 1983 is the most recent product of ongoing negotiations between DIAND and the Government of the Northwest Territories (GNWT). The proposal is significant in several respects, not the least of which is the obvious willingness of DIAND to negotiate, thereby displaying some flexibility.

The careful language and internal tension of the proposal suggest that its overriding purpose was to stake out territory and delineate the roles of, and relationships between, the two levels of government in implementing northern land-use planning. Considerable emphasis is therefore placed on reasserting the existing mandates and authorities of the federal government and the GNWT, which is, of course, an important precondition to the success of the programme.

In the March 1983 proposal, however, intergovernmental politicking has displaced discussion on matters of form and substance. The proposal falls well short of its own goal of outlining "a common position on the part of *all* parties to cooperate, participate and implement a practical and effective system of land use planning" (emphasis added). For example, beyond acknowledging the concern and aspirations of native peoples, and expressing an intent to seek their agreement to participate, it is silent on their possible role at the planning area level. More generally, although there is recognition that public participation and review are an "important element of the land use [planning] process," there is no discussion of how these functions are to be achieved.

The following sections can only touch on some of the points raised in the policy that are worthy of more detailed discussion.

Observations on Substance

The *Basis of Agreement* advances "land, land use and resources" as the primary focus of land-use planning, yet there is no discussion of what precisely this encompasses. Does it include both renewable and non-renewable resources, and both surface and sub-surface rights? And what of the relationship to surface waters that are so much a part of the northern landscape? Much more thought needs to be given to defining the physical compass of land-use planning.

"Social and economic factors . . . will receive attention, in so far as they relate to the focus of land use planning." Although this point is ambiguous enough for general interpretation, it implies a separation of land use from socio-economic policy. This is a false dichotomy. Land-use planning is in fact a tool for the resolution of conflict between social and economic policy options, and is therefore the geographic expression of socio-economic priorities. All participants in the process should ask themselves whether land-use planning has any meaning otherwise.

Given the potentially sweeping focus of land-use planning, and its intimate relationship with other areas of policy, priority emphasis must be given to means and mechanisms for co-ordinating the land-related mandates and activities of various agencies at all levels of government. What of the roles of DOE, EMR, and COGLA? Where does the territorial Department of Renewable Resources fit in? What amendments are planned for the Territorial Land Use Act and Regulations?

The March 1983 document still does not go beyond suggesting that both governments "would administer programs in harmony with the final plan to achieve the results intended." With its concern on reasserting existing institutional arrangements, this proposal seems insensitive to the potential for evolution of northern planning mechanisms to reflect the increasing maturity of northern government at the territorial and regional levels.

On a related matter, the proposal argues that "special legislation . . . is not essential to initiating the process at the present time." It is probably wise to develop a backlog of experience and experimentation in land-use planning prior to drafting legislation that might eventually be required.

In the absence of legislation, however, other mechanisms to ensure compliance with land-use planning by line agencies must be spelled out explicitly. No such mechanisms are advanced in this proposal, beyond bland assurances that "implementation and monitoring mechanisms will serve to ensure compliance occurs." This assurance is wholly inadequate given the dismal record of failure to monitor northern development projects to date.

. . . and on Form and Process

Several changes in the planning system outlined in the March 1983 proposal make it a significant advance over DIAND's October 1982 proposal. However, several ambiguities and institutional weaknesses remain.

First, both the minister of Indian Affairs and Northern Development and the minister of Renewable Resources, GNWT, would be politically responsible for overseeing the land-use planning process (as compared with only the federal minister in the October 1982 proposal). This shared mandate for providing the terms of reference and approving the plans is a welcome development, provided that explicit and open mechanisms are instituted for the resolution of political disputes.

Secondly, a single, presumably continuing, senior advisory committee is proposed. The previous discussion of my alternative model suggests the clear advantage of this approach over the multiple temporary policy committees suggested in the October 1982 proposal.

Thirdly, several options are suggested with respect to land-use planning commissions, from a single body for the Northwest Territories, to several. This is another welcome indication of flexibility at the senior government level. There is considerable confusion and overlap, however, in the suggested roles for the advisory committee and the planning commission(s). For example, the former would venture well beyond providing policy advice if its mandate were indeed to include "an essential role in ensuring that plans are carried out and implemented, in an effective, timely and coordinated manner." How does this dovetail with the commission's role in "plan development ensuring public participation, providing recommendations on plans, and monitoring implementation"?

This functional ambiguity must be clarified. An active role in implementation by the advisory committee might be seen as an attempt to assert federal control over the process. The policy committee should be constrained to advising on wide-ranging, socio-economic initiatives and to interpreting their implications for land-use policy to the ministers and the commission, and to developing resource management policy *per se*. The commission should focus on the practical matter of overseeing the development and implementation of the plan.

At the operational level, the March 1983 proposal provides for a director of northern land-use planning to be responsible for the actual preparation of plans under the direction of the commission. He would work out of a land-use planning office in Yellowknife, assisted by a small staff of planners and technicians. The director also would chair an inter-governmental (technical) committee of senior officials of government agencies with responsibilities related to land-use planning. This committee would facilitate co-ordination of government activities, plan implementation, etc.

There is absolutely no suggestion of an intent to develop local and regional institutions for land-use planning. There is also no hint whatever of the role of public participation in plan preparation. Meanwhile, planning is still seen as largely product rather than process oriented. For example, there is no reference to any process for appeals, amendment, updating, or periodic review.

One can only infer that, while temporary interdisciplinary planning teams (and perhaps the commission) may visit local planning areas, actual plan preparation and preliminary approval will take place in Yellowknife. This conclusion is reinforced by the proposal that:

> Once the draft plan is acceptable, the Commission would sponsor public meetings or hearings to discuss, review and receive comments and recommendations, and will ensure that appropriate modifications are made.

This principle further implies that the public's role is to be confined to the review of "acceptable" plans. Acceptable to whom? The operational mechanisms proposed in the March 1983 *Basis of Agreement* are therefore as "top down" in character as those originally proposed by DIAND in October 1982. The difference is that the top has been broadened to include the GNWT.

Conclusion

In spite of improvements over the October 1982 proposal, the process as advanced in the current *Basis of Agreement* may:

a. inhibit the full expression of community and regional interests and priorities in land-use plans, while fostering the centralist bias;

b. squander an opportunity for community-based learning about the issues, values, conflicts, techniques, and procedures of planning; and

231

c. lead to suspicion of, and hostility toward, the planning process at the local level, thereby increasing community alienation.

Clearly, much careful thought must yet be given to planning as process and the role of the public and local institutions. Appropriately designed, these factors can spell the success of northern land-use planning; ignored, they will be its undoing.

Press Release

The *Press Release* outlines basic principles determined by the major native organizations to be essential for their co-operation and participation in land-use planning. According to the *Press Release*, the meetings at which these were presented (ending 5 May 1983) were the first opportunity these groups have had to meet with government officials to discuss the issue of land-use planning.

Not surprisingly, some of the native peoples' principles differ in emphasis and substance from those advanced by the central governments, as shown by the following four examples:

- . . . land use cannot be planned and managed without reference to the human community. Accordingly, social, cultural and economic endeavours of the human community must be *central to land use planning* and implementation [emphasis added].
- The primary purpose for land use planning in the N.W.T. must be to protect and promote the existing and future well-being of the permanent residents and communities of the N.W.T. taking into account the interests of all Canadians . . . .
- The planning process must ensure land use plans reflect the priorities and values of the residents of the planning regions . . . .
- To be effective the public planning process must provide an opportunity for the active and informed participation and support of the residents affected by the plan. Such participation will be promoted through means including: . . . recruitment and training of local residents to participate in comprehensive land use planning.

The orientation here is toward effective recognition of northern and even local interests through land-use planning, with due regard to territorial and national concerns. This view is a complete reversal of the structural bias contained in the October 1982 and March 1983 proposals produced by government.

A response from Ottawa and Yellowknife consistent with these principles would necessarily represent a significant compromise. The way would then be clear for the development of a land-use planning system that would answer many of the criticisms raised against both the October 1982 and March 1983 position papers. In this light, it is encouraging that both levels of government have accepted the native peoples' principles in their entirety.

Opinion Paper

Northern Communities and Regional Planning

Maggie Jones
Urban and Regional Planning Department
Ryerson Polytechnical Institute

The purpose of this paper is to suggest some of the factors at the community level that will have implications for the Department of Indian Affairs and Northern Development's (DIAND) northern land-use planning policy and process and vice versa.[1] It is difficult, however, to predict what these implications might be, because of the ongoing land-claims negotiations and the presumed eventual settlement of those claims. DIAND's northern land-use planning policy proposes that the formulation of regional planning policy and the initiation of the regional planning process be carried out concurrently with claims negotiations. Further, consideration and possible approval of specific development projects is not to be halted during the regional planning phase.

Inevitably, under these conditions, there will be some confusion and conflict. Five factors that will affect the regional planning process are the present administrative structures and practices; land claims; attitudes toward planning; values; and the community boundaries issue.

Present Administrative Structures and Practices

The Community Level

It is the stated aim of the Government of the Northwest Territories (GNWT) to devolve powers to the local government at the community level. Local government is seen by the GNWT as being instrumental in developing political and social awareness, capability, and expertise at the community level. The present system of local government, however, based on a southern model, is inflexible and incompatible with the traditional social structure and decision-making process of the native peoples. Local autonomy is granted by the territorial administration in spirit but is not granted in fact. Authority and control over local matters is, in practice, centralized in Yellowknife.

Local councils have control over only those services and programmes designated by the territorial administration. These are defined by the municipal status of each specific settlement. By and large, the areas of authority that have been granted to local councils involve the physical operation of the settlements. Although the essential hard services are important, the native residents see other issues at the local level (social, economic, educational) as affecting them more profoundly.Yet, local control is not granted in these areas. Participation in local government therefore is not given a high priority and frequently is issue-generated rather than ongoing.

Another problem that arises is the excessive demands that are made on those in the community who do choose to participate. The plethora of meetings of various committees easily can result in "burnout," and the southern-style schedule of meetings with time limits for decisions is incompatible with the native decision-making process. Power can become concentrated in few hands—often the hands of those who have the tenacity or specific motives to "hang in."

Local council control is undermined by several special-purpose committees that exist at the local level independent of councils. Sectoral committees, such as the Housing Association, interact directly with their counterparts at the territorial government level; as a result, decisions that affect the community are fragmented and often inconsistent with one another. The result of this fragmented approach to local administration is that, in answer to a municipal problem or issue, often several approaches are developed, none of which truly represents the community. In the western Arctic this is complicated further by the existence of a band council in addition to the local municipal council.

Thus, the problems that must be faced at the community level are: first, generating and maintaining interest in the regional planning process; secondly, trying to avoid overloading community leaders; and thirdly, determining which authorities to work with to ensure that the true community interest is put forward and to avoid exacerbating the already fragmented nature of community decision making.

The Territorial Level

The territories are not yet self-governing, and several responsibilities granted to provinces are retained by the federal government through its ministries and agencies. The most important of these as far as planning is concerned are the control of Crown lands (99 per cent of land north of 60°) and the administration of non-renewable resource development.

The territories have been granted many areas of jurisdiction by the federal government. These powers are guarded jealously and exercised with rigour, and a federal regional planning policy and process that directly addresses the communities' interests likely will be viewed with hostility by the territorial administration. However, a regional planning process that ignores the communities or grants them little input will be ineffective at best. This dilemma is unique to the North. In no other region of Canada does it occur, so there are no precedents to follow in developing the multilevel intergovernmental communication and co-operation that are essential for effective regional planning.

Much territorial legislation, which was of necessity drafted hurriedly after 1967, is based on similar legislation in the provinces. It does not take into consideration the very different nature of the northern peoples and their environment, nor the regional variations in these elements that occur within the territories. As a result, there is a lack of flexibility in territorial approaches to municipal issues, including planning, that may inhibit the adoption of different approaches for the various regions in the course of the federal regional-planning process. The problems to be addressed at the territorial level include the understandable sensitivity of the territories to the exercise of power by the federal level of government, in particular DIAND; the development of intergovernmental procedures that will maximize communication and co-operation that includes the communities; and the adaptation of potentially differing approaches used in diverse regions to the inflexible, territory-wide provisions of the existing legislation with regard to planning and municipalities.

The Regional Level

The developing sense of regionalism in the N.W.T. is demonstrated by the evolution of several regional councils. Significantly, these councils have evolved spontaneously out of common community concerns; they have not been imposed. However, the GNWT has not, and will not in the near future, devolve any powers or responsibilities to the regional level. Powers may be transferred only from the local level up to the regional level. Given the few powers granted the local level, it is not likely that much power will be relinquished. So far, regional councils have played only an advisory and advocacy role.

The regional planning process and policy should take note of the common interests and concerns of the communities that have surfaced with the development of these councils. These groups could play an instrumental role in helping to define policy objectives at the regional level. The more-detailed policies and proposals should be discussed at the community level.

Land Claims

Assuming eventual settlement of claims, the administration of those claims likely will result in overlapping areas of jurisdiction, duplication of services, and multiple representation of some groups through several legitimate bodies. Claims settlements will necessitate changes in the relationships between the federal, territorial, and municipal levels of government.

Comprehensive regional land-use planning is seen by the native groups engaged in claims negotiations as a useful tool in the protection of lands on which their traditional lifestyle depends. Major representation on the proposed regional planning commissions is being sought by some native groups as one of the conditions of settlement. The native groups seek control over allocation of lands for various purposes, and they view land-claims settlement as being of paramount importance. This is their strongest commitment and until agreements are signed their energies and interest will not be readily available for regional planning.

If the regional planning process precedes claims settlement, the native peoples may well view any approved plan simply as closing off options for the future.

Attitudes toward Planning— The Community Experience

The experience of local communities in dealing with planning will affect their approach to the regional planning initiatives. This experience up to now has not been particularly good.

Authority for community planning was transferred from Ottawa to the GNWT in the late 1960s. Until that time the settlements had grown incrementally, each new element being added and fitted in as each new policy and associated programme emanated from Ottawa (housing, health, community power supply, etc.). These additional land uses and services were put in place without even a rudimentary land-use plan. Partly because of considerations of cost, expediency, and inertia, many inappropriate decisions were made about issues such as the siting of airstrips.

The first phase of community planning usually was carried out by southern consultants hired by the GNWT Department of Local Government. The consultants were to develop comprehensive plans for those settlements under pressure from development or rapid growth. The era of the "suitcase planner" had begun. The consultants spent little time or effort in trying to understand community problems and values, and rarely were sympathetic to native sensibilities. The legacy of mistrust between northern native and southern expert resulted in widespread suspicion of the consultant planner. Native peoples felt unable to explain their priorities, or felt that it was pointless to try because southerners would neither listen nor understand. The final plan produced as a result of this process had little local input, and usually was similar to a plan developed for a southern Canadian community. It rarely was translated into the native language, even in summary form. Not surprisingly, these plans rarely were implemented.

In the late 1970s, the GNWT Department of Local Government decided to phase out the consultants and to take upon itself the comprehensive planning of the settlements. Although this in-house approach was an improvement over the efforts of the consultants, it too had its shortcomings. Community plans now were being prepared in Yellowknife by persons of southern attitudes, education, experience, and professional persuasion. In some respects the approach and results were similar to those of the consultants. This time it was the territorial bureaucrats who visited the community, suitcases in hand, to have a cursory look at the settlement, meet with the local council and community residents, and then retreat to Yellowknife to draw up the plan. This routine, albeit slightly modified, still is followed today in many communities.

The community planning experience parallels that of many other activities initiated by senior levels of government. To overcome this negative legacy and the intense native scepticism of the southern expert, the regional planning bureaucrats and technicians will require endless goodwill, patience, and time—qualities that have been in short supply in the past.

Values

To plan effectively it is necessary to have some appreciation of the underlying philosophy and values of the society for whom the planning is being done. In the case of regional planning in the North, two sets of values come into conflict: those of the dominant "national" society, and those of the northern native peoples who are the majority residents. The two value systems are diametrically opposed.

The Working Groups

The northern land-use planning policy states that, in addition to local and regional interests, national interests and concerns are to be considered when allocating land for various uses. In no province are national interests placed on an equal footing with local and regional ones. In the North it is not clear which level of interest is pre-eminent, but, if past experience is any indication, national interests will take precedence over local and regional interests. In any event, the policy ensures that the two sets of values will continue to conflict.

The effects of southern culture on the northern native population have been massive and rapid, and the pressures to change and conform to the dominant culture still are accelerating. Nevertheless, native cultural values are held strongly and must be understood by planners in the field and by bureaucrats in head office.

The different native populations in the North hold similar, although not identical, views of their world. They view their world in a holistic way, and, thus, their attitude toward land and their concept of sharing have important implications for planning. Freedom of access and flexibility of use are at the base of the native view of land, which they believe cannot, and should not, be fragmented, subdivided, and categorized. Yet, drawing boundaries and designating specific uses is a favourite pastime of planners. Thus, the two cultures clash when planners attempt to explain which activities are allowed and which are prohibited.

Differing attitudes toward time also cause many problems and frustrations when both cultural groups are participating in the same planning process. Native peoples sense an appropriate time for things to be done and decisions to be made. Scheduled meetings, deadlines for submissions, and fly-in visits from experts rarely coincide with that appropriate time.

Native decision making is a complex and comprehensive, but non-linear, process. Decisions are arrived at through lengthy discussion of all facets of an issue, not through adversarial debate. Decisions are reached by consensus, not by simple majority.

These values have important implications for the public participation that is to be an integral part of the northern land-use planning policy. The various formats used extensively in the South (public hearings, technical reports, workshops, etc.) are inappropriate to the North. Innovative formats must be developed, possibly using radio, community television, and video-cassette. The various native broadcasting agencies and the Canadian Broadcasting Corporation (CBC) should be consulted early in the planning process, and should be encouraged to work along with the process.[2] Referendums on specific issues might prove useful. Above all, imagination is needed here.

The participation programme will be costly and time consuming both for the federal agency given the responsibility for it and for members of the public who wish to participate. Adequate funding must be made available to ensure a free two-way flow of information between planning agency and public. Public hearings, if used, must be accessible to all those affected by a plan who wish to have input. This can be achieved either by holding hearings in the affected communities, or by providing subsidies to individuals and groups for travel to a central location. Other forums may be more effective, however, and funding also should be available for experimentation and execution of these methods.

Northern communities have experienced tokenism many times, with the result that there exists a deep cynicism that is potentially destructive to any planning process.

Community Boundaries Issue

A specific concern of communities that will be affected by regional planning is the contentious issue of municipal boundaries. At present, these boundaries are geometric lines drawn around the "built-up area" for administrative purposes. They demonstrate no consideration for the social, economic, and environmental realities of community life in the North.

Northern communities are the focal points of the often-large geographic regions used by native peoples in pursuing the traditional lifestyle. Many of the activities that provide the community's economic base are carried on in this economic hinterland, over which the community has no control. Increasing participation in wage labour means that hunting trips often are shorter than they were previously. This can result in more-intensive use of those areas contiguous to the municipalities. Native peoples want a greater degree of control over land use and wildlife management in such areas—areas that they consider to be a part of their community.

Even such mundane matters as water sources, sewage and garbage disposal sites, and sand and gravel deposits were not taken into account when municipal boundaries were drawn. This problem is solved in part by the federal Block Land Transfer Program, which co-ordinated the transfer of administration and control of federal lands in and around northern communities to the GNWT; however, native communities fear that designating lands in this manner will preclude other options in the future.

Native communities are growing rapidly as a result of high birth rates; thus, the need to control land use within the municipal boundaries and the economic region will intensify. The regional planning process must be sensitive to this issue.

241

Conclusion

To introduce a regional planning process into the volatile territorial scene will be difficult, given the many contradictory objectives of the proposed policy. The communities themselves also are changing rapidly—socially, economically, and politically. Native groups are highly politicized and are increasingly well organized.

Because settlement is a relatively recent experience and the local level of government is weak, there is not yet a strong identification with the settlements as such. Rather, the commitment is to the region on which the community depends. Thus, any disposition or designation of lands within the region will be scrutinized closely; any activity of "outsiders" will be observed, and any disturbance noted. The process, therefore, must be open and informative; there must be no hidden agendas.

It is to be hoped that the planning process will allow, if not require, that the personnel involved will live in a community within the region being planned, as this would aid two-way communication and education.

The communities are afraid that the northern land-use planning policy will be another example of planning *for* the people. They dare not hope for planning *by* the people and so are keeping their fingers crossed for, at best, planning *with* the people. Surely, planners have a special responsibility to make sure that this will happen this time around.

Endnotes

1. The communities being addressed here are the small, scattered, predominantly native settlements, many of which are of relatively recent origin. This assessment is based on knowledge of the situation in the N.W.T. and therefore may not be applicable to the settlements in the Yukon.

2. An excellent example of public participation in the examination of a contentious issue is the series of video-tapes produced by the Inuit Broadcasting Corporation on the Kaminuriak caribou herd. An adaptation of the CBC's former "Radio Farm Forum" might prove useful both in educating the public and in eliciting feedback on the issues.

Background Paper

Land-use Planning in the Yukon

Lindsay Staples
Yukon Conservation Society
Whitehorse, Yukon

On 29 November 1982, the Yukon Territorial Government (YTG) tabled Bill 14—The Yukon Land Planning Act—for first reading in the legislature. In so doing, it became the first government in Canada to legislate comprehensive land-use planning north of 60°. Such an initiative was welcomed by many organizations and agencies across the country. The expressed intent of establishing a legislated base for comprehensive, integrated Yukon-based land-use planning was, on its own, acknowledged as a sign of perception and maturity toward the responsible allocation and management of resources.

Within the territorial legislature, however, strong opposition arose over the discretionary powers of the government, the lack of policy guidelines, the absence of firm guarantees for public consultation, the questionable distribution of powers and responsibilities within the planning structure, and the poorly defined nature of the process itself. Indeed, the deeper motives of the initiative were viewed by some as suspect, the act heavily compromised by political ends[1]—securing block land transfers and increased jurisdictional control behind the façade of a responsible planning initiative.

Within one week of its introduction, over strong criticism from the Council for Yukon Indians (CYI) and the New Democratic Party in opposition, Bill 14 was given final reading and carried to the commissioner of the Yukon for proclamation. An act deserving of close scrutiny and broad public comment was set aside quickly to languish quietly in the face of bewildered media and an ill-informed public.

In this paper, I consider some of the major deficiencies of the Yukon Land Planning Act within the context of policy and planning initiatives undertaken recently by both the YTG and other northern-based organizations and agencies. I seek to address the failures of land-use planning in the Yukon to date and, in so doing, to suggest what a co-operative, territorial-federal land-use planning process must consider and be responsible to.

Background

The *ad hoc* nature of decision making in respect to northern land-use planning is well documented.[2] The Territorial Land Use Regulations, enacted in 1971, are a frequently cited example of a short-sighted, piece-meal, reactive approach to land management. The ability of the regulations to protect the environmental landscape is seriously limited and is compromised by the fact that they do not apply to mining activities—the largest use of non-renewable resources in the Yukon. Also, the administration of the regulations has been questioned because the Department of Indian Affairs and Northern Development (DIAND) assumes dual and conflicting roles as both facilitator and regulator of northern development. The high degree of discretionary powers afforded the engineer, the lack of policy guidelines, and the "closed shop" approach of DIAND's land-use advisory committees require a significant leap of faith if one is to believe that the public good is being served, and the full range of environmental values considered, in the pursuit of balanced development.

Toward the end of the 1970s, increasing land-use conflicts across the North and heightened environmental concerns brought recognition of the need for comprehensive planning of land use guided by revised policies in the resource sector. Competing proposals for land use associated with transportation corridors, mineral and hydro-electric developments, off-shore oil, agriculture, tourism, conservation lands, and native land claims made the allocation of natural resources very difficult.

At the same time, native and non-native northerners have come to expect greater participation in the opportunities and benefits of development according to their own aspirations and choices. Besides this, they have a strong desire for the further evolution of self-government in the Yukon and in the Northwest Territories. Although much of this was recognized as early as 1972 in DIAND's "National Objectives," it was still regarded as inevitable that policies affecting northern resource development would be formulated in the South according to southern priorities.[3]

In 1980, the National Energy Program reiterated a role for northerners in northern development: "In the North, our national objectives are . . . to achieve resource development at a rate and in a manner compatible with a delicate social and environmental balance, recognizing that northerners will play a growing role in both the decisions and benefits associated with that development."[4]

Initial efforts at co-operative local and sub-regional planning in the North involving the two levels of government were limited.[5] In 1975, the Mackenzie Delta Gas Assessment Group (MADGAG), jointly adminis-tered by the Government of the Northwest Territories (GNWT) and

DIAND, met with early failure because of poor intergovernmental relations and confused native and community involvement.[6] In 1978, the Committee for Original Peoples' Entitlement (COPE) agreement in principle provided for the establishment of a western arctic land-use planning commission, with representatives from the Inuvialuit and from the federal and territorial governments, but without final agreement, the proposals are not in effect.

Co-operative land-use planning exercises in the Yukon have occurred under a series of *ad hoc* federal–territorial agreements. Sub-regional plans for East Kluane, and Whitehorse North and South, did solicit community participation in their development, but upon their completion they were never subject to public review. None of these plans has the approval of a federal or territorial minister; they serve principally as an internal framework for government planners with respect to the designation of agricultural and recreational lands in zoning exercises. Other significant areas proposed for planning or currently being planned under these *ad hoc* joint agreements include Mackenzie Pass, the Beaufort North Slope, the Alaska Highway pipeline corridor, and the Dempster Highway corridor.

The most extensive and comprehensive resource-use planning exercise in the Yukon today is the Yukon River Basin Study (similar to the Mackenzie River Basin Study in the N.W.T.) involving federal, territorial, and provincial governments. Again, the planning mechanism is an *ad hoc* creation of intergovernmental cost-sharing agreements. In all of these cases, the planning mechanism is not consistent from exercise to exercise. Planning guidelines are highly discretionary and reflect the concerns and interests of the governments involved. Public consultation often consists of an "open house" where the public is simply informed about the mandate and programme of a solidly entrenched planning exercise and given the opportunity to respond. It is frequently no more than an exercise in public relations.

Legally, DIAND, as the landlord of 99.8 per cent of the land in the Yukon, has the right to undertake land-use planning unilaterally. Practically, it is doubtful that such an attempt would be successful without the help of the territorial governments and other departments. Intergovernmental and interdepartmental administrative arrangements have provided information exchange and co-ordination of activities through a number of bodies and programmes such as the Arctic Waters Advisory Committee, the International Biological Programme (IBP), and the Arctic Land Use Research Program. The participation of public-interest groups such as the Yukon Conservation Society and the Canadian Arctic Resources Committee has been vital to the development and review of policy.

The Working Groups

The effectiveness of the planning process in natural resource management rests heavily upon the effectiveness of interagency and interorganizational co-operation and co-ordination. The Ibex Pass Resource Study and Management Alternatives prepared for the Northern Pipeline Agency and the Yukon Department of Renewable Resources makes this abundantly clear[7] and cites a number of obstacles that stand in the way of establishing management goals and objectives, let alone achieving them: the "uncertainty of native land claims"; "the absence of background data"; "the lack of general clearly defined planning programs or strategies"; and the "apportionment of jurisdictional powers and land management responsibilities among a range of federal, territorial and occasionally private organizations."[8] Problems associated with jurisdictional co-operation and responsibility clearly affect the means of implementing any management plan. The authors of the Ibex report suggest that jurisdictional problems preclude agreement in three particular areas:

- a comprehensive agricultural policy
- general goals and policy to guide the direction of land use
- a newly revised policy for managing quartz and placer mining.[9]

With the absence of a fully integrated and formalized co-operative approach to planning, the North has been devoid of major policies. No framework has existed to view such land-use application and assess the broad long-term cumulative and interactive effects of incremental development. The lack of such a regional land-use picture has prevented the just resolution of conflicting uses.

In the Yukon, the territorial government's Area Development Ordinance has been a powerful means of land-use regulation. Under the ordinance, the commissioner may designate as a development area any region within the territory that he deems in the public interest to regulate. As well, the ordinance provides for the administration of any development area through the commissioner's regulatory capability. Much of this amounts to a zoning function with a strong municipal orientation given to considering "the allocation of land in the area for agricultural, residential, business, industrial, educational, public or other purposes."[10] The broad definition given to powers of the commissioner in the ordinance has been interpreted by YTG officials as providing them with the authority to undertake land-use planning exercises, of which the most significant is the Dempster Highway management planning process.

Begun in 1958 and completed in 1979, the Dempster Highway was built as an incentive to development in the northern Yukon, without evaluation of its environmental effects and with little formal public examination of its related social and economic costs and benefits. Other than some hunting restrictions (mainly scheduling) along the highway corridor, no management policy for caribou existed until DIAND proposed management plans in 1978. In response, and under the authority of the Area Development Ordinance, the YTG initiated the development of its own plan.

The Dempster Highway Management Committee, established to oversee the interim plan and formulate the final management plan, is composed exclusively of government members, predominantly from the YTG. Community involvement has been absent in the formulation of the plan.

Five years after DIAND's first initiative, no management plan yet exists. In the face of the YTG's promotion of the Dempster Highway as a transportation corridor to developments in the Beaufort region, the closed nature of the planning process leaves many of the most basic questions unacknowledged and unanswered:

1. Will the Dempster Highway be used as a corridor for arterial road construction to mineral deposits or to Old Crow?
2. Will the YTG's proposal to link the Dempster Highway with King Point by road conflict with COPE's agreement in principle?
3. Will the management plan reflect and mitigate the effects of increased traffic on the Porcupine caribou herd?
4. Will the authority of a final management plan be extended to arterial roads emanating from the Dempster Highway's protected eight-km corridor, to ensure that migrating caribou are protected from unlimited access?
5. Will the final plan provide a mechanism for the joint territorial management of the caribou herd and include participation from the subsistence user groups?

The Dempster Highway management planning process exemplifies the highly discretionary and *ad hoc* nature of land-use planning under the YTG's Area Development Ordinance. It illustrates how environmental values can be compromised and community concerns ignored, even in circumstances where no specific development proposals have been presented for consideration.

In 1981, the short-lived Beaufort Sea Task Force set up by DIAND made the following observation of resource-use planning in the North:

> No regional development framework exists at present; thus, industrial projects cannot be viewed in a long-term, cumulative and comprehensive context so as to maximize regional and local socio-economic benefits and minimize environmental inpacts; the lack of such a planning framework could preclude future resource use options. Coupled with this is the lack of a focused forum within which conflicting interests may be openly debated and balanced; the interests of all those affected must be considered in the decision-making process. Fundamental questions on the pace, direction and framework for development must be addressed in a national, regional and local context.[11]

The rapid increase in Beaufort Sea exploration activity and proposed hydrocarbon developments offer the most recent indication of the potential land-use conflicts in the North, particularly in light of the National Energy Board's and Justice Berger's recommendations for the northern Yukon and Mackenzie Delta, which gave strong consideration to conservation and subsistence land use. After so many years of *ad hoc* resource-use planning across the North, however, the flurry of proposals to establish formal, comprehensive land-use planning that emerged through 1981–82 cannot be attributed solely to a rapid increase in proposals for northern development.

The DIAND Initiative and the Yukon Responses

The release of DIAND's "Northern Land Use Planning" discussion paper in July 1981 prompted a good deal of concern over co-operative land-use planning across the North.[12] The paper acknowledged the need to include native and territorial government organizations in the planning process. However, it gave simultaneous support for strong federal ministerial responsibility for planning and for Ottawa-based policy development— reiterated one year later in the October 1982 revised draft paper *Land Use Planning in Northern Canada* and the accompanying "Northern Conservation Policy and Strategy." This gave impetus to northern agencies and organizations to develop their own land-use policies and planning proposals at a time when devolution of powers, block land transfers, and the selection of lands associated with land claims were vital and immediate concerns to all northerners.[13]

In April 1982, the Yukon Territorial Government released *Land: A Yukon Resource—A Land Use Policy*. This document sketched out briefly a land-use planning structure that was to apply to all lands in the Yukon, and that was to serve as a vehicle for the transfer of lands in the devolution of federal responsibilities to the territorial government. Its opening statement left no doubt about its motivations:

> If there has been one paramount objective of every government since Yukon was created in 1898, it has been self-government. . . .
>
> This policy is a response to the federal position on land use planning, released on the 31st day of July, 1981. That policy was totally unacceptable. It emphasized federal control from Ottawa, and minimal territorial and local control. It would have created a bureaucratic layer between the Minister of Indian Affairs and Northern Development and our Government, slowing rather than facilitating the disposition of land to Yukoners.[14]

Soon afterward, in the late spring, the YTG entered a territorial election on the platform of "land for all Yukoners" advocating extensive land ownership for Yukoners under fully responsible self-government. Its land-use policy document of April 1982 not only established the basis for this platform, but also articulated the bottom line of its land-use policy, namely, land ownership:

> . . . the quid pro quo must be that the balance of Yukon lands would come under our jurisdiction following identification and protection of Indian lands.[15]

By August 1982, the Council for Yukon Indians (CYI) had published its own policy statements and proposals for a northern land-use planning mechanism in the Yukon. CYI's *Land Use Planning, Environmental Assessment and Land Ownership in Yukon* reaffirms the basic principles of the 12 December 1980 agreement in principle on land-use planning with DIAND and the YTG, but goes on to propose the mechanism by which land-use planning and environmental assessment would occur in the Yukon.[16]

In a letter to Chris Pearson, territorial government leader, on 17 September 1982, John Munro, Minister of Indian Affairs and Northern Development, clearly stated that the YTG's appeals for land transfer would be tied to the northern land-use planning process.[17] This was reiterated on 27 November 1982, when Munro addressed the Yukon legislature, stating that there would be "no transfers of land to the Government of Yukon before a comprehensive planning process was in place."[18] Two days later, the YTG introduced the Yukon Land Planning Act, declaring itself to be capable of planning and ready for ownership.

DIAND's response to the YTG's planning act was one of conditional support. In his letter of 17 September to Pearson, Munro had indicated his support for the YTG's planning initiative, in so far as it applied to commissioner's land—land representing less than 1035 km² (400 square miles), most of which lies within Yukon municipal boundaries. At this time he made known his expectations: that the YTG's planning process would be "developed in concert with the federal planning initiative and our respective planning initiatives will be integrated one with the other, so they are mutually complementary."[19] These statements of conditional support were repeated by Neil Faulkner, Assistant Deputy Minister of DIAND's Northern Affairs Program, at the time the act was passed.[20]

From the outset, the YTG had stated its commitment to a Yukon-based planning process that would plan all Yukon lands. With its own planning act in place and awaiting proclamation, its public response to DIAND's planning initiative was a single repeated message: the YTG already had a mechanism with which to conduct land-use planning; it simply needed land to plan.

This response was distinctly different from that of the GNWT. In spite of the unanimous opposition across the North to DIAND's *Land Use Planning in Northern Canada*, the territorial government in Yellowknife maintained its commitment to negotiating a joint policy and process. With native organizations prepared to discuss land-use planning outside the forum of land claims, tripartite discussions took place through the winter and spring between the GNWT, DIAND, and native organizations representing members of the Tungavik Federation of Nunavut, the Métis Association of the Northwest Territories, and the Dene Nation (including the Dene Regional Council) to achieve a co-operative agreement.

The opportunity to achieve a co-operative federal–territorial agreement for land-use planning in the Yukon, based on DIAND's planning initiative, was limited at best by the YTG's stance that its Land Planning Act would apply to all Yukon lands. Whatever likelihood of agreement existed quickly disappeared in December 1982, when the YTG decided to boycott land-claims negotiations, and effectively, all co-operative discussion between DIAND, the YTG, and CYI broke down.

Once again, the issue of land transfers and ownership was at the heart of the disagreement. The YTG held that the federal government had linked the transfers of land to the final settlement of the Yukon land claim.

DIAND maintained that the relationship between land transfers to the territorial government and the settlement of land claims was one of chronology, and not of intent. Although not ruling out transfers after land claims, DIAND maintained that discussion of land transfers could not take place until that time without compromising the integrity of the land claims themselves.

With the land-use planning policy and the act in place, and the perceived promise of wholesale transfer of land to Yukon jurisdiction after the settlement of land claims, the YTG's response to Munro's unwillingness to talk process and quantity with respect to land transfers was to "demand that some 3,000 square miles of land be transferred on or before the passing of Settlement Legislation and that a total of 15%–20% of Yukon's surface land be transferred by 1987."[21] As well, the YTG proposed the immediate creation of a joint committee with representation from federal and territorial governments to "expedite the transfer of surface lands to the control, management and administration of the Yukon Territorial Government with the ULTIMATE objective of transferring surface lands throughout Yukon to the Government of Yukon."[22]

These statements, adopted by the YTG as "Yukon's Position on Land," contained four points of contention with some significant changes from positions held earlier. First, land transfers would not await a final land-claims agreement; secondly, discussion of and planning for land transfers would occur prior to a final land-claims agreement; thirdly, rather than the transfer of all lands upon a final land-claims agreement, 15 to 20 per cent would be transferred between 1983 and 1987, with the vague implication that more lands (all?) would be transferred subsequently; and finally, no provision was made for CYI's participation on the transfer committee, contravening section 3.2.4.2 of the agreement in principle providing for 25 per cent CYI participation on any "body, board or committee."

Based on its unwillingness to address land transfers prior to a final settlement of native land claims, DIAND rejected the YTG's "position on land." The YTG, in turn, maintained its boycott of all land-claims discussions, and also refused to participate in any of the discussions associated with the negotiated revision of DIAND's *Land Use Planning in Northern Canada.*[23]

To date, the Yukon Land Planning Act stands as the only adopted mechanism for formal comprehensive land-use planning in the Yukon. Although CYI has proposed a mechanism for comprehensive land-use planning, in the face of the Yukon Land Planning Act, its real value now lies in its expression of native perceptions of adequate mechanisms for land-use planning and environmental assessment in the North. In the event of discussions into DIAND's land-use planning initiative for the Yukon, this document likely will serve as the basis for CYI's input and concerns.

To understand the YTG's Land Planning Act is to understand land-use planning as it exists for a government that proclaims itself to be ready to plan.

The Yukon Land Planning Act: Its Formulation and Intent

The approaches to the development of land-use planning policies and mechanisms adopted by the governments of the Yukon and Northwest Territories have been markedly different. Much of their difference depends on their differing perceptions of the means by which to achieve increased jurisdictional responsibility—an objective shared by both territorial governments. The GNWT has understood jurisdiction primarily as it applies to management regimes and, accordingly, has pursued a more equitable and more active role for itself in the development and administration of land-use planning mechanisms with the federal government. The question of land ownership stands as an important, but secondary, consideration. In contrast, the YTG has linked increased jurisdictional control primarily to land ownership and has sought the development of a mechanism for block land transfers. To be sure, the YTG has pursued a strong place for itself in any management exercise, but in the Yukon, discussion of land-use planning has been largely obscured by the debate over the timing of and vehicle for land transfers.

Land claims, the demand for agricultural lands and the Agricultural Development Act, and the Yukon Land Planning Act have all been viewed as means for accomplishing block land transfers. Each of these has been threatened with compromise in the service of the higher end of land ownership.

Land Claims

Although the YTG accepted the freeze on land transfers respecting native land claims, it also viewed land claims as a forum for linking block land transfers to agreements in principle with CYI. Federal government officials argued that once native claims and land selections were finalized, the YTG would secure its due, namely, the balance of Yukon lands. The refusal of the minister of Indian Affairs and Northern Development to admit any discussion of land transfers to the land-claims forum was based on the view that land claims were to be used strictly for land settlements with claims beneficiaries. The minister also argued that the YTG avoided the established mechanisms for block and spot land transfers through claims-induced transfers that gave no provision for prior resource assessment and consideration of land-use options essential to avoiding land-use conflicts.[24]

Ignoring questions pertaining to the adequacy of these mechanisms, the point remains that DIAND would not accept land claims as a vehicle for the discussion of territorial land ownership.

The Agricultural Development Act

In another vein, the YTG sought to secure interim land transfers through demonstrated need. After inviting applications for agricultural lands, YTG officials were able to announce, in November 1982, that 60 applicants awaited transfers from the federal government.[25] At the same time, the YTG announced a mechanism for the selection of agricultural land. The newly created Agricultural Development Council was given legislation enabling it to screen applicants and to advise the minister on agricultural policy.[26] In this way the YTG sought to demonstrate that it was not simply sponsoring land give-aways, and that a rational process existed for the selection of agricultural lands.

Whatever the shortcomings of the Agricultural Development Act—some of which are examined later—the minister of Indian Affairs and Northern Development clearly had a more comprehensive planning scheme in mind when he addressed the question of land transfers for agricultural land to the Yukon legislature: "I am prepared . . . subsequent to implementing a comprehensive and cooperative land planning process, to recommend the transfer of blocks of land for agriculture."[27]

Land-use Planning

With the relationship established by the federal minister between block land transfers and land-use planning, the YTG moved quickly to entrench its own co-operative and comprehensive land-use planning process. It acknowledged this linkage early on in its own land-use policy paper, although *Land: A Yukon Resource—A Land Use Policy* is noticeably thin on policy statements and discussion. Of the four basic policy guidelines set out in this document, three address land-use planning in the context of increased jurisdictional control and land ownership.[28] Much of the document comprises a description of a land-use planning mechanism, but any account or explanation of land-use planning as a process is virtually absent.

This same orientation carries over into the Land Planning Act. When questioned about the lack of a policy framework for the act, and the absence of any provision for a policy body in the planning process, the territorial minister of Renewable Resources, Howard Tracey, remarked: "I say that we do have a policy. Our policy is: land for all Yukoners. That is exactly what our policy is. Our intent is to make land available for all Yukoners."[29]

The idea here is that resource management and land-use planning are synonymous with land ownership, that the greatest expression of jurisdictional power lies in ownership, and that ownership in its own right implies responsible use. Thus, in seeking comprehensive land-use planning, one requires extensive land ownership.

None of this is to say that the Yukon demand for land ownership is not legitimate. The freeze on the transfer of lands associated with native claims has been a long one, and has been attended by a certain amount of frustration with the delays that have postponed a final settlement. The postponement of any discussion of land transfers until after a final settlement is but another delay, another tactic for refusing Yukoners what they want most, and an indication of DIAND's reluctance to relinquish any of the areas over which it holds jurisdiction.

Wildlife is the only resource over which the YTG holds legal jurisdiction. Its basic responsibility is to protect and maintain diverse species of wildlife at, or near, the carrying capacity of the land. This responsibility for maintenance of species is related intimately to the maintenance of land. Yet, the YTG has no jurisdiction to protect the land base, which puts territorial wildlife officials in a difficult position when it comes to habitat protection.

DIAND's outdated legislation and land-use statutes often work against the goals of territorial wildlife officials. The Quartz Act and the Placer Mining Act offer no protection of soil and vegetation, and the Fisheries Act, in spite of itself, gives recognition to the value of gold over fish. Clearly, mining and land-use legislation policies must be updated. The territorial government has every right to seek a greater role in the planning and management of the land base. Only in this way can wildlife management be truly integrated with more-comprehensive management of resources.

To date, problems of political interest and jurisdiction have resulted in the integrity of resource management and allocation being questioned. Gordon Hartman, former director of the Yukon Government's Wildlife Branch, wrote in 1980: "Yukon Government has legal jurisdiction over wildlife . . . . It is my impression after three years that in reality the jurisdiction is regarded by government as more important than the resource itself."[30]

The YTG has an interest in land, and an important and shared role to play in any land-use planning exercise. In pursuing land transfers and ownership through a hastily entrenched land-use planning act, the YTG has thrown into contempt the planning process that is the basis for sound resource management. The YTG invited neither public discussion of its land-use policy nor public input during the formulation of the land planning mechanism over some three years, and provided no public forum for review of the act. Many questions regarding planning policy, structure, and process have gone unacknowledged and unanswered. All that remains are the government leader's words of solace: "Why should anyone get uptight about a policy written by Yukoners, for Yukoners?"[31]

Structure and Decision Making

Legislative backing usually conveys a strong government commitment to the planning process. It takes more than statements of good intention to provide a set of guarantees as to how, and by whom, planning will take place, and to define its relationship to other programmes.

From the outset, the Yukon Land Planning Act is ambiguous, even with respect to the lands to which it applies. The act addresses land planning "districts," which include "any area, designated by any other name" (s.2(1)), and which are created by the executive council for any "purposes related to the administration of this Act" (s.36(1)). It remains unclear as to whether the jurisdiction being addressed here is federal or territorial. This ambiguity extends throughout the act. At no point is the question of split jurisdiction and related jurisdictional conflicts—real or potential—examined. No statements are given to define either the relationship between the federal and territorial governments with respect to land ownership and regulation; the recommendation-making powers of the land planning board *vis-à-vis* the two ministers; the decision-making powers of the ministers; or the final implementation of the adopted plan. The conviction, first articulated in *Land: A Yukon Resource—A Land Use Policy*, that a YTG planning proposal would apply to all Yukon lands, along with the assumption that a "co-operative" approach to planning could be secured with the simple allocation of several federal representatives to the land-use planning board and planning committees, can be seen as a transparent political response to DIAND's October 1982 proposal for northern land-use planning. In light of the history of jurisdictional disputes between Whitehorse and Ottawa, and the protracted negotiations over jurisdictional responsibilities between the GNWT and DIAND in their joint land planning proposals, the YTG's refusal to address any jurisdictional questions renders much of its planning act meaningless.

CYI has observed rightly that "the planning process has become a political debate for control, which is placing the whole process in jeopardy."[32] The failure of the YTG to confront jurisdictional questions in a way that pursues a truly co-operative and truly integrated process for land-use planning merely duplicates the very stance that it has accused DIAND of taking in its approach.

Under the Yukon Land Planning Act the influence of the territorial government throughout the planning process is extensive. The government appoints the planning board (s. 3(1)). The government appoints the chairman of the planning board, who in turn directs the work of the board and calls all meetings of the board according to his discretion (ss. 5(1); 9(1)). The government minister on the board can convene the board at his discretion, and can direct the board to consider matters referred to it by him (s.9(2)). The chairman of the board can vote twice in the event of a split decision. The second vote of the chairman will decide the matter (s. 10(2)). The government has the discretionary power to establish planning committees and to appoint the members to them (ss. 17(1); 18(1)). The government appoints the chairman of the committee, who directs the work of the committee and convenes its meetings at his discretion (ss. 19(1) and (2); 22(1)). The government may issue the terms of reference to the committee (s. 26(1)). The government may adopt plans that the board has recommended for adoption (s. 28(1)). The government may establish the planning districts (s. 36(1)).

The powers given to the YTG in the Land Planning Act were acknowledged by the minister of Renewable Resources as it was given final reading:

> [The Land Planning Act] gives this government a tremendous amount of power in the person of a member of the Executive Council . . . we already have on the books an act that is just as powerful—in fact, more powerful—than the one we are dealing with today. We have the Area Development Act, under which we could declare any area of this territory under the Area Development Ordinance and plan it. So, we already have the power to do our land use planning.[33]

Although the legality and authority of the ordinance referred to by the minister are questionable, the reference is an appropriate one. Both the Area Development Ordinance and the Land Planning Act provide the territorial government with a high degree of discretionary power. The Land Planning Act sets out a mechanism for land-use planning, but it is heavily compromised by the government's ability to exercise its discretionary influence upon it. For instance, through the powers of the chairman of the planning board, the government's view could easily prevail on a continuous basis. Because only the chairman and the minister have the power to direct the board and to convene meetings, the chairman could easily limit the effectiveness of the board. So, too, could the will of the government prevail through the power of the chairman to vote twice on split decisions.

Section 37(1) of the act provides the territorial government with basically the same broad powers of procedure as it gives the planning board in section 11: "The Commissioner in Executive Council may make regulations respecting the business and proceedings of the Board and Committees under this Act . . . and such other matters as he considers necessary for carrying the purposes and provisions of this Act into effect." It is difficult to conceive of what independent functions concerning procedure exist for the board under such a provision. Although "the board may make recommendations to the Executive Council Member respecting public participation in the preparation, review, adoption and implementation of plans" (s. 15(2)), again the decision is left to the executive council member who "may, by order, provide for public participation" (s. 30(1)).

Under the act, the planning board depends heavily upon the territorial government. The territorial government, on the other hand, can act independently of the recommendations of the planning board. Thus, the planning board cannot recommend a plan to the ministers before it has received the recommendations of the district planning committees, whereas there is nothing to suggest that the YTG cannot act largely unilaterally to legislate a land-use plan that ignores both the recommendations of the planning board and the concerns of the public at large.

The federal presence articulated in the Yukon Land Planning Act is, at best, a subdued one. On the planning board, the federal government is allotted two representatives of a membership of eight; on the planning committees, it is allotted one representative of a membership ranging from four to eight. The individual conspicuous by his absence throughout this process is the federal minister of Indian Affairs and Northern Development. At no point is any decision-making function attributed to him— even in a shared capacity. In the act, he is referred to only once, and there his role is passive. The planning board is called upon to make recommendations to him, and to the territorial minister, about land-use planning in the Yukon. Beyond receiving these recommendations, nothing is asked of him and nothing is expected from him.

The Yukon Land Planning Act essentially addresses planning as it relates to structure and product, of which the latter is subject to a YTG presence that dominates the planning structure. The absence of any examination or explanation of the planning process is general and, specifically as it relates to jurisdictional concerns and conflicts, renders the very practicality of the planning mechanism questionable.

Policy

The Yukon Land Planning Act is an act without policy framework, distinguished from other comprehensive planning initiatives across the North by its lack of attention to policy, and its failure to provide a mechanism for developing and interpreting policy relevant to land-use planning. The only provision given to policy considerations is in section 25(1), which calls upon the planning committee to "take into consideration . . . the objectives, policies and programs of the Government of Yukon brought to the attention of the Committee by the Executive Council Member or otherwise known to the Committee." Existing policies can hardly be considered if they have never been publicly and clearly articulated.

Little policy exists with respect to resource management and development and land-use planning within the YTG. The only document that has been released publicly and that has claims policy status is *Land: A Yukon Resource—A Land Use Policy*, in which three or four land-use policy statements speak to the issue of increased jurisdictional powers and land ownership, and the fourth simply recognizes the need for land-use planning across the Yukon.[34] To suggest that principles on land ownership and jurisdiction constitute a land-use policy not only is misleading, but also ignores the substantive question of how best to manage public resources.

The YTG's record in the policy area is dismal and is strongly indicative of the *ad hoc*, discretionary approach that has characterized government planning. To date, although this government has jurisdiction for wildlife, it has neither wildlife policy nor policy respecting conservation lands and heritage areas. It has a vested interest in development of the Beaufort region, yet has no policy on energy, resource development, or comprehensive regional planning. It actively pursues the transfer of lands for agriculture, yet has no agricultural policy. It has legislated land-use planning, yet has no land-use policy.

The efforts of the YTG to develop an agricultural policy are a case in point. In spite of statements by the government leader claiming the existence of an agricultural policy, no such policy has ever been released for public scrutiny or input.[35] The minister responsible for agriculture himself has cast doubts on the status of government agricultural policy, when he remarked: "how could you have an agriculture policy with no land?"[36] Although territorial officials may view the denial of lands by the federal government as precluding the development of agricultural or any other policies, it did not impede their efforts to legislate an act establishing a mechanism for agricultural land selections and an act establishing land-use planning.

The Agricultural Development Act provides a process for the selection of land through the creation of the Agricultural Development Council and effectively removes agricultural policy from public scrutiny. This body is empowered to develop policy and to make recommendations to the minister, but it is not accountable to the legislature, as it functions under the direction of the minister and the Cabinet. In this way, discussion of the effects on agricultural policy of competing land-use interests such as mining, wildlife, and agriculture becomes an internal government exercise whereby a minister can make a policy decision without consultation.

At present, no land-use policies exist to accompany land-use plans and no policy framework exists to guide planning. Where will land-use policies come from? Where will decisions about development strategies come from? With no provision for an advisory or a policy committee, the planning act directs the planning committees and the board to look only to the government, which makes decisions on policy internally without public review. In the forum of the land-use planning exercise, it appears likely that government policy might be made public as it is brought to the attention of the planning committees for consideration. Yet, under section 26(2), the government is empowered to provide terms of reference ensuring the confidentiality of the committee's reports if the government considers it advisable. Thus, the YTG policies can be brought to the attention of the planning committee through private and confidential correspondence, and the planning process reflects the private direction of a government that can resolve policy debates and conflicting interests internally. No body exists:

- to co-ordinate the terms of reference for the planning committees as set out by the planning board with government policy
- to co-ordinate departmental policies with the planning process
- to involve government agencies actively in the planning process
- to propose new policy arrangements for land-use planning

- to propose policy review in light of public input through the planning process
- to challenge the planning board as to its operations and procedures
- to review land-use plans to ensure that they reflect changing government policy.

Under the Land Planning Act, *ad hoc* government decision making will continue to guide planning. With no policy body in place to monitor and stimulate the planning process, planning will continue to be more reactive than anticipatory.

Public Participation and Balanced Interests

Public participation and involvement in the planning process are the means by which conflicting values are weighed and conflicting interests are judged in the political forum. They establish a public stage where the advocacy of interest groups can be subjected to broad scrutiny. If a full range of land-use options is to be considered, the options must be presented.

Public participation presupposes public information, without which the public cannot comment on planning and policy development, even through its elected representatives. Information on land-use issues, benefits, constraints, conflicts, hazards, and alternatives must be publicly available if the public is to affect the planning process through comment on land-use values and standards. Strong public involvement is the basis upon which the planning process will gain respect and land-use plans will enjoy community support.

The Yukon Land Planning Act offers no clear commitment to firm guarantees of public involvement. "The [Planning] Board may make recommendations to the Executive Council Member respecting public participation in the preparation, review, adoption and implementation of plans" (s. 15(2)). It will allot "such amount of time as the Board considers appropriate" (s. 15(3)), and give consideration in its recommendations to:

- any urgency that may affect the manner and extent to which the public should participate in the matter
- the apparent importance of, and public interest in, the matter for which the public participation is being recommended
- the estimated cost of the public participation being recommended

- the anticipated effectiveness of the proposed procedure for public participation in relation to its costs, public interest in the matter and the availability and effectiveness of alternative procedures
- how public participation, in respect of the matter, may take place most effectively at a cost appropriate to the importance of the matter (s. 15(4)).

The inadequacies of such an approach to public participation are significant. Meanwhile, participation remains discretionary and depends heavily upon political and bureaucratic will. To a great extent, the degree to which it is permitted seems to rest on a cost–benefit analysis of its merits. Institutional arrangements for public participation remain unclear, and the role of public involvement throughout the process remains ill-defined. No mention is made of the public's right of appeal. No direction is given as to how the input will be used. Much of the point of a public process is to resolve land-use conflict, yet no procedures are defined for its resolution.

Especially troubling is the matter of "urgency" as it affects the planning process. When a development proposal appears to carry attractive benefits, it is possible to envisage public participation being passed by in favour of the rapid adoption of a plan. Such a scenario becomes more plausible in light of recent statements by a senior government official who voted in support of the planning act: "[Land-use planning] is fine, for the long term, but there are things that should be allowed to proceed, and proceed fairly quickly, to get away from the red tape of government, and to get on and get the job done."[37]

He stated later: "I think it [land-use planning] is to everyone's benefit, as long as it is not seen that during the planning exercise that has to be gone through that it is going to hold up development which is perceived to be in the public interest."[38]

What we are left with in the short run, or when urgency warrants "development which is perceived to be in the public interest," is the same *ad hoc*, discretionary, in-house decision making that has characterized most territorial planning to date. In the past, it has been the very absence of a comprehensive planning process and of a regional framework within which to view development proposals that has led government leaders to jump to the tune of the first proposals to come along, fearing developers may go elsewhere. It has always been assumed that the kind of development that is in the public interest can be determined in advance, without any process of public consultation. Public hearings are seen as time-consuming exercises that merely confirm what all-knowing ministers have already prophesied. Public consultation is seen as an election once every four years.

The Working Groups

Under the Land Planning Act, the board can only recommend public participation to the executive council, but has no independent authority to conduct its own public participation programme. Neither is the government committed to public participation. These arrangements encourage strong interests to circumvent the formal planning process and its provision for public forums that democratize power, in favour of more private routes of access. If these routes prove equally effective as, or more effective than, the public forum at selling a particular point of view, they are hard to ignore for any group committed to advancing its interests.

The Land Planning Act sets out no minimum standards of accountability. With no guarantes of access to information, interested groups cannot make reasoned interventions respecting specific land-use proposals and any associated land-use conflicts. Under such circumstances, any information becomes "privileged," and those who have access to it hold a tremendous strength in presenting their case. Special interests establish themselves on the basis of privileged information and private access. Public servants come to be associated with a narrow range of interests by those standing outside the process.

The former director of the Yukon Wildlife Branch expressed his concern about the need for some basic standards of accountability, when he remarked:

Public participation and involvement is a critical element in resource management. I believe that resource managers in an area such as wildlife have to be free to discuss issues openly with the public. They should be free, in particular, to correct misinformation that reflects upon them . . . . In the field of resource management where tradeoffs have to be made, there will always be differing views among citizens and among public servants. Lively open discussion of such issues is not unhealthy. It provides all of us with the information that there is a conflict. It provides all of us with a chance to hear other views. Strong control of information and discussion does not allow this particularly well. Indeed, it may stop discussion after only one interest has been heard from.[39]

Balanced development rests upon a balance of interests, not simply between the natural environment and humans, but between persons. Public involvement and participation are the means by which human interests are balanced against one another. Land-use planners strive to achieve a balanced division among increasingly competitive users, but, in spite of their efforts, planning often falls well short of this goal. Land-use planning has been used by some to appease public concern, and a multiple-use policy has been employed to protect industrial interests. On occasion, with careful planning of the kind seldom seen, some competing uses can co-exist on the same tract of land. In practice, however, planners more often allocate large, poorly regulated tracts of land to major extractive users and then offer the remaining nooks and crannies to conservation interests.

The Yukon Land Planning Act makes no statement as to how conflicts are to be resolved. The choices are often harsh ones. In some areas where the land is low in productivity and the habitat fragile, and where populations require unobstructed space and are thus vulnerable to developments, achieving a balance between the interests may be difficult. Justice Berger observed:

> We should recognize that in the North, land use regulations, based on the concept of multiple use, will not always protect environmental values, and they will never fully protect wilderness values. Withdrawal of land from any industrial use will be necessary in some instances to preserve wilderness, wildlife species and critical habitat.[40]

Land-use planners, when considering multiple use and balanced development, must often compare values of different kinds. This difference is often resolved by converting all such values into economic terms. In the process, many social and environmental values become obscured. It is one thing to recognize that political decisions should be cost conscious, and it is another to accept the reduction of political decisions to market choices.

Although the Yukon Land Planning Act provides for consideration of a range of social, cultural, and economic values in the development of land-use plans, it offers no basic statements of commitment or of principle to the protection of the environmental integrity of the land and to the lives of the peoples who depend upon it. No acknowledgement is made of the importance of subsistence use, or of the native economy and social life. The only explicit reference to community involvement in the planning process, besides public participation, is the provision that requires the minister "to make a reasonable effort to nominate" a community resident (s. 18(2)). Thus, it is conceivable that participation by the residents of Old Crow could be limited to 25 per cent of the membership of the committee planning their district, i.e., the minimum representation to which CYI is entitled under the agreement in principle.

Some Closing Remarks

YTG's Land Planning Act is not law, for it has never been proclaimed, and the territorial government has made no announcement that proclamation is imminent.

On 15 May 1983, the YTG and DIAND signed a five-point document committing both the territorial and federal governments to joint land-use planning. Negotiations in Whitehorse are now underway [June 1983], with the recently signed GNWT–DIAND agreement in principle on land-use planning serving as a point of departure. To be sure, the agreement signed in Yellowknife needs significant development, but it represents a new opportunity for achieving responsible forward-looking land-use planning in the Yukon. It offers major improvements over many of the areas of deficiency in the Yukon Land Planning Act.

A co-operative YTG–DIAND land-use planning process raises a new set of questions in respect of planning in the Yukon:

- How will a YTG–DIAND planning mechanism affect the YTG's Land Planning Act? When adopted, will the new planning mechanism apply to all Yukon lands; to federal lands; to transfer lands?
- Will YTG officials be content to leave the Yukon Land Planning Act unproclaimed?
- Will block land transfers be tied to the adoption of land-use plans?
- In areas of overlapping territorial jurisdictions, how will the planning exercise be conducted?
- Will the Beaufort Sea and Mackenzie Pass regions be planned jointly by the YTG and the GNWT, or will one government take the lead and, if so, according to what criteria?
- What provisions will be made for planning in the interim?
- What will be the status of development proposals in the interim?
- What role will DIAND's regional office play with respect to the federal and territorial governments in the planning process?
- What will be the extent of CYI's formal participation in the planning process?

Endnotes

1. Dave Porter, Renewable Resources critic for the NDP, remarked in the legislature: "Some would think that the original impetus was to provoke an aggressive political campaign with the federal government." *Hansard,* The Yukon Legislative Assembly, no. 18, 2nd Session, 25th Legislature (1 December 1982), p. 342.

2. William E. Rees, "Development and Planning North of 60°: Past and Future," *Northern Transitions: Second National Workshop on People, Resources and the Environment North of 60°* (Ottawa: CARC, 1978), pp. 42–62; K.P. Beauchamp, *Land Management in the Canadian North* (Ottawa: CARC, 1975); A.R. Lucas and E.B. Peterson, "Northern Land Use Law and Policy Development: 1972-78 and the Future," *Northern Transitions: Second National Workshop on People, Resources and the Environment North of 60°* (Ottawa: CARC, 1978), pp. 63-93.

3. Jean Chrétien, *Canada's North: 1970-1980* (Ottawa, Department of Indian Affairs and Northern Development, 28 March 1972).

4. *The National Energy Program* (Ottawa: Energy, Mines and Resources, 1980), p. 76.

5. See N.H. Richardson Consulting, "Land Use Planning, Regional Planning, and Environmental Assessment: A Preliminary Review of Issues," (1982), pp. 2-5. Prepared for the Beaufort Sea Environmental Assessment Panel.

6. Rees, "Development and Planning North of 60°," pp. 49-53. See above, note 2.

7. Reid Crowther & Partners Ltd., *Ibex Pass Resource Study and Management Alternatives* (Whitehorse, 1983). Prepared for the Department of Renewable Resources, Yukon Territory, and the Northern Pipeline Agency Canada.

8. Ibid., s. 3.1

9. Ibid.

10. Area Development Ordinance, Government of Yukon, s. 4(1)(a).

11. *Report of Task Force on Beaufort Sea Developments,* by Olaf H. Løken (Ottawa, April 1981), s. 3.2.1.2. Submitted to the Senior Policy Committee, Northern Development Projects.

12. DIAND, "Northern Land Use Planning," Discussion Paper (July 1981).

13. DIAND, *Land Use Planning in Northern Canada,* draft (Ottawa: DIAND, 14 October 1982).

14. *Land: A Yukon Resource—A Land Use Policy* (Whitehorse: Government of the Yukon, 1982), "Introduction."

15. Ibid.

16. Council for Yukon Indians, *Land Use Planning, Environmental Assessment and Land Ownership in Yukon: A Discussion Paper* (Whitehorse: CYI, August 1982).

17. In his letter of 17 September to Pearson, Munro stated: "I anticipate that a comprehensive approach to land transfers will be developed in conjunction with the establishment of appropriate land use mechanisms in the territory." See *Hansard*, The Yukon Legislative Assembly, no. 18, 2nd Session, 25th Legislature (1 December 1982), p. 341.

18. See *Hansard*, The Yukon Legislative Assembly, no. 16, 2nd Session, 25th Legislature (29 November 1982), p. 287.

19. See *Hansard*, The Yukon Legislative Assembly, no. 18, 2nd Session, 25th Legislature (1 December 1982), p. 341.

20. Faulkner stated that a federal system involving territorial officials would apply to federal lands, thereby limiting the Yukon Land Planning Act to commissioner's lands—0.2 per cent of the Yukon's 1 248 380 km² (482 000 square miles). Both he and Munro invited the YTG to discuss the federal proposal. See *The Whitehorse Star*, 2 December 1982.

21. *Yukoners Deserve a Fair Deal: A Land Claims Information Package* (Whitehorse: Government of the Yukon, 1983), p. 36.

22. Ibid., p. 37.

23. In March 1983, the YTG extended its boycott to the DIAND-sponsored workshop in Whitehorse convened to discuss its draft discussion paper, *A Comprehensive Conservation Policy and Strategy for the Northwest Territories and Yukon* (Northern Environment Directorate, October 1982). Conspicuous by its absence, the YTG dismissed the opportunity to participate with a wide cross-section of representatives from government, industry, and native and conservation organizations in the formulation of a mechanism for developing a northern conservation policy with wide input and support.

24. See *Hansard*, The Yukon Legislative Assembly, no. 18 (1 December 1982), p. 341.

25. See *Hansard*, The Yukon Legislative Assembly, no. 16 (29 November 1982).

26. The Agricultural Development Act was tabled on 29 November 1982, the same day as the Land Planning Act.

27. See *Hansard*, The Yukon Legislative Assembly, no. 18 (1 December 1982), p. 337.

28. *Land: A Yukon Resource—A Land Use Policy* (Whitehorse: Government of the Yukon, 1982), p. 5.

29. Howard Tracey, *Hansard*, The Yukon Legislative Assembly, no. 18 (1 December 1982), p. 347.

30. Gordon F. Hartman, "Is there a future for Yukon Wildlife," *Northern Perspectives* 8:4 (Ottawa: CARC, 1980), p. 6.

31. Chris Pearson, in *The Whitehorse Star* (3 November 1982), p. 3.

32. Council for Yukon Indians, "Submission on Development in the Yukon Region." See this volume, pp. 653–656.

33. Howard Tracey, *Hansard*, The Yukon Legislative Assembly, no. 20 (6 December 1982), p. 378.

34. See above, note 28.

35. Chris Pearson announced to the legislature on 15 November 1982: "As all members are well aware, we now have an agricultural policy and we are hopeful that the Government of Canada will view that policy positively . . . ." *Hansard*, The Yukon Legislative Assembly, no. 8 (15 November 1982), p. 122. Ten days later he reported this statement. See *Hansard*, The Yukon Legislative Assembly, no. 15 (25 November 1982), p. 272.

36. Dan Lang, *Hansard*, The Yukon Legislative Assembly, no. 18 (1 December 1982), p. 335.

37. Dan Lang, *Hansard*, The Yukon Legislative Assembly, no. 3 (3 November 1982), p. 29.

38. Dan Lang, *Hansard*, The Yukon Legislative Assembly, no. 19 (2 December 1982), p. 359.

39. Gordon Hartman, *Northern Perspectives*, p. 8. See above, note 30.

40. Thomas R. Berger, *Northern Frontier, Northern Homeland: The Report of the Mackenzie Valley Pipeline Inquiry*, vol. 1 (Ottawa, Supply and Services, 1977), pp. xi–xii.

Background Paper

Land-use Planning in the North Slope Borough

Shehla Anjum
Planning Department
North Slope Borough
Barrow, Alaska

The history of the development of the North Slope Borough's Comprehensive Plan and Land Management Regulations is linked closely to the rapid exploration for and development of the oil and gas resources in the borough. Although oil and gas operations were initiated in 1944 with the U.S. Navy's programme in the western area of the borough, now known as the National Petroleum Reserve in Alaska, it was not until the 1960s that the pace quickened. In the early 1960s, there was further exploration under the aegis of the federal government on lands east of the National Petroleum Reserve and south of the present Prudhoe Bay oilfield, but commercial quantities of oil were not found.

In 1964, the State of Alaska initiated the leasing of lands in what is known as the mid-Beaufort area, bounded by the National Petroleum Reserve in the west and the Arctic National Wildlife Range in the east. The state conducted further sales in 1965, 1967, and 1969. In 1968, the Prudhoe Bay oilfield was discovered, the North Slope became an area of extremely high interest to the oil companies, and the Prudhoe Bay leases of the 1960s were further explored to delineate the Prudhoe Bay oilfield.

Plans to construct a pipeline to transport the oil from Prudhoe Bay were announced in 1960; but construction began only after the passage of the Alaska Native Claims Settlement Act in 1971 and the Trans-Alaska Pipeline Authorization Act in 1973. The Arctic Slope Regional Corporation, one of the 13 corporations created under the Native Claims Settlement Act, was incorporated in the summer of 1972, at the same time as the North Slope Borough.

The North Slope Borough is the largest municipality in the United States, covering 228 000 km² (88 000 square miles). The boundaries of the borough and the Arctic Slope Regional Corporation are roughly the same. The population of the borough is about 9000 individuals, which includes the workers in the Prudhoe and Kuparuk oilfields. The rest of the population lives in the eight villages of the North Slope, and in the military installations along the coast.

The resident population is mainly Inupiat. The Inupiat have inhabited the Arctic for more than 4000 years. The Inupiat way of life is linked closely to the harvesting of the renewable resources in the region. Both cultural and economic considerations support the continuation of this way of life and demand that future generations have access to the same species that are now in abundance. There is fear that uncontrolled development within the region will reduce the possibility for this way of life. This reduction could occur as a result of loss of habitat, forcing species to seek areas that are inaccessible to humans; as a result of an industrial accident, such as an oil spill, which would reduce the wildlife population drastically; or simply because access by humans to harvesting areas is restricted by the presence of oil-production pads, pipelines, gathering centres, camps, and roads. There is an additional conviction that state and federal regulations and enforcement would not be enough, and that the peoples of the North Slope should have a voice in how development proceeds within its boundaries.

Formation of the North Slope Borough

The North Slope Borough was formally incorporated as a first-class borough on 1 July 1972. Two main reasons justified the creation of this entity. First, there was now ample development at Prudhoe Bay to establish a tax base to enable the borough to generate revenues; and secondly, this government entity could regulate the pace of development by exercising its planning and zoning powers.

Predictably, the oil companies soon challenged the formation of the North Slope Borough. There was an attempt to delay the certification of the borough's organization election and, when this failed, a suit was filed to invalidate the formal incorporation of the North Slope Borough. The companies contended that the formation of the borough would not benefit them in any way, and they expressed doubts about the borough's ability to provide them with traditional municipal services such as water, sewer, electricity, and other utilities. The companies had no desire to subject themselves to regulations devised by this new government, and also maintained that although they would receive no benefits, taxes on the industrial property at Prudhoe Bay would provide the borough with revenues.[1] The borough withstood the legal challenges. In January 1974, the Alaska Supreme Court dismissed the companies' suits. The companies had prepared well for this eventuality, however, by seeking to restrict the borough's taxing authority. A special session of the state legislature in 1973 passed legislation that limited the ability of municipalities to collect taxes on oil and gas property. Ostensibly, the measures applied state-wide, but the intent was clearly to restrict the North Slope Borough.

While the oil companies were busy pursuing their challenges, the borough was quietly establishing its identity as the government for the North Slope. The Planning Department and the borough-wide Planning and Zoning Commission were among the first departments set up by the new government in 1974. There was also a transition from a first-class borough to a home-rule borough—a government structure providing far more extensive authority. The North Slope leaders recognized that a home-rule borough would provide them with more flexibility and a greater feeling of self-determination. The home-rule charter was drafted in 1973, and ratified by the electorate in 1974.[2]

Authority of Home-rule Boroughs in Alaska

As a home-rule borough, the North Slope Borough enjoys broad authority. The Alaskan Constitution provides a home-rule borough with basic zoning and police powers "not prohibited by law or by charter." Alaska Statutes, Title 29, further define the powers possessed by a home-rule borough. Under the Alaskan Constitution and statutes, the borough (absent state statutory provisions to the contrary), has broad powers to enact police and zoning ordinances for the protection of the health and welfare of the inhabitants of the borough.[3] Decisions of the State Supreme Court have generally favoured the broad exercise of legislative powers by local governments, although other interpretations have been made, and a case involving the North Slope Borough's zoning powers has yet to come before the court.

Planning in the North Slope Borough

The North Slope Borough's initial efforts in planning were directed at the implementation of the Capital Improvements Program to provide the residents with the basic necessities: schools, health facilities, village roads, and fire protection. The other major effort, which would culminate in the adoption of the Comprehensive Plan in December 1982, was the development of a North Slope Borough Coastal Management Plan.

The borough realized the need for a coastal management plan in 1977, when it recognized that development activities were no longer confined to the Prudhoe Bay area. Previously, the borough's planning efforts had been confined to the needs of the villages. As exploration and development activities proceeded outside the Prudhoe Bay area, however, the residents and the leaders recognized the potential for conflicts.

The North Slope Borough's Coastal Management Program was initiated in 1977. The purpose of this effort was to enhance the borough's ability to manage effectively and to plan for the balanced use of North Slope coastal resources. The coastal programme, when adopted, was to become an element of both the state's Coastal Management Plan and the borough's Comprehensive Plan. The local coastal programme would also help in the resolution of conflicts over the use of coastal resources while providing for both future growth and conservation in an acceptable manner.[4] There is a close connection between the Coastal Management Plan initiated in 1977 and the Comprehensive Plan begun in 1980.

It was also in 1977 that the federal government scheduled an Outer Continental Shelf lease sale in the Beaufort Sea. The sale was postponed, however, after the borough joined with the State of Alaska in objecting to it, on the grounds that the oil industry did not have the proper technology to operate in the severe ice conditions found in the region. The federal government decided instead to hold a joint lease sale with the State of Alaska. The sale took place in 1979.

Brief History of Coastal Management Planning

In 1972, the United States Congress passed the Coastal Zone Management Act, in response to the rapid development of the coastal areas and the resulting conflicts between the developers and local residents. The act established a system for providing guidance and assistance to the states and to local government units in developing coastal planning and management programmes.[5] The act also established a national programme for the management, beneficial use, protection, and development of the land and water resources of the coast.[6] Congress intended to achieve a balance between competing uses of the coastal areas, and to ensure that development could proceed yet would produce minimal disruption. There was obviously an awareness of the intense pressure that the coastal states were under. Before coastal zone management, there was no programme that dealt specifically with the special needs of these coastal areas.

The situation in Alaska was unique, in that formerly inaccessible areas were being opened up for exploration, and with this came the effects of development on the cultural, historical, and subsistence resources, as well as socio-economic problems. In 1977, the state passed the Alaska Coastal Management Act and started work on a Coastal Management

Program for the whole state. The Alaskan programme was approved by the U.S. Secretary of Commerce in 1979. The state then had the means to have some say on activities on federal lands within the coastal areas and offshore. Federal actions, or grants of permits by federal agencies, now have to be "consistent" with the coastal management programme approved for the state under federal law. The coastal state has the right to agree on whether the proposed federal action is consistent with the state's coastal management programme.

Approved local coastal programmes become an element of the state's programme, and actions within the coastal zone have to be consistent with both state and local programmes. The federal Coastal Zone Management Act gives unprecedented powers to state and local governments in federal coastal actions.

The North Slope Borough recognized the import of this "consistency determination," and that most of the development was going to occur in coastal areas. The size of the North Slope Borough and the impending offshore lease sale in 1979 led to a decision to develop the coastal management programme in four phases. The borough focused first on the mid-Beaufort area, which included the state lands leased in the 1960s as well as the area for the 1979 sale. The next phase was to be the Arctic National Wildlife Range. The third phase would be the National Petroleum Reserve to the west; and the last phase would be the remainder of the western arctic coast.

Point Thomson Sale—1978

In March 1978, the state announced its decision to hold a lease sale in the offshore area at Point Thomson, close to the village of Kaktovik, where residents had a long history of the use of this area for their subsistence activities. The area was also biologically sensitive, being in the delta of the Canning River—an anadromous fish stream.

The announcement by the state came at a particularly sensitive time. The state had been working with the federal government on the provisions of the joint sale to be held in 1979; this work included the drafting of stipulations for the lease tracts. Although the borough had been involved in this effort, the Point Thomson lease sale was regarded as "a serious breach of faith, a politically inspired effort to evade the State's new protective leasing regulations and which dishonours the principles of cooperative management inherent in the OCSEAP [Outer Continental Shelf Environmental Assessment] Program, the State-Federal joint sale agreement and the State's Coastal Zone Management Program."[7]

This incident heightened the need to have a regulatory scheme in place as soon as possible. The late borough mayor, Eben Hopson, asked the borough's attorney to draft an ordinance to try to zone drilling out of the most sensitive offshore habitat areas. The state cancelled the Point Thomson lease sale, and scheduled the area for later lease sales.

First Phase of the Borough's Coastal Management Program

In June 1978, the North Slope Borough published the first phase of its Coastal Management Program. It focused on the Prudhoe Bay area, because of the intensity of the development activities and the real possibility of future discoveries in the vicinity. This area included the acreage for the 1979 lease sale.

One of the problems was that, until 1978, documents had been lacking that could be used for discussion about development and planning in the Prudhoe Bay area. New policies were developed that acknowledged the potential for further resource development in the area, but were also tailored toward the perpetuation and enhancement of wildlife and wildlife habitat. Some of the policies were perceived by the companies as severely limiting their operations.

The October 1978 issue of the *Arctic Coastal Zone Management Newsletter*, published by the North Slope Borough, listed some of the salient points of the *North Slope Borough Coastal Management Program: Prudhoe Bay Area:*

1. Need for additional studies. In spite of the massive amount of research, study, and planning by local, state, and federal agencies, there are several issues not covered and which warrant further study: a) critical gravel and water resources, exploitation and impact; b) commercial fishery potential; c) bowhead whale management; d) Porcupine caribou herd management; and e) the Narwhal Island Boulder Field.
2. Need for a national and international Arctic policy that would establish firm guidelines for all agencies involved in the Arctic and would treat the Arctic as a single ecosystem.
3. Development of national alternatives to Arctic resources.
4. *Protection of Inupiat subsistence lifestyle has a priority in all consideration* [emphasis added]. Aggressive management of fish and wildlife should not be abandoned simply because petroleum development exists in that area. The Borough

believes that management and programs of habitat improvement should be more intensive during this period of habitat consumption and fish and wildlife disruption . . . .

5. NSB standards developed at the local level, being the most comprehensive and structured to attain Borough goals, must guide federal and state agencies in the attainment of those goals.

6. The Borough envisions that all lands and waters within the Borough, including the Prudhoe Bay area, with the exception of the village selections [under the Native Claims Settlement Act] will be zoned by the Borough as a wildlife enhancement zone requiring a conditional use permit for all industrial extraction activities, tourism, and recreation. Subsistence hunting and fishing would not require such a permit.[8]

Under normal circumstances, this document would have been the subject of public hearings within the borough, to be followed by its acceptance by both the North Slope Borough Planning and Zoning Commission and the assembly. The sudden announcement of the Point Thomson lease sale, however, diverted attention away from the Prudhoe Bay Area Coastal Management Program. It was not clear whether the state would approve a plan that covered only a portion of the coastline in any case, and the state's coastal management programme had not yet been approved by the federal government. Moreover, it was evident that the Alaska Coastal Policy Council (the policy group formed to guide the state coastal management programme) would not be able to act on the borough's plan in time for it to have any influence on the upcoming 1979 lease sale.

This situation led the North Slope Borough to hire an environmental law firm, Trustees for Alaska, to draft a municipal zoning ordinance based upon the borough's Prudhoe Bay programme. The clear aim of this action was to regulate land and water uses in the Prudhoe Bay area until the borough's coastal management programme was approved. The borough zoning ordinance, ancillary documents, and maps that evolved out of this process became known collectively as the Mid-Beaufort Coastal Management Program.[9]

The Mid-Beaufort Coastal Management Program

A rough draft of the ordinances governing the mid-Beaufort area was circulated within the state for comments from industry and government officials in early 1979. The reaction was swift, and the borough was immediately perceived as being too stringent and, frankly, out of line. The oil industry joined with the state to seek legislation to suspend the borough's planning and zoning authority in the mid-Beaufort area.

The oil companies and the state contended that the ordinances would unreasonably and arbitrarily restrict or exclude "uses of state concern," one of which was the development of oil and gas. There was also a suggestion that the ordinances did not meet the guidelines of the state's coastal programme. The oil companies went one step further, requesting the federal government to withhold approval of Alaska's programme until the state legislature could make the necessary changes. Their concern was that the state had delegated too much authority to local governments, both through the coastal management programme and through planning and zoning powers.

The state and industry were most concerned about the following aspects of the draft ordinance:

1. The zoning of the mid-Beaufort area into four sub-districts:
    a. Petroleum Service Base and Production District, which covered the existing oil fields;
    b. Conservation District, in sensitive areas where no industrial activity could be permitted;
    c. Geophysical Hazard District, encompassing the area seaward of the Barrier Islands where extreme ice hazards would permit only experimental drilling; and
    d. Deferred Development District, less-dangerous areas in which other than experimental operations will be deferred until 1984.

2. The establishment of a North Slope Borough permitting system within the mid-Beaufort area. The Planning and Zoning Commission would grant permits for non-oil-and-gas-related uses and for new pipelines to carry any oil and gas out of the coastal zone. Oil and gas projects were to be approved through the issuance of special use permits by a coastal management administrator. All oil and gas exploration, development, and production, including pipeline and road routing and construction, and all gravel mining would be covered by the use permits. The operators had to file detailed plans of their operations. The plan also had to be reviewed by the nearest village council as the first step in its approval by the borough's coastal management administrator.

The oil companies and some state agencies, including the Department of Natural Resources, viewed the borough as being arbitrary and capricious, and as burdening the industry unnecessarily with a cumbersome permit process. One of the companies even wanted borough planning staff to identify the areas where "restrictive zoning" might take place. The borough denied this request, stating that only the Planning and Zoning Commission was responsible for creating any types of zones, on the basis of input from all concerned citizens.

The borough attempted to draw both the oil industry and the state into this planning process, knowing that the development of a legally defensible ordinance was possible only with the co-operation of the state and the industry. This attempt was met initially with hesitation by both the industry and the state. The companies generally chose to participate formally, in record-building fashion. Their comments stressed the lack of borough authority on oil and gas leases, permit duplication, creation of an unwieldy bureaucracy, and the argument that state and federal regulations already provided the protections being sought by the borough.

Eventually, both the state and the companies realized that a dialogue with the borough might resolve some of the problems that they had identified. This became more evident after the first formal draft ordinance was circulated and formal comments were received from state and federal agencies and industry. The borough also acknowledged that the comments and the testimony received on the draft were helpful, and that much had been learned from them.

At about the same time, the borough announced its plans to oppose the upcoming joint state–federal lease sale, because it would take place before the borough's Mid-Beaufort Coastal Management Program was in place.

During August and September 1979, there were several negotiating sessions with both the state and the companies. The state was anxious about possible harm that the borough ordinances might do to the state tracts for the lease sale. The borough finished work on the coastal management plan and the ordinances by the end of August. The revised ordinance was modified drastically from the original version. It was the borough's intention to submit to the state for approval the Mid-Beaufort Coastal Management Program, upon which the ordinance was based, and to adopt the implementing ordinance under the planning and zoning powers given it under the state's municipal code.

Admittedly, the ordinance was still restrictive, and set up standards that would have been very hard to meet; enforcement would have been a major problem. The Planning and Zoning Commission, after further changes, approved the documents in September and forwarded them to the assembly.

Recognizing the need for further co-operation, the assembly conducted three workshops in Anchorage and a fourth in Barrow prior to giving conceptual approval to the Mid-Beaufort Coastal Management Program and the ordinances. The assembly met, in turn, with oil companies, environmental groups, and state and federal agencies, and finally, in a consolidation session, to make changes in the ordinances based on the dialogues with the other interested parties.

The assembly gave its conceptual approval to the Mid-Beaufort Coastal Management Program and forwarded it to the state for its action in December 1979. In January 1980, after hearings conducted by the state Coastal Policy Council, the borough withdrew the Mid-Beaufort Coastal Plan Program, realizing it would never get state approval in its present form. The borough then resorted to reliance on its municipal planning and zoning authority, and adopted the Interim Zoning Ordinances.

Interim Zoning Ordinances

The borough was aware of the criticisms to which the Mid-Beaufort Coastal Management Program had been subjected, and was certain that the state would not approve the plan unless it was virtually emasculated. Based on this awareness, the borough adopted the Interim Zoning Ordinances, asserting the borough's zoning and planning authority in the area.

The Interim Zoning Ordinances were an abbreviated version of the mid-Beaufort ordinances. They were designed to regulate development in the region, and they retained the sub-districts mentioned earlier. The ordinances were intended to remain in place until the final approval of the Mid-Beaufort Coastal Management Program. When the plan was subsequently withdrawn from state consideration, the Interim Zoning Ordinances remained in place until 1983, when they were replaced by the Comprehensive Plan and Land Management Regulations.

The ordinances set up a system of permits that closely paralleled four State of Alaska permits. The borough started issuing permits under the new system, while also commenting to state and federal agencies on their permits.

The Comprehensive Plan and Land Management Regulations

Withdrawal of the Mid-Beaufort Coastal Management Program affirmed the borough's continuing commitment to developing a workable local planning programme for the protection, development, use, and, where necessary, restoration and enhancement, of the biological and cultural resources of the North Slope. In late 1980, the borough embarked on the development of both a comprehensive plan–land-use ordinance for the entire borough and a coastal management programme for the North Slope coastline.[10]

It had been pointed out to the borough by industry and state agencies that the borough should develop a comprehensive plan, and that the coastal plan should be one of its elements. After the 1979 lease sale and with the interim ordinances in place (with no legal challenges), the borough recognized the need for a comprehensive plan. The borough's planning staff also recognized a major flaw in the development of the Mid-Beaufort Coastal Management Program—there had been little input from the villages in the Prudhoe Bay vicinity. The reason, of course, was the spectre of the lease sale. Hearings on the mid-Beaufort programme were held in Barrow and even in Anchorage, but somehow the villagers had been forgotten. This matter was foremost in the development of the Comprehensive Plan.

The Comprehensive Plan and the implementing regulations would cover all lands within the North Slope Borough, and offshore to the three-mile limit of state jurisdiction. The mid-Beaufort programme and the Interim Zoning Ordinances applied only to state land. The Comprehensive Plan and the regulations would also apply to lands owned by the federal government, including the National Petroleum Reserve in Alaska and the Arctic National Wildlife Range.

The planning process that led to the adoption of the Comprehensive Plan and Land Management Regulations was long and, at times, frustrating. There was a determination to evolve a plan that would carefully balance the conflicting interests and produce regulations that would withstand any legal challenges. At the outset of plan development, the borough realized it had to balance the subsistence use with the rapid development of petroleum resources. The borough did not wish to thwart the development activities, but wanted the ability to assure the residents of a comprehensive plan and regulations that would allay their fears about encroaching developments.

Developing the Comprehensive Plan and Land Management Regulations (1981–1982)

The North Slope Borough began to develop the Comprehensive Plan and Land Development Ordinances (later known as Land Management Regulations) in the spring of 1981. At the same time, work started on the borough-wide Coastal Management Program. It was anticipated that the Comprehensive Plan and the ordinances would be completed and adopted by the borough assembly before the Coastal Management Program.

The Comprehensive Plan and the ordinances were developed with input from borough residents, industry, and state and federal agencies. The borough was under no mandate or statutory requirement to keep the private sector and the government agencies involved as much as it did. This point was often missed by individuals who criticized the borough for not providing adequate time for analysing and commenting on the various drafts.

Along with the participation of the private sector and government agencies, the borough actively pursued input from the residents of the villages. The borough's planning staff and the consultants made several trips to all the villages and conducted meetings to explain why the Comprehensive Plan was being developed and how the plan and ordinances would benefit residents.

Role of the Villages

It was the borough staff's goal to find out the concerns of each village, its problems, its use of the area around the village for subsistence activities, and, finally, to explain the need for comprehensive planning. The latter was most important for those villages that were beginning to feel the effects of development.

Understandably, there were those within the borough who wished to see no development at all. It was therefore important to explain to residents that, although the adoption of the Comprehensive Plan and ordinances would provide them with a document that was tailored to their needs, it would not necessarily be the solution to all their problems. The meetings in the villages were a learning experience for all involved.

Input from the villages resulted in the delineation of an "area of influence" around each village. A large-scale map of the borough was taken to each village, and, at the conclusion of a village meeting, the public was invited to identify the areas around the village that were used by the residents for subsistence purposes. Lines were drawn on this map identifying the area. The purpose of the "area of influence" concept was to involve the residents of each village in all development decisions affecting their "area of influence." It was pointed out to the village residents that they would be informed of all development activity in their area and that they would have the opportunity to comment to the borough on the proposed activity. It was also explained that this did not mean the residents could veto the activity, and that the borough, in reaching its decision, was obliged to balance the local interest with the national and state interests.

The residents of the villages appreciated the opportunity to participate in this planning effort, for too often in the past they had been the last ones to be informed about an activity or a planning effort.

At times, it was very difficult to explain that although the borough was able to influence, and even to control, development to some degree, it did not have the power to stop it. The role of the federal and state governments was explained, as was the borough's interaction with the two entities. It was emphasized that the plan and ordinances were important tools; they provided a compendium of the borough's objectives, goals, and policies, and served to inform others of what the borough expected of them. Even if the jurisdiction of the borough regulations in federally owned lands was not clearly defined, it still served the borough's interest to make use of established precedents and to develop a plan encompassing all the lands within its boundaries.[11]

Role of Industry

The major oil companies also played an important part in developing the Comprehensive Plan and ordinances. The borough's experience with the Mid-Beaufort Coastal Management Program had made clear the importance of continuing industry's involvement. It was also important to bring the Arctic Slope Regional Corporation into this process. As one of the largest landowners within the borough, the regional corporation would have to abide by any ordinances adopted by the borough.

Throughout the next two years, the borough made available to industry all the drafts of the plan and ordinances and gave serious consideration to the comments that were received. As far as possible, the borough incorporated the suggestions made by industry and the regional corporation; but it also made it clear that the priority was still the same: preservation of the Inupiat character of life.

To solicit input from the private sector, the borough held workshops in Barrow and in Anchorage, and also several meetings with individual companies to resolve differences. These efforts resulted in the adoption of a Comprehensive Plan and ordinances which, for the most part, were acceptable to all the parties.

The Role of State and Federal Agencies

State and federal agencies also played a key role by providing technical assistance to the borough. Agencies such as the U.S. Fish and Wildlife Service and the Alaska Department of Fish and Game provided the borough with the necessary data regarding renewable resources. These agencies also verified and, at times, corrected information on birds, terrestrial mammals, and other biological resources.

Agencies primarily responsible for non-renewable resources were initially very critical of the borough's attempt to develop the Comprehensive Plan and ordinances. Among the most critical was the Alaska Department of Natural Resources. It feared that the borough regulations would arbitrarily restrict the development of oil, gas, and other mineral resources on the North Slope. A concerted effort on the part of the borough allayed these fears and ensured that leasing and development of oil and gas would not halt with the adoption of the Comprehensive Plan and ordinances.

The first drafts of the Comprehensive Plan and the ordinances were released in July and August 1981. The drafts were circulated to the agencies, industry, and the villages for their comments. The documents, although more detailed and covering the entire borough, were really an extension of the Mid-Beaufort Coastal Management Program.

Both the plan and the ordinances were not well received by several agencies and industry. The villages, on the other hand, liked the creation of the eight zoning districts, which had numerous criteria assigned to them. There were several districts where development was prohibited.

Workshops on the first draft were held in all the villages. The zoning districts were explained, as were the purpose and the importance of the documents. The boundaries of the village districts were adjusted in accordance with the information provided by the residents.

In addition to the village meetings, the borough also conducted workshops and hearings for industry and agencies. From the comments received at hearings, it was evident that this draft would not be accepted by the industry, the state, and the federal government. There was once again the realization that these documents would be the subject of legal challenges if adopted in the form of the first draft.

As a result of the meetings, workshops, and public hearings, several changes were made to the first draft, and revised drafts were published in March 1982. The borough staff reviewed these drafts and decided that the changes were not substantial, and that releasing the revisions to the public would result in the same reaction as before. Therefore, the borough did not make these drafts public. At the same time, a decision was made to change the direction of the Comprehensive Plan and the ordinances, and to integrate the Comprehensive Plan and the Coastal Management Program background information. Thus, phase two of the process was initiated in May 1982, and this resulted finally in the adoption of the plan and the ordinances.

Phase two began with a workshop held for the Planning Commission, which outlined to the commission the problems inherent in the first drafts and sought its approval to tailor the plan and ordinances to meet local needs, desires, and concerns, and also to make it acceptable to other parties. As a result, the borough had to move away from the zoning and the elaborate permitting system; not abandoning it, but making it simpler and more predictable. The first drafts had focused primarily on the development of oil and gas, and had not taken into account other development and planning efforts within the borough, such as the Capital Improvement Program, health services, activities by the individual village and regional corporations, and the desire of residents for full employment. Thus, the Comprehensive Plan was not truly comprehensive and did not fit well with the ordinances. The ordinances were similarly flawed; they sought to control development of oil and gas resources rigidly, but ignored other effects such as those of increased tourism and possible future development activities by the village corporations.

The next step was to return to all the villages to explain the revised scope of work and how a truly comprehensive plan could be created. Once more, input was solicited from the residents and they were assured of their concerns being addressed adequately in the documents.

The draft Comprehensive Plan was reviewed; a list of the plan elements was developed; existing data were reviewed; and the need for additional or new data was identified. All the existing borough policies were compiled, and the need for new policies was noted. Areas of special concern to the borough, such as offshore development and marine tanker traffic, were also identified. This revised scope of work was then presented to the Planning Commission and received its approval.

Further workshops were held with the Planning Commission to finalize the format for the plan and ordinances before the release of the first draft in September 1982. A joint study session between the Planning Commission and borough assembly was also held to ensure that the assembly was familiar with the plan and the ordinances before its hearing in November.

Also in September, the borough conducted a "policies workshop" in Barrow. The impetus for this workshop came from the fact that the Land

Management Regulations being developed bore little resemblance to a normal zoning ordinance—or even to the borough's former attempts at creating an ordinance. Instead, the policies in the Comprehensive Plan would be used to guide, direct, and regulate development decisions in the borough. The policies were grouped in several categories, such as local economic development, transportation, petroleum and mineral development, subsistence, etc. Participants in the workshop represented industry, local residents, borough employees, state and federal agencies, borough planning commissioners, and borough assembly members.

The participants were divided into small groups of six or seven and were given a workbook containing all the policies. Each group was assisted by a borough staff member or consultant. The groups were asked to rate each policy for either its relevance or its importance on a scale of one to four. It was most interesting to see oil company officials (from as far away as Houston) and government bureaucrats sitting down with local residents and discussing the policies. There were some heated debates, but the meeting resulted in elimination of some superfluous policies and in consensus on many others. Another result of the policies workshop was that the policies came out as strong as, or stronger than, the initial draft. There was also a high level of agreement on results: all groups were very close on the importance factors. If a policy was inappropriate or duplicative, it was usually eliminated by several groups, not by just one.[12]

The results from the small groups were correlated into a composite workbook, and the language of the duplicative policies was standardized. The revised policies became part of the second draft of the Comprehensive Plan. It was generally felt that the policies met the borough's goal for preservation of subsistence resources and the Inupiat character of life, and were also "livable" for industry and other interested parties. The policies were re-worded so that they used the same terminology as the Alaska Coastal Management Program Regulations.

The borough now had a set of policies that were more or less agreeable to all parties concerned, and that were also compatible with coastal management planning. The borough was on its way to realizing its goal of achieving products that were balanced, workable, legally defensible, and acceptable to those who would use them and to those who would be regulated pursuant to their provisions.

There were two more drafts of the Comprehensive Plan between September and the adoption of the plan and the regulations in December 1982. In between, there were public hearings and private negotiating sessions with the state and with the industry. Further changes were made as a result of discussion between the borough, industry, the state, and federal agencies. All changes were discussed with and approved by the Planning

Commission, which approved the documents in November and forwarded them to the assembly for its consideration. The assembly held its public hearing in December 1982, when, although it listened to the criticism from industry, it felt comfortable with the documents and adopted them. The Comprehensive Plan and regulations became effective on 1 January 1983.

A Brief Summary of the Elements of the Comprehensive Plan and Land Management Regulations

The Comprehensive Plan is most definitely a decison-making tool for the borough. It contains the policy basis for land-use decisions and data landmaps. The plan and the regulations will help developers to design their projects—keeping borough policies in mind—and will help the borough to review the projects. The plan is comprehensive, containing all the policy and data developed by the borough on various issues. Most important, it is a compendium of official borough land-use policies, which will provide useful leverage in working with state and federal regulatory agencies. Several laws, such as the Coastal Zone Management Act, defer to local plans in the establishment of regulations.[13]

The unique aspect of the plan and the regulations is the elimination of most of the former geographical zones with rigid prohibitions. The emphasis is now on performance. The policies and standards are employed to review applications. For the first time, it is not only industry that is being regulated, but also the residents of the villages, Barrow, and the borough itself. The plan is written for the peoples of the North Slope, but it also accommodates other interests.

There are only four districts pursuant to the plan:

1. *Village District*, which comprises the municipal limits of each incorporated village and the sites and immediate environs of unincorporated villages in the borough;
2. *Barrow District*, which takes into account the larger size and population of Barrow, and accommodates urban development;
3. *Resource Development District*, which acknowledges the presence of the petroleum resources on the North Slope. It encourages companies to submit master plans for the district, and thus leads to the creation of a very predictable permitting system. This district is designed to accommodate large-scale resource extraction and ancillary activities; and

4. *Conservation District*, which encompasses the entire area of the borough except for the foregoing districts. The intent of this district is to preserve the natural ecosystem for all the various species upon which the borough residents depend for subsistence. There are no prohibited uses. This district can accommodate resource exploration and development on a limited scale, on a case-by-case basis, but major resource development projects will find it advantageous to apply for re-zoning to a Resource Development District.

A synopsis of the content of the ten chapters of the plan was published by the North Slope Borough in the January 1983 issue of the *Arctic Policy Review*.

The salient feature of the regulations is the regulatory system they create. Under the new system, the borough is now issuing two types of permits.

The *use permit* is granted for those activities that have been identified on a master plan. At present, permits are being issued only for the oilfields that have been unitized and that either are producing (Prudhoe and Kuparuk) or soon will be (Milne Point). The operators of the unit have to submit a master plan clearly depicting roads, pipelines, etc. Upon approval of the master plan, the borough issues use permits for the construction of the facilities. It is basically a system that keeps the borough informed of what is taking place and whether an activity is the same as is shown on the master plan or is substantially different. Use permits are issued within five working days.

The *development permit* is issued for all activities that involve a major alteration from an approved master plan, or are not specifically exempted from the definition of development in the regulations. Examples of some activities within this category are: seismic operations, construction of a building, roads, gravel islands, schools, hospitals, and pipelines.

If the development permit is for an activity within the "area of influence" of a village or villages, then a public notice is sent to the village, and the appropriate state and federal agencies are also notified.

The development permit can be issued within 23 working days, and it may have relevant conditions attached to it. If a permit is denied, the applicant has the right to appeal to the Planning Commission and to the assembly if necessary.

The policies contained in the plan and the regulations are uniquely tailored to meet the requirements of the borough and fall into three categories.

Mandatory policies either require or prohibit some feature. If a development requires a variance from such a policy, it will be granted by the Planning Commission only after a public hearing.

Best-efforts policies require that developers use their best efforts in meeting the requirements of these policies, but they also provide an "out" if there is no "feasible and prudent alternative." These policies conform with the terminology of the Alaska Coastal Management Program.

Policies for the minimization of negative impacts are similar to best-efforts policies and are designed to encourage developers of the project to minimize the negative effects of certain specific activities such as roads and pipelines.

Besides these three types of policy, standards labelled "beneficial impacts" encourage the developer to take actions that would have beneficial effects; for example, a developer's commitment to hire local residents for the project, consolidating facilities, or accommodating free movement of caribou in the project area.

Present Status of Comprehensive Plan and Regulations

The plan and regulations have been in place since January 1983. To date [June 1983], the plan and regulations have been accepted by all parties, and there have been no legal challenges to the borough's permitting system.

Under the new system the borough has processed several applications, from oil companies, geophysical companies, and private individuals. The applications have been for activities in areas under federal jurisdiction (Arctic National Wildlife Range), state jurisdiction (the Prudhoe and Kuparuk oilfields), and within the municipality of Barrow (a multiple-housing unit).

The borough has shown that it will not act in an arbitrary and capricious manner, and that it recognizes the multiple use of the land within its boundaries.

Other Planning Efforts

Coastal Management Program

The borough has completed the "Public Hearing Draft" of the Coastal Management Program. The draft has been distributed widely to state and federal agencies, industry, the villages, and to other interested parties. The borough will respond to all written and oral comments on this draft and will then present it to the assembly for its conceptual approval. Finally, the whole package, including the comments and borough's response, will be submitted to the state. If the programme is accepted by the state, it will be in effect by January 1984.

The Coastal Management Program will then become a component of the Comprehensive Plan, and its implementation will be through the existing Land Management Regulations. Overlay zones containing special regulations to govern the coastal areas will be added to the existing zoning districts. There will be the addition of a "consistency determination" for all activities within the coastal zone with the borough's Coastal Management Program, by which the borough will rule on the consistency of federal and state permit applications with borough regulations.

Subdivision Ordinance

The borough recently completed work on a new subdivision ordinance to replace one that had been adopted ten years ago, and that is now inadequate. This ordinance is complete, and complements fully the Comprehensive Plan, Land Management Regulations, and the Coastal Management Program. It was adopted by the North Slope Borough Assembly on 5 April 1983, and became effective on 4 June 1983.

Geographic Information System

The Geographic Information System is being developed to assist the borough in general planning, oil and gas development, and other resource-use issues. When implemented, the system will be capable of producing maps and biological information as well as identifying the traditional land use by the residents. It will provide those using it with access to the information, and will aid in planning by identifying potential conflicts prior to submission of an application.

The history of land-use planning in the North Slope Borough typifies the many problems faced in the industrial development of the Arctic. It also highlights the effectiveness of local government as a forum for solving those problems, offering northern societies their best hope for cultural and economic survival.

Endnotes

1. Gerald A. McBeath, *North Slope Borough Government and Policymaking*, Man in the Arctic Program, Monograph no. 3 (Institute of Social and Economic Research, University of Alaska, 1981), p. 17.

2. Ibid., p. 19.

3. Wickwire, Lewis, Goldmark, and Schorr, *Report: Powers of the North Slope Borough to Regulate Activities in the North Slope Borough Coastal Zone* (Seattle, Washington, 1979), p. 13.

4. North Slope Borough, *North Slope Borough Coastal Management Program: Background Report* (Barrow: North Slope Borough, 1983), p. 1.

5. North Slope Borough, *North Slope Borough Coastal Management Program: Public Hearing Draft* (Barrow: North Slope Borough, 1983).

6. Ibid.

7. "State Pt. Thomson Sale Compromises New Arctic Offshore Safeguards," *Arctic Coastal Zone Management Newsletter* 12 (June 1978), p. 5.

8. "Prudhoe Bay CZM Program: First Phase of NSB Plan Published," *Arctic Coastal Zone Management Newsletter* 15 (October 1978), pp. 9–10.

9. North Slope Borough, *North Slope Borough Coastal Management Program: Background Report* (Barrow: North Slope Borough, 1983).

10. Ibid., p. 12.

11. Conrad Bagne, "North Slope Borough Legal Powers and Options on the Haul Road and Adjacent Federal and State Lands," *Report to the North Slope Borough* (Barrow: North Slope Borough, 1977).

12. Kirk Wickersham, "Informational Memorandum no. 2 re: Draft of Comprehensive Plan and Land Management Regulations to: North Slope Borough," 1982.

13. North Slope Borough, *Arctic Policy Review*, January 1983, p. 8.

Conservation of Environmentally Significant Areas

Chairmen: John Lambert
Chris O'Brien

Introduction

The need for a comprehensive environmental conservation policy for northern Canada has been recognized by native peoples, public-interest groups, and some federal and territorial government agencies for some time. The federal government's northern development strategy has both stimulated exploration for hydrocarbons beneath the Beaufort Sea and in the arctic islands and made the development of these resources possible, and has encouraged exploration for and development of minerals in the North. Notwithstanding its promises to "balance" northern development with conservation, the federal government has taken little action to conserve environmentally significant areas. Proposals to conserve areas such as Polar Bear Pass in the Northwest Territories and the North Slope of the Yukon have led to conflicts between federal and territorial government agencies, native organizations, the oil and gas and mining industries, and conservation groups. These conflicts have delayed progress toward identifying and conserving environmentally significant areas in the North.

In 1982, DIAND published a draft discussion paper *A Comprehensive Conservation Policy and Strategy for the Northwest Territories and Yukon*. At a conservation workshop in Whitehorse sponsored by DIAND in March 1983 to discuss this document, the participants urged the federal and territorial governments to establish a task force of government officials and other knowledgeable persons with two objectives: first, to identify appropriate conservation targets for implementation through 1985; and secondly, to advise these governments on the establishment of a mechanism for conservation with appropriate links to the proposed northern land-use planning process. As the Third National Workshop convened, DIAND was establishing the Task Force on Northern Conservation. The working group on conservation of environmentally significant areas focused its discussion on recommendations to the task force.

291

The Working Groups

The working group included:

Chairmen: **John Lambert**
Department of Biology
Carleton University

Chris O'Brien
Ecology North
Yellowknife, N.W.T.

Rapporteur: **Sabine Jessen**
University of British Columbia

Invited Participants:

Bill Erasmus
Dene Nation
Edmonton, Alberta

Paul Gray
Wildlife Service
Department of Renewable Resources
Government of the Northwest Territories
Yellowknife, N.W.T.

Ben Hubert
Boreal Ecology Services Ltd.
Yellowknife, N.W.T.

Julian Inglis
Northern Affairs Program
Department of Indian Affairs and Northern Development
Government of Canada
Ottawa, Ontario

Tom Kovacs
Parks Canada
Department of the Environment
Government of Canada
Ottawa, Ontario

292

Nancy MacPherson
Yukon Conservation Society
Whitehorse, Yukon

Gordon Nelson
Faculty of Environmental Studies
University of Waterloo

Paul Smith
Faculty of Environmental Studies
University of Waterloo

Kenneth Taylor
Polar Gas Project
Toronto, Ontario

John Theberge
Faculty of Environmental Studies
University of Waterloo

Alan Vaughan
Department of Economic Development and Tourism
Government of the Northwest Territories
Yellowknife, N.W.T.

Background documents used in the working group, in addition to those printed in these proceedings, included:

Banff Centre School of Management. *Northern Conservation Policy Workshop*, Whitehorse, Yukon, 27 February-2 March 1983. Proceedings.

"Biosphere Reserves." Ottawa: Canadian Man and the Biosphere Committee, 1982.

Department of the Environment. *Canada's Special Places in the North: An Environment Canada Perspective for the '80's.* Ottawa: Minister of Supply and Services Canada, 1982.

Fenge, Terry. "Towards Comprehensive Conservation of Environmentally Significant Areas in the Northwest Territories of Canada." *Environmental Conservation* 9:4 (Winter 1982), pp. 305-313.

The Working Groups

Nelson, J.G. and Sabine Jessen. *Planning and Managing Environmentally Significant Areas in the Northwest Territories: Issues and Alternatives.* Ottawa: Canadian Arctic Resources Committee, 1984.

Northern Environment Directorate, Northern Affairs Program, Department of Indian Affairs and Northern Development. *A Comprehensive Conservation Policy and Strategy for the Northwest Territories and Yukon,* draft Discussion Paper. October 1982.

Smith, Paul G.R. and John B. Theberge. "The Identification and Evaluation of Environmentally Significant Areas in the Northwest Territories." Canadian Arctic Resources Committee, unpublished.

Working Group Report
Conservation of Environmentally Significant Areas

Rationale

A policy for the use of northern renewable and non-renewable resources must ensure the wise stewardship of the northern environment. An essential component of such a policy is the identification and appropriate management of areas essential to sustainable resource use. These environmentally significant areas (ESAs) have special attributes (for example, wildlife) and uses (for example, hydrological, cultural) that are vital to those of the surrounding lands and seas.

Recommendations and Guidelines

Based on the preceding rationale, the working group on conservation of environmentally significant areas recommends that the newly established Task Force on Northern Conservation:

- provide copies of its reports simultaneously to DIAND, DOE, the territorial governments, and the public
- have representation from all interests
- be organized and staffed efficiently
- have the necessary commitment and resources to do its job
- provide resources to enable interested parties to present their views to the task force.

The working group recommends that the task force and other concerned parties adopt the following guidelines:

- Recognition of native ownership and use of northern lands is essential to establishing ESAs.
- ESAs that are owned privately can be managed successfully.
- ESAs should be managed according to biophysical characteristics and requirements.
- A process to review the creation, modification, and management of ESAs should be defined explicitly. This process should identify integrated systems of ESAs.

- Standard criteria should be used for selecting ESAs. The data acquired should be accessible to the public. An organization or classification system for ESAs should be developed so that each area will be managed appropriately (for example, as a national park, a wildlife area, etc.). Systems for land-use planning and environmental protection developed in other countries (for example, the Scandinavian nations) could be used as models for northern Canada.
- A system for the management of ESAs should include regular public participation, especially of those persons directly affected. It should provide for appropriate response from and accountability of the responsible agencies.
- Establishment, development, and management decisions should be made at the local level.
- A statement of political commitment to establish systems of ESAs should be forthcoming from the federal and territorial governments. The statements should include schedules for action to complete the designation of priority ESAs.
- ESAs should be managed so as to contribute to the continuation of traditional lifestyles and the conservation of renewable resources.
- Both natural and cultural features should be considered in creating ESAs.
- A process for identifying and managing ESAs should be established by the federal and territorial governments. The process should involve industry, native organizations, and other interested individuals, and should bring together regularly ESA managers and landowners to ensure comprehensive management.
- A bridging or co-ordinating body with headquarters in the North should be established to facilitate the creation and management of ESAs. It should include interested citizens and representatives of industry and government agencies.
- Bridging institutions and decision-making processes should reflect the regional differences in the North and the changing social and political circumstances.
- Support should be provided for the preparation and distribution of educational and evaluative information on ESAs.

Concerns of the Working Group

- Local residents should be involved actively in the management of ESAs (for example, two residents of Gjoa Haven have been accepted for training as wardens of the new Ellesmere Island National Park Reserve).
- Regardless of the involvement of local communities in the management of ESAs, these areas will require financial support from governments.
- The federal government must determine how the transfer of responsibility for ESAs will be carried out for lands included in native land-claims settlements and for lands transferred to regional and territorial governments.

Northern Conservation Policy Workshop: Action Plan for Northern Conservation

Whitehorse, Yukon
27 February–2 March 1983
The Banff Centre
School of Management

Workshop participants were asked to develop the elements of a conservation policy for the north and a long range action plan setting out goals for the implementation of such policy. A draft discussion paper, entitled "A Comprehensive Conservation Policy and Strategy for the Northwest Territories and Yukon" and released by the Northern Program of DIAND in October, 1982, provided the basis for the workshop discussion.

The workshop considered the subject from the standpoint of desirable futures. It then addressed the obstacles and constraints that could impede the attainment of the desired goals. Finally, the workshop looked at how those obstacles could be overcome and made recommendations as to how the goals and objectives of a comprehensive conservation policy could be achieved. But first, the workshop noted a long history of conservation achievements in the Canadian north. Game reserves, national park reserves, migratory bird sanctuaries, etc. had been established through the efforts of many persons and agencies throughout the Twentieth Century. However, more recent initiatives had failed to progress at a pace satisfactory to most interested parties, owing to an increasingly complex institutional environment.

This report follows the format of the workshop and deals with the subject under the headings described in the previous paragraph. The recommended Action Plan is intended to complement and encourage current conservation initiatives in northern Canada.

A. Desirable Futures

(1) Clarification of conservation concept:

Much of the inaction related to northern conservation is due to lack of understanding of what conservation really is. Thus conservation needs to be defined. Suggestions ranged from 'wise use' and 'the reduction of waste' to that adopted for the World Conservation Strategy.

Conservation reflects not only inherent natural values but also social, cultural and economic values.

Conservation is not simply the setting aside of special geographic areas but also comprises activities related to protection, managed use and restoration.

Conservation recognizes and reflects in an appropriate way local, territorial, national and international interests and responsibilities.

Finally, it should be noted that just as conservation includes an economic component (for example, sound forest management practice to ensure a sustained annual harvest), economic development ideally contains a conservation component.

(2) Northern conservation should be developed through a process in which:

— conservation decisions are linked to other decisions affecting the resource base;
— all interested parties are able to participate;
— community information programs are implemented;
— conservation strategy is a component of a land-use planning process;
— conservation strategy takes into account jurisdictional, cultural and economic differences between the two territories and the major geographic and natural differences in northern Canada;
— conservation strategy also takes into account local, territorial, national and international interests and mechanisms; and
— proposals for conservation or development are comprehensively evaluated with opportunities for public examination of costs, benefits and alternatives appropriate to the scale and importance of the proposal.

(3) Means to accomplish the designation of geographic areas for conservation purposes must be established. This must include steps to: identify; assess; select; proclaim; monitor and regulate delineated areas.

(4) Legislative and administrative mandates (inter- and intra-governmental) should be clarified and, where necessary, modified in order to effectively implement northern conservation strategy and policy.

(5) The success of policies, strategies and processes will be directly dependent on achieving broad acceptance and clear political commitment at all levels.

B. Obstacles, Difficulties and Constraints

(1) Concept of conservation:

— a lack of understanding as to what is meant by conservation (by industry resulting in some cases in confrontation and by the public resulting in lethargy and an absence of political will);
— no political articulation of conservation goals;
— no public consensus with respect to the value, costs and benefits of conservation; and
— lack of public recognition that conservation has an economic component (a cost rightfully belonging to the consumer may be passed on to the taxpayer).

(2) Public involvement:

— a feeling, by northerners, of a lack of influence upon the decision making process;
— inconsistent access to information and to the decision making process;
— poorly defined processes for intervenors or "competitors" to be heard; and
— no well established education program re conservation.

(3) Jurisdiction

— unsettled native land claims;
— fragmentation between federal and territorial government;
— inter- and intra-agency competition;
— questions of devolution of authority to territorial governments;
— the land transfer issue;
— questions of constitutional development and political evolution;
— multiplicity of legislation and regulation; and
— lack of appropriate "management"-type legislation.

(4) Site selection of special areas:

Apart from cases like the national park system, these are:

(a) identification and selection:
— little or no public involvement;
— lack of criteria;
— insufficient justification;
— lack of assessment;

(b) proclamation:
— perceived loss of economic benefits and/or opportunities;

(c) monitoring and management:
— little political commitment to ensuring that appropriate regulation takes place.

C. Dealing with the Obstacles and Constraints and Developing an Action Plan

(1) It is recommended that a slightly modified version of the World Conservation Strategy's definition of conservation be adopted, viz.:

The maintenance of representative ecosystems, their ecological processes and genetic diversity; and the management of human use of natural resources so that they may yield the greatest sustainable benefit to present generations while maintaining their potential to meet the needs and aspirations of future generations.

(2) It is recommended that the Minister of Indian and Northern Affairs, in consultation with the appropriate federal Ministers and the appropriate Ministers in each of the territorial governments, appoint a balanced Task Force of senior government officials and non-government persons who have appropriate qualifications.

The committee would operate until December 31, 1983 and, during that time, would: (a) identify appropriate conservation targets for implementation through 1985, and (b) advise on the establishment of an ongoing mechanism for conservation having appropriate links to the northern land use planning process.

The terms of reference of the permanent mechanism must take into account desirable futures described in Section A and constraints described in Section B above and also develop a strategy for northern conservation which:

— extends beyond DIAND's mandate and interacts with the responsibilities of other government departments and agencies;
— is transferable, thereby recognizing constitutional development and political evolution;
— is cognizant of the land issues and agreements related to the settlement of comprehensive native land claims;
— rectifies the current stalemate related to the dedication of conservation lands with a timetable so that real progress can be made in this part of the conservation program in the next two-year period; and
— reflects and involves a range of local, territorial, national, and international interests and mechanisms.

(3) Greater priority should be given to international northern conservation concerns and issues. The Canadian government is encouraged to sponsor a circumpolar conservation conference developed in co-operation with appropriate international agencies and groups.

Reprinted with kind permission of the Banff Centre School of Management.

Position Paper

Aboriginal Rights: The Development of Northern Conservation Policy

The Dene Nation

Introduction

The development of non-renewable resources north of 60° has proceeded at a far greater pace than the planning and implementation of management policies needed to control it. As a result, northerners have little control over land use and resource management, and increasing amounts of land are alienated. Concomitant with the alienation of land, the effects on the renewable resources and the peoples who benefit from them directly also have been great.

Traditionally, it is the Dene who have used and managed a vast area of the mainland N.W.T. and adjacent regions "since time immemorial," as they stated to the federal government in October 1976.

Today, although the economy of the Dene remains viable and, most important, tied to the land, it faces serious threats from the continued improper and uncontrolled development of northern resources. Such development has already drastically affected day-to-day life in the Dene communities throughout the Mackenzie Valley.

Many persons have voiced the urgent need to control the development of northern lands and resources. Many persons and interest groups now wish to express their opinions and to exercise their rights to ensure that, when a comprehensive land and resource policy is finally implemented, it will fairly represent the rights of all interested parties and benefit those affected.

Principles

In light of this need, and recognizing the aboriginal rights of the Dene people, the rights of northern residents, and the rights of all Canadians, this paper outlines four principles that should guide the establishment of a comprehensive northern land and resource management policy.

Control and Ownership of Land and Resources

Control and ownership of all northern land and resources must be determined ultimately through the aboriginal rights claims process.

One of the main objectives of the Dene in the claims process has been to incorporate into the final settlement a comprehensive policy for the management of land and resources. The Dene have become acutely aware that their rights require special recognition if those rights are to be protected. The constitutional guarantees now afforded will ensure that the terms of aboriginal rights settlements will provide that protection.

The Dene have the right to be involved in decisions made about the future of their land. If that right is to be protected from gradual erosion, then the role of the Dene in the decision-making process must be determined in the aboriginal rights claims forum where it will receive constitutional protection.

Northern land and resource policies and the aboriginal rights claims process cannot be considered as separate issues.

Protection of Land and Renewable Resources

Pending a final settlement of aboriginal rights claims, land and resources in the North will need to be protected from non-renewable resource development. The measures for protection must reflect the final settlement and be temporary in nature. Settlement of aboriginal rights in the North may require many years of negotiation. Therefore, it is necessary to develop protective measures in the interim to control the development of non-renewable resources and to ensure that special land and resource areas will be maintained in their natural state.

As these measures will, in all probability, lay the groundwork for comprehensive policies to be incorporated in the final aboriginal rights agreements, they must be temporary in effect, but must also reflect the aboriginal rights position. In this sense, land and resources must not be alienated from the claims process, or from active use by the Dene.

For example, the establishment of environmentally significant areas (ESAs), must be considered an interim and temporary measure only, and therefore the criteria governing ESAs must be developed in conjunction with the aboriginal rights claims process.

Access to Renewable Resources

Any interim measures taken to conserve northern lands and resources must in no way impede Dene access to the renewable resource sector. Rather, these measures must encourage and foster the Dene economy and ways of life, while providing adequate interim protection to land and resources. Regardless of past intrusions and impacts of the southern economy and values on the Dene economy, the land and its resources remain of prime importance to, and are still used extensively by, the Dene. This is especially true of the renewable resource sector (i.e., country foods, water, wood, etc.).

Consequently, the development of interim measures to protect land and resources must incorporate principles that will ensure that the Dene will have uninterrupted access to the renewable resource sector.

Participation by Northerners in Developing Policy

Efforts in developing interim northern policy must take place in the North, and must include fair and equal participation at all levels by the Dene and all northern residents, in conjunction with southern participation.

The only rational approach to northern policy development is through the co-operative efforts of all interested parties.

This approach, although often called for, has not been implemented fully in the past. More often, the Dene, and in essence, all northerners, have been viewed as constituting only another "interest group," and invited to participate only when it was convenient. Consequently, the development of northern policies, whatever they may entail, has taken place largely in the South, through the co-operation of primarily southern interests. Although these efforts are in many ways laudable and are appreciated by northerners, they will not be acceptable until northern participation is inherent.

The continuation of this "reactive" approach to northern policy development is not in the best interest of all Canadians, and more important, it will never reflect the aspirations and needs of northern residents.

An example of where northerners and, particularly, native groups can contribute a great deal to the planning process is in the identification of special areas requiring immediate protection. The Dene people living in the Mackenzie Valley possess the greatest amount of knowledge and expertise concerning land and resources there. To ignore this would be to compromise effective development of northern land and resource management policy.

Conclusion

Northern land and resource management policy must be developed through the aboriginal rights claims process. This does not mean that the public will not be invited to play a role in its development. Rather, only through a co-operative effort of all interested parties will the Dene be able to ensure the proper protection of northern lands and resources. In fact, only with public support of this approach can the "political will" needed to ensure its satisfactory completion be created.

Thus, only through the recognition of the legitimate role in northern policy development that northerners are entitled to play, and the subsequent co-operation of all interested parties, will our northern heritage be preserved, for the benefit of all Canadians.

Background Paper

Conservation of Environmentally Significant Areas

Tom J. Kovacs
Head
Northern Park Proposals
National Parks System Division
Parks Canada
Department of the Environment

Parks Canada is responsible for the conservation of natural areas of national significance and, as such, is an advocate of the national interest. Through its public and consultative process for the selection and establishment of parks, Parks Canada ensures that regional interests are heard and attempts to reconcile the two perspectives through public dialogue and negotiations.

Parks Canada has made some strides in developing appropriate policies for northern parks. More needs to be done in this area, particularly with respect to the use by native peoples of park resources in relation to protection of those resources. Policy development is expected to advance further over a period of time as field experience is gained and as consultations with native peoples continue. In these ways, Parks Canada attempts to contribute to the overall conservation of environmentally significant areas (ESAs) in the North and to reconcile the legitimate interests of both the nation and the region.

One of Parks Canada's mandates is to protect special resources such as natural areas of national significance. In the conservation of ESAs, its attention is focused specifically on the identification, selection, establishment, and management of those lands of national interest that best represent the natural diversity of Canada. New national parks are selected from areas identified by Parks Canada as natural areas of Canadian significance (NACS).

The identification of NACS in the North is nearly complete and the selection of candidate areas is well advanced. The establishment and management of new national parks is the major task ahead.

Progress in the selection and establishment of future national parks has been, and continues to be, affected by the evolving relationship between the federal and territorial governments, the settlement of native claims, and competing resource interests. Compliance with federal policies for balanced development in the North, for prior assessment of mineral and energy resources in proposed park areas, and for public consultative processes has been time consuming, and necessarily so. The lack of an overall strategy for northern conservation, to identify a comprehensive range of components and their policies, has hindered progress in northern conservation generally, although it has had only a limited effect on the establishment of new national parks.

The consultative and public nature of the process for establishing national parks requires that a variety of views and concerns be taken into account in the selection, establishment, and management of new parks. By design, therefore, the mechanism for establishing national parks is set up to bring together the national and regional interests. Further, it provides an opportunity for the expression of local views at a later stage as well, when plans for park management are prepared. In the North, consultations primarily involve the territorial governments, local residents, native organizations, and special-interest groups. Generally, Parks Canada and the conservation groups represent the national interest in the pursuit of new parks, whereas the others mentioned are concerned with the territorial or local viewpoint. For the purposes of this paper, territorial and local viewpoints are considered to be the regional interests. The different perspectives associated with national and regional interests have brought several different problems to the surface.

Appeal of Parks to Local Residents

The concept of a national park is alien to many northern residents, especially to local native persons. Understandably, they view parks with suspicion as yet another intrusion by a southern institution. When confronted with unsolicited proposals affecting their lives and livelihoods, local residents ask questions and want answers. The answers have not always been quick enough in coming.

Northern national parks are a relatively new institution to Parks Canada as well. Lack of experience with northern parks has constrained the ability of Parks Canada to predict what effects new parks may have on local ways of life. To some extent, northern park policies cannot be clarified until more practical experience is gained and until policies can be developed jointly with local residents.

Local residents are the persons most directly affected by the establishment of national parks and, consequently, they bear most of the social costs associated with them. Thus, parks cannot be expected to have much appeal to local residents on the grounds of national interest. To ensure the acceptability of new national park proposals, and a continuing good-neighbour relationship, parks have to represent a positive contribution to the lives of native peoples. The point is that national parks have to be a "good deal" for local residents to gain their support.

Role of National Parks

The different expectations of the federal and territorial governments of the role of national parks in the North is another key problem area associated with national and regional interests. Parks Canada's policy calls for the preservation of certain natural areas as national parks in a manner that causes minimum disruption to the lives of local residents. Territorial governments, particularly the Government of the Northwest Territories, hold the view that national parks are desirable provided that their social and economic value to territorial residents can be demonstrated. It is not surprising, therefore, that the territorial governments wish to have a say in the selection of new parks and to set conditions for their development and operation. Consequently, territorial governments seek guarantees to ensure that whatever economic benefit derived from the establishment and operation of parks will accrue to the peoples of the territories.

In an effort to secure the support of the territorial governments for northern park initiatives, Parks Canada has sought to accommodate the primary territorial concern for social and economic benefit. Much has been accomplished in this area, especially since ongoing consultative mechanisms are in place between Parks Canada and both territorial governments.

Indications are that a balance between the national interest in protection and the regional interest in economic and social benefit is possible through continued dialogue, negotiations, and a degree of flexibility on both sides. The aspirations of the territorial governments for the development of their own system of conservation has not yet been satisfied, although contiguous territorial and national parks have been discussed. The development of territorial parks concurrent with the growth of the national parks and other conservation initiatives would be a desirable component in any comprehensive plan for conservation in the North. It may be a prerequisite for the full co-operation of territorial governments.

The Working Groups

Parks Canada has recognized the existence of national and regional interests since the late 1960s, when the first public hearings on master plans for the parks were held. In accepting the validity of both and the need to deal with them, Parks Canada seeks to demonstrate that the two interests are reconcilable so that new national parks will be of value both to the nation and to local residents. With respect to local native persons, Parks Canada provides for local involvement in management, and for employment and training opportunities. Some benefits have yet to be explored fully with local residents and territorial governments. A good start in the required consultations was made in the six north-of-60° initiatives [Northern Yukon; Ellesmere Island; Northern Banks Island; Bathurst Inlet; Wager Bay; and one national landmark proposal—eds], and a useful exchange of ideas has since resulted in making both national and regional interests more sensitive to each other. Federal–territorial co-operation in achieving the withdrawal of lands on Ellesmere Island for a future national park with local support is an example of progress achieved to date. However, much remains to be done.

To advance conservation, it is necessary to establish a common goal to provide a basis for co-operation among governments, agencies, and interest groups. That common goal is the conservation of ESAs. Because of the varied interests and agencies involved in such a comprehensive goal, the respective mandates and policies of participating interests should be defined within the framework of an overall plan. An appropriate forum for striking an overall plan should emerge as a result of the Whitehorse Workshop on Northern Conservation Policy, held in March 1983. It should clarify northern conservation policies and identify the components, the schedule, and the means for accomplishing their implementation.

Parks Canada is ready to make a contribution to such a comprehensive plan. But the agency itself needs to develop further its northern policies and management philosophy to fit northern circumstances specifically. Two areas, resource use by native peoples and resource protection, require specific attention. Parks Canada will continue to conduct a dialogue with territorial governments and local residents on these issues.

As well, Parks Canada needs to communicate its overall plan for the North, defining those areas it wishes to select, establish, and manage as national parks. As stated earlier, much of the work behind the plan has been accomplished; however, it has to be reviewed in public, integrated with departmental plans, and worked into the comprehensive plan for northern conservation. Parks Canada's plan calls for a total of 15 national parks in the North, of which 4 already exist as parks or reserves, roughly 5 per cent of the territorial land mass.

Expanding public support for new northern parks would be desirable to facilitate political commitment and action at the various levels of government. One way of broadening the public support is through a clear indication of Parks Canada's plan for the North. Another is to demonstrate a responsible and capable approach to managing existing northern parks. The introduction of appropriate policies and management practices will assist in this effort. One of the proposed amendments to the National Parks Act is to legislate wilderness areas in northern parks, the dual purpose of which is, first, to strengthen Parks Canada's commitment to safeguard sensitive resources and, secondly, to reassure native peoples that their traditional way of life will not be threatened by the development of extensive facilities or by large numbers of visitors.

Further, Parks Canada is prepared to work toward the acquisition of new park areas within the framework of regional land-use planning. Areas identified as having significance for a number of different uses will be subjected to regional planning. Proposed national parks will have to be tested against other proposals to determine the best uses of lands.

As in the past, Parks Canada will continue to present proposals for national parks at native-claim negotiations to determine whether the establishment of new parks can be combined with settlement legislation. However, because of the need for northern national parks, its ability to work within the plans for regional land use or the process of native land-claims settlement is dependent upon reaching results within a reasonable time frame. If regional land-use planning is not implemented soon, or if native-claim negotiations fail to result in agreements before too long, Parks Canada should push for new parks or park reserves on its own. Reserve status would be assigned to areas affected by native claims in order not to prejudice the outcome of that process.

Much of the groundwork for planning the system of northern national parks has been completed. Wide-ranging public support for new northern park initiatives would permit the federal government to proceed with an ambitious programme of expansion. It is recognized, however, that developments in conservation in the North are best approached in a comprehensive fashion. Parks Canada is prepared to contribute to a co-operative intergovernmental, interagency, and public process that identifies the various conservation policies, components, and means of protecting specific geographical areas. It is also willing to participate in the native-claim negotiations and in regional land-use planning to achieve new park areas in a process that takes a variety of interests and regional concerns into account. Thus, Parks Canada supports approaches that will permit the parallel development of northern national parks and other conservation systems, including territorial parks.

Position Paper

Northern Conservation Lands

**National and Provincial Parks
Association of Canada**

Canadians have a rich northern natural heritage, a landscape of incredible beauty. From wave-battered polar seas, across rolling expanses of tundra, to rugged mountain peaks, Canada's northland encompasses great diversity. There are places in the North where caribou and musk-oxen roam, where great colonies of seabirds nest, and where migratory geese congregate—providing unsurpassed wildlife spectacles.

These places are not adequately protected. Governments at all levels have failed the peoples of Canada. Slowly, step by step, development by development, we are losing this heritage.

The National and Provincial Parks Association of Canada is calling for a strong united voice from conservationists and others concerned with the protection of this heritage, to make governments aware of our deep concern and to demand that they act now to reverse this incremental loss.

Our Targets

By the end of 1983, we ask that federal and territorial ministers responsible for any conservation lands issue press releases and policy statements, approved by their respective cabinets, that promise the Canadian public that they will establish the conservation lands under their jurisdictions by January 1988.

These statements should include a schedule of steps describing ways, means, and times of public input for completing this task. Specifically, the ministers should commit themselves as follows:

- that the federal minister of the Environment complete the system of national parks, marine parks, national landmarks, national heritage rivers, and national wildlife areas
- that the territorial ministers of the departments of Renewable Resources complete the system of territorial parks: historical, recreational, and day-use

- that the federal minister of Indian Affairs and Northern Development, as present landowner of all the potential conservation lands, support their transfer to the aforementioned jurisdictions, specifically for conservation purposes, and support the establishment of conservation lands as a key and fundamental component of land-use planning.

Our targets imply the settlement of native land claims.

The North—Our Precious Heritage

A system of protected conservation lands does not exist in northern Canada, even though the legislation that would enable the federal and territorial governments to do so has existed for several years. Consider the following:

- there is only one national wildlife area in the North—Polar Bear Pass, announced in 1982
- of 15 natural regions defined by Parks Canada, 11 are without parks
- only a few of the 151 ecological sites identified in the International Biological Programme are protected
- existing legislation for bird and game sanctuaries is not strong and fails to protect the habitats from development.

The delicate nature of arctic ecosystems is a familiar theme to many, but efforts to protect significant examples of these ecosystems have been rare and sporadic. The urgency is real and well documented. For more than a decade, the federal government has talked of "balanced development," and has poured millions of dollars into the North to stimulate exploration and industrial development. The government has done little, however, to protect areas of outstanding natural significance.

Growing Development

Many persons visualize Canada's North as a vast, empty land of ice and snow. In fact, there is little of the North that has not been explored. Much of this exploration, aside from the travels of native peoples, has been in the form of searches for non-renewable resources such as oil, gas, and coal. Other persons have surveyed the flora and fauna.

When individuals visit the North, they are frequently astounded by the amount of development that has already occurred. The Mackenzie Valley is a good example. Barges ply the river, and it is possible now to drive within a few kilometres of the Arctic Ocean. Supply ships, drillships, tugs, and other vessels frequent the offshore region. Tuktoyaktuk is a bustling hub of industrial and marine activity with fuel tanks, an airport, a dry dock, and facilities for several hundred persons.

The land is dotted with communities, both isolated native settlements and larger developed areas. The oceans and rivers carry more traffic than most Canadians realize. There are many mines in the Yukon and in the Northwest Territories, and the network of roads continues to spread as development increases.

The Framework of Government

The federal Department of Indian Affairs and Northern Development is both the land manager and the owner. Its mandate originates in various pieces of legislation such as the Territorial Lands Act. DIAND not only has authority over land disposition, but also is responsible for negotiating and settling native land claims.

The federal Department of the Environment is responsible for environmental matters. Included in its mandate is responsibility for establishing and managing national parks, national landmarks, national wildlife areas, and migratory bird sanctuaries.

The governments of the Yukon and the Northwest Territories act primarily through ordinances such as the Area Development Ordinance, the Game Ordinance, and the Parks Ordinance. These allow for the establishment of territorial parks both for the protection of important natural features and for recreation. However, to establish these, the land must be transferred from the control of the federal government.

Land-use planning, as proposed by the federal and Yukon governments, is an important programme currently underway to identify prime areas for various priority uses. The programme has great importance for the establishment of a system of conservation lands in the North. Currently, however, land-use planning has no legislative base or data base. Governments write position papers and talk about land-use planning, but the process of establishment has hardly begun. In Alaska, 25 per cent of the land is protected as national parks and wildlife refuges; but in the Canadian North, less than 2 per cent of the land is protected.

The Struggle for the Land

The activities of governments, developers, and individuals occur within a complex political framework. Perhaps the most prominent feature of this framework is the struggle for control over land and natural resources. The mining and petroleum industries clearly would prefer to be bound by as few restrictions as possible. The federal and territorial governments frequently seem to disagree on who the primary land manager should be. Native peoples are caught in the midst of these discussions with their very legitimate claims to land resources and to the protection of their culture. Agencies and individuals who are concerned about the protection of the environment struggle within the morass of political and regulatory conflicts. Time and time again, it is the environment that suffers.

Despite the complexities of land ownership and management, the essential missing ingredient to establishing conservation lands is political will. The key candidate areas for protection are all known. The technical work in identifying and classifying them is essentially complete. Nevertheless, at the point of political action, the process of protection has stalled. It is up to concerned persons to speak out on this issue. Otherwise, Canadians forfeit not only the immense treasure of a system of conservation lands to protect the northern natural heritage, but also the right to complain about the loss.

Background Paper

The History and Future of Parks in the Northwest Territories: A Government of the Northwest Territories Perspective

A. Vaughan
Superintendent of Parks
Department of Economic Development and Tourism
Government of the Northwest Territories

The Park System of the Northwest Territories

In the Beginning

On 24 January 1973, at the Legislative Assembly of the Northwest Territories, the Honourable T. Butters introduced a motion calling for the establishment of a system of territorial parks. After debate, the assembly agreed to support the motion in order to counterbalance the pressures of southern "conservationists," and to ensure that there would be parks to serve "the NEEDS of the PEOPLE—as well as of the birds, and the fish. . . ."[1]

An ordinance respecting the establishment, development, and operation of territorial parks was passed later that year by the assembly, spelling out two prime objectives—recreation and economic benefits—to be derived from tourism. Parks would be "developed to maximize public benefit and enjoyment of Territorial residents. Economic benefits may be expected to accrue directly to residents, to communities, and to the overall economy of the Northwest Territories. The growth of tourism is accelerating and parks are known to have attractive values for tourism."[2]

The essential desired characteristics of territorial parks, as they were envisaged then, were that:

- traditional rights and privileges of the indigenous peoples to hunt, fish, and trap in the parks would not be impeded

- the development potential of renewable and non-renewable resources would be assessed prior to delineation and designation of prospective park sites (Care would be taken not to include areas favourable for mineral exploitation)
- zoning would be introduced where necessary to permit the development of renewable resources "incorporating accepted resource management practices and . . . subject to legislation regulating resource use." Care would be taken in selecting sites to avoid potential mineral exploitation–recreation conflicts
- selected park sites not only should be attractive from a recreational viewpoint, but also should "be suitable for the development of accommodation and related visitor services"
- park sites "should have reasonable access in relation to the potential demand for recreation areas by population centres"
- public hearings would be held prior to designation of any major park.[3]

The Territorial Parks Ordinance, enacted in 1974, was intended to result in the creation of the following four types of parks:

1. *Natural environment recreation parks* would be selected from relatively untouched areas suited to "the more passive types of outdoor recreation activities," requiring only limited facilities (e.g., canoeing, back-packing, and fishing). No internal roads would be built, although access roads might be provided. No permanent dwellings or business establishments would be permitted in these parks.
2. *Outdoor recreation parks* would be selected from sites relatively accessible to major communities, and suitable to "the more active types of recreation pursuits" (e.g., power boating and waterskiing). Construction of access and internal roads and mooring and docking facilities was envisaged in these parks, as were permanent accommodation facilities and services for visitors.
3. *Highway and wayside parks* would be much smaller facilities providing day-use picnic sites and campgrounds for overnight accommodation along highways. They were to be sited in particularly scenic spots and were to contain selected facilities, such as boat launch areas, that would tend to enhance the travel experience.

4. *Community parks* were to be similar in size and nature to highway and wayside parks, but would be developed for the benefit of, and in consultation with, specific communities.[4]

After the preliminary stages of development were undertaken by the territorial government, arrangements were to be negotiated between the Government of the Northwest Territories (GNWT) and the communities involved, so that the communities could assume responsibility for management of the parks.

From 1974 to 1983

In 1974 there were 26 sites, all in either the wayside park or community park category, comprising a total of 600 ha (6.0 km²). By 1977 this had grown to 36 sites comprising 2910 ha (29.1 km²). Only 26 sites, totalling 1870 ha (18.7 km²), were equipped with facilities, however, and the remainder either had been discontinued or were in the early stages of development. Of the 1870 ha, two parks together—Reid Lake (1090 ha) and Whittaker Falls (360 ha)—accounted for the major part of the total area (1450 ha). The remaining 24 park sites comprised a total of 420 ha (4.2 km²). The Norah Willis Michener Territorial Park in the Mackenzie Mountains, which now is administered as a game preserve by the Department of Renewable Resources, comprises 13.0 km² of relatively inaccessible area on the N.W.T.–Yukon border.

Over the last two to three years, the Government of the Northwest Territories has taken steps to expand the system of parks, with the full support of nearby communities. Two new wayside parks are now operational along the Dempster Highway. Development is partially completed for an outdoor recreation park of some 14.3 km² at the mouth of the Blackstone River (near Nahanni National Park Reserve), and construction has just begun on another outdoor recreation park at Long Lake (6.2 km² within Yellowknife city limits).

The federal government has been asked to transfer responsibility for the management of the surface rights for two natural environment parks. One of these parks is located close to Inuvik in the Campbell Lake Hills (520 km²), and the other is located close to Yellowknife at Hidden Lake (130 km²). The Government of the Northwest Territories has expressed long-term interest in acquiring the surface rights for parks in several other locations, such as Dodo Canyon in the Mackenzie Mountains.

In January 1983, the first substantive change was made to the Territorial Parks Ordinance since its enactment in 1974. Legislation now permits the designation, commemoration, and operation of historic parks.

Consultations with the communities have been completed, and by this autumn [1983], an appropriate plan for development and operation will be completed for the first proposed historic park, at Peale Point, a Thule site near Frobisher Bay.

Consistent with the recent significant expansion of park facilities and growth in use of the parks in the Northwest Territories, the department's budget has grown substantially over the past four years. In 1975–76, total expenditure on the parks system was $159 000. In 1983, the maintenance budget was $636 000, and the capital construction budget was $1 202 000.

The Territorial Park System Today

Like the majority of resources in the Northwest Territories, the park system is not yet even partially developed, having no interpretive programmes and only one nature trail. However, territorial parks do provide both local residents and visitors with an inexpensive alternative to hotel or motel accommodation and with a place to spend a sunny summer afternoon on a lakeshore.

The following are some of the more interesting results of the first system-wide survey of park users, made in 1981:

- about 30 per cent of all summer visitor parties to the Northwest Territories used the campgrounds
- campers in the Northwest Territories spent about $35.00 per day (1981 dollars)
- 70 per cent of the park users were non-residents
- most park users would like the use of hot showers, and electrical outlets for their trailers and motor homes
- "campers" who fly to the Northwest Territories would like "simple cabin-like" accommodation to be provided in the parks.[5]

The 1981 survey clearly demonstrated the strong role that the park system plays in support of tourism. The 1982 survey, although not as exhaustive as the 1981 survey, provided similar answers to comparable questions.

The responsibility for the development and operation of the territorial park system has remained within the Department of Economic Development and Tourism. This reflects the government's past and present conviction that parks be established for the use and benefit of people. The park system complements tourism-related activities by providing sites for outdoor recreational activities.

Table 1

	1980/81	1981/82	1982/83	1983/84	1984/85
Square km	42.1	56.4	68.8	720.5	740
Campsites	500	525	580	605	650
Total Operations and Maintenance	$205 000	$270 000	$400 000	$636 000	N/A
Person Years	3.0	3.0	4.5	6.0	N/A
Capital	$465 000	$818 000	$922 000	$1 202 000	N/A

Notes:

1983–84 park lands data assume the addition of Hidden Lake (130 km²) and Campbell Lake Hills (520 km²). 1984–85 park lands data assume the addition of the Arctic Red River day-use area, Peale Point historic park, and boundary adjustments to Prelude Lake Park.

Lands set aside primarily for the purpose of preservation are administered by both the Department of Renewable Resources and the Department of Justice and Public Services. The specialized expertise of their staff in managing significant natural and cultural resources is used in the territorial park system when and as required.

Tomorrow

In May 1983, the Executive Committee of the Government of the Northwest Territories gave formal approval to key principles, objectives, and associated strategies for the Department of Economic Development and Tourism, which will provide guidance for the development and operation of the park system for the next several years. The following are relevant extracts from the goals and objectives of the department:

Key Principle

Parks are to assist in promoting, interpreting, and conserving the culture and land of the Northwest Territories.

Objective

Develop territorial parks to assist in meeting outdoor recreational needs, while assisting local residents in realizing park-related training, employment and business opportunities.

Strategies

- Provide a diversified system of all types and sizes of parks.
- Develop, through the Territorial Parks Program, significant visitors attractions/activities.
- Increase the numbers and length of stay of territorial park visitors.
- Facilitate the development and strengthening of service businesses near territorial parks.
- Provide local communities with the opportunity to participate in all aspects of the establishment, design, development and operation of nearby territorial park and outdoor recreation area related developments.
- Promote the Northwest Territories applicable social, environmental, and economic development goals in Parks Canada's programs.

Objective

Support and encourage traditional skills and pursuits in the economy of the Northwest Territories.

Strategy*

- Develop parks for interpretation and conservation and provide interpretive park programs to create interesting opportunities for both visitors and residents to learn and experience the Northwest Territories culture and its land.[6]

The department's objectives and associated strategies will be subjected to public review over the next 12 months, after which they will be rewritten if required. Also, over the next 12-18 months, work will be completed on developing policies, programmes, and priorities within the context of the approved objectives and strategies for the park system for the 1980s. Some of the required background work for preparing this proposed "Territorial Park Strategy" already has been completed.

- Consultants were hired to outline possible policies and operational procedures for natural and cultural park interpretive programmes.
- Staff from the Parks Branch of the Province of Alberta currently are assisting the GNWT in a critical review of the territorial parks operation and maintenance procedures.
- Staff on loan from Ontario Parks drafted proposed policy and implementation guidelines for marketing the N.W.T. parks.
- Pilot projects have been completed to assist in establishing guidelines for the boundary identification, development, and management of both natural environment and outdoor recreation type parks.
- A pilot study will be initiated this summer to help in drafting development and management guidelines for historic parks.
- As a specific priority project for the Executive Committee, this summer consultants will be hired to draft policies and guidelines for managing the natural and cultural resources located within N.W.T. parks. The second purpose of the study is to describe an appropriate zoning system for territorial parks.

*[Only the park-related strategy has been listed — author.]

The Working Groups

Through the work to date on the "strategy," nine key concepts have emerged:

1. Rather than adopting the many founding principles associated with southern park systems, the territorial park system must respond directly to the territories' unique social, political, and economic environment. The department does not accept the argument that establishing territorial parks must result in large tracts of land with fixed boundaries being reserved in perpetuity in the name of the Government of the Northwest Territories for a single and exclusive purpose—where local control, interests, and traditional uses are set aside.
2. Territorial parks should not be designated simply as a means for planning or regulating land uses—there are other more effective and direct land-use planning processes and regulatory regimes that should be used.
3. One of the prime functions of territorial parks should be to assist in developing and strengthening the economy of local communities. Within the context of sound land management practices, parks should be selected, designed, and operated to attract visitors and to play a major role in extending the lengths of stay of visitors in the region. Encouraging the use of the parks by those who wish to learn about, observe, or experience first hand the land, its peoples, and their heritage, will create local business and job opportunities.
4. Establishment of territorial parks should contribute to the preservation of significant territorial natural and cultural resources, and should assist in meeting the outdoor recreation needs of visitors and residents.
5. Territorial parks should not be established without the support of potentially affected communities, and all potentially affected communities should be provided with the opportunity to participate fully in the park development planning process.
6. Where there is sufficient interest, and to the extent feasible and practical, the operations of territorial parks should be controlled locally.
7. The establishment of a system of territorial parks should not prejudice the process of land claims.
8. The establishment and operation of territorial parks should not result in any undue interference with the exploration for or exploitation of any significant non-renewable resources in the Northwest Territories. Through dialogue, and based on

the government's acceptance of the value of the mining industry and the mining industry's acceptance of the value of maintaining the integrity of the N.W.T.'s more significant natural
and cultural resources, irreconcilable differences can be
avoided.

9. Territorial parks, as with national parks, normally should not
be established just to preserve nationally, territorially, or
regionally significant or representative features. Rather, territorial parks should be established in response to demonstrated
needs for outdoor recreation or needs for outdoor, on-site
interpretive conservation.

A Two-year Work Plan—Tasks and Priorities

The following eleven substantive targets and priorities have been established for the department's park programme for the next two years:

1. To obtain formal approval from the Government of the
Northwest Territories for a "Territorial Park Strategy." The
document will include policies and guidelines for the selection, development, and management of natural environment
parks; outdoor recreation parks; community parks; highway
and wayside parks; historic parks; landmarks; and waterways-
hiking trails.

2. To obtain formal approval from the Government of the
Northwest Territories for specific guidelines, policies, and
processes to facilitate turning over responsibility for the
operation of existing community parks to interested and
capable groups and communities.

3. To obtain necessary approvals for system-wide maintenance
and construction standards.

4. To implement a user self-registration system in all campgrounds that are not staffed with gate attendants.

5. To achieve 80 per cent visitor satisfaction (as documented by
surveys) with the level and quality of visitor services provided
in N.W.T. parks.

6. To encourage the federal Department of Indian Affairs and
Northern Development (DIAND) to develop and then to
publish mutually acceptable criteria for use in assessing the
degree of federal support for park proposals from the
Government of the Northwest Territories.

7. To encourage DIAND to develop and then to publish a workable process for the review of park proposals from the Government of the Northwest Territories, a process that leads to the transferring of authority for the administration of the surface rights for those proposed territorial park lands that meet established federal criteria.

8. To identify, carry out the public consultation, have designated, and complete the site development and operation planning for at least one sample natural environment park, outdoor recreation park, historic park, landmark, and waterway–hiking trail.

9. To provide on-site park interpretive activities and services in at least two parks in the Fort Smith Region and one park in the Inuvik Region.

10. To facilitate the successful completion of the negotiations associated with drafting a final agreement for the northern Ellesmere Island National Park Reserve.

11. To encourage and facilitate the site selection, public consultation, and development planning for at least one national historic park.

National Parks

The Setting

In 1922, Wood Buffalo National Park was established with about 9500 km² of its 45 000 km² located in the Northwest Territories. Nahanni National Park Reserve (4780 km²) and Auyuittuq National Park Reserve (21 500 km²) were both established in 1972. The lands for the East Arm of Great Slave Lake Reserve (7450 km²) were withdrawn in 1970, and for the Ellesmere Island Reserve (41 600 km²) in 1982. Together these withdrawals represent about 40 per cent of the entire land area contained within the national park system. This percentage will grow considerably if Parks Canada is successful in acquiring the additional ten or so areas within the Northwest Territories in which it has expressed interest.

Parks Canada, excluding the Crown itself, is now the largest single private or government agency using Northwest Territories' land (about three per cent of the total land area of the N.W.T.). Given the size and the historical presence in the Northwest Territories of Parks Canada, the residents of the Northwest Territories believe that they are familiar with its policies and management style.

National parks are viewed in different ways by Northwest Territories' residents and by their predominantly southern "users and champions." The "wilderness" park designation proposed by Parks Canada in the late 1970s antagonized many northerners, as did Parks Canada's method for announcing its proposed expansion programme for the national parks.

Historically, many northerners have viewed the national parks as a salve to the southern environmental conscience. They see lands in the Northwest Territories as being used to meet southern needs, with the Northwest Territories left to bear the significant problems (and costs) but to receive few, if any, offsetting benefits. Existing national parks are viewed traditionally by residents of the N.W.T. as causing the loss of opportunities for business and resource development, making only a minimal contribution to the economic health of nearby communities, and being managed under policies and guidelines that perhaps are more applicable to southern national parks. Less than one per cent of the visitors to national parks across Canada visited parks located in the Northwest Territories (7000 visitors in 1982).

The Honourable George Braden, Minister of Economic Development and Tourism, in a speech in 1980 to a group of international media representatives, stated:

In your northern travels thus far you have seen the vast expanse of land and water in our northern territory. Citizens of the North will describe to you in a variety of ways the attachment and feeling they have for the land . . . because in the North, it is impossible to become detached from that basic factor which makes 45 000 Inuit, Dene, Métis and non-native northerners believe so strongly in 1.3 million square miles [3.25 million km²] of land and water. If I can be brief, our northern land to some of our citizens is a resource which in turn has supported and become part of the culture of native people. It is a resource which can be further developed to meet the demands of the 20th century—and it is a source of challenge for northerners who were born here or who have moved north and chosen to remain.[7]

A position paper prepared by the Department of Economic Development and Tourism in 1981 stated that national parks represent only one of many alternative land uses and regulatory regimes and that Parks Canada therefore should be treated as any other potential user or administrator of Northwest Territories lands. As a proponent, it is Parks Canada's responsibility when soliciting support for its proposals to clearly identify its land requirements; the manner in which it intends to develop and administer its lands; and the likely impact of its proposals on the environmental, social, and economic health of the Northwest Territories. The position paper went on to say that although there is very broad support across the Northwest Territories for the concepts of preservation and conservation, and it is recognized that some natural and cultural resources do require protection, the methods for achieving preservation and conservation of resources in the N.W.T. should not be detailed using criteria that have evolved largely from a southern perspective, nor should they be left for application by well-meaning but often misguided southerners.

Parks Canada and the Government of the Northwest Territories began to discuss fully these and other related problems late in 1980 and throughout 1981. As a basis for discussions, the Government of the Northwest Territories indicated that "national parks, if appropriately located, developed, and operated, could make a significant contribution to the achievement of the environmental, social, and economic goals and objectives of the N.W.T." Parks Canada accepted that most of the concerns of the Northwest Territories could be accommodated fully within the context of its existing legislative and policy base. The role of the Government of the Northwest Territories, as the representative of all residents of the N.W.T. and their varied interests, also was accepted by Parks Canada.

Recent Agreements

Improving dialogue between senior officials of Parks Canada and of the Government of the Northwest Territories was the first priority. The Canada–Northwest Territories Consultative Committee Concerning Park Matters, established in 1980, now provides an excellent forum for regular discussions of issues of mutual concern associated with both existing and proposed national parks.

In 1981, the territorial government and Parks Canada reached agreement on the process that Parks Canada now uses to select, establish, and develop new national parks across the Northwest Territories. The process provides the Government of the Northwest Territories with a direct and meaningful voice in decision making. It also acknowledges the legitimate role of other interested groups in the process of establishing parks, including DIAND, the native organizations, resource development interests, and potentially affected communities.[8]

Following agreement on a process for selecting and establishing new national parks, the Government of the Northwest Territories formally and publicly presented Parks Canada with a series of principles concerning the establishment, development, and operation of new national parks in the Northwest Territories. These principles clarify the criteria that will be used for evaluating new proposals for national parks, and recommend ways in which new national parks in the N.W.T. should be established, developed, and operated.

1. Parks Canada, for each new park proposal, should clearly identify: the land requirements; the manner in which the park will likely be developed and administered; and, the likely impact of park establishment on the environmental, social, and economic health of the N.W.T.
2. A decision by Parks Canada to withdraw lands for the purposes of establishing a national park should be subject, in part, to receiving the support of the G.N.W.T. G.N.W.T. support for specific new Parks Canada initiatives will be dependent primarily upon:

   • the degree of support for the park proposal from any directly affected communities
   • the potential economic and social development opportunities associated with the park proposal to be created for the local communities
   • the potential contribution to the achievement of G.N.W.T. environmental, social and economic goals and objectives, that could result from park establishment
   • consideration of the potential economic (eg. lost resource development opportunities), social (eg. lifestyle) and financial (eg. infrastructure) costs associated with the park proposal.

3. Parks Canada should provide adequate opportunity for the G.N.W.T. and all potentially affected N.W.T. residents, communities and associations to fully participate in the planning and decision making processes associated with the selection, establishment, development and operation of proposed new national parks. Additionally, Parks Canada should develop and implement guidelines and procedures which permit the devolution of significant responsibility for park operations and resource management to the local people.

4. Establishment of national parks should not:

- prejudice the outcome of the land claims process
- or, result in the loss of potentially significant mineral or petroleum reserves (i.e. "blocked" or "locked-up" reserves)
- or, interfere with the continuation of resource harvesting by residents of nearby local communities.

5. The N.W.T. wildlife resource harvesting regulations and practices for General Licence Holders should be used as the basis for regulating the harvest of wildlife within proposed parks.

   The responsibilities of the Hunters' & Trappers' Associations should not be restricted through park establishment, without the prior consent of the potentially affected Hunters' & Trappers' Associations, and the G.N.W.T.
6. Parks Canada and the G.N.W.T. should work towards drafting an agreement for each proposed new national park, which sets out the conditions under which the establishment of that national park would likely be in the best interests of the two parties. Such inter-governmental agreements should be in place, prior to any withdrawal of lands for the purposes of establishing a national park.
7. Park development and management guidelines should reflect a commitment to ensuring that the residents of local communities are provided with real opportunities to derive all possible social and economic benefits potentially associated with the development and operation of the proposed new national parks.
8. Prior to the withdrawal of land, Parks Canada shall prepare a specific socio-economic "action plan" for the proposed park. The socio-economic action plan should include details concerning the steps that Parks Canada will take to ensure that the residents of local communities can derive all the possible benefits associated with the development and operation of the proposed national park (Parks Canada manpower training programs, preferential purchasing guidelines, etc.).
9. If so requested by the G.N.W.T. and local communities, Parks Canada should actively promote visitation to their proposed new park(s), and through appropriate development, facilitate and encourage park visitation.[9]

In February 1982, the results of meaningful dialogue, and an application of the process and principles papers, were first seen. The Northern Ellesmere Memorandum of Understanding is a historic document, because it reflects the interests of both northerners and Parks Canada.[10] Criticism of the Memorandum of Understanding by some southerners and the interest groups to which they belong perhaps is based on misunderstanding. Our local newspaper, in an editorial at the time, declared, "The tunnel vision actions of those who have a romantic notion of the High Arctic fail to take into account the people that live here, their needs, their aspirations and their opinions. . . ."[11] The Memorandum of Understanding demonstrates that agreement can be reached on how national parks can respond to both national and more-regional sets of objectives. National and regional objectives need not be viewed as being mutually exclusive.

In 1982, the Government of the Northwest Territories became involved formally for the first time in the various stages of a Parks Canada management planning process for an existing national park. A substantive brief concerning all aspects of the management (boundary adjustments, resource management practices, visitor services, local employment, etc.) of Wood Buffalo National Park was forwarded by the minister to his federal counterpart. Similar input was provided for Auyuittuq National Park Reserve.

In 1983, the territorial government will monitor and participate fully in the current management planning process for the Nahanni National Park Reserve. At the conclusion of the consultation programme, the formal position of the Government of the Northwest Territories will be forwarded to the federal minister responsible for Parks Canada.

Some Final Observations

Mr Braden, Minister of Economic Development and Tourism, in 1980 publicly stated that:

> we must, of course, continue to work with our federal counterparts to ensure northern interests are considered and respected in federal plans for national parks, heritage parks, wilderness preserves, heritage rivers, international biological sites and so forth. We must ensure that land is not set aside just for the sake of setting aside an area which will look nice when plotted on a map. We must ensure that present interests and our options for the future are not alienated because southerners in Ottawa want to create parks 3000 miles [4830 km] from their home.[12]

The Working Groups

The accords between the Government of the Northwest Territories and Parks Canada reached in 1981 and the Ellesmere Memorandum of Understanding of 1982 have demonstrated that the concerns of the assembly, and of the peoples that it represents, can be met.

There has been substantial improvement over the past three years in the relations between Parks Canada and the Government of the Northwest Territories, as is evidenced by several current joint ventures. This improvement results from a conviction that there is common ground in national and territorial interests. Working together is facilitating the achievement of the goals and objectives of both Parks Canada and the Government of the Northwest Territories.

The Government of the Northwest Territories is prepared to support publicly selected new national park initiatives, but only if, through the negotiating process, a formal agreement can be reached that ensures that Parks Canada's initiatives will result in minimal costs and significant measurable positive benefits (i.e., economic, social, and environmental).

The Government of the Northwest Territories is in the process of establishing a framework for a well-rounded system of territorial parks. Although officials are studying southern park systems, the system that is being developed will reflect perceived local needs, and it will be in keeping with the unique cultural, economic, and environmental setting of the N.W.T.

Conservation of the rich cultural and natural resources of the Northwest Territories has a very high priority within the current territorial government. Establishment of a complementary system of national and territorial parks that reflects the full range of interests of residents in the Northwest Territories will help to achieve that most important objective.

This is not the time for bold plans for the expansion of territorial parks. More-orderly growth, in response to substantive and well-defined need, is required. The proposed exercise in land-use planning between the Government of the Northwest Territories and the Department of Indian Affairs and Northern Development, discussions associated with DIAND's north of 60° conservation strategy, the land-claims settlement process, fiscal restraint, and common sense preclude rushing full speed ahead with a major plan for land acquisition.

Endnotes

1. *Council for the Northwest Territories Debates, Official Report*, 48th Session, 7th Council, 24 January 1973, pp. 137–139.

2. T. Auchterlonie, "Northwest Territories: Year in Review," from *Tourism and Parks, the Twelfth Federal Provincial Parks Conference*, 1973, p. 148.

3. Ibid., pp. 149–150.

4. Ibid., pp. 153–155.

5. *Northwest Territories Travel Surveys 1981–1982, Summary Report: Visitors, Park Users, Residents* (Deloitte Haskins & Sells Associates, June 1982, Vancouver).

6. "We've Rolled Up Our Sleeves . . . So You Can Go to Work" (Department of Economic Development and Tourism, GNWT, September 1983).

7. George Braden, World Heritage Media Luncheon, 31 July 1980, Yellowknife, N.W.T.

8. "National Park Selection and Establishment Process—The Involvement of the Government of the Northwest Territories," October 1981, signed by Assistant Deputy Minister, Parks Canada, and Deputy Minister of Department of Economic Development and Tourism, GNWT.

9. "Principles Concerning the Establishment, Development and Operation of New National Parks in the N.W.T." (Department of Economic Development and Tourism, Government of the Northwest Territories, 1981).

10. Canada, Department of the Environment, Parks Canada and the Government of the Northwest Territories, Department of Economic Development and Tourism, "Memorandum of Understanding for the Establishment of a Reserve for a National Park on Ellesmere Island" (Ottawa, 25 February 1982).

11. *News of the North*, "Editorial: Don't Fence Me Out" (5 March 1982, Yellowknife), p. A4.

12. George Braden. See above, note 7.

Mineral Development

Chairmen: Walter Kupsch
John Willson

Introduction

Tungsten, lead, zinc, silver, and gold are mined in the Northwest Territories and the Yukon. The mining industry is thus an employer and a contributor to local and regional economies in the North.

Mining activities in the Yukon and the Northwest Territories are influenced by several important factors. World-wide and national economic conditions have contributed to the closure of some mines and a reduction in the level of exploratory activity. The desire of northerners for greater control over northern development and the unsettled claims of northern native peoples to land and resources have led to increased levels of intergovernmental competition for the right to regulate, manage, and tax the use of mineral resources.

Three major interests—the native peoples, the territorial governments, and the federal government—claim rights to develop and benefit from the use of minerals. Jurisdiction is unlikely to be decided quickly. For some time now various interests have called for revision of the Yukon Quartz and Placer Mining acts to bring these land uses under the territorial land-use regulations. Little progress is evident or likely as the three-way struggle for resource control continues.

Regulation of the mining industry is thought by many to need review and revision. Notwithstanding a greater understanding of the ecological impacts of mining and a stronger regulatory process than ever before, serious damage to the northern environment continues to occur. Water quality, terrestrial habitats, and wildlife are affected adversely by exploration, development, production, refining, and transportation of minerals. The establishment of standards for environmentally sustainable mineral development and the capability to assess, monitor, and enforce them are therefore important environmental issues.

The Working Groups

There are many concerns about regulation of northern mining. Environmental groups argue that current regulations are neither sufficiently stringent nor adequately enforced. Many in the mining industry view regulations as bottlenecks and deterrents based on whim rather than on solid data. Resources are frequently too limited to enable officials to implement and enforce standards adequately and fairly. Regulatory processes can be too discretionary, too costly, too time consuming, duplicative, and guided by the project rather than by policy. These factors suggest that a review of regulations is needed. The mining industry is concerned particularly about access to land for mineral exploration. The establishment of northern national parks, wildlife reserves, and other conservation areas may reduce the amount of land available for mineral development. This issue is handled best through regional land-use planning.

A northern mineral policy currently is being developed by the Department of Indian Affairs and Northern Development (DIAND). Many interests, including the mining industry, have been advocating new policy initiatives for mineral development in the North for some time. The Northern Mineral Advisory Committee has outlined several federal government initiatives necessary to support northern mining and to link industry interests more closely to decision makers and the decision-making process.

The recommendations of the Northern Mineral Advisory Committee have yet to be related to the northern land-use planning policy approved by Cabinet in 1981. The prevailing view of the industry and its regulators seems to be that mineral development programmes can proceed independently of comprehensive land-use planning. The federal and territorial governments, however, are now moving to implement the 1981 northern land-use planning policy. It is therefore important that those discussing the future of northern mining deal with the need for an approach that is co-ordinated with comprehensive land-use planning.

The working group included:

Chairmen: **Walter Kupsch**
Department of Geology
University of Saskatchewan

John Willson
Cominco Ltd.
Yellowknife, N.W.T.

Rapporteur: **Jocelyn Lillycrop**
Natural Sciences and Engineering
Research Council (NSERC)
Ottawa, Ontario

Invited Participants:

Al Clark
Mineral Policy Sector
Department of Energy, Mines and Resources
Government of Canada
Ottawa, Ontario

Terry Daniels
Northwest Territories Chamber of Mines
Yellowknife, N.W.T.

David Emery
Giant Yellowknife Mines Limited
Yellowknife, N.W.T.

John Fraser
Mineral Policy Division
Department of Indian Affairs and Northern Development
Government of Canada
Ottawa, Ontario

John French
Minerals Adviser
Government of the Northwest Territories
Yellowknife, N.W.T.

The Working Groups

Robbie Keith
Faculty of Environmental Studies
University of Waterloo

Glen MacDonald
Yukon Chamber of Mines
Whitehorse, Yukon

Garnet Page
Calgary, Alberta

Bob Spence
Northern Mineral Advisory Committee
Department of Indian Affairs and Northern Development
Government of Canada
Ottawa, Ontario

Background documents used in the working group, in addition to those published in these proceedings, included:

DIAND. "Notes for an Address by the Honourable John C. Munro, Minister of Indian Affairs and Northern Development, B.C. and Yukon Chamber of Mines." *Communiqué*, 3 May 1982.

Energy and Resource Development Secretariat. "Resource Development Policy." Yellowknife: Government of the Northwest Territories, March 1983.

Report of the Northern Mineral Advisory Committee. Submitted by John Bruk, Chairman, to the Honourable Jake Epp, Minister of Indian Affairs and Northern Development. Ottawa, 15 August 1979.

Woods Gordon Management Consultants. Executive Summary of "An Evaluation of the Social and Economic Impact of Exploration, Development, and Production of the Mineral Resources in the Yukon and Northwest Territories on the Northern and National Economies," a study done for the Department of Indian Affairs and Northern Development. May 1982.

Working Group Report

Mineral Development

General Statement

Although the representatives of native groups invited to participate in this discussion were not present to express their important interests in mineral development issues, the working group had a reasonably open, rational, and unbiased discussion that made all participants aware of the complexities that face an expanding northern mining industry.

The importance of northern mineral development was acknowledged by all working group participants. The development of minerals and hydrocarbons is the only major growing source of wealth foreseeable in the North; therefore, mineral development is essential. The mining industry is a responsible industry; its development practices have been responsive to increasing public awareness of the environmental and social consequences of mineral development.

There is a need for an updated general northern policy with which the forthcoming northern mineral policy will be compatible. These policies must address the two main problems currently facing the mining industry: the competition between the federal and territorial governments for jurisdiction over resources and the lack of a streamlined process that will allow the timely involvement of any interested party in project implementation. Time is important to the success of any development. The working group accepted that the input process must be finite and that, in the end, decisions never can please all parties.

National Benefits

The national benefits of mineral development are related to the economy and to sovereignty. Notwithstanding the substantial past and present economic contributions of the mining industry to the economies of the Northwest Territories and the Yukon, both territories have been and still are burdens to the national economy. The size of the Northwest Territories, for example, requires a government bureaucracy more costly to maintain than the revenue it draws from the territory. Nevertheless, the Northwest Territories exists as a political and economic entity. A larger resource industry is needed to provide revenues equal to, and ultimately greater than, the cost of government so that the N.W.T. will be able to repay the current investment of all Canadians and become a net contributor to Canada's economy. Until that time, mineral rights should remain vested in the Crown in right of Canada. The transfer of mineral rights to the Crown in right of the Northwest Territories should take place only when the Northwest Territories has a responsible and stable government. This sequence of events occurred in some of Canada's provinces: Alberta and Saskatchewan, for example, were divided from the N.W.T. and made provinces in 1905, but did not have jurisdiction over natural resources until 1930.

Regional and Local Benefits and Costs

Benefits from mineral development include increased opportunities for employment, direct financial gain from municipal taxation of the mining installations and from fuel taxes, and revenue sharing. The costs of development include environmental disturbances, job-related health problems, and social problems attributed to changes in lifestyle.

If a mine project is located near an existing community, there will be employment opportunities for the local residents. Hiring local residents is a worthwhile and necessary undertaking of the mining industry. Local skilled labour can be trained and employed in this way. Legally binding quotas should not be introduced, however; a local employment policy should not go beyond guidelines, targets, or objectives.

In the past it has been necessary for the mining industry operating in the North to import skilled labour, but some companies have begun to hire local native residents and to train them in technical programmes that include modular training courses. The advantage of the modular courses is the ease with which they help workers to learn new skills. In the short term, and perhaps in the medium term, this practice has cost the mining industry more than importing labour. Because of hunting and family activities, many members of the northern labour force have not reported for work as regularly as the members of the labour force in southern Canada. Adjustments in work schedules at the Rankin Inlet Nickel Mine and other remote mines in Canada and Greenland, however, have been satisfactory to both local labour and management.

In addition to direct employment in mine projects, mineral development will create a need for additional community services (such as shops and schools) for the growing local population. These services will provide spin-off employment opportunities. Mining activities also will require the associated infrastructure (such as roads, power plants, and air strips) that will be paid for by industry, government subsidies, or both.

For mineral developments in areas remote from existing settlements, whether to use "fly-in, fly-out" workers or to construct a new community near the mine site is a serious question. The working group recommends a thorough study of these alternatives as soon as possible. The points to be considered in such a study include the desirability of frontier development, the costs of providing the needed infrastructure, the fate of the townsite when the mine closes, and the taxation of "commuting" workers.

The environmental, health, and social costs of mining activities must be assessed before any mining operation starts.

Solutions to Existing Problems

Mineral development conflicts can be solved best by working through existing government bodies and processes. These include Parliament and the legislative assemblies of the Northwest Territories and the Yukon. The territorial governments gradually will become leaders in the legislative and regulatory processes. At all times there should be close co-operation and consultation between various levels of government. In the past, such interaction has left much to be desired.

The regulations most acceptable to the mining industry are those that are stable for several (for example, ten) years, yet are flexible enough to allow adjustments to new circumstances. Many existing regulations can be streamlined and overlap can be diminished so that the regulatory processes will be more efficient and fair.

The greatest concern of the mining industry in the North is land-use policy. The working group participants were concerned that mineral exploration and exploitation may be excluded from or severely restricted in a large area of the North. Access to those lands currently open to mining activities should be guaranteed. Transportation corridors through alienated lands should be established where they are required. Exclusive-use designations may be necessary for areas most sensitive to environmental disturbance, but such areas should be as small as possible. Moreover, areas that have not been assessed thoroughly for mineral resource potential should not be alienated. In most cases, multiple-use regulations satisfy the mineral industry, but resource potential must be assessed before land-use decisions are made.

A thorough study of an area's renewable and non-renewable resource potential is impossible without biological and physical baseline data. These data must be acquired through systematic surveys well in advance of mineral development. Acquisition of such data is currently the responsibility of the federal government; this information therefore is in the public domain. Its dissemination to affected communities through the print and electronic media should be encouraged, and can be accomplished best by an existing agency such as the Science Advisory Board of the Northwest Territories. Some native organizations are contemplating establishing their own research groups. Native-controlled science policy and research institutions are already in place in Alaska on the municipal (borough) level.

Background Paper

Northern Mineral Policy: Selected Issues for Discussion

Dr J. Lazarovich
J.W. Fraser
Mining Management and Infrastructure Directorate
Northern Resources and Economic Planning Branch
Northern Affairs Program
Ottawa

Participation by the Department of Indian Affairs and Northern Development (DIAND) in a discussion of northern mineral development issues is timely in view of the work now underway in the department on the development of a northern mineral policy. Work on a northern mineral policy is being resumed following a period of about one year during which more urgent priorities forced a suspension of it.

Work on policy development began following an announcement by the minister of Indian Affairs and Northern Development at a meeting with the Northern Mineral Advisory Committee (NMAC) in October 1981. Copies of a preliminary outline were widely circulated to NMAC, the territorial governments, native organizations, the four chambers of mines, the Mining Association of Canada, organized labour, some major mining companies, and other federal departments. Inputs were received from most of those contacted. In addition, the department commissioned two consultant studies. In a speech to the British Columbia and Yukon Chamber of Mines in May 1982, the minister outlined some considerations that he wished to see addressed in the policy. Preparation of a discussion paper had begun when work was suspended in mid-1982.

DIAND is now reviewing and re-evaluating its previous approach to see if it is still relevant in light of the developments over the past year, during which the mining industry has suffered its worst depression in decades. DIAND views this workshop as an important part of the consultative process that is being followed in developing the northern mineral policy.

This paper identifies and provides comments on some of the major questions and issues involved in the development of northern resources. These are put forward to stimulate the debate on northern mineral policy development. They should not be construed, however, as representing federal government policy, because no formal northern mineral policy has, as yet, been approved by the federal Cabinet or even within DIAND.

Issues in Policy Development

Policy development requires that, at a number of key points, choices and decisions be made that influence not only the process of policy development but also, ultimately, the content of the policy itself. Three of the important considerations that shape policy development are the overall objective of the policy, the scope of the policy, and the specific issues considered in the policy.

Overall Objective of a Policy

The overall objective of a policy needs to be stated clearly and understood so that individual elements of the policy can be developed to achieve it. The perception of an appropriate objective for mineral policy undoubtedly varies, however, and may well be contradictory, among different groups such as governments, mining companies, northern residents, and interest groups, depending upon their particular interests and priorities. Setting the overall objective, therefore, is a major element in policy development.

How should the federal government's objective be established? In that it must try to achieve some balance between various interests, we would be very interested to learn what objective the participants at this workshop advocate as being appropriate for northern mineral policy.

Scope of a Northern Mineral Policy

The scope of a policy for the development of northern minerals, like the objective, governs the ultimate effect of the policy. In the territories, because of the pervasive influence of mining on the land, the peoples, and the economy, it is difficult to determine the appropriate scope and limits for mineral policy. It is relatively easy to identify some issues for inclusion, e.g., the updating or development of new mining regulations and legislation. There is a broad range of other issues, however, each of which bear directly on mining, or vice versa, that must be considered; for example, the provision of infrastructure, native land claims, and environmental protection. In many cases, policy development is also taking place simultaneously in these areas. The question then becomes one of how separate policy developments should be integrated.

Other questions that must be addressed in determining the scope of mineral policy concern the relative emphasis that should be placed on short-term problems as opposed to long-term considerations. Similarly, how far should a policy go in outlining specific measures as opposed to setting broad policy guidelines? What scope or limits do the participants at this workshop feel are appropriate for a northern mineral policy?

Policy Issues

In determining the issues to be covered in mineral policy, it is necessary to consider the particular characteristics of the northern mineral industry and the conditions under which it operates. Usually large, rich deposits are needed to make development in the North worth the risk involved. Major new mines require long-range planning, averaging six to ten years from discovery to mine production. The industry is capital intensive, requiring $150–300 million for major projects.

The industry is basically export-oriented and, therefore, being subject to work competition, is a risk taker. It faces several major disadvantages, however. First, northern mines are remote from major world markets. Secondly, mine sites may be located a long distance from sources of materials, services, and manpower, necessitating long transportation hauls for inbound shipments of supplies and outbound shipments of commodities.

The remoteness, severe climatic conditions, permafrost, and periods of darkness contribute to high capital and operating costs and create problems in attracting and retaining a skilled labour force.

Bearing in mind these characteristics, the following have been identified as being among the most important issues that should be considered in a northern mineral policy.

Government Attitudes toward Industry

The mineral industry is looking for a clear indication of government interest toward it. DIAND intends to send out a clear message that the federal government recognizes the fundamental role played by the mining industry in the northern economy. It is the federal government's intention to foster, to promote, and to encourage prospecting, exploration, and mining in the years to come.

Maximization of Economic Returns and Social Benefits from Mining

The mining industry provides significant benefits to both territories in terms of employment and support to other sections of the economy. Because of the nature of the goods and services demanded by the industry and the characteristics of the northern economy, however, there are limits to the benefits that can accrue to the northern economy and even to Canada as a whole. Therefore, the policy should ensure that economic and social benefits are maximized, consistent with other constraints.

Provision of Infrastructure

Availability of adequate infrastructure is a crucial element in developing northern mining, because, in some projects, infrastructure may account for more than 50 per cent of the capital costs. Whereas in other areas of Canada, or of the world, the required infrastructure may already be in place, its absence in the North could be a major factor affecting the competitive position of northern mines. The policy should address the degree to which infrastructure should be provided by government and under what conditions. The issue is complex because there are several types of infrastructure to be considered—roads, power, townsites. In addition there are different levels of responsibility for the provision of infrastructure, and policy development is underway in other sectors such as roads and energy.

Opinions on government's role in the provision of infrastructure range between two extremes. On the one hand, mining industry officials believe government should have complete responsibility for the provision of infrastructure. On the other hand, there are those who believe that provision of infrastructure is a cost of developing a resource, and that development should go ahead only if a project can bear the full costs. There may well be some intermediate course in which government would take the lead in developing key infrastructure to encourage development in the belief it will recoup the costs in the long run.

Administrative Regime

A stable administrative regime is necessary to create a favourable climate for investment in the North. Some elements of legislation are antiquated, however, and amendments or new legislation are required to take account of current conditions. Conflicts between pieces of legislation need to be resolved. Legislation should be amended to meet the overall objectives of mineral policy.

Fiscal Regime

Mining in the North is subject to several levels of taxation: federal, territorial, and municipal. Federal taxation cannot be addressed directly through a northern mineral policy, although territorial mining royalties under federal jurisdiction can. The appropriate level for northern royalties is a controversial issue. Operators in the North feel that the existing schemes are appropriate for northern conditions. Others, not involved in the North, object to the current royalties, which are the lowest in Canada. An appropriate mix of taxation that provides a fair return to government and at the same time maintains a favourable climate for investment is a major policy consideration.

Land Management and Environmental Protection

Although there is a need to encourage the mineral industry in order to sustain economic development in the North, it must be acknowledged that the industry must live and operate in harmony with others in the North. Thus, on the one hand, full consideration must be given to environmental and social concerns arising from new and existing mineral industry operations. On the other hand, the mineral industry has expressed concern about the scale of potential land withdrawals for parks, International Biological Programme (IBP) sites, game preserves, etc. Some reconciliation of those interests is required. A major element in improving resource management and planning will be the land-use planning process, which will help to resolve environmental and social concerns in advance of development, thereby reducing uncertainties for all involved. Progress has been made in the development of the land-use planning process in the period during which work on mineral policy was suspended. As a result, the implications of land-use planning for northern mineral policy, and the manner in which these policies will be integrated,have yet to be worked out in detail.

Policy and Regulatory Responsibilities

Although DIAND has the mandate for the control, management, and administration of virtually all Canada lands in the North, there are some areas of conflict and uncertainty between the federal and territorial governments. Mineral policy should establish clearly responsibilities for non-renewable resource management in the North. We think that the federal government's legislative authority will be recognized clearly.

Native Claims

The issue of native claims is very important and relevant to the northern mineral industry. The extent to and manner in which it will be incorporated into mineral policy remain to be developed, however, and undoubtedly will reflect the status of claims negotiations at the time at which the policy is released. Other related issues of concern to native peoples, such as investment opportunities, joint ventures, training, and employment, also must be addressed.

Labour–Management Relations

To remain competitive, northern operators must strive continually to reduce operating costs. The recent experience at Cyprus Anvil has shown how labour–management co-operation can help to lower operating costs and to improve the long-term viability of a mine. Because Canadian labour–management relations have a negative image in some foreign markets, visibly improved relationships may be essential in developing and maintaining markets for Canadian producers. Whether there is a role for government in this area is an issue to be addressed in a northern mineral policy.

Summary

The development of a northern mineral policy is a complex undertaking involving consideration of objectives, scope, and specific issues. The process is underway at DIAND, but much work remains to be done. The department looks forward to the results of the discussion at this workshop, which, we hope, will be helpful in the ongoing development of a northern mineral policy.

Opinion Paper

Northern Mineral Development

Robert W. Spence
Executive Secretary to the
Northern Mineral Advisory Committee

The New Year's Day edition of the *Dawson Daily News*, January 1901, had an interview with Dr Joseph B. Tyrrell, then Yukon resident geologist for the Geological Survey of Canada. He said, "As yet there are between one and three million square miles of country in Canada practically unprospected and the mineral wealth that lies hidden in this vast area will be an important factor in the progress of this northern continent." He even went so far as to predict that Canada's mineral wealth would equal, or even exceed, that of the U.S.A. Whether by the end of the century these predictions will have come true remains to be seen. The mining industry in the North faces many handicaps that, if left unchecked, could prevent it.

Among the many problems facing developers in the North has been the intercession of non-government organizations such as the Canadian Arctic Resources Committee (CARC). CARC's emotional campaign against Gulf Canada Resources' application for a marine support base at Stokes Point, Yukon, is a recent example. It is hardly surprising that developers resent this kind of "motherhood" approach to issues.

Whatever the justification for this interference, it not only makes it harder for developers but also could prevent the development of some mineral prospects. Besides CARC, industry locks horns with many other organizations including Project North, Canadian Coalition for Nuclear Responsibility, Greenpeace, World Wildlife Fund, and the Canadian Environmental Advisory Council, to name a few.

The Northern Mineral Advisory Committee (NMAC) was formed in October 1978 by the Honourable J. Hugh Faulkner, then minister of Indian Affairs and Northern Development, in response to the concerns expressed by the mineral industry about the lack of a meaningful consultative process between it and the federal government on mining in the North.

NMAC's first report, submitted on 15 August 1979 to the Honourable Jake Epp, then minister of Indian Affairs and Northern Development, by its chairman, John Bruk, then president of Cyprus Anvil Mining Corporation, recommended eight principles of policy to be adopted by the government:

1. It should foster, promote, and encourage prospecting, exploration, and mining in the two territories.
2. It should undertake to establish means for continued consultation with the mineral industry.
3. All mineral rights should remain vested in the Crown.
4. Access to mineral rights should be maintained.
5. Land-use policy should achieve and maintain a balance between economic development and environmental protection.
6. Incentives should be commensurate with the difficulties of finding, exploring, developing, and operating mines in Canada's North.
7. Northern residents should be encouraged, by both government and industry, to participate in northern Canada's mining industry.
8. The Government of Canada should assist in the development of efficient and economical modes of transport and other forms of infrastructure in the North.[1]

In response to the report, as well as to other stimulations, the Department of Indian Affairs and Northern Development (DIAND) has been preparing a northern mineral policy, a draft of which is expected to be ready this year. Naturally, the mineral industry expects the policy to address the eight principles recommended in the NMAC report. Considering the extent of the review outline for the northern mineral policy and the amount of consultation and input by industry, the policy statement should touch on all of the concerns and aspirations that have arisen. The mining industry's need to know the "rules of the game" should be fulfilled.

Another problem that has frustrated industry in the past has been that of how to satisfy regional interests. When a new development takes place in a remote and sparsely populated area, the problem appears not to be too serious. Even on the remote Little Cornwallis Island, however, Cominco had to inform, and consult with, all the arctic coastal communities about the Polaris Mine Project. The contest of competing authorities has exacerbated the problem. Industry always has known the value of the goodwill and participation of local residents, which is reflected in NMAC's seventh policy recommendation: "Northern residents should be encouraged, by both government and industry, to participate in northern Canada's mining industry." Native groups themselves are providing a unique solution to this issue, however, through the formation of native development corporations. The participation of Inuit in Cullaton Lake Gold Mines and Polaris, of the Dene and Métis at Norman Wells, of Inuvialuit in the Beaufort region, and the activities of the Yukon Indian Development Corporation are all examples.

As we approach the year 2000 and reflect on what Dr Tyrrell predicted nearly 100 years ago, we must recognize that the North may not be able to measure up to his expectations. The severe handicaps imposed by nature, coupled with those imposed by society, make it difficult to transform the North's resources into the nation's wealth.

Because mineral markets are international, it would be hard to smooth out the industry's badly cyclical nature. It might be possible, however, to provide industry with the means to cope. Although taxes clearly are necessary, those that are more of an impediment to national goals than a source of revenue should be changed. The cruelty of the northern climate will be lessened as our technical ability to cope improves. The jealousy of successful entrepreneurs always will be with us. Regulations that are unnecessary and punitive will be corrected by ongoing consultation between the regulators and the regulated. The aspirations of native groups are being realized and become less of an impediment to development. Public ignorance of the hazards of mining, and of certain minerals like uranium and arsenic, will have to be changed. The cost and frustration of the long delay between mineral discovery and production may be corrected by better technology and infrastructure. The quantity and quality of infrastructure in the North will depend upon the nation's will to provide it. The special problems of remote single-industry communities are being studied. Interference by outside organizations will continue. The lack of government policy is being corrected. Regional interests are being considered and served better than ever before.

The mineral industry of the two northern territories has expanded and prospered in the first eight decades of this century. During 1980 alone it added more than $750 million to the Canadian economy. Whether the industry will measure up to Dr Tyrrell's expectation by the end of the century will depend upon many things—not the least of which will be the will of the nation, the international economy, and good fortune.

Endnote

1. ["Report of the Northern Mineral Advisory Committee," Ottawa, 15 August 1979, see pp. 3-4 — eds]

[*The author's review of mining history in the Yukon and Northwest Territories has been omitted because of space limitations in these workshop proceedings—eds*]

Report of the Northern Mineral Advisory Committee: Summary

Submitted by
Mr John Bruk, Chairman
to
The Honourable Jake Epp
Minister of Indian Affairs and Northern Development
Government of Canada
Ottawa, Canada
15 August 1979

Policy

The Committee has formulated and presented to the Minister the following eight principles of policy:

1. Role of the Non-Renewable Resources

The Government of Canada will foster, promote and encourage prospecting, exploration and mining in the Yukon and Northwest Territories in recognition of the fundamental and major role of non-renewable resources in the economic and social development of the North. The Committee supports the principle that economic development of the North must proceed with full recognition of the legitimate interests of Northern people and the protection of the environment.

2. Consultation

In support of the above declaration, the Government of Canada undertakes to establish means for continued consultation with the mineral industry preceding and during the development of legislation and regulations related to Northern mineral development.

3. Mineral Tenure

A preferred option with respect to the reservation of surface lands for any parties is that all mineral rights remain vested in the Crown. Although some mineral alienation may occur in the Committee for Original Peoples' Entitlement (COPE) settlement, the Committee does not regard this part of the agreement as an essential element in land settlements. This is not inconsistent with achieving a broad equity between settlements, but such equity does not mean that any one settlement should be considered a precedent because of the wide variability of conditions throughout the North. The Committee recognizes that there will be areas where economic development is prohibited or restricted. These lands should consist of only the minimum area required to achieve the objective, and their selection should take into account their potential mineral value.

4. Access

Access to mineral rights and to non-alienated areas should be maintained, notwithstanding any subsequent alienation of the surface rights. On all lands where development is not prohibited, access should be assured for prospecting, staking, exploring and developing mineral resources.

5. Land Use

Land use policy should endeavour to achieve and maintain a balance between economic development and environmental protection. The Committee recognizes that reasonable and positive efforts must be made by all parties to minimize disturbance of the natural environment.

6. Incentives for Northern Mining

Administrative and fiscal terms and conditions established by the Crown with respect to the disposition and use of the mineral rights should provide to individuals and corporations incentives which are commensurate with the difficulties and risks of finding, exploring, developing and operating mines in Canada's North.

7. Participation by Northern Residents

Northern people will be encouraged by both government and industry to participate in Northern Canada's mining industry.

8. Infrastructure

The Government of Canada will assist in the development of efficient and economical modes of transport and other forms of infrastructure in the North.

The Minister's response to the eight policy elements appears in his letter of April 18, 1979.

Strategies

The following elements of strategy are recommended by the Committee:

1. Reorganization of the Department of Indian Affairs and Northern Development (DIAND)

The Committee recommends that:

(i) The Department be reorganized to give prominence to the Northern Development section by the appointment of an Assistant Deputy Minister of Northern Development, responsible for non-renewable resources, Northern pipelines, Northern water management, Northern lands management, Northern forests, regional directors and all subsidiary functions.

(ii) The position of Special Advisor, Mining, to the Minister be made a permanent one.

(iii) A three phase program be implemented for the evolving transfer of natural resources to the Territorial governments. After mechanisms for effecting such a transfer have been examined in the first phase, the second phase would see the actual transfer of administrative and management functions, followed finally by the transfer of ownership of resources when full responsible government has been attained.

2. Consultation

The Committee recommends that another consultative committee, similar in format to the Northern Mineral Advisory Committee, be formed to assist the Minister in making his decisions on mineral development and policy formulation in Canada's North.

3. Land Use

With respect to land use, the Committee makes the following recommendations:

(i) Report, Centre for Resource Studies

The principal findings of the report, *The Administration of Mineral Exploration in the Yukon and Northwest Territories*, prepared by the Centre for Resource Studies, Queen's University, Kingston, October, 1978 should be accepted and implemented.

(ii) Land Use Planning

Two independent advisory bodies should be created which, through public participation, would review and examine government proposals for constraints and withdrawals of land for single or limited-use purposes such as parks, sanctuaries and international biological project (IBP) sites. One of these bodies would be in place in the Yukon, and one in the Northwest Territories. This would follow the practice established in several provinces.

(iii) Land Use Regulations

(a) The ecological zoning of Northern lands should be examined and detailed in order that the terms and conditions of land use regulations can be properly tailored to meet the requirements for ecological protection in any given area. Zones might be established where no land use permits are required.

(b) The requirements for Class B land use operations should be redrawn so that users can proceed by simple prior notification to the proper authorities.

(c) Sections 8 and 9 of the Territorial Land Use regulations should be changed so that those undertakings that define Class B land use operations will be substantially increased.

(d) Section 28 of the Territorial Land Use regulations should be repealed so that administrating officials cannot arbitrarily raise Class B Land Use operations to Class A operations.

(e) The requirements for Class A land use operations should be changed so that permits can be issued within 10 days of application in those instances where the livelihood of nearby communities is not threatened. When the engineer decides that community livelihood is threatened and that consultation is desirable, permits should be issued within 42 days of application.

(f) Land Use Inspectors are to be trained in the objectives and methods employed in land use operations so that the land use policies will be implemented in a rational and efficient manner.

(iv) Thelon Game Sanctuary

(a) The status of muskox and other wildlife in the Thelon Game Sanctuary should be updated so that an intelligent decision can be made as to whether parts, or all, of the sanctuary can be considered for mineral exploration and development.

4. Participation by Northern Residents

The Committee recommends that the Mineral Industry continue its commitment to work toward the involvement of Northern residents in its activities.

5. Infrastructure

The Committee recommends that the Minister should encourage the development of new mines by directing that appropriate priorities and funds be applied to infrastructure support for resource development.

6. Mineral Legislative Amendments

The Committee recommends that immediate amendments be made in the Yukon Quartz Mining Act to improve its provisions respecting title, and that comprehensive amendments be made to the Territorial Coal Regulations as soon as possible to facilitate development of Territorial coal deposits.

7. Financial Incentives

(i) Mining Corporation Income Tax

The Committee recommends:

(a) Increasing the investment tax credit in the Yukon and Northwest Territories from the proposed level of 10% to a new level of 20% for the first $250 million of investment on a specific project.

(b) Elimination of the present provision of a five-year limitation on the carry-forward of investment tax credits earned on qualifying expenditures in the Yukon and Northwest Territories.

(c) Increasing the earned depletion rate to $1 for every $2 spent on all qualifying expenditures related to mining, including exploration and social assets, made in the Yukon and Northwest Territories.

(d) Increasing the 25% annual claiming rate for earned depletion to 50% on Class 28 assets in the Yukon and Northwest Territories, against resource income earned anywhere in Canada.

(ii) The Royalty Regime

The Committee recommends that a joint Federal Government/Industry Committee be established, which should, in consultation with the territorial governments, review the 1976 proposed revisions to the royalty regime (made by a federal interdepartmental committee) and make recommendations to the Minister.

The review of the Committee should take into account the high costs of operating in the North, and should be based on a careful consideration of the following:

(a) **Consistency with National Resource Taxation Objectives**

Royalty regimes for the Yukon and Northwest Territories should be consistent with the "Recommendations for Government Action to Work Towards Achieving Desirable Resource Taxation Objectives", contained in the report, *Federal–Provincial Resource Taxation Review, 1978.*

(b) **Legislation by the Parliament of Canada**

The royalty regime for those federal lands under the jurisdiction of the *Territorial Lands Act* should be legislated by the Parliament of Canada.

(c) **"Pits-Mouth" Tax Base**

The basis for calculating the royalty should be the "pits-mouth" concept. Processing allowances should remove entirely from royalty tax liability profits earned from processing assets.

(d) **Recognition of the Cyclical Nature of the Mining Industry**

The royalty regime should contain appropriate provisions to avoid taxation of cyclical-type profits by one or a combination of the following:

–averaging the value subject to royalty over a four-year period;

–loss carry-forward and carry-back;

–carry-forward of unused processing allowances.

(e) **Recovery of Capital**

Royalties should be kept to a minimum until the original invested capital is recovered, by:

–allowing the full write-off of all exploration, preproduction and development expenses at a rate of 100%; and

–allowing the depreciation of all new mine assets or major expansions at a rate of 100%; and

–allowing the depreciation of replacement assets at a rate of no less than 30%.

(f) **Interest Costs**

The deduction of interest costs related to mine development should be considered in royalty provisions.

(g) **Combined Marginal Tax Rate**

The combined marginal tax rate (income tax and royalties) should be competitive with provincial jurisdictions and respond to the concerns of the mining industry.

(h) **Discretionary Powers**

Discretionary powers of the Minister in administrating the royalties should be kept to a minimum.

(i) **Further Processing**

Further processing should be encouraged where economically feasible and of net benefit.

(j) **Royalty Rate Structure**

The relative merits of the following rate structures should be examined in detail:
–a flat rate royalty structure similar to that in some provinces;
–a graduated rate royalty structure similar to that in some provinces;
–a two-tier royalty rate structure similar to that in the proposed Canada Oil and Gas Act.

(k) **Royalty System Based on Modified Federal Income Tax Base**

The adoption of a modified federal income tax base as a starting point for determining mining income subject to royalty should be examined.

(l) **Existing Producers**

If a new or substantially modified royalty regime would result in an increase in the royalty payable by the established producers in the Yukon and Northwest Territories, then a transition period of about five years should be considered in order to permit a gradual adjustment.

(iii) The Prospector and Related Individuals

The Committee recommends that:

(a) The current interpretations applying to a prospector, as defined under the Income Tax Act, should be reviewed.

(b) The prospecting community and the mining industry should jointly develop an easy-to-understand guide to the financial options open to a prospector.

(c) A "Prospector Resource Sale Exemption" of $100,000 should be introduced for non-incorporated prospectors to be applied against the cumulative cash proceeds received from the sale of resource properties.

(d) The provision that all taxpayers be allowed to write-off immediately 100% of their exploration costs should be extended for a period of at least five years beyond the present expiry date of December 31, 1979.

(e) The deduction of earned depletion on exploration expenditures incurred in the Yukon and Northwest Territories should be allowed against any Canadian income.

(iv) Provisions for Northern Residents

The Committee recommends that:

(a) The Department of National Revenue should be requested to refrain from taxing any of the currently existing common and essential benefits and subsidies conferred upon both employees and their families living in the Yukon and Northwest Territories.

(b) The Federal and Territorial governments should undertake in consultation with northern employees, a review of the taxation of northern residents with a view towards replacing or substantially modifying present policies and practices.

Steps to a Northern Mineral Policy

Draft Presented to Minister, DIAND, 13 October 1978
in Yellowknife, N.W.T.

Step 1—Policy Statement

The Government of Canada recognizes that mining is important to Northern Canada, being the most significant industry, the largest employer, and a major contributor to settlement and transportation, and that mining can be expected to provide future economic growth and stability to the benefit of all Canadians.

Therefore, the Government of Canada is committed to foster, promote and encourage prospecting, exploration and mining in the Yukon Territory and Northwest Territories.

To effect this purpose:

1. The ownership of mineral rights in the Territories will remain vested in the Crown.
2. Access to minerals for the purpose of acquiring title, prospecting and mining will be assured.
3. Land use policies will not be formulated without considering their impact on mining.
4. Fiscal policies will stimulate northern mining.
5. Employment of northern peoples in mining will be encouraged.
6. Transportation, energy and other infrastructure will be sponsored to meet mining development.
7. The Department of Indian Affairs and Northern Development will be re-structured and will employ administrative regulations and practices to achieve this policy.

During the formulation and implementation of this policy, the Government of Canada will not make any land withdrawals for any purpose, and will not impede the normal business of prospecting and mining through the introduction and/or amendment of regulations and administrative practices.

Step 2—Reorganization of DIAND

Inasmuch as it is the objective of the Government of Canada to restore confidence and to promote a healthy mining industry in Canada's north which can benefit many Canadians both socially, and economically; and inasmuch as the resource sector is the largest industrial employer, the greatest source of new wealth, and the greatest potential source of new wealth, it is desirable that the department re-organize in such a manner as to exemplify the prominence of the Northern Development section of Indian Affairs and Northern Development. To this end, an Assistant Deputy Minister of Northern Development will be appointed who will be responsible for Resources and Economic Planning, Northern Pipelines, Northern Water Management, Northern Lands Management, Northern Forests, Regional Directors and all subsidiary functions.

Step 3—Consultation

The development of an effective Northern Mineral Strategy will require meaningful consultation and dialogue between Indian Affairs and Northern Development and the mining industry so as to foster an air of credibility and mutual trust.

This dialogue will take the form of ongoing consultation through the Chambers of Mines and the formation of a Northern Mineral Advisory Committee similar to that in effect at the annual joint chambers meeting. This advisory committee will meet on a regular basis with the Assistant Deputy Minister of Northern Development.

In addition to ongoing consultation, it will be necessary to establish a committee specifically for the purpose of developing the Northern Mineral Strategy. The committee will report its findings to the Minister for action, and will be comprised of appointees of the chambers, two from the N.W.T., two from the Yukon, one each from British Columbia and Alberta; one appointee by the Mining Association of Canada, and two or three appointees from the newly established Northern Development Division.

Northern Mineral Advisory Committee

Executive

Chairman	Mr John Bruk
Alternate Chairman	Mr R.J. Cathro
Executive Secretary	Mr W.T. Irvine
Recording Secretary	Mr R.A. Eastman

Committee Members

Mr Doug Bell
Deputy Commissioner
Government of the Yukon Territory
Whitehorse, Yukon

Mr John Bruk
President
Cyprus Anvil Mining Corporation
Vancouver, B.C.
Director
Mining Association of Canada

Alternate for Mr Bruk:
Mr John L. Bonus
Managing Director
Mining Association of Canada
Ottawa, Ontario

Mr R.J. Cathro
Archer, Cathro and Associates
Vice President
B.C. and Yukon Chamber of Mines
Vancouver, B.C.

Mr Ewan Cotterill
Assistant Deputy Minister
Northern Affairs Program
Department of Indian Affairs and
Northern Development
Ottawa, Ontario

Alternate for Mr Cotterill:
Mr D.G. MacKinnon
Acting Director-General
Resources and Economic Planning
Northern Affairs Program
Department of Indian Affairs and
Northern Development
Ottawa, Ontario

Alternate for Mr Cotterill:
Mr J.G. McGilp
Director-General
Northern Policy and Programming
Northern Affairs Program
Department of Indian Affairs and
Northern Development
Ottawa, Ontario

Mr R.P. Douglas
Group Vice President
Cominco Limited
Yellowknife, N.W.T.

Alternate for Mr Douglas:
Mr D.J. Emery
President
Giant Yellowknife Mines Ltd.
Yellowknife, N.W.T.

Mr Robert A. Eastman
ACND Secretariat
Department of Indian Affairs and
Northern Development
Ottawa, Ontario

Mr Ronald A. Granger
President
Yukon Chamber of Mines
Whitehorse, Yukon

Alternate for Mr Granger:
Mr Dick Joy
Yukon Chamber of Mines
Whitehorse, Yukon

Mr Ronald J. Hawkes
President
Northwest Territories
Chamber of Mines
Yellowknife, N.W.T.

Alternate for Mr Hawkes:
Mr Tony Shearcroft
Northwest Territories
Chamber of Mines
Yellowknife, N.W.T.

Mr Robert Hornal
Director, Northwest Territories
Region
Northern Affairs Program
Department of Indian Affairs and
Northern Development
Yellowknife, N.W.T.

Alternate for Mr Hornal:
Mr Murray Morison
Assistant Director
Non-renewable Resources
Northwest Territories Region
Northern Affairs Program
Department of Indian Affairs
and Northern Development
Yellowknife, N.W.T.

Mr W.T. Irvine
Special Advisor on Mining to the
Minister
Department of Indian Affairs and
Northern Development
Ottawa, Ontario

Dr W.G. Jeffery
Acting Assistant Deputy Minister
Mineral Policy Sector
Department of Energy, Mines &
Resources
Ottawa, Ontario

Alternate for Dr Jeffery:
Mr R.J. Shank
Director
Resources and Development
Department of Energy, Mines &
Resources
Ottawa, Ontario

Mr A.C. Ogilvie
Manager
Yukon Chamber of Mines
Whitehorse, Yukon

Mr John H. Parker
Commissioner
Government of the Northwest
Territories
Yellowknife, N.W.T.

Alternate for Mr Parker:
Mr Douglas Patriquin
Assistant Director
Economic Development
Office of the Commissioner
Yellowknife, N.W.T.

Mr J.M. Patterson
Chief
Mining Division
Northern Affairs Program
Department of Indian Affairs and
Northern Development
Ottawa, Ontario

Dr C.M. Trigg
Trigg, Woollett and Associates
Past President
Alberta Chamber of Resources
Edmonton, Alberta

Alternate for Dr Trigg:
Dr Ben Baldwin
Shell Canada Resources Ltd.
Calgary, Alberta

Mr Denis M. Watson
Director
Yukon Region
Northern Affairs Program
Department of Indian Affairs and
Northern Development
Whitehorse, Yukon

Dr H.W. Woodward
Director
Northern Non-renewable Resources
Branch
Northern Affairs Program
Department of Indian Affairs and
Northern Development
Ottawa, Ontario

Maximization of Benefits Accruing to Northern Natives from the Mining Industry North of the 60th Parallel: Conclusions

A Study Done for the Department of
Indian Affairs and Northern Development
K. Harper

In recent years, native peoples in the North have become increasingly aware of the effects of non-renewable resource development on their lives and cultures, and of the potential benefits that such development, including mining, can offer them. This new awareness has been created and spurred on by the attainment among young natives of higher educational levels, a generally higher level of political awareness, and the anticipation of land-claims settlements, which are expected to include financial compensation. Northern native peoples perceive widely that they have not received major benefits through employment in the mining industry, a view that is shared by government and is admitted generally by the industry. Native peoples continue to demand that industrial activities in their lands be structured and be conducted in such a manner that they will derive maximum benefit from the development. With their increased political and economic awareness, native peoples have now moved beyond an interest only in jobs and are now demanding other "pieces of the action" through participation in industry in ways other than as employees.

This desire for more participation in industry has resulted in the approaches being taken or being considered involving equity participation by native peoples in mining ventures.

The Council for Yukon Indians (CYI) has proposed a Yukon Resources Corporation, a tripartite corporation to be composed of Yukon Indians and the federal and territorial governments, created for the purpose of investment with industry in the development of the Yukon's resources [see this volume, pp. 427–433]. The Inuit Development Corporation (IDC) has entered into a financing agreement with Cullaton Lake

Gold Mines in which it will earn equity through the receipt of bonus shares and through the exercise of purchase options on other shares. The Dene Nation and the Métis Association of the Northwest Territories have considered equity participation in aspects of the Norman Wells project. Clearly, there is interest by native peoples in participating as partners in the development of non-renewable resources in the North. Spokesmen for the mining industry have indicated their support for participation by native corporations in mineral development, subject to certain conditions. The mining industry does not support the so-called carried-interest approach, or any legislated equity for native corporations. It believes that native peoples should be encouraged to invest as would other investors, and that profits made by participants should be commensurate with the degree of risk involved. The federal government, for its part, has given some consideration to analysing whether equity participation is in the best interests of native corporations.

Undoubtedly, mining companies feel that the federal government and its regulatory agencies might be more receptive to their proposals for development if they have significant participation by northern natives. Thus, they may assume that, although economic conditions for the industry generally are less attractive than they previously were, native involvement may lead to concessions being granted that will make projects more viable. It behooves companies, therefore, to enter into agreements and economic ventures with, and to the benefit of, native partners.

One gets the impression that most native suggestions concerning equity involvement have stressed the philosophy, rather than the economics, of involvement, and that the possibility exists that native peoples, in their desire for involvement, may enter into unprofitable ventures or become involved with unscrupulous operators. Although not all discussions mention compensation to be provided under a land-claims settlement as their source of funding for involvement in industrial ventures, it is assumed that some land-claims compensation money undoubtedly will be used for this purpose. The question arises then: Should land-claims compensation be invested in high-risk ventures?

IDC's equity in the Cullaton Lake mine has been achieved without using advances against land-claims compensation, but rather through an innovative financial arrangement with the company (Cullaton Lake Gold Mines). The nature of IDC's involvement with Cullaton Lake is known well throughout the North and there may therefore be pressure for it to serve, if not as a model, then at least as a type of precedent. Although other native corporations may not structure their involvement with industry exactly after the IDC–Cullaton Lake model, it can be expected that they will seek involvement that is equally innovative. There may be serious risks in using the IDC–Cullaton Lake relationship as a model or precedent. For one thing, hard facts on the details of the financial guarantees IDC gave to the lending bank are not known outside the corporation, and therefore it cannot be assumed that IDC's venture is without substantial risk. Were a serious loss to occur to the corporation or to other corporations entering into similar financial arrangements, it may have to be covered by payments from, or advances against, land-claims settlements, especially if letters of comfort have been given to lending institutions by native organizations attesting to the intent that the native development corporation will be the major beneficiary of a land-claims settlement. Ultimately, recourse may have to be made to government for payments to cover any such losses incurred.

Government is concerned lest native peoples enter into equity-participation agreements with the mining industry that turn out to be poor investments. However, government analyses have tended to look at standard equity-purchase arrangements rather than at the type of creative structuring worked out between IDC and Cullaton Lake Gold Mines. Mining companies, although insisting that native investors be given no preferential treatment, often have their own risk spread over a number of projects. Native corporations have few financial resources and any major investment may therefore represent a maximum risk.

The federal government should not feel compelled to restrict the uses to which land-claims compensation or other funds to which native peoples have access can be applied. Government should establish a structure within which native-controlled corporations can seek advice in the initial stages of their involvement with the mining industry, and assistance in determining the feasibility of certain financial ventures. Not all native corporations would avail themselves of assistance offered in this way, as some have their own financial advisers, but government assistance should be available to those who seek it. Any government structure established for this purpose, then, should include one contact at the federal level, whose role would be to put native organizations in touch with agencies or consultants who could perform the required feasibility studies. Funds should be made available to those native corporations requiring financial assistance to have these studies conducted. Sources of funding may be programmes such as DREE's (Department of Regional Economic Expansion) Special ARDA (Agricultural and Rural Development Act), if it is continued, or the Indian and Inuit Affairs Program's (Department of Indian Affairs and Northern Development) Native Economic Development Fund. As some native corporations may prefer to deal with the economic development departments of their territorial government in this regard, a territorial point of contact should be designated in each territory to receive these requests and to administer them, and that contact should liaise with the responsible federal contact. Native corporations should be encouraged to direct their requests for assistance of this nature to the appropriate territorial government. Until such time as significant revenue from resource development is turned over to the territorial governments, federal funds should support the necessary studies.

CYI, IDC, and the Dene Nation have suggested that native corporations should have the right to participate in mining and other industrial ventures in the North. None has suggested that it should have a carried interest or the right to "back in" to a project after the start-up costs have been covered by project initiators, but all seem to support the legislation of a preferential right for native corporations to participate in projects of their choosing. CYI proposes that legislation should permit the proposed Yukon Resources Corporation a preferential right to purchase equity in mining ventures, and that such legislation should be modelled after the Province of Saskatchewan's Mineral Disposition Regulations, 1981. Using this as a model, when an individual or corporation expects to spend more than a certain amount per year on mineral exploration or development, the appropriate native corporation would be offered the opportunity to purchase equity, to a certain level, in the project. Should the native corporation decide not to purchase equity in the project, it would have no further rights to purchase equity at a later date. The mining industry has stressed that no carried interest should be allowed, but has not addressed the subject of preferential rights for participation by native organizations during a project's early stages. The Government of the Northwest Territories (GNWT) also has indicated its interest in forming a development corporation to enter into joint ventures with industry; this would be a Crown corporation, perhaps with the involvement of the Dene or Métis organization, or both. The Yukon Territorial Government (YTG) is considering CYI's suggestion for a Yukon Resources Corporation but, as a conservative government, it may be expected to reject the suggestion of government investment in mining ventures.

Serious study will have to be given to whether native corporations should, or can, be given preferential rights to participate as investors in mining projects. Whereas the Saskatchewan model may be appropriate for the involvement of a government or a Crown corporation in industry, it is unclear whether in fact it would be legal for such a right to be extended to a native organization. Alternatively, some thought has been given in the context of land-claims discussions to whether native organizations and corporations should be given preferential rights to assume mineral leases in certain designated areas and within specified time limits. Much more consideration will have to be devoted to this subject of preferential rights for native investment, and the legal and economic ramifications of it will have to be investigated thoroughly.

Were legislation to be developed giving a preferential right to participate in ownership to a native corporation, a northern government, or Crown corporation, because of the high costs of exploration and development in the North, the level of annual expenditure that would trigger the right to purchase should be substantially higher than the Saskatchewan level of $10 000. Consideration will have to be given to the maximum extent of equity a company would be required to offer to a native corporation, northern government, or Crown corporation, to determine whether the Saskatchewan level of 50 per cent is appropriate under conditions in the N.W.T. and the Yukon. The mining industry probably will oppose such a regime if mining companies themselves are not allowed to retain majority interest in individual projects. On the other hand, it may not be in the interests of a native or Crown corporation to participate as anything less than an equal partner.

Concern has been expressed by native organizations that the economic and social benefits accruing from the development of non-renewable resources be shared equitably among the native peoples. Government shares this concern. There is a fear that investment by solely community-based corporations may lead to a division of the North into rich and poor communities. Nevertheless, those communities most directly affected by a development probably will be those in closest geographical proximity to it. Although they should not be the sole benefactors of a project, they should have a greater share in the benefits than will communities farther removed and therefore less affected by the project. How the economic benefits of such projects can be shared most equitably can be worked out best by the umbrella or parent native organizations and individual communities.

Government and other observers question also whether there is good accountability from the native development corporation to the individuals at the community level who are purported to be the ultimate benefactors of the development corporation's involvement with industry. IDC is not accountable to the political organization, Inuit Tapirisat of Canada (ITC), and the suggestion is made often that neither is it accountable to Inuit in the communities. The use of a native development corporation as the vehicle to ensure native involvement with, and benefit from, industry is justified only to the extent that linkages from that organization to the community level are in place.

Native corporations approach the achievement of equity participation out of a desire to be involved in development and in decision making on development, and to share in the benefits deriving from it. Yet, on the political level, native leaders begin with the premise that they own the land and its resources and should therefore control the nature and pace of development. A native corporation that has invested in certain ventures will not want to slow the pace of developments in which it has invested, and problems therefore can arise between the native political leaders and the native-owned corporation. This has been the case with ITC and IDC; although it is assumed that IDC will be the major financial beneficiary of the land-claims settlement that ITC is negotiating, IDC is not accountable to ITC and has taken an approach to investment in non-renewable resource development projects contradictory to ITC's basic tenet that no new development should precede the settlement of land claims. Other native organizations are aware of this situation, which they consider undesirable, and are studying the advisability of structuring their economic development corporations so that they will be accountable to the parent association. Success in this will avoid debate of the type that has occurred between ITC and IDC.

Native political leaders, in expressing their desire to control the pace and nature of development, anticipate that they will achieve this control with a successful conclusion to land-claims negotiations. One cannot predict at this time, however, whether this will be the case. Regardless of the nature of land-claims settlements, and in advance of their settlement, native peoples should be encouraged to exercise some control over development, including mineral development, through participation on regulatory boards and agencies. Natives must be appointed to full membership in such structures as water boards, environmental assessment review panels, land-use planning commissions, etc. They should be appointed to boards that have regulatory powers, and their appointments should be based on their ability to deal adequately and responsibly with subjects under the purview of such boards. This is not meant to imply that native persons should dominate or control these boards or agencies. There will remain, of course, a place for native persons to participate on the advisory boards that will continue to function in, and concerning, the North.

The GNWT has entered into socio-economic agreements with some mining companies in which goals are set out for the companies to strive to achieve in their relationships with communities and northern employees. Other agreements are being negotiated. Similar agreements will be negotiated in the Yukon Territory when new projects go ahead there. In the Northwest Territories, the cumulative learning from each successive negotiation contributes to making each new agreement more comprehensive.

Nevertheless, they are gentlemen's agreements and are, therefore, not really enforceable. Each territory should develop legislation under which the terms of its socio-economic agreements would be enforceable.

The GNWT is developing a socio-economic impact zones policy under which communities identified as having the potential to be affected by development will be allowed to participate in planning for that development. The type of planning that may ensue will be, in fact, sub-regional planning. The YTG has also been involved in the preliminary stages of such planning in one geographic area through its Macmillan Pass Task Force.

This type of participation by communities in planning for industrial development should be encouraged. Perhaps, through participation, communities can grapple with the problem already identified of promising students dropping out of the education system to take high-paying, short-term jobs during the construction phase of a project and then being unemployable as skilled workers in the longer term production phase. Another consideration is the problem of the detrimental effect on community leadership of the loss of community leaders who become workers on industrial sites.

Socio-economic agreements will require mining companies to consult with communities peripheral to proposed developments. Although a meaningful and comprehensive approach to community consultation is required, government must recognize, nevertheless, that junior mining companies do not have the financial resources or the federal financial incentives that oil and gas companies have, and may not be able to mount such impressive consultation schemes as do the oil and gas companies.

As a result of the controversy at Baker Lake over the effect of mineral exploration on caribou, the Department of Indian Affairs and Northern Development (DIAND) funded a film project, which facilitated dialogue between biologists and Inuit, and which resulted in a meaningful dialogue between the protagonists in the dispute. The department should take similar approaches to facilitating consultation and the resolution of conflict over the development of non-renewable resources in the future.

The territorial governments should be encouraged to maintain their opposition to the establishment of single-resource communities, except in exceptional circumstances.

Territorial governments will continue to provide apprenticeship programmes for their residents. It is important that mining companies identify to government, as early as possible, their anticipated job requirements on specific projects so that government can assist with developing comprehensive manpower plans that will encourage the maximum participation of northerners by identifying potential employees and the training that they require.

Industry has suggested that a modular training programme, similar to that offered by Falconbridge Nickel at Sudbury, Ontario, is needed in the North.[1] The territorial governments should assist with developing modular training programmes and with accrediting them. The GNWT and YTG should work jointly in this so that credentials will be recognized across the North.

A study should be conducted of individuals who have left employment at a specific mine site in the North, to determine to what extent those individuals have learned skills on the job that are transferable to other work situations, and to what extent those skills have been applied in other situations.

The mining industry opposes the imposition of quotas for native employment. As yet, no project on which a quota has been imposed has met that quota. With the failure of the Nanisivik mine at Strathcona Sound to meet its unrealistically high goal of 60 per cent native employment, the government has moved away from the imposition of quotas on more recent projects. Companies are expected to hire as many northerners as possible, and in certain geographic areas it is assumed that most of these northerners will be natives. The maximization of native employment can be handled through socio-economic agreements with the territorial governments, especially if these are supported by legislation giving them enforceability, and should not require the imposition of quotas that are demeaning and counter-productive. Quota systems for native employment should not be imposed.

Serious consideration should be given to alternative uses for mining towns and mine sites well in advance of the closure of a mine, to avoid serious disruption of the kind experienced by the native community with the closure of the nickel mine at Rankin Inlet in the 1960s. In particular, it is time now that planning begins for alternative uses of the townsite at Nanisivik when the ore body is exhausted in a few years.

Mining companies should be encouraged to hire native persons as native employment officers and counsellors. Cyprus Anvil Mining Corporation has experienced a marked increase in its number of permanent native employees since the hiring of its current native employment officer. Part of the success there is a result of having chosen the right person for the job, and care must be taken to hire an individual with the right attitudes and counselling skills. It also would benefit others if such individuals and their specific companies involved in such success stories would share their ideas and approaches at some time. Thus, consideration should be given by the territorial governments and the chambers of mines to sponsoring jointly a workshop of individuals employed by mining companies who are responsible for native employment and counselling so that they may benefit from one another's experience.

The taxation of northern benefits should be opposed strongly because of the adverse effect it will have on all northern workers, native and non-native, and the untenable position in which marginal northern businesses will be placed as a result of it.

No native organization has responded formally to the minister of Indian Affairs and Northern Development's request for input into the development of a northern mineral policy. For all native organizations, the negotiation of land-claims settlements is the first priority. Other priorities vary for different organizations, but in all native organizations, funding and, consequently, staff are limited. Governments at all levels must realize that the development of meaningful input into a policy as far-reaching and all-encompassing as a northern mineral policy will take both time and money. When government invites a native organization to participate in such an exercise, that invitation should be accompanied by an offer of funding to allow the native organization to marshall the human resources necessary to prepare a meaningful submission within a reasonable time frame.

Summary of Recommendations

1. Government should establish a structure within which native corporations can seek advice, assistance, and funding in determining the feasibility of specific opportunities for equity participation in mining ventures. Such a structure should consist of one point of contact at the federal level that will facilitate the native corporation's access to agencies or consultants able to conduct the required studies. The federal contact should liaise with officials of the economic development departments of the territorial governments in this regard. The federal government should encourage native corporations to direct their requests for assistance to the appropriate territorial government.

2. Further study should be devoted to the subject of preferential rights for involvement in the mining industry, to determine whether such rights should, or can, be extended to native corporations, or whether they should be extended to Crown corporations established by northern governments.

3. Native peoples should be appointed to full membership on the boards and agencies that regulate mineral development. This is not meant to imply that native peoples should dominate or control such boards and agencies.

4. Each territory should develop legislation under which the terms of its socio-economic agreements with mining companies would be enforceable.

5. Communities expected to be affected by the development of new mines should participate with the appropriate territorial government in planning for the development.

6. The territorial governments should continue to oppose the establishment of single-resource communities, except in exceptional circumstances.

7. Mining companies should identify to government as early as possible anticipated job requirements on specific projects so that government and industry can develop co-operatively comprehensive manpower plans that will maximize the participation of northerners.

8. Governments at all levels should use approaches similar to DIAND's initiative in using audio-visual techniques to facilitate consultation and resolution of conflict over the development of non-renewable resources.

9. The GNWT and the YTG should work jointly in assisting industry to develop modular training programmes and in accrediting such programmes.

10. A study should be conducted of individuals who have left employment at a specific mine site in the North, to determine to what extent those individuals have acquired skills on the job that are transferable to other work situations, and to what extent they have applied those skills in other situations.

11. Quota systems for native employment should not be imposed.

12. Mining companies should be encouraged to hire native persons as native employment officers and counsellors.

13. Consideration should be given to alternative uses for mining towns and mine sites well in advance of the closure of a mine. Planning should begin now for alternative uses for the Nanisivik townsite when the ore body is exhausted in a few years.

14. The territorial governments and the chambers of mines should sponsor jointly a workshop of individuals employed by mining companies as native employment officers or counsellors so that they may benefit from one another's experience.

15. The taxation of northern benefits should be opposed strongly.

16. When government invites a native organization to participate in an exercise such as the development of a northern mineral policy by providing input to be considered in the formulation of the policy, that invitation should be accompanied by an offer of funding to allow the native organization to marshall the human resources necessary to prepare a meaningful submission within a reasonable time frame.

Endnote

1. [A modular training programme trains miners in various skills (modules) such as drilling, blasting, mucking, etc. As the skills needed in mining change, a training module is added to the programme. The advantages of the programme are that it is flexible and portable—eds]

Reprinted with kind permission of the Department of Indian Affairs and Northern Development.

Renewable Resources Management

Chairmen: James Bourque
Milton Freeman

Introduction

Renewable resources remain a very important component of the northern economy, particularly in the small communities. Many native northerners maintain a close relationship to and an appreciation of the land. Wage employment, available through non-renewable resource development, is sought widely but hunting, fishing, and trapping continue to be important for nutritional, economic, social, and cultural reasons.

Greater attention to the renewable resources economy in the North has been urged upon government in recent years as a result of perceived conflicts between users of renewable resources and developers of non-renewable resources, fears of the over-harvesting of renewable resources, and new institutions for wildlife management proposed by native groups in land-claims negotiations. Managers of renewable resources face many technical problems yet must operate with incomplete wildlife inventories and inadequate knowledge of the biology and ecology of many harvested species. There is still too little information about the interaction between the use of renewable resources and the development of non-renewable resources. How species management can be part of land and water planning and management has been discussed only recently.

Land-claims negotiations have focused attention on the role of harvesters in managing resources. The Beverly and Kaminuriak Caribou Management Board is a recent attempt at more co-operative management between harvesters and government personnel, and it should be followed soon by a similar management structure for the Porcupine caribou herd. A central task for managers in the years ahead will be finding ways and means to manage renewable resources to ensure their continued availability to harvesters in the face of competing demands for land, water, and other resources.

The Working Groups

The working group included:

Chairmen: **James Bourque**
Department of Renewable Resources
Government of the Northwest Territories

Milton Freeman
Department of Anthropology
University of Alberta

Invited Participants:

George Barnaby
Fort Good Hope, N.W.T.

Steve Behnke
Division of Subsistence
Department of Fish and Game
Government of Alaska
Juneau, Alaska

Dave Brackett
Department of Renewable Resources
Government of the Northwest Territories
Yellowknife, N.W.T.

Linda Ellanna
Division of Subsistence
Department of Fish and Game
Government of Alaska
Juneau, Alaska

Harvey Feit
Department of Anthropology
McMaster University

Willie Joe
Council for Yukon Indians
Whitehorse, Yukon

Steve Kakfwi
Dene Nation
Yellowknife, N.W.T.

James Maxwell
Lands Directorate
Department of the Environment
Government of Canada
Ottawa, Ontario

Hugh Monaghan
Department of Renewable Resources
Government of the Northwest Territories
Yellowknife, N.W.T.

Jim Schaefer
Beverly and Kaminuriak Caribou Management Board
Fort Smith, N.W.T.

Charlie Snowshoe, Sr
Mackenzie Delta Dene Regional Council
Fort McPherson, N.W.T.

Doug Stewart
Department of Renewable Resources
Government of the Northwest Territories
Inuvik, N.W.T.

Peter Usher
P.J. Usher Consulting Services
Ottawa, Ontario

Background documents used in the working group, in addition to those published in these proceedings, included:

Berkes, Fikret. "The Role of Self-regulation in Living Resources Management in the North." *Proceedings: First International Symposium on Renewable Resources and the Economy of the North*, ed., M.M.R. Freeman, pp. 166–178. Association of Canadian Universities for Northern Studies; Canada Man and the Biosphere Program, 1981.

Theberge, John B. "Commentary: Conservation in the North—An Ecological Perspective." *Arctic* 34:4 (December 1981), pp. 281–285.

Working Group Report

Renewable Resources Management

Governments and all user groups in the North agree that the harvesting and management of renewable resources should be compatible with the conservation of these resources. Conservation is taken to mean the continued productivity of wildlife and fish populations and the protection of habitat necessary to ensure the integrity of ecological systems.

Users' access to renewable resources requires protection under the law. Existing "rights" and licensing systems do not provide the necessary protection. It is accepted generally that a more appropriate form of protection is to be achieved through the land-claims process; this process, therefore, is basic to the long-term resolution of northern land-use conflicts.

Effective management of renewable resources requires the greatest possible involvement of the users. History demonstrates clearly the high cost and ineffectiveness of management systems that do not involve the resource users. Moreover, much recent research demonstrates that traditional or customary systems of management based on the users controlling the local level of use are more effective.

Involvement of local resource users should extend to research and monitoring activities undertaken in support of resource management. This would enable managers to benefit from the users' extensive knowledge of local environmental issues, and would assure users of their specific perceptions and needs being addressed by the studies undertaken. Research priorities should include studies not only of the populations and habitats of wildlife resources, but also of social and management-related issues such as traditional and current land-use and resource-use practices, nutrition and health concerns related to the use of these resources, and the means by which traditional foods can be used more fully in the home and community to maximize conservation of resources as food preferences and culinary practices change.

Generally, it is desirable to establish responsibility for the management of renewable resources as close to the user groups as possible. Migratory animals present a difficult management problem, however, because they cannot be managed locally. The recently appointed Beverly and Kaminuriak Caribou Management Board is an innovative approach to the management of the migratory barren-ground caribou. Such management boards are a very promising development, fully compatible with the management principles agreed upon during the working group discussions.

Multiple uses of land, which are inevitable over time, are likely to cause conflicts between users of renewable resources and developers of non-renewable resources, and between competing users of renewable resources. These conflicts can be resolved only through open consultation between affected parties. Given the present and future value of renewable resources to northerners, the potential social and economic benefits of non-renewable resource development must be shown to outweigh the anticipated negative impacts of such developments on the continued use of renewable resources.

Where there is competition between users of a single renewable resource (for example, competition between commercial, sport, and subsistence users of a fishery), subsistence users should be given priority. This is the current arrangement in Alaska and Québec. Rigid categories of resource use such as "commercial," "sport," and "subsistence" can impede rational management of renewable resources. For example, "subsistence" users often must sell surplus production to finance their subsistence practices, a resource use that is allowed only to "commercial" users, and the use of "sport" fishermen's gear may be more efficient for the selective harvest of certain fish for subsistence use.

Comprehensive land-use planning that involves local residents can be an effective mechanism for minimizing impacts of developments on renewable resources. Should unanticipated negative impacts occur nevertheless, adequate compensation must be obtainable. Administrative procedures for compensation must be in place before development projects are allowed to proceed where renewable resources are harvested.

Background Paper

Property Rights: The Basis of Wildlife Management

Peter J. Usher

Introduction

The thesis of this paper is that resource management policies can be neither conceived nor implemented without reference to the system of property rights, which is in turn the fundamental political arrangement of any society. In elaborating on the traditional foundations of both western and native systems of property and management, my objectives are to show how prevailing game management policies in the North are rooted in our western system of property, and to suggest alterations to that system that will have beneficial results both for the conservation of fish and wildlife, and for those who depend on those resources. I shall refer to the situation in the northern parts of the provinces as well as in the territorial North.

It is common for resource managers to think of their work as a technical problem, to be solved by the application of scientific expertise and sound management technique. "We are responsible for resource management, not social programmes," "politics should be kept out of resource management," and "resource management is a scientific problem," are ideas commonly expressed by those who work for resource management agencies. The ideology of their professional training, and the bureaucratic nature of their work, encourage them to see their immediate task as a highly specialized one, distant if not disconnected from its social context.

It is true that there is no single, unified theory of resource management. Peter Pearse, for example, distinguishes between the perspectives of the conservationists, the technologists, and the promoters.[1] However, the tendency to divorce each of them from politics seems to be widespread among managers of diverse convictions.

Wildlife professionals favour the views of the conservationist and technologist, chiefly because they perceive most of the resources they study or administer to be scarce rather than abundant. Many wildlife professionals see themselves as custodians of a conservationist ethic that is above politics. This perspective sets them apart from those who manage resources such as timber, oil and gas, or minerals, although the promoter's view is not unknown in wildlife agencies when a particular resource appears to have great commercial possibilities.

Management for scarcity is the norm, however, and this requires both the allocation of scarce resources, and the limiting of human access and effort. This fact alone should dissuade us from accepting the idea that management can be divorced from politics.

More important, however, is that management is a prerogative that flows from the system of property. Every system of resource management is based on certain assumptions, frequently unstated, about social organization, political authority, and property rights, all of which are closely interrelated. As no two societies or cultures are identical in these respects, there can be no such thing as a scientifically or technically neutral management regime that is equally applicable and acceptable to both. Consequently, where two social systems share an interest in the same resources, there must be some accommodation in the sphere of property, as well as in the system of management, unless one is to be completely obliterated by the other.

Throughout northern Canada, the management, allocation, and use of fish and wildlife resources are matters of pressing public debate. There are two major reasons for this. First, there is a rising demand for these resources, both by a resident population that is growing in numbers as well as in the diversity of its interests, and by non-residents who are increasingly aware and concerned about the northern environment whether or not they visit the North. Thus there is perceived to be a conservation problem with fish and wildlife. Secondly, native northerners, who have always enjoyed some measure of special access to fish and wildlife under colonial rule, now seek to enlarge and entrench this status as a set of rights by means of the settlement of native claims. These rights are not, however, clearly or uniformly defined, nor is it clear what consequences will flow from the exercise of these rights, either for fish and wildlife populations, or for the use and enjoyment of these resources by non-natives. It is now generally recognized that the conservation problem and the native claims problem cannot be resolved independently of each other. Not everyone agrees that this connection is a good thing, however, and neither is there much agreement about how to proceed.

What is at issue is not simply the allocation of scarce resources among competing demands, although that is a thorny enough problem in any jurisdiction. In the North, the allocation issue cannot be resolved within a common conceptual framework of property rights. Who has rights to what resources, what manner of claim on these resources do these rights bestow, and what management prerogatives flow from these rights are questions also at issue. Management, after all, presumes a human presence, which is always a social rather than an individual one. Property rights, social organization, and resource management are but facets of the same human presence.

My point of departure for this discussion is, therefore, the connection between property rights and the problem of management. I believe that the importance of this connection has not been recognized sufficiently, in spite of the continuing and widespread debate over the future of wildlife management and of native claims in the North. Yet it is in that very connection that I believe we can find some workable solutions.

Property and Management

By property I mean not simply material goods that are owned, but also a system of rights: a set of generally held concepts, which are codified and enforced, about who has the right to use what, to dispose of what, to benefit from what, and within what limits. In every society each member, without much special training or even thought, has an inner concept of the basic system of property of that society. This is especially so where the range of things, owners, and uses is relatively limited, less so when the range is great. That is why complex societies rely so heavily on lawyers and judges who have specialized knowledge of these matters. Yet even the simplest societies rely on elders or similar authorities who can adjudicate disputes on the basis of their accumulated knowledge of custom, as well as their personal authority. For the most part, however, every member of society has sufficient practical understanding of the system of property rights so as to acquire, exchange, and use property in the normal course of affairs without creating undue social disruption.

Systems of property rights are, however, entirely a cultural artifact. There being no natural or immutable system of property rights, each system must have a justifying theory that is, on balance, accepted across the society, even though it may benefit individuals differently. If too many persons reject the prevailing theory, and together have the power to change the system of property rights, then they will in all likelihood do just that. C.B. Macpherson tells us that:

> Property is controversial...because it subserves some more general purposes of a whole society, or the dominant classes of a society, and these purposes change over time: as they change, controversy springs up about what the institution of property is doing and what it ought to be doing.

> ... any institution ... of property is always thought to need justification by some more basic human or social purpose. The reason for this is implicit in two facts ... about the nature of property: first, that property is a right in the sense of an enforceable claim; second, that while its enforceability is what makes it a *legal* right, the enforceability itself depends on a society's belief that it is a *moral* right. Property is not thought to be a right because it is an enforceable claim: it is an enforceable claim because it is thought to be a human right. ... Property has always to be justified by something more basic; if it is not so justified, it does not for long remain an enforceable claim. If it is not justified, it does not remain property.[2]

Anyone who has followed the native claims issue will not have failed to notice the profusion of justifying theories of property advanced by the participants. No one should dismiss these justifying theories as mere tawdry political gambits. They are, rather, essential to the resolution of the problem. Everyone, however, should try to judge the relative merits of these theories.

What are the implications of all this for resource management? Put very simply, anyone who seriously believes that it is a purely scientific or technical problem, separate from the political process, and separate from the sphere of property rights, is operating in a world of fantasy and will never develop a workable management regime. More important is that both traditional native concepts of management and modern scientific management are founded on their respective systems of property. Thus, any blending of the two management systems requires also a blending of the two systems of property. By the same token, one cannot transform the system of property rights without fundamentally altering the logic and viability of the management regime. To understand the system of property rights, which is the foundation of politics in any society, is to recognize the political base that underlies all of the technical and administrative details of management.

Two Systems of Property and Management

I shall now describe the two existing systems of property and management in the North—the aboriginal and the Canadian—with the intent not only to contrast them, but also to make them more intelligible to each other. To begin, I shall describe them as they have actually existed and worked, regardless of their legal standing in the courts of the land at this time.

To the extent that our preconceptions of native northerners are founded on popular culture, or even on a few undergraduate social science courses taken 10 or 20 years ago, we are poorly equipped to see what is really there. The very words "primitive" and "nomadic," which we use so easily, suggest hordes of individuals without culture or social organization roaming aimlessly about the land in search of sustenance. Living on the edge of survival, they had no time to create culture. Beset by superstition, they lived more as animals at the top of the food chain than as conscious and rational human beings capable of influencing the outcome of their affairs.

Although there is remarkable variation among northern native peoples, it is possible to make certain generalizations based on recent anthropological and other social scientific research. Across the North, there have existed discrete bands of peoples, each having a distinct social organization, and each occupying a certain territory in which they foraged for their subsistence. Each of these bands was characterized, first, by a systematic and more-or-less stable pattern of land use, in which co-residential groups used predictable areas or sites for foraging at certain times of the year, or over a cycle of years; secondly, by a system of local authority by which individuals, households, or other units within the band as a whole were acknowledged to have certain pre-eminent rights of use and occupancy to certain areas, which were again more or less stable over time; and thirdly, by a set of customs and rules that regulated their foraging behaviour so as to ensure the survival and harmony of the group.

Each of these territories was known and bounded: members of the band had the automatic right to hunt within the territory, whereas others might gain access only by arrangement. It is true that these boundaries sometimes changed over time, and it is also true that not all neighbouring bands had amicable relations with one another. That these boundaries occasionally changed by virtue of intrusive occupation or abandonment does not negate the historical existence of political societies with territorial boundaries in the North, capable of mediating their relations among themselves, any more than the much more prevalent occurrence of wars in contemporary international society negates the existence of organized, sovereign states. Persons did not rove the countryside aimlessly in some uncomprehending Darwinian struggle for individual survival. Every person carried a knowledge of the territorial extent of the group, or, if they did not as individuals use this entire territory, each could distinguish between the territory of a neighbouring member of the group and that of a quite different group to which he or she did not belong. That knowledge had a practical effect on their behaviour, whether or not they conceptualized boundaries in a formal or an abstract way.

The Working Groups

The means by which space was allocated among individuals within the band's own territory varied considerably across the North. Among the Inuit and the Dene, the common arrangement seems to have been subdivision by smaller co-residential groups for much, if not all, of the year. These groups would use certain areas collectively, in the sense that, for example, any individual could hunt caribou or moose anywhere within the group's area. Among the Algonkians in eastern Canada, there appears to have been a more specific and mutually exclusive territorial organization at the household level, although it is not clear whether this arrangement predated the fur trade or was an artifact of it. In all of these cases, there were complex social arrangements, for example, marriage rules, which served to govern the size and composition of the local groups.

Finally, each of these groups had a system of customs and rules, capable of enforcement, that served to regulate the manner in which each individual hunted, trapped, and fished. No individual did exactly what he pleased, in some lawless jungle in which the strong triumphed over the weak. Every person knew and observed a complex set of rules about how, where, and when to hunt and, importantly, not to hunt. These rules were commonly expressed in a metaphor of religion and spirituality, although the fact that a lot of them served in result, if not in conscious or well-articulated intent, to conserve both the resource base on which the group relied as well as harmony within the band, suggests that they had a material as well as an ideological basis. It is true that these rules did not work always or invariably, but it is ridiculous to suggest that substantiation of one or even several instances where they did not is grounds for completely rejecting their existence and function throughout the breadth and depth of native peoples' experience on this continent. It is unbecoming in the extreme when that suggestion comes from a society that, by virtue of its own alleged modernity and sophistication, has managed to obliterate more species on the North American continent in less than a century than had disappeared since the Ice Age.

The anthropological literature on the territorial arrangements of the eastern Algonkians, and on the band structure of the Dene and Inuit, dates back several decades, but there has been a great advance in documentation and interpretation in the last ten years, particularly as a result of the various studies of native land use and occupancy. The thrust of these research results is that the native peoples who now live in arctic and sub-arctic Canada not only occupied distinct territories according to systematic patterns since aboriginal times, but also had relatively stable systems of political authority, land tenure, and rules for resource harvesting, and if their continued existence over generations is anything to go by, these systems worked. Known to lawyers as *lex loci*, these systems may be conceived as the local equivalent of English common law. In the light of historic court decisions in the 1970s, it is now possible to assert that these groups "have a *lex loci* which is, on the evidence, of a class which can be presumed to have survived the assertion of a territorial sovereignty by the Crown. . . ."[3]

I stress these findings because they stand in contrast to the received wisdom of jurists, theologians, political theorists, and statesmen over centuries of colonization of North America. In his landmark judgement in the Calder case, Justice Hall wrote:

This concept of the aboriginal inhabitants of America led Chief Justice Marshall in . . . the outstanding judicial pronouncement on Indian rights to say . . ., "But the tribes of Indians inhabiting this country were fierce savages, whose occupation was war . . . ." We now know that this assessment was ill-founded. The Indians did in fact at times engage in some tribal wars but war was not their vocation and it can be said that their preoccupation with war pales into insignificance when compared to the religious and dynastic wars of "civilized" Europe of the 16th and 17th centuries. Chief Justice Marshall was, of course, speaking with the knowledge available to him in 1823.[4]

Unfortunately, the message, which is finally getting through to at least some of the courts and the legislatures of Canada, may not be making a similar impression on wildlife professionals. It is still possible to find statements in the current scientific literature such as the following:

There seems no evidence, then, that wildlife was purposefully managed by Amerindian populations in northern Canada at the time of contact. Instead, we may conjecture that the impact of hunting on wildlife stocks was limited only by the low technological level of the hunters and the fact that their populations were small and insecure. . . .

Wildlife management for sustained yield is today a sophisticated, scientific activity which seeks to accommodate social desires in wildlife without damage to the resource. Historically, however, it is a product of the feudal society, and began as an imposition on the wanting by the wealthy. It is a craft rooted in privilege and not in poverty.[5]

Early man often failed to conserve, too, because he lacked the two prerequisites for conservation of resources: perception of the danger of over-exploitation, and an option to do something about it. Concerning the former, early man had no ability to count wildlife abundance except locally, and was mobile enough to overcome local depletion by moving. Concerning the latter, when the resource in question is absolute availability of food, there is no option. Anthropologists have not described any behavioural self-regulatory mechanism or tradition to adjust natality to the realities of food supply, such as exists in man's co-predator, the wolf.[6]

Is it possible that those responsible for wildlife administration in northern Canada are still mired in the notion that aboriginal societies were nothing more than biological populations in a pure predator–prey relationship, having no culture, no historical experience, and no self-conscious or rational means for making their way in the world? Are there administrators who believe that these peoples are but ancestral relics, like Neanderthals in our midst, having no option but to rely on the wisdom of scientists for the management of their daily affairs? One can only hope that these are the views of a minority.

Property rights, in aboriginal society, can be said to have rested with the group. Each band or co-residential group maintained the right to use its territory by virtue of occupancy. The connection between the land and the group lay in knowledge, naming, travel, foraging, and residence. There were no attempts to alter or partition the landscape, or to appropriate sections or features of it into private hands in a manner that would exclude other members of the group. The land and its resources were, in effect, the communal property of the group, meaning that no member could be excluded from access. To the extent that peoples articulated their relationship with the land, they saw themselves as belonging to it, rather than it to them. Traditional cosmology did not share with western thought the clear subject–object distinction between man and nature: the idea that nature is but insentient stuff for man to dominate or master. The land provided home and sustenance, but could not be reduced to individual possession and could not be alienated. Land was neither a commodity nor a factor of production. Nor were animals property, but rather, existed in relation to man, and man could to some extent control that relationship through knowledge and deliberate action.

There existed as well the political means to ensure that individuals used the land in harmony rather than in conflict with one another, and that they did not use the land or its resources in such a way as to endanger the security of the group, in so far as that could be known. The longevity and stability of these systems is an indication that they worked well in practice.

Recalling C.B. Macpherson's comment on the need for justification of property institutions, it seems clear that the absence of well-articulated theories of that nature amongst aboriginal societies was not a result of their lack of civilization or intelligence, as earlier European theorists presumed, but rather of the fact that land and resources were held in common. If no class within native society could or did appropriate land to itself, there was no need of a justifying theory to advance or rebut that process. Now that southern society encroaches on their traditional lands by peaceful political processes of absorption, rather than through outright warfare, native peoples are rapidly elaborating theories that justify their title. Contemporary native perceptions of their property rights in land and resources seem to me to rest on their understanding of the consequences of losing these things. These consequences are seen in a collective as well as an individual way, as adverse effects on native communities and on native institutions, as well as on native individuals.[7] This concern is entirely consistent with aboriginal tradition and experience. It is not a subterfuge for grabbing oil revenues, nor was it mischievously invented by outsiders.

In contrast, let us now examine our own system of property rights. Many Canadians subscribe to democratic and individualistic notions about land and resource rights. Frontier areas, and especially the North, are regarded as lands of opportunity where the individual, regardless of class, may make his fortune or pursue his own goal of happiness and, in so doing, may strengthen and enrich society as a whole. Perhaps the source of these ideas lies in too much American TV, because the reality of the Canadian system of land and resource rights is far removed from this conception. The Crown owns the land and its resources, and alienates these piecemeal to private interests and only at such quantities and rates as further the collective interests of society as perceived by the state. We may disagree as to what those collective interests are, or we may point to the tendency of the state to identify the public interest with that of large corporate holders of land and resource rights, but legally not much can be done on northern lands in Canada without licence or authority from the Crown. The tradition that public lands should be transferred to private interests in full, and as fast as possible, is an American, not a Canadian, idea.

Whatever rights individuals hold in land, or in access to its resources, they do so by virtue of a deed, grant, or licence from the Crown. The Crown is divisible, in the sense that both the federal and territorial levels of government may have the authority to grant titles or interests in land. No other, smaller group within Canadian society has collective rights in land

and resources. The claim for such rights by aboriginal groups rests on their traditional use and occupancy prior to the assertion of European sovereignty. All the rest of us derive our titles and interests from the sovereign. These titles and interests carry certain rights, but obviously these too derive from the sovereign. Freehold title to land, or entitlements to particular resources, may be the private property of individuals (or of corporations, which are individuals under the law). Where they are transferable, these titles and interests have value as commodities, but because they are derived from the Crown, the Crown also may expropriate them.

There are several categories or levels of interest in land. These range from freehold title in which a person may transfer, assign, or dispose of his property as he pleases, to the barest of licence to engage in certain activities on a piece of land subject to relevant statutes and regulations. In between are grants such as easements, exploration permits, grazing or cutting rights, and production leases. In some cases these rights are transferable, whereas in others they revert to the Crown. To maintain the right in good standing, there may be performance requirements and the grant may be only for a limited time. If fee simple title is only to the surface (as is usually the case), then at least some of these other rights may be granted to other parties, solely at the pleasure of the Crown.

Thus we have a system of property in which lands and resources can be divided up both conceptually and legally in space and by attribute or use, and can be parcelled out to individuals. For a group to gain such rights, it must be incorporated and must have the legal standing and the liability of an individual. In this system, it is the Crown that has sovereignty over the land and that allocates land to its subjects on certain conditions and according to certain policies.

We have very few common property resources under our system. Fish and wildlife are such, not because everyone believes this is a good and functional arrangement, but because we have not been very successful in figuring out how to place them into private hands. Because of their mobility and wildness, fish and wildlife are not property under the common law until they have been reduced to possession by kill or capture. This raises another important theme in western thought: that property arises through the application of human labour. Labour is involved only in the capture or killing, not in the creation of wildlife. Wildlife therefore not only is not property, but also has no value, prior to the application of labour. Here we move from the legal to the economic aspects of the property system, however, and I shall return to the latter below.

In England, the Crown did not actually own wildlife, but had the right to reserve the taking of wildlife on Crown lands to itself by forbidding its subjects to do so. Wildlife was, therefore, not common property in the aboriginal sense, which meant that no member of the group could be excluded from using it. In North America, more-democratic ideas have prevailed. No one has the pre-eminent right to use fish and wildlife to the exclusion of others, except on private lands. In Canada, special access to and use of fish and wildlife on Crown lands have been granted to at least three categories of persons: native Indians and Inuit, scientists, and those deemed privileged by the Crown. In no case, however, is this privilege unrestricted and unregulated. Without exception, the prerogative to manage fish and wildlife rests with the Crown in right of Canada or of a province.

Management, in this system, must always keep certain objectives and problems in mind. The Crown, having overarching sovereignty, has an interest in its land and resources that may be separable from those of any particular set of individuals or groups. The Crown therefore not only mediates the interests of these parties, but also furthers its own interests, not the least of which is to maximize the flow of revenue from its assets.

Our modern conception of property is either that it is private, or that it belongs to the state. If it is neither, then it is not really property. Resources that are not amenable to private appropriation we call common property, but, contrary to aboriginal conceptions, by this we do not mean that it is collectively owned by a group. We mean that it is not owned by anyone, indeed that it is a free good, there for the taking. The prevailing view in our society is that this is a bad arrangement, to be remedied by subjecting common property to administrative arrangements that will make it akin to private property. The distinctive feature of private property in modern society is that it is alienable and marketable. Private property is the foundation of many social systems, but the transformation of land (and, for that matter, labour) into commodities to be exchanged on the free market is an institutional innovation linked to the transformation from feudalism and mercantilism to industrial capitalism. It is the creation of the market as the institutional device for allocating property, including land and resources, that Karl Polanyi referred to as the "Great Transformation" in European history.[8] I have argued that the same process is currently entraining a "great transformation" among native northerners.[9] Heilbroner refers to these events, and the rise of economics as a distinct field of inquiry, as "the making of economic society."[10]

This new discipline, asking such questions as "what is value?," "how is wealth created?," and "by what rational principles do we allocate scarce resources among economic ends?" has profoundly informed our ideas about resource management. Some economists like to think of their discipline as a science divorced from social, cultural, and historical reality, capable of deducing human nature from observations of economic behaviour. In fact, economics arises from, and is informed by, the property arrangements of modern society.

A final observation, in this comparative exercise, on the connection between property and management is that economics distinguishes between productive property—the means of production—and individual property—consumer goods. Because we generally regard the management of the latter as a private affair, public economic policy is concerned with the management of the former. Management skills are in great demand these days, in business, in factories, and in resource administration. The growth of management parallels the increasing functional separation of the ownership and administration of productive property in modern economies. The chief requirement of industrial organization, with its elaborate specialization of functions, and the chief consequence on the humanity of those who are employed in industry, is the separation of conception and execution in work.[11]

In traditional, simply organized societies, this division was within the person. The mind conceived and the hand executed. In industry, the division is within the workforce. The managers and the engineers conceive; the manual and clerical workers execute.

Stripped of conception, work becomes labour, which economists call a disutility. Large employers commonly refer to the entire range of pay, pensions, and benefits to their labour force as a compensation package. The value of this compensation is realized, however, in the course of time off work, which we generally call leisure. This distinction between work and leisure is largely an artifact of industrial society. Leisure, however, requires not only time but also space and resources. The need for wilderness parks, and for the recreational use of wildlife, well known to wildlife managers, is that of an industrial as opposed to an agrarian or a foraging society. Some social theorists, however, have suggested that leisure is not so much the opposite of work as it is its counterpart, and that modern industrial society finds need to manage our leisure experience no less than our work experience.

What is more-or-less unified in aboriginal cosmology is fragmented in our own. The division of knowledge into branches such as law, political theory, economics, and biology, the distinctions between work and leisure, between man and nature, among the attributes of land and the incidents of property, are essentially foreign to aboriginal tradition. That in itself, as well as the many specific comparisons I have drawn, contributes to the gulf between our different societies and heritages. My intention, however, is not simply to draw contrasts, but also to suggest where bridges might be built.

Property and Wildlife Management Policies

I shall now show how some of the fundamental tenets of wildlife management, as it has been practised by government agencies in the North, relate to these two systems of property. Let us begin with the concept of common property itself.

Canadian law does not recognize the right of ownership in any wild animal or fish until it is captured. These resources are therefore called common property resources, and their management and regulation is the responsibility of the state on behalf of its citizens. Common property is thus, in effect, state property. These resources were not always state property in the modern sense, however.

Originally, within each of a series of bounded territories, there was an organized society that had the effective right and ability to use and to manage fish and wildlife while these resources were present. Fish and wildlife were, in effect, communal property.[12] They became state property through various forms of expropriation, in that transfer of title everywhere took place against the wishes of native peoples, with or without their compliance or agreement. In the treaty areas, there is continuing debate about what was actually agreed to, and whether the terms of the agreements have been fulfilled. In the rest of the North, the debate is about whether or not expropriation has already legally occurred, and what the nature and amount of compensation should have been or should be. In practice these are such contemporary issues because the effective transfer of title has been quite recent. The state has chosen to exercise the powers and prerogatives of ownership, chiefly through the granting of competing interests in land, and the regulation of harvesting of fish and wildlife, only in the last generation or so in much of the North. It is these developments that have given such strong impetus to the native claims movement.

Our prevailing conception of common property as state property was imposed not on a lawless, free-for-all situation in which no one owned or had responsibility for anything, but rather on a functioning system of communal property that was in fact managed by the occupying group. We must therefore re-examine our assumptions about the management implications of common property, about the comparative achievements of management systems other than our own, and about the role of science in public administration.

Consider the highly influential essay by Garrett Hardin "The Tragedy of the Commons," in which a number of herdsmen have access to common grazing land. For each additional head of cattle the individual herdsman puts out, he receives all of the utility from its use or sale. The consequent effects of overgrazing are felt equally by all herdsmen, however, so that the disutility to that individual is only a small fraction of his utility. On balance, it is perfectly rational for each herdsman to continue putting more cattle on the commons, until the pasture is bare and can no longer support any cattle.

What is omitted from this scenario, however, is social organization and its mediating role between individuals and their environment. Instead, Hardin's portrait has atomistic herdsmen, each making individual calculations about his personal gain, "each pursuing his own best interest in a society that believes in the freedom of the commons. *Freedom in a commons brings ruin to all* [emphasis added]."[13] Hardin sees two options: sell the commons off as private property, or keep it as public property but allocate the right to enter, either of which will introduce the required element of individual responsibility. According to Hardin, these new social arrangements require mutual coercion, mutually agreed on.

The view that all arrangements other than individual property ownership lead to negative or even to tragic consequences is seductive, but is unsupported by historical and anthropological evidence. The reason is that in Hardin's commons, the social arrangements that have actually prevailed in most instances of common property tenure are absent. Gordon, one of many economists who, for different reasons, have excoriated common property arrangements, wrote that under feudalism:

> the manor developed its elaborate rules regulating the use of the common pasture, or "stinting" the common: limitations on the number of animals, hours of pasturing, etc., designed to prevent the abuses of excessive individualistic competition

and added that:

> stable primitive cultures appear to have discovered the dangers of common-property tenure and to have developed measures to protect their resources.[14]

Aboriginal and feudal systems of land tenure alike were characterized by similar restraints. Unrestricted individualistic competition was not a feature of traditional Inuit or Indian life. Indeed, those cultures were highly resistant to such personality traits, not least in the economic sphere. Further, it seems likely in both the feudal and aboriginal cases that these arrangements were achieved under the very conditions of social stability that Hardin supposed would remorselessly generate the tragedy of the commons.

Commons without law, restraint, or responsibility is an appropriate metaphor not for those societies, but rather for *laissez-faire* industrial capitalism and the imperial frontier, both of which provided the historical contexts for such events as the arctic whale fishery, the west-coast salmon fishery, and the buffalo and passenger pigeon hunts. Hardin's herdsmen were putting into practice not the economics of medieval times, but those of Adam Smith. Their behaviour is what we expect when community, and its restraining institutions, are absent.

It is therefore essential to distinguish between traditional communal systems of property, and what we now call common property arrangements. The latter are characteristic of rapid economic change, unstable social institutions, and the absence of local community control. The Pacific salmon fishery, which is, to biologists and economists alike, the classic illustration of the evils of common property tenure, resulted from the expropriation of historic local fishing systems and the deliberate creation of an economic free-for-all in which the spoils went only to the strong. It was, thus, the substitution of piracy for community, and it is the former condition, not the latter, that managers are, or should be, trying to overcome.

I am by no means suggesting that native peoples never found it convenient or necessary to behave as pirates once the institutions of community were overturned. Aboriginal *systems* of tenure must, however, be acquitted of the charge of lawless individualism. The ideas of biologists like Macpherson and Theberge can be rejected on the grounds that the propensity to conserve wildlife resources (or not to do so) is a function neither of the psychological nor genetic make-up of "human nature" but rather of social organization and the system of property rights.

Traditional systems of tenure and of customary law have been under substantial assault for many years in the North, so it might be wondered what relevance all of this has for future management strategies. It is not enough, however, for wildlife managers to blame causes such as the rise of commercialism and the decline of the old way of life and to claim that they now have no alternative but to clean up the mess with a healthy dose of scientific management. The history of fish and wildlife management in the North is founded at almost every turn on western notions of property rights, and the assumption that these were being imposed in the absence of stable and viable indigenous institutions. These institutions were thus either consciously or unconsciously suppressed by policies for wildlife management, as the following brief history indicates.

Fish and game management in the North had its practical beginnings around the time of the First World War. From the start, managers have distinguished between commercial and subsistence activity. This was an era in which native peoples were no longer alone in the North as hunters, trappers, and fishermen. The monopoly of the fur trade had long since passed, and there was everywhere an influx of mobile and individualistic commercial fishermen, trappers, and traders relying heavily on wild game for food. The management response was, usually belatedly, to restrict their entry, sometimes by season or gear, sometimes by categories of persons, sometimes by instituting private property-like arrangements.

The outstanding example of the last method was the registered trap-line system, which was introduced in British Columbia in 1926 and which was then widely adopted in such areas as Ontario, Alberta, the Yukon, and the Mackenzie River Delta in the 1940s and early 1950s. Files on the implementation of this system contain explicit claims about the superiority of private property relations as a means to resource conservation, not only over unlimited entry by non-natives, but also over native peoples' own practices. Many native peoples, however, did not view trapline registration so positively. Protection against the encroachment of outsiders was indeed desirable, but in practice, the system was seen as a disruption of their own tenure and conservation arrangements, as well as in some instances actually favouring white trappers in preference to themselves. Only in the N.W.T. were measures taken to exclude white trappers without recourse to the registration system.[15]

The regulation of commercial fishing has a somewhat different history. This activity was, in the twentieth century, more typically a non-native enterprise, relying on heavier capitalization and much faster and more reliable access to markets than did trapping. Native peoples therefore tended to enter the commercial fishery later, and in a subordinate or disadvantaged position, although in some cases special efforts were made to encourage Indian participation.

The policy of using wild game as a social overhead cost of pioneer settlement was, in Canada, short-lived (in contrast with the situation in Alaska, for example). From an early date, in most jurisdictions, wild game was reserved for native peoples' subsistence and for sport hunters.

Again, however, to read the views of those who made these policies is instructive. The commercial and subsistence use of fur, fish, and game was generally seen as a temporary phase. There was a widespread expectation that the transformation of the North into a frontier of timber, hydro, and mineral wealth would more or less put an end to development based on the exploitation of wildlife and, at the same time, put an end to native peoples' reliance on it for subsistence. The concern (where it was expressed) to reserve stocks of fish and wildlife for native peoples' use was motivated in no small part by a desire to keep them off the welfare rolls until jobs could be found for them. Similarly, in the years following the Second World War, when the old fur-trade system was collapsing, reserving traplines and commercial fishing licences for Indians was often seen as a temporary substitute for wage employment.

Where local non-natives had strong interests in the commercial exploitation of fish and wildlife, conflicts arose. Federal Indian agents and provincial resource administrators were sometimes at odds over licensing policies. The Crown in right of Canada had to consider the economic welfare of its Indian wards. The Crown in right of the provinces had to consider the economic return on its resource assets. In the longer run, however, the emphasis at both levels of government has been on the recreational use of fish and wildlife by both a growing resident population and a non-resident (or, in the provinces, a southern-based) urban industrial population. Whatever the allocation priorities are at any particular time, there appears to be a thrust in all fish and wildlife administrations (and in economic development administrations) to eventually phase out subsistence and commercial uses in favour of recreational use.

This thrust is supported by economic theories that are also grounded in our western notions of property. The labour theory of value, referred to earlier, derives primarily from the economics of Ricardo and Marx. Although neo-classical economics does not subscribe to a pure labour theory of value, the idea of labour as a justification for property is nonetheless a dominant theme in our political economy, whether we read the story of the little red hen or the writings of John Locke and Jeremy Bentham. Neo-classical economics has difficulty assigning value to wildlife for a different reason: not being property, it cannot be exchanged and therefore has no empirically observable market value. Welfare economics seeks to overcome this problem by imputing a value, or a shadow price, to wildlife by proxy transactions that do occur in the market place. All modern approaches to wildlife evaluation seek to determine the consumer's willingness to pay, and this in turn presupposes existing property arrangements. They assume not only that it is possible to measure all personal utility in dollars, but also that the consumer has no proprietary interest in wildlife, only a privilege granted by the state. They ask, in effect, what are persons willing to pay for that privilege, not necessarily to consume the resource itself, but to experience the chase. What is being measured here is not only the utility that users derive from consuming wildlife (or the "wildlife experience"), but also the economic rent the resource could yield to its owner, because the one question presupposes the other. The question of economic rent is of course very interesting to the Crown in its endeavour to maximize revenue from its assets. From the Crown's perspective, the distinction between the willingness to pay for the experience as opposed to the resource itself is an important one because many more persons will experience the chase than will consume the resource. Anyone who has a proprietary interest in a resource, however, is asked not what he is willing to pay for the privilege of using it, but what he is willing to accept as compensation for its loss.

As economics has grown in sophistication, the business of maximizing revenues from resource assets has grown in complexity. Once one can evaluate non-market goods, and hence the potential rent to their owner, the owner is in a position to evaluate alternative uses for his assets, and, in the case of land, the relative merits of choosing to maximize revenue from one resource or attribute rather than another. That is the objective of cost–benefit analysis, whether in its more primitive reliance solely on market values a generation ago, or in its more sophisticated contemporary attempts to evaluate non-market phenomena.

The legacy of these policies is very much with us today. One consequence is that native peoples' access to resources is seen by many as a social policy issue rather than a property right. Native peoples are finding out, however, that resource assets, the use of which rests on the interests of a governing party, do not provide the same security as those that rest on proprietary title. Where the prospect of the use and enjoyment of assets is not secure, the inclination to maintain and manage those assets for long-range benefit declines.

There are many instances in northern Canada in which native peoples have first been encouraged by governments to move somewhere or take up some new occupation based on fur, fish, and game, and have then been left high and dry when some new social or economic policy direction was implemented. Inuit were moved to the High Arctic to make a better living from hunting and trapping. If the development of oil and gas now threatens that livelihood, let them now get jobs in that industry. In the boreal forest, many Indian bands were encouraged to take up commercial fishing, or to rely for their livelihood on new programmes for beaver management. If the marshes and streams are later flooded or the waters are polluted by industrial development, let them also get jobs in those industries.

The problem is that, with few exceptions, native peoples have no recognized legal interest in the resources on which they have relied historically. Aboriginal and treaty hunting rights have been viewed as providing the barest of interest in the land. All they mean, it turns out, is that the Indian or Inuk who is hunting or fishing on unoccupied Crown land is not actually trespassing (although he may be violating the game laws). The overseas oil company granted an exploration permit yesterday has greater standing before the law than the Indian whose ancestors used and occupied the land for 10 000 years. The reason is that such devices as the Dominion Lands Act, the Territorial Lands Act, and the Canada Oil and Gas Act, were all intended to convey rights in land from the Crown to individuals. All the while, aboriginal rights, which preceded those of the Crown, were never properly codified so as to give their holders a legally enforceable and practically useful defence.

This situation has created two problems for native peoples. First, there is the question of the property interest that native peoples have in the land, and in fish and wildlife resources, *vis-à-vis* that of parties granted competing interests in the land. Secondly, there is the question of their rights *vis-à-vis* those of other parties to the fish and wildlife resources themselves. Governments that do not recognize the proprietary interests of native peoples in these resources can make only economic calculations about allocation. Whether on the narrow basis of direct rents, or on a broader basis of maximizing the yield of the resource to society, the state seeks to maximize the difference between the total value and the total costs of production. This level of output, assuming resource rents are properly calculated, is somewhat below the maximum sustainable yield. Although the economic maximization theorists pay lip service to the importance of other social goals—equity, social and cultural values, community viability, and so on—they almost invariably fall back on efficiency as the central criterion. This is especially so in commercial harvesting because efficiency is so much more readily measured in dollar terms. Once the issue is cast in terms of efficiency, native peoples, who are in aggregate a minority group with a minority way of life, and who are in their communities both geographically and socially isolated, inevitably become the losers. The efficiency criterion also explains the state's preference for recreational over subsistence or commercial use of fish and wildlife.

The Crown licenses economic activities on its lands to maximize its revenues, and social goals are invariably considered as secondary. Even allowing for social concerns, the theory of economic maximization suggests that the measurable social benefits of deviating from the goal of maximization must outweigh the cost burden on the resource. The way in which revenues are maximized from allocating resource rights to private interests is normally to make the grant, permit, or licence conditional on the performance of its holder. Thus, to be kept in good standing, mining claims, timber and grazing leases, and registered traplines must be used. The holder must be able to demonstrate the appropriate levels of labour and capital input, shown either by exploration expenditures per hectare, or by the trapping of a predetermined quota of beaver. Those most able to meet Crown performance requirements year after year are those who have chosen economic efficiency as their primary objective and who have the most efficiently capitalized and the most profitable operations. If the number of licences is restricted, then those who choose to maximize for any other goals, in addition to, let alone instead of, economic efficiency, will gradually lose access.

Between the biological conservationist and the economic maximizer, native peoples are caught in a double bind. They are said either to be harvesting too much (for example, caribou in Keewatin), which is seen as a reason to clamp down on them, or to be harvesting too little (for example, wild rice in northern Ontario), which is seen as a reason to allocate the resource to someone else.

Both apply utilitarian judgements to native peoples' use of resources. The conservationists suggest that native peoples do not really need their resources, and could substitute other things for them. Urban environmentalists tell the Newfoundland sealers that they should get jobs to replace their lost income, as though human well-being is totally and perfectly measurable by per-capita income. This is in spite of the fact that in contemporary social science the distinction between wants and needs is fraught with both theoretical and empirical difficulty.

The economic maximizers suggest that native peoples do not make efficient use of the resources to which they have been "given" access. They maintain that the fish taken home for domestic consumption would be better sold to the packing plant, because some dollars are better than no dollars. Even better, they claim, is that the fish sold to the packing plant should be left for the sport fisherman to take (or the polar bear whose hide is sold at auction left to the sport hunter to kill), because more dollars are better than fewer. To the economic maximizers, the changes engendered in the relations among persons, and in the organization of work, are of no consequence; nor even is the fact that the extra dollars may accrue to someone other than the hunter who has foregone his right, although here there is substantial contrast among jurisdictions. The N.W.T., for example, has a much better record of ensuring that the sportsman's dollar goes to the local community than does, for example, Ontario.

Not the least of the problems with the utilitarian economic approach is its denial of the sacred. In the perfect free market, all men's powers are commodities for sale. Nothing is exempt from private bid, or from state expropriation and compensation. Everything and every person must have a price. That is why the most-dedicated environmentalist, thrust into administrative power, has no choice but to wind up trading musk-oxen for oil. The notion that land and animals might have religious or sacred significance is untenable in a society where these things are routinely bought and sold. The sacred, in this system, can have material expression only in consumer goods, not in producer goods, because the latter case would constitute an intolerable interference with the free market. It is this feature of our western heritage that is so repugnant to many native persons, and, indeed, to many non-natives.

Finally, let me explore the theme of management as the separation of conception and execution, in the context of wildlife management. Perhaps no other society on earth has unified conception and execution in its daily economic activity to the same extent as have Canadian Indians and Inuit. The competent adult combined an accumulated knowledge of animal habitat and behaviour with high physical dexterity and simple, but efficient, technology for capture. Scientists, by different and, in terms of practical experience, much more remote techniques, have been able to duplicate some of this knowledge, and add to it other data unobservable by traditional hunters. Using modes of thought and analysis sometimes different from those of the hunters, scientists have reached certain conclusions about fish and wildlife. Some of these findings can be empirically verified time after time, and no hunter disputes them. Others are partly or largely speculative, and can be verified only by modifying the behaviour of those who use fish and wildlife.

Scientists and managers have thus been able to appropriate a good part, but certainly not all, of the collective knowledge of hunters, trappers, and fishermen. Having conceived their theories and policies, however, they must get others to execute their instructions so as to test the theories and to implement the policies. This means that managers must replace hunters' conceptions of how the world works with their own, or must convince them beforehand that they can produce desired results that hunters on their own cannot.

From where do managers get this power? It has been delegated to them by the Crown, which expropriated communal property and turned it into common (state) property. The results for hunters and trappers may (or may not) be more animals and more money at the end of the season, or at the end of next season in exchange for less at the end of this season. What is certain, however, is that some of their autonomy and their power has been stripped from them.

In Pennsylvania, in the late nineteenth century, an engineer by the name of Frederick W. Taylor revolutionized industrial production by appropriating the individual skills and knowledge of many autonomous artisans and tradesmen. Using time and motion studies, he fragmented the unified flow of thought and action, and reassembled the bits as prescribed routines for individuals to follow, over and over again. Output increased and costs decreased, as these workers were stripped of their skills and autonomy in the workplace. Within a generation, engineers and managers were planning the production routine in every factory to the minutest detail, and every morning the workers were given their instruction cards and told not to think or question, just to do.

This process has not been restricted to the workplace. In our leisure time, too, there is growing evidence of the managed recreational experience. Disneyland may be the extreme, but even in Canadian national and provincial parks visitors are told more and more where and when to go, how to conduct themselves, and how to interpret what they see. Many anglers today are told, as conditions of their licences, what lake to fish, what day to fish, what time to fish, what gear to use, how many fish to catch or possess, and what these fish may and may not be used for. I do not dispute the need for some such direction where property is common and community is absent. Native northerners, however, see more and more examples of detailed regulations on how to go about their business. They are assumed to be as personally incompetent and as socially unrestrained as other Canadians. True, not all of these regulations are zealously enforced, but one has only to peruse, for example, the Seal Protection Regulations under the Fisheries Act to imagine what it would mean to Inuit hunters in Labrador if they were. Excessive management seems liable to lead to the loss of native hunting skills and, as in the factory, to less rather than more responsible attitudes toward resources that are quite correctly perceived to be under the control of management.

Is There a Way Out?

I have emphasized the differences between the two traditions in the North, but I also think that it is possible to bridge them. Bridges require firm foundations, however. Are the institutional and ideological bases of the native tradition still sufficiently intact to provide that foundation? I think there is good evidence that they are, and further, I believe that we would be well advised to shore them up rather than to continue to erode them.

The directions I propose are in keeping with some general principles to which, I think, all interested parties currently subscribe, although I have not seen such a list written down in any one place. At a minimum, these principles would include the following:

1. There exists in law a category of rights known as aboriginal rights.
2. Whatever these rights might be understood to encompass, they most certainly have included the right of native peoples to hunt and fish in their traditional territories. This right has been recognized by the Crown in every major proclamation, treaty, and statement with respect to native peoples.

3. One of the objectives of settling native claims is to make these aboriginal rights recognizable to the legal and institutional arrangements of Canadian society.
4. Whatever arrangements emerge must be consistent with the conservation of biological resources and of their environments.

In the modern day, native hunting rights must accomplish three practical ends. First, they should provide native peoples with a proprietary interest that constitutes an enforceable claim against all others. Secondly, they should provide a fair and effective system for compensation in the event of nuisance or trespass by a third party, or expropriation by the Crown. Thirdly, they should provide a framework within which local customary law can operate with respect to the harvesting and management of resources and within which native peoples can have effective input to the policies and administration that affect their interest in the resource base.

A proprietary interest need not require full ownership of land in fee simple title, or of the resources themselves. A grant of interest in certain resources, in this case fish and wildlife, would suffice, but such a grant must carry with it something akin to a right of *profit à prendre*. This means not simply the right to hunt and fish, nor even the sole right to do so in the area of the grant, but also the right to enjoy the fruit (or "profit") of these resources, which is in principle measurable and predictable.

Such an interest is an enforceable claim on that land, which cannot simply be ignored when the Crown expropriates the interest, or grants a competing interest to a third party, or when a third party interferes with the interest. It puts the native hunter or fisherman on an equal footing with the holder of an oil and gas exploration permit or a mineral claim.

This arrangement is in stark contrast to the conventional system of hunting and trapping rights in which the licence holder (whether native or non-native) is deemed to have no interest in the land or resources as such, but a property right only in a fish or animal once it has been taken. If there are no longer any fish or animals to be taken, no right has been interfered with. What is proposed here is simply to raise hunting and trapping rights from the lowest form of interest in land to a higher, proprietary one.

There would be two important differences, however, between what I am suggesting and a conventional right of profit. First, because native peoples' use of fish and game is not exclusively, or even largely, commercial, the notion of *profit à prendre* must also encompass the subsistence interest. There must be a recognition that subsistence resources have value to native peoples, and that their loss has consequences that are, at least in part, measurable and compensable.

Secondly, these grants would be made on the basis of traditional use and occupancy (aboriginal title), rather than the Crown's prerogative to maximize the revenue from its assets. These grants would be the means by which a particular group is entitled to pursue its legitimate interests as recognized by the Crown, rather than the means by which the Crown implements economic development policy. Consequently, these grants would carry neither the relatively short time-limit nor the annual performance criteria for their maintenance in good standing normally associated with other types of resource rights. The only appropriate performance criteria these grants could carry would be those related to conservation, not maximization, and, thus, the exercise of the right must be consistent with the principles of conservation.

The implications for compensation are significant. At present, compensation to harvesters need be paid only if they have legal standing by virtue of a commercial trapping or fishing licence, and then only to the extent of actual property damage, i.e., traps, cabins, or animals actually caught. Some companies also pay a nominal sum for the fur bearer that could have been caught in a damaged trap, but this is not a legal requirement unless specified in a contract between the parties.

Under the proposed system, not only commercial but also subsistence harvesting would be eligible for compensation, and in the amount of what could have been taken in the area. The amount of compensation would be related not to actual previous harvests, but to potential ones on a sustainable yield basis, in the same way that payment of fair market value for expropriated land is based on its potential productive value to others, not on what the particular owner did with it in the past.

To avoid the uncertainties, expense, and delay of court proceedings, which would be the normal recourse of parties whose property rights have been violated, there should be an administrative system of compensation. Aside from property values, a compensation board could base its awards on such considerations as the additional costs to harvesters incurred by the need to travel farther in search of fish and game, or the need for increased protection from vandalism; the impairment (for example, by pollution) of the quality as well as the quantity of the harvest; and the impairment of physical and mental health and of the social well-being of native peoples and their communities. A compensation fund could be established, at least in part, from the posting of performance bonds by those granted competing land-use interests. Although some of these arrangements could also be effected by specific agreements between licensed operators and affected communities, a no-fault compensation system is necessary for two reasons. One is that certain types of damage may be neither acknowledged by, nor legally attributable to, a particular operator; the other is that a damage award against some fly-by-night or offshore operators might prove unenforceable.

An appropriate compensation regime should accomplish two things. First, it should deter both those granted competing land-use rights by the Crown and unauthorized trespassers from taking lightly the destructive risks of their activities. Secondly, it should ensure that if damage does occur, the losses and grievances of the individuals and communities affected are dealt with fairly, quickly, and effectively.

Finally, there must be more than advisory status granted to native harvesters. Grants of interest in fish and wildlife in specified areas, within which each community can be guaranteed a resource base appropriate to its needs, provide defined geographic territories within which there is much scope for local management, on a customary basis if that is desired. It may well be that this system could only work by assigning verifiable harvest quotas to each area. The determination and verification of these quotas might thus be the key link between local management authorities and territorial or provincial authorities. Within that system, however, the licence holders could be largely or entirely responsible for non-quota limitations, and it could be up to them to set restrictions on seasons, size, sex, and gear. As well, they could determine the use and disposition of the harvest. Within the quota allocation, local harvesters could consume or sell their catch, or assign the right to hunt or fish to others, as they pleased. Whether local communities or groups would maintain their licences on a group basis, or allocate them to individual members, could again be their decision.

What I am suggesting is by no means entirely novel, or without practical precedent. One need only refer to Sutton's work on trappers' rights in Alberta,[16] Brody's proposals for Indian hunting areas in north-eastern British Columbia,[17] and the Council for Yukon Indians' recommendations on trappers' compensation.[18] Group harvesting rights based on traditional occupancy already exist in the group-registered trapping areas in the N.W.T. and the Yukon, and, formerly, in the band fishing licences in Ontario. The proposed Indian fishing agreement in Ontario is based on similar principles. The hunters' and trappers' associations in the N.W.T. and the band fishing by-laws in British Columbia suggest that there is already an institutional basis from which to begin.

These proposals are not inconsistent with either native or non-native property concepts and institutions. Whether they are the best means of bridging the two traditions is for others to judge. However, if native and non-native peoples are to live together in the North in any kind of harmony, some innovative proposals and serious negotiations on both property and management issues will be necessary. Imposed solutions cannot conserve fish and wildlife, if by their very nature they replace security, confidence, and responsibility with dispossession, anger, and despair.

No amount of moralizing about what stake persons should feel they have in natural resources will affect their behaviour if the practical effects of the property system are to institutionalize a disproportionate flow of benefits. Sound management is not simply a matter of good science. Nor do I believe that management can be based on purely utilitarian considerations. It requires viable community institutions; a sense of dependence on the resource (perhaps I should say a sure recognition of the interdependence rather than the opposition of man and nature); and a system of ethics, whether expressed in philosophical, spiritual, or religious metaphor. Wherever these things already exist, it makes only common sense to foster them and build on them, instead of continuing to undermine them. A better understanding of both our heritages seems to me to be a good place to start.

Endnotes

1. P. Pearse, "Natural Resource Policies: An Economist's Critique," in R.R. Krueger and B. Mitchell, eds, *Managing Canada's Renewable Resources* (Toronto: Methuen, 1977), pp. 17–19.

2. C.B. Macpherson, ed., *Property: Mainstream and Critical Positions* (Toronto: University of Toronto Press, 1978), pp. 11–12.

3. G.S. Lester, "Primitivism Versus Civilization: A Basic Question in the Law of Aboriginal Rights to Land," in C. Brice-Bennett, ed., *Our Footprints Are Everywhere: Inuit Land Use and Occupancy in Labrador* (Nain, Labrador: Labrador Inuit Association, 1977), p. 367.

4. *Calder et al.* v. *AGBC* (1973) 4 *WWR*, 25. See Lester, p. 366 (see above, note 3).

5. A.H. Macpherson, "Commentary: Wildlife Conservation and Canada's North," *Arctic* 34(2):103–107 (June 1981), p. 104.

6. J.B. Theberge, "Commentary: Conservation in the North—An Ecological Perspective," *Arctic* 34(4):281–285 (December 1981), p. 281.

7. There is some evidence that justifying theories for differential access within native society are beginning to appear, in certain areas. See "Transcript of Discussion" on the reindeer industry in the western Arctic, in M.M.R. Freeman,

ed., *Proceedings: First International Symposium on Renewable Resources and the Economy of the North* (Ottawa: Association of Canadian Universities for Northern Studies; Canada Man and Biosphere Program, 1981), pp. 91–95; and on the emergence of class interests with respect to land in James Bay, I. La Rusic, *Negotiating a Way of Life*, report prepared for Research Division, Policy, Research and Evaluation Group, DIAND (Montreal: ssDcc inc., 1979).

8. K. Polanyi, *The Great Transformation* (Boston: Beacon Press, 1957).

9. P.J. Usher, "Assessing the Impact of Industry in the Beaufort Sea Region" (Ottawa: Beaufort Sea Alliance, 1982).

10. R.L. Heilbroner, *The Making of Economic Society* (Englewood Cliffs, N.J.: Prentice-Hall, 1968), 2nd ed.

11. I use "industry," and "industrial organization," in this context, to refer to the bureaucratic and hierarchical organization of society as a whole, or at least of the institutions, whether public or private, rather than specifically to blue-collar work, production lines, or individual factories.

12. I use the term "property" here to refer to native title, although "proprietary interest" might be more appropriate. I take this interest to be no less forceful a title than freehold ownership, but, unfortunately, it is very difficult for non-natives to transcend ethnocentric connotations of property that derive from an agrarian tradition of land use and a political philosophy of possessive individualism. Indeed, it has been argued that native title is an allodial one, existing independently of sovereign grant, and consequently a higher order of title than freehold (G.S. Lester, "The Territorial Rights of the Inuit of the Canadian Northwest Territories: A Legal Argument," doctoral thesis in law, Toronto: York University, 1981).

13. G. Hardin, "The Tragedy of the Commons," *Science* 162:1243–1248 (13 December 1968), p. 1244.

14. H. Scott Gordon, "The Economic Theory of a Common-Property Resource: The Fishery," *Journal of Political Economy* 62:124–143 (1954), pp. 135 and 134–135.

15. Especially the creation of the Arctic Islands Game Preserve in the 1920s, from which all but native Inuit and Indians were prohibited from hunting and trapping, and the restriction of the General Hunting Licence to native Inuit and Indians, and to non-natives who already held valid licences, in 1938.

16. G. Sutton, "Trappers' Rights," a report prepared for the Alberta Trappers' Central Association and Native Outreach, 1980.

17. H. Brody, *Maps and Dreams* (Vancouver: Douglas & McIntyre, 1981).

18. Council for Yukon Indians, "A Trapper Compensation Model," unpublished report, Whitehorse, 1979.

Background Paper

The Caribou Management Board and Its Early Growth

Hugh J. Monaghan
Assistant Deputy Minister
Department of Renewable Resources
Government of the N.W.T.

Introduction

In this paper I shall outline the events and considerations that led to the formation of the Beverly–Kaminuriak Caribou Management Board. I shall discuss the role of the board and its recent activities as a pragmatic example of resource management agencies and users joining forces to manage a common property resource in northern Canada. The paper highlights some reasons why early board growth has been successful.

Distribution and Importance of the Beverly and Kaminuriak Caribou Herds

The Kaminuriak caribou herd spends the summer in the south-central Keewatin District of the Northwest Territories and the winter in southern Keewatin and northern Manitoba (Figure 1). In some years, the herd winters as far west as the north-eastern corner of Saskatchewan. Since the late 1950s, the distribution of caribou in winter has slowly declined. In recent years, the peoples of northern Manitoba, who enjoyed the use of this resource as far south as latitude 57°N, have had little access to caribou.

The Beverly herd spends the summer west of the Kaminuriak herd, and winters in the southern Keewatin and south-eastern Slave region of the Northwest Territories and throughout northern Saskatchewan. At one time, a portion of the Beverly herd spent the winter in north-eastern

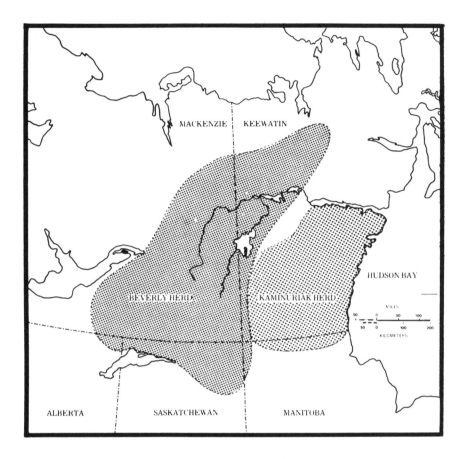

Figure 1 Present range of the Kaminuriak and Beverly caribou herds.

From: N. Simmons, D. Heard, and G. Calef, *Caribou: Kaminuriak Caribou Herd: Inter-Jurisdictional Management Problems* (Yellowknife: N.W.T. Wildlife Service, GNWT, 1979), Progress report no. 2, p.6.

Alberta. Many thousands of caribou are harvested from the Beverly and Kaminuriak herds each year. In general, the harvest is taken almost exclusively by native peoples. The caribou resource traditionally has been, and continues to be, a mainstay for the peoples of the region. A study conducted in 1977 valued the use of caribou at $6000 per household in Baker Lake.[1]

Background to the Formation of the Beverly–Kaminuriak Caribou Management Board

In response to the perceived decline of caribou during the 1950s, the federal government gathered biological information with the co-operation of the provinces of Manitoba and Saskatchewan, and considered management strategies. In general, the Canadian Wildlife Service led the research programme. Native users of caribou were encouraged by local wildlife officers and personnel of the federal Indian Affairs Branch to provide kill statistics. In some cases, they participated in projects such as caribou tagging. The communities usually were briefed informally on management initiatives; however, there was no standard forum for the native users to become directly involved in formulating management programmes.

Although a fully integrated management plan was not formulated, a series of actions was taken in the 1950s and 1960s by the federal, provincial, and territorial agencies to arrest the assumed decline of caribou in these two herds. The primary focus was to reduce mortality to the caribou herds by implementing a widespread wolf-poisoning programme in the caribou winter range, and to encourage hunters to reduce their kill voluntarily. In addition, a forest-fire control programme was implemented in the Northwest Territories portion of the Beverly caribou winter range.

Implementation of these measures and monitoring of herd status and harvest were viewed as tasks for governments. Users were encouraged to provide information on caribou movements and harvest. Interpretation of the data and subsequent recommendations were influenced by officers with practical experience, usually speaking for the perceived interests of users in that jurisdiction. The administrative structures involved in this process included a technical committee, which made recommendations to a management committee (Caribou Management Group) consisting of representatives from each government agency responsible for implementing research and management programmes on the caribou range. User groups were not represented on the management committee.

In general, it was believed that populations of barren-ground caribou on the mainland east of the Mackenzie River had declined radically between the late 1940s and mid-1950s, with an upward trend in the late 1950s.[2] The Beverly herd was thought to have increased to about 210 000 by 1971, but then declined to about 100 000 animals by 1981, with harvest exceeding natural replacement. During the same period, the Kaminuriak herd declined from a high of about 150 000 in 1955 to about 40 000 in 1980, at which point it was thought to be declining at a rate of roughly 2000 animals per year.

These data suggested that the Beverly herd had decreased by more than 50 per cent between the mid-1970s and 1980 and that, if the rate of decline persisted, within five years the herd no longer would be a significant resource. The Kaminuriak herd, although smaller in size, was declining at a precipitous rate (17 per cent over 25 years). The herd was no longer available to the Dene of Manitoba and Saskatchewan; if the rate of decline persisted, it would cease being a resource for Keewatin Inuit in fewer than eight years.

It was clear in the late 1970s that new efforts to develop an integrated and comprehensive resource management response were required if caribou were to be conserved. The dependence of northerners on these herds and their continuing decline highlighted the need for improved management. What was also clear was a growing appreciation by governments of the idea that effective management could occur only if management programmes were supported in principle by the users of the resource at a local level.

In essence, the management problem was that annual harvest exceeded recruitment into the caribou population. Although some management measures could contribute to herd recovery, these measures never could succeed without harvest management that had local support. Co-ordination of the government agencies could be organized, but this alone would not be sufficient for public understanding of the programmes necessary to permit the herds to recover.

Governments attempted to deal with the problem. Although Northwest Territories hunters' and trappers' associations had been actively involved in data collection and harvest allocation aspects of some management programmes, statements by government that caribou populations were declining were received with scepticism at best and, at worst, they were interpreted as outright deceit. Those who lived where the remaining caribou congregated found these statements about declining caribou herds hard to understand.[3] Many believed the caribou had moved elsewhere, particularly northward. Those who accepted that the herds might be declining blamed disturbances associated with the recent increase in mineral exploration near the calving areas. Some believed that such a decline, if it were indeed occurring, could affect negatively the position being advanced on behalf of native peoples in land-claims negotiations for greater responsibility in the area of wildlife management.

Residents of the region had moved into the communities, leaving the more rural life of the 1960s. During this period, there was unprecedented political development in the Northwest Territories, including the organization and growing sophistication of local and regional associations. Clearly, this environment was not conducive to building a bridge of understanding between the traditional and technological perspectives. Similar changes had occurred in the northern communities of Manitoba and Saskatchewan. In the provinces, the recognition of a "problem" in relation to caribou was clearer—often there simply were no caribou available. Even there, the reasons were less than apparent and suspicion toward governments prevailed.

In the Northwest Territories, legislation exists that permits the territorial government to restrict harvesting of caribou by native peoples. The application of such laws, however, would require acceptance by those who would be affected. There are two reasons for this. First, heavy enforcement is seen as regressive; enforcement is costly and difficult in a land as vast as the N.W.T., which is sparsely populated and where access is primarily by air. In the provinces, legislation does not exist at present to control hunting by native peoples on unoccupied Crown land. Secondly, and more important, management must involve those who are to be served— primarily native peoples. For example, population targets, selective harvest, and resource management tradeoffs must be chosen by those with a primary interest in the resource.

An interjurisdictional caribou management board, which represents governments and users, was suggested as a solution to the caribou management problem. Although both sides were keen to proceed, several native organizations were concerned that land claims would give them more control of wildlife management than would participation on a joint board, and that participation on a joint board before claims were settled could prejudice claim negotiations. Governments provided assurance that participation by native peoples would not be prejudicial to claims, but some natives thought they would be better off with a board consisting entirely of users. Government representatives were viewed as being protective of ministerial mandates and tied to preconceived ideas about bureaucratic structure and function.

Government agencies argued that management would be effective only if both users and agencies were represented on the board with shared responsibilities. Further, they argued, successful management could be achieved only if there were integration with other resource management programmes such as DIAND's fire management programmes.

A series of meetings led gradually to an accommodation of views and a general willingness to accept the problem as one that belonged to all those involved. Public meetings, public participation in field programmes, and a major film project were used to aid an exchange of views between governments and the public in the Keewatin. Each party achieved a better understanding of the positions of the others.

The Beverly-Kaminuriak Barren Ground Caribou Management Agreement

On 3 June 1982, the Beverly-Kaminuriak Barren Ground Caribou Management Agreement was signed by the governments of Manitoba, Saskatchewan, the Northwest Territories, and Canada, and witnessed by the native associations concerned. The agreement acknowledges the need for the "coordinated management, goodwill and cooperation amongst the . . . governments and the traditional users of these caribou," and notes that "a special relationship exists between traditional users and the caribou."[4]

The agreement enables the formation of a Beverly and Kaminuriak Caribou Management Board that consists of 13 members: five representatives of the government agencies; two community representatives each from northern Manitoba and northern Saskatchewan; two representatives from the N.W.T. Keewatin Wildlife Federation; and one each from the N.W.T. Dene Nation and Métis Association. The overall objectives of the board are:

- to co-ordinate the management of the herds primarily for traditional users on the caribou range
- to establish a process of shared responsibility for the development of management programmes between the agencies and traditional users
- to encourage communication between the agencies, groups, and public at large.

Specific recommendations for herd management that can be made under the agreement include the limitation of the annual harvest and the allocation of that harvest between jurisdictions; the encouragement of traditional users to participate in management programmes; and development and review of research proposals, harvest data collection systems, and predator management programmes. Recommendations for habitat management and public information are also within the purview of the board. The recommendations of the board are provided directly by the secretary of the board to the appropriate ministers. The board is funded by the government agencies and is required to file an annual report.

Land-claims negotiations in the N.W.T. have respected the principle of ministerial accountability for the conservation of wildlife resources and the need for governments to integrate those needs with other aspects of public government at the provincial, territorial, and federal levels. Within this broad responsibility, ministers are accountable for staff resources, facilities, and funds that they allocate to resource management programmes. This arrangement is respected by the agreement. To reinforce the role of the board, the interjurisdictional agreement and terms of reference of the board require that if a minister does not intend to respond positively to a recommendation, he must indicate his reasons to the board within a reasonable length of time.

The geographic limits of the board's concerns are defined by the traditional range of the caribou herds. The interest of the board must clearly extend to recommendations on any factors that could affect caribou management, such as land-use planning.

Regional associations, such as the coalition of South Slave Hunters' and Trappers' Associations and Bands and the Keewatin Wildlife Federation, bring their perspectives to caribou management. These groups are in a position to sub-allocate regional quotas to their respective communities based on their mandate from the local hunters' and trappers' associations and band councils.

Local and regional wildlife management structures already exist for most of the Northwest Territories. A territorial hunters' and trappers' federation is being formed. The work of these groups will be integrated to ensure that the interests of the northerners in wildlife management programmes are represented in all levels of decision making. The caribou management board will provide the connection between these territorial structures and government agencies and user groups from other jurisdictions. The link between the board and other public resource management committees and boards, such as the advisory committee on wildfire management, are now being established. As well, links are being forged with some committees internal to government, such as the Canada–N.W.T. Research Co-ordinating Committee.

An agreement in principle respecting wildlife has been negotiated between the federal government and Inuit. The terms of that agreement seem to be compatible with the mandate of the board. Specifically, that agreement gives a major role to a Nunavut Wildlife Management Board. However, this must be compatible with agreements negotiated between ministers and other jurisdictions involved in the management of shared resources. Native persons not resident within the caribou range are not, at present, considered to be within the management regime.

The interests of non-native northerners have not been given a high profile. It is important that responsibilities in this regard be clarified before future harvest allocations are made. Several options exist: government agencies may represent the interests of non-native northerners; these groups may appear and make their case before the board; or these groups may lobby with appropriate ministers directly.

Growth of the Caribou Management Board

Since the signing of the Beverly–Kaminuriak Barren Ground Caribou Management Agreement, native groups and government agencies have appointed their representatives and the caribou management board has had three meetings. These followed several informal meetings during the time the formation of the board was being considered. The board elected a user representative, James Schaefer, as chairman, and one of the administrators, Rich Goulden of the Manitoba government, as vice-chairman.

The usual approach of designating a standing technical committee to support the board in the role of a senior management committee has not been followed in this instance. Both user and agency representatives expressed concern that the technical group would be dominated by government personnel, further aggravating the gulf between technical adviser and user perspectives. Concern was also expressed that the availability of a standing technical committee encouraged time lags in decision making. The board chose an alternate approach—to provide firm leadership to small task groups whose composition varies with the issue of concern. These groups report their analyses and recommendations to the board, thereby increasing the learning opportunity for all concerned in decision making.

The board has decided to meet in communities on the caribou range to increase the board profile with its constituent groups. Communicative media, such as films, school programmes, and newsletters, are being developed. Conservation education has been the first priority of the board, and will be for some time.

A key priority has been the drafting of a management programme for the two herds. This task is being carried out primarily by three members of the board, with progress reports and further direction being provided at each meeting on the various aspects of the plan. The plan is being developed by consensus, and it will be the responsibility of board members to keep the communities informed of their progress and to facilitate community input.

The management plan eventually will include specific targets for population levels and quotas, habitat management plans, and the other requirements of a species management plan. The plan also will include elements geared to maximizing benefit of the use of the resource, such as improved storage and use of the harvested animals.

As the management plan develops, the board is confronted with the need to develop positions on related issues raised in other forums. At a recent meeting in Snowdrift, the board developed interim positions on fire management in caribou winter range in the southern Mackenzie and on the regulation of mining exploration on calving grounds in the Keewatin.

Although the board is still in its formative stage, it has, nevertheless, demonstrated considerable growth. There has been a reduction in the polarization of opinions as each party has gained an appreciation of the viewpoints of the others. A good portion of this growth can be attributed to the continuity of board membership; the general goodwill and growing realization that all board members are deeply committed to maintaining the resource; and the extensive preparation that precedes each meeting.

The board members have discovered two useful ways to cope with the frustration of grappling with so enormous a task. First, each meeting focuses on one primary theme. Secondly, the board is establishing operating procedures similar to *Robert's Rules of Order,* and meetings are physically structured so that observers sit apart from the board table.

The board has not experimented to any significant degree with the limits of its influence. During the next budget cycle, however, board members will discuss the allocation of resources available to tackle the problem, such as manpower, funding, and time. Just as there has been an acceptance of the problem as "our problem" rather than the problem of any one agency or user group, so there will be a growing sense that the resources available are "our resources." Meetings have not been used as forums to advance personal interests or to flex mandates.

There will be a time lag between when the board agrees on an issue and when the communities and the agencies support that agreement. Board members from the communities face the particularly challenging task of conveying the progress achieved at a meeting to the persons they represent. It is hoped that the newspaper *Caribou News* will contribute to a growing understanding of the issue, and that holding some of the board meetings in the communities will be helpful.

Conclusion

Progress will be made by the Beverly and Kaminuriak Caribou Management Board through a series of small successes, which will provide direct benefits to the communities while building the credibility and consensus that will be essential when the difficult decisions have to be made. The continuous updating and improving of elements of the plan will improve the board's effectiveness in satisfying the national interest in general, and local and regional interests in particular.

An entire management plan may never be in place. It is too early to point to the Beverly and Kaminuriak Caribou Management Board as a successful model of how to combine the requirements and contributions of northern traditional users of the resource with the benefits of current technological and integrated systems. This experiment is off to a good start, however, and I am optimistic that it will succeed. The key ingredients of continued progress will be good faith on the part of all those concerned, and a willingness to accommodate change when it is necessary for progress toward the goals of resource conservation and resource management in meeting the changing needs of northerners. We have had the courage to take the first step.

Endnotes

1. Interdisciplinary Systems Ltd., "Effects of Exploration and Development in the Baker Lake Area," vol. 1, *Study Report for Department of Indian Affairs and Northern Development* (February 1978). See also J. Stager, "A Background Report of Social and Economic Development," unpublished manuscript prepared for Polar Gas, 203 pp. (Baker Lake: 1977).

2. D.C. Thomas, "A Short Review of Caribou in Canada," *Annual Proceedings of the American Association of Zoological Parks and Requirements* (1975), pp. 20–28.

3. This problem has been compounded since by a radical anomaly in the 1982 survey of the Kaminuriak herd, during which an unusually large number of animals was observed. Whether or not the "increase" is real will be more certain after the 1983 survey.

4. The Beverly-Kaminuriak Barren Ground Caribou Management Agreement, 3 June 1982, a formal intergovernmental agreement between Canada (ministers of the Environment and Indian Affairs and Northern Development) and the provinces of Manitoba (minister of Natural Resources), Saskatchewan (minister of Northern Saskatchewan), and the Northwest Territories (commissioner); p. 2.

Position Paper

Submission on Renewable Resources Management

Council for Yukon Indians

Introduction

Recently, it has become necessary repeatedly to refute government, industry, or non-native arguments that Yukon Indians no longer depend upon renewable resources the way they did traditionally. Often at issue, as well, is whether wage labour will provide an appropriate alternative for hunting, fishing, and trapping activities. Another popular argument is that as soon as Indian harvesters acquire modern technology, they must, for the sake of wildlife conservation, be regulated in their endeavours.

To native peoples, however, since time immemorial, these resources have not been just commodities with little meaning beyond their nutritional or cash value. They formed, and still form, the basis of a way of life. Thus, the Indian environment never once was considered as one to be exploited at all costs. Rather, renewable resources were the means to ensure everyone's livelihood. Because these resources are replaced naturally, there is always some further stock available for future survival.

Needless to say, subsistence use of resources continues to play a strong central role in the lives of large numbers of Indian people—even today, under the enormous pressures brought to bear, on the one hand, by commercial and sport hunting and fishing, and, on the other hand, by parks and sanctuaries set aside to protect the "wilderness quality" of the Yukon.

When Yukon game laws have not been imposed on Indian providers, they have at least existed in an uneasy equilibrium with Indians' traditional harvesting rights. Although the Indian approach to the biosphere too frequently contradicts government policies, renewable resources themselves become mere pawns in a game of dispute over plans for land-use management. If all involved are not very careful, the renewable resources may be sacrificed in the process.

Concerning the ongoing subsistence harvest, CYI takes the position that the land base should remain as productive as possible, and that the total resource base should be integrated satisfactorily with social, cultural, and economic aspects of the Indian way of life. CYI cannot over-emphasize

427

that sensitive areas for calving, staging, overwintering, and spawning should all be specially protected locations. Wildlife management, moreover, should be based on habitat capability, for the carrying capacity of the Yukon's land base, after all, is limited.

Thus, CYI believes that evaluating the relationship of the Indian people and their subsistence requirements should constitute a major component of any realistic scheme for the protection and management of game in the Yukon Territory. In effect, this translates into four points, each of which is examined here.

First, an improved wildlife ordinance must include a clause for longer residency prior to the issuance of hunting licences; and the issuance of hunting licences should be based not only upon sufficient qualifications on the part of the hunter but also upon both a reasonable rationale for harvesting wildlife and the efficient consumption of meat or use of wildlife by-products.

Secondly, game management should include animal husbandry, the stocking of endangered species, the introduction of new species into the Yukon, and the means to remove ecological pressures on wildlife crucial to the needs of the Indian people.

Thirdly, a new and strong status should be accorded to wildlife planning, protection, and management in the Yukon for a better balance between renewable and non-renewable resources.

Lastly, training programmes in all aspects of wildlife management must be initiated for Yukon Indians.

Hunting, Fishing, and Trapping

The agreements in principle on Yukon Indian hunting, fishing, and trapping rights were signed in mid-December 1980. The fishing accord includes the definition and protection, in perpetuity, of certain fishing rights for Yukon Indians. Primarily, these rights involve the establishment of guaranteed levels of harvest for various species based upon the ratio of Indian to non-Indian catches in the 1979–1980 seasons. Indians shall retain the exclusive use of traditional fishing sites. The agreement also establishes that, where in conflict, the Indian food fishery as well as sport fishing shall take precedence over commercial fishing. Finally, the parties committed themselves to determining ways and means of facilitating access by Indians to the limited commercial fishing opportunities.

Regarding Indian trapping rights, the agreement in principle primarily entrenches, in perpetuity, the current ratios of Indian to non-Indian trapping. Thus, Yukon Indians will exercise a continuing right of first refusal to acquire up to 70 per cent of all traplines in the territory, the remaining 30 per cent, if and when they become available, being open to acquisition by any qualified trapper. The agreement also provides that the parties will, prior to the final agreement, decide upon the ways and means to finance enhanced Indian trapping programmes.

The hunting rights of Yukon Indians are easily the most controversial of the harvesting issues. Under existing laws, the non-status Yukon Indians, who number about 3000, have no special hunting rights. They are treated in the same manner as non-native Yukoners. For the status Indians, however, who also number about 3000, the situation is totally different. Section 17(3) of the Yukon Act provides that government may not pass any legislation that infringes upon the right of status Indians to hunt, year round, for food on unoccupied Crown land. The discrepancy between hunting rights for status and non-status Indians has been a source of friction for years and, therefore, a key objective of CYI's claims negotiators was to bargain for a package of uniform hunting rights.

The essential features of the Hunting Agreement, signed 12 December 1980, entail the abrogation of the section 17(3) rights on the part of status Indians in exchange for greatly enhanced rights on the part of non-status Indians. More specifically, the unlimited hunting rights of status Indians have been relinquished in exchange for a guaranteed quota, in perpetuity, of at least 50 per cent of the annual allowable harvest of moose and caribou. With respect to other game, such as bear, sheep, goat, and the Porcupine caribou, the parties agreed to determine quota levels, based primarily upon previous harvests, and to describe these quotas in the final agreement.

Yukon Indian people will retain the exclusive responsibility for allocating the Indian portion of the game quotas, and the Yukon Territorial Government will continue its responsibility for allocating the non-native quota. Subject to the Yukon Indian people's specified preferences regarding hunting seasons, methods of harvest, and age and sex of game, the laws of application will apply to all Yukoners.

Another central feature of the hunting package is the creation of a Wildlife Management Board comprising an equal number of representatives appointed by the territorial government and CYI. The board will advise on all matters associated with the management of wildlife, but will have a specific mandate to report on matters related to the division of harvesting rights between natives and non-natives throughout the Yukon.

The hunting, fishing, and trapping agreements are similar in a number of important ways. First, they acknowledge that, subject to the provisions contained in the agreements, the territorial government will retain legislative authority over fish and wildlife. Secondly, they enshrine certain rights in perpetuity. Thirdly, they establish uniform rights for both status and non-status Indians. Finally, the agreements have, for the most part, Yukon-wide applicability; they are not limited to so-called Indian lands except in so far as Yukon Indians, like any other landowners, will enjoy exclusive hunting rights on their property.

Porcupine Caribou

The Porcupine caribou herd and habitat in the northern Yukon have remained a priority resource of the Old Crow Indians. Annual harvest levels reportedly have remained constant throughout the centuries. In 1982, Gulf Canada Resources Inc. applied for approval to build a marine base at Stokes Point to support its Beaufort Sea exploration programme for the next five to seven years. The site lies only about two kilometres from caribou-calving grounds and other areas sensitive for wildlife.

In September 1982, not without foreboding of the disruptive consequences of a rush to develop hydrocarbons, but primarily with regard to protection measures in general, native user communities signed the Agreement on the Management of the Porcupine Caribou Herd within the Yukon and N.W.T., providing for the following:

- co-operative structures for management of the Porcupine caribou herd between the native peoples and governments of Canada, the Yukon, and the N.W.T.
- the protection of certain native harvesting rights and the allocation of annual harvest levels
- the management and training of native peoples to enable them to take advantage of economic opportunities that may arise from the conservation and habitat protection of the Porcupine caribou herd.

With several similar regional, national, and international draft agreements already tabled in both Canada and the United States, CYI and the N.W.T., as well as Alaskan native organizations, are now exploring the possibility of producing a workable international Porcupine caribou treaty at the earliest opportunity.

Pacific Salmon

As it now stands, the Agreement-in-Principle on Fishing calls for substantial changes in the management of the Yukon Indian salmon and coarse fisheries, requiring that certain rights to fish be defined quantitatively, that priorities be assigned among fisheries, and that Indians have the opportunity to participate in commercial fisheries and to be consulted in the development of a Yukon fishery policy.

Especially concerning Pacific salmon stock, a Yukon fisheries enhancement programme is the key factor in the contentious issue of available reserves. As a result of preponderent United States commercial interests, the solution to many problems hinges on the pending Canada–U.S. Pacific Salmon Treaty.

CYI expects the federal Department of Fisheries and Oceans to consider, not only in spirit but also to the letter, the agreement reached at the claims table when negotiating salmon quotas for the Canadian portion of the Yukon River system. A process of direct consultation with, or participation in the treaty negotiations by, CYI is viewed as a desirable option.

Migratory Birds

It has long been taken for granted that the right of native peoples to hunt migratory birds has been restricted by the Migratory Birds Convention Act. The ability of the federal government to restrict this right through federal legislation was upheld by the Supreme Court of Canada in several documented cases. It has been suggested, however, that the government legislatively restore these rights guaranteed by treaty, and that such rights be free from federal and provincial limitations. In 1971, as a result of pressure from various native organizations, the federal government enacted a new set of Migratory Birds Regulations by Order-in-Council PC 1971–1465. These provided certain exemptions for Indians and Inuit. Since then, the regulations have undergone several amendments. It now appears that Indians and Inuit can hunt migratory game birds in any area of Canada, without a permit, but only during open season.

Because migratory game birds are subject to international treaties similar to those that would be applicable to the Porcupine caribou herd or Pacific salmon, any change in existing regulations requires the consent of others besides the Canadian federal or provincial jurisdictions. In the matter of migratory game birds, the Canadian and U.S. governments involved are beset by internal political problems, which so far have prevented them from reaching a mutual understanding. Moreover, Canadian native peoples, either among themselves or in accord with U.S. native peoples, so far have failed to exchange their views on the amendments to the Migratory Birds Convention Act.

For Yukon Indians, the spring bird hunt provides traditional subsistence food just as it does elsewhere in Canada and the United States, even though it can be argued safely that the total local kill is of minimal proportions.

The federal government's main argument against amending the act seems to be that if sport hunters in Canada and the United States were to seek the same easement of restrictions for recreational hunting, no migratory bird population could withstand the combined effects even for a short time.

On the other hand, both Canadian and U.S. sportsmen's groups lobbied hardest against the amendments. The U.S. groups were the most vocal, one of their concerns being the prospect of a lower bag limit for recreational hunters.

In March 1983, the U.S. Fish and Wildlife Service (FWS) published a notice in the U.S. *Federal Register* of its intent to develop an agreement with the Canadian Wildlife Service (CWS) on the interpretation and implementation of the protocol amending the subsistence hunting provisions of the act. Because FWS seems to carry the momentum in this matter, CYI outlined the following three concerns with regard to the process from which, it is hoped, will eventually evolve an international agreement acceptable to both governments and to all native peoples involved.

First, CYI, on behalf of Yukon Indians, should be involved fully in developing a CWS position before FWS meets with CWS to negotiate an agreement.

Secondly, CYI, on behalf of Yukon Indians, should be afforded an opportunity to participate as observers during discussions between CWS and FWS concerning the negotiations of such an agreement.

Thirdly, if Yukon Indians are not given a meaningful role in the CWS regulatory process, and if they cannot accept the fundamental fairness of restrictions that regulations of the spring hunt will undoubtedly impose, then the hunt will be regulated on paper only. The reality on the ground will be, as before, that the hunt will continue in an unregulated fashion.

Water Resource Management

A preliminary CYI position paper on water resource management, first introduced to the land-claims negotiators in 1982, sums up three general points.

First, Yukon Indians have a special interest in the management of Yukon water resources because their lifestyle and lands are closely associated with the rivers, lakes, and wetlands of the territory.

Secondly, due to this long-established use of rivers, lakes, and wetlands for harvest, aesthetic, and resource purposes, Yukon Indians wish to retain these resources in a natural condition until it is deemed beneficial for the community as a whole to change their natural condition.

Finally, Yukon Indians accept the jurisdiction of the Yukon Territorial Water Board or its applicable legislation as the means to license water use, and, in view of their interest in water resources, Yukon Indians will designate some of the members of the board.

Background Paper

Conflict Arenas in the Management of Renewable Resources in the Canadian North: Perspectives Based on Conflicts and Responses in the James Bay Region, Québec

Harvey A. Feit
Department of Anthropology
McMaster University

Addressing the Mandate

The mandate of this working group is to identify national and regional interests and conflicts in the management of renewable resources and to explore the means available to reconcile or to deal effectively with such conflicts, highlighting those that are resistant to effective reconciliation. There are several perspectives from which the mandate could be addressed and around which discussion could be oriented.[1]

According to one perspective, there are no real conflicts at all. In this view, regional populations have no specific or special rights, and from a legal point of view, therefore, no interests that need significant special consideration in legal or administrative measures. Alternatively, it has been argued that whatever rights and interests northern peoples may have, they are ephemeral; the broad sweep of history dictates that, because of numbers or because of the "primitiveness" of their way of life, they will be wholly incorporated into those economic, political, social, and cultural structures that dominate the national arena in Canada.

This view dominated Canadian policy concerning Indian people for two centuries. The failure of this perspective to take into account the survival of diverse native populations, even in southern Canada, has done little to weaken the recurrence of such claims. They continue to be made in court cases and in various public statements, although no longer in national policy pronouncements, since court decisions in the 1970s gave credibility to recognition of distinctive aboriginal rights. This denial of a distinctive future for native peoples of the North is not solely associated with one political perspective. Although this view is most commonly expressed by some persons of small "c" conservative persuasion, it also has been expressed by some of small "s" socialist persuasion, the difference being signalled by whether northern peoples will be incorporated into the democratic free-market system or united with the working class.

These perspectives fail to recognize the extent to which northern indigenous peoples have retained a real but constrained control over their own lives during 350 years of interaction with world economic systems, and 50 to 100 years of interaction with the Canadian state. This history demonstrates that the almost universally stated desire of northern native peoples for continued relative autonomy within the Canadian state, with appropriate economic, political, and social linkages to national and international institutions, is a potentially viable alternative.[2] I stress the word "potentially" because the question remains whether that autonomy can continue to be made workable in practice.

A second perspective would address the mandate by recognizing that there are conflicts, but claiming that they are not so fundamental that they cannot be resolved effectively in the short or medium term. Judging from the experience in northern Canada, and in Québec in particular, I conclude that this is a useful perspective to explore, although it may not account for the total picture. I do not find the regional and national interests locked in such all-encompassing conflict that no progress or resolution is foreseeable. Many of the arenas of conflict do not involve direct head-on confrontations but, rather, differing interests that have complementary elements and can be reconciled practically with political, legal, and administrative measures.

There are compromises involved in such resolutions, however. Therefore, the resolutions can be reached only through direct negotiations among the protagonists, because only compromises that are acceptable to them can be workable.[3] *Acceptable reconciliation* is a key concept here. It is not good negotiating to compromise basic, long-term goals for short-term conciliation, so the tradeoffs must be struck by each party in the light of its long-term goals. Nevertheless, given the possibility of finding reconciliations that do not make compromises on major points, it may be essential to resolve reconcilable conflicts in the short term so as to increase the chances of being in a position to continue the pursuit of long-term goals. Given the nature of renewable resources in the North, immediate solutions to those resolvable problems faced by both national and regional interests will enhance considerably the chances of survival of the renewable resource base until other, more intransigent, problems may be addressed. In short, I would argue for compromise and reconciliation, but not capitulation.

In this respect, experiences with implementing different types of legal, political, and administrative measures in various jurisdictions need to be examined and assessed as an aid to those seeking workable solutions. The main body of this paper addresses one set of such compromise resolutions—those being tried in the James Bay region of Québec. I do not argue that these are models for other regions, only that there are important lessons to be learned from each experiment for finding workable solutions. The solutions sought will vary by region. By examining experiences in the N.W.T., Yukon, Alaska, and Québec, we may be able to take some useful initial steps to assess the effectiveness of various means of reconciling resolvable conflicts. Resolution rests with the protagonists, but detailed evaluations, rather than rhetoric, may provide some information useful to the process.

A third perspective on our mandate suggests that there is a limited number of highly important arenas of conflict wherein effective reconciliation cannot be foreseen now in the short or medium term. I have been impressed by how wrong various pronouncements have been about what conflicts were irreconcilable. On the other hand, my reading of the northern Canadian experience is that we may be able to identify arenas where various potential means of reconciliation have failed repeatedly. In these arenas, administrative and other means of implementing a reconciliation may be available, but parties to the conflict may not have been able, in fact, to strike acceptable compromises. Alternatively, they may have appeared to do so, but later may have found that the actions of one party were inconsistent with understandings of another.

In these cases, we have to ask how and whether changes in those basic interests themselves are possible. This could lead to consideration of the structural and ideological foundations that inform those interests. Such an analysis would lead to a consideration of how various groups could contribute to changes in basic interests of parties. This perspective involves looking at historical patterns and underlying processes. In some respects, this analysis is not part of the typical fare of pragmatic workshops. Nevertheless, I would argue that it is a key part of our mandate and that we should view these as the pragmatics of the longer term.

In summary, I would argue for the need to adopt at least two perspectives in our discussions. The first is addressed to the short and medium terms and involves evaluating experiences with various means available to parties desiring to reconcile resolvable conflicts. The second perspective involves identifying irreconcilable conflict arenas and seeking to understand how the interests in question are rooted, how they have changed in the past, and how they might be changeable in the longer term future.

The main body of this paper comments on the short- and medium-term experience and, more specifically, on the means being tried for reconciling conflicts in the James Bay region of Québec. My agenda for this part of the discussion comprises five arenas of conflict: the recognition and definition of the basic rights of native hunters; the management of the resources; the allocation of the resources among conflicting users; the provision of adequate cash incomes for indigenous hunters; and the protection of the renewable resources from the effects of non-renewable resource development. At the end of the paper I shall raise agenda items for discussion of irreconcilable conflicts.

Recognition and Definition of the Basic Rights of Native Hunters

Throughout much of Canada, no basic and inalienable right to harvest and use wildlife resources is recognized. Native peoples are accorded various rights to use renewable resources by the Crown; the rights so accorded are subject to change by the will of the Crown alone. In the past, the exercise of the Crown's authority has been constrained only partially, mainly by political considerations and certain treaty obligations. Indigenous peoples, on the other hand, have asserted their aboriginal rights consistently, which include a right to harvest and to use renewable resources not subject to government authority. Recently, the negotiation of aboriginal claims agreements, the restructuring of northern political arrangements, and the drafting of the Constitution have provided contexts in which a recognition of native hunting rights can be enshrined in a form that is more enduring and less subject to unilateral alteration.

The view that native peoples' rights should not be subject to unilateral alteration seems to be basic. All of us feel that we should have certain rights inalienably entrenched, as the inclusion of a Charter of Rights in the Constitution has again indicated. We may disagree about what those rights should be, but the need for such rights is acknowledged widely today. For native peoples, these inalienable rights would differ in content but would be equally necessary, and I assume that northern native peoples would include among their inalienable rights those relating to hunting.

The issue of whether such rights need to be enduring requires a brief comment. It may not be appreciated how often basic hunting rights have been changed in the past. A cursory review of the history of legislation relating to the use and management of wildlife resources in Québec reveals that the basic regulations have been overhauled once in every one or two decades in this century and that each major revision has altered significantly the bases and the principles on which use and management were recognized in practice. I suspect that a similar pattern has occurred in other jurisdictions with similarly long histories of legislative action. Although everyone recognizes the need for revision and change, the frequency of basic rewrites emphasizes the need to enshrine basic and enduring rights outside conventional legislative forms. This need arises, in the first instance, from the explicit and universal desire of native peoples to retain and to continue to develop the hunting cultures and economies that have been their heritage, and that they envisage in terms of generations rather than decades.

The contents of the rights that indigenous peoples seek will vary, but the need for new definitions is clear. The standard Canadian formula of hunting rights on unoccupied Crown lands is clearly inadequate for maintenance of renewable resource-based economies, as the history of non-native occupation of southern Canada has indicated. One possible direction for revision is indicated by the harvesting right enshrined in the James Bay and Northern Québec Agreement (JBNQA). This agreement specifies the content of the right, the limitations that apply to it, and the persons to whom the right applies. The JBNQA also states the need to recognize the Crees' own culturally defined system of rights and privileges.

The JBNQA provides for a native right to hunt, fish, and trap—called a right to harvest—all species of fauna, at all times, over all categories of land in the entire territory, wherever this activity is possible physically. The only general restrictions to this right are that it is subject to the principle of conservation, it cannot be exercised inside towns, and it is restricted when there is actual interference with the physical activities of others or with public safety. The latter restraints are specifically and narrowly defined. The right to harvest also explicitly includes the right to subsidiary activities and technology necessary to exercise harvesting rights, many of which have been and often are restricted by current provincial, territorial, and federal legislation. The right to harvest includes the right to conduct all of the hunting, fishing, trapping, and related activities that the Cree people now are pursuing and traditionally have pursued. This establishes a general right to hunt, intended to codify aboriginal hunting rights in modern terms and to give them legal force binding on governments at all levels.

The one new constraint on the right to harvest is that it is subject to the principle of conservation, which is specifically defined in paragraph 24.1.5 of the JBNQA:

"Conservation" means the pursuit of the optimum natural productivity of all living resources and the protection of the ecological systems of the Territory so as to protect endangered species and to ensure primarily the continuance of the traditional pursuits of the Native people, and secondarily the satisfaction of the needs of non-Native people for sport hunting and fishing.[4]

In essence, the principle of conservation provides that the right to harvest may be limited only under specific conditions in order to protect endangered species and ecological systems. These limitations are essential to the reconciliation of the interests of the provincial and federal governments and those of the regional population. The principle signifies the acceptance by all parties of the priority interest in protecting wildlife and environments.

To whom the rights apply and who can benefit from the products of the exercise of the rights have been the central questions argued in each legislative jurisdiction in the North. In the JBNQA, there is no basic subsistence means test. The right can be exercised by all Cree and Inuit beneficiaries, whether status or non-status. Harvesting in order to sell meat to non-natives is, however, effectively prohibited.

The right to harvest, as set out in the JBNQA, was intended to give legal recognition to Cree hunting and to provide the basis for hunters to pursue their way of life according to their own culturally ordered knowledge, decisions, and activities. The agreement does not try to codify or to define the cultural system, but recognizes its existence and its key structures: the system of hunting territories and of "owners" of territories, which are called, respectively, "traplines" and "tallymen" in the agreement.

A trapline is defined as an area in which harvesting is conducted under the supervision of a Cree tallyman. A tallyman is defined as a person responsible for a trapline and recognized by a Cree community. These definitions incorporate the essential cultural concepts and practices of the Cree in their use and management of renewable resources without forcing the specific features of the system into western legal concepts; these features, therefore, are left flexible for definition and adaptation by the Cree.[5] Usher has emphasized that such recognition is essential to the establishment and recognition of native rights.[6]

Finally, Usher has raised, in his paper for this workshop, an important question with respect to the legal nature of the right to wildlife resources *vis-à-vis* the rights to development and compensation [reproduced in this volume]. One attempt to redefine hunting rights has been explored in Québec through the use of the term "harvesting" in the JBNQA to define the native right to use wildlife. This term avoided the extensive judicial and legislative interpretations that attach to the terms "hunting," "fishing," and "trapping." If I understand Usher, however, he not only wants to distinguish a new right from previous rights, but also wishes specifically to identify its priority or inferiority to other land-use rights and to give it a higher priority than currently exists. This could provide new avenues for an attempt to resolve several of the types of conflicts discussed below.

Management of the Wildlife Resources

Management of wildlife resources inevitably raises the issue of conservation of the resources. Just as the scientific definition of conservation has been changed historically and has been debated frequently by scientists, so it varies among cultures. The cultural relativity of both values and concepts is a given for modern social science, and the fact that there is considerable variability in the definition and use of concepts is more than abundantly demonstrated. The implications in the northern Canadian context are that values, goals, and methods of conservation and wildlife management differ among the culturally distinct populations of the area, and that these differences need to be recognized. This variability further implies that the different systems need to be articulated.

First, however, I must argue that the recurrent claim, recently expressed by Theberge, that there are no behavioural self-regulatory mechanisms or traditions among hunting peoples to limit human natality with respect to food supply, or to conserve resources, is simply wrong on both counts.[7] There is an important literature on the limitations to the growth of hunter–gatherer populations.[8] More important for the present discussions, the existence of hunting territories among the Algonkian people of eastern sub-arctic Canada and the use of these territories to conserve key wildlife were described early in this century by Frank G. Speck.[9] These systems, which clearly predate government introduction and which may or may not predate the fur trade (I would claim the former), have been the subject of an extensive research extending over six decades.[10] Lest I appear to be choosing a single case, there have been periodic reviews of indigenous conservation systems by anthropologists over at least the last 25 years. More recently, Canada has been one of the main areas for quantitative work on indigenous management systems relating to beaver and moose populations,[11] fisheries,[12] and to waterfowl,[13] as well as to management of forest successions.[14] The significance of self-regulation has been emphasized in these recent articles and need not be repeated here.

My own research among the Waswanipi Cree of Québec emphasized several additional issues. First, indigenous systems not only serve to constrain the use of wildlife resources but also, at least under certain conditions, serve to manage the resource. Thus, the indigenous systems can control certain vital biological parameters of the resource and can do so to optimize the quantities or qualities of wildlife populations that are highly valued in a given indigenous cultural system. I have argued that Waswanipi Cree try to hunt moose and beaver so as to meet four objectives. Based on the statements of the Waswanipi Cree and the logic of their belief and spiritually sanctioned symbolic systems, I have phrased their goals in western technical terminologies as follows: to harvest these resources within sustainable yields so as to avoid depletion; to choose, from the variety of harvesting strategies that are compatible with sustained yields, the intensity and frequency of harvesting that relatively stabilize the biological populations and that also may make them relatively resilient to perturbation; to optimize the labour cost of hunting by using more efficiently harvestable resources in preference to less efficiently harvestable resources, whenever this is compatible with the foregoing objectives; and to produce as much food as is consistent with the foregoing goals and with cultural values of work intensity, social sharing obligations, and spiritual propriety.

In general, the research on Cree activities supports the conclusion that the Waswanipi actually seek these objectives in practice, and biological indicators support the conclusion that they usually achieve these objectives. An important factor in this success is the extensive knowledge that senior hunters have of the land and of the wildlife they hunt. This knowledge comes from observing trends in game population indicators and harvests over many years. Harvests are adjusted in response to these trends. The observed indicators of moose and beaver populations include trends in numbers of animal signs and sightings, numbers of moose yards and beaver colonies, sizes of aggregations or colonies, age and sex structures, frequency of births, the frequency of twinning in moose, and the size of cohorts among beaver (judged from observations of placental scars during butchering), and the general health of animals. These are precisely the kinds of data that non-native game managers try to get in order to manage moose and beaver populations. Senior Cree hunters who have returned frequently to the same hunting territories, and who know these distinct tracts (which average about 1200 km²) in great detail, have more knowledge of the game populations they hunt and manage than non-native game managers can have for the vast tracts under their management and intermittent observation.

The goals of management may vary among different native peoples, but the often extensive knowledge of these peoples needs to be recognized and their capabilities as managers acknowledged. Although there is important variability among indigenous cultures and societies in the Canadian North, I would suggest that a testable working hypothesis is that many northern hunters may share the goals of Waswanipi Cree on the whole, and that it is plausible that other northern hunters also can be successful at meeting these objectives. There is a significant difference between these native objectives and the goals of conserving resources and maximizing cash returns from them, cited by Usher as characteristic of non-native management systems. The two kinds of objectives clearly are based on different cultural values.

A second issue is that indigenous management systems are themselves highly resilient and adaptable. This, however, does not mean that they are not easily put under pressure or that they do not undergo changes. Berkes has identified several conditions under which indigenous management systems require alteration: loss of control over resources, rapid technological change, commercialization of subsistence uses, and rapid population growth.[15]

In northern Québec, the indigenous management system, based on hunting territories or traplines, has existed at least since the beginning of this century, and there is good evidence of its existence at the beginning of the last century as well as plausible grounds for assuming it to have existed under certain pre-contact conditions. During this period there have been successive intrusions by outsiders who have threatened, and occasionally have implemented, controls over resources. There has been extensive technological change, increased pressure for commercialization, and rapid population growth. As well, there has been the introduction of new consumer demands, non-native controlled education, more sedentary lifestyles, extensive land-based development, and increased bureaucracy. The wildlife management system has been maintained, however.

The Waswanipi Cree have fought both government and internal changes to maintain the system. Although it has not always been possible to maintain the system with respect to all species, they have abandoned it only in those times, under those circumstances, and for those species for which it temporarily was not possible to continue management practices. For example, when there were competing fur trappers in the 1920s and 1930s, the Waswanipi feared loss of control of the resource and trapped out beaver and marten. They did not over-hunt moose or other fur-bearers less easily depleted by non-native trappers, however. Simultaneously, they petitioned the government to restore their control over the resource so that they could re-establish the game populations and good management practices.

Various changes resulted from these events, some of which made it appear to outsiders that fundamental control of wildlife had shifted to the government. In practice, only the Cree had a sufficiently detailed knowledge of trends in local game populations to be able to manage them, and any local and detailed management by government agents was not enforceable in practice if it was not supported by the Cree tallymen. In the widely decentralized system of hunting territories—there are close to 300 in the James Bay region of Québec—only the most general and ineffective regulations can be enforced by a centralized authority. This situation provides an incentive for reconciliation amongst interests.

If the fact that it can be regulated only by decentralized "owners" of hunting territories is a strength of the Cree system as it has been tested and reshaped during recent history, this is not to say that it is, or can be, isolated from outside interventions. The same history shows that the actions of non-natives can disrupt and require alteration of the system. The historical weakness of the system lies in its ability to regulate only the activities of members of the indigenous community. This is why recognition of the system in the JBNQA was insufficient; means still were needed to regulate non-Cree use and effects of this use on wildlife. This situation provided additional incentive for reconciliation.

Although indigenous systems probably are widespread and resilient, there is still a need to articulate them with management systems designed for regulated non-native activities. There is, thus, a mutual benefit in recognizing both systems. Thus, the JBNQA, besides protecting hunters' autonomy by recognizing rights and the culturally defined Cree system, also recognizes that there will have to be new structures and principles for articulating that system with government powers.

Most of the specific provisions of the JBNQA are designed around this latter need. Given the effectiveness of indigenous management, the agreement recognizes that there should be as little interference as possible. Because harvesting is limited by the principle of conservation, so long as Cree conservation is working the Cree are complying with this condition. Interference with Cree practices can occur only if and when one party—native or government—claims (and can show plausibly) that a conservation problem exists, whether it is caused by native or non-native peoples. Depending on the nature of the problem, its solution may or may not involve alterations in Cree practices for the short or long term. When it does involve alterations, conservation decisions affecting native peoples will be implemented first through guidelines or advisory programmes or both, which amount to native self-regulation. If these mechanisms are not effective or if they are inappropriate, regulations may be used. Regulations will be used, however, to create a minimum of interference with native peoples and harvesting activities. If regulations do not conform to this pattern, they are unlikely to be fully or even extensively enforceable. The underlying assumptions are that the new structures will come into play only when problems arise and that, when they are needed, the Cree people and the appropriate governments will wish to see the problem resolved to protect the resource.

An obvious area of contention is the nature of the new structures that are to join indigenous management systems to those of wider application—in particular, the relative authority of native and non-native institutions in those processes. The JBNQA provided for equal representation on primarily consultative bodies, with the provincial and federal governments retaining a final authority for most, but not all, issues. This authority is constrained by a series of principles specifying native needs and by the procedural elaborations that are required to alter the initial advice. It is fair to say that although the key tests have not been made decisively, this system appears to be workable, but not necessarily desirable. The system is complex and bureaucratic; when it is not used in an atmosphere of goodwill, those using it can lose sight of issues in the plethora of procedures and rights. Other means of establishing joint exercise of management clearly need to be explored in other regions of the Canadian North. The nature of evolving government forms in the northern territories will provide an opportunity for establishing different structures and procedures.

Regulation of Conflicts between Native and Non-native Users

Conflicts between native and non-native users of wildlife are common in many, but not all, areas of the North, and raise the basic question of how the resource will be allocated. The first key to successful resolution of this conflict is agreement on the relative merits and strengths of the claims made by various user groups. This relative ranking is largely a political process, shaped at various times by legal and ideological features of both societies. In the last decade, the principle of a priority for native use has gained ground. It is still clouded, however, by questions of whether it applies equally to status and non-status peoples, whether there should be an economic means or subsistence test, whether the priority should include non-native peoples with similar lifestyles if not similar social communities, and whether the priority applies only to subsistence uses or includes various exchange, monetized, or commercialized uses. These issues will be resolved increasingly through aboriginal claims agreements, constitutional rights definitions, and the development of new government structures, and they will have to vary between regions. Recognition of native priority is likely to be a key to conciliation.

As priorities among resource users and uses are established, various mechanisms will have to be established to regulate conflicts and to allocate resources according to these priorities. One such set of mechanisms was developed in the JBNQA to establish the priority accorded to native harvesting. The JBNQA contained several provisions intended to regulate present and future conflicts between use of the wildlife resource by natives and use by sport hunters and fishermen, outfitters, and commercial fishermen. One provision was intended to limit the extent of potential conflict, the second was to establish a mechanism to put into operation the priority of native harvesting over sport hunting and fishing, and the third was to design an outfitting regime that would provide an important degree of practical native control over aspects of non-native hunting and fishing activities.

In general, the agreement limits potential conflicts between native and non-native sport hunters and fishermen to the species for which non-native use had been established already and to geographical areas less essential for native use. It also eliminates existing conflicts in areas of primary interest around native settlements. The goal of these provisions was to set aside several general species and geographical areas for exclusive native use.

Several mechanisms for putting a native harvesting priority into practice were discussed during the negotiations. One mechanism guaranteed a harvest per native hunter. Another guaranteed the native peoples a percentage of the total kill of a species. A third guaranteed the native peoples a fixed level of harvest, if permitted by animal population levels. The first option was dropped early in discussions because it was unacceptable to governments. Preference for the third mechanism was based on two convictions: first, that most resources subject to competing use were nearly fully harvested at that time and secondly, that the most sensitive period for the maintenance of subsistence production occurs when game populations decline, either for natural reasons or because of development or over-hunting.

It was considered preferable to guarantee a fixed harvest that would effectively cut off sport hunting or fishing when animal populations declined and would reserve the entire available catch for the native peoples, rather than simply guarantee a fixed percentage of a declining kill while non-native hunting continued. In the periods when populations were low, this would assure native hunters of a higher harvest of a species than would the alternative formula, thereby protecting subsistence production during the period of greatest vulnerability. This option also would place the initial burden of development-induced declines in jointly used resources on non-native users. The fixed-level guarantee, however, was acceptable to the native peoples only when it was linked to the additional provisions that larger kills were possible when warranted by game populations and that allocations above the guaranteed level would be based on need.

Because it is impossible in practice to guarantee actual harvests over time, the mechanism finally adopted provides for the governments and native peoples to establish fixed, guaranteed levels of allocations to natives. These levels are to be based primarily on the results of a joint research project concerning native harvests of wildlife during a seven-year period (James Bay and Northern Québec Native Harvesting Research Committee (JBNQNHRC), 1982).[16] Once the guaranteed level is established, it will determine partly how the permissible kill in any one year will be allocated between native and non-native users. When the estimated permissible kill from a wildlife population in a given year is equal to, or less than, the guaranteed level, the entire kill will be allocated to the native peoples. When the permissible kill of a wildlife population in a year is higher than the guaranteed level, the native peoples will be allocated at least the guaranteed level; the balance of the permissible kill then will be divided between the native peoples and non-natives according to their needs, provided that some of the balance is allocated to the non-natives.

This mechanism for giving priority to native harvesting will provide a major means of controlling the actual kill by sport hunters and fishermen and of limiting the conflicts with native hunters. The mechanism will be used only when conflicting uses create a conservation problem. Furthermore, although quotas are given priority as the means of implementing allocations, other management techniques can be used in ways consistent with these principles.

Other areas of native concern, with respect to non-native hunting and fishing, were to have some effective influence over the times, places, and ways in which non-natives hunted, and assurance of a higher share for native peoples of the economic benefits produced from outfitting for sport hunters and fishermen. The outfitting provisions established in the hunting, fishing, and trapping regime, therefore, require the following: that the numbers of non-native hunters, and the times and places where they may hunt or fish, shall be regulated, and that outfitting shall be a principal means of that control; that as the number of outfitting facilities grows, non-native hunters and fishermen increasingly shall be required to use such facilities; that native peoples shall have a right of first refusal, which they may exercise in seven of ten cases, of new or transferred outfitting establishments, and that this right shall continue for 30 years, at the end of which its continuation shall be reviewed; that non-natives shall be required to use native guides to the extent that this is possible.

It was thought that this combination of measures could regulate and restrict conflicts between native and non-native users. In practice, the verdict is not in yet, but two items have become problematic—the lack of personnel and funds for policing non-natives around large development sites, and the tardiness of the governments in enforcing the provisions.

The compromise provisions of the JBNQA are based, in part, on the assumption that governments and the native peoples take the conservation of renewable resources as an important objective. To the extent that provisions of the agreement have not been implemented quickly or fully by responsible governments, and particularly by the provincial government, this reflects the fact that the government sometimes has ignored its responsibility for the conservation of the renewable resources of the territory, or has made it subsidiary to departmental political interests. This has occurred not only in interdepartmental conflicts, but also within the departments whose primary responsibilities are for renewable resources. To the extent that this can happen elsewhere, it would require a re-evaluation of the kinds of compromises that may be workable. In the James Bay case, it already has required legal action to enforce certain provisions of the agreement, and more may be required in the future. Legal and political action will test the defensibility of the agreement provisions.

Provision of Adequate Cash Incomes

Native peoples in the Canadian North who continue to depend extensively on renewable resources also have come to depend on complex, extensive, and direct interactions with the Canadian market economy. This aspect of renewable resource use is sometimes overlooked as a major arena of conflict between native and non-native societies.

Native peoples now depend on imports of some, although clearly not all, important and sometimes specialized components of their hunting technology, and materials to operate and maintain these components. They depend on the use of various commercial services, particularly in transportation and communications. They depend on use of imported foodstuffs to make up any difference between harvestable resources and the subsistence requirements of a growing population. All these imports require substantial annual cash incomes.

Cash incomes have come from several sources. Income from the sale of harvested products—of which furs are the most important—is highly unstable because prices respond to unpredictable variations in international economic cycles, as well as to style shifts. Government transfer payments, since the 1940s, have cushioned the effect of the unregulated market cycle on incomes, but have not always kept pace with rises in import outlays. As well, governments have attempted repeatedly to use dependence on transfer payments as a lever to force northern native peoples to comply with government development policies. Because these policies typically have either sought or assumed the demise of the harvesting economy, the effects, in most cases, have been detrimental to the support and maintenance of income from harvesting. Some important counter-examples can be cited, such as federal assistance for Inuit hunting camps and Québec assistance for the organization of Montagnais caribou hunts. Such programmes are increasing, but some insulation from the economic effects of changes in government administration and policy is required.

Several proposals have been made in this regard. Few have been put forward as single comprehensive solutions, but each of the following proposals has been offered as a possible component of a larger solution: new government bush camp programmes; rents on the use of, and participation in the development of, non-renewable resources; compensation for damages to wildlife; and guaranteed income security programmes.[17] Each of these proposals has its advantages and its potential weaknesses and probably a "mix" will be desirable in most cases.

The economic problems of hunting were addressed in the JBNQA sections dealing with the Income Security Program (ISP), a Cree Trappers' Association (CTA), and the compensation provision for a corporation to undertake compensatory and remedial works relevant to the effects of the first stage of the hydro-electric development, the La Grande Complex Remedial Works Corporation (SOTRAC) [la Société des travaux de correction du complexe La Grande]. ISP is the key provision here, intended to provide sufficiently generous cash payments to Cree hunters to reduce their dependence on fur prices in the world economy, and on government-controlled transfer payment programmes. Section 30.1.8 of the JBNQA states the objective of the ISP as follows:

> The program shall ensure that hunting, fishing and trapping shall constitute a viable way of life for the Cree people, and that

individual Crees who elect to pursue such a way of life shall be guaranteed a measure of economic security consistent with conditions prevailing from time to time.

The ISP could be used to accomplish this objective, however, only because it was integrated into the JBNQA, which contained the other provisions briefly cited above. The effectiveness of a cash payment to hunters depended on their possession of a right to hunt that could not be removed at the initiative of governments; it depended on a continued priority access to wildlife resources and on limiting the effects of sport hunters and fishermen; it depended on continuing Cree wildlife management; and it depended on regulation of the effects of future development.

The general effectiveness of ISP payments depends also on the availability of the goods, services, and infrastructure necessary for hunters to make effective use of the funds available to them. This is the role of SOTRAC and the CTA, within the framework of the agreement. These organizations, individually and jointly, can provide infrastructure in the forms of access routes, improved bush camps, and bush communication systems; also they can provide needed goods and services such as fur sales co-operatives, bulk-purchasing and distribution facilities, bush pick-up and delivery facilities, airplane dispatching services, and wildlife and harvest monitoring services. SOTRAC is funded by the James Bay Energy Corporation. The CTA has been funded by joint contributions from the governments of Québec and Canada and from the Cree themselves.

Without these provisions of the JBNQA, the ISP could not contribute effectively to reducing the dependency of Cree hunters on world economic conditions and government welfare policies. Even with these other provisions, it can only reduce, not eliminate, such dependencies.

The incorporation of ISP into the framework of the Cree claims settlement made it possible for the programme to be structured in such a way that it would limit some of the dependencies inherent in other transfer payment programmes. The costs of ISP—both programme benefit costs and administrative costs—were to be paid by Québec under the terms of the agreement. In this sense, the ISP is another transfer payment programme and it ran the risk of creating dependency of the kind experienced by the Cree under the previous welfare programmes—dependency on funds controlled by changing government policies and politics.

When the Cree negotiated the ISP as part of the JBNQA, they attempted to use the negotiations and the agreement itself to limit this kind of dependency. First, the ISP exists not only in the agreement but also in Québec law, which gives legislative force to the terms of that agreement.

The legislation is subject to parliamentary politics and discretion. However, because this legislation does not replace the agreement, because the agreement states that the legislation must reflect the provisions of the JBNQA, and because the agreement is a legally binding contract between the Cree and the governments of Québec and Canada, any change in the programme must involve changes in the agreement. Changes can be made only with Cree consent. Recourse in the event of a breach of this contract would be to the courts.

Secondly, unlike most welfare recipients, the beneficiaries of the ISP have the right to benefits from the ISP as long as they meet the fixed criteria for eligibility for the programme. The benefits to be paid are based on fixed criteria for calculating the amounts due. Beneficiaries can appeal to the ISP board or can take legal action if those rights are violated.

Thirdly, the ISP is not administered by the government that funds it, but by a separate corporate entity, the Cree Income Security Board, made up equally of Québec and Cree appointees, with a rotating chairmanship. The board hires and employs its own staff, although those hired may be civil servants if the board so decides. The obligation of the Québec government is to transfer the funds needed each year to the accounts of the ISP board. In practice, the board members and the staff are closely associated either with the Cree Regional Authority or with the Québec government, and the balance is and has been maintained. The board is therefore not bound by the full range of government administrative norms. It is given considerable authority to implement and, where necessary, to interpret and to review the ISP and its operations, in accordance with the legislation and the agreement.

Fourthly, the board operates out of a regional office, but it must maintain staff and offices in each Cree community to assure the beneficiaries of access to the administrators of the programme.

To summarize, the incorporation of the negotiations over the ISP within the framework of the comprehensive aboriginal and land-claims negotiations permitted integration of the ISP into the package of regimes, programmes, organizational structures, and benefits thought to be necessary to ensure the economic viability of hunting. It also made it possible to establish a programme that, although funded by government, is significantly independent of government policy and politics, is jointly controlled and administered by the government and representatives of the beneficiary population, and legally encodes the specific rights of the individual beneficiaries.[18]

Protection of Renewable Resources from the Effects of Non-renewable Resource Development

There is clearly no long-term future for renewable resource based economies in the Canadian North if there is not, in fact as well as in policy, a real priority given to renewable resources in the decisions about how non-renewable resources and land are used in the North. Unless rights to have and to use renewable resources can be given more political weight, the recent history of northern development is not very promising for the future. There has been an extensive series of government policy statements and regulatory regimes designed to afford protection to at least some components of northern ecosystems. We also have seen the development and, in many cases, the adoption of a range of tools to assist with the making of decisions and choices among various development objectives such as multiple-use planning, land-use planning, environmental and social impact assessment, and a plethora of others. Yet the history of northern development has shown that the key considerations in decisions concerning whether, where, and how projects and explorations have been undertaken have not been environmental considerations.

A series of investigations over the last decade has made it increasingly clear that policy statements and tools of decision making and administration have not been effective means to do more than moderate and, where possible, to remedy the effects of non-renewable resource developments.[19] We have not yet seen the political will, nor a sufficiently large lever, to alter the balance. On economic, ecological, and social grounds, I see reasons to believe that controlled development could be quite extensive and yet still be compatible with needed environmental protection, as well as be of potential benefit to native peoples in the North. An effective way to ensure the establishment of this balance has been elusive, however. This is an instance in which a short- or medium-term reconciliation may not be possible.

In this respect, the one positive note is that there may be time for basic circumstances to be changed, albeit at the cost of the particular regions and resources that already have been, or may soon be, damaged.

A two-fold approach is essential, one part of which aims at changing basic circumstances and interests, in the long term, and another part of which seeks to increase the moderating and remedial provisions attached to ongoing developments in the shorter term.

Under these conditions it is clear that significant damages caused by development will occur in the future in the North. The key issue facing native peoples is whether conditions for maintenance of a viable native hunting society might be maintained in the medium term despite these developments. I remain hopeful that these societies can be maintained for a considerable time, while the effort to establish a basic balance of interests between conservation and development continues.

Several types of provisions were negotiated in the JBNQA in an attempt to help Cree hunters to continue their activities and economy despite the effects of development. As I have already indicated, harvesting rights were recognized as exercisable wherever physically possible, subject to certain limited restrictions. This recognition ensured that the legal taking of land for development purposes would not, in itself, preclude use of the land. The key problem was the actual physical transformation of the land and its wildlife resources by development activity, and the effects of such transformations on harvesting activities. Future development was subjected to social and environmental impact assessment and to ongoing environmental quality review, but final decisions on developments rested with the responsible governments. This regime has not been strong enough yet to establish an effective balance between wildlife conservation and large-scale development interests.

To survive the effects of the reduction of wildlife populations that would accompany even regulated development, native peoples clearly needed access to other currently under-used wildlife resources.

In the James Bay area of Québec, despite the maintenance of an intensive modern hunting society, despite the fact that all land was being used on some regular and recurring basis, and despite the fact that populations of some species were harvested very intensively, there remained significant opportunities to intensify the use of some renewable resources. There were important limitations on these possibilities as well, including limited biological productivity, low harvesting efficiencies, high cash costs, and cultural acceptability. There was no clear basis for claiming that the under-used resources were fully equivalent in quality to those damaged, nor was there any assurance of their being equal in quantity to those that could be made unproductive by continued development in the long term. The need to provide immediate access to those wildlife resources that were available and were desired by the Cree was clear, however.

Access to alternative wildlife resources could be provided in several ways. In the case of those species for which there was a substantial kill by non-natives as well as a native kill, any reduction of population levels as a result of development activity in the territory would result in a consequent reduction in sustainable yields. Given the principles of priority and guaranteed level of allocation to native harvesting, the reduced allocation would influence first the total kill by non-natives. Thus, for certain key species, effects on the total native kill could be moderated by the operation of the guaranteed allocation of harvests and the principle of priority to native harvesting, at least in the initial phases. This procedure has not yet come into operation.

This buffer will work only at a group level, however. It will not reduce the effects on individual native hunters whose traplines are disrupted by development. For these hunters, alternative means of hunting must be provided even though such alternatives cannot replace the loss suffered by destruction of land on which a lifetime of knowledge and care has been vested. Further, not all species that would be affected adversely sustain high kills by non-natives.

One response to these effects on individual Crees was to establish the guaranteed annual income programme, which provided a payment indexed to rises in the cost of living for all Cree hunters for whom wildlife harvesting is a way of life. This programme was established, in part, to provide these hunters with the means to maintain, to modify, or to expand harvesting activities in changing circumstances. The additional funds made available to hunters could be used to finance travel to more distant or isolated wildlife resources, to improve the efficiency of harvesting by improving equipment, and to provide an increased level of security in the bush during a time of disruption caused by development. Complementary infrastructures and services could be provided by SOTRAC and the CTA.

To date, these provisions appear to have worked; between 1974–75 and 1978–79 no downward trends in total available weights of food from harvesting occurred in the affected Cree communities, although the effects of future hydro-electric and other resource developments create uncertainty for the future.[20] It also needs to be emphasized that the major renewable resources the Cree use are species that either are relatively localized (e.g., moose, beaver, non-anadromous fish), in which case the effects of development so far also have been localized, or they are migratory species, such as geese and smaller populations of caribou, whose patterns have been affected only marginally by the developments to date. Future developments may alter this relative insularity for the Cree, just as current developments elsewhere in the North clearly and directly threaten other important renewable resources and the native peoples who depend on them. Thus, specific immediate opportunities for resource maintenance in the face of ongoing development need to be explored and used, while longer term efforts to find effective resolutions in this area of fundamental conflict continue.

Conclusion

This discussion began with the premise that the maintenance and enhancement of relatively autonomous indigenous cultures is a comprehensible and justifiable objective for the native peoples of the Canadian North. I have ended on the question of its practical plausibility, and the linked question of the plausibility of retaining extensive renewable resources in viable ecological systems in the North. Clearly there are areas and peoples whose isolation and autonomy will survive for a long time. The vital question is whether this will be a result of the happenstances of non-renewable resource distributions, economic conditions, and indigenous tenacity and adaptability. Or, whether basic political processes eventually will lead to effective regulation of development, with the result that continued maintenance of indigenous communities and economies and of ecological systems can be widespread and can respond both to the intentions of the native peoples and to what some of us think should be a more balanced national interest. The survival of native societies and cultures does not mean that they will not change, nor that non-renewable resource development will not occur. It does presuppose a new political will based on the plausibility of creating balanced developments, on ideological justifications for such an outcome, and on effective legal and administrative levers to produce such an outcome. Such changes necessarily will involve greater control of development at the local and regional levels.

It is hard to envisage precisely how fundamental changes in the national, provincial, and territorial interests could be brought about, but this does not alter the problem. Historical analyses show that these long-term processes are always going on and must be occurring today, despite the fact that they are hard to perceive and to participate in effectively. A variety of open-ended initiatives and explorations is therefore needed. The changes that we know are desirable and possible may not come to fruition, but efforts to bring about these possibilities require that groups with diverse interests pursue them by a variety of means.

In summary, there are aspects of the conflicts over renewable resources in the Canadian North that are resolvable in the short and medium terms, primarily through recognition and enhancement of local control. Meanwhile, there are aspects of the conflicts that really send us back to look at the long-term processes and the means of political, economic, and cultural change in the national interests.

Endnotes

1. The research project results reported in this paper were funded by a Social Sciences and Humanities Research Council research grant, a Killam Post-doctoral Research Fellowship, and a Canada Council Doctoral Fellowship. Portions of the paper are drawn from previous publications. Attendance at the Third National Workshop was made possible by funding from the Department of Anthropology and the Faculty of Social Sciences, McMaster University, and by the Canadian Arctic Resources Committee.

2. See H. Feit, "The Future of Hunters within Nation States: Anthropology and the James Bay Cree," in *Politics and History in Band Societies*, B. Leacock and B. Lee, eds (Cambridge: Cambridge University Press, 1982), pp. 373-411, and M.I. Asch, "Dene Self-Determination and the Study of Hunter-Gatherers in the Modern World," in *Politics and History in Band Societies*, pp. 347-371.

3. See H. Feit, "Negotiating Recognition of Aboriginal Rights: History, Strategies and Reactions to the James Bay and Northern Québec Agreement," *Canadian Journal of Anthropology* 1:2, pp. 159-172; and R.F. Salisbury, "Formulating the Common Interest: The Role of Structures in Cree Development," in R. Merrill and D. Willner, eds, *The Common Interest*, in press.

4. *The James Bay and Northern Québec Agreement* (hereinafter, JBNQA), 11 November 1975 (Québec City: Éditeur officiel du Québec, 1976).

5. See H. Feit, "The Future of Hunters within Nation States: Anthropology and the James Bay Cree," in *Politics and History in Band Societies*, see above, note 2; and F. Berkes, "The Role of Self-regulation in Living Resources Management in the North," in M. M. R. Freemen, ed., *Proceedings: First International Symposium on Renewable Resources and the Economy of the North* (Ottawa: Association of Canadian Universities for Northern Studies; Canada Man and the Biosphere Program, 1981), pp. 143-160.

6. Peter J. Usher, "Sustenance or Recreation? The Future of Native Wildlife Harvesting in Canada," in M.M.R. Freeman, ed., *Proceedings: First International Symposium on Renewable Resources and the Economy of the North*, pp. 56-71. See above, note 5.

7. John B. Theberge, "Commentary: Conservation in the North—an Ecological Perspective," *Arctic* 34:4, pp. 281-285.

8. For reviews, see R.B. Lee and I. DeVore, eds, *Man the Hunter* (Chicago: Aldine, 1968); James N. Anderson, "Ecological Anthropology and Anthropological Ecology," in John J. Honigmann, ed., *Handbook of Social and Cultural Anthropology* (Chicago: Rand McNally, 1978), pp. 179-239; and John L. Bennett, *The Ecological Transition: Cultural Anthropology and Human Adaptation* (New York: Pergamon, 1976).

9. Frank G. Speck, "Family Hunting Territories and Social Life of Various Algonkian Bands of the Ottawa Valley" (Ottawa: Geological Survey, Department of Mines, Memoir 70, 1915); and "Family Hunting Band as the Basis of Algonkian Social Organization," *American Anthropologist* 17:2, pp. 289-305.

10. See Edward Rogers, "The Hunting Group—Hunting Territory Complex among the Mistassini Indians" (Ottawa: National Museum of Man of Canada, Bulletin 195); and Harvey A. Feit, "The Hunting Territory: A History of Debate" (in preparation).

11. See H. Feit, "The Ethno-ecology of the Waswanipi Cree—or How Hunters Can Manage Their Resources," in *Cultural Ecology: Readings on the Canadian Indians and Eskimos*, Bruce Cox, ed. (Toronto: McClelland and Stewart Limited, 1978), pp. 115-125; "Waswanipi Realities and Adaptations: Resource Management and Cognitive Structure," Ph.D. dissertation (Montréal: McGill University, Department of Anthropology, 1978); and "Decision-making and Management of Wildlife Resources: Contemporary and Historical Perspectives on Waswanipi Cree Hunting," paper prepared for a symposium on "Natural Management Systems," International Congress of Anthropological and Ethnological Sciences, Québec City, 14-17 August 1983, unpublished.

12. F. Berkes, "An Investigation of Cree Indian Domestic Fisheries in Northern Québec," *Arctic* 32:1, pp. 46-70; and "Fisheries of the James Bay Area and Northern Québec: A Case Study in Resource Management," in M.M.R. Freeman, ed., *Proceedings: First International Symposium on Renewable Resources and the Economy of the North*, pp. 143-160. See above, note 5.

13. F. Berkes, "Waterfowl Management and Northern Native Peoples with Reference to Cree Hunters of James Bay," *Musk-Ox* 30, pp. 23-35; and C. H. Scott, "The Semiotics of Material Life among Wemindji Cree Hunters," Ph.D. dissertation (Montréal: McGill University, Department of Anthropology, 1983).

14. H. T. Lewis, *A Time for Burning* (Edmonton: University of Alberta, Boreal Institute for Northern Studies, 1982), Occasional paper no. 17.

15. F. Berkes, "The Role of Self-regulation in Living Resources Management in the North." See above, note 5.

16. James Bay and Northern Québec Native Harvesting Research Committee, *The Wealth of the Land: Wildlife Harvests by the James Bay Cree, 1972-73 to 1978-79* (Québec: JBNQNHRC, 1982).

17. See T. R. Berger, *Northern Frontier Northern Homeland: The Report of the Mackenzie Valley Pipeline Inquiry*, vols 1 and 2 (Ottawa: Minister of Supply and Services Canada, 1977); M. Watkins,*Dene Nation—The Colony Within* (Toronto: University of Toronto Press, 1977); M. I. Asch, "Capital and Economic Development: A Critical Appraisal of the Recommendations of the Mackenzie Valley Pipeline Commission," *Culture* 2:3, pp. 3-9; Usher, "Property Rights: The Basis for Wildlife Management," 1983 (reproduced in this

volume); and H. Feit, "The Income Security Program for Cree Hunters in Quebec: An Experiment in Increasing the Autonomy of Hunters in a Developed Nation State," *Canadian Journal of Anthropology*, 1982.

18. See C. H. Scott, *Modes of Production and Guaranteed Annual Income in James Bay Cree Society* (Montréal: McGill University Programme in the Anthropology of Development, 1979); I. E. LaRusic, *The Income Security Program for Cree Hunters and Trappers: A Study of the Design, Operation, and Initial Impacts of the Guaranteed Annual Income Programme Established under the James Bay and Northern Québec Agreement* (Montreal: McGill University Programme in the Anthropology of Development, 1979).

19. See P. Usher and G. Beakhust, *Land Regulation in the Canadian North* (Ottawa: Canadian Arctic Resources Committee, 1973); M.M.R. Freeman and L. M. Hackman, "Bathurst Island, N.W.T.: A Test Case of Canada's Northern Policy," *Canadian Public Policy* 1, pp. 402-414; J. B. Theberge, "Commentary: Conservation in the North—An Ecological Perspective," *Arctic* 34:4, pp. 281-185; and H. Brody, *Maps and Dreams* (Harmondsworth: Penguin, 1981).

20. James Bay and Northern Québec Native Harvesting Research Committee, *The Health of the Land: Wildlife Harvests by the James Bay Cree, 1972-73 to 1978-79*, see above, note 16; and F. Berkes, "The Role of Self-regulation in Living Resources Management in the North," see above, note 5.

Inland Water Resources

Chairmen: Dixon Thompson
Glenn Warner

Introduction

An upcoming review of placer mining guidelines in the Yukon and proposed hydro-electric power developments on the Slave and the Liard rivers within the Mackenzie River system recently have made northern inland waters the focus of considerable debate. The hydro-electric developments themselves would be south of 60°—on the Slave River in Alberta and on the Liard River in British Columbia—but many of the environmental, social, and economic impacts would occur downstream in the Northwest Territories.

Proposed and actual developments like these have altered Canadians' perception of inland waters—particularly of northern inland waters—as a limitless resource. Inland waters are beginning to be recognized as a renewable resource that must be managed not only to assure human users of continuous and clean supplies, but also to protect the wildlife and habitats that this resource supports.

In the Yukon and the Northwest Territories, federal water boards are responsible for licensing and regulating water uses. These boards are pressing for greater autonomy from the federal Department of Indian Affairs and Northern Development and for authority to manage, as well as to regulate, water use. The territorial governments currently advise the water boards on water-use issues affecting wildlife resources; they hope eventually to expand their informal advisory role into formal responsibility for water-use planning and management.

Northern native peoples' organizations, too, are proposing new water management institutions in their land-claims negotiations. Native peoples want greater recognition from all levels of government of indirect uses of inland water resources. For example, many native northerners harvest wildlife that rely heavily on wetland habitats. This use of water is not licensed by water boards, and therefore is often discounted.

The Working Groups

The management of northern inland water resources involves many problems of jurisdiction. The Mackenzie River system, for example, is subject to control and regulation by federal government agencies, territorial water boards established by federal legislation, both territorial governments, and three provincial governments. Two water policy conferences held recently at the Banff School of Management have illustrated the need for agreements between jurisdictions on northern water resource management. Such agreements are likely to occur only after much negotiation; therefore, water resource development projects that could have major impacts on northern communities and the northern environment may proceed before these agreements are reached.

The working group included:

Chairmen: **Dixon Thompson**
Faculty of Environmental Design
University of Calgary

Glenn Warner
Northwest Territories Water Board
Yellowknife, N.W.T.

Rapporteur: **Rosemary Wallbank**
Corporate Policy
Department of Indian Affairs and Northern Development
Government of Canada
Ottawa, Ontario

Invited Participants:

Walter Bilawich
Department of Economic Development and Intergovernmental Relations
Government of the Yukon
Whitehorse, Yukon

William Case
Northwest Territories Water Board
Yellowknife, N.W.T.

Dennis Davis
Inland Water Directorate
Department of the Environment
Government of Canada
Regina, Saskatchewan

Adrian D'hort
Slave River Basin Coalition
Fort Smith, N.W.T.

Irving Fox
Smithers, British Columbia

The Working Groups

Allan Jones
Northern Renewable Resources Directorate
Department of Indian Affairs and Northern Development
Government of Canada
Ottawa, Ontario

M. Helene Laraque
Yellowknife, N.W.T.

Violet Mandeville
Fort Resolution, N.W.T.

Lloyd Norn
Dene Nation
Yellowknife, N.W.T.

Gary Sykes
Noval Technologies Ltd.
Calgary, Alberta

Carson Templeton
C.H. Templeton & Associates
Victoria, British Columbia

Background documents used in the working group, in addition to those published in these proceedings, included:

The Banff Centre School of Management. *Water Policy for Western Canada: The Issues of the Eighties*, ed., Barry Sadler. Proceedings of the Second Annual National Resource Conference, The Banff Centre, 9-12 September 1982. Calgary: The University of Calgary Press, 1982.

Fox, Irving K., Peggy J. Eyre, and Winston Mair. *Yukon Water Resources Management Policy and Institutional Issues*. Vancouver: Westwater Research Centre, University of British Columbia, 1983.

Mackenzie River Basin Committee. *Mackenzie River Basin Study Report*. 1981.

MacLeod, William. *Water Management in the Canadian North: The Administration of Inland Waters North of 60°*. Ottawa: Canadian Arctic Resources Committee, 1977.

Northern Inland Waters Act, Chapter 28 (1st Supp.). Northern Inland Waters Regulations, SOR/72-382, 18 September 1972. *Canada Gazette* part 2, vol. 106, no. 19.

Planning Division, Alberta Environment. *Water Resources Management Principles for Alberta*. No date.

Working Group Report

Inland Water Resources

In response to the first of the four questions posed by CARC—What are the national and regional interests in northern resources?—the working group on inland water resources identified the major uses of and levels of interest in inland water resources.

Uses of Inland Water Resources:

- biophysical (insects, fish, wildlife)
- recreational
- subsistence hunting, fishing, and trapping
- domestic water supply and waste disposal
- agricultural
- industrial water supply and waste disposal
- placer mining
- hydro-electric power generation, flood control, and river engineering
- navigation

Managers of Inland Water Resources:

- water users (individual and industrial)
- municipalities and communities
- regional bodies (e.g., the Slave River Development Impact Zone Society)
- provincial and territorial government departments (e.g., the Northwest Territories Department of Renewable Resources)
- interjurisdictional bodies (e.g., Mackenzie River Basin Committee, Yukon River Basin Committee)
- federally established bodies (e.g., Northwest Territories Water Board, Yukon Water Board)
- international bodies

In response to the second question by CARC—What are the conflicts and compatibilities between the interests?—the working group designed a matrix using the nine identified uses.

Conflicts and Compatibilities between Uses

	Biophysical	Recreational	Subsistence	Domestic	Agricultural	Industrial	Placer Mining	Hydro-electric Power	Navigation
Biophysical		+	+	-	-	x	x	x	+
Recreational			-	-	-	x	x	x	+
Subsistence				-	-	x	x	x	-
Domestic					-	x	-	-	-
Agricultural						-	-	-	-
Industrial							-	-	-
Placer Mining								-	x
Hydro-electric Power									x
Navigation									

Legend: + compatible
              - undetermined
              x conflict

Using this matrix, the working group determined that the main sources of conflict between uses of inland water resources are the impacts of industrial, placer mining, and hydro-electric power uses on biophysical, recreational, and subsistence uses.

The third question posed by CARC was: Can the identified conflicts be resolved? The working group on inland water resources drew the following conclusions concerning the three major sources of conflict between water resource uses.

The Working Groups

Industrial Water Uses

There has been a history of conflict between industrial water uses and biophysical, recreational, and subsistence uses. Conflicts between industrial and other water resource uses eventually could be resolved through regional and land-use planning, but action to resolve these conflicts should not be delayed until the northern land-use planning policy is implemented. The development impact zone (DIZ) concept also may be a useful mechanism for resolving water resource conflicts. Individuals and communities should discuss their concerns with the companies involved; companies using water resources should discuss the projects and possible impacts with communities that may be affected. These discussions should help to resolve some conflicts before the water boards begin formal project review processes.

Placer Mining

Placer mining cannot be accomplished without creating conflicts with other resource uses. Placer mining degrades streams used by fish and other wildlife, and therefore conflicts with recreational uses and the harvesting of renewable resources. These conflicts are most apparent in newly developed areas and, in many cases, are irreconcilable.

Legislation governing placer mining currently is inadequate to resolve conflicts between water uses. The upcoming review in the Yukon of the placer mining regulations may help to resolve some of the conflicts between uses, but politicians must recognize and resolve the conflicts in the relevant legislation.

Hydro-electric Power

Conflicts between river engineering projects such as hydro-electric power developments and biophysical, recreational, and subsistence uses are difficult to resolve at best and are often irreconcilable. Developments such as hydro-electric dams often flood wildlife and recreation areas, and create environments (lakes) that seldom are as productive as those that have been lost or damaged.

The final question posed by CARC was: How can the conflicts between resource uses be reconciled to improve resource management? The working group on inland water resources made the following recommendations:

- Conflicts in all types of water use could be resolved better through the dissemination of more comprehensible information; the improvement of users' responses to community concerns; and the increased accountability of decision makers to the users.

- Measures taken to resolve conflicts should use existing legislation and institutions to avoid unnecessary increases in bureaucracy.
- The federally appointed water boards for the Yukon and the Northwest Territories never have used the Northern Inland Waters Act fully to set priorities for water uses. Recognition by the water boards and other water resource managers of biophysical, recreational, and subsistence uses is essential in setting priorities.
- The Slave River Basin Coalition should present its concerns about downstream impacts of the Slave River Dam directly to TransAlta Utilities Corporation and Alberta Power Ltd. An independent body should identify alternative means of satisfying the demand for electricity and assess the alternatives for decision makers.
- Unsettled land claims and the undefined nature of the Constitution's new provisions for aboriginal rights complicate the resolution of water-use conflicts, for native peoples eventually may control some northern water resources as well as lands through ownership or management responsibilities. These factors should be settled as quickly as possible.
- Residents of northern communities have valid concerns about inland water resource issues and how conflicts will be resolved. The devolution of authority and accountability to the regional and local levels of government will improve the ability of decision makers to find solutions that satisfy northern communities. It is inappropriate, for example, that the federal minister of Indian Affairs and Northern Development is responsible for municipal water uses in northern communities. Water boards should not be accountable to federal officials, but instead to elected officials in the North.
- Research is required to determine the cumulative effects of hydro-electric power development. There is concern among northern residents and other individuals that these developments may be causing environmental destruction by small increments.
- Research also is required to make known the environmental implications of licensing water uses according to the "total loading" capacity of a water resource, that is, its ability to support and assimilate various water uses fully.

The Working Groups

Bearing in mind the theme of the Third National Workshop—national and regional interests in northern resource development—the working group on inland water resources recognizes the importance of a clear and workable mechanism for resolving conflicts between jurisdictions, particularly in the Mackenzie River system. The working group endorses the recommendations of the Mackenzie River Basin Committee and the Agenda for Action prepared by the Banff Centre water policy conference, 26-29 May 1983 (see pp. 473-474 and 475-476 in this volume).

Statement by Chief Johnny Charlie of Fort Mcpherson Re: Slave River Dam– Mackenzie River Water Levels

As told to M. Helene Laraque
14 December 1982

The water is down on the Mackenzie River. A few years back, in the early sixties, we used to get high waters in the spring, when all the lakes used to flood, and this was good for the muskrats. But by that time, I guess, they put up the Bennett Dam on the Peace River, so every year the water seems to be going down more. We don't get the flood anymore, except for last spring. I don't know what happened.

Down in Arctic Red [River], I fished there every fall except this fall. Four years ago I set nets there in September and I hammered these sticks in for nets. The next year I went back, the water was about three to four feet below that stick from the last year. Now, this fall I went back, it was pretty near 15 feet lower than what it used to be four years ago. Maybe the Water Board knows this but they won't tell the people. They'll say, "Sure, the water level is the same every year." But it's not.

Now they're talking about working the Sans Sault Rapids. They're talking about damming the Slave River. Well, it's going to affect the Fort Smith people and all the way down along the Mackenzie, right down to the delta. It's going to affect the trappers. The government is not worried about the trappers.

We need the water. So if there's no water, that means more lakes dry out in the delta, which will affect trappers in the delta. So this is why we just wish that it won't happen.

I'm not against development because there are a lot of young people who make their living off working for companies, oil companies, but what we would like to see and what we are fighting for is this: Let's settle the land claims. Let's settle this land for the Dene and the Métis Association together and then go ahead with development if they still want to go through with it. But this is what the government doesn't like. They don't want to develop it after they settle the claims because they're going to be cutting through our land and that's going to cost them a lot of money. But right now they're cutting it up, it doesn't cost them anything because [the claims are] not settled.

Statement of Mrs Helen Cheezie
of Fort Smith (mother of 15)

As told to M. Helene Laraque
April 1983

We don't want a dam. No way! They took the land of the people of the North. That's enough. They should leave us alone now. I know many people in Alberta. They don't want to see changes in the Mackenzie. We don't need it.

White people should find other ways. When they found oil in MacMurray a lot of ducks died. The people lost a lot. They don't want to see these things happen here. If they build a dam, the fish and the animals will die, will be gone. Close [dam] the river—no good. They will kill a lot of animals. A lot of people will die too. What will we live on?

People who want the dam, they're born outside [the North]. Indians never trouble white people. They just want to leave everything alone the way it is. I want to talk for the people of the North because I too am born in the North. I want to help my people in the North. I will pray for this. Only God is boss. Good luck to all the people in the North.

Mackenzie River Basin Study
Report: Recommendations

A report under the 1978-81
Federal-Provincial Study Agreement
respecting the water and related resources
of the Mackenzie River Basin

Mackenzie River Basin Committee, 1981

1. It is recommended that the jurisdictions at an early date conclude an agreement through which trans-boundary water management issues such as minimum flows, flow regulation, and water quality can be addressed at jurisdictional boundary crossing points in the Mackenzie River Basin, and which establishes a permanent board to implement the provisions of the agreement.
2. It is recommended that the proposed integrated long-term network of hydrometric, snow, meteorologic, sediment, and water quality stations outlined in this report be implemented.
3. It is recommended that precipitation, streamflow, and lake levels be evaluated for the entire basin to determine variability over time and space, and that the relationships among all parts of the water budget be analyzed and modelled.
4. It is recommended that the computer model of the river system developed in this study be continually refined and updated as additional hydrometric data are collected and as changes occur on the river system.
5. It is recommended that the monitoring and analysis of the processes involved in spring breakup and sediment transport in selected streams in the Liard River Subbasin be continued until several high-flow years have been documented, and that the study area be extended to include the Mackenzie River from Fort Simpson to its mouth.
6. It is recommended that a comprehensive study of the Mackenzie Delta be undertaken to determine the relationships among the processes of delta change; and the vegetation, fish, and wildlife resources; and the hydrologic regime.
7. It is recommended that each jurisdiction in the Mackenzie River Basin, when considering a project proposal, follow an environmental assessment process that accommodates the interests in other jurisdictions in an equitable manner.

The Working Groups

8. It is recommended that the program of abstracting documents regarding water and related resources in the Mackenzie River Basin for entry in the national water document data base (WATDOC) be continued.
9. It is recommended that the jurisdictions recognize the increasing level of interest in the resources of the Mackenzie River Basin and ensure that any new information on the resources and their development is made available to each other and to the public in a timely fashion.

Reprinted with kind permission of the Mackenzie River Basin Committee.

Water Policy for Western Canada
Agenda for Action

The Banff Centre
School of Management
26-29 May 1983

Major water developments are under consideration for the Mackenzie River System that could seriously affect natural systems water use and rights within and across jurisdictional boundaries. Some preliminary bilateral discussions at the officials level are already underway;

We call upon the six governments involved in this shared resource, to move, as a matter of urgency, to implement the key recommendation of the Mackenzie River Basin Committee's study report and conclude a formal agreement or compact on the cooperative management of the water resource. Such an agreement would cover trans-boundary issues, such as flow regime and water quality at the jurisdictional crossing points of the Mackenzie system, and would establish a permanent agency to implement the provisions of the agreement. It would involve a commitment to a framework of goals and principles on future coordination.

The basic objective of the agreement would be to provide an umbrella under which the specific details on interjurisdictional coordination could be worked out in a way that preserves the rights and responsibilities of the participating governments, while recognizing the broader regional and national interest created by the interdependencies of natural systems use and management. A task force with representation from each of the jurisdictions should be formed to prepare and recommend to the governments an agreement incorporating the following *general principles*:

1) Wise stewardship, to ensure socio-economic development that is consistent with maintaining the productivity of the resource for future generations;
2) Fair use and enjoyment of the resource;
3) Recognition of native and other resident rights, entitlements, and interests, and encouragement of their understanding and participation;

4) Recognition that a coordinated approach to management involves reconciliation of upstream and downstream interests;
5) Recognition and conservation of the special bio-physical regimes of the basin.

At the earliest stage, there should be agreement on coordination and funding of the needed studies identified in the Mackenzie River Basin Committee study report.

The agreement should establish a board to implement the interjurisdictional agreement on the Mackenzie River Basin. Its functions should include the following:

a) Act as the vehicle for policy coordination and exchange of information among the member agencies;
b) Serve as mechanism for resolving trans-boundary issues through review and recommendations to the governments concerned;
c) Promote consistency with the umbrella agreement in on-going bilateral negotiations;
d) Provide for public consultation in decision making.

The board should be provided with the necessary resources for effective implementation of the agreement and discharging related functions, including technical support and assistance. To these ends, *we recommend* that the responsible ministers meet as soon as possible in 1983 to agree on a program of action leading to the establishment of an umbrella agreement.

We believe the urgency of the situation dictates the conclusion of such an agreement by the end of 1984.

Reprinted with kind permission of the Banff Centre School of Management.

Position Paper On
Resource Development

Slave River Basin Coalition

The Slave River Basin Coalition is a group of individual citizens and organizations that formed in response to proposed megahydro development in the South Slave region. Because of the territory-wide implications of this proposed development, and also because of our concern about resource development and political development in general throughout the Northwest Territories, we have a genuine interest in this discussion.

The stated goal of our contribution is to "identify pragmatic policy alternatives that will accommodate the growing demands of northerners for greater control while respecting the interests of all Canadians in the orderly development of northern resources." To us this goal implies the assumption that the accommodation of northerners' struggle for autonomy may not be compatible with the interests of all Canadians in the orderly development of our resources. It also reiterates the theme of provincial status for the Northwest Territories. Let us remember that the resources that we are discussing belong to the peoples of the N.W.T. and that this area can no longer be regarded as a grab bag of mineral wealth from which the provinces can draw.

The Slave River Basin Coalition takes as its basic position on issues concerning the management of resource development that full control of all management of, and benefits from, the resources must be assumed by the Government of the Northwest Territories (GNWT) as soon as possible. The move toward provincial status and full responsibility for resource management must be escalated. Only with full territorial responsibility for the management of our resources can we be assured that impending development will be in the interests of the citizens of the North and the rest of Canada. It is not in the interest of Canada to permit irresponsible exploitation of the North. We, as citizens of the North, to whom the consequences of irresponsible development must accrue, are the best ones to judge how our resources should be used.

The Working Groups

The position of the Slave River Basin Coalition on policy initiatives regarding the development of territorial autonomy in jurisdiction over resources is as follows:

1. We support GNWT initiatives to legislate and to implement its Resource Development Policy provided that the policy be amended to enable the GNWT to exercise complete control over resource management issues. The policy must, however, have more public input before it is legislated in its final form and we wish to contribute suggestions as to those amendments.
2. We call for the repeal or amendment of Bill C-48 to enable the GNWT to assume full control over, and to gain the full benefits of, resource development.
3. We support a continued lessening of the role of the commissioner of the Northwest Territories, and increasing political autonomy for the N.W.T., with the goal of full provincial status before 1990.
4. We support speeding up the transfer to the GNWT of jurisdiction over resource management and lessening the role of federal agencies such as the Department of Indian Affairs and Northern Development.
5. We support a commitment by the Government of Canada to continue negotiating land claims with the goal of achieving a prompt and equitable conclusion. Although we recognize that resource ownership and management issues are complicated by outstanding land claims, we do not see this as a legitimate or insurmountable obstacle to the transfer of resource jurisdiction to the GNWT in the interim.
6. We support the style of self-government as outlined in the Denendeh proposal [*Our Land: Public Government for the People of the North*] and call for more public consultation and participation in the policy decisions of the GNWT.
7. We support, as a priority of both the GNWT and the Government of Canada, the establishment of Nunavut, with full provincial status accruing to both jurisdictions to follow.
8. We call for the immediate establishment of a Mackenzie River Basin Water Board, similar in mandate to the Prairie Provinces Water Board. We assert that this board must be established prior to the consideration of any further developments affecting water quality and the hydrologic regime in the basin.

On Controlling Environmentally Sensitive Areas

Land under the Territorial Parks Ordinance is only "set aside" for park purposes, yet the right to dispose of any surface rights, to use or to occupy the surface of the land, or to conduct any business, commercial enterprise, or industry remains with the federal government. We note a needless duplication of effort here, however, as the commissioner of the Northwest Territories also may make territorial regulations regarding the uses on the same lands and may control the use and development of resources in a territorial park.

At this stage in the evolution of northern land-use administration, we consider that it is unnecessary to continue the duplication of administrative services now provided by the federal and territorial governments in matters of land administration except for national park lands. In federal–territorial and federal–provincial matters of study, recommendation, or resource development, our position is both comprehensive and integrative.

First, we believe that northerners must be included more effectively in the heritage rivers process, or any process affecting the resources in their lands, and we attach great significance to the fact that the heritage rivers proposal should include:

- participation by citizens as well as civil servants on heritage rivers committees
- opportunities for citizens or public-interest groups to nominate heritage rivers
- non-reversible designation of heritage rivers
- federal–provincial or federal–territorial co-operation in integrated planning of the entire watershed related to a potential heritage river
- effective enforcement processes and follow-up after designation.

Secondly, federal jurisdiction over environmentally significant areas such as the Peace–Athabasca, Slave, and Mackenzie river deltas is to be protectively legislated and enforced because these areas fit into a continental perspective. They are not, therefore, to be impaired or altered on a local, regional, or provincial level. At present, the Peace–Athabasca Delta protection is not seriously enforced, as one can see from B.C. Hydro's impairment of that delta's water quality and flow.

The Public's Role

Although we endorse the establishment of the two land-use committees, we believe that the public should take an active role in each.

a. Land-use advisory committees at present include as members only representatives of the Department of the Environment, the Department of Indian Affairs and Northern Development, and N.W.T. hierarchies. We feel that these committees should include citizens as members and the actual forwarding of nominations and designations of lands for specific use. Such citizens can be found in community and hamlet councils, band councils, trappers' associations, or public-interest research groups.

b. The Territorial Parks Committee has pseudo citizen participation, similar to the land-use advisory committees or heritage rivers proposal system. It examines only proposals for the establishment of territorial parks that have originated within the bureaucracy rather than from the citizenry. It is therefore our position that citizens be encouraged to contribute to making land-use decisions that must include:

- control of policy
- control of conduct (enforcement)
- hiring and administration by a policy board of citizens who depend heavily on the scientist–technician to describe systematically, and in a usable form, the capability and limitations of the land base.

Ocean Management

Chairman: J.M. Harrison

Introduction

In the last decade, petroleum exploration in the Canadian Arctic has been concentrated offshore and in the arctic islands. For the next two decades, proposed hydrocarbon development on the polar continental shelf will involve offshore drilling and production, year-round tanker traffic, and ports and harbours on the arctic coast. In northern coastal communities, current offshore exploration projects are creating opportunities for economic and social change. They are also provoking concerns about how the development of oil and gas will affect other natural resources and emphasizing the urgent need for public policies and management programmes to protect the arctic marine environment and conserve marine resources. As industrial, scientific, and military activities in these waters increase, so will the need for comprehensive national and international policies for ocean management.

There is currently a lack of a systematic effort in Canada to understand and address the domestic and international policy implications of issues such as accelerating offshore exploration, the need for co-ordinated scientific and technological research, Inuit claims to the offshore, changes in the international law of the sea, and proposals for year-round arctic marine transportation. In 1982, the Canadian Arctic Resources Committee (CARC) established the Arctic Ocean Programme in response to the many emerging issues of law, policy, and management relating to development in the Arctic Ocean.

As part of the Arctic Ocean Programme, background studies were undertaken on the following topics: the current ocean policy-making process in Canada; the new United Nations Convention on the Law of the Sea; Inuit use of the offshore; marine transportation; and ocean management. These studies were discussed in the working group on ocean management at CARC's Third National Workshop. The working group brought together members of the Arctic Ocean Programme Advisory Committee and other invited participants to discuss the background studies and arctic marine science and technology.*

*The proceedings of the working group on ocean management were published previously in *Ocean Policy and Management in the Arctic*. Ottawa: Canadian Arctic Resources Committee, 1984.

The working group included:

Chairman: **J.M. Harrison***
Science Advisory Board of the Northwest Territories
Ottawa, Ontario

Rapporteur: **Ken Beauchamp**
Director, Arctic Ocean Programme
Canadian Arctic Resources Committee
Ottawa, Ontario

Invited Participants:

Randy Ames*
Tungavik Federation of Nunavut
Ottawa, Ontario

Nigel Bankes
Canadian Institute of Resources Law
University of Calgary

Robert Burchill*
Legal Operations Division
Department of External Affairs
Government of Canada
Ottawa, Ontario

R. McV. Clarke*
Arctic Resource Assessment Section
Freshwater Institute
Department of Fisheries and Oceans
Government of Canada
Winnipeg, Manitoba

Murray Coolican*
Peters, Coolican & Associates Ltd.
Halifax, Nova Scotia

Harriet Critchley*
Northern Political Studies Program
University of Calgary

The Working Groups

R. Davis*
LGL Limited
Toronto, Ontario

William DuBay
North Slope Borough
Anchorage, Alaska

Gerry Glazier*
Petro-Canada
Calgary, Alberta

Peter Jull
Ottawa, Ontario

Cynthia Lamson
Dalhousie Ocean Studies Programme
Halifax, Nova Scotia

Hal Mills*
Halifax, Nova Scotia

Allen R. Milne*
Environmental Management
Sidney, British Columbia

A.E. Pallister*
Pallister Resource Management Ltd.
Calgary, Alberta

R.J. Paterson
Department of Fisheries and Oceans
Government of Canada
Ottawa, Ontario

Everett B. Peterson*
Western Ecological Services (BC) Ltd.
Sidney, British Columbia

T.C. Pullen*
Ottawa, Ontario

E.F. Roots*
Science Adviser
Department of the Environment
Government of Canada
Ottawa, Ontario

Judy Rowell
Labrador Inuit Association
Dartmouth, Nova Scotia

Omond Solandt
Bolton, Ontario

Wayne Speller
Petro-Canada
Calgary, Alberta

Carol Stephenson*
Coast Guard Northern
Department of Transport
Government of Canada
Ottawa, Ontario

*Member of CARC's Arctic Ocean Programme Advisory Committee

Working Group Report

Ocean Management

The ocean management working group discussions were based on six topics of arctic marine policy:

- the state of national ocean policy making
- international law and diplomacy
- Inuit interests in the offshore
- marine science policy
- marine transportation
- ocean management.

The theme throughout these discussions was comprehensive management of the Arctic Ocean and the co-ordination of government policies for the arctic region and its resources as a single, comprehensive Arctic Ocean policy.

National Ocean Policy Making

Canada must be able to make and implement ocean policy if it is to manage the arctic offshore effectively. The current policy-making process is inadequate.

Responsibility for ocean policy making in Canada currently is divided among many federal government departments and agencies. Each department makes marine policies to meet its own needs. The mandates of departments overlap and, although many interdepartmental co-ordinating committees have been established, departmental activities are poorly co-ordinated. A central policy-making system is needed to provide a more comprehensive view of marine activities in and uses of the Arctic Ocean so that management priorities can be determined.

No single department has a mandate to or is able to assume this role now. A Cabinet-level body, such as the Arctic Ocean policy council proposed by Hal Mills, could be created to co-ordinate ocean policies and direct the overall ocean policy-making process [See Hal Mills, "Ocean Policy Making in the Canadian Arctic," pp. 491–527 in this volume]. The proposed council would be made up of civil servants and other knowledgeable persons from outside government and would report to the federal Cabinet rather than to a department. The working group participants expressed two main concerns about establishing such a council: first, it would add one more committee to the existing number. Secondly, Cabinet would continue to avoid making policy choices because of the changing circumstances of arctic ocean development and the perpetual desire of decision makers for more information than is available.

Participants were frustrated with the inertia of the federal government in implementing schemes to integrate ocean policy making. Pressure from the public or from an external source such as a competing coastal state is needed for the federal government to act. An appropriate way for the public to influence decision makers and to convey the need for a comprehensive Arctic Ocean policy is through existing forums such as the Nunavut Constitutional Forum and land-claims negotiations. Prompt action is important because offshore development is taking place now without the necessary management process in place.

International Legal Issues

Official statements on the extent of Canadian claims in the arctic offshore are unclear. Canada's claim to internal waters in the Northwest Passage and arctic islands should be made formally through legislation. The occupation of the region by Inuit throughout history supports Canada's claim to sovereignty in these waters.

Canada must develop icebreakers that can occupy and control the use of Canada's arctic waters in support of its claims. The resolution of offshore claims is important if Canada is to take the lead in formulating a comprehensive policy for development and management in the arctic offshore.

Inuit Interests in the Offshore

Greater Inuit involvement in arctic marine management and policy making was a major concern of the working group. Many government agencies do not take the idea of Inuit involvement in offshore management seriously. Inuit are not merely a special-interest group; they possess aboriginal rights based on traditional use and occupancy of the arctic marine region. Inuit are not asking for total control in the offshore, but for a meaningful share in the decision-making process. The arctic marine environment should be managed not only in the national interest, but also for the benefit of persons living on the coast and using the waters. The federal government's acknowledgement of the Inuit interest in this region and its resources would allow Inuit to live as equal members of Canadian society.

Inuit are in a good position to take a leading role in some areas of ocean management—for example, management of marine mammals. The federal Department of Fisheries and Oceans is not ready to give up any of its authority for decision making, however, and prefers an advisory or consultative role for Inuit.

The impacts of shipping on their use of the land-fast ice is an important concern of Inuit. Both the federal government and Inuit can benefit from shared management of the land-fast ice—a region Inuit use for winter hunting and travelling. Some participants felt that it would not be possible for Inuit to have any authority for managing vessel traffic in the Arctic because activities that are related to national sovereignty and defence cannot be subject to local control. Other participants felt that native peoples can be involved in this decision-making process without limiting federal authority.

A comprehensive system of regional planning would give Inuit an active role in offshore and coastal zone management. Establishing an Inuit policy-making council that is linked to a similar federal government council may be another useful way to involve Inuit. Inuit and the federal government must consider how management of activities in and resources of the Arctic Ocean can be shared.

Arctic Marine Science Policy

Studies of arctic marine science policy and northern science policy have reached many of the same conclusions: there are serious gaps in baseline data; there is no systematic co-ordination of research; there is no effective means of disseminating information; and there never are sufficient funds.

The working group moved its discussion beyond these conclusions and identified three primary objectives of an arctic science policy:

- to conduct research in the interest of and for the benefit of persons living and working in the Arctic
- to involve northern residents, particularly Inuit, in research projects
- to assess research priorities according to the objectives rather than according to what is urgent.

Calling for more data has become a habit; the data now available could be used better. Good monitoring techniques for arctic activities would be more useful than more physical and biological inventories.

The primary reasons for carrying out arctic marine science are: to demonstrate sovereignty; to support national defence; to support resource development; to support transportation of supplies and resources; and to satisfy the "need to know." Those who sponsor and conduct arctic scientific research have a dismal record in involving northerners in activities other than consultation. Native peoples should be given the opportunities to apply their knowledge in setting priorities, doing research, and interpreting scientific data. An Arctic Ocean policy must enable northerners to contribute to research objectives.

Canadians should be concerned that other nations are preparing to provide the technology and transportation systems that will be needed to support Canadian oil and gas development in the arctic offshore. Increased research and the use of northern skills in resource development may be required if Canada is to compete sucessfully for its own business.

Arctic Marine Transportation

Conflicts between the residents of communities on the arctic coast are inevitable when year-round shipping begins in the Arctic. Mariners' traditional freedom to select routes will have to be modified by vessel management schemes for the safety of ships and to protect the environment and resources used by native peoples. Safe shipping in arctic waters will require a sophisticated traffic management system. This system need not add to existing regulations controlling arctic shipping; it should simplify the regulatory process. The involvement of Inuit in decisions about arctic transportation will not require creating additional authorities to control shipping activities; the powers necessary for their participation exist now in legislation such as the Arctic Waters Pollution Prevention Act (AWPPA). Neither the shipping nor the local (Inuit) interests can continue to take positions that are unwaveringly opposed. When offshore development in the Arctic proceeds, these groups will have to co-operate to determine acceptable routes for vessels.

Ocean Management

The new United Nations Convention on the Law of the Sea provides an opportunity for coastal states to implement national ocean management plans by extending coastal state jurisdiction offshore for specific uses. A comprehensive ocean management system must treat the marine environment as a single system in which resources, human activities, and administrative arrangements are closely related. In developing an ocean management programme, Canada must consider international law and its responsibilities to other circumpolar nations, as well as to the international community. Other nations are watching to see that Canada deals with the arctic offshore in a way that is consistent with its international obligations.

The working group endorsed the principles formulated at the Environmental Science Workshop for the Lancaster Sound Region organized by CARC in 1979, and drafted the following statement of principle for managing the arctic marine environment:

> The Arctic Ocean and adjacent waters have distinctive physical and biological characteristics that have important and dynamic influences on world climate and the economic and social activities of all northern nations. The arctic marine area contains resources that promise to be important to world economy and commerce, and its ecosystems constitute a sensitive world resource that is vital to northern peoples. Circumpolar nations have an obligation, as individual sovereign states and as members of the international community, to manage their activities in arctic marine areas in accordance with the World Conservation Strategy and in the interests of human safety, environmental quality, and optimum long-term benefit from all resources.

The participants defined "ocean management" as:

> comprehensive and systematic planning for the conservation and development of marine resources and the ordering of human activities in a way that is economically and environmentally acceptable in the national and regional interests and consistent with international rules and responsibilities.

The working group on ocean management concluded that a comprehensive approach to ocean management was not likely to be adopted in Canada until decision makers find it politically expedient to do so.

Ocean Policy Making in the Canadian Arctic

Hal Mills
Marine Policy Consultant

Introduction

Canada does not have an integrated Arctic Ocean policy. Policy making does occur, and policy elements can be identified, but it occurs in an *ad hoc*, fragmented fashion. This may have been acceptable in the past, but the current pace of development in the circumpolar North is such that it will no longer do. Within Canada, proposed activities such as the Arctic Pilot Project, oil and gas production in the Beaufort Sea, drilling in Lancaster Sound, and the prospect of year-round use of the Northwest Passage by ice-breaking supertankers are posing real hazards to the marine environment, the renewable resources, and the Inuit way of life. If guiding principles to chart future directions are not developed, Inuit and other Canadians could suffer unnecessarily damaging consequences. Without an integrated Arctic Ocean policy, we may choose the wrong options and foreclose the right options.

The term "policy making" refers to the statements, regulations, and actions that involve a choice between different courses of action. Policy making requires establishing principles, goals, and objectives. In the absence of a formal policy, however, a policy can be the result of a series of decisions or actions. Having an integrated Arctic Ocean policy will require definition of policy principles, establishment of priorities, formation of links between policy-making bodies, and development of a mechanism for implementing the policy.

The terms "Arctic Ocean" and "arctic waters" are used broadly to describe all non-inland waters in the North including the Arctic Ocean proper, the Beaufort Sea, waters between the arctic islands, Hudson Bay, Hudson Strait, Baffin Bay, Davis Strait, and the Labrador Sea. These marine areas are normally ice covered for much of the year and are adjacent to land occupied by Inuit.

Canadian arctic waters extend offshore to the 200-nautical-mile limit of the exclusive economic zone, and to offshore boundaries between Canada and Greenland and between Canada and the United States north of Alaska and the Yukon Territory (see Map 1). The boundary between Canada and Greenland in Nares Strait, Baffin Bay, and Davis Strait has been settled; however, the extension of this boundary into the Lincoln Sea and the Canada–U.S.A. boundary through the Beaufort Sea are in dispute. The marine areas traditionally used and occupied by Canadian Inuit are shown on Map 2.

The Present Regulatory Structure

Roles of Key Federal Departments

Administration of the uses of Canada's arctic marine waters and their resources lies almost entirely within the purview of federal departments and agencies. Although the territorial governments have some authority to regulate offshore activities, they do not play key roles.

The Department of Indian Affairs and Northern Development (DIAND), under the Department of Indian Affairs and Northern Development Act, has jurisdiction over the resources and affairs of the Northwest Territories and the Yukon Territory, and is responsible for co-ordinating federal activities and implementing policies and programmes for social, economic, and political development and protection of the northern environment. DIAND is responsible for land statutes, and, with federal Cabinet approval, for implementing a northern land-use planning programme for lands that include marine areas out to the legal limits of the continental shelf. DIAND also is responsible for non-shipping provisions of the Arctic Waters Pollution Prevention Act. These provisions forbid the unauthorized deposition of wastes into arctic waters. Through the Canada Oil and Gas Lands Administration (COGLA) and in co-operation with the Department of Energy, Mines and Resources (EMR), DIAND administers hydrocarbon resources on Canada lands pursuant to the Canada Oil and Gas Act and the Oil and Gas Production and Conservation Act, except in Hudson Bay and Hudson Strait where EMR has this responsibility.

The Department of Fisheries and Oceans (DFO), under the 1979 Government Organization Act, is responsible for sea-coast and inland fisheries, hydrography, and marine science, and for the co-ordination of policies and programmes for oceans. Under the Fisheries Act, DFO is responsible for the protection of fish and marine mammal resources and their habitats and, where necessary, for controlling the harvest of species. The department is responsible for conducting hydrographic surveys and

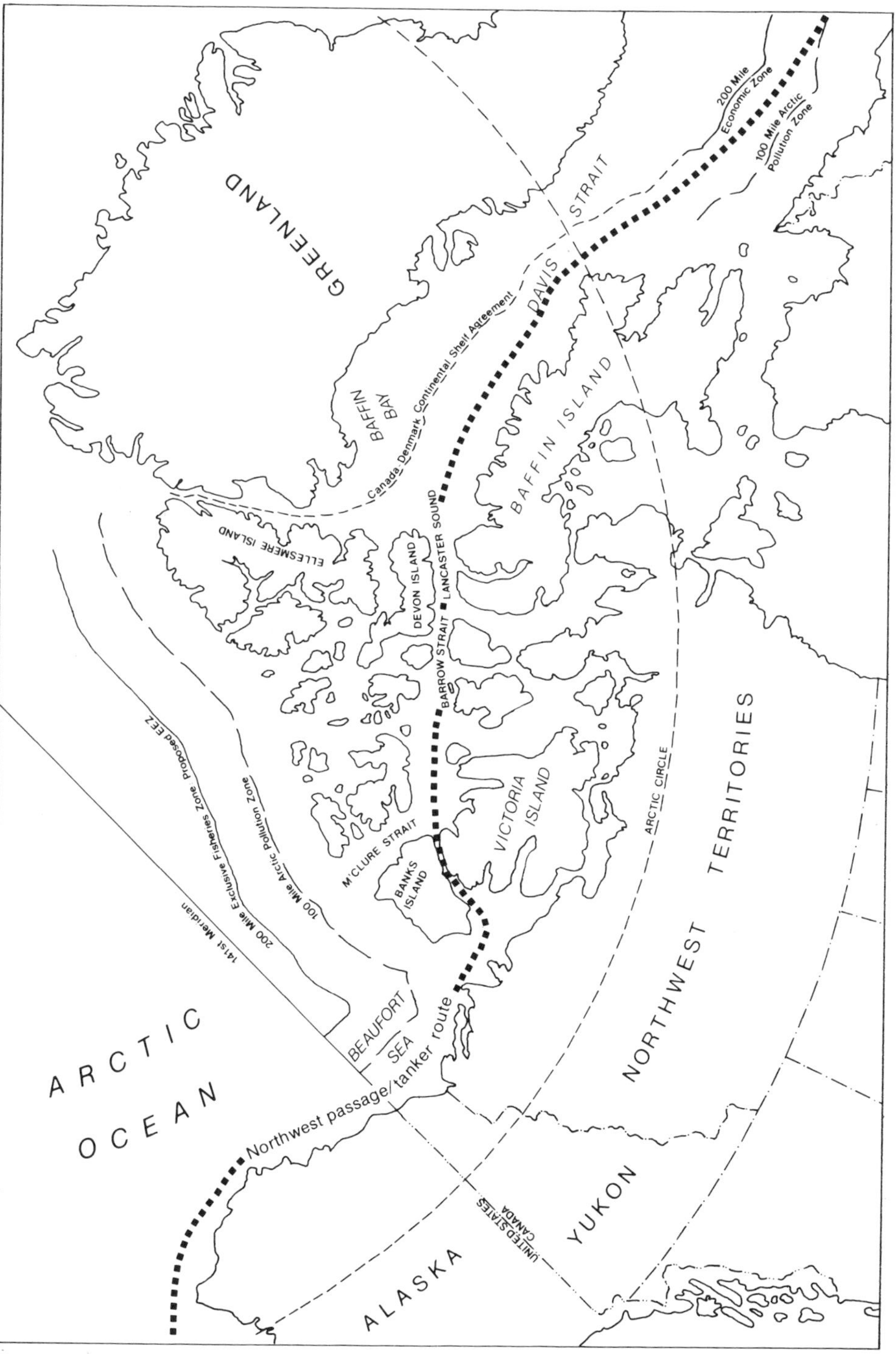

Map 1   Extent of Canada's Offshore Jurisdiction in Arctic Waters

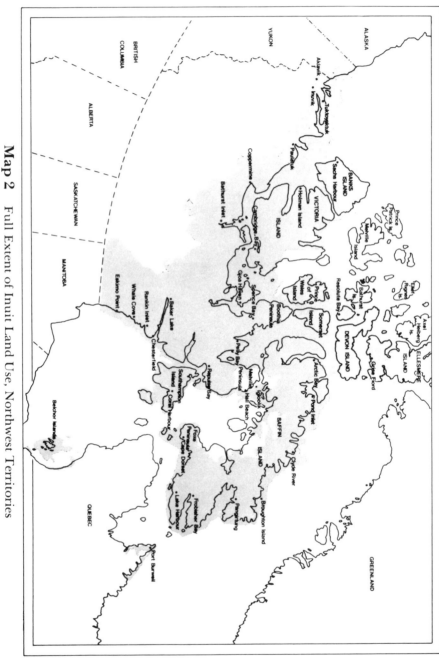

Map 2 Full Extent of Inuit Land Use, Northwest Territories

Based on Inuit Land Use and Occupancy Project. *Report: Inuit Land Use and Occupancy Project,* volume 3, *Land Use Atlas* (Ottawa: Minister of Supply and Services Canada, 1976), Map 153.

providing hydrographic charts in accordance with the Resources and Technical Surveys Act. A key role of DFO is to acquire scientific knowledge about arctic waters and ecosystems and to stipulate conditions for the protection of fish, marine mammals, and their habitats.

The Department of the Environment (DOE), under the 1979 Government Organization Act, is responsible for co-ordinating all policies and programmes of the Canadian government concerning the preservation and enhancement of the quality of the environment. It plays the role of environmental advocate in two ways: by advising industry, other departments, and the public of environmental implications of development projects, and by participating in northern planning activities. It may establish environmental guidelines for other departments and agencies through orders in council. This department administers the Ocean Dumping Control Act, which makes permits mandatory for dumping certain substances into the sea or onto sea ice. DOE also administers section 33.1(1) of the Fisheries Act concerning the deposition of deleterious substances into waters frequented by fish. Under the National Parks Act, DOE establishes and administers national parks for the benefit, education, and enjoyment of present and future generations. DOE's Atmospheric Environment Service provides meteorological and sea-ice information. Through Cabinet policy and the Federal Environmental Assessment Review Office (FEARO), the minister of the Environment is responsible for the Environmental Assessment and Review Process (EARP) as it applies to major projects that could have a significant impact on the arctic marine environment.

The Department of Transport (DOT) is responsible for the Canada Shipping Act and for the shipping provisions of the Arctic Waters Pollution Prevention Act (AWPPA). Pursuant to the AWPPA, the Canadian Coast Guard administers the Shipping Safety Control Zones Order, Arctic Waters Pollution Prevention Regulations, and Arctic Shipping Pollution Prevention Regulations. DOT also administers the Navigable Waters Protection Act, which was designed to protect the public right of navigation by requiring permission for the obstruction of navigable waters. DOT may use the TERMPOL Code (Code of Recommended Standards for the Safety and Prevention of Pollution for Marine Transportation Systems and Related Assessment Procedures) to assess plans for marine terminals. The Coast Guard has operational responsibilities defined by the Arctic Marine Emergency Plan and the interim Arctic Seas Contingency Plan. Additional Coast Guard responsibilities include ice-breaking and escorting services, ship and port safety, northern resupply, navigation aids, the voluntary vessel-traffic management system (NORDREG), and the Arctic Shipping Control Authority.

EMR has responsibilities under the Resources and Technical Surveys Act and the Energy, Mines and Resources Act for co-ordinating, promoting, and recommending national policies and programmes concerning production, transportation, distribution, and export of energy and minerals. Through COGLA, EMR administers hydrocarbon exploration and development on Canada lands in Hudson Bay, Hudson Strait, and offshore south of 60°. The minister of Energy, Mines and Resources is responsible for the Petro-Canada Act. EMR's operational responsibilities are carried out through the Energy Program and the Mineral and Earth Sciences Programs. The minister is also responsible for the National Energy Board, which has regulatory authority over offshore pipelines and hydrocarbon export licences.

The Department of External Affairs (EA) has a broad mandate that includes foreign policy and trade, arctic sovereignty issues, and the law of the sea. This mandate includes a role in developing the Joint Canada–U.S. Marine Pollution Contingency Plan and the Canada–Denmark Marine Environment Cooperation Agreement.[1]

Administrative Problems

The first problem with the regulatory structure for the Arctic Ocean is its remoteness from the area and resources it administers. The regulatory programmes are designed to serve the national interest in arctic marine resources, yet they are administered from Ottawa or other locations remote from the Arctic Ocean and from Inuit who depend upon the Arctic Ocean for their livelihood. DIAND's regional offices in arctic coastal communities have limited roles concerning the Arctic Ocean and marine resources.

The second problem is the overlapping mandates of federal departments. No fewer than five federal departments have legislative responsibilities for protection of the arctic marine environment. Three of these departments are responsible for co-ordinating federal policies and programmes: DIAND with respect to the North; DFO with respect to oceans; and DOE with respect to preservation and enhancement of the quality of the environment. It is not clear which department has the mandate to co-ordinate federal policies and programmes for the arctic marine environment. Without a clear mandate, no department will provide adequate leadership and control.

The third problem is expertise. So many departments have their fingers in the same pie that available expertise is diluted. Requirements for paperwork and co-ordination are increased, and there is less time to fulfil responsibilities.

The fourth problem is DIAND's dual role in the North: promoting development and protecting the environment and the Inuit culture. It is extremely difficult for any agency to fulfil mandates that are often in opposition. DIAND's internal struggles over these two mandates result in many programme delays and missed opportunities.

Co-ordinating Committees

Co-ordinating committees include the task forces, working groups, and advisory committees required by all regulatory structures to co-ordinate policies and programmes and to work with other such committees on matters of mutual interest. Given the administrative problems described above and the absence of a clearly stated Arctic Ocean policy, there are far too many co-ordinating committees for the Arctic Ocean.

The complex array of intradepartmental and interdepartmental committees that co-ordinate and implement policy and planning in the North has been well documented. In its presentation to the Special Committee of the Senate on the Northern Pipeline, DOE cited more than 50 committees concerned with northern environmental matters alone and estimated that, in all, the number of co-ordinating committees is more than twice that figure.[2] Some of these are short-lived committees that will disband after working on a single issue or project. Some are active standing committees, but others are non-functional standing committees, such as the Advisory Committee on Northern Development (ACND). Many of its 14 subcommittees seldom or never meet.

There are some co-ordinating committees of special importance to the Arctic Ocean regime:

- The Senior Policy Committee on Northern Resource Development Projects, chaired by DIAND, includes representatives from other federal departments and the territorial governments. Its role is to provide policy and planning advice on socio-economic and environmental aspects of major development projects, and to co-ordinate related government activities. Since its establishment in 1981, this committee has been involved with a number of marine activities including marine transportation administration planning, Beaufort Sea planning, and the Northern Oil and Gas Action Program (NOGAP).
- The Interdepartmental Environmental Review Committee (IERC), chaired by DIAND, includes representatives from DOE, DFO, DOT, and COGLA. IERC co-ordinates the review of potential effects of major resource exploration and development programmes on the northern environment and establishes environmental conditions for programme approval. DIAND's internal Regional Environmental Review Commit-

tee (RERC) screens applications of project proponents to determine whether they should be referred to FEARO.

- The Arctic Waters Advisory Committee, chaired by DIAND, co-ordinates offshore drilling requirements that seek to minimize environmental damage, and sees that pertinent sections of the AWPPA and the Fisheries Act are applied.

- The Arctic Marine Oilspill Program (AMOP) Management Committee, chaired by DOE, is responsible for managing and evaluating research on all facets of oil-spill prevention and clean-up, and on the fate of oil in ice-infested waters.

- The Regional Ocean Dumping Advisory Committee (RODAC), chaired by DOE, reviews applications for ocean dumping and recommends terms and conditions for such licences.

- The Arctic Offshore Developments Committee (ARCOD) is an internal DFO committee that co-ordinates responses to proposed offshore developments.

- The Arctic Resources Utilization Review Committee (ARUR), chaired by DFO, provides advice on fisheries management issues in the North.

- The Arctic Research Directors Committee is an internal DFO committee that co-ordinates research programmes.

- The Beaufort Sea Steering Committee is chaired by DIAND and its membership includes DFO, DOE, DOT, EMR, EA, and the Government of the Northwest Territories (GNWT). This committee and its three subcommittees present an annual report to the federal Cabinet on exploration activities in the Beaufort Sea.

- The COGLA Policy Review Committee develops policy guidelines and ensures that COGLA's actions are consistent with the requirements of energy policy and northern policy.

- The Environmental Advisory Committee on Arctic Marine Transportation (EACAMT) was established on the recommendation of the EARP panel reviewing the Arctic Pilot Project (APP). This committee, co-chaired by DOE and DFO, advises DOT on environmental concerns with respect to shipping in arctic waters and assesses alternative shipping routes from an environmental perspective.

- The Advisory Committee on Northern Development (ACND) was established in 1948 to provide a mechanism for interdepartmental planning and co-ordination of federal policies and programmes in the North. Chaired by DIAND, this committee gradually became an instrument to build support for DIAND's positions on controversial issues. It is now considered impotent.[3]

- The ACND Transportation Committee, chaired by DOT, recently developed an arctic marine services policy to provide a more adequate level of services in support of marine transportation and related activites.

- The TERMPOL Coordinating Committee, chaired by DOT, reviews ship terminal systems and assesses TERMPOL standards for minimizing pollution in these systems.

The impotence of ACND may have been partially responsible for the large number of advisory bodies and the fragmentation of regulatory responsibilities. In the absence of policy direction and co-ordination, the separate committees, depending on their degree of power and the initiative of the lead agency, make policy decisions *de facto*. Although this system has many good points and some committees do an excellent job, it also results in inefficiencies and regulatory confusion. As development activity increases in volume and extent, it undoubtedly will exceed the capability of the existing regulatory system.[4]

In its submission to the Special Committee of the Senate on the Northern Pipeline, Esso Resources Canada Limited cites 32 federal acts that could affect its northern operations, names 22 sets of regulations that apply to arctic shipping, and lists the many agencies and committees responsible for these acts and regulations. Esso's complaint concerns the difficulty of satisfying all the conditions and agencies involved and the cost and time required to do so.[5] DOE has recently identified an integrated management programme to streamline regulatory processes and co-ordinating mechanisms as essential for Beaufort Sea hydrocarbon development.[6]

An integrated regulatory structure is needed, not only to facilitate hydrocarbon production and to ease the regulatory burden on oil companies, but also to protect the peoples, environment, and resources of the Arctic Ocean from adverse impacts of hydrocarbon development and transportation activities.

Current Arctic Ocean Policy

Canada's Domestic Policies

Few of the formal policy statements that affect Canada's Arctic Ocean specifically address the marine environment; they are, instead, statements of northern policy. The cornerstone of Canada's northern policy is DIAND's 1972 statement, *Canada's North 1970–1980*, which declares that:

> People, resources and environment are the main elements in any strategy for northern development . . . the needs of the people in the North are more important than resource development and . . . the maintenance of ecological balance is essential. In the setting of objectives and priorities in the North, in line with national policy goals, the essence of choice for the Government is to maintain an appropriate degree of balance among those three elements.[7]

This policy statement identified several national objectives: improving the quality of northern life; protecting the northern environment as an essential element of northern economic and social development; and promoting meaningful progress toward responsible government in the North. The policy emphasized the importance of achieving a balance between these objectives while giving people and the environment priority over resource development.

In 1976, as a result of the energy crisis, the federal government introduced the document *An Energy Strategy for Canada: Policies for Self-Reliance*.[8] This document called for accelerated exploration to delimit Canada's hydrocarbon resources, commonly referred to as the "need-to-know" policy. This policy has had the effect of delaying many initiatives, such as the establishment of national parks in the North, until the need to know has been satisfied.

The National Energy Program, announced in 1980 and updated in 1982, reaffirmed the "need-to-know" policy concerning the location, size, and economic feasibility of hydrocarbon resources and defined three objectives for the North:

- to ease the energy cost burden for northern Canadians
- to achieve resource development at a rate and in a manner compatible with a delicate social and environmental balance
- to consult closely with northerners in establishing rules for northern energy projects.[9]

In his statement to the House of Commons during debate on the Canada Oil and Gas Act (Bill C-48), the Hon. John Munro, Minister of Indian Affairs and Northern Development, explained DIAND's northern policy:

> In carrying out [my] responsibilities, I want to emphasize that we must strive to achieve balance in development; balance between renewable and non-renewable resource development; balance between conventional wage employment activities and those that support the traditional native economy; balance between externally generated development and that from within; balance between using the land and resources and conserving them and, balance between protecting the environment and developing the natural resources available to us.[10]

This "balancing act" policy was questioned by Senator Doody during DIAND's presentation to the Special Committee of the Senate on the Northern Pipeline. Senator Doody questioned the compatibility of DIAND's objectives and asked whether energy and the national interest take priority over the environment and the social fabric of the North. Neil Faulkner, Assistant Deputy Minister of DIAND's Northern Affairs Program, replied:

> If it comes to that, then clearly that is political judgement. The policy clearly talks about being able to balance these things and being able to manage whatever it is. In particular, it has been the view that if one understands the various interactions involved there are ways to deal with them. When it relates to people, land and resources the critical policy that we are moving on, which I think will to some extent deal with the problem you raise, is land use planning, where there is a mechanism for assessing the various values and uses of these resources.[11]

Mr Faulkner's reply is almost an admission that there is not a government policy that defines priorities. DIAND is expected to muddle through by balancing objectives and by understanding interactions, and now sees land-use planning as the vehicle that will enable it to address issues and options in the future. However, land-use planning clearly is not a policy. At best, it is a programme proposal designed to meet certain departmental objectives, and, as such, can be compared with programmes and objectives formulated by other departments. All federal departments, in order to carry out their regulatory responsibilities and to obtain programme funding, formulate policy and programme objectives. These objectives follow, by and large, from the mandate of the department and do not chart new directions for government policy. Examples of these objectives are:

- the DFO policy and programme objective "to protect fish and marine mammal resources and habitat from man-made disturbances and thus ensure that options for future resource use are retained"[12]
- the DOT arctic marine services policy to "provide for marine transportation and related activities in the Arctic in a time-frame that is compatible with socio-economic development in the north"[13]
- the DOE northern objective "to promote the establishment of a comprehensive network of protected areas in the North to provide adequate protection and management for areas and sites of significance in the preservation of Canada's natural and cultural heritage, or in the provision of opportunities for public appreciation and enjoyment of the North's natural and cultural features"[14]
- the EMR Energy Program objective "to establish and maintain effective policies, strategies and programs for the supply and efficient use of energy resources, with due regard for other social and economic goals of the Government of Canada."[15]

In the absence of policy direction from above, it is a common practice of government departments to develop policy proposals from below. This is policy development by trial balloon; many of these policy proposals are shot down by other government departments or public-interest groups when their implications are made known. Other policy proposals stay at the draft stage for a long time. This is policy development by smoke and mirrors; the policy proposals may disappear or change tomorrow, but they serve a useful purpose for the department or the federal government today by giving the appearance that something is being done. Some of the current policy proposals are:

- Northern land-use planning—the implications of this DIAND policy initiative are discussed later in this paper.
- Environmental impact assessment—FEARO is preparing a new policy proposal for the EARP process.
- Comprehensive conservation policy—DIAND has prepared a discussion paper with the intent of developing a comprehensive conservation policy and strategy for the Yukon and Northwest Territories, including marine ecosystems.[16]

- Environmental policy for the North—DOE has released a discussion paper outlining future policy directions and a strategy for a larger role in northern environmental issues and planning.[17] It makes few specific references to the arctic marine environment, but one notable strategy it proposes is to use the Canada Water Act to co-ordinate the development of coastal zone management plans as components of regional land-use plans.
- Arctic marine habitat protection—DFO is working on a policy and programme proposal to identify critical habitats and protect them from hydrocarbon-development and transportation impacts.
- Arctic hydrocarbon facilities siting—DOE and DIAND are considering a policy proposal to assist in identifying sites for hydrocarbon facilities in the Arctic.

What is missing from this list is a framework for Arctic Ocean policy that integrates the other policy proposals. The "balancing act" policies of DIAND do not establish directions or priorities, and they provide little basis for conflict resolution. It is increasingly clear that we cannot proceed with arctic megaprojects without such a framework. In its report on the transportation of hydrocarbon resources in the North, the Special Committee of the Senate on the Northern Pipeline concluded that:

> a timetable for development that meets regional and national aspirations hinges on clear policies, identified priorities, good planning and effective regulation. Until the Federal Government clarifies its position relative to petroleum resource development by providing firm policy direction, neither industry nor those charged with its regulation will be able to proceed effectively. Unless these policy and planning measures are formulated expeditiously before development proceeds further, the Committee believes options in such matters as land use and resource and environmental management will be foreclosed and the priorities of northern peoples will be relegated to a secondary position.[18]

The committee recommended:

- that Federal Government policy and planning relating to such matters as northern energy, land use, environmental management, manpower training and infrastructure development be formulated early in 1983

503

- that the Federal Government give high priority to settling land claims and resolving issues relating to constitutional evolution.[19]

International Policies and Issues

Arctic Waters Pollution Prevention Act

The question of sovereignty over arctic waters, particularly in the Northwest Passage, is an important policy issue. Canada has consistently taken the position that the waters within the arctic archipelago are internal waters, subject to full Canadian sovereignty, and that the right of innocent passage does not apply to the Northwest Passage since it has never attained the status of an international strait through customary use, nor has it ever been defined as such by international convention.[20]

The voyages of the *Manhattan* provide the prime example of the importance of this policy issue. After oil was discovered at Prudhoe Bay, Alaska, in the late 1960s, an American consortium of petroleum companies, led by Humble Oil, announced plans for a test transit of the Northwest Passage by the *Manhattan*, an ice-strengthened supertanker. This was interpreted in Ottawa as a direct challenge to Canadian sovereignty and as a threat to the arctic environment. The *Manhattan*'s first transit, in 1969, prompted a number of diplomatic manoeuvres, and plans for the return voyage in 1970 moved Canada to pass the AWPPA. The United States tried to use the *Manhattan* incident to make the claim that the Northwest Passage is an international strait, an argument that still has not been resolved.[21]

Canada has never formally claimed these arctic waters as internal by drawing territorial baselines around them, but, according to reports, is prepared to do so should a sovereignty challenge arise. Canada is not opposed to the use of the Northwest Passage for foreign shipping so long as users acknowledge Canada's jurisdiction. In a diplomatic note to the United States, Canada reiterated "its determination to open up the Northwest Passage to safe navigation for the shipping of all nations subject, however, to necessary conditions required to protect the delicate ecological balance of the Canadian Arctic."[22]

The passage of the AWPPA was prompted by the *Manhattan* incident and by an oil spill resulting from the grounding of the tanker *Arrow* in Nova Scotia. This act was based on Canada's assertion of its right to defend itself against threats to the environment and on the vulnerability of the unique arctic environment to damage from pollution. The AWPPA established a 100-nautical-mile zone north of 60°; vessels are permitted to enter this zone only if they meet standards for construction, crew, design, navigation aids, and cargo controls. Since the act was implemented, critics have argued that those who drafted the legislation cared little and knew less about the arctic marine environment, and were using the act merely to establish jurisdiction in arctic waters. Nevertheless, the act did establish Canada's position regarding the arctic marine environment and eventually inspired Canada to negotiate international support for a special provision for ice-covered areas in the new draft United Nations Convention on the Law of the Sea:

> Coastal States have the right to adopt and enforce non-discriminatory laws and regulations for the prevention, reduction and control of marine pollution from vessels in ice-covered areas within the limits of the exclusive economic zone, where particularly severe climatic conditions and the presence of ice covering such areas for most of the year create obstructions or exceptional hazards to navigation, and pollution of the marine environment could cause major harm to or irreversible disturbance of the ecological balance. Such laws and regulations shall have due regard to navigation and the protection and preservation of the marine environment based on the best available scientific evidence.[23]

This diplomatic victory, combined with the extension of the territorial sea to 12 nautical miles through the AWPPA in 1970 and the enactment of legislation defining 200-nautical-mile fishing zones in 1977, has established for Canada a large degree of functional jurisdiction over arctic waters and marine resources. The current policy question is: Will Canada actually meet its responsibility to protect the arctic marine environment?[24] Land-based sources of pollution, hydrocarbon developments, and year-round tanker traffic may pose significantly greater threats to the environment than did the *Manhattan*.

Canada Oil and Gas Act

The new definition of "Canada lands" in the Canada Oil and Gas Act is borrowed from the United Nations Convention on the Law of the Sea.[25] The convention defines the legal limits of the continental shelf, including circumstances in which the shelf may extend more than 200 nautical miles offshore. The use of this definition gives the Canada Oil and Gas Act international credibility with respect to jurisdiction over the continental shelf, but also allows Canada flexibility with respect to policy for the continental shelf.[26] One major purpose of Canada's recent scientific expedition to study the Alpha Ridge was to determine whether a portion of the ridge can be claimed as Canada lands. If the Alpha Ridge, which extends north-west from Ellesmere Island, is composed of continental-type rocks, then Canada may be able to extend its jurisdiction beyond the 200-nautical-mile limit.

Multilateral Obligations

Policy issues may arise over Canada's multilateral obligations regarding arctic waters. Article 197 of the Convention on the Law of the Sea will create an international obligation for regional co-operation "for the protection and preservation of the marine environment, taking into account characteristic regional features."[27] This provision raises the question of whether the convention applies to the ice-covered Arctic Ocean, but there is reason to believe that it will apply. If it does, it will place obligations on Canada with respect to land-based sources of pollution, pollution from continental shelf activities, dumping, vessel-source pollution, monitoring, and environmental assessment.

Canada endorsed the World Conservation Strategy[28] in October 1981 after a DOE review of its implications. The review endorsed the strategy, "accepting the key principles of the Strategy and making a commitment to take action to lead and coordinate development and implementation of conservation strategies in areas of federal jurisdiction."[29] The aim of the strategy is to achieve three objectives of living resource conservation:

- to maintain essential ecological processes and life support systems
- to preserve genetic diversity
- to ensure the sustainable utilization of species and ecosystems.

The World Conservation Strategy advocates the development of regional strategies to help solve common problems and to advance the conservation of shared living resources. With respect to the Arctic Ocean, it proposes that:

> because the Arctic environment takes so long to recover from damage, the Arctic should be considered a priority sea. Within their Arctic territories the Arctic nations should systematically map critical ecological areas (terrestrial as well as marine), draw up guidelines for their long term management, and establish a network of protected areas to safeguard representative, unique and critical ecosystems.

The strategy identifies the following items of common concern for arctic nations:

> measures (including joint research) to improve protection of migratory species breeding within the Arctic and wintering inside or outside the region; studies on the impact of fisheries and other economic activities in the northern seas on ecosystems and non-target species; the possibility of developing agreements among the Arctic nations on the conservation of the region's vital biological resources, based on the principles and experience of the Agreement on Conservation of Polar Bears.[30]

Military and Strategic Uses

The use of Canada's arctic waters for military and strategic purposes is also a policy issue. Both Soviet and United States Navy submarines make transits of the Northwest Passage and Nares Strait, but such transits are not legal in the internal waters of Canada. Improved detection and surveillance capabilities in Canada's arctic waters clearly are required.[31] Canada has no winter ice-breaking capabilities for its arctic waters. Class 8 or Class 10 icebreakers could play an important role in establishing Canadian sovereignty in arctic waters.

On the topic of circumpolar issues, Franklyn Griffiths wrote:

> There is much to be done in the circumpolar North if Canada's varied interests are to be met to fullest advantage in the coming years. . . . it should be evident that a piecemeal, *ad hoc* approach to policy will no longer do. Canada's problems in the increasingly active circumpolar setting must be handled in an integrated fashion if missteps are to be avoided and opportunities fully exploited.[32]

Comprehensive Claims and Inuit Ocean Policy

Comprehensive native claims are based on traditional use and occupancy of the land since time immemorial and the historical assumption of an aboriginal title. In 1973, DIAND announced the willingness of Canada to negotiate land-claims settlements in those areas in which native rights based on traditional use and occupancy of the land had not been extinguished by treaty or superseded by law.[33] This policy was reaffirmed and guidelines were clarified in the 1981 publication *In All Fairness: A Native Claims Policy*.[34] This recent policy statement requires that the negotiation process and settlements be fair and thorough so that the claim will not arise again, and provides for settlement rights and benefits that may include lands, limited subsurface rights, wildlife rights, and monetary compensation.

The 1981 policy provides for negotiations on selection of traditional lands currently used or occupied by the claimants, and for meaningful involvement of the claimants in land-use planning and management decisions. There is no definition of "land" in the policy and its application to arctic waters is currently in dispute. Wildlife settlements, including those for fish and marine mammals, may prescribe preferential harvesting rights and native participation in wildlife management.

Inuit do not differentiate between land and sea ice in terms of use and occupancy. Traditionally dependent upon marine resources for sustenance, Inuit are able to document traditional and present-day use of arctic waters and sea ice in the land-fast ice area.[35] Inuit policy on this matter was enunciated recently by the Nunavut Constitutional Forum (NCF) in its proposals for the creation of the new territory Nunavut in the eastern Arctic. NCF proposed:

> that a Nunavut government have particular powers in relation to the fast ice zone, its management, exploitation within it and benefits from its development, and that a functional division of powers respecting the offshore be worked out with the federal government taking into consideration the marine nature of Nunavut, the revenue requirements of a Nunavut government, the dependence of Inuit on the arctic seas and the health of the marine environment, and the employment and economic benefits which could accrue to the people of Nunavut from offshore development.[36]

Inuit claim that a federal policy that recognizes aboriginal rights of Inuit to the land-fast ice area would strengthen Canada's claim to sovereignty over arctic waters through historic title.[37]

Regional Planning and Ocean Management

Northern Land-use Planning

In July 1981, John Munro, Minister of Indian Affairs and Northern Development, announced that the federal government had approved a new policy on comprehensive northern land-use planning.[38] The policy advocated a formal land-use planning system that would improve management of land resources in the North and help to resolve conflicting interests of the resource users, including native peoples, developers, and conservationists. An attachment to Mr Munro's *communiqué* explained that, for purposes of land-use planning, "land" includes those offshore areas adjacent to the coast of the Yukon and Northwest Territories out to the legal limits of the continental shelf.

This announcement followed Cabinet approval of a DIAND discussion paper on northern land-use planning[39] and approval in principle of substantial funding for a land-use planning programme: $2 million in 1981–1982, increasing to $4 million by 1983–1984. For years conservationists, native peoples, other government departments, and industry had been prodding DIAND to develop a programme for northern planning. The new policy on northern land-use planning therefore was well received by these groups, even though specific details about the system were lacking.

There were concerns about the policy in addition to the concern about the lack of detail. Although DIAND had hosted a public workshop at Mont Ste. Marie, Québec, in March 1981 on the theme of northern land-use planning, the details of the new policy were developed by DIAND with little reference to the workshop and with little or no consultation from native groups and territorial governments. John Amagoalik, President of Inuit Tapirisat of Canada, acknowledged that although an innovative planning approach for the North was "desperately needed," Inuit representatives had not been consulted on the new policy and could not support its implementation without more information about the proposed planning system and how it might affect aboriginal land claims.[40]

The policy announced by Mr Munro was not really a policy, but was instead a vehicle for developing one. The DIAND discussion paper admitted that, for land-use planning to be viable, there must be a hierarchical policy framework, and stated that: "The first requirement is for an overall federal government policy statement concerning [the government's] objectives as manager of federal lands and resources in the North."[41] That first requirement is still unfulfilled.

DIAND officials appeared not to know whether they were developing a comprehensive regional planning process or a more limited land-use planning process. The definition of "land" to include marine areas was not in the original draft discussion paper circulated to other departments for review and comment, and DOT was not pleased with this addition to the definition in the published version. The intention expressed in the document to conduct planning in the North conflicted with the highly centralized, DIAND-controlled planning structure. The territorial land-use commissions proposed were not really commissions, and, in place of commissioners, DIAND proposed a co-ordinating committee and a DIAND planning secretariat. The roles of the territorial governments, native groups, and the public in the proposed planning process appeared to be minimal and the intended use of the results of the planning process was not clear.

Despite Cabinet approval, funding, and a pressing need to implement a planning process for the Beaufort Sea region, DIAND was unable to decide what to do next. A consultant's study submitted in December 1981 recommended an implementation strategy focusing on the following points:

- opening up consideration of the proposed planning process to meaningful consultation with concerned interest groups and public agencies
- establishing a Task Force within DIAND to prepare for the full implementation of comprehensive land use planning in the North within a period of six months
- conducting a detailed analysis of the basic policy and program development issues confronting the federal government in establishing a system of comprehensive land use planning in the North
- finalizing the planning process and the organization to implement that process, based on the results of the consultations.[42]

DIAND was reluctant to act on these recommendations or to initiate meaningful consultation until it had published a brochure describing the proposed programme. Officials agonized over what to put in the brochure, which went through numerous drafts, the length of the "brochure" increasing with each draft. The result is the 160-page draft document *Land Use Planning in Northern Canada*.[43] In so many pages of information on a proposed planning process there is, predictably, much with which to find fault.[44] By failing to set up an effective consultative mechanism for developing and refining the proposed process at an early stage, DIAND had already ignored an important planning principle. Native groups and the territorial governments rejected the proposed structure and process and asked DIAND to return to the bargaining table to negotiate a consensus on principles for land-use planning. Although the publication is only a draft, and although DIAND has been holding consultations, two years have passed since Cabinet approved the policy and there has been little progress toward designing an acceptable planning system.

In its recent report on hydrocarbon transportation, the Special Committee of the Senate on the Northern Pipeline echoed the view of many persons:

> The Committee is convinced that the planning process must not just be a system of allocating land uses but must be developed within the context of comprehensive regional planning. Through this process regional goals can be formulated that address the concerns and aspirations of the region's people. Regional benefits in the future will largely depend on the success of land-use planning.[45]

In this report the Senate committee recommended:

> That the Federal Government expedite the regional planning process and that the Department of Indian Affairs and Northern Development inaugurate a planning mechanism to allow participatory regional planning to proceed effectively.[46]

Lancaster Sound

Exploration permits for hydrocarbon resources in Lancaster Sound were issued as early as 1968. A consortium of 12 companies formed under the name Magnorth Petroleum Ltd. to conduct an exploration programme, with Norlands Petroleums Ltd. as the chief operator. In 1973, following geophysical work that identified several hydrocarbon-containing geological formations, Norlands applied for approval to drill a single exploratory well at the Dundas K-56 site. Because of the potential for significant environmental impacts, the proposal was referred to the Environmental Assessment and Review Process (EARP).

In its 1979 report, the Lancaster Sound Environmental Assessment Panel recommended against drilling approval, concluding that a meaningful assessment of potential impacts could not be made in isolation from the broader issues of the area's biological uniqueness and the socio-economic concerns of the native residents.[47] The panel recommended that the federal government initiate a comprehensive review of the issues surrounding use of Lancaster Sound and seek advice from the national and regional publics to determine the best use of Lancaster Sound as a resource. The minister of Indian Affairs and Northern Development accepted the panel's recommendations and, in July 1979, inaugurated the Lancaster Sound Regional Study to prepare policy options.

The Working Groups

This initiative was hailed as an innovative form of regional planning by many observers of northern decision making. The Environmental Science Workshop for the Lancaster Sound Region was held at Kananaskis, Alberta, in November 1979 to bring together experts on various aspects of the Lancaster Sound issue in a non-adversarial forum early in the planning process. It was hoped that the workshop would bring out information about the environmental significance of the region and its relationship to impending social and economic changes. The workshop participants agreed on the following principles for planning and decision making:

- maintenance of biological productivity and environmental quality
- integrated environmental management
- interrelationships between biological, technical, and social concerns
- rights and responsibilities of northern residents
- protection of special areas
- regional and long-term management
- accident prevention and mitigation of environmental damage.[48]

DIAND gave the Lancaster Sound Regional Study two parallel goals. The first was to stimulate informed discussion on options for future use of the region's marine and land areas. The second was to provide the foundation and framework for a comprehensive regional planning process. The actual preparation and implementation of a regional plan was to follow completion of the study. DIAND organized the study in collaboration with DOE, DFO, EMR, DOT, and the GNWT, and established a senior steering committee to provide general direction to the study and a working group to conduct the study. There were no Inuk representatives or residents of the region on the steering committee or in the working group.

The Lancaster Sound Regional Study working group produced a draft green paper in December 1980,[49] held community hearings and public workshops in the North and the South, and produced the final green paper in 1982.[50] The final phase of public consultation on the green paper is still in progress. Neither the draft nor the final green paper was well received by the public concerning its content or the time taken to prepare it. One lesson still to be learned by government is that neither green papers nor discussion papers should be written by large committees of civil servants.

The Lancaster Sound Regional Study may earn higher marks for its contribution to a foundation and framework for a comprehensive regional planning process. As a result of its focus on the marine resources of the region, the dependency of Inuit on the marine resources, and the vulnerability of these resources to hydrocarbon development and transportation, a case could be made for integrated planning of the land and marine areas as a whole. The public review and consultation elements of the study also served to raise public expectations of involvement in some form of regional planning process.

The report submitted to DIAND by the chairman of the public review phase is an excellent summary of the issues and a statement of the need for both integrated policies and a planning process. In his letter of transmittal to Mr Munro, Peter Jacobs wrote:

An important and potentially significant initiative has been launched by your department with respect to the national concern for Canada's high Arctic. The Lancaster Sound Regional Study and the draft green paper derived from it are the first attempts by government to initiate a process of regional planning in the North. . . .

The first issue is the clear need for a national policy across all departmental sectors of government for Canada's high Arctic. The public expressed an urgent need for integrated national policies with respect to energy, transportation, conservation and development of the high Arctic.

The second issue is the pressing need to resolve native land claims in northern Canada. The strategic importance of this activity to the native peoples of Canada in general, and the Inuit of the Lancaster Sound region in particular, cannot be too strongly stressed. Mention of the issue and current negotiations must be contained in the green paper. . . .

Virtually unanimous agreement was achieved on the urgent need to establish a regional planning process for the high Arctic. Consensus on this issue is supported by a wide range of government departments, industry, informed northern experts and the citizens of the region. . . .

In the final section of this report I ask the question, How shall we plan? Consensus to plan is one of the many significant aspects of the public review of the draft green paper. But agreement to plan will not, *a priori*, resolve complex issues viewed from the two predominant cultural perspectives in the Lancaster Sound region. I argue that many of the basic tenets of the planning process, as understood and practiced in southern Canada, may not be appropriate for the high Arctic. . . .

All of us are faced with the challenge to develop an exemplary planning process for the high Arctic. This process must be attuned to national and regional interests. It must be perceived, understood and supported by all cultures of Canadians, in the North and the South. It must be viable as a means of conserving our rich biological heritage for sustainable development. Both the challenge and the process are exciting undertakings, indeed. Similarly failure to accept this challenge and to deal with it creatively and energetically may well result in environmental and social impacts that far exceed those discussed during the public review.[51]

The final green paper presents six options for future use of the Lancaster Sound region. These range from strict environmental protection to concerted economic development. The green paper states that options for a regional planning process must be capable of functioning within the framework of the northern land-use planning process, and suggests two interim alternatives. The green paper also proposes six interim steps to maintain the momentum of the green paper exercise and to facilitate the evolution of regional planning:

- announcement of a policy statement on the pace and timing of new resource use activities in the region
- formulation of a comprehensive conservation policy and strategy
- establishment in the immediate future of an ad hoc advisory committee with involvement of the Inuit residents
- initiation of an ongoing regional planning process before further project proposals are assessed
- provision for the modification of the membership and terms of reference of the planning body in accordance with a Nunavut claims settlement
- use of the tentative planning principles to evaluate all resource use options for the region.[52]

Four years have passed since the Lancaster Sound Regional Study was initiated. Determination of the best future use for the resources of Lancaster Sound may be further away now than it seemed in 1979. Public consultation on the green paper is still in progress [June 1983], and the minister of

Indian Affairs and Northern Development soon may have to choose between implementing a regional planning process or announcing his own choice among the green paper options. Magnorth Petroleum Ltd. returned to centre stage in 1982 when it submitted a detailed response to the green paper, arguing not only that exploratory drilling should be approved now, but also that it can proceed in conjunction with regional planning initiatives.[53] Can Petro-Canada be far behind?

Beaufort Sea

The prospect of discovering and developing the vast hydrocarbon resources in the Beaufort Sea–Mackenzie Delta is behind many policy and planning questions in the North. Geophysical work commenced in the 1950s and the first exploratory well was drilled in the delta in 1965. Imperial Oil Limited's discovery well H-25 was drilled at Atkinson Point in 1970. The first offshore well from an artificial island was drilled in 1973, and Dome Petroleum Limited's offshore drilling programme using drill-ships commenced in 1976. Of the approximately 185 exploratory wells that have been drilled to date, at a cost of more than $2 billion, at least 27 have successfully struck oil reserves.[54] Proven reserves are on the order of one billion barrels of recoverable oil and nine trillion ft^3 of gas, and potential reserves are much greater.*

The prospects for and requirements of Beaufort Sea exploration and development have had a strong influence on the National Energy Program, the "need-to-know" policy, and the Petroleum Incentives Program (PIP). The three principal operators—Dome, Gulf, and Esso—all are learning by doing in a situation where PIP grants cover about 93 per cent of their exploration costs, and are making great technical progress in their abilities to operate in this technically hazardous northern environment. There are, however, great social and environmental hazards associated with Beaufort Sea hydrocarbon developments, and there is no integrated policy and planning framework in place to deal with them.

The projects associated with Beaufort Sea hydrocarbon development have an estimated cost of $50.8 billion (1980 dollars).[55] The region already has been affected significantly by exploration activities, shore-based supply facilities at Tuktoyaktuk and McKinley Bay, and construction of artificial islands. Full-scale development, should it occur, would require modern ice-breaking tankers, arctic production and loading atolls, deep-water ports, sub-sea and surface pipelines, and greatly expanded support

---

*[1 barrel equals approximately 0.16 m^3. 1 ft^3 equals approximately 0.028m^3]

and supply facilities. The need for policy and planning initiatives to delimit these exploration, development, and production activities has been evident for some time.

There is no better example of this need than the current question of whether there will be a port at Stokes Point on the North Slope of the Yukon. In 1977, the Mackenzie Valley Pipeline Inquiry recommended that the Government of Canada reserve the northern Yukon as a wilderness park. The 1978 agreement in principle between the federal government and COPE on the land claims of the Inuvialuit of the western Arctic (COPE agreement in principle) provided for a national wilderness park along the entire arctic coast of the Yukon. In the same year the federal government, by order in council, withdrew the northern Yukon from new development because "the lands described in the schedule are required for a national park and other conservation purposes."[56] The national park has yet to be established. In 1982 Gulf informed DIAND that it intended to apply for permission to construct a deepwater port at Stokes Point. Government support for a port somewhere on the North Slope was evident,[57] but before Gulf's interest in Stokes Point, its preference had been for port facilities at McKinley Bay. Gulf formally applied for a land-use permit for a port facility at Stokes Point on 11 March 1983, but Mr Munro has delayed a decision because of strong opposition from native groups, conservationists, and the minister of the Environment [June 1983].

The issue of Beaufort Sea hydrocarbon production was referred to an EARP panel in July 1980. The panel was directed to consider the environmental and socio-economic effects of hydrocarbon production (not exploration) and transportation routes to southern markets. The evidence of the three proponents—Dome, Gulf, and Esso—was based on broad development possibilities rather than on specific projects. Their environmental impact statement (EIS) addressed impacts on the Beaufort Sea–Mackenzie Delta region, the Mackenzie Valley pipeline route, and the Northwest Passage tanker route north of 60°.[58] The EIS was submitted to the environmental assessment panel in October 1982 and distributed for public and government comment. In March 1983 the panel announced that it had found the EIS deficient in major ways and that public hearings would not be held until the deficiencies were corrected. The proponents were asked to prepare additional information on impact assessment methodology, cumulative impacts, socio-economic and environmental effects, oil-spill risks, and mitigation measures relating to their proposals for hydrocarbon development. They also were asked to revise the environmental impact statements for the three regions.

The urgent need for regional planning in the Beaufort region has been acknowledged by almost everyone: the COPE agreement in principle proposed the establishment of a regional planning commission; industry has urged DIAND to establish a regional planning process; the environmental assessment panel requested that DIAND develop a regional plan; the Task Force on Beaufort Sea Developments noted that, in the absence of comprehensive planning, there can be no integrated programme delivery;[59] and the Senate Special Committee on the Northern Pipeline recommended a regional planning process that would enable native groups to participate in planning for the region.[60] DIAND used the development proposals for the Beaufort Sea region as the principal rationale for its new policy on northern land-use planning and funded a planning appraisal for the region.[61] This study was completed in July 1982. It outlines action required for DIAND to draft an interim plan by March 1983 while proceeding with consultation concerning the implementation of a regional planning process. [As of June 1983, DIAND had not taken any action on the preparation of the interim plan.]

Arctic Coastal Zone Management

Coastal zone management (CZM) is a concept that recognizes the interactions between onshore and offshore uses and ecosystems, and employs planning and management tools that treat the coastal zone as a single unit. The concept was given legal status in the United States in 1972 with passage of the federal Coastal Zone Management Act (CZMA) and the provision of funding that encouraged state co-operation in the development of CZM programmes. Within Canada, the CZM concept has been promoted since the late 1960s. Its limited success can be attributed to several problems: the perceived intrusion of the CZM concept into existing provincial planning jurisdictions south of 60°; the distinction made in Canada between planners (who are considered land specialists rather than marine specialists) and marine specialists (who are considered scientists rather than planners); and the lack of legislation and funding for CZM.

In Alaska, the North Slope Borough recently has adopted a Coastal Management Program pursuant to the CZMA.[62] This programme was designed to help the Inupiat—the native people of Alaska's North Slope—to manage and plan for the balanced use of coastal resources. The programme attempts to resolve coastal resource-use conflicts while providing for future growth and conservation. A unique feature of the programme is its focus on policies, objectives, and standards for performance on permit applications, rather than on rigid zoning and regulations. Alaska state law will require that all agencies fulfil their planning responsibilities in a way that is consistent with the Coastal Management Program, once it becomes official.

It may be timely and appropriate now to introduce CZM planning in the Canadian Arctic. There are at present no conflicting planning mechanisms in place and the northern land-use planning programme and regional planning commissions are still malleable ideas. A wide range of ocean policy and management issues could be handled by a CZM framework for planning. As a people who live by the sea and use predominantly marine resources, Inuit may make better use of a CZM planning framework than of a land-use planning framework. The development of CZM concepts into a legally established and adequately funded regional planning mechanism could assist with the co-ordination of arctic policies and programmes. Establishment of a CZM planning commission for the Beaufort Sea–Mackenzie Delta shore zone was recommended in 1981.[63]

Through comprehensive-claims negotiations, Inuit are determined to secure rights to the land-fast ice area and to participate in wildlife management. Both of these goals could be achieved through a CZM planning framework. The Labrador Inuit Association has asked that its marine claims be negotiated as part of its land claims and that a comprehensive marine policy and coastal management plan be developed for Canadian arctic waters, Davis Strait, and the Labrador Sea.[64]

Arctic Ocean Policy Requirements

Assessment of the Present Structures

International

Ocean policy options are limited by the law of the sea, which has been evolving rapidly throughout recent negotiations at the Third United Nations Conference on the Law of the Sea (UNCLOS III). The Canadian delegation has served Canadians well; there is no doubt that Canada will be one of the major beneficiaries of the new draft Convention on the Law of the Sea that is the product of this conference. The Department of External Affairs has argued consistently in favour of functional jurisdiction over offshore resources and has kept concerns about arctic sovereignty very much in mind. Article 234 of the new convention gives Canada the right to adopt and enforce laws and regulations controlling vessels that pose pollution hazards to the arctic marine environment. The present regime therefore scores high marks for international policy negotiation.

An Arctic Ocean foreign policy is another story. The Arctic Waters Panel, chaired by External Affairs, has co-ordinated viewpoints on bilateral issues in an adequate but piecemeal way. Canada has never attempted to develop an integrated foreign policy for the Arctic Ocean, although there is an urgent need to do so. The circumpolar nations are using arctic waters for military purposes, scientific investigations, and hydrocarbon developments at an accelerating pace. Year-round shipping routes through the Northwest Passage are anticipated in the near future. Deep-seabed mining is a possibility for the future. These activities pose hazards to the arctic marine environment, its renewable resources, and the Inuit lifestyle.

Canada must meet its international obligations for regional co-operation in dealing with these concerns and has an international reputation to maintain as the champion of the arctic marine environment. This will require an integrated Arctic Ocean foreign policy for Canada, followed by the establishment of multilateral or bilateral mechanisms to promote regional co-operation. Because there is still little action from External Affairs on these structures, the present regime scores low marks for foreign policy.

Inuit, however, already have established their own forum for regional co-operation and consultation. The Inuit Circumpolar Conference (ICC) could have an innovative and effective role in many aspects of foreign policy concerning arctic waters, such as regional co-operation for the management and conservation of marine mammals. Canada could benefit substantially by recognizing and supporting Canadian Inuit participation in both the ICC and the development of an Arctic Ocean policy.

Domestic

The legislative basis for Arctic Ocean policy making within Canada is comprehensive compared with the international situation. Legislation is divided among numerous acts and sets of regulations, however, which confer responsibilities on a large number of federal and territorial departments and agencies. DIAND, DFO, DOE, DOT, EA, EMR, and COGLA all have large responsibilities for federal activities in the Arctic Ocean, but there is no workable mechanism to direct policy making and co-ordinate the various roles. There is, instead, a confusing array of co-ordinating committees that make policy in a piecemeal way. Mandates overlap or are too vague to give any single department a clear mandate to co-ordinate federal policies and programmes for the arctic marine environment. Because of this situation, and because the administrative structure for Arctic Ocean policies is so remote from the peoples and resources it administers, the present regime for domestic Arctic Ocean policy making scores very low marks.

Principles for Arctic Ocean Policy Making

Canada should develop an integrated Arctic Ocean policy in accordance with the following principles:

- The Arctic Ocean and adjacent arctic waters contain ecosystems that constitute an essential world resource. The circumpolar nations have an obligation to conserve this resource through state practices and through regional co-operation, in accordance with the World Conservation Strategy.
- The quality of the arctic marine environment and the sustainable use and conservation of species and ecosystems take precedence over development projects that may have unacceptable impacts on ecosystems.
- Inuit have an aboriginal right to use renewable resources from arctic waters. Along with this right they have a responsibility to conserve these resources through regional co-operation.
- Canadian sovereignty over arctic waters within and adjacent to the arctic archipelago, which is based in part on historic use and occupancy by Inuit, is of paramount importance.
- Development of Arctic Ocean resources is to proceed within the context of a comprehensive system of regional planning, which includes the meaningful participation of Inuit in the planning process.

Conclusions

Successful Arctic Ocean policy making has three institutional requirements. All three are non-existent in Canada. This explains the present lack of an integrated policy. Figure 1 shows a proposed institutional framework for making an Arctic Ocean policy.

The first requirement is for a senior body, such as an independent Arctic Ocean policy council, to advise the federal Cabinet on policy principles and directions. This council would help Cabinet to determine who should be responsible for co-ordinating and implementing elements of an integrated policy, and would ensure that Inuit have a policy role.

The second requirement is for an effective federal mechanism, such as an Arctic Ocean policy board, to integrate and direct the elements of an Arctic Ocean policy. This mechanism should not lie within any one

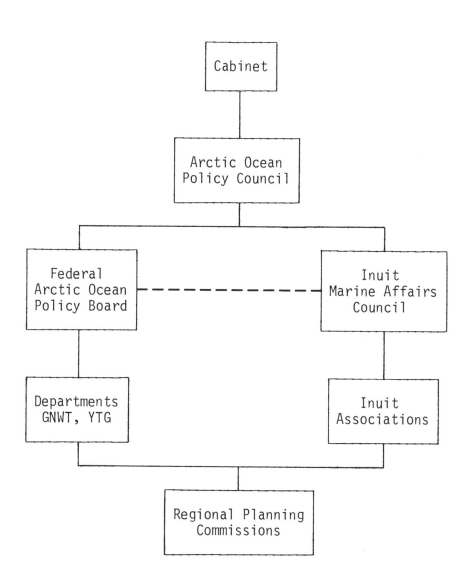

Figure 1   Proposed Arctic Ocean Policy Framework

department but, instead, should have the power to review and streamline the existing regulatory structure and to ensure that policies for energy, transportation, environmental protection, northern development, science, and so forth are consistent with one another. This Arctic Ocean policy board should have a direct connection with an Inuit marine affairs council for consultation and co-operation.

The third requirement is for a comprehensive regional planning process. This process is essential for balancing regional and national goals and for addressing planning issues in a systematic fashion. Regional planning commissions should employ a CZM approach that recognizes the interactions between onshore and offshore uses and ecosystems.

Inuit constitutional development and rights of self-determination are addressed at present through comprehensive-claims negotiations. It is expected that this process will result in determination of Inuit rights to lands and resources and their right to participate in management of these lands and resources. The CZM concept is particularly suited to Inuit needs, given their traditional use and occupancy of the coastal region and their dependence on marine resources. The resolution of Inuit claims is, therefore, an important requirement for the establishment of a regional planning process. Once this process is in place, and if there is meaningful Inuit participation, the requirements for Arctic Ocean policy implementation could be met.

Bureaucratic bungling, the maze of regulatory and co-ordinating committees, conflicting mandates, and a host of other problems often are cited as the causes of Canada's lack of both a northern policy and an Arctic Ocean policy. Bureaucratic bungling and the regulatory maze are merely symptoms of the problem, however, not its causes. DIAND is a relatively helpless victim of a government that finds it politically expedient to keep all its options open by not formulating a northern policy. Development of an Arctic Ocean policy cannot be accomplished from within DIAND. Canada requires an independent Arctic Ocean policy council, an effective federal mechanism for integrating and directing the various elements of an Arctic Ocean policy, and a comprehensive system of regional planning for implementing this policy that includes the meaningful participation of Inuit.

Endnotes

1. Agreement in the Form of an Exchange of Notes between the Government of Canada and the Government of the United States of America concerning the Establishment of a Joint Marine Pollution Contingency Plan, 19 June 1974; Agreement between the Government of Canada and the Government of the Kindom of Denmark for Cooperation Relating to the Marine Environment, Copenhagen, 26 August 1983.

2. See the presentation of DOE in *Proceedings of the Special Committee of the Senate on the Northern Pipeline*, Issue 37 (Ottawa: Senate of Canada, 16 September 1982), 37A:73.

3. Frances Abele and E.J. Dosman, "Interdepartmental Coordination and Northern Development," *Canadian Public Administration* 24:3 (Fall 1981), p. 431.

4. Northern Pipeline Agency, *Hydrocarbon Development in the Beaufort Sea–Mackenzie Delta Region: Review and Recommendations* (Calgary: Northern Pipeline Agency, 1983), p. 125. Submitted to DOE.

5. See the presentation of Esso Resources Canada Limited in *Proceedings of the Special Committee of the Senate on the Northern Pipeline*, Issue 17 (16 February 1982), 17A:96–101.

6. DOE, *Environment Canada's Proposed Response to Beaufort Sea Hydrocarbon Production* (Ottawa, July 1982). Position paper submitted to the Beaufort Sea Environmental Assessment Panel.

7. DIAND, *Canada's North: 1970–1980* (Ottawa: Information Canada, 1972), p. 6.

8. EMR, Energy Policy Sector, *An Energy Strategy for Canada: Policies for Self-Reliance* (Ottawa: Supply and Services Canada, 1976).

9. EMR, *The National Energy Program: 1980*, Report EP80-4E (Ottawa: Supply and Services Canada, 1980).

10. DIAND, "Notes for Remarks by the Honourable John C. Munro, Minister of Indian and Northern Affairs, in Debate of Bill C-48 in the House of Commons," *Communiqué* (Ottawa, 19 October 1981), p. 4.

11. See evidence given by Mr Faulkner in *Proceedings of the Special Committee of the Senate on the Northern Pipeline*, Issue 31 (22 June 1982), p. 31:24.

12. DFO, *The Implications of the Beaufort Sea Hydrocarbon Production Proposal to the Department of Fisheries and Oceans* (Ottawa, October 1982), p. 6. Submitted to the Beaufort Sea Environmental Assessment Panel.

13. DOT, *Canadian Marine Transportation Administration* (Ottawa, August 1982), pp. 10, A20. Position Statement to the Beaufort Sea Environmental Assessment Panel.

14. DOE, *Environment Canada and the North: The Perceptions, Roles and Policies of the Department of the Environment Regarding Development North of 60°*, Discussion Paper (Ottawa: DOE, July 1983), p. 29.

15. See the submission of EMR in *Proceedings of the Special Committee of the Senate on the Northern Pipeline*, Issue 32 (29 June 1982), 32A:4.

16. DIAND, *A Comprehensive Conservation Policy and Strategy for the Northwest Territories and Yukon*, Draft Discussion Paper (Ottawa, October 1982).

17. DOE, *Environment Canada and the North* (see above, note 14).

18. The Senate of Canada, *Marching to the Beat of the Same Drum: Transportation of Petroleum and Natural Gas North of 60°*, Report of the Senate Special Committee on the Northern Pipeline (Ottawa: Senate of Canada, 1983), p. 1.

19. Ibid.

20. Lancaster Sound Regional Study, *The Lancaster Sound Region: 1980-2000, Issues and Options on the Use and Management of the Region*, Green Paper (Ottawa: DIAND, January 1982), pp. 30-31.

21. For an analysis of the *Manhattan*'s voyages and policy implications, see Howard Hume, "Toward a Canadian Arctic Policy," *Marine Affairs Journal* 5 (January 1978), pp. 32-71.

22. See "Summary of Canadian Note Handed to the United States Government on April 16, 1970," in *House of Commons Debates* 6 (17 April 1970), Appendix, pp. 6028-6029.

23. United Nations Convention on the Law of the Sea (A/CONF, 62/122), opened for signature 10 December 1982, Montego Bay (hereinafter, UNCLOS). Reprinted in *International Legal Materials* 21 (1982), p. 1261. See art. 234.

24. For an overview of this policy issue, see Ted L. McDorman, *Record of an Environmental Nation: Canada 1967-1982* (Halifax: Dalhousie Ocean Studies Programme, Dalhousie University, 1981).

25. UNCLOS, art. 76(1).

26. Ted L. McDorman, "The New Definition of 'Canada Lands' and the Determination of the Outer Limit of the Continental Shelf," *Journal of Maritime Law and Commerce* 14:2 (April 1983), p. 220.

27. UNCLOS, art. 197.

28. International Union for Conservation of Nature and Natural Resources (IUCN), *World Conservation Strategy: Living Resource Conservation for Sustainable Development* (Gland, Switzerland: IUCN-UNEP-WWF, 1980).

29. DOE, Environmental Conservation Service, Policy and Economics Branch, *World Conservation Strategy: Federal Review* (18 December 1981), p. ii.

30. Both quotations are from IUCN, *World Conservation Strategy* (see above, note 28), 19:12.

31. Harriet Critchley, "Canadian Security in the High Arctic," *Technology* (March–April 1982), p. 119.

32. Franklyn Griffiths, *A Northern Foreign Policy*, Wellesley Papers 7 (Canadian Institute of International Affairs, 1979), p. 7.

33. DIAND, "Statement made by the Honourable Jean Chrétien, Minister of Indian Affairs and Northern Development on Claims of Indian and Inuit People," *Communiqué* (Ottawa, 8 August 1973).

34. DIAND, *In All Fairness: A Native Claims Policy, Comprehensive Claims* (Ottawa: DIAND, 1981).

35. See Inuit Land Use and Occupancy Project, *Report: Inuit Land Use and Occupancy Project*, 3 vols (Ottawa: Supply and Services Canada, 1976); and Carol Brice-Bennett, ed., *Our Footprints are Everywhere: Inuit Land Use and Occupancy in Labrador* (Nain: Labrador Inuit Association, 1977).

36. Nunavut Constitutional Forum, *Building Nunavut: A Discussion Paper Containing Proposals for an Arctic Constitution* (Ottawa: NCF, 1983), p. 41.

37. Marc Denhez, "Inuit Rights and Canadian Arctic Waters," in *Sikumiut: "The People Who Use the Sea Ice,"* eds, Alan Cooke and Edie Van Alstine (Ottawa: Canadian Arctic Resources Committee, 1984).

38. DIAND, "Northern Land Use Planning Policy Announced," *Communiqué* 1-8124 (Yellowknife, 30 July 1981).

39. DIAND, "Northern Land Use Planning," Discussion Paper (Ottawa: DIAND, July 1981).

40. Letter to Mr Neil Faulkner, Assistant Deputy Minister, Northern Affairs Program, DIAND, from John Amagoalik, President, Inuit Tapirisat of Canada, 27 October 1981.

41. DIAND, "Northern Land Use Planning" (see above, note 39), p. 7.

42. DPA Consulting Ltd., *Preliminary Planning for the Implementation of Comprehensive Land Use Planning in the Yukon and Northwest Territories* (December 1981), pp. 2–3. Submitted to DIAND, Northern Affairs Program.

43. DIAND, *Land Use Planning in Northern Canada*, draft (Ottawa: DIAND, 14 October 1982).

44. For a detailed review of problems with the proposed planning process, see William E. Rees, "Northern Land-use Planning: In Search of a Policy," in *National and Regional Interests in the North: Third National Workshop on People, Resources, and the Environment North of 60°* (Ottawa: Canadian Arctic Resources Committee, 1984).

The Working Groups

45. Senate of Canada, *Marching to the Beat of the Same Drum* (see above, note 18), p. 3.

46. Ibid.

47. Federal Environmental Assessment Review Office, *Report of the Environmental Assessment Panel: Lancaster Sound Drilling*, Report No. 7 (Ottawa: FEARO, 1979).

48. E.F. Roots, ed., *Lancaster Sound: Issues and Responsibilities* (Ottawa: Canadian Arctic Resources Committee, 1980), pp. 3-4.

49. Working Group on the Lancaster Sound Regional Study, *The Lancaster Sound Region: 1980-2000, Perspectives and Issues on Resource Use*, draft Green Paper (Ottawa: DIAND, December 1980).

50. Lancaster Sound Regional Study, *The Lancaster Sound Region* (see above, note 20).

51. Lancaster Sound Regional Study, *People, Resources and the Environment: Perspectives on the Use and Management of the Lancaster Sound Region, Public Review Phase*, by Peter Jacobs (Ottawa: DIAND, August 1981), pp. 3-5.

52. Lancaster Sound Regional Study, *The Lancaster Sound Region* (see above, note 20), p. 8.

53. Consolidex Gas and Oil Ltd., Magnorth Petroleum Ltd., and Oakwood Petroleums Ltd., *Response to the Lancaster Sound Regional Study Green Paper "The Lancaster Sound Region: 1980-2000"* (October 1982).

54. See the presentation of COGLA in *Proceedings of the Special Committee of the Senate on the Northern Pipeline*, Issue 35 (14 September 1982), 35A:31.

55. Major Projects Task Force, *Major Canadian Projects Major Canadian Opportunities: A Report by the Major Projects Task Force on Major Capital Projects in Canada to the Year 2000* (June 1981), p. 95. Submitted to the Honourable Herb E. Gray, Minister, Department of Industry, Trade and Commerce, and Chairman, Federal/Provincial Ministers of Industry Conference.

56. Order-in-Council SOR/78-568 in *Canada Gazette*, Part 2, 112:14 (1978).

57. Letter to Jim Fulton, M.P. Skeena, British Columbia, from John C. Munro, 15 November 1982: "I regard a requirement for a small marine support base, during the exploration phase of oil and gas activities as . . . something that government should reasonably allow to proceed in a carefully controlled manner."

58. Dome Petroleum Limited, Esso Resources Canada Limited, and Gulf Canada Resources Inc., *Environmental Impact Statement for Hydrocarbon Development in the Beaufort Sea-Mackenzie Delta Region*, 7 vols (Calgary: Dome Petroleum Limited, 1982).

59. DIAND, *Report of Task Force on Beaufort Sea Developments*, by Olav H. Løken (Ottawa, April 1981), s.2.2.2. Submitted to the Senior Policy Committee on Northern Resource Development Projects.

60. Senate of Canada, *Marching to the Beat of the Same Drum* (see above, note 18), p. 3.

61. DPA Consulting Ltd., *Beaufort Sea/Mackenzie Delta Planning Appraisal* (July 1982). Submitted to DIAND, Northern Affairs Program.

62. North Slope Borough, *Coastal Management Program, Public Hearing Draft* (North Slope Borough, Alaska, 1983).

63. J.G. Nelson and Sabine Jessen, *The Scottish and Alaskan Offshore Oil and Gas Experience and the Canadian Beaufort Sea* (Ottawa: Canadian Arctic Resources Committee, 1981), p. 108.

64. See Office of Native Claims, DIAND, presentation in *Proceedings of the Special Committee of the Senate on the Northern Pipeline*, Issue 37 (16 September 1982), 37A:37.

International Legal Issues in Arctic Waters

Ken Beauchamp
Director, Arctic Ocean Programme
Canadian Arctic Resources Committee

Introduction

In the Arctic, coastal states are looking to the polar continental shelf for energy resources and planning for year-round transportation in the ice-covered ocean waters. International legal questions relating to these waters have been debated for years, and the list of issues has grown with recent developments in international law for the oceans.

On 10 December 1982, in Montego Bay, Jamaica, the draft United Nations Convention on the Law of the Sea[1] was signed by 117 nations, an overwhelming majority of the 150 nations participating in the Third United Nations Conference on the Law of the Sea (UNCLOS III).[2] The United States is the only arctic circumpolar nation that has not signed. The convention will come into force one year after it has been ratified by 60 nations. There is no time limit for accession by other nations after the convention is in force.[3]

UNCLOS III has been called the greatest international law-making exercise of all time. The new Law of the Sea Convention is the culmination of 14 years of preparatory work and negotiations. It will extend the marine jurisdiction of coastal states, bringing 35 per cent of what were formerly high seas under coastal state control. It also contains new provisions for navigational freedoms that attempt to reconcile coastal state interests with those of the shipping nations, industrial and developing countries, and landlocked and otherwise geographically disadvantaged states. This paper provides a brief overview of some of these issues, but their importance to the Canadian national interest demands that they be given a timely and a full analysis.

Legal Status of Arctic Waters

The arctic marine environment has been referred to as a hypothetical ocean because 80 to 90 per cent of this region is permanently covered by ice. There is much debate about whether arctic waters are subject to the international law of the sea and, therefore, whether the freedom of the high seas prevails outside national jurisdictions. These questions can be addressed by considering the physical characteristics of arctic waters, the attitudes and practices of the circumpolar nations, and the attitude of the international community.[4] Different legal theories treat the ice as land or as an ocean in all respects.

The ice-as-land theory has received support from some scholars and, occasionally, from governments. Although the ice surface does possess some of the attributes of land, there are more compelling reasons for treating this area as ocean. The water column, seabed, and living resources below the ice and the frozen surface above cannot be used or administered in the same way as land. The polar ice cap is in constant motion, leads open in the ice, and, with melting during the summer months, some areas become ice-free for short periods of time. This physical instability of the sea ice would thwart any attempt to administer the ice as land. Moreover, technology now permits submarine navigation to the centre of the arctic basin and will provide icebreakers and ice-breaking tankers large and powerful enough to extend the area and season for surface shipping in arctic waters. Although there are still legal questions concerning whether this area should be treated as land or ocean, most arctic nations appear ready to treat it as an ocean and, therefore, as subject to the international law of the sea.[5]

Another view is that arctic waters are *sui generis* (in a class by themselves) and are not subject to international rules governing jurisdiction in the sea. This view treats the region as neither land nor sea but, instead, as something whose nature is yet to be determined by international agreement.

The Canadian position is that arctic waters are like other oceans in many ways, but that the ice cover should give these waters a special status under international rules relating to the ocean. Canada has not stated this position clearly, but seems to view all arctic offshore areas in this way, not only those areas claimed within national jurisdiction. This view imposes on arctic coastal states a different set of rights and responsibilities than exists for states bordering other oceans.[6] This special status has yet to be defined in legal terms. Canada has applied this special-status argument to support the Arctic Waters Pollution Prevention Act, which creates a functional jurisdiction for the control of marine pollution within 100 nautical miles of the Canadian Arctic coastline.[7]

Canada argued its view of arctic waters at UNCLOS III and succeeded in having a clause included in the new convention that supports it. Article 234 of the convention, commonly called the "Arctic exception clause," gives coastal states a special right to establish and enforce regulations for the prevention of marine pollution in ice-covered areas within a 200-nautical-mile economic zone. Approval of this clause by the international community can be taken as evidence of support for the Canadian view of a special status for arctic waters.

Other than article 234, the convention does not deal specifically with arctic waters. World opinion appears to be that this marine region should be treated as an ocean area that is unique but also subject to the law of the sea. However, as arctic offshore development accelerates and as coastal states begin to implement the new provisions of the Law of the Sea Convention, or as customary international law develops, it will be more important to have regional and international agreements that clarify the legal status of this area.

Jurisdiction and Sovereignty in Arctic Waters

Canada's Offshore Claims

Canada has established, by acceptable tests of international law, that the land areas of the North, including the islands of the arctic archipelago, are Canadian territory.[8] Canada also claims that the waters of the arctic archipelago, including the Northwest Passage, are internal waters subject to absolute territorial sovereignty.[9]

Canada has declared a 12-nautical-mile territorial sea on all its coasts.[10] In the Arctic, this zone lies beyond the internal waters of the arctic archipelago and along the mainland coast in the Beaufort Sea. In the territorial sea, a coastal state has sovereignty subject only to the right of innocent passage for foreign shipping. The right of innocent passage, which allows foreign shipping within another state's territorial seas, was codified in the Convention on the Territorial Sea and Contiguous Zone, one of four conventions resulting from the First United Nations Conference on the Law of the Sea held in Geneva in 1958. This convention states that passage is innocent "so long as it is not prejudicial to the peace, good order or security of the coastal state."[11] This right applies to both commercial and military vessels and to submarines only if they navigate on the surface. It requires foreign vessels to respect the laws of the coastal state while in passage, and may be suspended only if a ship's passage constitutes a threat to security.

In addition to the 100-nautical-mile pollution prevention zone, applicable only in arctic waters, Canada claims an exclusive fishing zone 200 nautical miles off all coasts for fisheries management.[12] These two zones currently are measured from the low-water mark on the Beaufort coast and the outer perimeter of the arctic islands.

Canada also claims sovereign rights over the continental shelf off its coasts. Canada has ratified the Geneva Convention on the Continental Shelf,[13] which grants a coastal state the right to explore and exploit the continental shelf beyond its internal waters and territorial sea to the continental margin—the point at which the geological rise meets the deep ocean floor (see Figure 1).

Canada's lateral maritime claims overlap those of two other coastal states in the Arctic—Greenland (Denmark) in the east and Alaska (U.S.A.) in the west. In 1973 the current Canada–Denmark boundary was settled by agreement on an equidistance line dividing jurisdiction in Davis Strait and Baffin Bay.[14] The extension of that boundary into the Lincoln Sea north of the arctic archipelago has yet to be negotiated but is not disputed now. In the western Arctic, Canada claims that the 141st meridian, which defines the land boundary between the Yukon Territory and Alaska, should be extended offshore as the maritime boundary. The United States disputes this claim and argues that the boundary should be based on an equidistance line.[15]

Canada bases these boundary claims on the assumption that arctic waters will continue to be treated in international law as part of the world ocean and, therefore, as subject to the law of the sea. The Canadian claims are founded in convention, in customary international law, and in principles now emerging as customary law. There will be no dispute over the seaward limits of the territorial sea and the exclusive fishing zone. Trends in international law evident in the new Law of the Sea Convention support Canada's claim to the pollution control zone. Canada's claim to the continental shelf also is acceptable in international law, but its outer limit may become an issue when the Law of the Sea Convention comes into force. The convention's formula for determining the outer limit of the continental shelf may raise questions such as whether submarine elevations and other features that extend far out into the Arctic Ocean are natural components of the continental shelf and, therefore, whether they are extensions of the Canadian claim.[16]

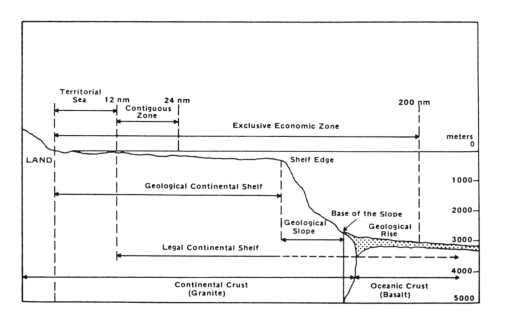

Figure 1   Zones of National Jurisdiction

Source: Robert D. Hodgson and Robert W. Smith, "The Informal Single Negotiating Text (Committee II): A Geographical Perspective," *Ocean Development and International Law Journal* 3:3 (© Crane, Russak & Company, Inc.), p. 254.

Unresolved Claims

The Waters of the Arctic Archipelago

It is Canada's position that the waters of the arctic archipelago, which include the Northwest Passage, lie entirely within the territory of Canada and are, therefore, internal waters. In international law, such waters can be considered internal if they fall within either of two categories: historic waters, or waters inside straight baselines.

To prove a historic claim, a state must show evidence of long and consistent dominion that has been accepted by a majority of nations and must prove its intention to treat these waters as internal. In law, internal waters are as much a part of a state's territory as is its land, and the right of innocent passage for shipping does not exist in such waters.[17] Canada has not declared and drawn baselines around the arctic archipelago; therefore, the Canadian claim to these waters as internal must be based on the rights gained through historic title. Canadian policy concerning this claim in the Arctic has not always been clear, nor has it been consistent. Although there have been demonstrations of Canadian sovereignty both in recent years and before control of this region was transferred from Britain to Canada, the case for historic title to these waters has not been presented or argued fully.[18] The usual criteria that can be used to support such a claim must be considered in light of the Arctic's unique features, such as remoteness, size, sparse population, and harsh climate. Important to the Canadian claim is that Inuit have lived and travelled on the waters and land-fast ice in the Arctic for thousands of years. This traditional use of waters between the arctic islands supports Canada's claim based on historic title.[19] But Canada is reluctant to use this argument because current federal government policies concerning northern development and the settlement of aboriginal claims do not officially recognize this claim.

Another way Canada could establish that the waters of the arctic archipelago are internal waters is to draw straight baselines around the arctic islands. Many states now measure their offshore zones of jurisdiction from the low-water mark, following the sinuosities of the coast,[20] but where a coastline is heavily indented and fringed with islands, straight baselines may be drawn. This practice originated in Norway, where straight baselines were drawn along rugged parts of the coast (see Figure 2). In 1951, in the Anglo-Norwegian Fisheries case, the International Court of Justice approved this practice where the baselines do not depart to an unreasonable extent from the general direction of the coast.[21] The Geneva Convention on the Territorial Sea and Contiguous Zone codified the rules established in the Fisheries case;[22] the new Law of the Sea Convention does not alter those provisions.[23] In the Anglo-Norwegian Fisheries case, the

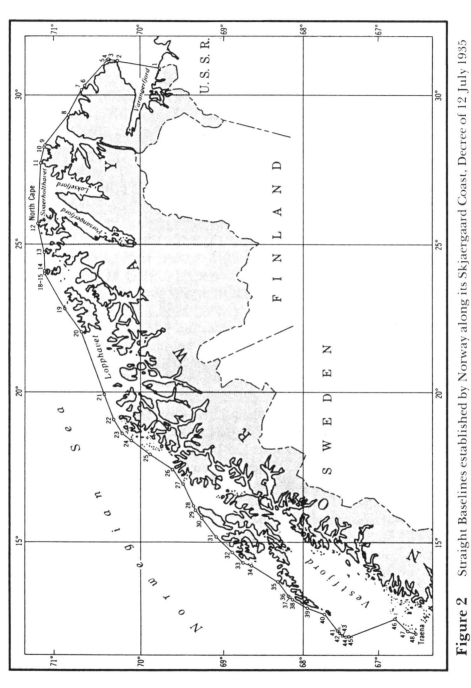

Figure 2 Straight Baselines established by Norway along its Skjaergaard Coast, Decree of 12 July 1935
Source: Aaron L. Shalowitz, *Shore and Sea Boundaries*, volume 1 (Washington D.C.: U.S. Government Printing Office, 1962), p. 69.

court upheld Norway's unusual baselines partly because of its historic use and control of these waters. Because of this historic use, the internal waters within Norway's baselines were subject to absolute territorial sovereignty and there was no right of innocent passage for foreign shipping. Reliance on the Law of the Sea Convention rather than on historic title as the sole authority for establishing internal waters means that the coastal state would have to permit innocent passage within waters enclosed by the baselines. Several important features of the Canadian arctic archipelago would meet the tests for baselines enunciated in the Anglo–Norwegian Fisheries case and in the Geneva Convention on the Territorial Sea and Contiguous Zone.[24] The Canadian government, for diplomatic reasons, still has not declared baselines around the arctic archipelago.

The Northwest Passage

The Northwest Passage is included among the waters of the arctic archipelago, but it is an especially important area because of its present and potential use as a route for surface shipping in the Arctic. This use raises the question of Canadian control over foreign shipping, since the status of the Northwest Passage will determine the type of passage available to foreign ships and the nature and extent of management that Canada can impose.

If the waters of the Northwest Passage, along with the other waters of the archipelago, are considered internal on the basis of historic claim, then foreign ships will not have the right to use the route without Canadian consent. If, on the other hand, these waters are not internal, then the 12-nautical-mile territorial sea would extend off the mainland and around each of the arctic islands. This would give Barrow Strait and Prince of Wales Strait the status of territorial seas. In these waters, foreign shipping would have the right of innocent passage.

The United States and other maritime powers take the view that the Northwest Passage is an international strait. In an international strait, there is a non-suspendable right of innocent passage that is tantamount to the freedom of the high seas.[25] An international strait joins two parts of the high seas or joins the high seas and the territorial sea of another state. The test in international law to designate international straits was stated in 1949 in the Corfu Channel case, which established that such a strait must have been a useful route for international maritime traffic.[26] Whether a strait is international, then, depends on its location and its actual use, rather than on its potential use.

The Northwest Passage has an appropriate location, but it would be difficult to argue that the test of use as a shipping route has been met because the route is so frequently impassable due to ice and because very few transits have been made. However, it would be dangerous for Canada to assume that the status of the Northwest Passage as internal waters or of parts of it as territorial seas is secure because there is potential for its increased use by maritime nations as an international shipping route. Shipping nations might argue that such activity establishes the status of the Northwest Passage as an international strait in customary law. It is the Canadian position that the Northwest Passage has not attained the status of an international strait through use, nor has it ever been defined as such by international agreement.

The Canada-Alaska Offshore Boundary

The western boundary of British possessions bordering the Beaufort Sea was established by treaty with Russia in 1825. Article III of that treaty defined the boundary as the 141st meridian "in its prolongation as far as the Frozen Ocean."[27] This boundary was not changed when the United States purchased Alaska from Russia. When the Yukon Territory was created in 1891, its western boundary was described in the Yukon Territory Act as "Beginning at the intersection of the 141st meridian of west longitude from Greenwich with a point on the coast of the Arctic Sea."[28] In 1906, Great Britain and the United States created a boundary commission to survey and map the 141st meridian of longitude.[29] The survey ended at the coastline of the Beaufort Sea and there never has been an agreement on the offshore boundary.

Canada consistently has taken the position that the 141st meridian, extended offshore, marks the western boundary of Canadian jurisdiction in the Beaufort Sea. Early maps of Canada show the 141st meridian on the west and the 60th meridian on the east as boundaries of Canadian territory extending to the North Pole. This practice appears to assert the sector theory of jurisdiction—a method of defining territory as the "sector" lying between lines of longitude. This theory has been advanced from time to time, but official Canadian claims have never been based on it. However, Canada is firm about the 141st meridian as the western limit of offshore claims to the continental shelf and superjacent waters. The Canadian government has issued oil and gas exploration permits in the Beaufort Sea using the 141st meridian as the western boundary for these permits. Moreover, when the Arctic Waters Pollution Prevention Act came into force in 1970, it defined Canada's offshore pollution control jurisdiction as an area bounded on the west by the 141st meridian of longitude.[30]

The United States favours an offshore boundary determined by an equidistance line (see Figure 3).[31] The area in dispute is 6180 square nautical miles.[32] The incentive for a resolution of this dispute will be the area's offshore hydrocarbon potential. Although the United States has issued overlapping exploration approvals, a Canadian protest has been sufficient to have these approvals withdrawn. Both countries are awaiting the outcome of the Gulf of Maine boundary case, a similar dispute that has gone to the International Court of Justice, before seeking a final resolution of the arctic maritime boundary.[33] The Gulf of Maine decision could be made by mid-1984 but it is not clear whether the Beaufort Sea boundary will be settled by negotiation or whether it will become the subject of another legal battle.

The Emerging Law of the Sea

The Legal Frame of Reference

Sovereignty over territory has always been a basic element in the coastal state concept of maritime jurisdiction. The narrow coastal belt of territorial sea, for many years, was defined by the three-mile cannon-shot range and was looked upon as a continuation of the state, subject only to the right of innocent passage. Within this area, a coastal state could deny entry for fishing, defend its shores, and manage its port and customs system. Until almost the middle of this century, claims to the ocean concerned only this narrow belt of coastal waters. Fishing, transportation, and defence were the ocean's main uses. The legal frame of reference for maritime jurisdiction was developed during this period and was influenced mainly by maritime commerce, which restricted coastal state jurisdiction to a narrow territorial sea and gave the powerful shipping nations freedom of the high seas that lay beyond.

The idea of a zone of maritime jurisdiction based on something less than territorial sovereignty began with the contiguous zone, a belt of water adjacent to and extending seaward from the territorial sea. Within the contiguous zone, a state could exercise a limited special jurisdiction to prevent violations of its customs, health, and sanitation laws. Waters within this zone still were considered high seas, however, and the concept represented, in part, a tradeoff of rights between the shipping nations and coastal states; some of these coastal states accepted the narrow territorial sea only on the condition that they have this further limited jurisdiction. The contiguous zone was first introduced by Great Britain in 1736, codified in 1958 in the Geneva Convention on the Territorial Sea and Contiguous

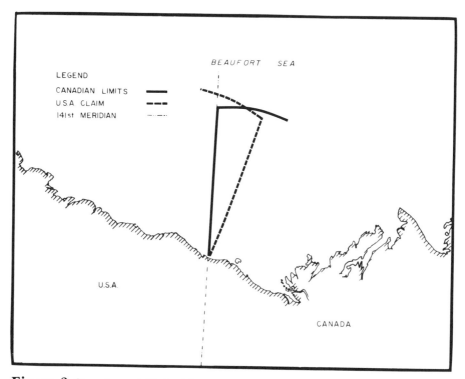

Figure 3 Canada and United States Coastal Boundary Claims: Beaufort Sea

Source: Erik B. Wang, "Canada–United States Fisheries and Maritime Boundary Negotiations: Diplomacy in Deep Water," in *Behind the Headlines* 38:6–39:1 (Canadian Institute of International Affairs, April 1981), p. 7.

Map courtesy of Canadian Hydrographic Service

Zone, and is maintained in the new Law of the Sea Convention.[34] It was the first functional zone of jurisdiction offshore, but was still related directly to the influence of maritime commerce.

An important change in the legal frame of reference for offshore jurisdiction took place with the Truman Proclamation on the Continental Shelf in 1945.[35] This proclamation caused a change in international legal thinking that was codified in 1958 in the Geneva Convention on the Continental Shelf. This convention created a functional zone over which the coastal state did not have sovereignty but in which it had exclusive rights to explore and exploit the shelf adjacent to its coast. In this zone, the superjacent waters retained the status of high seas; other nations could use the seabed to lay submarine cables and pipelines and to carry out scientific research with coastal state consent.

The 1958 United Nations Conference on the Law of the Sea produced four separate conventions that dealt with different areas and uses of the ocean: the territorial sea and contiguous zone, the continental shelf, the high seas, and conservation of living resources. The legal divisions still were based mainly on the simple distinction between territorial sovereignty and high seas, but the groundwork had been laid for a new approach to offshore jurisdiction based on functional management rather than on absolute sovereignty.

In the years preceding UNCLOS III, the number of coastal states making unilateral claims for functional fisheries jurisdiction was increasing. During UNCLOS III negotiations, a majority of coastal states began to support the idea of an exclusive economic zone (EEZ) that would provide a functional jurisdiction for a variety of purposes. The new Law of the Sea Convention will codify this concept of extended functional jurisdiction for coastal states. The validity of such a maritime jurisdiction now can be based in customary international law that has developed over the last decade. Whether or not the new convention comes into force, the trend in international law toward functional rather than territorial jurisdiction is evident.

Application to Arctic Waters

The application of the convention's provisions to arctic waters will raise questions for the circumpolar nations, individually and collectively, as well as for the international community.

The convention will provide for four zones of functional jurisdiction outside territorial waters: the contiguous zone, with a maximum width of 24 nautical miles;[36] the continental shelf, with a new formula for determining the outer limits;[37] the exclusive economic zone (EEZ) 200 nautical miles wide;[38] and the seabed beyond the continental shelf, called the "area."[39] The convention will raise several legal issues: the precise interpretation of article 234; implications of the new provisions for transit passage through straits[40] and of the new definition of "archipelago" for Canadian control over shipping in the Arctic;[41] and the influence of rules for delimiting maritime boundaries between opposite or adjacent states on the continental shelf and in the EEZ.[42] Moreover, individual arctic states will have to consider their duties under the convention for conservation and management of living resources of the high seas,[43] protection and preservation of the marine environment,[44] global and regional co-operation,[45] and marine scientific research.[46] These issues have some important implications for arctic waters.

Ice-covered Areas

Article 234 of the new Law of the Sea Convention states that:

> Coastal States have the right to adopt and enforce non-discriminatory laws and regulations for the prevention, reduction and control of marine pollution from vessels in ice-covered areas within the limits of the exclusive economic zone, where particularly severe climatic conditions and the presence of ice covering such areas for most of the year create obstructions or exceptional hazards to navigation, and pollution of the marine environment could cause major harm to or irreversible disturbance of the ecological balance. Such laws and regulations shall have due regard to navigation and the protection and preservation of the marine environment based on the best available scientific evidence.[47]

This article gives coastal states the right to set and enforce standards in ice-covered waters outside territorial and internal waters that may be more stringent than standards for other areas of the ocean. It appears to support Canada's Arctic Waters Pollution Prevention Act and could provide additional control over shipping, especially of hydrocarbons, in the Northwest Passage should these waters ever be classified as an international strait. This article would give Canada some control over shipping in those areas not part of the territorial sea; but if the waters of the arctic archipelago are internal, article 234 will apply beyond, up to 200 nautical miles into the Beaufort Sea, the Arctic Ocean, and Davis Strait.

There is considerable room for interpretation of article 234, and there will be questions about its influence on coastal state control over shipping for some time: Does it permit an absolute ban on shipping of hazardous substances? Does it apply only to pollution from the discharge of substances or does it apply to any environmental disturbance of the marine environment? Does it apply in international straits?[48]

The Exclusive Economic Zone

The exclusive economic zone (EEZ) will have the most direct influence on coastal state control. It will extend 200 nautical miles from the coast or straight baselines and will provide jurisdiction on the seabed, subsoil, and in the superjacent waters for the following purposes:

- exploring and exploiting, conserving, and managing both living and non-living natural resources
- exploring and exploiting the economic potential of the zone for purposes such as energy production from water, currents, and wind
- establishing and using artificial islands, installations, and structures
- marine scientific research
- protection and preservation of the marine environment.[49]

Other states will continue to enjoy traditional rights such as freedom of navigation and overflight and the right to lay submarine cables and pipelines within this zone. Landlocked and otherwise geographically disadvantaged states will have the right to share in the exploitation of surplus living resources of the zone.[50] This zone will give the coastal state effective jurisdiction over an area wide enough for comprehensive management of ocean resources and activities.

The scope of jurisdiction provided by the EEZ supports the Arctic Waters Pollution Prevention Act and the implementation of article 234 in ice-covered areas. In the EEZ, the coastal state also will have control over scientific research, which has always been one of the implied freedoms of the sea. The consent of the coastal state now will be required for all foreign scientific research activity in this zone. Although this requirement may cause disputes, it also might foster more scientific co-operation in the Arctic. It certainly will affect the activities of those states that do not become parties to the convention.

Marine Transportation

The Law of the Sea Convention will introduce a new category of ships passage called "transit passage."[51] This new status will apply in international straits used for navigation between one part of the high seas or an exclusive economic zone and another part of the high seas or an exclusive economic zone. The rights of transit passage will replace and extend the non-suspendable right of innocent passage that prevails in international straits under the current rules of international law.[52] These rights will permit innocent passage of all vessels, including submerged submarines,[53] and also will allow overflight of aircraft, a right that does not exist under current rules for international straits. These rights give ships in transit the freedom of the high seas. They are the result of important concessions made by coastal states to the maritime powers during UNCLOS III deliberations.

If the Northwest Passage ever is considered an international strait, then foreign ships will have the right of transit passage there; however, the new convention does not state clearly whether article 234 will apply in an international strait. Read together, the provisions for transit passage and the special provisions for ice-covered waters suggest that article 234 will apply, but that submarines will be able to make the transit submerged and that warships will have sovereign immunity.[54]

Limits of the Continental Shelf

The Geneva Convention on the Continental Shelf defined the outer limit of the continental shelf as the 200-metre isobath or the depth of exploitability.[55] The new convention's formula for determining the outer limit is somewhat less open-ended and attempts to accommodate the interests of those states that have very wide or very narrow continental shelves. Measuring seaward from the low-water mark or from straight baselines, this formula sets a minimum limit of 200 nautical miles and provides a formula for determining the outer limit in regions with a wide shelf or unusual subsurface features.[56] The convention also contains a revenue-sharing provision for exploitation of areas beyond the 200-nautical-mile limit.

Within ten years from the time the convention comes into force, coastal states will be required to submit details of the limit they seek on the continental shelf, beyond 200 nautical miles, to the United Nations and to the Commission on the Limits of the Continental Shelf. The convention is not clear about how a final decision will be made, but, if there is disagreement with the commission, negotiations may be necessary to establish the limits.

The outer limits of the shelf are to be 200 nautical miles or, where the shelf is wider, 350 nautical miles from the baselines from which the territorial sea is measured, or up to 100 nautical miles from the 2500-metre isobath. However, the convention states that "submarine elevations that are natural components of the continental margin, such as its plateaux, rises, caps, banks and spurs" are not restricted to the 350-nautical-mile limit.[57] Such elevations could add large areas to a state's continental shelf. The new convention will require that evidence to support extension of these limits be presented to the commission within ten years after the convention comes into force. A recent Canadian investigation of the Alpha Ridge, an underwater feature that extends far into the Arctic Ocean northwest of Ellesmere Island, may help to prove that this feature is an extension of Canada's continental shelf.[58] Further studies will be necessary for Canada to prepare its claim to the outer limit of its arctic continental shelf.

Canada already has incorporated the new convention's definition of the continental shelf into the Canada Oil and Gas Act, which governs hydrocarbon exploration and production on the continental shelf.[59] If the convention comes into force, Canada will be required to make payments or contributions in kind to signatories for the mineral resources exploited beyond 200 nautical miles.[60]

Maritime Boundaries

Principles for delimiting maritime boundaries have been based on state practice, the Geneva conventions concerning the territorial sea and the continental shelf, negotiated agreements, and third-party adjudications.[61] The rule that has emerged from custom and convention is that boundaries are to be determined in accordance with "equitable principles."

The new Law of the Sea Convention provides for delimiting boundaries between opposite and adjacent states for the territorial sea,[62] the EEZ,[63] and the continental shelf.[64] With respect to the EEZ and continental shelf, delimitation of boundaries is to be "effected by agreement on the basis of international law . . . in order to achieve an equitable solution."[65] This is not a formula, and the guidelines for delimitation established by earlier adjudications will have to be considered and debated. The new convention will confer on coastal states a broader offshore jurisdiction in which they can arrange for comprehensive management of marine resources and activities. This will make maritime boundary delimitation a more complex process than a simple division of territory. Adjudications that attempt to achieve such an "equitable solution" may provide clearer guidelines for settling boundary disputes, but negotiated agreements for offshore boundaries and resource jurisdiction are likely to provide more satisfying solutions.

Circumpolar Co-operation

The call for a new, comprehensive treaty for the oceans began in the 1960s with the realization that the marine environment is so important to a stable economic and political world order that oceans outside of national jurisdictions should be considered the "common heritage of mankind." Five years of preparatory work and almost ten years of negotiation have produced a comprehensive text that provides for this "common heritage" in the "area."[66] The basic elements in the common heritage concept are:

- all rights to resources in the "area" are vested in mankind as a whole acting through an international organization in which all states have the right to participate
- management, financial benefits, and technology are to be shared
- the "area" may be used only for peaceful purposes and transmitted environmentally unimpaired to future generations.

As a result of UNCLOS III, coastal states may extend their national jurisdictions. Since the "area" consists of the deep seabed beyond the continental margins of coastal states, its extent will depend on where the outer limits of national jurisdiction on the continental shelf are set.[67]

The economic attraction of this concept, especially for developing countries, is the potential for development of mineral resources, such as manganese nodules found in parts of the ocean floor. The geological profile of the arctic basin is still incomplete, but, whether or not there are commercially exploitable resources in the international seabed portion of the Arctic Ocean, implementation of the convention's provisions for exploitation of these resources will raise more questions about the status of the Arctic Ocean.

The continental shelf in the Arctic Ocean covers about one-third of the subsurface. Beyond the shelf, the arctic deep seabed should be considered part of the "area." However, these arctic waters are nearly enclosed by the circumpolar nations, and two of these nations are the world's superpowers. Sharing the "area" will require co-operation among the circumpolar nations because each will be constrained by the ocean policies and activities of others. The new Law of the Sea Convention does not stipulate the form such co-operation should take, but it does call for co-operation in establishing and maintaining the new legal order for the ocean.[68]

The convention defines a semi-enclosed sea as an area "surrounded by two or more States and connected to another sea or the ocean by a narrow outlet."[69] Arctic waters may fit this definition. In such seas, the convention promotes co-operation through a regional organization that would co-ordinate the management and conservation of living resources, protection of the marine environment, and scientific research. Any international seabed authority established to govern the "area" will have to acknowledge the activities of such a circumpolar regional network.

The impacts of offshore resource development by any of the arctic nations could be felt around the arctic basin. Some current bilateral initiatives address such problems. Canada and Denmark have signed an environmental agreement for the prevention, reduction, and control of pollution from offshore resource development and transportation activities.[70] This agreement will apply to Nares Strait, Baffin Bay, and Davis Strait, and will deal with any pollutant, not just hydrocarbons. Canada has signed the Joint Canada–U.S. Marine Pollution Contingency Plan, Beaufort Sea Annex, with the United States.[71] There is also a history of joint scientific research by circumpolar nations in the Arctic. This research may increase as a result of current efforts to develop an international arctic science network.[72]

Some of the disputes over use and development of arctic waters can be settled through bilateral arrangements such as those just described, but a multilateral initiative in the Arctic eventually will be required. The Agreement on the Conservation of Polar Bears signed in 1974 by Norway, Denmark, the United States, Canada, and the Soviet Union may be a precedent for such multilateral agreements.[73]

The idea of multilateral co-operation in a marine region is not new, nor is it limited to United Nations conventions. The World Conservation Strategy, issued by the International Union for Conservation of Nature and Natural Resources (IUCN), recommends co-operative regional planning in the arctic basin;[74] and the United Nations Environment Programme (UNEP) already has developed experience in multilateral co-operation through its Regional Seas Action Plans in other parts of the world.

Implications of Non-participation

The United States is the only arctic nation that has not signed the new Law of the Sea Convention. Canada can do little offshore without having to consider the position of the United States, which shares four of Canada's maritime boundaries. The world community can do little in maritime affairs without considering the commercial and maritime power of the United States. The decision of the United States, under the Reagan administration, not to sign the convention was a surprise to the participants and a setback for the conference. Some participants now feel that the international law-making process is irrevocably off the track and that the United States' refusal to participate has jeopardized the emerging law of the sea. Others expect that the convention will be implemented in a few years and believe that the United States has hurt its own interests and will have to conduct separate negotiations with various countries on maritime issues.

Nations that have not signed the convention have been unsatisfied primarily with the provisions for deep-seabed mining. This was the most controversial issue at the conference even though exploitation of these resources is unlikely to become economically viable until the turn of the century. The manner in which this issue was addressed by the participants was fundamental to the success of the conference.

In the "area"—the deep seabed beyond the claims of coastal states on the continental shelf—the mineral-bearing manganese nodules are to be mined under the control of the International Seabed Authority. This authority will issue licences to both private and state-owned companies, and also will operate an international mining company called the Enterprise. Mining companies receiving licences within the "area" will have to share profits and technology with developing nations through the International Seabed Authority.[75] These provisions draw clear lines between the interests of developing countries and major industrialized nations. Developing countries have proposed that this authority govern subsea mining, revenue sharing, and transfer of technology from the industrial nations. Some industrial nations want this authority to be merely a licensing body.

The Reagan administration complains that these provisions will restrict production, impose an unfair revenue-sharing scheme, and force the transfer of sensitive technology to some unstable Third World countries.[76] When a major power such as the United States refuses to participate in so comprehensive an agreement as the Law of the Sea Convention, legal issues will abound. Non-participants will have neither rights nor duties under the convention, but, because some provisions do no more than codify existing international law, it will be necessary to determine what status the non-participant has in relation to participating states on each issue.

Canada is one of the foremost producers on land of the minerals found in seabed nodules, and also possesses the technology required to enter the seabed mining industry. Nevertheless, Canada signed the convention believing that the compromise formula and the mechanisms for seabed mining operations are the only ways to ensure that land-based operations are not adversely affected. Unrestrained operations of the United States or of a consortium of like-minded nations that neither abide by the production limits set by the convention nor submit to its dispute settlement mechanisms could severely impair or destroy Canadian land-based mining operations. Such an approach could create conflicts over ocean space and mineral wealth and lead to serious regional and global economic and political instability. This situation also could undermine further the credibility of the United Nations and retard the advances in international law making achieved by UNCLOS III.

Although the seabed mining issue is believed to be the cause of the rift between the United States and other nations, it also is used to support a broader effort to maintain a traditional concept of freedom of the seas. The political and economic costs of the United States' non-participation may be felt around the world—not least of all, perhaps, by the United States.

The refusal of the United States to sign the Law of the Sea Convention will affect global, regional, and local ocean policy matters other than seabed mining. In the absence of specific bilateral or regional agreements with other states, it is likely that the United States will be involved in disputes over issues other than seabed jurisdiction: lateral and seaward limits of coastal state jurisdiction; protection of the marine environment; freedom of military and commercial navigation, particularly in ice-covered areas, straits, and other areas subject to special regulations; the conduct of marine scientific research; and the method of international dispute settlement. In some of these disputes, existing international law may secure for the United States all benefits it might have under the convention. In other disputes, however, the United States will not have some rights it would otherwise acquire as a party to the convention. These disputes probably will concern significant maritime issues such as freedom of navigation and marine scientific research.

If the convention comes into force within the next several years, the attitude of other states toward non-participants will be important. The convention is a complex and comprehensive document, designed by the world community to be an all-or-nothing package. Many states will assume that their interests have been harmed by the non-participation of other states, an assumption that will lead to unsatisfactory bilateral negotiations and agreements. As a coastal state that shares many interests in ocean affairs with the United States and other nations, Canada may feel pressure to take on the familiar role of honest broker in foreign affairs. Canada's initial task will be to analyse thoroughly the implications of the United States' decision for Canadian offshore interests. Arctic marine issues have a large potential for disrupting relations between Canada and the United States.

Canada's Role

Canada has signed the new Law of the Sea Convention and, upon ratification, will have an obligation to ensure that the domestic offshore legal regime complies with the new international rules. Canada's obligation is even greater than that of most coastal states, if credibility in the international arena is to be maintained, because this country was instrumental in drafting some of the important provisions, especially those relating to protection of the marine environment. These provisions are consistent with Canada's own objectives as a coastal state; having achieved so many of its objectives, Canada should not delay in bringing both spirit and letter of the convention into effect.

In some cases the only way to fulfil the intent of the convention will be through bilateral or multilateral action. During the period of implementation, neighbouring coastal states and regions will become aware of the need for co-operation in ocean management. The international benchmarks established by the convention not only will provide the guidelines for necessary revisions in each coastal state's ocean law and policy, but also will give each state a useful perspective of the ocean management philosophies of neighbouring countries.

The existing Canadian offshore legal regime is based largely on legislation that has been enacted to deal with separate ocean areas, uses, and problems such as fisheries management, marine transportation, and resource exploitation. When the EEZ concept is implemented, when precise outer limits to the continental shelf are set, and when straight baselines are declared, new legislation for these jurisdictions will be needed. With the current trend toward a multifunctional offshore jurisdiction that provides the basis for a system of management rather than regulation, there will be a need for legislation that integrates the various management processes. Enactment of such laws presupposes the development of an integrated ocean policy and of an operational planning process for management of the offshore. In the meantime, Canada and other coastal states will have to appraise existing legislation and judge its validity in light of international trends and rules, and the policies and programmes of neighbouring coastal states. This analysis will be a first step toward development of effective national and regional offshore legal regimes.

The Law of the Sea Convention does not require that signatories implement specific laws, but provides a framework and a tone for the legal and administrative changes necessary for each state to fulfil the principles and guidelines of the convention. If this is not done in a diligent way, the convention will be merely a prestigious document subject to conflicting interpretations and uncertain application.

Endnotes

1. United Nations Convention on the Law of the Sea (A/CONF. 62/122), opened for signature 10 December 1982, Montego Bay (hereinafter, UNCLOS). Reprinted in *International Legal Materials (ILM)* 21 (1982), p. 1261.

2. By June 1983, the number of signatories was 125 and there were eight ratifications.

3. The convention's provisions for signature, ratification, accession, and entry into force appear in UNCLOS, arts. 305-308.

4. See Donat Pharand, *The Law of the Sea of the Arctic: With Special Reference to Canada* (Ottawa: University of Ottawa Press, 1973), esp. pp. 145-179.

5. Ibid., p. 177.

6. J.A. Beesley, "Rights and Responsibilities of Arctic Coastal States: The Canadian View," *Journal of Maritime Law and Commerce* 3:1 (October 1971), pp. 1-12.

7. Arctic Waters Pollution Prevention Act, *Revised Statutes Canada (RSC)* 1970, c. 2 (1st Supp.) (hereinafter, AWPPA), s. 3(1).

8. The Canadian government has made definite statements on this claim. For example, see the "Policy Statement re: Canadian Sovereignty in the Arctic by Right Hon. P.E. Trudeau, Prime Minister," *House of Commons Debates* 8 (15 May 1969), p. 8720. This claim is now unchallenged by the world community.

9. Ibid.

10. Territorial Sea and Fishing Zones Act, *RSC* 1970, c. 45 (1st Supp.), s. 3(1).

11. Convention on the Territorial Sea and Contiguous Zone, opened for signature 29 April 1958, Geneva, in *United Nations Treaty Series (UNTS)* 516:205, art. 14.

12. Fishing Zones of Canada (Zone 6) Order, *Consolidated Regulations of Canada (CRC)* 18(1978), c. 1549, p. 13747. These regulations extended the exclusive fishing zone from 12 to 200 nautical miles.

13. Convention on the Continental Shelf, opened for signature 29 April 1958, Geneva, in *UNTS* 499:311.

14. Agreement between the Government of Canada and the Government of the Kingdom of Denmark Relating to the Delimitation of the Continental Shelf between Greenland and Canada, Ottawa, 17 December 1973, *Canada Treaty Series* (1974), no. 9.

15. The United States favours a boundary determined by a more complicated system that involves a line equally distant along its length from points on the coastlines of Alaska and the Yukon Territory. This line would lean to the east of the 141st meridian because of the southward curve of the Canadian coastline and would give the United States a larger offshore area.

16. The Canadian government recently has completed the Canadian Expedition to Study the Alpha Ridge (CESAR), which may prove that the geologic and geomorphologic structure of the Alpha Ridge links it to Canada's continental shelf. See "Unlocking Secrets of the Mystery Ocean," *Toronto Star* (26 March 1983), p. 26.

17. L. Oppenheim, *International Law: A Treatise*, vol. 1, *Peace*, ed., H. Lauterpacht, 7th ed. (London: Longmans Green and Co., 1948), p. 416.

18. Donat Pharand, "Canada's Jurisdiction in the Arctic," in *A Century of Canada's Arctic Islands 1880-1980*, ed., Morris Zaslow (Ottawa: Royal Society of Canada, 1981), pp. 121-123.

19. For a more-detailed discussion of this issue, see Marc Denhez, "Inuit Rights and Canadian Arctic Waters," in *Sikumiut: "The People Who Use the Sea Ice,"* eds, Alan Cooke and Edie Van Alstine (Ottawa: Canadian Arctic Resources Committee, 1984).

20. Oppenheim, *International Law*, vol. 1 (see above, note 17), pp. 443-444.

21. Anglo-Norwegian Fisheries Case (*U.K.* v. *Norway*), *International Court of Justice Reports (ICJ)* 1951, p. 116.

22. Convention on the Territorial Sea and Contiguous Zone (see above, note 11), arts. 4, 5(2).

23. UNCLOS, arts. 7, 8.

24. Pharand, *The Law of the Sea of the Arctic* (see above, note 4), pp. 97, 98.

25. See C. John Colombos, *The International Law of the Sea*, 6th ed. (London: Longmans Green and Co. Ltd., 1967); K.L. Koh, *Straits in International Navigation: Contemporary Issues* (New York: Oceana Publications, Inc., 1982); and Roger D. McConchie and Robert S. Reid, "Canadian Foreign Policy and International Straits," in *Canadian Foreign Policy and the Law of the Sea*, eds, Barbara Johnson and Mark W. Zacher (Vancouver: University of British Columbia Press, 1977), pp. 158-201.

26. Corfu Channel Case, [1949] *ICJ* 1, pp. 358-366.

27. Convention between Great Britain and Russia, 28 February 1825, reported in Lewis Hertslet, *A Complete Collection of the Treaties and Conventions and Reciprocal Regulations, at Present Subsisting between Great Britain and Foreign Powers, and of the Laws, Decrees, and Orders In Council, Concerning the Same*, vol. 3 (London: Henry Butterworth, 1827), p. 362.

28. Yukon Territory Act, *Public General Acts*, vol. 1 (Ottawa: Queen's Law Printer, 1898), c. 6, schedule.

29. Convention between the United Kingdom and the United States of America Respecting the Boundary between the Dominion of Canada and Alaska, 21 April 1906, in *Treaties and Other International Agreements of the United States of America 1776-1949*, ed., Charles I. Bevans, vol. 12 (Washington D.C.: Department of State, 1968), p. 276.

30. AWPPA, s. 3(1).

31. See above, note 15.

32. Erik B. Wang, "Canada-United States Fisheries and Maritime Boundary Negotiations: Diplomacy in Deep Water," in *Behind the Headlines*, 38:6/39:1 (Canadian Institute of International Affairs, April 1981).

33. For a general discussion of the Beaufort Sea boundary dispute, see Karin L. Lawson, "Note—Delimiting Continental Shelf Boundaries in the Arctic: the United States-Canada Beaufort Sea Boundary," *Virginia Journal of International Law* 22 (1981), pp. 221-246.

34. Sayre A. Swartzrauber, *The Three-Mile Limit of Territorial Seas* (Annapolis: Naval Institute Press, 1972), pp. 70-71. See also Convention on the Territorial Sea and Contiguous Zone (see above, note 11), art. 24; and UNCLOS, art. 33.

35. Shigeru Oda, *The International Law of the Ocean Development: Basic Documents*, vol. 1 (Netherlands: A.W. Sijthoff International Publishing Company N.V., 1972), p. 341.

36. UNCLOS, art. 33.

37. Ibid., arts. 76-85.

38. Ibid., arts. 55-75.

39. Ibid., arts. 133-155.

40. Ibid., arts. 37-44.

41. Ibid., arts. 46-54.

42. Ibid., arts. 74, 83.

43. Ibid., arts. 116-120.

44. Ibid., arts. 192-196.

45. Ibid., art. 123.

46. Ibid., arts. 238-265.

47. Ibid., art. 234.

48. For a detailed assessment of the scope of art. 234, see D.M. McRae and D.J. Goundrey, "Environmental Jurisdiction in Arctic Waters: The Extent of Article 234," *University of British Columbia Law Review* 16:2 (1982), pp. 197-228.

49. UNCLOS, arts. 56-58.

50. Ibid., art. 62.

51. Ibid., art. 38.

52. Convention on the Territorial Sea and Contiguous Zone (see above, note 11), art. 16(4).

53. UNCLOS, art. 39(1)(c).

54. Donat Pharand, "The Northwest Passage in International Law," *The Canadian Yearbook of International Law* 17 (1979), pp. 99-133 (p. 123).

55. Convention on the Continental Shelf (see above, note 13), art. 1.

56. UNCLOS, art. 76.

57. Ibid., art. 76(6).

58. See "Unlocking Secrets of the Mystery Ocean," *Toronto Star* (see above, note 16).

59. Canada Oil and Gas Act, *SC* 1980-81-82-83, c. 81.

60. UNCLOS, art. 82.

61. North Sea Continental Shelf Cases, [1969] *ICJ* 3; Anglo-French Arbitration, (1978) *British Treaty Series* (command no. 7438).

62. UNCLOS, art. 15.

63. Ibid., art. 74.

64. Ibid., art. 83.

65. Ibid., art. 74(1).

66. See UNCLOS, arts. 133-191. For a discussion of the "common heritage" concept, see Arvid Pardo, "The Evolving Law of the Sea: A Critique of the Informal Composite Negotiating Text (1977)," in *Ocean Yearbook* 1 (Chicago and London: University of Chicago Press, 1978), p. 9.

67. UNCLOS, art. 134(4).

68. See, for example, ibid., arts. 123, 197-201, 202, 203, 242-244.

69. Ibid., art. 122.

70. Agreement between the Government of Canada and the Government of the Kingdom of Denmark for Cooperation Relating to the Marine Environment, Copenhagen, 26 August 1983.

71. Agreement in the Form of an Exchange of Notes between the Government of Canada and the Government of the United States of America for a Joint Marine Pollution Contingency Plan, Beaufort Sea Annex, 19 June 1974.

72. *Northern Science Network Newsletter* 1:1 (Edmonton: UNESCO-MAB Northern Science Network Secretariat, April 1983), pp. 2-6.

73. Agreement on the Conservation of Polar Bears, 1974, *United States Treaties and Other International Agreements (UST)*, vol. 27, part 4 (1976), p. 3920.

74. IUCN, *World Conservation Strategy: Living Resource Conservation for Sustainable Development* (Gland, Switzerland: IUCN-UNEP-WWF, 1980).

75. UNCLOS, arts. 133-191.

76. Testimony of James L. Malone before the U.S. House Committee on Foreign Affairs, 29 April 1981, reprinted in David L. Larson, "The Reagan Administration and the Law of the Sea," *Ocean Development and International Law: The Journal of Marine Affairs*, ed., Daniel S. Cheever (New York: Crane Russak, 1982), pp. 304-305. The main concerns of the United States government were stated by Mr Malone, Assistant Secretary of State and chairman of the U.S. delegation to UNCLOS III, in his testimony:

— The Draft Convention places under burdensome international regulation the development of all the resources of the seabed and subsoil beyond the limits of national jurisdiction, representing approximately two-thirds of the earth's submerged lands. . . .

— The Draft Convention would establish a supranational mining company, called the Enterprise, which would benefit from significant discriminatory advantages relative to the companies of industrialized countries. . . .

— Through its transfer of technology provisions, the Draft Convention compels the sale of proprietary information and technology now largely in U.S. hands. . . .

— The Draft Convention limits the annual production of manganese nodules from the deep seabed, as well as the amount which any one company can mine for the first twenty years of production. . . .

— The Draft Convention creates a one-nation one-vote international organization which is governed by an Assembly and a 36-member Executive Council. In the Council, the Soviet Union and its allies have three guaranteed seats, but the U.S. must compete with its allies for any representation. . . .

— The Draft Convention provides that, after fifteen years of production, the provisions of the treaty will be reviewed to determine whether it has fulfilled overriding policy considerations, such as protection of land-based producers, promotion of Enterprise operations and equitable distribution of mining rights. If two-thirds of the States Parties to the treaty wish to amend provisions concerning the system of exploitation, they may do so after five years of negotiation and after ratification by two-thirds of the States Parties. . . .

— The Draft Convention imposes international revenue-sharing obligations on seabed mining corporations which would significantly increase the costs of seabed mining.

— The Draft Convention imposes an international revenue-sharing obligation on the production of hydrocarbons from the continental shelf beyond the 200-mile limit. . . .

— The Draft Convention contains provisions concerning liberation movements, like the PLO, and their eligibility to obtain a share of the revenues of the Seabed Authority.

— The Draft Convention lacks any provisions for protecting investments made prior to entry into force of the Convention.

Mr Chairman, on the basis of the foregoing difficulties and others that I have not taken the time to mention, *it is the best judgement of this Administration that this Draft Convention would not obtain the advice and consent of the Senate.*

Mr Malone's last comment on the Senate's probable response may give pause to those who feel that a change in the U.S. administration is all that is needed to solve the problem.

Inuit Interests in the Arctic Offshore

Peter Jull
Political and Constitutional Adviser to Inuit Organizations

and

Nigel Bankes
Research Associate
Canadian Institute of Resources Law

Introduction

The term "land claims," which has become so much a part of the Canadian vocabulary in recent years, obscures a much more general political concept: the regaining of control of their lives and livelihoods by northern aboriginal peoples. Other northerners in Canada, the persons of European background, have come to use "provincehood" as a code word for similar aspirations. Both groups are expressing political aspirations in the terms of their own cultures and social traditions.

Identification with the land and waters of their homelands was defined as a basic characteristic of aboriginal peoples and their outlook in 1975 at a gathering in Port Alberni, British Columbia. The purpose of this gathering was to create the World Council of Indigenous Peoples. This characteristic also was written into the charter of the Inuit Circumpolar Conference (ICC) adopted at the ICC's second general assembly, held in 1980 in Nuuk, Greenland. Although identification with both land and water has fundamental importance in the lives of Inuit and other peoples, this concept has not yet been wholly understood or adequately accepted by the European peoples who govern the northern circumpolar countries.

In Canada, for instance, governments have adopted various principles for the discussion and negotiation of aboriginal land claims. These principles invariably have been resisted by Inuit and other native groups, who view them as too limiting and feel that they imply a compartmentalization of values in a way that is meaningless, naïve, or mischievous. Because

557

native groups approach politics from the ground upward rather than impose political theories or structures from the top downward, government-native relations at times have seemed a dialogue of the deaf.

When Inuit recently began to remind the public and governments in the South that the seas and sea ice are as much a part of their traditional homeland as is the land, they did not receive serious attention. The Canadian population, already choked with unfamiliar aboriginal concepts, either did not take note of this "new" dimension or passed it off as some sort of bargaining ploy. To this day, it has been taken seriously in no official forum. This paper, therefore, provides an important but preliminary discussion of this concept.

Inuit have played the most consistent role of all Canada's aboriginal peoples in promoting constitutional reform as a means of advancing aboriginal claims. On 22 June 1982, at a meeting to prepare for the first major constitutional conference involving Canada's heads of government and aboriginal leaders, Inuit leaders told Prime Minister Pierre Trudeau that they regarded their claim to the marine environment as a fundamental constitutional question. They have pressed consistently for inclusion of this subject on agendas and often have presented their claim to the offshore as a matter of economic development rather than as a matter of constitutional right—a point of view that they believe may be more acceptable and understandable to governments. In a letter to the prime minister concerning the constitutional agenda, the co-chairmen of the Inuit constitutional negotiating committee—the Inuit Committee on National Issues (ICNI)—outlined three principles that form the basis of Inuit concerns. One of these is:

> the recognition of our economic rights to our lands and waters,
> their resources and their benefits, as a base for self-sufficiency and
> the development of native communities and families, including
> the protection of our traditional livelihoods.[1]

This principle includes both economic development and environmental protection—especially protection of the environment of the sea mammals that form a large part of the Inuit livelihood.

A reworded version of this statement of concerns was accepted by the federal government as its own position.[2] The federal government adopted the three Inuit principles at the federal-provincial ministers' meeting preceding the First Ministers' Conference on Aboriginal Constitutional Matters with the native leaders. At the conference, in response to recurring Inuit expressions of concern, Newfoundland's Premier Brian Peckford said that his government was prepared to settle Inuit claims, keeping in mind the "special relationship of our [Inuit] people to the land and the adjacent sea."[3]

Since 1979, Inuit leaders have pressed the federal and provincial governments, privately and through the constitutional process, to acknowledge Inuit interest in international relations, particularly in the international management of marine species. Ottawa already has begun to study this matter in response to Inuit requests. Although a constitutional remedy seems unlikely, administrative arrangements are possible. In the past, Inuit have been included in Canadian delegations to the International Whaling Commission because of this interest. More recently, they have represented Canada abroad on sealing and other wildlife issues.

Northern political development, notably the campaign for creation of two new governments to replace the present Northwest Territories administration in the Canadian Arctic, has been much concerned with the Inuit claim to marine areas. On 14 April 1982, a resounding majority of Inuit voted in favour of creating the new jurisdiction of Nunavut in the eastern Arctic. ("Nunavut" is Inuktitut for "our land.") During the campaign preceding the plebiscite concerning the creation of Nunavut, Inuit leaders made much of the point that Inuit are a maritime people and that their interests and needs demand better management of marine areas than can be entrusted to a jurisdiction whose primary interest is inland along the Mackenzie Valley. Although the greatest possible control and benefit from offshore resources is a goal for Nunavut, there is no indication yet that Ottawa is prepared to concede more than an advisory role to a Nunavut government. In its announcement of approval in principle for Nunavut, Ottawa was silent on the issue of resource revenue sharing and on all other resource issues.[4] This silence was an immediate focus of criticism from northern leaders, both native and non-native.

The Nunavut Constitutional Forum (NCF) is the vehicle through which the elected leaders of Nunavut are developing detailed proposals for the creation of a Nunavut government. In May 1983, NCF released a statement containing its offshore proposals. This statement argues that the land-fast ice zone is useful as a management area because of its coincidence with the area Inuit use offshore. The statement recommends:

that a Nunavut government have particular powers in relation to the fast ice zone, its management, exploitation within it and benefits from its development, and that a functional division of powers respecting the offshore be worked out with the federal government taking into consideration the marine nature of Nunavut, the revenue requirements of a Nunavut government, the dependence of Inuit on the arctic seas and the health of the marine environment, and the employment and economic benefits which could accrue to the people of Nunavut from offshore development.[5]

The Working Groups

In designing these proposals, NCF calculated that a demand for complete Nunavut jurisdiction over the land-fast ice zone might be rejected by the federal government but that discussions might lead to an agreement similar to that between the governments of Canada and Nova Scotia with respect to the offshore.[6]

The ability of Nunavut to support the modern Inuit society as it did the ancient one is the objective of all Inuit political interests. The progressive loss of control of their homeland in recent times has led Inuit to pursue a restoration of their rights through several channels. Formal land-claims negotiations are but one of these channels. There are several other important aspects of the Inuit claim.

In formal land-claims negotiations, the marine issue has been most fully pursued by Inuit of Québec in their 1975 agreement with the federal and provincial governments.[7] The offshore component was not settled at that time, however, and negotiations have been pending for some years. In 1979, Prime Minister Joe Clark stated that the status of Inuit and Indian claims in coastal areas would have to be considered in the implementation of agreements on provincial jurisdiction over mineral resources offshore.[8] This statement was made in response to protests from Inuit and other groups then negotiating land claims in areas the Clark government was preparing to transfer to provincial control. Offshore concerns are important elements in all Inuit land claims, but they are not accepted as such by the current federal government.

Participation in resource projects, both onshore and offshore, has been advanced by governments, industry, and some Inuit as a way Inuit can be compensated for outside exploitation of the arctic environment, or even as a "modern" way for Inuit to make the most of available opportunities. Inuit development corporations have been established with these two aims in mind. Such corporations nevertheless represent a distinctively different philosophy from that of ordinary corporations and they usually are seen as vehicles for the collective management of land-claims "compensation" funds. A few Inuit leaders in Canada also have seen the activity of such corporations as a way to wield economic power for a variety of collective ends, a view that has prompted the current debate among Inuit on economic philosophy. This approach is favoured by many policy makers in Ottawa as a way of giving Inuit "a piece of the action" in return for the dropping of claims. It would make "cowboys" of the "Indians" and bypass the novel legal and political proposals of native associations.

Even small enterprises may become important elements in the effort to have offshore claims recognized. Imaqpik Fisheries Incorporated, a Québec Inuit fishing enterprise (a subsidiary of Makivik Corporation) hoping to pioneer a Canadian Arctic fishery for shrimp, failed in part because it was denied a licence to test this resource base. The reason for denial given by federal officials was that the formation of one Inuit fishing company might create a precedent for other Inuit claims to exclusive ownership of marine resources.

Intervention in regulatory processes has become an important tool used by Inuit to press their land and resource claims. The most celebrated example of the use of this method is the joint effort by Inuit of Canada and Greenland to halt the Arctic Pilot Project (APP) through presentations to Canada's National Energy Board (NEB). In such interventions, Inuit are faced with the need to supply detailed critiques of project proposals that threaten to alter their lives. Inuit feel that this means of coping with development is utterly unsatisfactory and frustrating.

Lobbying and public relations are major activities of Inuit organizations on behalf of all Inuit. Conservationists, particularly those interested in wildlife, have criticized Inuit and cast doubt on the strength of their commitment to responsible management of living species. Inuit find that making their views understood on such matters is very difficult and time consuming. The Inuit attempt to explain their seal harvests is one example of the problem. One newspaper article devoted five columns to a wildlife researcher who said that "viscerally we think" Inuit are eliminating the polar bear in areas near communities.[9] It is difficult to counter visceral thinking at the best of times, but Inuit, by virtue of their northern location and lack of access to Canada's principal media, are especially ill-placed. Inuit organizations have not been as effective as they might have been in developing their ability to respond to these situations, yet an unbiased public and government perception of Inuit conservation ethics is crucial for the future of environmental management in the Arctic.

International action is a relatively new way in which Inuit have expressed their claims. The international ICC was founded in 1977, largely because the Inupiat of Alaska were concerned about environmental standards in the Beaufort Sea. The co-operation of Greenlandic and Canadian Inuit in response to the APP proposal has been the ICC's most notable achievement. The international team working on this issue brought forward important information about marine science and traditional use of marine resources. This presentation made a major contribution to the development of arctic marine science. The evidence provided by the ICC revealed not only the deficiencies of existing scientific assessments, but also reminded public authorities that persons who use these resources have a vital role to play even in highly technical fields. Asked how Canadian Inuit could co-operate with Greenlanders, the premier of Greenland replied that Inuit must be "the soldiers and police of the arctic environment because, without the good health of that environment, Inuit cannot survive."[10]

561

After all, that environment is international, its limits defined as much by ocean currents and migrating species as by jursidictional lines drawn on maps by latecomers and their governments.

Inuit view their right to use the seas and the land as one that is fundamental and woven into the fabric of their lives. They view their environment and their own place in it as a whole. They do not make the arbitrary distinctions made by scientists or administrators in the European tradition. When public authorities, private interest groups, or critics tackle questions relating to the Inuit use and perception of the seas, they may not meet with the technical response they expect, but instead they may discover a perception that is complex and difficult to comprehend. The inability of outsiders to understand how Inuit perceive their own world is at the root of most of the present conflicts between Inuit and governments.

Inuit in Circumpolar Affairs

The importance of the arctic seas in the international concerns of Inuit is evident in the words of the late Eben Hopson, former mayor of Alaska's North Slope Borough, in his welcoming address to the first gathering of the Inuit Circumpolar Conference:

> Our language contains the memory of four thousand years of human survival through the conservation and good management of our arctic wealth. Ours is the language of the very environment that challenges the environmental safety of existing offshore technology. Our language contains the intricate knowledge of the ice that we have seen no others demonstrate. Without our central involvement, there can be no safe and responsible resource development. The ultimate result of our land claims movement will be the development of strong local government all across the North American Arctic. The defense of the world's Arctic environmental security must rest upon the strength of local home-rule government. The motivation behind the North Slope Borough's work in the planning and conduct of this conference should be clear to all. The environmental security of our long municipal coastline depends upon the strength of home-rule government in Canada and Greenland. Only when there is effective home-rule government for our people in Canada and Greenland will we be able to really trust any offshore operation in the Beaufort Sea, or in the Davis Strait.[11]

Mayor Hopson's energy and vision had been the driving forces that first made an international Inuit organization possible. In his address to the ICC, he went on to say that "peace with the oil industry" was the goal, and that this industry should be glad that stronger local governments would facilitate the planning and other contexts that would make resource development "a good business investment."

At the second gathering of the Inuit Circumpolar Conference, in 1980, Jimmy Stotts of the North Slope Borough, a leading member of the ICC executive, carried on the Alaska initiative:

> The environmental consequences which once appeared reasonably local with onshore development now with offshore development obviously threaten the entire circumpolar region. Offshore development not only places more pressure upon the caribou, fish and waterfowl in the coastal zone onshore, but it threatens the life providing habitat of the sea mammals, polar bears, fish and a variety of birds used [by Inuit] for subsistence purposes. . . . Political boundaries are meaningless to these migrating species. In the Inuit circumpolar region, policies and actions of one country regarding development can have serious impacts upon the habitat and subsistence resources of neighbouring countries.[12]

Mr Stotts also called for the "construction of a uniformly protective coastal-zone management program with the maximum of local control to be exercised as an international Inuit instrument."

The ICC began to take on a permanent form at the second assembly. The organization's charter was adopted after many months of hard work by representatives of Inuit groups in Canada, Greenland, and the United States, and by some outside experts. Both the preamble of the charter and its purposes emphasize environmental themes and the often uncomfortable relationship of Inuit to development activities in the Arctic, although the words are general and the seas are not dealt with specifically. Nevertheless, whenever these issues were discussed at the assembly or in its many subgroups and workshops, they were discussed invariably in terms of activities offshore.

Following the second ICC assembly, a variety of committees began work, guided by the resolutions of the assembly. Some committees were more industrious than others, but, as time went on, it became clear that the offshore question and the APP were the subjects on which the ICC could work most effectively and agree most easily. The APP was a proposal to extract Canadian natural gas from the high arctic islands and ship it south in tankers through Davis Strait as liquefied natural gas. This proposal required the approval of Canada's National Energy Board, and the approval process provided a focus for Inuit activity. Inuit associations of Baffin Island and Labrador—the Canadian regions that would be affected by the project—and the Inuit Tapirisat of Canada (ITC), as well as the ICC and the Greenland authorities, pooled their staff and ideas. The campaign to defeat the APP involved publicity, lobbying, and the mobilization of high-quality scientific, legal, and political expertise. The co-ordinating group, established under the aegis of the ICC, made the project a *cause célèbre*. It received assistance and moral support from Alaskans, especially from the North Slope Borough. The appearance of Greenlanders as witnesses at the Canadian hearings created a precedent and made a considerable impression. Inuit in all countries were satisfied when approval for the project was denied, temporarily at least, by the NEB in mid-1982.

The future of Inuit international action is uncertain. Inuit of Canada, Alaska, and Greenland are concentrating primarily on problems at home and are divided by different economic philosophies and political cultures. However, they are all skilled practitioners of the political action that is possible in liberal democracies. The inability of Canadian Inuit to raise funds to contribute to the ICC has been a painful and problematic issue within the organization. Unlike Alaskan and Greenlandic Inuit, who have government resources and land-claims settlements to work with, Canadian Inuit (apart from the Québec land-claims corporation, Makivik, which has contributed handsomely in the past) must rely on special-purpose grants from the federal government to operate at all.

The North Slope Borough has played a special role in the Inuit circumpolar movement, just as it has in the history of native claims in Alaska. The North Slope Borough's staunch and maverick tactics gave the final push and shape to Alaska's legislation for the settlement of native claims after a break with the collective strategy of other native groups in the state.

The residents of the North Slope Borough live in the area that appeared to have the greatest potential for development (this area includes Prudhoe Bay); therefore, they had both leverage and a sense of urgency during their claims negotiations. Some Canadian observers have likened this situation to that of the Committee for Original Peoples' Entitlement (COPE), the independent-minded Canadian organization representing the Inuvialuit—the native people in Canada's western Arctic—in their claims negotiations.

After bringing Inuit together at Barrow for the first circumpolar gathering, the North Slope Borough provided financial and administrative support for the ICC. In 1980, when Inuit gathered in Greenland for a second general assembly to consolidate the many ideas that had begun to develop from the first meeting, the North Slope group organized the event. Since then, the North Slope Borough consistently has provided financial aid for Inuit projects and groups in both Canada and Greenland.

The Greenland situation is different from that of Alaska or Canada. Home rule came into effect in 1979 after years of intensive and well-publicized work. It placed the question of control and use of the offshore in a different context. The Greenland government is composed entirely of Greenlandic (Inuit) elected members. Both Greenland and Denmark have the power to veto policies and projects for non-renewable resource development onshore and offshore. This double-veto system requires discussion and negotiation through a committee made up of an equal number of members from Greenland and from Denmark. The chairman, appointed by the queen of Denmark, is the premier of Greenland. The governing Siumut party, re-elected in April 1983, is adamantly opposed to offshore drilling, and none is foreseeable. Although the home-rule system forbids Greenlandic initiatives in foreign affairs—a point of great sensitivity to the Danish authorities—the Danes assist the Greenlanders in specific and practical matters of foreign affairs. The Greenlanders' involvement in the ICC (which is staffed entirely by Greenlanders) and their energetic and skilful member of the European Parliament provide other opportunities for international activities.

Greenland's economy centres on the fishing industry of the south-west coast. For this reason the Greenlanders are highly sensitive to marine activities in these waters. The Arctic Pilot Project, proposed by Canadians, created a sensation in Greenland. The APP was seen as a test case for the larger oil-tanker traffic that might follow, and the Greenlanders organized to fight the project.

Greenland Inuit already had displayed their determination to protect marine resources in their response to another offshore issue. Unhappy with European fishing in Greenland's waters, they had waged a long campaign to withdraw from the European Economic Community (EEC). Even though the EEC made many concessions to Greenland in relation to fishing and other matters, and despite a large annual grant to Greenland from EEC funds, a plebiscite held early in 1982 confirmed the Greenlanders' desire to leave the EEC.

Greenland shares important marine interests—notably fisheries—with other North Atlantic communities, including Iceland, Denmark's Faroe Islands, and Norway. It also shares historical, second-language, and political-culture ties with these communities. As small countries just outside the EEC's perimeter, their common interests may emerge more clearly and co-operation may bloom. In November 1982, at a meeting in Copenhagen, the ICC executive approved a Circumpolar Environmental

Commission to be composed of two representatives from each of the three participating ICC countries. This body had originated in the work to oppose the APP. Its members had learned one important lesson from that experience: Inuit must establish their own expertise and do some of their own planning. This commission replaced a number of special-purpose committees, notably two committees devoted to marine issues. Canadian Inuit are in a position to make an important contribution to the work of the Circumpolar Environmental Commission.

After the harrowing and expensive battle over the APP, the Inuit Tapirisat of Canada decided to study all aspects of arctic seas. It was agreed that a marine environment group should be assembled to work on emerging marine issues and to facilitate planning for the arctic seas environment, and that this group should consist of several specialists with access to additional contract expertise. At a time when Inuit organizations are especially hard-pressed for funds, this effort is no mean commitment. Experts from across Canada have begun to help the new body to organize. Canadian Inuit have committed this new group to support the ICC's Circumpolar Environmental Commission. With this expert staff and with the help of the Alaskan Inuit, the ICC is not likely to be short of skills in marine environmental studies.

The ICC has facilitated and encouraged contact among Inuit of Greenland, Canada, and Alaska. No contact has been made yet with Soviet Inuit; the Soviet government continues to forbid them to attend ICC gatherings even as observers. A glossy, multilanguage newsmagazine—*Inuit Arctic Policy Review*—routinely has devoted more than half of its space to offshore and resource-related issues. A growing number of Inuit prominent within Canada, Alaska, or Greenland are seeking political and administrative experience among their Inuit neighbours. The ICC's rapidly increasing use of co-operative broadcasting and other communication ventures is providing greater opportunities for awareness among circumpolar Inuit communities.

Mayor Hopson saw home rule as the solution for arctic marine problems: the fruits of his vision have developed unevenly across the Arctic. Canadian Inuit are contributing to this vision through land-claims settlements and through discussions concerning regional and national constitutions. The Nunavut constitutional proposals contain a section relating to international relations that suggests that Canadian Inuit might play a special role in circumpolar affairs on behalf of all Canadians and that their international contacts should be supported.[13]

In the summer of 1983, the third ICC assembly will be held in Canada in Frobisher Bay, N.W.T. The meeting will elaborate a circumpolar Arctic development policy in which development refers in large measure to the offshore. Whatever the difficulties in preparing global statements, given a specific threat to the marine environment such as the APP, Inuit have no difficulty working together internationally. The importance of the marine environment to Inuit survival requires that they do work together.

Legal Basis of an Aboriginal Offshore Claim

Offshore Claims under the Common Law

The legal basis of an aboriginal offshore claim does not differ in principle from the legal basis of a terrestrial claim. Under Canadian law it appears that aboriginal title to a particular area may be based upon either the Royal Proclamation of 1763 or common law.[14] The application of the Royal Proclamation to offshore regions in the North is doubtful because it repeatedly refers to lands rather than to lands and waters, and probably does not apply to lands or waters unexplored in 1763.[15] This discussion therefore will concentrate on the establishment of aboriginal title under the common law.

It is an established principle of both international law and Anglo-Canadian constitutional law that when a nation acquires territory through peaceful occupation and discovery, that nation becomes subject to and respects the pre-existing property rights of the inhabitants,[16] although these property rights are held at the goodwill of the sovereign. This principle should apply also to offshore areas claimed in modern times as internal or territorial waters. In these waters, the sovereign nation has the right to explore and exploit the resources of the seabed and the adjacent waters.[17] In other words, as a coastal state Canada may claim offshore rights, but in doing so it is obliged to respect existing property rights.

It now is recognized under international law that the coastal states have full sovereignty over internal and archipelagic waters. The coastal states also have sovereignty over 12-nautical-mile territorial seas subject to the United Nations Convention on the Law of the Sea and other rules of international law. Seaward of their territorial seas, coastal states have exclusive sovereign rights to explore and exploit the natural resources of the continental shelf as well as:

> sovereign rights for the purpose of exploring and exploiting, conserving and managing the natural resources, whether living or non-living, of the waters superjacent to the sea-bed and of the sea-bed and its subsoil, and with regard to other activities for the

economic exploitation and exploration of the [exclusive economic] zone, such as the production of energy from the water, currents and winds.[18]

Coastal states also have regulatory powers over the exclusive economic zone that include special powers over ice-covered areas.[19] All these rights may be burdened by an unextinguished aboriginal title.

Establishing Inuit Aboriginal Property Rights

In the case of *Calder, et al.* v. *Attorney-General of British Columbia*, the leading Canadian case concerning aboriginal title, Mr Justice Judson stated, "Although . . . it is clear that Indian title in British Columbia cannot owe its origin to the Proclamation of 1763, the fact is that when the settlers came, the Indians were there, organized in societies and occupying the land as their forefathers had done for centuries."[20] The right to live on the land as their forefathers had done persisted until it was lawfully extinguished. In his ruling in the Calder case, Mr Justice Hall emphasized possession of the land from time immemorial and the existence of "a distinctive cultural entity with concepts of ownership indigenous to their culture and capable of articulation under the common law."[21] An indigenous group claiming an aboriginal title must be able to establish that it has developed a concept of property. The common law does not recognize these rights for groups that have not developed concepts of property in their social organization. To claim title to a marine area under the common law, a group would have to be able to provide evidence of an assertion of proprietary rights over the area claimed.[22]

In Canadian law, it does not appear to be necessary for the government to recognize aboriginal title. In the Calder case, the Nishga Indian claim included marine as well as terrestrial areas. The declaration sought in this case included within its scope Observatory Inlet, Portland Canal, and Portland Inlet. Evidence supporting the Nishga claim included references to Nishga use of clam beds and the hunting of sea mammals.[23] In the judgements of the Supreme Court, no distinction was made between marine and terrestrial areas.

In the case of *Hamlet of Baker Lake, et al.* v. *Minister of Indian Affairs and Northern Development, et al.*, Mr Justice Mahoney considered elements of cases from the United States, Canada, and the Commonwealth that could be used to establish a four-fold test for aboriginal title under the common law:

1. That [the current aboriginal inhabitants] and their ancestors were members of an organized society.
2. That the organized society occupied the specific territory over which they assert the aboriginal title.
3. That the occupation was to the exclusion of other organized societies.
4. That the occupation was an established fact at the time sovereignty was asserted by England.[24]

It appears that "occupation" in this context is to be given a relatively broad meaning, incorporating use as well as continuous physical occupation.[25] Certainly the court hearing the Calder case seemed prepared to accept relatively unintensive use of parts of the region claimed as sufficient grounds for aboriginal title.[26]

Prerequisites of Inuit Aboriginal Title in Offshore Areas

The Baker Lake case concerned the status of an aboriginal title in an inland area and therefore is not pertinent to this discussion. In this particular case, however, Mr Justice Mahoney concluded that title could be established throughout most of the area included in the claim on the basis of archaeological and geographical evidence.[27]

Evidence for an Inuit aboriginal claim to offshore regions was considered at the Sikumiut Workshop sponsored by the Canadian Arctic Resources Committee and McGill University's Centre for Northern Studies and Research in 1982. This evidence did not concern a particular geographical area, which limits its usefulness in any specific claim, but the material presented does indicate that evidence is available concerning the extent of Inuit use of the marine and sea-ice areas.[28] However, this material presents a limited view of useful evidence. To establish aboriginal title to an area, Inuit need only to establish that they have used or occupied the area. It does not matter whether that area is ice-covered or open water. Inuit are able to use the sea ice in more intensive, varied, and permanent ways.

Substantial documentary evidence of Inuit use and occupancy of marine areas also can be found in land-use and occupancy studies conducted for both the Eastern Arctic Region[29] and Labrador Inuit.[30] Inuit use of the sea ice in Alaskan waters also has been described extensively.[31]

Archaeological Evidence

In summarizing the archaeological evidence presented in the Baker Lake case, Mr Justice Mahoney concluded that although the pre-Dorset culture (2000 to 1000 B.C.) was oriented to the land, the Dorset culture (1000 B.C. to A.D. 800) "disclosed a strong orientation to the hunting of sea mammals, on land and on the ice. Most known sites are coastal."[32] The Thule culture also was based on the coast and "was marked by advanced navigation, larger boats and the hunting of large sea mammals on the water and, for the first time, the use of dogs as traction animals."[33]

Dr George Wenzel identified three types of archaeological evidence that support Inuit use of the sea ice: "sea-ice living or house sites, faunal remains specific to the sea ice, and artifacts specifically related to the sea-ice environment."[34] Evidence of house sites is sparse due to the transitory nature of the *iglu* and the ice environment, although Thule whalebone sledshoes provide strong evidence of house sites. Artifacts associated with the toggle-head sealing harpoon are found throughout the Dorset and Thule periods and provide evidence of the use of marine fauna.

Historical and Anthropological Evidence

The historical record provided by explorers and writers such as Franz Boas, Vilhjalmur Stefansson, and members of the British arctic expeditions confirms Inuit folk memories of their once-intensive use of the sea ice.[35] Current Inuit use of the sea ice has been confirmed in Alaska, Greenland, Labrador, and the Canadian Arctic.[36] Extensive use of marine areas in the Lancaster Sound region also has been confirmed.[37]

Conclusion

The evidence discussed above clearly suggests that aboriginal use of the sea ice can be documented adequately to establish an Inuit aboriginal title. In the Baker Lake case, Mr Justice Mahoney appeared to have been satisfied that the Inuit claim was legitimate, although there was very little evidence of an organized society. It was sufficient that the Baker Lake Inuit were "organized to exploit the resources available on the barrens and essential to sustain human life there."[38]

Aboriginal use and occupancy is not confined to the sea ice. Within their own regions, Inuit use the entire marine environment. The most concentrated Inuit use of the marine environment probably occurs at the interface between land-fast ice and open water, either where a lead is opening up or where there is a permanent polynya (a space of open water).

Such a polynya occurs at the north-east end of Lancaster Sound. Inuit use is concentrated in these areas because of the high biological productivity of the sea-ice interface.[39]

Limitation or Extinguishment of an Inuit Aboriginal Title

Aboriginal title may be extinguished by purchase (treaty), conquest, or legislation. In the Calder case, Mr Justice Hall asserted that "once aboriginal title is established, it is presumed to continue until the contrary is proven."[40] Mr Justice Judson does not appear to have addressed directly the burden of proof that must be met prior to extinguishment of aboriginal title but, in agreement with the trial judge and the British Columbia Court of Appeal, he held that legislation of the Colony of British Columbia had extinguished aboriginal title because it established a "unity of intention to exercise . . . absolute sovereignty."[41] The better view is that a statutory provision that specifically extinguishes aboriginal title must be shown to exist, although the exercise of rights inherent in aboriginal title may be limited by applicable federal legislation. In the Baker Lake case, Mr Justice Mahoney ruled that aboriginal title had not been extinguished but that federal mining regulations had diminished the rights to hunt, trap, and fish held with aboriginal title.[42]

Extinguishment of aboriginal offshore rights raises questions about when the imperial and federal governments established sovereignty or sovereign rights over particular offshore areas. These questions are beyond the scope of this paper. Answering them would require an investigation of the legal status of the waters of the arctic archipelago.[43] Are they within the territories and, therefore, subject to general federal legislation, or are they subject only to legislation that applies specifically to offshore areas?[44]

The scope of an aboriginal offshore title is extraordinarily difficult to define.[45] At the very least, the title encompasses the rights to occupy and use the area and to hunt, trap, and fish.[46] In Canada, these rights may be limited by federal legislation such as the Fisheries Act and Regulations but it does not follow that rights to the area that conflict with aboriginal rights may be granted by the Crown. This distinction seems to have escaped Mr Justice Mahoney in the Baker Lake case. Nevertheless, a question remains about the extent to which aboriginal title reinforced by the 1982 Constitution Act may be used to restrain activities, access, and grants of title by the Crown that are inconsistent with the exercise and maintenance of aboriginal rights.[47]

Political Context of Aboriginal Claims

Government Reaction to Aboriginal Claims

Following the Supreme Court decision on the Calder case, the federal Department of Indian Affairs and Northern Development (DIAND) agreed to negotiate comprehensive claims to aboriginal title, but government policies say nothing about claims to marine areas.[48] Nevertheless, claims to renewable marine resources—rights to hunt and fish—are clearly negotiable.[49] In the one comprehensive claim negotiated to date—The James Bay and Northern Québec Agreement—offshore rights are not considered and the agreement extinguishes the aboriginal title of the Cree and Inuit only within Québec and "the Territory" as defined in the agreement.[50] Claims to the Hudson Bay area have been made by Québec Inuit but negotiations have not yet begun in earnest.

The Inuvialuit of the western Arctic, through the Committee for Original Peoples' Entitlement (COPE), have signed an agreement in principle with the federal government on their land-rights claim.[51] This agreement offers little information about the federal government's attitude toward offshore claims. On the one hand, it applies to the entire Western Arctic Region, which includes offshore marine areas, and grants preferential rights for the use of marine mammals and fish to the Inuvialuit throughout the region. On the other hand, the agreement does not grant any offshore property or mineral rights to the Inuvialuit.[52]

The clearest information about federal government policy on offshore claims is found in position papers on land selection as part of the process of settling claims. For example, a position paper by DIAND's Office of Native Claims lists the following "criteria for and constraints on land selection" for negotiations with Inuit of the eastern Arctic:

- All water, both fresh and salt, shall remain in Crown ownership and control.
- The beds of all salt water bodies, and tidal estuaries, shall remain in Crown ownership.
- The beds of all inland waters shall remain in Crown ownership. Exceptions may be considered where the ratio of water to land is so high as to make the separation impracticable.
- The proportion of coastline under native ownership will be subject to negotiation.[53]

So much for free negotiations.

Political Development in the Northwest Territories

The Inuit claim strategy has followed several tacks, including participation in the First Ministers' Conferences on Aboriginal Constitutional Matters, political development of the N.W.T., and creation of the new territory Nunavut. The move to create Nunavut as a separate territory is probably the most significant development for offshore claims, since it is likely to lead to a clear definition of territorial boundaries. At present, the seaward extent of the N.W.T. is not defined clearly.[54] This question probably will be answered definitively when the N.W.T. is divided. The provinces in Canada, however, have had a remarkable lack of success in appropriating offshore jurisdiction and property rights held by the federal government.[55] Unless the boundaries of Nunavut are based on the existing boundaries of the N.W.T., or unless Canada claims the waters among the arctic islands as internal waters under international law, the Nunavut boundaries, and therefore Inuit offshore claims, probably will be restricted to land areas.

Offshore Claims and Canadian Sovereignty

When a state acquires sovereignty or sovereign rights through international law or by virtue of uncontested or successful claims, these rights are subject to pre-existing property rights.[56] Consequently, Canada's international offshore claims and rights in the Arctic and off the west and east coasts are subject to pre-existing aboriginal property rights under domestic law. These aboriginal rights do not limit Canada's sovereignty *vis-à-vis* other nations, but, before they are extinguished, they do limit the freedom with which Canada can exercise its rights.

At the same time, Canada has obligations under international law; for example, Canada must permit innocent passage through its territorial waters. In settling aboriginal claims, Canada must take care not to violate its international obligations; therefore, Inuit may not be granted the right to exclude vessels from marine areas. One way in which Canada may circumvent this particular limitation of its power to grant rights to Inuit is to argue that traditional aboriginal use of offshore areas justifies a claim by the coastal state that these waters are historic waters. Under international law there is no right of innocent passage through historic waters.[57]

A Functional Resolution [58]

In the document *In All Fairness: A Native Claims Policy*, DIAND describes aboriginal claims negotiation as a process of translating the uncertain elements of aboriginal title into "concrete rights and benefits."[59] This description implies that rights held through aboriginal title are not real rights at all (even though such rights are recognized in the Constitution Act, 1982).[60] In this policy statement, DIAND argues that if northern aboriginal peoples wish to have any security of tenure they must give up their aboriginal title in exchange for limited tracts of land with limited ownership rights, hunting rights, monetary compensation, and aboriginal membership "on those appropriate boards and committees whose decisions affect the lives of their communities."[61] This limited view of the strength of aboriginal rights is appropriate only if these rights have, in fact, been diminished by legal decisions.[62] In the Baker Lake case and in other similar rulings, the courts recognize aboriginal title, but the title apparently is an empty one because the federal government continues to alienate resource rights prior to settling or extinguishing the claim. The existence of an aboriginal title does not appear to limit the actions of the federal government in this way. Consequently the negotiating positions of Inuit and other aboriginal peoples are weak and participation in the claims negotiation process may be fruitless.

Against this dismal imbalance between federal and aboriginal negotiating positions, any proposals for a functional resolution to Inuit aboriginal claims look overly optimistic—the more so for marine claims. Establishing the existence of an aboriginal title is only a beginning point. The strength of the title must be ascertained in order to bargain.

Tungavik Federation of Nunavut Negotiating Position

Since 1982, Inuit of the eastern Arctic have been represented in their aboriginal claim negotiations by the Tungavik Federation of Nunavut (TFN). Until recently, the TFN position for negotiating aboriginal claims was described best as a functional position: Inuit eschewed the traditional settlements of land, money, and hunting and trapping rights on the grounds that these would not be adequate to protect their interests. Inuit believed that they would never obtain title to lands adequate for hunting, trapping, and economic development through a settlement of their aboriginal claims. It is likely that, had they been interested in these traditional settlements, they would have been granted ownership of relatively small tracts of land with surface title only. Consequently, Inuit would have had no control over developments on adjacent lands and waters that might isolate and damage the lands and resources gained through such a traditional settlement.

Instead, TFN negotiators developed proposals that they felt would protect and enhance vital Inuit interests. In these proposals, Inuit differentiate between two types of entitlement to land. First, communities should own the land upon which they are built because they are communities, not because they are inhabited by Inuit who have unextinguished title to land. Secondly, in settling their land claims, Inuit should be able to select lands that are important to their needs. These proposals also call for clearly defined Inuit hunting and trapping rights, Inuit participation in the management of wildlife through a wildlife management board, and Inuit influence upon the use of non-Inuit lands.[63] The proposals suggest the following means for Inuit influence upon uses of non-Inuit lands:

- participation in local and regional planning agencies responsible for developing and implementing regional and local plans
- participation in a lands authority responsible for disposing of public land and resource rights[64]
- participation on an impact review board to consider the environmental and social impacts of major projects
- participation on a water board responsible for disposing of public water rights and reviewing major water-use proposals
- negotiation of development agreements among project proponents, Inuit, and affected communities.

In these proposals, TFN suggests that a share of the government royalty interest in Crown minerals and oil and gas, and a portion of the "Crown share" reserved under the Canada Oil and Gas Act, be used for Inuit economic development.[65] Entitlement to these shares would provide Inuit with revenue, a low-risk investment, and the right to participate in resource development. To balance deferred revenues from such shares in resource development, Inuit also propose monetary compensation.

Application of the TFN Negotiating Position to the Offshore

The rights claimed by TFN on behalf of the eastern Arctic Inuit fall into two categories. The first comprises property rights based on ownership (proprietary rights) such as the ownership of Inuit lands, royalty interests, and hunting and trapping rights. The second comprises management rights that can be fulfilled through participation in management agencies and authorities and on management boards. Management rights normally are the exclusive preserve of government, and public participation usually is limited to those interest groups that are consulted by government, but these rights are essential for Inuit to control the use of the environment in which they live.

Inuit of the eastern Arctic are addressing the issue of their right to participate in resource management from another direction. They propose that the Northwest Territories be divided and that the new territory of Nunavut be created in the eastern Arctic. The TFN negotiators argue that land claims can be applied to offshore as well as to land areas. They prefer not to let the question of offshore boundaries wait until the boundaries of Nunavut are defined; because of the current provincial–federal disputes over offshore jurisdiction, it is not realistic to assume that the federal government will be more willing to grant offshore jurisdiction to the territory of Nunavut.

The TFN negotiators argue that the seabed can be owned just as land can be owned, and that the various boards and agencies established for mineral and resource disposition, planning, wildlife management, and impact review can exercise jurisdiction over the waters of Hudson Bay and the arctic archipelago as effectively as they do over land uses. This approach is supported by current practices of the federal government. For example, the federal Environmental Assessment and Review Process (EARP), National Energy Board legislation, and the Canada Oil and Gas Act apply equally to onshore and offshore areas and activities.

Transportation and Navigation

The TFN proposals for settling aboriginal claims directly address most of the major uses of arctic marine regions. These major uses include exploitation of renewable and non-renewable resources, navigation and shipping, ports and harbours, Inuit hunting and fishing, protection of marine wildlife and environments, tourism, and national security. Under the TFN proposals, renewable resource exploitation in marine areas would be subject to the wildlife agreement, Inuit harvesting rights, and a wildlife management board. Non-renewable resource exploitation would be subject to the resource disposition agency, the planning authority, and the impact review procedures. However, Inuit proposals for management and ownership of land and resources have one major weakness—they do not suggest how Inuit may participate in managing marine transportation and navigation.

Navigation through ice-covered areas would affect current Inuit use of these areas. The Lancaster Sound green paper summarizes Inuit concerns about navigation in ice-covered waters.[66] These concerns include inadequate environmental safety measures for year-round shipping, the effect of ships' tracks through the ice on hunting patterns, and the potential for oil spills from oil-tanker traffic. Moreover, the effect of noise from these ships on marine wildlife has been identified as a major concern in the Arctic Pilot Project hearings.

It is unlikely that Inuit will obtain a veto, based on proprietary rights, management control, or devolution of federal powers to Nunavut, over the use of ice-covered areas for transportation and navigation. The Constitution Act of 1867 grants jurisdiction over marine transportation and navigation to the federal government,[67] and this control is unlikely to be diminished.

As an alternative to a veto, Inuit could propose the creation of an arctic marine transportation authority (AMTA), to which both Inuit and federal representatives would be appointed.[68] An AMTA would be like other agencies proposed for resource disposition and impact review. Such agencies would have federal, Inuit, and territorial representatives. Territorial representation may not be appropriate, however, because marine transportation and navigation are under federal jurisdiction. Inuit representation on an AMTA could be justified on the following grounds:

- aboriginal use and occupancy of offshore areas
- protection of hunting, fishing, and trapping rights
- access across the ice
- the right of residents to protect and influence the environment in which they live
- Inuit experience in the sea-ice environment.

Most of the jurisdiction exercised by an AMTA would be derived from jurisdiction currently exercised by the governor-general in council pursuant to the Arctic Waters Pollution Prevention Act.[69] An AMTA would have the power to:

- specify shipping control zones
- prohibit navigation by specific types of ships, or all ships, at certain times of the year
- prescribe construction and navigation standards, and types of cargo
- prescribe routes for particular vessel types
- control the establishment of major ports and harbours in arctic regions.

An AMTA would be expected to base its decisions on environmental and social, as well as technical, information. For example, an AMTA could prohibit all navigation through particularly sensitive marine habitats at certain times of the year. Consequently, an AMTA could regulate shipping in a way that would be compatible with management of the marine environment for purposes other than shipping.

The establishment of such an authority to control and regulate shipping through arctic marine waters would complement other agencies proposed by TFN. It would permit Inuit representatives to participate in management of marine areas and marine development without direct control based on proprietary right or title.

A Fall-back Position for Offshore Claimants

If the onshore and offshore regulatory agencies proposed by TFN are accepted, Inuit and the territorial governments will have a voice in all northern development decisions for the eastern Arctic. Inuit will be involved in important resource development decisions such as planning, resource disposition, environmental review, transportation proposals, water use, and effluent disposal. These proposals probably are too comprehensive, and give Inuit more control than will be accepted by the federal government.

As a possible fall-back position, Inuit could identify more precisely those offshore regions in which they have a special interest and include these areas in their aboriginal claims. The Inuit Land Use and Occupancy Study suggests that there is a good correlation between offshore areas used by Inuit and the land-fast ice areas, particularly the land-fast ice–sea interface.[70] Inuit use this area most intensively because it is more biologically productive than other areas. The way Inuit use this area and the physical characteristics of land-fast ice may allow it to be treated as land rather than as marine in the aboriginal claims process. Therefore, even if the TFN proposals for settling offshore claims are not acceptable for the entire offshore area, a good argument can be made that they should be accepted at least for the land-fast ice region and the sea–ice interface. Although it might be difficult, in practice, to draw boundaries between the land-fast ice and the open sea, this position may be an appropriate compromise between existing Inuit offshore claims and the federal government's unwillingness to consider offshore areas in claims negotiations.

Still another alternative to the TFN proposals is a coastal zone management authority. This authority would have jurisdiction over an area partly terrestrial and partly marine. The seaward boundary of such a coastal zone could be defined as the seaward limit of the land-fast ice. The landward boundary would be more difficult to define. Proposals for such coastal zone management schemes have suggested that this boundary be defined either as the watershed boundary or the high-water mark.

The coastal zone management authority might exercise some of the powers currently proposed for both the Nunavut Planning Board and the Nunavut Impact Review Board. Although such an authority might not itself control land and resource disposition within the coastal zone, the land managers would be expected to work within coastal zone plans.

Settlement of Offshore Claims in Alaska

In contrast to the Canadian Inuit struggle to include offshore claims in aboriginal title negotiations, the Inupiat of Alaska are pursuing their offshore claims in the courts. The 1971 Alaska Native Claims Settlement Act extinguished aboriginal title in the State of Alaska,[71] but the Inupiat of the North Slope currently are claiming before the U.S. courts that their aboriginal title to offshore areas beyond the three-mile state boundary has not been extinguished. The Inupiat claim sovereign rights and unextinguished aboriginal title to an area between 3 and 65 nautical miles offshore in the Beaufort and Chukchi seas of the Arctic Ocean. Defendants in the action include the United States government and numerous oil companies. The Inupiat argue that their claim "establishes rights to the surface of the sea, the water column beneath it, the seabed, and the minerals lying beneath the seabed within the geographic boundaries of their claim."[72] They therefore sought an injunction to restrain the sale of leases for the Beaufort Sea outer continental shelf and also are seeking damages and a declaration of their title to the area claimed.

The Inupiat requested a trial to resolve these claims but the defendants asked the court for a judgement on the pleadings. The United States District Court held that the federal government has supreme powers over the seas adjacent to the nation's boundaries—powers that are essential to national sovereignty. Any non-federal claim to sovereign powers (and, apparently, to property rights offshore) therefore must fail because it would be inconsistent with national sovereignty. Subsidiary Inupiat arguments, based on the federal government's responsibility to respect aboriginal title and on the right to protect Inupiat religious beliefs, also were rejected by the courts. The Inupiat have appealed this judgement to the United States Court of Appeal for the Ninth Circuit.

The Inupiat example suggests still another alternative for Canadian Inuit attempting to settle aboriginal claims. To date, Canadian aboriginal groups have been unwilling to litigate their claims. But the ability of Inuit to pursue their claims in the courts rather than around the negotiating table is bolstered by the 1982 Constitution Act.[73] In the absence of a *bona fide* federal government intention to negotiate all aspects of aboriginal claims, Inuit may have to consider litigation of their claims.

Endnotes

1. Letter to the Right Honourable Pierre E. Trudeau from Charlie Watt and Tagak Curley, co-chairmen, Inuit Committee on National Issues, 25 January 1983.

2. Minister of Justice and Attorney General of Canada, *Communiqué* (28 February 1983).

3. Proceedings of the First Ministers' Conference on Aboriginal Constitutional Matters, 15-16 March 1983, unpublished.

4. John C. Munro, Address to the Legislative Assembly, Yellowknife, 26 November 1982.

5. Nunavut Constitutional Forum, "Building Nunavut: A Discussion Paper Containing Proposals for an Arctic Constitution" (May 1983), p. 28.

6. Agreement between the Government of Canada and the Government of Nova Scotia Relating to Oil and Gas Resource Management and Revenue Sharing, 2 March 1982, Department of Energy, Mines and Resources.

7. The James Bay and Northern Québec Agreement (hereinafter, JBNQA), 11 November 1975 (Québec City: Éditeur officiel du Québec, 1976).

8. Office of the Prime Minister (The Rt. Hon. Joe Clark), *Communiqué* (3 Oct. 1979, 10:30 a.m. E.D.T.).

9. Ian Mulgrew, "Inuit Rights May Harm Bears: Biologist," *The Globe and Mail* (7 February 1983), p. 9.

10. Private interview between Greenland Premier Jonathan Motzfeldt and Peter Jull, Nuuk, Greenland, March 1981.

11. Eben Hopson, Sr, Welcoming Address, First Inuit Circumpolar Conference, Barrow, Alaska, 12-19 June 1977. See *The Arctic Policy Review* (North Slope Borough, June-July 1983), p. 2.

12. Jimmy Stotts, "The Need for an International Arctic Coastal Management Program," Second Inuit Circumpolar Conference, Nuuk, Greenland, 28 June-1 July 1980. See *The Arctic Coastal Zone Management Newsletter*, no. 29 (North Slope Borough, August 1980), p. 28.

13. Nunavut Constitutional Forum, *Building Nunavut: A Working Document with a Proposal for an Arctic Constitution* (Ottawa: NCF, 1983), pp. 42-43.

14. *Calder, et al. v. Attorney-General of British Columbia*, [1973] *Western Weekly Reports (WWR)* 4, pp. 1-91; *Hamlet of Baker Lake, et al. v. Minister of Indian Affairs and Northern Development, et al.*, (1980) *Dominion Law Reports* (Third Series) (*DLR* (3d)), 107, pp. 513-563.

15. See Royal Proclamation, 7 October 1763, *Revised Statutes Canada (RSC)* 1970, Appendix 1, p. 123. Concerning the geographical application of the Royal Proclamation, see the ruling of Mr Justice Judson, *Calder, et al.*, pp. 2-24; and *Sikyea* v. *The Queen*, [1964] *Supreme Court Reports* (Canada) *(SCR)*, pp. 642-646.

16. Geoffrey S. Lester, "Primitivism versus Civilization: A Basic Question in the Law of Aboriginal Rights to Land," in *Our Footprints are Everywhere: Inuit Land Use and Occupancy in Labrador*, ed., Carol Brice-Bennett (Nain: Labrador Inuit Association, 1977), pp. 360-363; see also the ruling of Mr Justice Hall, *Calder, et al.*, p. 60.

17. United Nations Convention on the Law of the Sea (A/CONF 62/122), opened for signature 10 December 1982, Montego Bay (hereinafter, UNCLOS). Reprinted in *International Legal Materials (ILM)* 21 (1982), p. 1261. See arts. 2, 3, 56, 77. The convention has not yet entered into force and is unlikely to do so for several years. Basic concepts, such as the continental shelf and exclusive economic zones, however, are now accepted as customary international law.

18. Ibid., art. 56.

19. Ibid., art. 234.

20. *Calder, et al.*, p. 11. In the Calder case, the Nishga Indians of north-western British Columbia sought a declaration that their aboriginal title had never been extinguished lawfully. The Supreme Court of Canada split three-three in voting on this question; the seventh judge decided the question against the Nishgas on a technical point of procedure.

21. Ibid., p. 49.

22. Although the aboriginal property system must be capable of articulation, it need not be capable of abstract definition under the common law. See *Re Southern Rhodesia*, (1919) *Appeal Cases (AC)* 211, p. 233.

23. *Calder, et al.*, pp. 37, 39.

24. *Hamlet of Baker Lake, et al.* In the Baker Lake case, the Inuit plaintiffs asserted an existing aboriginal title to a portion of the Northwest Territories around the Hamlet of Baker Lake. They contended that the defendants—federal government officials and mining companies—permitted or engaged in activities that interfered with the plaintiffs' aboriginal rights.

25. On Inuit use of the sea ice see George Wenzel, "Nunamiut vs Sikumiut: Prehistoric Canadian Politics," in *Sikumiut: "The People Who Use the Sea Ice,"* eds, Alan Cooke and Edie Van Alstine (Ottawa: Canadian Arctic Resources Committee, 1984).

26. See evidence of Dr Wilson Duff reproduced in *Calder, et al.*, pp. 37, 38.

27. *Baker Lake, et al.*, pp. 544, 547.

28. See Alan Cooke, "Historical Evidence for Inuit Use of the Sea-ice Environment," in *Sikumiut* (see above, note 25).

29. Inuit Land Use and Occupancy Project, *Report: Inuit Land Use and Occupancy Project*, 3 vols (Ottawa: Supply and Services, 1976).

30. Carol Brice-Bennett, *Our Footprints are Everywhere* (see above, note 16).

31. Richard K. Nelson, *Hunters of the Northern Ice* (Chicago and London: University of Chicago Press, 1969).

32. *Baker Lake, et al.*, p. 519.

33. Ibid.

34. George Wenzel, "Archaeological Evidence for Prehistoric Inuit Use of the Sea-ice Environment," in *Sikumiut* (see above, note 25).

35. Alan Cooke, "Historical Evidence for Inuit Use of the Sea-ice Environment," in *Sikumiut* (see above, note 25).

36. Milton M.R. Freeman, "Contemporary Inuit Exploitation of the Sea-ice Environment," in Alan Cooke, *Sikumiut* (see above, note 25).

37. K. Harper and G.G. McLean, *Socio-Economic Characteristics and Conservation Interests of the Lancaster Sound Region*, Lancaster Sound Regional Study Background Report 3 (Ottawa: DIAND, 1980), pp. 29–31.

38. *Baker Lake, et al.*, p. 544.

39. M.J. Dunbar, "The Biological Significance of Arctic Ice," in *Sikumiut* (see above, note 25).

40. *Calder, et al.*, p. 70.

41. Ibid, p. 15.

42. *Baker Lake, et al.*, p. 557. Although this case may be consistent with other cases such as *Regina* v. *Derriksan* ((1977) *DLR* (3d) 71, pp. 159–160) it supports an extremely worrisome doctrine. It stands for the proposition that, even when aboriginal title has not been extinguished, the federal government may legislate in conflict with aboriginal title although such legislation would not be specific enough to extinguish title. In this way, aboriginal title may be whittled away with no need for the government to comply with any specific forms and procedures. A different conclusion might be reached now following entrenchment of aboriginal rights in the constitution: see Kent McNeil, "The Constitutional Rights of the Aboriginal Peoples of Canada," *Supreme Court Law Review* 4 (1982), p. 257.

43. See, for example, Donat Pharand, *The Law of the Sea of the Arctic: With Special Reference to Canada* (Ottawa: University of Ottawa Press, 1973).

44. Legislation is far less likely to have extinguished offshore aboriginal claims than terrestrial claims because federal legislation generally was not considered to apply to the offshore and provincial legislation could not apply beyond territorial borders.

45. See *St. Catherine's Milling and Lumber Co.* v. *The Queen in Right of Ontario*, (1888) *App. Cas. (AC)* 14: 46 (Privy Council).

46. *Baker Lake, et al.*, p. 547.

47. Constitution Act, 1982, ss. 35, 52(1). For a discussion of the effect of section 35 of the Constitution Act on existing and aboriginal treaty rights see Kent McNeil, "The Constitutional Rights of the Aboriginal Peoples of Canada" (see above, note 42) and Slattery, "The Constitutional Guarantee of Aboriginal and Treaty Rights," *Queen's Law Journal* 8 (1983), p. 232. Early indications are that the courts will take a very restrictive view of these sections. For example, in *Bear* v. *The Queen*, [1983] *Canadian Native Law Reporter (CNLR)* 3:57 (Sask. QB) it was held that treaty-based hunting rights continue to be subject to regulation under the Migratory Birds Convention Act.

48. See, for example, DIAND, *In All Fairness: A Native Claims Policy, Comprehensive Claims* (Ottawa: DIAND, 1981).

49. DIAND has issued a series of maps under the title "Comprehensive Native Claims in Canada." These maps show that large marine and terrestrial areas will be considered in land-claims negotiations.

50. JBNQA (see above, note 7).

51. Committee for Original Peoples' Entitlement and the Government of Canada, represented by the Minister of Indian Affairs and Northern Development, Inuvialuit Land Rights Settlement, Agreement-in-principle, Sachs Harbour, 31 October 1978 (hereinafter, COPE agreement in principle).

52. Ibid. There is some ambiguity about the definition of the Western Arctic Region in the COPE agreement in principle. The definition section suggests that this region also has to be within the current boundaries of the N.W.T. It is not clear that the N.W.T., as defined by the Northwest Territories Act (*RSC* 1970, c. N-22), includes offshore areas in the Beaufort Sea.

53. Office of Native Claims, DIAND, "Position Paper on Land Selection Criteria for I.T.C. Claim" (Ottawa, November 1980), p. 5. In May 1983, TFN and the federal government negotiated an agreement in principle to guide the selection of lands and resources. This new arrangement is considerably less restrictive than that described in the Office of Native Claims position paper.

54. Two cases that take an expansive view of the seaward extent of the N.W.T., and are therefore important for the future boundaries of Nunavut, are *Regina* v. *Tootalik E4-321*, (1970) *WWR* 71, pp. 435–444, and *B.P. Exploration Company (Libya) Limited* v. *Hunt*, [1981] *WWR* 1, pp. 209–247. In *B.P. Exploration, etc.*, v. *Hunt*, the court held that federal exploration permits for areas some 20 nautical miles out in the Beaufort Sea were within the boundaries of the N.W.T. In *R.* v. *Tootalik*, the court held that an infraction of the N.W.T. Game Ordinance occurred on the sea ice in Pasley Bay.

55. On the west coast, the federal government has both the property rights to and legislative jurisdiction over those waters off the west coast of Vancouver Island; see *Reference re: Offshore Mineral Rights of British Columbia*, (1967) *SCR*, pp. 792–822. The status of Georgia Strait is currently uncertain. The British Columbia Court of Appeal determined that these areas were within the province but the judgement of the Supreme Court of Canada is pending on this matter; see *Reference re: Ownership of the Bed of the Strait of Georgia and Related Areas*, (1977) *British Columbia Law Reports* 1 (British Columbia Court of Appeal), pp. 97–141. The Newfoundland Court of Appeal recently has determined that the seabed and subsoil of a three-nautical-mile territorial sea off the Newfoundland and Labrador coast were vested in the Crown in right of Newfoundland, but that the continental shelf was not; see *Reference re: Mineral and Other Natural Resources of the Continental Shelf*, (1983) *DLR* (3d), vol. 145, pp. 9–41. This decision is currently under appeal. The federal government also has initiated a reference to the Supreme Court of Canada on the Hibernia region seeking to clarify the application of federal and provincial jurisdiction in the area.

56. The authority for this proposition is derived primarily from the Royal Proclamation of 1763 and later rulings on its application (see above, note 15). Acquisition of territory in this manner is closer to acquisition by peaceful occupation than to acquisition by conquest.

57. On the question of historic waters, see Donat Pharand, *The Law of the Sea of the Arctic* (see above, note 43), pp. 98–144. This is clearly a way in which aboriginal use and occupancy of the offshore could help the federal government to extend its claims to coastal jurisdiction.

58. In this context, a functional approach is one that considers the diverse aims and purposes (functions) of offshore claim negotiations and translates these aims into specific participation rights, such as the right to receive revenue, the right to harvest resources, and the right to participate in marine planning and management through boards and authorities.

59. DIAND, *In All Fairness* (see above, note 48), p. 19.

60. Constitution Act, 1982, s. 35.

61. DIAND, *In All Fairness* (see above, note 48), p. 23.

62. See, for example, *Baker Lake, et al.*; *R. v. Derriksan* (note 42); and *Kruger and Manuel* v. *The Queen*, [1977] *WWR* 4, pp. 300–310. In *R. v. Kruger and Manuel*, the Supreme Court of Canada held that Indians not relying upon treaty rights were subject to generally applicable provincial game laws. Mr Justice Dickson ruled that "Assuming, without deciding, that the theory of aboriginal title . . . is available in respect of present appellants, it has been conclusively decided that such title, as any other, is subject to regulations imposed by validly enacted federal laws."

63. See "Summary of Wildlife Agreement-in-Principle," *Nunavut Newsletter* 2 (15 July 1982), pp. 7–9.

64. The idea for a joint lands authority is supported by the recent Canada–Nova Scotia Agreement Relating to Oil and Gas Resource Management and Revenue Sharing (see above, note 6). The agreement establishes a joint Canada–Nova Scotia board to exercise the discretions of the minister under the Canada Oil and Gas Act (*SC* 1980-81-82-83, c.81). Such a board could be formed for territorial and offshore areas in the North, and the agreement could allow for gradual devolution of power to northern residents. The agreement has been criticized because power, under the agreement, effectively remains with the federal government. At best, Nova Scotia has the power to delay offshore activities but not to veto them. The territories currently have no control over resource disposition, and therefore view such an agreement as a major step forward.

65. Canada Oil and Gas Act, *SC* 1980-81-82-83, c. 81, s. 37. The TFN claim to royalty interest was expressed as a claim to a share of the production reserved by and payable to the Crown rather than a claim to the lessees' share. The Crown share is a 25 per cent share reserved by the Crown when it grants exploration agreements under the Canada Oil and Gas Act. This share is "carried" because the Crown does not have to pay its 25 per cent share of the costs until a production scheme is authorized by the minister.

66. Lancaster Sound Regional Study, *The Lancaster Sound Region: 1980-2000, Issues and Options on the Use and Management of the Region*, Green Paper (Ottawa: DIAND, 1981), p. 21.

67. Constitution Act, 1867, s. 91.10.

68. An arctic marine transportation authority has been created within the federal Department of Transport. However, the term "authority" is a misnomer because this agency is no more than an interdepartmental co-ordinating committee.

69. Arctic Waters Pollution Prevention Act, *RSC* 1970, c.2 (1st Supp).

70. Inuit Land Use and Occupancy Project, *Report* (see above, note 29).

71. Alaska Native Claims Settlement Act, (1971) *USC* 43:1601.

72. *Inupiat Community of the Arctic Slope, et al.*, v. *United States of America, et al.*, (F. Supp.) 548:182 (D. Alaska 1982), p. 185.

73. Constitution Act, 1982, ss. 25, 35.

Arctic Marine Transportation: A View from the Bridge

Captain T.C. Pullen
Marine Transportation Consultant

Introduction

Modern marine transportation in Canada's Arctic began in the 1950s with the building of the Distant Early Warning (DEW) line. During the summers of 1955, 1956, and 1957, 324 ships delivered 1.25 million metric tons of dry cargo and more than 10.25 million barrels* of oil to destinations north of the Arctic Circle from Barrow, Alaska, east to Greenland. In 1962, with the discovery of the Mary River iron-ore body on Baffin Island, the possibility was first considered that very large ice-breaking ore carriers could be built to deliver this rich, direct-shipping ore to Europe. This has yet to happen. The pace of arctic development has accelerated significantly since then, beginning with the discovery of oil in Prudhoe Bay in 1968. The successful navigation of the Northwest Passage by the 155 000-metric-ton steam tanker *Manhattan* and the more recent Canadian efforts to locate commercial quantities of oil and gas in the Beaufort Sea region have added to this increased interest in arctic marine shipping. These activities have created the need to plan for marine transport of resources.

There never has been year-round movement of ships of any sort, including icebreakers, anywhere in Canada's arctic waters. Annual resupply of remote settlements, regular delivery of cargoes to exploration companies, and scientific investigations of arctic oceanography, hydrography, and seismology by private companies and government agencies all are undertaken during the summer navigation season. This is the time when nature relents and some ice cover breaks and melts, permitting ships to penetrate some arctic waters to meet their commitments. Such seasonal shipping has been going on for years—the resupply of settlements for many years—and it employs a variety of vessels including icebreakers, ice-strengthened and unstrengthened ships, tugs, and barges.

*[1 barrel equals approximately 0.16 m³]

Impact of Year-round Traffic

Recent events such as the drop in world oil prices, the discovery of oil off Newfoundland, and the discovery of gas off Nova Scotia will slow production plans for arctic oil and gas. The prospect remains, however, that arctic oil and gas eventually will be transported to southern markets. The economics of oil and gas production and transportation require continuous delivery, year round. Year-round shipping will require special ships that have tremendous size, strength, and power. In general terms, the larger the ship, the more cargo she can carry at less cost. In the Arctic, this size–profit ratio pays another dividend: massive ships make superb icebreakers. Success in breaking polar ice is as much a matter of mass as of power or thrust. The more massive the vessel, the better an icebreaker it is. If year-round navigation through portions of the Northwest Passage is necessary, then only ice-breaking commercial giants will be capable of doing the job.

The prospect of year-round traffic through Canada's arctic waters raises several questions that are of concern to northerners and mariners alike. What will be the effect on the undisturbed winter-ice regime when the ice is sundered by these great vessels? Will ships use the tracks opened by other ships, thus adding to the icy rubble, or will it be easier to break a fresh channel on each pass? How long does it take for this icy débris to refreeze? What impact will this activity have on northerners who have traditionally used the smooth, land-fast ice as a winter highway? Can an ice sheet with a 60-metre-wide channel cut through it come together again instead of refreezing? This process creates ridges and, if repeated over the winter, could convert a level ice surface to a rafted and hummocked jumble of ice blocks. No one knows how ship traffic might affect springtime break-up patterns of land-fast ice. Answering these questions will require on-site investigations and experiments using ships—a role for a Coast Guard polar icebreaker. This is not possible now because of the inadequacies of the present Canadian fleet.

Foreign Interest in the Northwest Passage

Year-round navigation of the Northwest Passage does not hinge necessarily on the fate of Canadian projects in the Beaufort Sea and among the arctic islands. Canadians know that other countries have an interest in the availability of northern resources and a determination to take advantage of these resources in the future. Japan and the United States are two front runners in this regard. In a world where a secure and reliable source of oil is crucial, Japan is more vulnerable than any other developed nation. Japan is entirely dependent on imports but is far removed from its major supplier, the Middle East, which is in perpetual turmoil. It is therefore understandable that Japan is turning more and more to Canada as a closer and more reliable source of energy resources. For years, coal has been exported to Japan from British Columbia, and coal exports may be followed by liquefied natural gas (LNG) from the west coast. Japanese companies also have invested $400 million in Beaufort oil exploration, which is to be repaid later from production revenues.

Canada must achieve energy self-sufficiency before oil can be exported, but future prospects for shipping Canadian oil to Japan cannot be ignored. The Beaufort Sea is only 3600 nautical miles from Yokohama; this is approximately half the distance from Yokohama to the Persian Gulf. Japanese experts are said to have an interest in the eastern approaches to the Northwest Passage through Baffin Bay and Davis Strait. It seems reasonable to infer from this interest that movement of oil by ice-breaking tankers sailing under Japanese flags from, for example, the Hibernia field off Nova Scotia through the Northwest Passage could be in the cards. The distance, after all, is only 6300 nautical miles—virtually the same distance as that separating Yokohama from the Persian Gulf.

Ever since the discovery of oil in Prudhoe Bay, the United States has considered seriously the year-round use of the Northwest Passage to transport oil to its east coast. The voyages of the *Manhattan* represented a first step toward this goal. The decision to build the Trans-Alaska pipeline instead does not mean that U.S. plans to use the Northwest Passage have been shelved permanently. It is possible that by the year 2000, when oil production may rise to, say, two million barrels per day along the North Coast of Alaska, the use of U.S.-flag ice-breaking tankers could become a reality.

The U.S. Coast Guard currently is testing its two new icebreakers, *Polar Sea* and *Polar Star*, off the north coast of Alaska and in the Northwest Passage. It remains to be seen whether these ships can navigate these waters successfully in April and May, when arctic ice is thickest. Displacing just 12 000 metric tons but developing 60 000-shaft horsepower (with excursions to 75 000-shaft horsepower), these icebreakers lack the weight needed to break through thick, hummocked ice. These ships obtain their high horsepower with gas turbines, which are notoriously fuel-thirsty at high powers. A prolonged struggle through ice could cause problems: dwindling fuel reserves would be a source of anxiety, and, when ships consume large quantities of fuel, they ride higher in the water, become less effective as icebreakers, and risk damage to propellers and rudders.

Sovereignty in Arctic Waters

Whatever the status of the Northwest Passage, whether or not it is universally accepted as internal waters of Canada, Canada must be able to deploy convincing evidence of sovereignty if and when ships sailing under foreign flags attempt to navigate these waters. The Canadian Coast Guard should have ready all the plans and specifications necessary to contract, without delay, the construction of Canada's first 100 000-shaft horsepower polar icebreaker.

The Canadian Coast Guard currently is replacing its ageing fleet of so-called front-line icebreakers. Three of the four ships in the present fleet are more than 25 years old. First, *d'Iberville* was declared surplus, and *Labrador*, built in 1953, probably will be next. To replace these ships and expand the fleet, the Coast Guard is deploying ships of a new design—the R. Class. Three of these new ships—*Pierre Radisson*, *Sir John Franklin*, and *Des Groseilliers*—are in service now and are reported to be very successful. But no matter how satisfactory these new vessels may be, the Coast Guard is replacing inadequate old ships with inadequate new ships. An R. Class ship, with twin screws and a centreline rudder, is more difficult to manoeuvre and more vulnerable to crippling damage from ice than are the older ships. In fact, the deeper-draft veterans *John A. Macdonald* and *Louis S. St-Laurent* are heavier and more powerful, and have the significant advantage of three rather than two propellers.

The world leader for number and size of icebreakers is the Soviet Union. The first surface vessel ever to navigate the Arctic Ocean and attain the North Pole was the U.S.S.R.'s *Arktika*. This feat demonstrated that larger, heavier, and more powerful icebreakers are able to operate farther north for more of the year—even all year—than are the smaller ships Canada is building as replacements. Large Soviet icebreakers are propelled by self-contained generators (and therefore have unlimited endurance), displace more than 30 000 metric tons, and develop 75 000-shaft horsepower. Canada, on the other hand, seems content to meet its arctic responsibilities, at least for the next ten years, with ships that displace 7600 metric tons and develop only 13 600-shaft horsepower.

If there is a requirement for ships capable of operating in Canada's part of the Northwest Passage, then a large, powerful, polar icebreaker also is needed. As long ago as 1971, the *Vancouver Sun* editorialized as follows:

> The difficulty of establishing and maintaining Canada's sovereignty in the Arctic is well understood in Ottawa .... if there is any nation ready to dispute Canada's claims to the Arctic more than any other, it is the U.S. ... Canada's chances of dealing with

pollution in the Arctic are not bright unless it can assert its sovereignty over the waters there. . . . Canada needs muscle. One way to get it is to build ships, especially icebreakers, of sufficient power and range.[1]

In the same year, the federal government announced plans to construct a large new icebreaker. The House of Commons Standing Committee on Indian Affairs and Northern Development urged its construction,[2] but the planning continues.

Submarine Transportation of Cargo

The feasibility of using submarines to transport cargo through arctic waters is a question that frequently arises. General Dynamics, one of the chief proponents of the use of submarines to deliver arctic oil and LNG to market, makes the following argument:

> The primary advantage offered by a submarine system over a surface ship system is the ability to deliver a constant cargo volume at uniform, predictable schedule intervals year-round, regardless of surface ice and weather conditions.[3]

Nor would the shallow straits of the Northwest Passage be a major problem, according to General Dynamics:

> Water depths of 200 fathoms [366 metres] or more would permit a submarine tanker to maintain cruising depth and speed over practically the entire length of any proposed shipping route. Only in the western Barrow Strait, where depths as shallow as 300 feet [91 metres] are experienced, would a submarine be subject to operational constraints.[4]

This choke-point in Barrow Strait, however, would seriously restrict the movements of the large vessels General Dynamics is considering.

General Dynamics avoids this problem with its claim that "for several years nuclear-powered submarines have routinely cruised Arctic waters year-round without difficulty."[5] To compare the U.S. Navy submarines such as *Skate* and *Seadragon* with the monsters proposed by General Dynamics is to compare minnows with whales. *Skate* is 183 metres long and displaces 4280 metric tons. The General Dynamics leviathans would be nearly 448 metres long and would have an incredibly large submerged displacement of 860 650 metric tons.

The prospect of these enormous vessels groping their way safely through Barrow Strait, where as little as ten degrees' change of trim from straight and level would result in grounding on the rocky seabed or colliding with the overhead ice canopy, is justifiable cause for concern. If the economics of bulk transportation are favourable, cargo-carrying submarines of this sort might be better deployed on transpolar routes in the Arctic Ocean where there is ample clearance in all directions.

The State of Arctic Marine Hydrography

In September 1969, the 155 000-metric-ton *Manhattan* was west-bound in the Beaufort Sea, trailed by a Canadian icebreaker. The *Manhattan* sailed unknowingly over an uncharted shoal, on which she was within seven metres of impaling herself. It was subsequently established that this shoal is a pingo-like feature similar to the large mounds of ice covered by soil found on land in some arctic areas. There are 1500 or more pingoes on land in the Tuktoyaktuk area, but the *Manhattan*'s near-miss was the first indication that similar formations also exist offshore.

The Canadian Hydrographic Service (CHS) has surveyed the area since 1969 and has found several hundred similar features in the Beaufort Sea. If ships drawing more than 20 metres routinely travel through these waters, it may be necessary to confine their movements to "safe" or "swept" channels until thorough surveys of the entire area are completed. Because of the extensive hydrography required to make arctic waters safe for these great ships, it may be necessary as a first step to survey channels for navigation until resources are available for area surveys.

The *Manhattan*'s near-miss is one example of the shipping risks that are to be found throughout arctic waters. A great deal of hydrographic work is needed still if vessels of any size—particularly the big ships—are to navigate these waters safely. In considering arctic marine transportation, those with landlocked minds dwell overmuch on the obvious hazard—ice of every sort. But the chief danger is the uncharted underwater pinnacle. If these obstructions are hazards for surface-travelling ships, then they will be even greater hazards for huge cargo-carrying submarines. It will be crucial for navigators of submarines to know not only about the icy stalactites above, but also about the undulations and rocky stalagmites below.

Many arctic charts still used for navigation are based on reconnaissance data more suitable for smaller ships that draw less than 10 metres. The experience of the *Manhattan* supports the pressing need to accelerate arctic hydrography. It will be necessary first, however, to support the CHS in acquiring the resources it needs to accomplish this goal. That service is now fully committed.

Canada's disputed claim to sovereignty over arctic waters, particularly over those of the Northwest Passage, is unlikely to be honoured if a thorough and accurate survey is further delayed. The task is a large one, the conditions are difficult, and the time needed for completion of this task should not be underestimated. The amount of work that can be accomplished in a year in southern waters will take three or more years in the North.

Control of Shipping

The traditional freedom of shipmasters to guide their ships where they wish may need modification in arctic waters. Sensitive environments, such as Lancaster Sound at certain times of the year, might have to be avoided deliberately even though they may lie along the best route for a ship seeking the easiest path through pack ice. Notices to Mariners, the customary method for passing important navigation information, in future could include environmental cautions and warnings advising shipmasters of the need to avoid specific sensitive areas.

Mariners and environmentalists should be able to co-operate more effectively to resolve the legitimate concerns of both parties. Conflicts must be resolved between environmentalists and the mariners who will be sailing the great ships year round through arctic straits and sounds. Environmentalists wish to control and regulate year-round shipping through the Northwest Passage. They propose traffic lanes and "no go" zones. Mariners, however, cannot manoeuvre their ships along such "tram lines" because ice prevents this in many instances. To find the route of least resistance, icebreakers must steer a crooked and unpredictable course. This practice conflicts with the concept of traffic lanes and traffic control. Shipmasters must continue to have some freedom to manoeuvre. In many circumstances, ice conditions may allow ships to avoid a sensitive wildlife area, but shipping in the arctic, unlike shipping in more temperate waters, does not lend itself to the management of vessel traffic.

Greenlanders have voiced loudly their concerns about arctic shipping, particularly in response to the Arctic Pilot Project (APP), a proposal to ship liquefied natural gas from producing fields on Melville Island to markets in eastern Canada. The APP proposes to use two Arctic Class 7 ships (an Arctic Class 7 ship has the ability to make continuous progress through ice seven feet thick). Greenlanders fear that year-round traffic of these large ships passing close to the west coast of Greenland will interfere with traditional over-ice hunting routes. They also are apprehensive about the effect of propeller noise on marine mammals. Inuit of eastern Baffin Island have joined this protest.

At the National Energy Board (NEB) hearings into the APP's application to proceed with this plan, project sponsors produced diagrams that showed, in error, that the routes the ships would take going into Melville Bay ran very close to the Greenland coast. It is reported that these route diagrams were the result of a faulty computer programme. Why those representing the APP would have made such an error is not known.

Arctic Class 7 ships can navigate multi-year ice in Viscount Melville Sound. There is no need for these ships to take an inshore route off Greenland. The ice in Baffin Bay and Davis Strait is primarily first-year ice; these icebreakers easily would be capable of steering a course through the middle of Baffin Bay, where they would be 150 nautical miles away from both Greenland and Baffin Island. Small ships favour the eastern side of Baffin Bay where there is open water and loose pack ice.

The issue of propeller noise is more difficult to address. It has not yet been proved that a problem exists.

Impact of New Technology

Given that an environmentally safe Arctic class tanker can be built, and that professionally able and dedicated persons can be trained to handle such a ship in the demanding circumstances of arctic shipping, there remains the matter of safe and timely delivery of cargoes. A knowledge of the climate and environments with which shipmasters will have to cope, and the ability of shipmasters to navigate their ships safely and handle them effectively, will be aided by new technology.

An accurate record of a ship's position is difficult to maintain if she is zig-zagging to avoid heavy ice and cannot obtain frequent and reliable position information. In the wide expanses of Baffin Bay, Davis Strait, and the Beaufort Sea, land features are not within sight or radar range. Many shipmasters rely on dead reckoning until they make a landfall. Celestial navigation is difficult in high latitudes and, in any case, is often impossible due to whiteouts, fog, and indeterminate horizons. Hyperbolic navigation methods, such as Loran-C and Omega, are available but unreliable and inaccurate because of atmospheric influences of the aurora borealis and the Greenland ice-cap.

The satellite navigation (Satnav) system is now available to shipmasters. It is accurate, reliable, compact, and inexpensive. Satellites in polar orbits provide position data every 30 minutes and dead reckoning is sufficient within these brief intervals. Even this short gap in precise position information from satellite signals can be offset by extremely accurate speed information from Doppler sonar, another new technology. These new technologies can provide a continuous and accurate record of a ship's position in the sea approaches to the arctic islands, regardless of weather and atmospheric conditions.

Although the Satnav system is accurate to within a few metres, it has little practical value if navigators must plot the data on charts that may be as much as ten nautical miles in error because they are based on reconnaissance data that are less accurate than the Satnav data. When a ship is beyond radar range of land, the Satnav system would be useful. Within radar range of land, it is more prudent to rely on radar. Among the arctic islands, land is usually within visual and radar range.

In recent years, there have been many improvements in methods for detecting and classifying ice. Satellite imagery, laser profilometers, infrared sensors, low-light-level television, and side-looking airborne radar are some of the new developments to help navigators detect and differentiate among the many forms of ice: icebergs, bergy bits, growlers, pack ice, land-fast ice, and ice islands, to list a few. Long-range, fixed-wing, ice-reconnaissance aircraft, each fitted with every imaginable piece of new equipment, patrol the northern seas. The information they gather, together with satellite imagery, provides detailed ice reports for forecasters ashore and ships at sea.

Forward-looking sonars for ice detection have not been developed for icebreakers because it is difficult to protect the associated transducers from being damaged by the ice they are intended to locate, and because their mountings may weaken the hull, where strength is crucial. Modern echo-sounders supply accurate digital and graphic depth information and warn navigators of shoaling water and other hazards. They also have built-in alarms to alert an inattentive or harassed mate on watch that his ship has entered shallow waters.

The struggle of man against ice is centuries old, but the modern navigator in ice-filled waters has an impressive array of technical marvels available to him; he may have more than he needs. Every new "black box" installed on the bridge is one more piece of equipment that requires his attention. He must understand the technical intricacies of each, must calibrate and tune them all, and must have the sense to know whether the information they provide is accurate and useful.

Marine Transportation Needs: A Summary

The voyages of the *Manhattan* in 1969 and 1970, and concerns about damage to the arctic environment from oil spills, have received national attention. In 1970, the federal government passed into law the Arctic Waters Pollution Prevention Act. This act is implemented, with regard to shipping, through the Arctic Shipping Pollution Prevention Regulations and the Shipping Safety Control Zones Order. These regulations divide the Arctic into 16 zones and define the periods during which ships of all sorts, from unstrengthened vessels to Arctic-Class-10 icebreakers, are permitted to operate within these zones.

Although these regulations were drafted in haste, they are, in general, well conceived and realistic. As arctic shipping experience is gained, these regulations should be modified to reflect improved knowledge of ice, ship performance, and construction standards. In addition to these regulations, there is a need for guidelines that will satisfy the real concerns of conservationists and environmentalists, not so much with respect to pollution, which has already been addressed, but with respect to the operations of ships in those areas that should be avoided.

Those unfamiliar with marine shipping but who are responsible for its regulation, especially in the Arctic, often respond to concerns about the possibility of some disaster by insisting that shippers use more navigational aids. Overkill should be resisted. The utility of sophisticated gear is more important than quantity and variety.

The Canadian Coast Guard has, and will continue to have, an adequate icebreaker force for its summer commitments in the North. But it must have icebreakers equal to or better than Arctic Class 7 to meet its year-round commitments in the Arctic. Until at least one of these powerful vessels is in use, it will not be possible to answer the numerous questions concerning the challenges of arctic shipping between October and July.

It is important that the status of Canadian sovereignty in the waters of the Northwest Passage be resolved before year-round shipping begins. Canada must have ready the icebreakers, navigational aids, charts, sailing directions, and tide tables necessary to assist and control arctic shipping. There also should be international acceptance of Canada's regulatory measures for the safe conduct of ships through its waters, whatever the status of Canada's sovereignty within the Northwest Passage may be at that time.

Special qualifications and certification should be required of ship-masters and mates engaged in year-round operations in the Arctic. A headquarters for regulation of arctic shipping should be established in the North. But unnecessary regulation should be avoided.

Endnotes

1. Editorial, *Vancouver Sun* (17 November 1971).

2. House of Commons, *Minutes of Proceedings and Evidence of the Standing Committee on Indian Affairs and Northern Development*, Issue 25 (Ottawa House of Commons, 15 June 1971), pp. 25:3–25:4.

3. General Dynamics Corporation, *A Submarine LNG Tanker Concept for the Arctic*, by P. Takis Veliotis and Spencer Reitz, revised (1 October 1981), p. 1.

4. Ibid.

5. Ibid.

Ocean Management:
A Theoretical Perspective

Ken Beauchamp
Director, Arctic Ocean Programme
Canadian Arctic Resources Committee

Introduction

The idea of managing the ocean and its resources is relatively new. It would be wrong to assume that the legal and administrative mechanisms that have been applied to the use and management of land and land-based resources are directly adaptable to the ocean. It is an environment that is very different from land. Use of its resources involves different interests, is subject to different legal principles, has different requirements for science and technology, and often has international implications.

The practice of controlling ocean uses has been carried on for a long time through national legislation that regulates separate uses and activities in the very narrow territorial seas; however, control of offshore activities has never addressed the problem of "managing" the ocean as a total system. The term "ocean management," as it is used now by the international community and by national ocean-policy agencies, means a systematic and comprehensive process of planning that takes into account the relationships between the natural ocean system, its resources, human uses, and regulatory programmes. This concept of management has not yet been developed adequately or applied in any programme now operating. There is still much that is not known about the natural ocean system and, until now, there has not been an international legal order that provides the opportunity and incentive for coastal states to manage the offshore properly. The new draft United Nations Convention on the Law of the Sea does this by creating a legal basis for larger offshore zones in which coastal states have limited rather than absolute jurisdiction.[1] Canada and other coastal states will be acquiring extended jurisdictions offshore; therefore each state must begin to address the responsibilities and opportunities and the economic and political changes that will accompany the new law of the sea.

This paper will examine ocean management from a theoretical perspective. This should help to identify problems with existing offshore regulatory programmes and to assess appropriate alternatives. The goal is not to prescribe what ocean management is, but to examine whether it is needed, why it is needed, and what form it might take. This inquiry also will consider what is to be managed, who is to manage, and the relationship with existing management programmes. Both national and international interests are involved in questions of ocean management; therefore an examination of ocean management at the national level always must be done against the broader background of international rules and constraints. This process will help to define criteria for what would constitute good or adequate ocean management.

This discussion can benefit from building upon what we have learned from land-based resource management, particularly north of 60°. A sound and consistent ocean management policy is needed to provide a practical guide for long-range, comprehensive, and systematic planning. Such planning is essential for rational, balanced development of ocean resources that will provide optimum social and economic benefits, resolve conflicts among resource users, and protect the ocean environment. In the arctic offshore, in particular, current industrial activities and development proposals, the status of government ocean policies, conflicts between user groups, and some unique issues of international law and foreign policy make ocean management essential. Implementation of a national ocean management programme will be a function of government policy. This paper begins, therefore, with a brief discussion of the state of ocean policy in Canada. This discussion is followed by an overview of the current legal, political, economic, and scientific conditions in the world community that make ocean management necessary. The elements of an ocean management process are then discussed and several institutional and administrative options for implementing such a process are presented.

Ocean Policy: A Matter of Choice

The Process

Ocean policy has been defined in simple terms as "the relationship between government and the ocean environment" and, more precisely, as "a set of goals, directives, and intentions formulated by authoritative persons and having some relation to the marine environment."[2]

A systematic approach to policy making involves a choice by the policy maker between different courses of action. This requires that the ocean interests involved be identified clearly. The growing pressures to develop the offshore regions and the trends in the emerging international legal order for the ocean give rise to a multitude of national and international ocean interests. As nations develop their ocean space and begin to implement the rules providing for extended jurisdiction, they will have to choose between different objectives for use of the offshore and plan a course of action to achieve those selected as desirable. The process of making ocean policy will be governed by the nature of decision making and implementation in the coastal state. Because a national ocean policy must be implemented within the framework of international law, policy makers will have to account for international as well as national ocean interests. When defining ocean policy, then, it is necessary to make a distinction between foreign policy and domestic policy. Both are essential components of a national ocean policy.

The foreign-policy component of the Canadian ocean policy-making process has been described in the following way:

> Within the Canadian Government, law of the sea policy has been formulated and implemented through a highly centralized foreign affairs bureaucracy. This may be explained in terms of the political salience of law of the sea, of the parliamentary system, of the small size of the Canadian bureaucracy and of the preponderance of interests tending in a single direction.[3]

The Canadian national interest in the ocean since the 1958 and 1960 United Nations conferences on the law of the sea has been a coastal state interest. This was made very clear recently during negotiations at the Third United Nations Conference on the Law of the Sea (UNCLOS III) and is reflected in Canada's claims to greater national control over resources and activities in a broader coastal zone. These claims are for functional jurisdiction rather than for exclusive property rights; functional jurisdiction provides the control necessary for specific purposes such as fisheries management, exploration and exploitation of the continental shelf, and control of marine pollution. The Arctic Waters Pollution Prevention Act (AWPPA) is a good example of this type of claim. This act gives Canada power to regulate sources of pollution within a 100-nautical-mile zone off the arctic coast.[4] Canada's ocean policy making at the foreign-policy level has been cohesive because it has been developed with Canada's objectives as a coastal state firmly in mind. This aspect of the Canadian policy-making process was so effective at UNCLOS III that it is known to have played a role in shaping some parts of the new convention.[5]

To obtain the domestic benefits expected from the national ocean policy that was articulated at UNCLOS III, Canada will have to devise an integrated domestic ocean policy to guide the development and management of the ocean area under its jurisdiction. An integrated ocean policy is necessary if national decisions on marine affairs are to produce effective and equitable results. Canada's internal ocean policy is severely fragmented due to the *ad hoc* and incremental development of regulatory programmes relating to ocean matters, and the profusion of agencies responsible for various ocean activities.[6] This situation, in itself, reflects a policy choice and is evidence that, among the many national policy goals, a domestic ocean policy simply is not a priority for the federal government.

The Content

A policy for ocean development and management must be linked to other national policies. In the Arctic, a policy to guide national ocean development should involve government policies for science, foreign affairs, energy, transportation, and northern development, to list a few. These policy areas apply to separate systems of activities that relate to the offshore as well as to land. Because there are marine elements in many public policy areas, we have to ask some fundamental questions. Can or should the marine elements be isolated from national policies for land? Do land and sea require separate treatment? If so, how can ocean-related programmes be integrated with the existing management institutions?

An example of this problem in Canada is the National Energy Program (NEP), which applies to all of the Yukon Territory, Northwest Territories, and the offshore on three coasts. Through monetary incentives, new legislation such as the Canada Oil and Gas Act,[7] and direct involvement of the government through Petro-Canada, the NEP encourages frontier exploration and accelerates development in the North. This policy clearly commits national resources to early production of arctic offshore hydrocarbons. However, the NEP does not make any distinction between land and marine activities, does not allow for planning Arctic Ocean or Canadian offshore development, does not provide guidance on a mode of transportation to market, does not concern itself with adverse impacts of development on the ocean environment, and does not address foreign policy relating to coastal state jurisdiction. The NEP does not give a long-term, comprehensive context in which to view the offshore activities it encourages. Moreover, in the North, development is influenced by many different policies, including a foreign policy, a transportation policy, a science policy, and a general northern development policy. This raises the questions of how to define an ocean policy and what its content should be.

A tenable ocean policy-making process should identify the marine features of other public policies and the connections between them.[8] There are some obvious connections between the policy areas that currently influence development in the North and between the marine elements of each policy. This suggests that marine affairs cannot be treated as independent of other major public policies. Because interests in the offshore are primarily economic, ocean development in coastal states will be tied more and more to many national goals and aspirations. However, the ocean environment is different from land and it would be wrong simply to extend land-based policies and processes to the ocean. A recognition of the relationships between various policy areas will allow decision makers to anticipate the consequences of their decisions regarding ocean policy. This is the basis for any system of management.

There have been some efforts to address the need for a domestic ocean policy for Canada, mainly as it would concern science and technology. In 1971, the Science Council of Canada published a background study on marine science and technology.[9] This study was followed in 1979 by a study of ocean information systems for the Ministry of State for Science and Technology[10] and, more recently, by a study of ocean information services undertaken by the Department of Fisheries and Oceans.[11] Although a great capability for offshore research and development is needed to develop and support a programme for ocean management, there is now a clear need to study the relationships between science and technology, law, and policy making as they relate to control over offshore resources and activities.

As we have seen and are still experiencing north of 60° on land, when it is necessary to choose between conflicting national, regional, and local ocean interests, the *ad hoc* approach is not adequate. It is time to clarify goals for ocean development and to establish the principles by which these goals will be achieved. As a major beneficiary of the new Convention on the Law of the Sea, Canada has national and international obligations to begin this task and an incentive to formulate a workable ocean policy. In the Arctic, the international aspect is especially significant. As a major arctic power, Canada's role will be determined largely by its ability to develop an integrated ocean policy and an effective programme of ocean management. A sound ocean policy would benefit Canada's economy and would give Canada the credibility and sense of purpose it needs to promote co-operative management in the Arctic Ocean among the circumpolar nations.

Rationale for Ocean Management

The Nature of Offshore Jurisdiction

The ocean as a resource is common property among nations. Some of the ocean's features held in common are fisheries, seabed resources, vessel traffic routes, waste disposal capacity, strategic value, and climate control. The view that the ocean is common property follows from the traditional concept of freedom of the seas, which originated under Roman law. The ocean was *res nullius* (it could not be appropriated or owned) and *res communis* (open to all people).

The concept of common property is summarized aptly by the expression "everybody's property is nobody's property." The essential feature of property that is owned or subject to a specific jurisdiction is control over its use and allocation. In the case of common property, access without restraint leads to overuse or misuse of the resource, inequitable distribution of the benefits, and competition among the users. These results are losses to all users because there is no incentive for users to take a long-term view of the consequences of the overall pattern of use.[12]

The 1958 Geneva conventions on the law of the sea maintained the concept of freedom of the seas and continued to restrict coastal state jurisdiction to a narrow territorial belt.[13] Offshore development continued as an extension of some unsatisfactory land-based practices in frontier and colonial resource development, characterized by expropriation of ocean areas for exclusive and unconstrained use by a single nation. Such practices can continue only until some users impinge sufficiently on others to force a change.

The problems of this approach to ocean development were not addressed until the last decade. Coastal states are claiming jurisdiction over wider zones of the offshore for a greater variety of uses. Increasing development and use of the offshore regions has made the common-property approach untenable, and the inequities that resulted have forced the world community to consider legal and institutional changes: what was common property will be subject to a system of regulation. The new legal order that recently has emerged for the ocean through both custom and negotiations at UNCLOS III introduces a form of control over a vast expanse of ocean that formerly was considered high seas and, as such, common property. Coastal states will have a multifunctional jurisdiction in the surface, water column, and seabed out to 200 nautical miles, and further out on the seabed for states with wider continental shelves. Although there still will be areas of ocean that are high seas, even the mineral potential of the deep seabed will be subject to international control and regulation.

Acquisition of these exclusive or semi-exclusive rights to ocean space and resources, and the legal authority to enforce these rights, will eliminate the common-property nature of these ocean areas. These rights will give coastal states the ability and the incentive to control access, regulate use, and distribute benefits. They will give coastal states the opportunity to initiate and develop policies for ocean management. Whether or not the problems of treating the ocean as common property are solved in this way will depend on the policy choices made by coastal state governments.

Even under the emerging international legal order, however, there will remain common-property aspects of the ocean that can be addressed only through co-operative efforts. Resources such as fish stocks straddle the division between national jurisdictions and high seas. The traditional and continuing use of the high seas as common property will influence any national decisions and make effective control by the coastal state alone impossible to maintain. This also will be true where adjacent coastal states share an offshore boundary. If offshore management is to be effective, there must be bilateral or multilateral jurisdiction and control in some areas.

Advances in Ocean Science and Technology

As land resources have become depleted or as their production has become uneconomic or incompatible with other interests, and as world resource requirements have increased, ocean reserves have been tapped. It is inevitable that this trend will continue and intensify, and that the only limit will be technological capability.

Technological advances that permitted offshore drilling for hydrocarbons and led to the 1945 Truman Proclamation on the Continental Shelf are technologies of a bygone era.[14] Current technology permits offshore exploration to depths and in environments never contemplated when the Geneva Convention on the Continental Shelf was written. Most areas of the continental shelf are now accessible and extraction of its resources within the technological capability of industry. Offshore production is increasing and now accounts for approximately one-quarter of world hydrocarbon production.[15] In Canada, a great reliance is placed on the potential of offshore hydrocarbon reserves, particularly in the Arctic and on the east coast, where recoverable oil potential is estimated to exceed that of conventional land-based reserves.[16]

Technology now permits the mining of manganese nodules in the deep seabed beyond the continental shelf. These formations contain copper, lead, cobalt, nickel, and manganese, and could meet current world demand for these resources for centuries.[17] This industry awaits only commercial viability—a function of markets, alternate supply, and demand—and agreements on seabed jurisdiction by the international community. This new technology also will permit mining of other minerals on the continental shelf. Mid-ocean ridges contain large deposits of minerals, making future exploitation of these areas likely. Processes for extracting minerals and chemicals from sea-water are available and already are operating in some areas.[18]

About 85 per cent of the world fish catch comes from the ocean and an estimated 72 per cent of that catch is used for human consumption.[19] If the world human population, now four billion persons, increases to six and one-half billion by the year 2000 as expected, this resource will be harvested more intensely. Most of this catch is taken within the 200-nautical-mile jurisdiction of many of the coastal states. Developed coastal states are employing new technologies to increase efficiency, and developing coastal states are entering the fishery, in many cases with the help of technology from other nations. New electronic and computer-aided techniques for locating and catching fish, and larger vessels with greater storage and processing capabilities, increase the prospect of maximum catches.[20] Extension of the coastal fisheries jurisdiction will mean that maritime nations no longer will have access to traditional fishing grounds; some of these nations may travel to different regions and develop new fisheries such as those for krill and squid in the Antarctic.[21]

Since 1945, world sea-borne trade has expanded six-fold and the current volume is expected to double by the end of this century.[22] Economic expansion in both industrial and developing countries will have a significant effect on future patterns of ocean transportation. New materials and techniques permit production of larger ships that require less maintenance. Cargo handling has become more sophisticated and efficient. Ship-board automation and use of computers, satellite communication, long-range weather forecasting, and nuclear power will result in shorter turn-around times, faster hauls, and lower costs, all of which will increase traffic in shipping lanes. Safety and efficiency will require national and international reviews of traffic control and new schemes for compulsory routing, traffic separation, and priority lanes for dangerous cargoes.[23] By the end of this century, such schemes may have to deal with submarine as well as surface shipping.

Air transportation planners have known for a long time that the shortest routes between some major industrial centres pass through the Arctic. Resource activities in the arctic offshore will increase marine traffic, and advanced ice-breaking technology and submarine routing could make year-round shipping both technologically feasible and economic. In the Canadian Arctic, the petroleum industry is proposing to use ice-breaking tankers to deliver liquid hydrocarbons to market. This would require year-round shipping in the Beaufort Sea and through the Northwest Passage.[24]

The increase in shipping and offshore petroleum exploration at greater depths and in harsh environments, such as the Arctic, will increase the threat of marine pollution. A further threat is dumping of waste and radioactive material in the oceans, a current practice of governments.

There is more pressure on coastal zone areas for commercial, shipping, and resource development purposes and, in some areas, for residential and recreational uses. This land–sea interface clearly is within limits of national jurisdiction, but individual state practices in the coastal zone can have implications of international significance. National policies on coastal zone management will affect the management of other ocean zones and raise boundary issues with adjacent states. In the Arctic, the coastal zone is inhabited by Inuit, who make no distinction between the land-fast ice and the land. Petroleum development offshore, the siting of port and storage facilities, and overland transportation systems in this zone will require rigorous management programmes.

The ocean continues to be important for military purposes, although the traditional role of the surface fleet has changed. Nuclear power, computer navigation, satellite observation, and submarine-based missile systems are modern technologies that allow for high mobility, long patrol periods with concealment, and the ability to penetrate and operate in the ice-covered polar regions. Surrounded by Europe, Asia, and North America, the Arctic Ocean has a well-recognized strategic value. Sovereignty and control over new zones of jurisdiction in the Arctic Ocean are crucial issues.

Energy production from the sea is possible through tidal power, wind generation, and solar energy conversion. New scientific technologies such as floating and fixed manned and unmanned research stations, and habitats on the surface and the seabed, will allow access to ocean regions never used before. This access will raise questions about jurisdiction over living and non-living resources, sharing research data, and boundary locations.

The result of these advances is likely to be an increased level of ocean use. Developments in marine science and technology have made possible activities that pose new questions for law and policy. In response, the world community has formulated a new legal order through the new United Nations Convention on the Law of the Sea. As coastal states begin to implement the new rules, marine science and technology will have to provide answers to new questions. Coastal states will need to define new jurisdictional limits. Accurate boundary demarcation to 200 nautical miles will require computer and laser technology, and advanced hydrography and cartography. Demarcation and policing of offshore boundaries will require seabed sonar systems or remote-sensing techniques via satellite or land-based facilities.

Technology has pushed nations into some offshore activities that are beyond the scientific knowledge and technical skill available to control them. Comprehensive ocean management would include a science policy to ensure that management capability keeps pace with new technology.

Incremental Development of Existing Regimes

The 1958 Geneva Conference on the Law of the Sea produced four separate treaties that dealt with discrete ocean areas: the territorial sea and contiguous zone; the continental shelf; the high seas; and living resources in the water column.[25] This separation of areas perpetuated a fragmented international system of law for the ocean. These treaties did not account adequately for interdependencies between ocean areas and the influence of human uses on the physical system. In the years following the Geneva conference, the United Nations established many agencies to deal with ocean matters. Each agency was organized to address a particular area of marine interest, and there was no formal co-ordinating function outside the unworkable forum of the General Assembly. The direction taken by the United Nations has been described as:

> haphazard, random and piecemeal, unmindful of the need for a system rather than a sectorial approach to ocean space, for operational co-ordination, and for a comprehensive base of scientific, technical and economic facts for sound decision making.[26]

The international situation is partly responsible for the attitude of coastal states toward their offshore interests. There has been little incentive to initiate integrated programmes for ocean use because the narrow limits of national sovereignty do not permit the implementation of effective management schemes, and because the contiguous zone beyond the territorial sea does not provide sufficient jurisdiction for management. For these reasons, a multiple-use concept for offshore areas has been slow to develop. Legislation and policy in coastal states have been influenced by these international problems, resulting in fragmented procedures for control within national ocean limits. The incremental growth of offshore authorities in Canada, the U.S., and other major coastal states has allowed these authorities to address issues only as they arise.[27] The adequacy of single-purpose laws administered on a case-by-case basis must be examined as sea-borne commerce increases, as petroleum exploration accelerates, and as fishing and other activities expand in the 200-nautical-mile zone.

The approach to ocean policy at the international level is being changed by the concepts and rules defined through negotiations at UNCLOS III. Implementation of these new rules will be the responsibility of each individual state. Canada, like other coastal states, will have to define its ocean objectives and determine how to implement them *vis-à-vis* the objectives of other nations. The objectives expressed through existing legislation make it clear that a system for management does not exist in Canada. Without a management system, can Canada achieve its national ocean goals and fulfil its national and international responsibilities?

The Emerging International Legal Order

The development of the traditional legal order for the ocean began with agreements and customary practice, dominated by the few industrialized shipping nations. After 1945, there emerged many developing countries that never would achieve the maritime commercial status of the industrialized shipping nations. There are now more than 150 nations with ocean interests, the majority of which are developing coastal states. The international legal order that was the product of the Geneva law of the sea conventions was based on a simple and traditional distinction between the high seas and territorial seas. This system of laws has been inadequate to deal with the complexity and diversity of the relationships between the components of the ocean system. UNCLOS III has provided a new set of international rules to satisfy the need of coastal states to control ocean use in wider zones.

Prior to UNCLOS III negotiations, which began in 1974, and throughout the conference itself, coastal states were beginning to view maritime jurisdiction as functional control for management purposes rather than as territorial control or ownership. The most common example has been the claim for a unifunctional, exclusive fishing zone. Canada declared a 200-nautical-mile fishing zone around its coasts in 1977.[28] By 1979, 79 claims had been made for 200-nautical-mile jurisdictions.[29] These claims were for unifunctional fishing zones, multifunctional economic zones, and territorial seas. If the new Law of the Sea Convention comes into force, it will impose a uniform limit on these claims to extended jurisdiction. Even if it does not become binding soon, custom and state practice are persuading coastal nations to enforce uniform rights within this limit.

Once all eligible states have claimed a 200-nautical-mile exclusive economic zone, approximately 35 per cent of what formerly were high seas will be subject to national jurisdiction.

The Geneva law of the sea conventions, in a limited way, recognized the concept of functional (as opposed to territorial) jurisdiction by codifying the concepts of the contiguous zone and the continental shelf. The new convention retains the contiguous zone, with an increased maximum width of 24 nautical miles, in which the coastal state will have control sufficient to prevent violations of its customs, fiscal, immigration, and health laws.[30] The formula for locating the outer limits of the continental shelf is redefined, but the nature of a coastal state's jurisdiction will not change, although coastal states will have a responsibility to contribute revenue to geographically disadvantaged states from exploitation that occurs on the shelf beyond 200 nautical miles.[31]

The new functional jurisdictions found in the convention are the "area" and the exclusive economic zone (EEZ).[32] The "area" is defined as the seabed and subsoil beyond the national limits of the continental shelf and the EEZ. An international authority will be established to manage the exploitation of resources there. It will be the only zone under a global jurisdiction.

The most significant functional zone that the convention proposes is the EEZ, which will extend 200 nautical miles from the coast. Although this type of zone has become accepted through state practice over the last several years, the new convention will codify it and stipulate the nature of coastal state jurisdiction within it. Within the EEZ, the coastal state will have jurisdiction over the seabed, subsoil, and superjacent waters for the following purposes:

(a) exploring and exploiting, conserving, and managing both living and non-living natural resources;
(b) exploring and exploiting the economic potential of the zone for purposes such as energy production from water, currents, and wind;
(c) establishing and using artificial islands, installations, and structures;
(d) marine scientific research;
(e) protection and preservation of the marine environment.[33]

Unlike sovereignty in the territorial sea, functional jurisdiction is not absolute. Instead, it provides control for a limited purpose or purposes. Other nations may carry out, in the same area, activities that are different from the specific activities for which functional jurisdiction is claimed. Therefore, in the EEZ, other states will continue to enjoy the rights of navigation that exist for the high seas, the right of overflight, and the right to lay submarine cables and pipelines. One feature of the EEZ that is very different from earlier functional zones is that it provides rights in the zone not only for the coastal state but also for the international community. Landlocked and other geographically disadvantaged states will have the right to share in the exploitation of any surplus of the living resources in the zone beyond the needs of the coastal state.

Although the emerging legal order for the ocean will be applicable world wide, it is not a global scheme of management. However, it does create a global framework within which individual nations may take the steps needed to establish an ocean management programme for the ocean space allocated to them. It also provides formulae for the distribution of benefits in a way that is intended to be equitable. Article 234 of the new Law of the Sea Convention gives special rights to coastal states in ice-covered regions and sets the tone for a management approach for the arctic marine environment. The Arctic Ocean is nearly enclosed by the circum-polar nations. Activities of any one state in such a body of water will have an impact on the others. Therefore, these coastal states must co-operate to ensure that individual and collective responsibilities are fulfilled. While the emerging legal order does not impose such co-operation in law, it creates the framework for co-operation. Because the new convention will give coastal states jurisdiction over a greater area of the ocean and more of its resources, it also imposes on these states greater management responsibilities and promotes the national, regional, and global co-operation required for effective ocean management.[34]

Ocean Management

Concept and Definition

The rate of change that society must cope with today has given a large role to management processes. This applies to the area of ocean development.

Management, in simplest terms, means direction or control. In operation, it is a series of actions designed to formulate and attain particular objectives. The criteria for management have been identified as:

(1) a process of organized activity
(2) directed toward an objective
(3) by establishing certain relationships among the available human, material, and financial resources,

The Working Groups

(4) working through an effective division of labour, and

(5) being actively involved with the decision-making process —having the responsibility for evaluation and selection of alternatives in a complex environment.[35]

The systems approach to management is useful to identify the desired objectives, to determine procedures for achieving them, and to identify methods for resolving conflicts. This approach stresses interactions and interdependencies among the components that make up the system. The systems approach to management is a common-sense approach in that it requires decision makers to take as large a view as possible of the total system. The first step in this approach is identification of subsystems, or system components. The next step is to identify the interactions among the subsystems in order to design and implement procedures that account for and control the interactions. This approach recognizes that these interactions may be synergistic—that the whole system may be quite different from the sum of the components.

This systems approach to management is appropriately applied to the ocean, which is a classic system made up of separate yet interdependent subsystems. The ocean is both a single resource and the source of living and non-living natural resources. A complex, but comprehensive and helpful, definition of resource management has been proposed:

> Resource management . . . may be defined as a process of decision making whereby resources are allocated over space and time according to the needs, aspirations, and desires of man within the framework of his technological inventiveness, his political and social institutions, and his legal and administrative arrangements. Resource management should be visualised as a conscious process of decision involving judgement, preference, and commitment, whereby certain desired resource outputs are sought from certain perceived resource combinations through the choice among various managerial, technical, and administrative alternatives. . . . Resource management involves strategies of action involving computations of tactics and methods and a variety of objectives. The emphasis is upon flexibility and the minimisation of long-term environmental catastrophes, while maximising net social welfare over time. The allocation process is dominated neither by the market place nor by the quasi-political forum, but by a combination of social, cultural, economic, and institutional processes that strive for the best solution, but which inevitably must seek compromise.[36]

In theory, rational management can only mean management of the whole system. In practice, however, management choices are not always made with information about the effect of action in one area upon the others.

In Canada, ocean policy making currently is directed to separate components of the ocean system so that activities such as petroleum exploration, fishing, shipping, coastal zone use, and environmental protection are regulated by separate authorities that often do not co-ordinate these management efforts. Because the ability to control a system requires an understanding of how internal and external forces affect it, the systems approach would give policy makers a feeling for the long-range and cumulative consequences of decisions made within the system. In this way, policy makers will be more able to define desired objectives.

Once a coastal state has defined its national objectives for ocean management, the necessary scope and degree of control also can be defined. Decision making without objectives is not management because there is no effort to direct or control. Neither is heavy regulation, in itself, necessarily management, and it may work against the management objective.[37] However, there are many management possibilities, ranging from limited to comprehensive.

The federal government in Canada manages the ocean on the basis of single ocean uses such as shipping, fishing, and petroleum exploration. This management approach could be based instead on special values such as environmental protection, conservation, or national security, or it could emphasize special geographic areas such as biologically rich Lancaster Sound, the land-fast ice zone used by Inuit, or areas of concentrated shipping activities. A coastal state also might manage ocean resources based on the uses, values, and special areas together. In Canada, the federal government is struggling to reconcile conflicting uses and interests in the arctic marine environment. The different bases for management are alluded to in several government documents and policies;[38] however, none of them addresses a comprehensive approach to management that would recognize the interactions of the various subsystems that are the subjects of these reports or policy statements. As a coastal state, Canada must examine the concept of ocean management and select the degree of management necessary for the system to be managed. Canada also must articulate the principles and process of management that will achieve its objectives for that system.

Principles and Process

Management has been described as "a *process* that begins with *goal setting*, and extends through the functions of *information systems, research, planning, development, regulation* and *financing*."[39]

Ocean management begins with a choice of public policies relating to objectives for the marine environment. This is the goal-setting function. At this stage, the management philosophy will be formed and based on uses, values, special areas, a combination of these, or will be a comprehensive approach.

The next two functions—information systems and research—involve the collection, storage, distribution, and analysis of data. These functions will indicate the level of ocean management required to attain the national ocean objectives. A capability in marine science and technology, a specific goal of these functions, enables an evaluation of consequences, benefits, and options, and permits a rational judgement of what is acceptable and what is not. The data base is made up of political, legal, economic, cultural, and scientific information.

The planning function serves to clarify for the policy maker the relationships within the system that is to be managed. Planning can be carried out only within the context of a clear policy and stated objectives. As a continuous part of the management process, planning will keep the decision makers in touch with the future management requirements of the system and help to generate timely and relevant changes in policy. The systems approach to ocean management emphasizes the importance of planning. When decisions are made or actions are taken that can lead to a chain of responses within the system, policy makers must consider potential consequences if they are to avoid foreclosing options. Options can be foreclosed when the ocean system is so affected by some activity that it cannot be restored to a state in which public benefit is maximized; for example, the genetic pool of a species may be lost, the attributes of the environment may have changed, or the activity may have become uneconomic. Planning can be done by decision makers who administer single-purpose programmes, but planning at this level is not sufficient for a comprehensive management process. Within a comprehensive management process, however, planning leads to co-ordination and a sense of direction in keeping with national ocean objectives. Comprehensive planning and co-ordination are essential to a systems approach.

The development function of management begins the implementation stage. Development can proceed only when the previous management functions have been performed. At this stage legislation will be drafted and programmes will be initiated. The development function also will determine what mechanisms will be used to achieve the degree of management desired. Management mechanisms include controls such as economic sanctions, environmental impact assessment, ocean-area zoning, and limited coastal access to offshore areas.[40] Selection of these mechanisms will depend on the goals, such as sustained yield, optimum yield, multiple use, or best use. These goals will have to be compatible with the coastal state's overall ocean management objective.

The regulation and financing functions are the administrative part of the management process. They include standard setting, zoning, licensing, revenue collection, enforcement, monitoring, and conflict resolution. Management requires the combination of all these functions. Together they allow decision making and implementation to proceed with the necessary administrative skills and infrastructure.[41]

Coastal states are beginning to assert control over 200-nautical-mile multifunctional zones either under the provisions of the new United Nations Convention on the Law of the Sea or on the basis of state practice leading to customary international law. An ocean management process, therefore, will be important to the pursuit of national ocean objectives. Planning for offshore development will be essential as states assess their own capability to manage, and the costs and benefits of managing, these multifunctional zones. Coastal states must have a strategy for developing such a management process.

A Strategy for Management

The first step in developing a management strategy is to demonstrate that an ocean management system is necessary to achieve national ocean objectives. This could commence with the following procedures:

(1) an analysis of current conflicts among uses competing for ocean resources;
(2) an evaluation of existing programs which rely on integrating various marine authorities into a management program; and
(3) a survey of existing legal and administrative authorities that pertain to the marine environment.[42]

This analysis will reflect the current state of ocean policy, show what management requirements are not being fulfilled, and provide a point of departure for modifications in policy, institutional structure, and administrative authority.

The analysis of ocean uses will provide a valuable inventory of all current and potential uses and resources within the jurisdiction of the coastal state and will identify the relationships among the uses as well as the conflicts that need resolution. Such an inventory will also be useful in defining the boundaries of the management area.

The evaluation of existing programmes will indicate the features that are valuable in any new scheme for ocean management. Existing programmes also may serve as models for new programmes. In Canada, study of existing programmes also would have to take into account the constitutional division of powers in a federal state. That issue has become important on the east and west coasts of Canada, where offshore resource control is a subject of federal–provincial conflict. It also will be important north of 60° as territorial powers change and native interests play a greater role in resource management decisions.

This analysis, overall, may demonstrate that a massive overhaul of institutions and legislation is not required, and that effective ocean management will be achieved through co-ordination and integration of existing programmes. On the other hand, the analysis may show the need for a management system and suggest specific changes.

If the results of the analysis suggest that a system for ocean management must be developed in order to achieve national ocean objectives, it can be helpful to refer again to the systems approach to management. There are three steps in developing such a programme: (1) analysis; (2) development; and (3) management.[43] An inventory of activities within those functions provides an action plan that a coastal state might follow to establish a comprehensive ocean management programme (see Table 1).

Actors and Interests

The application of a national management programme to the ocean may require decisions that foreclose some options in favour of others, but this would be part of the planning process and would result from informed decisions based on relevant scientific, economic, and social data. Inadvertent foreclosure of options is anathema to the concept of management. Decision makers, therefore, must identify all the interests in ocean development in order to recognize the basic policy questions. Public, private, development, and conservationist interests have legitimate concerns in the development of ocean policy and management. An objective of ocean management will be to accommodate these interests.

Ocean users will have to be identified and their interests assessed in light of long-term planning goals. Ocean users such as the fishing, petroleum, and shipping industries are concerned primarily with development.

Table 1

Proposed Action Plan for Establishing a National Ocean Management Programme

Stage 1: Analysis

A. Area
1. Select interim ocean management zone
2. Identify constraints imposed by international law
3. Identify constraints imposed by neighbouring states
4. Assemble data on natural marine processes

B. Resources
1. Inventory existing and potential resources
2. Assess existing and potential conflict between resources
3. Relate resources to natural marine processes
4. Relate resources to uses and identify impacts
5. Relate resources to legislation and programmes

C. Uses
1. Inventory existing and potential uses
2. Assess existing and potential conflicts between uses
3. Relate uses to natural marine processes
4. Relate uses to resources and identify impacts
5. Relate uses to legislation and programmes

D. Actors
1. Identify public-sector actors
2. Identify private-sector actors
3. Relate public interests to private interests
4. Relate public interests to resources and uses
5. Relate private interests to resources and uses

E. Authorities
1. List primary legislation relating to ocean use
2. List secondary legislation relating to ocean use
3. Identify public authorities and describe marine programmes
4. Identify and describe private marine programmes
5. Relate legislation to resources and uses
6. Relate marine programmes to resources and uses

Table 1 (continued)

    7. Relate legislation and authorities to international law
    8. Identify common goals with other nations
    9. Identify authorities, programmes, and legislation of neighbouring coastal states
  10. Identify divergence in ocean policies with other nations
  11. Identify existing links in public and private sectors with other nations
  12. Assess adequacy of co-ordination

Stage 2: Development

    1. Formulate objectives for ocean management
    2. Recommend changes in national law and policy
    3. Develop policy on priority uses and areas of concern
    4. Suggest methods of improving co-ordination
    5. Recommend procedure for public participation and information sharing
    6. Recommend changes in national ocean-policy process
    7. Consult with neighbouring coastal states
    8. Recommend priorities to harmonize programmes with other nations
    9. Foster exchange of information with other nations
  10. Prepare interim management plan
  11. Recommend national decision-making structure for ocean management
  12. Recommend binational or regional structure for ocean management
  13. Recommend funding programme

Stage 3: Management

A. Administrative

    1. Co-ordinate marine agencies and programmes
    2. Administer subordinate agencies
    3. Administer ocean management structure
    4. Consult with neighbouring coastal states
    5. Co-ordinate activities of lead agencies in other nations
    6. Integrate programmes with other nations

Table 1 (continued)

B. Planning
1. Hold hearings
2. Classify priority uses
3. Classify ocean areas
4. Exchange information with other nations
5. Develop scientific capability
6. Prepare final ocean management plan

C. Regulatory
1. Prepare regulations in line with management objectives
2. Co-ordinate other agencies
3. Enforce management legislation

D. Dispute settlement
1. Hold public hearings
2. Disseminate information
3. Hear appeals or objections to classification
4. Co-ordinate enforcement capability of other agencies and with other nations

There is not an organized constituency that can represent the entire range of interests in the ocean, and the existing programmes for the regulation of ocean use have developed mainly in response to the specific needs of industry. Individual interests probably are better served under this arrangement than they would be under a multi-use programme that has a mandate to balance resource developers' goals with other interests.[44] Resource interests are visible and powerful and the federal government, as the primary authority in managing Canada's ocean areas, will have to ensure that other interests are considered in the development of an ocean management plan.

In Canada, federal, provincial, and territorial governments will have an interest in resource revenues and mineral rights in the ocean. Provincial governments in the South and the federal and territorial governments in the North also will be concerned with long-term effects of resource development on the environment and on coastal communities. North of 60°, Inuit claim aboriginal rights to ocean resources and, therefore, have a legitimate interest in ocean management. Ocean management is a political process, and a successful management programme first must be accepted at that level by all actors and interests.

Management Zones

Ocean space is divided into six zones under international law: territorial sea, contiguous zone, economic zone, continental shelf and subsoil, high seas, and deep ocean floor. For management purposes, these zones must be defined in political and administrative terms such as international, national, and transboundary zones. The international zone includes the deep ocean floor, the high seas, and the airspace above the high seas and economic zones. National zones for a coastal state include the territorial sea and airspace above it, the contiguous zone, the economic zone, and the continental shelf and subsoil. Transboundary zones are administrative concepts, such as the interfaces between national and international zones or between two or more national zones.

Although most states will participate in management of international zones, all coastal states will have management responsibilities in national and transboundary zones. In these areas, decisions will have to be made regarding the appropriate unit of ocean space for application of a management programme. Within national jurisdictions, the outer limits will be from the coastal zone seaward to 200 nautical miles on the surface and in the water column, and further on the seabed in those areas where the continental shelf is broader than 200 nautical miles. Boundary arrangements with adjacent coastal states will determine the lateral extent of the national management zone, although joint activities with neighbouring states may allow integrated management functions in transboundary areas.

Some further analysis is required to provide indicators of the appropriate physical and geographical limits of a management zone. A management zone definition will have to account for a complex network of local, national, regional, and international ocean interests. Any spatial definition will have to account for the geographic, ecological, political, legal, and administrative conditions peculiar to the area.[45]

A management zone should be defined by the national ocean objectives and by the management needs of the area. These can be identified at the analysis stage in the exercise described in Table 1 to establish an ocean management system. Information on natural marine processes, resources, and human uses and activities will indicate what the management needs are. The next step is to decide whether fulfilment of the objectives requires national, regional, or international action.

In the Arctic, Canada has settled one lateral boundary with Greenland by an agreement made in 1973.[46] This agreement divides the two jurisdictions in Davis Strait and Baffin Bay, but the northernmost boundary in the Lincoln Sea has yet to be settled. Canada's lateral boundary with Alaska in the Beaufort Sea is still disputed and its resolution probably will await the decision of the International Court of Justice on the disputed Canada–U.S. boundary in the Gulf of Maine. Seaward, Canada has claimed a 200-nautical-mile fishing zone and a 100-nautical-mile pollution-control zone, both of which include the water column. Canada also has claimed jurisdiction to the outer limits of the continental shelf. These limits have not yet been defined.

Within Canadian marine jurisdiction north of 60°, a management programme may require the definition of several new zones. Zones are provided for in the federal government's proposed land-use planning policy, but they are not designed for a marine management programme. One functional unit that might be considered as a logical marine management area in the North is the seasonal land-fast ice that covers arctic waters along the shoreline for much of the year. These are the areas Inuit use most for travel and hunting, and are important marine areas for wildlife.

A functional zone is an abstract entity. Therefore, any spatial definition of such zones will be somewhat arbitrary. Effective management of the ocean will require new methods of administration at the national level and co-operation at the international level to the extent necessary to overcome the difficulty of defining management boundaries in the fluid ocean system.

Institutional Options for Ocean Management

Ocean policy makers eventually must choose an appropriate administrative and institutional structure to develop and implement policies for managing national ocean space. This assumes that the coastal state has a clear idea of its ocean management objectives. The choice will be determined, to a large extent, by the objectives.

Some fundamental questions must be considered in this exercise. Is it possible or practical to have a central authority governing all of the management functions? Will the focus or mandate be national, regional, or local? Will the mandate be for collecting scientific data alone or will it include policy making? Will the organization have power to regulate and enforce, or merely to advise? Will the organization be politically neutral? Will it be a departmental or an independent organization? Some options for ocean management call for action at the national level and, in regions such as the Beaufort Sea and Davis Strait, where neighbouring coastal state activities impinge one on the other, for joint action by the two coastal states.

National Ocean Management

Many ocean resources and uses have an international aspect, but some are mainly national in character. In any event, a successful, binational arrangement would have to be based on effective ocean management structures at the national level of government.

An integrated national ocean policy might be achieved by taking one or both of two general approaches—central policy making and education, and institutional reform.[47] In the first approach, the central political authority could formulate an ocean policy and then order all government agencies involved to act according to the new policy. This method would require that bureaucrats learn to appreciate the effect of their decisions within the system and to take a broad view of their functions relating to ocean matters. This method also would be an element of any institutional reform. The second approach is to reorganize the institutional structure. This can be accomplished by:

(1) redefining the competence of existing authorities;
(2) designating the agency with primary responsibility;
(3) increasing resources and funding to one agency over others;
(4) creating a new institution—either a superagency or a prestigious advisory and co-ordinating body.[48]

A combination of the educational approach and some form of institutional change probably would be most effective in both the short and the long term.

Options for Institutional Change

Some options that the federal government may employ to change its institutional and administrative structures for more effective ocean management are described below.

Option A: Central Policy Formulation and Directives

Having formulated a comprehensive ocean policy, the federal government could amend existing legislation and regulations to have all government departments and agencies act in accordance with the stated policies. This alone would not achieve the co-ordination and planning essential to the systems management approach, nor would it involve territorial, provincial, or municipal institutions. It also would not involve direct participation of the public and industry. Moreover, the policy could set out principles too vague to provide the guidelines necessary to achieve the policy objectives, and very precise rules may be impossible to follow without changes in the existing institutional structure.

Option B: Strengthen an Existing Lead Agency

The federal government could select an appropriate existing government department or agency to be the lead agency within the bureaucracy for marine affairs. Increased funding and resources, and new legislation, would give this agency a clear mandate and the power and authority to implement it. The Department of Fisheries and Oceans Act suggests that the Department of Fisheries and Oceans (DFO) could undertake such a lead role,[49] but the mandate would have to be defined more clearly than it is now to take on the dominant federal position in marine affairs.

Option C: A New Lead Agency

The federal government could create a new departmental agency and give it the mandate and resources necessary to assume leadership in marine affairs.

Option D: A Cabinet-level Ocean Affairs Department

The federal government could create a new ocean affairs department with a strong mandate to operate at the cabinet level and independently of the existing bureaucracy. This would differ from the line position now held by DFO, and would give ocean affairs a high priority that would not be affected by the constant balancing of priorities with those of other departments. Such a department would assume the responsibilities of existing departments or their branches for ocean matters. Because there would be conflicts between development functions and a pollution control jurisdiction, the Department of the Environment (DOE) should remain independent of this new department, with, perhaps, a clearer and stronger authority for all federal marine pollution legislation.

Option E: An Executive-level Advisory and Co-ordinating Group

The federal government could create a strong policy advisory and co-ordinating task force within the prime minister's office. This task force would require a staff and budget adequate for research, and would monitor existing ocean agencies to ensure complete and effective implementation of ocean policy.

Option F: An Interjurisdictional Independent Co-ordinating and Advisory Agency

The federal government could create a non-departmental, or independent, agency with representatives from the federal and territorial departments and Inuit coastal communities. This agency would co-ordinate involvement of these groups and advise the agency responsible for ocean management.

Option G: An Interjurisdictional Independent Superagency

A federal–territorial board could be formed that would be responsible for policy, planning, and regulation of marine affairs. The board would behave as a quasi-judicial, administrative tribunal capable of research, planning, and assuming delegated powers. This would require many changes in the present distribution of power among the federal and territorial departments and agencies currently responsible for ocean affairs.

Models for a Management Structure

Model One: Interdepartmental Offshore Resources Planning Committee

This model requires federal initiative only.[50] Its objective is to integrate policy at the federal level. The committee would be composed of senior representatives from all federal departments responsible for marine affairs. It would be a permanent body in order to fulfil its planning mandate. All ocean policy would be integrated at the committee level before going to Cabinet for a decision. Responsibility for ensuring that approved programmes are carried out would be left with the originating department. This model would provide a multidisciplinary approach to ocean management problems.

Model Two: Maritime Resources Board

This model was proposed in 1977 by the federal government and the Atlantic provinces of Nova Scotia, New Brunswick, and Prince Edward Island as a means of resolving the federal–provincial dispute over offshore jurisdiction.[51] The Maritime Resources Board was designed to deal with mineral resources of the continental shelf but, given broader scope, it has value as a model for a more comprehensive ocean management programme.

A maritime resources board north of 60° would be composed of representatives from the territories, the Inuit coastal communities, and the federal government. A resource administration line would be drawn offshore at an agreed distance. Landward of this line, the territories and Inuit communities would share 100 per cent of all revenues; seaward of this line, a percentage would go to the federal government. The board would have jurisdiction from the line out to the continental margin, and a specific mandate to:

(1) issue rights to resources;
(2) set terms and conditions for issuance;
(3) commission studies related to offshore resources; and
(4) review policies, administration, and management of the resources and make recommendations to both levels of government.

Because the offshore area is under federal jurisdiction, this board would perform some of the present functions of DIAND and the Canada Oil and Gas Lands Administration (COGLA). It also would assume some functions of DFO. However, the day-to-day administration would be done by the existing federal agencies.

The advantage of this model is that it renders academic the question of which party should have offshore mineral jurisdiction. By virtue of the revenue-sharing feature, it also provides an economic base for future territorial development. This board would settle some of the conflicts between federal, territorial, and Inuit interests, but it would not necessarily set up further arbitrary seaward boundaries offshore if it was delegated administration of the area landward of the resource administration lines. Interterritorial boundaries might be resolved by a formula for revenue sharing.

With additional powers and a broader mandate to deal with other resources and activities, this could be a very useful model for a national-level ocean management scheme in the Arctic. The authority to oversee the management activities of all existing departments and agencies that deal with ocean matters would be one step toward the integration necessary for effective operation. Because the federal government has overriding authority under these terms of reference, the model's success would depend on how the board's recommendations are treated. This model eventually would have to be modified with respect to representation and revenue sharing to accommodate greater territorial autonomy and new political divisions of the territories.

Model Three: Regional Ocean-resource Councils

Regional ocean-resource councils, with representation from federal, provincial, industry, and public groups could be set up on each coast of Canada.[52] An arctic council with territorial and Inuit representatives, for example, would be an advisory body reporting directly to the federal Cabinet. It would have several primary functions:

(1) advising government agencies and user groups on a solicited or unsolicited basis;
(2) collecting and disseminating data pertaining to the ocean area;
(3) planning and co-ordinating ocean uses in liaison with existing agencies, and defining priorities for development;
(4) promoting and facilitating scientific research and readiness for marine disaster;
(5) involvement in specific processes such as allocation of surplus living resources and definition of shipping lanes; and

(6) setting up mechanisms for adjudicating conflicts between uses and marine agencies. This function would be contingent on the council being quasi-judicial rather than strictly advisory.[53]

Model Four: Coastal Zone Commission

This form of management structure was considered in a study concerning the process of coastal zone management.[54] In that study the coastal zone was defined to include the ocean from the coast seaward to the limits of national jurisdiction.

Applied to the Arctic, a coastal zone commission would consist of representatives of the federal and territorial governments, with appointed representatives from local governments and the private sector. The management structure has four levels, and each successive level has a larger area to manage and a wider set of management objectives. The commission would form the fourth and highest level, and would be responsible for the entire arctic region. The nature of these commissions was described in that study as follows:

> The mandate of the Commissions would be to identify, appraise, and articulate the needs of the coastal zone in each region with a view to influencing policy discussion at all levels of government that would have an impact on the coastal zone, and to gradually create a climate of opinion and practice in which coastal zone management is a reality. Furthermore, it would be a responsibility of the Coastal Zone Commissions to seek to obtain throughout the regions under their jurisdictions, a heightened degree of inter-governmental and inter-agency co-operation in the development and implementation of coastal zone administrative operations....
>
> It would not undertake the implementation of programs throughout the region. It would, however, seek to establish the alternatives for management open to government and to develop those alternatives into a general plan.... The details of implementation, the fleshing out of the plan, would be entrusted to the participating governments and specifically to their agencies having more precisely defined functional responsibilities within the zone.[55]

The coastal zone commission would be a comprehensive planning body, and its main function would be to establish guidelines for ocean management. The commission would not change the present ocean affairs bureaucracy but, instead, would supplement it. The commission's prestige and effectiveness could be enhanced through direct communication with the federal and territorial executive through standing cabinet-level committees.

Model Five: Joint Federal-Territorial Ocean-use Planning Commission

This model involves an intergovernmental commission composed of an equal number of federal and territorial representatives, with federal and territorial co-chairmen.[56] As the offshore beyond the low-water mark is under federal jurisdiction, the federal government could enact legislation creating such a commission. Changes in territorial status might require similar territorial legislation, and both levels of government then would delegate to the commission the powers required for its operation.

This commission would have a broad mandate to advise, but would not have power to regulate or to enforce. To achieve its purpose, the commission would be divided into two subgroups—a resource planning team and an advisory committee. The resource planning team would have a strong scientific capability and would act at the direction of the commission. Its initial task would be an inventory of all ocean resources and uses, which the commission would use as a comprehensive data bank. This inventory would accumulate resource, environmental, and socio-economic information for the arctic region, and would include the fishery zone and seabed to the continental margin. The data could be compiled according to hydrographic subregions for planning purposes. Existing data systems such as that of DFO's Arctic Data Compilation and Marine Environmental Data Service would be used to assist the resource planning team. The resource planning team would analyse present and potential resource uses, identify where data are inadequate, and predict the most likely and important conflict areas.

The advisory committee would have representatives from federal and territorial governments and ocean users, both industry and Inuit, from all subregions. This committee would keep the commission informed of local changes that should be recorded in the information bank, and would supplement public participation in regional planning. The mandate of such a commission should include:

(1) a process of ocean-use planning involving identification of resource and use conflicts, designation of ecologically sensitive areas, and selection of priority or best-use areas;
(2) monitoring and reviewing existing ocean management processes to identify gaps and duplication of effort;

(3) establishing procedures for obtaining the widest range of views on the ocean management programmes, including public hearings;

(4) making recommendations to the federal and territorial executive regarding changes in laws and policies to achieve effective ocean management; and

(5) making recommendations to improve co-ordination and consultation between federal and territorial governments.

Binational Ocean Management

For those ocean management issues that cross offshore boundaries between coastal states, policy, planning, and management first will have to be negotiated and then jointly co-ordinated. Some form of bilateral institution will have to be designed to manage a programme that encompasses separate and sovereign jurisdictions. The breadth of the programme's mandate and the extent of its authority will depend on the extent to which the two states are willing to give up some of their sovereignty.

If such a joint programme is workable, Canada and the United States would be an almost-ideal combination; they are both developed nations with the technical, scientific, and financial abilities to be equal partners in implementing a systems approach to the management of ocean uses. The hydrocarbon potential of the Beaufort Sea region and the importance of environmental protection in this area are incentives for the development of such a programme. There has been a history of good relations and co-operation through the International Joint Commission. However, the failure of the East Coast Fishery Agreement in 1981,[57] followed by the recent refusal of the United States to participate in the new United Nations Convention on the Law of the Sea, indicates that a co-operative approach to ocean management is not ensured.

The current lack of success should not deter the development of a joint ocean management programme. There currently is no institutional arrangement between the countries to deal with offshore development; any current joint efforts are made on an *ad hoc* basis to meet situations as they arise. This will have to change. If the proposed industrial development in the Beaufort Sea region proceeds, it could provide sufficient incentive to devise co-operative arrangements for ocean management.

Endnotes

1. United Nations Convention on the Law of the Sea (A/CONF. 62/122), opened for signature 10 December 1982, Montego Bay (hereinafter, UNCLOS). Reprinted in *International Legal Materials (ILM)* 21(1982), p. 1261.

2. John King Gamble, Jr, *Marine Policy: A Comparative Approach* (Toronto: Lexington Books; D.C. Heath and Company, 1977), p. 6.

3. Ann L. Hollick, "United States and Canadian Policy Processes in Law of the Sea," *San Diego Law Review* 12:3 (April 1975), p. 519.

4. Arctic Waters Pollution Prevention Act, *Revised Statutes Canada (RSC)* 1970, c. 2 (1st Supp.) (hereinafter, AWPPA).

5. See Barbara Johnson and Mark W. Zacher, eds, *Canadian Foreign Policy and the Law of the Sea* (Vancouver: University of British Columbia Press, 1977).

6. See Hal Mills, "Ocean Policy Making in the Canadian Arctic," pp. 491-527 in this volume.

7. Canada Oil and Gas Act, *Statutes Canada (SC)* 1980-81-82-83, c. 81.

8. See John King Gamble, Jr, *Marine Policy* (see above, note 2), pp. 3-7.

9. R.W. Stewart and L.M. Dickie, *Ad Mare: Canada Looks to the Sea, A Study on Marine Science and Technology,* Background Study for the Science Council of Canada, Special Study 16 (Ottawa: Information Canada, 1971).

10. Philip A. Lapp, *Report of the Interdepartmental Study Group on Ocean Information Systems* (Ottawa, March 1979). Prepared for the Ministry of State for Science and Technology.

11. Department of Fisheries and Oceans, *Ocean Information Services,* Canadian Special Publication of Fisheries and Aquatic Sciences 53 (Ottawa: Minister of Supply and Services Canada, 1980). Report to the Ad Hoc Interdepartmental Committee to Discuss the Requirements and Availability of Ocean Information Services.

12. See Robert Dorfman and Nancy S. Dorfman, eds, *Economics of the Environment: Selected Readings* (New York: W.W. Norton & Company Inc., 1972); see also Francis T. Christy, Jr, "Property Rights in the World Ocean," in *Natural Resources Journal* 15:4 (October 1975), pp. 695-712.

13. Convention on the Territorial Sea and Contiguous Zone, opened for signature 29 April 1958, *United Nations Treaty Series (UNTS)* 519/205; Convention on the Continental Shelf, opened for signature 29 April 1958, *UNTS* 499/311; Convention on the High Seas, opened for signature 29 April 1958, *UNTS* 450/82; Convention on Fishing and Conservation of Living Resources of the High Seas, opened for signature 29 April 1958, *UNTS* 599/285.

14. "Proclamation by President Truman of 28 September 1945 on Policy of the United States with respect to the Natural Resources of the Subsoil and Sea Bed of the Continental Shelf," Executive Proclamation 2667, *Stat.* 59 (1945), p. 884.

15. Elizabeth Mann Borgese and Norton Ginsburg, eds, *Ocean Yearbook 3* (Chicago: University of Chicago Press, 1982), p. 540.

16. See R.M. Procter, et al., *Canada's Conventional Oil and Gas Resources* (Geological Survey of Canada, EMR, March 1981).

17. Georges Brondel, "Offshore Oil and Gas," in *Technology Assessment and the Oceans*, eds, Philip D. Wilmot and Aart Slingerland, ISTA Documentation Series 1 (Surrey, England: IPC Science and Technology Press Limited, 1977), p. 102.

18. See Michael S. Baram, et al., *Marine Mining of the Continental Shelf: Legal, Technical and Environmental Considerations* (Cambridge, Mass.: Ballinger Publishing Co., 1978), pp. 27, 88, 89.

19. Food and Agriculture Organization EEZ Programme, "World Fisheries and the Law of the Sea" (United Nations, 1979).

20. Technological spin-offs from advances in the aircraft, space, and computer industries are making it possible to locate fish by satellite and laser search from aircraft. Species can be identified by odour using gaseous spectrophotometrics. Detection devices on ocean platforms soon may combine weather reports with fish forecasting. See Jon L. Jacobson, "Future Fishing Technology and its Impact on the Law of the Sea," in *Law of the Sea: Caracas and Beyond*, eds, Francis T. Christy, Jr, et al. (Cambridge, Mass.: Ballinger Publishing Co., 1975), pp. 237-250.

21. Krill, found in antarctic and sub-antarctic waters, is a major potential source of protein. It is estimated that the annual potential yield of the krill fishery is five times that of the total fish catch world wide. Russia and Japan already have begun to exploit this fishery. Squid is another enormous potential source of protein but, because squid live at a great depth, they have not been fished as intensively as they might be in the future. See Baram, et al., *Marine Mining of the Continental Shelf* (see above, note 18), pp. 49-50.

22. Thorsten Rinman and Rigmor Lindén, *Shipping: How it Works* (Gothenburg: Rinman & Lindén AB., 1978).

23. Current shipping traffic has caused the International Maritime Organization (IMO), formerly Intergovernmental Maritime Consultative Organization (IMCO), to publish "Ships Routing Schemes" for major shipping lanes and port areas of the world, pursuant to the International Collision Regulations. These are not compulsory; states are invited to use them. For a discussion of the IMO and its functions in shipping, see Bernhard J. Abrahamsson, *International Ocean Shipping: Current Concepts and Principles* (Boulder: Westview Press, Inc., 1980), pp. 134-140; see also R. Michael M'Gonigle and Mark W.

Zacher, *Pollution, Politics, and International Law: Tankers at Sea* (Berkeley and Los Angeles: University of California Press, 1979), c. 3, pp. 39–77.

24. For details of this proposal, see Dome Petroleum Limited, Esso Resources Canada Limited, and Gulf Canada Resources Inc., *Environmental Impact Statement for Hydrocarbon Development in the Beaufort Sea-Mackenzie Delta Region*, vol. 2, *Development Systems* (Calgary: Dome Petroleum Limited, 1982), c. 6.

25. See above, note 13.

26. Edward Wenk, Jr, "International Institutions for Rational Management of Ocean Space," *Ocean Management* 1 (1973), p. 17; see also D.M. McRae, "The Law of the Sea Draft Convention and International Organizations," *Marine Policy Reports* 3:2 (1980).

27. See the Traverse Group, Inc., *Ocean Management: Seeking a New Perspective*, by John M. Armstrong and Peter C. Rymer (Washington D.C.: U.S. Government Printing Office, n.d.).

28. Territorial Sea and Fishing Zones Act, *RSC* 1970, c. T.7 (as amended). Designation of fishing zones is by order in council. The arctic fishing zone is established under the Fishing Zones of Canada (Zone 6) Order, *Consolidated Regulations of Canada (CRC)* 18 (1978), c. 1549, p. 13747.

29. Robert D. Hodgson and Robert W. Smith, "Boundary Issues Created by Extended National Marine Jurisdiction," *Geographical Review* 69:4, pp. 423–433 (October 1979) p. 426.

30. UNCLOS, art. 33.

31. Ibid., arts. 76, 82.

32. Ibid., arts. 136, 137; arts. 55, 56, 57, 58.

33. Ibid., art. 56.

34. Ibid., arts. 123, 197-201, 242-244, 270-274.

35. David I. Cleland and William R. King, *Management: A Systems Approach* (New York: McGraw-Hill Book Company, 1972), pp. 4-7.

36. Timothy O'Riordan, *Perspectives on Resource Management* (London: Pion Limited, 1971), p. 19.

37. The Senate of Canada, *Marching to the Beat of the Same Drum: Transportation of Petroleum and Natural Gas North of 60°*, Report of the Senate Special Committee on the Northern Pipeline (Ottawa: Senate of Canada, 1983).

38. The management requirements of these different approaches are discussed, for example, in: Federal Environmental Assessment Review Office, *Report of the Environmental Assessment Panel: Lancaster Sound Drilling* (Ottawa: FEARO, 1979); the proceedings of the National Energy Board on the Arctic

Pilot Project; DIAND, "Northern Land Use Planning," Discussion Paper (Ottawa: DIAND, July 1971); DIAND, *A Comprehensive Conservation Policy and Strategy for the Northwest Territories and Yukon*, Draft Discussion Paper (Ottawa, October 1982); A.R. Lucas, et al., "Regulation of High Arctic Development," in *Marine Transportation and High Arctic Development: Policy Framework and Priorities* (Ottawa: Canadian Arctic Resources Committee, 1979), pp. 98–176; and reports cited in notes 24 and 37. These management approaches are not linked, however, in a way that satisfies requirements for a systems approach.

39. J.W. MacNeill, *Environmental Management* (Ottawa: Information Canada, 1971), p. 5.

40. Traverse Group, Inc., *Ocean Management* (see above, note 27), pp. 59–76.

41. For a good discussion of management principles as they relate to coastal zone planning, see Douglas M. Johnston, et al., *Coastal Zone: Framework for Management in Atlantic Canada* (Halifax: Institute of Public Affairs, Dalhousie University, 1975).

42. John T. Epting and David W. Laist, "Perspectives on an Ocean Management System," *Ocean Development and International Law Journal* 7: 3–4 (1979), p. 259.

43. Cleland and King, *Management* (see above, note 35), p. 18.

44. Peter Harrison, *Managing Canada's Ocean Area: Institutions, Client Groups, and Co-ordination*, Research Notes No. 26 (Ottawa: University of Ottawa, 1971), pp. 13–17.

45. For a discussion of management units in relation to the coastal zone, see Johnston, et al., *Coastal Zone* (see above, note 41), pp. 2–13 and 151–155.

46. Agreement between the Government of Canada and the Government of the Kingdom of Denmark Relating to the Delimitation of the Continental Shelf between Greenland and Canada, Ottawa, 17 December 1973, *Canada Treaty Series (CTS)* (1974), no. 9.

47. Arild Underdal, "Integrated Marine Policy: What? Why? How?," *Marine Policy* 4 (July, 1980), pp. 166-168.

48. Ibid.

49. Department of Fisheries and Oceans Act, *SC* 1978-79, c. 13, s. 5.

50. This type of arrangement is suggested and discussed by Felix Kwamena, *Canada's Offshore Resources: The Problem of Integrated Planning in Canada's 200-Mile Economic Zone*, Research Notes 27 (Ottawa: University of Ottawa, May 1979).

51. Memorandum of Understanding in Respect of the Administration and Management of Mineral Resources Offshore of the Maritime Provinces, February 1977.

52. This type of arrangement has been suggested and discussed by Harrison, *Managing Canada's Ocean Area* (see above, note 44), pp. 25-28.

53. Ibid., pp. 26-27.

54. Johnston, et al., *Coastal Zone* (see above, note 41), pp. 151-163.

55. Ibid., pp. 162, 154.

56. This structure is suggested by the provisions of the Alaska Native Claims Settlement Act (*Stat.* 85:688), which created a Joint Federal-State Land-use Planning Commission.

57. Agreement between the Government of Canada and the Government of the United States of America on East Coast Fishery Resources, signed in 1979, was not ratified by the U.S.

Development in the Beaufort Sea Region

Chairmen: Jack Heath
David Brooks

Introduction

Northern development and government policies that promote development have affected the Beaufort Sea region profoundly. Oil and gas exploration began onshore in the Mackenzie Delta in the 1960s and moved offshore in the late 1970s. In the 1980s, exploration has been promoted and subsidized by the federal government through the National Energy Program. Reserves sufficient for commercial production have not been proved, but both industry and government are preparing for hydrocarbon production by the late 1980s.

Offshore hydrocarbon development in the Beaufort Sea region was referred to the federal Environmental Assessment and Review Process (EARP) in mid-1980. The three major proponents—Dome Petroleum, Esso Resources Canada Limited, and Gulf Canada Resources Inc.—produced a seven-volume environmental impact statement (EIS) in 1982 outlining the possible environmental, social, and economic implications of commercial hydrocarbon production from the Beaufort Sea region. The recommendations of the Beaufort Sea Environmental Assessment Panel, due in 1984, will influence future government and industry efforts to manage development.

The national interest in the Beaufort Sea region is seen by many Canadians to be the development of a large and reliable source of hydrocarbons, but fair settlement of native land claims in this region and conservation of important wilderness areas such as the Yukon's North Slope, which encompasses the calving grounds of the Porcupine caribou herd, also are matters of national interest and concern. Ways and means must be found to serve these national interests and to integrate them with local concerns and aspirations.

The Working Groups

Residents of communities in the Beaufort Sea region look forward to the economic benefits, so often promised, of hydrocarbon developments "in their own backyards." They are concerned, however, about how these developments will affect renewable resources that now are an important part of their culture and economy, about the larger communities and greater number of local businesses that will result from development, and about how these will fare when development is finished. The Beaufort Sea Development Impact Zone Society has been formed recently to give residents a direct role in managing development. The governments of the Yukon and the Northwest Territories are pressing developers to hire northerners and pressing the federal government to implement policies that will maximize benefits to northerners. The regional land, water, and wildlife management institutions likely to result from the settlement of aboriginal land claims of the Committee for Original Peoples' Entitlement (COPE) will provide another way for local residents to participate in management decisions.

The Beaufort Sea region is likely to be the first area in which DIAND's 1981 northern land-use planning policy will be implemented. Land-use planning is intended to integrate local, regional, and national concerns and therefore will require the co-operation of federal and territorial government agencies and the participation of local residents and other interests.

The working group included:

Chairmen: **Jack Heath**
Northwest Territories Public Utilities Board
Inuvik, N.W.T.

David Brooks
Beaufort Sea Alliance
Ottawa, Ontario

Rapporteur: **Winston Mair**
Victoria, British Columbia

Invited Participants:

Hiram Beaubier
Northern Affairs Program
Department of Indian Affairs and Northern Development
Government of Canada
Yellowknife, N.W.T.

Ewan Cotterill
Northern Policy and Employee Relations
Dome Petroleum Ltd.
Calgary, Alberta

Dennis Lang
Dome Petroleum Ltd.
Calgary, Alberta

Jim Lee
Esso Resources Canada Ltd.
Calgary, Alberta

Simon McInnis
Energy Strategy Branch
Department of Energy, Mines and Resources
Government of Canada
Ottawa, Ontario

The Working Groups

Brett Moore
Department of the Environment
Government of Canada
Edmonton, Alberta

Bill Oppen
Intergovernmental Relations
Government of the Yukon
Whitehorse, Yukon

Bob Simpson
Fort McPherson, N.W.T.

Nancy Weeks
Committee for Original Peoples' Entitlement
Inuvik, N.W.T.

Background documents used in the working group, in addition to those published in these proceedings, included:

Government of the Yukon. *Government of Yukon Position on Beaufort Development Proposals*, Submission to Beaufort Sea Environmental Assessment Review Panel. August 1982.

Working Group Report

Development in the Beaufort Sea Region

The working group on development in the Beaufort Sea Region identified three possibilities for hydrocarbon development in the Beaufort Sea–Mackenzie Delta region:

- small-scale phased development of oil and gas reserves in small quantities in shallow water or in the delta
- large-scale development of oil and gas reserves in large quantities offshore
- small-scale phased development extended to many small pools of oil and gas offshore.

Large-scale development of hydrocarbon resources is of concern to local, regional, and territorial interests. Small-scale phased development is more compatible with territorial and local interests. The working group looked at jurisdictional problems and concluded that they were largely problems of management and decision making.

The Interests

The working group defined the national interests as the delineation of frontier resources, the impacts of development on the environment and the economic development of the region. The territorial interests were defined as: first, economic development of the region, jobs, and conservation; and secondly, serving the national interests. Local and regional interests are economic development, jobs, the establishment of infrastructure, impacts on the environment, land-use conflicts, and social change.

Native peoples engaged in land-claims negotiations also have an interest in the development of hydrocarbon resources in the Beaufort Sea region, but this interest was not defined by the working group.

The federal government, representing the national interest, has the controlling role in resource development in the North through legislation, finance, and the administration of natural resource use. The territorial government, representing the territorial interests in social and economic development, requires greater involvement in managing resource development to fulfil its role. The local and regional interests require participation in planning processes to find ways to accommodate developments and to respond to proposals for energy development.

Conflicts and Compatibilities

The national, territorial, regional, and local interests in resource development in the Beaufort Sea region all require a role in resource management. Although these roles need not be incompatible, it is inevitable that conflicts will arise over specific development issues and management responsibilities. Conflicts over jurisdiction between and within levels of interests will delay decision making and damage the credibility of those involved.

Conflict Resolution

Many of the anticipated conflicts can be resolved through discussion and by improving the management process if all levels of interests are involved. Powerful interests should be discouraged from circumventing the planning process by seeking political solutions to questions of planning and management.

Required Research and Policy Initiatives

Although the working group's discussion of resource management problems in the Beaufort Sea region concluded that conflicts exist, none were identified clearly. Identifying key conflicts in resource management and examining the existing information on these issues is therefore a first step in improving the management of resources in the Beaufort Sea region, and the forthcoming report of the Beaufort Sea EARP panel should do so. The working group did not propose priorities for research.

The three levels of government and industrial interests must find an appropriate way to identify issues and to agree upon action. Carried out conscientiously, this process could resolve many, if not most, of the problems of resource management in the Beaufort Sea region. It should not require new management institutions.

Resource management decisions must be made. If these decisions are made after the available information has been assessed and after concerned parties have had sufficient opportunity to be involved, the final decision must be accepted by all parties.

Background Paper

Development in the Beaufort Region: from EARP to Regional Planning

Terry Fenge
Director, Policy Studies
Canadian Arctic Resources Committee

Introduction

Most Canadians are familiar with the extensive exploration for and proposed exploitation of hydrocarbons in the Beaufort region. Fewer realize that this activity is occurring without a plan or a planning process in place to ensure the balanced development of the region, that is, to accommodate various, and often conflicting, values and interests.

The oil and gas industry is now the main force directing social, economic, and environmental change in the Beaufort region. The industry's long-term presence here seems assured, for the federal government's National Energy Program encourages exploration for hydrocarbons in frontier areas. This presence is likely to become overwhelming, however, when exploration leads to the production and transportation of hydrocarbons. Lasting development, nevertheless, is based on diversity and balance, in which renewable as well as non-renewable resources are valued. Similarly, the issue of development cannot be divorced from the question: Development for whom and by whom? The roles of the persons directly affected by externally induced change, particularly the control and management they exert over that change, largely determine the ability of development to serve local, regional, and national interests simultaneously.

The scale and pace of hydrocarbon development in the Beaufort region will reflect many factors, including the rate of discoveries, the productivity of wells, total reserves, market demand, regulatory measures, and social and environmental constraints, but the proponents have recently outlined massive development scenarios. Hydrocarbon production could begin as early as 1986 or 1987 and expand throughout the 1990s. Pipelines up the Mackenzie Valley and ice-breaking tankers along the Northwest Passage are being proposed as modes of transportation by Esso and Dome Petroleum, respectively. Shore-based facilities may be proposed for many locations, from Herschel Island on the North Slope of the Yukon to Cape Parry, near Paulatuk, N.W.T. The scale of the proposed development is truly daunting; by the year 2000, total development expenditures could reach $100 billion.

A Redirection in Thinking?

Exploration for hydrocarbons in the Beaufort region has proceeded by small increments. The federal government has dealt with industry's proposed plans in an *ad hoc* manner, confining its responsibilities to monitoring and regulating. These increments accumulate quickly, however, and often create additional and unforeseen changes elsewhere. It is clear now that incremental change in the Beaufort region is leading toward massive change.

Industry perceives change in a long-term context and fits together individual pieces of the development jig-saw puzzle in a sequence and fashion that rapidly completes the puzzle according to industry's design. Government seems to view change as a short-term phenomenon, and reacts to each proposed development as if it were a new puzzle. Government has yet to appreciate the immense magnitude and scope of proposed long-term development in the Beaufort region. Existing management institutions and processes do not provide direction on the best ways to complete the puzzle, for they do not operate from a model of the probable future. This lack of preparedness is surprising, for hydrocarbon exploration in the Beaufort region has long been fuelled by tax incentives and other inducements provided by the federal government, and current proposals by industry are only logical extensions of earlier exploratory activities.

Major decisions will be made soon on the types of technology required to produce and to transport hydrocarbons, and on the siting of production and support facilities. These decisions should be made within a broad context of planning if the federal government's avowed aim of balanced and harmonious development for the North is to be served. Government should sponsor public planning processes to develop preferred futures for the Beaufort region. An early product of such planning should be a set of development principles to consult when specific projects are proposed, and to guide discussion on the appropriate scale and pace of the exploitation of hydrocarbons. The task facing government, industry, native organizations, community residents, and others with interests and concerns in the region is to think in broad terms and to establish public and private institutions to manage and to direct change in accordance with predefined goals.

A number of policy initiatives suggest that both the federal and territorial governments are beginning to recognize the magnitude of likely development in the Beaufort region and the planning and management roles that each should perform. The federal government's 1981 Northern Land Use Planning Policy, the current attempts of the Department of Indian Affairs and Northern Development (DIAND) to establish a comprehensive environmental conservation policy and implementation strategy, the 1982 Resource Development Policy established by the Government of the Northwest Territories (GNWT), and the land and resource assessment policies of the Yukon Territorial Government (YTG) represent efforts to improve governments' abilities to manage change in the region.

It will take many months for these policy initiatives to affect the manner in which the development jig-saw puzzle is pieced together. In fact, these initiatives may wither in the rough and tumble of intergovernment and interagency politics and may never alter the rules of the game. The Beaufort Sea Environmental Assessment and Review Process (EARP), however, could contribute to the implementation of these broad management policies through its public hearings on industry's development proposals and its formal recommendations to the minister of the Environment.

It will be difficult for the Beaufort Sea EARP to evaluate governments' abilities to regulate, plan for, and manage development, and for it to recommend institutions and processes needed for management. Nevertheless, should it succeed, it will ensure this EARP's lasting impact on events in the region. It would be particularly beneficial if the Beaufort Sea EARP supported the emerging policy initiatives for planning, conservation, and resource development and if it advocated clearly both locally and regionally based management authorities.

The Northern Land Use Planning Policy

DIAND announced a Cabinet-approved Northern Land Use Planning Policy in July 1981. It hoped that land-use planning would help to:

  a. avoid or minimize land use conflicts arising from the inability of different land uses . . . to be accommodated on any area of northern lands;
  b. ensure the integration of the management of northern land resources;
  c. enable northern lands to be allocated and used in an optimum way, taking into account local, regional and national interests and concerns and the physical and biological characteristics of northern lands and the resources they support;

d. enable public participation in the decision-making process concerning allocation and best use of northern lands.[1]

The intent of the policy is to anticipate conflicts in land use and, through allocation of land based on public planning processes, to direct development, conservation, and related land uses.

Progress in implementing the planning policy has been agonizingly slow, but negotiations are now underway between the federal and N.W.T. governments, the Dene Nation, Inuit Tapirisat of Canada (ITC), the Métis Association of the N.W.T., and the Committee for Original Peoples' Entitlement (COPE) to determine appropriate principles, structures, and processes for northern land-use planning. The Yukon Territorial Government feels that land-use planning in the Yukon should be its responsibility, and it passed a Yukon Land Planning Act in response to the federal policy. In the N.W.T., however, negotiations between the federal and territorial governments and native organizations have focused on the appropriate degree of northern control over, and participation in, land-use planning.

A discussion paper released by DIAND immediately following the announcement of the planning policy envisaged a federally based planning process with territorial governments and northerners generally relegated to advisory and technical pursuits. Although virtually all organized interests and northern governments supported the concept and principle of land-use planning, they demanded a devolved, northern-based process. In October 1982, DIAND released a draft implementation strategy for land-use planning that marginally increased the role for northerners. This strategy was greeted with widespread condemnation by northern groups, and DIAND was cajoled into rethinking the institutional base to implement the policy.

In March 1983, DIAND and the GNWT agreed to implement the planning policy jointly through land-use planning commissions and a policy advisory committee. Northern native organizations are to have representation on both structures. Although the GNWT has secured a considerable role in implementing this policy, how communities and regional governments will participate in developing land-use plans remains unclear. This is likely to become a major question in the Beaufort region, where northern land-use planning will be attempted first.

A Comprehensive Environmental Conservation Policy

In announcing the Northern Land Use Planning Policy, DIAND accepted that certain areas should be reserved for conservation purposes in advance of industrial development:

> Northern Canada possesses unique biological and physical attributes that must be preserved from degradation and protected from any threat of diminution or extinction. The difficulties lie in trying to objectively balance the two by identifying and evaluating trade-offs that may have to be made in the public interest, and doing so in a systematic and open manner. A land use planning approach provides a means for such decision-making.[2]

In October 1982, DIAND published a draft discussion paper on comprehensive environmental conservation. This was followed by a workshop on conservation policy in Whitehorse to formulate the elements of a potential policy and a long-range plan of action setting out conservation goals and objectives. The minister of Indian Affairs and Northern Development recently approved the concept of a task force to:

1. recommend appropriate conservation targets for implementation through 1985; and
2. recommend on the establishment of a strategy and an ongoing mechanism for implementing a northern conservation programme linked to the new northern land-use planning process.[3]

Although a policy for northern conservation has yet to be established, the recent flurry of activity in this area of policy contrasts with previous years of lethargy and reactive thinking. It is still unclear how such a policy will be implemented and what will be the probable role for northern governments. Potential management institutions have still to be discussed, but the attempt to generate a conservation policy is most welcome. Environmentally significant areas (ESAs) in the Beaufort region require management to safeguard their natural values. The number, size, and appropriate management designations for such areas are still unknown, but it is important to note that the concept of conserving ESAs prior to industrial development is a cornerstone of the emerging policy.

Resource Development Policy

The 1982 GNWT Resource Development Policy supports development when its "overall economic, social and environmental implications are judged to result in a net benefit to the people of the Northwest Territories."[4] The aim is to enable the territorial government to make decisions on resource development in a comprehensive and integrated manner, yet the policy promotes local and regional processes to assist in the management of development.

Development impact zones (DIZ) composed of communities likely to experience the effects of resource development are to be established. Each zone is to have a "group that is representative of the public interests in the area and relies on existing bodies such as municipal, band and regional councils, as well as native organizations, for overall local identification and resolution of issues associated with the perceived impacts of resource development."[5] A Beaufort–Mackenzie Delta Development Impact Zone Group is being formed.

Yukon Land Planning Act

The YTG released a land-use policy in April 1982, and passed a Land Planning Act last autumn. Both are essentially political statements in response to the federal planning policy. Nevertheless, they endorse the principle of land allocation based upon comprehensive planning processes and make an explicit connection between social and economic development and land-use planning.

The policy outlines the setting up of a proposed Yukon land-use planning board and land-use planning committees, the division of the Yukon into planning districts, and the transfer of land from federal to territorial jurisdiction as land-use plans are adopted. Majority representation by northerners is envisaged on all land-use planning institutions. Central to the YTG position is that land be transferred to the territorial government as a result of planning activities, and that continued evolution of the YTG be linked with ownership and control of land.

For development in the Beaufort region, the YTG wishes to implement a land-use plan based on principles outlined in the 1980 *Northern Yukon Resource Management Model*. This model proposes a national park in north-western Yukon, west of the Babbage River, a territorial historic park on Herschel Island, and a multiple land-use zone elsewhere. A committee is envisaged to advise government on the management of the area.

The planning, conservation, and resource development policy initiatives of the federal and territorial governments reflect the growing awareness of the need to have management institutions and processes in place before the exploitation of resources occurs. Each policy reflects anticipatory as well as reactive thinking and seeks to preserve future development options that may otherwise be pre-empted by large-scale exploitation of non-renewable resources. The intent of these policy initiatives is fairly clear, but major unanswered questions concern how, and by whom, they will be implemented, and their ability to control completion of the development jig-saw puzzle.

The Beaufort Sea EARP

Currently, public attention on the region is focused through the Beaufort Sea Environmental Assessment and Review Process (EARP), administered by the Federal Environmental Assessment and Review Office (FEARO). This process was initiated in July 1980, before the aforementioned policy initiatives were underway. Since then, the Beaufort Sea EARP has navigated a complex course and is soon to enter the highly visible phase of public hearings on a seven-volume environmental impact statement (EIS) produced by Dome Petroleum, Gulf, and Esso, who are the major proponents of development.

The avowed purpose of EARP is to ensure the assessment of environmental consequences of all projects, programmes, and activities that benefit from federal funds, and to include the results of such assessments in decision making and project implementation. The process is normally reactive to industry's proposals and evaluates primarily industry's perceptions and advocacy. The Beaufort Sea EARP is the only major public forum inquiring into development in the region, hence the majority of interests affected by events there will participate in its deliberations. It has been provided with unusually broad terms of reference and has made procedural innovations in response to criticisms of earlier assessments. These factors provide this EARP with an opportunity to document the need for, and to hasten the adoption of, broad planning and management processes.

The ability of the Beaufort Sea EARP panel to play this role partially reflects the advice and recommendations it receives from interested parties. Its public meetings in autumn 1983 on the EIS will illustrate how the panel views its bridging function to subsequent planning and management processes. If the panel adopts a passive, honest-broker role during public hearings, then it is unlikely to stimulate discussion on broad problems of management and on the directions it could take, and will be poorly equipped to make recommendations on planning and management. If, however, the panel recognizes the importance of *process* in what it does, treats the public meetings as opportunities to experiment with ideas on how to manage for development, and takes an active role in drawing out participants on this crucial issue, then it could assume a useful bridging role.

The Subject and Terms of Reference of the Beaufort Sea EARP

The Beaufort Sea EARP is dealing with the *concept* of developing hydro-carbons over a very large area, for industry has yet to bring forward specific proposals. The EIS provides only an overview of industry's thoughts on the probable interaction between the region's natural and social environments and the potential siting of production facilities for hydrocarbons and the scale and pace of their development.

Most environmental assessments focus on effects that may be experienced in the near future. The Beaufort Sea EARP panel, however, has requested that the EIS project possible effects of development to the year 2000. Both the mandate of the panel and the scope of the review are extremely broad in recognition of the conceptual nature of the proposal:

> the Panel is to identify major developmental effects, both positive and negative, upon the physical, biological and human environments and recommend ways and means of dealing with them.

> The Panel review is to include all related activities north of 60° of the proponent's proposal associated with or resulting from the commercial production and shipment of hydrocarbon resources from the Beaufort Sea area. This includes possible on-shore and off-shore oil and gas production facilities in the Canadian Beaufort Sea area and subsequent transportation of oil and gas to southern markets by ice-breaking tankers or pipeline(s) or by both means. The exploration component is not part of the Panel's review.[6]

The panel is also to consider "previous and possible future northern activities which are relevant to this specific proposal," and "the capacity of Governments to control Beaufort Sea oil and gas developments."[7] Recommendations for additional public reviews of the proposed development are also solicited. Clearly, this panel is being asked to review and to assess the broad spectrum of regional, environmental, and socio-economic issues that are raised by development. The panel has an unusual opportunity to contribute to balance and diversity in the Beaufort region by recommending institutions and processes to manage the area's future.

Besides its generous terms of reference, the panel has made procedural innovations that enable the review to focus on process as well as product:

- The panel is composed solely of private citizens rather than employees of the federal civil service. Moreover, most of the members reside north of 60°. It is hoped that this representation will make the panel more independent and aggressive than its predecessors.

- Funding for interveners has been obtained from Treasury Board by FEARO and DIAND. Almost $1 million has been allocated to northern communities, native peoples' groups, public-interest groups, and others to enable their participation in the process.
- The panel has retained a particularly wide variety of technical specialists to assist with the review of the EIS.
- The panel intends to hold both community and general meetings to allow the presentation of local knowledge based on experience, as well as of scientific knowledge.
- In keeping with the panel's broad terms of reference, government agencies have been asked to provide position statements on the interaction between departmental policies and programmes and hydrocarbon production from the Beaufort region.

The Beaufort Sea EARP is a hybrid incorporating elements of traditional project-specific environmental assessment, regional land-use planning, and policy analysis. Its recommendations could reflect all these elements, and if so, key policy questions raised by development, such as aboriginal land claims, regional land-use planning, environmental conservation, government evolution, and potential institutions to direct and manage change, could be addressed. Institutions must be designed to fit these policy areas into a management perspective if the elusive "balance" sought by all concerned with development in the Beaufort region is to be attained. The Beaufort Sea EARP should make recommendations on how this could be done.

A Comparative Study Revisited

In 1981, CARC published a study that compares offshore oil and gas development in Scotland, Alaska, and the Canadian Beaufort Sea. *The Scottish and Alaskan Offshore Oil and Gas Experience and the Canadian Beaufort Sea* illustrates how other jurisdictions have coped with massive change very similar to that now occurring in the Beaufort region.[8] The Shetland Islands and Alaska's North Slope Borough resemble the Canadian Beaufort region in a number of ways. Each has a small population, little urbanization, a traditional dependence on fish and other renewable resources, distinctive indigenous populations, and a historical vulnerability to "boom and bust" patterns of economic growth. The Canadian

Beaufort situation is, however, different in one key way: it lacks the type of powerful regional governments employed in Alaska and Scotland to moderate offshore oil and gas development in the regional and local interest.

The book outlines how an effective local response to petroleum development has been achieved in the Shetlands through the Shetland Islands Council and groups such as the Sullom Voe Harbour Authority and the Shetland Oil Terminal Environmental Advisory Group (SOTEAG). SOTEAG, a co-ordinating body that brings together representatives from the Shetland Islands Council, the oil companies, the University of Aberdeen, the Scottish Development Department, the Nature Conservancy Council, and a number of similar agencies, is of particular interest as a model for the Beaufort region. Along with comparable groups such as the Alaska Coastal Policy Council, these organizations support the authors' conclusion that self-government, land ownership, and coastal zone management must be strengthened in the Canadian Beaufort region. They recommend:

- the strengthening of local government by means of a regional structure linking western arctic communities such as Inuvik and Tuktoyaktuk
- the provision of a comprehensive project approval system linking senior and local governments
- the allocation of land to the native peoples and to territorial and local governments to counterbalance the power of the federal government and the legal and financial leverage of industry
- the establishment of a Canadian Beaufort Sea–Mackenzie Delta shore-zone planning commission to co-ordinate, through research and monitoring, the diverse industrial interests in the area
- the creation of an Arctic Environmental Forum for the exchange of information between all interested parties
- the improvement of Canada's overall shore-zone co-ordination system.[9]

Summary

The Beaufort region is experiencing tremendous change as a result of exploration for hydrocarbons. Ambitious development scenarios would industrialize the region during the 1980s and 1990s. Broad land-use planning and management must be instituted well before the production and transportation of hydrocarbons if the values placed on the conservation of the region's renewable resources are to be maintained. The federal and territorial governments appear to be adopting policies that favour planning and management for development, but such processes should not be implemented from afar. They should be based within the region. Experience in Alaska and in Scotland shows that local peoples and communities can manage the large-scale development of hydrocarbons that proceeds under the imperative of national interest. Residents of the Beaufort region are capable of planning for and managing their region, but they need the support and encouragement of senior members of governments.

It seems crucial that, if they are to plan for and manage development, institutions should support and serve further political evolution in the region. Regionally based planning and management should become accountable to local residents through local and regional governments. Progress must be made on the political and government fronts if broad planning and management, based in the region, is to work. Similarly, land claims by COPE, the Dene Nation, and the Council for Yukon Indians, all of which will have an impact on the region, have to be resolved. Outstanding land claims and the absence of regional governments will hinder the implementation of broad planning and management processes.

These policy areas are now interlocked like a log jam but have little effect on industry's timetable for industrializing the region. The log jam has to be removed, and only the federal government has the power to do this. Into this complex situation, in which too many interests expect others to make the first move, is injected EARP. Whereas EARP is usually a process to evaluate specific projects, the Beaufort Sea EARP is reviewing the *concept* of development in a large region. The ability of government, at whatever level, to regulate, plan for, and manage development is the key issue facing the Beaufort Sea EARP panel. How this issue is dealt with will determine EARP's contribution to the region's future. Is it possible for the Beaufort Sea EARP, like the first stones that begin an avalanche, to press for regionally based planning and management processes that will serve local, regional, and national interests?

Endnotes

1. DIAND, "Northern Land Use Planning," Discussion paper (Ottawa: DIAND, 1981), p. 8.

2. Ibid., p. 6.

3. DIAND, "Task Force on Northern Conservation Announced," *Communiqué* 1-8328, p. 4.

4. GWNT, "Resource Development Policy," (Yellowknife: Energy and Resource Development Secretariat, GNWT, 1983), p. 2.

5. Ibid., p. 3.

6. Beaufort Sea Hydrocarbon Production Environmental Assessment Panel, "Terms of Reference," June 1981, p. 2.

7. Ibid., p. 3.

8. J.G. Nelson and S. Jessen, *The Scottish and Alaskan Offshore Oil and Gas Experience and the Canadian Beaufort Sea* (Ottawa: Canadian Arctic Resources Committee, 1981).

9. Ibid., pp. 107-111.

Position Paper

Submission on Development in the Yukon Region

Council for Yukon Indians

Land-use Planning in Northern Canada

For the past number of years, the increased pace of industrial development in Canada's North, particularly in the non-renewable mineral and oil and gas sectors; the continued and growing reliance of the aboriginal peoples on renewable resource harvesting; and the increased awareness by all parties of the relationships between resource development, traditional land-use activities, and conservation have led to the conclusion by all parties that these wide and varied interests cannot be accommodated by unilateral action by any party.

These parties conclude that there is a need to resolve these differences through a process that must be co-ordinated, co-operative, and comprehensive in nature. There is consensus that, to promote the orderly development of all sectors of northern interests, land-use planning is the key.

The process of land-use planning is widely accepted as the basis for making decisions about the location of undertakings and activities on the land; for resolving competing demands with regard to the use and disposition of the land; and for resolving competition between related resources based on predetermined policies and objectives. The idea of comprehensive planning, which is generally accepted by all parties in the North, embodies the co-ordination of public policies and programmes for the social, economic, and physical development of a particular region toward predetermined goals.

The major problem facing the comprehensive process of land-use planning and environmental assessment in the North, however, is the number of and the widespread competing interests, which include the federal and territorial governments, aboriginal and non-aboriginal northerners, resource developers, conservationists, and, last but not least, the Canadian consumer. Although their interests vary and compete, it is argued that a considerable degree of consensus exists among the parties on the process itself and on many of its objectives, specifically on the following points:

- the existing processes and regimes are inadequate for dealing with many of today's issues concerning land and resources
- the effects of megaprojects undertaken in the national interest must also be in the regional interest
- land-use activities must be minimized to ensure proper conservation
- the process must involve public participation
- planning in the North must be done by both aboriginal and non-aboriginal northerners and must make allowances for their goals and aspirations
- the process must be multilateral and multidisciplinary
- the socio-economic and environmental integrity of the North must be protected.

If consensus exists on so many fundamental, northern-oriented issues *vis-à-vis* the process of land-use planning and environmental assessment, then the art of reaching consensus should be used as the mode of planning. Truly co-operative and comprehensive planning requires compromise in making decisions, which lends itself readily to arriving at consensus. This approach, although anticipatory in nature, contributes to ensuring that all parties' views and, and therefore, alternative land uses, are first assessed and then addressed. In this way, those land uses best suited to a certain location will develop.

Unfortunately, arriving at consensus takes time. Considering the great pressure to develop the Beaufort Sea, it is possible that *ad hoc*, reactionary planning will prevail in the coastal Yukon region. Consensus on interim planning would help to alleviate this situation.

The issue of control in the planning of northern land use presents another problem. The planning process has become a political contest for control, which is placing the whole planning process in jeopardy. Political debating must be removed from the process of land-use planning and environmental assessment. Again, consensus offers an interesting and effective way of deciding who controls what and, therefore, of keeping all players involved.

Development in the Coastal Yukon Region, Land-use Planning, and Yukon Indian Land Claims

The Council for Yukon Indians (CYI) looks back on a decade of experience at the negotiations table—negotiating within a confusing array of political claims, negotiating formats, and industrial and government development activities. Not surprisingly, CYI has had to modify its initial claims proposal, so as to march with the changing times. Perhaps it is just too simple to say that the prerogatives of land claims need to be defined independently of the perspectives of either industry or government. However, land claims do need to be given fair political, economic, and social recognition—an acknowledgement of the legitimacy of Indians' beliefs in themselves and in their future. Land claims never will be settled if settlement is thought to mean laying land claims to rest. On the contrary, the settlement should not exist to obliterate claims, but rather should serve to translate them out of their present legal and administrative entanglement into effective social, economic, and political forums. Land claims *per se* have become a nucleus for the entire North. Unfortunately, to developers of non-renewable resources and promoters of premature provincial status for the Yukon alike, the claims also represent something of an impediment.

The issue of greatest priority and urgency, then, although it is seldom viewed as such in the context of land-use planning, is that of land claims.

Regardless of the morality of placing the exploitation of oil and gas above the necessity of first settling outstanding native claims, it is paramount that land claims be recognized as part of land-use planning. It is also imperative, not only for governments and other interest groups but also for industry, to respond to the prerogatives of land claims so as to create a context in which land claims can be accepted as a premise of northern development. In fact, land claims *are* northern development, and as such, northern development and land-use planning should be grounded on the probability of land claims, not on the possibility of hydrocarbon development. Thus, the difference in attitude between those interests that take the North for a frontier and those that own it as a homeland, must be incorporated and dealt with in the context of planning.

The essential element here is that land-claims settlements have a more precise and permanent reality for the North than do hydrocarbon development proposals because land claims provide a more coherent, comprehensive, and imaginative vision of land-use planning. Land claims are the means of ensuring that aboriginal peoples can plan and develop their own permanent land uses, rather than merely participate in temporary schemes devised and controlled in southern boardrooms. These differences and antagonisms between land claims and hydrocarbon development simply have to be recognized, accounted for, and made part of the Canadian North of tomorrow.

Stokes Point

A marine base at Stokes Point supportive of exploration activities alone might cause only negligible effects on the social and environmental fabric of the northern Yukon, if there were not the real danger that the Stokes Point facility is only part of a larger plan. Questioned on the possibility, Gulf Vice-President Motyka acknowledged this to be "a justifiable concern," but he noted: "Had the North American Indian done a socio-economic study on the Europeans landing on North American shores, we would not have gotten here."

This "foot-in-the-door" expansionism extrapolated to Stokes Point explains too well that if exploration is successful and leads into the later phases of development and production, the requirements for shore-based industrial sites will mushroom proportionately, thereby increasing potential conflicts in land use. This, of course, is a major concern to the Old Crow Indians specifically, and to CYI generally.

The Old Crow Indian Band, in a letter to John Munro, Minister of Indian Affairs and Northern Development, recently opposed publicly the development of Stokes Point until: first, the land claims of the Old Crow people have been addressed and resolved through agreements in principle; secondly, there has occurred a satisfactory public inquiry into the proposed development of Stokes Point, particularly with respect to the implications of such development for the long-term viability of the Porcupine caribou herd; and, finally, the role of the Old Crow people in land-use planning and environmental assessment in the northern Yukon has been satisfactorily resolved.

Government of Yukon Position on Beaufort Development Proposals

**Submission to
Beaufort Sea Environmental
Assessment Review Panel
August 1982**

Summary

Yukoners have been involved in Beaufort Sea activities since the whaling expeditions of the early 1900s. They have been involved in hydrocarbon transportation since the building of the Canol pipeline, and in exploration and drilling since the push into Eagle Plains in the 1950s and the drive across Northern Yukon in the late 1960s. Yukoners come to the present phase of Beaufort development then, with considerable experience in hydrocarbon activities and with a sense that they have a strong role to play in the latest series of work opportunities in the Beaufort.

The Government of Yukon, holding the political and legislative mandate for socio-economic affairs in Yukon, is pursuing employment, training and business opportunities for Yukoners who wish to participate in Beaufort hydrocarbon activities. It argues that Yukoners, as northerners, will bear many of the direct and indirect social costs of oil and gas developments on their doorstep and Yukoners, consequently, should have an equitable share in these developments. The Government of Yukon is committed to working cooperatively with industry, the federal government and GNWT toward ensuring the participation of Yukoners in Beaufort work and toward the smooth integration of much of the growing Beaufort workforce into the Yukon population. The Government of Yukon's work in this regard is conducted within the framework of its move toward full political responsibility and is done with the recognition of the separate objectives of its NWT neighbours regarding their involvement in Beaufort activities.

The Government of Yukon has the mandate for wildlife management and protection in Yukon. It is aware that development in Northern Yukon, whether this development involves periodic activities such as quarrying and pipeline construction, or long term activities such as the operation of shore bases, harbour facilities and connector roads, will place considerable stress on the environment and the wildlife species dependent on the environment. The Government of Yukon is resolved to manage development in Northern Yukon in a manner that will minimize negative impacts on the area. It will require additional wildlife survey data in order to develop effective management regimes. However, it has already developed a process for formulating and implementing such management plans. This process is described specifically in the *Northern Yukon Resource Management Model* and more generally in *Land: A Yukon Resource*.

The Government of Yukon looks forward to the opportunities that Beaufort development will offer to the north and to Canada in general. It is prepared and anxious to participate fully in the complex planning required to achieve the timely and carefully managed production of Beaufort oil and gas. It supports the Beaufort Environmental Assessment Review Process as a critical step in the move toward the full development of the Beaufort Sea's important hydrocarbon resources.

Reprinted with kind permission of the Government of the Yukon.

Background Paper

Points for Discussion: Development in the Beaufort Sea Region

P.H. Beaubier
Department of Indian Affairs and Northern Development

The issues associated with exploration and development in the Beaufort Sea region are as complex as any in Canada today. They go far beyond questions of "resource management" in the strict application of this expression and affect essential threads of the national, regional, and local fabric. As in all complex issues, there is a range of concerns, many of which conflict and require decisions that are both political and technical in nature. The responsibilities for making these decisions are equally complex. Governments, industry, interest groups, and individuals all have an interest and a role to play. Decisions relating to the Beaufort region will be made not by a single agency or government structure, but by a wide variety of public and private institutions, as well as by individual citizens. These will range from decisions of the federal Cabinet on the conditions of Beaufort development and international jurisdictions, to decisions made by individuals about employment or business opportunities.

Decisions about development in the Beaufort region are required in these uncertain times, when it is very difficult to predict the international and national climate with any confidence. One simply needs to recall the fluctuating oil prices and political instability of the last decade to appreciate the complexity of long-term planning. Ten years is not an exceptional lead time when considering energy projects. The magnitude of the resources is another unknown factor. The proven and probable reserves in the Beaufort are estimated to exist on the order of 111 million m^3 (700 million barrels) of oil and 255 billion m^3 (nine trillion ft^3) of gas. The 1982 drilling season identified fewer reserves than had been anticipated, and threshold reserves have not yet been discovered.

Optimism for the future remains generally high, however. Innovation, technological advancement, and accelerated capital investment have all contributed to increased exploration in the Beaufort Sea. These have increased the capacity to lengthen the drilling season, and have hastened the search for additional reserves of hydrocarbons. This exploration has been encouraged to enhance the knowledge of the resource potential of the North. The value of super-depletion allowances for northern hydrocarbon exploration activities over the period 1977 to 1980 is estimated to be on the order of $1.8 billion. The National Energy Program set a goal of oil self-sufficiency by 1990, and established an effective system of incentives to encourage increased investment in the exploration and development of new oil reserves to meet domestic requirements. Petroleum incentive payments now average 80 per cent of every dollar invested in development, resulting in anticipated payments on northern operations of several hundred million dollars per year. The public and private investment in these activities has been very high, but no direct returns have yet been generated, and production reserves remain undelineated.

The accelerated pace of northern exploration has, however, led to the discovery of significant reserves of oil and gas. It is widely anticipated that reserves to support commercial production will be located soon. Major industrial investments continue to be made. Planning for the development of northern hydrocarbons has reached a critical stage, where significant financial commitments by industry soon will be required for the preparation and construction of support facilities to meet anticipated production schedules. Companies are proceeding on the assumption that once sufficient reserves have been identified, the necessary approvals will be granted for production.

Northern residents and public-interest groups have expressed concerns about the pace of hydrocarbon development and have identified the need to safeguard northern interests. Of particular concern to northerners is the implementation of effective socio-economic planning and environmental control. Northern native groups have raised the subject of resource development as an integral part of land claims. It is considered essential by the federal government that hydrocarbon production be planned and controlled in a manner that would permit it to accommodate northern interests and to proceed at the same time as the resolution of land claims.

The management and structuring of decisions relating to the development of oil and gas is difficult when key reference points such as reserves, prices, and production models are uncertain. Yet specific processes and guidelines are required to respond to public concerns and the expectations of industry. A smooth transition from exploration to production will depend largely on the success of preparations made by governments and industry and on adequate information. To provide a more rational basis for responding to opportunities and influences, and to encourage general readiness for development in the Beaufort Sea region, a number of initiatives have been introduced by the federal government.

Northern Hydrocarbon
Development Strategy

On 30 September 1982, the federal Cabinet approved a planning strategy for the development of northern hydrocarbons that will allow production, when it occurs, to proceed in a phased manner by initially developing proven commercial reserves on a small-scale demonstration basis, subject to the established regulatory and review process.[1] This strategy provides a clear framework against which those involved in, or affected by, production in the Beaufort region can base decisions. At the same time, approval was given for the implementation of a co-ordinated and accelerated five-year socio-economic, environmental policy, and technical planning and research programme involving departments of the federal and the territorial governments. Its specific objective is to achieve a state of preparedness for production of northern hydrocarbons.

The programme will be separate from, but complementary to, those generated under the Environmental Studies Revolving Funds (discussed later in this paper), and will focus on studies that are the single responsibility of governments.

Environmental Assessment
and Review Process

The ongoing Environmental Assessment and Review Process will be refined further with respect to proposals for how hydrocarbons might be developed and transported from the Beaufort and Mackenzie River delta area. The progress of those hearings and the eventual report and recommendations should yield valuable information about specific projects, engineering design, environmental risks, and social and economic requirements. The hearings and the report will provide an opportunity to advance the debate that must be promoted concerning the necessary conditions under which development might take place. The report should be instructive also in terms of government research and monitoring activities, and should provide guidelines for general preparation for hydrocarbon production in the North.

Exploration Agreements

The Canada Oil and Gas Act provides further opportunities for anticipating exploration and development and for generating some of the data necessary to guide decisions. Under this legislation, exploration agreements spanning a five-year term are struck with companies operating in the Beaufort Sea and other northern locations.

The chief effect of these formalized commitments is to achieve a more predictable level of exploration activity by defining the land on which exploration will take place, the minimum amount of work, timing, and approximate costs. The general knowledge and control of hydrocarbon exploration allows all concerned with Beaufort development to benefit from defined time frames, to advance planning and research activities, and to manage decisions essential to their areas of concern.

Canadian and Northern Benefits

The Canada Oil and Gas Act also provides the opportunity for determining what national and regional benefits can be achieved from oil and gas activities. The Canadian and northern benefits relating to business and employment opportunities are an important component of the exploration agreement. These statements provide a further mechanism by which advanced planning and the accommodation of concerns relating to Beaufort exploration and development can be achieved.

Environmental Studies Revolving Funds

The Canada Oil and Gas Act allows for specific programmes of studies and data collection. Under this legislation, the northern Environmental Studies Revolving Fund provides $15 million for the examination of issues of an environmental or social nature relating to exploration and development of oil and gas. A wide range of agencies and associations are eligible to receive funding for studies. These funds should assist in the assembly of data for proper planning.

Land-use Planning

Finally, a land-use planning programme, currently under development, will provide an additional framework for accommodating activity in the Beaufort Sea region. The planning programme is being set up to establish goals, objectives, and guidelines relating to land use, land disposition, and resource management, allowing specific decisions to be made in an orderly, rational, and open manner. Land-use planning has as its primary focus land, land use, and resources. The purpose is to plan ahead and to anticipate, to resolve, and to minimize competing demands or land-use conflicts, to determine the best use of resource lands, and to ensure integrated management of resources. In the process, social and economic factors and implications will receive attention in so far as they relate to the focus of land-use planning. This programme, in operation, will be one of the cornerstones for a complex range of decisions and interests relating to the Beaufort Sea region.

Conclusion

The complexity of issues surrounding Beaufort Sea development and the very significant unknowns make fundamental decisions about production and long-term planning difficult. It is, therefore, necessary to ensure that adequate processes are in place to provide timely refinement of information and to encourage advance preparation. Several important steps have been taken in this regard. Government has expressed its intention to moderate potential effects by applying the principle of phased development, in which demonstration projects would precede full-scale development. Other initiatives include development of a land-use planning programme, the Environmental Assessment and Review Process, opportunities provided by the Canada Oil and Gas Act, and the five-year strategy to refine data and policies under the Northern Hydrocarbon Development Strategy. Other steps being considered to assist in refining the knowledge and planning framework relating to the Beaufort Sea region include extensive environmental monitoring programmes, a comprehensive review of northern regulatory processes, and the consideration of developing sub-agreements for the Beaufort Sea region under the Economic Development Agreement. All of these initiatives will provide the framework within which planning can be done and choices made. They should encourage a more measured and reasonable foundation upon which all interested groups, governments, industry, and the public can build decisions in response to the challenges of Beaufort development.

Endnote

1. *Northern Hydrocarbon Developments: A Government Planning Strategy, A Discussion Paper* (Ottawa: DIAND, May 1982).

Position Paper

Project Management Philosophy in Canadian and Northern Settings

J.E. Lee
Production Development Manager
Esso Resources Canada Limited

Esso has been active in northern Canada for many years, starting in 1919 at Norman Wells and the early 1960s in the Mackenzie Delta–Beaufort Sea area. From extensive consultation with the many interested and concerned stakeholders and from our on-site operating experience during this period, we have gained an in-depth appreciation of the many challenges and issues associated with operating in northern Canada.

We continually modify our operating plans and philosophies to reflect new information and experience, and thus, participation in workshops like this provides an opportunity for all of us to exchange ideas and discuss our aspirations, hopes, concerns, and experiences.

There is little doubt in anyone's mind that because of declining production from currently developed western Canadian reserves, Canada will need to develop significant new reserves of hydrocarbons over the next 10 to 20 years to provide for its longer term energy security. There is also little doubt in anyone's mind that the potential hydrocarbon resources in northern Canada can play a significant role in helping Canada to achieve its goal of energy security.

Finally, it is the aspiration of many of the participants of this workshop that, as the hydrocarbon resource potential of northern Canada is developed, it should be developed in such a way as to provide opportunities for all Canadians, not only southern Canadians but also northern Canadians, the local residents, to participate and to benefit. To help to ensure that all Canadians will have this opportunity, we need to build our plans on a firm base.

To do this, it is important that all understand clearly how Esso currently manages its activities in northern Canada and agree on the strengths and weaknesses of these current practices. It is only by moving from a strong base of commitment and understanding that we shall achieve the desired results in the future.

With this in mind, I shall review briefly the two major projects that Esso is operating in northern Canada, namely the Beaufort Exploration Agreement Project and the Norman Wells Expansion Project, and then I shall describe how Esso, through its project planning and project execution process, attempts to ensure that concerns and aspirations of affected parties are reflected in its approach to developing Canada's hydrocarbon resources. I shall discuss the major elements of Esso's project planning and management process and give examples of results achieved in the past relative to each element.

Beaufort Exploration Agreement Project

Turning first to the Beaufort Exploration Project, in April 1982, Esso signed six exploration agreements with the federal government covering all of the land that Esso had under permit in the Mackenzie Delta–Beaufort Sea area (Figure 1). The signing of these exploration agreements committed Esso to drill five wells in the Beaufort Sea offshore area and four wells in the Mackenzie Delta–Tuk Peninsula onshore area between April 1982 and the end of 1986.

Simultaneously, we concluded a Beaufort farm-out agreement with a number of Canadian companies whereby they would earn 50 per cent of Esso's interest in this area by drilling seven wells in the offshore and six wells in the onshore and funding up to a maximum of 90 per cent of the programme.

The exploration programme involves drilling the West Atkinson, Itiyok, and Nipterk wells from islands constructed by what are referred to as sacrificial beach construction techniques, i.e., dredging sand from the ocean floor directly onto the adjacent island site. A new method, the caisson retained island (CRI), will be used to support drilling operations at the Kadluk, Amerk, and Minuk islands. Development of the CRI concept was pioneered by Esso Resources. The current plan is to use a drillship to complete the seventh offshore well at Kaubvik in the summer of 1984.

The onshore wells at Natagnak, Pikiolik, and South Tuk, all on the Tuk Peninsula, as well as a sixth onshore well located on Richards Island, will use conventional winter drilling and construction techniques (Figure 2).

Besides the drilling and construction programmes, we shall conduct an extensive seismic programme in the onshore areas during the winter and in the offshore areas in the summer.

The expenditure profile for the Beaufort Exploration Project is anticipated to total $855 million.

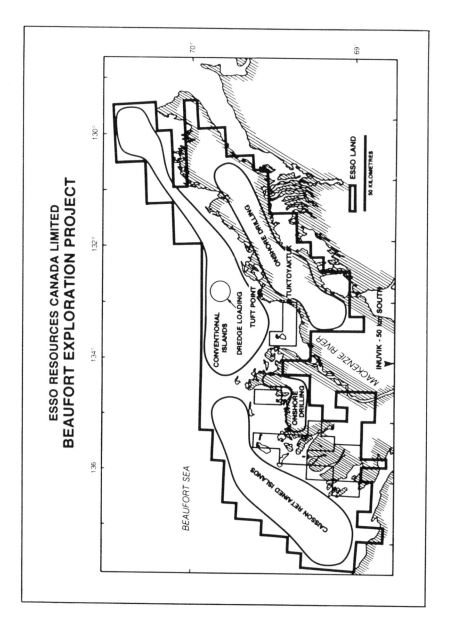

Figure 1

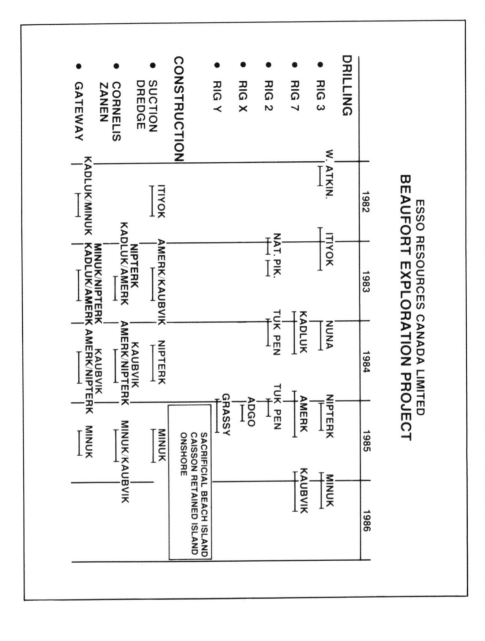

Figure 2

Norman Wells Expansion Project

Esso's second major northern project is located some 480 km (300 miles) south of the coast, in the Mackenzie Valley at Norman Wells (Figure 3). This project has two major components. The first phase, which is managed by Esso Resources, involves construction and drilling at Norman Wells to provide for expansion from the current production of about 475 m³ per day (3000 bpd [barrels per day]) to over 3975 m³ per day (25 000 bpd) by mid-1985. The second phase, which is managed by Interprovincial Pipe Line (NW) Ltd., involves the construction of a 12-inch-diameter (300 mm), buried, ambient-temperature, oil pipeline from Norman Wells to the Zama terminal in Alberta.

The oilfield at Norman Wells was discovered by Imperial Oil Limited as a result of drilling a well during the winter of 1919–1920 on the north shore of the Mackenzie River at Norman Wells. For several years after 1920, the field was operated on an intermittent basis to provide petroleum products from a small distillation plant for the local logging operations, mission stations, and communities (Figure 4). As mining activities in the area picked up in the 1930s, demand for petroleum products increased somewhat and production became more stable at higher production rates.

In the early 1940s, the "Canol Project" resulted in a major expansion of the oilfield. This project was supported by Imperial Oil, the Canadian government, and the U.S. Army with the goal of providing petroleum products to the U.S. Air Force. The project included the drilling of a number of wells at Norman Wells, the laying of a four-inch-diameter (100 mm) pipeline from Norman Wells to Whitehorse, and the construction of a small refinery at Whitehorse to provide aviation and diesel fuel to the U.S. Air Force in Alaska.

Shortly after the completion of drilling about 60 wells at Norman Wells, the construction of the pipeline from Norman Wells to Whitehorse, and the commencement of the refining operation at Whitehorse, the Second World War ended. This eliminated the need for the refining operation at Whitehorse. Thus, production and refining operations at Norman Wells fell back to their pre-war levels.

From the mid-1940s to the present, the Norman Wells oilfield has continued to operate at about 475 m³ per day (3000 bpd), providing petroleum products to many northern communities.

Following the rapid increase in the price of crude oil in the early and mid-1970s, Imperial Oil undertook a study in 1978 to determine the economic feasibility of expanding production at Norman Wells and transporting the increased production to southern markets through a small-diameter pipeline up the Mackenzie Valley to tie into existing pipeline

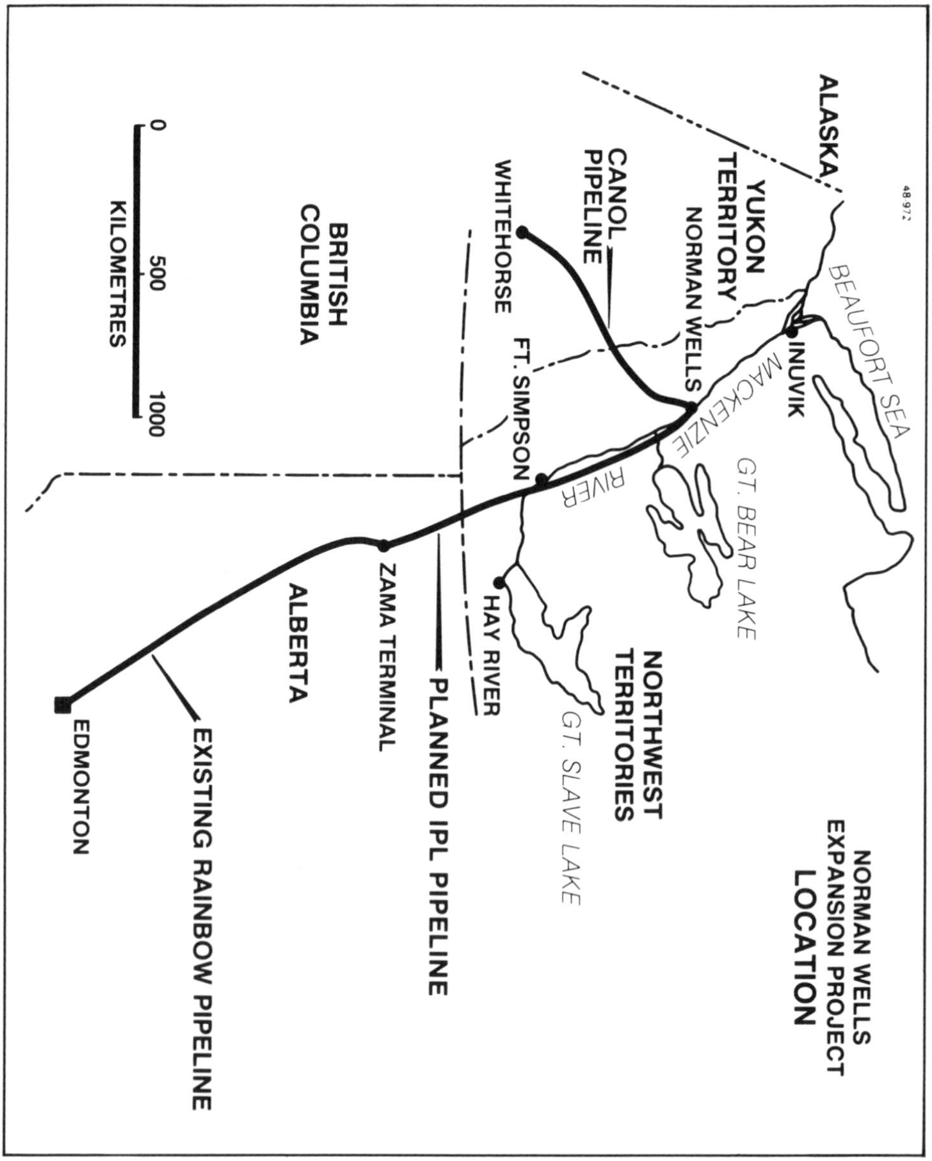
NORMAN WELLS
EXPANSION PROJECT
LOCATION
ALASKA
YUKON
TERRITORY
NORMAN WELLS
CANOL
PIPELINE
WHITEHORSE
BRITISH
COLUMBIA
0
500
1000
KILOMETRES
BEAUFORT SEA
INUVIK
MACKENZIE
RIVER
FT. SIMPSON
GT. BEAR LAKE
NORTHWEST
TERRITORIES
GT. SLAVE LAKE
HAY RIVER
PLANNED IPL PIPELINE
ZAMA TERMINAL
ALBERTA
EXISTING RAINBOW PIPELINE
EDMONTON
48 972

Figure 3

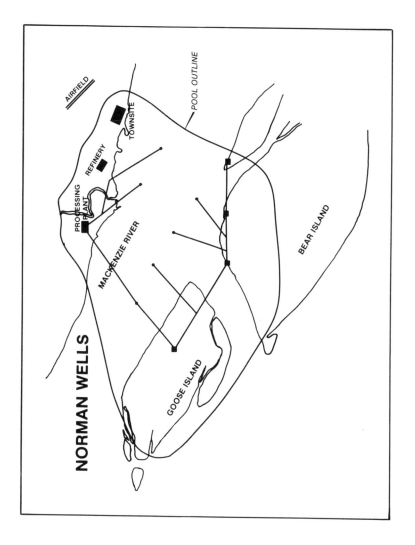

Figure 4

systems in northern Alberta. That analysis indicated that it was likely that such an undertaking would be both economically attractive and technically feasible. Thus, we undertook more-detailed studies and started to consult with the various government agencies and northern communities to plan a project that would also be acceptable from an environmental and socio-economic standpoint.

The culmination of these studies and consultations was the filing of a development application with the Department of Indian Affairs and Northern Development, in the spring of 1980, to expand production at Norman Wells. Simultaneously, Interprovincial Pipe Line (NW) Ltd. filed an application with the National Energy Board for the construction of a small-diameter pipeline up the Mackenzie Valley from Norman Wells to Zama, Alberta (Figure 5).

These applications were reviewed in public hearings conducted by the federal government in a number of northern communities and in a few southern communities during the summer and autumn of 1980. Federal government approval for the project and the associated pipeline was granted in July 1981. Shortly thereafter, the Imperial board approved the expenditures for this undertaking.

Since mid-1980, a continuing engineering effort has been underway to design facilities and drilling programmes that will be cost effective, environmentally sound, and will provide opportunities for northern communities to participate.

In the latter half of 1982, construction and drilling equipment, associated camp facilities, and materials required for the drilling and construction activities were moved by barge to Norman Wells. In the summer of 1982, Esso began a two-rig drilling programme with wells being drilled from two natural islands in the Mackenzie River and from the mainland area on the north shore of the river.

Esso also commenced construction in Edmonton of 64 modules that will make up the production plant at Norman Wells after being barged down the river and assembled on piles at Norman Wells.

This winter and summer, Esso will be completing four of the six permanent production islands to be constructed in the river at Norman Wells to provide access to the oil beneath the Mackenzie River. The remaining two islands will be completed in the winter and summer of 1984.

This past winter, Interprovincial Pipe Line (NW) Ltd. completed 70 per cent of the right-of-way clearing for the pipeline. The main pipeline construction will take place in the winters of 1984 and 1985.

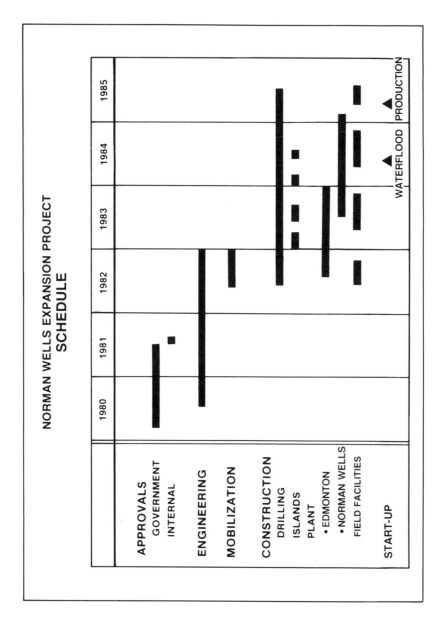

Figure 5

Esso anticipates that it will commence injection of water at Norman Wells in the summer of 1984 to repressure the field to original pressures, and that it will commence the increased level of oil production in the summer of 1985.

The current forecast expenditure profile for the Expansion Project, excluding the pipeline, totals some $640 million over the life of the construction activities.

Thus, between these two projects, Esso Resources and its associates will be spending nearly $1.5 billion on activities directed at petroleum exploration and development in northern Canada during the period from 1982 to 1986.

Elements of Project Planning and Management

There are many aspects to the management of large projects like these. Esso Resources' philosophy in undertaking major resource development projects is to ensure that plans for executing the project are in place to cover all key elements well in advance of major activities taking place. The key elements of Esso's project planning process are summarized in Figure 6.

First, it is essential that good cost estimates and activity schedules be developed to ensure that the planned project will be economic and that the funds, materials, equipment, and workforce will be available to execute the activities. Unless the economic viability of a project is sound and the proponent has sufficient funds available to finance it, there is little value in developing detailed plans to cover the subsequent elements of the project plan.

Secondly, after establishing the economic viability of a project, it is important to ensure that the technology to be used is sound so as to yield safe and effective facilities, and that the construction activities will not adversely affect either the environment or the local residents.

Thirdly, Esso places the highest priority on the safety of its operations and has developed extensive programmes to ensure that its employees, as well as all persons associated with a project, are not exposed to unsafe situations.

Fourthly, protection of the physical environment is also essential, especially in northern Canada where there are many unique conditions, one of the more important being the presence of permafrost.

Fifthly, to ensure that Canadian and local businesses are able to participate effectively in Esso's activities, it must communicate its needs for various services and materials to the business communities well in

Esso Resources Canada Limited Elements of Project Planning and Management

- Cost, Schedule, and Quality Control
- Technology Utilization
- Total Loss Control (Safety)
- Environmental Protection
- Industrial Development
- Employment and Training
- Local (Northern) Consultation

Figure 6

advance, so that they can present their best proposals for providing these services and materials during the tendering process. However, Esso needs to be careful not to create false expectations; thus, considerable judgement needs to be exercised in determining the appropriate time to begin the communication process. This consideration is especially important for many northern businesses, which have not had the amount of experience in dealing with the oil industry that many southern contractors have had.

Sixthly, to ensure maximum opportunity for local residents, and indeed for all Canadians, to participate in, and to benefit from, job opportunities associated with projects, we have developed an employment programme that provides information about the opportunities for employment on the project to those interested. The programme also needs to address the training needs of those who have not yet acquired the skills required for the jobs associated with such a project, or who wish to advance to jobs requiring higher skills. This training can be provided on-site and through off-site government-sponsored training programmes.

Finally, Esso must maintain close contact with the local communities, government agencies, and the many other organizations that are affected by, and vitally interested in, its projects.

Thus, it is desirable that these plans be in place before on-site activities are undertaken so as to provide the maximum opportunity for interested parties to participate in, and influence, the plans.

Esso has developed policies relative to each of these key components of a project plan; below are a few examples of how Esso has been achieving desirable results in each.

Cost and Schedule Engineering

Principles

Esso's approach to project management is to ensure that planning is completed for each of the activities necessary to complete the job. This allows for the clear assignment of responsibilities as to the monitoring of costs and schedule performance relative to the plan.

Esso's planned projects must have a sound economic basis and they must be executed in the most cost-effective fashion in keeping with sound engineering principles. Thus, it is essential that costing and scheduling of all project activities be completed in a very disciplined and thorough manner to ensure not only the economic success of the project, but also the success of all other elements of the project plan (Figure 7).

Esso Resources Canada Limited Cost and Schedule Engineering Principles

- Ensure that cost and schedule services are utilized by project managers to assist in optimizing, evaluating, developing, and controlling projects by using:

  - latest data and techniques (e.g., IVA)
  - experienced and trained costing and scheduling staff
  - established procedures for AFE approval and cost management

- Provide management with an independent assessment of cost and schedule performance through audit techniques
- Assign dedicated cost and schedule engineers to all major projects.

Figure 7

It is a well-established fact that, on average, 80 per cent of all cost savings on a major project are achieved during the planning for the project. Only 20 per cent of any cost savings are realized during its execution. Thus, it is important, especially in times like the present when funds are scarce, that the very best cost and schedule engineering services are used to ensure that project execution schedules are optimized and that cost-control procedures are in place.

In some cases, it can also be helpful to use an independent assessment to check that cost and schedule performance is as planned by means of on-site and office audits during the execution of the project. Of course, it goes without saying that to achieve the above it is essential that cost and schedule engineers be dedicated to the projects and not be provided on an *ad hoc* basis.

Results

Esso has seen some very positive results from using these techniques on the Norman Wells Expansion Project. When we appropriated the project our original cost estimate was $806 million; our current estimate, after completing about one-third of the project, is that we shall be able to complete it for about $640 million—$166 million (more than 20 per cent) less than the original estimate. We estimate that about one-third of the cost reduction at Norman Wells has been achieved because of the general slowdown in the economy; however, more than two-thirds of the savings has resulted from improvements in productivity and from efforts in cost management planning and scheduling.

Technology Development and Use

Policy

We at Esso realize that the strength of any industrial society is often strongly dependent on its research activities. Therefore, we support strongly the identification of new technology that can contribute to the effectiveness of our operations and we endeavour to develop this new technology in a way that allows Canadian engineering and construction firms to participate in the development and use of new technology (Figure 8).

Esso Resources Canada Limited Technology Development and Utilization Policy

Esso Resources will identify new technology that may contribute to the efficiency of its operations in a cost-effective manner and endeavour to develop that new technology in a co-operative approach with Canadian engineering and construction firms and to provide for joint utilization of that newly developed technology.

Figure 8

For our efforts in this area to be effective, we realize that there is a need for close liaison with many government agencies, universities, and the research arms of engineering firms to ensure they are aware of the areas where Esso believes the greatest gains from new technology can be realized.

Results

To ensure that our northern programmes are cost effective and to ensure that we do not affect the physical environment adversely, Esso has had to research and to develop considerable new technology, some examples of which are:

- the development of onshore seismic techniques to account for the presence of permafrost and to minimize damage to tundra
- the determination of the properties and behaviour of Beaufort Sea ice
- the development of construction procedures for man-made islands for use as drilling platforms
- the determination of marine mammal populations and their distributions.

The overall result of Esso's northern R&D programmes, which have been a joint effort with Canadian engineering and construction firms, is that Canada is now viewed as a world leader in design and construction of man-made islands for use as drilling and production platforms in offshore areas.

Loss Control (Safety) Programme

Philosophy

From its many years of experience in operating in the often harsh northern environment, Esso has gained a keen awareness of the need for safety consciousness in all its northern operations. We continually communicate our philosophy on safety, not only to personnel directly employed by Esso, but to all contractors' personnel who are working for Esso.

Esso's safety programmes are tailored to individual operating conditions and are based on the underlying principle that an effective loss-control programme relies on the understanding and commitment of all personnel involved. Our primary goal is to ensure that the commitment of each individual is in place before he or she undertakes field activities. All our safety programmes are developed on the basis of the five principles outlined in Figure 9.

Results

One of the key indications of the effectiveness of any loss-control programme is an organization's accident frequency rate. Figure 10 shows the results Esso has achieved over the past two years. We have shown a steady improvement in our performance over this period. Compared with the general drilling and construction industry, our performance is two or three times better.

Environmental Protection

Policy

The many studies in which Esso has participated in order to learn about the northern environment, as well as its many years of experience in operating in northern Canada, have led us to realize that there are many unique aspects of the northern Canadian environment. To protect this environment adequately from adverse effects of our operation, our programmes must be planned to ensure that procedures are in place that will minimize such effects. In the past, Esso has worked closely with a number of government agencies and environmental groups to improve our understanding of the environment. We continue to pursue this co-operative approach.

Our plans for protection of the environment in any area where we undertake operations are based on a number of fairly basic principles, which are summarized in Figure 11.

Results

In conducting its northern programmes over the past number of years, Esso has participated in a number of environmental studies, some of which are summarized in Figure 12.

In the field of marine biology, our programme has been aimed at monitoring and counting various mammals in the northern environment and undertaking specific research into the effects of our programme on the behaviour and life-cycle of these mammals. We have also researched

Esso Resources Canada Limited
Loss Control (Safety) Philosophy

- The safety of all personnel, the protection of the environment, and the protection of physical assets at all sites are of utmost importance in the conduct of our business.
- Management is responsible for providing a safe work environment and for ensuring that work is performed to accepted standards.
- Each employee is responsible for working safely with equal concern for the safety of all co-workers.
- All risks can be avoided or controlled.
- Safety excellence can be achieved through careful planning and the support and active participation of everyone.

Figure 9

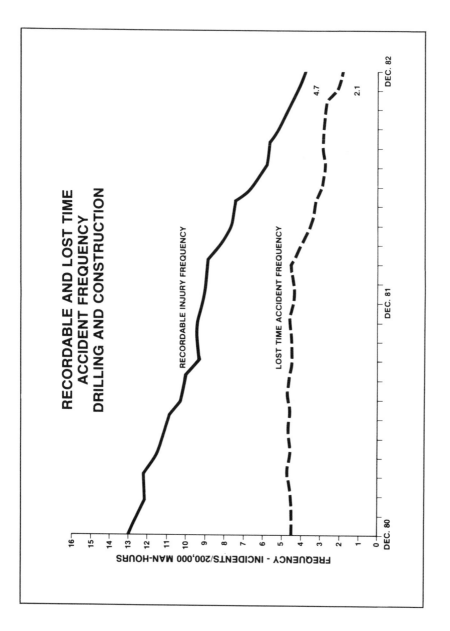

Figure 10

Esso Resources Canada Limited
Environmental Protection
Policy Statement

- Ensure that hazards to public health and damage to the environment, attributable to company activities, are minimized.
- Comply with all applicable laws, regulations, and standards.
- Provide additional environmental protection beyond that required by law, when the benefits to society justify the costs.
- Ensure that employees understand and accept responsibility for monitoring and protecting the environment.
- Provide future environmental protection requirements in design and long-range planning.
- Encourage, support, and conduct environmental research.

Figure 11

Esso Resources Canada Limited Mackenzie Delta-Beaufort Sea Environmental Studies

- Marine Biology
  - marine mammals, birds, fish
  - impacts of dredging and drilling

- Physical Environment
  - ice, waves, wind, ocean currents
  - revegetation and permafrost
  - design criteria

- Oil Spill Research
  - fate and effects
  - new equipment
  - contingency plans and training

Figure 12

changes in the physical environment resulting from our operations, such as the effects of dredging operations or the potential effects of different drilling fluids used in our programmes.

In studying the physical environment, we have gathered extensive data on the properties of ice and on wind, wave, and current patterns and their characteristics to aid in the design of structures.

Most important, we have studied the potential effects of oil spills on the aquatic environment.

On the basis of these and similar studies, we are convinced that development of the hydrocarbon resource potential of the Mackenzie Delta–Beaufort Sea area, at least within the confines of Esso-operated lands, can be undertaken in a safe and environmentally acceptable manner.

Industrial Development

Policy

We at Esso recognize the need for a strong industrial base to support our operations, and also recognize our responsibility in providing opportunities for the industrial sector to participate in providing goods and services to our programmes. To ensure that maximum opportunities are made available to Canadian and local firms to participate in our programmes, we have developed and publicized our policies relative to supporting development and maintenance of a strong industrial base in Canada.

The key principles of this policy are summarized in Figure 13, which states that Esso will provide maximum opportunity to Canadians to benefit from its operations through provision of goods and services on a competitive basis.

To ensure that this occurs, Esso is committed to packaging its tender requests in a way that provides the maximum opportunity for Canadian and local firms to be competitive and also to provide the required lead times for them to prepare their bids. In our tenders, we request information on the Canadian and local content of the bid proposal together with potential future Canadian benefits associated with undertakings by the vendors. In addition, we undertake to review with the unsuccessful bidders and appropriate government agencies the reasons why businesses were not successful in being awarded tenders. However, we do maintain all tender information on a confidential basis.

Relative to our northern programmes, we have tailored our planning in the area of industrial benefits to ensuring that there is a maximum opportunity for local northern businesses to participate and to benefit from our ongoing programmes. This has been achieved through the use

Esso Resources Canada Limited
Industrial Development Policy Statement

- Maximize opportunities for Canadian industrial benefits when procuring goods and services.

- Support and encourage development of competitive Canadian products and services.

- Select consultants and contractors competitively, ensuring greatest practicable industrial benefits to Canada.

- Support Canadian suppliers of all sizes to foster development of comprehensive and competitive domestic supply capability.

- Require Canadian content quotations in tenders for supplies and services being offered.

- Monitor corporate activities to maximize opportunities for Canadian industrial benefits and Canadian supplier development.

- Be prepared to discuss confidentially with appropriate government authorities the reasons for major awards to foreign-based firms.

- Encourage international affiliates to purchase Canadian goods and services when competitive and provide appropriate supply information.

- Maintain confidentiality of all tender information except as required to be disclosed to appropriate government authorities.

Figure 13

of business seminars, the distribution of brochures that tabulate the business opportunities associated with our programmes, and one-on-one meetings with northern businesses and northern government agencies to ensure that the maximum information is provided on a timely basis to the business community in the North about opportunities within Esso's programmes.

Results

I believe that Esso's northern projects are providing real benefits to Canadians and northerners who provide goods and services to its operations. In 1982, Esso's expenditures on northern projects totalled $269 million, with an associated 85 per cent Canadian content (Figure 14). There was also much participation by northern businesses in the programme, with some 215 northern firms providing goods and services. These firms represented 14 communities throughout the western Arctic and they received payments from Esso of $42 million, which represents over 15 per cent of our total expenditures on northern programmes in 1982.

Employment and Training

Policy

We at Esso recognize and willingly accept our responsibility to ensure that programmes we undertake in Canada, and specifically in northern Canada, provide maximum opportunities for local residents and other Canadians to participate. This can be a very vital aspect in maintaining a healthy national and local society, especially in these days of economic slowdown.

Esso's employment programmes are based on the principle of equal opportunity for all Canadians to participate (Figure 15). However, we recognize that there can be traditional and systemic barriers that will prevent some groups from benefiting to the same extent as others. Therefore, we have tailored programmes to eliminate these barriers.

From our long experience in the oil industry, we have observed in all areas in which we operate that on-the-job training as well as off-the-job training of our workforce pays large dividends. We have also found that training programmes need to be tailored to the specific situation. Thus, we have tailored our employment and training programmes to meet specific needs of the northern population. We view this not only as a corporate responsibility but also as a sound business practice; i.e., it is more economic to obtain our workforce from the local communities than to transport it long distances from other parts of the country or of the world.

Esso Resources Canada Limited
1982 Northern Business Record

	Norman Wells	Beaufort	Total
• Charges to Projects-$M	156	113	269
• Canadian Content-%	91	77	85
• Northern Participation			
• Number of Businesses	123	134	215
• Number of Communities	12	11	14
• Expenditures-$M	33	9	42

Figure 14

Esso Resources Canada Limited Employment and Training

Employment Policy

- Esso is an equal-opportunity employer
- Maximize employment opportunities for northern residents
  - corporate responsibility
  - sound business practice
- Priority to employment planning with federal and territorial governments, contractors, and northern communities

Training Practices

- Encourage employees to reach growth potential
  - Promote safe, supportive work practices
  - Joint management–employee responsibility
  - Employee orientation programme
  - Cross-cultural training

Figure 15

We recognize that for our plans in employment and training to be effective, we have to be well co-ordinated with the federal and territorial governments, our contractors, and the individual communities in which we work. Thus, we give priority to consultation with all of these groups in our planning.

Our training practices are aimed at encouraging all employees to reach their potential and to work in a safe and supportive manner. We recognize that this is a joint management–employee responsibility. We have special programmes in place aimed at encouraging individuals to participate in the training programmes through such means as employee orientation programmes and cross-cultural training programmes for our supervisors.

Results

We believe that our efforts in providing employment opportunities for northerners and other Canadians in our workforce are being effective, as the results summarized in Figure 16 indicate.

During 1982, 773 person-years of work effort were required to execute our northern programmes, of which more than 99 per cent was provided by Canadians. Northern communities provided some 356 person-years of support to our programmes, or about 46 per cent of the total workforce, with an associated northern payroll of $11 million. During 1982, our northern workforce came from some 27 northern communities, providing a fairly widespread benefit to the peoples of the western Arctic.

Summary

In summary, we at Esso tailor our northern project plans to provide maximum opportunities for all Canadians to participate in, and to benefit from, the activities associated with these projects. We attempt to achieve the desired results through three major focuses.

Consultation

We maintain open and timely consultation with all local communities and organizations. We encourage two-way consultation so that not only does Esso communicate its position and information, but it also hears the aspirations and concerns of the local residents so that its programmes can be tailored to address these needs.

Esso Resources Canada Limited
1982 Northern Employment Record

	Norman Wells	Beaufort	Total
• Total Work Effort			
Person-years	495	278	773
Per cent Canadian	100	98	99+
• Northern Participation			
Person-years	240	116	356
Per cent of Total	48	43	46
• Northern Payroll—$M	7.3	3.7	11

Figure 16

Employment Opportunities

Our employment programmes are tailored to meet the specific needs and concerns of the southern and northern workforce and to assist the northern workforce as it moves from a traditional lifestyle toward a lifestyle related to a wage economy.

Business Opportunities

We are committed to providing maximum opportunities for the use and development of Canadian businesses so that they can support and benefit from our northern programmes on a fair and competitive basis.

Background Paper

Mackenzie Delta–Beaufort Sea: Their Roles in Canada's Oil Supply Options

Simon McInnes
Senior Adviser
Northern Energy Strategies and Initiatives
Energy Strategy Branch
Department of Energy, Mines and Resources

Introduction

Energy policy since October 1980 has emphasized security of oil supply, increased participation by Canadians in the oil and gas industry, and fairness both in prices to consumers and in revenues for governments and industry.[1] These goals, by now well known, have been reaffirmed in *The National Energy Program: Update 1982* and in subsequent ministerial statements.[2]

In this brief paper I address the first goal: in particular, the contribution that the onshore and near-shore Mackenzie Delta and the offshore Beaufort Sea oil reserves can make to ensuring that Canadians have adequate supplies of oil. I first discuss the broader issue of Canadian oil supply and related variables that have an effect on the Delta–Beaufort, and secondly, tackle the factors that form the immediate context of Delta–Beaufort hydrocarbons.

In 1982, Canada produced 217 000 m^3/day of oil, and exported 25 000 m^3/day of oil (primarily heavy) [1 cubic metre (m^3) equals 6.2926 barrels]. Gross imports of oil for domestic use, excluding exchanges, amounted to 40 000 m^3/day. On a net basis, oil imports were only 12 000 m^3/day. Domestic production from western Canada was 198 000 m^3/day, and synthetic oil from the tar sands was 19 000 m^3/day. Domestic oil consumption in 1982 was 239 000 m^3/day. Norman Wells' contribution to Canada's supply is about 500 m^3/day, but its output is expected to increase about eight-fold once field expansion has been completed.

The importance of oil is apparent when it is remembered that Canada depends on oil for nearly 40 per cent of its total energy consumption. This percentage has dropped since 1979 because of conservation measures, conversion to other fuels, and general economic conditions; this downward trend is expected to continue. Nevertheless, for many years to come, oil still will be a significant component of Canada's energy supply.

To answer the question of where Canadians will obtain the oil to meet their needs over the next 15 years requires anticipating how much they might want. Thanks to accelerating frontier exploration both off the east coast and in the North, and present activity in the western basin, the supply picture is quite well known. Let us discuss supply then, before turning to demand.

Supply

Overall productive capacity of world oil outside centrally planned economies is projected to remain fairly stable at around 8 000 000 m^3/day, climbing to 8 500 000 m^3/day (50 to 53 million barrels/day) by 2001, according to the International Energy Agency (IEA).[3] In Canada, supply from established conventional reserves in western Canada will continue to decline, despite new discoveries and enhanced recovery from existing reservoirs. Existing synthetic (tar sands) plants will increase their output slightly. Whether development of new tar sands and major upgrader projects for heavy oil take place depends, of course, on international prices, the perceived economic viability of those projects, and fiscal policy. However, the Department of Energy, Mines and Resources (EMR) forecasts one or two new developments in this century.

Table 1 shows the last official Energy, Mines and Resources supply–demand balance as projected in mid-1982, although conditions have changed since then.[4] International prices have dropped, but they now appear to be holding steady. In January 1983, the official Organization of Petroleum Exporting Countries (OPEC) selling price was US$208.30/$m^3$, whereas the spot (free market) price was about US$187.50/$m^3$ (US$33.10 versus US$29.80 per barrel). In mid-April, both the official OPEC selling price and the spot price were hovering in the US$176 to $182/$m^3$ range (US$28 to $29/barrel). Demand for OPEC oil has dropped further than EMR anticipated during summer 1982, primarily because of poor international economic conditions, increased international conservation and substitution efforts, and industry depletion of stocks on hand. The amount of oil supplied from non-OPEC sources has increased, however.

The Oil Supply-Demand Balance*

	Quantity in Year:					
	1975	1979	1981	1985	1990	2000
DEMAND	264†	290	265	242	233	247
SUPPLY						
Conventional areas						
old oil	244	241	202	135	84	40
NORP oil**	0	0	0	44	74	88
Existing synthetic	7	15	17	26	28	28
Frontier/additional oil sands	0	0	0	0	47	99
Total	251	256	219	205	233	255
Balance	-13	-34	-46	-37	0	+8

†All quantities are in x 10^3 m^3/day.

*Balance cannot be directly translated to gross imports, because the balance consists of both exports and imports.

**The pricing of crude oil and natural gas in Canada is governed by a number of agreements between the federal government and the producing provinces, the most important of which is the Memorandum of Agreement between the Province of Alberta and the Government of Canada, originally signed in September 1982 [amended on 30 June 1983]. To encourage the development of Canada's vast crude oil potential, a new oil reference price (NORP) is provided to new discoveries after 1980: synthetic crude oil, frontier oil, incremental production from enhanced recovery schemes, experimental projects, oil from wells suspended for at least three years, and oil from infill wells. Also receiving the NORP is oil from discoveries made between 1974 and 1980. The NORP is scheduled to increase to $79.10/barrel delivered to Montréal by July 1986, subject to a ceiling of the actual cost of imported oil at Montréal. Since 1981, the NORP has been essentially the same as the world price.

Table 1

Besides reassessing the potential contribution of new tar sands and upgrader plants to Canadian oil supply, probably some adjustment to the picture is necessary given further reservoir and economic knowledge gained over 1982–83.

Demand

The Government of Canada is, in June 1983, revising its supply–demand forecast, and, with producing provinces, is reviewing the pricing and revenue arrangements that were reached in 1981. Demand declined in 1982, and probably will continue to decline in 1983, more sharply than was anticipated in May 1982. In general, this trend is expected to be followed by a relatively flat demand, increasing slightly through the 1980s. EMR expects the level in 1990 to approximate that of the 1982 forecast, but the evolution of demand during the 1980s may be slightly different. Any significant adjustment of Canadian oil and gas prices will affect the demand for oil.

The federal government knew in 1982, as is known now, that if Canada is to lessen its reliance on oil imports and to achieve oil self-sufficiency, a contribution will have to be made at some point from east coast and northern frontier reserves, and from tar sands–heavy oil projects. Although permanent structural changes in the use of liquid fuel have occurred because of the 1973 and 1979 international oil supply and price shocks, and although conservation and substitution measures will continue to play an important role in lowering oil's share in the use patterns of energy, government policy recognizes the need to bring frontier and synthetic oil supplies on stream to meet Canadian needs and to achieve oil self-sufficiency. This is important also in light of the IEA's projection that the present international oil surplus is temporary and that international supply could tighten over the next 15 years. The IEA suggests that growing margins of excess demand could create substantial international price pressures later this decade and in the next.[5]

Frontier Supply

Oil supplies from both the frontier and the tar sands will be required to reach oil self-sufficiency (Table 1); achieving this requires an additional supply of at least 47 000 m³/day by 1990 and more thereafter. Table 2 shows estimates of Canada's potential oil reserves. From a reserves perspective, the Mackenzie Delta–Beaufort area is as important as the east Newfoundland shelf area to Canada's oil requirements. East coast oil supply would include Hibernia. Proven reserves at Hibernia are about 206 000 000 m³, and peak production could be 48 000 m³/day. The proven supply in the

Estimated Recoverable Reserves
of Canada's Oil*

Area	Quantity Area	$(10^6 m^3)$ Regional Total	Percentage Area	(%)** Regional
North of 60°				
Delta–Beaufort	1500		25	
Mainland				
Territories	100		2	
Arctic Islands	790		13	
Hudson Bay	130		2	
Total	2520	2520	42	42
Eastern Canada				
Labrador	80		1	
East Newfound-				
land Shelf	1340		22	
Scotian Shelf	290		5	
Other	340		6	
Total	2050	2050	34	34
Western Canada				
Mainland	1370		23	
West Coast	50		1	
Total	1420	1420	24	24
Total for Canada		5990		100

*45 per cent probability
**rounded

Table 2

delta (onshore and near-shore) is estimated at 48 000 000 m³, with peak production at 8000 m³/day. Offshore reserves are still being proven beneath the Beaufort Sea, but proven reserves are now about 46 000 000 m³, and it is anticipated that additional reserves will be established over the next few years.

Frontier Variables and Factors

What, then, are the major variables that influence frontier and tar sands developments? Furthermore, what immediate factors must be assessed accurately before decisions can be made on bringing these new reserves to market?

The two primary variables are probably *demand* and *price*. As mentioned before, the IEA predicts growing margins of excess demand, creating upward price pressures on the international market later in the 1980s and through the 1990s. The increasing domestic and foreign demand, and the resulting increase in prices, could make economically viable many oil production plans that are now only marginal. This applies to the Mackenzie Delta–Beaufort region, upgrader projects, and tar sands developments. The problem is that major project planning calls for relatively stable economic conditions; industry, government, and Canadians, however, are obliged to make decisions in a less-than-certain world. It is a gamble (but part of this business) to make decisions in 1983 or 1984 about levels of demand and prices for major oil production six or more years away.

A third variable is *non-frontier domestic supply*. How many small oil booms, such as the one brought about by the discoveries at Waskada, Manitoba, may be anticipated in the next 15 years, and how much will they contribute to Canada's overall supply situation? What new techniques may be invented that will boost recovery of existing western Canada reserves?

These three variables are the chief determinants of large-scale frontier and tar sands hydrocarbon developments. As can be seen, the uncertainty of each variable combines to create an unstable decision-making framework.

An implicit fourth variable is *time*. It is easier to predict accurately the market conditions for a small-scale project that can be brought on stream in two to three years, than to do the same for a large-scale development requiring a lead time of half a decade, or longer. The fact that these circumstances exist in the case of frontier and tar sands production should not, however, deter the Canadian government from making decisions to safeguard future Canadian energy interests.

Beyond these four variables, there are six factors that have an immediate bearing on frontier and tar sands developments. First, the *environment* must be a consideration. Government, industry, those most immediately affected in the vicinity of projects, and Canadians in general have a stake in ensuring that potential environmental effects of major projects are minimized and are judged acceptable by national and local standards.

The second factor, an extension of the first, is to ensure that *wildlife and wildlife habitats* are accorded similar treatment. Energy policy is committed to achieving resource development at a rate and in a manner compatible with a delicate social and environmental balance.[6] The Beaufort Sea Environmental Assessment and Review Panel and additional environmental and geoscience research by government and industry will further this commitment.

Thirdly, *aboriginal land claims* have to be respected. Both in ministerial statements and in legislation, it has been indicated that no action will be taken under the Canada Oil and Gas Act (COGA) that will prejudice land-claims settlements. In addition, provisions in COGA enable the minister of Energy, Mines and Resources to establish advisory committees on oil and gas developments. The Hudson Bay Oil and Gas Advisory Committee, with representatives from Hudson Bay area Inuit associations and local governments, was established in 1983.[7]

Fourthly, the *role of other governments* is crucial. Major frontier and tar sands projects are difficult to bring to fruition without close collaboration between federal, provincial, and territorial governments. Development of the Hibernia field is being held back by a dispute over offshore jurisdiction. The revenue-sharing and offshore management agreement with Nova Scotia in 1982, however, has spurred considerable activity in the Nova Scotian and Canadian economies. Close co-operation between the federal government and the Government of the Northwest Territories is equally essential in the development of the Delta–Beaufort region.

Fifthly, the *participation of northerners* is essential for projects north of 60°. The federal government is committed to consulting closely with northerners in establishing ground rules for northern energy projects, and to recognizing the growing role northerners will play in decisions about the development of energy.[8]

Sixthly, consideration for *northern and national economic benefits* will play a significant role in decisions about frontier production. Major projects mean jobs for both northerners and other Canadians.

A final observation before turning to the issue of the Delta–Beaufort region is that although Energy, Mines and Resources establishes and maintains policies, strategies, and programmes for the supply and efficient use of national energy resources, it does not act alone. For Canada lands north of 60°, the participation of many departments and agencies—the Department of Indian Affairs and Northern Development (DIAND), the Government of the Northwest Territories (GNWT), the Canada Oil and

Gas Lands Administration (COGLA), and the Department of the Environment (DOE), to name only a few—is necessary for the orderly development of energy resources.[9]

Frontier Production in the Mackenzie Delta-Beaufort Region

The demand for Delta-Beaufort oil, in addition to the need for frontier supply discussed earlier, also depends upon the timing of tar sands projects, heavy oil upgrader plans, and Hibernia production. For instance, a slower pace in establishing the extent of Hibernia and nearby fields puts more pressure on the other three; difficulties associated with tar sands projects and upgraders have a similar effect upon Hibernia and the Delta-Beaufort region, and disappointing delineation results from Delta-Beaufort fields such as Tarsiut affect the other three. For the federal government it is very difficult to know which of these four, what mix of these four, or even whether all of these sources of oil can be counted upon, and when, and to what degree, they can be counted upon to contribute to Canada's oil supply.

A second specific issue that affects the Delta-Beaufort region, as well as Hibernia, upgraders, and tar sands, is technological advancement. In the past 15 years, tremendous strides in exploration technology have enabled areas of Canada to be explored more effectively than was hitherto possible. Similar advances in development and production technology can be expected. The Beaufort Sea-Mackenzie Delta environmental impact statement discusses in general the operators' plans, but new ideas are expected over the coming years.[10] It will be important to retain flexibility in development and production plans to take advantage of this new technology, which may have beneficial environmental effects and decrease production costs. Canada should not become wedded immutably to current technologies, which may become outmoded several years hence. This belief applies not only to the Delta-Beaufort region, but equally to Hibernia, tar sands, and upgrader projects.

The third specific issue is the mode of transportation of oil. Current schemes are variants of two basic themes: tankers versus pipelines. Canada has had more experience with pipelines than with very large crude carriers (VLCCs). Perhaps this explains why more data on pipelines are available. It is fair to say that there exists a considerable range of opinion about the conditions under which the delivery of Delta-Beaufort oil to market by pipeline becomes economically feasible. Table 3 shows estimates of a minimum size of pipeline to handle daily oil quantities required. These vary from 3200 m^3/day using a 300-mm pipe to 95 000 m^3/day using a

Estimated Productive Capacity
Required for Pipelines

Oil Quantity $10^3 m^3$/day	Pipe Diameter (mm)	Source of Data	Date of Estimate
3.2	300	Beaufort EIS*	October 1982
4.7	300	Esso Resources	July 1982
12.0	400	Path Economics	February 1983
56.0	914	Dome Petroleum	March 1982
95.0	914	Dome Petroleum	September 1982

*EIS: environmental impact statement

Table 3

914-mm pipe. This is not a criticism of the estimators, but it illustrates, perhaps, that more information is needed to predict the break-even point.

The fourth specific issue is what will be the route of transportation of oil? Will it be by tanker to Montréal or to Vancouver, or by pipeline up the Mackenzie Valley to Edmonton, or both? Will it be by tanker to export markets in, say, Japan? Can these questions be decided today in the face of the many imponderables outlined in this paper? Yes, they can, and there is still time to obtain more information that will enable Canada to make more accurate decisions.

Finally, what will be the cost of oil per cubic metre delivered to Vancouver, Edmonton, or Montréal? Answers to this question, like answers to those preceding, depend on many interrelated factors.

Conclusion

I have attempted to show that uncertainty is the prevailing condition governing frontier production.

To demonstrate and analyse this uncertainty is not to avoid responsibility for finding answers. Rather, it tells us that although easy and definite answers cannot be found, the Government of Canada, other levels of government, northerners, and all Canadians are engaged in a multi-dimensional exercise to ensure that Canada has an adequate supply of energy to meet future demand. Achieving this requires flexibility of decision making in all sectors of society; these may be either individual or collective decisions to conserve or to substitute in order to reduce the demand for oil, or industry and government decisions to ensure future oil supply.

The uncertainty is, however, balanced by opportunity. Canada is involved in exploration in the Delta–Beaufort region because of the enormous potential contribution the region could make to our oil supply. Development of this potential could produce jobs for northerners, economic benefits for the North and for Canada as a whole, and could raise the incomes of Canadians substantially. These potential benefits outweigh the ever-present uncertain economic conditions. Regardless of how uncertain the picture may be now, Canadians would be derelict in their duty to tomorrow's generations if they let uncertainty reduce us to a state of indecisiveness.

Endnotes

1. *The National Energy Program: 1980* (Ottawa: Supply and Services, 1980).

2. *The National Energy Program: Update 1982* (Ottawa: Supply and Services, 1982).

3. *World Energy Outlook: Summary and Conclusions* (Paris: International Energy Agency, October 1982), p. 9.

4. *Presentation by Energy, Mines and Resources to the Special Committee of the Senate on the Northern Pipeline* (Ottawa: Energy, Mines and Resources, 29 June 1982), mimeo, p.13.

5. *World Energy Outlook: Summary and Conclusions* (Paris: International Energy Agency, October 1982), p. 15.

6. *The National Energy Program: 1980* (Ottawa: Supply and Services, 1980), p. 76.

7. See ss. 5(6), 5(8), 10(2)(d), and 10(4) of the Canada Oil and Gas Act for references to aboriginal peoples.

8. *The National Energy Program: 1980* (Ottawa: Supply and Services, 1980), pp. 76-77.

9. For a description of more than 40 departments, agencies, administrations, Crown corporations, and government committees with energy responsibilities, see Appendix II, *Presentation by Energy, Mines and Resources to the Special Committee of the Senate on the Northern Pipeline* (Ottawa: Energy, Mines and Resources, 29 June 1982), mimeo.

10. *Hydrocarbon Development in the Beaufort Sea-Mackenzie Delta Region: Environmental Impact Statement* (Calgary: Dome Petroleum Limited, Esso Resources Canada Limited, and Gulf Canada Resources Inc., 1982).

Background Paper

Black Gold Redrilled: Are the Economics of Beaufort Sea Oil Getting Better or Worse?

David B. Brooks
Executive Director
Beaufort Sea Alliance

Introduction

Two years ago, my article entitled "Black Gold: the Beaufort Oil Rush"[1] brought together information on the economics of producing oil from beneath the Canadian Beaufort Sea. Its conclusions can be summed up in three points. First, any statement about costs of production in the Beaufort region is subject to great uncertainty. Secondly, the only certainty is that, no matter how large the field or how successful the technology, Beaufort Sea oil will be expensive. Thirdly, assuming, nevertheless, that large pools can be tapped from single sites, there is a good possibility that oil from the Beaufort Sea region could be produced at a profit for the then world price of $40 (Canadian) per barrel.

The foregoing conclusions were not meant to argue for production from the Beaufort region. Indeed, I went on to suggest that, even if Beaufort Sea oil was potentially profitable, its costs seemed likely to be higher than those of other Canadian opportunities, notably offshore East Coast (Hibernia) and synthetic crudes from tar sands and heavy oils. Moreover, environmental and social dangers also seemed likely to be greater in the Arctic than in other areas. On the other hand, the Canadian government might opt to promote production from the Beaufort region in the name of industrial development, renewed exports, or fiscal gain. (Land claims aside, the Beaufort Sea is the only one of the three areas to lie exclusively within federal jurisdiction.)

How does Beaufort Sea oil look today? To what extent have the answers to questions about economics gathered in late 1980 changed over the last two years? Briefly, we know little more about the costs of producing oil from the Beaufort region now than we did then, but, if anything, statistics and such new information as has become available since that time suggest that the economics have become worse, not better.

In trying to make independent cost estimates, the July 1982 "Carin report" for the Department of Energy, Mines and Resources (EMR) and the Department of Indian Affairs and Northern Development (DIAND) began with a *caveat lector*, which stated that the estimates "are the result of a creative rather than an analytic exercise."[2] The situation is still so fluid that the environmental impact statement (EIS) submitted to the forthcoming Beaufort Sea EARP hearings highlights a production system—the Arctic Production and Loading Atoll (APLA)—that, in the meantime, Dome Petroleum has decided is infeasible. Perhaps the only point that has become absolutely clear in the last two years is that the goal is oil, not gas. With an abundance of low-cost gas available in southern Canada, domestic markets growing only slowly, and export licences unused, there is no reason to move high-cost arctic natural gas south.

Five economic factors will play strong roles in determining whether Beaufort Sea oil is produced. More or less in order of increasing uncertainty, these are: on the demand side, questions of markets and uses for oil and of the price of oil; on the supply side, questions of the volume of oil reserves beneath the Beaufort Sea and of costs of production; and finally, the policy regime within which production will take place.

This review covers only the first four factors. The policy framework for Beaufort Sea oil is a topic worthy of at least as much space as that devoted here to economics. Although the National Energy Program (NEP) cleared up many uncertainties about taxes and incentives, even greater uncertainties continue to surround export policy, native peoples' land claims, and regional planning.

Markets and Uses for Oil in Canada

There is no question that markets for oil exist and that they remain strong. As a portable source of energy, oil is remarkable. One barrel (0.16 m³) contains as much energy as 170 m³ of natural gas or 2000 kW.h of electricity, and neither of those common forms of energy is very convenient to carry around. As yet, oil has no peer as a transportation fuel, and it should continue to dominate transportation markets until after the turn of the century even if it is gradually squeezed out of its current heating and industrial markets.

A need for oil, however, does not imply a need for oil from all sources and certainly not for oil from the Beaufort region. A survey of oil demand projections done for the Beaufort Sea Alliance (the successor to the Beaufort Sea Coalition) found projections for the use of oil in Canada in the year

2000 that ranged from 1000 to 4000 petajoules per year (roughly 500 000 to 2 million barrels per day). Even the lowest of the National Energy Board's (NEB) projections of oil production from existing sources would be sufficient at the low end of this range. At the higher end, oil production would be sufficient if existing sources are supplemented by either oil sands or offshore production. Given that forecasts for the use of oil in Canada in the year 2000 have fallen by half in just ten years, one has to conclude that demand projections in the lower end of the range are more likely than those in the upper end. Both EMR and the NEB anticipate the possibility of producing Beaufort Sea oil, but such production would exceed comparable demand projections from the same agencies (a situation that implies renewed exports although the agencies never explicitly address this policy issue). Thus, there will be markets for oil, but they are not unlimited, and certainly they do not require that oil be produced from the Beaufort region.

Oil Prices

Two years ago, the world was still recovering from the second round of price increases imposed by the Organization of Petroleum Exporting Countries (OPEC), and the National Energy Program had just announced its schedule of oil prices increasing to more than $60 per barrel in 1990. It seemed that we were irrevocably in a world of high-priced oil.

In the longer term, we certainly are. Nothing has indicated any great increase in the ultimate resources of oil available in the world, and, even with declining consumption, the tendency will be for those resources to become more valuable with time.

In the shorter term, the situation is less certain. On the one hand, current oil prices are softening as the oil-producing nations scramble among themselves to get a larger share of a shrinking market. Cartels have seldom been able to enforce the internal discipline needed to keep market prices high for very long. On the other hand, the heart of this cartel lies in what is arguably the least stable region in the world. War or revolution in any of several countries could knock out a substantial share of world oil production, and prices could climb quickly once again.

So far as Beaufort oil is concerned, the price prospect over the long term is certainly good—something that is essential if any project in the far North is to be profitable—but whether price will be high or low when any specific project comes into production, particularly any project aimed at the 1980s or early 1990s, is anybody's guess.

Oil Reserves in the Beaufort Region

How much oil is there in the Canadian Beaufort region? Far from enough drilling has been done as yet even to approach a clear answer. Moreover, existing answers depend on radically different interpretations of the geology. According to the Geological Survey of Canada (GSC), the sediments once formed a delta, and the oil will likely be found in a multitude of relatively small pools. According to Dome Petroleum, however, the sediments are marine, and the oil-bearing formations should thicken and become more continuous as drilling moves to the north (and into deeper water). As a result, the GSC estimates that ultimate reserves will be around 9 billion barrels, whereas Dome estimates 40. About the same factor separates the low from the high estimates of the quantity of oil that has been discovered already—from around 500 to perhaps 3 billion barrels of recoverable oil. The lower end of the range appears to be quite firm but may not be enough to justify production, whereas the upper end is enough to justify production, but is anything but firm. It is agreed generally that close to one billion barrels of proven reserves would be necessary before investment in production systems could be contemplated.

Recent drilling in the Canadian Beaufort region has not identified as much oil as had been expected. Two years ago, the Kopanoar well was expected to be the first big producer, but later drilling was disappointing. More recently, Tarsiut was promising, but did not produce the anticipated drilling results. In neither case were the reserves small; they just were not big enough for the mammoth investments required to develop the Beaufort region.

Costs of Production

How big are those investments? How much is it going to cost to find enough Beaufort Sea oil, get it out of the ground, and move it to markets in southern Canada or, possibly, in Europe or Japan? We are little better off in answering this question now than we were two years ago. "Black Gold" gave a stage-by-stage assessment of costs and compared what was known of them to costs in other producing areas. Little has appeared in the interim to supplement that information. An environmental impact statement some 25-cm thick, an even thicker set of presentations to the Special Committee of the Senate on the Northern Pipeline, and hundreds of technical reports are all equally devoid of any but the vaguest cost figures.

Inflation alone would suggest that costs are now perhaps 20 or 25 per cent higher than those cited two years ago. One is left with little more than speculation along the following lines:

- The EIS shows economic benefits to Canada amounting to $6 billion in the year 2000. Assuming that the usual multipliers were used (total effects cumulating to about twice direct effects), this suggests direct expenditures on production from the Beaufort region of $3 billion. Dividing by an intermediate production rate of 600 000 barrels per day, this suggests direct costs of production averaging $20 per barrel.
- In October 1982, Jack Gallagher, Chairman of the Board of Dome Petroleum, told the Ninth National Northern Development Conference in Edmonton that, to make Beaufort Sea oil profitable, the federal government would have to eliminate essentially all oil taxes and royalties.[3] Considering the package of incentives given to Canadian firms exploring for oil in the Arctic, the statement suggests that Dome needs at least $40 per barrel.
- Gallagher also indicated that the cost of developing Kopanoar to produce 410 000 barrels per day would be $6 billion. Using his 20 per cent discount rate and his operating cost and profit figures, one can calculate total costs (exclusive of transportation) of $24 per barrel.
- A recent report on transportation costs prepared for EMR and DIAND attempts to estimate unit costs for a variety of scenarios, including pipelines and tankers, domestic use and exports, and ultimate production rates ranging from 200 000 to 1 million barrels per day. The report emphasizes the enormous uncertainties but concludes that, for transportation only, costs would range from nearly $5 to $15 per barrel to move oil south (eight per cent discount rate).

Proposals to produce oil from the Beaufort region may be damned by their own grandeur, for, of all the megaprojects, the current Beaufort Sea proposal is the "mega-est." However, the day of megaprojects may have passed. A great deal of what is happening in the economy—by no means exclusively in the area of energy—suggests that we have gone too far toward large scale, that by assuming that bigger is cheaper we have built an economic system that is inflexible in the extreme just at a time when changing markets and uncertainties throughout the world economy require a maximum of flexibility.

Even the economic benefits alleged by Dome and the other proponents can be questioned. For example, the proponents take credit for regional development by emphasizing the potential for constructing tankers in Canadian shipyards, but the "Carin report" points out that a shipyard in the Maritimes does not automatically yield positive national industrial benefits unless the shipyard is profitable over its full life, which means that it would have to attract continued business after the tankers are built.[4] Moreover, a report prepared for the Beaufort Sea Alliance suggests that many of the industrial benefits in the North are offset, at least in part, by individual and community costs.[5]

On the other hand, perhaps the assumption that production from the Beaufort region will have to be large to be profitable can itself be questioned. By thinking big we may have neglected some smaller scale alternatives that might be lower in cost and less damaging both socially and environmentally. Information prepared by Dome suggests that production might range between the "lowest economically feasible rate" at around 150 000 barrels per day and the "high technically achievable rate" at around 2 200 000 (and then goes on to assure us that "the likely production rate" will "probably" fall between the two). Privately, Dome officials have talked about production rates as low as 20 000 barrels per day, based on the development of a single offshore system and summer-only delivery by tankers to southern ports. Contrary to statements by Dome and the Senate Committee, however, an economic analysis prepared for the Beaufort Sea Alliance concludes that a small-scale (i.e., 16-inch) pipeline connecting onshore fields and one shallow field makes more economic sense than do tankers.[6]

Confirmation that there may be something to the idea of thinking small (or smaller) has come from Esso Resources, which has proposed to go forward with its "phased development concept" involving production from two small onshore fields (one on the Tuk Peninsula and one on the outwash of the Mackenzie River) and the construction of a small-diameter pipeline capable of moving 25 000 to 50 000 barrels per day.[7] Because the oil discovered to date in the Beaufort region is low in waxy constituents, it flows easily without heating, which means that small-diameter pipelines can be buried entirely, even in permafrost. Such a pipeline would obviously link with Esso's pipeline being built southward from Norman Wells. Although Esso does not claim that the small pipeline is an alternative to the larger scale transportation systems required for extensive off-shore production, it is well known that Esso favours pipelines over tankers; Esso notes that its small pipeline would provide "real time" experience for design of the larger one. It would also, of course, push off construction of that larger pipeline into the indefinite future, which fits in with Esso's probable game plan and likely would be better for everyone else as well.

Conclusion

Two years ago it was possible to be cautiously optimistic about the possibilities for profitable production of oil from beneath the Canadian portion of the Beaufort Sea. Since then, so far as one can infer from the paucity of new information, oil prices have fallen and costs have probably increased. Compounding the problems for the proponents of Beaufort production are the high investment requirements and the complexities and vulnerability of megaprojects, making them less attractive both to industry and to government. Thus, production of oil from the Beaufort region appears to be less likely today than it did in 1980. If production does come about, it will almost surely be at a much lower rate than that talked about two years ago. Hence, it is on such smaller scale alternatives that socio-economic and environmental evaluation should now focus.

Endnotes

1. David Brooks, "Black Gold: The Beaufort Oil Rush," *Northern Perspectives* 8:6 (1980), p. 1.

2. B. Carin, K. Barrey, and R. Mackay, "Beaufort Sea Oil Transportation Alternatives," a report to the departments of Energy, Mines and Resources and Indian Affairs and Northern Development, 16 July 1982, p. 3-1.

3. Jack Gallagher, Speech to the Ninth National Northern Development Conference, Edmonton, 28 October 1982.

4. "Carin report," p. 7-1. See above, note 2.

5. P.J. Usher, "Assessing the Impact of Industry in the Beaufort Sea Region" (Ottawa: Beaufort Sea Alliance, 1982).

6. Path Economics Ltd., "An Analysis of the Minimum Economic Scale of Developing Beaufort Sea Oil Reserves" (Ottawa: Beaufort Sea Alliance, 17 February 1983).

7. Gordon Haight, Esso Resources Limited, *Proceedings of the Special Committee of the Senate on the Northern Pipeline*, 16 February 1982, Issue no. 17, pp. 17a:90–17a:93.

IV
CONCLUDING
PLENARY SESSION

Concluding Plenary Session

Chairman's Opening Remarks

Alastair Lucas

This concluding plenary session of the workshop is the moment where we attempt some synthesis, take a hard look at what actually went on in the working groups over the last day and a half, attempt to clarify further as many issues as we can, and perhaps even resolve a few things. There will be two short presentations. They will attempt to synthesize, and to draw themes and issues out of, the workshop activity.

George Francis is a professor at the University of Waterloo. He has worked extensively for many years in the field of planning and environmental management—particularly in the planning and management of complex resource systems and in environmental assessment work. John Bayly is a Yellowknife lawyer who has worked primarily in the areas of native law and environmental law for a number of years. He has worked directly with several of the native groups, including serving as general counsel to the Dene Nation. He has also been involved with the federal Department of Justice, so he brings a varied legal background to the issues under consideration here.

Professor George Francis: When CARC was organizing this workshop it thought it might be helpful to have a couple of persons who would browse through the background papers for the various working groups, circulate among the working groups, and sit in for brief periods to tune in to the conversations—all of this with a view to doing three things: First, to try to identify some particular themes or points of emphasis that were recurring in the discussions of a number of working groups. Secondly, having identified themes, to see how these might be related to policy-oriented research CARC might consider undertaking in the future; and thirdly, to try to get a sense of the mood of the workshop, particularly to see whether there was some sense in having this kind of forum where persons with diverse interests in related issues in the North could come together to exchange views and opinions and whether this was perceived as a helpful process in terms of facilitating communication and maybe even reconciling some differences of opinion. I shall try to sketch what I saw to be the three main themes permeating the discussions of a number of groups, and then to indicate what I think might be some of the policy-oriented research opportunities that CARC, or anybody else, might wish to take up. Then John Bayly will take a look at the various kinds of answers that came out of the groups to the four questions that they were all asked to address.

The first theme was that of trying to come to grips with the various implications of the political developments that are now going on in the North. As you are all aware, this refers to the inter-related sets of changes that are associated with land claims, including the territorial governments' interest in getting jurisdiction over resources and the various strategies that are being pursued for developing new structures for governance. There are some variations there, including the apparent approach of the Yukon —striving for the provincial status that would be very familiar to those of us from the South—but also the more innovative arrangements for self-government that are proposed for the Nunavut constitutional group. A further issue is the way these developments might be integrated into the new Constitution, especially with regard to aboriginal rights. It appears that these processes are well underway, although many individuals who are directly associated with them are finding a certain amount of frustration in the process, inherent in the pacing of developments, and perhaps at times a certain worry about the direction of developments. Maybe if we could adopt a historical perspective on all this, we might see this to be a period of very rapid change and transformation of the basic political and administrative structures for governance.

We also recognize the central importance of resource ownership and management. There is a lot of discussion of the importance not just of ownership, but also of shared management or maybe direct management by other jurisdictions of the pace of resource development and the whole question of the sharing of revenues from resource development. Revenue sharing is a well-known point of tension amongst all known federalisms. The working group on natural resource jurisdiction and political development dealt with this issue quite directly. It urged that the process be supported and allowed to carry on and evolve. The working group on regional planning and land-use planning also faced these questions—but perhaps more indirectly, even though just as centrally. In other words, whatever arrangements are arrived at for planning, if they are to be acceptable to all concerned, will have to be rooted in the new structures for governance that are now in the process of being redefined and developed.

There are several implications of this observation for all the issues that were raised in the various working groups. First, the only clear trend in these political developments is that they are leading to much more influence and control over policy, planning, and management decisions by peoples in the North through institutions that are being developed by them in the North. This will determine the acceptability and the outcome of whatever gets proposed for resource management, by the working groups or whomever. The second implication, which was quite clear, is that the present situation should be viewed essentially as an interim one. It will change, it has to change, as a result of the negotiations. It may be useful to note that, until more permanent agreements or arrangements are arrived at, there is going to be an air of added uncertainty. Thus, resource management proposals of any kind probably will succeed only if they have the flexibility to adapt to the changes that are yet to come in the months or years ahead. Thirdly, as was evident in the discussions in a number of the groups, a lot of attention goes to trying to understand the implications of the various events in each process, and particularly to their significant implications as perceived by the various parties to the negotiations. What this may mean, in terms of a role for CARC in policy-oriented research, is that it would still have quite a helpful role to play by undertaking certain studies that could assess the policy implications of the particular positions taken by negotiating parties as the political development process unfolds.

The second theme that was quite evident was that of looking for effective and equitable planning and management arrangements that can be applied to resource decision making in the North. This theme came out in a number of the working groups dealing especially with the resource management issues, and for a number of different reasons. Some saw it in terms of perceived weaknesses in the existing arrangements. This weakness was noted for all of the resource sectors, and was related for the most part to the limitations inherent in management that relies largely on regulations coming from several different agencies. Others saw the question more in terms of the need to take into account the political developments noted earlier, because these are really changing the context in which planning and management have to be done. A third reason comes from the recognition that resource decisions involve a number of government agencies and other groups that all have a stake in whatever decisions get made. So the question, then, is how all that can be handled effectively.

The working groups addressed this theme in various ways. Some were able to take a hindsight perspective on the lessons of experience. The Beaufort Sea working group was able to do that. Others adopted a more anticipatory perspective. The group on northern land-use planning was doing that in trying to look at workable frameworks for planning in the North. Others reviewed the current state of the art or practice for resource management. The group dealing with environmentally significant areas (ESAs) did that and, to a large extent, so did the group dealing with renewable resources.

Some of the outcomes of those discussions just reaffirm some of the basic principles that should underlie all planning and management systems for resources—such as the right to know and its implications for access to information, communication, and consultation amongst all concerned. Other groups arrived at some general guidelines or principles that could guide the development of planning and management systems and could also serve to evaluate policy options. The working group on ESAs produced an interesting set of principles with that in mind, as did the working group on ocean management. Other groups were looking for good working models, or at least leads on working models, for effective planning and management systems—in part by reviewing the experience of others, especially in neighbouring jurisdictions. I can recall a number of discussions in which participants from Alaska were called upon to share their experiences in handling some of the issues facing the territorial jurisdictions in the North.

Such discussions often led quite directly into the main questions posed to the working groups. In the course of those discussions, two other types of things came up. One was the importance of having arrangements that really come together, make sense, and are acceptable to all concerned "on the ground," right there where the issues have to be addressed. It is not sufficient just to have some neat co-ordinating arrangement in some administrative agency somewhere at headquarters or a regional office or wherever. That probably would be desirable but, in itself, it is not sufficient. Another issue that came up directly in a few cases, but perhaps implicitly in others, was a suggestion that government agencies need now to see their role much more as the facilitators of good planning and management processes and much less as the high authorities imposing their own particular ideas of what is good or right for all of us.

A number of opportunities for policy-oriented research are raised by the discussions around this theme. How about assessing innovative approaches to the management of renewable resources—for example, in Alaska or other jurisdictions—as these might be applied to situations here in the North? What about reviewing attempts elsewhere in Canada, and maybe elsewhere generally, to develop effective means whereby a number of organizations—government, industry, citizens' groups, the same mix of representation as we have here at this workshop—come together to co-operate on issues that no single organization can handle alone? They have neither the mandate, the expertise, nor the interest to do so.

How about picking up and elaborating on some of the suggestions made in the working groups—for example, the issues that would be associated with a proposed Mackenzie Basin Committee, which was endorsed in principle by the inland waters working group? There is, as many of you know, quite a wealth of experience in the concept of organizations for river basin planning and management in North America. From that experience we should be able to identify some of the factors that could lead to effective organizations, and some arrangements that are, in effect, programmed to fail. What about picking up on a question raised at least by the mineral development group: the feasibility of looking into fly in–fly out mining operations *vis-à-vis* the rather standard practice of relying upon mining to become the focus for regional development? It works well, of course, as long as the mines do—but then what? Maybe we should be raising the issue here of a development strategy that would be based more on the renewable resource sector and should be relying on the non-renewable resource sector, given a flexibility to sort of ride the fluctuations of the market without some of the social costs inherent in being so dependent upon them. Maybe there are other studies that could be picked up with regard to the suggestion from the land-use planning group of looking into pilot projects for testing out these new kinds of arrangements and processes in the North.

So there is a rich array of possibilities here. The third theme that was evident in some discussions was that of incorporating quite different styles of organization and decision making into the thinking about arrangements for resource management. The issue here is how you can acknowledge and accept the approaches derived from the native cultural traditions as something that might again be appropriate for resource management in the North. This possibility was addressed quite well in a couple of the background papers, yet there seemed to be considerable ambivalence about the opportunities that the cross-cultural heritage in the North could bring to, and could mean for, resource management. The problem of acknowledging this potential contribution was revealed indirectly by the kind of discussion that went on about planning and management, which said, "Yes, by all means native peoples, native groups, should be involved in the process at all stages." Yet the process being talked about implicitly was one where the kinds of administrative management systems and decision styles that are very familiar to those of us from the South were retained. What about other kinds of management decisions and organizational arrangements that would be more comfortable, shall we say, and consistent with the cultural traditions of the native groups themselves? There seems to be little apparent recognition yet for the idea of communal management or self-management of resources such as wildlife, as at least a component in overall management or perhaps, in some cases, as a viable alternative to it. Maybe CARC would have an opportunity here, if it wished to take it up, for looking into that question a little bit more thoroughly.

Concluding Plenary Session

Finally, we all appreciated the challenge of having working groups involving anywhere from 20 to 45 persons, many of whom had never had occasion to meet before. For the first while there was a certain amount of announcing positions, of exchanging information, of individuals trying to get a sense of the meeting and of what was likely to be expected of them. Once that phase was past, however, the mood of the working groups was relaxed and very positive, although perhaps a bit reticent at times. Maybe that was the way implicit conflicts of views were handled. The chairmen of all working groups concluded that in their view, and the view of those participants with whom they talked, the discussions were certainly useful; they were often very informative; and in some cases there were some rather pleasant surprises concerning the cherished stereotypes that some groups hold about others. They did not seem to hold true in this particular meeting. I think the message here for CARC is that from time to time having forum events of this sort is perceived to be fairly useful and maybe, in due course, it should be done again.

John Bayly: My job was to go over the reports of the working groups to see whether the workshop had answered the four questions that had been put to you before you came here. I must say that as I read these reports, the attempts made by the eight groups to answer the four questions reminded me of my first murder trial in the North. It was about nine years ago, in Clyde River, and the court party had never been there before. It had no experience with courts. I remember a very nervous young man who gave his evidence and then hurried back to work. We heard later that his boss, who was the manager of the Hudson's Bay Store, asked him how things had gone. "Well," he said, "I was called as a witness and I won." "Well that doesn't make any sense," said the manager, "how can you win if you are a witness?" "Well," the young man said, "when the lawyers had finished asking their questions I still had some answers left." If that is a criterion for winning, the working groups have outdone that witness. Not only do they have plenty of answers left, but many of them did not, or could not, answer the questions that were posed. In fact, when I sat in on the land-use planning working group, some of the participants did not seem to know what was meant by "local" and "regional." They were helped out by a delegate from the Government of the Northwest Territories. He defined "local" as "smaller than big" and "regional" as "smaller than territorial." Other groups used the term "regional interest" to signify anything smaller than the national interest.

In another group, we were given a clue to the formation of government policy by a former assistant deputy minister, who revealed why the national interest is so difficult to figure out. He said, and I am paraphrasing him, that governments will identify three priorities—development, peoples, and the environment—but they will not state any order of priority of these three, so we look in vain. It became easier, therefore, to see why these apparently simple questions are not so simple when you get down to them and try to address them in terms of the theme of the workshop. If the working groups did not always answer the questions, they did try to deal with the ideas and issues surrounding them.

The theme of the first question was the roles of the two levels of government and the regional and local interests. There was general agreement in the working groups that the existing levels of government will have continuing policy and management roles to play in all the topic areas. Some groups suggested continuing to try to use existing mechanisms in preference to inventing and experimenting with untried approaches. It was recognized, however, that political and constitutional change toward provincial status or something like it and the creation of regional governments would alter dramatically the balance of power and responsibility in favour of territorial residents. Regional and local interest groups, including those of community residents, governments, native groups, conservation societies, etc., were seen as having interests and unrealized aspirations that added to political tensions and complicated problems. Most groups recognized that local, regional, and especially aboriginal interests have not in the past been given enough weight when decisions have been made. Most working groups acknowledged that aboriginal interests as expressed constitutionally, legally, and through land claims could not be ignored, and indeed should not be ignored. Most groups also acknowledged that the land-claims issue was important, but that translating it into roles was beyond them.

The second question was, if there is a variety of interests, are the interests compatible. Most working groups considered this, in one fashion or another. The groups found that, in some cases, interests, activities, and projects could be compatible but that others were, and would continue to be, irreconcilable. In the water management group, for example, the users and the managers of water were identified. A matrix was used to show areas of conflict and compatibility between users. The adverse effects of industrial uses were seen as the main sources of conflict with environmental integrity and with subsistence and recreational uses of the resource. The Beaufort Sea group seemed to come to a similar recognition. In its discussions, it raised the question of whether the selection of an oil port on the North Slope, which might be a poor choice environmentally but an important choice industrially, is amenable to the search for a "right" solution in which apparently conflicting interests can accommodate one another. Its conclusion was that, in some cases, such conflicts could not be resolved by a "right" decision. In land-use planning and in renewable resource management, similar conflicts and irreconcilabilities were identified.

The third question asked about the resolution of conflicts by the use of information and discussion. This was a difficult one. On the one hand, there was general agreement that having accessible, usable information is necessary for all who are concerned about, and affected by, decisions. Some discussions concluded that information and discussion will not in themselves reconcile real conflicts, nor will the provision of a fair hearing or due process satisfy those who feel that their legitimate interests have been sacrificed to other, apparently higher, interests. These concerns were expressed not only by local, regional, native, and that sort of interests but also by representatives of the mining and oil and gas industries. Territorial governments felt that their interests as well were often ones that were not satisfied in the decisions.

That took me back a number of years to meeting halls like this, where Mr Justice Berger observed during his inquiry that there were certain fundamental questions that were irreconcilable through debate. Persons with deeply held convictions, and with different world views, could not convince one another. As one participant observed in the Beaufort Sea working group: "Someone has to bite the bullet." That is all very well to say—but who? The working groups groped for an answer to this question. Most groups acknowledged that there should be more local, regional, and aboriginal say in decisions. All groups realized at the same time that the so-called national interest casts a long shadow across the northern landscape. At one end of the spectrum, the mining working group said that this is how things ought to be, at least until the North can pay its way into confederation. At the other end, the natural resources and political development working group agreed upon a consensus statement urging province-like status, land and resource control, and protection of aboriginal rights for northern peoples in the near future. I am sorry that these two working groups could not have been combined. We could have all benefitted from their exchange of ideas and points of view.

The last question dealt with what research and information are currently needed and what policy and institutional initiatives must be taken to reconcile conflicts and to implement policy. This question was addressed by all the working groups—frankly, much more directly than they addressed the other three. The group dealing with ESAs suggested a small task force with a balanced representation, and that it adopt a set of 13 guidelines to identify and establish ESAs. The mineral working group suggested studies into the comparative benefits of townsite and camp development in relation to mining. It recommended that a biological survey be set up on the model of the Geological Survey of Canada to provide publicly available data well in advance of development debates and decisions.

The ocean management working group offered a definition of ocean management and a set of principles for management of the arctic marine environment. The land-use planning working group reproduced the Bill Rees model as a structure for land-use planning, to be considered as a guide for establishing land-use planning in the territories. That group also suggested a pilot planning project for immediate implementation. It further recommended that senior levels of government foster regional associations (by which I think it meant regional governments, although it did not say so), define planning area priorities, and recognize land-claim priorities in any land-use exercise.

The Beaufort Sea group felt that it had not identified or cited key issues and, therefore, that this was a priority. That group acknowledged that decisions would be made, might be unpopular, and had to be lived with. Not having identified any issues, however, it could not say why. It expressed the belief that if the three levels of government and industry sat down to discuss interests, to identify issues, and to agree upon action, many, if not most, of the problems discussed would disappear. Again, it did not say why. I would like to have been in that discussion at that point.

The renewable resources working group recommended that renewable resource management north of 60° should be the responsibility of northern governments, requiring speedy transfer of responsibility for fisheries and marine mammal management from the federal level, except in the case of endangered or migrating species, where the federal government should remain involved. This group also recommended comprehensive land-use planning as an effective mechanism for minimizing the adverse effects of development on renewable resources. Similar recommendations to these were made by the inland water resources working group. It recommended successful regional planning; the full or fuller use of the Northern Inland Waters Act and its provisions, especially for setting water-use priorities; use of the development impact zone concept more fully; and the vital importance of a clear, workable mechanism for the resolution of interjurisdictional matters in the Mackenzie River system. In that regard, the group endorsed the draft statement of 26–29 May 1983 from the Banff conference on water issues, which urged action on the "Mackenzie Basin Committee Report" and proposed a plan of action for its implementation. The working group recognized two outstanding problems, one being native claims, that are not yet resolved, and the other being the new, undefined nature of the constitutional provisions concerning aboriginal rights—which may lead to claims to, and rights to, the waters themselves. It saw the upcoming hearings on placer mining in the Yukon as holding promise for the resolution of identified problems, but acknowledged problems stemming from conflicts between the Yukon Placer Mining Act and the Northern Inland Waters Act. That group again acknowledged that native communities have major concerns about water resource issues, and attached the statements of two native residents to its summary report. It recommended immediate devolution of powers and accountability for water to regional and local levels. It saw no reason why water boards should not be accountable to elected officials in the North.

The working group on natural resource jurisdiction and political development recommended a three-stage transfer of natural resources to northern peoples and to their governments: First, transfer of management and regulation; secondly, revenue sharing; thirdly, provincial status and ownership. Because a variety of processes are in operation, including political and constitutional forums and land-claims talks, it was thought that the national constitutional talks could be an integrating factor. In conclusion, that working group agreed on the following consensus statement:

> Democratic political rights are an important component of the fundamental human rights of Canadians. These rights should apply equally to all citizens. A primary expression of these rights in Canada has been the right of persons in a region to have their government attain provincial-like powers and jurisdictions, control over natural resources and land being of fundamental importance.
>
> This working group reports to the plenary session of the CARC Third National Workshop in its consensus statement that it calls on the existing federal and provincial governments in Canada to support the evolution of the territories north of 60° to provincial status in the near future and to protect effectively aboriginal rights in the transfer of powers to the new provincial governments of the North.

Well, I am sure my bias has come out in the summaries I have made. I may have over-emphasized some recommendations and under-emphasized others. I have tried to restrain myself from commenting.

I was at CARC's 1978 workshop. Like many northerners who participated in that workshop, I am grateful that such a distinguished collection of Canadian and American thinkers and doers has shown, and continues to show, a sustained and sustaining interest in northern Canada. You may detect a feeling of ambivalence toward your interest and advice from some northerners. Part of this may be your manner of speaking in what John Blake of Fort McPherson calls "twelve-cylinder words." Northern peoples are learning the meaning of such words but they still value plain, straight-forward talk. I wish to make three suggestions before I close: First, come and give advice as soon as you see we might be having problems that your experience might assist with. Secondly, put your coveralls on; we may need your help to try out the solution you propose, and you might have to get your hands dirty. Finally, try to make sure that you understand what is going on in the North from a northern perspective as well as from a southern perspective before you venture to give your advice, because things seen through our eyes look quite different sometimes.

Discussion

Terry Fenge, Director of Policy Studies, CARC: One of the things that came through to me in a number of the working groups was the frustration of many persons about the length of time it takes to make decisions. Many seem to characterize this almost as an inability to make decisions and to live by them. I also noticed in a number of the working groups that the discussion focused very much upon institutional structures and what sort of representation from various groups should be in structures to make decisions. Very, very little discussion focused on process—that is, on how things are going to be done. This came through extraordinarily clearly in the land-use planning group. It seemed that the discussion on how to implement the 1981 northern land-use planning policy, which has been around for nearly two years now, is still stuck at the institutional structure and representation stage. We have yet to begin delving into the meat of the problem: namely, how we are actually going to do it. I felt that we were very frequently stuck in first or second gear, still talking about structure and not yet talking about process. I am interested in hearing from anyone who may have had a similar feeling from some of the other working groups.

Alistair Crerar, Environment Council of Alberta: I might comment as the chairman of the regional planning and land-use planning group. Part of our prescription was in fact engendered by the kind of frustration that Terry mentioned. We looked at and considered the structure, the represen-tation on it, and what it means in terms of whether everybody is properly represented, and so forth. There were problems with it and there were ways in which we could improve it, but we felt that we should go with the models that have been partially agreed to by the Government of the Northwest Territories—which we are using as a model—and the federal government. It is more important to get on with and actually to start doing some planning, because many of the questions will be resolved only by discussions and decisions at the local levels in relation to the territories and the federal government. Our solution for trying to get out of the bind in which we find ourselves when talking about process is actually to get out and start planning, and then to use the results of doing it to improve the process. We think it is more important to start practising it than to try to refine it a little bit more. Let's take it out and let it fly for a while and see. If it crashes, well, it crashes. If it flies, maybe we can improve it as it goes—you know, you can sort of get out on the end of the wings and bend them up a bit or something like that.

Carson Templeton, Templeton Facilities Ltd.: I have been surprised at the strong, sometimes rather bitter, criticism of the federal government—which I think is uncharacteristic of Canadians. Perhaps we, the population, think that government should manage, whereas the persons in the various departments think that their job is to administer an act and talk about their mandate. I think government should set a goal, a social goal, working out the means by which to achieve that goal using time and money budgets, public participation, and any other tools that are available. Then it should have its progress reviewed from time to time by its peers—whom I think are the Canadian public. Don Gamble's comments were pretty strong in asking why there is not a goal for settling the land claims, with a time budget on it. If we could get a means by which the departments come together publicly and make the tradeoffs, I think Canadians would perhaps accept better some of the decisions—or lack of decisions, which seems to be the new Canadian way of making a decision. We would not be faced with what we have in western Canada today, where a poll published by the Canada West Foundation recently said that about three per cent of Canadians believed the federal government.

Chairman: One of your comments, Carson, addresses what appears to be a lack of pressure, and a lack of things putting pressure, on those responsible for making the kind of decisions that you are talking about. That came out very clearly in the context of the land-claims process. We were talking about a process of negotiation in which there was very little pressure of any sort on the key party in the process actually to sit down and to negotiate, much less to negotiate in good faith. There seems to be a distinct lack there, and in a number of the other areas we have looked at, of what American environmental administrators, at least prior to the Reagan administration, used to call "action-forcing mechanisms."

Milton Freeman, Anthropology Department, University of Alberta: In response to Terry's question about structure and process, it was quite apparent in the renewable resources working group that our concern with structure was because of the inappropriateness of the existing structures and our concern not to replicate them, not to introduce into the new North, the politically evolving North, the technocratic, bureaucratic structures, or the talk-down approach. We had an example—a case study, if you like— before us: the Caribou Management Board. The management of caribou is a very, very difficult, refractory problem that is incapable of solution under the existing process. We heard that that particular approach to managing a migratory renewable resource with many different interest groups, and an animal that crosses various jurisdictional boundaries, should be approached with a whole new structure.

The interesting thing is that that structure carries with it a new process that falls into place quite normally. In other words, they work it out as they go along, because it is not an imposed alien type of structure. Let me be more specific on that point. Normally, when you set up game management boards you have the managers making decisions—advisory decisions to a minister or to a higher authority—and then underneath that group of managers you have technical committees. It is the technical committees who come up with "twelve-cylinder words," who eventually get their way, and who, thus, are forcing a lot of the pace. Well, if users manage the resource—which from our working group's point of view is the only way to do it, because it works—then to have this type of technical structure schematically underneath you but basically dictating the way you go is not going to work. If, in fact, the board constitutes its own technical commit- tees, using the technical expertise of its own members, they can always bring in new participants if they want them on a one-shot basis, and in this way the structure does not get institutionalized and rigid or become the tail wagging the dog. We were not too concerned about talking about process because process will flow automatically from the most appropriate structure.

Chairman: I should like to give the working group chairmen a chance to share their innermost thoughts and frustrations. In some cases, as I think John Bayly quite fairly pointed out, working groups have slid away from addressing some of the key issues, particularly this question of "national interest." I want to invite working group chairmen to respond. What were the questions that in your view really were not quite addressed, or did not quite come through, in the working group reports? What were the sticky issues that you tended to slide around and slide off for a day and a half?

Andrew Thompson, Chairman, Natural Resource Jurisdiction and Political Development Working Group: In the working group on natural resource jurisdiction and development of government, the question of regional and national interests was central. You will have noted a consensus statement in favour of provincehood as soon as possible. That does not tell you a lot about the intricacies of the discussion, so I think that we should take this opportunity to elaborate to avoid leaving the impression that we simply came up with a glib statement about the desirability of provincehood. Considerable time was spent in trying to define national interests with respect to natural resource developments. A list of national interests and objectives was laid out quite clearly. Energy security was very high on the list, because we have not yet forgotten the experience of a few years ago when we all sensed that we faced global disaster in terms of energy shortages. There were international responsibilities, a northern ocean to be looked after, and all kinds of things.

When the question turned to which national interest requires that the development of government in the North be different from the development of government in the South, however, there never did emerge from the group any identifiable national interest except an emergency (unspecified) that could justify an evolution of government different from that in the past in the South.

On the other hand, participants were invited to think: Suppose you were sitting in Prime Minister Trudeau's office and you had this kind of an analysis? It was recognized that the federal government is bound to proceed cautiously. I suppose the analogy is to a parent with a 13- or 14-year-old who knows that with the grace of God that child will become an adult at some time in the future. In the meantime, however, that parent is going to exercise a little restraint because caution is not a bad idea and the child's time will come. I think the federal responsibility and position is recognized in that kind of an analogy. On the other hand, of course, there are lots of parents who never let their kids grow up. Maybe in the North there is a sense that the time has come when the federal government ought to recognize adolescence approaching adulthood in the very near future.

Walter Kupsch, Chairman, Mineral Development Working Group: After some discussion, our working group came to the conclusion that as far as the mineral resource is concerned there is an overriding national interest, and the local interest is connected only with the benefits that accrue from the exploitation of that resource. The local benefits are seen to be in jobs, in revenue sharing, and so on. It is most important for the nation as a whole to develop certain mineral resources—the reason is, minerals are exported in the main, and we have difficulties with the balance of payments. From the federal point of view and that of the rest of Canada, these resources belong to all of Canada. Certain things follow from this. Our working group was very firmly of the opinion that mineral rights should remain with the Crown. There are, of course, all kinds of possibilities that once there is a claims settlement in place, the mineral rights in small parcels of lands will be alienated and go toward the settlement. In the main, we believe that the resources belong to the whole of Canada.

We also looked briefly at the history of western Canada. When Saskatchewan and Alberta were carved out of the Northwest Territories in 1905, the mineral resources were not transferred immediately. It took another 25 years until Alberta and Saskatchewan obtained mineral rights. We cannot see that there is any realistic expectation on the part of the peoples in the North to get the mineral rights immediately. Even if there were to be a settlement of land claims and evolution in the government structure toward complete responsible government, that does not mean that the natural resources would be turned over immediately. I think that is a false expectation.

Jim Harrison, Chairman, Ocean Management Working Group: The ocean management working group was somewhat different from all the rest in the sense that it involved only one native group, Inuit, and that ocean resources are almost totally undeveloped. The term "resources" in this case means the whole spectrum of activities that can take place in the arctic marine waters or the Canadian arctic marine environment. The major recurring theme was the need to involve Inuit people and to obtain their advice and knowledge on the marine environment so as to include it adequately in any plans or projections for development. This theme came up several times in every session. One of the difficulties is the multiplicity of federal agencies that have responsibilities, or as many of them like to say, a mandate, which could be interpreted to mean "right" rather than "responsibilities." Anyway, it became clear that Inuit and other native peoples feel that by participating in some of the studies that may lead to development they may be prejudicing their own place in the land-claims settlements, or whatever other settlements or government developments are going to come up, so they tend to withdraw from such activities. Thus we are faced with an unfortunate situation where the native groups feel that they cannot participate, and yet they have a great deal to offer in any of the planning or projections that are going to be developed. We concluded—at least I concluded—that CARC could offer one of its very best supports for government service because it can deal directly with native peoples in a way that government cannot. CARC could, therefore, take a point of view to government deliberations that might not otherwise be available.

Kevin McNamee, National and Provincial Parks Association: I would like to clarify a remark made by Mr Bayly. I was in the ESA working group, and we produced a number of recommendations to the Task Force on Northern Conservation. Mr Bayly's remarks have left the impression that these recommendations were to develop another task force to look at ESAs. That was not the point. These recommendations are directed to the specific task force that has now been established. His last point on having necessary resources and commitment to the job—and this point was voiced strongly by the working group—implied participation in this task force by native groups and other interest groups. I think that is consistent with, and that it would demonstrate a commitment to, what we have been saying today about participation and about voices being heard.

Jean Morisset, Département de geographie, Université du Québec à Montréal: CARC has presented itself for many years as an independent and critical group, but then—and this session is a very good example—it follows exactly the same pattern as the federal government does. Thus, the so-called Canadian way becomes the CARC way.

I shall give you some examples. First, on the subject of the North, for your information, the border of the Northwest Territories goes as far south as James Bay. You have been speaking of the Northwest Territories all the time as north of 60°. Yet because of the very thing that CARC wanted to tackle this year, political development, in the way you have been working—through a biological detour, like caribou and land management and the rest of it—has regressed as compared with what was taking place a few years ago.

Secondly, there is no translation here for anyone who does not speak CARC's language, which is neither Inuktitut—because I have not heard it—nor Dene, nor French. You will be answering all the time that you need money, that you do not have enough money. It is easier to speak of caribou management for some reason, because you do not have to learn the language of caribou.

Thirdly, if I look at the panel as it is, one of the persons in front of us is for water management, another is for mining, another .... It is just a replica of the federal departments. There is no one for Indian affairs— maybe for the next meeting. Everyone has been saying that land claims and

aboriginal rights are important, but no new forms of political development were discussed because the CARC organization is based on biological
priorities. Therefore the workshop invites participants if they have some
biological bias, so you do not find any persons among your guests here
who will speak on a socio-economic or socio-political basis.

I am challenging CARC, if it pretends to speak also about political
development, to organize a workshop on that topic and to invite persons
who have something to say on those aspects. Otherwise it is just a nice
exercise for persons to come up North and to speak about their vision of the
North without involving those who speak languages other than the management language. We end up by being a replica of the system that you
want to criticize, and CARC becomes a by-product of the federal
government.

Chairman: Your charges are difficult to deny. There is no doubt that
CARC, like most other public organizations in this country, suffers—in its
membership at least—a surfeit of lawyers and aspiring, failed, or retired
politicians. In that sense, it is probably a fair reflection of most Canadian
public organizations. There has been a great deal of debate in the committee over the years about several of the points you raise—namely, the "north
of 60°" question as well as the matter of more extensive communications
both in our other national language and in the aboriginal languages. In
some of the CARC publications that have been specific or pointed, publication has been arranged in Inuktitut, for example, and I suppose the odd
rather perfunctory French-language abstract has been produced.

I think on that point you probably provided part of the answer to your
question when you mentioned money. CARC is basically a public-interest
organization that has to fund itself as it goes. There have always been
priorities upon priorities. Basically the same answer goes as far as the
admittedly arbitrary line drawn at the 60th parallel. You are right; it is no
less a convenient political boundary than the map boundaries that have
been drawn for the Northwest Territories and the Yukon. It has simply
been a matter of allocating scarce resources within the committee, and this
has been a method—though admittedly an artificial one—of working out
priorities. The committee is certainly sensitive to the issues that you raise.
Perhaps pleading lack of funds is not a complete answer, but it is certainly
part of the answer. Perhaps I can ask one or more of the members of the
panel to respond to the suggestion that you are really a bunch of surrogate
federal bureaucrats in your respective areas.

Concluding Plenary Session

Milton Freeman: I shall not respond to that charge, but rather to the one that the socio-economic side was not dominant, or that we are just a bunch of caribou biologists, or something like that. We found we had a tremendous meeting of minds in our working group on renewable resources management. The fact that we did have persons who could be accused of being "Ottawa persons"—professional biologists, government officials, whatever—did not stand in the way of our realizing very quickly that caribou management is a human problem. It is a political problem; it is not a technical-biological problem. We got beyond that very, very quickly. In fact, our working group report speaks of this political concern. We are very unconcerned about the technical aspects of caribou management. It is a non-problem basically if you have appropriate management structures, namely, the appropriate persons doing the job. Our working group lent itself very easily to that type of solution because renewable resources are very close to many other concerns. If you are involved with them you are very involved with the problem of renewable resources management. You become, in the northern context, very close to the peoples who have that dependence and reliance and concern with those resources. In some of the other working groups it was not so easy to reach that conclusion quickly, because the issue in question was more of a technical problem, but certainly from our working group's point of view, there was not, in any sense, a division, or hierarchy, or any technocratic or bureaucratic overbearing. It just was not seen as that sort of a problem and it certainly is not amenable to that sort of solution.

Jim Deranger, Cross Cultural Consultants Ltd.: I am a native business person. I am a Dene. I did live the traditional lifestyle. I trapped, fished, and hunted for a living, and today I do it differently. I would like to make one recommendation that CARC should consider seriously. There are enough native business and professional persons out there who could hold the position that the panelists are now, and who could address the sensitive issues that are changing the North both socio-economically and politically. The next time you plan such a workshop you should look for these persons because we are out there. I am sure that our input would address the sense of issues that we did not agree on in principle, but in which we have come to an understanding. I am sure that this can be brought forward in the next CARC workshop.

Nigel Richardson, N.H. Richardson Consulting: I attended CARC's Second National Workshop, in Edmonton in 1978, and at that time I knew absolutely nothing about Canada north of 60°. It is debatable whether I have learnt much since. At that time I was working in northern Ontario. I went to the workshop thinking and hoping that I would learn some things that would be useful in my work, and indeed I did. I suggest to CARC that, in turn, it might find it useful to pay greater attention to what happens in some parts of the country south of the 60th parallel. As I think everybody in this room is well aware, there are some very strong similarities. That parallel is not a real thing, it is a geographical and political convenience. There is a lot for peoples in the Northwest Territories and the Yukon and for CARC to learn from various kinds of experiences in the provinces. I can quite understand CARC's concern about lack of resources, but I suggest to CARC that that might be offset by stronger and wider support if CARC turned its attention to the northern parts of the provinces.

Willie Joe, Council for Yukon Indians: It has always been the policy of the Council for Yukon Indians to encourage as well as to participate in discussions like this, and to do so in the hope that we may provide solutions to the problems we all face in this part of Canada. I, for one, believe we have begun to recognize the geographical, political, and social differences of the Northwest and Yukon territories. Although Indian people constitute a smaller percentage of the total Yukon population as compared with the Northwest Territories, a message well ingrained into your minds by the Yukon Territorial Government, the Indian people's problems are very similar on both sides of the border and, to date, going to the polls every four years has not resolved them. Indian people have had a vote in the Yukon, I believe, since 1957 and those problems are still very inherent in their day-to-day lifestyles.

In the Yukon, the Indians are negotiating for certain rights to these homelands. We staked our past, our present, and our future on the comprehensive-claims negotiations process with the Government of Canada and the Government of the Yukon. The overall agreement in principle has come within reach. Some of the major outstanding issues such as constitutional development and the sharing of non-renewable resources, however, have yet to be resolved. These twin components are vital for the settlement to be successful. Inherent in and imperative to constitutional development is the guarantee of our participation with both the territorial and federal governments.

With regard to non-renewable resources, we have challenged the federal government to deviate from its status quo and to put forward a policy in recognition of Yukon Indian rights to share in the ownership, management, and benefits of revenues from minerals, oil, and gas. We have come a long way, for instance, by developing a very innovative, responsible, and fair position. I cannot emphasize strongly enough that the failure or success of the Yukon settlement rests ultimately with the negotiated one-government model as well. It implies nothing less than the sharing of jurisdictional powers of both levels of government with the Yukon Indian people, and if in return we agree to the extinguishment of our aboriginal rights, then the price we will have to pay could surely not be any higher. I should like to reaffirm CYI's commitment to the resolution of the Yukon Indian land claims and trust that the respective governments will commit the same.

Winston Mair, Victoria: I am the rapporteur for the Beaufort Sea working group. The point that comes particularly to my mind with our working group is the question of the paralysis, real or perceived, that is a consequence of the uncertainties surrounding the energy picture. This was discussed in very considerable detail, and it was pointed out that everything cannot stand still awaiting certainty. Individuals, local groups, and governments must make decisions.

We did have considerable discussion on the usefulness of having a federal co-ordinator, or a single-window agency, or something of that sort to effect better co-ordination and decision making. I might say that no consensus was reached by the group. We also had considerable discussion of land-use planning, regional planning, and the development impact zones of the N.W.T. as a means of achieving regional and local inputs and co-ordination. The uncertainty that inevitably surrounds the energy picture at the present moment was a very serious problem.

Under the discussion of required research and information, it was the feeling of our group that too frequently we use research to avoid either coming to grips with the problems or making decisions. We probably already know a great deal more than we are using, and before we rush off to do more research we need to isolate what are some of our key problems and then to sit down and look through what information we already have and determine whether we are able to reach an intelligent decision at that point. Then we can decide whether more research is required.

On the question of the failure of our group to identify issues, it was made perfectly clear that there were many issues—there have to be; there are so many problems there have to be some issues someplace. If I may use one example I shall try to point out to you what we mean. We had a very heated discussion about Stokes Point and the proposed land-based facilities there. The question was raised, however, whether Stokes Point is an issue or a conflict. There is a suggestion that the real issue is: Do you need a port on the Yukon coast? Do you need more than one port at some point on the Yukon coast? If you need ports, are the companies going to be required to share those facilities?

That decision then becomes very crucial. For instance, it would alter entirely the position of the Yukon Territorial Government. It sees the Beaufort region as important and it would like to benefit economically from it, and it would like to have jobs for Yukoners, but it is in a sense a bit peripheral. If, however, there are going to be facilities, are they going to be temporary or are they going to be permanent and major on its coastline because, depending on the answer, its interest is quite different, drastically different. This is why it was thought that we tend to expend a great deal of energy taking sides and arguing about certain things that may not really be the basic issue, the key issue. It would move everything forward if we were to take the time to sit down and pull out the key points, and address ourselves to those.

Finally, Mr Bayly raised our recommendation of having the several levels of government and industry sit down so that many of the problems could be resolved. This recommendation arose directly out of a situation that now exists at Tuktoyaktuk, which seems to have assumed considerable proportion when, on examination, all agree there really is not that much reason why it should. If the three levels of government—I am including the local council—had sat down together with industry, it seems pretty certain that the issue could have been resolved very quickly. There are certainly many problems of that sort that get blown up into larger things; then we start looking for changes in structure and all sorts of exotic approaches, when it simply requires that well-meaning individuals sit down, quit defending their particular positions, and agree to find a compromise or common solution.

John Lambert, Chairman, Conservation of Environmentally Significant Areas Working Group: The point was raised that possibly Mr Bayly had misinterpreted one of the ESA working group's statements, that he saw it as requiring a new task force. This was not the point. What we considered in our deliberations was where we could be most effective. On the basis of the outcome of the meetings in Whitehorse earlier this year where the government had agreed and where it was recommended that DIAND set up a task force that would look at this conservation strategy, we felt that we could best help that task force if we considered how we could help it through ESAs. Therefore, all of our thoughts and recommendations here went toward that task force.

We had a very good meeting. We were in agreement. We had a great range of interests—territorial, federal, native, non-native, northern individuals, southern individuals—and there was no basic disagreement. There was a great deal of compromise, or willingness to compromise. We did not look at the picture of ESAs from a national or international point of view, although we did talk about those views at the very beginning. We considered it as basically a regional problem, and therefore stressed throughout the recommendations that the task force should consider that regional interests are most important and that the involvement of local peoples is important. It is well known that the local native peoples have much expertise in, and knowledge of, these ESAs and their biological uniqueness, that they have to be included. At the same time, one of the things that bothered me was that we did not come to grips with any process here. It seemed as though we are more worried about structure right now and shall be until we have this task force put together, and know exactly what it is going to do, and it comes up with some recommendations to the governments. We hope that these governments will act, and it is at that time that the process will be set into motion. I think that we felt in agreement amongst ourselves that we were doing the right thing in attempting to assist this task force.

Mike Holloway, Friends of the Earth, Alaska: The emphasis here has been on regional and national interests; we come bringing the emphasis of international interest as well. Our position on Stokes Point is that it might be used as a model to work through the difficulty of how to protect these areas. The peoples of Alaska are concerned about the rational development of northern resources and have long supported the work of CARC. We wish to express our support for the position of COPE, the Council for Yukon Indians, and the Dene Nation on the issue of the Stokes Point proposal. We feel that plans for development of facilities in the northern Yukon have proceeded without proper consideration for public policy, which includes the following: the Stokes Point proposal violates the 1978 order in council that recognizes the request of the Mackenzie Valley Pipeline Inquiry conducted by the Honourable Justice Berger and the COPE agreement in principle. It jeopardizes years of work and international co-operation to protect the range of the Porcupine caribou herd. On the U.S. side, this work has resulted in the creation and protection of the 7.2-million-ha (18-million-acre) Arctic National Wildlife Range, after one of the most bitter environmental fights in the U.S. Congress. The Stokes Point proposal jeopardizes the ongoing efforts of local peoples and the governments of the U.S., Canada, and the State of Alaska to develop an international management regime for the Porcupine caribou herd. Further, it violates international regard for aboriginal rights and the ongoing process of Canadian land-claims settlement. We feel very strongly that the land-claims settlement should come before facility sitings are chosen. Finally, the proposal violates those principles and policies regarding the need to manage development of the Arctic as a single ecological unit under co-operative management. Such an international arctic management regime would necessarily include delay of all development in those areas where land claims are not settled and where local communities have not yet put in place the civic structures for the management of industrial development.

We urge the Canadian and Yukon governments to consider the international importance of the northern Yukon and the need to proceed in the framework of rational planning and commitment to these stated international and national policies. For this purpose we recommend strongly that all action on the Stokes Point application be delayed until a site plan for arctic industrial facilities can be formulated with the full participation of those communities that will be affected by these developments.

Chairman: CARC certainly has had, and continues to have, very strong international interests; I think that came through in a number of the working groups, perhaps particularly those on the Beaufort Sea and the Arctic Ocean. CARC has a particular interest in circumpolar issues as well.

Herb Norwegian, Dene Nation: Most of you took part in a discussion session that dealt with the whole question of the land-claims policy. For the peoples in the Northwest Territories and other areas where land claims are being looked at seriously, we concluded that the whole question of land-claims policy is really vague. I think that we need to look at overhauling the land-claims policy. The reason I say this is that just the title "land claims" itself, from the government's perspective, means that the native or aboriginal peoples are claiming land. Our position has always been that the Dene are not claiming land. We own the land. It is the government and the institutions and the corporations that are claiming land.

We want to make very clear that any kind of policy that would be formulated would have to demonstrate clearly that we are in a position that we want to sit down reasonably and talk about the kinds of things that are before us. When we talk about a reasonable arrangement, I think a situation has to be created where the native peoples would have an opportunity to sit down with senior persons within government—the ministers—to present our case. One of the things that we have to make very clear is that we are not giving up land, nor are we giving up rights as the land-claims policy spells out. The intent of that particular policy is to extinguish or to exchange rights. Our approach has always been that that is not what we are talking about. If we are in a position where we are to negotiate, then what we must be looking at is a shared arrangement. I think that the negotiator from the federal government on the Tungavik Federation of Nunavut claim mentioned that briefly. The position of the Dene 62 years ago, when our leaders sat down with the federal government to work out that arrangement, was that: We are not giving up land, nor are we giving up rights, nor are we giving up the rights to govern ourselves. Instead what we are saying is that non-Dene peoples would have the opportunity to live amongst us, in our homeland, freely, and to be able to share with us the resources we now enjoy. I think that we take that same concept that our elders put forth during those sessions and we bring it into day-to-day practice. We are not talking about giving up rights. We want to share resources with the rest of Canada. The first thing that has to be dealt with, however, is our interest. The interest of the permanent population, the interest of the aboriginal peoples, has first got to be protected. This policy itself definitely has to be modified to a degree where it puts the aboriginal peoples in a position where they feel that they have something to bargain with. So far this has not been the case.

In the land-claims policy itself there is no clear statement as to what should happen with political development. The experience that we have had through the last few years, in relation to that particular subject, is that when we sat down with the federal government, the first position that the federal government took was: "Well, we are not here to talk about political development; we are not here to talk about the Denendeh government; we are here to talk about the present programmes that you people enjoy. Those are the kinds of things that we would like to talk about. We would like to talk about your present hunting and trapping rights."

These kinds of things we already have. Why negotiate something that we already enjoy? So what we would like to look at is to make a clear statement and have the whole question of political development included in land-claims policy—because you cannot talk about political development separately from the other aspects of land claims. We have always taken the position that land, resources, and political rights are all entangled. You cannot separate them.

I noticed in the land-claims plenary that there was a good discussion on the land-claims policy, the direction that aboriginal rights are going, and what it means to Canada as a whole. There has to be some serious discussion of the land-claims policy. I would have liked to see the whole question of land-claims policy, of aboriginal rights, as one of the key sessions—a plenary session. After that, the groups could have broken up into sessions, and this would have been dealt with as one particular working group item. Then I think we could have said that this workshop was successful.

Nevertheless, the other aspects that were dealt with throughout the last few days contributed quite a bit. I know that, five or six years ago, if we were trying to organize a similar kind of workshop—where you brought together different interest groups, different peoples, from all walks of life—it would have been a failure. I do not think that it would have worked. In today's society, however, we see that there is definitely a need for public consultation and for public dialogue. This particular workshop has demonstrated that. These kinds of things have to be ongoing. This also demonstrates that the Northwest Territories, the whole question of the land-claims area, and the aboriginal interests that lie within Canada are a priority and they have to be dealt with. As a result of that, I feel pleased that individuals are raising this as a major concern and it demonstrates clearly that there is support for this whole process to be resolved. We definitely have to keep going with these kinds of discussions.

Chairman: Your point is underlined by the fact that every single one of the working groups, whether it was dealing with minerals, land-use planning, or water resources, banged head-on into the subject of native claims. I think without exception those working groups found that to be one of the most difficult problems to deal with in looking at each of those areas. That suggests that it is a problem that is really all encompassing and cannot be avoided whether you are talking about minerals, water, political development, or whatever.

Howard Tracey, Yukon Territorial Government: I think the tone of the workshop has been very beneficial to the North and to the peoples who live in the North. The only concern I did have was with one of your working groups—the colonial attitude that came out of the mineral working group that we should maintain the control of the resource in southern Canada for the benefit of Canadians as a whole rather than having the devolution of those resources to northerners.

Jim Kowalsky, Tanana Chiefs' Conference in the Interior of Alaska: The Tanana Chiefs' Conference does support officially the negotiation and ratification of a formal agreement for a binational management of the Porcupine caribou herd. To some extent, this workshop fell just a little bit short, in as much as the participants were not directed to focus somewhat on the binational or the international interest in the case of the Porcupine herd, which ranges extensively through the Yukon, through the northwestern part of the Northwest Territories, and also north-eastern Alaska, and is used primarily—almost exclusively—by the native peoples of those regions.

Concluding Plenary Session

With respect to the discussions in the working groups about the devolution of authority, I would just like to add a note of caution. The users have chartered their own Porcupine Caribou Commission with four members from each side of the border. In a sense, we could say that that commission—although it consists only of users from amongst all native peoples, not of biologists—is a type of caribou board although it is informal and has no legal or governmental authority or standing. In any case, it is the grass-roots, bottom-up initiative with its thrust and energy that has gone into trying to build a case for international management since at least 1978. Although the State of Alaska, which is comparable to a regional government here, has attempted in the recent past under the Hammond administration to negotiate a memorandum of understanding with the Yukon government—to somewhat throw a sop to us who were creating pressure for a formally negotiated agreement—this approach is unacceptable. Perhaps there is goodwill; I called it a sop. In Alaska, we call the Alaskan attempt a clumsy effort—so much so, in fact, that it has angered the State Department and our senior U.S. senator, who has now asked for formal negotiation of some kind of an agreement at the federal government level. The users who form the International Caribou Commission recognize that negotiation of this sort can appropriately be carried forth only by the federal governments. Only they have the authority to do that.

Our working group did touch on that, and there is one slight reference to it in the final report. I want to emphasize that we have a truly grass-roots effort. However, that grass-roots organization is looking to the federal government as the proper authority or the proper body to conduct the negotiation of an agreement that means something. A memorandum of understanding may in fact be useful—the drafts that we have seen dealt with scientific matters and research. This is all very necessary, but it does not include the Northwest Territories and it has no force of law because a formal convention—at least in our case, and I guess in yours too—has to be ratified by the legislative body of the land, in our case the Congress. I would like to have CARC address international or binational management for a truly binational resource in the future.

Bill Erasmus, Dene Nation: I would like to address the matter that Mr Lambert mentioned concerning ESAs. I was in that working group for the last couple of days and I would like to add a qualifier to what he mentioned about the idea of talking about international versus regional concerns, not only with respect to ESAs but with respect to the whole area of environmental issues. In our working group we split into different groups; we did talk about the international aspect. We talked about the importance of things that happen on an international basis. So it is a concern. We did not deal specifically with it because the task force that is being set up to address concerns specifically with ESAs is concerned mainly about the Northwest Territories. The international aspect will come in. At that time, when we address the task force after it is set up, we shall bring out our international concerns. I wanted to qualify that for the Alaskan members. We are concerned on a regional basis—but when we talk about "regional" diversity and "regional" differences, the term "regional" is used to emphasize that the Yukon is different from the Northwest Territories. They are two different entities.

In the Northwest Territories, political development is moving in such a way that we shall have two different entities, one in the west and one in the north and east. We are calling them Denendeh and Nunavut. They are the only two serious proposals on paper at this time, so we are moving in that direction. That is what we meant in our discussion, as I understood it, when we talked about regionalism. It did not exclude anyone outside our boundaries. We cannot help but support the Yukon and the Alaska native concerns and environmental concerns because the native peoples had no participation in the boundaries that were set, not only in that direction but also in the rest of the country. To us, the boundaries are lines that were set up to please governments, to please the other society, and so those lines do not exist in our minds in the same way that they exist in other peoples' minds.

Irving Fox, Westwater Research Centre, University of British Columbia: I participated in the inland waters group. I would like to comment, however, on a concern that has been expressed here again and again. It is part of the theme of the workshop. That is the lack of voice on the part of the peoples of the territories, in particular, in decision making related to natural resources management. I make my comments in view of a feeling that the whole process of achieving provincial status may be a rather rocky road and may take considerable time. If that concern is true—and we have seen some evidence in previous remarks that this is recognized as a serious problem—then, if we do not find some alternative, we are going to see a continuing period in which the peoples of the territories still will not have a politically accountable voice in decisions related to natural resources, at least to the extent that it would be desirable.

I am going to focus my comments in light of my experience in the Yukon; I hesitate to comment with regard to the N.W.T. because I have not had much experience here. It seems to me that there is a need now for a larger political voice on the part of the peoples of the Yukon in decision making, and I think that could be achieved without upsetting, you might say, the current relationship between the federal government and the territory. I would suggest that there could be established immediately, without too much ado, a joint resource policy board—one that is formally established, that is visible to the electorate, and that is much more accountable to the electorate than the existing arrangements we have for policy formation. I say "joint" because I think the territorial government should have full representation on such a board. This board could establish policy with regard to the major natural resource matters that confront the territory; furthermore, it could guide the resource planning activity that has been discussed here and see that action is taken with regard to the results of such plans. I think that is lacking from the existing framework that is now envisaged, because we still have to go through the existing bureaucratic structure.

My second point with regard to immediate action to give a greater voice to the peoples of the territory in resource management decision making would be to delegate responsibility for administration or management to the territorial government in the same manner as wildlife management has been delegated to the Yukon at the present time. In other words, let the management activity be taken on by the territory. Policy still could be established by the joint board, in which the federal government would have a full voice. I think that those two steps would be a movement toward achieving the provincial aspirations of the territorial governments, at the same time not leaving us with the current situation in which the voice of the territory is limited in these resource management matters—a situation that may continue while this whole matter of provincial status is being negotiated.

Hal Mills, Halifax: We have been talking about national versus regional interests in the North and, in general, looking toward what the future of the North is to be. I would like to question the role of CARC in this. CARC has been getting accolades for getting people together in this forum. Certainly I have found it very useful, and I expect that most others have as well. In the past, CARC has undoubtedly been the most effective public-interest group with respect to northern issues. After being a thorn in the side—not that it is not still—but after being just a thorn in the side of government for years, CARC has certainly achieved a high degree of credibility to the extent that I understand that the organizers of next week's Lancaster Sound Workshop are upset that CARC is not going to be there because they are afraid that the credibility of their workshop will be undermined. I think that is an interesting turn of events. One of the panel members observed earlier that the peoples of the North, the different native groups and so on, are really talking on different wave-lengths from the government, and that CARC should take on the role in the future of speaking to native groups more and of trying to act as the intermediary. I would like to caution CARC, in case anyone took that seriously, that trying to take on any special status within the North could be a very serious mistake. If you look at the membership of the board of CARC, and if you look at the panel here, it is fairly clear that CARC does not have and, in my opinion, should not have in the future, any special status in the North. Certainly, if it wants to take that on, it had better start thinking carefully about how that will relate to native groups in the North and about the structure of the board that it would have to create.

I think CARC will have a role for some time to come—perhaps, I hope, forever—in terms of acting as an effective lobby group in the South. To do that CARC will need to have a close dialogue with all parties in the North. I think CARC's past success and potential success lies in being an effective, but not over-ambitious, lobby group.

Chairman: As you know, CARC's original rationale for being was that there were gaps in the decision-making process, particularly related to northern resource decisions, and that, particularly in the early 1970s, the mechanisms for getting information out to the public and facilitating and encouraging debate were not there. The essential role of CARC has always been as a facilitator; that is the role the committee sees at the moment and it is a role that is expressed in workshops such as this. CARC does not have any particular status to put on workshops or sponsor seminars, but it is something with which we have had some experience and that we intend to continue.

Peter Burnet, Executive Director, CARC: I should like to add a few reassuring remarks about formal status. I believe that it was suggested by someone in the working group on land-use planning that CARC wants to be involved in land-use planning. It was pointed out that we made a decision several months ago that even if we were invited to participate in the Lancaster Sound Workshop, we would not participate. One of our reasons was the feeling that CARC's role, in the sense that there is a vacuum there, is to bring an issue to the attention of government and to try to promote a better and more open analysis of that issue. Once that is done, it is time to get out. We feel we have said what we had to say about Lancaster Sound. As it turned out, we were not invited to the workshop.

You said you did not know how long CARC would be around. You said you hoped "forever." I sincerely hope not. I think most of the committee members hope that CARC is not around forever. It is a group that came together in response to a particular problem it saw in the North—a political problem. CARC has been working hard to push not a specific resolution, but specific directions toward the resolution that is in fact occurring with some of the political development that is proceeding—tortuously slowly, but proceeding nevertheless. I hope we shall all live to see the day when CARC disbands because there is no more particular concern in the North that gave rise to the organization in the first place.

Chairman: CARC works on a five-year plan, and in fact this workshop is part of the kick-off for the next five-year plan. Very serious consideration was given to disbanding the organization; as Peter says, the organization will be disbanded—and that is a certainty—when it appears to members of the committee that it has no further role. As political development proceeds, and as the various interests and the various players in the North become more sophisticated, the role of the committee even in performing functions such as organizing workshops of this kind clearly is going to diminish. So the long-term objective is to work ourselves out of a role.

George Barnaby, Fort Good Hope: I did not hear too much from the communities' points of view at this workshop. I heard some participants saying that peoples in the North should have more say, but the way that they have their say is where we disagree. In our working group on renewable resources, we recommended that local residents should have a lot of say and quite a bit of control over what goes on locally. That is what we agree with in [Fort] Good Hope. We want to have a lot of say in what goes on in the area of land that we use. We live about 100 miles south of Norman Wells, where there is a big project going on with islands being built in the river and a pipeline being built. All these decisions were made between the federal government and Esso Resources Canada.

We are the persons who will be most affected by any accidents that happen from that project. We are trying to get some agreement with the company to protect ourselves. I recommend here that communities should have a negotiating position, the same as the federal government and the companies, when they are talking about projects. The persons most affected should be involved right there in making the decision; they should be involved in monitoring the work that goes on; and in regular inspections. They could work along with the government and the company. There should also be agreements on compensation for any interference with the way that residents are living. The work we are doing at this time is along these lines.

We are hearing a lot of persons talking, but not the persons who will be affected by what is going on in the North. The changes that we are asking for are not changes from one location to another—like from Ottawa to Yellowknife—but changes in the system under which the decisions and the controls would be exercised.

Robert MacQuarrie, Legislative Assembly of the Northwest Territories: I should like to comment first on a statement that was made by Herb Norwegian of the Dene Nation—namely, if I understand it correctly, that the federal land-claims policy should be revised to make provision for the negotiation of constitutional development through that forum. If Mr Norwegian is talking about Dene government for the Dene, I have no problems with that. If he is talking about the development of a public government for the western Arctic territory, then I do have problems with that. Two years ago, in a letter to the minister, I challenged that position. I feel that if we are to have public government, all parties who will be subject to the authority of that government must have a direct and full say in what kind of government it is going to be. The Eighth Assembly of the Northwest Territories attempted to wrap up constitutional development on its own, not directly involving the native peoples of the Northwest Territories. I rejected that position. That is the major reason that I ran for the assembly in 1979. However, I also reject the position that public government should be negotiated in a land-claims forum. We now have a Western Constitutional Forum, which comprises the parties of interest in the territories. Each effectively has a veto over constitutional developments in that western territory. I cannot see a better means than that of resolving the very difficult problems that we face. It is a process full of promise.

I note and regret, both here in the plenary session and in the working groups, the absence of a federal political presence. I do not know whether CARC invited federal politicians; if it did not, then that was, in my opinion, a serious omission. If it did, and the invitations were not accepted, then I find that inexcusable. In one of the working groups I found myself, as a territorial politician, trying to interpret and, in fact, to speak for, the national interest. Some amongst us feel that there really is not a national interest in political and economic development in the North. I cannot agree with that; I think there is indeed a national interest. I think it is important that it be addressed. I am painfully aware, however, that it is not defined very precisely, and perhaps is not being advanced effectively, which absolutely needs to be done.

Having said that, I am concerned about—or rather interested in, and sensitive to—the concerns of other Canadians about what is happening in the North. Their concerns have to be respected and dealt with.

Finally, I am not a rabid regionalist but at the same time I must take issue with the summation from the minerals working group. The statements were made that minerals must remain with the Crown, and that northern resources are owned by all Canadians. I say that is much too simplistic. Even though I am not one who is insistent, I am not a hard-liner on the ownership of northern resources or the immediate need for provincial status in the North, I will not accept that point of view. There is much more involved than merely benefits or jobs for northerners. If ownership is not to be conferred, we need a direct and full presence in the planning and management of mineral and other resources. We need a measure of control; we need resource revenue sharing to ensure that we are not looked upon as welfare recipients relying merely on handouts from the Government of Canada, and eventually we need ownership of sufficient resources to ensure that the peoples of the North can live in dignity and in equality with the other peoples of Canada. I do not want the public to think that the statement from that working group was the last word on mineral development in the North. I can assure you it is not. You will be hearing more from us on that.

Chairman: No specific invitation was, in fact, issued to federal politicians, although they were certainly invited. Perhaps you are right that, in retrospect, it was a tactical error. I guess the feeling of the organizers was that the presence of a federal politician would dilute the regional emphasis of the workshop. At any rate, that was the planning strategy for the workshop. Your point is a good one. No invitations were sent to any of the provincial premiers. We have found it very useful to have participants from other regions: from Québec, Saskatchewan, and northern Ontario. Your participation has been very much appreciated and welcomed, but no effort was made to turn this into a sort of para-constitutional conference by extending invitations not only to federal politicians but also to provincial premiers. I thank all of you, and, on behalf of the Canadian Arctic Resources Committee, I now close this Third National Workshop.

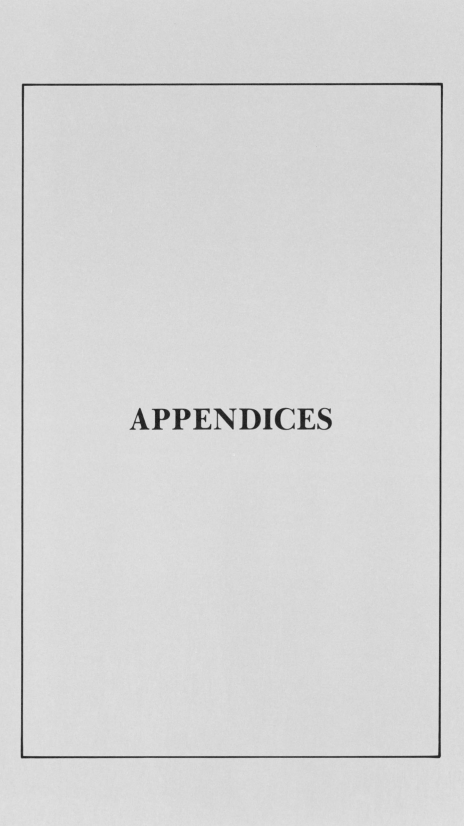

APPENDICES

Appendix I

Registered Participants

Albert Adams
Senator Willie Adams
Rebecca Aird
P.J. Airhart
Randy Ames
Tom Andrews
Shehla Anjum
D'Arcy Arden
Margaret Ault

Nigel Bankes
George Barnaby
Tony Baron
John Bayly
P.H. Beaubier
Steven Behnke
Robert Bell
Frank Belyea
Dennis Bevington
Walter Bilawich
Dan Billing
Gina Blondin
Joachim Bonnetrouge

R. Michel Bourassa
James Bourque
Arthur Boutilier
David Brackett
Meriel Bradford
W.D. Brakel
Mimi Breton
Desmond Brice-Bennett
Robin Bricel
David B. Brooks
Steve Brooks
Jon Buchholdt
R.W. Burchill

Ed Caldwell
William Case
Robert Childers
A. Clark
R. McV. Clarke
Cindy Clegg
Judy Collard
Murray Coolican
Ewan Cotterill
Byron Cox

Anne Crawford
Alistair Crerar
Harriet Critchley
Marg Crombie

Sonya Dakers
Terry Daniels
John Darling
D.A. Davis
R. Davis
J.L. Deakin
Michael Dehn
Clovis Demers
Jim Deranger
Adrian D'hort
Ron Doering
John Donihee
Pegi Dover
Bruce Downie
Jane Dragon
William DuBay
Yvon Dubé
Jeanne Dubé
Sid Dutchak

Appendices

Peter Eaton
Linda Ellanna
David Emery
Bill Erasmus

Neil Faulkner
Harvey Feit
Warren Fenton
Peter Ferguson
Chris Findlay
Donald R. Flook
Irving Fox
George Francis
John Fraser
Milton Freeman
John French
Stephen Fuller

Lucie Gagnon
Bob Gamble
Don Gamble
Jacques Gérin
Cindy Gilday
Bruce Gillies
J.G. Gilmour
Gerry Glazier
John Goddard
Lorne Gold
Yvonne Gosselink
Mary Jane Goulet
Paul Gray
Bob Greyell
John Gullion

R.A. Hale
Ann Hanson
Bea Hardy
J.M. Harrison

Art Hay
Jack Heath
Laurie Henderson
Mr Hill
Gregg T. Hill
Rod Hines
A. Hodgson
Manfred Hoefs
Mike Holloway
B.A. Hubert
Monte Hummel
Bonnie Hurlock
Bob Huxley

Julian Inglis
Kate Irving
Steve Iveson

Joe Jack
Ted Jackson
Lynn Jamieson-Clark
Sabine Jessen
Willie Joe
Phil Johnson
Allan Jones
Maggie Jones
Peter Jull

Stephen Kakfwi
Robbie Keith
Dennis Kelso
Bren Kolson
Tom J. Kovacs
Jim Kowalsky
Walter Kupsch
Ed Kustan

J.D.H. Lambert
Cynthia Lamson
Dennis Lang
M. Helene Laraque
J. Lazarovich
James E. Lee
Robert Lemaire
Brian Lendrum
C.A. Lewis
Jocelyn Lillycrop
Peter Liske
Ron Livingston
Alastair Lucas

Glen MacDonald
Dan MacKinnon
Letha MacLachlan
Andrew Macpherson
Nancy MacPherson
Sheila MacPherson
Robert MacQuarrie
Natasha MacVicar
C. McCauley
Kevin McCormick
Charles McGee
Margaret McGee
John McGrath
Dawn McInnes
Simon McInnes
Kevin McNamee
David S. McRobert
Winston Mair
Modeste Mandeville
Violet Mandeville
David Marshall
Lorne Matthews
Jennifer Mauro
James Maxwell
Hal Mills

Allen Milne
Robert Mitchell
David Moll
Hugh Monaghan
Brett Moore
Colleen Moore
Jean Morisset
Dave Muirhead
Bill Musgrove

Richard Nancarrow
Gordon Nelson
Hon. Richard Nerysoo
B. Neufeld
Lloyd Norn
Dwight Noseworthy

Chris O'Brien
Lynn O'Farrell
W. Oppen
Bob Overvold
Charles Overvold

Bob Page
Garnet Page
A.E. Pallister
John Parker
W.R. Parks
Denis Pascal
R.J. Paterson
R. Payne
Hon. Chris Pearson
E.B. Peterson
Dave Porter
Dan Prima

Dennis Prince
T.C. Pullen
Arthur Redshaw
Bill Rees
Brian Render
A.R.V. Ribeiro
Nigel Richardson
Jeff Richstone
E.F. Roots
James Ross
Judy Rowell
R.D. Roycroft
Harriet Rueggeberg
Nancy Russell LeBlond

Robert Scace
Jim Schaefer
Bernie Scott
Roland Semjanovs
Patrick Shaw
Gregg Sheehy
Marilyn Simms
Bob Simpson
L.G. Smith
Paul Smith
Charlie Snowshoe, Sr
Omond Solandt
Dick Spaulding
Wayne Speller
Bob Spence
Don Stalker
Lindsay Staples
Carol Stephenson
Doug Stewart
Ruth Stewart
Steve Stockermans
Dave Sutherland
Gary Sykes

Kenneth Taylor
Carson Templeton
John Theberge
Andrew Thompson
Dixon Thompson
Gerry Thorne
Howard Tracey
Dietmar Tramm
Arnold Tusa

Mr Unka
Peter Usher

N. Van Den Assem
Jacques van Pelt
Alan Vaughan

Murray Wagner
Rosemary Wallbank
P.J. Walsh
Glenn Warner
Pat Watson
J.H. Wedel
Nancy Weeks
Martin Weinstein
M.S. Whittington
Tony Williamson
John Willson
Kelly Willson
Brian Wilson
Marie Wilson
Jackie Wolfe
Larry Wolfe

Keith Yonge

A.R. Zariwny

Appendix II

Members of the Canadian Arctic Resources Committee 1983-1984

Murray Coolican
Peters, Coolican & Associates
Halifax

Ron Doering
Kelly, Doering & Morrow
Ottawa

Maxwell Dunbar
Marine Sciences Centre
McGill University

Hon. Hugh Faulkner
Alcan Aluminum
Montréal

Kirk Foley
Urban Transportation Metro Canada
Toronto

Don Gamble
Alaska Native Review Commission
Anchorage

Terry Godsall
Toronto

Stephen Goudge
Cameron, Brewin & Scott
Toronto

Peter Jacobs
Faculté de l'Aménagement
Université de Montréal

Peter Jull
Ottawa

Robbie Keith
Department of Man-Environment Studies
University of Waterloo

Alastair Lucas (chairman through June 1983)
Faculty of Law
University of Calgary

Ian McTaggart Cowan
University of Victoria

Allen Milne
Environmental Management
Sidney

Appendices

Eric Molson
The Molson Companies Ltd.
Montréal

Everett B. Peterson (current chairman)
Western Ecological Services (BC) Ltd.
Sidney

William Rees
School of Community & Regional Planning
University of British Columbia

Einar Skinnarland
Toronto

Andrew R. Thompson
Westwater Research Centre
University of British Columbia

Edie Van Alstine
Low, Québec

Kitson Vincent
Norfolk Communications
Toronto

Janet Wright
Toronto

Appendix III

Acknowledgements

The Third National Workshop on People, Resources, and the Environment North of 60° was made possible through the generous support of the following:

The Bay
Bell Canada
Canadian Corporate Management Company Limited
Carson Templeton
Environment Canada
Edmonton Journal
Explorer Hotel, Yellowknife
Government of the Northwest Territories
Government of Saskatchewan
Hiram Walker & Sons Limited
Investors Syndicate Limited
Kenting Limited
Lochiel Exploration Limited
National Research Council Canada
Northwest Territories Housing Corporation
NOVA, an Alberta Corporation
Okanagan Helicopters Ltd.
Pacific Western Airlines Limited
Rothmans of Pall Mall Canada Limited
Telesat Canada
Xerox of Canada Inc.

The following contributed to the Third National Workshop through their generous support of CARC's research programmes: the Donner Canadian Foundation through the Northern Decisions Study; the Max Bell Foundation through the Arctic Ocean Programme; and the Richard and Jean Ivey Fund through Conservation and the North in a Decade of Uncertainty.

Appendices

The Third National Workshop and these proceedings are the result of the efforts of many persons. The following deserve special recognition: Terry Fenge, who organized the structure and content of the workshop and was an indispensable adviser to the editors of these proceedings; Ann Ray, who arranged journeys, facilities, and accommodations, and responded with characteristic calm to the inevitable crises; Albert Eggenberger and Joan Remmers of Raven Tours in Yellowknife, who found ways to meet every need, from typewriters to a picnic wind shelter; Jane Buckley of Gilpen Services, who did the large share of the manuscript editing under a punishing deadline; Edie Van Alstine, who checked the manuscripts and galley proofs with her usual care for detail; Anne Kneif, who designed and produced this volume with dependable flair, notwithstanding the flight to France awaiting her on the tarmac; and the citizens of Yellowknife, who turned out their best welcome, if not their best weather, for the more than 200 visitors who joined them at CARC's Third National Workshop.

Peter Burnet, Executive Director
Danna Leaman, Publications Manager
Canadian Arctic Resources Committee

758